# PSYCHOLOGY

Mary Cassatt
*Two Women Reading*, 1901
Oil on canvas

*Mary Cassatt (1844–1926), an American impressionist painter, is known particularly for her paintings of women and children, often infants in their mothers' arms. Her genius lay in her ability to show us ordinary people, engaged in everyday activities in conventional settings, in a way that enables us to see the remarkable harmony between them and their environment. As we look longer and closer at this painting, or at the detail of it on the book's cover, the ordinary becomes increasingly extraordinary. In a similar way, the longer and closer we study human behavior, the more our admiration and interest grow as we see the myriad ways in which people relate to one another and to their environment.*

# PSYCHOLOGY

## PETER GRAY

Boston College

Worth Publishers, Inc.

*To Anita and Scott*

**PSYCHOLOGY**

Copyright © 1991 by Worth Publishers, Inc.

All rights reserved

Manufactured in the United States of America

Library of Congress Catalog Card Number: 90-71171

ISBN: 0-87901-480-6

Printing:   2 3 4 5–95 94 93 92 91

Development editor: Phyllis Fisher

Design: Malcolm Grear Designers

Art director: George Touloumes

Production editor: Karen Landovitz

Production supervisor: Barbara Anne Seixas

Layout: Patricia Lawson

Photographs: Barbara Salz

Fine art consultant: Steven Diamond

Line art: Warren Budd and Demetrios Zangos

Composition and separations: TSI Graphics, Inc.

Printing and binding: R. R. Donnelley & Sons Company

Cover: Mary Cassatt, *Two Women Reading* (detail), 1901

Private collection. Photo courtesy of Valley House Gallery, Dallas, Texas.

Illustration credits begin on page IC-1, and constitute an extension
of the copyright page.

**Worth Publishers, Inc.**

33 Irving Place

New York, New York 10003

# ABOUT THE AUTHOR

During his undergraduate and graduate years, at Columbia and Rockefeller Universities, Peter Gray supported himself by teaching nursery school, coaching basketball at youth centers, supervising a summer program in biology for inner-city high school students, and teaching psychology courses at Hunter College and City College of New York.

Since 1972 Dr. Gray has been at Boston College, serving in the past as Psychology Department Chair. He has taught a wide range of courses in the undergraduate and graduate curricula while pursuing research in physiological psychology and (more recently) in child development, cognition, and their relation to education. He continues to teach the introductory course regularly, and has been active in a program designed to help students from disadvantaged educational backgrounds gain more from their college experience.

In order to write an introductory textbook that shows students how psychologists think and work, Dr. Gray has educated himself deeply in every area. For 15 years he has immersed himself in the literature and avidly followed developments in each subfield, from its roots up to work currently being done. This broad knowledge, acquired through curiosity and persistence, has given him a unique perspective on the whole field. Peter Gray's *Psychology* has the authority and currency of a textbook written by a team of experts, yet it has the advantages of a single authored book: continuity, logic, and personality.

Peter Gray brings to his readers an accessible book that is intelligent and thought-provoking, warm and engrossing. His enthusiasm for psychology is evident in every chapter and in the reason he gives for writing this book: *"Understanding, organizing, summarizing, and retelling to students what human beings have learned about human behavior is the most exciting task that I can imagine."*

# Contents in brief

**PART 1**
**BACKGROUND TO THE STUDY OF PSYCHOLOGY** 1

CHAPTER 1
THE HISTORY AND SCOPE OF PSYCHOLOGY 3

CHAPTER 2
METHODS OF PSYCHOLOGY 25

**PART 2**
**NATURE, NURTURE, AND BEHAVIORAL ADAPTATION** 45

CHAPTER 3
GENETICS OF BEHAVIOR 47

CHAPTER 4
THE ADAPTIVENESS OF BEHAVIOR I: EVOLUTION 81

CHAPTER 5
THE ADAPTIVENESS OF BEHAVIOR II: LEARNING 121

**PART 3**
**PHYSIOLOGICAL MECHANISMS OF BEHAVIOR** 163

CHAPTER 6
THE NERVOUS SYSTEM 165

CHAPTER 7
MECHANISMS OF MOTIVATION, SLEEP, AND EMOTION 197

CHAPTER 8
SENSATION 239

**PART 4**
**COGNITIVE MECHANISMS OF BEHAVIOR** 281

CHAPTER 9
PERCEPTION 283

CHAPTER 10
MEMORY 323

CHAPTER 11
THE HUMAN INTELLECT 365

**PART 5**
**GROWTH OF THE MIND AND PERSON** 409

CHAPTER 12
COGNITIVE DEVELOPMENT 411

CHAPTER 13
SOCIAL DEVELOPMENT 449

**PART 6**
**THE PERSON IN A WORLD OF PEOPLE** 489

CHAPTER 14
SOCIAL COGNITION 491

CHAPTER 15
SOCIAL INFLUENCES ON BEHAVIOR 527

**PART 7**
**PERSONALITY AND DISORDERS** 561

CHAPTER 16
THEORIES OF PERSONALITY 563

CHAPTER 17
MENTAL DISORDERS 605

CHAPTER 18
TREATMENT 643

STATISTICAL APPENDIX A-1

GLOSSARY G-1                REFERENCES R-1

ILLUSTRATION CREDITS IC-1

NAME INDEX NI-1            SUBJECT INDEX SI-1

# CONTENTS

PART 1
BACKGROUND TO THE STUDY OF PSYCHOLOGY    1

CHAPTER 1
THE HISTORY AND SCOPE OF PSYCHOLOGY    3

Before Psychology:
Preparing the Intellectual Ground    4
  Philosophical Developments: From Spirit to Machine    4
  Nineteenth-Century Physiology:
    Learning About the Machine    6
  Darwin and Evolution:
    A New Unity of Person and Nature    7

The Evolution of Psychology:
A History of Alternative Perspectives    8
  The Origin of Experimental Psychology    8
  Early Structuralism    9
  Early Functionalism    9
  Gestalt Psychology    10
  Psychoanalysis    12
  Behaviorism    13
  Ethology    14
  Physiological Psychology    16
  Cognitive Psychology    16

The Scope of Psychology Today    19
  The Connections of Psychology
    to Other Scholarly Fields    19
  The Questions of Psychology as
    Arranged in This Book    20
  Psychology as a Profession    21
Concluding Thoughts    22
Further Reading    23
Looking Ahead    23

CHAPTER 2
METHODS OF PSYCHOLOGY    25

Lessons from Clever Hans    25
A Taxonomy of Research Strategies    28
  Research Designs    28
  Data-Collection Methods    31
  Research Settings    32
Statistical Methods in Psychology    33
  Describing the Central Tendency
    and Variability of a Set of Data    33
  Describing a Correlation    34
  Inferential Statistics    35
Sources of Error and Bias
in Psychological Research    36
  Problems with the Measurement Procedure    36
  Observer-Expectancy Effects    38
  Subject-Expectancy Effects (Placebo Effects)    38
  Problems in Generalizing from
    a Sample to a Larger Population    39
Ethical Issues in Psychological Research    40
Concluding Thoughts    42
Further Reading    43
Looking Ahead    43

## PART 2
### NATURE, NURTURE, AND BEHAVIORAL ADAPTATION   45

## CHAPTER 3
### GENETICS OF BEHAVIOR   47

**Principles of Gene Action and Heredity**   48
*How Genes Affect Physical
   Development and Behavior*   48
*Sexual Reproduction and Patterns of Heredity*   49

**Single-Gene and Chromosomal Effects on Behavior**   53
*Mendelian Inheritance of Behavioral
   Traits in Dogs: Scott and Fuller's Study*   54
*Mendelian Disorders in Humans*   56
*Chromosomal Disorders in Humans*   58

**Polygenic Effects on Behavior**   61
*The Concept of Heritability*   62
*Selective Breeding for Behavioral
   Characteristics in Animals*   64
*The Heritability and Environmentality of IQ*   67
*Genetic Influence on Risk for Schizophrenia*   73

**Concluding Thoughts**   77        **Further Reading**   79
**Looking Ahead**   79

## CHAPTER 4
### THE ADAPTIVENESS OF BEHAVIOR I: EVOLUTION   81

**Basic Concepts: Natural Selection
and Evolutionary Adaptation**   81
*The Process of Evolution by Natural Selection*   81
*Evolutionary Adaptation*   85
*Some Precautions Concerning
   Adaptational Thinking*   87

**Ethology: The Study of Species-Specific
Behavior Patterns**   89
*Describing Species-Specific Behaviors*   89
*Development of Species-Specific Behaviors:
   The Role of the Environment*   91
*Tracing the Evolution of Species-Specific Behaviors*   93
*Human Emotional Expressions as
   Species-Specific Behaviors*   97

**Sociobiology: The Comparative Study
of Animals' Social Systems**   104
*Patterns of Mating*   105
*Patterns of Aggression*   110
*Patterns of Helping*   112
*Sociobiological Thought About Human Behavior*   113

**Concluding Thoughts**   118
**Further Reading**   119
**Looking Ahead**   119

## CHAPTER 5
### THE ADAPTIVENESS OF BEHAVIOR II: LEARNING   121

**The Behavioral Perspective:
Acquiring New Responses to Stimuli**   121
*Classical Conditioning*   122
*Operant Conditioning*   130

**The Cognitive Perspective:
Acquiring Information About the World**   143
*Cognitive Views of Conditioning*   143

*Place Learning*   150
*Observational Learning*   151

**The Ecological Perspective: Filling the
Blanks in Species-Specific Behavior Patterns**   153
*Learning What to Eat*   153
*Other Examples of Selective Learning Abilities*   157

**Concluding Thoughts**   159

**Further Reading**   160

**Looking Ahead**   161


**PART 3**
**PHYSIOLOGICAL MECHANISMS OF BEHAVIOR**   163

**CHAPTER 6**
**THE NERVOUS SYSTEM**   165

**Neurons: The Units of the Nervous System**   165

**Functional Organization of the Nervous System**   172
*The Peripheral Nervous System*   173
*Functional Approach to the
    Central Nervous System*   175
*The Spinal Cord and Reflex Mechanisms*   175
*Subcortical Structures of the Brain*   177
*The Cerebral Cortex*   180
*Hierarchical Organization in the
    Control of Movement: A Summary*   185

**Hormones, Drugs, and
Their Interactions with Neurotransmission**   187
*Hormones*   187
*Drugs*   190

**Concluding Thoughts**   194

**Further Reading**   195

**Looking Ahead**   195

**CHAPTER 7**
**MECHANISMS OF MOTIVATION,
SLEEP, AND EMOTION**   197

**Motivation and Reward**   197
*The Physiological Approach to the Study of Drives*   199
*Hunger*   202
*The Sex Drive*   208
*Reward Mechanisms and
    Their Relationship to Drives*   214

**Sleep**   216

**Arousal and Emotionality**   226
*High Arousal and Stress*   226
*The Relationship Between
    Physiological Arousal and Emotion*   229

**Concluding Thoughts**   236

**Further Reading**   236

**Looking Ahead**   237


**CHAPTER 8**
**SENSATION**   239

**Overview**   240

**Hearing**   244

**Vision**   251

**Pain**   266

**Psychophysics**   270

**Concluding Thoughts**   277

**Further Reading**   278

**Looking Ahead**   279


**PART 4**
**COGNITIVE MECHANISMS OF BEHAVIOR**   281

CHAPTER 9
PERCEPTION    283

**Perceiving Patterns and Recognizing Objects**    284
*Holistic Perception and Top-Down
    Analysis of Stimulus Input*    285
*Feature Detection and Bottom-Up
    Analysis of Stimulus Input*    290

**Attention: The Selectivity of Perception**    295

**Perceiving Objects in Relation to Space:
Depth, Size, and Motion Perception**    303
*Perceiving Depth*    304
*Perceiving Size*    306
*Perceiving Motion*    311
*Two Perspectives on the Use of Relational Information:
    Unconscious Inference and Direct Perception*    313

**Concluding Thoughts**    319        **Further Reading**    321
**Looking Ahead**    321


CHAPTER 10
MEMORY    323

**An Information-Processing Model of Memory**    323
**Sensory Memory: The Preattentive Store**    328
**Short-term Memory and
Encoding into Long-term Memory**    331
*Rote Rehearsal*    331
*Beyond Rote Rehearsal*    334

**Representation and Organization
in Long-term Memory**    340
*The Problem of Representation*    340
*Organization of Knowledge*    345

**Problems of Retrieval from Long-term Memory**    349
*Why Do We Forget?*    349
*Memory Construction as a Source of Distortion*    354
*Effects of Hypnosis on Memory*    356

**Neuropsychological Evidence for Multiple Memory
Systems**    357
**Concluding Thoughts**    361        **Further Reading**    362
**Looking Ahead**    363


CHAPTER 11
THE HUMAN INTELLECT    365

**Conceptions of Intelligence**    365
*The Psychometric Approach to Intelligence*    366
*The Information-Processing
    Approach to Intelligence*    373
*The Neuropsychological Approach to Intelligence*    377
*The Ecological Approach to Intelligence*    383

**Logical Reasoning and Problem Solving**    385
*Elements of Logic*    386
*Some Strategies for Solving Problems*    390

**Language and Its Relationship to Thought**    394
*Language as a Cognitive System*    394
*The Relation of Language to Thought*    401

**Concluding Thoughts**    406        **Further Reading**    407
**Looking Ahead**    407


PART 5
GROWTH OF THE MIND AND PERSON    409

CHAPTER 12
COGNITIVE DEVELOPMENT    411

**Some Basic Issues in the Study of Development**    411
**Development of Perception and
Knowledge in Infancy**    414
*Perceptual Development*    414
*Early Knowledge*    417

**Development of Language**    420
*The Course of Language Development*    420
*Internal and External Supports
    for Language Development*    425
*Teaching Language to Chimpanzees*    428

**Development of Logical Thought**    431
*Piaget's Studies of Reasoning in Children*    431
*Piaget's Theory of Mental Development*    435
*The Information-Processing Perspective*    440
*The Sociocultural Perspective*    443

**Concluding Thoughts**    446
**Further Reading**    447
**Looking Ahead**    447

CHAPTER 13
SOCIAL DEVELOPMENT   449

Perspectives on Social Development   449
*Theories Emphasizing Drives and Mental Conflicts*   449
*Theories Emphasizing Cognitive Growth*   451
*Theories Emphasizing the Social Environment*   451

Infancy: Attachment to Caregivers   454

Childhood: Becoming Socialized   460
*Parenting Styles*   460
*Theories About the*
*Developmental Functions of Play*   463
*School as a Socializing Force*   464
*Gender as a Factor in Socialization*   466

Adolescence: Finding Oneself   470
*Relationships in Adolescence*   470
*Sexuality*   472
*Self-Concept and Identity*   473
*Moral Reasoning*   475

Adulthood: Caring and Working   479
*Family*   479
*Employment*   481
*Growing Old*   483

Concluding Thoughts   486          Further Reading   487
Looking Ahead   487

PART 6
THE PERSON IN A WORLD OF PEOPLE   489

CHAPTER 14
SOCIAL COGNITION   491

Perceiving Others   491
*Basic Processes of Person Perception*   492
*Biases in Person Perception*   494

Perceiving and Presenting the Self   501
*The Self as a Social Product*   501
*The Social Presentation of the Self*   506

Meanings of Friendship and Love   510

Attitudes   513
*Functions and Origins of Attitudes*   513
*Cognitive Dissonance as a Force*
*for Attitude Consistency and Change*   516
*Why Don't People Always Behave*
*According to Their Attitudes?*   519

Concluding Thoughts   523
Further Reading   525
Looking Ahead   525

CHAPTER 15
SOCIAL INFLUENCES ON BEHAVIOR   527

A Perspective: The Person in a Field of Social
Forces   527

Influence of Others' Requests   530
*Some Principles of Compliance*   530
*Obedience: Milgram's Experiments and Beyond*   535

Influence of Others' Presence or Examples   540
*Audience and Coparticipant Effects*   540
*Conformity*   545
*Group Discussion and Decision Making*   548
*Group Versus Group*   552

Concluding Thoughts   558          Further Reading   559
Looking Ahead   559

PART 7
PERSONALITY AND DISORDERS   561

CHAPTER 16
THEORIES OF PERSONALITY   563

Freud's Psychodynamic Theory   564
*Freud's Model of the Mind*   564
*Freud's View of Personality Development*   570
*Personality Research Based on Freud's Theory*   572
*Critique of Freud's Theory*   574

Post-Freudian Psychodynamic Theories   576

Humanistic Theories   578
*Basic Tenets of Humanistic Psychology*   579
*Rogers's Theory*   581
*Maslow's Theory*   582
*Critique of Humanistic Theories*   584

**Social Learning Theories** 585
*Basic Tenets of Social Learning Theories* 585
*Two Cognitive Constructs:*
*Locus of Control and Self-efficacy* 586
*Critique of Social Learning Theories* 589

**Trait Theories and Psychometric Research** 590
*Basics of the Trait Approach* 590
*A Sampling of Trait Theories* 592
*Questions About the Consistency of Traits*
*Across Situations, Time, and Generations* 595
*Critique of Trait Theories* 600

**Concluding Thoughts** 602
**Further Reading** 603
**Looking Ahead** 603

**CHAPTER 17**
**MENTAL DISORDERS** 605

**Basic Issues and Problems** 605
*What Is a Mental Disorder?* 605
*Perspectives on Mental Disorders* 606
*Categorization and Diagnosis of Mental Disorders* 609

**Anxiety Disorders** 615

**Somatoform and Dissociative Disorders** 619
*Somatoform Disorders* 620
*Dissociative Disorders* 622

**Psychoactive Substance-Use Disorders** 624

**Mood Disorders** 627
*Depression* 628
*Bipolar Disorders* 632

**Schizophrenia** 633
*Characteristics and Variations of the Disorder* 634
*Potential Causes* 638

**Concluding Thoughts** 640      **Further Reading** 641
**Looking Ahead** 641

**CHAPTER 18**
**TREATMENT** 643

**Care as a Social Issue** 643
*What to Do with the Seriously Disturbed?* 643
*Structure of the Mental Health System* 646

**Clinical Assessment** 649

**Psychotherapies** 652
*Psychoanalysis and Other*
*Psychodynamic Therapies* 653
*Humanistic Therapy* 659
*Cognitive Therapy* 662
*Behavior Therapy* 666
*Evaluating Psychotherapies* 671

**Biological Treatments** 675
*Drugs* 675
*Other Biologically Based Treatments* 678

**Concluding Thoughts** 680
**Further Reading** 681
**Looking Ahead** 681

**STATISTICAL APPENDIX** A-1

**Organizing and Summarizing a Set of Scores** A-1
**Converting Scores for Purposes of Comparison** A-5
**Calculating a Correlation Coefficient** A-7
**Supplement on Psychophysical Scaling** A-9

**GLOSSARY** G-1

**REFERENCES** R-1

**ILLUSTRATION CREDITS** IC-1

**NAME INDEX** NI-1

**SUBJECT INDEX** SI-1

# PREFACE

My immodest goal has been to write an introduction to psychology that describes the main ideas of the field, and the evidence behind them, in as logically coherent and intellectually stimulating a manner as possible—one that will excite students' interest through appealing to their intelligence. As cognitive psychologists have shown repeatedly, the human mind is not particularly good at absorbing and remembering miscellaneous pieces of information. It is designed for thinking, figuring out, understanding; and it remembers what it understands. I want students to join you and me in *thinking about* behavior—its functions, causes, and mechanisms.

Toward achieving this goal, I have approached each domain of psychology with the aim of identifying its main questions, its main approaches to answering questions, and its most important and interesting theories and findings. I have striven to describe these as clearly as possible and have provided concrete, real-life examples to help readers see their relevance. The book is organized in a way that brings together similar questions and ways of thinking about behavior, so as to maximize the opportunities to present extended arguments while still covering the traditional ground of the introductory course. Margin notes continuously call attention to the main ideas and lines of evidence. Throughout the book I have aimed to depict the science of psychology as a human endeavor in which progress comes through the work of thoughtful, if fallible, people who make observations, conduct experiments, reason, and argue about behavior.

One of my dearest aims has been to achieve some small measure of the personal touch that William James accomplished so masterfully in *The Principles of Psychology*—the book that still stands, in my mind, as far and away the best introduction to psychology ever written. (I keep reminding myself that James had it easier—psychology was only a few years old at the time.) I hope students will read this text—as anyone must read James's—not as Truth with a capital *T*, nor as an unbiased distillate of all of psychology, but rather as one person's honest attempt to understand the field and to convey that understanding as best he could. Toward that end, in writing the book I constantly imagined myself carrying on a dialogue with an inquiring, thinking, appropriately skeptical student.

I must also confess (as you will find it out anyway in reading the text) to sharing two of James's biases—rationalism and functionalism. As a rationalist, I am uncomfortable presenting findings and facts without trying to make sense of them. Sometimes in our teaching of psychology we overplay the methods for gathering and analyzing data and underplay the value of logical thought. I want students always to think about findings in relation to larger ideas and not to gain the impression that the discipline is simply a piling of fact upon fact. As a functionalist, I want to know why, in terms of survival or other benefit, people (or animals) behave as they do. This latter bias does not dominate the book, but it certainly seeps through in many places. It is part of the reason why the first major unit (following the brief *Background to the Study of Psychology* unit) is entitled *Nature, Nurture, and Behavioral*

*Adaptation* and deals with behavioral evolution and learning in back-to-back chapters. Natural selection and learning are the two reasons why behavior is functional, and I want students to know something about those processes, and their interaction, right from the start. This functionalist orientation also leads me, in the second half of the book, to pay more than the usual amount of attention to cross-cultural research and to behavioral processes as they operate in the contexts of people's everyday lives.

An important issue faced by any textbook author is that of deciding how much attention to pay to current as opposed to classic work. Clearly, a prime task of any introductory psychology text published today is to represent the field as it is in the 1990s, but, in my view, that task cannot be achieved without a historical perspective. One cannot adequately depict psychology for the future by providing a snapshot of the present. Ideas and approaches in psychology or any scholarly field emerge and evolve over time, and a reasoned presentation must portray something of that evolution. This book contains plenty of current research, but it sets that research in the context of ideas that have been around for a long time and are associated with such names as Darwin, Pavlov, Piaget, Lewin, and Freud.

## Organization

Over the decades, a relatively uniform way of dividing up and arranging topics has emerged and taken hold in introductory psychology. For the most part, I have followed that standard organization: It is comfortable; it fits reasonably well with the ways that research psychologists divide up the discipline; and it makes considerable logical sense. My slight departures reflect three important developments in contemporary psychology: (1) Knowledge of heredity and evolution is increasingly recognized to be important as a background for thinking about basic psychological processes. (2) Developments in the study of basic learning processes (which has always been conducted largely with nonhuman animals) link that field more closely than ever to an evolutionary perspective. (3) Developments in cognitive psychology link its attempts to understand the components of the mind more meaningfully than in the past to the more traditional psychometric approach to the human intellect.

The book is divided into seven units, or parts, each of which consists of two or three chapters.

Part 1, *Background to the Study of Psychology*, has two relatively brief chapters. The first, on the history and scope of psychology, shows how some of psychology's most basic ideas and ways of conducting research have developed over time; and the second, on methods, lays out some general elements of psychological research that will be useful to students in later chapters. (If you prefer a more thorough discussion of statistics than Chapter 2 contains, you may wish to supplement it with the first three sections of the Statistical Appendix.)

Part 2, *Nature, Nurture, and Behavioral Adaptation*, is devoted explicitly to two fundamental themes that reappear frequently in the book: (1) Behavioral mechanisms are formed through an interplay between genetic inheritance (nature) and environmental experience (nurture); and (2) behavior can be understood as adaptation to the environment, which occurs at two levels—the phylogenetic level (through natural selection) and the individual level (through learning). These themes are developed in three chapters. The first is on behavioral genetics; after laying out the fundamentals of the nature-nurture issue and the behavioral genetic approach, this chapter explores research on the heritability of intelligence and schizophrenia as well as various single-gene traits. The second chapter, on the evolution of behavior, includes the idea that even behaviors that are most highly prepared by evolution must develop, in the individual, through interaction with the environment. The third chapter, on basic processes of learning, includes the idea that learning mechanisms themselves are products of evolution.

Part 3, *Physiological Mechanisms of Behavior*, is a three-chapter discussion of the attempt to explain behavior in terms of the neural and hormonal mechanisms that produce it. The first chapter is a functional introduction to the nervous system and to the actions of hormones and drugs. The second is about basic mechanisms of motivation and arousal; here the ideas about the nervous system and hormones developed in the previous chapter are applied to the topics of hunger, sex, reward mechanisms, sleep, and emotionality. The third chapter is on sensory mechanisms, focusing mainly on hearing, vision, and pain. Although this unit emphasizes physiological mechanisms, it is not exclusively physiological. For example, the discussions of motives and emotions pay ample attention to the role of environmental influences, and the discussion of sensation includes psychophysical methods and findings.

The sensation chapter at the end of Part 3 flows logically into the perception chapter at the beginning of Part 4, *Cognitive Mechanisms of Behavior*. Like the physiological approach, the cognitive approach attempts to explain behavior in terms of inner mechanisms; but it is concerned with mechanisms that are too complex to understand physiologically, and are therefore discussed in the metaphorical terms of information-processing models. The second chapter of this unit is on memory, the core topic of cognitive psychology, and the third is entitled *The Human Intellect*. This somewhat unusual chapter deals with three topics that are becoming ever more closely associated in contemporary psychology: (1) the structure of human intelligence, (2) the cognitive components of problem solving, and (3) the cognitive components of language ability and the relation of language to thought. Throughout these chapters, the information-processing approach is highlighted but is tempered by ecological discussions that draw attention to the functions of each mental process and the environmental contexts within which they occur.

In sum, Parts 2, 3, and 4 are all concerned with basic psychological processes, and each part deals with those processes from a different explanatory perspective. Part 2 takes a functionalist, or adaptationist, perspective; Part 3 takes a physiological perspective; and Part 4 takes an information-processing perspective. This arrangement allows me to develop coherent arguments and to avoid the confusion that often comes when very different modes of explanation are mixed together. The remaining three parts are concerned with understanding the whole person and the person's relationships to the social environment.

Part 5, *Growth of the Mind and Person*, is a two-chapter unit on developmental psychology. The first chapter, on cognitive development, deals with the same large processes—thought and language—as did the last chapter of Part 4, but now from a developmental perspective. A major goal here is to show how the adult mind can be understood by identifying and describing the steps through which it is built in the developing child. The second chapter, on social development, is concerned with the changes in social relationships and life tasks that occur through the life span. This chapter also sets the stage for the next pair of chapters.

Part 6, *The Person in a World of People*, is a two-chapter unit on social psychology. The first chapter, on social cognition, is concerned with the mental processes involved in forming judgments of other people, perceiving and presenting the self in the social environment, and forming and modifying attitudes. The second chapter, on social influence, deals with compliance, obedience, conformity, group decision-making, and intergroup conflict. A theme running through this chapter is that of contrasting the normative and informational influences that stem from observing other people's behavior. The unit on social psychology is placed before the one on personality and mental disorders because the insights of social psychology—especially those pertaining to social cognition—are increasingly becoming incorporated into personality theories and approaches to understanding and treating mental disorders.

Part 7, *Personality and Disorders*, consists of three chapters on topics that students most strongly identify as "psychology" before they enter the course. The first chapter, on personality theories, focuses on the main explanatory concepts and lines of evidence underlying (a) Freud's theory, (b) post-Freudian psychodynamic theories, (c) humanistic theories, (d) social learning theories, and (e) trait theories of the person. The second chapter, on mental disorders, begins by discussing the problems involved in categorizing and diagnosing disorders, and then, through the discussion of specific disorders, emphasizes the notion of multiple causation and the theme that the symptoms characterizing disorders are different in degree, not in kind, from normal psychological experiences and processes. The final chapter, on treatment, offers an opportunity to recapitulate many of the main ideas of earlier chapters—now in the context of their application to therapy. Ideas from Parts 2, 3, 4, and 6 reappear in the discussions of biological, behavioral, and cognitive therapies, and ideas from the personality chapter reappear in the discussions of psychodynamic and humanistic therapies.

Although this ordering of topics makes the most sense to me, I recognize that other sensible arrangements exist and that time limits may prevent you from using the entire book. Therefore, each chapter is written so that it can be read as a separate entity, independent of others. Links are often made to material presented in another chapter, but most of these are spelled out in enough detail to be understood by students who have not read the other chapter. The only major exception falls in the physiological unit: Chapters 7 and 8, on motivation and sensation, assume that the student has learned some of the basic information presented in Chapter 6, on the nervous system.

## Features

The main pedagogical feature of this or any other textbook is, of course, the narrative itself, which should be clear, logical, and interesting. Everything else is secondary. I have avoided the boxes and inserts that are often found in introductory psychology texts, because such digressions add to the impression that psychology is a jumble of things that don't fit together very well. I have aimed, to the degree that the field allows it, to produce a logical flow of ideas.

One nondisruptive feature I have included is *margin notes*, each of which calls attention to the main idea, line of argument, or evidence addressed in the adjacent paragraphs of text. Each note contains an implicit question; to make the question clear, most of the notes begin with the words *How, Why, The difference between*, or *Evidence that*. As described in the *To the Student* section, these notes are designed both to promote active, focused reading and to provide a guide for review. To review, the students need only re-read the margin notes and study again the accompanying text in those places where he or she cannot answer a note's implied question. I owe the idea to my son, Scott, who found that his understanding of a book of philosophical dialogues was enhanced by similar notes that helped him to keep track of the developing arguments.

Because the margin notes make a traditional end-of-chapter review unnecessary, I am able to conclude each chapter with a section called *Concluding Thoughts*. This section expands on the broad themes of the chapter, points out relationships to ideas discussed in other chapters, and sometimes even offers a new idea or two for students to consider as they reflect on the chapter. *Concluding Thoughts* is followed by a brief section called *Further Reading*, which contains thumbnail reviews of several relevant and interesting books that are sufficiently nontechnical to be read by the first-year student. At the very end of each chapter, a tiny section called *Looking Ahead* is designed to entice the reader into the next chapter and to show its relationship to the chapter just read.

## Supplements

An excellent study guide called *Focus on Psychology* has been prepared to accompany this text. Its author, Mary Trahan, is a cognitive psychologist at Randolph-Macon College who has a special interest in applying the insights of her field to the teaching of psychology. Trahan's guide is designed to be used in parallel with the reading of each textbook chapter, helping students to focus their attention on and think about its main ideas. Students who have pretested the guide have praised it highly.

For instructors, a very useful *Instructor's Resource Manual* has been prepared by Timothy M. Osberg, a specialist in developmental and clinical psychology, and Burt Thompson, a specialist in perception and learning, both at Niagara University. For each chapter, Osberg and Thompson describe interesting class demonstrations and activities, with handouts, for class participation; provide writing exercises to test students' mastery of concepts; suggest ways to elaborate on some of the textbook's key ideas; and recommend relevant films and videos, including modules from The Brain and The Mind series. They also suggest appropriate programs from *PsychSim II: Computer Simulations in Psychology*, the award-winning software with accompanying student worksheets, developed by Thomas Ludwig at Hope College. I have also contributed an introductory chapter to the manual, offering some general thoughts about teaching introductory psychology and using this text. An extensive set of transparencies, available on request, has been made from charts, graphs, and illustrations from the textbook and other sources. Also available is a carefully developed *Test Bank* of multiple-choice and essay questions, prepared by Mary Trahan and Norman Simonson, a clinical psychologist at the University of Massachusetts, Amherst.

## Acknowledgments

Nobody writes a textbook alone. Hundreds of people have contributed to the development of this one, of whom I can list only a few here.

Herbert Terrace's inspiring introductory psychology course at Columbia University enticed me, at age 18, to turn away from a planned career in physics toward one in psychology. In graduate school at Rockefeller University, I was inspired and taught by Neal Miller, Jay Weiss, Bruce McEwen, William Estes, Peter Marler, and many others. My outlook has also been strongly influenced by my colleagues at Boston College, some of whom have contributed in very direct ways to the development of this book. They include (in alphabetical order) Greg Ball, Ali Banuazizi, Norm Berkowitz, Hiram Brownell, Donnah Canavan, Randy Easton, Marc Fried, Murray Horwitz, Marianne LaFrance, Ramsay Liem, Michael Moore, Gilda Morelli, Michael Numan, Bill Ryan, Karen Schneider-Rosen, Jeanne Sholl, Joe Tecce, and Ellen Winner. Of these, I owe special thanks to my friend Michael Moore, who worked closely with me on early drafts of the cognitive and developmental units, and who carefully read and brilliantly critiqued early drafts of the other units.

Another group who deserve special thanks, but are too numerous to name, are the hundreds of students in my sections of Introductory Psychology, who read chapter drafts as part of their course assignments, and whose feedback was invaluable in my writing of final drafts. I also thank Jane Manwaring, Dawn Derienzo, and Bianca Dinapoli for their help in the preparation of materials. I thank, too, my friends Daniel and Hanna Greenberg, educational innovators and philosophers who have contributed greatly to my own thinking in both psychology and education. And, more than anyone else, I thank my wife, Anita, and my son, Scott, who have put up with me through all this and have contributed immeasurably to my growth and to the development of the ideas in this book. It is dedicated to them.

How can I appropriately thank Phyllis Fisher, my wonderfully demanding and intellectually inspiring developmental editor? Our working arrangement has been one of continuous dialogue and debate. In the process, Phyllis has taught me not only to be a better writer, but also a better thinker and psychologist than I was before we met. She shared all of my initial goals and insisted that I stick with them, but she also led me to adopt some new goals. For example, she made me far more sensitive than I had previously been to issues pertaining to gender and culture, and this sensitivity has become an important part of the book.

As part of her task, Phyllis coordinated the process by which experts in each area of psychology and notably successful teachers of the introductory course reviewed each draft of the text. I was greatly impressed by the seriousness with which the reviewers approached this task; they taught me a great deal, and each one influenced the final outcome. A reviewer whose wise, gentle suasions were especially valuable is Peter Platenius, of Queen's University, Ontario. For their thoughtful, sometimes challenging, and always helpful reviews, I thank:

George W. Albee, *University of Vermont*
Lewis M. Barker, *Baylor University*
John B. Best, *Eastern Illinois University*
Sharon Brehm, *State University of New York, Binghamton*
Nathan Brody, *Wesleyan University*
Michael F. Brown, *Villanova University*
Robert B. Cialdini, *Arizona State University*
Stanley Coren, *University of British Columbia*
Katherine Covell, *Brock University*
Martin Daly, *McMaster University*
Richard B. Day, *McMaster University*
V. J. DeGhett, *State University of New York, Potsdam*
Timothy J. DeVoogd, *Cornell University*
Donald D. Dorfman, *University of Iowa*
David C. Edwards, *Iowa State University*
Gilles O. Einstein, *Furman University*
Nancy Eisenberg, *Arizona State University*
Owen R. Floody, *Bucknell University*
Janet J. Fritz, *Colorado State University*
Mary Gauvain, *Scripps College*
Don J. Gawley, *AT&T Bell Laboratories*
Daniel Gilbert, *University of Texas, Austin*

G. P. Ginsburg, *University of Nevada, Reno*
W. Larry Gregory, *New Mexico State University, Las Cruces*
Ed Hass
Benjamin Harris, *University of Wisconsin, Parkside*
Bryan Hendricks, *University of Wisconsin, Marathon Center*
Stephen P. Hinshaw, *University of California, Berkeley*
Jill M. Hooley, *Harvard University*
Valerye A. Hunt, *Fraser Valley College*
John C. Jahnke, *Miami University of Ohio*
Sybillyn Jennings, *Russell Sage College*
Saul M. Kassin, *Williams College*
Terry J. Knapp, *University of Nevada, Las Vegas*
Mary F. Lombard, *Regis College*
Alan Marks, *Berry College*
Donald H. McBurney, *University of Pittsburgh*
David B. Miller, *University of Connecticut, Storrs*
Douglas Mook, *University of Virginia*
Greg Moran, *University of Western Ontario*

Daniel D. Moriarty, Jr., *University of San Diego*
Harry G. Murray, *University of Western Ontario*
Lynn M. Musser, *Purdue University*
John B. Nezlek, *College of William and Mary*
Julie K. Norem, *Northeastern University*
Tibor Palfai, *Syracuse University*
Peter Platenius, *Queen's University*
Dennis R. Proffitt, *University of Virginia*
Leon Rappoport, *Kansas State University*
Marc Riess, *Middlebury College*
Joseph F. Rychlak, *Loyola University of Chicago*
Neil J. Salkind, *University of Kansas*
Steven M. Smith, *Texas A & M University*
Kathryn T. Spoehr, *Brown University*
James R. Stellar, *Northeastern University*
Ross Thompson, *University of Nebraska, Lincoln*
Mary Trahan, *Randolph-Macon College*
Eric Turkheimer, *University of Virginia*
Jonathan Vaughan, *Hamilton College*
W. Scott Wood, *Drake University*
Murray S. Work, *California State University, Sacramento*

Many people at Worth Publishers in addition to Phyllis Fisher deserve my heartfelt thanks. These include Anne Vinnicombe, whose energy, commitment, and intelligence in supervising all aspects of this project made the book a reality; and Karen Landovitz, whose thoughtful, careful work improved the text immensely as she turned it from manuscript to final film in her role as production editor. Thanks also to Patricia Lawson for page layout, Barbara Anne Seixas, production supervisor, and the many others who helped make this book a work of art.

*Framingham, Massachusetts*
*January 1991*

Peter Gray

# To the student

Welcome to your psychology textbook. I hope you will enjoy it. It is about a question that, to me, is one of the most fascinating anyone can ask: What makes people feel, think, and behave the way they do? That, really, is what psychology is about. In this book you will read, in different units, about different approaches to answering that big question; and you will discover dozens of specific findings and ideas that help to answer it.

I hope that as you read this book you will allow yourself to become intrigued by psychology; that you will not focus too narrowly on getting a good grade; that you will think about, challenge, and discuss with others the book's ideas; and that you will keep constantly in mind that ideas in psychology come from people who are basically no different from you—so your own insights, questions, and thoughts are legitimate. Psychology is a science, and the essence of science is this: We do not accept anything on authority. It doesn't matter *who* says that something is or isn't true; what matters is the *evidence*—the facts and logic upon which the ideas are based, which are open for evaluation by any thinking person. In this book I have tried to present both the main ideas in psychology and some of the evidence. Each page is offered for your consideration, not for your unquestioning acceptance.

You may find it useful to know about some of this book's special features before you begin your study. Perhaps the most useful of these is the *margin notes*, which occur at a rate of about one per page of text. Each note points out the main issue or argument in the paragraph or paragraphs that follow it. For example, if you turn to page 3, you will find that the book's first margin note reads as follows: ■ *A succinct definition of psychology and three ways of expanding on it.* That note tells you exactly what the following paragraphs are about. If you read it first, before reading the paragraphs, it will help you to focus your attention; you will read with the goal of discovering how psychology is defined and three ways in which that definition can be expanded. As you continue on through the book, you will find that these notes serve not only to help you to read actively—for the explicit purpose of answering their implied questions—but also to review. When you have completed a section of the chapter, go back and re-read the margin notes. If you can answer the implied question in each note, you have understood what you have read; if you cannot, you should probably read the relevant paragraphs again.

I would also like to draw your attention to the *numbered figures* in each chapter. In some cases a figure will help you understand a point that would be difficult from the text alone, and in other cases it will provide you with information that supplements or complements what is in the text. Whenever the text says, "see Figure _____," take a few moments to study that figure and read the caption. Many of the figures are graphs, with data that back up an idea described in the text. If you have not had much experience reading graphs, please do not feel embarrassed about mentioning that to your instructor. He or she might then present some sample graphs in class and explain how to read them.

Another feature is the use of **bold italics** to highlight important terms. I suggest that you *not* devote much effort, on your first reading, to learning term definitions. Rather, read with the aim of understanding and thinking about the main *ideas* and the lines of evidence supporting or refuting them. In that process you will learn many of the terms, in the context of the ideas, without explicitly trying to learn them. The bold italics may be useful, however, in your later review. As you are reviewing the margin notes, look also for each of the bold italics terms and check your knowledge of its meaning. These terms are also defined in the *glossary* at the back of the book. If an important term has been defined in an earlier chapter, it is sometimes, but not always, defined again when it reappears. If it is not defined, you can use the glossary to find both the term's definition and the number of the page on which it was first used.

A feature that this book shares with other books and articles in psychology is the use of *reference citations*, which can be found in the narrative on nearly every page. Each citation consists of the name of one or more researchers followed by a year. Sometimes both the name (or names) and the year are in parentheses, such as *(Jones & Smith, 1984)*, and other times, when the name or names are part of the sentence, only the year is in parentheses, such as *According to Alice Jones (1987)*. . . . In either case, the year refers to the year of publication of an article or book, by the person or persons named, which describes more fully the idea or the research study being mentioned or discussed. The full reference to that article or book can be found in the *References* section at the back of the textbook. At first you may find these citations disruptive to the flow of your reading, but you will soon learn to read right through them. Their purpose is to give credit to the people whose work or ideas are being described and to give you the opportunity to look up, and read more about, any ideas or research findings that intrigue you. In addition, at the end of each chapter, in a section called *Further Reading*, you will find brief reviews of several interesting books that you might use to supplement your study of specific areas of psychology.

An excellent study guide, called *Focus on Psychology*, has been written by Mary Trahan to accompany this textbook. The study guide will help you learn and remember the main ideas as you read each chapter of the textbook. It also contains practice tests you can use to determine your mastery of the material.

Finally, I suggest that you turn to page 336, where, in the context of a general discussion of research on memory, you will find some ideas about reading any textbook that will help you to remember its contents.

And now—let's discuss psychology.

*Peter Gray*

# PART 1   BACKGROUND TO THE STUDY OF PSYCHOLOGY

## THE HISTORY AND SCOPE OF PSYCHOLOGY

## METHODS OF PSYCHOLOGY

*You and I stand at a moment in time that is preceded by Aristotle, Descartes, Freud, and millions less known. Psychology, today, is the accumulated and sifted ideas of all people before us and with us who have attempted to fathom the mysteries of the human mind. It is also, by its own definition, a science, using methods that are as objective as the subject matter will allow. In this background unit, we examine the history and methods of psychology.*

# CHAPTER 1

Before Psychology: Preparing the
Intellectual Ground

The Evolution of Psychology:
A History of Alternative Perspectives

The Scope of Psychology Today

# THE HISTORY AND SCOPE OF PSYCHOLOGY

*A succinct definition of psychology, and three ways of expanding it*

The human being, as far as any human being can tell, is the only creature that contemplates itself. We are the only creature that not only thinks, feels, dreams, and acts, but wonders why and how we do these things. Such contemplation has taken many forms, ranging from just plain wondering, to folk tales and popular songs, to poetry and literature, to formal theologies and philosophies. Most recently—extending back a little more than a century—human self-contemplation has taken a scientific turn, and we call that science *psychology*.

**Psychology** is the science of behavior and the mind. **Behavior**, in this definition, refers to the observable actions of an individual person or animal. **Mind** refers to an individual's sensations, perceptions, memories, thoughts, dreams, motives, emotional feelings, and other subjective experiences. The other important term, **science**, can be defined as an approach to answering questions that is based on the systematic collection and logical analysis of objectively observable data. The data in psychology are about an individual's behavior—and not about one's mind—because behavior is objectively observable, but psychologists often use these data to make inferences about the mind. Most psychologists study human behavior, but some study the behavior of other animals, either to learn about animal behavior for its own sake or to learn about basic processes and mechanisms that are shared by other animals and humans.

Extending the simple definition just presented, there are many ways to characterize psychology. Here are three of them:

1. *Psychology is a set of questions*. Psychology is the set of all questions about behavior and mind that are potentially answerable through scientific means. Some of the questions are very broad, with answers that are necessarily complex, qualified, or tentative: What is the nature of human intelligence? How are memories stored and retrieved? In what ways are people influenced by their perceptions of what other people think of them? Other questions are narrower, with more specific or definite answers: Why does a mixture of blue light and yellow light look white to people? What parts of the brain are most directly involved in the ability to understand and produce language? At what age do children begin to fear strangers?

2. *Psychology is a set of procedures for answering questions*. Psychology, like any science, contains a body of theoretical perspectives, methods, and tools that guide and aid psychologists in answering questions about behavior and mind.

3. *Psychology is a product of history*. Like any other organized human endeavor, psychology is what it is today because of a historical evolution. Viewed this way, psychology is the set of questions, methods, perspectives, and tentative answers that have been passed on and modified through successive generations. To understand psychology today it is necessary to know something of that history.

This chapter is about the history of psychology, and is an important foundation for the chapters that follow. In reading the history, don't think of it simply as a record of the past, but as an explanation of the present. Your goal is to understand psychology today, but that goal is unachievable without some knowledge of its history.

Before a science of psychology could come to pass, human beings had to conceive of and accept the idea that questions about human behavior and the mind can in theory be answered scientifically. This idea had become well established in intellectual centers in Europe and North America by the last half of the nineteenth century, which is when psychology was founded as a formally recognized scientific endeavor. Then came an evolutionary period in which various competing schools of thought arose, each offering a new view as to just what subject matter and methods were appropriate to this new science. As in most intellectual disagreements, there was a degree of truth on every side, and psychology today can be understood as a synthesis of what had seemed to be contradictory ideas in the earlier turmoil of its development. In what follows we will look first at some of the thought and research that led to the founding of psychology, and then at some of the conflicting schools that emerged and led to what psychology is today. The chapter ends with a brief section that outlines the domain of psychology today, as a research area and as a profession.

## Before Psychology: Preparing the Intellectual Ground

Psychology arose in the nineteenth century out of developments in philosophy, physiology, and evolutionary biology that paved the way toward acceptance of the idea that it is possible to study the human mind and behavior scientifically.

### Philosophical Developments: From Spirit to Machine

**Figure 1.1** *René Descartes*

*Descartes's speculations, in the seventeenth century, about reflexes and the interaction of the body and soul in controlling voluntary behavior were an important step in the direction of a scientific analysis of human behavior.*

For the philosophical roots of psychology one could easily go back to the ancient Greeks, who speculated about the senses, the human intellect, and the physical basis of the mind in ways that often seem remarkably modern. But such ideas became dormant in the Middle Ages and did not begin to sprout again until about the fifteenth century (the Renaissance) or to take firm hold until the eighteenth century (the Enlightenment). A key thinker in the transition between prescientific and scientific views of the human being was the French mathematician and philosopher René Descartes (1596–1650). As a mathematician Descartes developed what is still studied today as Cartesian geometry, and as a philosopher he speculated about human behavior and the mind.

Descartes's theory of human behavior is called *dualism*, because he proposed that two distinctly different systems are involved in the control of behavior—the body and the soul. The body is a purely physical "machine," which operates according to natural laws and can be understood through the means of science. The soul, on the other hand, is a spiritual entity, characterized by free will rather than obedience to natural laws, and it cannot be understood through the means of science. Descartes's theory is also called *interactionism*, because he maintained that the body and the soul, though distinct, interact with one another. The soul takes into account information received from the body in making its free decisions, and it acts upon the body in ways that result in muscle movements, thereby adding the element of free will to human action.

Descartes was by no means the first dualist. The aspect of his theory that was radical in his time was the great emphasis he placed on the role of the body. He held that a great deal of human behavior occurs purely mechanically, through

■ *How Descartes's version of dualism helped pave the way for the scientific study of behavior*

**Figure 1.2 *Descartes's depiction of the reflexive withdrawal response***

*Descartes believed that reflexes occur through purely mechanical means. In describing this figure, Descartes (1637/1972) suggested that the fire causes movement in the nearby particles of skin, pulling on a "thread" (marked cc) going to the brain, which in turn causes a pore to open in the brain, allowing fluid to flow through a "small conduit" to the muscles that withdraw the foot. What Descartes called a "thread" and a "small conduit" are today called nerves, and we now know that nerves operate through electrical means, not through physical pulling or the shunting of fluids.*

bodily processes that don't involve the soul at all. In his *Treatise of Man*, Descartes (1637/1972) presented detailed descriptions of the machinery of the body to show how behavior might be controlled mechanically. Although little was known about the nervous system in his time, Descartes's basic idea about the mechanical control of movement bears some similarity to our modern understanding of reflexes, which are involuntary responses to stimuli (see Figure 1.2).

In Descartes's view the essential things that humans can do that other animals cannot are to think and to use thoughts to guide their actions. Thinking, according to Descartes, is a function of the soul, which he believed to reside in a small organ buried between the two hemispheres (halves) of the brain (see Figure 1.3). Nerves bring sensory information by physical means into the brain, where the soul receives the information and, by nonphysical means, thinks about that information. On the basis of those thoughts, the soul then wills movements to occur and executes its will by initiating physical activity in nerves that in turn act upon muscles.

Descartes's theory is appealing to many people even today, because it takes into account the roles of sense organs, nerves, and muscles in behavior, and at the same time it does not violate people's intuitive feeling that at least some of their behavior results from their freely made decisions. But the theory has serious limitations, both as a philosophy and as a foundation for a science of psychology. As a philosophy it stumbles on the question of how a nonmaterial entity (the soul) can have a material effect (move the body), or how the body can follow natural laws and at the same time be moved by a soul that does not follow natural laws (Campbell, 1970). As a foundation for psychology it sets strict limits, which few psychologists would accept today, on what can and cannot be understood scientifically. The whole realm of thought, and all behaviors that are guided by thought, are out of bounds for scientific analysis if they are the product of a willful soul.

■ *Why Descartes's theory, though intuitively appealing, is unsuitable as a foundation for a complete psychology*

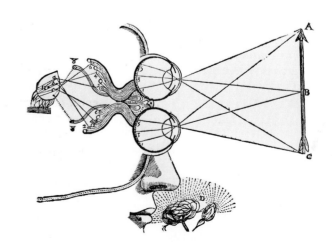

**Figure 1.3 *Descartes's depiction of how the soul receives information through the eyes***

*Descartes believed that the human soul is housed in the pineal gland, depicted here as the tear-shaped structure in the center of the head. In describing this figure, Descartes (1637/1972) suggested that light from the arrow enters the eyes and opens pores in structures that we now know as the optic nerves. Once opened, fluid flows from the eyes through the pores, causing movement in the pineal gland, which, in Descartes's terms, "renders the idea" of the arrow to the soul.*

At about the same time that Descartes was developing his interactionist theory of dualism, an English philosopher named Thomas Hobbes (1588–1679) was going much further. Hobbes argued that spirit, or soul, is a meaningless concept and that nothing exists but matter and energy, a philosophy known as ***materialism***. In Hobbes's view, all human behavior, including the seemingly voluntary choices that we make, can in theory be understood in terms of physical processes in the body, especially the brain. Conscious thought itself, he argued, is purely a product of the brain's machinery. Most of Hobbes's work was directed toward the implications of materialism for political science, but his ideas helped initiate a school of thought about the mind known as *British empiricism*, which was carried on by such English philosophers as John Locke (1632–1704), David Hume (1711–1776), and James Mill (1773–1836).

*Empiricism*, in this context, refers to the idea that all human knowledge and thought ultimately comes from sensory experience (vision, hearing, touch, and so forth). The British empiricists' central idea was that the human mind consists of basic units, or elementary ideas (such as the idea of a chair), which stem from sensory experiences. These elementary ideas become associated (linked together) in certain ways based on the pattern of one's sensory experiences, and those links in turn provide the basis for the chaining together of ideas into the flow that we call *thought*. You will read more about empiricist philosophy in later chapters and see it contrasted with ***nativism***, the view that elementary ideas are innate to the human mind and do not need to be gained through experience. The important point for now is simply that the empiricist philosophers believed that thought is not a product of free will, but rather a reflection of one's physical experience in the physical world. From this point of view, unlike Descartes's, thought can be studied scientifically.

### Nineteenth-Century Physiology: Learning About the Machine

The nineteenth century was a time of great advance in physiology, the science of the body's machinery. One especially important development for the later emergence of psychology was an increased understanding of reflexes. The basic arrangement of the nervous system—consisting of a central nervous system (brain and spinal cord) and peripheral nerves connecting the central nervous system to sense organs and muscles—was well understood by the beginning of the century. In England in 1811, Charles Bell demonstrated that nerves entering the spinal cord contain two separate pathways, one for carrying messages into the central nervous system from the skin's sensory receptors, and one for carrying messages out to operate muscles (Hothersall, 1990). In experiments with animals, scientists began to learn about the neural connections that underlie simple reflexes, such as the withdrawal response to a pin prick, and also found brain areas that, when active, could either enhance or inhibit such reflexes.

*▪ Reflexology as an account of human behavior based on a nineteenth-century conception of the nervous system*

Some of these physiologists began to suggest that all human behavior occurs through reflexes, that even so-called voluntary actions are actually complex reflexes involving higher parts of the brain. One of the most eloquent spokespersons for this view, known as ***reflexology***, was the Russian physiologist I. M. Sechenov. In a monograph entitled *Reflexes of the Brain*, Sechenov (1863/1935) argued that every human action, "[b]e it a child laughing at the sight of toys, or . . . Newton enunciating universal laws and writing them on paper," can in theory be understood as reflexes. Whenever anyone does something, he claimed, it is because some stimulus or set of stimuli in the environment acts on the person's sensory receptors, setting into motion a chain of events in the nervous system that eventuates in the muscle movements that constitute the action. Reflexology was an important predecessor to a school of thought in psychology called *behaviorism*, about which you will read in a few pages.

■ *How discoveries of localization of function in the brain helped establish the idea that the mind can be studied scientifically*

Another important development in nineteenth-century physiology was the concept of **localization of function** in the brain—the idea that specific parts of the brain serve specific functions in the control of mental experience and behavior. In Germany, Johannes Müller (1838) published the idea that the different qualities of sensory experience come about because the nerves from different sense organs excite different parts of the brain. Thus, we experience vision when one part of the brain is active and hearing when another part is active. In France, Pierre Flourens (1824) performed experiments with animals showing that damage to different parts of the brain results in different kinds of deficits in animals' ability to move. And Paul Broca (1861), also in France, published clinical evidence showing that people who suffer damage to a very specific area of the brain's left hemisphere lose the ability to speak without losing other mental abilities. All such evidence concerning the relationships between mind and brain was important to the founding of a scientific psychology, because it gave substance to the idea of a material basis for mental processes. The discovery of localization of function also led to the idea that there may be natural divisions among various mental processes, and that the mind can be understood by identifying those basic processes and discovering how they interact. As you will see later, this is an idea that is especially important today in the psychological approach called *cognitive psychology*.

### Darwin and Evolution: A New Unity of Person and Nature

■ *How Darwin's theory of natural selection offered a scientific basis for functional explanations of behavior*

In 1859 the English naturalist Charles Darwin (1809–1882) published *The Origin of Species*, which was destined to revolutionize biology, mark a new age in philosophy, and provide, along with the developments in physiology, a scientific grounding for psychology. Darwin's most important idea was that living things have arrived at their present shape through a long evolutionary process involving natural selection, in which those individual organisms whose inherited characteristics were best adapted to their environment survived and reproduced while others died. Because of evolution, each part of any given plant or animal can be examined for its role in allowing the individual to survive and reproduce in its natural environment. To understand, for example, why one species of bird has a stout beak and another has a slender beak, one must know what foods the birds eat and how they use their beaks to obtain those foods. The same principle applies for behavior patterns as for anatomy. Through natural selection, living things have acquired innate predispositions to behave in ways that promote their survival and reproduction in their natural environment. A key word here is *function*. While the physiologists were concerned with the neural mechanisms of behavior, Darwin was concerned with the functions of behavior, that is, with the ways in which an individual's behavior functions to help the individual survive and reproduce.

**The expression of emotion**
*There is no doubt about the emotion shared by this happy pair. Research by contemporary psychologists supports Darwin's notion that expressions such as joy and sadness have an evolutionary basis. You will find a discussion of this interesting topic in Chapter 4.*

In *The Origin of Species* Darwin discussed only plants and nonhuman animals, but in later writings he made it clear that he viewed humans as no exception. Humans also evolved through natural selection, and human anatomy and behavior could be analyzed in the same terms used to analyze those of other living things. In a book entitled *The Expression of the Emotions in Man and Animals*, Darwin (1872/1965) illustrated how evolutionary thinking can contribute to a scientific understanding of human behavior. There he argued that human emotional expressions (such as laughter and crying) are predisposed by heredity, as are those of other animals, and may have evolved because of survival advantages associated with the ability to communicate one's emotions or intentions to others of one's kind. Darwin, perhaps more than anyone else, helped convince the intellectual world that human beings, despite their pretensions, are as much a part of nature as any other creature and can be understood through the methods of science. The world was ripe for psychology.

# The Evolution of Psychology: A History of Alternative Perspectives

### The Origin of Experimental Psychology

■ *The first psychologists performed laboratory experiments to identify elementary processes of sensation, memory, and judgment*

The first research psychologists were Germans who were impressed by the success of laboratory methods in physiology and wished to apply similar methods to the study of the mind. Their view was that the proper place to begin this study was with the simplest kinds of mental processes—simple sensations, memories, and judgments. If these could be understood, then the science could progress to more complex processes. Among these first psychologists were Ernst Weber (1795–1878) and Gustav Fechner (1801–1887), who founded a subfield of psychology called *psychophysics*, the study of the relationship between conscious sensory experiences and the physical stimuli that produce the experiences. As you will see in Chapter 8, they were interested in such issues as the degree to which two physical stimuli (such as two sounds) must differ before a person can tell them apart, and they expressed their answers to such questions in mathematical terms. Another was Hermann Ebbinghaus (1850–1909), who hoped to find simple laws of memory. Using himself as his only subject, Ebbinghaus performed dozens of experiments in which he would memorize lists of nonsense syllables and test himself at various times afterwards to see how many he could still recall. You will read more about his work in Chapter 10. But the German who is most often credited as the founder of our science was Wilhelm Wundt (1832–1920).

In 1879, Wundt opened a laboratory of experimental psychology at the University of Leipzig; that event is commonly used to mark psychology's official birth. Wundt and other Germans had been conducting psychological experiments for about two decades prior to that date, but the Leipzig laboratory was important because it represented the official acceptance of this new science by a respected university (Blumenthal, 1985). The first official graduate students of psychology were Wundt's students.

**Figure 1.4  *Wilhelm Wundt***
*Wundt's opening of a laboratory of experimental psychology at the University of Leipzig in 1879 is often taken to mark the birth of psychology as a science.*

Before starting his psychological research, Wundt had worked as an assistant to the eminent physiologist Hermann von Helmholtz on projects such as measuring the speed of neural impulses. An important insight that Wundt took from such work was that mental processes, as products of the nervous system, do not occur instantaneously but rather take time. One of his aims in psychology was to measure the speed of simple mental processes. The fastest-occurring processes would be the most elementary, the "atoms of the mind." After identifying these he could begin to test hypotheses about how these elements combine to form more complex mental processes.

■ *How Wundt measured the speed of simple mental processes*

One of Wundt's methods was to test people in two reaction-time tasks, one slightly more complex than the other, and to subtract the shorter time from the longer to determine the time required for the mental step or steps that differentiated the two tasks. Thus, in one experiment (see Kendler, 1987), the simple task was to release a telegraph key (which looks like a large typewriter key) as quickly as possible when a light came on. This took an average of 0.20 second. In the more complex task, the person was to release a telegraph key, held down by the left hand, if the light was red, and a different key, held down by the right hand, if the light was green. The average reaction time for this was 0.29 second. Subtracting the former from the latter, Wundt determined that the time needed to categorize the color and decide which key to release was 0.09 second. By comparing this with times for other kinds of judgments, Wundt could rank different judgments in terms of their simplicity, where simplicity was defined as the quickness with which they could be performed. The idea that complex mental processes can be understood as sequences of more elementary processes and the use of reaction time to measure the latter are still important today in cognitive psychology.

**Figure 1.5  Edward Titchener**
*A student of Wundt's, Titchener was one of
the first psychologists in North America. He
coined the term* structuralism *to refer to his
approach to learning about the structure of
the mind, through introspective analysis of
its parts.*

■ *Why Titchener's introspective
approach to the structure of the
mind failed as a scientific method*

### Early Structuralism

Following psychology's founding, alternative schools of thought arose as to how
the mind could best be characterized and studied. The school that descended
most directly from Wundt's approach is called *structuralism*, a term coined not
by Wundt but by one of his students, Edward Titchener (1867–1927). Titchener,
an Englishman educated at Oxford, went to Leipzig to earn a Ph.D. degree in
psychology under Wundt and then moved to the United States to head the newly
established department of psychology at Cornell University. It was at Cornell that
he began to refer to his approach as *structuralism*. Like Wundt, Titchener believed that the proper goal of psychology is to identify the basic elements of the
mind and to determine how they combine with one another. Titchener's aim was
to learn about the *structure* of the mind through analyzing elementary conscious
experiences, which he considered to be the mind's building blocks.

Although Titchener was influenced by Wundt, he was no carbon copy. He
was also heavily influenced by British empiricist thought, and this led him to believe, unlike Wundt, that all of the basic elements of the mind could be tied directly to sensory experience. Thus, Titchener's goal was to identify the most elementary sensory experiences. His prime method was *introspection*, a method that
Wundt had occasionally used but had more often opposed as unscientific (Blumenthal, 1985). *To introspect* literally means *to look inward* to examine one's own
conscious experience. Titchener believed that through careful training people
could learn to introspect objectively and scientifically. He and his students would
listen to simple sounds or look at simple sights and try to separate their experience of the sound or sight into its basic elements. Through such work, Titchener
concluded that every sensation has four basic dimensions: quality, intensity, duration, and clarity (Kendler, 1987). Thus, he might describe the sensation produced
by a particular flash of light as blue, strong, brief, and clear.

Although many psychologists today admire Titchener's goal of understanding
the elements of the mind, there is universal agreement that his method failed.
Wundt had been right in warning about the limitations of introspection. Suppose
that you, a student of Titchener's, look into your mind while gazing at a flash of
light and decide that the sensation it produces has four elemental qualities, and
that I, trained in introspection by another master, look into my mind while gazing
at the same flash and decide that there are only three. To you, the clarity and intensity of the patch are two separate elements, but I claim they are one. How can
we resolve our disagreement? Whose introspection is best? Are we just using
words differently, or do our two minds really differ in some fundamental way? I
can't look into your mind to see what you see when you look at the flash, and you
can't look into mine. The basic problem is that introspection is a private technique, and science requires public techniques. A public technique is one that produces data that are available to an outside observer, not just to the individual user
of the technique.

### Early Functionalism

A contemporary of Titchener's in American psychology was William James
(1842–1910), who held professorships at Harvard in both philosophy and psychology (the latter beginning in 1889). James is famous as a great thinker, writer, and
teacher who helped make psychology known and who established some of its
philosophical foundations. He had a small laboratory at Harvard, primarily for
teaching purposes, but was not by nature a laboratory scientist. In describing the
work of the German experimentalists, James (1890/1950) wrote, only half in jest,
"This method taxes patience to the utmost, and could hardly have arisen in a
country whose natives could be *bored*." More important, James opposed Wundt's

and Titchener's view that the structure of the mind can be understood by analyzing its elementary parts. In one article, he compared their approach to that of a person attempting to understand a house by analyzing the content of each of its bricks (James, 1884). James argued that to understand a house or a mind one must first ask what it is for, and then must look at the whole thing and its larger parts to see how it fulfills its purposes. Because of his emphasis on the purposes and functions of the mind, James's psychological approach is called *functionalism*.

■ *James's functionalism, and why it demands that one look at consciousness and behavior broadly rather than at their parts*

While the structuralists were most influenced by physiology, which attempted to understand the elementary machinery of behavior, James and other functionalists were most influenced by Darwin, who had shown that it is possible to explain behavior in terms of its purposes without analyzing the elementary mechanisms through which it occurs. To James, purposes or goals are the most important aspects of human consciousness and actions, which must be understood broadly and cannot be characterized as products of more elementary conscious experiences. To illustrate this perspective, in the first chapter of his classic textbook *The Principles of Psychology*, James (1890/1950) contrasted Romeo and Juliet's attraction to each other with that between iron filings and a magnet:

> Romeo wants Juliet as the filings want the magnet; and if no obstacles intervene he moves toward her by as straight a line as they. But Romeo and Juliet, if a wall be built between them, do not remain idiotically pressing their faces against the opposite sides like the magnet and the filings with the card. Romeo soon finds a circuitous way, by scaling the wall or otherwise, of touching Juliet's lips directly. With the filings the path is fixed; whether it reaches the end depends on accidents. With the lover it is the end which is fixed, the path may be modified indefinitely.

**Figure 1.6  William James**

*A contemporary of Titchener's in North American psychology, James is considered to be the founder of the school of philosophical and psychological thought called* functionalism. *He believed that the main objective of psychology should be to understand the mind's functions, not its structures.*

James was eclectic in his views about methods. He respected the experimental method, but his own contributions were more philosophical. He relied heavily on introspection, but used it more loosely and broadly than did Titchener, as a source of ideas rather than proof, and made no claim that he was being rigorously scientific. To develop a theory about emotions he looked into his own mind while in various emotional states and described what he was feeling; and to get ideas about the concept of the self (what people mean when they say *I* or *me*) he thought about the various meanings this concept had to him and the functions it served in his daily life. You will read more about James's view of emotions in Chapter 7 and his view of the self-concept in Chapter 14.

James's functionalism did not lead to a lasting, unified school of thought in psychology, partly because it was based so heavily on introspection, but it provided a core of ideas that have since been pursued by others who used more rigorous means. One of the many students inspired by James was Edward Thorndike (1874–1949), who studied under James for a while at Harvard and then went to Columbia University for a Ph.D. and a long career as a professor of educational psychology. Thorndike was one of the first psychologists to perform systematic experiments on the learning process, with both animals and humans. As you will see in Chapter 5, his main contribution was to develop an explicitly functionalist theory of learning, describing the learning process in terms of its value to the learner.

### Gestalt Psychology

■ *How a perceptual effect, the phi phenomenon, helped promote Gestalt psychology as an alternative to structuralism*

In 1912, two years after James's death, a German psychologist named Max Wertheimer (1880–1943) published an article on a perceptual effect that he labeled the *phi phenomenon*. The phenomenon can be described as follows: Take a single light and blink it at a certain rapid rate (about 20 times per second) against a dark background. What you see (no surprise) is a single blinking light. Now add a second light, near the first, and blink it at the same rate but in alternation with the first, so that when the first is on the second is off and vice versa. The sensory

*Art and perceptual experience*

*Long before Gestalt psychologists considered the question of part-whole relationships, artists were exploring this and other perceptual experiences. In his painting* The Garden, *Giuseppe Arcimboldo (1527–1593) takes advantage of the viewer's tendency to look at the whole. For a clearer impression of the parts, turn the book upside down.*

result is not what you would expect if you consider the two lights separately. You do *not* see two blinking, stationary lights, but rather a single, unblinking light moving rapidly back and forth. In his paper on this phenomenon, Wertheimer (1912) pointed out that it violates the atomistic view of perception favored by Wundt and Titchener. The two blinking lights together produce in the observer a sensory experience of movement that does not exist in the physical lights themselves or in the sensory experience that either light produces alone. The movement can be understood only as a sensory product of the whole complex stimulus—both blinking lights together.

Based on this and other studies that followed, Wertheimer and a group of other Germans—including Kurt Koffka, Wolfgang Köhler, and Kurt Lewin—founded a school called **Gestalt psychology**. *Gestalt* is a German word that can be translated roughly as *organized shape*, or *whole form*. The basic premise of this new school was that the mind must be understood in terms of organized wholes, not elementary parts. A melody is not the sum of individual notes, a painting is not the sum of the individual dots of paint, an idea is not the sum of elementary concepts that make up the idea. The meaningful units of consciousness are whole, organized constructs—whole melodies, whole scenes, whole ideas—that cannot be understood by analyzing elementary judgments and sensations of the sort that Wundt and Titchener studied.

Most early research in Gestalt psychology was in the area of perception. As you will see in Chapter 9, the Gestaltists identified many perceptual phenomena that, like the phi phenomenon, show that whole objects and scenes take precedence over component parts in conscious experience. For example, when looking at a chair, people perceive and recognize the chair as a whole before noticing its arms, legs, or other parts. Moving away from the area of perception, Köhler (1917/1973) performed experiments on problem solving with chimpanzees. He argued that these animals hit upon solutions through sudden flashes of insight, in which the whole solution (such as moving a box to a position underneath a banana dangling on a string in order to reach it) comes at once rather than in bits and pieces. Other Gestalt psychologists, including Kurt Lewin, took their principles into the realm of social psychology in ways that you will read about in Chapters 14 and 15.

Gestalt psychology started in Germany, but by the mid-1930s, with the increased threats against Jews and their sympathizers that accompanied German Nazification, all of its founders—including Wertheimer, Koffka, Köhler, and Lewin—had moved to the United States and established research laboratories in various colleges and universities here (Ash, 1985). Gestalt psychology eventually lost its position as a discrete school of thought, but it became integrated into many different lines of psychological work.

### Psychoanalysis

**Freud's conception of an unconscious mind that influences conscious thought and action**

**Figure 1.7 Sigmund Freud**
As a Viennese physician specializing in neural disorders, Freud came to believe that many of his patients' physical and mental problems originated as a way of keeping certain disturbing memories out of consciousness. He went on to develop a theory of the mind and approach to psychotherapy called psychoanalysis. Here he is shown in his office in Vienna in May 1938.

**Freud's approach to the study of the unconscious mind, and why his approach is criticized**

Sigmund Freud (1856–1939) was a creative thinker whose work and ideas were outside of the mainstream of academic research and thought. Unlike the other pioneers we have been discussing, Freud was not a university professor. He was a physician who specialized in neurology and, from 1886 on, worked with patients at his private office in Vienna. He found that many people who came to him had no detectable medical problems, but seemed to suffer from their memories, especially their memories of disturbing events in their early childhood. In many cases they could not recall such memories consciously, but cues in their behavior led Freud to believe that disturbing memories were present nevertheless, buried in what he referred to as the *unconscious mind*. From this insight, Freud developed a method of treatment in which people would talk freely about themselves, and Freud would analyze what they said in order to uncover the buried memories that were disturbing them. The goal was to bring the memories to the patient's conscious attention, so his or her conscious mind could then work out ways of dealing with them.

Freud coined the term **psychoanalysis** to refer both to his method of treatment and to his theory of the mind. Although most of his data came from his work with patients, Freud developed his theory to describe the structure and development of the human mind in general, not just the source of mental disorders. His most important concept was that of the unconscious mind. While Wundt, Titchener, James, Wertheimer, and others had defined the mind entirely in terms of conscious experience, Freud argued that the conscious mind is only the tip of the iceberg, and that the bulk of the mind is unconscious. The unconscious mind not only contains buried memories, but it is also the source of instinctive wishes or drives, particularly sexual and aggressive drives. Although the conscious mind has no direct access to the contents of the unconscious, it is nevertheless strongly affected by the unconscious. Conscious thoughts and wishes can be understood as products of the unconscious mind that have been modified to become acceptable to the conscious mind. For example, a child's wish to kill a parent might be so terrifying that it would be converted unconsciously into an obsessive conscious fear that the parent might die. The child would never be aware of the original wish unless it arose in the course of psychotherapy.

Freud's basic approach was to collect clues from what a person says and does, and put them together, like a detective, in order to make inferences about the contents of the person's unconscious mind. Dreams and slips of the tongue provided especially important clues, because they are instances in which unconscious wishes and memories slip into consciousness in the least disguised form. In general, every aspect of conscious behavior and thought that seems irrational—that is, that would not be produced through conscious logic—was seen by Freud as evidence of the unconscious mind. Freud considered his method to be scientific, but relatively few psychologists in academic circles have ever agreed with him on that. Most have argued that his approach leaves too much room for interpretation. There are too many plausible alternative ways of putting the clues together to be certain that any given analysis is not at least as much the analyst's creation as a true account of the mind of the person being analyzed.

Although most psychologists today do not accept the details of Freud's theory, most do accept his general view that unconscious mental processes influence conscious thought and action. His work also helped focus attention on a wide range of topics that had been largely ignored by previous psychologists. The role of childhood experiences in later development, the sexual drive and its various manifestations, and the whole realm of irrational, emotional behavior and thought became appropriate subjects for psychological research.

**Figure 1.8 Applying alternative perspectives**
Some of the schools of thought described in this chapter have led to therapies that are useful in treating different types of mental disorders. Part 7 looks at theoretical explanations of what can go wrong in personality development and how such difficulties can be treated.

■ *The principles of behaviorism, as set out by its founder, John B. Watson*

### Behaviorism

Every school of psychology described above—structuralism, functionalism, Gestalt psychology, and psychoanalysis—defined psychology as the science of the mind. For the first three it was the science of the conscious mind, and for the last it was the science of the conscious and unconscious mind. In 1913, an American psychologist at Johns Hopkins University named John B. Watson (1878–1958) published an article entitled "Psychology as the Behaviorist Views It," which was intended as a manifesto for a new approach in psychology, an approach that would define psychology as the science of *behavior*, not of the mind.

Watson was one of an expanding group of psychologists studying nonhuman animals. In the dozen years preceding 1913 he had performed experiments with monkeys, chickens, dogs, cats, frogs, and fish (Hothersall, 1990), but his usual research animal was the rat, which he studied using mazes and similar apparatus. He was impressed with the amount he could learn about an animal's behavior with no consideration of the animal's mind. Laws of behavior could be described that related changes in behavior directly to changes in the environment to which the animal was exposed, with no mention of thought or other mental processes. For example, a rat's route and rate of movement through a maze toward food could be predicted on the basis of where food had been placed in the maze during a previous trial, without reference to the rat's "knowledge," "perceptions," "decisions," or other mental events. In fact, Watson was convinced that any reference to the mind only obscured the explanation, because there was no direct way to observe the animal's mind. All one could observe were the external environmental conditions (such as the shape of the maze and the type of reward in its goal box) and the animal's muscular actions. Watson also studied human behavior, and he became convinced that here too the use of mental concepts was of no scientific value. The human has access to his or her own mind through introspection, but, like other critics of Titchener, Watson argued that introspection is not a scientific technique and can only lead to irresolvable debate. Science, argued Watson, must limit itself to what can be publicly observed.

The new approach that Watson advocated was called **behaviorism**. Its fundamental tenets, as set out in the 1913 article, can be summarized as follows:

1. The proper subject of study in psychology is not the mind but *behavior*, defined as the observable actions of people and other animals.

2. The appropriate goal of psychology is to understand the environmental conditions that cause an individual to behave in a particular way.

3. The achievement of this goal does not require that we attempt to explain the environment-behavior relationship in terms of the mind or other unobservable events occurring within the individual. In fact, such explanations should be avoided.

4. There is no fundamental difference between human behavior and that of other animals, nor between the methods that should be used to study humans and other animals.

Many psychologists throughout North America responded enthusiastically to Watson's ideas. They wanted to throw out the armchair philosophy and convoluted terminology that they saw as carry-overs from stuffy European traditions. Within a decade after Watson's 1913 article, behaviorism replaced Titchener's structuralism as the dominant school in North American psychology, and it remained in that position into the mid-1960s. Watson himself, however, was forced to leave the academic world before the school that he had founded reached full bloom. In 1920, an extramarital affair with his research assistant Rosalie Rayner became public, and the scandal was cause for Johns Hopkins University to fire him and for no other university to pick him up. He continued publishing books and articles on behaviorism, and he and Rayner (whom he later married) conducted some highly publicized research with nursery school children. But his main employment after 1920 was in the advertising world. In an autobiographical sketch, Watson (1936) wrote, perhaps wistfully, "I began to learn that it can be just as thrilling to watch the growth of a sales curve of a new product as to watch the learning curve of animals and men."

Of the many behaviorists who succeeded Watson, by far the most famous is B. F. Skinner (1904–1990). As a graduate student at Harvard, Skinner developed a new kind of apparatus for studying learning in animals and a new way of describing the learning process. You will read about both in Chapter 5. In 1938, he published a book entitled *The Behavior of Organisms*, based mostly on work he had done as a graduate student. The book brought him instant fame among psychologists, and from shortly after its publication until his recent death he was the recognized leader of behaviorism. Like Watson, Skinner had a knack for stating his case strongly, clearly, and sometimes in terms that seemed deliberately designed to provoke controversy. The mere title of one of his books, *Beyond Freedom and Dignity* (1971), elicited a storm of protest. His basic argument in that book was that concepts like freedom and dignity, like other concepts referring to the mind, have no scientific explanatory value. Skinner's constant message was that human behavior is a product of the environment in which a person grows and lives, and terms like *freedom, dignity, willpower, decisions*, and so on only obscure our understanding of the lawful relationships between environment and behavior.

The pristine brand of behaviorism advocated by Watson and Skinner, which called for avoidance of speculation about processes occurring inside the animal or person, is often called *radical behaviorism*, to distinguish it from modified forms of behaviorism developed by other theorists. It is also sometimes called *S-R psychology*, where *S* stands for stimulus and *R* for response. Watson, Skinner, and their followers stated their research findings, and the laws they developed from such findings, purely in terms of stimuli (observable events in the world that affect behavior) and responses (observable behavioral acts). Other psychologists who called themselves behaviorists—such as Edward Tolman (1886–1959) and Clark Hull (1884–1952)—talked about hypothetical intervening variables that underlie the connections between stimuli and responses. Their brand of behaviorism is sometimes called *S-O-R psychology*, where the *O* stands for hypothetical processes occurring inside the organism. They were getting back gingerly to the concept of the mind, in a way that did not depend on introspection, and their views helped lead to the development of the approach that is today called *cognitive psychology*.

### Ethology

Meanwhile, back across the Atlantic, an approach to the study of animal behavior that was in some ways the opposite of America's behaviorism was taking hold in

**Figure 1.9  B. F. Skinner**

*Skinner, who devoted a long career to the study of animal learning and to wide-ranging speculation about human behavior, was the acknowledged leader of behaviorism for the past four decades or so. Much of his basic research on learning used pigeons as subjects.*

■ *The distinction between the radical behaviorism of Watson and Skinner and the more moderate behaviorism of others*

**Konrad Lorenz and followers**

*Ethologists have described a behavior known as imprinting in which some newborn animals follow and become attached to the first moving thing they see or hear. These geese, which were hatched by Lorenz in an incubator, responded to him as if he were their mother. You will learn more about ethologists' research on mechanisms of learning in Chapter 5.*

■ *How ethology and behaviorism differed, but then began to merge*

Europe in the 1930s. The leaders of this movement—most notably Konrad Lorenz (1903–1989) in Austria and Nikolaas Tinbergen (1907–1988) in Holland—were genuine animal enthusiasts who studied animals for their own sake, not as substitutes for humans. Rather than focusing on domesticated breeds in laboratory apparatus, they preferred to study wild animals in their natural settings—woods, fields, and ponds. Lorenz named this science *ethology*, a term that today can be defined simply as the study of animal behavior in the natural environment (Gould, 1982). Ethology originated as a branch of zoology, not psychology. But neither nature nor good scientists respect the arbitrary disciplinary boundaries that universities have established for administrative purposes. Ethologists and psychology's behaviorists were studying the same thing, animal behavior, and it was inevitable that the two would begin to interact.

At first the interactions between ethologists and behaviorists took the form of arguments. They were both studying animal behavior, but from entirely different points of view and with very different methods. The behaviorists were interested almost solely in learning. They brought into their work a long-standing philosophical bias, dating back to British empiricism, holding that behavior is a reflection of previous experience and that the way to understand it is to understand learning. In the laboratory they were impressed by the degree to which they could train animals to behave in very unnatural ways by controlling their environment. Skinner even trained pigeons to play a version of Ping-Pong. In contrast, ethologists were most strongly influenced by Darwin, and when they observed animals in the natural environment they were impressed by the highly complex and adaptive behavior patterns that animals show without any apparent learning, at least not learning as defined by behaviorists. Lorenz studied courtship patterns in ducks and geese, and Tinbergen studied mating rituals in stickleback fish and various species of gulls. They showed in experiments that these behaviors occur in essentially normal form even in animals that had never previously observed them and never been provided with rewards for practicing them. Lorenz and Tinbergen developed the idea that many survival-related behavior patterns are "wired into" the animal's nervous system and are triggered at the appropriate time through an interaction between events in the environment (such as the sight of an appropriate mate) and events inside the body (such as the heightened production of sex hormones in the spring).

By the 1960s, developments in both ethology and behaviorism began to bring the two schools together in cooperative ways. Behavioral researchers were increasingly reporting on biologically based constraints on animals' learning abilities, and they were describing differences among different species in the kinds of responses they could learn (Shettleworth, 1972). For example, they reported that migratory birds are biologically predisposed to learn landmarks that help guide their migratory flight, and that seed-eaters are predisposed to learn the locations of seeds. They increasingly accepted the idea that learning itself is a set of processes that came about through evolution, and that quite different learning mechanisms may have evolved to serve different survival needs. At the same time, some ethologists began to turn their attention to mammals, and they found mammal behavior to be far more flexible and dependent on prior experiences than that of insects, fish, and birds, which had been the focus of earlier ethological studies. As you will see in Chapter 4, some ethologists even went on to study humans, and they helped develop new insights about the interactions between innate predispositions and environmental experiences in human behavior.

### Physiological Psychology

**Physiological psychology** is not a school of thought in the sense of the schools described above. It has no specific birth date and no specific founders, and there has been little controversy as to whether it is an appropriate approach or not. Rather, it is the direct extension into psychology of studies of the nervous system that were begun in the nineteenth century, before psychology was a formally recognized science. It can be defined as the attempt to understand the physiological mechanisms, in the brain and elsewhere, that mediate behavior and psychological experiences. Most physiological psychologists work with laboratory animals, usually rats. Their basic approach is to interfere in carefully controlled ways with specific physiological processes in these animals. For example, they may damage a particular part of the brain or inject a drug that is known to modify specific brain processes in specific ways to see how this manipulation affect's the animal's movement, motivation, sensory ability, or learning ability in behavioral tests.

Closely related to physiological psychology is **neuropsychology**, which is the study of how the nervous system organizes and controls behavior that is specifically human. Neuropsychologists study people who have suffered brain damage due to injury or disease, both to help these patients and to learn about the psychological functions performed by different parts of the brain. Paul Broca's research on language loss after damage to a specific area of the left hemisphere was pioneering in this area.

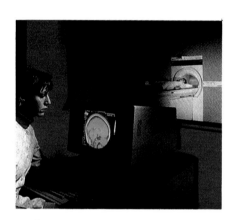

**Looking into the brain**

*The understanding of brain disorders has advanced rapidly as a result of new computerized techniques for viewing the brain.*

### Cognitive Psychology

By about 1960 behaviorism began to lose its dominance in North American psychology. Research with nonhuman animals moved in a biological direction, toward physiological psychology on the one hand and a modified ethology (more often simply called *animal behavior*) on the other. At the same time, research with humans moved in a *cognitive* direction, meaning that the mind was readmitted as a focus of study. From the 1960s to today, **cognitive psychology** has increased in influence, and for the past two decades it has been considered the dominant approach. The term *cognition* refers to knowledge, and cognitive psychology can be defined as the study of people's ability to acquire, organize, remember, and use knowledge to guide their behavior. Although cognitive psychologists study the mind, they do not do so through introspection, but rather through inferences based on observable behavior. Cognitive psychologists develop models or theories about mental processes that mediate behavior, and test them in controlled situations where people would be expected to behave in one way if the model is correct and a different way if it is incorrect. Although cognitive psychology began to come into its own in the 1960s, it was not suddenly born then. Many of the S-O-R behaviorists, alluded to earlier, would today be called *cognitive psychologists*, because their goal was to understand mental processes (the *O*) through observations of behavior. Going back further, it is reasonable to suggest that Wilhelm Wundt, the commonly acknowledged founder of psychology, was also the

*An early analogy*
*The use of analogies to understand the brain can go beyond machines. In the 1930s a children's encyclopedia used the notion of a factory to represent the complex information-organizing activities of the brain.*

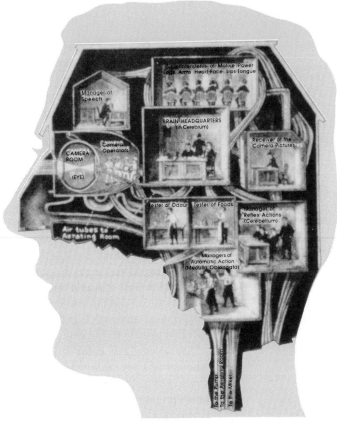

■ *How the computer analogy contributed to the rise of cognitive psychology*

founder of cognitive psychology (Blumenthal, 1985). Wundt considered psychology to be the study of the mind and, as you recall, his favored approach to the mind was the objective recording and timing of people's performance on various mental tasks.

Why did cognitive psychology begin to blossom in the 1960s and continue to grow in influence? Perhaps the most important reason has to do with computer technology. In every age the concepts that people have of the brain and mind are influenced by the kinds of machines that are available as analogies (see Rose, 1973). Descartes explicitly compared mechanical aspects of human behavior with the hydraulic mechanisms used to move the robot-like statues that decorated public gardens in seventeenth-century France. Nineteenth-century reflexologists compared the brain to the telephone switchboard, an analogy that was also implicit in the theories of some of the early twentieth-century behaviorists. Today the machine that most influences people's conception of the brain is the computer. A computer receives coded information (the input), reorganizes the information, compares it to other information stored in its memory, performs calculations on it, and uses the results to determine what signals to send to the computer's output system. All this is analogous to what the brain does: input is analogous to the receipt of information by sensory systems, output is analogous to behavioral action, and everything in between is analogous to thought.

There are two quite different ways to understand how a computer works. One is to learn about its hardware, that is, the electrical system through which it operates; this is analogous to learning about the physiology of the brain. The other is to learn about its software, that is, its program or set of programs. A computer program can be understood as a set of clearly specified steps for operating on specific kinds of information. The steps have to be written in such a way that the machine can follow them, but they can also be translated into English so that we can understand them without knowing the computer's language. We can write them out in the form, "First do _____, then _____, then _____. . . ." When cognitive psychologists talk about understanding the mind, they are usually talking about something similar to specifying the steps of a computer program. They

*The importance of the work of
Piaget and Chomsky in the cognitive
revolution*

are asking: Through what steps is information transformed as a person perceives, remembers, thinks, and makes decisions?

Aside from the role of computer technology, the cognitive revolution was also spurred by several interesting lines of psychological research and theory about the mind. Among these was the work of Jean Piaget (1896–1980), a Swiss psychologist who studied children's reasoning abilities. Based on objective data collected in hundreds of experiments, Piaget developed the idea that children undergo a series of mental metamorphoses, from infancy through adolescence, at each of which they become able to reason in a qualitatively different and more advanced way than they had at the previous stage. He attempted to describe the manner of thinking that characterizes each stage of this development in terms of hypothetical mental constructs called *schemes*. Roughly, a scheme can be thought of as a mental blueprint for acting upon the world and for using information about the world to control those actions. By 1960 American psychologists were aware of Piaget's work, and many began to perform experiments to try to test some of his ideas. Although Piaget's specific way of describing schemes (which was highly mathematical) did not catch on, his general approach of trying to explain behavior in terms of internal mental constructs has been widely adopted and has contributed greatly to the cognitive movement.

A second name for special mention is that of Noam Chomsky (1928–  ), who is not a psychologist but a linguist. In 1957, Chomsky published a book entitled *Syntactic Structures*, which spurred a revolution in linguistics and had an enormous impact on psychology as well. In this book, and even more explicitly in later writings, Chomsky argued that language must be understood as a system of mental rules, not as stimulus-response chains as behaviorists had proposed, and that these rules are at least partly founded on the innate capacities of the human mind. Thus, Chomsky attacked behaviorism on its two most vulnerable fronts at once: the cognitive front, in arguing that language must be understood in terms of mental rules, and the biological front, in arguing that these rules are in part wired into the brain as a result of evolution.

Ironically, 1957 was also the year that B. F. Skinner published a book entitled *Verbal Behavior*, in which he attempted to explain human language purely in the stimulus-response terms of behaviorism. Skinner's simplistic account was altogether too easy for the young Chomsky to attack, and attack it he did (see, for example, Chomsky, 1959). Many psychologists eagerly began to test Chomsky's ideas experimentally, contributing to the rapid growth of *psycholinguistics* (the study of the psychological bases for human language), which was very much a part of the cognitive revolution. Today many psycholinguists maintain that Chomsky went too far in his arguments for innate processes, and they place more emphasis on learning. However, their way of describing learning, in terms of the construction of mental rules, is very different from the behaviorists' approach.

Cognitive psychology cannot be described as a single approach or school of thought. Rather, it is an entire constellation of approaches that are unified only in their attempt to explain observable behavior by reference to hypothetical mental structures or processes. Some cognitive psychologists, who call themselves *information-processing theorists*, make direct use of the computer analogy and even try to spell out their theories of the mind in terms that a computer can follow. Others warn that the computer analogy can be misleading. The human being is not just an "information-processing device," but also a biological survival machine with motives and emotions that are foreign to computers but color all aspects of human thought and behavior. Some psychologists have even proposed that Freud's psychoanalytic theory falls within the range of cognitive psychology; they have argued that a full account of human behavior must, as Freud tried to, account for the irrational as well as rational aspects of our behavior (see Erdelyi, 1985).

## The Scope of Psychology Today

Psychology today is an extraordinarily vast and diverse field. The historical account that you have just read describes not just an evolution but a mushrooming. Each school of thought brought with it new questions about the mind and behavior, and new techniques for trying to answer them. Psychology today is an amalgam of all of those questions and techniques.

### *The Connections of Psychology to Other Scholarly Fields*

One way to picture the domain of psychology is to think of it in the context of the spectrum of academic disciplines that form the departments of a typical college of arts and sciences. As shown in Figure 1.10, the disciplines are roughly divisible into three broad areas. One division is the *natural sciences*, the sciences of nature—including physics, chemistry, and biology—shown in the left-hand side of the figure. The second is the *social sciences*, the sciences of society and the individual's relationships to society—including sociology, anthropology, political science, and economics—shown in the right-hand side of the figure. The third is the *humanities*—including languages, philosophy, art, and music—shown in the lower part of the figure. The humanities represent things that *humans* do. Humans, unlike other animals, talk to one another, develop philosophies, and produce art and music.

Now, where does psychology fit into this scheme? As shown in the figure, it fits right in the center, tied to all three of the broad divisions. On the natural science end it is strongly tied to biology by way of physiological psychology and ethology, and on the social science end it is strongly tied to sociology by way of social psychology. In addition to bridging the natural and social sciences, psychology ties the whole spectrum of sciences to the humanities, through its interest in how people produce and understand languages, philosophies, art, and music.

If you were to look at the research activities of psychologists, you would find that some behave like natural scientists. They have labs, wear white coats, perform experiments, and spend a good deal of time over in Biology, Chemistry, and

■ *How psychology links the three main divisions of academic studies*

**Figure 1.10** *Connections between psychology and other scholarly areas*

*Psychology bridges the natural and social sciences, and it also has strong connections to the humanities. In this sense it lies in the center of the academic pursuits of the university.*

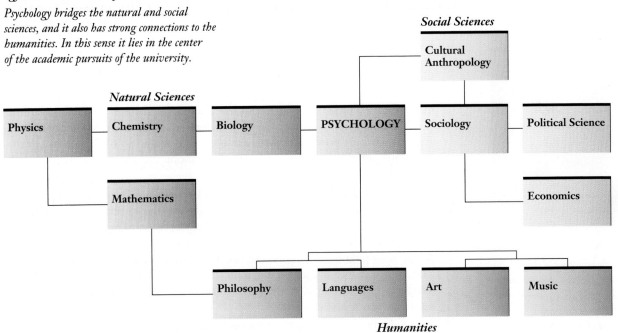

Physics exchanging ideas and equipment. Others behave more like social scientists. They use surveys, historical documents, and interviews as sources of data, and they find intellectual companionship in the various social science departments. The distinction between these two groups, however, is often a fuzzy one. As you will see, there are social psychologists who have labs and fancy data-collecting equipment, and there are biopsychologists whose data come mainly through their own two eyes, out in the field.

The link between psychology and the humanities is provided by people who ask questions about *how* and *why* people do such things as talk, philosophize, and produce art or music. For example, consider the link between psychology and the study of languages. If you are interested in describing the structure of one or another of the world's languages, you are a *linguist*. But if you are interested in how people are able to learn and use that structure, and how this may affect other aspects of their behavior, you are a *psycholinguist* (a psychologist of language). Similarly, there are psychologists who are interested in the hows and whys of art and music, and many who are interested in the hows and whys of people's reasoning and ways of explaining the world (their philosophizing), who provide links to the other humanities.

### The Questions of Psychology as Arranged in This Book

Another way to get an idea of the scope of psychology today is to preview the contents of this book. After two chapters of background, the remaining chapters are divided into six parts that can be viewed as large subdivisions of the set of questions that make up psychology as a whole. The first three parts (2, 3, and 4) are about the fundamental processes that underlie behavior and thought; the last three (5, 6, and 7) are about the person as a whole entity and the real-life contexts in which human behavior and thought occur. Here is a brief overview of each part:

■ *One way to divide the vast disciplines of psychology into parts*

- *Part 2: Nature, Nurture, and Behavioral Adaptation* How do genes influence our behavior? In what ways does an understanding of evolution by natural selection inform our understanding of ourselves? How do we learn? What is the relationship between our learning ability and our inborn behavioral tendencies? This set of chapters is about genetics and evolution, on the one hand, and learning, on the other, and how they work together to promote the individual's ability to survive in a partly stable and partly changing environment.

- *Part 3: Physiological Mechanisms of Behavior* In what ways does an understanding of the nervous system, especially the brain, contribute to an understanding of behavior? How do hormones and drugs affect behavior through action in the brain? What is known about the physiological bases of sleep or arousal, of emotional states, or of drives such as hunger and sex? How do the sensory systems work to provide us with a useful representation of the external environment? This set of chapters is mostly about the physiological underpinnings of behavior.

- *Part 4: Cognitive Mechanisms of Behavior* How can mental processes too complex to be understood physiologically be understood in terms of information-processing steps? For example: How do we perceive (make sense of) our environment? How do we form memories and recall them at a later time? How do we manipulate information in our mind to solve problems or make decisions? How do we use and understand language? This set of chapters is about psychologists' attempts to describe and explain the ability to perceive, remember, think, and converse.

- *Part 5: Growth of the Mind and Person* How do people change, psychologically, as they grow from infancy through adulthood? Can we understand adult abil-

**Exploring the mysteries of sleep**
*No one knows exactly why people sleep, but researchers, using devices like the one shown here, have learned a good deal about the rhythms of sleep. Chapter 7 includes a discussion of this area of physiological psychology.*

ities better by observing how they grow in the infant and child? What are the environmental prerequisites for healthy psychological development? This pair of chapters concerns the broad field of *developmental psychology*. One chapter is about the development of perception, language, and thought; the other is about the development of people's social relationships and their way of understanding themselves and others.

■ *Part 6: The Person in a World of People* The human being is a social animal, whose abilities and understanding come from interaction with others. How do people form impressions of other people? How are people influenced by others' impressions of them? How do people perceive their relationships to each other? In what ways is human behavior influenced by the demands, requests, examples, or simple presence of other people? This pair of chapters concerns the broad field of *social psychology*. One chapter is about basic thought and perceptual processes as applied to the social world, and the other is about the ways that people are influenced by social pressures, such as the pressure to comply with others' requests or to conform to group norms.

■ *Part 7: Personality and Disorders* How can individuals be described and understood in terms of their overall style of behavior? Along what psychological dimensions do people differ from each other? Can the differences be measured? When is a difference harmful, warranting the label *psychological disorder*? Can such disorders be classified in useful ways? What are the origins of disorders, and how can they be treated? The final three chapters are devoted to three closely related fields of psychology: (a) *personality psychology*, the attempt to describe and explain the most general psychological differences among people, (b) *abnormal psychology*, the attempt to describe and explain the various mental or emotional problems or disorders that trouble people, and (c) *clinical psychology*, the attempt to help people cope with or overcome such problems or disorders.

### Psychology as a Profession

■ *Where psychologists work and what they do*

Psychology is not only an academic discipline, but also a profession. It is a profession made up of men and women who, on the academic end, are trying to answer the kinds of questions outlined above, and who, on the practical end, are applying psychological knowledge in clinics, businesses, and other settings. In 1983 the American Psychological Association conducted a massive survey of all psychologists residing in the United States (Stapp & others, 1985). The survey revealed that there were slightly over 100,000 people employed as psychologists at that time. Of these, 67 percent held doctoral degrees and almost all of the rest held master's degrees; 41 percent were involved in research, 64 percent in teaching and other educational activities, and 66 percent in health and mental health services (the percentages add up to more than 100 percent because many psychologists were involved in more than one activity). The main settings in which psychologists work, and the kinds of services they perform in each, are as follows (also see Table 1.1):

■ *Academic departments in universities and colleges* Here psychologists are employed to conduct basic research and to teach psychology courses.

■ *Elementary and secondary schools* Psychologists here work as guidance counselors and as supervisors of programs for children who have special needs, and they may also use their knowledge of learning and child development to help teachers develop more effective classroom techniques.

■ *Independent practice* Most in this category are self-employed clinical or counseling psychologists, who work with clients who have psychological problems or disorders.

**Table 1.1** *Percentage of U.S. psychologists employed in various settings*

| Primary employment setting | Percentage in each setting |
|---|---|
| Academic departments in universities and colleges | 29.3% |
| Elementary and secondary schools | 14.9 |
| Independent practice | 17.5 |
| Hospitals, mental health centers, clinics, and counseling or guidance centers | 24.9 |
| Business, government, and other organizations | 13.4 |
| Total: | 100.0% |

*Source:* From "Census of psychological personnel: 1983" by J. Stapp, A. M. Tucker, & G. R. VandenBos, 1985, *American Psychologist, 40,* pp. 1326–1327.

- *Hospitals, mental health centers, clinics, and counseling or guidance centers* Most here are also clinical or counseling psychologists, employed by an institution to work with people who have psychological problems or disorders.

- *Business and government* Psychologists are hired by businesses and government agencies for a wide variety of purposes. Some conduct research, such as evaluating human services programs or assessing consumers' reactions to products. Some help screen candidates for employment in jobs requiring high emotional stability, such as police work or aviation. Still others help design more pleasant and efficient work environments, or serve as counselors to personnel who have work-related problems.

The decision to major in psychology in college, incidentally, does not necessarily imply a choice of psychology as a career. Most students who major in psychology do so primarily because they find the subject interesting and fun to learn and think about. Most go on to careers in other fields—such as social work, law, education, and business—where they are quite likely to find their psychology background to be helpful (see Woods, 1987).

## Concluding Thoughts

At the end of each chapter I offer two or three (occasionally more) "concluding thoughts," which in some cases might help you organize your review of the chapter and in other cases might add an insight or two to those that you generate yourself as you think about the chapter's contents. Here are two concluding thoughts for the chapter you have just read:

**1. Ways to characterize the mind** The history of psychology can be viewed in part as a history of alternative ways of characterizing the human mind. Most of the early psychologists were interested primarily in conscious, rational thought. Following the lead of philosophers before them, their broad question was, "How is it that people can think?" Wundt and Titchener (structuralists), in their different ways, tried to understand thought in terms of its elementary parts. That tradition persists today in cognitive psychology, which studies elementary processes involved in perception, memory, judgment, and so on. James (a functionalist), on the other hand, felt that thought loses its very essence if it is broken down. He characterized thought as a continuous flow, which must be understood in terms of its broad goals or purposes rather than its parts. The Gestaltists also argued that thought must be understood in wholes rather than parts. Freud (a psychoanalyst) added a new twist to the problem, arguing that it is not enough to study conscious thought, since unconscious, irrational thoughts affect the conscious ones and also influence behavior in ways that bypass conscious thought. Finally, Watson and Skinner (radical behaviorists) rejected the issue of thought entirely, changing the question from "How is it that people can think?" to "How is it that the environment controls people's behavior?"

**2. The value of a historical perspective** There is a temptation, stronger today than in times past, to think of everything that is old as obsolete. In psychology, that temptation is manifest in the tendency to avoid reading the works of the early psychologists and other thinkers who set forth the questions and pioneered the methods that constitute the field of psychology as we know it today. But those who do read such works are often amazed by the breadth of mind, clarity of vision, and sheer intelligence of such pioneers as Charles Darwin, William James, and Edward Thorndike. Sometimes psychology seems to be a hodgepodge of specific facts, findings, theories, and techniques; to elevate one's vision above that jumble, it is useful to think of the broader questions, raised by the pioneers, that set psychology along the roads leading to the more specific issues. One work to which I will refer occasionally throughout this book is William James's two-volume *Principles of Psychology*, first published in 1890. Take a look at that work in your library, or maybe even buy a copy (it's available in paperback). If you do buy it, you might very well enjoy reading it along with this textbook. As you go from topic to topic in this book, look up what James had to say on the topic and see if there has been progress or not. On some topics you might be quite impressed with how far the field has moved in a hundred years, and on others you might well decide that the field has barely begun to budge.

## Further Reading

**David Hothersall** (1990). *History of psychology* (2nd ed.). New York: McGraw-Hill.
*This lively historical account begins with the psychological theories of the ancient Greeks and ends with the behaviorism and neobehaviorism of the mid-twentieth century.*

**Howard H. Kendler** (1987). *Historical foundations of modern psychology.* Philadelphia: Temple University Press.
*This is not just a history, but also an insightful analysis of the ideas, methods, and findings of past psychologists and psychological schools, emphasizing their contributions to contemporary psychology.*

**Paul J. Woods** (Ed.) (1987). *Is psychology the major for you?* Washington, DC: American Psychological Association.
*This booklet contains useful information about careers that psychology majors go on to, both in and out of psychology; about preparing for graduate training in psychology; and about ways to maximize one's undergraduate education.*

## Looking Ahead

As described earlier in this chapter, psychology has from its outset been defined as a science. Psychology became a formally recognized area of study when people accepted the idea that behavior and the mind are in the realm of phenomena that obey natural laws. The goal of psychology has always been to understand those laws through scientific methods. But what is meant by scientific methods, and what are the special problems of applications of those methods in psychology? These are the main questions of the next chapter.

# CHAPTER 2

Lessons from Clever Hans

A Taxonomy of Research
Strategies

Statistical Methods in Psychology

Sources of Error and Bias
in Psychological Research

Ethical Issues in Psychological
Research

# METHODS OF PSYCHOLOGY

In the last chapter, psychology was defined as the *science* of behavior and the mind. But what does it mean to say that psychology is a science? Science entails a concerted, organized effort to be objective, unbiased, and logical. In addition, it usually entails the systematic collection and analysis of publicly observable data (data whose raw form can be agreed upon by all reasonable observers). In psychology, the data usually consist of some form of behavior produced by human or animal subjects, collected in accordance with a carefully prescribed procedure. There are special problems associated with collecting such data, and, as in all sciences, with drawing conclusions from the data once collected.

This chapter is about scientific methods as applied to psychology. You will read sections on research strategies, statistical procedures, sources of error and bias, and ethical issues in research design. But first, to ease ourselves into the topic, here is a story about a horse . . . and a psychologist.

## Lessons from Clever Hans

This story, a true one, took place in Germany near the beginning of the twentieth century. The horse is Clever Hans, famous throughout Europe for his ability to answer questions, and the psychologist, who turns out to be cleverer than Hans, is Oskar Pfungst. I tell the story here because it contains some important lessons about scientific attitude and methods, but it would be worth telling even if it had no lessons. In a preface to the original account (Pfungst, 1911/1965), James Angell wrote, "Were it offered as fiction, it would take high rank as a work of imagination. Being in reality a sober fact, it verges on the miraculous."

Hans's owner, Mr. von Osten, was an eccentric retired schoolteacher and devoted horseman who had long believed that horses would prove to be as intelligent as people if they were only given a proper education. To test his thesis, von Osten spent 4 years tutoring Hans in the manner employed in the best German schools for children. Using flash cards, counting frames, and the like, he set about teaching his horse reading, arithmetic, history, and other scholarly disciplines. He always began with simple problems and worked to more complex ones, frequently rewarding Hans with much praise as well as carrots. Since von Osten knew that his horse lacked the vocal apparatus for speech, he taught Hans to spell out words using a code in which the letters of the alphabet were translated into hoof taps, and to answer yes-no questions by tossing his head up and down for yes and back and forth for no. By the end of 4 years of this training, Hans was able to answer practically any question that was put to him in either spoken or written German, whether about geography, history, science, literature, math, or current events. Re-

**Figure 2.1** *Clever Hans at a mathematics lesson*
*Mr. von Osten believed that his horse was intellectually gifted, and so did many other people until the psychologist Oskar Pfungst performed some simple experiments.*

markably, he could also answer questions put to him in other languages, even though he had never been trained in other languages.

Now you might think that von Osten was a charlatan, but he wasn't. He genuinely believed that his horse could read and understand a variety of languages, could perform arithmetical calculations, and had acquired a vast store of knowledge (see Figure 2.1). He never charged admission or sought other personal gain for displaying Hans, and he actively sought out scientists to study the animal's accomplishments. Indeed, many scientists, including some rather eminent zoologists and psychologists, came to the conclusion that von Osten's claims were true! Perhaps the most convincing evidence to them was that Hans could answer questions even when von Osten was not present, a finding that seemed to rule out the possibility that he depended on secret signals from his master. Moreover, several circus trainers, who specialized in training animals to give the appearance of answering questions, studied Hans and could find no evidence of trickery.

Hans's downfall finally came, however, when the psychologist Oskar Pfungst performed a few simple experiments. Pfungst (1911/1965) found that Hans could not answer any questions if he was fitted with blinders so that he could not see any of the people who were present, and that even without blinders he could not answer questions unless at least one person in his sight knew the answer. From this, Pfungst hypothesized that the horse obtained cues as to when to start and stop tapping by observing some subtle aspects of the behavior of the questioner or others who knew the answer. With further study, Pfungst discovered just what the signals were.

Immediately after asking a question that demanded a hoof-tap answer, the questioner and other observers would naturally turn their heads down just a bit to observe the horse's hoof. This, it turned out, was the signal for Hans to start tapping. To determine whether Hans would be correct or not, the questioner and other observers would then count the taps, and unintentionally make another response as soon as the correct number had been reached. This response varied from person to person, but a common component was a slight upward movement of either the whole head or of some facial feature, such as the eyebrows. This, it turned out, was the signal for Hans to stop tapping. Hans's yes-no head-shake responses were also controlled by visual signals. Questioners and observers would unconsciously produce slight up-down head movements when they expected the horse to answer yes and slight back-forth head movements when they expected no, and Hans would shake his head accordingly. All of the signals that controlled Hans's responses were so subtle that even the most astute observers had failed to notice them until Pfungst pointed them out. And Pfungst himself reported that the signals occurred so naturally that, even after he had learned what they were, he had to make a conscious effort to prevent himself from sending them after asking a question.

For 4 years von Osten had believed that he was communicating scholarly information to Hans, when all he had really accomplished was to teach the horse to make a few simple responses to a few simple, though minute, gestures. Hans was no intellectual. He did not really understand any questions or know their answers. His cleverness lay in his ability to notice very subtle changes in the posture of his examiners and use those to guide his quest for carrots and praise.

One lesson of this story has to do with human gullibility and the value of skepticism. People are naturally drawn to the extraordinary and to claims that violate mundane views about how the world is organized. We often act as if we want to believe such claims. This is as true today as it was in the time of Clever Hans. We have no trouble at all finding otherwise intelligent people who believe in astrology, psychokinesis, water divining, telepathy, or other occult phenomena, despite the fact that all such phenomena have failed when subjected to controlled tests of the sort that Pfungst gave to Clever Hans (see Singer & Benassi, 1981). Von Osten clearly wanted to believe that his horse could do all sorts of amazing things, and so to a lesser degree may have the scholars who had studied the horse before Pfungst. Pfungst learned the truth partly because he, unlike the others, was highly skeptical of such claims. Instead of setting out to prove them correct, he set out to prove them wrong. His skepticism led him to look more carefully, to notice what others had missed, to think of an alternative, more mundane explanation, and to pit the mundane explanation against the paranormal one in controlled tests.

The importance of skepticism applies not only to extraordinary claims that come from outside of science, but also to the usually more sober claims or theories produced by scientists themselves. The ideal scientist always tries to disprove theories, even those that are his or her own. The theories that scientists accept as correct, or most likely to be so, are those that potentially could be disproved but have survived all attempts so far to do so.

A second lesson has to do with the importance of careful observations under controlled conditions. Pfungst solved the mystery of Clever Hans by isolating the conditions under which the horse could and could not respond correctly to questions. He tested Hans repeatedly, with and without blinders, recording the percentage of correct responses in each condition, and this led him to hypothesize that the animal relied on visual signals. He then pursued this hypothesis by carefully observing Hans's examiners to see what signals they might be giving off. And when he had an idea what the signals might be, he performed further experiments, in various controlled ways, and recorded their effects on Hans's tapping and head-shake responses. Careful observation under controlled conditions is a hallmark of the scientific method.

A third lesson concerns *observer-expectancy effects*, which plague a great deal of psychological research (Rosenthal, 1965, 1976). A general problem in studies of humans and other sentient animals is that researchers may quite unintentionally communicate to the subjects their expectations as to how they "should" behave, and subjects, intentionally or not, may respond by doing just what the experimenter expects. The same is true in any situation in which one person administers a test to another. Have you ever taken an oral quiz and found that you could tell whether you were on the right or wrong track by noting the facial expression of your examiner? By fishing around, trying different tracks, you may have finally hit upon just the answer that your examiner wanted. Clever Hans's whole cleverness depended on picking up such cues. We will return to the issue of expectancy effects later, in the context of a more general discussion of sources of error and bias in psychological research.

■ *How the Clever Hans story illustrates the value of skepticism, controlled experimentation, and the need to rule out observer-expectancy effects*

# A Taxonomy of Research Strategies

Throughout this book you will be reading about research evidence for or against one or another idea or hypothesis, and it will be useful to enter armed with some general knowledge of the different kinds of research strategies you will encounter. One approach to categorizing research strategies in psychology is to think of them as varying along three separate dimensions (suggested by Hendricks & others, 1990). One dimension is the *research design*, of which there are three basic types—experiments, correlational studies, and descriptive studies. The second dimension is the *data-collection method*, of which there are two basic types—observation and self-report. And the third dimension is the *setting* in which the study is conducted, of which there are again two basic types—laboratory and field. Each of these dimensions can vary independently of the others, resulting in twelve different varieties of studies, each defined by its combination of design, data-collection method, and setting (see Figure 2.2). I will first discuss the three types of designs, and then turn briefly to the other two dimensions.

**Figure 2.2  *Three dimensions of research strategies***

*The three categories of research designs, combined with two categories of data-collection methods and two categories of research settings, yield twelve different types of research strategies. These research strategies are described in detail in the following pages, and specific examples are given of each. (Adapted from Hendricks & others, 1990.)*

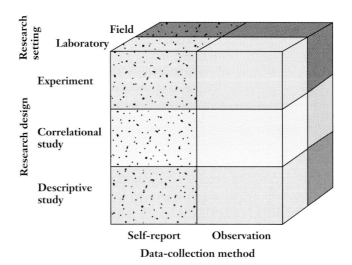

## *Research Designs*

**Experiments**   An experiment is the most direct and conclusive approach to testing a hypothesis about a cause-effect relationship between two variables (a variable is simply anything that can vary). In describing an experiment, the variable that is hypothesized to cause some effect on another variable is called the **independent variable**, and the variable that is hypothesized to be affected is called the **dependent variable**. The independent variable is called "independent" because its dependence on other variables is not the issue being tested, and the dependent variable is called "dependent" because the aim of the experiment is to learn how it depends on the independent variable. In psychology, dependent variables are usually measures of behavior, and independent variables are factors that are hypothesized to influence those measures.

■ *How an experiment tests causal hypotheses*

■ *Two sample experiments, illustrating the meaning of independent and dependent variables*

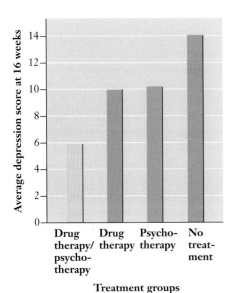

**Figure 2.3** *Effect of treatment condition on depression*

*The graph shows that those clients who received both drugs and psychotherapy were the least depressed at the end of the 16-week treatment period (based on results of a standard interview procedure scored on a 17-point scale). In contrast, those who received no scheduled treatment were the most depressed. (From DiMascio & others, 1979.)*

More specifically, an experiment can be defined as a procedure in which a researcher systematically varies (manipulates) one or more independent variables while looking for changes in one or more dependent variables, keeping all other variables constant. The reason for keeping other variables constant is to insure that any change observed in a dependent variable is really caused by the change in an independent variable, not by some other factor that happened to vary between the different tests.

To make all of this more concrete, consider how these terms would apply to one of Pfungst's experiments with Clever Hans. To determine if visual cues were critical to Hans's ability to respond correctly to questions, Pfungst tested him sometimes with blinders and sometimes without. In that experiment the independent variable was the presence or absence of blinders, and the dependent variable was the percentage of questions responded to correctly. The experiment could be described as a study of the effect of blinders (independent variable) on Hans's percentage of correct responses to questions (dependent variable). Pfungst took care to keep other variables, such as the difficulty of the questions, constant across the two test conditions. This experiment is an example of a *within-subject experiment*, since the different conditions of the independent variable were applied to the same subject (Hans).

As a second example, consider an experiment in the area of clinical psychology conducted by Alberto DiMascio and his colleagues (1979). These researchers identified a group of patients suffering from major depression (defined in Chapter 17) and randomly assigned them different treatments. One group received both drug therapy and psychotherapy, a second received drug therapy alone, a third received psychotherapy alone, and a fourth received no scheduled treatment (though they were assigned to a psychiatrist whom they could call when needed). The drug therapy consisted of daily doses of an antidepressant drug, and the psychotherapy consisted of weekly sessions with a psychiatrist focusing on the person's social relationships. As one measure of the effect of different treatments, the researchers rated the patients' degree of depression after 16 weeks of treatment using a standard set of questions about mood and behavior. Thus, in this experiment, the independent variable was the kind of treatment given, and one dependent variable was the degree of depression after 16 weeks of treatment.

This is an example of a *between-groups experiment*, because the different conditions of the independent variable (that is, the different treatments) were applied to different groups of subjects. Notice that the researchers randomly assigned the subjects to the different treatment groups. Random assignment is important in between-groups experiments, because other methods could bias the results. For example, if the subjects had chosen their own treatment, it is possible that those who were most likely to improve even without treatment would have chosen one treatment and others would have chosen a different treatment. Then one could not know whether greater improvement in one group compared to the others was due to that initial likelihood or to treatment.

The results of this experiment are shown in Figure 2.3. Following a common convention in graphing experimental results, to be used throughout this book, the figure depicts variation in the independent variable along the horizontal axis and variation in the dependent variable along the vertical axis. As you can see in the figure, those in the drug treatment plus psychotherapy condition were the least depressed after the 16-week period, and those in the no-treatment condition were the most depressed. The results support the hypothesis that both drug therapy and psychotherapy help relieve depression, and that the two together have a greater effect than either alone.

**Correlational Studies**   In an experiment, as you just read, the researcher deliberately manipulates one variable (the independent variable) to determine its effect on another variable (the dependent variable). But many of the questions that psychologists ask are about relationships between variables over which the researcher has no reasonable means of control. In such cases an experiment is not possible, but a **correlational study** is. A correlational study can be defined as any study in which the researcher does not manipulate any variable, but observes or measures two or more variables to find relationships among them. While correlational studies can identify lawful relationships, they do not tell us in any direct way whether change in one variable is the cause of change in another.

Sometimes correlational studies look quite similar to experiments and are analyzed statistically in the same way as experiments, but one must be cautious about interpreting them in cause-effect terms. An example is a classic study by Diana Baumrind (1971) on the relationship between parents' discipline style and behavioral characteristics in their young children. Through questionnaires and home observations, Baumrind classified discipline styles into three categories: *authoritarian* (high exertion of power), *authoritative* (a more democratic style, but the parents are still in charge), and *permissive* (parental laxity in the face of their children's disruptive behaviors). She also rated each child on several dimensions of behavior, such as cooperation and friendliness, through observations in their nursery schools. The main finding was that children of authoritative parents performed better on the measures of behavior than did children of authoritarian or permissive parents.

Notice how tempting it is to treat Baumrind's study as if it were an experiment and to interpret the results in cause-effect terms, viewing parental style as the independent variable and the children's behavior as the dependent variable, and concluding that the differences in parental style caused the differences in the children's behavior. But other cause-effect interpretations are also possible. Perhaps the differences in children's behavior caused the differences in parental styles. Perhaps some children are better behaved than others for reasons quite separate from parental style, and perhaps parents with well-behaved children simply glide into an authoritative mode of parenting, while those with more difficult children fall into either of the other two modes as a way of coping. Or perhaps the causal relationship goes in both directions—parents affect children and children affect parents. Still another possibility is that other variables independently influence both parental style and children's behavior. For example, anything that makes families feel good about themselves (such as having good neighbors, good health, and an adequate income) might promote an authoritative style in parents and, quite independently, also lead children to behave well. In many correlational studies one causal hypothesis may seem more plausible than others, but that is a judgment based on reasoning about possible causal mechanisms, or on evidence from other sources, not from the correlational study itself.

In Baumrind's study, one variable (parental style) was used to place subjects into discrete groups and the other (children's behavior) was compared across those groups. Many correlational studies are analyzed in that way, but in many others both variables are measured numerically and neither is used to assign subjects to groups. In the latter case the data are assessed by a statistic called the *correlation coefficient*, which we will discuss later, in the section on statistical methods.

**Descriptive Studies**   Sometimes the aim of research is to describe the behavior of an individual or set of individuals without systematically investigating relationships between specific variables. A study of this sort is called a **descriptive study**. Descriptive studies may or may not make use of numbers. As an example of one involving numbers, researchers might survey the members of a given community to determine the percentage who suffer from various mental disorders. This is a descrip-

■ *How correlational studies differ from experiments, and why caution must be exerted in inferring causal relationships from them*

**What causes what?**

*Although many correlational studies have found a relationship between the viewing of televised violence and aggressive behavior, such studies cannot tell us whether television inspires the aggressive behavior or whether aggressive individuals are more likely than others to watch violent TV.*

■ *How descriptive studies differ from experiments and correlational studies*

tive study if its aim is simply to describe the prevalence of each disorder without correlating the disorders to other characteristics of the community's members. As an example of a descriptive study not involving numbers, an ethologist might observe the courtship behavior of a duck species to describe the sequence of movements that are involved. Some descriptive studies are narrow in focus, concentrating on just one specific aspect of behavior, and others are very broad, aiming to learn as much as possible about the habits of a particular group of people or species of animal. One of the most extensive and heroic descriptive studies in history is Jane Goodall's of the behavior of wild chimpanzees in Africa, which has been going on now for about 30 years and has provided a wealth of information about every aspect of these animals' lives.

### Data-Collection Methods

We turn now from research design to the second dimension shown in Figure 2.2, the data-collection method. Regardless of the research design, there are two broad categories of data-collection methods, self-report and observational.

*Self-report methods* are those in which the people being studied are asked to rate or describe their own behavior or mental state in some way. This might be done through a *questionnaire*, in which people check off items on a printed list, answer multiple-choice questions, or write out answers to essay questions aimed at producing a self-description. Or it might be done through an *interview*, in which people describe themselves orally in a dialogue with the interviewer. An interview may be tightly structured, with the interviewer asking questions according to a completely preplanned sequence, or it may be more loosely structured, with the interviewer following up on the subject's earlier responses with additional questions. Researchers have developed numerical methods for scoring some structured interviews, as in the case of the method used to rate depression in the experiment depicted in Figure 2.3.

*Observational methods* include all of the procedures by which psychologists directly observe the behavior of interest rather than rely on subjects' self-descriptions. In one subcategory of such methods, *naturalistic observation*, the researcher avoids interfering with the ongoing flow of the subject's behavior. Examples of naturalistic observation are an ethologist unobtrusively watching a duck's courtship behavior, or a developmental psychologist watching children through a one-way window into a laboratory playroom. In the other subcategory, *tests,* the researcher deliberately presents stimuli or problems for the subject to respond to. Examples of tests include reaction-time tests, in which a person is asked to respond in a particular way as quickly as possible when a specific stimulus is presented, and problem-solving tests, which might be in written form for people or in the form of maze problems or other such tasks for animals.

None of these data-collection methods is in any absolute sense superior to another. Each has its purposes, advantages, and limitations. Self-report measures are limited by the subjects' honesty and by their ability to observe and remember their own behaviors or moods. Naturalistic observations are limited by the great amount of time they take, by realistic constraints on a researcher's ability to observe ongoing behavior without disrupting it, and by the difficulty of coding results in a form that can be used for later statistical analyses. Tests are convenient and objective, but by nature artificial, and the relationship between test results and everyday behaviors is not always clear. What is the relationship between a rat's ability to run a maze and the kinds of behaviors that rats engage in normally? What is the relationship between a person's score on an IQ test and his or her ability to solve the problems of daily living? These are the kinds of questions that psychologists must try to answer whenever they generalize from test results to behaviors beyond the test environment.

■ *Two kinds of self-report methods, two kinds of observational methods, and the limitations of each*

*An observational technique*

*In most studies using a one-way window, subjects know that they are being watched. With the researcher hidden, most people find it relatively easy to forget that they are being observed and behave naturally.*

*The advantage and disadvantage of laboratory studies compared to field studies*

## Research Settings

The third dimension shown in Figure 2.2 is the research setting, which can be either the laboratory or field. A *laboratory study* is any research study in which the subjects are brought to a specially designated area that has been set up to facilitate the researcher's ability to collect data, or to manipulate an independent variable. A *field study* is any research study conducted in a setting other than the laboratory. Laboratory and field settings offer opposite sets of advantages and disadvantages. The laboratory allows the researcher to collect data under more uniform, controlled conditions than are possible in the field. On the other hand, the strangeness or artificiality of the laboratory may induce behaviors in subjects that obscure those that are of interest to the researcher. Thus, a study of parent-child interactions in the laboratory might produce results that reflect not so much the subjects' normal ways of interacting as their reactions to a strange environment in which they know that they are being observed. To counteract such problems, some researchers combine laboratory and field studies. If the same conclusions emerge from tightly controlled laboratory studies and less controlled but more natural field studies, they can be more confident that the conclusions are meaningful.

Experiments are most likely to be conducted in laboratories, and correlational and descriptive studies are most likely to be conducted in field settings. But any of the three research designs can be, and often are, carried out in either type of setting. For example, a *field experiment* can be conducted by manipulating some aspect of the natural environment in a controlled way. In one field experiment (which you will read about in Chapter 14), school teachers were instructed to praise some of their students, selected at random, about their ability in math and not to praise others, and the effect of this manipulation on the students' scores on subsequent math tests was observed (Miller & others, 1975). This is a field study, because it was conducted in the children's regular classrooms, but it is also an experiment, with an independent variable manipulated by the researchers (praise or no praise) and a dependent variable hypothesized to be affected by the independent variable (grades on subsequent math tests).

*A field study*

*Social psychologist Harold Takooshian and his colleagues found that passersby rarely intervene when they observe a man apparently attempting to break into a car. Staged incidents are often part of field studies in social psychology.*

## Statistical Methods in Psychology

When the data in any research study have been collected, they must somehow be summarized and interpreted. Statistical procedures are mathematical aids for summarizing and interpreting data. They can be divided into two categories: (a) *descriptive statistics*, which are used to summarize a set of data, and (b) *inferential statistics*, which help the researchers decide how confident one can be in drawing specific conclusions (inferences) from the data. We will look here at some commonly used descriptive statistics and then at the basic rationale of inferential statistics. A more detailed, mathematical discussion of some of these procedures can be found in the Statistical Appendix at the back of this book.

### Describing the Central Tendency and Variability of a Set of Data

■ *A set of scores can be characterized by its central tendency and variability*

Descriptive statistics include all of the methods for summarizing a set of data. If the study involved classifying people according to whether or not they showed some specific behavior, the data might be summarized by calculating the percentage of people who showed it. If the data are numerical in form (such as depression ratings), they might be summarized by calculating either the mean or median. The *mean* is simply the arithmetic average, determined by adding together the scores and dividing by the number of scores. The *median* is the center score, determined by ranking the scores from largest to smallest and finding the score that falls in the exact center of the list. (The Statistical Appendix explains when it is better to use the mean or the median.) The mean or median tells us about the central tendency of a set of numbers, but not about its variability. Variability refers to the degree to which the numbers in the set differ from one another or from their mean. In Table 2.1 you can see two sets of numbers that have identical means but different variabilities. In Set *A* the scores cluster close to the mean (low variability), and in Set *B* they differ widely from it (high variability). A common measure of variability is the *standard deviation*, which is calculated by a formula (described in the Statistical Appendix) that takes into account the difference between each individual score and the mean, and combines those differences to produce a single measure. As illustrated in Table 2.1, the greater the average difference between each score and the mean, the greater the standard deviation.

**Table 2.1** *Two sets of data, with the same mean but different amounts of variability*

| Set *A* | Set *B* |
|---|---|
| 7 | 2 |
| 7 | 4 |
| 8 | 8 |
| 11 | 9 |
| 12 | 14 |
| 12 | 16 |
| 13 | 17 |
| *Median = 11* | *Median = 9* |
| *Total = 70* | *Total = 70* |
| *Mean = 70/7 = 10* | *Mean = 70/7 = 10* |
| *Standard deviation = 0.98* | *Standard deviation = 2.22* |

### Describing a Correlation

A descriptive statistic used in correlational studies is the **correlation coefficient**, which measures the strength and direction of the correlation between two variables that have been measured numerically. Correlation coefficients are calculated by a formula (described in the Statistical Appendix) that produces a result ranging from +1.00 to −1.00. The sign (+ or −) indicates the direction of the correlation (positive or negative). A positive correlation is one in which an increase in one variable coincides with a tendency for the other variable to increase also, and a negative correlation is one in which an increase in one variable coincides with a tendency for the other variable to decrease. The absolute value of the correlation coefficient (from 0 to 1.00, irrespective of sign) indicates the strength of the correlation. A correlation is strong if it is possible to predict quite reliably one measure by knowing another, and weak if it is not.

As an example, consider a study correlating high school students' scores on a standard intelligence test (IQ scores) with their grade point averages (GPAs), in which the raw data consist of an IQ score and a GPA for each of fifteen students. To visualize the results, the researchers might produce what is called a *scatter plot*, in which each student's pair of scores is represented by a single point on a graph. The scatter plots for four different hypothetical sets of results are shown in Figure 2.4. Plot *A* illustrates a *moderate positive correlation*. Notice that each point depicts both the IQ (marked on the horizontal axis) and GPA (marked on the vertical axis) for a single student. Thus, the point indicated by the arrow represents a student whose IQ is 112 and GPA is 3.60. By looking at the whole constellation of points, you can see that, in general, higher GPAs correspond with higher IQs. This is what makes the correlation positive. Plot *B* illustrates a *strong positive correlation*. Notice that here the points fall very close to an upwardly slanted line. The closer the points are to forming a straight line, the stronger the correlation. The stronger the correlation, the more accurate you would be in predicting someone's GPA from his or her IQ, or vice versa. Plot *C* illustrates a *moderate negative correlation*. In this case, GPA tends to fall as IQ rises. Finally, Plot *D* represents *uncorrelated data*—a coefficient close to or equal to 0. Here there is no relation between the two variables; knowing a person's IQ does not help you predict GPA, or vice versa. (In case you are curious, actual studies of the correlation between IQ and GPA usually produce moderate positive correlations, with coefficients ranging from about +0.30 to +0.70 in different studies [Jensen, 1980].)

■ *How a correlation coefficient describes the direction and strength of a correlation*

**Figure 2.4** *Scatter plots relating grade point average to IQ*

*Plot* A *represents a moderate positive correlation* (a), *Plot* B *a strong positive correlation* (b), *Plot* C *a moderate negative correlation* (c), *and Plot* D *a correlation close to zero* (d). *(The actual correlation coefficients calculated for the data shown here are +0.52 for A, +0.89 for B, −0.52 for C, and +0.08 for D. The data are hypothetical.)*

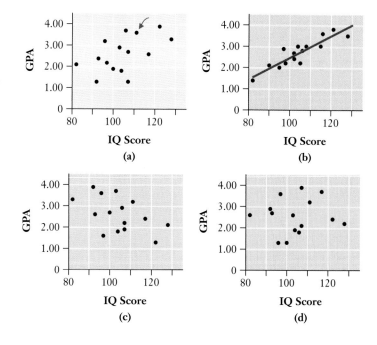

### Inferential Statistics

In any given set of data, collected in any given research study, there will be some degree of variability that can be attributed to chance. Thus, in the experiment comparing treatments for depression (shown in Figure 2.3), the different depression ratings obtained for the different groups reflect not just the effects of treatment, but also random effects caused by uncontrollable variables. For example, more people who were predisposed to improve could by chance have been assigned to one treatment group than to another, even with random assignment. As another example, random measurement error introduced by defects in the rating procedure could have contributed to differences between the group means. If the experiment were repeated several times, the results would be somewhat different each time due to these uncontrollable random variables. Given that results can vary due to chance, how confident can a researcher be in inferring a general law based on the study's data? Inferential statistics are procedures that make use of the laws of probability to answer that question.

The inference at issue in any given study can be called the *research hypothesis*. In an experiment, the research hypothesis is usually that the independent variable has some consistent effect on the dependent variable. In a correlational study, the research hypothesis is usually that two measured variables are correlated in some way. Inferential statistics, applied to either an experiment or a correlational study, are procedures for determining the probability that the data could have come out as they did if the research hypothesis is *wrong*. The lower that probability is, the more confident the researcher can be that the research hypothesis is correct. A long-standing convention in psychology is to label results as **statistically significant** if the probability is less than 5 percent that the data could have come out as they did if the hypothesis is wrong. Stated differently, the results of a research study are usually considered to be statistically significant if they indicate that there are fewer than 5 chances in 100 that the research hypothesis is wrong (or more than 95 chances in 100 that it is right).

As an example, the inferential statistics reported by DiMascio and his colleagues (1979) for the results shown in Figure 2.3 revealed that there was less than a 5 percent chance that the observed difference between groups receiving drug treatment and those not receiving drug treatment could have occurred by chance if in fact the drug had no effect. They also revealed that there was less than a 5 percent chance that the observed difference between groups receiving psychotherapy and those not receiving psychotherapy could have occurred by chance if in fact psychotherapy had no effect. Thus, both the effect of drugs and the effect of psychotherapy were statistically significant.

What are the elements that go into a test of statistical significance? One element, clearly, is the *size of the observed effect*, as determined by the descriptive statistics. Other things being equal, the larger the observed difference in the dependent variable between groups in an experiment, or the larger the correlation coefficient in a correlational study, the more significant the results. A second element is the *number of individual subjects or observations* in the study. Other things being equal, the greater the number of subjects or observations, the more likely the results are to be significant. If that number is huge, even very small effects will be statistically significant. A third element, applicable when the data are numerical in form and are summarized as means, is the *variability* of the data within each group. Variability within the group can be thought of as a direct assessment of the degree of randomness operating on the dependent variable. For example, in the experiment on the effects of treatments on depression, greater variability in depression scores within each treatment group would reflect greater randomness. Other things being equal, the lower the variability, the more likely the results are to be significant.

▨ *The meaning of statistical significance, and the factors that go into calculating it*

Thus, the formula for assessing the statistical significance of differences between group means takes into account (a) the size of the difference between the means, (b) the number of subjects in each group, and (c) the variability of the data within each group. (An example of such a formula, for a test of statistical significance called the *t* test, can be found in any textbook on psychological statistics.)

The method for assessing the statistical significance of a correlation coefficient takes into account just two factors—the absolute size of the correlation coefficient (its distance above or below 0) and the number of pairs of correlated observations. As the number of subjects grows, the size of the correlation coefficient needed for statistical significance declines. Thus, in the study of correlation between GPA and IQ, a correlation coefficient of 0.30 would be statistically significant if many subjects were sampled, but not if few were sampled.

## Sources of Error and Bias in Psychological Research

■ *The difference between error and bias*

Inferential statistics can be used to assess the likelihood that a particular set of results came out in the direction it did because of chance, but they cannot correct for flaws in the research study itself. Researchers must take care to minimize possible sources of error and bias in their studies. *Error*, as a technical term, refers to increased randomness in results. The greater the error, the greater will be the random variability in the results, and hence the less will be the chance of obtaining statistical significance. *Bias*, as a technical term, refers to nonrandom (directed) effects, caused by some factor or factors extraneous to the research hypothesis. Bias is a more serious problem than error, because it can lead to the false conclusion that the research hypothesis has been supported when in fact the results came out as they did for a different reason. Inferential statistics cannot tell us whether the results that they identify as significant stem from bias or from the truth of the research hypothesis.

Thus, while error can lead a researcher to believe that a true research hypothesis is not true, bias can lead a researcher to conclude that a false research hypothesis is true. Here are some of the main sources of error and bias in psychological research, and ways to guard against them:

### Problems with the Measurement Procedure

An important limiting factor in psychological research is the ability to measure the behavior or characteristic that is of interest. A good measurement procedure has three characteristics: reliability, sensitivity, and validity.

■ *How lack of reliability and sensitivity contribute to error, and lack of validity contributes to bias*

A measurement procedure is *reliable* if it gives similar results each time it is used with a particular subject under a particular set of conditions. Measuring height with an elastic ruler would not be as reliable as measuring it with a stiff ruler, because the elasticity would cause the results to vary from one time to the next. A paper-and-pencil test of intelligence is not reliable if the answers depend more on the momentary whims of the individual than on something more stable about the person. Typically, the reliability of a measure is assessed by using the same measure (or different versions of it) at least twice with the same subjects and then calculating the test-retest correlation. If the correlation is high (meaning that each person tended to score about the same each time), the test is considered to be reliable.

A measurement procedure is *sensitive* if it is able to pick up fine differences across individuals or test conditions. If a procedure doesn't pick up any differences, it is completely insensitive. For example, if your psychology professor gave a midterm exam and everyone got the same score no matter how well they knew the

*Measuring what babies see*

*Donald Duck is the lab assistant as researchers record the responses of this 7-month-old's brain to visual stimuli flashed on a screen. Donald, who is connected to the singer in the background, keeps the infant's attention focused on the lights. The electric device attached to her head records her responses. As you read about sources of measurement error and bias, think about the ways in which this clever device helps circumvent those pitfalls.*

material, the test would be completely insensitive. This is what would happen if every question was either so easy that everyone got it right or so hard that everyone got it wrong (in the latter case you might say that it was insensitive in more ways than one). Low reliability and low sensitivity are both sources of measurement error, and hence both reduce the likelihood of finding statistical significance in a research study.

A measurement procedure is **valid** if it measures what it is supposed to measure. It is possible for a procedure to be reliable but not valid. For example, assessing intelligence by measuring thumb length is highly reliable (you would get nearly the same score each time), moderately sensitive (people do differ on this measure), but almost certainly not valid (thumb length probably has nothing to do with intelligence). If common sense tells us that a procedure measures what we wish it to measure, the procedure has *face validity*. A paper-and-pencil test of the ability to solve logical problems has relatively high face validity as a measure of intelligence, but thumb length does not. Another, more certain index of validity is *criterion validity*, which is assessed by correlating the measure with other measures of the characteristic that we wish to assess. Thus, suppose intelligence were defined as that quality of mind that allows a person in appropriate circumstances to achieve greatness in any of various realms of human endeavor, including business, diplomacy, science, literature, and art. Then we might identify a group of people who have achieved such greatness and a group who, despite similar environmental opportunities, have not achieved such greatness, and see if they differ in the measure of intelligence. To the degree that they differ, the measure would be said to have criterion validity. If thumb length turned out to distinguish the two groups better than did the paper-and-pencil test of logic, then it would have greater criterion validity despite its lower face validity.

Validity is a major problem in psychological measurement. The assessment of validity requires the researcher to define clearly the psychological characteristic that he or she wishes to measure and to show that the measure really predicts behavior relevant to that characteristic. Lack of validity is a source of bias. Because an invalid procedure measures something different from the characteristic posed by the research hypothesis, it may reveal differences between groups that are statistically significant for reasons having nothing to do with that hypothesis. Suppose, for example, that the interview procedure used in the depression study (illustrated in Figure 2.3) was not a valid measure of depression, but rather reflected subjects' desires to appear depressed or not. In that case the results would still be statistically significant, but the researchers' conclusion (that treatment affects depression) would be mistaken. A more accurate conclusion would be that some treatments lead to a stronger desire to appear not depressed than do others.

### Observer-Expectancy Effects

■ *Two ways by which an observer's expectations can bias results, and how blind observation prevents such bias*

Being human, researchers inevitably have wishes and expectations that can affect how they behave and what they observe when recording data. The resulting biases are called ***observer-expectancy effects***. A researcher who desires or expects a subject to respond in a particular way may unintentionally communicate that expectation and thereby influence the subject's behavior. As you may recall, Pfungst discovered that this sort of effect provided the basis for Hans's ability to answer questions. In a between-groups experiment, a researcher who expects subjects in one group to behave one way, and those in another group to behave another way, may send different signals to the two groups and thus elicit the expected difference. In addition to influencing subjects' behavior, observer expectancy can also influence the observer's perception or judgment of that behavior. For example, an observer who expects to find that people smile more in one condition than in another may interpret an ambiguous facial expression as a smile in the one condition and as something else in the other.

The best way to prevent observer-expectancy effects is to keep the observer ***blind***, that is, uninformed, about those aspects of the study's design that could lead to differential expectations. Thus, in a between-groups experiment, a blind observer would be uninformed as to which treatment any given subject had received. Not knowing who is in what group, the blind observer has no basis for having different expectations for different subjects. In the study of treatments for depression (illustrated in Figure 2.3), the clinicians who evaluated patients' depression at the end of the treatment period were blind to treatment condition. To keep them blind, patients were instructed not to say anything about their treatment during the evaluation interview.

### Subject-Expectancy Effects (Placebo Effects)

Subjects also have expectations that can affect their behavior. If different treatments in an experiment produce different expectations, then observed behavior differences between groups may be due to those expectations. Effects of this sort are most well known in drug studies. People who take a drug, or who believe they are taking one, may subsequently behave in a certain way simply because they expect the drug to cause such behavior. To control for such effects in drug studies, subjects in the nondrug group are given an inactive substance, called a ***placebo***, which looks like the drug, and no subjects are told whether they are receiving the drug or the placebo. Other sorts of treatments besides drugs can also influence subjects' expectations. For example, subjects receiving psychotherapy may improve simply because they believe that psychotherapy will help them. In psychological research, the term ***placebo effect*** refers to any effect that stems from subjects' expectations.

■ *Placebo effects, and the value of a double blind experiment*

Ideally, to prevent bias due to placebo effects, subjects should be kept blind regarding the treatment they are receiving or its possible effects. An experiment in which both the observer and the subject are blind with respect to the treatment condition is called a ***double blind experiment***. Of course, it is sometimes impossible to keep the subject blind. For instance, you can't give psychotherapy to people without their knowing it. In some psychotherapy experiments (as you will see in Chapter 18), subjects in the nonpsychotherapy group are given a fake form of therapy designed to induce subject expectancies equivalent to those induced by psychotherapy. Incidentally, the subjects in the depression experiment described earlier were not blind concerning their treatment. Those in the nondrug groups did not receive a placebo, and those in the nonpsychotherapy groups did not receive fake psychotherapy. Thus, the results depicted in Figure 2.3 could, at least in theory, be placebo effects.

### Problems in Generalizing from a Sample to a Larger Population

The set of people or animals in any study are only a subset, or *sample*, from some larger population. If researchers want to make claims about the larger population, their sample should be representative of that population. A sample that is not representative of the population that the researcher thinks he or she is studying is called a **biased sample**. A notorious example of research that went awry because of a biased sample was the *Literary Digest*'s poll of U.S. voters in 1936, which led the *Digest* to announce that Alf Landon would beat Franklin D. Roosevelt in the presidential election that year by a margin of 2 to 1 (Huff, 1954). It turned out that their conclusion could not have been more mistaken—Roosevelt won by a landslide. The *Digest* had conducted its poll by telephoning magazine subscribers. In 1936, in the midst of the Great Depression, people who could afford magazine subscriptions and telephones may indeed have favored Landon, but the great bulk of voters, as the election showed, did not.

A great deal of psychological research employs college students as subjects. College students are convenient, since most research is conducted on college campuses. For some studies, such as those of basic sensory processes, there is probably little problem in generalizing from college students to other groups. But for others, such as studies of values, goals, achievement motivation, and the like, what is true of college students may not be true of people in general. Psychologists who wish to generalize their findings about such processes beyond the college population must often go to considerable trouble to study people in other settings. The same issue applies at an even broader level when psychologists wish to generalize their findings to other parts of the world. A psychological law that holds up for people reared in North America or Western Europe may not apply to people reared in the Orient. You will find examples of such cross-cultural differences sprinkled throughout later chapters of this book.

■ *Why a telephone poll failed, and why researchers must be cautious about extending their conclusions beyond the group studied*

*A cross-cultural difference*
*In most non-Western cultures, young children are kept much closer to their caretakers than in the West. This may provide a basis for cross-cultural differences found in studies of attachment.*

# Ethical Issues in Psychological Research

Because their research is with human beings and other sentient animals, psychologists must consider ethical as well as scientific issues in designing their studies. DiMascio and his colleagues (1979) might, from a scientific vantage point, have improved their study of treatments for depression by using a placebo in the nondrug conditions and a fake form of psychotherapy in the nonpsychotherapy conditions, to try to equate the level of expectancy across groups. But the researchers felt that their subjects should know what form of treatment they were getting, so they could make an informed decision as to whether or not to participate, and also so they would have a basis for understanding possible side effects as treatment progressed. The researchers also felt that it was important to change the treatment for any patient who by the end of 8 weeks had not shown evidence of reduced depression. In those cases they used the depression score at 8 weeks in the final data analysis (combining it with the 16-week data on the other subjects). These characteristics somewhat weaken the scientific merit of the study, but the researchers felt that this compromise was essential from an ethical standpoint.

*Privacy, discomfort, deception, and animal welfare as ethical issues*

In research with humans, ethical considerations revolve around three interrelated issues: (1) the person's right to privacy, (2) the possible discomfort or psychological harm that a research procedure could produce, and (3) the use of deception that characterizes some research designs. Concerning the first two of these issues, the usual ethical safeguards include obtaining informed consent from subjects before they take part in a study, informing subjects that they can quit the study at any time (and respecting their right to do so), and keeping records and reports in a way that ensures subjects' anonymity. In addition, whenever there is the possibility of discomfort or harm, researchers are obliged to determine if the same question could be answered in a study that involves less risk, and, if the answer is no, to demonstrate that the human benefits of the study outweigh any possible costs. In reality, the great majority of psychological studies involve completely harmless procedures, such as reading rapidly flashed letters, memorizing lists of terms, or carrying on a discussion with other subjects.

The most controversial ethical issue in human psychological research concerns deception. In some experiments the independent variable involves a lie. Subjects may be falsely told or led to believe that something is happening, or going to happen, in order to study their reactions to that belief. Some psychologists believe that any research that involves deception is unethical (see Carroll & others, 1985). They argue that deception (a) is intrinsically unethical no matter what its ends; (b) undermines the possibility of obtaining truly informed consent (subjects cannot give informed consent if they are not told the truth about the study before it begins); and (c) could undermine the validity of psychological research in the long run, because it might lead people to assume that they are likely to be tricked whenever they participate in a study, which in turn could affect their behavior and bias the findings.

Other psychologists justify deception on the grounds that certain important psychological processes cannot be studied effectively without it. They counter the above charges by responding that (a) research deception usually takes the form of benign "white lies," which are cleared up when the researcher informs the subject of the true nature of the study in a debriefing session after the experimental session has ended; (b) informed consent can still be obtained by telling subjects that some details of the study must be withheld until the data have been collected and by informing them of any realistic dangers that could be involved; and (c) the great majority of psychological studies do not involve deception, so there is little danger that people will regularly expect it to occur. In Chapter 15, you will read about some classic studies that involved deception, and it will be interesting then to think again about its pros and cons.

The use of nonhuman animals in research presents another area of ethical controversy. There are many good reasons why some psychologists study animals. With animals one can employ procedures that cannot be employed with humans. One can breed them in controlled ways, raise them in controlled environments, and surgically intervene in their physiology. Basic biological mechanisms underlying animal behavior are similar to those underlying human behavior, so such research contributes to our understanding of humans as well as the species studied. On the other hand, there is no doubt that research on nonhuman animals can sometimes cause them to suffer, and any researcher employing animals has an ethical obligation to balance the animal's suffering against the potential gains that can come from the research. Animals must be well cared for and not subjected to unnecessary deprivation or pain. Some people argue that animals should never be kept in cages and studied in laboratories, but those who defend such practices point to the enormous gains in knowledge and reduction in human (and animal) suffering that have come from them (see Miller, 1985).

**White rat with electrode**

*Physiological psychology experiments frequently involve operations on an animal's brain. In performing such experiments, researchers must balance the benefits of their possible findings against the costs to the animal.*

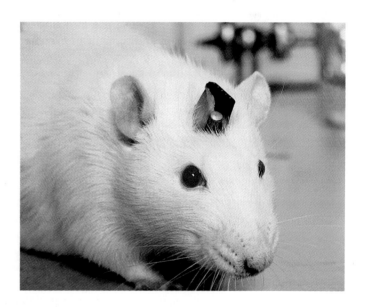

The American Psychological Association (1981, 1982) has established ethical guidelines for psychological research, which deal more elaborately with all the issues raised here. Moreover, in the United States and many other countries today research institutions that receive public funding are required by law to have ethics review panels, whose task is to review all proposed studies that have any potential for ethical controversy. Such panels quite often turn down research proposals, and one result is that some studies that were once seen as quite acceptable would not be conducted today. Among them are a few studies that are considered classics and, hence, occupy a place in most general psychology textbooks, including this one. As you read of some of the studies in the chapters to follow, questions of ethics may well occur to you from time to time. Such questions are always legitimate, as are questions about the scientific merit of a study's design and the validity or generality of its results. Psychology needs and usually welcomes people who raise these kinds of questions.

## Concluding Thoughts

**1.  The relationship of science to everyday observation and thought**  There is no sharp distinction between science and the kinds of observation and thought that all of us use every day to learn about the world around us. In our everyday learning, we begin with the data of our senses, and we use these data to draw tentative conclusions (make inferences) about specific aspects of our world. For example, we might one day observe someone from Town $X$ act politely and someone from Town $Y$ act rudely, and infer from that pair of observations that people from $X$ are more polite than people from $Y$. Most of us make such inferences all the time, often on scarcely more evidence than that. Science is simply the attempt to improve upon our natural ways of learning by formalizing the data-collection procedures, controlling conditions to be more certain which variables are having which effects, striving to eliminate sources of bias, deliberately thinking of alternative explanations, and using statistical procedures to assess the degree of confidence we should have in our tentative conclusions. As you review each of the main concepts discussed in the sections on research strategies, statistical methods, and sources of error and bias in this chapter, you might think about how that concept applies—somewhat less formally—to the distinctions between good and poor observation and thought in everyday life. We are observing and thinking poorly when we jump to conclusions with too little evidence, or fail to think about alternative explanations, or fail to see what is really there because of our biased expectations.

**2.  What is a science of psychology for?**  I remember, as a college freshman on a visit home, flaunting my pride a bit overbearingly about an $A$ that I had received in calculus. My mother, hearing me brag, and having a knack for diffusing undue pride and putting things into perspective, asked a simple question: "What is calculus for?" I was floored. I could rattle off terms and equations about calculus, and I could solve the problems as they were given to me in the class, but I had no understanding at all of what calculus was for. Perhaps that is why, by a few months after the class had ended, I had completely forgotten the terms, the equations, and how to solve them. So what is a science of psychology for?

Some people think of psychology purely in applied terms. They see its purpose as that of trying directly to solve human problems. The study on treatments for depression (illustrated in Figure 2.3) fits well with their view of the science, but these people may not quite appreciate Wundt's desire to measure the speed of human judgments, or Lorenz's desire to describe the courtship behaviors of ducks (both noted in Chapter 1). Do the ducks have a problem that needs solving? The same issue applies in other sciences as well. What good does it do us to know what the other side of the moon looks like?

For the most part, people go into psychological research, or any other research field, because they are curious, or because they are thrilled by the prospect of being the first to uncover some mystery of nature, large or small. So psychology, like any other science, has two purposes: to solve practical problems and to satisfy the human quest for knowledge. It is hard to separate the two, however, because very often research done solely to satisfy curiosity sometimes turns up findings that solve problems that at first seemed unrelated to the research. As you read the remaining chapters of this book, I hope you will allow yourself to become engaged by the questions for their own sake, regardless of whether you think they have practical applications. Each chapter contains mysteries, some solved, some not.

## Further Reading

**Theodore X. Barber** (1976). *Pitfalls in human research.* New York: Pergamon.
*This slender volume outlines, and illustrates with specific examples, ten different categories of mistakes in designing and conducting a research study, each of which can lead researchers or consumers of research to false conclusions.*

**Darrell Huff** (1954). *How to lie with statistics.* New York: Norton.
*This witty paperback, filled with anecdotes and cartoons, has a serious message. It tells you how not to lie with statistics, and how to spot lies when they occur. It is guaranteed to make you a more critical consumer of statistical information. Don't be put off by its date; it is reprinted regularly and widely available.*

**Mary Ann Carroll, Henry G. Schneider, & George R. Wesley** (1985). *Ethics in the practice of psychology.* Englewood Cliffs, NJ: Prentice Hall.
*This book begins with a chapter on philosophical approaches to ethics, and then discusses ethical principles as applied to various aspects of psychological research and practice. The appendix contains a complete reprint of the American Psychological Association's "Ethical Principles of Psychologists."*

**Robert J. Sternberg** (1988). *The psychologist's companion: A guide to scientific writing for students and researchers* (2nd ed.). Cambridge: Cambridge University Press.
*Psychologists, like scholars in every field, must communicate their ideas and findings in writing. This book, by one of the most prolific writers among contemporary psychologists, is a very practical guide to the writing of psychological papers of all types, ranging from library papers and lab reports by first-year college students to papers for publication by full-fledged researchers.*

## Looking Ahead

This is not the only chapter of this book that deals with methods. In a very real sense, all of the chapters to follow are about methods, because our knowledge in every area of psychology is inseparable from our ways of knowing. In each chapter, I will attempt to give you at least some ideas of the methods used to test the ideas being described, and the results of such tests. You will sometimes read relatively full accounts of specific studies, or see graphs summarizing the data; and in other cases you will find only hints of these. The concepts described in the present chapter will be useful in each chapter to follow. It will be especially useful to remember (a) the difference between an experiment and a correlational study; (b) the meaning of correlation coefficient, statistical significance, measurement validity, and double blind experiment; and (c) the problem of generalizing from a sample. These issues will all come up repeatedly, either explicitly or implicitly in discussions to follow.

And now, we move from background to the first chapter dealing substantively with the content of psychology. It is about the role of heredity in behavior.

# PART 2   NATURE, NURTURE, AND BEHAVIORAL ADAPTATION

**GENETICS OF BEHAVIOR**

**THE ADAPTIVENESS OF BEHAVIOR I: EVOLUTION**

**THE ADAPTIVENESS OF BEHAVIOR II: LEARNING**

*Our genetic structure has been shaped by millions of years of evolution, adapting us to the general conditions of human life on earth. As part of that shaping, we have acquired an immense capacity to learn. This unit consists of three chapters. The first examines the interplay between genes and environment in determining differences among individuals. The second has to do with inherited behavioral tendencies, and with the attempt to understand them in terms of evolutionary history. The third deals with elementary processes of learning, which modify behavior to meet the conditions of individual life.*

# CHAPTER 3

**Principles of Gene Action and Heredity**

**Single-Gene and Chromosomal Effects on Behavior**

**Polygenic Effects on Behavior**

# GENETICS OF BEHAVIOR

In 1582, Richard Mulcaster, an English educator, introduced into the world's literature a harmonious pair of terms, **nature** and **nurture**, to refer to what he regarded as twin forces in the development of a child's mind (see Teigen, 1984). By *nature* he meant the child's inborn biological endowment (what we would now call *genetic inheritance*), and by *nurture* he meant all the environmental conditions (including schooling) in which the mind develops. To Mulcaster the poetic flow of this pair of terms captured the harmony in which these forces work together. In an essay on the education of boys, he wrote, "Nature makes the boy toward, nurture sees him forward" (Mulcaster, 1582). Some 30 years later, William Shakespeare used the same terms, in a similar way, in *The Tempest*. Then, in the second half of the nineteenth century, the English scientist Francis Galton (1822–1911) picked up and popularized the terms, but he seemed to pit them against one another rather than emphasize their harmony.

Galton was interested in differences of many sorts among people, especially differences in intellectual achievement. What, he asked, explains the wide differences in achievement among people of the same social class? Theorizing that the source of the differences could be biological heredity (nature) or environmental conditions (nurture), he initiated a research program to determine which played the larger role in accounting for the differences. Galton's research marked the start of the so-called **nature-nurture debate** in psychology, which in various guises has been important throughout psychology's history. In essence, the question of the debate is this: Are psychological differences among people primarily the result of differences in their genes or in their environments?

Scientists today know far more about genes than did Galton and his peers. In fact, there is now a subfield in psychology called **behavioral genetics**—the study of the effects of genes on behavior. This chapter begins with a brief summary of gene biology, followed by a discussion of some of the most clear-cut effects of genes on behavior (involving single-gene inheritance or abnormal numbers of chromosomes). Then, the final section discusses research on behavioral differences that are affected by many genes. There we will return to the nature-nurture question, examining some of the misconceptions that have fueled the debate, and considering two topics that have attracted research and controversy from Galton's time until today: the application of the nature-nurture question to intelligence (as measured by IQ tests) and to susceptibility to schizophrenia (a class of mental disorder). An important theme throughout the chapter is that genes express themselves through interaction with the environment and, thus, all conclusions about gene effects on behavior are relative to the range of environmental conditions in which the organisms developed.

# Principles of Gene Action and Heredity

### *How Genes Affect Physical Development and Behavior*

At base, genes direct the synthesis of *protein molecules*, on which all physical development depends. A class of proteins called *structural proteins* forms the structure of every cell in the body, and another class called *enzymes* controls the rate of every chemical reaction in every cell. We are what we are, biologically speaking, because of our proteins, and the genetic differences among us are all mediated through the production of proteins.

How do genes direct the synthesis of proteins? The answer has been worked out in wondrous detail by molecular biologists, but here a rough sketch will suffice. Physically, the genetic material is an extremely long molecule called *DNA* (deoxyribonucleic acid). DNA, which exists in every cell, serves as a template (that is, a mold or pattern) for producing *RNA* (ribonucleic acid), another molecular substance, and RNA serves as a template for producing protein molecules. A protein molecule consists of a long chain of smaller molecules called *amino acids*, which come in about twenty different varieties. Different sequences of amino acids can form an almost infinite variety of protein molecules. Thus, the main job of the gene is to control, through the RNA mediator, the sequence of amino acids in a protein molecule. DNA molecules contain the codes for many different protein molecules. From a molecular vantage point, a gene can be defined as the portion of a DNA molecule containing the code for one specific type of protein molecule.

■ *How genes affect behavior by building a body with certain capacities and response characteristics*

The key point here is that genes affect behavior through one, and only one, means—the manufacture of proteins. Through building proteins they contribute to the anatomy and physiology of the body, and through that they affect behavior. Sometimes, as a sort of shorthand, people speak of genes "for" particular behavioral traits, but in reality there are no genes for behavioral traits that are separate from genes for anatomy and physiology. Thus, a gene might influence musical ability by promoting the development of a brain system that analyzes sounds, or by promoting certain physical aspects of the vocal cords. Similarly, a gene might affect aggressiveness by promoting the growth of systems in the brain that respond to irritating external stimuli and organize aggressive behavior. In a sense all genes that contribute to the body's development are "for" behavior, since all parts of the body are involved in behavior. Especially relevant for behavior, however, are genes that contribute to development of sensory systems, the nervous system, and motor systems (muscles and other organs involved in movement).

■ *Gene-environment interaction, and the difference between genotype and phenotype*

At every level of analysis, from biochemical to behavioral, the effects of genes are entwined with the effects of the environment. The term *environment*, as used in this context, refers to every aspect of an individual and his or her surroundings except the genes themselves. It includes the nourishing womb and maternal bloodstream before birth; the internal chemical environment of the developing individual; and all the events, objects, and other individuals encountered after birth. Foods—a part of the environment—supply genes with amino acids, which they need to manufacture proteins. Environmental effects also turn genes on and off. For example, physical exercise changes the chemical environment of muscle cells in a way that activates genes that promote further growth of the muscle. One's body and behavioral capacities result from a continuous and highly complicated interplay between genes and environment (see Figure 3.1). In no sense can one be said to be more basic than the other.

Geneticists use the term **genotype** to refer to the set of genes that the individual inherits and **phenotype** to refer to the observable properties of the body and behavioral traits. The same genes can have different effects depending on the environment and the mix of other genes. Two people with the same genotype can be

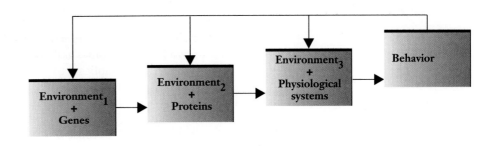

**Figure 3.1 *Route through which genes affect behavior***

*Genes build proteins, which form the body's physiological systems, which produce behavior. Each step in this process involves interaction with the environment. Environment₁ and Environment₂ represent the internal chemical environment that affects gene and enzyme action, and Environment₃ represents the external environment. The behavioral response in turn can affect each level of the environment.*

quite different in phenotype. As an obvious example, identical twins (who have the same genes) will differ phenotypically in muscle strength if one exercises a lot and the other doesn't. You will see other examples as the chapter progresses.

### Sexual Reproduction and Patterns of Heredity

**Chromosomes, and Genetic Recombination in Sexual Reproduction** The genes are not only templates for producing proteins, but are also the units of heredity. To understand patterns of genetic inheritance, it is useful to know something about the arrangement of genes in the cell and what happens to that arrangement in sexual reproduction.

The genetic material (long strands of DNA) exists in each cell in structures called ***chromosomes***, which are usually dispersed throughout the cell nucleus and not visible. However, just prior to cell division the chromosomes condense into compact structures that can be stained, viewed with a microscope, and photographed. The photographic representation of chromosomes in a single cell is known as a ***karyotype***. As you can see in Figure 3.2, the normal human male karyotype consists of 23 pairs of chromosomes, 22 of which are called ***autosomes*** and numbered 1 through 22, from largest to smallest. The remaining pair, the ***sex chromosomes***, includes a large ***X chromosome*** and a much smaller ***Y chromosome***.

***Identical twins***

*These 13-year-old girls have the same genes, but they obviously differ in at least one aspect of their phenotype.*

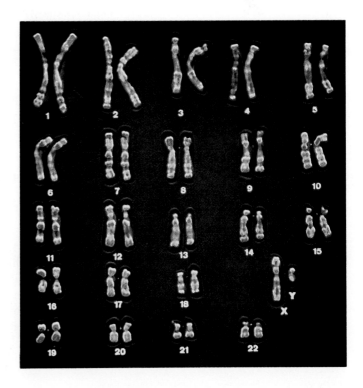

**Figure 3.2 *Normal human male karyotype***

*The 22 numbered pairs of chromosomes are called autosomes, and the remaining 2, labeled X and Y, are called sex chromosomes. The female karyotype, not shown, is identical to the male's except for the existence of a second X and no Y.*

The normal human female karyotype is identical to the male's except for the existence of two X chromosomes and no Y.

Cells can divide (duplicate themselves) in two ways: mitosis, which is involved in normal body growth, and meiosis, which produces the egg and sperm cells used in sexual reproduction. In **mitosis**, each chromosome precisely replicates itself and then the cell divides, with one copy of each chromosome moving into each of the two cells thus formed. Because of the faithful copying of genetic material in mitosis, all of your body's cells (except for egg or sperm cells) are genetically identical to each other. The differences among different cells in your body—such as liver cells and skin cells—arise from the differential activation of their genes, not from different gene content.

**Meiosis**, on the other hand, produces cells that are not genetically alike. Meiosis operates on precursor cells in the female's ovaries to produce egg cells, and in the male's testes, to produce sperm cells. To begin this process, the two members of each pair of chromosomes in the precursor cell line up next to one another, and each chromosome reproduces itself, resulting in sets of four identical-looking chromosomes (see Figure 3.3). Then the cell divides, with two chromosomes from each set of four going to each of the two cells thus formed. These cells then divide again, with one chromosome from each set going to each of the new cells. The result is four egg or sperm cells, each of which has half the normal number of chromosomes, one member of each original pair.

**Figure 3.3  *Schematic representation of meiosis***

*Each chromosome of the precursor cell reproduces itself once, but then the cell divides twice, resulting in four egg or sperm cells, each of which has one member of each original pair of chromosomes.*

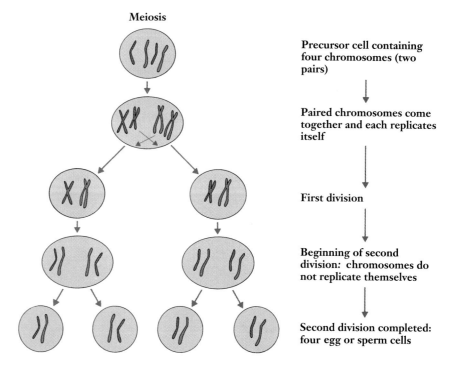

Meiosis

Precursor cell containing four chromosomes (two pairs)

Paired chromosomes come together and each replicates itself

First division

Beginning of second division: chromosomes do not replicate themselves

Second division completed: four egg or sperm cells

■ *How meiosis results in genetically diverse egg or sperm cells, and why such diversity is an advantage*

A given person's egg or sperm cells look alike in terms of the number and shape of their chromosomes except that half of the male's sperm cells have an X chromosome and the other half have a Y, but they are all different from one another in the genes they contain. To understand this, you must first realize that paired chromosomes, despite looking identical, do not have identical genes. During meiosis, after the chromosomes have reproduced but before the first cell division, sections of DNA are interchanged between chromosomes within each set of four in a random manner, a process called **crossing over** (illustrated in Figure 3.4).

**Figure 3.4 *Schematic representation of crossing over during meiosis***

*This drawing illustrates the effect of crossing over at one place on one pair of chromosomes. Crossing over actually occurs in multiple places. The result is that the chromosome in each cell is different from that in each other cell. (Adapted from Plomin & others, 1990.)*

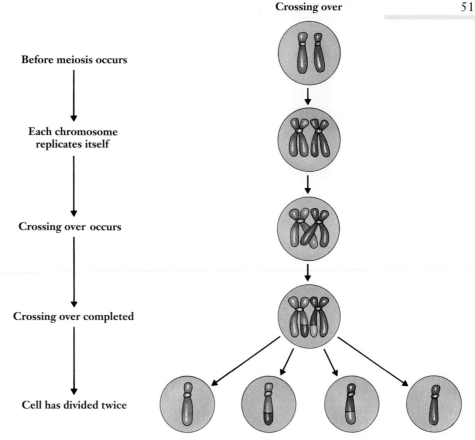

Before meiosis occurs

Each chromosome replicates itself

Crossing over occurs

Crossing over completed

Cell has divided twice

Then, during each meiotic cell division, the chromosomes within each set are randomly divided between the new cells thus formed. Because of both crossing over and the random assortment of chromosomes, the DNA content of a precursor cell can be divided among the resulting egg or sperm cells in a virtually infinite number of ways. Thus, the chance that a person will produce two identical eggs or sperm is, for all practical purposes, nil.

It may seem ironic that the very cells you use for "reproduction" are the only cells in your body that cannot, in theory, reproduce you. They are the only cells in your body that do not have all of your genes. In sexual reproduction you are, of course, not really reproducing yourself. Rather, you are creating a new individual who is genetically different from, though in some ways similar to, both you and your partner. When a sperm and egg unite, the result is a single new cell, the ***zygote***, which contains the full complement of 23 paired chromosomes, one member of each pair coming from each parent. The zygote then grows, through mitosis, eventually to become a new adult. Because each sperm and egg (even from the same parent) is different from any other sperm or egg, each zygote is different from any other. The purpose of sexual reproduction—as opposed to asexual reproduction, or *cloning*—is to produce offspring that are genetically diverse. That is, sex is a contrivance that came about in the course of evolution because of the advantage inherent in genetic diversity. In a world where the environment keeps changing, genes have a better chance of surviving in the long run if they get rearranged at each generation in many different ways, to produce different kinds of bodies, than if they are all put into the same kind of basket, so to speak. If one kind of body can't survive a particular environmental change, another kind may.

■ *The difference between identical and fraternal twins*

The only people who are genetically identical to each other are ***identical twins***. They are formed when two bundles of cells separate from one another during the early mitotic divisions following the formation of a single zygote. Because they originate from one zygote, identical twins are also known as *monozygotic twins*. ***Fraternal twins***, or *dizygotic twins*, on the other hand, originate from two zygotes, formed when two different eggs are each joined by a different sperm. Fraternal

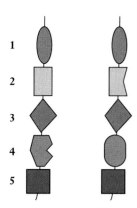

**Figure 3.5** *Schematic illustration of gene loci on a pair of chromosomes*
*Successive genes are depicted here as beads on a string. This pair is* homozygous *at loci 1, 3, and 5 (the paired genes there are identical) and* heterozygous *at loci 2 and 4 (the paired genes there are not identical). Nonidentical genes that can occupy the same locus are called* alleles.

■ *The meaning of dominance and recessiveness of genes*

■ *The meaning of percent relatedness*

twins are no more or less similar to one another genetically than are any pair of nontwin siblings. More will be said about these two classes of twins later in the chapter, as they provide a unique resource for studying both genetic and environmental contributions to variability in human characteristics.

**Consequences of the Fact That Genes Come in Pairs**    You have seen that genes exist on long DNA strands in chromosomes, something like beads on a string, and that chromosomes come in pairs. The two genes that occupy the same *locus* (location) on a pair of chromosomes are sometimes identical to one another and sometimes not. When they are identical the individual is said to be *homozygous* at that locus, and when they are not identical the individual is said to be *heterozygous* at that locus (see Figure 3.5). Different genes that can occupy the same locus, and thus can potentially pair with one another, are referred to as *alleles*.

For example, a gene for brown eyes and a gene for blue eyes in humans are alleles because they can occupy the same locus. If you are homozygous for brown eyes, you have two copies of a gene that manufactures an enzyme that makes your eyes brown. What if you were heterozygous for eye color, with an allele for brown eyes paired with one for blue eyes? In this case, you would have brown eyes, phenotypically indistinguishable from what would happen if you were homozygous for brown eyes. This fact is described by saying that the allele for brown eyes is *dominant* and the one for blue eyes is *recessive*. A dominant gene (or allele) is one that will produce its observable effects in either the homozygous or the heterozygous condition, and a recessive gene (or allele) is one that will produce its effects only in the homozygous condition. But not all pairs of alleles manifest dominance and recessiveness. Some pairs blend their effects. For example, if you cross red four-o'clocks (a kind of flower) with white four-o'clocks, the offspring will be pink, because neither the red nor the white allele is dominant over the other.

The fact that genes come in pairs provides the basis for calculating what geneticists call *percent relatedness*. Imagine that you have a particular rare gene. Because it is rare, it usually exists in heterozygous form (paired not with itself but with a different allele). Since any child that you produce will receive just one of each of your paired genes, there is a 50 percent chance that the child will receive the rare gene in question. This is the basis upon which geneticists say that parents and children are 50 percent related to one another. An extension of this reasoning can be used to calculate the percent relatedness of other relatives (see Table 3.1). It is important to realize that 50 percent relatedness does not mean that two people share only 50 percent of all their genes—any two people chosen at random share

**Table 3.1**  *Genetic relatedness expressed as a percentage of rare genes shared by the pair*

| Relationship | Degree of relationship | Percent relatedness |
|---|---|---|
| Identical twins | | 100.00% |
| Parent/child<br>Full brothers, full sisters<br>Fraternal twins | First degree | 50.00 |
| Grandparent/grandchild<br>Uncle or aunt/nephew or niece<br>Half-brothers, half-sisters | Second degree | 25.00 |
| First cousins | Third degree | 12.50 |
| Second cousins | Fourth degree | 6.25 |

far more genes than that. It only means that they share 50 percent of their rare genes. Everyone has a good number of rare genes, and these are important determinants of the differences among people. That is why percent relatedness calculations are useful.

**Mendelian Patterns of Heredity**   You may already know of the famous experiments with peas conducted in the mid-nineteenth century by a Czechoslovakian monk named Gregor Mendel. In a typical experiment, Mendel would start with two purebred strains of peas, differing in one or more easily observed traits, and cross them to observe the traits of the offspring, called the $F_1$ (first filial) generation. Then he would breed the $F_1$ peas among themselves to produce the $F_2$ (second filial) generation. For example, in one experiment Mendel crossed a strain of peas that regularly produced round seeds with a strain that regularly produced wrinkled seeds. His famous finding was that all of the $F_1$ generation had round seeds, and three-fourths of the $F_2$ generation had round seeds, while the other one-fourth had wrinkled seeds.

■ *Why three-fourths of the offspring of two heterozygous parents show the dominant trait and one-fourth show the recessive*

On the basis of our knowledge that genes come in pairs, how can we explain Mendel's finding? If we consider seed texture to be controlled by a single (paired) gene locus, with the allele for round dominant over that for wrinkled, Mendel's findings make perfect sense. Let us use the capital letter $R$ to stand for the dominant, round-producing allele and the small letter $r$ for the recessive, wrinkle-producing allele. The purebred round strain is homozygous for the "round" allele ($RR$), and the purebred wrinkled strain is homozygous for the "wrinkled" allele ($rr$). (A purebred strain is homozygous for all observed traits.) Since one allele must come from each parent, the only possible result for the $F_1$ generation, produced by crossing the two purebred strains, is the heterozygous condition ($Rr$). This explains why all of the $F_1$ peas in Mendel's experiment were round. On the other hand, when $Rr$ peas are crossed to produce the $F_2$ generation, there are four equally likely results: (1) an $R$ from each parent ($RR$); (2) an $R$ from the female parent and an $r$ from the male ($Rr$); (3) an $r$ from the female parent and an $R$ from the male ($rR$); or (4) an $r$ from each parent ($rr$). (See Figure 3.6.) Since only one of these possible outcomes ($rr$) is wrinkled, the expectation is that one-fourth of the $F_2$ generation will be wrinkled and the other three-fourths round. This, of course, is just what Mendel found.

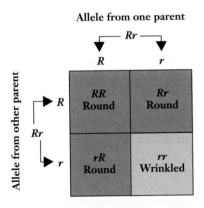

It is important to note that while the $Rr$ peas look the same as the $RR$ peas, they are not genetically the same. In other words, though they have the same phenotype, they have different genotypes. An $Rr$ pea plant, if crossed with either an $Rr$ or $rr$ variety, is capable of producing offspring with wrinkled seeds ($rr$). An $RR$ plant, on the other hand, can produce only round-seeded offspring ($Rr$ or $RR$) no matter what the variety with which it is crossed.

**Figure 3.6** *Explanation of Mendel's ratio*

*When two pea plants that are heterozygous for round versus wrinkled seeds are cross-bred, there are four possible gene combinations. Here R stands for the dominant, round-producing allele, and r for the recessive, wrinkle-producing allele. In three cases the phenotype of the offspring will be round, and in one case wrinkled. This 3:1 ratio was Mendel's famous finding.*

## Single-Gene and Chromosomal Effects on Behavior

One approach in behavioral genetics is to look for behavioral characteristics or disorders that are either inherited in Mendelian fashion, indicative of single-gene control, or that are related to observable abnormalities in the karyotype. Such studies represent the most clear-cut demonstrations that genetic variation can affect behavior, and they also serve as a first step toward understanding the biochemical routes through which specific genes can affect behavior. In humans, research of this sort has focused mostly on behaviorally important genetic disorders or diseases, and in some cases has led to effective modes of treatment. In this section we will look first at a classic study of differences in dog breeds, and then at some genetic disorders in people.

**Figure 3.7  Dogs used in Scott and Fuller's research**

*At left are a male basenji and a female cocker spaniel; at right are two F₁ hybrids resulting from a basenji-cocker cross.*

## Mendelian Inheritance of Behavioral Traits in Dogs: Scott and Fuller's Study

Some years ago, John Paul Scott and John Fuller (1965) performed an extensive study of the behavior of various breeds of dogs and their mixed-breed offspring. In one especially interesting series, they crossed cocker spaniels with basenji hounds. Basenjis are very timid dogs, showing fear of people until they have been much handled and gentled. Cockers, on the other hand, show little fear under normal rearing conditions. In a standard test with 5-week-old puppies, Scott and Fuller found that all of the basenji puppies yelped and/or ran away when approached by a strange person, whereas only a few of the cocker puppies showed these reactions. When cockers and basenjis were crossbred (see Figure 3.7), the offspring ($F_1$ hybrids) were like basenjis in this test: all showed signs of fear when approached. Since this was as true of hybrids raised by cocker mothers as those raised by basenji mothers, Scott and Fuller concluded that the effect stemmed from their genes and not from the way they were treated by their mothers.

The fact that the $F_1$ hybrids were as fearful as the purebred basenjis suggested to Scott and Fuller that the difference in fearfulness between the two purebred strains might be controlled by a single gene locus, with the allele promoting fear dominant over that promoting confidence. If this were so, then mating $F_1$ hybrids with each other should produce a group of offspring ($F_2$ generation) in which three-fourths would show basenji-like fear and one-fourth would show cocker-like confidence, the same ratios that Mendel had found with seed texture in peas. Scott and Fuller did this experiment, and in fact found ratios very close to those predicted. In addition, they also performed what are called *backcrosses*, mating $F_1$ hybrids with purebred cockers. In this case they found that about half of the offspring were basenji-like in fear and the other half were cocker-like in confidence. Again, this is just what would be expected if the difference in fearfulness between cockers and basenjis is controlled at one gene locus, with the "fear" allele dominant over the "nonfear" allele (see Figure 3.8).

Another reliable difference between cockers and basenjis is in their tendency to bark. Cockers are noisy dogs, easily provoked to barking, while basenjis almost never bark. Scott and Fuller found that this difference was also inherited in a pattern indicative of a single-gene effect. The $F_1$ hybrids of cockers and basenjis barked just as much as purebred cockers, indicating that the allele promoting barking is dominant over that promoting silence. Thus, although the $F_1$ hybrids were like basenjis in timidity, they were like cockers in noisiness. When $F_1$ hybrids were mated with other $F_1$ hybrids to form the $F_2$ generation, the offspring showed all

**Allele from cocker-basenji hybrid**

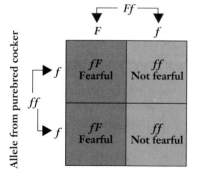

**Figure 3.8  Explanation of Scott and Fuller's results for backcrosses between basenji-cocker hybrids and purebred cockers**

*The finding that half of these offspring were fearful and half not makes sense if fearfulness results from a dominant allele (F) and lack of fearfulness from a recessive allele (f). Since half of the offspring receive F and the other half receive f from their hybrid parent, and all receive f from their cocker parent, half of the offspring will be Ff (phenotypically fearful) and the other half ff (not fearful).*

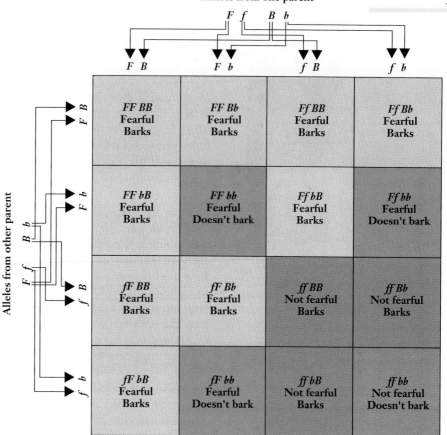

**Figure 3.9** *Possible genotypes and phenotypes for fear and barking for F$_2$ generation of basenji-cocker hybrids*

*Assuming that the alleles for fear and barking occupy separate gene loci (and hence can go separate ways in the process of meiosis), each F$_1$ basenji-cocker hybrid parent can produce 4 different combinations of fear and barking alleles in their egg or sperm cells (FB, Fb, fB, and fb). The pairings of each of these from one parent with each from the other parent produce the 16 possible results shown in the grid. Notice that phenotypically 3/4 are fearful and 1/4 are not; and 3/4 bark and 1/4 don't. Concerning both traits combined, 9/16 are fearful and bark, 3/16 are fearful and don't bark, 3/16 are not fearful and bark, and 1/16 are not fearful and don't bark.*

■ *How Scott and Fuller inferred that basenji-cocker differences in barking and fear are controlled by different gene loci*

■ *Why it would be wrong to conclude that fear in dogs is due to a single gene, or due to genes and not environment*

possible combinations of the traits of the original breeds. Some were noisy and fearful, some were noisy and confident, some were silent and fearful, and some were silent and confident. In other words, the tendency to bark was inherited independently of the tendency to show fear in the behavioral test. As shown in Figure 3.9, these results would be expected if the tendency to show fear and the tendency to bark are affected by dominant genes occupying different chromosomal loci.

In sum, Scott and Fuller's work shows how behavioral-genetics experiments can demonstrate not only the pattern by which a given trait is inherited, but also the dependence or lack of dependence of one trait upon another. From observing purebred basenjis and cockers, one might assume that fearfulness and silence in dogs necessarily go together, or that confidence and barking do; but Scott and Fuller showed that such is not the case. They showed that the tendency to bark or not is inherited independently of the tendency to show fear or not.

It is important not to misinterpret these findings. They concern the differences between two breeds of dogs in certain behavioral tests. It is surely not the case, for example, that fear itself, in all of its various forms, is controlled by a single gene. Thousands of different genes must contribute to the tendency to show fear (for example, by producing the complex neural structure necessary to organize fear behavior). What Scott and Fuller's work indicates is that the difference between cocker spaniels and basenji hounds in a particular test of fear is controlled by a single gene. It is also important to realize that their studies do not negate the importance of environmental effects on fear and barking in dogs. Scott and Fuller were able to pick up the genetic effects in a clear-cut way because they raised all of the dogs in similar environments. In other research, Scott (1963) showed that any puppy isolated from people for the first four months of life will be fearful of humans. Had Scott and Fuller isolated the cockers from all human contact and given the basenjis lots of kind handling before the behavioral test, they might well have found the cockers to be more fearful than the basenjis despite the genetic predispositions toward the opposite.

**Figure 3.10** *Triplets, two with PKU and one without*

*The two children at the right are genetically identical and have PKU. Their arm posturing is typical of severely affected PKU individuals. Since PKU is caused by a recessive allele, on average one out of every four children born to two parents who are heterozygous for the allele will have the disorder. Today the most severe effects of PKU are prevented by starting affected individuals on a diet low in phenylalanine immediately after birth.*

■ *How knowledge of the genetic basis of PKU has led to an environmental treatment*

■ *Why males have more genetic disorders than females*

## Mendelian Disorders in Humans

Many human disorders that have important consequences for behavior are passed from generation to generation by single-gene inheritance. These are called *Mendelian disorders*, because they are inherited in patterns like those that Mendel found for wrinkled or smooth peas. The following examples illustrate different patterns of heredity and some further principles concerning the ways that genes can influence behavior.

**PKU as an Example of a Recessive Disorder**   Phenylketonuria, usually called *PKU*, is an example of a disorder caused by a recessive gene located on an autosome (any of the nonsex chromosomes). The disorder occurs in about 1 out of every 10,000 newborn babies. If untreated, it usually results in reduced brain size, poor motor coordination, and severe mental retardation, including, in many cases, an inability to speak or understand language (Hay, 1985). (See Figure 3.10.) The gene responsible for this disorder is a defective allele at the locus that normally directs the synthesis of an enzyme that controls the body's use of phenylalanine (an amino acid present in milk and other protein-containing foods). In the absence of this enzyme, phenylalanine is converted to an acidic substance that, in high quantities, is poisonous to the brain and other tissues.

PKU is an excellent example of a disorder that, though inherited genetically, can be treated by environmental means. Because scientists understand the biochemical basis for PKU, they can minimize the faulty gene's damaging effects by controlling the biochemical environment. Most hospitals today routinely test newborn babies for PKU and immediately place affected infants on a diet that is low in phenylalanine. With low phenylalanine intake, little of the poisonous acid is created, and the baby can grow up quite normally. The diet must be started soon after birth, because the most severe and irreversible effects of the acid on brain development occur in infancy. Later in life it is less important to stay on the diet, though pregnant PKU women must go back onto it as early as possible to prevent brain damage to their infant during prenatal development.

To say that PKU is controlled by a recessive allele is to say that the disorder (at least in anything like its full form) appears only in people who are homozygous for that allele. Thus, a child can be born with the disease only if both parents carry the allele. Let us use the capital letter *P* for the dominant normal allele and the small letter *p* for the recessive PKU-producing allele. If two parents who don't have PKU have a PKU baby, they must both be heterozygous (*Pp*) carriers of the disease, which in turn means that there is 1 chance in 4 that any future child they have will be born with PKU (as was shown in Figure 3.6 for wrinkled peas).

Most single-gene disorders are like PKU in that they are caused by recessive alleles. In other words, most faulty genes create serious trouble only if they exist in the person in the homozygous condition. It is fortunate that genes come in pairs. If one is defective, then its mate on the homologous chromosome can usually make up for the deficit. It's like carrying a spare tire. Only if *both* members of a gene pair are defective will the person be seriously harmed. On the other hand, a small degree of damage can occur to heterozygous carriers for some recessive disorders, including PKU. People who are heterozygous (*Pp*) for PKU have a slight problem metabolizing phenylalanine, and on a statistical basis they have slightly lower IQs than the general population (Bessman & others, 1978).

**Red-Green Color Blindness as an Example of a Sex-Linked Disorder**   An important exception to the rule that genes come in pairs exists for genes located on the X chromosome in males. The Y chromosome, which males have instead of a second X, is very small (see Figure 3.2) and does not contain genes to match all of those on the X. The interesting result is that males, genetically speaking, are more fragile than females. If a female has something wrong on one of her X chromosomes, the matched gene on the other X will usually be normal and produce a normal phenotype. But a male who has a defective gene on his X is in trouble. He has no spare.

Recessive traits controlled by the X chromosome are said to be *sex linked*, because they are far more likely to show up in men than in women. One relatively benign example is red-green color blindness (the inability, under certain conditions, to distinguish between red and green). We shall use $C$ to stand for the dominant allele, which promotes normal color vision, and $c$ to stand for the recessive allele, which promotes red-green color blindness. Since this gene is located on the X chromosome, and a male has only one, a male can be genotypically either $C$ or $c$. If 1 out of 10 X chromosomes in the population contains the recessive allele (a figure that is approximately accurate), then 1 out of 10 men will be red-green color blind. A female, on the other hand, who has two X chromosomes, can be genotypically $CC$, $cC$, $Cc$, *or* $cc$. Only in the last case ($cc$) will she show the trait phenotypically. If 1 out of 10 X chromosomes in the population contains the recessive allele, then the chance that both X chromosomes in a given female will contain the recessive allele is 1 out of 100. (The probability of two independent events occurring together is equal to the probability of one times the probability of the other. In this case, $\frac{1}{10} \times \frac{1}{10} = \frac{1}{100}$.) Incidentally, there is evidence that red-green color blindness comes in various forms, due to different sorts of abnormalities on the X chromosome that lead to faulty photochemicals on receptor cells in the eyes (Nathans & others, 1986). The figures just presented are for all forms taken together.

**Huntington's Disease as an Example of a Dominant Disorder**   Huntington's disease is one of the relatively few debilitating single-gene disorders that are caused by a dominant rather than recessive allele. Its symptoms usually first appear when the person is about 35 to 45 years old, at which time cells in the brain begin to atrophy, causing progressive debilitation in intellect, personality, and muscle control, and leading to death within 10 to 20 years. Because the disorder is due to a dominant gene, the victim suffers the additional knowledge that each of his or her children has a 50 percent chance of inheriting it. Each child has a 50 percent chance of receiving the chromosome that has the disordered gene, and, since the gene is dominant, every child who receives it will eventually manifest the disorder. Fortunately the gene is rare, occurring in 1 person out of 16,000 (Hay, 1985).

The time course of Huntington's disease illustrates an important point about dominant disorders. A lethal dominant disorder can be transmitted from one generation to the next only if it manifests its most debilitating effects after childbearing age. If Huntington's disease struck earlier, its victims would generally not have children, and the disease would not be carried on to the next generation. This fact is not true for recessive disorders, because the genes for recessive disorders continue to be passed on from one generation to the next by healthy heterozygous carriers, regardless of how lethal the genes may be in the homozygous condition.

A few years ago, using modern methods for mapping genes, geneticists discovered that the Huntington's gene is located near one end of chromosome 4. This in turn led to a means of determining if a person has the gene (Gusella & others, 1983). One member of the team that discovered the gene's location, Nancy Wexler, is herself the daughter of a Huntington's victim, and when the test became available she was faced with the same dilemma that now faces everyone with a Huntington's parent: Did she really want to know? Of course, she would want to know that she *didn't* have it, but what if she *did*? What would life be like knowing for sure that the disease would strike? She decided not to take the test, at least not yet (Lander, 1987). The predicament for people at risk for Huntington's is that science can now detect the disorder but cannot prevent it. However, knowing the gene's location has opened up new lines of attack toward understanding its action,

*Why lethal dominant disorders, unlike recessive disorders, can persist only if they manifest their effects after early adulthood*

*Nancy Wexler*

*As part of ongoing research on Huntington's disease, the researcher is testing the motor abilities of one of her Venezuelan subjects. Wexler has also been lecturing widely to call attention to the ethical dilemmas raised by genetic research.*

which may lead to a treatment. One present advantage of the test is that it can help a person at risk decide whether or not to have children. The issue of how to use our growing ability to detect genetic defects in potential parents and in embryos has raised a host of ethical questions, much discussed these days in magazines, churches, conferences on biomedical ethics, and elsewhere.

### Chromosomal Disorders in Humans

Some genetic disorders come not from single genes but rather involve whole chromosomes or relatively large chunks of chromosomes. Sometimes, in the process of meiosis, both copies of a chromosome will end up in the same egg or sperm cell, leaving another egg or sperm cell with no copy of that chromosome. Other times a piece of a chromosome will separate from the rest during meiosis, causing a portion of the chromosome to exist in duplicate in one egg or sperm cell and to be absent in another. Usually such egg and sperm cells are not viable; they either fail to form a zygote when they join with their complement, or they form a zygote that is so abnormal that it dies and is spontaneously aborted (miscarried). But a few chromosomal abnormalities are compatible with survival. About 1 out of every 200 infants is born with a detectable chromosomal abnormality, most of which involve either a sex chromosome or chromosome 21 (Plomin & others, 1990).

**The meiotic origin of abnormal numbers of chromosomes**

**Variations in the Number of Sex Chromosomes**    As pointed out earlier, the normal female karyotype has two X chromosomes and the normal male has an X and a Y. The most common variations in sex chromosome number compatible with survival are: (a) XXX, (b) X0 (a single X chromosome and no complement—the 0 stands for the absence of a chromosome), (c) XXY, and (d) XYY. Since the absence or presence of a Y chromosome determines phenotypic sex, XXX and X0 individuals develop as females, and XXY and XYY as males. In general, XXX females and XYY males undergo normal sexual development. They are usually fertile, and they have normal children because the extra chromosome is usually lost during gamete formation. On the other hand, X0 females and XXY males are usually underdeveloped sexually and infertile. Incidentally, the X0 disorder is also known as *Turner's syndrome*, and the XXY is known as *Klinefelter's syndrome*.

*Living with Turner's syndrome*
*Barbara Tiemann, president-elect of the Turner's Syndrome Society, is shown on her way to work in Boston. Because women with Turner's syndrome look a little different and because their condition is called a "syndrome," many people mistakenly think that they are intellectually slow. The society serves as a support group to help members deal with this kind of prejudice.*

■ *How theories about XYY and imprisonment illustrate indirect routes by which genes can affect a particular class of behavior*

Most individuals with any of these chromosomal disorders fall within the normal range of mental development, though the rate of mild mental retardation is considerably higher among XXX women and XYY men than in the general population (Stewart & others, 1982). Also, for unknown reasons, X0 women as a group perform below average on tasks involving spatial ability (such as completing picture puzzles) but not on tasks involving verbal ability (such as defining terms), and XXY men show the opposite pattern—below average on verbal but not spatial tasks (Netley, 1983).

An interesting controversy was stirred up some years ago when it was discovered that men with the XYY karyotype have a somewhat greater likelihood of ending up in prison than do XY men (Hook, 1973; Jacobs & others, 1965). Scientists developed a number of theories (reviewed by Witkin & others, 1976) to try to explain why this occurs. The earliest theory suggested that the extra Y chromosome increases aggressiveness through some direct (though unspecified) physiological means. That theory, however, was soon refuted by evidence that the increased imprisonment of XYY men is almost entirely due to property crimes, not crimes of violence. Another theory held that increased criminality of XYY men might be a secondary effect of their height (the average XYY man is 6 feet, 3 inches tall). Perhaps because they are tall, people react to them in some way that promotes criminality. But if that were true, tall men in general should end up in prison more often than do other men, which is not the case. A third theory held that increased imprisonment might be a secondary effect of the below-average intelligence of many XYY men. According to this view, low intelligence may lead to criminal behavior, or it may simply lead those who engage in such behavior to be caught and convicted more often. This theory received partial support from a study that looked at the imprisonment rate for karyotypically normal (XY) men with IQ scores as low as the average for XYY men. These men also show a higher than average rate of imprisonment, but still not as high as that for XYY men (Witkin & others, 1976). In the end, there will probably be no single explanation for the statistical association between the XYY karyotype and imprisonment. The extra Y probably produces a constellation of physiological effects, that, in concert with various aspects of the social environment, increase somewhat the probability of criminal behavior or conviction for such behavior.

**Figure 3.11** *A child with Down syndrome*

*Down syndrome children benefit greatly from a supportive and stimulating home environment. For this family, cognitive stimulation seems to be enriching all of their lives.*

■ *Possible link between the mental retardation of Down syndrome and too much production of a particular protein*

**Down Syndrome**   The most common chromosomal disorder that doesn't involve a sex chromosome is ***Down syndrome***, which occurs in about 1 out of every 700 live-born infants (Therman, 1986). Another name for this disorder is *trisomy-21*, reflecting the fact that the abnormality in the karyotype is usually an entire extra chromosome 21 (a triplet rather than the usual pair), although sometimes only a portion of an extra chromosome 21 is present. Many physical ailments (especially heart abnormalities) accompany this disorder, which often reduce the life span. Most Down children can be recognized by their physical appearance. Typical (but not inevitable) signs include short stature; a thick, short neck; stubby hands and fingers; a flattened nose bridge; a protruding tongue; and a fold of skin over the inner corner of each eye. In the past, Down children were commonly considered uneducable and placed in institutions, where they were often neglected. This belief had the effect of a self-fulfilling prophesy: when neglected, most people with Down syndrome remained extremely retarded throughout their lives. It is now clear that such people do far better if raised in a supportive environment and given special education (see Figure 3.11). With that support, some achieve IQs in the low normal range (70 or 80) and become able to care for themselves and find gainful employment, though there is a great deal of variability from person to person (Cicchetti & Beeghly, 1988; Cohen, 1984).

Recent research has shown that people with Down syndrome develop abnormal protein coats (called *amyloid plaques*) on nerve cells in their brain, and that the code for this protein lies at a specific gene locus on chromosome 21 (see Loehlin & others, 1988). Although many different genes on the chromosome are responsible for the constellation of symptoms in Down syndrome, this gene may be most responsible for the mental retardation. The same gene is also apparently involved in Alzheimer's disease, a disorder involving severe mental deterioration that strikes in old age. People with Alzheimer's develop the same kind of brain plaques as those with Down syndrome, and there is evidence that in both diseases the amyloid-producing gene is more active than normal (Delabar & others, 1987; St. George-Hyslop & others, 1987).

The incidence of Down syndrome, as well as certain other chromosomal disorders, increases with the age of the mother. It is not certain why this is so, but possibilities include hormonal and other physiological changes that accompany aging, and the accumulated effects of years of exposure to environmental radiation, which may adversely affect the precursor cells that divide to form eggs (Therman, 1986). Although most attention has been paid to the mother, there is also evidence that the father's age is relevant. In about 20 percent of cases the extra chromosome 21 comes from the sperm, and the likelihood of this occurring increases with the father's age (Therman, 1986).

## Polygenic Effects on Behavior

Thus far our concern has been with rather clear-cut genetic effects that are either inherited in a Mendelian fashion, indicative of single-gene control, or associated with an abnormal karyotype. Though these are clinically important, and they illustrate basic principles of heredity, they tell us relatively little about normal variability in behavior. Most measurable differences among people cannot be explained in terms of single genes or abnormal numbers of chromosomes, but rather lie in the combined effects of many genes and their interactions with the environment.

For any measurable behavioral characteristic, in any given group of individuals, one finds a certain range of variability. Some mice are more active than others, some rats learn mazes more quickly than others, some people score higher on IQ tests than others. The differences on such measures are not sharp, or step-like, as would be the case if they were heavily influenced by a single gene but, rather, are *continuous*, meaning that any possible gradation within the observed range can occur. Most often the set of scores obtained on such measures approximate a *normal distribution*, meaning that most scores fall near the middle of the range and the frequency tapers off toward the extremes (see Figure 3.12). Any characteristic that varies in a continuous way is presumably affected by many genes and hence is referred to as a *polygenic* characteristic (the prefix *poly-* means many). The same characteristics are also influenced by the environment, so the variability observed in a graph such as that in Figure 3.12 is due to a combination of genetic differences at many gene loci and a wide variety of environmental differences. A nonbehavioral example of a polygenic characteristic is height in humans. Many gene loci are involved in producing variations in height, and any given person's height depends on the relative number of alleles promoting tallness or shortness that occupy these loci, as well as on environmental factors (such as nutrition).

The behavioral-genetics study of polygenic effects is necessarily more abstract than that of single-gene or chromosomal effects. It is usually not possible, with present means, to identify the specific genes involved in such effects, to specify the biochemical routes through which they act, or to predict patterns of heredity within a family. Rather, behavioral geneticists attempt to understand the degree to which average differences among individuals in the phenotypic characteristic are due to genetic as compared with environmental differences among the individuals. This approach is called *quantitative genetics*, because it relies on statistical methods and mathematical models (see Plomin & others, 1990). Here we will not concern ourselves with specific formulas and mathematical models, but rather with the overall logic of this approach and some specific research findings and controversies.

■ *Continuous, normal distributions and polygenic characteristics*

**Figure 3.12** *Normal distribution*

*When many individuals are tested for a polygenic characteristic, such as height or performance on a psychological test, the majority usually fall in the middle of the range of scores and the frequency tapers off toward zero at the extremes. Mathematically, this defines a normal curve.*

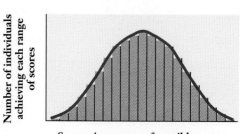

**Successive ranges of possible scores**

*The Concept of Heritability*

A central, often misunderstood concept in quantitative genetics is that of **heritability**. Heritability refers to the proportion of the variability in a particular characteristic, in a particular group of individuals, that is due to genetic compared to environmental differences among them. Stated somewhat differently, it refers to the proportion of variability that can be passed on genetically from one group of individuals to their offspring. It is measured by a statistic called the **heritability coefficient**, abbreviated $h^2$, defined by this formula:

$$h^2 = \frac{\text{Variance due to genes}}{\text{Total variance}}$$

The denominator (total variance) is simply a measure of the degree to which the individuals being studied differ from one another in the characteristic that was measured. It can be calculated directly from the set of scores obtained from the individuals in the group (the formula for variance can be found in the Statistical Appendix). The numerator (variance due to genes), on the other hand, cannot be calculated directly, but must be estimated by comparing sets of individuals who differ in their degree of genetic relationship to one another. Behavioral geneticists who work with animals use selective breeding (to be described below) as a means of estimating variance due to genes, and those who work with people use such procedures as comparing identical and fraternal twins (also to be described below). Examination of the formula shows that the heritability coefficient can in theory vary from 0.00 to 1.00. A coefficient of 0.00 means that none of the observed variance in the characteristic is due to genes (all of it is due to environmental differences), a coefficient of 1.00 means that all of the variance is due to genes, and a coefficient of 0.50 means that half of it is due to genes.

Because any method for calculating heritability depends on assumptions that may not be fully correct, a calculated heritability coefficient is at best a rough approximation. For that reason, some behavioral geneticists prefer not to use numbers to describe it. Yet, whether expressed quantitatively or not, the basic concept of heritability lies behind all studies aimed at comparing the degree to which genetic diversity and environmental diversity contribute to the observed variation in a characteristic. It is important, therefore, to understand what the concept means and what it *doesn't* mean. In particular, the following points are critical:

*Heritability applies to groups, not to individuals.* Sometimes people mistakenly assume that heritability refers to the degree to which a particular characteristic within an individual is determined by genes compared to the environment. For example, if they hear that the heritability for IQ scores for a set of people is 0.60, they might assume that 60 percent of a person's intelligence is caused by genes and the remaining 40 percent by the environment. But if you think about it, you will realize that such an assumption makes no sense. It is meaningless to try to quantify the contribution of genes or environment to any characteristic within an individual. With no genes there would be no person and hence no intelligence, and with no environment there would also be no person and no intelligence. Intelligence is fully due to genes and fully due to the environment. The same is true for any other characteristic of an individual. A useful analogy concerns the contribution of length and width to the area of a rectangle (suggested by Hebb, 1958). It makes no sense to say that the area of any given rectangle is due more to its length or its width. Shrink either to zero and the area goes to zero. But if you have a group of rectangles that differ in area you can sensibly ask whether the *differences* among their areas are due more to *differences* in their length or their width. In Figure 3.13 you can see two groups of rectangles of varying areas. In Group *A* the variability is due primarily to the differences in length, and in Group *B* it is due primarily to differ-

GROUP *A*

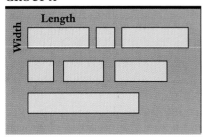

GROUP *B*

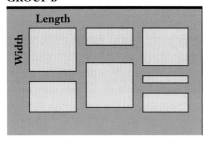

**Figure 3.13  *Width and length analogy to genes and environment***
*It makes no sense to ask whether a given rectangle's area is due more to its width or its length, but one can sensibly ask whether variation in area in a specific group of rectangles is due more to differences in their length or their width. In Group A above, variation in area is due to differing lengths, and in Group B it is due to differing widths. Similarly, for variation in a characteristic such as IQ, one can imagine one group of people where variation is due mostly to their differing genes and another where it is due mostly to their differing environments.*

■ *Why heritability applies to groups and not to individuals*

ences in width. Similarly, you might imagine two groups of people, *A* and *B*, each of which vary in IQ scores. In Group *A* that variability might be due mostly to genetic differences (high heritability), and in Group *B* it might be due mostly to environmental differences (low heritability).

■ *Heritability increases as genetic diversity increases.* This statement follows directly from the definition of heritability and the formula for measuring it. The numerator in the formula can be high relative to the denominator only if the individuals in the group being studied differ from one another in their genes (look again at the formula). If you were to study heritability of tomato size in a group of cloned (genetically identical) tomato plants, you would necessarily find a heritability coefficient of 0.00 (see Figure 3.14). That doesn't mean that their genes don't contribute to their tomato sizes; it only means that the differences among different plants have to be due to environmental differences (such as soil fertility), because the genes do not vary from plant to plant. On the other hand, if you started with a genetically diverse group of plants, you would find the heritability for tomato size to be greater than 0.00. The greater the genetic diversity, the greater is the numerator in the ratio that defines the heritability coefficient. The same applies for IQ scores in people or any other measurable characteristic.

■ *Heritability decreases as environmental diversity increases.* This statement also follows directly from the definition and formula for heritability. Increased environmental diversity adds to the denominator (total observed variance in the characteristic measured) without adding to the numerator (variance due to genes), thereby decreasing the heritability coefficient. If you raised a group of tomato plants under exactly the same environmental conditions (assuming that were possible), then whatever differences you found among them in tomato size would have to be attributed to genetic differences; the heritability

■ *How heritability changes as genetic or environmental diversity changes in the group studied*

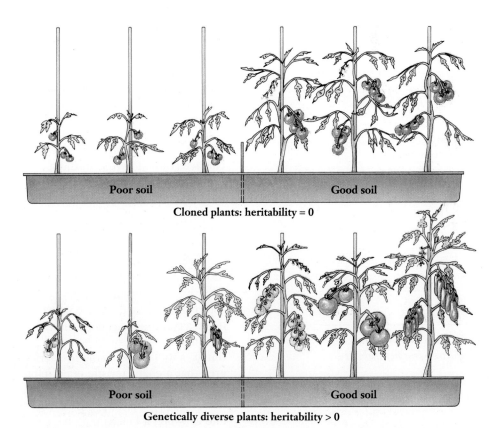

**Figure 3.14** *How genetic diversity affects heritability*

*The differences in the cloned tomato plants (top) are due to environment alone. Because the plants are genetically identical, the numerator in the heritability formula must be 0.00, and heritability must be 0.00. In contrast, the differences among the genetically diverse plants (bottom) are due to both genetic and environmental differences. Thus, the heritability coefficient for that group must be greater than 0.00 and less than 1.00.*

Poor soil    Good soil

**Cloned plants: heritability = 0**

Poor soil    Good soil

**Genetically diverse plants: heritability > 0**

*A great pumpkin*
*With the right combination of genes and environment, anything is possible!*

coefficient would be 1.00. On the other hand, if you raised them in highly diverse conditions—some in rich soil, others in sand, some with lots of moisture, others with little—large differences would be caused by the environmental differences, increasing greatly the denominator of the heritability formula and leading to a small heritability coefficient. Again, the same principle is true for any measurable characteristic in any group of individuals.

■ *Environmentality as the complement of heritability*

Some researchers prefer not to use the term *heritability* because it focuses too much attention on genes and not enough on the environment. As we have seen, the heritability coefficient is actually as much a measure of the environmental contribution to variability as it is a measure of the genetic contribution. For example, a heritability coefficient of 0.40 means that 40 percent of the measured variance is due to genetic variation and 60 percent is due to environmental variation. To create greater equity in focus, some behavioral geneticists have proposed that the term ***environmentality*** be used to refer to the proportion of variance that is due to environmental variation (Fuller & Thompson, 1978). Thus, a heritability coefficient of 0.40 would correspond to an environmentality coefficient of 0.60.

### Selective Breeding for Behavioral Characteristics in Animals

**The Rationale of Selective Breeding**   Polygenic effects on behavior in nonhuman animals can be studied through ***selective breeding***, defined as the deliberate mating of individuals that score toward one end or the other on some measurable characteristic. There is nothing new about the basic principles of this procedure. For thousands of years before there was a formal science of genetics, plant and animal breeders used selective breeding to produce new and better strains of every sort of domesticated species. Grains were bred to have fatter seeds, cows to be docile and produce greater quantities of milk, horses along separate lines for work and racing, canaries for their song. Dogs were bred along dozens of different lines for such varied purposes as following a trail, herding sheep (running around them instead of at them), and providing gentle playmates for children. The procedure in every case was essentially the same: Those members of each generation that best approximated the desired type were mated to produce the next generation, resulting in a continuous genetic molding toward the varieties that we see today.

■ *Selective breeding as a means of assessing heritability*

In the hands of behavioral geneticists, selective breeding is, among other things, a tool for assessing the heritability of behavioral characteristics. To the degree that a characteristic is heritable, the offspring of selected parents should be more like their parents than like the general population, and to the degree that it is not heritable, the offspring should be more like the general population. Thus, the rate at which a behavioral characteristic can change over generations of selective breeding is one measure of its heritability.

**Tryon's Classic Study and Its Aftermath**   The first long-term, systematic study of selective breeding in psychology was begun in the 1920s by Robert Tryon (1942), partly in reaction to the claim of some behaviorists that all important differences among individuals are environmental in origin. One of Tryon's goals was to show that a type of behavior frequently studied by psychologists could be strongly influenced by variation in genes.

Tryon began by testing a genetically diverse group of rats—formed by mixing breeds collected from various laboratories—for their ability to learn a particular maze. Then he mated those males and females that made the fewest errors in the maze to begin what he called the "maze bright" strain, and those that made the most errors to begin the "maze dull" strain. When the offspring of succeeding generations reached adulthood, he tested them in the same maze and mated the best-performing members of the "bright" strain, and worst-performing members of the "dull" strain, to continue the two lines. Some of his results are shown in Figure 3.15. As you can see, with each generation the two strains became more and more distinct, until by the seventh generation there was almost no overlap between them. In fact, almost all seventh-generation "bright" rats made fewer errors in the maze than even the best "dull" rats. To control for the possibility that the offspring were somehow learning to be "bright" or "dull" from their mothers, Tryon used a cross-fostering procedure, in which some of the offspring from each strain were

■ *How Tryon produced "maze bright" and "maze dull" strains of rats and showed that the difference was due to genes, not rearing*

**Figure 3.15** *Selective breeding for "maze brightness" and "maze dullness" in rats*

*The top graph shows the percentage of rats in the original parent stock that made each possible range of errors in the maze. Subsequent graphs show the percentage of "bright" and "dull" rats that made each possible range of errors. With successive generations an increasing percentage in the "bright" breed made few errors and an increasing percentage in the "dull" breed made many errors. (From Tryon, 1942.)*

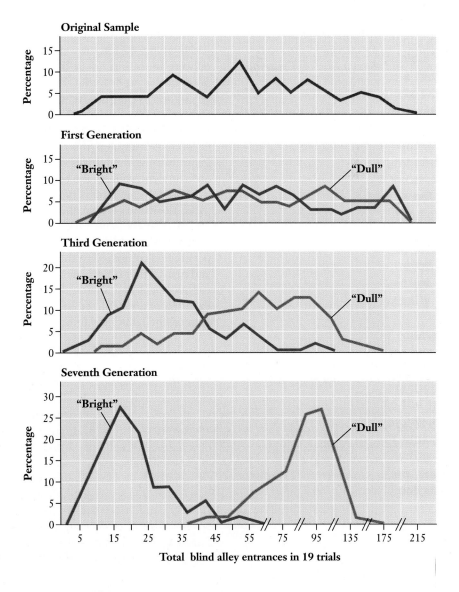

raised by mothers in the other strain. He found that rats in the "bright" strain were equally good in the maze, and those in the "dull" strain equally poor, regardless of which mothers raised them.

Tryon did not calculate a heritability coefficient from his data. He was satisfied to show that maze learning is to some degree heritable and that quite large differences can be produced over several generations of selective breeding. Since his time, behavioral geneticists have performed dozens of similar experiments on a wide variety of behaviors in several different species. Fruit flies have been bred to move instinctively either toward or away from a source of light, mice to be either more or less likely to fight, rats to show either more or less fear in an unfamiliar environment, and so on (Broadhurst & Fulker, 1974; Wimer & Wimer, 1985). On this basis, some behavioral geneticists have concluded that any behavioral characteristic that can be measured and that varies among members of a species can be affected by selective breeding. This is not really a surprising conclusion, as it follows logically from the fact that all behaviors depend in some way on sensory, motor, and neural structures, all of which are affected by heredity.

Once a strain has been bred to show some behavioral characteristic, the question arises as to what other behavioral or physiological changes accompany it. Tryon referred to his two strains as "bright" and "dull," but all he had measured was their ability to learn a particular type of maze. Performance in the maze no doubt depended on many sensory, motor, motivational, and learning processes, and specific changes in any of these could in theory have mediated the effects that Tryon observed. In theory, Tryon's "dull" rats could simply have been those that had less acute vision, or were less interested in the variety of food used as a reward, or were more interested in exploring the maze's blind alleys. It is interesting to note, in this regard, that Tryon's "dull" rats were found by another researcher to be as good as the "bright" ones, and sometimes even better, in other learning tasks (Searle, 1949).

In addition to the type of learning task employed, another important condition in Tryon's study was the environment in which he bred and raised his rats. Since genes express themselves through interaction with the environment, a change in environment could have changed the relative performances of the two strains of rats. Some years after Tryon's study, R. M. Cooper and John Zubek (1958) compared the maze performances of other rats that were bred for "maze brightness" or "maze dullness" and raised in varying environments. Some in each strain were raised in normal laboratory cages, others in cages that were either enriched or impoverished compared to the normal. The enriched cages contained tunnels, ramps, and many other objects designed to stimulate activity and learning, and the impoverished cages contained nothing but a food box and water pan. The results of the experiment are depicted in Figure 3.16. As you can see, the "bright" strain outperformed the "dull" strain only when raised in the normal laboratory environment.

*Evidence that effects of selective breeding can be specific to the bred-for task and the conditions of rearing*

**Figure 3.16** *Interaction of genes and environment in maze performance*

*Cooper and Zubek (1958) found that a difference between "maze bright" and "maze dull" strains of rats in maze learning occurred only when the rats were raised in normal laboratory cages. The breeds they used were not the same as those developed by Tryon, but were the result of another selective breeding program at McGill University. (Data from Cooper & Zubek, 1958.)*

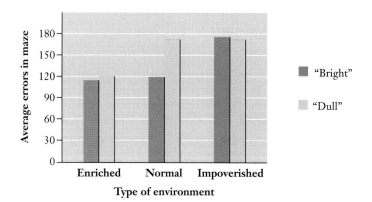

In the enriched environment both strains performed as well as the "brights" did in the normal environment, and in the impoverished environment both performed as poorly as the "dulls" did in the normal environment. Stated differently, enriching the environment caused the "dulls" to improve but not the "brights," and impoverishing the environment caused the "brights" to worsen but not the "dulls." Thus, in this case, the effect of selective breeding might be viewed as an ability to develop good maze-learning ability when raised in normal laboratory cages.

### The Heritability and Environmentality of IQ

With humans, of course, the heritability of polygenic traits cannot be studied by selective breeding. Instead, it can be studied by selectively comparing people who have different degrees of genetic relationship with one another. Using this method, researchers have studied the heritability of such personality characteristics as extroversion, anxiety, aggressiveness, ambitiousness, and persistence in completing tasks (all measured by self-report questionnaires), and have calculated heritability coefficients ranging from 0.35 to 0.65 for most characteristics (Goldsmith, 1983; Tellegen & others, 1988). That is, on average, given the conditions of the studies, somewhere between one-third and two-thirds of the variance among people in such measures appears to stem from genetic variation (to be discussed further in Chapter 16).

Of all human characteristics that have been studied from a behavioral genetics perspective, by far the most studied and debated is intelligence, as measured by standard IQ tests. In fact, the whole issue of heritability first arose in relation to debates about individual differences in intellectual ability. Let's look at a bit of that history, and then at more recent studies of the heritability of IQ.

**Historical Perspective: Galton, Mill, and the Nature-Nurture Debate** As noted earlier, in the nineteenth century Francis Galton initiated a program of research on the nature-nurture question as applied to human intellectual achievement. Inspired by the evolutionary theory that his cousin Charles Darwin had published in *The Origin of Species* (1859), Galton developed the idea that differences in human mental abilities may be inherited, and he set about trying to prove it. His basic question was this: Are the observed differences in people's intellectual achievement more the result of differences in their heredity (nature) or in their environments (nurture). Or, in more modern terms: Is heritability for intellectual achievement high (supporting the nature side) or low (supporting the nurture side)?

Using such sources as biographical dictionaries and historical texts, Galton identified about a thousand eminent men who had become famous through extraordinary achievements in such areas as diplomacy, science, literature, and art. In his book, *Hereditary Genius* (1869), he showed statistically that a disproportionate number of these men were related to one another. For example, in one analysis he looked at the relatives of the 100 most eminent men in his list and found that about 30 percent of their first-degree male relatives (brothers, sons, and fathers) and 7 percent of their second-degree male relatives (uncles, nephews, grandfathers, and grandsons) had achieved sufficient eminence to be in the top 0.025 percent of the male population as a whole.

Galton was aware that to some degree these results might be due to the privileged environments shared by eminent men and their relatives, but he argued (not very convincingly by today's standards) against the importance of that factor. His most interesting argument was based on his calculations concerning the eminence—or lack of it—achieved by the adopted kinsmen of Roman Catholic popes. Over the centuries, popes had adopted many boys and raised them as if they were their sons. These adoptees, according to Galton, were surrounded by eminent people and received the best of educations, yet, in contrast to the biological sons of

*Galton's invention of the adoptive and twin methods for studying heritability*

eminent men, very few achieved eminence themselves. Galton's argument here is also not particularly convincing—there may have been many factors about life as a papal adoptee that were very different from the typical environments of the biological sons of the eminent men in Galton's sample—but it is historically interesting as the first use of what today is called the ***adoptive method*** for studying heritability. This method involves comparing the similarity of adoptive relatives with that of biological (birth) relatives. To the degree that a trait is heritable, adoptive relatives should be less similar to one another than are biological relatives.

After publishing *Hereditary Genius*, Galton (1876) went on to study the contributions of nature and nurture to psychological characteristics using what is now called the ***twin method***. Galton was aware that twins come in two types, identical (from a single fertilized egg) and fraternal (from two fertilized eggs). Using self-report questionnaires and other biographical materials, he studied many sets of twins and concluded that those who were reported to have been "alike at birth" (who he assumed to be identical twins) remained similar psychologically throughout their lives, even after they left home and entered different environments. By contrast, those who were reported to have been different at birth (who he assumed to be fraternal twins) remained dissimilar throughout their lives. As you will see later, the twin method is used in a more quantitative fashion today to estimate heritability coefficients for IQ and other behavioral measures.

■ *Galton's more cautious and less cautious conclusions about the preponderant influence of nature*

On the basis of such research, Galton (1907) wrote, "There is no escape from the conclusion that nature prevails enormously over nurture when the differences of nurture do not exceed what is commonly to be found among persons of the same rank in society and in the same country." Many commentators today looking at Galton's studies and aware of the complexities involved in such research would disagree with his conclusion. But, even so, it is important to notice Galton's own qualification of his conclusion. He did not conclude that variability among any randomly chosen group of people is due more to nature (genes) than nurture (environment), but only that the variability found within a given range of environments is. More precisely, his conclusion might be restated as follows: psychological differences among upper-class British males are due more to differences in their genes than to differences in their environment.

But in other writings, where he strayed from the data, Galton was not so circumspect. He often implied that differences between social classes, as well as within them, are due to genetic differences; and he advocated a program of *eugenics*—which essentially means selective breeding—to improve human stock

*Like father, like son*

*As Galton pointed out long ago, eminent men often have eminent sons. In this 1965 photograph, the young Peter Serkin, a concert pianist, discusses a score with his father, the distinguished pianist Rudolf Serkin.*

(Fancher, 1985). In an article published in a popular magazine, Galton (1865) wrote enthusiastically of a future Utopia in which all young men and women would take an intelligence test; those who scored highest would be encouraged by the state through monetary incentives to marry each other and produce many children. Those who scored low would be discouraged from marrying or having children. He even suggested that the low scorers might gladly help finance the education of the high scorers' children, since that, he argued, would be "true charity." Perhaps you can see why discussions of the heritability of intelligence have always been hotly tinged with emotion. From Galton's time until today the issues have never been purely scientific, but have been wrapped in political ideology about social class, measures of human worth, and appropriate routes to human betterment.

For the contrasting nurture side of the nature-nurture debate, one need only look to another nineteenth century Englishman, John Stuart Mill (1806–1874). Mill was one of the British empiricist philosophers (mentioned in Chapter 1), and as such was interested in the ways that the human mind is built up through life's experiences. He applied this emphasis also to his thoughts about his own development and to his political philosophy (Fancher, 1985). He was acutely aware of his privileged environment, which included inherited wealth that gave him the opportunity to study and travel and a famous father (the philosopher James Mill) who took the time to tutor him throughout his childhood. James and John Mill were among the father-son pairs in Galton's study of hereditary genius (Fancher, 1985), but, while Galton credited their shared genes, John Mill credited their shared environment. Politically, Mill was an ardent democrat, who argued forcefully against the unequal conditions that society had established for different classes or groups of people. He was outspoken against slavery in the United States, and he wrote a lengthy essay, "The Subjection of Women" (1869/1980), that is still considered to be one of history's most powerful statements favoring gender equality. Mill's opinion of the political ideology favored by Galton is nicely captured in the following quote, written some years before Galton's first book (Mill, 1848/1978): "Of all the vulgar modes of escaping from the consideration of the social and moral influences on the human mind, the most vulgar is that attributing the diversities of human conduct and character to inherent original natural differences."

Prominent modern writings on the nature-nurture issue are imbued with much the same mix of science and politics as they were at the time of Mill and Galton. For a modern rendition of Mill's positions you might read *Not in Our Genes*, by R. C. Lewontin, Steven Rose, and Leon Kamin (1984); and for a modern rendition of Galton's you might read Richard Herrnstein's *IQ in the Meritocracy* (1971) or Hans Eysenck's *The Inequality of Man* (1973).

**Family-Relationship Studies of IQ**    Now let us turn to some of the actual data concerning the heritability of IQ. For the past 60 years, studies of the heritability of intelligence have relied almost exclusively on standardized IQ tests as the measure of intelligence. We will not concern ourselves here with the question of whether or not IQ tests are valid measures of intelligence (that will be taken up in Chapter 11). Suffice it to say for now that IQ scores do correlate moderately well with at least one aspect of life deemed important in our society, performance in school. The question at hand is this: To what extent are observed variations in IQ scores affected by variation in genes as compared with variation in environment?

In 1981, Thomas Bouchard and Matthew McGue summarized the results of all studies that they were able to find in the world's literature on the heritability of IQ (omitting only those studies that were believed to be fraudulent). In each study, researchers had calculated correlation coefficients for IQ scores for various categories of pairs of relatives, such as identical twins, fraternal twins, and nontwin siblings, who were reared in the same home or adopted at an early age and reared in

*How John Stuart Mill differed from Galton on the nature-nurture issue and in his politics*

different homes. As you may recall from Chapter 1, correlation coefficients can run from 0.00 to either plus or minus 1.00. A correlation of 0.00 in this case would mean that the IQs for the pairs in a study are no more alike on average than those of two people chosen at random. At the other extreme, a correlation of +1.00 would mean that their IQs are perfectly positively correlated; by knowing one person's IQ you could predict the other's exactly. The results for some of the most interesting categories of relatives are summarized in Figure 3.17.

Notice, as you look at the figure, how widespread the different findings are for any given class of relatives (each dot represents a different study). The differences from one study to another may reflect differences in the population studied (such as their age or social class), the type of IQ test used, or other methodological variations. Yet, all in all, the results show a strong genetic contribution to variation in IQ. For pairs of siblings reared in the same family, the closer the biological relationship the higher the IQ correlation: the average coefficients (in the right-hand column) are +0.86 for identical twins, +0.62 for same-sex fraternal twins, and +0.34 for unrelated (adopted) siblings. Perhaps even more impressive, the average correlation for identical twins *reared apart* (+0.72) is higher than that for fraternal twins reared together (+0.62).

■ **How evidence for both genetic and environmental contributions to variability in IQ can be found in family-relationship studies**

On the other hand, the data also show a strong environmental contribution to variation in IQ. Unrelated individuals reared in the same family have an average correlation of +0.34, well above the 0.00 that should be true of unrelated individuals chosen randomly. Moreover, although the extent of their genetic relatedness is the same, fraternal twins show a higher correlation in IQ than do nontwin siblings (+0.60 compared to +0.47). This finding may reflect the similarity in twins' environments. Unlike nontwin siblings, twins enter each developmental stage together and have the same number of older and younger siblings.

Various methods can be used to derive heritability coefficients from correlations such as those in Figure 3.17. The correlation for reared-apart identical twins is itself sometimes used as an estimate of heritability (Loehlin & others, 1988), because that correlation would theoretically be 1.00 (identical IQs for each pair of twins) if all IQ differences were due to genes and 0.00 if all IQ differences were due to environment. By that measure, based on the data in the figure, heritability is 0.72. A more recent report, which adds considerably to the total number of

**Figure 3.17  *Familial correlations for IQ***

*Each dot in the row for a given class of relatives represents the correlation coefficient found in a separate study, and the vertical bar in each set of dots indicates the median for all studies combined. The average correlation for each class of relatives (weighted in accordance with the number of pairs of relatives in each study) is shown in the right-hand column. (Adapted from Bouchard & McGue, 1981.)*

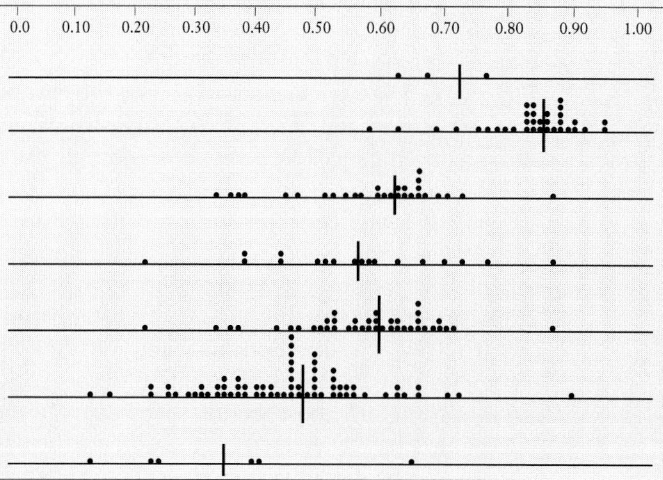

| Type of relationship | Correlation in intelligence | | Number of Correlations | Number of Pairings | Weighted average |
|---|---|---|---|---|---|
| | 0.0  0.10  0.20  0.30  0.40  0.50  0.60  0.70  0.80  0.90  1.00 | | | | |
| Identical twins reared apart | | | 3 | 65 | 0.72 |
| Identical twins reared together | | | 34 | 4,672 | 0.86 |
| Same-sex fraternal twins reared together | | | 29 | 3,670 | 0.62 |
| Opposite-sex fraternal twins reared together | | | 18 | 1,592 | 0.57 |
| Same- and opposite-sex fraternal twins reared together | | | 41 | 5,546 | 0.60 |
| Sibling pairs reared together | | | 69 | 26,473 | 0.47 |
| Nonbiological (adopted) sibling pairs reared together | | | 6 | 369 | 0.34 |

■ *Two ways to estimate heritability coefficients from correlation coefficients for twins, and reasons why the estimates may not be accurate*

reared-apart identical twins studied thus far, produced almost exactly the same result—0.71 (Lykken, 1982). In another method, based on the premise that fraternal twins are half as genetically related as identicals (as is shown in Table 3.1) but equivalent in environmental similarity, heritability is calculated by doubling the difference between the correlations for reared-together identical and same-sex fraternal twins. (The full rationale for this formula is beyond our present scope, but can be found in Plomin & others, 1990.) By this method, using the data in Figure 3.17, heritability = 2(0.86 − 0.62) = 0.48. The same calculation performed on studies conducted since 1981 puts the heritability coefficient somewhat higher—closer to the value found using reared-apart identicals (see Loehlin & others, 1988). The majority of estimates of IQ heritability in family-relationship studies, using various formulas and data sets, fall within the range of 0.50 and 0.75, indicating that somewhere between 50 and 75 percent of the variance in IQ found in such studies is due to genetic variability (see Plomin & others, 1990).

In considering these findings, it is important to realize that all present methods for estimating IQ heritability are based on assumptions that may not be true, so there is wide range for possible bias. For example, use of the correlation for reared-apart identical twins to estimate heritability is based on the assumption that the environments of reared-apart twins differ on average as much as those of two people chosen randomly. But that assumption is easily challenged. Adoption agencies place children only in homes that meet certain requirements, and twins adopted through the same agency are especially likely to be taken into rather similar homes. Moreover, many twins in such studies were actually reared by relatives, sometimes living in the same small town (Kamin, 1974; Taylor, 1980). When only those twins who were brought up in very different homes (city versus country, or rich versus poor) are included, the IQ correlation drops dramatically—to as low as 0.26, according to one recalculation (Bronfenbrenner, 1975).

On the other hand, certain other problems inherent in the studies tend to bias heritability estimates toward the low side (see Plomin & others, 1990). One such problem is measurement error. Variability that stems simply from the lack of perfect reliability of IQ tests adds to the environmental component in heritability estimates, so correcting for that would raise the estimates. As you can see, there is plenty of fodder for argument for those who think the heritability estimates should be pushed either downward or upward from those typically calculated. Almost everyone today agrees that both genetic and environmental sources contribute substantially to the IQ variability observed in such studies, but there is still much room for disagreement about the relative strengths of their contributions.

**Cultural and Racial Studies of IQ**   Many studies have shown average differences in IQ between members of different racial and cultural groups. For example, in the United States, Jews and Asian-Americans regularly score somewhat higher than do other groups (Willerman, 1979). The differences that have attracted by far the most attention, however, are the lower average scores obtained by the lower compared to upper socioeconomic classes in Europe, and by Blacks compared to Whites in the United States. There has been much debate about whether such differences result partly from genetic differences between the groups or result entirely from environmental differences.

An example of the argument for a genetic component to the differences can be found in an article published in the *Harvard Educational Review* some years ago by Arthur Jensen (1969), an educational psychologist. Jensen's thesis—which elicited a storm of controversy—was that compensatory educational programs aimed at raising the academic achievements of Blacks and other economically deprived groups are likely to fail because the differences are more genetic than environmental in origin. He admitted that he had no direct evidence for that claim, but rather was reasoning indirectly, primarily from family-relationship studies of the sort illustrated in Figure 3.17. Others (such as Lewontin, 1970), however, were quick to respond to Jensen's article by pointing out that even if the heritability coefficients derived from family-relationship studies are accurate, they have nothing to do with differences between social or cultural groups. In family-relationship studies the correlations are between pairs of people who share similar environments (they are brought up in the same home or in rather similar adoptive homes), while racial or social class comparisons are between groups who differ greatly in environment.

*How it is possible to have high heritability within groups and zero heritability across them*

To understand how it is possible to have high heritability within groups and zero heritability across them, imagine planting a genetically diverse packet of tomato seeds in two different fields, *A* and *B*, which differ from each other in soil fertility. Within either field, differences in tomato size could be entirely due to genetic differences among the seeds, leading to a heritability coefficient of 1.00. Yet, since the seeds planted in the two fields come from the same package, any average difference between the two fields in tomato size would have to be due to the environmental difference—a heritability of 0.00. Those who argue that the IQ differences between Whites and Blacks, or between rich and poor, are entirely environmental in origin argue that the environments of the two groups are different enough to produce the IQ differences even if everyone came from the same "packet of seeds."

*Two approaches that have shown no genetic contribution to cultural or racial IQ differences*

To test the genetic versus environmental explanations of group differences in IQ, researchers have looked at the IQs of children adopted at an early age into a group different from that of their genetic parents. Findings from several studies of this type support the environmental explanation. In one study, in France, lower-class children who were adopted at an early age into middle- or upper-class families had an average IQ of 109, which was 14 points higher than the average for lower-class children reared by their biological parents and not significantly different from that for middle- and upper-class children overall (Schiff & others, 1978). In another study, in the United States, Black children raised by White, middle- and upper-class adoptive parents had an average IQ of 106, which was significantly higher than that for the population at large and not significantly different from that of White adopted children reared by similar middle- and upper-class families (Scarr & Weinberg, 1976).

In other studies of Black-White IQ differences, researchers have compared the IQs of individuals who are socially defined as Blacks, but who vary in their ratio of African compared to European ancestry. Culturally, people in the United States are generally identified as Black if they have any detectable African ancestry. Thus, they may vary from as low as 25 percent (or even less) on up to 100 percent African ancestry. If the genetic theory of race differences in IQ is correct, Blacks who have high IQs should be found to have more European ancestry than those who have lower IQs. Many years ago, Paul Witty and Martin Jenkins (1935) tested this hypothesis in a study of school children in Chicago. They identified Black school children who had IQs in the superior range (125 or better) and then interviewed their parents to see if they had more European ancestry than did the general Black population. The results were negative. The proportion of European ancestry in the high-IQ Black children was neither more nor less than that in the Black population at large. (The highest IQ of all in that study, a whopping 200, was scored by a young Black girl with 100 percent African ancestry.) More recently, Sandra Scarr and her colleagues (see Scarr & Carter-Saltzman, 1983) used biochemical methods to determine the degree of African and European ancestry in a group of socially defined Blacks, and looked for a correlation between this and IQ score. They found no correlation and concluded, as did Witty and Jenkins, that the *social* designation of Black, not biological ancestry, is the critical variable in determining the Black-White IQ difference.

■ *Why all the fuss?*

**A damaging environment**
*When behavior geneticists speak of environmental effects, they don't just mean learning. Poor nutrition and lead poisoning are two of many ways a poor environment can slow intellectual development. Prior to lead paint laws, many children suffered brain damage from eating lead paint.*

■ *Evidence that schizophrenia runs in families, and why that by itself doesn't prove heritability*

To many people there is something disquieting about such research. Why this preoccupation with race? The range of IQ scores within any group greatly outweighs the average difference between groups, so why should it matter whether small average differences between groups are or are not partly genetic in origin? To a large extent, the excitement generated by cultural and racial studies of IQ differences has always been more political than scientific in nature. The presence of average IQ differences between groups, coupled with a view that such differences are genetic in origin, has long been used, in various guises, to justify economic and social inequalities. Because of this, those who wish to eradicate inequalities between the rich and poor, or Blacks and Whites, are politically motivated to show that IQ differences are *due* to economic and social inequalities, and are not the cause of the inequalities. The Galton-Mill debate continues, and perhaps it will not abate until the world truly offers equivalent opportunities for all.

### Genetic Influence on Risk for Schizophrenia

Another realm in which the nature-nurture controversy has been much apparent is that of mental or emotional disorders. Why do some people have psychological breakdowns while others don't? According to the nature side of the controversy, the answer lies in genes—some people are genetically more prone to such breakdowns than others. According to the nurture side, the answer lies in the environment—those who have breakdowns have been exposed to more stressful environments than those who don't. At this point you will perhaps not be surprised to learn that the weight of evidence, for almost every class of mental disorder that has been studied, indicates that both sides of the classic debate are partly correct, with lots of room for argument about degree.

By far the most extensive research in this realm has been concerned with **schizophrenia**, a serious class of mental disorder that usually first appears in young adulthood and is characterized by disrupted perceptual and thought processes. Common symptoms include hallucinations (such as hearing voices that aren't there), delusions (clearly false beliefs, such as the belief that one's movements are controlled by radio waves), and either the absence of emotional responsiveness or inappropriate emotionality (such as laughing while describing a very sad event). You will read much more about the varied symptoms of schizophrenia and the problems of diagnosing it in Chapter 17. For the present our concern is with studies of its heritability.

It has long been clear that schizophrenia tends to run in families, though not in the same clear-cut pattern as single-gene disorders such as PKU or Huntington's disease. The chance that a child will eventually develop schizophrenia is less than 1 in 100 if the child has no close relatives with the disorder, but is about 1 in 10 if the child has a parent or sibling with the disorder and almost 1 in 2 if the child has two parents with the disorder (Gottesman & Shields, 1982). On the face of it, such results might seem to support a genetic explanation for variation in susceptibility to schizophrenia, but at least in theory the results could be explained purely environmentally. Members of the same family share similar environments, so they may be exposed to the same environmental factors that either produce or protect against schizophrenia. Moreover, parents with schizophrenia might provide a disorganized and stressful home, which might promote the disorder in their children. Clearly, other data are needed to decide whether the family-resemblance findings are due primarily to shared genes or shared environment. Those data, as in the case of studies of IQ heritability, have come from adoption and twin studies.

**Adoption Studies of Schizophrenia** If family similarity in the presence or absence of schizophrenia is due principally to shared genes, then adopted children

■ *How Kety and Rosenthal provided strong evidence for the heritability of schizophrenia, and why they used blind assessment procedures and a control group of adoptees*

should be more like their biological than their adoptive relatives in this characteristic; but if it is due principally to shared environment, the opposite should be true. Based on this rationale, Seymour Kety and David Rosenthal directed a study in Denmark—where birth, adoption, and mental-hospitalization records are more readily available than in the United States (Kety & others, 1976). They began by identifying thirty-three adults who had been adopted in infancy and who later (in adolescence or adulthood) were hospitalized for schizophrenia. For comparison, they also selected a control group of adoptees, who did not have schizophrenia or any other diagnosed mental disorder but were similar to those in the schizophrenia group in other ways, such as age and socioeconomic class. Then they tracked down the biological and adoptive parents, siblings, and half-siblings of both groups and asked them to participate in an extensive psychiatric interview. The purpose of the interview (unknown to the interviewee) was to look for signs of schizophrenia. To prevent bias, the interviews were conducted and evaluated by a team of psychiatrists who were blind (uninformed) as to whether the interviewee was a biological or adoptive relative, or was related to an individual who did or did not have schizophrenia. The main results are shown in Figure 3.18. Only the biological relatives of the schizophrenic adoptees manifested significantly more evidence of schizophrenia than any other group, and they were about four times as likely as the others to show such symptoms.

**Figure 3.18** *Results of an adoption study of the heritability of schizophrenia*

*Kety, Rosenthal, and their colleagues looked for signs of schizophrenia in the biological and adoptive relatives of adoptees who either had or had not become schizophrenic. The results here are the percentage of relatives who showed either schizophrenia or a milder disorder now called* schizotypal personality disorder. *(Data from Kety & others, 1976.)*

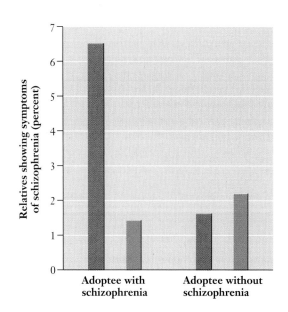

■ Biological relatives
■ Adoptive relatives

You might wonder why Kety and Rosenthal included relatives of non-schizophrenic adoptees in this study. Suppose they had not, and had found (as they did) that the biological relatives of people with schizophrenia showed more signs of the disorder than the adoptive relatives. In that case it could be argued that their findings might be due to a difference between people who give up a child and people who adopt one. That is, perhaps people who give up a child are predisposed toward mental disorders, while those who adopt a child are especially healthy psychologically. As you can see in Figure 3.18, the results for the relatives of the control adoptees negate this explanation. The biological relatives of the control adoptees did not show more evidence of schizophrenia than did the adoptive relatives.

A person bent on finding a nongenetic explanation for Kety and Rosenthal's results might also argue that the predisposition toward schizophrenia arose from the preadoption environment, either in the womb or shortly after birth. To test this possibility, Kety and Rosenthal compared the prevalence of schizophrenic symptoms in biological half-siblings of the two groups of adoptees, using only those who were related to an adoptee on the father's side and not the mother's. This is a particularly useful comparison, because, although genetically related to the adoptees, the half-siblings were born of different mothers and thus did not have the same prenatal or early postnatal environment. Kety and Rosenthal found significantly more signs of schizophrenia in those who were half-siblings to a person with schizophrenia than in those who were half-siblings to a member of the control group. All in all, the study provides compelling evidence that family resemblance with respect to schizophrenia is due more to genetic than environmental similarity. More recent adoption studies, involving additional controls to rule out the possibility of bias or alternative explanations, have also strongly supported that conclusion (Kety, 1988; Loehlin & others, 1988).

**Twin Studies of Schizophrenia**   Another way to assess the role of genetic variation in determining who does or doesn't develop schizophrenia is to find people who have the disorder and who also have either an identical or fraternal twin. In studies of this sort, the original group identified as having the disorder are referred to as the *index cases*. The relatives of the index cases can then be studied to see what percentage of them have the disorder. This percentage is referred to as the **concordance** for the disorder, for the class of relatives studied. A separate concordance measure can be calculated for identical and fraternal twins (or any other class of relatives studied) and used to estimate heritability.

An exemplary and now classic study of this sort was directed by Irving Gottesman and James Shields (1966, 1973) in England. For a period of 16 years, all patients admitted to the psychiatric unit of the Maudsley Hospital in London were asked if they had a twin of the same sex. Those who did, and who themselves were diagnosed as having schizophrenia, constituted the index cases. Then the twins were tracked down, and those who could be found and were willing to participate (most of them) were studied to determine (a) if they were identical or fraternal twins of the index cases, and (b) if they showed symptoms of schizophrenia. Gottesman and Shields ended up with 22 pairs of identical and 33 pairs of fraternal twins. The judgments as to whether the twins of the index cases had schizophrenia or not were made on the basis of psychiatric tests and interviews by a team of psy-

■ *The meaning of concordance, and how Gottesman and Shields found higher concordance for schizophrenia in identical than fraternal twins*

*The Genain quadruplets*

Nora, Iris, Myra, and Hester Genain are identical quadruplets who have all been diagnosed with schizophrenia. Two of the sisters have more debilitating forms of the disorder than do the other two. The differences among them must stem from environmental influences.

chologists and psychiatrists who did not know whether the person they were evaluating was a fraternal or identical twin of someone with schizophrenia. The results were as follows: of the 22 identical-twin index cases, 11 (concordance = 50 percent) were judged to have schizophrenia; and of the 33 fraternal twins, only 3 (concordance = 9 percent) were judged to have schizophrenia, which is about the same as the concordance for schizophrenia that is generally found in nontwin brothers and sisters. Many similar studies have since resulted in quite similar findings. The average concordances found in these studies, for other relatives as well as for the two classes of twins, are shown in Table 3.2.

**Table 3.2** *Concordance rates for schizophrenia*

| Relationship to a person who has schizophrenia | Average percentage found to have schizophrenia (concordance) |
| --- | --- |
| Relatives in same generation | |
| Identical twin | 46% |
| Fraternal twin | 14 |
| Nontwin brother or sister | 10 |
| Half-sibling | 4 |
| First cousin | 2 |
| Relatives in later generation | |
| Child of two parents with schizophrenia | 46 |
| Child of one parent with schizophrenia | 13 |
| Grandchild of one person with schizophrenia | 4 |
| Niece or nephew of one person with schizophrenia | 3 |

*Source:* From *Schizophrenia: The epigenetic puzzle* (pp. 85 and 104) by I. I. Gottesman & J. Shields, 1982, Cambridge: Cambridge University Press.

■ *How twin studies show an environmental as well as a genetic contribution to variability in who does or doesn't develop schizophrenia*

The twin studies, like the adoption studies, show strong evidence for the importance of genetic differences in determining who does or doesn't develop schizophrenia, but unlike the adoption studies they also point to an environmental influence. Of particular interest is the fact that concordance for identical twins is much less than the 100 percent that would be predicted if genetic variation alone were involved. To some degree reduced concordance could come from misdiagnosis, because any errors in diagnosing either the index cases or their twins would reduce the measured concordance below its true value. But some pairs of discordant identical twins have been studied over many years, and there can be no doubt in those cases that one manifests the disorder while the other doesn't (Wahl, 1976). Using statistical procedures too complex to describe here, some behavioral geneticists calculate from the sort of concordances shown in Table 3.2 that the heritability for the *liability* (risk) for schizophrenia is about 0.70 (Plomin & others, 1990). It is important to realize, though, that this refers to the heritability not of diagnosed schizophrenia but of a hypothetical underlying susceptibility for it. Although some research has suggested that this risk might stem primarily from a single dominant gene, the bulk of the evidence now suggests that many genes are involved and that no single gene plays an overwhelming role (Farone & Tsuang, 1985; Kennedy & others, 1988).

**The Search for Prevention by Environmental Means: An Analogy to TB**   The studies just described indicate that in existing environments the development of schizophrenia depends to a great extent on genetic differences among people.

**■** *How an analogy to TB shows that high heritability does not imply that a purely environmental solution can't be found*

Does this mean that it is useless to try to find environmental means to prevent the disorder? No, certainly not. To illustrate why, it would be instructive to consider some findings about the heritability not of schizophrenia but of tuberculosis (TB).

In the 1930s and early 1940s, when TB was much more common than it is today, F. R. Kallman performed an extensive study of twins and other relatives to assess the heritability of the risk for this disease. He found, incredible as it may seem, that 87 percent of the identical twins, 25 percent of the fraternal twins or ordinary siblings, and 11 percent of the half-siblings of index cases eventually came down with the disease (Roth, 1957). At the time of the study, 1.4 percent of the general population came down with TB at some time in their lives. The evidence was overwhelming that genetic differences among individuals, not environmental differences, played the largest role in determining who got sick and who didn't. Should that have led scientists to conclude that the only way to solve the TB problem would be through genetic control? Certainly not. Today few people get TB, because TB depends not only on genetic predisposition, but also on exposure to the TB bacillus, the germ that causes the disease. TB was reduced not by changing people's genes, but by cleaning up the environment to get rid of the bacillus. In the 1930s almost everyone was exposed to the TB germ, so determination of who got TB and who didn't depended more on genetic susceptibility than on exposure to the germ. But today very few people are exposed to the TB bacillus, so genetic susceptibility is relatively unimportant.

**■** *The promise of ongoing studies of people who are at risk for schizophrenia*

Today something like two dozen different long-term studies of children who are genetically at risk for schizophrenia are underway in various parts of the world (Asarnow, 1988). One of the major goals of the studies is to identify environmental conditions that, in combination with genetic predisposition, bring on the disorder. The studies are not likely to bring an environmental solution as easy or as effective as that for tuberculosis, but they are turning up some helpful leads. There is evidence that children predisposed to schizophrenia often have difficulty focusing their attention or dealing with more than one source of environmental input at a time, and there are hints that they are more likely to develop overt symptoms of schizophrenia in highly stimulating or emotion-provoking homes than in those that are more orderly and calm (Asarnow, 1988). Research of this sort may eventually lead to an understanding of the different environmental needs of children with different inborn temperaments or tendencies. This is one of the most interesting future promises of the field of behavioral genetics.

## Concluding Thoughts

In looking back at this chapter, four important ideas stand out, which are worth re-iterating and elaborating on a bit more.

**1. Genes influence behavior through protein synthesis.** Sometimes when people talk about the role of genes in behavior they lose sight of how indirect that role is. Genes do not have eyes, ears, muscles, or minds. They are not little demons that sit inside a person and pull strings to make the person act according to their wishes. They are simply DNA molecules, which provide the code for building the body's proteins. Variations in that code from person to person can affect behavior to the degree that they affect the sensory, motor, neural, and other physiological systems involved in behavior. Genetic effects on human behavior are most apparent when an abnormality in the code leads either to the absence of some important protein (as in the cases of PKU and red-green color blindness) or to the overabundance of a protein that produces harmful effects (as in the case of Down syndrome, where a gene on chromosome 21 produces a protein that forms plaques in the brain).

**2. Single-gene effects can be inferred from patterns of heredity.** The concept of the gene was formulated by Mendel at a time when nothing was known about DNA or protein synthesis. Mendel inferred the existence of genes and their paired nature from patterns of heredity. By assuming that genes come in pairs, that variations (now called *alleles*) can exist within a given pair, and that some variations are dominant over others in their effect, he was able to explain the ratios that he found in the inherited characteristics of hybrid peas. Since then, researchers—such as Scott and Fuller in their work with dogs—have used patterns of heredity to infer that single-gene differences underlie certain stepwise behavioral differences among individuals. The same is true for many genetic disorders in humans. In reviewing the chapter you might see if you can explain the patterns of heredity leading to the inference of (a) a single dominant gene located on an autosome, (b) a single recessive gene located on an autosome, and (c) a single recessive gene located on an X chromosome.

**3. The nature-nurture debate is about heritability, and has to do with groups, not individuals.** Some people misinterpret the nature-nurture debate in a way that leads them to conclude that there is nothing to debate. The misinterpretation is to assume that the question is whether genes or environment contributes most to an individual's characteristics (psychological or otherwise). The debate would be foolish indeed if that really were its question. Obviously, neither genes nor environment can be more important than the other in the development of an individual's characteristics, since both of them working together are absolutely essential. With no genes there would be no person (and no characteristics), and with no environment there would again be no person (and no characteristics). The nature-nurture debate is not about characteristics within an individual, but about differences among individuals. To what extent are differences among people in, say, IQ or liability for schizophrenia due to genetic compared to environmental differences among them? That is a potentially answerable question, which quantitative geneticists address by calculating heritability coefficients from selective breeding studies with animals and adoption and twin studies with people. As you have seen, however, the answer is not fixed. Heritability depends not just on the characteristic studied, but also on the genetic and environmental diversity of the specific group studied. Heritability for any given trait might be high in Group *A* and low in Group *B*. If you understand the heritability concept you should be able to explain the differences between two groups that could lead to high heritability in one and low heritability in the other.

**4. The optimal environment may be different for individuals who have different genes.** The interplay of genes and environment in the development of behavioral characteristics becomes most apparent when a genetic effect on behavior is reduced or abolished through an environmental change. Infants with PKU become mentally retarded if they have the same diet that most infants thrive on, but they don't become retarded if they have a restricted diet. Cooper and Zubek found that their "maze dull" rats were less adept than the "maze bright" rats in learning a maze if both groups were reared in normal cages, but were not worse if both groups were reared in more stimulating cages. Apparently, as measured by maze-learning ability, the "dulls" benefited more from extra stimulation than did the "brights." Returning to humans, most people can develop and function well in stimulating and emotion-provoking homes, but long-term studies of people genetically at risk for schizophrenia suggest that such people may need a calmer environment for optimal development. In more subtle ways, genetic differences among all of us may lead each of us to seek different environmental conditions, most conducive to our own development.

## Further Reading

**Robert Plomin, J. C. DeFries, & G. E. McClearn** (1990). *Behavioral genetics: A primer* (2nd ed.). New York: Freeman.

*This textbook, by three highly respected behavioral geneticists, is an excellent source for the student who wishes to explore more deeply any of the topics touched on in this chapter. (Don't let the word* primer *fool you. This book will challenge the serious student.)*

**Raymond E. Fancher** (1985). *The intelligence men: Makers of the IQ controversy.* New York: Norton.

*This lively book, by one of the best writers among modern psychological historians, traces the history of the nature-nurture debate on IQ through biography, from Mill and Galton in the nineteenth century through Kamin and Jensen in our time.*

**J. P. Scott & J. L. Fuller** (1965). *Genetics and the social behavior of the dog.* Chicago: University of Chicago Press.

*In this fascinating book, two of the pioneers of behavioral genetics describe the methods and findings of their 13-year-long research project on genetics, social behavior, and learning in dogs. The student can see here how one question leads to another in a long-term research program.*

## Looking Ahead

Behavioral genetics emphasizes the differences among individuals. But any two randomly chosen members of a species are far more alike than different, and genes are at least as responsible for the similarities as for the differences. If there is such a thing as human nature, spanning history and cultures, it stems from our shared genes, which build into us a common set of capacities, tendencies, and proclivities. Those genes have been accumulated in the course of evolution, through a long weeding-out process, in which genes that built bodies that survived and reproduced were passed along and those that didn't weren't. In the next chapter we will look at the behavioral characteristics that unite and help define a species, and we will attempt to understand them in terms of evolution.

# Chapter 4

**Basic Concepts: Natural Selection and Evolutionary Adaptation**

**Ethology: The Study of Species-Specific Behavior Patterns**

**Sociobiology: The Comparative Study of Animals' Social Systems**

# THE ADAPTIVENESS OF BEHAVIOR I: EVOLUTION

In 1859, a book was published in England that helped change the way people think about themselves and the organic world in which they live. That book, *The Origin of Species*, by Charles Darwin, set forth a theory of evolution that restructured biological thought, had an enormous impact on philosophy, and provided one of the key foundations for the emergence of a scientific psychology (see Chapter 1). The basic idea of evolution—that modern forms of life came about by change from earlier forms—had been around for centuries before, but only after *The Origin of Species* was published did the idea begin to gain wide acceptance in the intellectual world. The book had a strong impact for two reasons. First, it set forth massive amounts of evidence—based partly on patterns of variation that exist in present-day forms of life and partly on the fossil record—for an evolutionary process. Second, and even more important, it spelled out a mechanism by which evolution could occur—natural selection.

This chapter is about evolution by natural selection, its implications for the study of animal and human behavior, some of the findings and ideas that have emerged from behavioral research inspired by evolutionary thought, and some of the pitfalls that can accompany the evolutionary approach. It is also the first of a two-chapter sequence on the *adaptiveness of behavior*, the second of which is on learning. Adaptation refers to modification to meet changed life circumstances. Evolution is the long-term adaptive process, spanning generations, that equips each species for life in its natural habitat. The chapter begins with a general discussion of natural selection and the meaning of adaptation; then looks at research concerning the evolution of specific movement patterns in humans and other animals; and finally it delves into research and controversies concerning the evolutionary basis for social relationships in humans and other animals.

## Basic Concepts: Natural Selection and Evolutionary Adaptation

Natural selection and evolutionary adaptation are so often misunderstood that it is important to begin our discussion with a careful review of what these concepts mean and don't mean.

### The Process of Evolution by Natural Selection

■ *The similarity and difference between natural selection and artificial selection*

**Natural Selection Is Selective Breeding in Nature**   Darwin himself introduced the idea of evolution through natural selection by devoting Chapter 1 of *The Origin of Species* to a more familiar concept, evolution by human-induced selection, or what he called *artificial selection*. Artificial selection is the process of selective breeding, discussed in Chapter 3, through which domesticated strains of such creatures as chickens, cattle, and dogs have been produced and modified. At each generation, the individuals that best approximated the desired type were mated to produce the next generation.

Darwin went on to point out that breeding in nature is also selective and can also produce changes in living things over the course of generations. Selective breeding in nature, which Darwin labeled *natural selection*, is dictated not by the needs and whims of humans, but by the obstacles to reproduction that are imposed by the natural environment. Those obstacles include predators, limited food supplies, extremes of temperature, difficulty in finding mates for sexual reproduction—anything that can cut life short or otherwise prevent an organism from producing offspring. Animals that have characteristics that help them overcome such obstacles are, by definition, more likely to have offspring than those that don't.

Darwin's essential point was this: Not all individuals survive and reproduce, and the determination of which do and which don't is based partly on the individual's inherited characteristics. Any inherited characteristics that increase the likelihood of survival and reproduction are selected for by nature, and any that decrease that likelihood are selected against. Thus, as long as heritable differences exist among individuals in an interbreeding population, and as long as some of those differences affect survival and reproduction, evolution will occur.

**The Synthesis of Darwin and Modern Genetics**   Darwin knew nothing of genes, or of what produces the heritable source of variation in plants and animals upon which natural selection acts. Mendel's work on heredity, which was the first step toward a knowledge of genes, was not discovered until 1900. Our modern understanding of evolution, which combines Darwin's principle of natural selection with knowledge of genes, is referred to as the *modern synthesis* (Mayr & Provine, 1980). From the perspective of the modern synthesis, what changes from generation to generation in evolution is the frequency of specific genes in an interbreeding population. Those genes that improve an individual's ability to survive and reproduce in the existing environment increase from generation to generation, and those that impede that ability decrease from generation to generation.

The genetic variability that provides the fodder for evolution comes from two main sources: (1) the reshuffling of genes that occurs in sexual reproduction (discussed in Chapter 3), and (2) *mutations* (Futuyma, 1986). Mutations are errors that occasionally and unpredictably occur during DNA replication, causing the "replica" to be not quite like the original. In the long run of evolution, mutation is the ultimate source of all genetic variation. All gene differences in any species are believed to have originated from mutations. As would be expected of any random change, new mutations are more often harmful than helpful, so natural selection usually works to weed them out. But occasionally a mutation is useful, producing a protein that affects the organism's development in a way that increases its ability to survive or reproduce, and the gene arising from that mutation increases in frequency from generation to generation. At the level of the gene, that is evolution.

Prior to the modern synthesis, many people believed that changes in an individual that stem from practice or experience could be inherited and provided the basis for evolution. For example, some argued that early giraffes, by continuously stretching their necks to reach leaves in trees, slightly elongated their necks in the course of their lives, and that this change was passed on to their offspring, resulting, over many generations, in the long-necked giraffes we see today. That idea, referred to as the *inheritance of acquired characteristics*, is most often attributed to Jean-Baptiste de Lamarck (1744–1829), though many other evolutionists, both before and after Lamarck, held the same view (Futuyma, 1986). Even Darwin did not reject that idea, but rather added to it the ideas of random change and natural se-

■ *The modern synthesis, and its solution to the question of what provides the original source of variation on which natural selection can act*

lection. Now, however, with the modern synthesis, we know that evolution is based on genes alone, and that nothing that happens in an individual's life changes the individual's genes. Random change followed by natural selection, not directed change stemming from individual experience, provides the basis for evolution.

**The Role of Environmental Change in Evolution**   If the environment did not change over time, organisms might become as adapted to it as they could and evolve no further. But the environment keeps changing. Climates change, new sources of food come and go, new predators come and go, and so on. When the conditions of life change, what was previously a useful characteristic may become harmful, and vice versa.

A nice example of small-scale, rapid evolution that illustrates this point is the change in peppered moths living in and around London over the past 150 years or so (Bishop & Cook, 1975). Prior to the Industrial Revolution of the mid-nineteenth century, the moths were mostly light in color, the same shade and mottling as the lichen that grew on the trees on which they spent most of their time. Their coloring thus helped protect them from being seen and eaten by birds (see Figure 4.1). At each generation, a few mutant moths that were dark in color would hatch, but—as experiments later showed—these would have been easily seen and eaten by birds, so they did not send their genes on to the next generation (Kettlewell, 1973). After industrialization, however, the air in and around London became so polluted that the lichen could not grow and the trees took on the darker color of their bark. In this environment, the dark moths were most likely to survive and have offspring, while the lighter ones were gobbled up. By 1950, 90 percent of the peppered moths in and around London were of the dark variety. More recently, antipollution laws have cleaned up the air in London, the lichen are growing again, and the light moths are making a comeback (Cook & others, 1986).

Darwin believed that evolution is a slow and steady process. But today we know that it can occur relatively rapidly, slowly, or almost not at all, depending on the rate and nature of environmental change and on the degree to which genetic variability already exists in the population (Gould & Eldredge, 1977). Environmental change spurs evolution *not* by causing the appropriate mutations to occur, but by promoting the process of natural selection. Thus, the presence of darker

**Figure 4.1** *Light and dark peppered moths*

*You have to look hard to see the light moth on the lichen-covered bark, or the dark moth on the dark bark. The evolution from light to dark (or back again) in this case involves change at just one gene locus, which is part of the reason why it can occur so rapidly. More complex evolutionary changes—such as in the evolution of an eye or a wing—involve an accumulation of the effects of many gene changes, each of which adds some degree of survival advantage.*

tree trunks did not cause more mutations in the direction of the gene for darker color, but only changed the selection criteria, so that those that did have this gene—whether from a new mutation or inherited from parents—were more likely to survive and reproduce.

*Three mistaken beliefs about evolution, all related to the misbelief that foresight is involved*

**Evolution Has No Foresight**   People sometimes mistakenly think of evolution as a mystical force working toward some planned end. One manifestation of this belief is the idea that evolution could produce changes for some future purpose, even though in the present environment these changes serve no function or are even harmful. But evolution has no foresight. Only those genetic changes that are immediately beneficial to the organism, in the sense of increasing survival and reproduction, will increase through natural selection.

Another manifestation of the belief in foresight is the idea that present-day organisms can be ranked in accordance with which of them are "most evolved," that is, according to which have moved the furthest toward some planned end. For example, some may think of humans as the most evolved creatures, with chimpanzees next, and amoebas way down on the list. But evolution has no planned ends. The three just-named creatures have taken their different forms and behavioral characteristics because of chance events that led them to occupy different niches in the environment, where the selection criteria differed. The present-day amoeba is not an early step toward humans, but rather a creature that has been evolving as long as humans have and is as complete and adapted to its environment as we are to ours. The amoeba has no more chance of evolving to become like us than we have of evolving to become like it.

A third manifestation of the belief in foresight is the idea that natural selection is a moral force, that is, its operation and products are in some moral sense right or good. In everyday talk, people sometimes imply that whatever is natural (including natural selection) is good, and that evil stems from society or human contrivances that go beyond nature. But nature is neither good nor bad, moral nor immoral. To say that natural selection led to such and such a characteristic does not mean that there is any moral virtue to that characteristic. As you will see later, fighting is as much a product of evolution as is cooperation, but that is no reason to consider them morally equivalent.

**Natural Selection of Behavior-Producing Mechanisms**   An organism's ability to survive and reproduce depends on its behavior as much as anything else, and, as you know from Chapter 3, behavior can be changed through selective breeding. Just as Tryon was able to breed rats, through artificial selection, to be better at learning a maze, natural selection breeds animals to become better at doing what they must to survive and reproduce in their natural environments. The consequence is that behavior evolves—or, to be more precise, the *mechanisms* for producing behavior evolve. These range from simple reflex mechanisms, such as the withdrawal response to a painful stimulus, on through the most complex learning mechanisms.

Your ability to read and make sense of these words is not just a result of natural selection, of course. You had to learn English, you had to come into contact with certain ideas, and so on. But the fact that you, given certain environmental conditions, can understand these words, while a chimpanzee or an amoeba could not do so under any conditions, *is* the result of natural selection. The massive human brain, with its billions of neurons and trillions of connections—which enable motivation, emotion, sensation, perception, and reasoning to occur, and to occur in certain ways and not others—is a product of evolution by natural selection. Our brain and the rest of our behavioral machinery came about for one and only one reason: to promote our ability to survive and reproduce in the context of the environment in which we evolved.

*A "cultural" tradition*

*Humans are not the only species that pass ideas from generation to generation. About 30 years ago scientists on the Japanese island of Koshima began leaving sweet potatoes on the beach for a group of macaque monkeys. Soon a female began to rinse off the sand in the sea—a practice that spread among the group. Today, all the macaques of Koshima wash their potatoes, and some of them, having acquired a taste for salt, dip them between bites.*

■ *The meaning of adaptation at the evolutionary, individual, and cultural levels, and implications for thinking about the functions of behavior*

### Evolutionary Adaptation

**The Meaning of Adaptation and Its Occurrence at Three Levels** To *adapt* is to change to suit new conditions. In psychology it is useful to think of three levels at which adaptation occurs. One level is evolution itself, by which change in genetic makeup over generations allows organisms to continue to survive and reproduce as the environment changes. A second level is that which occurs within individual lifetimes, including all of the moment-to-moment and year-to-year adjustments that individuals make to the fluctuations in their environment. This level includes such changes as hormonal responses to environmental stresses; increased or decreased strength stemming from use or disuse of muscles; and, most important for psychology, the entire class of changes that are labeled *learning*. Adaptation at the second level is not independent of adaptation at the first. The machinery that permits individual adaptation to occur is itself the result of evolution.

When we think about humans it is important to add a third level of adaptation. We not only learn, but we code what we have learned into words and pass it on from generation to generation. This ability has spawned a new way of adapting, *cultural adaptation*. Human cultures are made up of large numbers of interacting individuals, who speak the same language and share the same accumulated information. As the information is passed from generation to generation, it is modified in ways that suit the culture's changing needs and purposes; this is what is meant by cultural adaptation. This level of adaptation makes use of the individual level. New ideas and tools developed by individuals are added to the culture when they are useful, thereby affecting future generations, and older, less useful ideas and tools gradually drop out. The time scale of this evolutionary process is much faster than biological evolution. Essentially all of the dramatic change that has occurred over the past 10,000 years or more in the way that people live is due to cultural evolution. The amount of biological evolution that has occurred in humans in that time is miniscule.

**Thinking About Behavior in Terms of Its Function** Each level of adaptation promotes behaviors that serve specific purposes, though the behaving individual need not be aware of them. Natural selection leads to behavioral mechanisms that promote the individual's ability to survive and reproduce. Learning supplements this process by providing responses that help surmount the specific obstacles and achieve the specific goals that present themselves in the course of a lifetime. And cultural evolution—through traditions, religions, and laws—can lead to behaviors that serve the larger purposes of the culture, which in some cases may run counter to the more individually selfish ends promoted by biological evolution.

The *functionalist approach* in psychology—which today is not a distinct school of thought but is integrated into many areas of psychology (see Chapter 1)—is to try to understand specific behavioral actions or tendencies in terms of their adaptive functions. How does this or that behavior help promote (a) the long-term survival or reproduction of the individual (evolutionary adaptation), or (b) the individual's ability to solve a particular problem unique to its life (individual adaptation), or (c) the needs of the culture in which the person lives (cultural adaptation)? This approach is often difficult to apply to human behavior, because it is often hard to disentangle the different levels of adaptation. What one person interprets as an evolutionary adaptation may be interpreted by another as cultural.

When applied at the evolutionary level, the functionalist approach in psychology is essentially the same as the functionalist approach in anatomy: Why do giraffes have long necks? Why do humans lack fur, which is common to other mammals? Why do male songbirds sing in the spring? Why do humans have such an irrepressible ability to learn language? The anatomist trying to answer the first two questions, and the behavioral researcher or psychologist trying to answer the last two, would look for the role that each trait played in the ability of ancestral members of the species to survive and reproduce.

■ *How ultimate explanations pertain to evolutionary function, and how they differ from proximate explanations*

*A redwinged blackbird at home*
*This male's singing warns other males of the species to stay away.*

**Ultimate Compared to Proximate Explanations of Behavior**   Biologists and psychologists who think in evolutionary terms find it useful to distinguish between two different kinds of explanations of behavior—ultimate and proximate (see Barash, 1982). *Ultimate explanations* are functional explanations at the evolutionary level; that is, they are statements of the role that the behavior plays in the animal's survival and reproduction. *Proximate explanations* are explanations that deal not with function but mechanism; they are statements of the immediate conditions that bring on the behavior.

Consider, for example, the question of why male songbirds (of many species) sing in the spring. An ultimate explanation might go something like this: Over the course of evolution, songbirds have adapted to a mating system that takes place in the spring. Their song serves (a) to attract a female with which to mate and (b) to warn other males to stay away from the singer's territory in order to avoid a fight. In the evolutionary history of these birds, males whose genes promoted such singing produced more offspring (more copies of their genes) than those whose genes did not promote such singing. A proximate explanation, in contrast, might go as follows: The increased daylight and growth of vegetation that occur in the spring trigger, through the birds' visual system, a physiological mechanism that leads to the increased production of testosterone (a male hormone), which in turn acts on a certain area of the brain (which we might call the "song area"), promoting the drive to sing. Notice that there is nothing incompatible about these two kinds of explanation. The ultimate explanation states the survival or reproductive value of the behavior, and the proximate explanation states the stimuli and physiological mechanisms through which it occurs.

Of course, it is one thing to offer an explanation that sounds plausible, and another to establish its scientific validity. To test any explanation scientifically, one must make systematic observations or perform experiments to see if specific predictions based on that explanation hold up. That is as true of ultimate explanations as it is of proximate explanations. The ultimate explanation offered in the example above is supported by experiments showing that recorded bird songs do indeed attract females and/or repel males of the same species (see, for example, Yasukawa, 1981); and the proximate explanation is supported by physiological investigations of the sort to be discussed in Chapter 7.

### *Some Precautions Concerning Adaptational Thinking*

It is rather easy to make up ultimate explanations and more difficult to prove them. Richard Lewontin and Steven J. Gould (1978) have referred to some of the ultimate explanations developed by biologists and psychologists as "Panglossian myths," named after the optimistic Dr. Pangloss of Voltaire's novel *Candide,* who believed that every detail of everything on earth was placed there to serve a useful function. For example, according to Pangloss, the human nose has its peculiar shape to enable us to wear glasses. Of course, Pangloss's explanations were based on a different conception of life than that of natural selection. (No modern evolutionist would accept Pangloss's explanation of the nose, because human noses were around long before glasses, and evolution has no foresight.) But the basic error of overextending functionalist explanations is the same. To avoid creating Panglossian myths, it is important to base ultimate explanations on appropriate evidence and to realize that not every individual characteristic of humans or other animals is adaptive. Here are three reasons why characteristics cannot always be explained in adaptational terms.

■ *Three alternatives to evolutionary adaptation to explain genetically based characteristics of a species or population*

**Genetic Drift**   When one finds a genetic difference between two populations of a given species that occupy different locations, there is a strong and often reasonable temptation to attribute the difference to natural selection. The differing locations set different selection criteria; as a consequence, evolution can take different directions for the two groups. But there is another possible explanation—simple chance. Individuals that appear in one location may happen to have an unusual set of genes compared to those in another location. As long as the genes are not strongly maladaptive, they will be passed along from generation to generation at a high level. All forms of chance events that can lead to different gene pools in different populations of a species are referred to as *genetic drift.* Perhaps the most potent form of genetic drift is the *founder effect*—the genetic difference between two populations that occurs when one was founded by a small group of individuals that migrated to a new area and happened to have some unusual genes.

An example of a population difference that might be explained either by natural selection or the founder effect is this: Schizophrenia exists at about a 1 percent rate among people in most parts of the world, but at about a 3 percent rate among people living north of the Arctic Circle in Sweden. Why? Some years ago a group of researchers led by Julian Huxley and Ernst Mayr—two venerated pioneers of the modern synthesis—suggested an interesting adaptational answer. They suggested that while the genetic predisposition for schizophrenia may be maladaptive under most conditions, it may actually promote survival under the physically harsh but psychologically less complex conditions of life in northernmost Sweden (Huxley & others, 1964). That is, in the history of this group, people with genes that promote schizophrenia might have been more likely to survive and produce offspring than those without. In support of this view, they cited other research suggesting that people with schizophrenia are unusually resistant to certain kinds of physical shocks, wounds, and diseases. But an alternative explanation, also mentioned by Huxley and his colleagues, is the founder effect. The Arctic population was founded by a small group of Swedish migrants, who might by chance have had a higher proportion of schizophrenia-promoting genes than the population at large.

Still a third possibility, of course, is that the difference could be purely environmental in origin. The harsh Arctic environment might bring on schizophrenia in people who would not manifest that disorder elsewhere. This third possibility might be verified by determining if newer migrants to this part of the world, who have not interbred with the longer-established residents, also have an unusually high rate of schizophrenia. If they don't, that would tend to support either of the two genetic theories. It would be harder, though, to find data to determine which of the two genetic theories is more applicable.

**Correlates of Structure**    Darwin was aware that often a particular characteristic can evolve as a nonadaptive side effect of some other adaptive change. He referred to such changes as ***correlates of structure***, implying that the nonadaptive and adaptive changes are linked in the organism's biological structure. An example that might be explained in these terms concerns a characteristic of the spotted hyena that has intrigued naturalists since the time of Aristotle (see Gould, 1983). The female of this species has an enlarged clitoris, almost indistinguishable in size and shape from the male's penis. Why? Based on studies of the animals' behavior, Hans Kruuk (1972) proposed a possible ultimate explanation. He found that spotted hyenas live in clans but often separate and travel far distances alone. When two individuals meet they perform a greeting ceremony, which involves lifting a leg and sniffing and licking each other in the genital area. Kruuk suggested that this ceremony may help spotted hyenas recognize their kin and keep their clan together, and that the female's clitoris evolved over time so that she would have as conspicuous a structure for this ceremony as does the male.

But Gould (1983), looking at the same question, has suggested a different answer involving a correlate of structure. Most anatomical differences between males and females in any mammalian species are due to the presence or absence of a class of hormones called *androgens* (including testosterone) during fetal development and later. Spotted hyenas are unique in that the female, beginning in fetal development, produces as high a level of androgens as the male (Racey & Skinner, 1979). That is the proximate explanation of her enlarged clitoris. Androgens in fetal life can make the clitoris in the female of any mammal grow large and look like a penis. Now the question becomes: Why does the female spotted hyena produce a high level of androgens?

Kruuk's explanation would hold that natural selection favored high androgens because they resulted in the enlarged clitoris. But Gould suggests what may be a more plausible scenario. Natural selection favored a high level of androgens because it increased the body size and muscular strength of the female spotted hyena, and enlargement of the clitoris was a side effect. The spotted hyena is one of the few mammals in which the female is larger than the male and leads the clan in hunts and aggressive encounters with other clans. If Gould is correct, that is the phenomenon that begs for an ultimate explanation. Why is it advantageous for female spotted hyenas to be large and strong relative to males? The important point here is that an understanding of proximate mechanisms is often a key step toward determining just what it is that needs explanation in ultimate terms. According to Gould, people who think about behavior from an evolutionary perspective often jump too quickly to ultimate explanations without thinking about the proximate.

**Putting an Organ to Use for Purposes Beyond Those for Which It Evolved**
Suppose Gould is right, that the female spotted hyena's enlarged clitoris came about as a side effect. Even so, Kruuk's explanation could still be partly correct. Once the clitoral enlargement began to occur, the female may have found a use for it in the greeting ceremony, either through learning or further evolutionary change. Whatever structures one has are part of the conditions of one's life, around which further adaptive change can occur.

Now consider the human brain. The basic form of this organ certainly did not come about as a side effect. It must have evolved because the behavioral characteristics it made possible were valuable to the survival and reproduction of our ancestors. But that doesn't mean that everything people now do with their brains has a direct evolutionary, adaptational explanation. You may use your brain to write computer programs, compose sonnets, or figure out your taxes, but that doesn't mean that the human brain evolved because it allowed our ancestors to do those things. The brain evolved its complex set of characteristics and potentials to solve the kinds of problems that were critical to survival in an earlier time, but now that

***On point***

*The art of ballet gives the audience enormous pleasure but at considerable physical cost to the dancer. The foot can adapt to ballet positions, but ultimately that adaptation leads to physical deformity.*

we have it we can use its characteristics for all sorts of other purposes, some of which promote our survival and reproduction and some of which don't.

## Ethology: The Study of Species-Specific Behavior Patterns

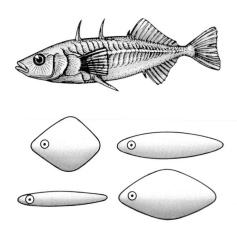

**Figure 4.2** *Stickleback models used in the test of sign stimuli*

*Models that had a red belly provoked aggression in male sticklebacks no matter how crude they were, whereas even a perfect replica of a male stickleback with no red belly did not. (From Tinbergen, 1951.)*

Suppose you saw an animal that looked exactly like a dog, but it went "meow," climbed trees, and ignored the mail carrier. Would you call it a dog or a cat? Clearly, we identify animals as much by their behavior as by their anatomy. Behavior patterns that are so characteristic of a given species of animal that they can be used to help identify that species are called *species-specific behaviors*. Meowing, tree climbing, and acting aloof are species-specific behaviors of cats. Dam building is a species-specific behavior of beavers. Talking and two-legged walking are species-specific behaviors of humans.

The field of behavioral study that has concentrated most explicitly on species-specific behaviors is *ethology*, which originated in Europe in the 1930s as a branch of zoology concerned with animal behavior in the natural environment (see Chapter 1). In contrast with psychologists, who studied animals in mazes and other artificial contrivances and who were looking for general principles of learning that cut across different species, ethologists were more interested in the behavioral differences among species, which they attributed to their differential evolutionary histories. Ethologists were (and still are) interested in (a) identifying and describing species-specific behaviors, (b) understanding the environmental requirements for the development of such behaviors in the young animal, and (c) understanding the evolutionary pathway through which the genetic basis for the behavior came about. Let us look now at all three of these enterprises.

### Describing Species-Specific Behaviors

**Fixed Action Patterns and Sign Stimuli**    The early ethologists, including Konrad Lorenz and Nikolaas Tinbergen (the field's main founders), focused on various species of insects, fish, reptiles, and birds, and found that these animals are quite predictable in some aspects of their behavior. Different members of the same species produce identical responses to specific environmental stimuli. The ethologists referred to such movements as *fixed action patterns*, a term designed to emphasize the idea that the movements are controlled by mechanisms that have been "fixed" in the animal's nervous system through heredity and are relatively impervious to modification through learning. Any stimulus that could elicit a fixed action pattern they termed a *sign stimulus*. The relationship between a sign stimulus and a fixed action pattern is essentially reflexive, except that the response to a sign stimulus is usually more complex than that of a reflex and only occurs when the animal is in an appropriate physiological condition.

Tinbergen (1951, 1952) studied fixed action patterns and sign stimuli in a little European fish, the stickleback. During the breeding season, the male stickleback's belly turns from dull gray to bright red, and he builds a nest and defends the area around it by attacking other male sticklebacks that come too close. To determine what triggers the attack on other males, Tinbergen made stickleback models of varying accuracy and trailed them on thin wires through a male's territory. He found that any model with a red belly, no matter how little it resembled a real stickleback in other respects, would elicit a vigorous attack from the defending male (see Figure 4.2). On the other hand, a model without a red belly, no matter how much it resembled a real stickleback in other respects, failed to elicit an attack. Thus, Tinbergen showed that the red belly is the sign stimulus for the attack response in the male stickleback. (He even observed male sticklebacks attacking in the direction of a red van driving past their glass-walled aquarium.)

■ *How Tinbergen identified the sign stimuli for the attack response and the zigzag dance in the male stickleback*

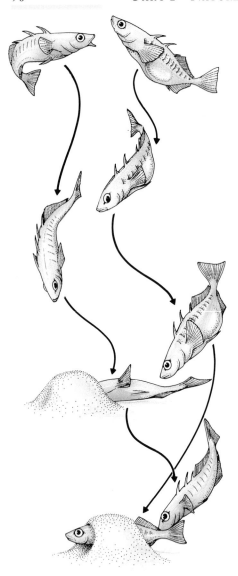

**Figure 4.3** *Courtship behavior of sticklebacks*

*After performing the zigzag dance in her presence, the male stickleback leads the female into the nest he has constructed, where she lays her eggs. (Adapted from Tinbergen, 1951.)*

■ *How the concept of* species-specific behavior *can be characterized as biological preparedness, and why it is a relative, rather than absolute, concept*

Tinbergen also determined the sign stimulus for a different stickleback fixed action pattern, the *zigzag dance*, by which the male lures the female into his nest and prompts her to lay eggs where he can fertilize them (see Figure 4.3). Again using dummies attached to wires, Tinbergen found that the sign stimulus for the zigzag dance is the female's swollen belly. Dummies without swollen bellies did not elicit the dance, and those with swollen bellies did.

**A More Liberalized View: Biological Preparedness**   In their early writings, ethologists tended to discuss all species-specific behaviors in the terminology of fixed action patterns and sign stimuli, but as they began to study mammals it became clear that many species-specific behaviors are more flexible in form and less tightly controlled by specific stimuli than is implied by those terms. This is particularly true of mammals, especially primates, and most especially humans. A scientist from outer space making a study of earthly life would almost certainly point to two-legged walking and use of a grammar-based language as among the species-specific behaviors of humans, but these certainly are not rigid in form or tightly controlled by environmental stimuli. They involve a great deal of learning, as anyone knows who has ever watched a child in the early stages of walking or talking. At the same time, it is clear that humans are biologically predisposed to learn and to engage in these behaviors.

Regarding walking, evolution has provided humans with anatomical systems—such as strong hindlimbs with feet, weaker forelimbs without feet, and a short, stiff neck—that combine to make it more convenient for us to walk upright than on all fours. Moreover, and less obvious, we are born with neural systems in the brain and spinal cord that give us the potential to move our legs and other body parts correctly for coordinated two-legged walking, and with neural structures that help provide the incentive to engage in that behavior at a certain time in development. Consider the difference between two-legged walking in humans and in dogs. Dogs are capable of learning to walk in this way, and much is made of that fact by circus trainers, but they are never very good at it. They do not have the appropriate muscular and skeletal systems to coordinate the behavior properly, and they have no natural impulse to walk in this manner. A dog, unlike a human child, will practice two-legged walking only if it receives immediate rewards such as food for doing so. Thus, two-legged walking is not a species-specific behavior in dogs.

The same is true for talking. Humans are born with anatomical structures (including a tongue and larynx) that are well designed for producing a wide range of sounds, and with a brain that has special neural centers for understanding and producing language (to be discussed in Chapter 11). Infants begin talking at a certain (approximate) age, just as they begin walking at a certain age; and they do this with little outside inducement (to be discussed in Chapter 12). Of course, to acquire a language a child must hear others use it and have others around with whom to speak it. But the fact that learning is involved does not negate the point that talking is a species-specific behavior. The natural environment of the human being, the one in which we have been evolving for millions of years, is one in which children are surrounded by adults who communicate through spoken language. Through structured training involving lots of rewards, chimpanzees can be taught to simulate some aspects of human language, just as dogs can be taught to walk on their hind legs, but they are never very good at it. We will pursue these issues in later chapters, but the point for now is that grammar-based language is a species-specific behavior in humans and not in chimpanzees.

Having characterized the concept of species-specific behavior in terms of biological preparedness, I must now add that the concept is clearly relative rather than absolute. No behavior stems just from biological preparation; some sort of experience with the environment is always involved. Conversely, any behavior that an animal can produce—no matter how artificial it may seem or how much training is necessary to produce it—must make use of the animal's inherited biological capacities. The concept of species-specific behavior is useful as long as we do not try to make it a discrete category or get into arguments about whether one or another behavior really should or should not be called species-specific. *Big* and *little* are useful terms in our vocabulary, but there is no point in arguing about whether a bread box is properly called one or the other. Two-legged walking is more species-specific for humans than for dogs, as a bread box is bigger than a book of matches.

The important question to ask when we study a particular behavior is not: Is this a species-specific behavior? Rather, the important questions are: What are the environmental conditions needed for the full development of this behavior? What internal mechanisms are involved in producing it? What is its function in the individual's daily life? In the course of evolution, why would the genes that make this behavior possible have been favored by natural selection? These questions can in principle be asked of any behavior, whether or not the behavior is thought of as species-specific.

### Development of Species-Specific Behaviors: The Role of the Environment

**The Rationale of Deprivation Experiments**   After identifying various species-specific behaviors, ethologists became interested in questions about the development of such behaviors in the lifetime of the individual. What aspects of the animal's natural environment are needed for a behavior to develop in its typical, species-specific form? To answer this kind of question, ethologists began to perform *deprivation experiments*, raising animals in ways that deprive them of some of their usual environmental experiences, to see what experiences are essential for the behavior to develop.

In some cases such experiments have shown that a particular species-specific behavior can develop quite normally in animals that have had no opportunity to observe the behavior in others. For example, Irenäus Eibl-Eibesfeldt (1961)—one of the first ethologists to focus on mammals—found that rats that were raised in isolation from other rats, and had never observed rats fight, nevertheless fought the very first time they were placed in a cage with another rat, using the same postures and movements as do normally reared rats (see Figure 4.4). This result, of course, does not mean that fighting in rats does not depend in any way on experience. It is impossible to deprive an animal of all experience. The isolated rats had experience moving and exercising their muscles in various ways in their cages, for example, which no doubt contributed to the development of their ability to fight. Moreover, once rats do begin to fight, their experiences can modify their likelihood of future fighting and also lead to further refinements in their skill. But the study does show that the basic pattern of movements in rats' fighting is genetically prepared in such a way that it can occur without observational learning.

■ *How deprivation experiments help determine what experiences are necessary for a species-specific behavior to develop*

**Figure 4.4 *Species-specific fighting postures of rats***
*When aggressive rats meet, they (a) first circle one another with arched backs, and then (b and c) rise into a boxing-like position, pushing each other with their paws. They fight in this way whether raised in isolation or with other rats. (From Eibl-Eibesfeldt, 1961.)*

(a)

(b)

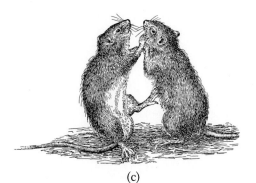

(c)

In other cases, deprivation experiments have helped pinpoint experiences that are necessary for a particular species-specific behavior to develop. For example, Peter Marler (1970) found that white-crowned sparrows develop the ability to sing their species-specific song only if they are permitted to hear that song during their first summer after hatching. Indeed, populations of that species living in different areas have somewhat different dialects, and a white-crowned sparrow learns to sing the dialect of the adult that it hears. Yet there is a strict limit on the range of possible songs that the birds can learn. No matter what environmental experiences it has, a white-crowned sparrow cannot learn to sing like a canary, or like any species other than a white-crowned sparrow.

**Emlen's Study of Migratory Flight in the Indigo Bunting**   My favorite example of a deprivation experiment is a study conducted by Stephen T. Emlen (1975) with indigo buntings. The indigo bunting is a small songbird that spends its summers in the eastern United States and Canada and its winters in the Bahamas and Central America. Like most songbirds, it migrates only at night. Without the sun as a guide, how does it know which way is north and which is south? That is the question that Emlen wished to answer.

If indigo buntings are kept in cages and exposed to natural seasonal changes in the daily hours of light, they get restless during the migrating seasons, making many futile movements to get out of their cages. Emlen found that if the birds are caged in such a way that the stars are in view, their restless movements are directed south in the fall and north in the spring. If the stars are not in view, their movements are directed randomly. Apparently, they use the stars to tell direction. Emlen next found that if he blocked from view the area of the sky that includes Polaris (the North Star) and the constellations around it, the birds directed their movements randomly, but if he blocked other portions of the sky, preserving the view of Polaris and the surrounding constellations, they directed their movements appropriately. Apparently, indigo buntings use Polaris as their guide. This is quite a "logical" choice, because Polaris is the only clearly visible star in the Northern Hemisphere that maintains a fixed compass position throughout the night. All of the other stars move across the sky as the earth rotates on its axis.

So, buntings migrate away from Polaris in the fall and toward it in the spring. But how do they know that it is Polaris, and not some other bright star, that should serve as their guide? Is this knowledge inborn, or do they somehow have to learn that Polaris is the one fixed spot in the night sky? This is where the deprivation experiment comes in.

*How Emlen discovered that indigo buntings must learn which star is stationary, and a possible evolutionary explanation of why they need to learn it*

Emlen raised three groups of indigo bunting nestlings in a laboratory, carefully controlling their visual experience. Group 1 was never exposed to any representation of the stars throughout the summer months. Group 2 was allowed to view a representation of the true night sky in a planetarium. Group 3, the most interesting group, was allowed to view, in the same planetarium, a false representation of the night sky, in which all of the stars rotated around Betelgeuse (a bright star in the constellation Orion) rather than Polaris. When the birds began to show migratory restlessness in the fall, all groups were placed in the planetarium with a representation of the true night sky. The results were that Group 1 showed no consistency in their orientation, Group 2 oriented directly away from Polaris as expected, and Group 3 oriented directly away from Betelgeuse! Thus, Emlen found that indigo buntings are not born (or rather hatched) with the knowledge that they must fly away from Polaris in the fall. Instead, their genes help equip them to know that (a) they must fly away from the fixed star in the fall, and (b) before that time they must learn, through observation, which star that is.

Why must each new generation of buntings learn the sky? Why haven't they evolved the innate knowledge to use Polaris as their guide? Emlen suggests an interesting answer to that question. The heavens are not fixed; each year the earth's

Vega   Polaris (North Star)

Earth's axis

**Figure 4.5** *Evolutionary advantage of indigo buntings' learning which star is stationary*

*Whichever star lies most directly over the earth's North Pole will be the most stationary star in the Northern Hemisphere, and hence the most reliable guide for migratory flight. Today that star is Polaris. But the earth spins on an axis that wobbles in a cycle that takes 26,000 years to complete. Thus, 13,000 years ago the fixed star was not Polaris but Vega, and in the interim since then a succession of other stars have occupied that status. (Adapted from Emlen, 1975.)*

axis of rotation changes very slightly. Polaris was not positioned over the North Pole 13,000 years ago, but rather it was about 43° away from it (see Figure 4.5). At that time, Polaris would have been a poor choice as a navigational guide, and another star would have been better. For indigo buntings to survive over thousands of years (a speck of time considering the millions of years required for them to evolve their present form), a flexible system for choosing the fixed star, which can accommodate the millennial changes in the heavens, is apparently more efficient than a genetically rigid system that must re-evolve every few thousand years. If Emlen is correct, then ancestral buntings who held a genetically fixed image of the sky would, with time, have gone off course and perished, while those that had a more flexible system, allowing them to adjust which star to use as their guide, would have continued to make it to their southern destination. This nicely illustrates the ethologists' idea that specific learning mechanisms arose in evolution to meet specific survival problems that could not be met through less flexible means (a point to be pursued in Chapter 5).

### Tracing the Evolution of Species-Specific Behaviors

Scientists who are interested in the origins of anatomical traits, especially bones, can dig up fossils and try to reconstruct the evolutionary pathway by comparing fossils of different ages. But behavior does not fossilize (except occasionally in remnants such as footprints, or, for humans, in products of behavior such as stone tools). How can ethologists make reasonable inferences about the evolutionary pathway of species-specific behaviors? The answer, as pointed out by Darwin and pursued by the pioneering ethologists, is through the systematic comparison of behaviors in present-day species.

*How to tell a homology from an analogy, in behavior as well as anatomy*

**Two Forms of Cross-Species Comparisons: Homology and Analogy**   To understand the logic of comparing present-day species to infer an evolutionary pathway, it is necessary to distinguish between two conceptually different classes of similarities among species—homologies and analogies. A **homology** is any similarity that exists because of common ancestry. If we look back far enough, all animals are related to one another, so it is not surprising that some homologies—such as the basic structure of the DNA molecule and of certain enzymes involved in

**Figure 4.6 *Analogous wings***
*Similarities in the wings of birds, bats, and butterflies are considered to be analogies, because they arose independently in evolution. Though similar in function and gross structure, the three types of wings are very different in the finer details of their structure, as is characteristic of analogies. The movements involved in flying in these animals are also analogous—similar in function and gross form, but different in detail and physiological mechanism.*

■ *How Darwin used comparison by homology to infer the evolutionary steps through which honeybees acquired their hive-making ability*

metabolism—can be found between any two species. But the more closely related two species are, the more homologies they will show. In fact, it is through assessment of homologies that biologists have traditionally measured the degree of relatedness of different species. An ***analogy***, in contrast, is a similarity that stems not from common ancestry but from *convergent evolution*. Convergent evolution occurs when different species, because of some similarity in their habitat or lifestyle, independently evolve some common characteristic.

As an illustration, consider comparisons that one might make among different species that can fly. Flying has arisen separately in three different taxonomic groups—birds, some insects (such as butterflies), and some mammals (bats). Similarities across these three groups in their flying motions, and in the anatomical structures that permit such flight, are examples of analogies because they do not result from common ancestry (see Figure 4.6). On the other hand, similarities among species within any of these groups, such as among birds or butterflies, are likely to be homologies.

Aside from evidence based on already existing knowledge about the relatedness of the species being compared, analogies and homologies can often be distinguished by the nature of the similarity involved (Lorenz, 1974). Analogies entail similarity in the function and gross form of the structures or behaviors being compared, but lack of similarity in their details or in the underlying mechanisms of their control. Thus, the wings of birds, bats, and butterflies are all similar in the sense that they provide broad, flappable surfaces, but they are very different in their finer details. Similarly, the specific movements involved in flight in these three groups are quite different in detail and are controlled by different neural mechanisms. In contrast, because homologies arise from shared genes, they entail similarities in the finer details and physiological mechanisms, even when, because of divergent evolution, large differences have emerged in gross form or function (for example, see Figure 4.7).

Analogies are useful as cues in understanding the evolutionary function of a species-specific behavior (as you will see later), but only homologies are useful in inferring the actual pathway of change through which it evolved. The pioneer in the use of this method was Darwin himself, so it seems most fitting to illustrate it by describing one of Darwin's studies, taken from his chapter on instinct in *The Origin of Species*.

**Darwin's Study of Hive Building in Bees**   Have you ever examined the hive that honeybees make? It is a marvelous piece of work, which the bees build with wax secreted from special glands in their bodies. Each comb in the hive consists of a double layer of thin-walled, hexagonally shaped cells, with their bases beveled to enable the two layers of cells to fit together perfectly (see Figure 4.8a). Mathematicians in Darwin's time had shown that this construction is the most efficient design possible, allowing for the storage of the greatest amount of honey and larvae with the least use of wax. This, plus the fact that the cells look as if they would be extraordinarily difficult to build, was used as evidence in Darwin's time that a divine and un-

**Figure 4.7 *Homologous forelimbs***

*Similarities in the forelimbs of different species of mammals are considered to be homologies, because they arose from common ancestry. Though the limbs of the (a) whale, (b) human, and (c) bear differ in function and gross structure (one is a flipper, another is an arm, and the third is a leg), they are similar in certain of their structural details, as is characteristic of homologies. Behaviors too can be homologous, and a key to their homology is similarity in mechanism and detail, even when function differs. (Adapted from Lorenz, 1974.)*

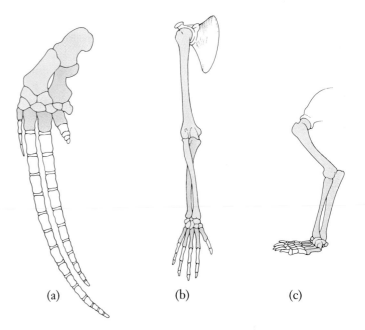

(a)          (b)          (c)

**Figure 4.8 *Cells built by honeybees and bumblebees***

*The hexagonal cells of the honeybee's hive (a) are the optimal shape for storing large amounts of honey and larvae using the least amount of wax. Darwin suggested that ancestors to modern honeybees built their hives in a way similar to that of modern bumblebees (b), but, through evolution, began placing their cells closer together, patching up the points of intersection, resulting eventually in the kind of hive they build today.*

fathomable intelligence lay behind their construction. Darwin knew that if his theory of evolution was going to succeed, he would have to show how such a marvelous behavior as this, in such a simple animal as the bee, could have come about through natural selection.

Darwin began his study of the honeybee's hive building by surveying the types of storage structures built by other living bee species. He discovered that these structures could be arranged in a series from very simple to complex. The simplest were those produced by bumblebees, consisting of small clusters of spherical cells (see Figure 4.8b). Darwin noted that spherical cells are easy to build, and that insects usually build them by sweeping their body, or some part of their body, compasslike around a fixed point. Another species of bee, *Melipona domestica*, which is anatomically more similar to the honeybee than is the bumblebee, builds much larger clusters of spherical cells that are more closely compacted than those of the bumblebee. Darwin noted that this species builds its cells in essentially the same way as does the bumblebee, but closer together, patching up intersecting cells with flat walls. This insight provided him with the key to explaining the honeybee's hive-building ability.

(a)

(b)

Darwin reasoned that if a group of honeybees began building spherical cells a certain distance apart (which they could do by using their own bodies as a measure), and then patched up the points of intersection between adjacent cells with flat walls, doing this in two layers, they would produce precisely the structures one finds in the honeybee hive. In other words, they did not need to calculate the sizes of the planes and angles of hexagonal prisms in order to build them, but simply had to add another, not terribly complex step (that of building cells equidistant apart) to the behaviors already present in the *Melipona* bees. Subsequently, Darwin developed a method to observe honeybees directly as they built their combs, and he confirmed that this indeed was how they worked.

On the basis of his comparisons of different bee species, Darwin proposed that the early ancestors of honeybees built spherical cells, like present-day bumblebees, but in the course of evolution gradually came to position their cells closer together, so that more walls were shared in common, until finally arriving at the "perfect" form of the present-day comb. Each small step in this process would represent a selective advantage to the bees, allowing for the construction of more cells (so as to store more honey and house more larvae) with less expenditure of precious wax.

*How comparison by homology can be used to infer the original function of a behavior that is now vestigial*

**Vestigial Behaviors**   Some species-specific behaviors do not make sense as adaptations to the present environment, but do make sense as adaptations to conditions present at an earlier time. These behavioral remnants of the past are called *vestigial* characteristics, and they can often be understood through homologies. An interesting example is the *grasp reflex*, by which newborn human infants close their fingers tightly around objects placed in their hands. This reflex may well be useful in the development of the infant's ability to hold and manipulate objects, but that does not explain why prematurely born infants will grasp so strongly that they can support their own weight, or why they will grasp with their toes as well as their hands (see Figure 4.9), or why the best stimulus to elicit the response is a clump of hair (Eibl-Eibesfeldt, 1975). These aspects of the reflex make more sense when we observe the homologous behavior in other primates. To survive, infant monkeys and apes must be able to cling tightly to their mother's fur while she swings around in trees or goes about her other daily business. In the course of our evolution from ape-like ancestors we lost our fur, so our infants can no longer cling to us in this way, but the grasp reflex remains.

**Figure 4.9** *Premature infant clinging with hands and toes*
*This ability may be a vestigial carryover from an earlier evolutionary time, when the infants of our ancestors would cling to their parents' fur.*

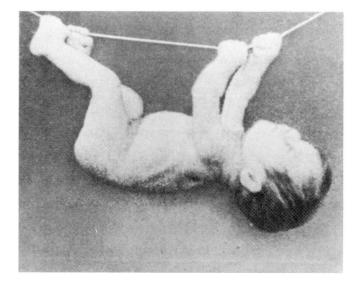

The issue of vestigial traits becomes quite important when we extend it from reflexes to our inherited drives or motives. Because of culture, our habitat and lifestyle have changed dramatically in just a few centuries, a speck of time compared to the time scale of biological evolution. The great bulk of our evolution occurred in a world that was very different from the one we inhabit today, and some of our inherited tendencies may be not only nonfunctional but harmful. An example is our taste for sugar. In the world of our ancestors sugar was a rare and valuable commodity. It existed primarily in fruits and provided the energy needed for life in the wild, as we can see by looking at the eating patterns of present-day monkeys and apes. But today, in our culture, sugar is readily available, and life (at least for some of us) is less physically strenuous. We need less sugar, yet our taste for it persists, as strong as ever. We also have access to more of it, and so we suffer such consequences as tooth decay and obesity.

### Human Emotional Expressions as Species-Specific Behaviors

Humans communicate their moods and behavioral intentions to each other not just through words, but also through bodily postures, movements, and facial expressions, which together comprise what is called ***nonverbal communication***. While verbal communication (communication with words) is unique to our species, nonverbal communication occurs regularly in other animals as well, and the specific movements it involves can often be analyzed in evolutionary terms. When Darwin turned his attention to human behavior, he was strongly drawn to nonverbal communication. In 1872, he published a book entitled *The Expression of the Emotions in Man and Animals*, making the case that (a) specific, objectively describable facial expressions reliably accompany specific emotional states in humans; (b) some of these expressions are universal, occurring in people of every age, race, and culture, and even in people who were born blind and thus could not have learned them through observation; and (c) the evolutionary origins of some of these expressions can be understood by comparison with expressions of other animals. A number of ethologists and psychologists have picked up where Darwin left off, and the evolutionary analysis of nonverbal expressions has become a rather active area of research. We will start here with three general principles concerning the evolution of nonverbal signals, outlined by Darwin, and then turn to studies of human emotional expressions.

**Darwin's Three Principles Concerning the Evolution of Nonverbal Signals**
Darwin (1872/1965) proposed three principles concerning the evolutionary origin of nonverbal signals, and these principles are still considered to be among the most useful generalizations on the topic. They are as follows:

*How communicative signals arise through ritualization, antithesis, and direct action of the nervous system*

1. *The principle of ritualization* Darwin's first principle, which he called "the principle of serviceable associated habits," but which today is referred to as ***ritualization***, was that many signals evolved from behaviors that originally served functions other than communication. The process involves the following steps: (a) A behavior that originally served some noncommunicative function begins to take on a communicative function, because other individuals, seeing the initial movements of the behavior, can use them as clues in predicting what the actor will do next. (b) If that communicative function benefits the individual manifesting the behavior, natural selection modifies the behavior, along with associated anatomical structures, in a way that enhances its communicative function. (c) The noncommunicative function of the behavior may gradually decline or disappear, in which case the behavior finally functions either mostly or solely as a signal.

As an example, consider the evolution of aggressive signals, or threats, in animals. Darwin pointed out that the displays that most animals use to threaten one

**Figure 4.10** *Threat display shown by a northern gannet*

*As a rule, the nonverbal signals with which animals threaten one another evolved from, and bear a physical resemblance to, the movements involved in actual fighting.*

another contain obvious elements of the behavior patterns involved in fighting. An animal about to attack another animal must first face the other and expose its weapons (beak, antlers, teeth, claws, or whatever). Originally, facing the enemy and exposing the weapons were part of the act of attacking, but they evolved, in some species, into signals of threat (see Figure 4.10). Since there is an advantage in knowing when one is likely to be attacked, animals acquired the ability (through natural selection or learning or both) to recognize the cues that another animal is about to attack. This in turn resulted in a selective advantage to those individuals that manifested their aggressive intentions most clearly—for example, by staring for a longer time or showing their weapons more conspicuously—as they could best intimidate others without actually fighting, and thereby get their way with minimal risk of injury. Thus, as evolution proceeded, what was initially a battle of tooth or claw increasingly became a battle of bluff, a way of communicating aggression and accomplishing one's aggressive ends with less actual fighting.

Ritualization can occur through learning and cultural tradition as well as through natural selection. Many human nonverbal signals that may or may not be entirely learned seem to be ritualized forms of behaviors that originally served purposes beyond signaling (see Eibl-Eibesfeldt, 1989). For example, the side-to-side shaking of the head to signal no may have originated from the movements by which an infant who has had enough to eat turns away from the mother's breast or another source of food. Similarly, tongue protrusion as a general signal of rejection may have originated from the tongue movements by which infants physically reject food that has been placed in their mouths.

*2. The principle of antithesis* If a species communicates a particular message with a particular movement or posture, natural selection or learning or both may lead it to adopt the opposite movement or posture to communicate the opposite message. This is what Darwin called the principle of **antithesis**. Among the best examples of this principle are signals of nonaggression or submission. To appear submissive, one must first and foremost *not* appear aggressive, so natural selection would favor signals that involve hiding the signs of aggression or behaving in ways opposite to those of aggression. Thus, gulls that express aggression by pointing their beaks at one another express nonaggression by pointing their beaks directly away from each other (Tinbergen, 1960), and primates that signal aggression by a direct stare signal nonaggression by very conspicuously looking away (Redican, 1982). Darwin's own illustration of the principle, applied to dogs, is shown in Figure 4.11. In the nonaggressive state, practically all moving parts of the dog are oriented in a direction opposite to the way they are oriented when the dog is in an aggressive state.

**Figure 4.11 *The principle of antithesis***

*As depicted in this woodcut from Darwin (1872/1965), the hostile and submissive dogs show opposite postures and movements. The hostile dog has its ears forward, back up, hair up, and tail up; the submissive dog has its ears back, back down, hair down, and tail down.*

3. *The principle of direct action of the nervous system* The response systems of the body can be divided into two classes: the *somatic* or *skeletal*, which includes the muscles attached directly to bones; and the *autonomic*, which includes glands and the muscles not attached to bones, such as the muscular walls of the heart, blood vessels, and digestive tract. Nonverbal signals that arise from ritualization or antithesis generally involve the skeletal muscles. Other signals, however, arise from the involuntary autonomic responses that accompany physiological arousal; this is what Darwin meant by direct action of the nervous system. Trembling when frightened and blushing when ashamed are among the examples of human autonomic responses that are visible to another person and can signal one's emotional state. It is not clear to what extent such signals have been modified over evolutionary time explicitly to serve a communicative function, and to what extent they occur only as a side effect or because they serve other, noncommunicative functions. There has been relatively little research on autonomically mediated signals.

**Ekman and Friesen's Atlas of Basic Human Emotional Expressions** Darwin believed that precise description is as important to the study of human facial expressions as to that of any other biological phenomenon. His book on emotional expressions includes descriptions of the muscles of the face and how they move during various expressions. The most thorough modern extension of Darwin's work along this line is that of American psychologists Paul Ekman and Wallace Friesen (1975, 1982). They have produced an atlas containing both verbal descriptions and pictures of the facial expressions that accompany what they consider to be the six basic emotions—surprise, fear, disgust, anger, happiness, and sadness. Ekman and Friesen developed the verbal descriptions by measuring the relative positions of the moveable parts of the face in photographs and films of dozens of people who were experiencing each emotion, and by using statistical means to find the positions that were most typical of each. Then, to produce standard pictures for their atlas, they asked models who were skilled at facial movements to contract just those muscles dictated by the verbal description. In Figure 4.12 you can see the full-faced expression of each of the basic emotions, as shown by one of the models. As you study the figure, keep in mind that the model was *not* asked to feel or act out an emotion, but only to contract certain facial muscles. Even so, it is hard to look at the photographs without attributing an emotion to the model.

**Figure 4.12 *Basic human emotional expressions***

*These are the six basic, universal emotional expressions depicted in Ekman and Friesen's atlas. They were produced by a model who was asked to move specific facial muscles in specific ways. As you study each figure, try to describe in words the exact facial positions for each expression. For example, surprise can be described as follows: (1) the brows are pulled upward, producing horizontal wrinkles across the forehead; (2) the eyes are opened wide, revealing white above the iris; (3) the lower jaw is dropped; and (4) there is no tension around the mouth.*

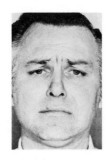
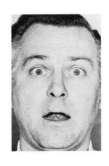
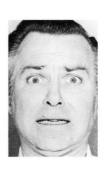

(a)                                    (b)

**Figure 4.13 *Blends of anger-fear and sorrow-happiness in humans***

*People often show blends of emotions by manifesting one emotion in the upper part of the face and the other in the lower part, as illustrated here for (a) anger-fear and (b) sorrow-happiness.*

■ *How basic emotional expressions can be understood as muscle movements, and how these combine to form more complex expressions*

**Blends and Deceptions**   We rarely express emotions in the pure forms depicted in Figure 4.12. This is at least partly because we rarely feel just one emotion at a time. More commonly we feel several emotions at once, and ***blends*** of two or more may appear on our face. For any two of the six basic emotions, you can probably imagine a situation that would elicit both at once. For example, surprise can blend with fear, disgust, anger, happiness, or sadness, depending on whether the unexpected encounter is with a fierce bandit, a disemboweled pig, a despised enemy, a dear friend, or a loss of fortune. Anger and disgust is a common blend, since things that make us angry often disgust us, and vice versa. Even the seemingly opposite emotions of sadness and happiness can blend, as, for example, when enjoying the company of a friend who is very ill, or when reminiscing over the sweet, lost days of childhood. According to Ekman and Friesen (1975), blends are most often expressed by showing one emotion in the lower part of the face and the other in the upper part, as shown in Figure 4.13. Blends can also be found in the emotional expressions of other animals, as shown for the dog in Figure 4.14.

Felt emotions can be expressed involuntarily, that is, without conscious control, but we also have voluntary control over the muscles used for emotional expression, and thus can inhibit true expressions and substitute false ones. There are many innocent as well as not so innocent reasons for doing this. For example, an ill or frightened person may fake an expression of happiness to reassure a friend or,

**Figure 4.14 *Blend of anger-fear in dogs***

*Dogs also manifest emotional blends in their faces. Increasing hostility in the dog is shown here from left to right, and increasing fear from top to bottom. The lower right-hand dog is simultaneously strongly hostile and fearful. (From Lorenz, 1966.)*

on the other hand, may intensify an expression of sadness or fear to gain attention. Ekman (1985) has described a number of clues for distinguishing true expressions from false ones. According to him, people are better at faking emotions with the lower part of the face than the upper part. Thus, a person who tries to look happy to mask anger may produce a good smile, but the anger may still leak through in the form of a lowered brow. A problem, of course, is that the smiling mouth and lowered brow could also represent a true blend of anger and happiness (sometimes we enjoy being angry, and other times we are angry at ourselves for being happy). Another clue to deception is the occurrence of *microexpressions* of the real emotion, lasting for about 1/20 of a second, which occasionally interrupt the deceptive expression. Ekman identified microexpressions by viewing, in slow motion, films of people who were deliberately falsifying their emotions, but he also found that with practice he could detect them even at normal speed.

Some people are much better than others at seeing through masks and detecting true emotions; the difference may result largely from practice. For example, when Ekman (1985) showed a film of a very depressed woman pretending she was happy, most people were taken in by her deception, but experienced psychotherapists usually were not. People commonly attribute skill in detecting true emotions to "intuition," and even those who are most skilled usually don't know how they do it. But in reality, whether they are aware of it or not, they must be using cues such as those described above and probably many others.

**The Universality of Emotional Expressions**   Do people everywhere express emotions in the same basic ways? Darwin (1872/1965) himself attempted to answer that by surveying missionaries and government officials who worked in various parts of the world among people who had minimal previous contact with Europeans. His survey contained such questions as: (1) "Is astonishment expressed by the eyes and mouth being opened wide, and by the eyebrows being raised?" (2) "When in good spirits, do the eyes sparkle, with the skin around and under them a little wrinkled, and with the mouth drawn back at the corners?" From the responses to this survey, Darwin concluded that the basic emotional expressions are universal, but his study has justly been criticized because the questions he asked clearly described the results that he expected. It is well known that observers of behavior, particularly relatively untrained observers such as those that Darwin relied on in this study, often "see" what they are expected to see. Thus, observers who expect to see the eyes and mouth opened wide in the expression of surprise may think they have seen this when they really haven't, or may notice it when it occurs while overlooking some other expression that better represents surprise in the person being studied. This problem can be circumvented by using observers who are unaware of the hypothesis being tested. (Observer-expectancy effects and double blind methods are discussed in Chapter 2.) Recent cross-cultural studies that have been conducted in ways that prevent observer bias have generally confirmed Darwin's conclusion.

*How Ekman and Friesen verified Darwin's suggestion that basic emotional expressions are universal*

Among the most careful of such studies were those performed by Ekman (1973) and his colleagues to assess the universality of the expressions described in their atlas (also see Ekman & Friesen, 1982). They showed their atlas photographs to individuals in many different countries—including members of a preliterate tribe in the highlands of New Guinea who had little previous contact with other cultures—and found that in every culture people described each depicted emotion in a way that was consistent with descriptions in the United States. In a reversal of this procedure, they also photographed members of the New Guinea tribe who had been asked to act out various emotions and showed the photographs to college students in the United States. The college students were as accurate in labeling the emotions portrayed by the New Guineans as the New Guineans had been in labeling those of people from the United States.

(a)                                                                                          (b)

**Figure 4.15** *The eyebrow flash*

*This universal signal of greeting is shown here in photos of a* (a) *French woman,* (b) *Yanomami man (of the Brazil-Venezuela border),* (c) *!Kung woman (of the central Kalahari, in Africa), and* (d) *Balinese man.*

Another scientist who studies human nonverbal communication cross-culturally is ethologist Irenäus Eibl-Eibesfeldt. After spending two decades studying nonhuman animals, he turned his attention for another two decades (so far) to a worldwide study of species-specific behaviors in humans. One of his interesting findings concerns a signal that he labeled the **eyebrow flash**, a momentary raising of the eyebrows, lasting about ⅙ of a second, usually accompanied by a smile and an upward nod of the head (see Figure 4.15). He has observed this response in every culture he has studied—including cultures in New Guinea, Samoa, and various parts of Africa, Asia, South America, and Europe—and has concluded that it is a universal sign of greeting among friends (Eibl-Eibesfeldt, 1989). It is interesting to note that raised eyebrows are also a component of the emotional expression of surprise (look back at Figure 4.12), so the eyebrow flash with its accompanying smile might be interpreted as a nonverbal way of saying, "What a happy surprise to see you."

Eibl-Eibesfeldt (1975) has also filmed children who were born blind, or both blind and deaf, and found that they manifest emotions in the same basic ways as sighted children do (see Figure 4.16). Such observations provide the most direct evidence that at least some human expressions do not have to be learned through observing them in others or hearing descriptions of them.

Taking all this evidence together, there can be little doubt that we come into the world genetically prepared to express certain emotions in certain species-specific ways. It is also clear that we come into the world genetically prepared to learn ways of controlling and modifying our emotional expressions and to learn new ones. Even researchers who focus on universal expressions are quick to point out many cross-cultural differences. For example, Eibl-Eibesfeldt (1975) found

**Figure 4.16** *Some emotional expressions need not be learned through observation*

*This young girl, manifesting joy, has been blind and deaf from birth.*

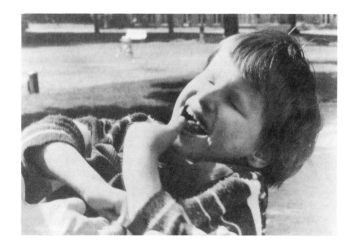

(c)

(d)

■ *Grounds for speculating that the human greeting smile and the human happy smile have separate evolutionary origins*

that despite its cross-cultural similarity in form and general meaning, large cultural differences exist in the use of the eyebrow flash. The Japanese, who are reserved in social expressions among adults, use it mainly when greeting young children, while Samoans, at the other extreme, greet nearly everyone in this way.

**Possible Primate Homologies of Smiling and Laughing**    Partly on the basis of his own observations at zoos, Darwin (1872/1965) pointed out many similarities between human emotional expressions and those of monkeys and apes. He suggested that they may have a common evolutionary origin (that is, they may be homologies), an idea that has found support in subsequent research. Perhaps the best evidence concerns the human smile and laugh.

The human smile is a component of the expression of happiness; it also serves, even when one is not particularly happy, as a friendly greeting signal. Most monkeys and apes produce facial displays that look similar to the human smile. In fact, many species, including chimpanzees, show two different smile-like displays, which are believed by some researchers to be evolutionarily related to the two different versions of the human smile (van Hooff, 1976).

One is the *silent bared-teeth display*, believed to be related to the greeting smile in humans. If you have ever watched macaque monkeys in a zoo, you have almost certainly observed this display, a grimace shown usually by the more submissive of two monkeys as it glances nervously toward the more dominant. A direct stare in macaques (and other primates) is an aggressive signal, which precedes attack and can precipitate an attack by the other, and the silent bared-teeth display seems to have evolved as a means for a more submissive monkey to look at a more dominant one without provoking a fight. If it could be translated into words, it might be rendered as, "I'm looking at you but I'm not going to attack, so please don't attack me." J. A. van Hooff (1972, 1976) studied this display in chimpanzees (our closest animal relatives) and found that among them it takes on a new function, more similar to that of the human smile of greeting. *Both* the more submissive and the more dominant of two chimpanzees show the display upon meeting, and it usually precedes friendly interaction between them. From such observations, van Hooff proposed that the silent bared-teeth display originated in monkeys as a submissive gesture, but evolved in chimpanzees, and even further in humans, into a general form of greeting. As used by the less dominant of two individuals it may retain its original meaning, "Please don't attack me," but as used by the more dominant it may mean, "Rest assured, I won't attack," and by both it may mean, "Let's be friends."

The other primate smile-like response is the *relaxed open-mouth display*, which occurs mostly in young primates when they are engaged in playful fighting and chasing and is believed to be related to the smile that accompanies human laughter and happiness. In chimpanzees it is often accompanied by a vocalized "ahh ahh ahh," which sounds like a throaty human laugh. Van Hooff believes that

104

*Possible homologues to the human smile of greeting and the human laugh and smile of pleasure*

*The silent bared-teeth display (a), shown here by a pygmy chimpanzee, is believed to be homologous to the human greeting smile. The relaxed open-mouth display (b), shown here by a pygmy chimpanzee, is believed to be homologous to the human laugh and smile of happiness.*

(a)

(b)

this display originated as a means for young primates to signal to each other that their aggressive-like behavior is not to be taken seriously; nobody will really get hurt. Interestingly, in human children laughter accompanies playful fighting and chasing more consistently than any other form of play (Blurton-Jones, 1967); and even among us "sophisticated" adults, pie throwing, chase scenes, mock insults, and other forms of fake aggression are among the most reliable ways to elicit laughter. Thus, our laughter is not only similar in form to the relaxed open-mouth display of other primates, but at least in some cases seems to serve a similar function. The smile that accompanies nonlaughing happiness in humans is similar in form to the smile that accompanies laughter, so it too may have originated from the relaxed open-mouth display (Redican, 1982). There is, it seems to me, some poetry in the thought that the smile of happiness may have originated from a signal indicating that, while the world can be a frightening and aggressive place, the aggression going on now is just in fun and we are safe.

## Sociobiology: The Comparative Study of Animals' Social Systems

An animal alone is in some ways not a complete animal. That is certainly true of the highly social species, from honeybees to humans. A bee without other bees cannot build a hive or tend a queen. A human without other humans cannot build a village or exchange ideas. Recognizing the close interdependence of animals with others of their own kind, many ethologists and other animal behaviorists have concentrated on the study of social systems in animals, a study called *sociobiology*.

As a school of thought, sociobiology arose partly from ethology, but it has taken on a somewhat different flavor. While ethology has tended to focus on the specific movement patterns involved in species-specific behaviors, sociobiologists have focused more on the ultimate functions of such behaviors. Not surprisingly, they have paid most attention to patterns of mating, aggression, and cooperation—patterns that are central to the functioning of social groups and are quite clearly related to the individual's goal of survival and reproduction. Why do some animal species bond as male-female pairs for an extended period of time, while others don't? Why do some animal species spread themselves out over the available territory, while others live in large groups? Why do animals sometimes compete and other times help one another in their struggle for survival? These are the kinds of questions that sociobiologists address.

A standard approach in sociobiology is that of comparison by analogy. If different species have independently evolved a particular social system, then those species can be compared to see what other commonalities of their habitat and lifestyle might have caused that particular social system to be adaptive. This process necessarily entails a good deal of guesswork, and to be reasonable the guesses must be based on a great deal of knowledge about the species that are studied. Social patterns that on the surface look similar can serve different functions in different species. Also, many species—especially many primate species—show considerable variability in their social behaviors, from group to group and time to time, so what might look like an evolutionary adaptation of the species as a whole can sometimes be a learned adaptation characteristic of the particular group that is being studied. The following sections discuss mating systems, aggression, and cooperation in nonhuman animals from a sociobiological perspective, and then turn to issues concerning the application of this perspective to human behavior.

## Patterns of Mating

A wide variety of male-female arrangements have come about in different animal species for the purpose of sexual reproduction. Some animals form male-female *mating bonds*, which may last for the duration of a breeding season or longer. A mating bond implies some degree of prolonged association between the individuals and some degree of exclusivity in copulation, the latter of which may apply to just one of the two sexes or to both. Three broad classes of such bonding can be distinguished: (1) *polygyny*, in which one male bonds with more than one female; (2) *polyandry*, in which one female bonds with more than one male; and (3) *monogamy*, in which one female and one male bond only with each other (see Figure 4.17). Other animals do not form mating bonds; their mating system, in which both sexes may copulate with many individuals during the course of a breeding season, is referred to as *promiscuous*. Why have different species evolved these different mating systems, and what are some of the consequences of the different systems for other aspects of their lives?

**Parental Investment, and Its Relation to Polygyny, Polyandry, and Monogamy**
In one of the most frequently quoted papers in sociobiology, Robert Trivers (1972) outlined a theory relating courtship and mating patterns to sex differences in *parental investment*. Parental investment can be defined roughly as the time, energy, and risk to survival that are involved in producing, feeding, and otherwise caring for each offspring. More precisely, Trivers defined it as the loss, to the adult, of future reproductive capacity that comes from the production and nurturance of any given offspring. Every offspring in a sexually reproducing species has two parents, one of each sex, but the amount of parental investment from the two is usually not equal. The essence of Trivers's theory can be stated as follows: *In general, whichever sex manifests the greater parental investment will be the sex that is more competed for by members of the other sex for purposes of mating, and will also be the sex that exerts the greater discrimination in determining with which individual to mate.* To illustrate and elaborate on this theory, let us apply it, as many sociobiologists have (for example, Daly & Wilson, 1983), to evolutionary thinking about polygyny, polyandry, and monogamy.

■ *Polygyny is related to high female and low male parental investment.* Polygyny is the most common mating system in mammals, and Trivers's theory helps explain why. Mammals, for whatever reason, have evolved in such a way that the female necessarily invests a great deal in any offspring she produces. The young must first develop for a period of weeks or months within her body, and then, for at least some period after birth, must (in most species) obtain nourishment from her in the form of milk. Because of her high investment, the number of offspring that a female mammal can produce in a breeding season or a lifetime is limited. For example, a female whose gestation and lactation periods are such that she can produce at most four young a year can produce no more than that number, regardless of whether she mates with one male or twenty. Things are different for the male, however. His involvement with off-

**Polygyny**

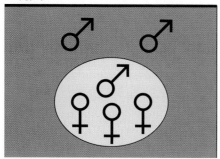

**Polyandry**

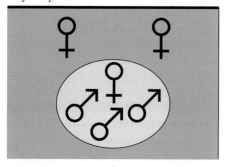

**Monogamy**

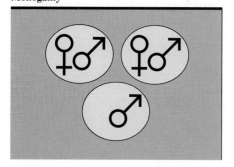

**Figure 4.17 Three mating systems**
*In a polygynous system the unmated males represent a threat to the mated male, and in a polyandrous system the unmated females represent a threat to the mated female.*

*An evolutionary account of the relationship between high female parental investment, polygyny, and sex differences in body size*

spring is, at minimum, simply the production of sperm cells and the act of copulation. These require little time and energy, so his maximum reproductive potential is limited not by parental investment but by the number of fertile females he mates with. A male that mates with twenty females, each of which can produce four young, can in theory produce eighty offspring a year. Thus, there is a greater evolutionary advantage to the male for multiple matings than there is to the female, which leads to a pattern in which males compete with one another to mate with as many females as they can.

Among mammals, male competition for females often takes the form of out-and-out battles, which the larger, stronger male is more likely to win. This leads to a selective advantage for increased size and strength in males, up to some maximum beyond which the advantage of greater size in obtaining mates is outweighed by disadvantages, such as problems in finding sufficient food to support the large size. In general, the more polygynous a species is, the greater is the average size difference between males and females. An extreme example is the elephant seal. Males of this species fight one another, sometimes to the death, for mating rights to groups of up to fifty females, and the males outweigh females severalfold. In the evolution of elephant seals, those males that had genes that made them large, strong, and successful in defeating other male elephant seals sent many copies of their genes onto the next generation, while those whose genes made them smaller, weaker, and unsuccessful in combat usually sent on no copies of theirs.

For the same reason that the female mammal usually has less evolutionary incentive than does the male to mate with many individuals, she has more incentive to be discriminating in her choice of mate (Trivers, 1972). Because she invests so much, risking her life and decreasing her future reproductive potential whenever she becomes pregnant, her interests lie strongly in producing offspring that will have the highest possible chance themselves of surviving and reproducing. To the degree that the male affects the young, either through his genes or through any care he provides, females would be expected to select males whose contribution will be most beneficial. The direction that such selection takes depends on other characteristics of the species or the environment in which it lives (as you will see later). In highly polygynous mammals, such as elephant seals, it is presumably to the female's evolutionary advantage to mate with those males that win battles with other males, because they are most likely to have genes that will produce sons that will win battles in the future and produce many young themselves. In other words, once a particular form of male behavior is established as a criterion for reproduction, it is to the female's evolutionary advantage to select males that best manifest that behavior. The elephant seal's system of polygyny could not persist if the females were not motivated to mate with the male that won the most battles. A single male could not possibly hold fifty females together, and mate with them, if they preferred to go off and find other males with which to mate.

*Polyandry is related to high male and low female parental investment.* Polyandry does not exist as the primary mating pattern in any mammal, but it is the primary pattern in many nonmammalian species. It is more likely to make its appearance in species that lay eggs than in mammals, because in egg layers a smaller part of the reproductive cycle is tied to the female's body. Once eggs are released from the female they can be cared for by either parent, and, depending on other conditions, evolution can proceed in a direction that leads to greater male than female investment. An example of a polyandrous species of fish is the seahorse, which has evolved a reversed form of sex (compared to mammals), in which the female deposits her eggs in a pouch in the male, who fertilizes them and carries them with him until the young are ready to swim off on their own (Daly & Wilson, 1983). (See Figure 4.18.) Because the female

**Figure 4.18** *Male seahorse with young*
*Among seahorses, the male's parental invest-ment is greater than the female's. Shown here are young short-snouted seahorses emerging from their father's pouch.*

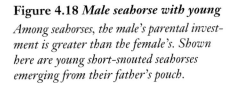

seahorse can produce far more eggs than one male can handle, the limit to her reproductive capacity is the number of males with which she mates, and as a consequence female seahorses are the more aggressive courters and males exert the greater selectivity in choice of mate. Several species of birds are also polyandrous, and they too show a pattern of increased size and courtship aggressiveness in the female compared to the male (Trivers, 1972; Erckmann, 1983).

*Monogamy is related to equivalent male and female parental investment.* According to Trivers's theory, when the two sexes are approximately equal in parental investment, their degree of competition for mates will also be approximately equal. This is a condition conducive to monogamy. Equal parental investment, and hence monogamy, seems to come about in evolution when other aspects of the lifestyle or environment of a species make it difficult or impossible for a single adult to raise the young, but quite possible for two adults working together to raise them (Dewsbury, 1988). Under these conditions, if either the mother or father abandons the young they may fail to survive, so there is selective pressure for the two parents to stay together and care for the young. Because neither sex is much more likely than the other to fight over mates, there is little selective pressure for sex differences in size and strength, and, in general, the males and females of monogamous animals are nearly identical to each other in these characteristics.

Consistent with the view that monogamy arises from the need for more than one adult to care for offspring is the fact that over 90 percent of bird species are monogamous (Lack, 1968) compared to only about 3 percent of mammalian species (Kleiman, 1977). The reproductive system of birds is such that it would be much harder for a single adult to raise the young than is usually the case for mammals. Most bird species must incubate and protect their eggs until they hatch, and then they must both guard the hatchlings and fetch food for them until they are able to fly. One parent alone would not be able simultaneously to guard the nest and leave it to obtain food, but two working together can. Thus, in the evolution of birds, genes leading both parents to stay together and care for the young would be passed along to their surviving young, while genes leading either to stray would die out as their young starved or froze in the nest or fell victim to predators.

**Why monogamy is more common in birds than in mammals, and why it occurs in some carnivores and primates**

In mammals, monogamy seems to have arisen most often in those species that are like birds in the sense that the young must be provided with food other than milk, of a type that the male is capable of providing. The best-known examples are certain carnivores, including foxes and coyotes (Barash, 1982). It takes much more skill to catch animals for food (as carnivores do) than to feed on vegetation, so carnivores must usually be fed by their parents for a longer period than is the case for other mammals. Young foxes and coyotes are fed meat by both parents until they have acquired the necessary strength, agility, and skills to hunt on their own. But need for this kind of adult care does not inevitably lead to monogamy. Some carnivorous species, such as lions, solve the same problem by living in small groups in which closely related females, usually sisters, assist one another in the care of the young.

Monogamy is also quite common in primates, occurring in approximately 18 percent of all species of monkeys and apes (Hrdy, 1981). According to an analysis by Sarah Hrdy (1981), a shift from polygyny toward monogamy in these species can often be understood as a process initiated by females and, in a sense, forced upon males. Imagine a species of monkey in which the female can raise some young on her own, but could raise more young, or more fit young, with the help of a male. Any change in her reproductive strategy that would induce a male to stay and help care for the young would be to her evolutionary advantage. One possible strategy is to live separately from other females, defending a territory by aggressively driving other females away, and requiring the male to stay with her for a period of time before she will copulate with him. This system makes it harder for the male to find other females or to copulate with them, so it may now be to his advantage to shift some of his resources away from that strategy and toward some investment in child care. Once that begins to happen, the female can produce more or larger young than she could before, which she cannot raise on her own. Eventually, over evolutionary time, the male monkey finds himself in essentially the same situation as the male bird or fox. If he leaves the young they may die, so evolution leads further in the direction of male fidelity. Consistent with this analysis, Hrdy (1981) cites evidence that females of monogamous primates do typically defend separate territories and produce larger young than do polygynous species.

**The Evolution of Promiscuity**   Few, if any, so-called monogamous species are completely so. The bird, fox, or monkey that bonds with one individual will often take the opportunity to copulate with another if it arises. Such behavior may make evolutionary sense for the male, because the extra copulation produces little loss to him, and it could possibly produce viable offspring. This is especially true if the female is bonded with another male that will help care for those offspring. Such behavior may also make evolutionary sense for the female, because it (a) increases the genetic diversity of her offspring (Dewsbury, 1988), and (b) may reduce the likelihood that a neighboring male will treat her offspring hostilely, because the male may be genetically primed to behave toward the young of any female with which he has copulated as if they were his own (Hrdy, 1981).

In primates, promiscuity is greatest in those species that live in large troops or colonies containing many males and females. One such species is our closest relative, the chimpanzee. A female chimp in estrus (the fertile period of the ovulatory cycle) develops a prominent pink swelling on her rump, which lasts several days and which she displays to advertise her sexual condition. During that time she is likely to mate with most of the adult males in the colony (Goodall, 1986). As Hrdy (1981) has argued, the advantage of female promiscuity in chimpanzees and other group-living primates may stem from its preventing males from knowing which offspring are or are not their own. Because almost any male in the colony could be

■ *Why promiscuity may be an evolutionary advantage to female primates that live in multimale groups*

**Jane Goodall and friend**

*For the past 3 decades, Goodall has been studying wild chimpanzees in their natural East African environment. The mutual trust that is evident in this recent photograph has permitted Goodall to uncover a wealth of information about chimpanzee social and emotional life.*

the father of almost any female's young, the male's evolutionary interest lies not in attacking any young but in helping to protect and care for the group as a whole, which helps make group living possible.

Just as monogamy rarely comes in a pure form, neither does promiscuity. This is especially true in primates, including chimpanzees. Sometimes a male and female chimp will form what Jane Goodall (1986) calls a *consortship*, which can be thought of as a bit of monogamy inserted into a basically promiscuous system. Through frequent grooming and other favors given to the female, and actively driving off other males, a particular male may successfully monopolize the sexual activity of a particular female throughout an ovulatory cycle, and thus assure his paternity of her next offspring. Some chimps become specialists at consortships, while others do not attempt this difficult task at all. Goodall reminds us constantly that there are few hard-and-fast rules governing the behavior of our closest animal relatives. Important individual differences exist within colonies, and different colonies may have different traditions passed on by learning rather than genes.

**Avoidance of Incest**   There is an evolutionary disadvantage to incest (mating with close genetic relatives), especially to sibling or parent-child incest. As pointed out in Chapter 3, genetic disorders often arise from recessive genes, which produce their harmful effects only if inherited from both parents. A closely related male and female are more likely to share the same defective genes than are an unrelated pair, so their offspring are more likely to have a genetic disorder. Thus, in the course of evolution, individuals with a genetic tendency to avoid incest would, on average, have produced healthier offspring than those that didn't have such a tendency. Research has shown that a wide variety of incest-avoidance mechanisms have arisen in the animal world, most of which can be placed into two broad categories: (1) recognition of close relatives and rejection of them as sexual partners; and (2) migration of either males or females away from the place where they were born, making it unlikely that they would encounter kin of the opposite sex after reaching sexual maturity (Partridge & Halliday, 1984).

Goodall (1986) has found that both of these mechanisms operate in chimpanzees. Even if a female chimp in estrus actively courts all of the other males in the colony, she will avoid her own brothers and adult sons, and successfully resist them in those rare instances in which they do attempt to copulate with her. The only incestuous mating that she cannot avoid by this strategy is that with her father, since daughters do not know which chimps their fathers are, or vice versa. There is some evidence that female chimps tend to avoid mating with males that are old enough to be their father (Pucey, 1980), but according to Goodall a more important mechanism for avoiding father-daughter incest is a general tendency for females to move out of their colony of birth and join a different colony when they become sexually mature. This process is aided by a complementary tendency, the *strange female effect*, for male chimps to show more interest in mating with females that have just entered their colony than with those that have always been with them (Goodall, 1986).

## Patterns of Aggression

Aggression, as the term is used by ethologists and sociobiologists, refers to fighting and threats of fighting among members of the same species. Physiological mechanisms that enable aggressive behavior to occur have presumably come about in evolution to the degree that they help animals acquire and retain the resources needed for their survival and reproduction. As already mentioned, a good deal of animal aggression centers on mating. Polygynous males fight over females, polyandrous females fight over males, and monogamous individuals of both sexes aggressively drive potential sexual competitors away from their partners. Aggression can also serve the function of protecting a feeding ground for oneself and one's offspring, of driving away individuals that may be a threat to one's young, and of elevating one's status within a colony. Here we will look at two broad classes of aggressive behavior—one aimed at defending a territory for oneself or one's group, and one having to do with status within the group.

▨ *How territorial signaling and the home-court advantage help reduce bloodshed in territorial animals*

**Territorial Aggression**   Many species of animals establish home territories, either permanently or for the duration of a breeding season, which they defend from others of their kind. Monogamous birds and mammals defend the territory around their nest or den partly to keep away potential sexual competitors, but also to preserve a feeding ground for themselves and their young. Animals that live in large groups—including wolves, macaque monkeys, and chimpanzees—often defend large feeding ranges, sometimes many square miles in size, from invasion by other groups of their kind. At times of food shortage or overpopulation, territorial battles can be bloody. But at other times battles are usually avoided by a combination of territorial signaling, through which residents warn others not to enter, and a tendency of others to respect the signals and stay out of occupied territories.

Methods of territorial signaling vary from species to species. Such diverse groups as birds, crickets, and alligators loudly announce, by song, that they are home and defending their area. Territorial troops of monkeys often warn off other approaching troops by running up into trees and shaking the branches loudly. Certain other mammals mark their territories with odor trails deposited either in their urine (as in the case of bears and wolves) or from special scent glands (as in the case of badgers and rabbits). When you walk your male dog and observe him urinating on every lamppost and fire hydrant in the neighborhood, you are observing a vestige of the territorial-marking behavior of his wolf ancestors.

In some species, prolonged fights are also avoided by a tendency for individuals that find themselves in another's territory to become psychologically transformed, such that they are less aggressive and more inclined to flee than they would be in their own territory. When fights do occur, the territorial owner fights more viciously than the intruder and usually succeeds in driving the intruder out, even if the intruder is the larger of the two. As an example, Lorenz (1966) described the behavior of two cichlid fish in a tank. When first placed into the tank, Fish *A*, the bigger of the two, drove Fish *B* into a tiny corner near the water surface (the most dangerous place for a fish to live in nature, where predatory birds can attack them) and forced it to stay there for several days. Gradually, however, *B* expanded its territory until it occupied approximately half the tank. After that the two fish coexisted peacefully, fighting only when one by chance swam over the boundary into the territory of the other. When *A* swam into *B*'s territory, *B* would drive *A* out, and when *B* swam into *A*'s territory, *A* would drive *B* out. This example is typical of much (though not all) animal territorial aggression: the defender wins, the invader retreats, and no blood is spilled in the process.

**Aggression and Dominance Within the Colony**   Animals that live in large groups may on the surface appear to get along peacefully, but closer examination often reveals an enormous amount of within-group bickering. They squabble almost continuously over such resources as food, mates, and the best location in the group (they usually prefer the center because it offers the most protection from predators). When group members fight, however, they must have a means of terminating the fight other than one in which the loser flees to another territory. The loser's interest lies in remaining in the group and the winner's interest lies in allowing the loser to remain (otherwise there would be no group). To permit fights to terminate without the loser running far away, a variety of submissive signals have evolved that allow one animal to signal to another that it has lost and will no longer challenge the victor (see Figure 4.19).

Aside from submissive signals, another great aid in reducing fighting within a colony is memory. Animals recognize other colony members and remember the results of their previous aggressive encounters; this provides the basis for ***dominance*** in relationships. If *A* has previously beaten *B* in a fight, then *B* will be less inclined to challenge *A* the next time, thereby establishing that *A* is dominant over *B*. In some species, including barnyard chickens, rather strict ***dominance hierarchies*** are established, in which the individuals in the group can be ranked, from alpha down to zeta, with each being dominant over those lower in rank and submissive to those higher. In other species, however, dominance hierarchies are not that rigid

**Figure 4.19 *Submissive response in a wolf***

*Animals that live in groups have evolved signals to terminate or prevent fights, so that the loser need not flee and can remain in the group. Here a wolf shows its submissive status by rolling over on its back in a defenseless posture. Dogs also show submission in this manner.*

and are not always based on individual fighting ability. In chimpanzees, cleverness can play a role. Goodall (1988) observed a relatively small male chimp achieve dominance over the entire colony by charging at the other chimps while banging together empty kerosene cans, which he had stolen from Goodall's camp. In other cases, she saw chimps raise their rank by forming coalitions and challenging a more dominant chimp together.

■ *How dominance status is passed from mother to young in the Japanese macaque*

In most group-living primates, females as well as males form dominance hierarchies, and in at least some species the female hierarchy lies at the core of the troop's social organization. An example is the Japanese macaque monkey, extensively studied by G. Gray Eaton (1976). On the surface, the male hierarchy would seem to be the more important in this species, because the males are larger than the females and almost any male could easily defeat almost any female in a one-on-one battle. But closer analysis shows that the female hierarchy provides the key to understanding the male hierarchy, because the young males (and the young females) inherit the dominance status of their mothers—not through genes but through learning and social tradition. When young macaques get into scraps, their mothers run quickly to their aid and fight their battles for them, either by themselves or by inducing one or more other adults to help. The most dominant female is the best at helping her young in this way, and soon the other young monkeys learn not to attack her young. The effect of this learning persists into adulthood, such that sons and daughters of dominant mothers move into dominant positions within their respective hierarchies without serious challenge. Meanwhile, because of their dominance, other monkeys form coalitions with them and will back them up if they are challenged. As a result of this system, it is possible for a relatively weak male, poor at fighting, to achieve and retain the most dominant position in the male hierarchy.

### Patterns of Helping

Animals of the same species bicker, fight, and sometimes even kill one another in their competition for resources, but they also help one another. From an evolutionary perspective, *helping* can be defined as any behavior that increases the survival chance or reproductive capacity of another individual. Given this definition, it is useful to distinguish between two categories of helping—cooperation and altruism.

*Cooperation* occurs when an individual helps another while at the same time helping itself. This sort of helping occurs all the time in the animal world. It occurs when a mated pair of foxes work together to raise their mutual young, or a pack of wolves work together to kill an antelope, or a troop of macaque monkeys work together to repel a troop invading their territory. Most of the advantages of social living lie in cooperation. By working with others for common ends, each individual has a better chance of survival and reproduction than it would have outside of the social group. There is nothing anti-Darwinian about cooperation. It is selfish. It is a way of obtaining resources that one cannot obtain alone. Whatever costs accrue are more than repaid by the benefits.

*Altruism*, in contrast, occurs when an individual helps another while at the same time *decreasing* its own survival chance or reproductive capacity. Animals do behave in ways that at least appear to be altruistic. For example, some animals, including ground squirrels, emit a loud, distinctive call when they spot an approaching predator, which warns others of the predator's approach and at the same time tends to attract the predator's attention to the caller (Sherman, 1977). (See Figure 4.20.) It would seem that the selfish response would be to remain quiet and hidden, or to sneak off quietly, rather than risk one's own detection by warning others. How can such behavior be explained from an evolutionary perspective? As Trivers (1971) has pointed out, any evolutionary account of apparent altruism must operate by showing that from a broader perspective the behavior is not truly altruistic.

**Figure 4.20** *An alarm-calling ground squirrel*

*When they spot a predator, female ground squirrels often emit an alarm call, especially if they are living in a group of close kin. Males are less likely to live near close kin and do not show this response.*

■ *Two evolutionary theories designed to take the altruism out of altruism*

Sociobiologists have developed two broad theories to account for apparent acts of altruism in animals—the kin selection theory and the reciprocity theory.

The **kin selection theory** holds that apparent acts of altruism come about evolutionarily because they are most likely to help close relatives, that is, most likely to help those that have the same genes (Hamilton, 1964). What actually survives over evolutionary time, of course, is not the individual but the individual's genes. Samuel Butler once wrote, "The chicken is only one egg's way of making another egg," and contemporary biologists have modernized this to read, "The organism is only DNA's way of making more DNA" (Wilson, 1975). The point is this: Any gene that promotes the production and preservation of copies of itself can be a fit gene, from the vantage point of natural selection, even if it promotes the self-destruction of an individual carrier of the gene.

Imagine an individual ground squirrel with a rare gene that promotes the behavior of calling out when a predator is near. The mathematics of inheritance are such that, on average, one-half of the children or siblings of the individual with this gene would be expected to have the same gene, as would one-fourth of the nieces or nephews and one-eighth of the cousins (refer back to Table 3.1). Thus, if the altruist sacrificed its own life while saving the lives of more than two children, or more than two brothers and sisters, or more than four nieces and nephews, or more than eight cousins, the gene would increase in the population from one generation to the next. Such a gene is clearly *fit* in the evolutionary sense.

The kin selection theory suggests that animals should be more likely to behave altruistically toward kin than toward others of their species. Consistent with this, ground squirrels living with kin are more likely to produce alarm calls than those living with nonkin (Sherman, 1977). On the other hand, the kin selection theory does not imply that helpers will always discriminate between kin and nonkin. In theory, the tendency to respond to predators with an alarm call *whenever* others of one's species are nearby could evolve if, on a statistical basis, the others are often enough kin that, over time, the gene preserves copies of itself more often than it self-destructs.

The **reciprocity theory** provides an account of how apparent acts of altruism can arise even in situations where nonkin are helped as often as kin. According to this theory, behaviors that appear to be altruistic are actually forms of long-term cooperation (Trivers, 1971). Through computer simulations of evolution, Robert Axelrod (1984) has shown that a genetically induced tendency to help nonkin can evolve if that tendency is tempered by (a) an ability to remember which individuals have reciprocated such help in the past, and (b) a tendency to refrain from again helping those individuals that failed to reciprocate. The reason it evolves is because such behavior induces others to reciprocate. That is, the reward for helping is the increased likelihood of receiving help in the future. A considerable amount of behavior that fits this pattern seems to go on in the animal world, especially among primates, which can best remember previous helpers or nonhelpers and can provide quite flexible modes of reciprocation (see Axelrod, 1984).

### Sociobiological Thought About Human Behavior

Can a sociobiological analysis—of the kind applied above in understanding mating, aggression, and helping in animals—shed any light on human social interactions? That is a question that can raise considerable passion, especially among people who are aware of ways in which evolutionary ideas have been misapplied, either for political ends or out of naive overexuberance.

In the nineteenth and early twentieth centuries a philosophical movement called *social Darwinism* employed a rough analogy between biological evolution and capitalism to justify extreme forms of the latter. The principal philosopher of the movement, Herbert Spencer, popularized the phrase "survival of the fittest" and applied it to human social systems. To him the fittest were those who rose to the top in unchecked capitalism, and the unfit were those who fell into poverty or starvation. He also believed that women are inherently inferior to men and meant by nature to occupy subordinate positions in society (Hofstadter, 1955). Some years later, a still more perverted form of evolutionary thinking played a role in Nazi philosophy—the purification of humanity was to be achieved by eliminating inferior races. Because of its association with Nazi racial theories, the whole enterprise of thinking evolutionarily about human behavior became distasteful for a period after World War II, but in the 1960s it began to reappear, sometimes in a more cautious, reasoned form, and sometimes in a form reminiscent of social Darwinism. As an example of the latter, in popular books entitled *African Genesis* (1961) and *The Territorial Imperative* (1966), Robert Ardrey—a playwright turned social commentator—seemed to revel in the idea that aggressiveness and territoriality are natural and unchangeable in human males. (He had little to say about females.)

**Some Common Fallacies**   Given this history, the need for caution and scientific skepticism is even more apparent in human sociobiology than in other realms of thought about human behavior. Here are three kinds of fallacies or errors that often creep into such thought:

■ *How the deterministic fallacy, the naturalistic fallacy, and the too-easy analogy can distort thought about human social behavior*

*The deterministic fallacy*   The deterministic fallacy is the belief that genes control behavior in a way that can be little affected by changes in the environment in which the individual develops. The very title of Ardrey's book, *The Territorial Imperative*, is an instance of deterministic fallacy. The word *imperative* means obligatory or necessary, and the implication of both the title and the text is that human evolution has involved natural selection for territoriality (an idea for which there is scant and mixed evidence), and therefore human beings (more specifically, human males, according to Ardrey's argument) *must* behave in a territorial manner. But that position is not even true of nonhuman animals. Territorial birds, for example, defend territories when the environmental conditions are ripe for them to do so. Birds raised by humans under a different set of conditions do not defend territories. If birds had the human capacity to modify their environments, and the human capacity to decide (for whatever reason) that they no longer want to fight for territories, they could in theory change those conditions so that the territorial urge would no longer be elicited.

As applied to humans, the deterministic fallacy usually entails a gross underestimation of the role of culture in human behavior. Long ago our species embarked on an evolutionary path that led away from rigid instincts and toward unprecedented capacities for learning, inventing, thinking, and talking, all of which are adaptations for culture. Culture, in turn, has led to enormous changes in human habitats and lifestyles. Cross-cultural studies show that humans can be warlike or peaceful; defend territories or not; organize in communities based on principles of equality or principles of hierarchy; and establish either quite similar or very different social roles for males and females.

*The naturalistic fallacy*   The naturalistic fallacy is the view that whatever is "natural" is right (Alexander, 1987). It is a confusion of biology and morality. Social Darwinists could be accused of this fallacy in assuming that, because natural selection can be construed as survival of the fittest, survival of the fittest is a moral principle that should guide our conscious choices about government and other social institutions. But there is nothing moral or immoral about the natural world. Morality is a product of the human mind. We have, for whatever reason in our evolution, acquired the capacity to think in moral terms and to develop moral philosophies that can go in any of various directions, including directions that place constraints on individual self-interest for the good of the larger community.

**Figure 4.21** *Male hamadryas baboon dominating three females*
*Male baboons are much larger than females and often behave quite ruthlessly toward them. Perhaps because of the extreme male dominance, female baboons, unlike the females of other primate species, do not form strong social bonds with one another. The bowed, turned-away head is a signal of submission.*

*The too-easy analogy* By picking and choosing, one can find in nature almost any kind of social system one wishes to find. In *African Genesis*, Ardrey hit upon the hamadryas baboon, of all creatures, as the species to focus on to understand humans. Why the baboon? It is not even an ape, but a monkey, no more closely related to us than dozens of other monkey species. Ardrey built his case for this comparison on scanty and now largely discredited evidence that baboons, more than any other primate, have adapted to a lifestyle like that of early humans. One cannot help but wonder if Ardrey's choice of the baboon was not at least partly influenced by its fitting his preconception of the "natural" human being. Ardrey's baboon is a cunning animal that lives in large troops and defends territory against other troops, and that has a within-troop social system centering on male dominance hierarchies and male dominance over females (see Figure 4.21).

Comparison by analogy is a useful approach as long as its limitations are kept in mind. As we have seen, analogies based on comparisons across many species have produced some interesting generalizations. An example is the generalization that monogamy tends to occur in species in which the young need extensive care that one parent alone cannot provide, and that monogamy is associated with lack of sex differences in size. But those generalizations do not hold up for every species. Not all species solve the problem of providing multiadult care for the young through monogamy, and not all species in which the male and female are the same size are monogamous. Moreover, in some cases where the correlation does hold, the adaptive explanation may be different from that which applies in other cases. As Tinbergen (1968) pointed out long ago, comparison by analogy provides no real short cut to understanding any particular species. It can be a basis for developing hypotheses, but the hypotheses must then be tested through detailed study of the species one wishes to understand.

**Some Sociobiological Hypotheses About Human Social Relationships**   Despite these caveats, and despite the politically motivated or naive abuses of the approach, the sociobiological analysis of human behavior—carried on by a growing group of responsible scientists, including an increasing number of women as well as men—is a fascinating endeavor that is here to stay. We are animals; we have an evolutionary history guided by natural selection; and our patterns of social behavior, while extremely modifiable by learning, are not infinitely so. It is almost inconceivable that evolution would somehow have left our species, alone among all the others, with no built-in biases concerning our ways of interacting with one another. The broad

■ *Some hypothesized biological biases in human social interaction, supported by cross-cultural evidence and sociobiological reasoning*

aim of sociobiology as applied to humans is to identify and understand those biases. What follows are hypotheses about what some of those biases may be. As you read them you should keep in mind that none of these hypotheses implies that every person's behavior is consistent with the bias, or that the bias cannot be counteracted through learning.

■ *The tendency to live in communities*  Humans seem to be strongly biased toward living in groups (Breuer, 1982; Chagnon & Irons, 1979). In no part of the world do people live like orangutans (an ape species for which the only social group is the mother and her children plus the occasional coming together of a male and female for mating). Human societies are everywhere more like the gregarious chimpanzee model. People everywhere live in at least moderately large communities, with smaller groupings of various types forming within the community. In non-Western, nonindustrialized cultures, most people live in tribes or villages consisting of a few dozen up to a few hundred individuals. People everywhere feel lonely when alone too long, and loneliness drives them to seek other people much as hunger drives them to seek food. There is no population of human beings anywhere who are unconcerned about making friends. Hermits exist, but are everywhere regarded as peculiar. It is uncertain what factors in our evolution led to our tendency to live in groups, but observations of present-day villages suggest that these include cooperation in hunting and gathering food; cooperation in child care; cooperation in building dwellings; cooperation in defense against predators; and, most human of all, the sharing, through language, of information that bears on all aspects of the struggle for survival.

■ *The tendency toward monogamy and/or polygyny*  Though we live in groups a bit like chimpanzees, we do not appear anywhere to be quite as sexually promiscuous as chimpanzees. In every culture people tend to form mating bonds, often but not always legitimized through some sort of culturally recognized marriage contract, and males in most cultures play at least some role in caring for their children (see Eibl-Eibesfeldt, 1989; Dewsbury, 1988). Anthropological studies indicate that the majority of non-Western traditional cultures, where Western influence has not made polygyny illegal, practice a mixture of monogamy and polygyny (Murdock, 1981). In such cultures, men with sufficient wealth or status have more than one wife, while the majority of men have either one wife or none. The moderate size discrepancy between human males and females is also consistent with the idea that we are a partly monogamous, partly polygynous species (Dewsbury, 1988).

■ *The tendency for males to be more violent than females*  Among mammals generally, and primates in particular, males and females are equally competitive, but commonly exert their competitiveness in different ways. Females tend to be more subtle in their jostling for resources and power, while males tend more often to be overtly violent (Hrdy, 1981). Cross-cultural studies show that, everywhere, human males are also more violent, more likely to maim and kill, than human females. In fact, in a survey of cross-cultural data on this issue, Martin Daly and Margo Wilson (1988) were unable to find any society in which the number of women who killed other women was even one-tenth as great as the number of men who killed other men. On average, in the data they examined, male-male killings outnumbered female-female killings by more than 30 to 1. One might construe a scenario through which such a difference in violence would be purely a product of learning, in every culture, but the hypothesis that the difference resides at least partly in biological sex differences seems more plausible.

■ *The tendency to avoid incest*  It is almost impossible to obtain reliable data on the actual incidence of sexual intercourse between human first-degree relatives (parent-child or brother-sister). But cross-cultural studies indicate that the great majority of people in every culture that has been studied view such unions as something to be either condemned or pitied (Thornhill & Thornhill, 1987; Berghe, 1983). This is true even in cultures that do not specifically outlaw such incest, and even where people have no knowledge that it can have deleterious effects on offspring. In our own culture, research suggests that the most common violation of incest avoidance occurs in father-daughter relationships, with the abusive (often alcoholic) father taking advantage of the dependent position of his daughter (see Meiselman, 1978; Berghe, 1983). This pattern is consistent with the sociobiological view that females—the most discriminating sex when it comes to mating (in most mammals)—avoid incest more avidly when they can than do males.

One line of support for the idea that we are biologically biased toward avoiding incest comes from studies indicating that unrelated children, who know they are unrelated, but who were raised together in intimate proximity as children, generally do not become romantically or sexually involved with each other even when there are no social prohibitions against it (see Berghe, 1983). For example, studies of dating and marriage patterns in Israeli kibbutzim—cooperative communities in which children are raised together somewhat as one big family—indicate that individuals who grow up in the same kibbutz rarely date or marry each other, even though the elders in the community may encourage them to do so (Tiger & Shepher, 1975). By their own preference, young kibbutzniks almost always look elsewhere for their boyfriends and girlfriends or husbands and wives. It seems reasonable to suggest that a biological tendency to avoid brother-sister incest works by identifying anyone with whom one was raised as *not* an appropriate sexual partner. Consistent with this view is evidence from studies in the United States that romantic attachment is much more likely to occur between a brother and sister who were raised in separate families, and who met as adults (knowing full well that they are brother and sister), than between those who were raised in the same family (see Berghe, 1983).

*The tendency toward nepotism (helping kin more than nonkin)* In accordance with the kin selection theory, nonhuman animals usually help their close relatives more than nonrelatives. Cross-cultural studies of humans have repeatedly shown that the same is true of our species (Essock-Vitale & McGuire, 1980). If a mother dies or for other reasons is unable to care for a child, the child's grandmother, aunt, or another close relative is by far the most likely adopter (Kurland, 1979). Close kin are also most likely to share dwellings or land, hunt together, or form other collaborative arrangements. In communal societies deliberately designed to abolish or minimize the importance of blood ties, strong tendencies to slide back toward them frequently emerge (Spiro, 1979). On the other side of the same coin, studies in Western culture indicate that genetic kin living in the same household are less likely to be violent toward each other than nonkin living in the same household (Daly & Wilson, 1988); and studies in other cultures have shown that villages in which most people are closely related have less internal friction than those in which people are less related (Chagnon, 1979).

What does one do with ideas like these? One thing is to study them further, challenging them or probing their limits, as any good scientist should concerning any broad generalizations. To the degree that the ideas are true they add to our understanding of ourselves and to our potential to use such understanding to make the world better. The mistake would be to assume that what are here called "tendencies" or "biases" represent either inflexible imperatives or moral virtues. We should avoid the deterministic and naturalistic fallacies.

## Concluding Thoughts

In these concluding paragraphs, it would be worthwhile to reflect on some very general lessons in psychology that have come at least partly from evolutionary thinking or from research inspired by such thinking. Here are four:

**1. The importance of studying behavior in the natural environment before dissecting it in the laboratory** Behavioral mechanisms evolve and develop to deal with the problems that animals routinely face in their natural environments. When animals (or people) are tested in unnatural settings, their behaviors may make little sense. This is a point that the early ethologists often made in their arguments with psychologists, who often limited themselves to laboratory studies. If Tinbergen had begun his research on sticklebacks by testing them in isolated laboratory aquaria, his discovery that males attack any red object that they see would have simply been a source of puzzlement. But because he began the other way around, first learning all he could about their mating habits and other aspects of their natural lives, this otherwise odd behavior made sense. Psychologists who study humans are usually concerned with behaviors that depend much more on learning than do the behaviors of sticklebacks, but the principle still applies. People have acquired their behavioral patterns in the contexts of their lives, and often those patterns don't make sense in the stark or strange conditions of the laboratory. Today psychologists, like ethologists, are increasingly concerned with the natural contexts and real-life meanings of the behaviors that they study. The laboratory is a fine place to perform controlled experiments aimed at understanding causal mechanisms, but not such a great place to learn about the real-life functions of behavior.

**2. The importance of careful descriptions of behavior** The early ethologists thought of behavior as something like anatomy. They saw it as having form, and they were very concerned about describing that form in detail. By adopting this same approach, psychologists Ekman and Friesen were able to produce a more objective description of the way that people express emotions than had previously been produced, which in turn led to further understanding of how various expressions are combined in blends, and how emotional expressions can leak through in people who are trying to mask them. In many other realms of psychology, too, careful description is an important first step to further discoveries about a category of behavior.

**3. A rationale for comparing human behavior to that of other species** Psychologists have long been interested in the behavior of animals as one route to understanding behavior in humans. Evolutionary thinking not only provides a general rationale for that enterprise, by pointing out our relatedness to other animals, but can also to some degree help guide the kinds of comparisons one makes. If a researcher wishes to understand the underlying mechanism of some form of human behavior by studying it in an animal, it is important that the animal's behavior be homologous—not just analogous—to the human's. As you will see in Chapters 7 and 8, physiological psychologists have learned a great deal about basic motivational and sensory mechanisms in humans by studying their homologous forms in other mammals. Analogies are useful for developing hypotheses about the adaptive value of a form of behavior, but they are not so useful for learning about mechanisms, since convergent evolution can produce superficially similar behaviors by means that involve very different mechanisms.

**4. A framework for thinking about psychological mechanisms** The basic psychological mechanisms that underlie motivation, emotion, sensation, perception, memory, and reasoning are all products of evolution by natural selection. They evolved because they enabled our ancestors to solve the kinds of real-life problems, in their real-life environments, that threatened their survival and reproduction.

That insight can provide some guidance in the development of more specific theories about such mechanisms. We can expect motivational and emotional mechanisms to be biased toward survival-promoting and reproductive goals; and sensory, perceptual, memory, and reasoning mechanisms to be biased toward picking up and using information that is most important for achieving those goals. In the sociobiology discussion in this chapter you have seen some examples of such thinking in a realm where it has been most controversial, that of theories about human social relationships. As we proceed through chapters on the more basic psychological mechanisms just listed, you will see examples of evolutionary theories that are more widely accepted.

## Further Reading

**Charles Darwin** (1859; reprinted 1963). *The origin of species.* New York: Washington Square Press.

*Darwin was an engaging writer as well as a brilliant thinker. Why not read at least part of this important book? The most relevant chapter for the psychologist is Chapter 8, entitled "Instinct," which includes Darwin's research on hive building in bees, as well as many other insights about the behavior of both wild and domesticated animals.*

**Jane Goodall** (1988). *In the shadow of man* (rev. ed.). Boston: Houghton Mifflin.

*Goodall's 3-decade-long study of wild chimpanzees, begun in 1960, surely rates as one of the most courageous and scientifically important studies of animal behavior ever undertaken. This book, first published in 1971, provides an account of her early struggle to locate the animals and find ways of studying them, and of some of her pioneering findings about their behavior. For a more complete and scientific account of her research, I recommend Goodall's 1986 book,* The Chimpanzees of Gombe.

**Sarah Blaffer Hrdy** (1981). *The woman that never evolved.* Cambridge, MA: Harvard University Press.

*Despite its clever title, this is a serious analysis of the evolution of behavior in primates. In an attempt to counter the bias of many previous accounts, which focused on males and tended to treat females as passive carry-alongs in the evolutionary process, Hrdy centers her attention on females. She builds a case that female activities and strategies are most central to behavioral evolution, because females most directly control reproduction.*

**Martin Daly & Margo Wilson** (1988). *Homicide.* New York: Aldine de Gruyter.

*Many interesting and provocative books have examined various human behaviors from a sociobiological perspective, and this is one of them. Daly and Wilson look at worldwide data on homicide from a sociobiological vantagepoint, and they argue that the patterns that they find are consistent with sociobiological theories concerning such issues as sex differences, sexual jealousy, family relationships, and struggles for status.*

## Looking Ahead

Among the products of evolution are the basic mechanisms of learning, mechanisms that allow people and other animals to benefit from experience and adapt within their own lifetimes. The study of learning has been one of the most central activities of psychology. We turn to it in the next chapter.

# CHAPTER 5

The Behavioral Perspective:
Acquiring New Responses to
Stimuli

The Cognitive Perspective:
Acquiring Information About
the World

The Ecological Perspective: Filling
the Blanks in Species-Specific
Behavior Patterns

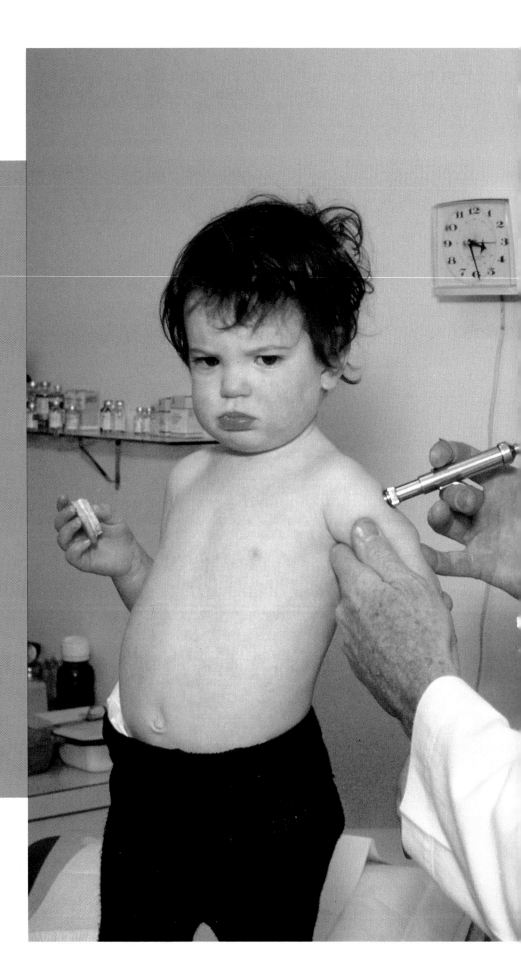

# The adaptiveness of behavior II: learning

*Learning* is a kind of adaptation to the environment that occurs within the lifetime of the individual. It can be defined as the process or set of processes through which sensory experience at one time can affect an individual's behavior at a future time. *Sensory experience* here refers to any effects of the environment that are mediated by the individual's sensory systems (vision, hearing, touch, smell, and so on). *Future time* in this definition does not mean the period immediately after the sensory experience, but rather a period some hours or days after that experience. If I make a clicking sound and then flash a bright light in your eyes, the immediate effect of the light on your behavior (blurring your vision) does not exemplify learning, but your tendency to blink when I make the same clicking sound tomorrow does.

Most of psychology is in one way or another concerned with learning. That is, most of psychology deals with ways by which experiences at Time *A* can affect behavior at Time *B*. Social psychologists are interested in the ways that social experiences at one time affect social behavior at another time. Clinical psychologists are interested in the ways that experiences at one time can affect the likelihood of having emotional problems at another time. Cognitive psychologists are interested in the basic perceptual, memory, and thought processes that are involved in people's ability to learn. Thus, most of the chapters in this book, or in any other introductory psychology text, are in one way or another about learning.

This chapter concerns the most basic attempts to characterize or describe the learning process. It looks at learning from three different perspectives: (1) the *behavioral perspective*, which attempts to characterize learning in terms of observable stimuli and responses, without reference to events occurring inside the individual; (2) the *cognitive perspective*, which attempts to characterize learning in terms of hypothetical mental entities, such as expectancies and cognitive maps; and (3) the *ecological perspective*, which attempts to identify separate, specialized learning mechanisms that have been built through evolution to meet specific survival needs. As you will see, much of the research within each perspective has been conducted with nonhuman animals. Research on basic learning processes has focused on nonhumans partly because of the greater control that can be exerted over their environments, and partly because of the assumption that basic learning mechanisms can be more easily uncovered in animals whose nervous systems and behavioral repertoires are less complex than ours.

## The Behavioral Perspective: Acquiring New Responses to Stimuli

*Behaviorism*, as described in Chapter 1, is the approach in psychology that attempts to understand behavior in terms of the relationship between observable *stimuli* (events in the environment) and observable *responses* (unitary behavioral actions). The early behaviorists were in the forefront of the effort to make psychology an objective science, and, in support of objectivity, they proposed dropping from psychology terms that refer to unseen, inner, mental entities such as thoughts or feelings. As John B. Watson (1913), the acknowledged founder of behaviorism, put it, "In a system of psychology completely worked out, given the response the stimuli can be predicted, and given the stimuli the response can be predicted." Neither Watson nor other behaviorists after him denied the existence of processes inside the organism, but they believed that these are too obscure to be studied scientifically.

In addition to their concern for objective, stimulus-response descriptions of behavior, the early behaviorists clearly established the topic of learning as their central focus. They believed that a person's behavior at any given time is the product of that person's past experience in the environment. In a famous boast illustrating this view, Watson (1924) wrote, "Give me a dozen healthy infants, well-formed, and my own specified world to bring them up in and I'll guarantee to take any one at random and train him to become any type of specialist I might select—doctor, lawyer, artist, merchantchief, and, yes, even beggar-man and thief, regardless of his talents, penchants, tendencies, abilities, vocations, and the race of his ancestors." Of course, Watson did not mean his boast to be taken literally, but simply as a dramatization of his view that the important behavioral differences among people come from their varying experiences, mediated by learning.

As behaviorism developed, its main goal became that of identifying basic learning processes that could be described in stimulus-response terms. By 1938, B. F. Skinner, the successor to Watson as behaviorism's most recognized leader, was able to describe, in such terms, what he took to be two separate learning processes (Skinner, 1938). One, now most often called *classical conditioning*, is a process by which a stimulus that previously did not elicit a response comes to elicit a response, in reflexlike fashion, after it is paired for one or more trials with a stimulus that already elicits a response. Your blinking to a clicking sound that was previously paired with a bright flash of light is an example of classical conditioning. The other learning process, which Skinner emphasized most strongly and labeled *operant conditioning*, is a process by which the consequences of a response increase or decrease the likelihood that the response will occur again. Your increased rate of smiling at people if that behavior brings you favorable consequences is an example of operant conditioning. The main task of behaviorism throughout its history has been to discover and apply basic principles associated with classical and operant conditioning. Let us look now at those principles.

### Classical Conditioning

*What a reflex is, and how it can change through habituation*

Classical conditioning has to do with the learning of reflexes. A **reflex** is a simple, relatively automatic, stimulus-response sequence mediated by the nervous system. If your knee is tapped with a rubber mallet, your leg will jerk. If a bright light is flashed in your eyes, you will blink. If lemon juice is squirted into your mouth, you will salivate. If a loud alarm suddenly clangs, your muscles will tighten. In each of these examples, a particular, well-defined bit of the environment, a *stimulus*, results in a particular, well-defined bit of behavior, a *response*. The tap on the knee, the flash of light, the squirt of lemon juice, and the sudden alarm are stimuli. The leg jerk, the eye blink, the salivation, and the tightening of muscles are responses. It is not surprising that behaviorists, early on, were interested in reflexes. With reflexes, the rather vague and wishy-washy statement "behavior is influenced by the environment" can be replaced by the more specific and stronger statement "a response is caused by a stimulus." Some early behaviorists hoped to be able to characterize all behavior in terms of reflexes.

To be counted as a reflex, the response to a stimulus must be mediated by the nervous system. Messages carried by nerves from the eyes, ears, or other sensory organs enter the spinal cord or brain and act there to produce messages in nerves running outward to muscles and glands. If something hits you and you fall down due to the direct force of the impact, that is not a reflex. But if something hits you and your muscles respond in a way that tends to keep you from falling down, that is a reflex. Because reflexes are mediated by the nervous system, they can be modified by experience.

One simple effect of experience is **habituation**, defined as a decline in the magnitude of a reflexive response when the stimulus is repeated several times in succession. Not all reflexes undergo habituation. One that does is the startle response to a loud sound. You might jump the first time the sound occurs, but each time the sound is repeated you respond less and soon show no visible response at all. In some cases habituation persists over long periods, and thus can be considered to be a simple form of learning. But habituation does not produce a new stimulus-response sequence, only the weakening of an already existing one. Classical conditioning, in contrast, is a form of reflex learning that does produce a new stimulus-response sequence. Classical conditioning was first described and most extensively studied by a Russian physiologist, Ivan Petrovich Pavlov.

**Pavlov's Discovery, and the Basic Terminology of Classical Conditioning**    Ivan Pavlov (1849–1936) was one of those scientists who become the fodder of myths about the dedicated scientist. By the time of his most famous research on classical conditioning, he was already in his fifties and had earned a Nobel prize for studies of the reflexes involved in digestion. His research so engulfed his life that he is said to have hardly noticed such events as the Bolshevik Revolution of 1917, which transformed his country. One former co-worker (Gantt, 1975, as quoted by Hothersall, 1990) recalled, many years later, Pavlov's angry scolding of an assistant who arrived 10 minutes late to start an experiment: "But Professor," exclaimed the assistant, "there's a revolution going on with shooting in the streets." To which Pavlov replied, "What the _____ difference does that make when you've work to do in the laboratory? Next time there's a revolution, get up earlier!"

Pavlov's initial discovery of what we now call classical conditioning emerged out of his earlier studies of digestive reflexes in dogs. Using ingenious methods for collecting salivary and stomach juices from dogs without disturbing them, he and his team of researchers had found, for example, that a dog salivates differently when different kinds of food are placed in its mouth. Juicy meat triggers a very thick saliva, dry bread a wetter saliva, and acid a wetter one yet. In a fine-grained

■ *How Pavlov discovered the conditioned reflex, and how he then systematized the process of conditioning and labeled the relevant stimuli and responses*

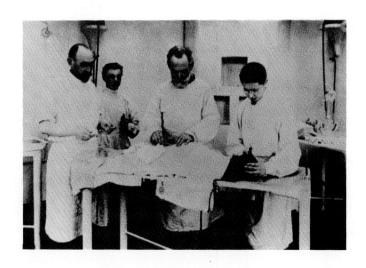

*Ivan Petrovich Pavlov*

*The scientist was a skilled surgeon who honed his craft while carrying out studies of the physiology of digestion. In his conditioning research, he typically connected one of his dog's salivary ducts to a tube and measuring device. An early version of such a device is shown in Figure 5.1.*

analysis, then, these represent three different reflexes, with three different stimuli eliciting three measurably different salivary secretions (see Figure 5.1).

In the course of these studies, Pavlov encountered a problem. After a dog had been given food on several occasions in the experimental apparatus, it would start to salivate *before* food was placed in its mouth. Apparently, signals that regularly preceded food, such as sight of the food or the sound associated with its delivery, alerted the dog to the upcoming stimulation and caused it to salivate. At first Pavlov was content to treat this simply as a source of experimental error. He called it "psychic secretion," implying that it was something outside of the physiologist's realm of study, and he attempted to eliminate it by developing ways to introduce the food into the dog's mouth without any forewarning. But then it occurred to Pavlov that this might well be a phenomenon that could be studied physiologically. Rather than call it psychic secretion, perhaps he could consider it a reflex and analyze it objectively, just as he had analyzed the reflexive salivation response to food in the mouth. It was this insight that led Pavlov to his first experiments on conditioned reflexes (see Pavlov, 1927/1960).

To study this phenomenon, Pavlov deliberately controlled the signals that preceded food. For example, in one experiment he sounded a bell just before placing food in the dog's mouth. After several such pairings of a bell with food, the dog would salivate in response to the bell sound alone; no food was necessary. Pavlov referred to this new reflex as a **conditioned reflex**, because it depended on the unique *conditions* present in the dog's previous experience—the pairing of the bell sound with the food-in-mouth stimulus. He referred to the stimulus in a conditioned reflex (the bell sound, in this case) as a **conditioned stimulus**, and to the learned response to it (salivation) as the **conditioned response**. Likewise, he referred to the original, unlearned reflex as an **unconditioned reflex**, and to its stimulus (food placed in the mouth) and response (salivation) as an **unconditioned stimulus** and **unconditioned response**. For a diagram of Pavlov's basic procedure, called **classical conditioning**, see Figure 5.2.

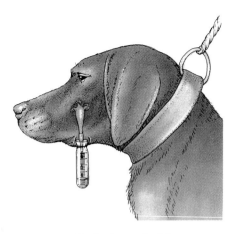

**Figure 5.1  *Pavlov's method for measuring salivation***

*The dog's saliva drains directly into a glass tube. In his early experiments, Pavlov learned that dogs produce different salivary secretions in response to different kinds of food, and later he learned that these could be conditioned to occur in response to stimuli that reliably precede the presentation of food. (Adapted from Yerkes & Morgulis, 1909.)*

**Figure 5.2  *Classical conditioning procedure***

*A neutral stimulus initially does not elicit a response. After it is paired for several trials with an unconditioned stimulus, however, it becomes a conditioned stimulus, and then it does elicit a response.*

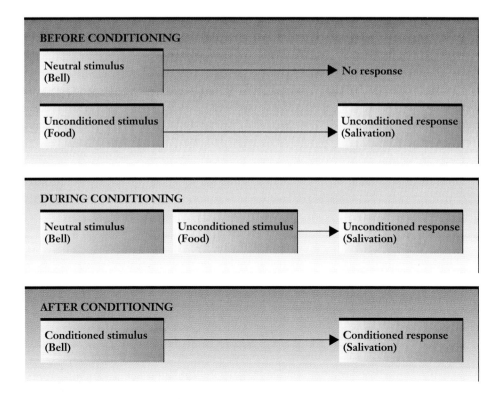

Pavlov (1927/1960) was impressed in these studies by the similarity between the dog's salivary response to a conditioned stimulus and its response to the unconditioned stimulus. For example, if the bell had been paired with meat, its sound elicited a thick saliva, similar to that elicited by meat; and if the bell had been paired with bread, its sound elicited a thinner, wetter saliva, similar to that elicited by bread. In other words, the same conditioned stimulus could result in different conditioned responses, depending on the nature of the unconditioned stimulus with which it had been paired.

In other experiments, Pavlov and his colleagues varied the stimulus used as the conditioned stimulus. They concluded that essentially any environmental event that the animal could detect could become a conditioned stimulus for salivation. Sounds produced by bells, buzzers, metronomes, or tuning forks were highly effective and used most often, because they were the easiest to control. But Pavlov's group also obtained conditioning by using visual stimuli, such as a black square or circle; olfactory stimuli, such as the odor of camphor; and tactile (touch) stimuli, such as pressing a particular point on the animal's skin. In each case, the stimulus initially did not elicit the salivary response, but it did after it was paired with food a number of times. Pavlov's team even found that a moderately painful stimulus, such as an electric shock or puncture of the skin, could be used as a conditioned stimulus for salivation. Such stimuli were initially unconditioned stimuli themselves for vigorous withdrawal responses, but after repeated pairing with food the withdrawal stopped and the dog no longer seemed to experience pain (Pavlov, 1927/1960).

Of course, classical conditioning is not limited to salivary responses. Researchers have shown this in hundreds of laboratory experiments, and you have undoubtedly experienced it dozens of times in the course of your everyday life. The sound of a dentist's drill may elicit a conditioned cringing response, because of its previous pairing with pain. The mere smell of coffee may help wake you up, because of its previous pairing with coffee's effects. The sight of the toilet when you enter a bathroom to comb your hair may elicit a previously unfelt urge to urinate, due to previous pairing of that sight with that urge. If you once had an automobile accident at a curve in the road on a wet day, each new encounter with such a curve, on such a day, may elicit a conditioned tensing of muscles. If you go through a day recording instances of conditioned responses, you will find that the list quickly becomes quite long.

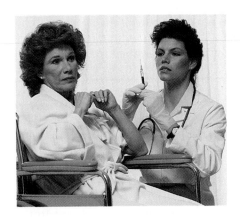

**Conditioned fear**

*For most people the mere sight of a hypodermic needle is enough to arouse a conditioned anxiety response because of previous pairing of the needle with pain.*

■ *How classical conditioning can be seen as an objectification of the philosophers' law of association by contiguity*

**The Importance of Pavlov's Discovery in the Emergence of a Science of Learning**    Pavlov's work on conditioning provided an objective method to study learning. To understand the importance of this discovery, it is useful to view his work in the context of earlier, philosophical thought. For centuries before Pavlov, one of the most important ideas about learning was the *law of association by contiguity*, originally proposed by Aristotle (see Hothersall, 1990). *Contiguity* means closeness in space or time, and the law of association by contiguity can be stated as follows: If a person experiences two environmental events (stimuli) at the same time or one right after the other (contiguously), those events will become associated in the person's mind, such that the thought of one will, in the future, tend to elicit the thought of the other. For example, if your thought *ice cream* is more often followed by the thought *spoon* than by the thought *pencil*, that is because in your past experience ice cream has been more often accompanied by a spoon than a pencil. As another example, if the sound of the word *ball* evokes in a child's mind an image of a spherical object, that is because in the child's past experience that sound had been often paired with the sight of a spherical object. Thus, according to Aristotle and subsequent philosophers, association by contiguity plays a major role in determining the flow of a person's thoughts, and it is involved in all sorts of learning, including the learning of language.

Now, consider the similarity between the philosophers' law of association by contiguity and Pavlov's principle of conditioning (outlined in Figure 5.3). Both propose that learning occurs when two stimuli are paired in a person's experience. The essential difference is that in the philosophers' formulation one stimulus comes to elicit a *thought* that was previously elicited just by the other, while in Pavlov's formulation one stimulus comes to elicit a *behavioral response* that was previously elicited just by the other. The great advantage of Pavlov's formulation is that a response is publicly observable, whereas a thought is not. A researcher using Pavlov's method can look at an animal or person and see the change in response and use it to chart the course of learning. While philosophers could speculate about the association of thoughts, Pavlov could do experiments. He could vary the conditions and objectively measure the effects on an individual's behavior. This idea, of course, was not lost on American behaviorists, such as John B. Watson. To them it was a step that helped make a *science* of learning possible.

**Figure 5.3  *Comparison of the law of association by contiguity with the principle of classical conditioning***

*Philosophers, from Aristotle on, argued that if two stimuli are paired in a person's experience, then the recurrence of one will tend to elicit the thought of the other. Pavlov's principle of conditioning parallels the philosophers' law, with the one important difference that, because Pavlov began with a stimulus that reflexively elicited an observable response, the learning process could be objectively observed.*

*Law of Association by Contiguity*

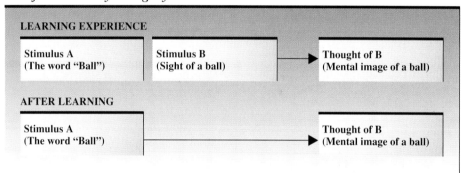

*Principle of Classical Conditioning*

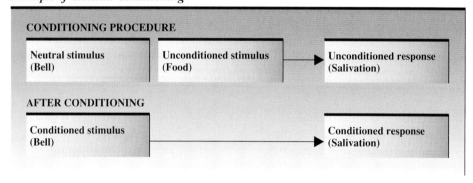

Pavlov and his associates went on, after their initial discovery, to do hundreds of experiments on classical conditioning (see Pavlov, 1927/1960). They identified and studied in detail many important phenomena related to conditioning, which are still very important in psychology today. Let us look now at some of them.

■ *How a conditioned reflex can be extinguished, and Pavlov's evidence that extinction does not return the animal to the untrained state*

**Extinction and Recovery from Extinction**   One question that interested Pavlov had to do with the permanence, or lack of permanence, of a conditioned reflex. Once a dog has learned to salivate to a bell, will this reflex continue to occur if the bell is sounded for many trials without the unconditioned food-in-mouth stimulus? Pavlov's group found that under these conditions the bell elicits less and less salivation on each trial, and eventually none at all, a phenomenon that they labeled ***extinction***. But they also found that extinction does not really return the animal to the unconditioned state. The mere passage of time following extinction can par-

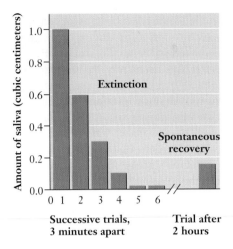

**Figure 5.4** *Extinction and spontaneous recovery of conditioned salivation*

*The conditioned stimulus in this case was the sight of meat powder, presented repeatedly at 3-minute intervals. Extinction was complete by the fifth and sixth presentations, but when 2 hours were allowed to elapse before the seventh presentation, the reflex was partially renewed. (Data from Pavlov, 1927/1960.)*

■ *How conditioned reflexes generalize to other stimuli, how generalization can be abolished by discrimination training, and how the latter can be used to assess an animal's sensory capacities*

tially renew the conditioned reflex, a phenomenon now known as ***spontaneous recovery*** (see Figure 5.4). And a single pairing of the conditioned stimulus with the unconditioned stimulus can fully renew the conditioned reflex, such that another series of extinction trials is necessary to abolish it. Based on such findings, Pavlov (1927/1960) reasoned that the conditioned reflex is not truly lost during extinction, but is somehow inhibited, and can be disinhibited by the passage of time or a single reinforced trial.

Subsequent research has shown that some conditioned reflexes are more difficult to extinguish than others. In particular, conditioned changes in heart rate, blood pressure, and certain other internal responses are much harder to extinguish than conditioned movements that involve the skeletal muscles (the muscles attached to bones). For example, electric shock to a person's arm produces an increased heart rate and a flinching away from the source of shock (a skeletal response), both of which can be conditioned to a new stimulus with just a few reinforced trials. Following such conditioning, the conditioned flinch disappears after only two or three extinction trials, but the conditioned heart-rate response usually persists even after dozens of such trials (Gantt, 1953). This may help explain why people can appear calm on the outside while experiencing turmoil inside, leading to such fates as chronically high blood pressure and ulcers.

**Generalization and Discrimination**   After conditioning, stimuli that resemble the conditioned stimulus will elicit the conditioned response even though they themselves were never paired with the unconditioned stimulus. This phenomenon is called ***generalization***. The magnitude or likelihood of response to the new stimulus is correlated with its degree of similarity to the original conditioned stimulus. Thus, a dog conditioned to salivate to a 1000 Hz (cycles per second) tone also salivated to tones of other frequencies. But the further the tone was in frequency from the original conditioned stimulus, the less the dog would salivate to it (Pavlov, 1927/1960).

Generalization between two stimuli can be abolished if the response to one is reinforced while that to the other is extinguished, a procedure called ***discrimination training***. To illustrate this procedure, Pavlov's group used a dog whose conditioning to the sight of a black square had generalized to a gray square. After a series of trials in which presentations of the gray square were never followed by food and presentations of the black square were always followed by food, the dog stopped salivating to the gray square and continued to salivate to the black one. The researchers continued this procedure with ever-darker shades of gray, until they eventually conditioned the dog to discriminate a black square from a gray one that was so nearly black that a human observer had difficulty telling them apart (Pavlov, 1927/1960).

Classical conditioning coupled with discrimination training provides an excellent tool to study an animal's sensory capacities. You cannot ask a dog what it can or cannot hear, but you can find the answer by doing a conditioning experiment. Pavlov's team conditioned dogs to salivate to tones that were of such high pitch as to be completely inaudible to humans, and to discriminate between pitches less than one-eighth of a note apart. In one experiment with a dog that had previously been conditioned to discriminate between tones coming from the right or the left, the researchers cut the nerve fibers connecting the right and left halves of the higher parts of the brain. After the surgery, the dog continued to salivate to tones, but could no longer discriminate between tones coming from different locations, and could not be retrained to do so. From this, Pavlov (1927/1960) concluded that the ability to localize sounds depends on the integrated activity of the two halves of the brain. This sort of experiment on the physiology of perception would have been impossible without the conditioned reflex as a tool.

■ *How one conditioned reflex can be used to produce a new one*

**Higher-Order Conditioning**   Once a conditioned reflex has been established, it can be used, without the original unconditioned stimulus, to produce a new conditioned reflex, a process called ***higher-order conditioning***. As an illustration, Pavlov (1927/1960) and his team conditioned a dog in the usual way to salivate to a buzzer, and then conditioned the dog to salivate to a black square by pairing it with the buzzer on several trials without the food-in-mouth unconditioned stimulus. As you might expect, they found such *second-order conditioning* to be rather fragile, since each reinforced trial for the new stimulus (black square) was an extinction trial for the previous stimulus (buzzer). Can second-order conditioning provide a basis for conditioning to yet another stimulus? Pavlov's group were unable to obtain *third-order conditioning* with salivation, but did obtain it with another response, a leg-withdrawal response for which electric shock was the unconditioned stimulus. Even in this case, however, they were unable to obtain *fourth-order conditioning*.

**Conditioned Emotional Responses**   We move temporarily from Pavlov's laboratory to that of John B. Watson, who was one of the first psychologists to describe human learning explicitly in Pavlovian terms, and was also one of the first to demonstrate directly how an emotional response—that of fear—can be conditioned in human infants. Consistent with his behavioral perspective, Watson (1924) defined *fear* not as a feeling, but as a set of observable responses: "a catching of the breath, a stiffening of the whole body, a turning away of the body from the source of stimulation, a running or crawling from it." Based on this definition, Watson found two unconditioned stimuli for fear in young infants—loud noise and sudden loss of support (as when a baby slips out of a person's hands). Other stimuli, he argued, come to elicit fear only as a result of conditioning. In a classic demonstration of such conditioning, Watson and Rayner (1920) conditioned an 11-month-old baby named Albert to fear laboratory rats. At first Albert played happily with a rat that was placed in front of him, showing no fear. Then, to condition the fear, the experimenters produced a loud sound, by striking a steel bar with a hammer, on two different occasions when Albert was paying close attention to the rat. Each occurrence of the loud sound elicited the fear response, and after the second occurrence Albert showed the fear response each time he saw the rat even though the loud sound was not repeated. Thus, in the terminology of classical conditioning, the rat had become a conditioned stimulus for fear through being paired with a loud sound, which was an unconditioned stimulus for fear.

■ *How Watson demonstrated that an emotional reaction can be conditioned*

You might wonder about the ethics of this experiment. In fairness to Watson, it should be noted that his main interest in fear concerned how to eliminate unwanted fears, not how to produce them. In Chapter 18, you will see how Watson's research and ideas helped lead to clinical methods to extinguish irrational fears through exposing the person to the fear-producing stimuli, at gradually increasing magnitudes, in a safe, relaxing context.

*Little Albert and Watson*

*After Albert was conditioned to respond fearfully to a white rat, he also cried at the sight of other furry objects including the rabbit shown here.*

*Forewarned is not necessarily forearmed*

*In natural environments classically conditioned responses have functional value. The animal learns negative responses toward harmful stimuli and positive responses to those that are beneficial. In contrast, when advertisers attempt conditioning, the results may be quite harmful to unwary "subjects."*

Fear, of course, is not the only emotional response that can be conditioned through Pavlovian procedures. When beer and car advertisers pair their products with scenes of beautiful people having wonderful times, they are trying to get you to drool with pleasure, like Pavlov's dogs, whenever you see their product.

**Conditioned Drug Reactions**  In one of their most intriguing experiments, Pavlov's group conditioned a dog to show a drug reaction to a nondrug stimulus. After repeated pairing of a tone with injection of a drug that elicited restlessness and vomiting, the dog began to show those responses to the tone alone (Pavlov, 1927/1960). This discovery suggests that stimuli that are normally present when a drug is taken may, through conditioning, come to induce the symptoms of the drug. Because of conditioning the sight of a coffee cup or the smell of coffee, for example, might give you a lift; a visit to a hospital where you were previously given a sedative might make you feel sleepy.

More recent research has shown that with some drugs the conditioned response is *opposite* to the most noticeable unconditioned effect of the drug. For example, the drug morphine has an unconditioned effect that includes a reduction in sensitivity to pain. When rats are repeatedly injected with morphine in a distinctive environment, and then are placed in that environment without morphine, they become temporarily more, not less, sensitive to pain (Hinson & others, 1986). What happens in such cases might be understood as follows (see Siegel & others, 1988): The drug produces two effects—a direct effect (which in this case includes reduced pain sensitivity) followed by a reflexive physiological response that tends to counteract the direct effect (tends to increase pain sensitivity). But only the reflexive counteractive effect becomes conditioned, so, when the cues are present without the drug, pain sensitivity increases rather than decreases.

*How the conditioning of counteractive drug effects helps explain why an addict's usual dose can sometimes be an "overdose"*

The discovery of conditioned counteractive effects of drugs may help explain an important observation associated with human drug abuse. A study of heroin overdose cases revealed that quite often the "overdose" was not actually any larger than the addict's usual drug dose, but was taken in an unusual environment (Siegel, 1984). Apparently, when an addict takes a drug in the usual drug-taking environment, cues in that environment, because of past conditioning, produce a counteractive physiological reaction that allows the addict's body to tolerate a large dose of the drug. If the addict takes the same amount of the drug in a novel environment, where the conditioned cues aren't present, the full impact of the drug kicks in before a counteractive reaction begins—resulting in extreme illness or death. Consistent with this interpretation, rats that had previously received many morphine injections in a specific, highly distinctive cage were much more likely to survive a high dose of the drug if given to them in that same cage than if given in a different setting (Siegel, 1976, 1984).

Little in psychology is simple, and as you will see later (in the section on the cognitive perspective), classical conditioning is not as mechanical and automatic as might be suggested by what you have just read. But now let us turn to the other kind of conditioning emphasized by behaviorists.

## Operant Conditioning

We are pulled as well as pushed by events in our environment. That is, we do not just react to stimuli; we also behave in ways that seem designed to *produce* or *obtain* certain environmental changes or stimuli. My dog rubs against the door to be let out. I flip a switch to illuminate a room, press keys on my computer to set up words on a screen, and say "please pass the potatoes" to get potatoes. Most of my day seems to consist of behaviors of this sort, and I expect that most of my dog's day would too if there were more things that she could control. Surely if Pavlov's dogs had some way to control the delivery of food into their mouths, they would have done more than salivate—they would have pushed a lever, perhaps, or bitten open a bag, or done what they must to get the food.

Actions such as those just listed—that is, actions that seem to be performed because of their effect—are called *instrumental responses*, because they function like *instruments*, or tools, to work some change on the environment. They are also called **operant responses**, referring to the fact that they *operate* on the world to produce some effect. B. F. Skinner (1938) coined this term, as well as the term **operant conditioning**, which refers to the learning process by which the consequence of an operant response affects the likelihood that the response will occur in the future. Before turning to Skinner and more about his way of describing operant conditioning, let us look at some research by an earlier pioneer.

**Thorndike and the Law of Effect**    At the same time that Pavlov initiated his first studies of conditioning, a young American student of psychology, Edward Lee Thorndike (1898), published a report on his own learning experiments with various animals, including cats. Thorndike's training procedure was quite different from Pavlov's, and so was his description of the learning process. His apparatus was a *puzzle box*, a small cage that could be opened from inside by some relatively simple act, such as pulling a loop or pressing a lever (see Figure 5.5).

In one experiment Thorndike deprived several cats of food for some time, then placed them inside the cage, one at a time, with food just outside it. When first placed inside, the cat would engage in many behaviors—such as clawing at the bars or pushing at the ceiling—in an apparent attempt to escape the cage or get at the food outside. Finally, apparently by accident, the cat would pull the loop or push the lever that opened the cage and permitted freedom and access to food.

 *How Thorndike's training procedure differed from Pavlov's and led him to formulate the law of effect*

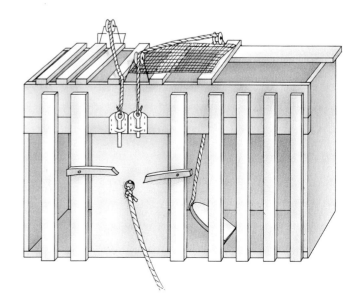

**Figure 5.5  *One of Thorndike's puzzle boxes***
*In each trial, a cat was placed inside and could open the box through some specific action, in this case pushing the lever on the floor. Before each trial, the clips on either side of the door would be turned up and the left-hand bolt would be released. Thus, when the cat pressed the lever, pulling the right-hand bolt up, the door would fall forward. (From Thorndike, 1898.)*

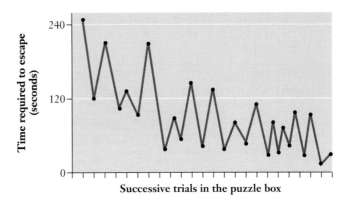

**Figure 5.6** *Typical learning curve for a cat in Thorndike's puzzle box*

*As illustrated here for a single cat, Thorndike found that cats usually took less time to escape from the box on successive trials, though there was a great deal of variability from trial to trial. (Adapted from Thorndike, 1898.)*

Thorndike repeated this procedure many times with each cat. He found that on early trials they made many useless movements before happening on the one that released the escape device, but, on average, they would escape somewhat more quickly with each successive trial. After about twenty to thirty trials, most cats would trip the latch to freedom and food almost as soon as they were shut in (see Figure 5.6). An observer who happened along and saw one of Thorndike's cats on Trial 31 might have been quite impressed by the animal's intelligence; but one who had sat with Thorndike through the earlier trials would have been less inclined to rhapsodize. In fact, as suggested by Thorndike himself, the latter observer might have been far more impressed by the creature's stupidity than its intelligence. In any event, Thorndike came to view learning as a trial-and-error process, through which an individual gradually becomes more likely to make those responses that produce beneficial effects.

It would be useful now to compare Thorndike's basic training procedure with Pavlov's. Pavlov could directly *elicit* the response he wished to condition in his animal. For example, he could elicit salivation by putting food in the dog's mouth. His conditioning method was to pair a new stimulus with a stimulus that already elicited the response. Thus, Pavlov was concerned only with environmental events that *preceded* the response that he wished to condition, not with the effect or consequence of the response. With Pavlov's procedure, the animal can be thought of as a passive, responsive machine: Push button *X* and get response *Y*. Thorndike, on the other hand, could not directly elicit the response he wished to condition. There was no known unconditioned stimulus, no button Thorndike could push, that would make the animal open the latch. With Thorndike's procedure, the animal has to be thought of as an active creature, one that produces or *emits* various responses, seemingly of its own accord. Most of the cat's initial movements in the box were ineffective, and Thorndike had to wait patiently until the animal emitted the correct one. To gain some control over the cat's behavior, Thorndike had arranged the environment in such a way that only one type of response would open the box. Thus, with Thorndike's method, the important environmental event (the opening of the box) was a *consequence* of the response, not something that occurred before the response.

Partly on the basis of his puzzle-box experiments, Thorndike (1898) formulated the **law of effect**, which can be stated, in somewhat abbreviated form, as follows: *Responses that produce a satisfying effect in a particular situation become more likely to occur again in that situation, and responses that produce a discomforting effect become less likely to occur again in that situation.* In Thorndike's puzzle-box experiments, the *situation* presumably consisted of all the sights, sounds, smells, internal feelings, and so on that were experienced by the hungry animal in the box. None of these initially elicited the latch-release response in reflex-like fashion; rather, taken as a whole, they set the occasion for many possible responses to occur, only one of which would release the latch. Once the latch was released, the *satisfying effect*, including freedom from the box and access to food, caused that response to become more firmly bonded to the situation than it was before, so the next time the cat was in the same situation, the probability of that response's recurrence was increased

**Figure 5.7** *Thorndike's law of effect*
*According to Thorndike, the stimulus situation (being inside the puzzle box) initially elicits many responses, some more strongly than others, but the satisfying consequence of the successful response (pressing the lever) causes that response to be more strongly elicited on successive trials.*

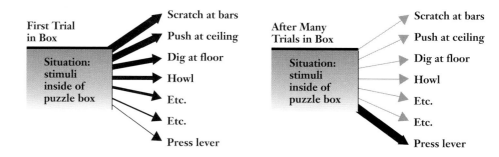

(see Figure 5.7). Of the many different responses that initially occurred in the puzzle box, the one that changed the environment in a satisfactory way was more likely to occur the next time.

■ *How Skinner's method for studying learning differs from Thorndike's, and why he preferred the term* **reinforcer** *to Thorndike's* **satisfaction**

**Skinner and the Basic Terminology of Operant Conditioning**    The psychologist who did the most to extend and popularize the law of effect for more than half a century is Burrhus Fredric Skinner. As a graduate student at Harvard around 1930, Skinner developed an apparatus for studying learning in animals that was considerably more convenient than Thorndike's puzzle boxes. His device, commonly called a Skinner box, is a cage with a lever or other mechanism in it that the animal can operate to produce some effect, such as delivery of a pellet of food or drop of water (see Figure 5.8). The advantage of Skinner's apparatus is that the animal, after completing a response and experiencing its effect, is still in the box and free to respond again. With Thorndike's puzzle boxes and similar apparatuses such as mazes, the animal has to be placed back into the start place at the end of each trial. With Skinner's apparatus the animal is simply placed in the cage and left there until the end of the session. Throughout the session there are no constraints on when the animal may or may not respond. Responses (such as lever presses) can easily be counted automatically, and the learning process can be depicted as change in the rate of responses (see Figure 5.9).

Skinner not only developed a more efficient apparatus to study such learning, but also a new vocabulary for talking about it. As a confirmed behaviorist, he wanted to describe learning purely in terms that refer to observable stimuli and responses, avoiding any terms that refer to mental events. As mentioned earlier, he coined the term *operant response* to refer to any behavioral act that has some effect on the environment, and *operant conditioning* to refer to the process by which the effect of an operant response changes the likelihood of the response's recurrence in the future. Thus, in a typical experiment with a Skinner box, pressing the lever is an operant response, and the increasing rate of lever pressing that occurs when each such response is followed by a pellet of food exemplifies operant conditioning. Applying the same terms to Thorndike's experiments, the movement that

**Figure 5.8** *Skinner box, or operant conditioning chamber*
*When the rat presses the lever, it operates an electrical relay system that causes the delivery of a food pellet or drop of water into the cup next to the lever. Each lever press can be automatically recorded to produce a cumulative record, such as that shown in Figure 5.9.*

**Figure 5.9** *Typical cumulative response curve for a rat learning to press a lever in a Skinner box*

*This graph is called a* cumulative response curve, *because the height of the curve at any point indicates the total (cumulative) number of responses that the rat has made up to that time. The graph is automatically produced, while the rat is responding, by a recording machine outside of the Skinner box. A pen moves horizontally across a roll of paper at a constant rate, and each lever press made by the rat produces a slight vertical movement of the pen. Thus, the degree to which the curve slopes upward is a measure of the animal's response rate. Note that early in learning the response rate was very low, and then it gradually increased to a fast, steady rate.*

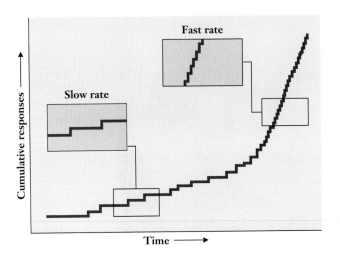

opens the latch is an operant response, and the increased speed of making that movement from trial to trial exemplifies operant conditioning.

Skinner (1938) proposed the term *reinforcer*, instead of such terms as *satisfaction* or *reward*, to refer to a stimulus change that occurs after a response and tends to increase the likelihood that the response will occur again in the future. Thus, in a typical Skinner-box experiment, the delivery of a pellet of food or drop of water following a lever-press response is a reinforcer. In Thorndike's experiment, the opening of the cage, such that the cat could escape its confines and obtain the food outside, was the reinforcer.

**The Scope of Operant Conditioning, and Some Applications**    To Skinner and his followers, operant conditioning is not simply one kind of learning to be studied, but represents an entire approach to psychology. In his many books and articles, Skinner argued that essentially everything we do, from the moment we arise in the morning to the moment we fall asleep at night, can be understood as operant responses that occur because of their past reinforcement. In some cases we are clearly aware of the relationship between our responses and reinforcers, as when we place coins in a vending machine for a candy bar, or study hard to obtain a good grade on a test. In other cases we may not be aware of the relationship, yet it exists and, according to Skinner, is the real reason for our behavior. To Skinner, awareness—which refers to a mental phenomenon—is not an issue worth debating, because we cannot observe it directly in others. We can never be sure what a person is aware of, but we can directly see the relationship between responses and reinforcers, and use that to predict the person's behavior.

■ *How Hefferline conditioned people to make a tiny thumb twitch, and the relevance of this for understanding the acquisition of motor skills*

A nice illustration, showing how a subtle response can be conditioned in human subjects, apparently without their awareness, comes from an experiment conducted many years ago by Ralph Hefferline and his colleagues (1959) at Columbia University. In this experiment, adult subjects sat in comfortable chairs for an hour and listened to music, and static was occasionally superimposed on the music. Unbeknownst to the subjects, they could turn off the static by making an imperceptibly small twitch of the left thumb. Through an electrical recording system, each thumb twitch of the appropriate size produced a signal that the experimenter, sitting in another room, used as a cue to turn off the static for a set period of time. Some subjects (the completely uninformed group) were told that the experiment had to do with the effect of music on body tension; they were told nothing about the static or how it could be turned off. Others (the partly informed group) were told that static would sometimes come on, that it could be turned off by some specific response, and that their task was to discover the response and keep the static off.

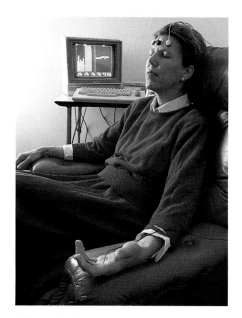

**Biofeedback training**

*In this procedure, sensors record scalp-muscle movements and finger temperature. (Muscle contractions are a source of tension headaches, and cold fingers often indicate tension.) Learning to control these physiological reactions has proved to be an effective means of warding off tension headaches.*

■ *How biofeedback training can be explained as operant conditioning*

The result was that all subjects in both of these groups learned to make the thumb-twitch response, thereby keeping the static off for successively longer periods as the session progressed. But, when questioned afterwards, none appeared to be aware that they had controlled the static with thumb twitches. Subjects in the completely uninformed group said that they had noticed that the static decreased over the session but were unaware that anything they had done had caused the decrease. Most subjects in the partly informed group said that they had not discovered what response controlled the static, even though they noticed it decreasing. Only one subject believed that he had discovered the effective response, and he claimed that it involved "subtle rowing movements with both hands, infinitesimal wriggles of both ankles, a slight displacement of the jaw to the left, breathing out, and then waiting"! While he was consciously making this response, he was also apparently unconsciously learning to make the thumb twitch.

If you think about it, Hefferline's finding should not come as a great surprise. We constantly learn finely tuned muscle movements as we develop skill at the violin, riding a bicycle, hammering nails, or whatever. The reinforcers, presumably, are the improved sound from the violin, steadier movement on the bicycle, or the straight downward movement of the nail we are pounding; but we often do not know just what we are doing differently to produce these good effects. Our knowledge is often similar to that of the neophyte carpenter who said, after an hour's practice at pounding nails, "The nails you're giving me now don't bend as easily as the ones you were giving me before."

Aside from its importance as a concept for understanding everyday behavior, operant conditioning is used by some clinical psychologists, called *behavior therapists*, to help their clients change their behavior in desired ways. From an operant perspective, many of the problems that lead people to seek therapy are best thought of as bad habits, learned and maintained because they are reinforced in the short run, even though they are harmful in the long run. Such behaviors as overeating, overdrinking, and smoking are obvious examples. Ultimately, these are unhealthy, but the immediate effect of each bite of food, each sip of alcohol, or each drag on the cigarette is pleasure, relief from discomfort, or both, and that is why the behaviors continue. To help a client give up such habits, a behavior therapist suggests ways to change the reinforcement contingencies, so that more immediate reinforcement will be obtained through other, more healthful pursuits and less will be obtained through the harmful ones. (Much more about behavior therapy will be found in Chapter 18.)

Even physiologically based problems, such as high blood pressure and migraine headaches, can sometimes be controlled through an interesting variation of operant conditioning, **biofeedback training**. In this procedure, a signal, such as a tone or light, is made to come on whenever a certain desirable physiological change occurs, and the person is instructed to try to keep the signal on for increasing periods of time. For example, a man being trained to decrease his blood pressure might hear a tone every time his pressure falls below a certain level. The tone allows him to detect a favorable consequence (reduced blood pressure) that he otherwise would not be able to sense. In operant terminology, the tone is a reinforcer (assuming that the subject is motivated to succeed at the task) for the response of decreasing blood pressure. As was the case for the subjects in Hefferline's thumb-twitch experiment, the client need not discover or be aware of just how he is reducing his blood pressure for successful learning to occur. Using a similar method, biofeedback trainers have also reported success in teaching people with irregular heart rates to produce more regular heartbeats and people who suffer from headaches to reduce muscle tension in the scalp and hence the incidence of headaches (see Mercer, 1986).

Having glimpsed the broad applicability of operant conditioning, let us now look at some basic processes associated with this form of learning.

**How to use operant conditioning to get an animal to do something that it presently doesn't do**

**Shaping**   In operant conditioning, the reinforcer comes only after the subject emits the desired response. But what happens if that response never occurs? Suppose you put a rat in a Skinner box and it never presses the lever, or a cat in a puzzle box and it never pulls the loop. The solution to this problem is a technique called *shaping*, in which successively closer approximations to the desired response are reinforced until the response finally occurs.

Imagine that you wish to shape a lever-press response in a rat whose initial rate of lever pressing is zero, or so low that you don't have the patience to wait for the response to occur. First you might present the reinforcer (such as a pellet of food) whenever the rat goes anywhere near the lever. As a result, the rat will soon be spending most of its time near the lever and occasionally will touch it. When that happens, you might provide the reinforcer only when the rat touches the lever, which will increase the rate of touching. Some touches will be more vigorous than others and produce the desired lever movement; when that has happened a few times you can stop reinforcing any other response—your animal has now been shaped. It is not hard to see that we all use this technique, more or less deliberately, when we teach new skills to people. For example, in teaching a novice to play tennis we tend at first to offer praise for any swing of the racket that propels the ball in the right general direction, and as training progresses we gradually restrict praise for closer and closer approximations to an ideal swing.

**Extinction, and Schedules of Partial Reinforcement**   An operantly conditioned response declines in rate and eventually disappears if it no longer results in a reinforcer. Rats stop pressing levers if no food pellets appear, cats stop scratching at doors if nobody responds, and people stop smiling at those who don't smile back. The lack of reinforcement of the response, and the consequent decline in response rate, are both referred to as *extinction*, which is analogous to the same term in classical conditioning.

In many cases, both in the real world and in laboratory setups, a particular response only sometimes produces a reinforcer. This is referred to as *partial reinforcement*, to distinguish it on the one hand from continuous reinforcement, where the response is always reinforced, and on the other hand from extinction, where the response is never reinforced. In initial training, continuous reinforcement is most efficient, but once trained an animal will continue to perform for partial reinforcement. Skinner and other operant researchers have distinguished among four basic *schedules* of partial reinforcement. They have shown that each has a different, quite predictable effect on an individual's rate and pattern of responding. As you read the description of each schedule, look also at the appropriate part of Figure 5.10, which depicts the typical response pattern of an animal that is reinforced on that schedule.

**Figure 5.10** *Typical cumulative response curves for rats well trained on four different schedules of reinforcement*

*As explained in Figure 5.9, the slope of the curve represents the response rate. Here each downward mark indicates the occurrence of a reinforcer. Ratio schedules (whether fixed or variable) typically produce faster response rates than do interval schedules; and variable schedules (whether ratio or interval) typically produce steadier response rates, with fewer postreinforcement pauses, than do fixed schedules.*

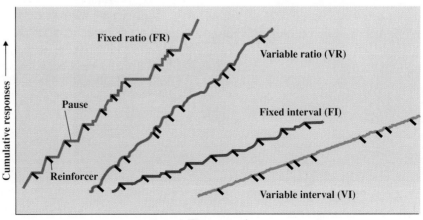

*How the four partial schedules of reinforcement affect (a) the response rate and response steadiness while the schedule is in effect, and (b) the amount of responding during later extinction*

*Fixed-ratio (FR) schedule*  With this schedule, the response must be emitted a certain fixed number of times before a reinforcer occurs. If a rat must make twenty lever presses before obtaining a pellet of food, the schedule is FR-20. If a garment worker must sew five dresses before getting paid, the schedule is FR-5. A fixed-ratio schedule can be thought of as the same as continuous reinforcement, but with a more complex response that consists of a series of repeated movements. An animal on a fixed-ratio schedule in a Skinner box typically produces a burst of lever presses until the reinforcer appears, and then, after a pause that may sometimes be of considerable duration, produces another burst (see Figure 5.10). The response rate during the burst is usually constant, which is consistent with the idea that the animal is treating the series of lever presses required for each reinforcer as one behavioral act.

*Variable-ratio (VR) schedule*  With this schedule, the response must be emitted a certain *average* number of times before a reinforcer will appear, but the number needed on any given instance varies randomly around that average. If a rat must make an average of ten responses for each pellet of food, but the actual number required for a given pellet is unpredictable, the schedule is VR-10. Many human gambling systems can be described as variable-ratio schedules. For example, the reinforcement schedule for betting heads in a coin-flipping game is VR-2, and that for betting on a particular lay of a six-sided die is VR-6. Slot machines also operate on variable-ratio schedules. A variable-ratio schedule typically produces a rapid, steady rate of responding, with shorter postreinforcement pauses than occurs with a fixed-ratio schedule (see Figure 5.10). Because one reinforcer sometimes comes immediately after another, this schedule provides greater incentive to resume responding right after receiving a reinforcer than does the fixed-ratio schedule. According to Skinner (1953), compulsive gambling occurs partly because people become hooked by the variable ratio. Since the very next response may pay off regardless of how long it has been since the last response paid off, the gambler keeps responding.

*Fixed-interval (FI) schedule*  With this schedule, a fixed period of time must elapse after each reinforced response before another reinforcer can be

*Partial reinforcement in daily life*

*Winning at bingo occurs on a variable-ratio schedule, which produces a rapid, steady style of play. Success at reaching a previously busy telephone number occurs on a variable-interval schedule, which results in a slow and steady rate of redialing.*

obtained. Thus, if a rat must wait 30 seconds after receiving a pellet of food before a lever press will produce another pellet, the rat is on an FI-30-second schedule. Similarly, if you are baking cookies a batch at a time in a small oven, your response of checking the oven with each batch to see if they are done is reinforced after rather constant intervals. A fixed-interval schedule induces a scallopedlike rate of responding, in which the subject pauses for a period of time after each reinforcer and then responds at an accelerating rate until the fixed interval is up and another reinforcer is received (see Figure 5.10). If your rate of study in college accelerates near midterm and finals time, that may indicate that the main reinforcers controlling your study are tests that occur at those fixed intervals.

- *Variable-interval (VI) schedule*   With this schedule, an unpredictable amount of time, varying around some average, must elapse between the presentation of one reinforcer and the availability of another. For example, if a pellet of food becomes available at unpredictable intervals averaging 30 seconds, the lever-pressing rat is on a VI-30-second schedule. A nonlaboratory example is that of repeatedly dialing a busy telephone number. At some point the line will become free and the call will go through, but there is no way to tell just when. Subjects well trained on a variable-interval schedule typically respond at a slow but steady rate (see Figure 5.10). Because reinforcement availability is based on time rather than the number of responses, and because a reinforcer *may* occur at any time, the slow and steady rate is most efficient.

The different response patterns produced by the different schedules make sense from the viewpoint of adaptiveness. Ratio schedules (whether fixed or variable), where the number of reinforcers received is proportional to the number of responses made, produce faster response rates than interval schedules, where a certain amount of time (fixed or variable) must elapse after each reinforcer before another can be received. And variable schedules (whether ratio or interval), where one cannot predict when a reinforcer will appear, produce steadier response rates, with fewer postreinforcement pauses, than fixed schedules, where one reinforcer never comes immediately after another.

One important consequence of partial-reinforcement schedules, especially variable-ratio and variable-interval, is that they make the behavior more resistant to extinction, a phenomenon known as the *partial-reinforcement effect*. If a rat is trained to press a lever only on continuous reinforcement, and then shifted to extinction conditions, it will typically make a few bursts of lever-press responses and then quit. But if the rat has been shifted gradually from continuous reinforcement to an ever-stingier variable schedule, and then finally to extinction, it will often make hundreds of unreinforced responses before quitting. So, quite often, will a human gambler, as many casino owners know full well. It is not hard to imagine why this effect should occur. Subjects who have been reinforced on stingy variable ratios, or long variable intervals, have, in their past experience, received reinforcers after long periods of no reinforcement, so they have learned (for better or worse) to be persistent.

**Stimulus Control of Operant Behavior**   Thus far in discussing operant conditioning I have paid attention to reinforcing stimuli, which follow the response, but ignored stimuli that precede and set the occasion for the response. A rat trained in a Skinner box has not merely learned to make a lever-press response, but has learned to make it in a particular *context*, which includes being inside the Skinner box. The rat does not go foolishly about making lever-press responses in its home cage or in other places where the response has never been reinforced.

In his original formulation of the law of effect, Thorndike (1898) emphasized the importance of the *situation* in which the animal is trained, saying, "Of several responses made to the same situation, those which are accompanied or closely followed by satisfaction to the animal will, other things being equal, be more firmly connected with the situation, so that when it recurs, they will be more likely to recur." The set of stimuli inside a puzzle box or a Skinner box are examples of a Thorndikian situation (look back at Figure 5.7). Only in the presence of those stimuli is the response reinforced, and therefore the response becomes likely to occur when those stimuli are present.

Through *discrimination training* (which has a meaning in operant conditioning analogous to that in classical conditioning), it is possible to bring an operant response under the control of a more specific stimulus than the entire inside of a Skinner box. The essence of this procedure is to reinforce the animal's responses when the specific stimulus is present and extinguish the response when it is absent. Thus, to train a rat to respond to a tone by pressing a lever, you could alternate between reinforcement periods with the tone on (during which the animal gets food pellets for responding) and extinction periods with the tone off. After considerable training of this nature, the rat will begin pressing the lever as soon as the tone comes on and stop as soon as it goes off. The tone in this example is called a **discriminative stimulus**. A discriminative stimulus is a cue that a particular response will be reinforced. It is a little like a conditioned stimulus in classical conditioning, in that it promotes a particular response as a result of the subject's previous experience, but it does so in a less reflexive way. It *sets the occasion* for responding, rather than reflexively eliciting the response.

▪ *How to turn a neutral stimulus into a discriminative stimulus to control an operant response*

*A discriminative stimulus*

*The pigeon is learning that its pecking will be reinforced with food only when a disk is lit. In this form of operant conditioning, the light is the discriminative stimulus.*

Operant discrimination training, like the analogous procedure in classical conditioning, can be a powerful tool for learning about the sensory abilities of animals and human infants who cannot describe their sensations in words. In one experiment, for example, researchers trained 1-day-old human babies to turn their heads in one direction—using a sip of sugarwater as the reinforcer—whenever a tone was sounded, and in the other direction whenever a buzzer was sounded (Siqueland & Lipsitt, 1966). This demonstrated, among other things, that newborns can hear the difference between the two different sounds.

■ *How a discriminative stimulus can become a secondary reinforcer and link two operant responses together*

**Chaining, Secondary Reinforcement, and Tokens** Let's return to the rat that has been conditioned to press a lever whenever a tone comes on. Because the tone sets the occasion for receiving a reinforcer, the tone itself acquires reinforcing value. If you arrange the environment such that the tone comes on whenever the rat pulls a string, the rat will learn to pull the string. After such training, the animal's behavior in the Skinner box consists of a chain of two operant responses, linked together by the tone, which serves as a reinforcer for one response (the string pull) and a discriminative stimulus for the next (the lever press):

string-pull response → tone → lever-press response → food

With further training, this chain could be extended by establishing a discriminative stimulus for the string-pull response (say, a green light) and then using that as the reinforcer for yet a new response (say, turning a wheel). By this stepwise procedure, rats have been trained to complete chains of as many as a dozen discrete responses to obtain in the end a pellet of food or drop of water (Pierrel & Sherman, 1963). Similar techniques have been used to train severely retarded people to complete such response sequences as those involved in dressing themselves. First the person learns the last step in the sequence, for some reinforcer, and then new steps are added on, each of which is reinforced by the opportunity it provides to perform the next step.

As shown in the above example, almost any kind of stimulus can become a reinforcer. A ***primary reinforcer*** is a stimulus, such as food or water, that is innately reinforcing, and a ***secondary reinforcer*** is a stimulus, such as the tone in the above example, that has acquired its reinforcing value through previous training. According to one widely accepted theory, the usual route by which a previously neutral stimulus becomes a secondary reinforcer is through first serving as a discriminative stimulus for some other reinforced response (Keller & Schoenfeld, 1950). In the example just discussed, the tone could be used as a secondary reinforcer for the string-pull response because it had been a discriminative stimulus for the lever-press response. From this perspective, a secondary reinforcer is reinforcing because it permits an individual to obtain a primary reinforcer. Operant theorists point out that much human behavior is reinforced by secondary reinforcers—such as money, certificates, grades, and praise—which have acquired their reinforcing value because in the past they have served as discriminative stimuli for other reinforced responses. If I have money in my hand, I can buy food; therefore, I will work for money:

work → money → buy food → food

In this chain, unlike the one described above for the rat, a considerable delay may occur between one response (working for money) and the next (using the money to buy food). A secondary reinforcer, such as money, which can be saved and turned in later for another reinforcer, is called a ***token***.

In a classic experiment with chimpanzees, J. B. Wolfe (1936) demonstrated that humans are not the only animals who can learn to work for tokens. Wolfe first trained chimpanzees to place poker chips into a machine that dispensed grapes. Because poker chips alone could activate the machine, they became discriminative stimuli for the response that led to grapes. Trained chimpanzees would not try to operate the machine unless they had a poker chip, and they would readily learn a new response to obtain poker chips, showing that these had now become secondary reinforcers. Interestingly, the chimpanzees would work for poker chips even when the grape machine was not present and the chips could not be used immediately to get grapes, indicating that the chips now functioned as true tokens. The chimpanzees would save them, cashing them in for grapes when the machine again became available.

*In a token economy*

*These volunteers at the Brooklyn Developmental Center (New York) wait on "customers" at the Center's "store." Staff members give tokens to their severely retarded clients to reward and motivate them for learning, maintaining, or improving a skill. Clients can then use the tokens to purchase different items at the store.*

■ *How negative reinforcement differs from positive reinforcement*

**Negative Reinforcement and Avoidance Learning** In Skinner's terminology, *reinforcement* refers to any process that increases the likelihood that a particular response will occur. Reinforcement can be positive or negative. ***Positive reinforcement***, the type that you have been reading about so far, occurs when the *arrival* of some stimulus following a response makes the response more likely to recur. The stimulus in this case is called a ***positive reinforcer***. Food pellets, grapes, money, words of praise, and everything else that organisms will work to obtain are positive reinforcers. ***Negative reinforcement***, in contrast, occurs when the *removal* of some stimulus following a response makes the response more likely to recur. The stimulus in this case is called a ***negative reinforcer***. Electric shocks, loud noises, unpleasant company, scoldings, and everything else that organisms will work to get away from are negative reinforcers. The one example of negative reinforcement discussed so far was Hefferline's thumb-twitch experiment. People learned to make the thumb-twitch response because each occurrence of that response resulted in temporary removal of unpleasant static. Notice that *positive* and *negative* here do *not* refer to the direction of change in the response rate—that increases in either case. Rather, they refer to whether the response causes a particular stimulus to appear (positive) or disappear (negative).

■ *The difference between escape and avoidance, and how the latter is explained as a combination of classical and operant conditioning*

An operant response that is reinforced by the removal of a negative reinforcer is called an ***escape response***. Psychologists often study escape learning in rats and other animals using a two-compartment apparatus such as depicted in Figure 5.11. When an electric shock comes on in the compartment where the rat is standing, the rat can escape by running into the other compartment. Most rats learn this response quite quickly. If conditions are then modified so that some signal, say, a light, comes on just before the shock, the animal will learn to run to the other compartment as soon as the light comes on, and before the shock. The response is now an ***avoidance response***, because it enables the animal to avoid the shock entirely. Avoidance learning is extremely important in everyday life. We do not just learn to escape unpleasant or life-threatening situations that we find ourselves in, but we learn to avoid those situations in the future. Having capsized in rough seas and escaped, we learn to head for shore as soon as storm clouds appear, before the sea is rough.

According to the *two-process theory*, a widely accepted theory initially proposed by O. Hobart Mowrer (1947), avoidance learning involves a combination of classical and operant conditioning. The first phase is classical conditioning, in which the individual learns to respond with fear or some other negative emotion to cues asso-

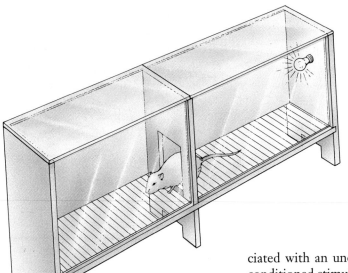

**Figure 5.11 *Two-compartment escape and avoidance apparatus***
*Electric shocks can be provided to the floor of either compartment. If no signal precedes the shock, the animal learns to escape the shock by running from one compartment to the other when the shock comes on. If a signal (such as a light) precedes the shock in every trial, the animal learns to avoid the shock by running from one compartment to the other as soon as the signal comes on.*

ciated with an unconditional unpleasant event. Thus, the signal light becomes a conditioned stimulus for fear in the example depicted in Figure 5.11 because of its prior pairing with shock, an unconditioned stimulus for fear. Subsequently, the rat learns the operant response of running away from the light, because that response is reinforced by reduction in fear.

In a classic experiment supporting Mowrer's theory, Neal Miller (1948) showed that avoidance learning can occur under conditions in which the classical and operant conditioning stages are clearly separated. Miller used a two-compartment apparatus similar to that shown in Figure 5.11, except that one compartment was painted black and the other white. In the first stage of training (classical conditioning), each rat received electric shocks in the white compartment, with the door closed so that escape was not possible. The purpose was to condition the animals to manifest a fear response to the cues inside the white compartment. Then, in the second stage (operant conditioning), the rats were again placed in the white compartment. Now, no shocks were given, but the apparatus was set up so that by turning a wheel the rats could open the door separating the two compartments and, in that way, leave the white compartment and enter the black one. The only reinforcer in this case was the opportunity to get away from the white compartment and thereby reduce the fear response that it elicited. Miller found that the animals readily learned this response.

Mowrer's two-process theory can be applied to almost any example of fear-related learning. Think back to Watson and Rayner's experiment with little Albert. Through classical conditioning, in which the sight of a rat was paired with a loud sound (an unconditioned stimulus for fear), Albert acquired a conditioned fear response to the sight of the rat. Later, when the rat was presented again, Albert not only showed a reflexive fear response, but also crawled away from the rat, which would be interpreted in Mowrer's theory as an operant response reinforced by the reduction in fear.

■ *How punishment differs from reinforcement, and how the two kinds of punishment parallel the two kinds of reinforcement*

**Punishment** In Skinner's terminology, ***punishment*** is the opposite of reinforcement. It is the process through which the consequence of a response *decreases* the likelihood that that response will recur. As with reinforcement, punishment can be positive or negative. In *positive punishment*, the *arrival* of a stimulus, such as electric shock for a rat or scolding for a person, decreases the likelihood that the response will occur again. In *negative punishment*, the *removal* of a stimulus, such as taking food away from a hungry rat or money away from a person, decreases the likelihood that the response will occur again. Both types of punishment can be distinguished from extinction, which, you recall, is the decline in a previously reinforced response when it no longer produces any effect.

To picture the distinction between positive and negative punishment, and to see their relation to positive and negative reinforcement, look at Figure 5.12. The terms are easy to remember if you recall that the positive and negative always refer to the arrival or removal of a stimulus, and that reinforcement and punishment always refer to the direction of change in the likelihood that the response will recur.

**Figure 5.12** *Two types of reinforcement and two types of punishment*

*Reinforcement (whether positive or negative) increases the response rate, and punishment (whether positive or negative) decreases the response rate. Positive and negative refer to whether the reinforcing stimulus appears or disappears when the response is made.*

| | | Response rate | |
|---|---|---|---|
| | | Increases | Decreases |
| Response causes stimulus to be | **Presented** | Positive reinforcement (Lever press → Food pellet) | Positive punishment (Lever press → Shock) |
| | **Removed** | Negative reinforcement (Lever press → Turns off shock) | Negative punishment (Lever press → Removes food) |

The figure also makes it clear that the same stimuli that can serve as positive reinforcers when presented can serve as negative punishers when removed; and the same stimuli that can serve as positive punishers when presented can serve as negative reinforcers when removed. It is easy to think of the former as "desired" stimuli and the latter as "undesired," but Skinner urged us to avoid such mentalistic terms. He argued that the only way we can tell whether a stimulus is "desired" or "undesired" is by observing the manner in which it serves as a reinforcer or punisher to the individual in question, so the mentalistic terms add nothing to our understanding.

Punishment is interesting to many people because of its common use to control children's behavior. Skinner (1953) and many other psychologists (see Newsom & others, 1983) have argued that caregivers would do better to make more deliberate use of positive reinforcement and less use of punishment.

Suppose a mother and father want to teach their child good table manners. They might try to do this by punishing the child's bad manners, but problems that could arise from this procedure include the following: (a) Punishment produces negative emotional reactions, such as anger or fear, which can lead to other unwanted behaviors at the dinner table or elsewhere. (b) Through classical conditioning, any stimuli present during the punishment—such as the parents themselves—may become conditioned stimuli for the negative emotions. This would be an unwanted side effect; parents certainly don't want their child to react negatively to them or to meals. (c) Through observational learning (to be described in the next section), the parents' use of punishment may inadvertently teach the child to use punishment to control others' behavior, which may have undesirable consequences. (d) Punishment may lead the child to refrain from those specific ill-mannered actions that have been punished, but it does not build good-mannered actions. The child may not show any obvious bad manners, but he or she may not behave very pleasantly, either. Thus, according to Skinner and others, a better method might be to positively reinforce the child—maybe with praise and privileges—for showing increasingly good manners at each meal, until the bad manners are simply pushed out by the good.

Nevertheless, in some cases punishment can be an effective, perhaps necessary means to get rid of a particularly harmful form of behavior. As an example, Thomas Sajwaj and others (1974) have described a therapeutic use of punishment that enabled a baby girl to overcome a form of behavior called *rumination*, which involves compulsively moving the tongue to the back of the mouth to induce vomiting after swallowing any fluid or food. In other children, such behavior has some-

■ *Some practical problems with the use of punishment to improve a child's behavior*

**Stove safety**

*In situations where a child's well-being is at stake, punishment may be unavoidable. In such cases, a calm demeanor and a clear explanation of the rationale for the punishment will increase its effectiveness.*

times led to death from dehydration or malnutrition. To get the baby girl to stop doing this, the therapists squirted tart lemon juice into her mouth (a mild, immediate punishment) each time she began to show the muscle movements that preceded vomiting. After several weeks of such treatment, she stopped producing those muscle movements and no longer vomited, and she eventually regained her health.

# The Cognitive Perspective: Acquiring Information About the World

The behavioral perspective, in the pure forms advocated by Watson and Skinner, avoids any reference to unseen events in the mind or brain; it seeks to describe learning and other behavioral processes in terms of observable stimuli and responses. In the foregoing, I have tried to be true to that perspective (though I may have slipped a bit on occasion). But many of Watson's and Skinner's contemporaries, who called themselves *liberalized behaviorists* or *S-O-R theorists*, argued that it is useful to describe behavior in terms of unseen mental constructs that are inferred from observed behavior. They pointed out that many constructs in science—such as gravity and the idea of force—are not directly observable, but are inferred from the way things behave and are useful in predicting future behavior. The *O* in *S-O-R* stands for *organism*, or, more precisely, for some sort of interpretation of the stimulus that occurs inside the organism:

$$\text{stimulus} \rightarrow \text{interpretation} \rightarrow \text{response}$$

Today the approach advocated by those liberalized behaviorists is called **cognitive psychology** (see Chapter 1). Cognitive psychology is the attempt to understand the behavior of humans and other animals in terms of hypothetical mental entities that are inferred from observable behavior. You will read much more about cognitive psychology in later chapters (especially Chapters 9–14). The present discussion of this perspective is limited to its application toward understanding basic learning processes. First, we will look again at classical and operant conditioning, but now from a cognitive perspective. Then we will turn to studies of place learning (learning where things are) and observational learning (learning by watching others), which are not easily described in stimulus-response terms and almost require cognitive explanations.

## Cognitive Views of Conditioning

According to cognitive theorists, many phenomena associated with classical and operant conditioning make sense only if we assume that a good deal of mental activity occurs before a response is made. That mental activity includes such events as interpretation of stimuli that are present, anticipation of stimuli that are about to occur, and activation of knowledge about how to make certain stimuli appear. In the following paragraphs, we will look at some of the evidence that favors this way of thinking about conditioning.

**The Cognitive Nature of Stimuli**    As you have seen, a fundamental concept in the behaviorist's view of learning is that of the *stimulus*. But what is a stimulus? Cognitive theorists argue that, to understand the role of stimuli in conditioning, one must consider not just their physical aspects but also their *meaning* to the individual being conditioned. To predict how a given individual will respond to a stimulus, you must know how that individual will interpret that stimulus, and to know that is to know something about the structure of the subject's mind—a cognitive problem.

**Evidence from people and pigeons that conditioned and discriminative stimuli are interpreted before they are responded to**

**Figure 5.13 Tree pictures similar to those used to study concepts in pigeons**

*Pigeons that had been trained to peck whenever a slide contained a tree, or part of a tree, pecked when they saw slides such as these and refrained from pecking when they saw similar slides that did not contain a tree.*

Consider, for example, an experiment on classical conditioning conducted many years ago by Gregory Razran (1939), who used college students as subjects, a squirt of lemon juice into the mouth as the unconditioned stimulus, and printed words as conditioned stimuli. By pairing each word with a squirt of lemon juice, Razran conditioned students to salivate to the words *style, urn, freeze,* and *surf.* He then tested them to see if the conditioned response would generalize to other words that had never been paired with lemon juice. Of most interest, he found that the students salivated more to the words *fashion, vase, chill,* and *wave* than to the words *stile, earn, frieze,* and *serf!* That is, the conditioned response generalized more to words that were similar to the original conditioned stimuli in meaning than to those that were similar in physical appearance or sound. Thus, the true conditioned stimuli were not the physical sights or sounds of the words, but the subjects' interpretation of them.

An even more dramatic demonstration of stimulus generalization based on word meaning was conducted by a Soviet psychologist (Volkova, 1953). First, a Russian schoolboy was conditioned to salivate to the Russian word for *good* and, by discrimination training, not to salivate to the word for *bad.* When the discrimination was well established, the boy was found to salivate copiously to such statements as *The Soviet Army was victorious,* and not at all to statements such as *The pupil was fresh to the teacher.* In other words, those statements that the boy, from past experience and training, interpreted as good elicited salivation, and those that he interpreted as bad did not. A child who had a different set of conceptions of what is good or bad might not have salivated to the statement about the Soviet Army, or might have salivated to the statement about the fresh student.

But we do not need to look to humans or language to make the point that stimuli are interpreted before they are responded to. Consider an experiment conducted by Richard Herrnstein (1979, 1984), who operantly conditioned pigeons to peck a key for grain, using slides depicting natural scenes as discriminative stimuli. Herrnstein divided the slides into two categories—those that had at least one tree or portion of a tree somewhere in the scene and those that didn't (see Figure 5.13). The pigeons received grain for pecking the key when a "tree" slide was shown and nothing when a "nontree" slide was shown. In the first phase, 80 slides were presented each day, 40 of which contained trees and 40 of which didn't. By the end of 5 days of such training—that is, after 5 presentations of all 80 slides—all of the birds were successfully discriminating between the two categories of slides, pecking when the slide contained a tree and not pecking otherwise.

Now, the question is, what did the pigeons learn in Herrnstein's experiment? Did they learn each slide as a separate stimulus, unrelated to the other slides, or did they learn a rule for categorizing the slides? Such a rule might be stated by a person in the following terms: "Respond whenever a slide includes a tree or part of a tree, and don't respond otherwise." To determine whether the pigeons had acquired such a rule, Herrnstein tested them with new slides and found that they immediately pecked at a much higher rate with new slides containing trees than with those that did not contain trees. In fact, they were as accurate with slides that they had never seen before as they were with slides that had been used during training. Thus, the pigeons apparently based their responses on a ***concept*** of trees. A concept, as the term is used here, can be defined as a rule for categorizing stimuli into groups. The pigeons' tree concept, in this case, must have guided their decision to peck or not peck.

How might one describe the pigeons' tree concept? That is an interesting question, not easily answered. It is *not* the case, for example, that the pigeons simply learned to peck at slides containing a patch of green. Many of the nontree slides had green grass, and some of the tree slides were of fall or winter scenes in New England, where the trees had red and yellow leaves or none at all. In some cases only a small portion of a tree was apparent, or the tree was way back in the background. Thus, the way in which the pigeons distinguished tree from nontree slides cannot be stated in *simple* stimulus terms, though ultimately it must be based on the birds' analysis of the stimulus material. The point here is that, even for pigeons and certainly for humans, to predict how an individual will respond to a stimulus one must know something about the concepts or rules by which the individual classifies stimuli into different groups. To really understand how a pigeon learns about its world, one must be able to answer not just "How does it respond to conditioned stimuli?" but also such questions as "How does it tell trees from nontrees?"

**Classical Conditioning Interpreted as Stimulus-Stimulus Association**   What does an animal learn in classical conditioning? Watson (1924) and other early behaviorists believed that the animal learns a new reflex, that is, a new stimulus-response connection. From this view, Pavlov's conditioned dog salivated to the bell because of a direct, learned connection between the bell and salivation. This *stimulus-response (S-R) theory* of classical conditioning is diagrammed in the top part of Figure 5.14. It is interesting to note that Pavlov (1927/1960) himself had a different theory. Consistent with the earlier associationist philosophers, Pavlov believed that the animal does not learn a direct stimulus-response connection, but rather learns a connection between two stimuli, the conditioned stimulus and the unconditioned stimulus. Because the bell and food have been paired in past experience, a physiological bond is formed between their representations in the brain, such that the sound of the bell now activates the part of the brain that was formerly activated by food, and that in turn elicits salivation. Using mental rather than physiological terms, we could say that the dog salivates to the bell because the bell sound makes the dog think of food (bell → thought of food → salivation). This *stimulus-stimulus (S-S) theory* of classical conditioning is illustrated in the bottom part of Figure 5.14.

Many experiments have been conducted over the years to test the *S-R* and *S-S* theories of classical conditioning, and the weight of evidence favors the latter (see Domjan & Burkhard, 1986). As an illustration, consider the following experiment

**Figure 5.14** *Comparison of* S-R *and* S-S *theories of classical conditioning*

*According to the* S-R *theory, conditioning produces a direct bond between the conditioned stimulus (CS) and the response (R). According to the* S-S *theory, on the other hand, conditioning produces a bond between the CS and the unconditioned stimulus (UCS). Support for the* S-S *theory comes from experiments showing that weakening the unconditioned reflex (through habituation), after conditioning, also weakens the conditioned reflex.*

**S-R** *Theory of Classical Conditioning*

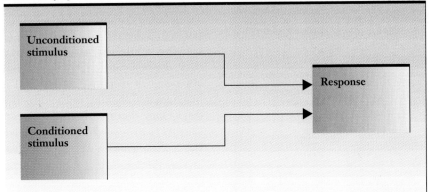

**S-S** *Theory of Classical Conditioning*

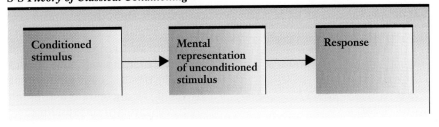

■ *How it is possible to test the*
**S-R** *and* **S-S** *theories of classical
conditioning, and how an experiment
involving habituation supported the
latter*

conducted by Robert Rescorla (1973), one of today's leading researchers on classical conditioning. Rescorla used rats as subjects, a loud sound that elicited freezing (a fear response in which the rats would stand motionless) as the unconditioned stimulus, and a signal light as the conditioned stimulus. By pairing the signal light with the loud sound, he conditioned the rats to freeze when the signal light came on. Now, the question was this: Did the rats freeze in response to the signal light because of a direct, learned connection between light and freezing, in accordance with the *S-R* theory (light → freezing)? Or did they freeze in response to the signal light because of a learned connection between the light and the loud sound, in accordance with the *S-S* theory (light → mental representation of loud sound → freezing)?

To answer this question, Rescorla habituated the response to the loud sound in half of the rats. That is, he presented the loud sound many times until they no longer froze in response to it. Then he again tested the rats with the signal light. Would the rats that no longer froze in response to the loud sound continue to freeze in response to the light? Notice that the *S-R* and *S-S* theories make different predictions. According to the *S-R* theory, they should continue to freeze in response to the light, because learning entailed a direct connection between light and freezing. But according to the *S-S* theory, they should not freeze in response to the light, because learning entailed a connection between the light and the loud sound. Since they no longer froze in response to the loud sound, they should no longer freeze in response to the light either. Rescorla's results supported the *S-S* theory. The habituated rats froze in response to the light much less than did the unhabituated rats.

■ *How differences between the
conditioned and unconditioned
response are explained by the
expectancy theory*

**Classical Conditioning Interpreted as Learned Expectancy and Prediction**   The *S-S* theory of classical conditioning, by its nature, is more cognitive than the *S-R* theory. It holds that the observed stimulus-response relation is mediated by an inner, unseen representation of the original unconditioned stimulus. Cognitive theorists argue that the inner representation may be best understood as an *expectation* of the unconditioned stimulus. From this view, Pavlov's dog learned to *expect* food when it heard the bell.

The *expectancy theory* helps make sense of the observation that a conditioned response is often quite different from the unconditioned response. Consider again a dog being conditioned to a bell that precedes food. In response to food, the dog not only salivates, but also chews (if it is solid food) and swallows. Salivation becomes conditioned to the bell, but chewing and swallowing usually do not. Moreover, the bell comes to elicit not only salivation, but also responses that do not usually occur in response to the food-in-mouth stimulus—such as tail wagging, food begging, and looking in the direction of the usual source of food. According to the expectancy theory, all of these responses, including salivation, occur *not* because they were previously elicited by the unconditioned stimulus, but because they are the dog's responses to the *expectation* of food:

bell → expectation of food → tail wagging, food begging, salivation, etc.

Rescorla (1988) has summed up his cognitive view of classical conditioning with the following words: "[Classical] conditioning is not a stupid process by which the organism willy-nilly forms associations between any two stimuli that happen to co-occur. Rather, the organism is best seen as an information seeker using logical and perceptual relations among events, along with its own preconceptions, to form a sophisticated representation of its world." Support for Rescorla's view comes from research showing that classical conditioning occurs only, or at least mainly, when the new stimulus provides information that the animal can use to *predict* the arrival of the unconditioned stimulus, and thus prepare itself for that event. Here are three classes of such findings:

**In rapt contemplation**

*There is nothing inscrutable about this
young tiger cat. Cognitive theorists explain
her conditioned response on the basis of
expectancy: The sound of the can being
attached to the opener permits her to predict
the arrival of food.*

■ *Three ways to pair stimuli without getting classical conditioning, and how these support the idea that conditioning comes from the animal's active attempt to predict important events in its environment*

1. *Ineffectiveness of simultaneous and backward conditioning*  Classical conditioning is most effective if the conditioned stimulus slightly precedes the unconditioned stimulus, and commonly doesn't occur at all if the conditioned stimulus comes either simultaneously with or just after the unconditioned stimulus (see Domjan & Burkhard, 1986). This observation makes sense if the animal is actively seeking predictive information: A stimulus that does not precede the unconditioned stimulus is useless as a predictor, and thus is ignored by the animal.

2. *Ineffectiveness of conditioning when the animal already has a good predictor*  A number of experiments have shown that if one conditioned stimulus reliably precedes an unconditioned stimulus, the animal will not become conditioned to another conditioned stimulus that occurs simultaneously with the first one. For example, Leon Kamin (1969) showed that if a sound reliably precedes the onset of a shock, and on later trials a light is added such that both the light and sound come on simultaneously just before the shock, a rat does *not* develop a conditioned response to the light. A cognitive interpretation of this is that the rat has already solved the problem of predicting shock (by listening for the sound) and thus has no reason to learn a new way of predicting it. Only if the sound were to become an unreliable predictor would the animal look for another predictor, and then it would be ripe to learn to respond to the light.

3. *Ineffectiveness of conditioning to stimuli that have been presented often without the unconditioned stimulus*  Not all stimuli that are present just prior to an unconditioned stimulus become conditioned stimuli. Conditioning is much more likely to occur to a *new* stimulus than to one that was previously presented many times in the absence of the unconditioned stimulus (Rescorla & Wagner, 1972; Rescorla, 1988). Thus, conditioning is not a function just of the pairing of the conditioned and unconditioned stimulus, but also of the reliability by which the first predicts the other. It is as if the animal learns to ignore stimuli that in the past have been unreliable predictors, and to attend only to reliable predictors and novel stimuli that may turn out to be reliable predictors.

**Operant Conditioning Interpreted as Means-End Knowledge**   Historically, theories about operant conditioning have paralleled those about classical conditioning. According to the *S-R* theory, held by many behaviorists (for example, Guthrie, 1952), operant conditioning entails the strengthening of a bond between the reinforced response and stimuli that are present before the response is made (the discriminative stimuli). Thus, for a rat learning to press a lever in a Skinner box, the learned connections can be described as:

stimuli inside Skinner box → lever press

Or, if a more specific discriminative stimulus, such as a tone, is used, it can be described as:

tone → lever press

According to this view, the reinforcer, which follows the response, enters into learning only in that it stamps in the connection between the antecedent stimuli and the response. Other theorists, however, emphasized the importance of the learned *S-S* relationship between the discriminative stimuli and the reinforcer (Mowrer, 1960; Spence, 1956), or the learned *R-S* relationship between the response and the reinforcing stimulus (Mackintosh & Dickinson, 1979).

Cognitive theorists typically hold that *all* of the above relationships are learned and are integrated into the animal's knowledge in a way that allows the animal to obtain reinforcers in an efficient way (see Rescorla, 1987; Dickinson, 1989). In one early description of operant conditioning in cognitive terms, Edward Tolman

■ *How the view that operant conditioning involves means-end knowledge can be experimentally tested, and the results of one such test*

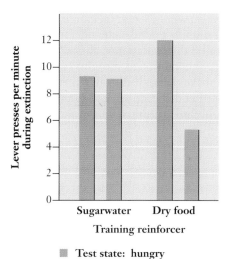

**Figure 5.15** *Evidence that rats learn what reinforcer a response produces*

*All of the rats were trained to press the lever when hungry. Some had received drops of sugarwater (sucrose) as their training reinforcer, and others had received dry food pellets. When tested under extinction conditions (no reinforcer given), the animals that had been trained with sugarwater made about the same number of responses whether they were thirsty or hungry. In contrast, those that had been trained with food pellets made fewer responses when thirsty than when hungry. These results suggest that the rats had a conception of the reinforcer that the response had previously produced, and knew whether it would satisfy both thirst and hunger or only hunger. (Adapted from Dickinson & Dawson, 1987.)*

▪ *How reward contrast effects are explained from a cognitive perspective, and evidence that they depend on brain structures not present in fish and reptiles*

(1959) discussed it as the learning of *means-end relationships*. A means-end relationship is the animal's knowledge or belief that in a particular situation a particular response will have a particular effect. Thus, according to Tolman, if a rat is reinforced for pressing a lever when a tone is on, the rat acquires the knowledge that pressing the lever when the tone is on will produce food. In the future, the occurrence of the tone does not automatically produce a lever press response as the *S-R* theory would hold, but rather activates the animal's knowledge that a lever press response will bring food. The animal can then use that knowledge, depending upon its current disposition toward the food. Thus, in Tolman's view, the rat's behavior is best understood as follows:

tone → knowledge that lever press will now bring food → decision to press lever or not depending on whether food is desired

This cognitive view of operant conditioning is supported by evidence that animals that have learned an operant response will vary their responses in ways that are predictable on the premise that they have a mental conception of the means-end relationship (Dickinson, 1989; Rescorla, 1987). For example, in one experiment, hungry rats were trained to press a lever either for sugarwater or dry food pellets as a reinforcer (Dickinson & Dawson, 1987). Later they were tested under extinction conditions (no reinforcer given), after having been deprived of either food or water. The interesting result was that when tested in the new drive state (thirst), those that had previously been reinforced with sugarwater (a substance that would satisfy thirst as well as hunger) pressed at a high rate, and those that had previously been reinforced with dry food pellets (which would not satisfy thirst) pressed at a low rate (see Figure 5.15). The most direct way to explain this difference is to assume that the rats had acquired knowledge of the kind of reinforcer they would receive for pressing the lever and were able to use that knowledge to decide if it would satisfy their current drive state. As in all cognitive theories, there is no supposition that the rats are conscious of such knowledge and decision. It is enough to say that they behave *as if* the knowledge is activated and a decision is made.

**Reward Contrast Effects in Operant Conditioning**    Many other phenomena associated with operant conditioning are consistent with the idea that subjects learn to expect a certain reinforcer or reward for making a certain response. Good examples are *reward contrast effects*, which involve shifts in the response rate when the size of the reward changes. As an illustration, imagine that two groups of rats are trained to press a lever with different reward sizes. If the rats in one group receive a large reward (five bits of food) for each response, and those in another group receive a small reward (one bit of food), then those receiving the large reward typically respond at a somewhat faster rate than those receiving the small reward. So far, this is consistent with *S-R* theory. Presumably, the *S-R* connection built by a large reward is stronger than that built by a small reward, resulting in a higher response rate. But now suppose the rats receiving the large reward are suddenly shifted to the small reward. According to the *S-R* model, they should continue, at least for a while, to respond at a higher rate than the other rats, because of the stronger *S-R* connection built during the first phase of the experiment. But what actually happens is the opposite. Rats shifted from a large to small reward show a sharp drop in their response rate, to a lower rate than is shown by those that had been in the small-reward condition all along. This illustrates the **negative contrast effect**. Conversely, rats shifted from a small to large reward show an increase in their response rate, to a higher rate than that of rats that had been in the large-reward condition all along. This illustrates the **positive contrast effect**.

It is easy to see an analogy between these effects in animals and effects of pay shifts in people. If you have been getting $1 per page for typing term papers, you

**Vacation reading**

*This young man's absorption in his book suggests that he deeply enjoys reading. Research on overjustification predicts that if he were rewarded for this activity, he might begin to see it as work.*

■ *Why the overjustification effect is called the overjustification effect*

will probably be delighted to discover that your pay is now $2 per page, and you may type with renewed vigor; but if you have been getting $4 per page, that same discovery (that you are now only getting $2) may lead you to quit. Clearly, our experience of reward size is relative to what we are used to receiving. From a cognitive perspective, these contrast effects—in rats as in humans—are explained by assuming that the animal (a) has learned to expect a certain reward, and (b) is able to compare the present reward to the expected one. If the comparison is favorable, the animal increases its response rate, and if unfavorable it decreases its rate. The animal is constantly out to do better, and if a particular response leads to less reinforcement than it did before, it may pay to spend less time at it and look around for other activities.

Reward contrast effects have been observed in many species of mammals and in pigeons (see Flaherty, 1982, 1985). On the other hand, according to a series of experiments conducted by M. E. Bitterman (1975), such effects do not occur in fish and reptiles. For example, Bitterman found that fish that had been trained to push a key for a large reward (forty worms per response) continued to respond at a faster rate when switched to a small reward (four worms per response), compared to fish that were initially trained with a small reward. In certain other ways, too, Bitterman found that fish and reptiles behave in ways more in line with *S-R* predictions than do mammals and birds. Perhaps, in the evolution of mammals and birds from their reptilelike ancestors, changes occurred in the brain that permitted more complex cognitive processes, including the ability to compare present rewards with past ones, and these were added on to a basic *S-R* learning mechanism. This view finds support in an experiment showing that rats treated with amobarbital, a drug that reduces neural activity in some of the higher parts of the brain, failed, like Bitterman's fish and reptiles, to show the negative contrast effect, while undrugged rats clearly showed it (Rosen & others, 1967).

**The Overjustification Effect: When Rewards Lead to Reduced Performance**  In humans, rewards can affect one's likelihood of engaging in a particular form of behavior by changing the person's understanding of the meaning of that behavior. Consider an experiment conducted with nursery school children as subjects (Lepper & Greene, 1978). Children in one group were rewarded with an attractive "Good Player" certificate and praise for drawing with felt-tipped pens. This had the immediate effect of leading them to spend more time at this activity than did children in the other group (who were not rewarded). Later, however, when certificates were no longer given for this activity, the previously rewarded children showed a sharp drop in their use of the pens—to a level well below that of children in the unrewarded group.

Other researchers have found that the drop in performance due to a period of reward occurs only for tasks that are initially seen as ends in themselves, that is, as the kinds of activities that one engages in for one's own pleasure, rather than for some other end (Newman & Layton, 1984). This decline is called the *overjustification effect*, because the reward presumably provides an unneeded justification for engaging in the behavior. The result, according to the usual cognitive interpretation, is that the person comes to see the task as work (the kind of thing that one does for external rewards) rather than play (the kind of thing one does for its own sake). The overjustification effect has important consequences for schooling. For example, rewarding children for reading might cause them to think of reading as work rather than fun, which could decrease the amount of reading they do on their own. The broader point here is that one must take into account the cognitive consequences of rewards in predicting the long-term effects they will have on people's behavior. The law of effect, or principle of operant conditioning, applies to human behavior only when elaborated on with qualifications and exceptions.

### Place Learning

Much of the early impetus for a more cognitive view of learning came from research by Edward Tolman and his students, using rats in mazes. Behaviorists at Tolman's time (the 1920s–1940s) often interpreted maze learning in stimulus-response terms. They believed that the animal learns a sequence of responses—such as turn right, go forward, turn left—each signaled by stimuli that are present at the critical choice points in the maze. Tolman's research led him to reject that view. He proposed instead that animals that are allowed to explore either a maze or a more natural terrain do not learn a specific sequence of responses, but rather acquire a *cognitive map*—a mental representation of the spatial layout of the maze or terrain. He also proposed that they acquire that representation just from exploring, whether or not they find any rewards.

**Evidence That Animals Learn Cognitive Maps**    Tolman and his students showed that, when faced with a change in their starting place, or with blockades placed in their usual routes, rats behave *as if* they are able to consult a map and work out the best available route to the goal (Tolman, 1948). In one experiment, for example, Tolman and Honzik (1930a) used the maze depicted in Figure 5.16, which contains three possible routes from the start box to the goal box (and food). After sufficient training, rats showed a strong preference for Route 1 (the shortest), a weaker preference for Route 2 (the next shortest), and weakest for Route 3 (the longest). In the critical phase of the experiment, Route 1 was blocked in one of two points, as shown in Figure 5.16. If the block was at Point *A*, most rats would run down Route 1, reach the block, and then go back and take Route 2. But if the block was at Point *B*, most rats would run down Route 1, reach the block, and then go back and take Route 3, previously their least preferred route. By inspecting Figure 5.16 (which literally is a map), you can see that this is exactly what an intelligent rat with maplike knowledge of the maze would be expected to do in this situation. The block at Point *B* blocks both Routes 1 and 2, so now only Route 3 leads to the goal. According to Tolman, such behavior—occurring as it did the first time the rats were faced with the blockade—cannot be interpreted in terms of learned stimulus-response habits, but must be understood as insight based on maplike knowledge of the maze.

   More recently, researchers have studied place learning in rats by using a Morris water maze, a circular tank filled with water that has been made opaque (usually by adding powdered milk), so an animal can't see through it (Morris, 1981; Rudy & others, 1987). The maze includes a small, slightly submerged platform, located somewhere in the tank, that the animal can climb onto to keep its head and most of its body above water. During training, each rat is placed into the tank at a given starting place, and it must swim until it finds and climbs onto the platform. After several such training trials, the rats are tested from different starting places. The typical finding is that from any starting place most rats swim directly to the hidden platform. How do they know which way to swim? They can't see, smell, hear, or in any other way directly sense the platform from the starting place. Richard Morris (1981) and others argue that during their training the rats must learn the location of the platform relative to cues in the room in which the tank is located, and then they must use that maplike knowledge to swim toward the platform.

**Evidence That Place Learning Does Not Require Reward**    Do animals learn the spatial layout of their environment only when they receive some reward, such as food or escape from water, for finding a particular location, or do they learn it even without such rewards? To answer that question, Tolman and Honzik (1930b) tested three groups of rats in a complex maze under different reward conditions. Group 1 received one trial per day in the maze with no food or other reward in the

■ *How Tolman showed that rats use cognitive maps and that they learn such maps whether or not they are rewarded*

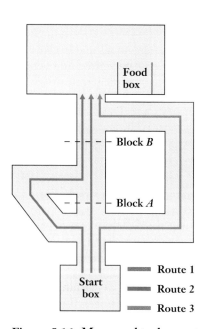

**Figure 5.16** *Maze used to demonstrate insightful use of cognitive maps*

*Rats well trained in this maze normally took Route 1, the most direct route to the food. If a block was placed at Point A, they would run back and take Route 2, the shortest unblocked route. If a block was placed at Point B, rather than A, they would run back and take Route 3, the only unblocked route. Since most rats made these adaptive responses on the first trial that the block appeared, Tolman and Honzik concluded that the rats had spatial knowledge (a cognitive map) of the maze, which they could use intelligently. (Adapted from Tolman & Honzik, 1930a.)*

**Figure 5.17  *Latent learning of a maze***
*Each rat received one trial per day in the maze, with or without a food reward in the goal box. The group that received its first reward on Day 11 performed as well on Day 12 (and thereafter) as the group that had received a reward every day. From this, Tolman and Honzik concluded that the rats had learned the spatial layout of the maze even without a reward and then were able to use that knowledge when a reward appeared. (From Tolman & Honzik, 1930b.)*

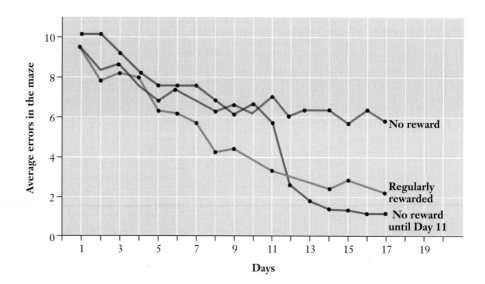

goal box. As expected, these rats showed very little improvement from day to day in the time it took them to reach the goal box (the goal box contained no "goal" for them). Group 2 received one trial per day with food in the goal box. As expected, they improved considerably from day to day. The interesting group was Group 3. These rats received one trial per day with no reward for 10 days, like Group 1, but beginning on the eleventh day they received one trial per day with a food reward, like Group 2. These rats improved dramatically between Days 11 and 12. On Day 11 they were no better than the other unrewarded group (Group 1), but on Day 12, after just one experience with the reward, they were as fast at reaching the goal box as the rats that had been rewarded all along (see Figure 5.17).

On the basis of this and other experiments, Tolman (1948) argued that rewards affect what animals *do* more than what they *learn*. Animals learn the location of distinctive places in their environment whether or not they have ever found rewards there, but they do not run directly to those places unless they have found rewards there. Tolman used the term ***latent learning*** to refer to learning that is not immediately demonstrated in the animal's behavior. In the experiment just described, the rats in Group 3 learned the maze in the first ten trials, but that learning remained *latent*, not manifested in their behavior, until the addition of a reward in the goal box gave them a reason to make use of their cognitive maps to run quickly to that location.

### Observational Learning

If you look at learning as it occurs in everyday human life, you cannot help but notice that people learn to a great extent by watching other people. Imagine what life would be like if such skills as driving a car or performing surgery were learned purely by trial and error! Fortunately, people learn such skills partly by observing closely and mimicking the behavior of those who have already mastered them. On a grander scale, learning by watching others seems to be a prerequisite for human culture. The skills and rituals acquired by each generation are passed on to the next not so much because the older generation deliberately trains the younger (though that is part of it), but more because each younger generation intently observes their elders—or at least some of their elders—to learn to behave as they do. Learning by watching others is called ***observational learning***, and the person watched in such learning is called the *model*.

While observational learning is especially apparent in humans, it can be seen to some degree in other creatures as well. It is well known that apes "ape" one another, and even dogs and cats can learn new responses by observing others of their kind perform them. In one experiment, for example, kittens learned very rapidly to press a lever for food if allowed to watch their mother perform the response, less rapidly if only allowed to watch a strange cat perform it, and they completely failed to learn if trial and error (with no shaping) was their only teacher (Chesler, 1969).

**Observational Learning of Both Specific Skills and General Behavioral Styles**
Albert Bandura (1977)—the psychologist who, over the years, has most vigorously studied observational learning in humans—has emphasized that people observe others to learn not just specific motor skills (such as driving a car or performing surgery), but also more general modes or styles of behaving. When you enter a new situation, you probably look around to see what others are doing before doing much yourself. When you do begin to act, you may mimic rather precisely some of the actions you have observed—such as the activity needed to get a cup of coffee from the new-fangled coffee maker in the room. But beyond that (unless you are a clown) you probably don't imitate many of the exact actions of others. Rather, you adopt a general style of behavior that fits in with what seems to be acceptable in the setting—such as being serious and intellectual.

Bandura has demonstrated both of these two functions of observational learning—that of acquiring specific actions, and that of learning general styles of behavior—in experiments with kindergarten children. In one experiment, for example, one group of children observed an adult behaving very aggressively toward a large inflated Bobo doll (Bandura, 1969). The aggressive actions included specific verbal insults and physical acts, such as banging the doll with a mallet, hurling it down, kicking it, and bombarding it with balls. A second group watched the adult model behave in a gentle manner toward the doll; and a third group was not exposed to any model. Later, when each child was allowed to play in the room with a variety of toys, including the Bobo doll, those in the first group behaved more aggressively, and those in the second group behaved more gently, than those in the third group. The children in the first group not only mimicked many of the same aggressive actions that they had observed in the adult model, but also improvised with many new aggressive actions of their own, directed toward other toys as well as toward the Bobo doll. They had learned not only specific ways of being aggressive, but also the more general message that an appropriate way to play in this particular playroom is to act aggressively.

**Bandura's Cognitive Theory of Observational Learning**    Bandura's theory of observational learning is an explicitly cognitive one. Just as Tolman posited that rats actively explore mazes to develop cognitive maps, Bandura (1977, 1986) proposes that people actively observe the behavior of other people to gain knowledge about the kinds of things that people do. Bandura theorizes that, to understand observational learning, one must take into account four interacting mental processes. These are: (1) *attention*—the learner must perceive the model and, for one reason or another, find the model to be interesting; (2) *memory*—the learner must encode the information obtained from observing the model in a form that can be used at a later time; (3) *motor control*—the learner must be able to use this coded information to guide his or her own actions; and (4) *motivation*—the learner must have some reason or inducement to perform the modeled actions. These processes must be involved in *any* complex form of behavior that depends on information gained from the environment, not just observational learning. The four components of the theory—attention, memory, motor control, and motivation—are discussed extensively in later chapters.

■ *What children learned when they saw an adult beating up a Bobo doll*

"The Far Side" cartoon is reprinted by permission of Chronicle Features, San Francisco.

■ *How Bandura's theory illustrates the idea that learning cannot be understood in isolation from other mental processes*

# The Ecological Perspective: Filling the Blanks in Species-Specific Behavior Patterns

The behavioral and cognitive approaches to learning both emphasize processes that are assumed to operate across a wide range of learning situations, and for that reason they are both considered to be part of a *general-process perspective*. Behaviorists have looked for general laws related to classical and operant conditioning, expressible in stimulus-response terms, that apply to all sorts of learning situations. And cognitivists have tried to identify general mental constructs, such as expectancies, that likewise apply to all sorts of learning situations. The alternative to the general process perspective is sometimes called the *specific-process perspective*, though it is more often called the **ecological perspective** (Johnston & Pietrewicz, 1985).

According to the ecological perspective, learning must be understood in relation to the natural environment, or ecology, in which the species evolved. Through natural selection, animals acquired instinctive species-specific behavior patterns (discussed in Chapter 4) that help them survive and reproduce in their natural environment. The mechanisms that promote such behaviors evolved in such a way that they are not rigid, but can modify themselves in response to specific aspects of the animal's experience. Thus, the abilities of animals to find food, avoid predators, find mates, raise their young, and do whatever else they must to survive genetically depend on inborn behavioral tendencies coupled with inborn means to modify or refine those tendencies. The latter, taken together, make up the collection of different mechanisms called *learning*. Each learning mechanism evolved to meet a different survival-related purpose, and to understand how the mechanism works we must think about it in relation to that purpose.

In Chapter 4 the white-crowned sparrow's ability to learn its parents' song and the indigo bunting's ability to learn the night sky were cited as examples of specific learning mechanisms designed to supplement specific instinctual tendencies. In Chapter 12 the idea that human language is acquired through a unique, specialized learning ability will be discussed. Now we will look in some detail at the learning of food aversions and preferences, and then, more briefly, at a few examples of other specialized learning mechanisms.

### Learning What to Eat

For some animals, learning what to eat is not a problem. Koalas, for instance, eat only the leaves of eucalyptus trees. Through natural selection, they have evolved a food-identifying mechanism that tells them that eucalyptus leaves are food and everything else is not. That simplifies their problem of food selection, but if eucalyptuses were to vanish so would the koalas. Other animals are more flexible in their diets. Most flexible of all are omnivorous creatures, such as rats and humans, which treat almost all organic matter as potential food and must *learn* what is safe to eat. Since eating is essential to survival, it is not surprising that omnivorous animals have, through natural selection, acquired special mechanisms for learning what to eat.

**Food-Avoidance Learning**   If rats become ill after eating some novel-tasting food, they will subsequently avoid that food (Garcia & others, 1972). In experiments demonstrating this, researchers induce illness by adding a toxic substance to the food or by administering a drug or high dose of x-rays after the food is eaten. Similarly, people who by chance get sick after eating some unusual food often develop a long-term aversion to the food (Bernstein & Borson, 1986; Logue, 1988). For years as a child, I hated the taste and smell of a particular breakfast cereal,

■ *How the ecological perspective differs from the behavioral and cognitive perspectives*

because one of the first times I ate it happened to precede, by a few hours, my developing a bad case of a stomach flu. I knew, intellectually, that the cereal wasn't the cause of my illness, but that didn't help. The learning mechanism kicked in automatically and made me detest that cereal.

Is it possible to describe such cases of food-avoidance learning in the terminology of either classical or operant conditioning? It is, but only if we are willing to stretch the concepts considerably and acknowledge that conditioning works quite differently in this situation compared to others. In classical conditioning terms, we might say that the x-ray treatment (or whatever else is used to induce illness) serves as an unconditioned stimulus for a feeling of revulsion or illness, and that the smell and taste of the food become conditioned stimuli for that feeling. But in more typical cases of classical conditioning, such as those studied by Pavlov, conditioning occurs only when the unconditioned stimulus follows immediately (within a few seconds) after the conditioned stimulus. Yet food avoidance has been demonstrated even when the x-rays were given as much as 24 hours after the animal had eaten the food (Etscorn & Stephens, 1973). Food-avoidance learning might also be described in operant terms, with illness serving as a punisher for the act of consuming a particular food. But again, in more traditional cases of punishment training the punisher (such as an electric shock or loud noise) is effective only if it immediately follows the response.

Another special characteristic of food-avoidance learning is that it is selective for the smell and taste of a food but not for other qualities, such as its visual appearance. Rats that have become ill after eating a particular food subsequently avoid food that smells and tastes like that food, even if it looks different; but they do not avoid food that looks like that food if it smells and tastes different (Garcia & others, 1968).

The distinguishing characteristics of food-avoidance learning make excellent sense from a vantagepoint emphasizing the function of such learning in the natural environment. In general, poisons and bad foods do not make an individual ill immediately, but only after many minutes or hours. Moreover, it is the chemical quality of a food, detectable in its smell and taste, not the visual quality, that affects health. For example, a food that has begun to rot and makes an animal sick may look just like one that has not begun to rot, but its smell and taste are quite different. Thus, to be effective, a learning mechanism for food avoidance must tolerate long delays and be tuned especially to those sensory qualities that correspond with the food's chemistry.

**Food-Preference Learning**   The other side of the coin from avoiding bad foods is that of specifically choosing foods that satisfy a nutritional requirement. In a series of experiments on food-preference learning, researchers deprived rats of thiamine (one of the B vitamins, essential for health) for a period of time, and then offered them a choice of foods, only one of which contained thiamine (Rozin & Kalat, 1971; Overmann, 1976). Each food had a different flavor, and thiamine—which itself has no flavor—was added to a different food for different rats. The result was that, within a few days of experience with the foods, most rats strongly preferred the thiamine-containing food.

How did the rats "figure out" which food contained the thiamine? Close inspection of their eating patterns suggests an answer (Rozin & Kalat, 1971). When first presented with the choices, a rat usually did not eat all of them, but rather ate just one or two. Then, typically after several hours, the rat would switch to a different food or two and just eat that. Such behavior—eating just one or two foods at a time—seems ideally suited for isolating particular foods that lead to an increase or decrease in health. If the rat sampled all of the foods at once, there would be no basis for knowing which had an effect on its health. Paul Rozin and James Kalat (1971; Kalat, 1985) have suggested that food-preference learning of this sort is

*Two characteristics of learned food avoidance that make it different from other examples of avoidance learning*

*How rats find vitamins, and how a baby cured himself of rickets*

actually a special case of food-avoidance learning. Since the animals are ill from lack of a vitamin to begin with, they continue to feel ill after eating any food that does *not* contain the vitamin, and hence develop an aversion to that food and try something different. Finally, they come to the food with the vitamin and after eating it do not feel as ill as before, so they stick with that food.

**A Food-Selection Experiment with Human Infants** In the 1920s, before food-selection experiments with rats had been performed, a pediatrician named Clara Davis performed a bold experiment on food selection with human infants—so bold, in fact, that it would probably not pass the ethics review board of a modern research institution (which helps explain why the experiment has never been repeated). The subjects were newly weaned baby boys whose mothers consented to their participation in the experiment, and the object was to determine whether the babies would feed themselves a nutritionally balanced diet if they could choose their own foods (Davis, 1928). For 6 months or longer, beginning at the age of 35 weeks, the babies lived in the children's ward of a hospital. At each meal a tray containing about a dozen different foods was placed before each infant. The choices were all natural foods, including cereals, fruits, ground meats, fish, eggs, and vegetables. Although only wholesome foods were included, no single food contained all of the needed nutrients. To remain healthy, the infants would have to select a variety of foods. One baby suffered from rickets (due to lack of vitamin D) at the beginning of the study, and a bowl of cod-liver oil (a substance high in vitamin D and generally held by children to taste terrible) was included among his choices. At first a nurse had to help the babies eat, but she was only allowed to feed a baby the food that he had chosen through reaching or pointing. Within a few weeks, all of the babies had learned to feed themselves, usually with their fingers, and the nurse's assistance was no longer needed.

The results of the experiment can be summarized as follows: The babies all developed clear food preferences, but the preferences varied from time to time such that over the long run each infant ate a nutritionally balanced diet. At any given meal an infant would usually eat just two or three foods in quantity and might stick to those for as long as a week or so, but then would switch to other foods and stick with them for a similar period. The baby with rickets, remarkable as it may seem, self-selected cod-liver oil until his rickets was cured, and then never touched the stuff after that.

All in all, the babies' behavior was rather similar to that of rats in food-selection experiments. It was as if they were following a logic that goes like this: Eat only a few foods at a given time; if you feel well later stick with those foods, but if you begin to feel less well switch. Of course, if the babies could talk, they would probably tell us a different logic, something like: "Last week I loved the applesauce, but this week it tastes awful and the mashed eggs are great." The assumption here, consistent with the rat studies, is that the loss of preference for one food, after several days of eating it, came from association of that food's taste and smell with a slight decline in health that began to occur due to the limited diet and was reversed when the infant switched to a new food.

(Perhaps you are wondering why many parents seem to have to struggle with their children to get them to eat a balanced diet. Here are two thoughts: First, if parents looked for balance over the long run rather than at every meal, there might be less struggle. Second, foods such as cupcakes and fudge bars were not available to the children in Davis's experiment. Very sweet foods might override the food-learning system, which, after all, evolved before such foods were invented.)

**Food Learning Through Observation** In humans, of course, cultural tradition plays an important role in food selection. It is not necessary for each generation to learn anew what is healthy and what is poisonous, because that can be passed on by

*Observational learning has its limits*
*Children acquire the food preferences of their culture through observing their elders, but sometimes it takes a while. This young boy may enjoy most of the dishes at this family celebration, but he holds his nose to the gefilte fish—a fish preparation that has a very fishy smell.*

word of mouth. Rats, too, are capable of a sort of cultural transmission with regard to food selection, though of course not by word of mouth. Newly weaned wild rats don't go out on their own to forage, but rather follow older rats in the colony around and eat what they eat, until their own food habits are well established (Galef, 1985). Through this means, they can avoid even tasting a food that older animals have already learned is poisonous (Galef & Clark, 1971). Young human children, between 1 and 4 years old, have also been found to be more willing to taste a new food if they see an adult eat it first (Harper & Sanders, 1975). Turning to yet another species, researchers have found that blackbirds avoid an otherwise attractive food if they have seen another blackbird get sick after eating it (Mason & Reidinger, 1982).

▓ *What natural selection has taught young omnivores*

**Summary of Rules for Learning What to Eat**    Suppose you were a wise teacher of young omnivorous animals and wanted to equip your charges with a few rules for food selection that could be applied in any environment, no matter what potential food materials were available. Two that you would probably come up with are: (1) When possible, eat what your elders eat. Such food is probably safe, as evidenced by the fact that your elders have most likely been eating it for some time and are still alive. (2) When you eat a new food, remember its taste and smell. If you don't feel sick within a few hours, continue choosing foods of that taste and smell, but if you do feel sick, avoid such foods.

Notice that these rules don't specify just what to eat, but rather specify *how to learn* what to eat. The first rule is a variety of observational learning, and the second is a particular kind of associative learning in which the stimuli to pay attention to are spelled out in a way that makes the learning most efficient. As you have just seen, rats in fact do behave in accordance with these rules, and young humans may also. Of course, we assume that these rules have been imparted not by a wise teacher of young omnivores, but by natural selection, which has shaped the brain to operate in accordance with the rules. Again, over evolution, animals have acquired instincts to learn about food in particular ways.

### Other Examples of Selective Learning Abilities

Food selection is by no means the only functional area in which special learning abilities have apparently come about through evolution. Here are some other well-studied examples.

**Innate Biases in Fear-Related Learning**   Earlier, this chapter discussed fear learning as containing elements of both classical and operant conditioning. Animals and people can learn, through classical conditioning, to fear a previously unfeared stimulus if it is paired with an unconditioned stimulus for fear; they can also learn, through operant conditioning, to make a response that is reinforced by termination of a fearful stimulus. There is reason to believe, however, that both of these aspects of fear learning are constrained in important ways by instinctual tendencies.

With regard to classical conditioning, some stimuli can apparently become conditioned fear stimuli much more easily than others. Remember the demonstration by Watson and Rayner, in which little Albert was conditioned to fear a white rat through pairing the rat with a loud noise? Several years later, Elsie Bregman (1934), a graduate student working with Thorndike, tried to repeat that demonstration with one important modification. Instead of using a rat as the conditioned stimulus, she used various inanimate objects, including wooden blocks and pieces of cloth. Despite numerous attempts, with fifteen different infants as subjects, she found no evidence of conditioning. What are we to make of this apparent discrepancy? One possibility, suggested by Martin Seligman (1971), is that people are biologically predisposed to classify certain kinds of objects—rats among them—as potentially dangerous, and to associate those objects, but not others, with fear-provoking events that they experience.

More recently, Arne Öhman (1986; Öhman & others, 1976) has performed experiments on classical conditioning of fear-related responses in adult humans, using pictures of various objects as conditioned stimuli and shock as the unconditioned stimulus. He has found that such responses are more easily conditioned, and much less easily extinguished, if the conditioned stimulus is a picture of a snake, spider, or angry human face than if it is a picture of a flower, house, or happy human face. This finding could be evidence of an instinctive tendency to treat certain kinds of events differently from others (which is Öhman's interpretation), or it could be the result of previously learned associations.

Turning now to operant conditioning, to escape fearful situations animals can learn certain responses much more easily than other responses. Rats can easily learn to stay motionless, or run from one place to another, or attack another rat or some other object, for the reinforcement of terminating a fearful stimulus, such as an electric shock. But they have great difficulty learning to press a lever for that reinforcement, even though they can easily learn to press a lever for food pellets or drops of water. On the basis of such evidence, Robert Bolles (1970, 1984) has argued that avoidance learning must be understood in relation to the animal's innate *defense reactions*, the animal's inborn ways of reacting to fearful stimuli. The particular defense reaction—freezing, fleeing, or fighting—produced in any given fearful situation depends on a variety of conditions, including past experience in that situation. Thus, according to Bolles, escape or avoidance learning in nature is usually a matter of discovering which innate defense reaction will be successful in a given situation, not a matter of associating just any response with a reduction in fear. Lever pressing is not an innate defense reaction, but is more akin to the kinds of behaviors that in natural situations might occur when searching for food.

**Imprinting in Precocial Birds**   Some of the earliest evidence for specialized learning abilities came from studies of young precocial birds. Precocial birds are those species—such as chickens, geese, and ducks—in which the young can walk

■ *A possible reason for Bregman's failure to replicate Watson and Rayner's results, and why rats have a hard time learning to press a lever to escape shock*

■ *How the young fowl's instinct to follow is supplemented by a bit of genetically guided learning*

When imprinting studies go awry . . .

almost as soon as they hatch. Because they can walk, they can easily get lost from their mother, and because of that it is important that evolution has provided them with an efficient means to recognize their mother and remain near her. In the nineteenth century, a naturalist named Douglas Spalding (1873/1954) observed that newly hatched chicks that saw Spalding rather than their mother move past their nest shortly after they hatched followed him as if he were their mother. They continued to follow him for weeks thereafter, and once attached in this way they would not switch to following the mother hen. Some 60 years later, Konrad Lorenz (1935) made essentially the same discovery with newly hatched goslings. He labeled the phenomenon *imprinting*, a term chosen to indicate the very sudden and apparently irreversible nature of the learning process involved.

One interesting feature of imprinting is the rather restricted **critical period** during which it can occur. Spalding (1873/1954) found that if chicks were prevented from seeing any moving object during their first 5 days after hatching, and then he walked past them, they did not follow him but rather showed "great terror" and ran away. In more detailed studies, Eckhard Hess (1958, 1972) found that the optimal time for imprinting mallard ducklings is within the first 18 hours after hatching, and that by 30 hours after hatching most ducklings cannot be imprinted at all.

Although early studies suggested that young birds could be imprinted on humans or other moving objects as easily as on their own mothers, later studies proved otherwise. Given a choice between a female of their species and some other object, young birds invariably choose to follow the female of their species. An important characteristic affecting this choice is the call made by the moving object. In one experiment, newly hatched birds were exposed to a moving replica of a female duck that emitted, through an internal speaker, the normal call of either a mother mallard duck or a mother chicken. The result was that mallard ducklings were much more likely to follow the replica if it produced the mallard call, and chicks were much more likely to follow if it produced the chicken call (Gottlieb, 1965). Once again, we see a specialized learning ability in which the effects of experience are guided and constrained by heredity.

◼ *How the ecological perspective helps make sense of an "error" that rats often make when first learning a maze*

**Place Learning Revisited**   Previously we looked at some of Tolman's research on place learning as support for a cognitive view of learning. Place learning provides many further examples of special learning abilities that are best understood in relation to the animal's natural ecology. Consider the behavior of a rat in a simple T-shaped maze. If a rat has, on one trial, found food in the right arm, what should the rat do on the next trial—turn right or turn left? A straightforward application of operant conditioning theory would have the rat turn right, because it was rewarded for that response on the previous trial. But if you think of this behavior in relation to normal foraging, turning right does *not* make the most sense. The rat has just cleaned out all the food hidden in the right compartment, and in nature food doesn't magically replenish itself in a given place within seconds or minutes after it has been removed. After removing food from one place, it makes sense for the rat to look anywhere other than that place to find more food. How do rats actually behave in such situations? In general, early in training, they behave in accordance with the ecological prediction, not the operant prediction. They tend to avoid the arm in which they have already been, whether or not they found food there, and choose the other arm (see Olton, 1979). Only after many trials in the maze do they learn to go always to the same arm if the reward is always in that arm.

Some research on maze learning has employed conditions more in keeping with natural foraging conditions. David Olton uses a radial maze in which each arm leads away from a center platform like the spokes on a wheel and food is hidden at the end of each arm. When the food is found and eaten in a particular arm it is not replaced, so efficient behavior in this case involves avoiding those arms in which food has already been found. Rats quickly learn to behave extremely efficiently in this task, rarely returning to an arm from which they have already taken food until all of the other arms have been explored, even when there are as many as seventeen arms to remember (Olton, 1979). Olton and his colleagues have shown that this efficient behavior is accomplished not by smelling or in some other way directly sensing the location of food, nor by a motor strategy such as taking one arm at a time in order, but by remembering the spatial location of each place that they have been, using visual cues, and avoiding that location.

In other species, even more dramatic evidence of specialized learning abilities has been discovered. As one example, Clark's nutcrackers (a species of bird inhabiting the southwest United States) bury food in literally thousands of different sites, to which they return during the winter when the food is needed (Shettleworth, 1983). Experiments have shown that their ability to find each site depends on their memory of visual landmarks, such as stones, near the site. A quite different example is the extraordinary ability of Pacific salmon to find their hatching place. Salmon that hatch in small streams in the northwest United States migrate into the Pacific Ocean, where they swim around for 5 years or more carrying with them a memory of the exact smell of the water in which they hatched. Then, when they are ready to spawn, they use their sense of smell to find their way hundreds of miles back to the same stream from which they had originally come (Hasler & Larsen, 1955).

While the cognitive perspective often emphasizes the general intelligence of an animal (its ability to bring sophisticated cognitive processes to bear on a learning problem), the ecological perspective reminds us that animals appear much more intelligent when faced with problems similar to those posed by their natural environment than when faced with other problems. The intelligence does not come from a general ability to reason things through, but from specialized learning abilities that have evolved over thousands of generations in the wild. This will be an interesting point to keep in mind when reading about human intelligence in Chapters 11 and 12. Might it be that we humans, too, have not one general intelligence, but various specialized intelligences that came about to solve different kinds of problems in the environment in which we evolved?

## Concluding Thoughts

You have read about learning from three different perspectives. What is a *perspective*? It is a point of view, a framework, a set of ground rules and assumptions, that the scientist brings to bear on the topic studied. It helps determine the kinds of questions that scientists ask, the kinds of evidence they regard as important, the kinds of experiments they conduct, and the vocabulary they use in talking about the phenomena studied. Perspectives are not right or wrong, but they may be more or less useful. As you review the chapter, think about how each boldface term and margin note is related to the larger perspective within which it falls. Here are some further thoughts about each perspective.

**1. The behavioral perspective** As we have seen, behaviorists such as Watson and Skinner began with the assumption that learning is best described in terms of stimuli and responses, without reference to inner events. That does not mean that they believed that nothing happens inside us when we learn. It simply means that they assumed that those inner processes are too obscure to study scientifically, by available means, and that lawful relations between stimuli and responses can be identified without worrying about the inner events that mediate them. Borrowing from Pavlov's lexicon related to classical conditioning, and adding a parallel set of terms for operant conditioning, the behaviorists brought to psychology a rich, objective vocabulary for talking about learning and many learning-related phenomena. That vocabulary is still very much a part of psychology. As you review the terms and concepts in the behavioral section, try to avoid the temptation to translate them into mental terms. Try to define each in terms of observable changes in stimulus-response relationships.

**2. The cognitive perspective**  This perspective grew out of the behavioral perspective by way of psychologists, like Tolman, who called themselves *S-O-R* behaviorists and began doing experiments to understand the *O*. These psychologists argued that you can go just so far without talking about inner processes. You can set out very general principles, but you can't predict how they will apply in a given situation. For example, you can set out the principle of stimulus generalization in classical conditioning, but you can't predict to what degree an individual will generalize from one stimulus to the next unless you understand something about the individual's mental concepts, which can lead the individual to perceive one stimulus as like another even if they aren't physically alike. Other cognitive constructs—such as expectancies, predictions, means-end relationships, and cognitive maps—can also be inferred from subjects' behavior and used to make better predictions about their future behavior. As you think about these constructs, try to imagine them not as conscious thoughts but as the kinds of rules for guiding behavior that one might program into a computer. That is how cognitive psychologists would like you to think of them.

**3. The ecological perspective**  This, of course, is the perspective that most closely unites the two chapters on adaptation—the previous one on evolution and the present one on learning. While behaviorism and cognitivism have roots in empiricist philosophy, which attempts to understand human behavior and the human mind in terms of general principles (such as the law of association by contiguity), the ecological perspective grew out of biology, which recognizes the diversity of life processes. The view that learning mechanisms are a product of natural selection implies that they should be especially designed to solve biologically important problems, related to survival and reproduction. Different animal species, whose ecological niches pose different problems, may have evolved different species-specific learning mechanisms to solve those problems. This idea seems most obvious when looking at nonhuman animals, less so when looking at humans. Increasingly, however, psychologists are looking for special learning mechanisms to characterize different aspects of human learning. Humans may have relatively separate learning mechanisms for such domains as language, spatial relations, motor skills, and emotionality, just as for food selection. The future, I think, will bring closer ties between the cognitive and ecological perspectives in all realms of psychology.

## Further Reading

**B. F. Skinner** (1978). *Reflections on behaviorism and society*. Englewood Cliffs, NJ: Prentice-Hall.

*Skinner—who wanted to be a novelist before he went into psychology—is always fun to read, and there is no better place to begin than with this collection of some of his essays. The titles include: "Human behavior and democracy," "Why I am not a cognitive psychologist," "The free and happy student," "The force of coincidence," and "Freedom and dignity revisited." You will find here Skinner's basic philosophy about psychology and his suggestions for using behavioral learning principles to improve society.*

**Harry I. Kalish** (1981). *From behavioral science to behavior modification.* New York: McGraw-Hill.

*This is a fine source for the student who wants to find out about practical applications of classical and operant conditioning principles. It includes chapters on the elimination of fears, operant methods in classrooms, operant methods in mental hospitals, self-control, and biofeedback training.*

**Charles F. Flaherty** (1985). *Animal learning and cognition.* New York: Knopf.

*This is a straightforward, clearly written overview of the main principles that have emerged from the long history of experimental research on animal learning. Most of the book is devoted to principles of classical and operant conditioning, but the last two chapters are concerned with cognitive processes and species-specific learning mechanisms.*

**Robert C. Bolles & Michael Beecher** (Eds.) (1988). *Evolution and learning.* Hillsdale, NJ: Erlbaum.

*This collection of chapters, each authored by different specialists, nicely shows how the traditions of behaviorism and ethology have merged in recent years and begun to provide rich detail about species-specific learning processes. The book begins with historical chapters about the relationship of learning theory to evolutionary theory, and then turns to contemporary research on learning in such biologically important domains as feeding, defending against predators, and sexual behavior.*

## Looking Ahead

The behavioral machinery that our genes produce and that is a product of natural selection, that can learn, and that is constantly refining its fit with its environment, is the flesh, blood, and nervous system of the human body, especially the nervous system. To that we turn.

# PART 3 PHYSIOLOGICAL MECHANISMS OF BEHAVIOR

THE NERVOUS SYSTEM

MECHANISMS OF
MOTIVATION, SLEEP, AND
EMOTION

SENSATION

*Behavior is a product of the body's machinery, especially the nervous system. The nervous system receives information about the internal and external environments, integrates that information, and controls the body's movements. This unit consists of three chapters. The first examines the overall structure of the nervous system and its principles of operation. The second is concerned with the neural and hormonal mechanisms underlying motivation, sleep, and emotion. The third deals with the neural processes that allow us to see, hear, and in other ways sense the world around us.*

# CHAPTER 6

Neurons: The Units of the
Nervous System

Functional Organization of
the Nervous System

Hormones, Drugs, and
Their Interactions with
Neurotransmission

# THE NERVOUS SYSTEM

A human brain is, I must admit, somewhat disappointing to look at. It is about the size and shape of a cantaloupe, but more gnarled in appearance. To the eye it seems quite dormant, even when viewed in a living person. Aristotle and many of the other ancient Greeks—who were among the first to try to figure out what the various parts of the body are for—were not very impressed by the brain. They noticed that the blood vessels leading into it are much larger than those entering other organs its size, which suggested to them that its main function might be to cool the blood. They were much more impressed by the heart, an obviously dynamic organ, and proposed that the heart and blood are the source of feelings, thoughts, and all else that we today call "psychological."

But not all of the ancients agreed with the heart theory of psychology. One who didn't was Galen, a physician of the second century A.D. Galen worked at the royal court in Rome, treating gladiators, among others, and perhaps he noticed that head injuries can create peculiar psychological disturbances in people. He also is known to have practiced his surgical skills on animals, and in one experiment he found that when he cut a particular structure (which we would now call a *nerve*) that ran from a pig's brain to its vocal cords, the pig no longer produced vocal sounds (Robinson & Uttal, 1983). Perhaps because of observations such as these, Galen maintained that the brain is the organ that thinks and feels, and that it controls behavior through a system of connections to the various other organs. Galen was right, of course, and that is why essentially every introductory psychology text ever written, from William James's (1890) classic on, has somewhere early within it a chapter about the nervous system.

This chapter begins with a discussion of neurons, the basic building blocks of the nervous system. It then turns to the larger structures of the nervous system, which are made up of neurons, and develops a broad theory about the way these structures work together to control the body's actions. Finally, the last section discusses how hormones and drugs influence behavior by interacting with the nervous system. Much of the basic information in this chapter will be used and expanded upon in chapters to follow.

## Neurons: The Units of the Nervous System

All of the seeming magic of the nervous system—its ability to provide the basis for our feelings, thoughts, and actions—is mediated at the cellular level by processes that are in themselves no more mysterious than any of the other processes of life. The basic units of the nervous system are **neurons**, or nerve cells. Neurons are cells that have become specialized for carrying information rapidly from one place to

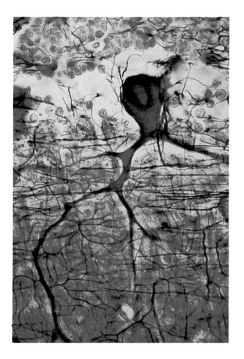

**A neuron**

*In this electron micrograph you can clearly see the cell body and the thin, branching dendrites.*

another and integrating information from various sources. The human nervous system contains billions of such cells, and their combined action provides the underlying physical basis of the human mind. Here we will look at the main functional types of neurons and at the chemical mechanisms through which they act.

**The Basic Structure and Function of Neurons** There is no such thing, really, as a typical neuron. Neurons come in hundreds of different shapes and sizes. But many of them do have certain parts in common, which you can see depicted for one kind of neuron in Figure 6.1. The ***cell body*** is the widest part and contains the cell nucleus and other basic machinery common to all cells. The ***dendrites*** are thin, tubelike extensions, which often branch repeatedly near the cell body, forming a bushlike structure. Their function is to increase the surface area of the cell, allowing for receipt of signals from many other neurons. The ***axon*** is another thin, tubelike extension, designed to carry the neuron's messages to other cells. Although microscopically thin, the axon is in some cases extraordinarily long. For example, you have axons extending all the way from your spine down to the muscles of your big toe—a distance of over a meter. The axon usually branches some distance away from the cell body, and each branch ends with a small swelling, the ***axon terminal***, which is designed to release a chemical substance onto another cell (either another neuron, a muscle cell, or a gland). The axons of some neurons are surrounded by a casing called the ***myelin sheath***, made of fatty cells that are wrapped tightly around the axon.

**Figure 6.1 *One type of neuron***

*The parts common to many neurons can be seen in this diagram of a motor neuron. The neuron receives input from other neurons on its dendrites and cell body, and sends its own output down the axon to the axon terminals. The myelin sheath is not part of the neuron; it is formed of separate cells that are wrapped around the axon.*

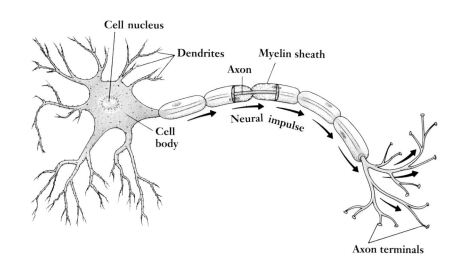

To understand more about the structure and function of individual neurons, we must visualize them in relation to the nervous system as a whole, as illustrated in Figure 6.2. The brain and spinal cord together make up the ***central nervous system***. Extensions from the central nervous system, called ***nerves***, make up the ***peripheral nervous system***. It is important to distinguish a nerve from a neuron. A nerve is a large bundle containing the axons of *many* neurons, which connect the central nervous system with the muscles, glands, and sensory organs. Within this general scheme, there are three main functional classes of neurons (see Figure 6.3):

1. ***Motor neurons*** These neurons carry messages from the central nervous system to the body's muscles and glands. The pioneering neurophysiologist Charles Sherrington referred to motor neurons as the *final common path*, be-

■ *How motor neurons, interneurons, and sensory neurons differ from each other in their structure, function, and prevalence*

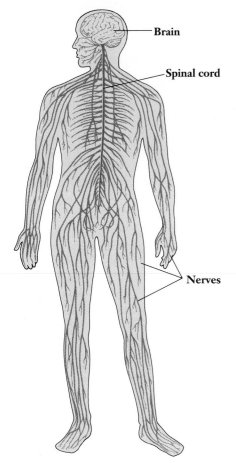

**Figure 6.2 *The human nervous system***

*The central nervous system consists of the brain and spinal cord, and the peripheral nervous system consists of the entire set of nerves, which are extensions from the brain and spinal cord that connect the central nervous system to the sensory organs, muscles, and glands.*

cause, in the end, all behavior occurs by way of their activity. The rest of the nervous system can be thought of as an elaborate device for determining what messages should be sent through the motor neurons. The cell body and dendrites of each motor neuron exist within the central nervous system, and the axon runs out, by way of a cranial or spinal nerve, with different branches terminating on different muscle cells.

2. ***Interneurons*** These exist entirely within the central nervous system and carry messages from one set of neurons to another. While there are "only" something like 2 or 3 million motor neurons in the human nervous system, there are something like *100 billion* interneurons (Nauta & Feirtag, 1986). Interneurons come in an enormous variety of shapes and sizes. Some are tiny, with hardly any branching extensions; others, at the other extreme, have dendrites and axons that run long distances within the central nervous system. As shown in Figure 6.3, some interneurons are similar in shape to motor neurons, except that the axon typically branches closer to the cell body, and each branch terminates on another neuron rather than on a muscle cell.

3. ***Sensory neurons*** These neurons carry information from the sensory organs to the central nervous system. The sensory neuron shown in Figure 6.3 carries information about touch. As you can see, its structure is quite different from that of the motor neuron or interneuron. Its cell body exists outside of the central nervous system, its axon extends out in both directions from the cell body, and its dendrites are branches at one end of the axon (the end in the skin) rather than direct protrusions from the cell body. In this cell, the tips of the dendrites are specialized to respond to physical stimulation of the skin, and the axon is designed to carry impulses, initiated by that stimulation, past the cell body, into the central nervous system. The total number of sensory neurons in the human is comparable to the number of motor neurons—a few million.

**Figure 6.3 *Three functional classes of neurons***

*This diagram shows the positions in the nervous system of the three functional classes of neurons. On the right is the central nervous system, and on the left are muscles and skin in the periphery.* Motor neurons *send messages from the central nervous system to muscles.* Sensory neurons *send messages into the central nervous system from sensory organs, such as the skin. And* interneurons, *located entirely within the central nervous system, carry messages between neurons.*

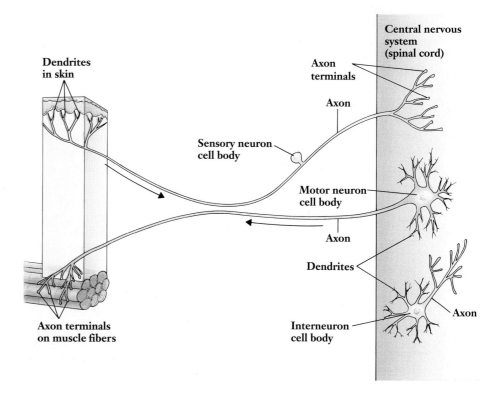

Although neurons are the main functional cells of the nervous system, they are not the most numerous cells in that system. The latter distinction belongs to *glial cells*, or *glia*, which in the central nervous system outnumber neurons by about 10 to 1 (Steward, 1989). Different varieties of glia serve different functions. Some form the myelin sheaths around neuron axons (as shown in Figure 6.1). Others form barriers around blood vessels in the brain, helping to protect the nerve cells in the brain from poisons that could otherwise reach them from the blood. Still others help clean up waste products in the nervous system or help provide nutrients to neurons.

**The Molecular Basis of the Neural Impulse, or Action Potential**   The messages that are sent along axons are called *action potentials*. They are all-or-nothing electrical bursts that begin at one end of the axon and move, in one direction only, to the other end. To say that they are "all or nothing" means that each action potential produced by a given neuron is the same strength as any other action potential produced by that neuron; there is no such thing as a partial action potential. In motor neurons and interneurons, action potentials begin at the place where the axon leaves the cell body, then move out, along each branch of the axon, to the axon's terminals. In sensory neurons, they begin at the dendritic ends of the axon, located in the skin or other sensory tissue, and travel along the axon to its terminals within the central nervous system.

To understand action potentials, you need to know something about the functioning of the *cell membrane*. The membrane is a porous "skin" that permits certain chemicals to flow in and out of the cell and blocks others. You can think of the neuron as a membrane-encased tube filled with a water solution, called *intracellular fluid*, and bathed on the outside by another water solution, called *extracellular fluid*. The flow of the chemicals dissolved in these fluids through the cell membrane provides the basis for action potentials.

Among the various chemicals dissolved in the intracellular and extracellular fluids are some that have electrical charges. These include: *soluble protein molecules*, which have negative charges and exist only in the intracellular fluid; *potassium ions* ($K^+$), which are more concentrated in the intracellular than the extracellular fluid; and *sodium ions* ($Na^+$) and *chloride ions* ($Cl^-$), which are more concentrated in the extracellular than the intracellular fluid. The balance of these charged particles is such that there are somewhat more negatively charged particles inside the cell than outside, resulting in an electrical charge across the membrane, with the inside typically about –70 millivolts (a millivolt is a thousandth of a volt) relative to the outside. This charge across the membrane of the inactive neuron is called the *resting potential*. Just as the charge between the negative and positive poles of a battery is the source of electrical energy in a flashlight, so the resting potential is the source of electrical energy that makes an action potential possible.

An action potential is initiated at one end of the axon and moves along the axon through a chain reaction that is sometimes likened to a row of dominoes falling after the first is tipped. As the action potential occurs at any given place on the axon (akin to the falling of one domino), millions of tiny pores in the axon's membrane open up, allowing some of the positively charged sodium ions in the extracellular fluid to pass into the intracellular fluid (see Figure 6.4). Two forces tend to drive sodium into the cell when the pores are open: (1) a concentration force, which stems simply from the fact that more sodium ions exist outside the cell than inside; and (2) an electrical force, which stems from the fact that like charges repel each other, so the positive electrical environment outside the cell pushes the positive sodium ions inward. As a result of these two forces, enough sodium moves inward to cause the electrical charge across the membrane to reverse itself, becoming momentarily *positive* inside relative to outside. This sudden shift constitutes the *depolarization phase* of the action potential.

*How an imbalance of dissolved particles provides a constant electrical charge (the resting potential) across the neuron's membrane, and how the opening of pores produces an action potential*

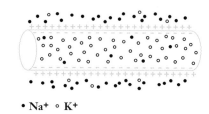

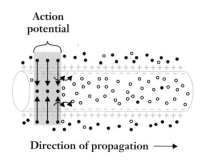

• Na⁺  ○ K⁺

Direction of propagation ⟶

**Figure 6.4** *The action potential*

*The axon can be visualized as a fluid-filled tube with the cell membrane as its skin. Among the materials dissolved in the fluids inside and outside the cell are sodium ions (Na⁺) and potassium ions (K⁺). The movement of these ions across the membrane is controlled by chemical gates that open or close pores in the membrane. There is always more Na⁺ outside the cell than inside and more K⁺ inside the cell than outside. When an action potential is triggered, pores that allow Na⁺ to pass through open, and enough Na⁺ enters the cell to make it temporarily positive inside (negative outside). That electrical change is the action potential. Once an action potential occurs at one end of the axon, it triggers sodium pores to open in the part of the axon just ahead. Thus, the action potential moves down the axon. In the wake of the action potential (not shown here), other pores open, which allow K⁺ to move out of the cell, restoring the original charge across the membrane (outside positive).*

■ *How the neuron keeps recharging itself*

■ *How an axon's conduction speed is related to its diameter and the presence or absence of a myelin sheath*

As soon as this shift occurs, the pores that permitted sodium to pass through close up, and pores that permit only potassium to pass through open (Stevens, 1979). Since potassium ions are more concentrated inside the cell than outside, and since they are repelled by the temporarily positive environment inside the cell, they are pushed outward. In this process, enough positively charged potassium ions move outward to reestablish the original resting potential. This constitutes the *repolarization phase* of the action potential. The entire action potential, from depolarization to repolarization, takes less than a millisecond (a thousandth of a second) to occur at any given point on the axon.

Knowing that some sodium moves into the cell, and some potassium moves out, each time an action potential occurs, you might wonder why a cell doesn't "wear down" after producing a certain number of action potentials. Actually, only a small amount of sodium and potassium moves with every action potential. (It takes only a tiny change in the balance of ions to reverse the electrical polarity.) But the question is still a good one, because neurons often produce several hundred action potentials per second, and eventually so much sodium could move in, and potassium out, that no more action potentials could occur. The answer is that the cell membrane continuously reestablishes the original balance of sodium and potassium with a *sodium-potassium pump*. The pump is actually a chemical mechanism, built into each part of the cell membrane, which moves sodium out and potassium in whenever the original balance is disrupted. One can think of it as the neuron's battery recharger. Like any recharger, it requires energy; to keep the pump going the neuron constantly needs food materials and oxygen, which come from the blood. (Remember the ancient Greeks' observation that the brain has particularly large blood vessels entering it? You now know a reason why.)

**The Movement of Action Potentials Down the Axon**    Action potentials are triggered at one end of the axon by any influences that tend to reduce the electrical charge across the membrane at that point. The axon's membrane is constructed in such a way that *depolarization*, or reduction in charge, to some critical value results in the sudden change in the membrane that produces an action potential. This critical value (for example, to –60 millivolts inside, compared with a resting potential of –70 millivolts inside), is referred to as the cell's *threshold*. Once an action potential occurs at one end of the axon, it depolarizes the area of the axon just ahead of where it is occurring, thus triggering the membrane's sodium pores to open up there. In this way the action potential keeps renewing itself and moves continuously down the axon. When an axon branches, the action potential follows each branch and thus reaches each of the possibly thousands of different axon terminals.

The speed at which an action potential moves down an axon is affected by the axon's diameter. Large-diameter axons present less resistance to the spread of electric currents and therefore conduct action potentials faster than thin ones. Another feature that helps speed up the rate of conduction in many axons is the presence of a myelin sheath, such as that depicted in Figure 6.1. The cells that form the sheath insulate the axon's membrane, so ions can move through only at spaces (nodes) between adjacent cells. Each action potential skips down the axon, from one node to the next, faster than it could move as a continuous wave. The thickest and most thoroughly myelinated axons in the nervous system can conduct action potentials at a velocity of about 100 meters per second (that translates into about 250 miles per hour). Thus, it takes about one-hundredth of a second for an action potential to run along such an axon from the central nervous system to a muscle about a meter away (a toe or finger muscle, for example). Very thin axons without a myelin sheath, on the other hand, may conduct at rates as slow as 1 or 2 meters per second. When you poke your finger with a pin, you feel the pressure of the pin before you feel the pain. That is partly because the sensory neurons for pressure are large and myelinated, and those for pain are thin and mostly unmyelinated.

■ *How neurotransmitters at excitatory and inhibitory synapses affect the rate of production of action potentials*

**Synaptic Transmission**   Neurons exert their influence on other neurons or muscle cells at *synapses* (see Figure 6.5). Although there are many kinds of synapses (including synapses of dendrites upon dendrites and axons upon axons), the classic, most well understood synapses are those that exist between an axon terminal and either a muscle cell or the dendrite or cell body of another neuron. The axon terminal is separated from the membrane of the cell that it influences by a very narrow gap, the *synaptic cleft*. The membrane of the axon terminal that abuts the cleft is the *presynaptic membrane*, and that of the other cell, on the other side of the cleft, is the *postsynaptic membrane*. Within the axon terminal are hundreds of tiny globe-like *vesicles*, each of which contains several thousand molecules of a chemical substance referred to as the **neurotransmitter**, or *transmitter* (Stevens, 1979).

**Figure 6.5** *Transmission across the synapse*

*When an action potential reaches an axon terminal, it causes some of the synaptic vesicles to spill their neurotransmitter molecules into the synaptic gap. Some of the molecules diffuse across the gap and bind at special binding sites on the membrane of the postsynaptic cell, where they act to modify the activity of the cell (a neuron or muscle cell).*

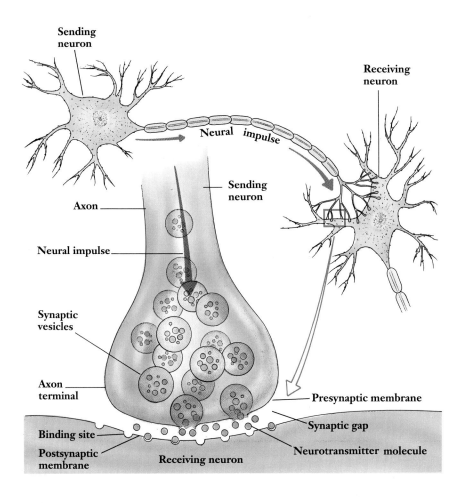

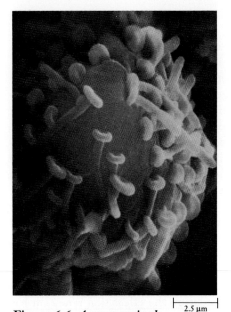

**Figure 6.6 *Axon terminals***

*In this electron micrograph you can see the terminals of many axons forming synapses on the cell body of a single neuron. Synaptic vesicles, filled with neurotransmitter molecules, reside within the button-like swelling of each axon terminal. In the central nervous system, the cell bodies and dendrites of motor neurons and some interneurons are blanketed with thousands of such terminals.*

When an action potential reaches the axon terminal, it causes some of the vesicles to spill their neurotransmitter molecules into the cleft. The molecules then diffuse across the cleft and become attached to specialized binding sites on the postsynaptic membrane, where they act to influence that cell. If the postsynaptic cell is a muscle cell, the transmitter triggers a process that causes the cell to contract. If the postsynaptic cell is a neuron, the transmitter triggers a process that alters the rate of action potentials produced by that neuron. At an *excitatory synapse* the transmitter increases the rate of action potentials, and at an *inhibitory synapse* the transmitter decreases the rate of action potentials.

To understand how excitatory and inhibitory synapses influence the postsynaptic neuron, it is important to realize that any given neuron receives input from many synapses. In fact, the cell body and dendrites of some neurons are completely blanketed with axon terminals from thousands of other neurons (see Figure 6.6). Some of these synapses are excitatory and some inhibitory, and at any given moment transmission is occurring at some but not all of them (see Figure 6.7). At each excitatory synapse, the transmitter opens up pores in the postsynaptic membrane, allowing sodium ions to enter the cell. At each inhibitory synapse, in contrast, the transmitter opens up different pores, allowing potassium ions to leave the cell.

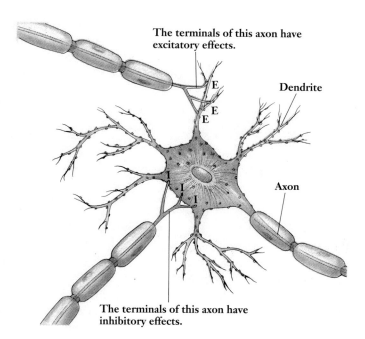

The terminals of this axon have excitatory effects.

Dendrite

Axon

The terminals of this axon have inhibitory effects.

**Figure 6.7 *Excitatory and inhibitory synapses***

*Neurons in the central nervous system receive many synapses from other neurons, some excitatory and some inhibitory. All synapses from any single neuron are either excitatory or inhibitory, as shown here.*

Thus, activity at an excitatory synapse increases the number of positive charges inside the cell body, and activity at an inhibitory synapse decreases that number. The more positive charges there are inside the cell body, the lower will be the electrical charge across the cell body's membrane. If the charge is reduced below the threshold level, action potentials will be triggered at a steady rate at the junction between the cell body and the axon (and they will move down the axon). The further the charge is below the threshold, the faster will be the rate at which action potentials are triggered. In this way, transmitters at excitatory synapses increase the rate at which the neuron sends action potentials, and those at inhibitory synapses decrease the rate.

The transmission processes just described are what happen at *fast synapses*. They are called "fast" because the electrical change induced by the transmitter occurs almost instantaneously and disappears within a few milliseconds. More recently, other kinds of synapses have been discovered, where transmitters can produce more prolonged excitatory or inhibitory effects. At these *slow synapses* the transmitter initiates biochemical processes that can increase or decrease the activity of the postsynaptic neuron for minutes or even hours (Bloom, 1981). In general, as you might guess, fast synapses are important for rapid neural processes, such as those involved in analyzing incoming stimulus information or producing muscular movements; and slow synapses are important for more sustained processes, such as sleepiness or changes in mood.

**A Neuron's Message Lies in Its Frequency of Action Potentials**   Although each action potential produced by a given neuron is an all-or-nothing event, identical to any other action potential produced by that neuron, the effect that a neuron has upon other cells is *not* all or nothing. The important information coming through an axon at any given time resides in the *frequency* at which action potentials follow one another down the axon. This can vary from zero on up to several hundred per second. Each action potential releases more transmitter molecules from the axon terminal, which have cumulative effects on the postsynaptic neuron or muscle cell.

As we have seen, the frequency of action potentials produced by a motor neuron or interneuron at any given time is a function of the balance of activity at excitatory and inhibitory synapses at that time. But other cellular processes can also affect the rate of action potentials produced by a neuron. Some neurons in the central nervous system, called **rhythm generators**, undergo a continuous, repeating cycle of change in electrical charge controlled by chemical processes built into the neuron itself (Llinás, 1988). The rate of action potentials produced by these neurons varies in a rhythmic pattern even in the absence of external influences. Rhythm generators are believed to help govern certain rhythmic behavioral processes, such as breathing (to take a rapid-cycle example) or the 24-hour sleep-wake cycle (to take a slow-cycle example). Although rhythm generators have their own intrinsic rhythms, they can also be influenced in either transient or sustained fashion by synaptic input from other neurons.

Thus far we have been discussing the controls over neural activity in motor neurons and interneurons. What about sensory neurons? Action potentials are initiated at the dendritic ends of these neurons by the particular physical stimulus (touch, sound, light, or tasty or odorous molecules) that the sensory neuron is designed to pick up. In some cases this process is quite direct, and in others it involves intervening steps (discussed further in Chapter 8). In every sensory system, the more intense the stimulus, the faster is the frequency of action potentials carried by individual neurons into the central nervous system.

*How the rate of action potentials is controlled in rhythm generators and sensory neurons*

## Functional Organization of the Nervous System

The amazing abilities of the nervous system reside not in the individual neuron, but in the organization of the billions of neurons that make up the nervous system as a whole. The following paragraphs and accompanying figures are designed to paint a picture of that organization. We will begin with the peripheral nervous system (cranial and spinal nerves), and then we will turn to the central nervous system (spinal cord and brain), working upward from the more primitive lower parts to the more recently evolved higher parts. As you read about each part, pay particular attention to its main functions in the control of behavior and try to think about it in relation to other structures already described.

## The Peripheral Nervous System

As mentioned earlier, the peripheral nervous system consists of the entire set of *nerves*. A nerve, once again, is a bundle of axons of neurons existing anywhere outside of the central nervous system. Nerves connect the central nervous system with sensory organs and with muscles and glands. Thus, they provide the vehicle through which the central nervous system receives sensory information and affects the body.

**Cranial and Spinal Nerves**   *Cranial nerves* come directly from the brain, and *spinal nerves* come directly from the spinal cord. Like most other structures in the body, nerves exist in pairs; there is a right and left member in each pair. In humans there are twelve pairs of cranial nerves and thirty-one pairs of spinal nerves. With their various branches, these nerves form an enormous network, extending to all portions of the body (look back at Figure 6.2).

Some pairs of cranial nerves are highly specialized. Three pairs are purely sensory—one pair conveys input just from the nose, another just from the eyes, and another just from the ears. Five other pairs are purely motor—three pairs are involved exclusively in controlling eye movements, another controls tongue movements, and another controls the neck muscles that move the head. The remaining cranial nerves and all of the spinal nerves, however, contain axons of both sensory and motor neurons. The spinal nerves convey motor output to muscles and glands below the neck, and they convey sensory input from below the neck for the set of senses collectively referred to as **somatosensation**. *Soma* means body, and somatosensation is the set of senses that derive from the whole body—such as from the skin, muscles, and tendons—as opposed to those that come from the special sensory organs of the head.

■ *How the autonomic and skeletal motor systems differ from each other*

**The Autonomic Compared with the Skeletal Motor System**   The structures that motor neurons operate can be divided into two broad classes. One class is the *skeletal muscles*, the muscles attached to bones, which produce externally observable movements of the body when contracted. The other class includes the *visceral muscles* and *glands*. Visceral muscles include such internal muscular structures as the heart, arteries, and gastrointestinal tract; glands include such structures as salivary glands and sweat glands. Neurons that operate skeletal muscles make up the *skeletal* portion of the peripheral motor system, and those that operate visceral muscles and glands make up the *autonomic* portion.

The skeletal and autonomic motor systems differ anatomically. As you saw in Figure 6.3, skeletal motor neurons have cell bodies in the central nervous system and send axons all the way out to the muscle cells that they operate, with no intervening synapses. In the autonomic system, motor connections are not as direct. Autonomic motor neurons with cell bodies in the central nervous system send their axons not directly to a muscle or gland, but rather to a *ganglion* (a group of neural cell bodies that exists outside of the central nervous system), where they form synapses with a second set of neurons. The second set then send their axons to the muscle or gland.

An important functional difference between the skeletal and autonomic systems is that the autonomic *modulates* (modifies) rather than initiates activity in the muscles that it acts upon. Whereas skeletal muscles are completely inactive in the absence of neural input, visceral muscles have built-in, non-neural mechanisms for generating activity. The heart continues to beat, and the muscular walls of such structures as the intestines and arteries continue to contract in response to local influences, even if all the nerves to these organs are destroyed. Significantly, most visceral muscles and glands receive two sets of neurons, which produce opposite effects and derive from two distinct divisions of the autonomic system—the sympathetic and parasympathetic (see Figure 6.8).

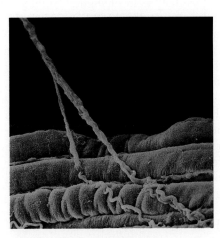

**The axon of a motor neuron**
*This electron micrograph shows an axon and three skeletal muscle fibers.*

**Figure 6.8** *The autonomic nervous system*

*The autonomic nervous system modulates the activity of visceral muscles and glands. Its sympathetic and parasympathetic divisions commonly have opposite effects on any given organ. As a rule, the sympathetic division promotes bodily arousal and the parasympathetic division promotes relaxation, digestion, and bodily restoration.*

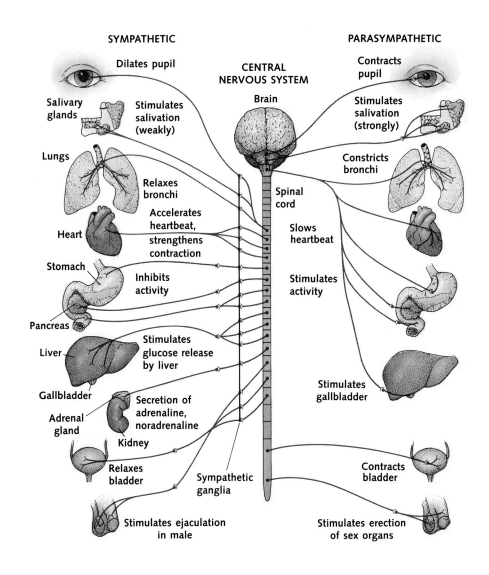

SYMPATHETIC

PARASYMPATHETIC

Dilates pupil

CENTRAL NERVOUS SYSTEM

Contracts pupil

Brain

Salivary glands

Stimulates salivation (weakly)

Stimulates salivation (strongly)

Lungs

Constricts bronchi

Relaxes bronchi

Spinal cord

Accelerates heartbeat, strengthens contraction

Heart

Slows heartbeat

Stomach

Inhibits activity

Stimulates activity

Pancreas

Liver

Stimulates glucose release by liver

Gallbladder

Stimulates gallbladder

Adrenal gland

Secretion of adrenaline, noradrenaline

Kidney

Relaxes bladder

Sympathetic ganglia

Contracts bladder

Stimulates ejaculation in male

Stimulates erection of sex organs

**How the sympathetic and parasympathetic portions of the autonomic system differ from each other**

The **sympathetic** division mediates many of the body's immediate responses to stressful stimulation, preparing the body for possible "fight or flight." Among its effects are (a) increased heart rate and blood pressure, (b) the release of energy molecules (sugars and fats) from storage deposits to permit high energy expenditure, (c) increased blood flow to the skeletal muscles, and (d) inhibition of digestive processes (which helps explain why a heated argument at the dinner table can lead to a stomachache). Conversely, the **parasympathetic** division serves regenerative, growth-promoting, and energy-conserving functions. Its effects are generally the opposites of those just listed for the sympathetic division. If you are relaxed as you are reading this book, your parasympathetic activity probably predominates over your sympathetic, so your heart is beating at a slow, normal rate and your digestion is working fine. On the other hand, if you are engaged in last-minute cramming for an important midterm exam, your sympathetic system may be going full blast, and perhaps you can feel its consequences in your gut and pounding heart. The sympathetic response is not always adaptive in today's world, where stressful stimuli often call for a response quite different from fight or flight. Some nonadaptive consequences of too much sympathetic arousal are discussed in Chapter 7. (For a summary of the subdivisions of the nervous system, see Figure 6.9.)

**Figure 6.9** *Divisions of the nervous system*

*The nervous system as a whole can be divided into the central and peripheral portions, and the peripheral portion can be further divided as shown.*

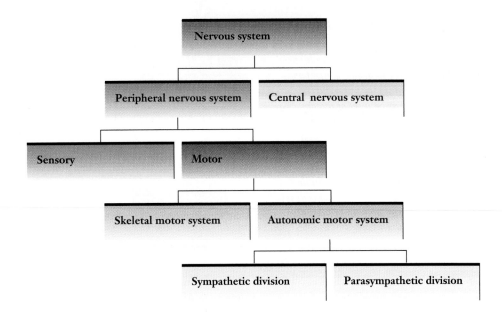

■ *How the presence of tracts and nuclei makes brain science possible*

### Functional Approach to the Central Nervous System

The human central nervous system has been called the most complex living structure in the known universe (Bloom & Lazerson, 1988), though that might reflect a human-centered bias (the central nervous systems of whales and dolphins are bigger than ours and may be equally complex). Our central nervous system contains billions of neurons and trillions of synaptic connections, most of which are in the brain. It would be hopeless to try to work out its complete wiring the way we might with a machine, such as a radio or even a computer. Fortunately, though, for those who wish to work out parts of it, there are certain patterns to the trillions of connections. Axons do not run willy-nilly; they usually run in bundles connecting one cluster of cell bodies with another. A bundle of axons coursing together in the central nervous system is called a ***tract*** (a tract in the central nervous system is analogous to a nerve in the peripheral system). A cluster of cell bodies in the central nervous system is called a ***nucleus*** (not to be confused with the cell nucleus within each cell). The myelin sheaths around axons cause tracts to appear relatively white, so tracts are referred to as *white matter*. Nuclei, which appear relatively darker, are referred to as *gray matter*. In general, neurons whose cell bodies occupy the same nucleus, and whose axons run along the same tract, have similar functions. Moreover, groups of nuclei that exist in the same area of the brain or spinal cord often have functions that are closely related to one another. Because of this we can talk about the functions of various relatively large anatomical structures within the central nervous system.

The following sections discuss the general functions of the largest subdivisions of the central nervous system—moving from the spinal cord up to the anatomically highest part of the brain, the cerebral cortex. The focus will be on the human central nervous system, but the same basic parts, serving the same basic functions, exist also in other mammals, such as rats and cats. In fact, as you will see, much of what we have learned about the human central nervous system comes from studies of other mammals.

### The Spinal Cord and Reflex Mechanisms

The spinal cord serves as a conduit between the spinal nerves and the brain. Within the spinal cord are *ascending tracts*, which carry somatosensory information

176

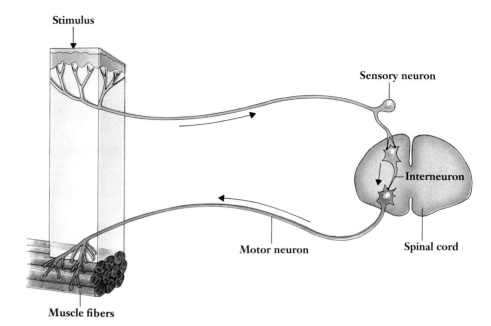

**Figure 6.10** *Neural connections for a simple spinal reflex*

The simplest spinal reflexes involve input from a set of sensory neurons, which form synapses on a set of spinal interneurons, which form synapses on a set of motor neurons, which form synapses on muscle cells. The flexion and crossed-extension reflexes described in the text are more complex than this. The interneurons organizing those reflexes have multiple branches, which activate motor neurons to flexor muscles in one limb and to extensor muscles in the opposite limb.

■ *Adaptive functions of the flexion and crossed-extension reflexes, and how the same neural systems that produce these reflexes are used in walking*

brought in by spinal nerves up to the brain, and *descending tracts*, which carry motor-control information down from the brain to be carried out by spinal nerves to muscles. If a person has an accident that completely severs the spinal cord at some point, the person will be completely paralyzed, and without sensation, in those parts of the body that are innervated by spinal nerves that come from below the place of injury. As you can see by looking back at Figure 6.2, the closer the place of injury is to the neck or head, the greater is the number of spinal nerves cut off from the brain, and the greater, therefore, will be the extent of paralysis and insensitivity. Thus, if the spinal cord is completely cut through in the upper part of the neck, the paralysis and insensitivity will include the arms, trunk, and legs; but if the cut is farther down, it may include only the legs.

In addition to serving as a conduit between the spinal nerves and the brain, the spinal cord exerts some control over behavior independently of the brain; it contains the neural organization for a number of important reflexes. These are typically studied in animals whose spinal cords have been surgically separated from the brain. (One might question the ethics of animal experimentation of this sort, but, in its defense, it has produced valuable information for helping people who have injured spinal cords.) After the cut is made, the animal—now referred to as a *spinal animal*—cannot maintain a standing position and, of course, is not capable of brain-directed movement of muscles below the neck. But certain reflexes, collectively called **spinal reflexes**, can nevertheless be elicited in parts of its body below the neck. All such reflexes involve a set of sensory neurons synapsing within the spinal cord upon a set of interneurons, which, in turn, synapse upon a set of motor neurons (see Figure 6.10).

If the paw of a spinal cat (cats are most commonly used) is poked with a pin, the animal does *not* hiss or show facial signs of pain as a normal cat would, because the stimulus input cannot reach the pain and vocalization centers of the brain. The animal presumably cannot feel sensations from below the neck, because feeling is mediated by the brain. Nevertheless, the animal's paw quickly withdraws from the pin. All of the joints of the stimulated limb flex simultaneously, causing the limb to fold in toward the body, a movement called the **flexion reflex**. At the same time, the joints of the corresponding limb on the other side of the body extend, a movement called the **crossed-extension reflex**. (*Flexion* refers to the bending of a limb at a joint, and *extension* refers to the straightening of a limb.)

The advantage of the *flexion reflex* is obvious: It quickly and automatically removes the limb from potentially damaging stimuli. Notice that this occurs in the spinal animal even though pain is not felt, and it occurs in the normal animal before pain messages are processed by the brain. To understand the advantage of the *crossed-extension reflex*, imagine what would happen to a normal, standing animal that suddenly flexed a foreleg without simultaneously extending and stiffening the other foreleg. The animal would fall forward, because the other foreleg would not be prepared to support the additional weight. Thus, the crossed-extension reflex enables the animal to retain a standing position when one leg is flexed.

Most interesting, for our present purpose, is evidence that the same interneurons in the spinal cord that organize the flexion and crossed-extension reflexes are also involved in the control of walking (Easton, 1972). Walking, of course, consists of a repeated cycle of movements in which first one leg extends while the other flexes and then the reverse occurs. Thus, each half-cycle of walking involves the same basic movement pattern as the flexion and crossed-extension reflex just described. The continuous alternating output needed to sustain walking is believed to be produced by rhythm generators in the spinal cord, which themselves are turned on or off, or modulated in frequency, by neurons descending from the brain (Ito, 1986). Thus, we have here an example of *hierarchical control*, in which a higher structure exerts its effects by operating on one or more lower structures. The brain controls walking by activating rhythm generators in the spinal cord, which in turn act on the same set of interneurons in the spinal cord that are involved in the flexion and crossed-extension reflexes.

### Subcortical Structures of the Brain

The term *subcortical* refers to all parts of the brain that lie under the cerebral cortex. Let us work our way up through these structures, beginning with those most directly attached to the spinal cord.

**The Brainstem and Thalamus**   As the spinal cord enters the head it enlarges and becomes the *brainstem*. The parts of the brainstem, beginning closest to the spinal cord and going upward (and toward the front of the head), are the *medulla*, *pons*, and *midbrain* (see Figure 6.11). The brainstem is functionally and anatomically quite similar to the spinal cord, though it is more elaborate. Just as the spinal cord is the site of entry of spinal nerves, the brainstem is the site of entry of most (ten of twelve pairs) of the cranial nerves. Just as the spinal cord contains ascending (sensory) and descending (motor) tracts connecting nerves to higher parts of the central nervous system, so does the brainstem. And finally, just as the spinal cord is capable of a certain amount of behavioral control independently of higher parts, so is the brainstem.

■ *Similarities between the brainstem and the spinal cord*

**Figure 6.11** *The brainstem and thalamus*

*This figure makes it clear why the medulla, pons, and midbrain are collectively called the* brainstem. *They form a stem-like continuation from the spinal cord, to which other brain structures are attached. Also shown here is the thalamus, attached most directly at the head of the brainstem.*

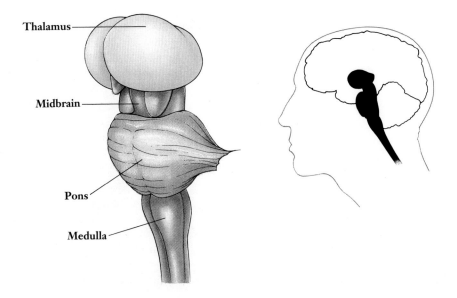

The medulla and pons organize many reflexes that are more complex than spinal reflexes, including *postural reflexes*, which help one maintain balance while standing or moving. In addition, the midbrain contains neural centers that organize basic movement patterns. For example, the neurons that act on rhythm generators in the spinal cord to control walking are located in the midbrain (Ito, 1986). An animal (usually a cat) whose central nervous system is cut completely through just above the midbrain can right itself if knocked over, and, given the appropriate stimulation, it can walk, run, jump, and climb (Schmidt, 1986). But none of these actions ever occurs spontaneously or in a goal-directed fashion. If the animal is placed on a pole, it will climb, but it does not itself *choose* to climb a pole that has food at the top or avoid one that doesn't. Thus, the midbrain and structures below it contain neural systems that organize movements, but they do not contain neural systems that permit deliberate decisions to move or to refrain from moving.

Directly atop the brainstem (and forward in the head) is the **thalamus** (see Figure 6.11). This structure is, among other things, a sensory relay station, connecting incoming sensory tracts to special sensory areas of the cerebral cortex (to be described below). For each sense there is a particular nucleus in the thalamus, which receives input from that sense and sends output to an appropriate area of the cerebral cortex. For example, one nucleus in the thalamus (called the *lateral geniculate*) receives visual input that has entered the brain by way of the optic nerve and sends its output to the visual area of the cortex.

**The Cerebellum and Basal Ganglia**    The term *cerebellum* means little brain, and the **cerebellum** indeed looks something like a smaller version of the rest of the brain, riding piggyback on the rear side of the brainstem (see Figure 6.12). Its most important function is to help initiate and control very rapid movements of the limbs—movements that are too fast to be modified by sensory feedback once they are initiated. Humans with damage in the cerebellum are often incapable of such rapid movements as kicking or throwing, but can still make slower movements of the same limbs, such as walking or reaching (Kornhuber, 1974). It is noteworthy that both birds and monkeys have particularly large, well-developed cerebellums. Birds must continuously make rapid, well-timed movements in flying, and monkeys must do the same in leaping about in trees. The cerebellum has been likened to a highly sophisticated computer. It receives and integrates information from all of the senses, including visual information about relevant objects in the external

■ *How the cerebellum and the basal ganglia are functionally similar though anatomically distinct*

**Figure 6.12** *The cerebellum and basal ganglia*

*These two structures are important for initiating and coordinating movements.*

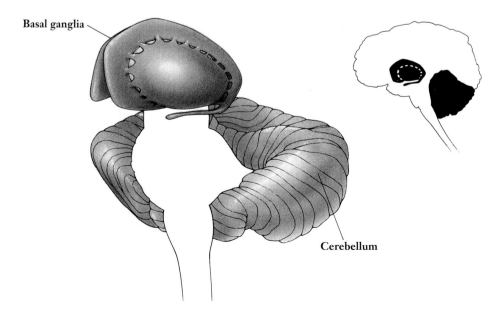

Basal ganglia

Cerebellum

world and somatosensory information about the current positions of the limbs, and it makes rapid-fire calculations as to just what muscle groups must be activated, and by just how much, to leap over a hurdle, hit a baseball, or swing from branch to branch in the treetops.

The **basal ganglia** are large masses of gray matter lying on each side of the thalamus (see Figure 6.12). They are important motor centers, playing a role that is complementary to that of the cerebellum. While the cerebellum is most important for rapid movements, the basal ganglia are more important for slower, deliberate movements, such as reaching for an object or walking (Kornhuber, 1974). Parkinson's disease, which is characterized by difficulty in starting and stopping deliberate movements and by involuntary muscle tremors, results from deterioration of certain neurons that run from the brainstem into the basal ganglia (Sourkes, 1989).

**The Limbic System and Hypothalamus**    The term *limbic* comes from the Latin word *limbus*, meaning border or edge. The **limbic system** can be thought of as the border dividing the evolutionarily older parts of the brain, below it, from the newest part (the cerebral cortex), above it. The limbic system consists of several distinct structures—including the *amygdala* and *hippocampus*—which interconnect with one another in a circuit wrapped around the thalamus and basal ganglia (see Figure 6.13). These structures have long been known to play important roles in the regulation of basic drives and emotions (to be discussed in Chapter 7). The limbic system is believed to have evolved originally as a system for the sophisticated analysis of olfactory input (Thompson, 1985), and its connections with the nose remain strong. This may help explain the special influence that smells—such as the aroma of good food or perfume, or the stench of vomit—can have on drives and emotions. But the limbic system also receives input from all of the other sensory systems. In addition, the limbic system is intimately connected to the basal ganglia, and those connections are believed to be important in the translation of emotions and drives into bodily movements.

At least one part of the limbic system, the hippocampus, is also critical to the formation of memories. People who have suffered a large amount of damage to the hippocampus on both sides of the brain are able to remember events that occurred before the damage but are unable to form new, long-term memories of events that occur after the damage. You will read in Chapter 10 of a man who sustained such damage to his hippocampus and could read the same story day after day without realizing that he had read it before.

■ *Why the limbic system is called the limbic system, and what functions it performs*

**Figure 6.13  *The limbic system and hypothalamus***

*The most conspicuous structures of the limbic system are the hippocampus and amygdala, which have strong connections to the hypothalamus. The pituitary gland is not technically part of the brain, but it is strongly tied to the hypothalamus and is controlled by it.*

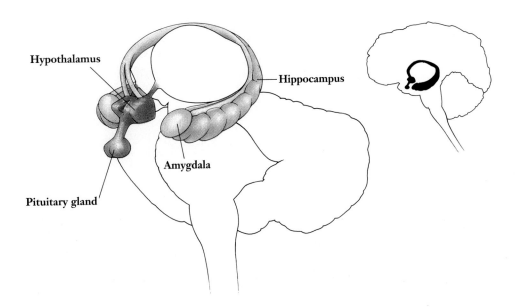

**Three ways by which the hypothalamus controls the body's internal environment**

The **hypothalamus** is a small but extraordinarily important structure. It receives its name from the fact that it lies directly underneath the thalamus (*hypo* in this case means underneath). (See Figure 6.13.) The hypothalamus is intimately connected to all of the structures of the limbic system, and indeed it is sometimes classed as part of that system. It is most directly involved in regulating the internal environment of the body, which it accomplishes by (a) influencing the activity of the autonomic nervous system, (b) controlling the release of certain hormones (to be described later), and (c) influencing certain drive states, such as hunger and thirst. In addition, through its connections with the limbic system, the hypothalamus helps regulate emotional states, such as fear and anger. You will read much more about the hypothalamus's role in drives and emotions in Chapter 7. If I had to give up a cubic millimeter (a tiny speck) of tissue from some part of my brain, the last place I would want it taken from is the hypothalamus. Depending on just which part was taken, I could be left without one or more of my basic drives, or without a normal cycle of sleep and wakefulness, or without the ability to regulate my body metabolism.

### The Cerebral Cortex

We move now up to the evolutionarily newest and anatomically topmost part of the brain, the **cerebral cortex**. *Cerebrum* is the Latin word for brain (the term is now sometimes used to refer to all parts of the brain other than the brainstem and cerebellum). *Cortex* is the Latin word for bark, and in anatomical usage it refers to the outside layer of any structure. The cerebral cortex, therefore, is the outer layer—the bark—of the brain. It is by far the largest part of the human brain, accounting, remarkably, for something like 80 percent of its total volume (Kolb & Whishaw, 1990). Its surface area is much greater than it appears to be, due to the fact that it folds inward in many places. Approximately one-third of the surface of the human cortex is visible in a view of the undissected human brain, and the remaining two-thirds lies buried within the folds. The entire cerebral cortex is divided into left and right *hemispheres*, and each hemisphere is further divided into four lobes demarcated at least partly by rather prominent folds. The lobes, whose positions you can see in Figure 6.14, are the **occipital, temporal, parietal**, and **frontal lobes**.

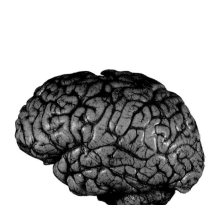

**A cerebral cortex and cerebellum**

*What you can see here is only one-third of the cortex mass. The remaining two-thirds is hidden in the folds and fissures.*

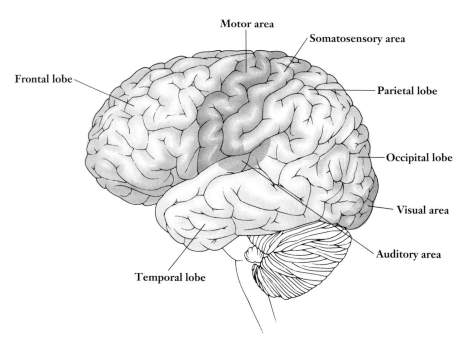

**Figure 6.14  The cerebral cortex**

*This figure shows the four lobes of the cortex, as well as the locations of the visual, auditory, somatosensory, and motor areas.*

■ *Four general principles concerning the organization of the cerebral cortex*

**Principles of Cortical Organization**   As further introduction to the cerebral cortex, it is useful to note four general principles concerning its organization:

1. *Functional specialization*   Different areas of the cerebral cortex serve different functions. The ***primary sensory areas*** receive rather direct input from sensory nerves and tracts by way of the relay nuclei in the thalamus. As shown in Figure 6.14, these include the *visual area* in the occipital lobe, the *auditory area* in the temporal lobe, and the *somatosensory area* in the parietal lobe. Directly in front of the somatosensory area, in the rear part of the frontal lobe, is the ***motor area***, which sends axons down to motor neurons in the brainstem and spinal cord. Other parts of the cortex, not labeled in the figure, include *secondary sensory areas*, which receive input from primary sensory areas for further analysis, and ***association areas***, which receive inputs from sensory areas for more than one sensory modality (such as vision and hearing) and are involved in associating these with each other and with stored memories, in the processes that we refer to as perception, thought, and decision making. The bulk of the human cortex is occupied by the association areas. As you can see in Figure 6.15, the amount of association cortex increases dramatically, relative to that devoted to specific sensory and motor processes, when going from simpler mammals (such as the rat and cat) on to more complex ones (such as the monkey and human).

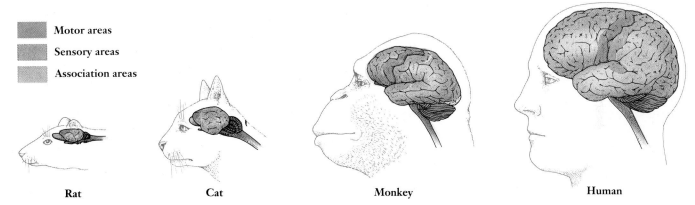

Motor areas
Sensory areas
Association areas

Rat          Cat          Monkey          Human

**Figure 6.15 *Comparison of the brains of four mammals***
*These brains all contain the same structures, but the monkey and human have much more cortical space devoted to association areas than do the rat and cat.*

2. *Topographic organization*   The sensory and motor areas of the cortex are organized in such a way that adjacent neurons receive input from, or send output to, adjacent portions of the sensory or muscular tissue to which they are ultimately connected. This fact is referred to as the *principle of topographic organization*. For example, neurons that are near one another in the visual cortex receive input from receptor cells that are near one another in the retina of the eye. Similarly, neurons that are near one another in the somatosensory cortex receive input from adjacent areas of the skin, and neurons near one another in the motor cortex send output to adjacent sets of muscle fibers. It is possible to map onto the somatosensory cortex the part of the body from which each portion of the cortex receives its input, or onto the motor cortex the part of the body to which each portion sends its output (see Figure 6.16).

The maps in Figure 6.16 show a distorted view of the human body. This is because the amount of cortex devoted to each part of the body does not correspond to the size of the body part, but rather to the degree of sensitivity of that part (in the case of a sensory map) or the fineness of its movements (in the case of a motor map). As you can see in Figure 6.16, huge areas of the human motor cortex are devoted to control of the fingers and vocal apparatus, where fine

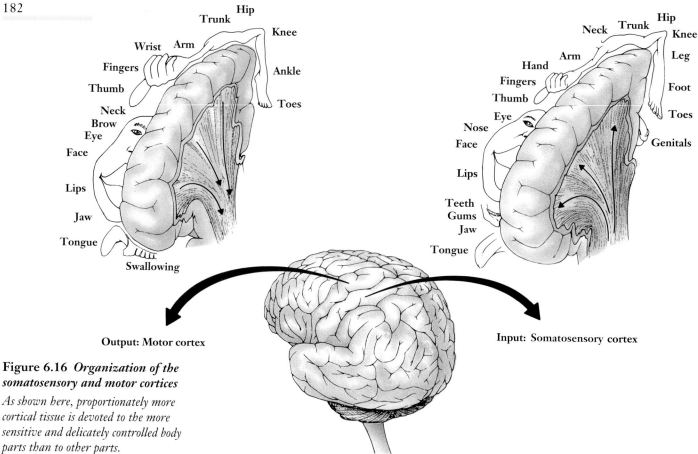

Wrist Arm Trunk Hip Knee Ankle Toes — Fingers Thumb Neck Brow Eye Face Lips Jaw Tongue Swallowing

Neck Trunk Hip Knee Leg Foot Toes Genitals — Arm Hand Fingers Thumb Eye Nose Face Lips Teeth Gums Jaw Tongue

**Output: Motor cortex**

**Input: Somatosensory cortex**

**Figure 6.16** *Organization of the somatosensory and motor cortices*

*As shown here, proportionately more cortical tissue is devoted to the more sensitive and delicately controlled body parts than to other parts.*

control is needed. In other animals, other body parts have greater representation, depending on the range and delicacy of their movements. For example, the somatosensory and motor areas of the cortex in a cat have large portions devoted to the cat's whiskers, and those of a spider monkey—a creature that uses its tail as a fifth arm and hand—have large areas devoted to the tail (Walker, 1973). Some experiments with animals have shown that these maps are not entirely fixed by heredity, but can be modified as a result of the extent to which the individual has used the body part in question (see Edelman, 1987).

3. *Contralateral connections* The most direct connections between sensory or motor areas of the cortex and body structures are crossed, or *contralateral*, meaning that the right side of the cortex is most strongly connected to the left side of the body, and vice versa. For this reason, damage in the motor or somatosensory area of one hemisphere interferes most strongly with the ability to move muscles on, or feel somatosensory input from, the opposite side of the body. But the two hemispheres are not isolated from one another. They are connected by a massive bundle of axons called the ***corpus callosum*** (see Figure 6.17). In the undamaged brain, sensory information that reaches one hemisphere passes through the corpus callosum and in that way reaches the other hemisphere as well. Thus, the two hemispheres normally share their information and work as a unit in controlling behavior.

4. *Asymmetry of higher functions* In their sensory and motor areas, the two hemispheres are quite symmetrical. The right and left motor areas, for example, perform basically the same functions, though for different halves of the body. But the symmetry breaks down in association areas. The most dramatic and fully studied asymmetry is in language analysis and production. Large areas in the left hemisphere are devoted to language functions, while comparable areas in the right are devoted less to language and more to other functions, such as analyzing visual and spatial information. Some of the evidence for this comes

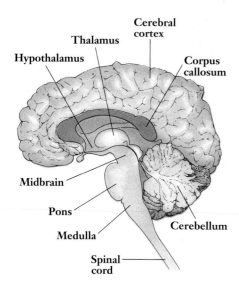

Cerebral
cortex

Thalamus

Hypothalamus

Corpus
callosum

Midbrain

Pons

Medulla

Cerebellum

Spinal
cord

**Figure 6.17 *The corpus callosum***
*The corpus callosum is a huge bundle of axons connecting the right and left halves of the cerebral cortex. You can see it here in an inside view of the right hemisphere of a human brain that has been cut in half. This photograph and matched diagram also allow you to see an inside view of other brain structures.*

▪ *Evidence that the motor cortex comes relatively late in the chain of command preceding an action, and that its function is to refine the more delicate parts of the action*

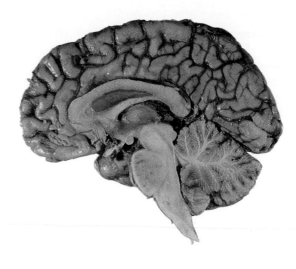

from observations of people who, for medical reasons (to control epileptic seizures), have had the corpus callosum cut. After this so-called split-brain operation the two hemispheres can no longer communicate directly with one another, and information that reaches just one hemisphere is treated quite differently from information that reaches just the other. For example, if you blindfold a woman who has had such an operation and put something in her right hand (connected to her left hemisphere), she can say what it is, but if you put something in her left hand (connected to her right hemisphere), she cannot. Yet, in certain nonlinguistic ways, such as putting puzzle pieces together (still blindfolded), she can perform better with objects in the left hand than the right, even though she cannot say verbally what she is doing. (These and other findings concerning cortical asymmetry are discussed in more detail in Chapter 11.)

**Cortical Control of Movement**   You will read more about the role of the cerebral cortex in sensation and thought in later chapters. For the present, I will focus on its role in the control of movement.

One area of the cortex important for movement control is, as I already mentioned, the motor cortex. This structure receives input from the basal ganglia and cerebellum, and it is specialized to fine-tune the signals that go out to the smaller muscles that must operate in a finely graded way. Experiments in which monkeys must make well-controlled hand movements to obtain a food reward have shown that each movement is preceded first by a burst of activity in the basal ganglia and then by a burst of activity in the motor cortex (Kornhuber, 1974; Evarts, 1979). This is evidence that activity in the motor cortex comes later in the chain of command than activity in the basal ganglia and cerebellum. Some of the output from the motor cortex occurs by way of extremely long neurons, whose cell bodies are in the motor cortex and whose axons terminate directly on motor neurons in the brainstem and spinal cord. These point-to-point connections, from cells in the motor cortex to small sets of motor neurons, help make delicate motor movements possible.

Electrical stimulation of specific small areas of the motor cortex, through thin wires inserted into it, can produce twitches of single small muscles without activating nearby muscles (Asanuma & Sakata, 1967). It is through such experiments that the motor map shown in Figure 6.16 was produced. Other experiments have shown that monkeys that have been deprived of their motor cortex in both hemispheres behave normally in most respects but are unable to make delicate hand movements, such as those needed to lift a small piece of food out of a narrow hole (Passingham & others, 1983).

**Figure 6.18** *Control of movement by the cerebral cortex*
*The frontal lobe association areas integrate information received from other brain areas and make a general plan for action. The premotor and supplementary motor areas convert this plan into neural programs for movement, which are then executed through connections to the motor cortex or through downward connections to the cerebellum and basal ganglia.*

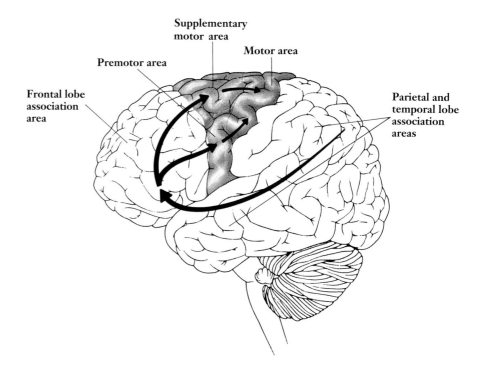

■ *Evidence that the premotor and supplementary motor areas of the cortex help set up programs for skilled actions*

■ *General roles of (a) the frontal lobe association areas, and (b) the parietal and temporal lobe association areas in movement control*

Directly in front of the motor cortex lie two other cortical areas devoted to motor control—the *premotor area* and the *supplementary motor area* (see Figure 6.18). These are both known to be important in the initiation and coordination of learned, skilled movements (see Ghez, 1985b), and they exert their control, at least partly, by acting on neurons in the motor area. Monkeys with damage to these areas, for example, can perform a learned task that requires just one hand but are unable to perform a learned task that requires the coordinated action of both hands together (Brinkman, 1984).

Other experiments, with human subjects, have taken advantage of techniques for monitoring the degree of neural activity in specific cortical regions by measuring changes in the flow of blood to those regions. Using such a technique, Per Roland and his colleagues (1980) in Denmark have found that neural activity in the supplementary motor area precedes the performance of a skilled, learned motor task, and the more complex the task the greater is the degree of neural activity in that area. These same researchers also found, most interestingly, that when people were simply asked to rehearse a motor task mentally, without actually performing it, they also showed a large amount of activity in the supplementary motor area. Perhaps when skilled divers or gymnasts "visualize" their performance before they act, what they are doing, at least partly, is warming up the neurons in the supplementary motor area—in that way setting up the neural program that will eventuate in the perfect dive or vault.

The various association areas of the cortex also contribute to the development of plans for action, but they do so in ways that are more complicated and less well understood than those just described. To get an idea of the general flow of information in the cortex in the control of movement, notice the arrows in Figure 6.18. Association areas in the rear parts of the cortex, especially the parietal and temporal lobes, are involved in the analysis of information that comes to them from sensory areas. These areas in turn send output to the association areas of the frontal lobe, which also receive information about the internal environment through strong connections with the limbic system. Combining all of this information, the frontal association areas set up general plans for action that can be put into effect through connections to the premotor and supplementary motor cortex, and also through downward connections to the basal ganglia.

Consistent with this interpretation, damage to the frontal lobes of the cortex does not, as a rule, harm one's ability to extract information from the environment, but it does harm one's ability to use that information effectively to control behavior. Depending on the location and extent of the damage, it can destroy either short-range planning, such as working out the series of movements needed to get through a maze or operate a lever, or long-range planning, such as organizing one's day, one's week, or one's life (Kolb & Whishaw, 1990).

### Hierarchical Organization in the Control of Movement: A Summary

In preceding discussions, I have emphasized the role that each part of the nervous system plays in the control of movement. From an evolutionary perspective, control of movement is the overarching purpose of the nervous system. The nervous system integrates information to provide a basis for effective, life-preserving movement. The simplest nervous systems—found in the simplest invertebrate animals—control movement largely through means that can be described as reflexes. A stimulus produces a response, with relatively little intervening processing of the stimulus information. The evolution of more complex movement-control systems occurred not so much by replacing earlier systems as by building onto them. Thus, the human nervous system can be viewed as a *hierarchy* of systems, ranging from the most primitive, reflexive levels in the spinal cord up to the most complex, analytical levels involving association areas in the cerebral cortex. The higher and evolutionarily newer levels to a large degree exert their effects by controlling the activity of lower, older levels.

To review the functions of the various parts of the nervous system, and to visualize how they interact as a whole, it is useful to use the diagram shown in Figure 6.19 (based partly on Schmidt, 1986, and Ghez, 1985a). Structures are organized in this figure according to their general roles in controlling movement, not according to their anatomical position. At the top are structures involved in motivation and planning, and proceeding down are structures involved in refining and executing the plans, that is, turning them into action. Notice that structures deeper in the brain (shown on the left side of the diagram) and structures in the cortex (shown on the right side of the diagram) are involved at each of the top three stages in the hierarchy.

■ *An evolutionary rationale for viewing the nervous system as a hierarchy of movement-control mechanisms*

**Figure 6.19   *A hierarchy of motor control***

*This figure summarizes the broad functions of various structures of the nervous system in the control of movement. The structures shown higher up are involved in the more global aspects of an action, and those shown farther down are involved in the finer details of carrying it out. Notice that both subcortical and cortical structures exist at each of the top three levels of the hierarchy. While there are flaws in this portrayal, it is useful in thinking about the flow of information from the planning of an action to its execution.*

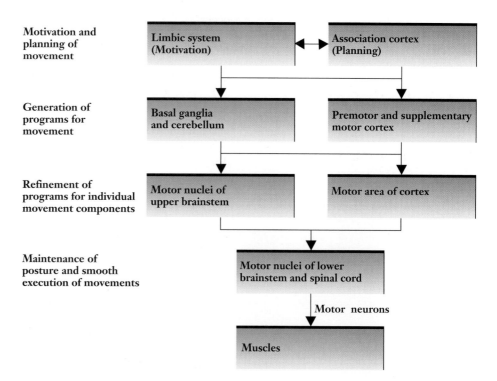

Motivation and planning of movement | Limbic system (Motivation) ⟷ Association cortex (Planning)

Generation of programs for movement | Basal ganglia and cerebellum | Premotor and supplementary motor cortex

Refinement of programs for individual movement components | Motor nuclei of upper brainstem | Motor area of cortex

Maintenance of posture and smooth execution of movements | Motor nuclei of lower brainstem and spinal cord

Motor neurons

Muscles

■ *An imaginative tour through the nervous system of a person who decides to eat some peanuts*

To illustrate the hierarchy further, let's imagine events occurring in the nervous system of a hungry person who sees some peanuts. At the top of the hierarchy, the limbic system (which most directly monitors the internal state of the body) senses that food is needed and sends a message of "hunger" to the cortical association areas with which it is connected. These areas, which share the top of the hierarchy with the limbic system, analyze information coming to them from the visual cortex and determine that there are some peanuts in a bowl across the room. Other information is also considered by the association areas, including memories about the taste of peanuts, about how to eat them, and about the propriety of eating them in this room at this time. Such information is integrated by association areas in the frontal lobes, leading to a global decision to cross the room, take a few peanuts, and eat them.

At the second level, the basal ganglia and cerebellum, as well as the premotor and supplementary motor areas of the cortex, receive the broad program from the limbic system and association cortex. They also receive direct somatosensory input concerning the exact position of parts of the body and visual input concerning the exact spatial location of the peanuts. They use this information to refine the motor program, working out the specific timing and patterning of the movements to be made.

At the third level, the motor program is conveyed through two parallel pathways for further refinement. The program for larger movements, such as walking toward the peanuts, is conveyed by a pathway involving many way stations in the upper part of the brainstem. The program for delicate movements, such as removing the peanuts from their shells, is conveyed to the motor cortex, which in turn sends its output down to the brainstem and spinal cord. The motor cortex also receives sensory feedback from the fingers, through direct connections with the somatosensory cortex, which helps it make fine adjustments in the finger movements needed to shell the peanuts.

Finally, at the fourth level of the hierarchy are the motor neurons of the lower brainstem and spinal cord, which serve as the "final common pathway" in the movement-control system. In addition to the input that these neurons receive from the higher brain structures, they also receive input from stretch receptors, which helps them smooth out irregularities of movement that could otherwise occur.

■ *The difference between "where" and "how," and why brain science hasn't replaced other approaches to understanding basic psychological processes*

**A Word of Caution**  The hierarchy just described is useful as a first approach to understanding the nervous system, and it accurately reflects the kinds of behavioral deficits that occur when different parts of the nervous system are damaged. However, there is a possible danger in this portrayal: It can seduce us into believing that we know more than we actually do know. Specifically, the knowledge that certain parts of the brain are critical for certain aspects of behavioral control to occur can be mistaken for knowledge about *how* those processes are accomplished. But the discovery of "where" does not answer "how." In describing the hierarchy, I spoke of a "global decision" made in association areas of the cortex, and of "programs of action" developed and refined by other brain areas. What do such statements mean? They only mean that individuals who suffer damage in one part of the brain lose the ability to make good choices for action, and those who suffer damage in another part retain the ability to make good choices but lose the ability to carry them out in a coordinated manner. Such statements leave unanswered the far more difficult question of how the association cortex makes decisions, or how various other structures develop and refine action programs. There is a temptation to think of a *homunculus* (little person) residing in each structure (especially in the association cortex), who analyzes input and makes decisions. But the homunculus theory doesn't help at all, because then we would have to explain how each homunculus does its job.

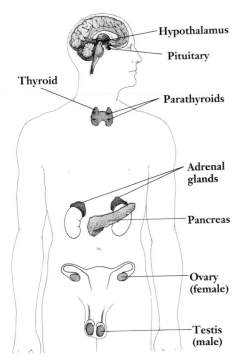

**Figure 6.20** *Endocrine glands*
*These are some of the glands that secrete hormones into the bloodstream. The pituitary, which is controlled by the brain, secretes hormones that in turn control the production of hormones by the thyroids, adrenals, and ovaries or testes.*

Hypothalamus

Pituitary

Thyroid

Parathyroids

Adrenal glands

Pancreas

Ovary (female)

Testis (male)

■ *Similarities and differences between hormones and neurotransmitters, and their possible common origin*

In later chapters (Chapters 9–11) you will see theories about how information is analyzed and how decisions are made, but the theories will not be at the level of neurons and action potentials. They will be general depictions, analogous to computer programs, of the stages through which information might be coded and interpreted. Detailed, explicit, neural-based theories cannot be presented here—not for lack of space or interest, but because they have not yet been developed. Brain science has progressed a long way since the time of Galen, but it still has a long way to go before it can explain, in purely physiological terms, how you or I decide to eat some peanuts.

## Hormones, Drugs, and Their Interactions with Neurotransmission

When the ancient Greeks argued that the heart is the seat of thought, feeling, and behavioral control, they were not entirely without reason. Like the brain, the heart is an organ that has long protrusions from it (blood vessels, in this case), connecting it with other parts of the body. Blood vessels are easier to see than nerves; and because they can be found in all of the sense organs and muscles, as well as in other tissues, it was quite natural that early theorists believed them to be the conduits of sensory and motor messages. Today we know that the circulatory system indeed *does* play an important communicative role in the body. A slower messenger system than the nervous system, it carries chemicals that affect both physical growth and behavior. Among these chemicals are hormones, which are secreted naturally into the bloodstream, and drugs, which may enter the blood through various routes.

### Hormones

*Hormones* are chemical messengers that are secreted into the blood, are carried by the blood to all parts of the body, and affect specific parts of the body referred to as *target tissues*. Dozens of different hormones have been identified. The classic hormones—the first to be identified and the best understood—are secreted by special organs called *endocrine glands* (see Figure 6.20). But many other hormones are secreted by organs not usually classified as endocrine glands, such as the stomach, intestines, kidneys, and brain. Most hormones act simultaneously in more than one target tissue.

**Similarities Between Hormones and Neurotransmitters**   In chemical structure, some hormones are identical to neurotransmitters. For example, the chemical *norepinephrine* is a hormone when it is secreted into the blood by the adrenal gland (shown in Figure 6.20), but it also serves as a neurotransmitter. It is a neurotransmitter released by sympathetic motor neurons of the peripheral nervous system upon visceral muscles and glands; and it is also a neurotransmitter in certain pathways in the brain. It is interesting to note that in each of these roles norepinephrine helps arouse and alert the body. As a hormone and sympathetic transmitter it has such effects as increasing the heart rate, and as a brain transmitter it helps produce a state that we experience psychologically as high arousal or alertness.

Another example of chemical sameness between hormones and transmitters can be found in the *endorphins*. These are a set of closely related chemicals that serve both as hormones, released by the pituitary and adrenal glands into the blood, and as neurotransmitters, released by neurons in certain parts of the brain and spinal cord (Snyder, 1985). Both as hormones and as transmitters, these substances are important in reducing the sense of pain (Henry, 1986). You will read more about them in Chapter 8.

Because of their chemical similarity, many scientists believe that hormones and neurotransmitters originated, evolutionarily, from the same, more primitive system of communication among cells in simpler organisms. As organisms became more complex, with circulatory systems and nervous systems, the primitive communication system adapted via two routes. One route involved the blood, which permitted widespread, relatively slow communication; this became the system of hormones. The other route involved the nervous system, which became ever more capable of rapid, detailed communication; this became the system of neurotransmitters. While a hormone must travel long distances through the blood to reach its target tissue, taking anywhere from seconds to hours to have its effect, a neurotransmitter must travel only across the tiny synaptic gap and can have its effect within a thousandth of a second from the time it is released.

The most obvious link between hormones and transmitters can be found in *neurohormones*. These are chemicals that are like neurotransmitters in that they are secreted from axon terminals, but they are hormones because they are secreted into blood vessels rather than onto other neurons. Neurohormones are involved in the brain's mechanism for regulating the production of other hormones.

**Control of Hormones by the Brain**    The pituitary gland, which sits at the base of the brain (see Figure 6.20), produces hormones that in turn stimulate the production of hormones by other endocrine glands. In particular, the pituitary produces hormones that control hormone production in the thyroids, adrenals, and gonads (ovaries in the female and testes in the male). Because of its control over other glands, the pituitary is sometimes called the "master endocrine gland." But it might be more accurate to say that the brain is the master endocrine gland, because it, through neurohormones, controls the pituitary.

To visualize the intimate relationship between the brain and the pituitary, look at Figure 6.21. Notice that the rear part of the pituitary, the *posterior lobe*, is in fact a part of the brain. It consists of modified neurons, referred to as *neurosecretory cells*, which extend down from the hypothalamus and secrete hormones into a bed of capillaries (tiny blood vessels) in much the same way that other neurons secrete

■ *How secretions produced by brain cells control the action of several endocrine glands*

**Figure 6.21** *How the hypothalamus controls pituitary hormones*

*Neurosecretory cells, specialized neurons in the hypothalamus, control the activity of the pituitary gland. Some neurosecretory cells secrete hormones directly into capillaries in the posterior pituitary, where they enter the general bloodstream. Others secrete hormones, called* releasing factors, *into a special capillary system that carries them to the anterior pituitary, where they stimulate the release of hormones manufactured there.*

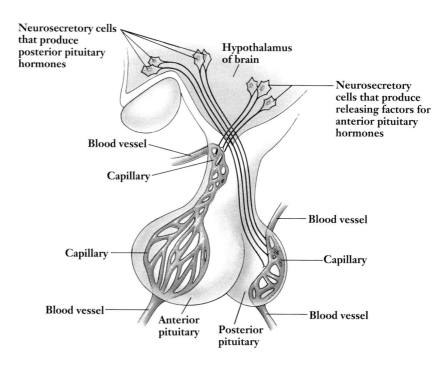

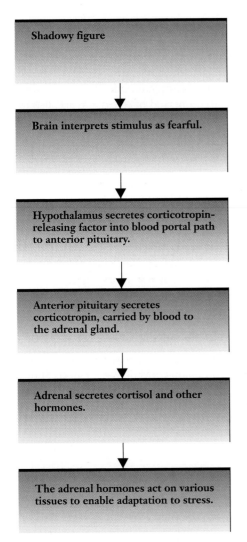

Shadowy figure

↓

Brain interprets stimulus as fearful.

↓

Hypothalamus secretes corticotropin-releasing factor into blood portal path to anterior pituitary.

↓

Anterior pituitary secretes corticotropin, carried by blood to the adrenal gland.

↓

Adrenal secretes cortisol and other hormones.

↓

The adrenal hormones act on various tissues to enable adaptation to stress.

**Figure 6.22 *Brain-pituitary-adrenal response to a fearful stimulus***
*This is one example of a brain-mediated hormonal response to sensory stimulation.*

■ *How hormones can produce either long-term or short-term behavioral effects, acting either in the periphery or in the brain*

neurotransmitter molecules into synaptic gaps. Once these hormones get into the capillaries they are transported into the rest of the circulatory system to affect various parts of the body. The remainder of the pituitary, the *anterior lobe*, is not actually part of the brain as the posterior lobe is, but it is intimately connected to it by a specialized set of capillaries, as shown in Figure 6.21. Neurosecretory cells in the brain's hypothalamus produce *releasing factors*, neurohormones that are secreted into the capillary system and carried to the anterior pituitary, where they cause the synthesis and release of pituitary hormones. Different releasing factors, produced by different sets of neurosecretory cells in the hypothalamus, act selectively to stimulate the production of different anterior pituitary hormones.

As an example of a sequence of hormonal events triggered by the brain, consider the following (shown in Figure 6.22): (1) A shadowy figure is seen at night and interpreted as fearful. (2) The association cortex sends a neural message to the viewer's hypothalamus, causing secretion of *corticotropin-releasing factor*. (3) The specialized capillary system transports this releasing factor to the anterior pituitary, where it causes the release of another hormone, *corticotropin*, into the bloodstream. (4) From the bloodstream, corticotropin enters the adrenal cortex (the external layer of the adrenal gland), where it causes the release of a number of adrenal cortical hormones, including *cortisol*. (5) These adrenal hormones are carried throughout the body and help prepare it for a possible emergency. Of course, at the same time that all of this is happening, many other brain-controlled effects—including the development of plans for escape and activation of the sympathetic portion of the autonomic nervous system—are also occurring to deal with the possible emergency.

In addition to controlling the release of hormones in response to sensory stimuli, as just described, the brain also helps govern longer-term, cyclic changes in hormone production. For example, corticotropin is released not just in response to fear-inducing stimuli; it is also released in smaller amounts that vary throughout the 24-hour day, increasing during sleep and peaking shortly before waking up. Through its effect on cortisol and other adrenal hormones, corticotropin helps keep blood sugar levels sufficiently high during sleep, and it may also help prepare the brain for waking up (McEwen, 1989).

**How Hormones Affect Behavior**    Hormones influence behavior in many different ways. One route is through stimulating growth processes that produce relatively permanent anatomical changes. For example, the increase in sex hormones at puberty (especially estrogen in the female and testosterone in the male) stimulates different sets of growth processes in females and males, which in turn have both direct and indirect effects on behavior. Thus, men usually have deeper speaking voices than women, because of a permanent effect that testosterone has on the growth of the larynx (the vocal apparatus in the throat). At an earlier life stage, before birth, hormone production by the fetus also affects many aspects of development in a permanent way. Essentially all of the anatomical differences between newborn boys and girls are caused by hormones—primarily by the presence or absence of testosterone, which is produced by the male fetus but not the female. Among these anatomical differences are differences in the brain (Feder, 1984), which are known to have important behavioral consequences in other mammals, and may or may not have important consequences in humans (to be discussed in Chapter 7).

Hormones also have shorter-term effects, ranging from those that last only a few minutes to those that last many days. Consider again the effects of the hormones released from the adrenal cortex in response to a stressful or frightening stimulus. These hormones act on tissues throughout the body to help prepare it for a possibly prolonged period of energy expenditure and possible wounds. For example, they promote the release of sugar and fat molecules into the blood for energy and, if a wound occurs, help suppress inflammation at the wound site. In addition, experiments with rats and other animals show that these same hormones are taken up by neurons in the limbic system, especially in the hippocampus (McEwen & others, 1986). Just what role they play there is not yet certain, but there is some evidence that they help the animal calm down after a period of stress and are also involved in the formation of long-term memories related to the stressful experience (McEwen, 1989).

At a molecular level of analysis, hormones can work on cells in a variety of ways. Most hormones fall into one of two chemical classes: *peptides*, which are short-chain protein molecules, and *steroids*, which are chemically related to cholesterol. Neurohormones and the hormones produced by the anterior pituitary are peptides; hormones produced by the adrenal cortex and the gonads are steroids. Peptides do not easily cross through cell membranes, so they usually exert their effects by attaching to the outside of the cell membrane and stimulating biochemical processes there. In the nervous system, peptides can act like neurotransmitters, causing pores to open up in cell membranes, and in that way changing the electrical charge across the membrane and affecting the rate of neural activity. They can also stimulate more sustained changes in the neuron, by activating other messenger systems that work inside the neuron. Steroids, on the other hand, easily pass through cell membranes and commonly exert their effects within the cell nucleus. There they may activate or inhibit specific genes, and in that way increase or decrease the production of specific protein molecules (McEwen, 1989). Thus, steroids can alter either cell growth, in a long-term manner, or cell activity, in a short-term manner.

### Drugs

The difference between a hormone and a drug is that the former is produced within the body and the latter is taken in from the outside. Like hormones, drugs are carried by the blood and are taken up in target tissues in various parts of the body.

**Drug Administration and the Blood-Brain Barrier**   To be carried to potential sites of action, a drug must first get into an individual's blood. Sometimes drugs are injected directly into the blood, by intravenous injection, but more commonly they are administered by routes that bring them into contact with capillaries, where they are gradually absorbed into the blood. Drugs are absorbed by capillaries in the intestines if taken orally, by capillaries in the lungs if taken by inhalation, by capillaries in the rectum if taken by rectal suppository, or by capillaries under the skin or in the muscles if taken by subcutaneous or intramuscular injection. The preferred route of administration depends largely on the properties of the drug and the desired time-course of action. A drug that is destroyed by digestive juices in the stomach, for example, cannot be taken orally; a drug injected intravenously will act more quickly than one taken by any other route.

If a drug is going to act on the brain, it must pass from the blood into the extracellular fluid that surrounds neurons in the brain. The capillaries in the brain are much less porous than those in other tissues. In addition, they are tightly surrounded by the fatty membranes of a certain variety of glial cells. The tight capillary walls and the surrounding glial cells provide a ***blood-brain barrier***, which helps protect the brain from poisons. To act on the brain, a drug (or hormone) must be able to pass through this barrier. In general, fat-soluble substances pass through easily, and other substances may or may not pass through, depending on other characteristics of their chemistry.

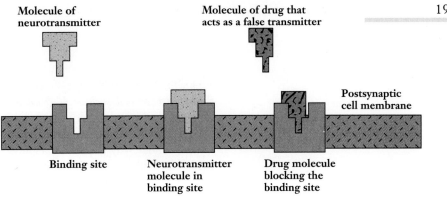

Molecule of neurotransmitter  Molecule of drug that acts as a false transmitter

Postsynaptic cell membrane

Binding site  Neurotransmitter molecule in binding site  Drug molecule blocking the binding site

**Figure 6.23** *Lock-and-key view of drug effects in the synapse*
*The binding site on the membrane of the postsynaptic cell can be thought of as a keyhole, and the neurotransmitter molecule as a key that fits into it and opens the lock (causing pores to open up in the cell membrane). A drug can serve as a substitute key, producing the same effect as the neurotransmitter; or it can serve as a broken key (as shown above), occupying the keyhole without activating the lock, thereby preventing the neurotransmitter from acting.*

■ *Three ways by which drugs can alter activity at a synapse*

■ *How the effects of curare, L-dopa, and psychoactive drugs can be interpreted in terms of the hierarchical model of movement control*

**How Drugs Can Alter Synaptic Transmission**   Many different drugs are used in psychiatry and neurology to alter a person's mood or behavioral capacities. Nearly all such drugs work by enhancing or blocking synaptic transmission somewhere in the nervous system (Snyder, 1985). In normal synaptic transmission, as you may recall, neurotransmitter molecules released from the presynaptic neuron cross a narrow synaptic gap, and then bind to the membrane and alter the activity of the postsynaptic cell (look back at Figure 6.5). Three general ways (though not the only ways) that drugs can influence activity at a synapse are the following: (1) They can act on the presynaptic neuron to either facilitate or inhibit release of the transmitter, thereby affecting the amount that enters the gap. (2) They can act in the gap to either facilitate or inhibit the processes that normally terminate the action of the transmitter once it has been released, and thus either prolong or shorten the amount of time that the transmitter remains in the gap and exerts its effects. (3) They can act directly on postsynaptic binding sites, either producing the same effect as the transmitter or blocking the transmitter from having its normal effect.

To understand how the third, and best understood, of the effects just listed can occur, it is useful to visualize the binding site as a lock and the transmitter molecule as a key that fits into the lock and opens it (see Figure 6.23). A drug molecule that diffuses into a synapse may act as a substitute key, producing the same effect as the transmitter would, or it may act as a broken key, filling the keyhole for a period of time but not turning the lock, thereby preventing the transmitter from having its normal effect. There are many different transmitters in the nervous system, and a particular drug may produce one or more of the above effects for just one or for many different transmitters. Thus, drugs can be more or less specific, affecting either a small class of synapses or a large class, and hence can be more or less specific in the effects they produce on behavior.

**Drugs May Act at Different Levels of the Behavior-Control Hierarchy**   Drugs may act at any of the levels of the neural hierarchy depicted in Figure 6.19, influencing the behavior-control processes that occur at each level. *Curare* is an example of a drug that acts at the lowest level, at synapses between motor neurons and skeletal muscle cells. This poison, long used by certain South American Indians on the tips of their arrows for hunting, paralyzes the animal that is hit. Curare produces paralysis by blocking the postsynaptic binding sites for *acetylcholine*, which is the transmitter released by skeletal motor neurons on muscle cells. Since the motor neurons can no longer release acetylcholine onto muscle cells, the muscles can no longer contract, and the animal is unable to move. Acetylcholine is also a transmitter at many places within the central nervous system, but curare does not act in those places because it cannot pass the blood-brain barrier.

An example of a drug that acts somewhat higher in the movement-control hierarchy is *L-dopa*, which is used to treat victims of Parkinson's disease. As noted earlier, Parkinson's disease—which is characterized by muscle tremors and severe difficulty in initiating movements—is caused by the degeneration of certain neurons whose axons terminate in the basal ganglia. The neurotransmitter released by these neurons is *dopamine*. L-dopa is a precursor in the synthesis of dopamine, and it increases the level of dopamine in those neurons to the basal ganglia that are still intact, thereby helping to counteract the loss due to the neural degeneration. You might wonder why dopamine itself is not used in the treatment of Parkinson's disease. The reason is that it cannot cross the blood-brain barrier. L-dopa can cross the barrier, and once in the brain it is converted to dopamine.

Incidentally, L-dopa is often not a satisfactory treatment for Parkinson's disease over the long run, because of its cumulative side effects. A great deal of research has been conducted to find alternatives. One of the most interesting possible alternatives—still in the experimental stage, but already tried with some success in a few patients—involves the transplantation of dopamine-producing cells directly into the basal ganglia (Lewin, 1987). This work has generated quite a stir in the scientific and medical worlds, because it is among the first indications that cells transplanted into the brain can take hold and grow, becoming part of the brain itself. Such research opens up the possibility of a new approach to treating many kinds of brain disorders, not just Parkinson's disease. (The work has also caused an ethical stir, because the cells that work best are taken from aborted human fetuses.)

Drugs that work still further up in the behavior-control hierarchy may alter mood or general arousal, or affect one's thoughts and perceptions. These drugs are called *psychoactive drugs*, because they influence processes that we think of as psychological. In Chapter 18 you will read about some of the clinical uses of psychoactive drugs—in the treatment of anxiety, depression, schizophrenia, and other emotional or thought disorders. Meanwhile, Table 6.1 shows one way of categorizing psychoactive drugs and what is known about the action mechanism of some of them, including such everyday examples as caffeine and nicotine.

**Tolerance, Withdrawal Symptoms, and Addiction**   Some drugs produce smaller physiological and behavioral effects if taken repeatedly, a phenomenon known as **drug tolerance**. Because of tolerance, people who regularly take a drug may need to increase their dose over time to continue to achieve the original effect. In addition, repeated use of some drugs can produce **withdrawal symptoms** when drug use is stopped, which can be very disturbing and in some cases life-threatening. Withdrawal symptoms are commonly opposite in direction to the initial direct effects of the drug. Thus, anticonstipation drugs tend to increase constipation on withdrawal, sleep-inducing drugs tend to produce insomnia on withdrawal, drugs taken to prevent headaches tend to produce headaches on withdrawal, and antianxiety drugs tend to increase anxiety on withdrawal. As a rule (though not an inviolable one), the same drugs that produce tolerance when taken repeatedly also produce withdrawal symptoms when stopped (Julien, 1985).

> *How drug tolerance and withdrawal symptoms may be explained in terms of physiological adaptation to a drugged state*

A general theory to explain both tolerance and withdrawal symptoms relates them both to long-term adjustments that the body makes to adapt itself to a drugged condition. During prolonged drug use, physiological changes occur that serve essentially to *counteract* the effects of the drug, permitting the individual to function more normally while in the drugged state. These changes may involve a reduction in the activity of physiological systems that are excited by the drug, or an increase in the activity of systems that are depressed by the drug. Because of these long-term compensatory changes, a continuously higher dose is needed to achieve the original drug effect, and absence of the drug results in an unbalanced state in which the long-term compensatory changes are not counteracted by the drug.

> *A possible molecular explanation for tolerance and withdrawal symptoms produced by amphetamines*

To illustrate how tolerance and withdrawal symptoms may develop, consider *amphetamines*, a class of drugs that are often used (and abused) to sustain wakefulness or produce a psychological feeling of elation (a drug "high"). Amphetamines promote the release of the neurotransmitter *norepinephrine* into synapses in the brain, and this provides at least part of the physiological basis for the arousal and

**Table 6.1** *Categories of psychoactive drugs based on their main behavioral effects*

1. **Behavioral stimulants and antidepressants**
   Drugs that increase alertness and activity level and elevate mood. Some examples of these are:
   - *Amphetamines and cocaine*  Often abused because of the psychological "high" they produce, these drugs increase the release of *norepinephrine* and *dopamine* into synapses and prolong their action there.
   - *Clinical antidepressants*  These counteract depression but do not produce the sleeplessness or euphoria that amphetamines and cocaine produce. These also increase activity at *norepinephrine* synapses. (See Chapters 17 and 18.)
   - *Caffeine*  Found in coffee, tea, and cocoa beans, this drug increases neural activity throughout the brain by a variety of means that are not well understood.
   - *Nicotine*  Found in tobacco, this drug increases neural activity by stimulating neurons where *acetylcholine* is the transmitter, including in the cerebral cortex (which may increase mental alertness) and in the sympathetic ganglia of the autonomic nervous system (producing such effects as increased heart rate).

2. **Tranquilizers and central-nervous-system depressants**
   Drugs that counteract anxiety and/or decrease alertness and activity level. Included in this category (and further described in Chapter 18) are:
   - *Benzodiazepines*  Prescribed to counteract anxiety, these drugs (including diazepam, sold as Valium) act on postsynaptic receptors to make them more responsive to *GABA*, which is an inhibitory transmitter. Increased responsiveness to GABA causes a decrease in neural activity in those parts of the brain where it is present.
   - *Alcohol and barbiturates*  These often-abused drugs depress neural activity throughout the brain by a variety of means that are not well understood. Low doses may produce relief from anxiety, and higher doses produce sedation, sleep, unconsciousness, coma, and death, in that order. Their antianxiety effects are believed to work in the same way as that of benzodiazepines.

3. **Opiates**
   These include *opium*, a crude extract from the opium plant; *morphine*, the most active ingredient in opium; *codeine*, an extract from opium that is chemically similar to morphine but less active; and *heroin*, which is synthesized by chemical modification of morphine. All are potent pain reducers and can also produce feelings of euphoria. They produce at least some of their effects by activating neurons that normally respond to *endorphins*, a class of slow-acting transmitters that are part of the body's natural system for relieving pain. (See Chapter 8.)

4. **Antipsychotic drugs**
   Prescribed mostly to treat schizophrenia, these drugs (including chlorpromazine and haloperidol) are believed to work by decreasing activity at synapses where *dopamine* is the transmitter. (See Chapters 17 and 18.)

5. **Hallucinogenic drugs**
   These induce hallucinations and other sensory distortions. Some, such as *mescaline* and *psilocybin*, exist naturally in plants and have a long history of use among various peoples, including Native Americans, in religious rites. Others, such as *LSD* (lysergic acid diethylamide), are synthetic compounds. Most are structurally similar to neurotransmitters, and they are believed to act either by mimicking or blocking transmitters that they resemble. Both LSD and psilocybin resemble the transmitter *serotonin*.

*Source:* Adapted from *A primer of drug action* (4th ed.) by R. M. Julien, 1985, San Francisco: Freeman.

mood elevation. With prolonged use of an amphetamine, tolerance develops (higher doses are needed) and withdrawal symptoms—including extreme fatigue and psychological depression, which of course are opposite to the direct effects of the drug—begin to appear during periods of abstinence (McKim, 1986). Research suggests that both the tolerance and the withdrawal symptoms come about at least partly because the brain, reacting to the repeated, drug-induced oversupply of norepinephrine, begins to produce a specific chemical that blocks the postsynaptic binding sites for norepinephrine, by the broken-key method illustrated in Figure 6.23 (Caldwell & others, 1980). Because many of the binding sites are blocked, a larger than normal amount of norepinephrine is needed in the synapse to activate the postsynaptic neurons. Thus, a higher dose of amphetamine is needed to achieve the effect that was once achieved by a low dose, and, when no amphetamine is taken, the postsynaptic neurons are unusually inactive, accounting for the fatigue and depression. After a sufficient period of drug abstinence, however, the brain stops making the blocking chemical, and the person can once again achieve a normal mood and alertness without the amphetamine.

Thus far I have avoided the term *addiction*. People are said to be addicted to a drug if, despite contrary intentions, they cannot refrain from continuing to take it. Physiological withdrawal symptoms can certainly provide part of the basis for addiction. In some cases a person may be taking a drug almost entirely to alleviate the withdrawal symptoms that emerge when the drug is not taken. But addiction can also occur when there is no evidence of physiological withdrawal symptoms. Perhaps the person cannot resist the good feelings, or the escape from the pains of real life, that the drug produces. Crack—the cocaine preparation that produces an extraordinarily rapid high and is currently ruining many people's lives—seems to induce addiction well before it produces long-term changes of the sort that cause tolerance or withdrawal symptoms.

In Chapter 17 you will read more about addiction, including evidence that it is a product not just of the direct biological effects of a drug, but also of the learned expectancies and values concerning the drug, which people acquire from their social experience. In Chapter 5 evidence was presented that classical conditioning can also affect the way a person reacts to a drug, so that the same drug dose can have different effects, depending on the environment in which it is taken. Whether we are talking about drugs or any other class of influences on human behavior, the effect can be fully understood only by considering it in the context of a great deal of other information about the person and his or her experiences.

## Concluding Thoughts

Galen was right: The brain is the organ of the mind. The mind is a process, or set of processes (feeling, thinking, initiating action, and so on), carried out by physical activities in the brain and interfered with by lesions in the brain. The brain, of course, doesn't work in isolation from the rest of the body or the environment. It needs input from sensory nerves, it is affected by chemicals carried in the blood, and it acts through motor nerves and (to a smaller degree) hormones. Yet the brain is the center of all that we call the mind: It contains the mechanisms needed to analyze all inputs and organize all outputs.

In reviewing this chapter, so full of terms and details, you may find it useful to keep the following broad points in mind:

1. **The value of a functional perspective** As you list the structures described in this chapter—ranging from the little ones, such as *synaptic vesicles* or *neurohormones*, on up to the big ones, such as the *limbic system* or *autonomic nervous system*—ask yourself, for each: What is it for? That is, what role does it play in the larger machine that is the human being? How is it related to other parts of the machine, and how can variations in it affect human behavior? The structures are a lot easier to remember, and certainly more interesting, if you think of them in terms of their role in a larger system rather than as isolated entities.

2. **Uses of the hierarchical model** The hierarchical model described in this chapter (summarized in Figure 6.19) provides a way to organize thinking about the nervous system. It is a useful memory scheme, because it allows us to see each part in relation to the whole. It summarizes, in a very general way, the effects of damage to different parts of the nervous system. It also summarizes, again in a general way, the effects of drugs that act in different parts of the nervous system. As you review the discussion of the central nervous system, and the later discussion of drugs, tie the bits and pieces together into the hierarchical model.

3. **Thinking of brain science in relation to the rest of psychology** As more is learned about the brain, knowledge about it becomes relevant to broader areas of psychology. In later chapters you will be reading about the brain in relation to psychology's attempt to understand basic processes of motivation, sensation, memory, and thought. Still later, you will read of brain-based theories of mental disorders and of drugs that are believed to alleviate specific mental disorders through their interactions with neurotransmitters. Your review of the present chapter may be more interesting, and more effective, if you try to anticipate the ways that each topic discussed here might be relevant later. Ask yourself: Why might a *psychologist* want to know about this structure or process? You may surprise yourself with the frequency with which you come up with a good answer.

## Further Reading

**Floyd Bloom & Arlyne Lazerson** (1988). *Brain, mind, and behavior* (2nd ed.). New York: Freeman.

*This is a beautifully illustrated, clearly written introduction to the topics listed in its title. It begins with chapters on basic neural mechanisms and proceeds to chapters on the brain's involvement in sensation and movement, motivation, behavioral rhythms, emotions, learning, thought, and psychopathology.*

**Richard Thompson** (1985). *The brain: An introduction to neuroscience.* New York: Freeman.

*This is a thoughtful introduction to the nervous system and ways of learning about it, written by an eminent physiological psychologist. It includes chapters on basic neural mechanisms, sensory and motor systems, and developmental changes that occur in the brain over the life cycle.*

## Looking Ahead

There were hints, in the chapter you just finished, about the physiological underpinnings of motivation, sleep, and arousal. The goal of the next chapter is to add substance to those hints. What happens inside to make a person hungry, or sleepy, or emotionally excited, and how are those internal happenings governed by things happening outside?

# CHAPTER 7

**Motivation and Reward**

**Sleep**

**Arousal and Emotionality**

# Mechanisms of motivation, sleep, and emotion

In the kaleidoscope that makes a day or year of mental life, there are fast-moving and slower-moving components. The fast-moving parts are the sensations, perceptions, thoughts, and actions that flit continuously across our consciousness and behavior. The slower-moving parts are the more sustained changes, called *states*, which help modulate and direct the faster-moving parts. They include states of motivation, of sleep and arousal, and of emotion—the topics of this chapter.

Changing metaphors from a kaleidoscope to a television set, you might think of the fast-moving components as the sounds and sights that a TV produces as it responds to signals in the air, and the slower-moving components, the states, as those produced when you operate the controls that change the channel, volume, or hue. A channel change causes the set to become attuned to different signals in the air, somewhat as you and I become attuned to different signals when hungry than when not. A change in volume is a bit like the change you and I undergo as we become more alert or sleepy. And a change in hue is somewhat akin to a change in emotional state, which colors our daily experience. This chapter begins with a section on the channel changer (motivation), then turns to a section on the volume control (sleep and wakefulness), and finally moves to those hue knobs that seem so hard to keep set on any TV (emotion). The main questions throughout are: What happens inside the person (or animal) to produce changes in state? How do the channel changer, volume control, and hue knobs work in the living being?

## Motivation and Reward

**The broad meaning of** motivation, **and the somewhat narrower meanings of** drive **and** incentive

To *motivate*, in the most general sense of the term, is to set in motion. In psychology, the term **motivation** is often used to refer to the entire constellation of factors, some inside the organism and some outside, that cause an individual to behave in a particular way at a particular time. Motivation defined this way is a very broad concept, almost as broad as all of psychology. Every chapter in this book deals with one or another facet of motivation. Genes, learning, physiological variables, perceptual and thought processes, developmental variables, social experiences, and personality characteristics are all constructs that psychologists describe as contributors to motivation.

A better label for the specific topic of our present discussion is either **motivational state** or **drive**. These terms, which I will use as synonyms, refer to the internal condition, which can change over time in a reversible way, that orients an individual toward one or another category of goals. There are different drives for different goals. *Hunger* is a drive that orients one toward food, *sex* is a drive that orients one toward sexual goals, *curiosity* is a drive that orients one toward exploration of novel stimuli, and so on. For the most part, drives are thought of in psychology as hypothetical constructs. The psychologist does not observe a state of hunger, thirst, or curiosity inside the animal, but rather infers that state from the animal's behavior. An animal is said to be hungry if it behaves in ways that bring it closer to food, to have a sex drive if it behaves in ways that bring it into contact with a sexual partner, to be curious if it seeks out and explores new environments. To say that the drive varies over time is to say that sometimes the animal will work harder, or accept more discomfort, to attain the goal than at other times. The assumption is that something inside the animal changes, causing the animal to behave differently in the same environment at one time than at another.

But the inside interacts constantly with the outside. Motivated behavior is directed toward **incentives**, objects or ends that exist in the external environment. Incentives are also called *reinforcers* (the term used in Chapter 5), *rewards*, or *goals*. The motivational state that leads you to stand in line at the cafeteria is presumably hunger, but incentives for doing so are the good-tasting hamburger and french fries that you intend to purchase.

It is useful to think of drives and incentives as complementary and interacting components of the motivational process. Whether or not you will wait in line at the cafeteria depends on the mix of drive and incentive. If you know that the cafeteria serves a very good hamburger (high incentive) you will wait even if your hunger drive is weak, but if their hamburger tastes like cardboard you will wait only if your hunger drive is strong. Conversely, just as a strong drive can increase the attractiveness of particular incentives, an attractive incentive can increase the strength of a drive. Thus, the aroma of a really good hamburger wafting your way as you wait in line might increase your hunger, which might in turn induce you to eat something that previously wouldn't have interested you, if, by the time you get to the grill, they are out of hamburgers.

In the following pages we will look first at physiological theories and methods in the study of basic drives, then at hunger and sex as two examples of drives, and finally at the neural basis of reward. I have chosen to focus on hunger and sex partly because they are the drives that have been most fully studied physiologically, and partly because of their obvious importance in the lives of humans as well as other species. Please do not assume from this that I or other psychologists believe that drives like hunger and sex are all that motivate human behavior. Later chapters, particularly those dealing with social psychology and personality theories, discuss drives that are more specific to humans, such as those for achievement and self-esteem.

Even hunger and sex in humans always occur in a context of social influences, values, and beliefs that goes way beyond the basic biological influences discussed in

*A matter of time and place*

*Victorians were probably somewhat less concerned with propriety, and contemporary couples are probably somewhat more ambivalent about freedom, than these illustrations suggest. Nevertheless, permissible sexual behavior has changed dramatically over the past century, and the differences underscore the socially constructed nature of human sexuality.*

this chapter. People don't just eat, they *dine*, which connotes all sorts of social and cognitive influences. And people don't just copulate; they fall in love, compose romantic sonnets, promise to be faithful, have affairs, suffer guilt, and engage in long, intimate discussions with their beloved. Moreover, human beings have enormous powers of conscious control over even their most basic drives, as witnessed in those who voluntarily undergo starvation to protest political repression or in those who choose a life of chastity, whether from religious conviction or prudence (especially in this era of AIDS). We will not review these social and cognitive influences in this chapter, but we should not forget them either.

### The Physiological Approach to the Study of Drives

The very notion of drives, as defined above, almost begs us to look inside the organism to see what has happened there to cause a change in behavior. The goal of the physiological approach to the study of drives is to try to give substance to the hypothetical inner state, to make it no longer hypothetical. What really happens inside to make a person hungry, or driven in some other way? Some have searched for *central* changes, that is, changes in the brain. Others have searched for *peripheral* changes—bodily changes outside of the brain, such as chemicals in the blood or the activity of such organs as the stomach or liver. The search for peripheral changes has often been based on the concept of homeostasis.

**Drives as Tissue Needs: The Concept of Homeostasis**  In an influential book entitled *The Wisdom of the Body* (1932), Walter B. Cannon—a famous physiologist of the early twentieth century—described simply and elegantly the requirements of the tissues of the human body. For life to be sustained, certain substances and characteristics within the body must be kept within a restricted range, going neither too high nor too low. These include body temperature, oxygen, minerals, water, and energy-producing food molecules. Physiological processes, such as digestion and respiration, must continually work toward achieving what Cannon termed **homeostasis**, the constancy of internal conditions that the body must actively maintain. Most important, Cannon pointed out that maintenance of homeostasis involves the organism's outward behavior as well as internal processes. To stay alive, individuals must find and consume foods, salts, and water and must maintain their body temperature through such means as finding shelter. Cannon theorized that the basic physiological underpinning for some drives is an upset in homeostatic balance, which induces behavior designed to correct the imbalance.

Following Cannon, psychologists and physiologists performed experiments showing that animals indeed do behave in accordance with their tissue needs. For example, if the caloric (energy) content of its food is increased or decreased, an animal will compensate by eating less or more of it, keeping the daily intake of calories relatively constant regardless of the food available. As another example, removal of the adrenal glands causes an animal to lose salt in its urine (because one of the adrenal hormones is essential for conserving salt), and this loss of salt dramatically increases the animal's drive to seek out and eat extra salt, which keeps the animal alive as long as salt is available (Richter & Eckert, 1938; Stricker, 1973).

The force of homeostasis in human behavior was dramatically and poignantly illustrated by the clinical case of a boy, referred to as D. W., who when 1 year old developed a great craving for salt (Wilkins & Richter, 1940). His favorite foods were salted crackers, pretzels, potato chips, olives, and pickles; he would also take salt directly from the shaker. When salt was denied him he would cry until his parents gave in, and when he learned to speak, "salt" was one of his first and favorite words. D. W. survived until the age of 3½, when he was hospitalized for other symptoms and placed on a standard hospital diet. The hospital staff would not yield to his demands for salt, and he died within a few days. An autopsy subsequently revealed that his adrenal glands were deficient; only then did D. W.'s doc-

*The meaning of homeostasis, and its demonstration in a little boy who needed salt*

tors realize that his salt craving came from physiological need. His strong drive for salt and his ability to manipulate his parents into supplying it, even though they were unaware that he needed it, had kept D. W. alive for 2½ years—powerful evidence for "the wisdom of the body."

**Limitations of Homeostasis: Regulatory and Nonregulatory Drives**   Homeostasis is a useful concept for understanding thirst, hunger, and the drives for salt, oxygen, and temperature control, but not for understanding certain other drives. Consider sex, for example. People are highly motivated to engage in sex, but there is no tissue need for it. No vital bodily substance is affected by engaging in sexual behavior; nobody can die from lack of sex (despite what an overly amorous someone may have told you). In their desire to develop a unitary theory of drives, some psychologists proposed hypothetical needs for sex and other drives for which there is no observed tissue need. But by doing so they were destroying the original advantage of the homeostatic theory. If needs cannot be identified in the body, independently of the behaviors they are believed to motivate, then the concept of need is not an objective explanation. In fact, it is no explanation at all, as the term "need" in that case is simply a substitute for the term "drive." Psychologists today find it useful to distinguish between regulatory drives and nonregulatory drives. A *regulatory drive* is one, like hunger, that helps preserve homeostasis, and a *nonregulatory drive* is one, like sex, that serves some other purpose.

**Drives as States of the Brain**   If drives are inner states, how can they best be described physiologically? Early theories, based on the concept of homeostasis, attempted to define drives as tissue needs. But such definitions were never fully satisfactory, even when applied to regulatory drives. For example, under certain conditions hunger can be high when the tissue need for more food is low, or low when the need for food is high. Most physiological psychologists today think of drives not as states of peripheral tissues, but rather as states of the brain. According to most versions of this *central-state theory of drives*, different drives correspond to neural activity in different sets of neurons in the brain (Stellar & Stellar, 1985). The set of neurons in which activity constitutes a drive is called a *central drive system*. Although the central drive systems for different drives must be at least partly different from one another, they may have overlapping components. For example, because hunger and sex are different drives, the neural circuits for them cannot be identical, yet they may share some parts. Thus, they might share components that keep the animal alert and increase its general level of motor activity.

What characteristics must a set of neurons have to serve as a central drive system? First, concerning input, it must receive and integrate all of the various signals that can raise or lower the drive state. For hunger, these signals include chemicals in the blood, the presence or absence of food in the stomach, and the sight and smell of food in the environment. Second, concerning output, a central drive system must act on all of the neural processes that would be involved in carrying out the motivated behavior. It must direct perceptual mechanisms toward stimuli related to the goal, cognitive (thought) mechanisms to work out strategies to achieve the goal, and motor centers of the brainstem and spinal cord to produce the appropriate movements. Look back at Figure 6.20, which depicts a hierarchical model of the control of action, with mechanisms involved in motivation and planning at the top. The central drive systems are part of that top level of the hierarchy. To affect behavior (for example, to cause a hungry person to cross a room for some peanuts), they must influence the activity of motor systems that occupy lower levels of the hierarchy.

There is reason to believe that a hub of many central drive systems lies in the hypothalamus. Anatomically, this brain structure is ideally located to play such a role (see Figure 7.1). It is centered at the bottom of the brain, just in front of the midbrain, and contains tracts that interconnect many areas of the brain. It also has

---

■ *The difference between regulatory and nonregulatory drives*

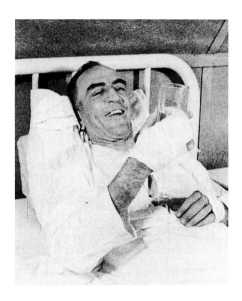

**Consuming thirst**

*Twenty-one days on a life raft in the Pacific is enough to drive a man to drink. And, in fact, once World War II Captain Eddie Rickenbacker was rescued, he said, "Water was the only thing on my mind." Thirst is not discussed in this chapter, but, like hunger, it is a regulatory drive involving an elaborate interplay of neural and hormonal mechanisms.*

■ *The definition of a central drive system, and the characteristics it must have to motivate behavior*

■ *Some characteristics of the hypothalamus that make it suited to be a hub of central drive systems*

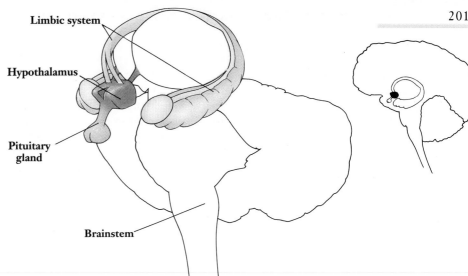

**Figure 7.1 *Location of the hypothalamus***

*The hypothalamus is ideally situated to serve as a hub for central drive systems. It has strong connections to the brainstem below, the limbic system and cerebral cortex above, and the circulatory system (by way of the capillaries that penetrate it and its tie to the pituitary gland).*

direct connections to nerves that carry sensory input from, and autonomic motor output to, most of the body's internal organs. It has many capillaries and thus is more sensitive to hormones and other substances carried by the blood than are other brain areas. Finally, through its connections to the pituitary gland, it controls the release of many hormones. Thus, the hypothalamus has all of the inputs and outputs that central drive systems would be expected to have. And, as you will soon see, small disruptions in particular parts of the hypothalamus can have dramatic effects on an animal's drives.

**Brain Lesions and Stimulation as Ways to Locate Central Drive Systems**   To identify the functions of specific nuclei (groups of neural cell bodies) or tracts (groups of axons running together) in the brain, researchers may either damage or stimulate them and assess the effect on the animal's behavior.

Specific brain areas can be damaged either through electrical or chemical means. To produce an area of damage, or ***lesion***, electrically, a thin wire called an *electrode* is lowered into the brain with the help of a *stereotaxic instrument* (see Figure 7.2), and an electric current is sent through it with enough intensity to destroy the neurons adjacent to its tip (the rest of the electrode is electrically insulated). To produce a lesion chemically, a tiny tube called a *cannula* is lowered into the brain, again using a stereotaxic instrument, and a small amount of a chemical that is poisonous to neurons is injected through the cannula, destroying neurons whose cell bodies are located near the cannula's tip. Lesions usually are made *bilaterally*, in the same area in both the right and left halves of the brain, because the right and left halves of such structures as the hypothalamus and limbic system usually serve identical functions; to eliminate a function, the same part of the structure must be destroyed on both sides. If, after a bilateral lesion, an animal no longer shows a particular drive (for example, no longer responds to food but does respond to other incentives), the inference can be made that the destroyed area is a critical part of the central system for that drive.

**Figure 7.2 *Method for making lesions in or stimulating a rat's brain***

*A stereotaxic instrument, depicted at left, is used to insert an electrode into a precise location in the anesthetized (unconscious) animal's brain. To produce a lesion, a relatively large electric current is sent through the electrode, and then the electrode is removed. To prepare the animal for electrical brain stimulation, on the other hand, the electrode is cemented in place, as shown in the drawing at right, so that it can be stimulated through wire leads during behavioral tests after the animal has recovered from surgery.*

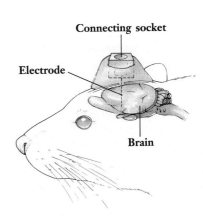

**How and why localized areas of the brain are damaged or stimulated in the study of drives**

*Stimulation* of specific areas of the brain can also be accomplished either electrically or chemically. To stimulate neurons electrically, an electrode is permanently implanted in the brain, as shown in Figure 7.2. The electrode can be activated at any time after surgery, through either a wire connection or radio waves. The electrical current used for stimulation is much weaker than that for producing a lesion—it is strong enough to activate, but not strong enough to destroy, neurons near the electrode's tip. To stimulate neurons chemically, a cannula is permanently implanted in the brain, and shortly before behavioral testing a tiny amount of a transmitter or other chemical known to activate neurons is injected through it. If electrical or chemical stimulation of a specific brain area elicits a drive (for example, if a previously nonhungry animal responds to the stimulus by seeking food and eating), the inference can be made that the stimulated area is part of the central system for the drive elicited.

### Hunger

Hunger is the drive that has been most fully studied physiologically. In fact, a major impetus in the development of the central-state theory of drives was the demonstration, about 50 years ago, that small lesions in the hypothalamus can drastically alter an animal's tendency to seek food and eat (Morgan, 1943). Yet an enormous amount remains to be learned about the physiological control of hunger. The hundreds of experiments conducted so far demonstrate wonderfully the adage that the more we learn, the more we become aware of how little we know. In the following paragraphs, we will look first at hypothalamic involvement in hunger, then at studies of the signals that presumably act on the brain to increase or decrease hunger, and finally at some ideas about weight control in humans.

**An old and elegant, but too-simple, theory about the hypothalamus and hunger**

**The Involvement of the Hypothalamus in Hunger**   About 2 or 3 decades ago, a simple theory would have been described under this heading. Its essence would have been that (a) the *lateral area* of the hypothalamus is a hunger center, which induces food seeking and eating when its neurons are active, and (b) the *ventromedial area* of the hypothalamus is a satiety center, which reduces hunger through inhibitory connections to the lateral area (to see the relative positions of these parts of the hypothalamus, see Figure 7.3). The theory would also have included the idea that glucose, a sugar molecule that is the main source of energy for the brain, reduces hunger by directly activating neurons of the ventromedial hypothalamus. Conversely, when blood glucose is low—according to the theory—hunger increases, because the ventromedial cells become less active and no longer inhibit

**Figure 7.3  *Diagram of some parts of the hypothalamus***
*This schematic diagram shows the relative location of some of the parts of the hypothalamus where lesions or electrical stimulation have dramatic effects on behavior. To interpret the diagram, imagine that you are looking straight down through the top of the animal's head and can see an x-ray view of the lower part of the hypothalamus, at the very bottom of the brain. The paired central structures lie along the midline of the brain, and the paired lateral areas lie to their right and left. To make a bilateral lesion, both the right and left structures must be damaged.*

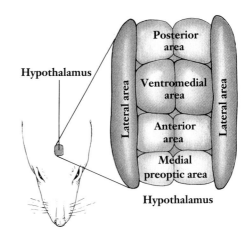

**A newer theory about why lesions in the lateral hypothalamus abolish hunger**

**Evidence salvaging the idea that some neurons in the hypothalamus are specific to hunger**

the lateral area. Unfortunately for the sake of elegance, research since then has shot some holes in that theory. Today, what we know about the role of the hypothalamus in hunger is more complicated than what I read about as a college student first becoming intrigued by the brain.

Consistent with the early view that the lateral hypothalamus is a hunger center, animals with bilateral lesions in this area neither seek food nor eat that which is placed in front of them; they would die from starvation if not force-fed through a tube. Conversely, electrical stimulation in this area causes previously sated animals to eat. Complications arose, however, when tests with incentives besides food revealed that animals with lesions in the lateral hypothalamus lacked not just hunger but many other drives as well, including thirst, sex drive, and parental drive (they would no longer build nests or retrieve their young). Moreover, electrical stimulation in this area was found to increase behaviors related to all of these drives, the specific behavior depending upon what incentives were available (Stricker, 1982). Thus, if only food was available the animal would eat in response to the stimulus, but if another incentive was available—such as water or a sexual partner—the animal was equally likely to behave in a goal-directed way toward it.

Other experiments, aimed at understanding which neurons are involved in these effects, revealed that the most critical neurons are not those with cell bodies in the lateral hypothalamus, as had previously been believed, but rather those whose cell bodies exist elsewhere and whose axons form a tract through the hypothalamus, connecting parts of the brainstem (below the hypothalamus) with the basal ganglia (above the hypothalamus). Lesions or electrical stimulation anywhere along this tract, including in the brainstem or at its entrance to the basal ganglia, were as effective as those in the lateral hypothalamus in abolishing or stimulating drives (Grossman, 1979). Researchers now believe that this tract through the lateral hypothalamus is part of a general motor-activation system, which prepares the basal ganglia to initiate deliberate movements regardless of the specific drive. Electrical stimulation of this tract seems to give the animal the message, "Do something," leaving the animal to respond to whatever incentives are present in the environment.

But all is not lost for the theory that some lateral hypothalamic neurons are specifically involved in hunger. Using chemical rather than electrical means to produce lesions in the lateral hypothalamus, researchers can destroy neurons whose cell bodies are located there without destroying neurons whose axons pass through the area (the chemical must contact the cell body in order to destroy the neuron). Such lesions greatly reduce hunger (though do not abolish it), whereas they have much less of an effect on other drives (Stellar & Stellar, 1985). Other evidence comes from another way to explore the brain, that of *recording* activity in single neurons, through permanently implanted microelectrodes (very tiny electrodes). Using this method, Edmond Rolls (1982) found a set of neurons in the lateral hypothalamus in monkeys that produced bursts of action potentials only when the monkey was both hungry (from having been deprived of food) and exposed to food-related stimuli. The cells would become active when the hungry monkey saw or smelled food, or saw a conditioned stimulus that had previously been used to signal the delivery of food, but not when exposed to stimuli that had never been associated with food.

Rolls's study is especially interesting because it provides a clue concerning the physiological basis for the interaction of drives and incentives. The motivational state of hunger apparently includes, as one of its components, the sensitization of certain neurons in the lateral hypothalamus, such that they respond to an incentive (food signals) to which they would not respond otherwise. Rolls also found that these same neurons send their axons to the association areas in the frontal lobes of the cerebral cortex, which are known to be important for planning and organizing goal-directed movements. Work of this sort helps validate the theory that motiva-

■ *A newer theory about why lesions in the ventromedial area cause overeating and obesity*

**Figure 7.4** *Effect of a lesion in the ventromedial area of the hypothalamus*
*After receiving a bilateral lesion, this rat overate and gained weight to the point where it tipped the scale at 1080 grams— about three times what a normal rat weighs.*

■ *How receptors sensitive to the availability of food inside and outside of the organism can alter the hunger drive*

tional mechanisms in the hypothalamus and limbic system work closely with planning mechanisms in the cerebral cortex when an individual chooses a course of deliberate action (such as moving toward and consuming food). (See Figure 6.20.)

What about the ventromedial hypothalamus? Does research still support the idea that activity there suppresses hunger by directly inhibiting the lateral hypothalamus? Bilateral lesions in the ventromedial area do cause animals to eat more and become obese (see Figure 7.4), but there is reason to believe that this effect is mediated by changes in digestion and metabolism rather than by direct action within the brain. The ventromedial hypothalamus is an important control center for the parasympathetic portion of the autonomic nervous system, and its destruction causes parts of the parasympathetic system to become overactive. As a result, food is digested more rapidly than normal (Duggan & Booth, 1986) and food molecules in the blood are converted very quickly to fat, leaving less for use as fuel for other tissues in the body (King & others, 1984). The result is that messages are sent from the body's tissues to the brain that more food is needed. Occasionally a tumor at the base of the brain causes, in humans, damage to the ventromedial hypothalamus, and in such cases the person becomes obese, apparently for the same reasons that experimental animals do (Bray & Gallagher, 1975).

**Stimuli That Act on the Brain to Increase or Decrease Hunger**    In the early days of hunger research, many researchers hoped to find *the* signal to the brain that turns hunger on or off. Some thought it might be glucose (as mentioned before) or some other sugar molecule in the blood. Others thought it might be signals from the stomach. Today, researchers know that the central nervous system is responsive to a wide variety of influences, none of which has full control. Among these influences are the following:

  ■ *Feedback indicating stomach distension*    Most people believe that an empty stomach signals hunger and a full stomach signals satiety, and this is one instance where the popular view is supported by research. Sensory neurons that respond to distension of the stomach run from receptor cells in the stomach walls directly to the brain by way of a cranial nerve (Gonzalez & Deutsch, 1981). When those neurons are stimulated by inflating a balloon in the stomach with water, rats eat less than usual and lose weight (Geliebter & others, 1987). Conversely, when those neurons are destroyed by cutting the nerve from the stomach, rats eat more than usual and gain weight (Gonzalez & Deutsch, 1981). Thus, neural input to the brain signaling a full stomach tends to decrease hunger, and the absence of such input tends to increase it.

  ■ *Feedback indicating the amount of food molecules in the blood*    After being partially digested in the stomach, food passes into the small intestine for further digestion down to its molecular components, and then the molecules enter the bloodstream and are carried to all of the body's tissues. Receptors in various tissues may be sensitive to the level of food molecules in the blood, but an area of special sensitivity appears to be the liver. Researchers have found that food molecules (such as glucose) injected into the liver cause a previously hungry dog or rat to eat much less than it otherwise would. This effect is apparently mediated by sensory neurons that run from the liver to the brain by way of a cranial nerve (Russek, 1971; Novin & others, 1983). The food molecules *decrease* the rate of action potentials in these sensory neurons (Niijima, 1982). Thus, a high rate of action potentials in neurons from the liver is believed to stimulate the hunger mechanism in the brain, and a low rate is believed to dampen it.

  ■ *Feedback indicating the amount of fat in the body*    Hunger regulates not only the short-term supply of energy molecules, but also body weight. In both rats and humans, weight tends to remain relatively stable throughout adult life (except for a gradual upward drift, in both species, from youth through middle age). Individuals find a particular weight, referred to as the *set point*, easiest to maintain. Rats that have been slimmed down below their set point by food deprivation, or fattened up above it by forced feeding through a tube, subsequently eat more or less than normal until their weight returns to the set point (Hoebel & Teitelbaum, 1966). Most weight changes over time are due to increased or decreased fat, stored in special fat cells under the skin. The amount of fat in such cells apparently contributes to hunger or satiety in a way that tends to return weight to the set point. During the period between meals, as the food molecules from the previous meal are used up, fat molecules enter the blood from fat cells and supply most of the energy needed to keep the body going until the next meal. When one's weight is below the set point, fat cells become less likely to give up their stored fat, so receptors sensitive to low blood levels of food (such as those in the liver) become active and stimulate hunger sooner after a meal than they otherwise would.

*The appetizer effect*  The signals described so far all come from inside the body and have to do with the actual need or lack of need for food. Food in the stomach, blood, and fat cells decreases hunger, and lack of food in those places increases hunger. But hunger is also affected by external stimuli. Any stimulus that reminds one of good food can increase the hunger drive—a phenomenon known as the *appetizer effect*. This effect is probably mediated partly by processes occurring entirely within the brain, but it may also be mediated partly through reflexes involving peripheral digestive and metabolic processes (see Powley, 1977). For example, one reflexive response to external cues is the secretion of insulin, a hormone that stimulates the transfer of glucose and other food molecules from the blood to storage cells in various parts of the body. Thus, insulin reduces the level of food in the blood, which in turn may increase hunger through the means already described.

**Theories About Human Obesity**  Magazines and self-help books are full of new ways to lose weight. In part, the desire to be thin is related more to current societal notions of beauty than to health needs. Still, many of us *do* weigh more than is healthy, sometimes considerably more. Why is it that many people can't seem to lose excess weight and keep it off, despite their fervent desire to do so? Studies comparing obese people (usually defined as those whose weight is more than 20

*A cultural paradox*

*Members of our affluent society are constantly bombarded with food-related cues. And, no matter how "relaxed" the jeans, our culture conspires to make the wearer feel uptight about excess weight.*

percent above average for their sex, height, and bone structure) and nonobese people have revealed no consistent differences in willpower or other personality characteristics (Leon & Roth, 1977). Thus, current research on obesity focuses not on general personality characteristics, but on the more specific ways that obese individuals differ from the nonobese in their responses to, and metabolism of, food.

Two theories about obesity that have provoked a good deal of research are (1) that the obese are more likely than the nonobese to eat in response to stressful events in their lives, and (2) that the obese are more responsive than the nonobese to external food-related cues (the appetizer effect) and less responsive to internal cues signaling the actual need or lack of need for food. Let us look at experiments supporting both of these theories, and then at a possible alternative explanation of the findings.

Supporting the stress-eating theory are experiments in which obese and nonobese people were given an opportunity to eat under either stressful or relaxed conditions, without being told that their food intake was being measured. In one experiment, obese and nonobese subjects participated in a "taste test" of chocolate-chip cookies (McKenna, 1972). Some subjects, in the *stress condition*, were told that after the taste test they would have to give a rather large sample of blood for physiological analysis, and others, in the *nonstress condition*, were given no such information. Consistent with the theory, anticipation of giving blood caused obese subjects to eat more cookies, and nonobese subjects to eat fewer cookies, than did obese and nonobese subjects in the nonstress condition. Thus, in the nonstress condition the two groups did not differ in the number of cookies eaten, but in the stress condition the obese ate many more cookies than did the nonobese.

Supporting the cue-sensitivity theory are a series of experiments performed by Stanley Schachter (1970) and his colleagues. In one experiment, obese and nonobese college students took part in a "taste test" of crackers. Some subjects were required to eat roast-beef sandwiches before the test, and others were not asked to eat anything before the test. Consistent with Schachter's theory, prefeeding reduced the number of crackers eaten by nonobese subjects, but it had no effect on the number eaten by obese subjects (see Figure 7.5a). In another experiment, obese and nonobese students were told that their task was to sit at a table and "think," and they were invited to snack from a bowl of peanuts if they wished to during their thinking time. For some subjects, the nuts were brightly illuminated by a table lamp, and for others they were dimly illuminated. As predicted, nonobese subjects ate about the same number of nuts in either condition, whereas obese subjects ate many more nuts when they were visually prominent than when they weren't (see Figure 7.5b). Thus, the first experiment supported Schachter's view that obese individuals fail to respond to internal cues (the satiating effect of food in the stomach), and the second supported his view that they overrespond to external cues (the prominent display of peanuts).

■ *Evidence for the (a) stress-eating and (b) cue-sensitivity theories of obesity*

**Figure 7.5 *Responsiveness of obese and nonobese subjects to internal and external cues for eating***

*Schachter and his colleagues found that (a) obese college students ate about the same number of crackers whether or not they had been preloaded with roast-beef sandwiches and (b) they ate more peanuts if the peanut bowl was brightly illuminated rather than dimly illuminated. In contrast, nonobese students ate less after preloading, and they were not affected by the illumination of the peanut bowl. Other researchers have suggested that these differences might not correspond with obesity per se, but might be due to the greater number of dieters in the obese group. (From Schachter, 1970.)*

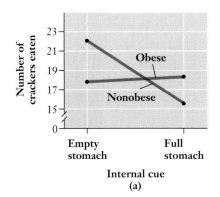

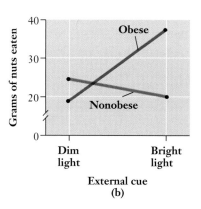

Experiments such as McKenna's and Schachter's are appealing because of their cleverness and because they seem to support the self-reported experiences of many overweight people. Yet the theories that obese people in general overeat in response to stress or external cues remain unproven. Experiments similar in design to those just described have not always produced the same results (see Spitzer & Rodin, 1983), and other experiments have suggested that the tendency of obese individuals to overeat in response to stress or external cues may be more a *consequence* of obesity than a cause.

One consistent difference between obese and nonobese people—in our culture, at least—is that at any given time more obese people are likely to be on a diet, consciously trying to lose weight by restricting their food intake. Experiments similar in design to McKenna's and Schachter's have shown that dieters, *whether or not they are obese*, are more likely to eat in response to emotion-provoking and strong external cues than are nondieters, and less likely to eat in response to internal signals (Herman, 1980; Spitzer & Rodin, 1983). Dieters may learn to resist their internal hunger cues, but in emotional situations, or in the presence of really strong external cues for eating, this resistance may break down, accounting for the well-known "binge" (Rodin, 1981). Thus, it is possible that the findings of McKenna and Schachter could have resulted from there being more dieters among the obese subjects than among the nonobese.

- **An alternative explanation of the findings that supported the stress-eating and cue-sensitivity theories**

- **Heredity, fat cells, and the ratchet effect—why weight tends to change in only one direction**

Heredity plays an important role in who becomes obese and who doesn't, as indicated by studies showing that adopted children are more similar to their biological parents than to their adoptive parents in weight (Foch & McClearn, 1980). Other research suggests that the number of fat-storage cells (fat cells) that one has is an important determinant of body weight, establishing the set point that I mentioned earlier (see Faust, 1984). Obese rats and humans have more fat cells than do nonobese individuals; when they lose weight they do not lose these cells, but rather each cell becomes abnormally thin, which in turn may stimulate hunger (as described earlier). The number of fat cells one has seems to be determined mainly by heredity, but it may also be affected—in one direction only—by the amount of food intake. While there is no evidence that the number of fat cells decreases when one diets, there is, alas, evidence that the number increases when one overeats for a prolonged period. This may be the mechanism that explains why the set point does not go down when one eats less than usual for a period of time, but does go up when one overeats for a period of time—a phenomenon known as the *ratchet effect*. In one experiment, rats placed on a high-fat diet gained weight, and examination of their fat cells showed that the gain was due partly to an increase in the size of each cell and partly to an increase in number (Faust, 1984). When the rats were subsequently returned to a normal diet they lost some of the weight they had gained, but not all of it. The amount that they lost was accounted for by the return of their fat cells to normal size, and the amount *not* lost was accounted for by the increased number of fat cells (see Figure 7.6).

**Figure 7.6 *Effect of a high-fat diet on fat cells***

*As illustrated by this schematic diagram, when rats were placed on a high-fat diet their fat cells increased in both number and size. When they were subsequently returned to a normal diet, their fat cells returned to normal size but did not decrease in number. The result was that the rats remained heavier than they would have been had they never been on the high-fat diet.*

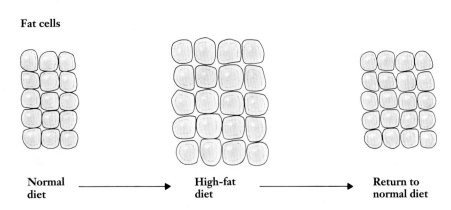

**Fat cells**

Normal diet → High-fat diet → Return to normal diet

■ *How a shift in basal metabolism helps keep weight at the set point*

The tendency for weight to stabilize at the set point is mediated not just by changes in food intake, but also by changes in basal metabolism (the rate at which calories are burned up during rest). When weight in animals or humans is reduced below the set point, their metabolic rate slows down, so weight gain can occur with less food than it otherwise would (Keesey & Corbett, 1984). Recent studies with humans have shown that by measuring basal metabolism it is possible to predict with reasonable accuracy who will gain weight. In one study, babies who had lower metabolic rates than average at the age of 3 months gained more weight by the age of 1 year than did those with higher rates (Roberts & others, 1988). In another study, adults with low metabolic rates gained more weight over both a 2- and 4-year period than did those with higher rates (Ravussin & others, 1988). Many obese people believe that they gain weight without eating more than nonobese people, and these recent studies suggest that they could well be right.

Does all of this sound discouraging to those who want to lose weight? Here's an encouraging idea with which to end this section: No matter how overweight a person is, the biggest health gain comes from the first 5 to 15 pounds lost, and most people *can* lose and keep off that much just by avoiding high-fat foods, which have a bigger effect on fat cells than do other foods. Also, of course, some people *do* manage to take off lots of weight and keep it off, despite the odds. People vary in their reasons for being overweight and their ability to lose weight, just as they vary in other realms.

### The Sex Drive

Most of our knowledge of the brain mechanisms of the sex drive comes from laboratory studies with animals, especially rats. In the case of this drive, much more than in that of hunger, one must be cautious in extending findings from animals to humans. Aside from the important role of social and cognitive processes in human sexuality, humans differ from other species even in the basic, biological aspects of sexual physiology and behavior. Modification of the ways in which sexual behavior is controlled and expressed was probably an important part of human evolution.

One basic difference between humans and other species is in the realm of hormonal control of sexual behavior in the female. The females of nearly all other mammals are sexually motivated only during a specific time in their hormonal cycle, which is not true for human females. Another difference lies in the nature of sexual behavior itself. In other animals, including other primates, sexual behavior occurs in a stereotyped way, with one set of postures and movements for the female and a different set for the male (see Figure 7.7). In humans, however, there are no rigidly determined sexual patterns or postures, even for copulation.

Despite our unique sexual characteristics, we humans certainly have not lost all traces of the biological determinants of sexual behavior found in other species, and studies of other species provide clues to such determinants in humans. In the fol-

**Figure 7.7  *Copulation in rats***
*Rats, like other nonhuman mammals, have a stereotyped (unvarying) pattern of copulation, with clearly different postures for the female and the male.*

lowing sections I will first summarize what has been found with other species and then discuss evidence concerning how such findings may apply to humans. More on some of the uniquely human aspects of sexuality, with an emphasis on social influences, can be found in Chapter 13.

■ *Evidence that different parts of the hypothalamus are involved in the male and female sex drives in nonhuman mammals*

**Brain Mechanisms and Early Developmental Effects of Hormones**    Lesion and electrical-stimulation studies, with rats and other mammals, reveal that different neural systems are involved in the control of male and female sex drives. The brain area most critical to the male's sex drive is the *medial preoptic area* of the hypothalamus (look back at Figure 7.3). Lesions there abolish, and electrical stimulation there increases, the male but not the female sex drive (Heimer & Larsson, 1967; Van Dis & Larsson, 1971). The same procedures show that the brain area most critical to the female sex drive is the *ventromedial area* of the hypothalamus (Powers & Valenstein, 1972; Pfaff & Sakuma, 1979). Such brain manipulations truly affect drive, not simply reflexive copulation, as they influence the animal's tendency to seek out and approach a member of the opposite sex, not just the tendency to copulate when presented with a sexual partner (Clark & others, 1981).

■ *Evidence that the presence or absence of testosterone before birth predisposes male or female brain development*

Other research with rats has shown that the male-female brain differences that account for different adult sexual behaviors are determined by the presence or absence of the hormone *testosterone* during a critical period of development beginning before birth. As described in Chapter 3, the only *genetic* difference between the two sexes is that females have two X chromosomes, whereas males have one X and one Y. A specific gene on the Y chromosome causes the growth of testes (the male gonads) from structures that would otherwise grow into ovaries (the female gonads) (Page & others, 1987). The testes begin to produce testosterone before birth, which acts on the brain as well as on other body structures to create malelike growth. In the absence of this hormone, the structures grow in the female direction. Thus, rudimentary external genitals differentiate into the penis and other male structures if testosterone is present, or into the clitoris and other female structures if testosterone is absent. Within the brain, testosterone produced before birth acts on the hypothalamus to promote growth of neurons involved in the male sex drive and to inhibit growth of those involved in the female sex drive (Feder, 1984). Thus, genetically female rats treated with testosterone during this period grow up predisposed to show male sexual behavior, and genetically male rats deprived of testosterone during this period grow up predisposed to show female sexual behavior.

Perhaps you are wondering why a male, rather than a female, hormone plays the key role in early sexual differentiation. The answer is that female hormones, produced by the mother, are available to all young mammals during the prenatal period. The mother produces large amounts of progesterone (one female hormone) throughout pregnancy, and large amounts of estrogen (another female hormone) near the end of pregnancy; these hormones enter the bloodstream of the developing fetus. Thus, if female hormones promoted growth of female structures during the prenatal period, both males and females would be born looking like females. It is interesting to note that in birds and reptiles—which develop in eggs outside of the mother's body—early sexual differentiation is determined by the presence or absence of the female hormone estrogen, not testosterone (Adkins-Regan, 1981).

■ *Evidence that prenatal stress can affect the sexual development of male rats, and a possible explanation of how this happens*

In a fascinating series of experiments, Ingeborg Ward and her colleagues (1985) showed that stressful events experienced by pregnant rats can influence the future sexual behavior of their male offspring, apparently by reducing the level of prenatal testosterone. When the researchers subjected pregnant rats to bright lights and physical restraint, the rats' male offspring manifested less male sexual behavior and more female sexual behavior in adulthood than did the male offspring of unstressed mothers. In further studies, these researchers showed that males born to stressed mothers had unusually low levels of testosterone in their blood at the time of birth. Apparently, in response to stress the mother secretes hormones that inhibit the production of testosterone in male fetuses, which in turn causes their brains to be less masculinized, and more feminized, than would otherwise be the case.

*Reasons for thinking that sharp brain differences in the control of male and female sex drives may not hold for humans*

Experiments such as Ward's show how behavior throughout life can be influenced by events that occur before birth. On behavioral grounds alone, it seems unlikely that the sharp differentiation between male and female sex drives that exists in other mammals would also be found in humans. In humans, unlike other species, there are no sexual behaviors that uniquely and universally characterize one sex or the other. Moreover, experiments have shown that men and women manifest similar patterns of peripheral physiological changes during sexual arousal and climax (Masters & Johnson, 1966) and describe their subjective feelings during sex in similar ways (Vance & Wagner, 1976). With such similarity at the behavioral and peripheral physiological levels, it seems unlikely that sharply different brain mechanisms would be involved. On the other hand, the possibility of some sex difference in the human brain's organization of sex drive is suggested by the fact that men are predominantly more sexually attracted toward women than toward men, and vice versa. There is some evidence (reviewed by Ellis & Ames, 1987) that this difference is at least partly mediated by the presence or absence of testosterone, produced by the male fetus and not by the female, during the prenatal period.

*Evidence, however, that prenatal stress in humans may have an effect analogous to that in rats*

Several studies have suggested that stress experienced by the mother during the middle 3 months of pregnancy may affect sexual orientation in human males somewhat as it does in other species (Ellis & Ames, 1987; Ellis & others, 1988). In one such study, researchers asked nearly 300 mothers of adult sons and daughters to fill out a questionnaire concerning stressful experiences that occurred during their pregnancy, and they asked the sons and daughters to fill out a separate, confidential questionnaire concerning their sexual orientation. The main finding was a small but statistically significant relationship between stress experienced by the mother during the middle 3 months of pregnancy and homosexuality in the sons (Ellis & others, 1988). On a four-point scale, the mothers of homosexual males rated their stress level during those 3 months as 2.3, compared to 1.2 for the mothers of heterosexual males. Consistent with Ward's finding, no such relationship occurred with daughters. As the authors of this study point out, the results certainly do not imply that homosexuality in human males results simply from prenatal stress, but they do suggest that prenatal stress may be a contributing factor in some cases, perhaps through the same hormonal mechanism that Ward discovered in animals.

**Hormonal Effects on the Sex Drive After Puberty**   At puberty, in both humans and other mammals, the production of sex hormones greatly increases. In men, increased testosterone at this time stimulates such changes as beard growth and the male pattern of muscle development; in women, increased estrogen stimulates such changes as breast growth. As will be discussed in Chapter 13, these peripheral changes affect the way that other people react to the individual, and in that way change the developing person's self-concept and behavior. But our concern now is with the possibility that the increase in hormones also affects behavior more directly, through acting on brain mechanisms for the sex drive. We will look at this phenomenon first in the male and then in the female.

*Evidence that testosterone is needed to maintain the male's sex drive, and that, in animals, it does so by direct action in the hypothalamus*

In male animals, castration (removal of the testes and hence the main supply of testosterone) causes a marked decline in sex drive—not all at once, but gradually over time (it takes days to occur in rats, weeks in dogs, sometimes months in monkeys) (Feder, 1984). But the injection of testosterone into the bloodstream of castrated animals fully restores their drive. Sex drive can also be restored by implanting a tiny crystal of testosterone in the medial preoptic area of the hypothalamus, whereas the same amount of testosterone placed anywhere else does not produce this effect (Davidson, 1980). Thus, testosterone apparently augments and maintains the sex drive in males by acting directly on cells in the medial preoptic area, the same area where brain lesions destroy the drive. Other experiments have shown that neurons in this area contain testosterone receptors, where the hormone acts to modify neural activity (Pfaff & Modianos, 1985).

Testosterone is also important for maintaining the sex drive in human males. Men castrated in an accident or for medical reasons almost always experience a decline (though often not a complete loss) in sex drive and behavior, but their drive is usually fully restored if they take injections of testosterone (Money & Erhardt, 1972). In other studies, testosterone injections sharply increased sexual behavior in noncastrated men whose testes were producing abnormally low amounts of the hormone; this effect was more on drive than on sexual ability (Davidson & others, 1979; Davidson & Myers, 1988). Men with abnormally low levels of testosterone were apparently fully capable of the mechanics of sexual behavior—including erection and ejaculation—but had little desire for it until injected with testosterone. Since the subjects in this research did not know when they were receiving testosterone and when they were not, the results must have been due to the effects of the hormone, not to their expectations.

It should be emphasized that this effect of injected testosterone has been documented only in men whose original testosterone level was very low. There is little evidence that variation in testosterone level within the range produced by gonadally normal men affects sex drive (Feder, 1984). Apparently, some minimal level of the hormone is needed for full sex drive, and testosterone beyond that level has little if any further effect.

*Evidence that estrogen is needed to maintain the female sex drive in other mammals, but not in humans, and that it does so by direct action in the hypothalamus*

What about females? Here, as I noted earlier, there is a clear difference between humans and other mammals in the role of hormones in sex drive. After puberty, estrogen and progesterone are produced in cyclic fashion, accounting for the cycle of physiological changes referred to as the *menstrual cycle* in humans and the *estrous cycle* in other mammals. In both humans and nonhumans, this cycle controls ovulation (the release of one or more eggs, so that pregnancy can occur). In most nonhuman animals, it also tightly controls the sex drive—which ranges from very strong at the time of ovulation to nonexistent during other phases. Removal of the ovaries (the main source of estrogen and progesterone) completely abolishes the sex drive in such animals, and injection of hormones fully restores it. For some species an injection of estrogen alone is most effective, and for others (including the rat) a sequence of estrogen followed 2 or 3 days later by progesterone is most effective. Just as testosterone increases the male sex drive by direct action in the medial preoptic area, estrogen increases the female sex drive by direct action in the ventromedial area of the hypothalamus. A tiny amount of estrogen inserted into this area renews the sexual behavior of female animals whose ovaries have been removed (Matthews & Edwards, 1977; Floody & others, 1987).

In contrast, the hormonal changes accompanying the human menstrual cycle play relatively little if any role in women's sexual motivation. A few studies, in which women kept records of their daily sexual activities or thoughts, have shown a somewhat enhanced sex drive around the time of ovulation (see, for example, Adams & others, 1978), but such results have not been widely replicated (Davidson & Myers, 1988). Moreover, if hormonal changes during the menstrual cycle do play a role, the most relevant hormone is probably neither estrogen nor progesterone, but testosterone. Testosterone is usually thought of as a male hormone, but it is produced in small amounts by the adrenal glands in women and undergoes a cyclic change that mirrors the cycle of estrogen during the menstrual cycle. One study, in which women kept records of their self-initiated sexual activity, showed a correlation between the peak level of testosterone, occurring around the time of ovulation, and sexual activity throughout their cycle (Morris & others, 1987). That is, those women who had the highest testosterone levels around the time of ovulation tended to have the highest sex drive at all times in the cycle. One possible interpretation of this is that the testosterone peak produces a prolonged effect on the sex drive, which persists at least until the next testosterone peak.

Regardless of whether fluctuations in testosterone over the menstrual cycle affect sex drive, a certain minimum baseline level of this hormone *does* seem to be important in women, as it is in men. Women whose adrenal glands have been removed, for medical reasons, often report a decline in sex drive, whereas women whose ovaries have been removed usually report no such decline, and injection of testosterone reliably increases the sex drive in low-sex-drive women (Bancroft & Skakkebaek, 1978; Feder, 1984). The apparent role of testosterone in women's sex drive provides further support for the view that sex differences in the physiological control of sex drive are less marked in humans than in other species.

■ *Evidence that testosterone affects the sex drive in women as well as men*

**The Role of External Stimuli**   Brain structures primed with hormones provide the physiological *potential* for the sex drive. But the actual induction of the drive at any given time requires, in addition, sensory stimulation—usually some aspect of the sight, sound, smell, or touch of a potential sexual partner (or, in humans, the fantasy of such stimulation). The interplay between a drive (an inner, motivational state) and an incentive (an outer stimulus) is even stronger in the case of sex than in the case of hunger. Most animals have anatomical structures and behaviors that distinguish one sex from the other and serve innately to stimulate sexual interest. The huge tail feathers of the male peacock, fanned out to excite the female, and the female chimpanzee's display of the red swelling of her rump when in heat are examples. Concerning humans, we do not know to what degree biological distinctions between men and women (such as genital differences, or the woman's rounder form compared to the man's more angular form) innately serve as sexual stimuli, and to what degree such cues depend on learning. The fact that standards of sexual beauty vary greatly across cultures, and even from individual to individual within a culture, shows at least that human biology permits a great deal of flexibility in the kinds of stimuli that can become cues for sexual attraction.

*More than skin deep*

*Physical attractiveness plays a major role in the initiation of intimate relationships, although standards of beauty vary across cultures. These men reside in (left to right) central India, North America, and central Africa.*

One long-standing belief (supported by Kinsey & others, 1953) is that men are sexually more aroused by visual cues, such as the sight of a nude member of the opposite sex, than are women. Does this belief have a basis in fact? The main evidence for this is that men are the chief consumers of sexually explicit films and magazines. But there are lots of possible social explanations for such a difference. For example, women are usually expected to be sexually more demure, which may dissuade them from seeking explicit forms of erotic material. In addition, the frequent link between pornography and the abuse of women could make such material particularly distasteful to women (Lott, 1987).

**Does pornography promote antisocial behavior?**

*Women who protest pornography believe that it contributes to violence against women, and they particularly object to images that show women being dominated or coerced sexually. For them, the issue is not whether pornography is sexually arousing, but whether it is sexist and degrading.*

A more direct approach to answering this question is to see how men and women actually respond to erotic material in laboratory tests. A number of such studies have been conducted, in which sexual arousal was assessed both physiologically, by devices that measure changes in blood flow in the penis or vagina, and psychologically, through the subjects' reports about their feelings. The results have shown surprisingly little difference between men and women in the kinds of stimuli that induce sexual arousal (see Griffitt, 1987; Lott, 1987; Rosen & Beck, 1988). Contrary to popular belief, women, like men, were more sexually aroused by explicit sexual stimuli—such as nude individuals engaged in clearly sexual activities—than by tender, romantic scenes of clothed individuals kissing or touching. The only clear sex difference in such studies was the unsurprising observation that women were usually more aroused by erotic pictures of men, and men were usually more aroused by erotic pictures of women.

One cannot caution too often about possible misinterpretations of all such research. Human sexuality is certainly a lot more than stimulus-induced, reflexive changes in blood flow. It is certainly significant that in our culture men are by far the leading consumers of pornography and women are by far the leading consumers of romance novels. But issues of that sort go beyond the ken of the present chapter; they require an analysis of sexuality in the context of the larger social environment in which both sexes develop.

### Reward Mechanisms and Their Relationship to Drives

Pleasure, rewards, reinforcers. These terms are certainly related to one another and relevant to any full discussion of motivation. Subjectively, we humans experience pleasure when we achieve ends or goals related to our drives. As a rule, the stronger the drive, the stronger the pleasure upon achieving the goal. For example, we enjoy food more when we are hungry than when not. Psychologists have no way of knowing if other animals experience a similar subjective feeling (though it is hard for me to watch my dog eat her dinner without believing that she does). But a reward clearly has different effects on an animal's behavior, depending on the drive. A hungry rat that receives a food pellet for pressing a lever will press again, whereas a nonhungry rat will not. The food pellet serves as a reinforcer for the hungry, but not the nonhungry, rat. We don't know what the rat subjectively feels, but there is no reason to think that the effect in its brain is qualitatively different from that underlying what humans call pleasure. Now let us turn to some research on the neural mechanisms of rewards or pleasure.

■ *How reward areas of the brain are identified by the self-stimulation technique*

**Rewards from Electrical Stimulation of the Brain** In the early 1950s, James Olds and Peter Milner made a remarkable discovery. They observed, quite by accident at first, that rats that received electrical stimulation in certain brain areas behaved as if they were trying to get more of it. For example, if a rat happened to receive the stimulation while exploring a particular corner of the cage, the animal would return repeatedly to that corner. To determine systematically if the brain stimulation was serving as a reward, Olds and Milner tested rats to see if they would stimulate their own brains by pressing a lever (see Figure 7.8). With certain electrode placements, rats learned very quickly to press the lever and would continue to press at high rates, sometimes for many hours without stopping (Olds & Milner, 1954). Olds and Milner's finding was the first clear indication that rewards can occur in the absence of any external stimulus change (such as the delivery of food). It suggested, too, that the rewarding effect of natural rewards such as food may occur through the activation of specific reward circuits in the brain—circuits that Olds and Milner had stimulated directly.

In the 1960s, a number of clinical researchers tried electrical stimulation in the brains of human patients as a possible treatment for various disorders, including epilepsy and severe schizophrenia (reviewed by Valenstein, 1973). With some electrode placements (mostly in the limbic system), patients reported that stimulation was highly pleasurable, and, given an opportunity, they would stimulate their own

**Figure 7.8** *Lever pressing for electrical stimulation to the brain*

*Each time this rat presses the lever it receives a brief pulse of electrical current through an electrode implanted in its brain. Some rats continued to lever press for 24 hours without rest, pressing as often as 5000 times per hour. (From Olds, 1956.)*

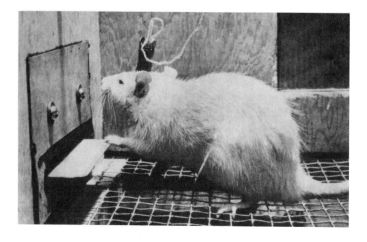
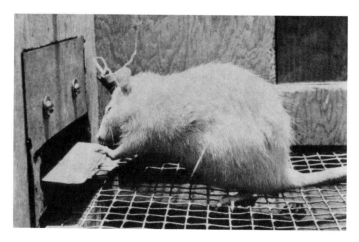

brains through the electrode. In no cases did this procedure produce compulsive brain stimulation. The patients liked it but they could leave it. However, none of the electrodes were in the brain areas known to be most effective in rats for self-stimulation. A few patients spontaneously equated the pleasure evoked through the electrode with that achieved through natural rewards, saying in some cases that it was like a sexual orgasm, or in others that it was like a good meal when hungry. Other patients, however, spoke vaguely of warm, pleasurable feelings. Still others thought the sensation was not so much pleasurable as "interesting," and they wished to explore it further by giving themselves the stimulation again. Patients who had electrodes in more than one brain area usually described the feeling differently, depending on which electrode was stimulated. Today, such studies have been discontinued for humans, apparently because the procedure is not sufficiently useful therapeutically to justify the risks involved.

*Evidence that dopamine is a neurotransmitter in a reward pathway, and that the same pathway is involved in the rewarding effect of some drugs*

Research with rats has shown that the most effective reward areas in the brain—those that animals will work fastest and longest to stimulate—lie along a pathway that runs from certain areas of the brainstem, through the lateral hypothalamus, on up into specific parts of the limbic system and the frontal lobes of the cerebral cortex (Routtenberg, 1978; Stellar & Stellar, 1985). Many of the neurons in this pathway use dopamine as their transmitter, and drugs that selectively block dopamine transmission also block the rewarding effect of brain stimulation in this pathway (Wise & Bozarth, 1984). This finding is particularly interesting in view of the fact that these same dopamine-blocking drugs also block the rewarding effect that comes from cocaine, amphetamines, and certain other drugs that are often abused for the temporary "high" that they produce (Stewart & others, 1984). Thus, the same neurons that mediate the rewarding effect of electrical brain stimulation may also mediate the rewarding effect of certain drugs.

**The Relationship Between Brain-Stimulation Rewards and Natural Drives**
The complex neural circuitry that provides the basis for the reward effects just described did not come about evolutionarily to respond to cocaine or to electrical stimulation through wires inserted into the brain. It must have evolved as part of the brain's mechanism for motivating behaviors, such as eating and copulating, that promote the animal's ability to survive and reproduce.

*Evidence that a dopamine-using pathway is involved in the rewarding effect of food*

Roy Wise and his colleagues (1978) found that the same dopamine-blocking drugs that inhibit the rewarding effect of brain stimulation or cocaine also inhibit rewards that come through a more natural route. They trained rats to press a lever for food pellets. Then, at a time when the rats were hungry, they injected some with a dopamine-blocking drug and tested their rate of lever pressing. The drugged rats started off by pressing the lever and consuming pellets at the same high rate as did the undrugged rats, suggesting that they were motivated for food. But within a few minutes their rate of pressing and eating slowed down, eventually falling nearly to zero. Apparently, the drug deprived the rats not of hunger but of the rewarding experience that normally comes from consuming food when hungry. Hence, their lever pressing underwent extinction, similar to that of undrugged, hungry rats whose lever presses brought no food.

*A seemingly paradoxical relationship between the rewarding effect of brain stimulation and its effect on natural drives, and a possible resolution of the paradox*

Other experiments have more directly shown a link between electrical stimulation and natural drives. For example, D. L. Margules and James Olds (1962) implanted electrodes in the lateral hypothalamus in a group of rats and then tested each electrode to see if (a) its stimulation would cause the animal to eat if food were available, and (b) the rat would press a lever repeatedly to self-stimulate through the electrode. They found, remarkably, that *every* electrode that elicited feeding also elicited self-stimulation and that most electrodes that did not elicit feeding did not elicit self-stimulation. Subsequent experiments showed that rats would self-stimulate more rapidly in the lateral hypothalamus if they were made hungry by food deprivation, and more slowly if anything was done that would reduce their hunger (Olds & Fobes, 1981). At first such results seem paradoxical. If stimulation of the lateral hypothalamus makes the rat hungry, why should it choose to stimulate its lateral hypothalamus? Is hunger pleasurable? One might imagine that a little hunger is pleasurable, but then why should rats that have already been made moderately hungry by food deprivation stimulate at a faster rate than those that are not already hungry? Is a lot of hunger more pleasurable than a little hunger?

This apparent paradox is resolved if we assume that the neurons associated with drives and rewards are closely intermingled in the lateral hypothalamus, and that electrical stimulation there activates both sets (first proposed by Deutsch, 1963; also see Stellar & Stellar, 1985). Thus, in the eating test, where the experimenter stimulates the animal's brain while food is available, the animal might experience a drive to eat coupled with a strong but fleeting sense of the reward (pleasure?) that comes from eating, which would add even further to its motivation to eat. In the self-stimulation test, on the other hand, where the animal can stimulate its brain by pressing a lever, the same set of sensations (a drive to eat plus a strong but fleeting sense of reward) may lead the animal to press the lever again rather than eat, because the electrode-induced reward is quicker and probably stronger than that which comes from eating food pellets. Finally, the already hungry animal may press at a faster rate than the nonhungry animal because hunger may entail, among other things, sensitization of the reward neurons—making their stimulation (through eating or through the electrode) all the more rewarding.

Several experiments have shown similar relationships between brain self-stimulation and drives other than hunger. In one, rats with electrodes in different locations in the lateral hypothalamus, which could be activated by pressing different levers, chose to self-stimulate through one electrode when deprived of food and another when deprived of water, suggesting that there may be separate reward systems related to hunger and thirst (Gallistel & Beagley, 1971). In other experiments, male rats self-stimulated through electrodes in brain areas where stimulation promotes the male sex drive; their rate of self-stimulation decreased when they were castrated and increased again when they were treated with testosterone (Caggiula & Hoebel, 1966). Here again we see that variables affecting the level of drive also affect the rate of self-stimulation.

There is much more to be learned about both the anatomy and functioning of reward systems in the brain. But results so far seem consistent with the ecological theory of learning discussed in Chapter 5—the theory that different learning and reward mechanisms, with different operating characteristics, came about in evolution for different survival-promoting purposes. Thus, the reward system for each drive may be partly different, in anatomy and function, from that for other drives, and the difference may provide the basis for the different ways that learning occurs in relation to different drives.

# Sleep

Sleepiness can be thought of as a drive. A sleepy person is motivated to go to sleep, and will expend some effort to reach a safe, comfortable place to do so—preferably one where the sheets are clean. Achieving this goal and drifting off to sleep provide a sense of pleasure, different from, yet analogous to, the pleasure that comes from eating when hungry. But sleep is more than the end state of a drive: It is an altered state of consciousness, in which the brain for a time gives up some of its functions, leaving the person in a condition of reduced activity and responsiveness to the environment. Most of us spend about a third of our lives in this state. How, more precisely, can sleep be described? What is its function? What causes it? During sleep we dream. What are the function and cause of dreams? These are the questions that are addressed in the following discussion.

**The Electroencephalographic Description of Sleep and Its Stages**    Because sleep is a state in which people show little overt behavior and cannot answer questions, scientists who study it must focus on subtle behavioral and physiological changes. The most valuable index of sleep is a measure of brain activity called the *electroencephalogram* (abbreviated as *EEG*).

■ *What the EEG actually measures, and how the EEG differs in two awake states and four stages of sleep*

As you know (from Chapter 6), neural activity is electrochemical activity and can be measured as an electrical change. The brain, with its billions of neurons, produces constant electrical "chatter," which to some degree penetrates the overlying skull and scalp. With electrodes on the scalp it is possible to detect and amplify these signals. The amplified signals can move pens up and down on a roll of paper that moves continuously under the pens, resulting in a permanent record of the signals. This record is the EEG (see Figure 7.9).

**Figure 7.9 *Recording an EEG in a sleep laboratory***
*Electrodes pasted to this woman's scalp pick up weak electrical signals from her brain, which are then amplified and used to produce an EEG (ink tracings on the continuously moving roll of graph paper in the foreground). Other physiological changes, such as eye movements, can also be electrically recorded in this way.*

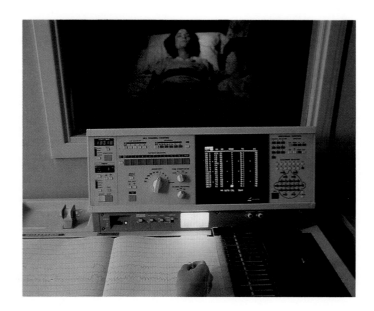

It is important to realize that the EEG is a very gross index of the activity of the brain, representing a sort of average of activity of billions of neurons, with the greatest weight given to those lying closest to the recording site. As one group of electroencephalographers put it, "We are like blind men trying to understand the workings of a factory by listening outside its walls" (quoted by Hassett, 1978). You can't tell how the machines inside a factory work by listening outside the walls, but you can get some idea of the total amount of activity. You can tell, for example, when things have partly shut down and when they are going full steam ahead. If you listen long and hard enough you may begin to make finer distinctions than that, and if you also observe the outputs of the factory you may be able to determine which sounds correspond with which outputs. Similarly, by correlating the types of ink squiggles recorded in the EEG with subjects' overt behavior or reported moods, psychophysiologists have developed a basis for using the EEG as a rough index of psychological states.

When a person is relaxed but awake, with eyes closed, and not thinking of anything in particular, the EEG typically consists of large, regular waves called *alpha waves*, which occur at a frequency of about 8 to 13 cycles per second (see Figure 7.10b). These relatively slow waves are believed to stem from a spontaneous, syn-

**Figure 7.10** *EEG waves of waking and sleep stages*

*In general, as one goes from an alert to a relaxed state, and then to ever-deeper stages of sleep, the EEG waves become slower in frequency and higher in amplitude. (From Snyder & Scott, 1972.)*

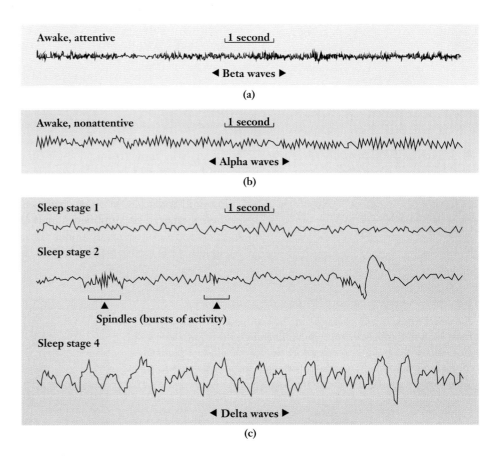

chronized pulsing of neurons that occurs in the absence of focused mental activity or emotional excitement. When a person concentrates on an external stimulus, or tries to solve a problem, or becomes excited, the EEG pattern changes to low-amplitude, fast, irregular waves called *beta waves* (see Figure 7.10a). The low amplitude of beta waves is believed to indicate that neurons are firing in an unsynchronized manner, such that their contributions to the EEG tend to cancel one another out. Whereas alpha waves are analogous to the large, regular waves that occur on a pond undisturbed by anything but the wind, beta waves are more akin to the effect that would occur if a million pebbles were suddenly tossed onto the surface of the pond. The crests of the ripples created by some pebbles would cancel out the troughs created by others, resulting in a chaotic, high-frequency, low-amplitude pattern of ripples.

When a person falls asleep, the EEG goes through a fairly regular sequence of changes (see Figure 7.10c). First, the alpha rhythm of the awake but nonalert state is replaced by irregular, low-amplitude waves. After some seconds, these waves become slower and somewhat higher in amplitude and are interrupted by brief bursts of rapid waves called *sleep spindles*, which most reliably indicate the onset of sleep. As sleep continues, sleep spindles diminish, and very slow, irregular, high-amplitude waves called *delta waves*, with a frequency of 0.5 to 3 cycles per second, begin to appear in the EEG and eventually dominate it.

Although these changes in the EEG are gradual and continuous, sleep researchers find it convenient to divide them into four stages, using a system first devised by William Dement and Nathaniel Kleitman (1957). *Stage 1* is the brief transition between wakefulness and sleep, when alpha waves decline and are replaced with unsynchronized activity; *stage 2* is the period when sleep spindles appear; *stage 3* is the period during which 10 to 50 percent of the EEG shows delta waves; and *stage 4* is the period during which more than 50 percent of the EEG shows delta

**■ *How REM and slow-wave sleep differ, and how they cycle through the night***

waves. Stages 2 through 4 represent successively deeper stages of sleep. Muscle tension, the heart rate, the breathing rate, and other physiological indices of arousal decline with each successive stage, and the sleeping person becomes increasingly hard to awaken.

Having reached stage 4 a person does not remain there for the rest of the night. Instead, after about 80 to 100 minutes of total sleep time, sleep rapidly lightens, returning through stages 3 and 2, and then a new, quite fascinating stage of sleep appears for a period of about 10 minutes or more. During this new stage the EEG is unsynchronized, looking much like it would during alert wakefulness. Based on the EEG alone, one might think that the person had awakened, but direct observation shows that the person is sound asleep, and the record of muscle tension shows that the muscles are more relaxed than at any other sleep stage. Yet, consistent with the unsynchronized EEG, there are other indices of high arousal: Breathing and the heart rate are more rapid and less regular than in other sleep stages; penile erection occurs in males (even in infants and young boys); twitching movements occur in the small muscles of the fingers and face; and, most indicative of all, the eyes can be observed to move rapidly back and forth and up and down under the eyelids. These eye movements, which can be recorded electrically along with the EEG, give this stage of sleep its name, ***REM sleep*** (rapid eye movement sleep). As you may have guessed, REM sleep is when dreams occur—a topic to which we will return. REM sleep is also sometimes called *emergent stage 1*, because, even though it is different from the original stage 1, it marks the onset of a new sleep cycle. The other stages—2, 3, and 4—are referred to collectively as ***slow-wave sleep***, because of the slow EEG waves that characterize those stages.

In a typical night's sleep, a person goes through four or five sleep cycles, each involving gradual descent into deeper slow-wave sleep, followed by a rapid lightening of slow-wave sleep, followed by REM sleep (Hobson, 1987). Each complete cycle takes about 90 minutes. As you can see in Figure 7.11, the deepest slow-wave sleep occurs in the first cycle or two. With each successive cycle, less time is spent in deep slow-wave sleep (stages 3 and 4) and more is spent in light slow-wave sleep (stage 2) and REM sleep.

**Figure 7.11 *The cycle of sleep stages through a night***

*People usually go through four or five sleep cycles per night, each ending with a period of REM sleep. With successive cycles, less time is spent in deep slow-wave sleep (stages 3 and 4) and more is spent in light slow-wave sleep (stage 2) and REM sleep. (Adapted from Snyder & Scott, 1972.)*

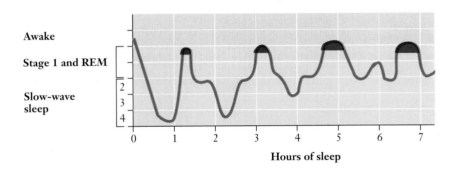

**The Function of Sleep**   Why must we sleep? Many children have asked that question to protest their parents' desire to put them to bed, and many scientists have asked it, too (though usually for a different reason). Researchers have proposed two different theories to explain why a tendency to sleep came about in evolution, both of which probably contain more than a grain of truth.

**■ *Two theories about the function of sleep, and evidence supporting each***

The *restoration theory* is the one that most people intuitively believe. It is the theory that your parents probably repeated to you as their reason for requiring you to go to bed at a certain hour. According to this view, the body wears out during the day and sleep is necessary to put things back in shape. Scientific support for this theory includes the following: (1) Sleep *is* a time of rest. The muscles are relaxed, the metabolic rate is down, and the rate of neural activity in the brain is reduced (though only by about 10 percent, according to recordings from individual neu-

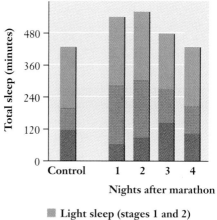

**Figure 7.12** *Effect on sleep of running a marathon*

*Shown here is the average time spent in each sleep stage by athletes on each of 4 nights following a 92-kilometer marathon, compared to control nights (2 weeks before and 2 weeks after the marathon). Notice that the main effects were an increase in the time spent in deep slow-wave sleep (stages 3 and 4) and a decrease in REM sleep on the first 2 nights after the marathon. (From Shapiro & others, 1981.)*

rons in various brain structures (see Hobson, 1987). (2) The secretion of *growth hormone* from the pituitary gland is triggered by the onset of each cycle of slow-wave sleep throughout the night. Because growth hormone promotes the synthesis of protein molecules in muscles and other tissues, its high presence during sleep is consistent with the view that body repair is occurring at that time. (3) Extreme physical exercise, which would be expected to increase the need for restoration, is generally followed by increased depth of sleep and, to a smaller degree, increased sleep duration (for an experiment showing this, see Figure 7.12).

The *preservation and protection theory* is less intuitive than the restoration theory and is based primarily on comparisons of sleep patterns in different species of animals. It posits that sleep came about in evolution to preserve energy and protect the individual during that portion of each 24-hour day when there is relatively little value and considerable danger in moving about. An animal needs only a certain number of hours per day to do those things that are necessary or useful for survival, and the rest of the time, according to this theory, it is better off asleep—quiet, hidden, and protected from predators and other possible dangers.

Support for this theory comes from evidence that variations in sleep time among different species do not correspond with differences in physical exertion while awake, but they do correspond with feeding habits and ways of achieving safety (Allison & Cicchetti, 1976; Webb, 1982). At one extreme, large grazing animals such as bison and horses average only 2 or 3 hours of sleep during every 24-hour period. Because they eat grass and other vegetation, which are extremely low in calories, they must spend a tremendous amount of time each day eating, and thus they have little time to sleep. Moreover, because of their size and the fact that they cannot burrow or climb trees, such animals are not adept at finding safe nooks in which to sleep. Thus, they are safer when awake. (The fact that such animals sleep at all might be taken as evidence that some minimal amount of sleep is necessary for restorative functions.) At the other extreme, opossums and bats spend an average of 20 hours or more asleep each 24-hour day. These two species need only a couple of hours per day to obtain food (such as high-calorie insects), and they are adapted to hide in out-of-the-way places. Presumably, they sleep so much because they have no need to be awake for long and because they are protected from predation while asleep.

In addition to explaining species differences in total amount of sleep, the preservation and protection theory also helps explain differences in the time of day at which different species sleep. Animals that rely heavily on vision generally forage in the day and sleep at night. Conversely, animals such as mice and rats that rely more on other senses, and are preyed upon by animals that use vision, generally sleep in the day and forage at night. The theory also offers an explanation for the fact that infants in most species sleep much more than adults. Infants who are being cared for by adults do not need to spend time foraging, and sleep protects them from wandering away into danger. Their sleep also gives their caregivers an opportunity to rest or attend to other needs.

It is interesting to speculate, in this vein, about the evolutionary conditions that may have led to the 8-hour nighttime sleep pattern that characterizes adult humans throughout the world. Humans are highly visual creatures who need light to find food and do other things necessary for survival. At night it may have been best, throughout most of our evolution, for humans to be asleep, tucked away in a cave or other hiding place, so as not to be tempted to walk about and risk falling over a cliff or being attacked by a nighttime predator. Only during the past few centuries—an insignificant speck of evolutionary time—have lights and other contrivances of civilization made the night relatively safe. According to this line of thinking, our pattern of sleep might be in part a vestigial trait, a carryover from a period when the night was a time of great danger; or, to the degree that nighttime is still more dangerous than daytime, it may continue to serve an adaptive function.

**Sleep as a Biological Rhythm** One approach to understanding sleep is to view it in relation to other biologically based changes that accompany the 24-hour cycle of day and night. The day-night cycle has been a stable feature of our planet since its beginning, and all plants and animals have mechanisms that accommodate it. Among the physiological changes in humans that follow a daily rhythm are body temperature, which falls at night and increases during the day, and secretion of the adrenal hormone cortisol, which follows an opposite pattern.

Experiments with animals have shown that cyclic changes in temperature, hormones, and behavioral activity (indicative of sleep or wakefulness) continue even when the animals are maintained in a time-free environment, that is, an environment in which there is no regular change in lighting or other cues that could indicate the time of day. In such an environment the cycle length is usually somewhat longer than 24 hours, and it varies somewhat from individual to individual, but it is remarkably constant within a given individual (Takahashi & Zatz, 1982). Similar experiments have been done with human volunteers who have agreed to live for days or weeks in rooms with no windows, clocks, or other time cues, with results quite similar to those found with animals. Temperature, cortisol production, and sleepiness continue to oscillate at close to a 24-hour period (see Figure 7.13).

The technical term for any rhythmic change that continues at close to a 24-hour cycle in the absence of external 24-hour cues is *circadian rhythm* (from the Latin words *circa*, meaning about, and *dien*, meaning day). Such rhythms are governed by cyclic changes in activity in the nervous system that can occur independently of external cues.

■ *Evidence that sleepiness is affected by an internal clock that can operate in the absence of external time cues but is continuously reset by daily changes in light*

**Figure 7.13** *Human circadian rhythm in a time-free environment*

*These data are from a single male subject. Each horizontal bar represents one circadian period of wakefulness followed by sleep, with successive periods drawn below each other. The triangles indicate the time of minimal body temperature in each period. Notice that during the period of isolation from time cues, the cycle period was somewhat longer than 24 hours, so the subject fell asleep and woke up later each day. (Adapted from Aschoff & Wever, 1969.)*

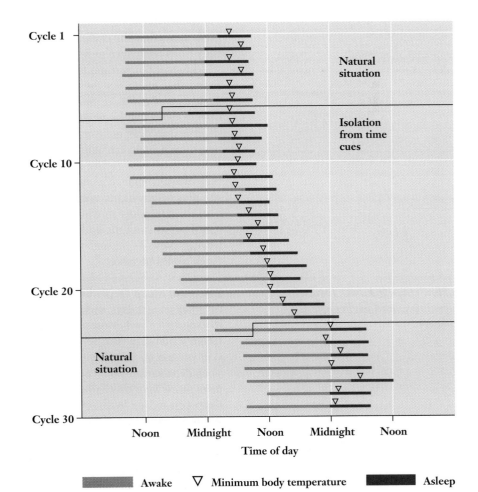

**Figure 7.14** *Resetting the circadian clock*
*The woman shown here is being treated by Charles Czeisler for a sleep problem. Before treatment, she would routinely drop off to sleep at about 9 P.M. and awaken at about 4 A.M. After treatment—3 evenings of bright lights—she would fall asleep at about 11 P.M. and awaken at about 7 A.M., her preferred schedule. If her circadian clock were to drift back, it could be reset with another evening or two of lights. Other research by Czeisler and his colleagues suggests that even normal room lights can influence the circadian clock, but the very bright lights shown here are more effective.*

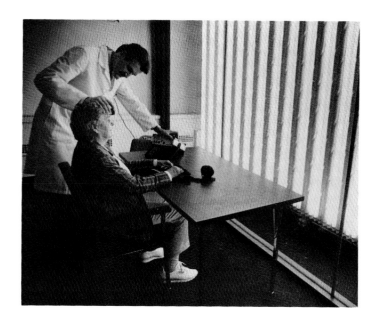

The environmental day-night cue that normally resets the circadian clock each day, so that rhythms occur in periods of exactly rather than approximately 24 hours, is daylight. Experiments with animals show that the cycle can be shortened or stretched somewhat, say, to a 22-hour or 26-hour period, by artificially changing the period of light and dark. And experiments with humans as well as other animals show that the cycle can be reset—to any setting one chooses—through carefully timed exposure to bright fluorescent lights.

In recent experiments with humans, Charles Czeisler and his colleagues (1989) found that just a few hours of bright fluorescent lighting at night, coupled with avoidance of daylight, over 3 successive days is enough to reverse a person's circadian clock so that he or she becomes sleepy during the day and alert at night. Some sleep researchers believe that this technique could be put to many practical purposes, such as to (a) help people whose circadian cycle is out of kilter with those around them (see Figure 7.14), (b) help night workers adapt their circadian cycle to their work hours (they should avoid the morning sun and seek the late-afternoon sun plus bright lights at night), and (c) help overseas travelers avoid jet lag (a New York businesswoman who wants to be at her best at a 4-day conference in Tokyo could avoid sunlight and receive night doses of artificial light for 2 days before leaving New York, and then, on the third day, enjoy Tokyo sunlight—and her clock would be reset).

■ *How staying awake through several days and nights affects behavior*

**Effects of Sleep Deprivation**   In a number of experiments, people have voluntarily gone several days without sleep. After 3 or 4 such days, people sometimes begin to experience rather dramatic mental upsets, such as distorted perceptions and extreme irritability (Borbély, 1986). Yet if asked to work at tasks requiring physical skill or mental judgment, they show an ability that is remarkably unaffected by sleep deprivation. As a rule, sleep deprivation hurts performance on simple, boring tasks more than on challenging ones (see Horne, 1979, 1988); this observation led sleep researcher William Dement (1979) to suggest that impaired performance, when it occurs, is mainly caused by subjects dozing off for brief periods during boring tasks. Evidence that even extreme sleep deprivation does not necessarily impair physical coordination or judgment comes from Dement's observation of the world-record-setting vigil of a young college student named Randy Gardner. During the final hours of an 11-day period without sleep, Gardner played a penny ar-

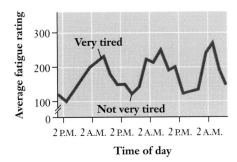

**Figure 7.15  Rhythm of fatigue during 72 hours of sleep deprivation**

*In this experiment, fifteen women went for 72 hours without sleep. Every 3 hours they rated their subjective feeling of tiredness on a scale on which 100 meant "normal fatigue" and 200 meant "twice as fatigued as normal." Notice that in each successive 24-hour period, the maximal fatigue ratings occurred around 2 to 6 A.M. and minimal ratings occurred around 2 to 8 P.M. (From Akerstedt and Fröberg, 1977.)*

■ *The difference between nonsomniacs and insomniacs*

■ *Evidence that true dreams accompany REM sleep, while other forms of sleep thought can occur in other sleep stages*

cade baseball game 100 times with Dement and won every one. Before going to bed, after 264 hours of no sleep, Gardner held a news conference at which he was "very coherent and conducted himself in impeccable fashion" (Dement, 1972).

The most reliable effect of sleep deprivation is sleepiness itself. (This is also the most dangerous effect, because it can cause one to fall asleep at the wrong time, such as when driving.) Yet even this effect is not simply related to the amount of time that one has gone without sleep. During sleep deprivation the circadian rhythm maintains its 24-hour cycle, so subjects who manage to remain awake all night usually find it much easier to remain awake after daybreak than before (see Figure 7.15).

Other research on variations in sleep patterns has focused on *nonsomniacs*, people who naturally sleep very little. Ray Meddis (1977) identified a number of individuals who slept much less than the typical 8 hours per day and rarely felt tired. If 8 hours of sleep were essential for physical restoration, we would expect that nonsomniacs must be extremely inactive during the day or that they must suffer in some way from their lack of sleep. But according to Meddis, the opposite seems to be true. Nonsomniacs as a group appear to be unusually vigorous and healthy. One such individual was a nurse who reported that for most of her life she had slept about 50 minutes per night. She was very active during the day and would usually spend the night in quiet activities, such as reading or painting. To verify her nonsomnia, Meddis tested her in the sleep lab. She slept not at all the first three nights in the lab, remaining cheerful and talkative throughout. Finally, on the fourth night, she slept a total of 99 minutes and awoke feeling fully rested.

Lest you gain the impression that the usual 8 or so hours that most people sleep per night is not necessary, I hasten to add that for most of us it *is* necessary. It is important to distinguish nonsomniacs from *insomniacs*. An insomniac is someone who has a normal desire for sleep but who, for some reason (such as worry), is unable to sleep at night. An insomniac, unlike a nonsomniac, feels tired all day as a result of not sleeping. And so do most people who voluntarily reduce their sleep. Again, the desire to sleep can be thought of as a drive, similar in some but not all ways to hunger. To oversimplify somewhat, we sleep because we have a mechanism in the brain that makes us *want* to sleep at certain periodic intervals. If we yield to this want, we experience pleasure as we drift off, and if we resist it we experience discomfort and an increased craving to sleep until we finally give in. The strength of this drive varies from person to person. Most of us have a drive that can be satisfied by about 8 hours per night, but some have a stronger drive, requiring more sleep, and others have a weaker drive, requiring less.

**Dreams and REM Sleep**   Dreams have always been a great mystery to people. In sleep one travels to distant places, speaks with friends long-since dead, and performs impossible feats as if they were commonplace. People at various times and places have believed that dreams foretell the future or are instructions from the spiritual world. Others (notably Sigmund Freud, as you will see in Chapter 16), less mystically inclined, have held that dreams express deep, hidden wishes and can be used to unlock the secrets of the unconscious mind. Today our knowledge of dreams has been advanced by studies in sleep laboratories, where sleep stages are monitored physiologically and people are periodically awakened to report what was on their mind just before awakening.

When people are awakened during REM sleep they usually (in about 90 percent of the cases) report a mental experience that researchers call a ***true dream*** (Foulkes, 1985). A true dream is experienced as if it were really happening, rather than something merely imagined or thought about. The dreamer has the feeling of actually seeing or in other ways sensing various objects and people, and of actually moving and behaving in the dream environment. Moreover, the true dream usually involves a progression of such experiences, woven together in a somewhat coherent though often bizarre story. The longer the sleeper engages in REM sleep before awakening, the longer and more elaborate is the reported dream. Studies show that essentially everyone dreams several times a night. People who believe that they rarely dream, or who can recall only fragments of dreams upon normal awakening in the morning, describe vivid, detailed dreams if awakened during REM periods. Dreams are fleeting experiences, quickly lost from memory unless we catch them and think about them immediately upon awakening.

When people are awakened during slow-wave sleep, they report some sort of mental activity just before awakening in roughly 60 percent of the cases (Foulkes, 1985). Such reports are usually not of true dreams but of *sleep thought*, which lacks the vivid sensory and motor hallucinations of true dreams and is more akin to daytime thinking. Often the subject of sleep thought is some problem that had been of concern during the day. For example, a student who had been cramming for a math exam might report working on a calculus problem while sleeping. The main difference between sleep thought and daytime thought is that sleep thought doesn't usually further us along; while the sleeper may feel that he or she is solving a calculus problem, questions upon awakening indicate that no real progress was made (Hobson, 1987).

■ *How dreams may be a side effect of REM sleep, which itself may have evolved to exercise brain circuits*

Thus far, research has not answered the question: What are (true) dreams for? But theories about this that have emerged from the sleep labs are more mundane than those that others have sometimes proposed. One prevalent view today is that dreams don't serve any special purpose at all, but are side effects of physiological changes in REM sleep that do serve a purpose (Foulkes, 1985; Hobson, 1988). According to one version of this view, the purpose of REM sleep is to provide regular exercise to groups of neurons in the brain. Neural connections can degenerate if they go too long without being active (Edelman, 1987), so neural activity during REM sleep may help preserve important circuits. Some of the neurons are in perceptual and motor circuits, and perceptual and movement hallucinations may be inevitable consequences of their activity. In research done many years ago, electrical stimulation in portions of the cerebral cortex produced dreamlike hallucinations in people who were awake (Penfield & Perot, 1963). It is quite likely that a similar phenomenon occurs in REM sleep. In addition to producing hallucinations, the brain continues in REM sleep to engage in some degree of thought, just as it does in slow-wave sleep. But now the thought becomes wrapped up in trying to make sense of the hallucinations. The result is the weaving of a story, of sorts, connecting one hallucination to the next—hence, the dream. Because of reduced mental capacity during sleep, the story is less logical than one the awake brain would develop, but it still contains some degree of logic.

Consistent with the view that the purpose of REM sleep is to exercise brain pathways, with dreams as a side effect, is the observation that REM sleep occurs in mammals besides humans, and to a much greater degree in fetuses and infants of all species than in adults (see Figure 7.16). In fact, the peak of REM sleep in the human occurs in the 30-day-old fetus, who spends almost 24 hours a day in this state (Parmelee & others, 1967). Why should fetuses spend so much time in REM sleep? Perhaps as their brains are developing in the relative isolation of the womb they need to exercise important sensory and motor pathways, and REM sleep is their means for doing that (Hobson, 1988). In the fetus, REM sleep is also accompanied by body movements such as kicking and twisting, which are apparently triggered by the bursts of activity in motor areas of the brain. By the time of birth a neural inhibitory system matures, which inhibits most motor neurons during REM sleep and thus prevents most movements that would otherwise occur. The motor neurons to the eyes, however, remain uninhibited, so eye movements remain as a visible effect of the brain's activity.

Sometimes the side-effect theory just described is interpreted as an argument against the psychoanalytic view that dream analysis can be useful for understanding

**Figure 7.16** *Changes in sleep over the course of life*
*As shown here, both the total daily sleep time and the percentage of sleep time spent in REM sleep decrease as a person gets older. If the curves were extended to the left, they would show that prior to birth REM sleep occupies most of each 24-hour day. (Adapted from Snyder & Scott, 1972.)*

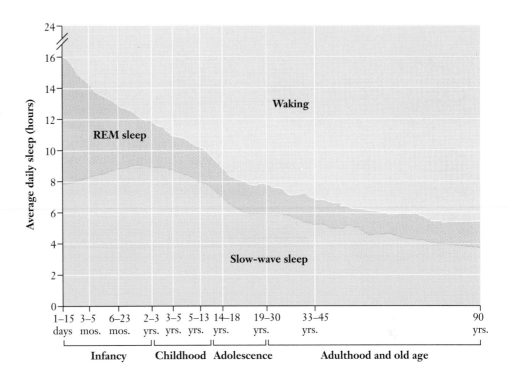

the mind. But, on the face of it, that interpretation seems unjustified. Even if dreams are triggered by random events in the brain, the actual images, emotions, and story lines that constitute the dream are not random. They certainly contain elements based on the dreamer's previous experiences, and, because they occur at a time when the brain is less logical, ideas or feelings normally suppressed by logic could emerge and could, possibly, be useful in psychoanalysis. Evidence for or against this view would have to come from studies in which dream experiences are correlated in meaningful ways with other aspects of a person's life.

**Brain Mechanisms Controlling Sleep** Are there special neural systems for inducing sleep, analogous to those for inducing drives such as hunger? In the early days of sleep research, some researchers believed that sleep is the natural state that the brain slips into when not aroused by external stimulation, and that there is no need to posit special sleep-inducing mechanisms. But such a view is inconsistent with the observation that sleepiness sometimes overwhelms us even when external stimulation is high, and other times we can't sleep no matter how quiet, dark, and unstimulating the environment. We now know that the early theory was mistaken, and that sleep is actively promoted by special neurons in the brain. In fact, based on experiments with animals, researchers have identified three separate but interacting brain systems involved in sleep. These are:

■ *Evidence that the circadian clock is in the hypothalamus and that more specific centers for slow-wave and REM sleep are in the brainstem*

1. *Circadian rhythm generators in the hypothalamus* The circadian clock is apparently located in a specific nucleus of the hypothalamus (called the suprachiasmatic nucleus). If this nucleus is damaged, animals lose their regular rhythms and fall asleep or wake up at rather random times over the 24-hour day. This nucleus contains rhythm-generating neurons, which gradually increase and decrease their rate of action potentials over an approximately 24-hour cycle, even when surgically isolated from other parts of the brain (Takahashi & Zatz, 1982). This neural rhythm presumably accounts for the circadian rhythm of sleep-wakefulness that occurs in a time-free environment. The same nucleus also receives direct input from the eyes by way of a special set of neurons in the optic nerve, and it is apparently through this pathway that daily changes in

sunlight synchronize the circadian clock to the 24-hour pattern of the earth's rotation (Takahashi & Zatz, 1982).

2. *A neural center for slow-wave sleep in the brainstem*    The brain area that most directly brings on slow-wave sleep is an interconnected set of nuclei (collectively called the *raphé nuclei*) in the medulla and pons of the brainstem. Neurons with cell bodies in these nuclei send their axons to all parts of the cerebral cortex and release the transmitter *serotonin*, which has an inhibitory effect, causing the reduced cortical activity that characterizes slow-wave sleep (Lindsley, 1983). Damage to these brainstem nuclei, or drug-induced depletion of serotonin in the brain, reduces or abolishes sleep in animals (Jouvet, 1967; Lindsley, 1983). These nuclei receive input directly from the rhythm generators in the hypothalamus, which accounts for the circadian change in sleepiness; but they also receive input from other brain areas, which may help explain why sleepiness can come and go at times that are out of sync with the circadian cycle, depending upon one's experiences during the day or night.

3. *Neural centers for REM sleep in the brainstem*    The shift from slow-wave to REM sleep seems to involve two interconnected sets of neurons in the pons. One set generates the increased brain activity that occurs in REM sleep, and the other produces the extreme loss of muscle tension that occurs at that time, by inhibiting motor neurons. Cats with lesions in these inhibitory neurons begin to move about every time they fall into REM sleep, waking themselves by their own movements (Jouvet, 1972). If these neurons were damaged in you or me, we would probably produce in fact the movements that we dream we are producing during REM sleep. In some people—who suffer from a rare disorder called *cataplexy*—the inhibitory brainstem center becomes active at random times during the day, with the result that their skeletal muscles become limp and they collapse, unable to move for several seconds or minutes, though otherwise wide awake (Chase & Morales, 1987). Perhaps you have experienced something akin to a cataplectic attack yourself when, while you were trying to sleep, your brain shifted into an REM mode while you were still half awake and you could sense the condition of being temporarily paralyzed.

## Arousal and Emotionality

Midterm exams are just around the corner, your family is after you to get your life in order, your lover has just left you for someone else, the surgeon says your nose and left ear will have to go, and a hungry tiger is crouched behind you about to pounce. Are you awake? All of these events have something in common: All are likely to be psychologically disturbing, and all may—in some people at least—produce a pattern of physiological reactions referred to as *high arousal*. In this section we will look first at the arousal response and its effects, and then at the psychological experience called *emotion*. (By the way, I was only kidding about your left ear.)

### *High Arousal and Stress*

**The Arousal Response and Its Effects on Behavior**    The *arousal response* is a pattern of measurable physiological changes that helps prepare the body for "fight or flight" (to use Walter Cannon's famous phrase). The pattern varies from person to person and situation to situation, but commonly includes the following elements: (1) Skeletal muscles become tense, and blood is diverted from other parts of the body to muscles, preparing them to spring into action. (2) The heart rate, blood pressure, and breathing rate increase, and sugar and fat molecules are released into the blood from storage deposits—all of which help prepare the body

**An unsympathetic situation**

*The physical changes that prepare the body for combat or retreat from a threatening situation are found in nonhuman animals as well as humans. For this bird, "flight" would be a lot easier if its body were built for the air or if an aquatic escape route were available.*

metabolically for a possibly prolonged expenditure of energy. (3) Changes occur in the blood that enable it to clot more easily, and pain-relieving hormones called *endorphins* (to be discussed in Chapter 8) are released—both of which help prepare the body for possible injury. (4) Alerting mechanisms of the brain are strongly activated, and cognitive processes are narrowly focused on the arousing stimulus or thought. This pattern seems nicely designed to cope with the proverbial tiger about to attack, or with a bully at the neighborhood playground. But it can also occur in response to such challenges as midterm exams or asking someone out on a date, where neither fight nor flight is called for, and in these cases it may do more harm than good.

Many experiments have been performed, both with humans and other animals, to determine the effects of the arousal response on the performance of various tasks. The usual finding is that high arousal is beneficial for tasks that require a good deal of physical energy, or where performance of the task is instinctive or very well practiced, but is often harmful for tasks that call for novel (unpracticed) movements, creativity, or careful judgment. In other words, for any given task there is some optimal level of arousal (at which task performance is best), and this optimal level is lower for intellectually difficult tasks and higher for tasks that are limited more by endurance or persistence than intellect (see Figure 7.17).

■ **When high arousal is helpful, and when it is not**

**Figure 7.17** *The relationship between the cognitive difficulty of a task and the optimal level of arousal for task performance*

*As shown by these hypothetical curves, humans and other animals typically perform cognitively easy tasks best when their arousal level (as measured, for example, by the heart rate) is very high and cognitively difficult tasks best when their arousal level is lower. This relationship is often called the* Yerkes-Dodson law.

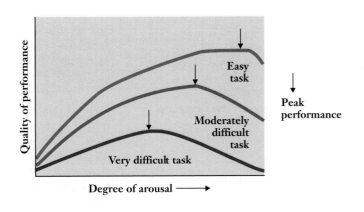

This relationship between optimal arousal and type of task is often called the **Yerkes-Dodson law**, because a version of it was first proposed by Robert Yerkes and John Dodson (1908). These researchers performed experiments in which mice could avoid electric shocks by entering the brighter of two compartments. They varied the arousal level in the mice by varying the intensity of the shocks used, and they varied the task difficulty by varying the contrast in brightness between the two compartments. When the task was easy (a big difference between the two compartments), the mice did best with high arousal (from a strong shock). But when the task was difficult (little difference between the compartments), the mice performed best with lower arousal (from a low shock). Chapter 15 discusses experiments showing a comparable effect in people—where arousal was manipulated not by shocks but by the presence or absence of an audience. An audience, as the Yerkes-Dodson law would predict, typically improves performance on routine tasks and worsens it on tasks requiring calm judgment or creativity.

**Debilitating Effects on the Body of Prolonged or Repeated Arousal**   The concept of arousal is often associated with that of stress. *Stress* is a much abused term in psychology and medicine, used in such a vast number of different ways as to have become almost meaningless. (I once heard a psychologist argue, quite seriously, that "everything in life is stress." It seemed to me that she had stretched the term quite beyond any useful purpose.) For our purposes, *stress* can be defined as the process or set of processes through which some stimulus or change in the environment can result in long-term debilitation to the individual—either physically or in the form of a psychological breakdown. Given this definition, the arousal response is properly called stressful if it has a long-term debilitating effect; otherwise, it is not properly called stressful. Chapter 17 (on mental disorders) is concerned with stress as applied to psychological breakdown. Here our concern is with observable effects in the body.

The concept of stress first became popular in psychology and medicine in the 1950s, spurred largely by the work of a Canadian physiologist, Hans Selye. Selye (1956/1976) studied the physiological changes that occur in laboratory animals subjected to prolonged disruption of normal physiological functioning, from such sources as wounds or temperature extremes. He found that if such disruption is sufficiently extreme the animal will go through a reliable sequence of changes, which he referred to as the **general adaptation syndrome** and broke down into three stages. The first is the *alarm stage*, during which bodily arousal reaches a peak and all of the animal's energy is devoted to coping with the source of stress. Then comes the *stage of resistance*, during which physiological adjustments occur that enable the animal to exist relatively normally for a period of time despite the stressful situation. Finally, if the stressful situation is sufficiently severe and prolonged, comes the *stage of exhaustion*, in which resistance breaks down in the form of damage to various body tissues, resulting in illness or death. It is now known that some of the debilitating effects in the stage of exhaustion (such as heart damage and stomach ulcers) are mediated by prolonged overactivity of the sympathetic nervous system, and others (such as increased susceptibility to infection) are mediated by suppression of the immune system, stemming at least partly from the prolonged secretion of cortisol and other hormones from the adrenal cortex (Solomon & others, 1985).

Following Selye's ground-breaking work, other research has indicated that in humans prolonged or severe psychological stressors can have debilitating effects similar to those that Selye observed with physical stressors (see Burchfield, 1985). Some studies have shown that such stressful events as the loss of a job or death of a spouse increase one's susceptibility to various diseases, including cancer. Other studies have compared people who have different styles of coping with disruptive events in their lives. Such studies suggest that those who cope in a passive way, such as by denying the stressful situation, tend to suffer from diseases indicative of

*The harmful bodily effects of psychological stressors, and evidence that these may depend on aspects of personality*

a suppressed immune system (Cox, 1984), while those who cope by fighting or trying to control the situation are more likely to suffer from disorders induced by too much sympathetic arousal, such as high blood pressure and heart disease (see Burchfield, 1985).

Particular attention has focused on people who show a pattern of behavior referred to as *Type A*. These are people who not only have the fighting and controlling mode of coping, but also interpret situations as disruptive that others would not find disruptive. They are competitive, impatient, and often tense—the kind who get riled when caught in a traffic jam. The opposite, more relaxed approach to life is referred to as *Type B* behavior. A number of long-term studies—mostly with White, middle-class males—have found that Type A individuals are about twice as likely as Type B individuals to develop heart disease or have a heart attack (Haney & Blumenthal, 1985; Matthews & Haynes, 1986).

In addition to these long-term studies, dozens of short-term experiments have compared Type A and Type B individuals with respect to their physiological arousal in response to psychological challenges in the laboratory—such as taking a history quiz or being mildly insulted by the experimenter. When all such studies are combined, they show a clear effect for men, but not for women (Harbin, 1989). Type A men have manifested greater increases in their blood pressure and heart rate than Type B men in such tests, but there has been no difference between Type A and Type B women. At this time it is not clear why this difference between the sexes should occur. One possibility is that the questionnaire and interview procedures used to categorize Type A and Type B individuals, which were originally developed for studies of men, simply fail to categorize women in a meaningful way (Harbin, 1989).

Many procedures have been developed to help people modulate their responses to disturbances in their environment. These include biofeedback techniques (described in Chapter 5), meditation, and cognitive means of reinterpreting experiences (cognitive therapies are described in Chapter 18). There is evidence that all such techniques can be helpful in reducing the arousal response and/or the long-term debilitation that accompanies it (Benson, 1984; Burchfield, 1985; Johnston, 1985).

### The Relationship Between Physiological Arousal and Emotion

Stimuli that produce high physiological arousal also produce strong emotional feelings, such as terror, rage, or passion. An *emotion*, as I will use the term, is a subjective feeling, and it is usually accompanied by an aroused physiological state. While emotions and drives are often discussed separately, the concepts are not fully separable. Emotions are drives to the extent that they orient us toward particular paths of action. Drives, on the other hand (at least in humans), are usually suffused with emotion. Drive and emotion might be thought of as two aspects of the same inner state, so that when emphasizing the effect of a state on behavior, the state is called a drive, but when emphasizing subjective feelings, it is called an emotion. Thus, *fear* is a drive when researchers are focusing on the avoidance behavior it induces but an emotion when they are focusing on the feeling of fear. As another example, psychologists usually think of *hunger* as a drive because their emphasis is on its role in directing behavior toward food. But if they were to focus on the feelings that accompany hunger, such as the desire for food or joy upon receiving it, they would call it an emotion.

As in the case of drives, there is no end to the possible number of different emotions that we might attribute to human beings. The number depends on how finely graded a taxonomy we wish to create. You may recall (from Chapter 4) that Ekman and Friesen believe that there are six basic emotions for which there are unique facial expressions and that most other emotions can be thought of as either blends or variations of those six. Another way to divide emotions is illustrated in

**Figure 7.18** *Spectrum of positive and negative emotions*
*Emotions can be thought of as varying on a two-dimensional grid. The degree to which they are associated with approach or avoidance is one dimension, and the level of bodily arousal associated with the emotion is the other. (From Kissin, 1986.)*

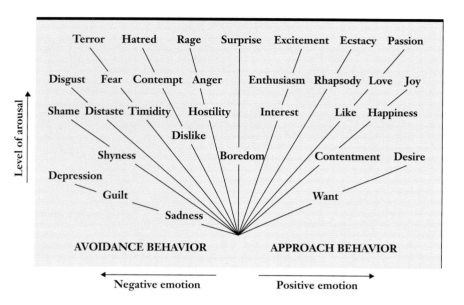

■ *James's theory that emotion follows arousal, and his evidence in support of the theory*

Figure 7.18, which portrays various emotions in a two-dimensional array. One dimension is the degree to which the emotion is associated with approach or avoidance, and the other the degree of bodily arousal associated with it.

**The James-Lange Theory of Emotion**   Because strong emotions are commonly associated with a high degree of bodily arousal, psychologists have long wondered about the causal relationship between the two. Which comes first, the arousal or the emotion?

In his famous textbook, *The Principles of Psychology*, William James (1890) argued that arousal causes emotion. More specifically, he argued that bodily arousal occurs immediately in response to the perception of certain kinds of environmental events, and that emotions are one's sense of arousal. In James's words,

> Our natural way of thinking . . . is that the mental perception of some fact excites the mental affection called the emotion, and that this latter state of mind gives rise to the bodily expression. My theory, on the contrary, is that *the bodily changes follow directly the perception of the exciting fact, and that our feeling of the same changes as they occur IS the emotion.* Common sense says, we lose our fortune, are sorry, and weep; we meet a bear, are frightened, and run; we are insulted by a rival, are angry, and strike. The hypothesis here to be defended says that this order of sequence is incorrect . . . and that the more rational statement is that we feel sorry because we cry, angry because we strike, afraid because we tremble, and not that we cry, strike, or tremble, because we are sorry, angry, or fearful. . . . Without the bodily states following on the perception, the latter would be purely cognitive in form, pale, colorless, destitute of emotional warmth. We might then see the bear, and judge it best to run, receive the insult, and deem it right to strike, but we should not actually feel afraid or angry.

This theory is commonly called the ***James-Lange theory of emotion,*** because Carl Lange, a Danish physiologist, proposed a similar theory at about the same time as James. James's evidence was not based on experiments (nor was Lange's), but rather on introspection—his looking inward at his own emotions. James concluded that when he felt an emotion what he really felt was a set of bodily changes. When fearful he felt a quickened heart, shallow breathing, goose-bumpy flesh, and trembly limbs. When angry he felt a seething chest, flushed face, dilated nostrils, and clenched teeth. James believed that he could identify a different constellation of bodily changes for each emotion, and that if he could not feel these changes he would not feel the emotion. Shortly, we will look at some experiments that have a bearing on the James-Lange theory, but first let's compare this theory with some alternatives.

**Common Sense Theory**

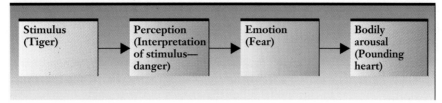

**James-Lange Theory**

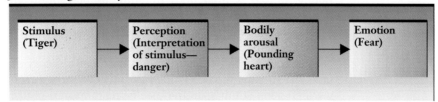

**Schachter Theory**

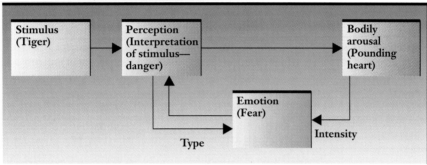

**Fully Interactive Theory**

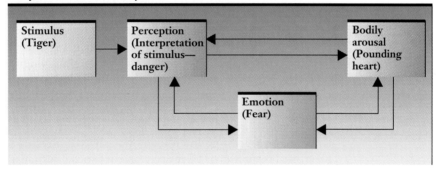

**Figure 7.19  Four theories of emotion**
*Each theory proposes a somewhat different set of causal relationships among perception of the stimulus, bodily arousal, and emotion.*

■ *How Schachter's theory and the fully interactive theory add additional causal relationships to that proposed by James*

**Alternatives to the James-Lange Theory**  Figure 7.19 portrays four different models of the relationships among perception, bodily arousal, and emotion. The first is the *common sense theory*, which James argued against in the above quotation: Perception of the stimulus causes the emotion, which then causes bodily arousal. The second is the James-Lange theory: Perception of the stimulus causes bodily arousal, which then causes the emotion. The third, the *Schachter theory*, is named after Stanley Schachter, who first proposed it (this is the same Schachter whose theory of obesity was discussed earlier). According to this theory, emotion is influenced by both perception of the external stimulus and one's sense of bodily arousal. Perception of the stimulus influences the *type* of emotion felt, and the degree of bodily arousal influences the *intensity* of the emotion. Thus, in the case of seeing a tiger, the perception that the tiger is dangerous determines that the emotion felt will be fear, and the perception of one's own beating heart, sweating, and so on determines how much fear will be felt. An additional feature of the Schachter theory is that the emotion in turn influences perception of the stimulus. According to this theory, high arousal due, say, to having consumed too much coffee could increase emotional intensity, which could cause the person to perceive the tiger as more dangerous than he or she otherwise would.

Finally, the fourth model in Figure 7.19, which I have labeled the *fully interactive theory*, is my interpretation of the way many researchers today view emotions. In this model all of the arrows in the triangle of perception, arousal, and emotion run in both directions. Each process is directly influenced by each of the others. Bodily arousal is influenced by stimulus perception and emotion, emotion is influenced by stimulus perception and bodily arousal, and stimulus perception is influenced by bodily arousal and emotion. Here the relationship among the three processes is that of a continuous cycle rather than a chain, and the cycle runs in both directions. Notice that the fully interactive theory contains all of the interactions specified by the other theories and adds some new ones as well. The following discussion emphasizes the specific relationships predicted by the James-Lange and Schachter models, but the sum result of all of the experiments to date is support for the fully interactive theory.

**Effects of Bodily Arousal on Emotional Intensity**   One prediction that is consistent with all of the theories in Figure 7.19 except the common sense theory is that an artificially induced increase in arousal, such as from a drug, should increase the intensity of the emotion felt in an emotion-inducing situation. Schachter (1971) tested this prediction in experiments that formed part of the basis for his theory. He injected people with either epinephrine (which produces arousal by stimulating processes normally activated by the sympathetic division of the autonomic nervous system) or a placebo (an inactive substance). His main finding was that epinephrine by itself did not produce any particular emotion (the subjects just said they felt jumpy), but when it was combined with emotion-inducing environmental stimuli it increased the intensity of the subjects' emotions. Thus, epinephrine-injected subjects manifested and reported more anger when insulted, more fear when watching a frightening film, and more hilarity when watching a slapstick comedy than did placebo-injected subjects. This emotion-enhancing effect only occurred if the subjects had *not* previously been informed of the physiological effects of epinephrine. Thus, according to Schachter, high physiological arousal increases emotion only when people believe that the arousal is caused by the external situation.

*Evidence for the theory that emotional intensity is influenced by the perception of an aroused bodily state*

Another prediction of both the James-Lange and Schachter theories is that a person who shows no physiological arousal to a stimulus should experience no emotion, or at least no intense emotion. It is impossible to find people who show no arousal response, or to entirely prevent such a response with drugs. But George Hohmann (1966) pioneered a partial test of this prediction by interviewing men who, in adulthood, had suffered spinal cord injuries. Because of the injuries, the men were insensitive and paralyzed in large areas of their body below their neck, and thus they could not feel any arousal from those areas.

When Hohmann asked these men to describe their emotions since their injury, as compared to before, most reported that although they still *acted* as if they experienced intense emotions they didn't really *feel* them in the way that they had before. For instance, one man described his anger as follows: "Sometimes I act angry when I see injustice. I yell and cuss and raise hell, because if you don't do it sometimes I've learned people will take advantage of you, but it doesn't have the heat to it that it used to." Another, in response to questions about fear, said, "I say I am afraid, like when I'm going into a real stiff exam at school, but I don't really feel afraid, not all tense and shaky, with that hollow feeling in my stomach like I used to." One emotion that the men reported to be *not* reduced was that of sentiment or tenderness, which may normally depend more on thought processes and physiological arousal in the head (such as tears, or a sense of choking in the throat), which were still fully intact in these men. As you can see in Figure 7.20, the higher the height of their spinal cord damage (and hence the greater the paralysis and loss of sensation), the greater was the decline in reported intensity of anger and fear. Incidentally, Hohmann is partially paralyzed himself, which he says gave him a special rapport with the people he studied.

**Figure 7.20** *Change in reported emotional intensity following spinal cord injuries*

*Hohmann interviewed five different groups of men who had spinal cord injuries. Group 1 had damage in the lower part of the spinal cord, leaving intact most sensation and muscle control above the waist. At the other extreme, Group 5 had damage in the cervical (neck) portion of the spinal cord and had no muscle control or sensation below the neck. The numbers on the vertical axis refer to subjects' self-reported change in the intensity of two emotions (anger and fear) since the accident as compared to before. The scale was such that +1 = moderate increase, 0 = no change, −1 = moderate decrease, and −2 = large decrease. As you can see, the higher the site of the lesion, the greater was the decrease in self-rated feelings of anger and fear. (Adapted from Schachter, 1971, based on data in Hohmann, 1966.)*

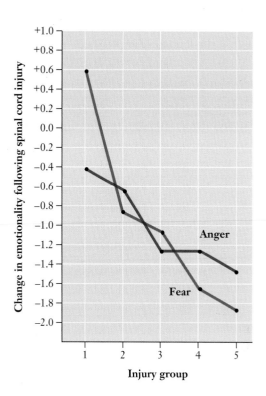

Not all studies have supported the view that varying peripheral arousal influences the intensity of emotion. Some experiments similar to Schachter's original experiments have failed to produce similar results (Reisenzein, 1983). In addition, as intriguing as Hohmann's findings with spinal-damaged patients are, they must be interpreted cautiously. If Hohmann's mode of questioning led the men to equate emotionality with bodily arousal, then by definition those with reduced bodily arousal would report reduced emotion. It is also possible that these men, because they could no longer act out emotions in all the ways they could before their paralysis, had *learned* to suppress emotional feelings as a way of coping with their condition. Precisely because emotion is defined as a subjective feeling, it is difficult to achieve a firm answer to questions about factors that influence it. All in all, however, consistent with the fully interactive theory, a reasonable conclusion from research in this area is that bodily arousal contributes to, but is not the only contributor to, the intensity of an emotion.

**Evidence for a Role of Facial Expressions in Emotion** Responses mediated by the autonomic nervous system are not the only responses that occur automatically in emotion-inducing situations. Chapter 4 presented evidence that different facial expressions innately tend to accompany different emotions. The possibility arises, consistent with the James-Lange theory, that these expressions not only express the emotion but also contribute to the emotional feeling. If you form your face into a smile, will you feel happier? A Pollyannish suggestion, perhaps, but a number of experiments suggest there is some truth to it.

In one experiment, subjects were induced to move certain facial muscles in such a way as to mimic either a smile or a frown (Laird, 1974). They were not told that the purpose was to produce a smile or frown, nor that the study had anything to do with emotions, but rather that the study had to do with the relationship between muscles and perception. (To mislead them, researchers pasted electrodes on each subject's face, as if recording muscle activity was the main purpose.) The subjects were asked to examine a picture while holding the induced facial position. Then, as if it were incidental to the experiment, they were asked to fill out a questionnaire designed to assess their mood. The kind of picture they saw had the

■ *Evidence that molding the face into an emotional expression can affect mood, and that it may do so partly by producing changes elsewhere in the body*

**Figure 7.21** *Effect of facial molding on self-reported happiness and anger*

*Adult subjects were asked to contract certain facial muscles, which effectively molded their faces into either a smile or frown, while viewing a picture of children at play. The smile increased self-reported happiness and the frown increased self-reported anger. (Data from Laird, 1974.)*

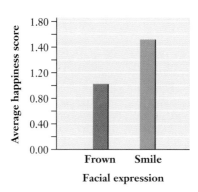

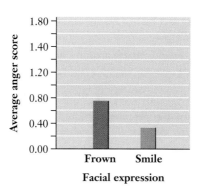

biggest effect on mood, but the artificially induced facial expression also had an effect, as you can see in Figure 7.21. Those whose face had formed a smile were happier, and those whose face had formed a frown were angrier, as measured by the mood questionnaire. In another experiment, people reported themselves to be happier after repeating the vowel sound of a long *e*, which forces the face into a smile, than after repeating other vowel sounds (Zajonc, 1989).

Other research has shown that forming the face into an emotional expression can produce effects on the rest of the body that are similar to those produced when the emotion is felt. Paul Ekman and his colleagues (1983) asked subjects to move specific facial muscles in ways designed to mimic each of the six basic emotional expressions in Ekman and Friesen's atlas of expressions (see Figure 4.12 and Figure 7.22). For comparison, they asked other subjects to feel each emotion, by mentally reliving an event in which that emotion had been strong. While the subjects performed these tasks, the researchers assessed each subject's pattern of physiological arousal. The main finding was that different emotions coincided with somewhat different patterns of arousal, and the pattern for a given emotion was the same whether the subject had been asked to relive the emotion or simply to move certain facial muscles. In particular, skin temperatures increased more when the face mimicked the expression of anger than when it mimicked that of fear (consistent with other evidence that blood tends to flow into the skin in anger and away from it in fear), and the heart rate increased more when the face mimicked either anger or fear than when it mimicked other emotions (see Figure 7.23). Thus, consistent with the James-Lange theory, Ekman and others believe that producing the facial expression appropriate to a particular emotion can cause the rest of the body to respond in a way that is consistent with that emotion, which in turn contributes to the person's psychological experience of the emotional state.

**Figure 7.22** *Inducing a fear expression*

*Shown here are frames from a videotape of a man following the instructions used by Ekman and his colleagues (1983) to induce a fear expression: (a) "Raise your brows and pull them together," (b) "now raise your upper eyelids," and (c) "now stretch your lips horizontally, back toward your ears." Other instructions were used to induce other emotional expressions, producing the results shown in Figure 7.23.*

(a)          (b)          (c)

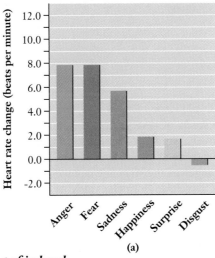
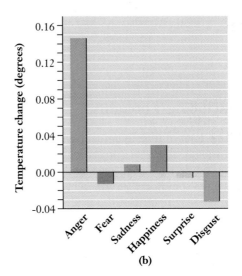

(a)　　　　　　(b)

**Figure 7.23** *Effect of induced emotional expressions on the heart rate and skin temperature*

*Ekman and his colleagues (1983) found that (a) the heart rate increased most when the induced facial expression was of anger, fear, or sadness, and (b) the skin temperature increased most when the induced expression was of anger. (From Ekman & others, 1983.)*

**Figure 7.24** *Two kinds of attack shown by cats*

*In experiments with cats, J. P. Flynn (1967) found that electrical stimulation in one area of the hypothalamus elicited the "hot," noisy variety of attack depicted in the photo on the left, which cats usually use in attacking other cats, and electrical stimulation of another area of that structure elicited the "cold," stealthy variety of attack depicted in the photo on the right, which cats usually use in attacking mice or other prey. Thus, the two attack responses not only look different, but are apparently organized by different neural circuits in the brain.*

**Emotions as Brain States** Our discussion in this section has been about the relationship between peripheral bodily changes and emotions, but I will conclude by reminding you of the role of the brain. The brain is, of course, central to all the processes that I have been describing. It receives and interprets emotion-inducing information from the environment, controls the peripheral responses to such input (such as changes in the heart rate and facial expressions), receives feedback from the responses it produces, and organizes all such information in a way that results in the emotion.

There are many different ways to study the role of the brain in emotional processes. Physiological psychologists have identified brain areas critical for the expression of fear and aggression in animals in the same way that they have identified those critical for hunger and sex. Although we cannot know if other animals feel emotions in the sense that humans do, stereotaxic lesions and electrical stimulation of certain areas of the hypothalamus and limbic system dramatically alter an animal's tendency to either flee or attack (see Figure 7.24). A few clinical studies involving electrical stimulation in the human brain (in the same series that identified pleasure areas in the human brain) have shown that stimulation in specific regions of the limbic system can produce feelings of anxiety, fear, rage, or sexual passion, depending on the area stimulated (see Valzelli, 1981). Other studies, comparing people who have suffered brain damage in either the right or left cerebral cortex, have indicated that the right cortex is more involved in emotions than the left (to be discussed in Chapter 11). In addition, an enormous amount of work has been devoted to identifying neurotransmitters and other chemicals that modulate emotions through their action in the brain. I already said something about such work in Chapter 6, and more will be said in Chapters 17 and 18 in relation to the attempt to understand and treat specific emotional disorders.

## Concluding Thoughts

**1. The goal of physiological psychology in the study of states** This chapter has been mostly about the physiological approach to the study of motivation (specifically hunger and sex), sleep, and emotion. All of these are *behavioral states*. They all involve somewhat sustained but reversible changes in the way one behaves in a given environment. But the goal of physiological psychology in the study of such states is to equate them with *physiological states*. That is, the goal is to identify the somewhat sustained but reversible physiological changes that modify the behavior-producing mechanisms and thereby create the behavioral states. It is a fascinating but difficult goal, because the machine being studied is so extraordinarily complicated. As you think about each state discussed in this chapter, ask yourself: What have researchers discovered about the physiological change that corresponds with this behavioral state? This broad question will be useful for organizing your review.

**2. Two categories of methods in the physiological study of states** In their attempt to relate behavioral states to physiological ones, researchers use two broad categories of methods. One category is to *intervene* in some way in ongoing physiological processes to see what happens to the behaviorally measured state. What happens to hunger, or the sex drive, or sleep, or an emotion if this part of the brain is destroyed, or stimulated, or if the supply of this hormone is cut off, or increased? As you review the chapter, notice how often such methods were mentioned. Intervention is a powerful way to identify causal relationships between physiology and behavior. But most intervention procedures are harmful or at least risky to the subject, so they are used more often in studies of other animals than of humans. The intervention approach is approximated, however, in studies of people whose natural physiology has been disrupted through an accident or disease—as in Hohmann's study of people with spinal cord injuries.

The other category is to *measure* physiological processes in some way and *correlate* those measures with changes in behavioral state. Do natural changes in hormones, brain waves, the heart rate, or other physiological variables accompany natural changes in the behavioral state? Most measurement procedures are safe and can be used with humans. Notice, as you review the chapter, how often this correlational approach was used in the human studies described. It helps identify reliable relationships, but it does not, by itself, tell us about cause and effect. If brain waves slow down during sleep, or skin temperature goes up during anger, that does not tell us that slow brain waves *cause* sleep, or that high skin temperature *causes* anger. Do you see why it is so tempting for scientists to find some way to intervene, to test cause-and-effect hypotheses once they have found a correlation?

## Further Reading

**Alexandra Logue** (1986). *The psychology of eating and drinking.* New York: Freeman.
*This is an interesting introduction to the variables, both inside and outside the body, that affect hunger, thirst, and the ways they are expressed. The last unit is devoted to malfunctions of these processes, including anorexia and bulimia, overeating, and alcohol abuse.*

**K. Kelly** (Ed.) (1987). *Females, males, and sexuality: Theories and research.* Albany, NY: State University of New York Press.
*In this book, various experts describe contemporary research and theories dealing with biological and social aspects of human sexuality.*

**J. Allen Hobson** (1988). *The dreaming brain*. New York: Basic Books.

*This fascinating book on a fascinating topic, by a leading researcher on sleep and dreaming, begins with a review of the ways that dreams have been understood in the past, and then moves to modern studies of the biology of sleep and dreaming.*

**Neil McNaughton** (1989). *Biology and emotion*. Cambridge: Cambridge University Press.

*This is a thoughtful, highly readable, up-to-date integration of evolutionary and physiological approaches to the understanding of emotion.*

**James Stellar & Eliot Stellar** (1985). *The neurobiology of motivation and reward*. New York: Springer-Verlag.

*For the student who wants to go beyond an introduction and see how contemporary physiological psychologists talk about motivation and reward, this is an excellent source. Though technically oriented, its clear prose is such that the nonexpert who has some familiarity with the brain can read it profitably.*

## Looking Ahead

Many issues concerning drives and emotions that are hinted at in this chapter are discussed more fully in chapters to come. The role of social factors in human sexuality is discussed in Chapter 13. Freud's idea that the sex drive underlies behaviors that are not explicitly sexual, and also his theory of dreams, are discussed in Chapter 16. Human motives having to do with affiliation, achievement, and self-esteem are important themes running through the chapters on social psychology and personality (Chapters 14–16). Emotional problems and treatments for them are the subjects of Chapters 17 and 18.

But now we turn from the slower-moving components of the kaleidoscope to the fast-moving components. The next chapter is on sensation.

# CHAPTER 8

Overview

Hearing

Vision

Pain

Psychophysics

# SENSATION

What would mental life be like if you had no senses? What if, from birth, you could not hear, see, touch, taste, smell, or in any other way sense the world around you? You would not be able to react to anything, because reactions require sensory input. You would not be able to learn anything, because learning begins with sensory input. Would you be able to think? What could you think about with no knowledge gained from the senses? Philosophers, from Aristotle on, have pondered these questions and have usually concluded that without sensation there would be no mental life. It is no wonder that the study of the senses has always been a fundamental part of the science of psychology.

This chapter is on sensation, and the next is on perception. *Sensation* refers both to the experience associated with a sound, light, or other simple stimulus and to the initial steps by which the sense organs and neural pathways take in stimulus information. *Perception* refers to the subsequent organizing of that information and to the meaningful interpretation (such as "That object before me is a coffee cup") extracted from it. This distinction between sensation and perception is convenient as a basis for organizing chapters, but, as you will discover, it is somewhat arbitrary. The organization of stimulus information, in ways useful for extracting meaning, actually begins during the early steps of taking it in.

Sensation is the area of psychological study that has enjoyed the longest and happiest marriage with physiology. In the mid-nineteenth century, around the time when psychology was just beginning to emerge as a recognized science, an esteemed German physiologist, Hermann von Helmholtz, became intrigued with certain elementary *psychological* questions about sensation. How is it that we can hear sounds as having different pitches? How is it that we can see objects as having different colors? Why do we see certain mixtures of colored lights as having a color entirely different from that produced by the original lights alone? He went on to develop theories about how structures in the ears, eyes, and nervous system might respond differently to different aspects of sound and light stimuli in ways that would permit different psychological experiences to occur. Subsequent research confirmed and extended Helmholtz's early theories.

From Helmholtz's time until today, sensory psychology and physiology have been happy partners, making many discoveries and winning many Nobel prizes together. The simple reason is that sensation is easier to study physiologically than are other psychological processes. Many of the processes that control sensations occur in the sense organs themselves—in the ears, eyes, skin, tongue, and nose —and it is much easier to study sense organs than to study the brain. Information about the world is coded in the sense organs into neural messages that are sent to the brain for decoding and analysis. As you will discover in this chapter, much has been learned about the coding and relatively little has been learned about the decoding and analysis.

This chapter is divided into five main sections. The first provides an overview of basic questions, approaches, and processes important to the study of sensation. The second and third are devoted to hearing and vision, respectively, which are the two most studied senses. The fourth is on pain, which can be thought of as both a sense and a motivating force. And the fifth is concerned with psychophysics, a non-physiological approach to describing relationships between physical stimuli and the sensory experiences they produce.

## Overview

*How the process of sensation can be depicted as a chain of three different kinds of events*

Most broadly, the process to which this chapter is devoted can be diagrammed as follows:

physical stimulus → physiological response → sensory experience.

We have here three classes of events: (1) The *physical stimulus* is the matter or energy that impinges on sense organs; (2) the *physiological response* is the pattern of electrical activity that occurs in sense organs, nerves, and the brain as a result of the stimulus; and (3) the *sensory experience* is the subjective, psychological sensation—the sound, sight, taste, or whatever—that is experienced by the individual whose sense organs have been stimulated.

To be studied scientifically, events must be measurable. The first two classes of events in this chain can be measured directly by physical means, such as with light meters and recording electrodes. The third class cannot be measured directly—there are no meters that can be plugged into the head to read out sensory experiences—but it can be measured indirectly through observing behavior.

*A sensational device*

Modern technology has made it relatively easy to measure physical stimuli and the physiological responses to those stimuli. Here an electroencephalograph records the response of an infant's brain to sound. The technique is particularly useful for testing hearing in infants, who cannot yet describe their subjective experiences.

*How sensory experience can be measured through observing behavior*

The most useful indices of human sensory experience are verbal answers to carefully worded questions about stimuli presented under controlled conditions. If we show two patches of light to a person, and the person repeatedly says that Patch *A* is brighter than Patch *B*, we can conclude that the person experiences some difference between the two patches on a dimension that he or she has learned to call *brightness*. If other people make the same judgment, we can conclude that brightness is a sensory experience that is regularly affected, in people, by whatever is the difference between Patches *A* and *B*. In studies of nonhuman animals or human infants, we can obtain information about sensory experiences through nonverbal means. For example, we might train a pigeon to peck one key when one stimulus is present and a different key when another stimulus is present. Whether working with humans or other animals, it is not raw sensory experience that is assessed, but the individual's ability to use that experience to guide a behavioral choice.

**Domains of Questions**    The basic questions in the study of sensation can be categorized into three domains, each concerning a different one of the three possible relationships that can be derived from the chain of events described above. These are the following (see Figure 8.1):

1. *Sensory physiology*  This domain deals with the relationship between the stimulus and the physiological response. The questions asked here are of the following general form: If such-and-such a stimulus is present, what physiological response will occur in a sense organ, or in the nerve from that organ, or in neurons in the brain? Thus, a sensory physiologist interested in color vision might present lights that are seen as different colors and try to determine how cells in the eye or brain respond differently to them.

2. *Sensory physiological psychology*  This domain deals with the relationship between the physiological response and the sensory experience. The basic question here is this: What physiological occurrences are essential for a particular sensory experience (measured behaviorally) to occur? A common approach to answering this type of question in nonhuman animals is to destroy or temporarily inhibit the action of some specific part of the sensory system and assess the resultant deficits in sensory experience. A variant of this approach, common in human research, is to study individuals who are already missing some component of the normal sensory machinery. Thus, a scientist interested in color vision might identify people who, for genetic reasons, are missing a particular kind of cell in the eye and then test them to see just which colors they can and cannot distinguish from each other. Another approach is to try to induce particular sensory experiences by electrically stimulating parts of a sensory system. For example, electrical stimulation of the auditory nerve (which runs from the ear to the brain) results in the sensation of sounds whose pitch depends on which part of the nerve is stimulated.

3. *Psychophysics*  This domain deals with the relationship between the stimulus and the sensory experience, ignoring the physiological response that mediates that relationship. (You can remember *psychophysics* by recalling that it relates the *psychological* sensory experience to *physical* characteristics of the stimulus.) Questions in psychophysics take the following form: If the physical stimulus is changed in such-and-such a way, how will the sensory experience change? Thus, a psychophysicist studying color vision might present lights that vary physically in known ways. The researcher might then have people state the color they see, or match each light's color to another stimulus, to determine what sorts of physical changes produce changes in one's experience of color.

■ *The questions of sensory physiology, sensory physiological psychology, and psychophysics*

**Figure 8.1** *Three domains in the study of sensation*
*Sensory physiology, sensory physiological psychology, and psychophysics are concerned with the relationship between different pairs of the three classes of events involved in sensation. (Adapted from Uttal, 1973.)*

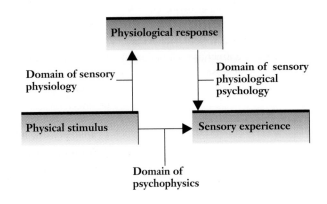

**The Various Human Senses and Their Basic Anatomy**   Ever since Aristotle, people have spoken of the *five senses*, counting them as hearing, vision, touch, taste, and smell. Actually there are more than five senses, and any attempt to tally them up to an exact number is arbitrary, because what one person thinks of as one sense may be thought of as two or more by another. For example, our skin is sensitive not just to touch but also to temperature and pain, neither of which is included in Aristotle's five senses. Other senses omitted by Aristotle have to do with body position and the body's internal environment. We have a sense of balance mediated by a mechanism in the inner ear, a sense of limb position and movement mediated by receptors in muscles and joints, and senses pertaining to homeostatic needs (such as sensitivity to the inner supply of food molecules, discussed in Chapter 7).

Each sense has its own set of ***receptors***, specialized structures that respond to the physical stimulus by producing electrical changes that can initiate neural impulses, and its own set of ***sensory neurons***, which carry neural impulses from the receptors to the central nervous system (the structure of sensory neurons was described in Chapter 6). For some senses the receptors are simply the sensitive ends of sensory neurons, and for other senses they are separate cells, which form synapses upon sensory neurons. For some senses the receptors all exist in a specific, localized sensory organ, such as the ear, eye, or nose, and for others they exist in a wide variety of locations. For example, pain receptors exist not just in the skin, but also in muscles, tendons, joints, and many other places. The stimuli, receptors, and peripheral nerves involved in the most well studied senses are identified in Table 8.1. Regardless of whether they come from one location or many, the neurons for a particular sense lead to sensory-specific pathways in the central nervous system. These pathways in turn lead, for most senses, to specific ***sensory areas*** in the cerebral cortex, designed to receive and analyze the neural input (for depictions of sensory areas, see Figure 6.14).

■ *Common elements of all of our senses: receptors, sensory neurons, and pathways in the central nervous system*

**Table 8.1**  *Stimuli, receptors, and the pathways to the brain for various senses*

| Sense | Stimulus | Receptors | Pathway to the brain |
|---|---|---|---|
| Hearing | Sound waves | Pressure-sensitive hair cells in cochlea of inner ear | Auditory nerve (8th cranial nerve) |
| Vision | Light waves | Light-sensitive rods and cones in retina of eye | Optic nerve (3rd cranial nerve) |
| Touch | Pressure on the skin | Sensitive ends of touch neurons in skin | Trigeminal nerve (5th cranial nerve) for touch above the neck. Spinal nerves for touch elsewhere. |
| Pain | Wide variety of potentially harmful stimuli | Sensitive ends of pain neurons in skin and other tissues | Trigeminal nerve (5th cranial nerve) for pain above the neck. Spinal nerves for pain elsewhere. |
| Taste | Molecules dissolved in fluid on the tongue | Taste cells in taste buds on the tongue | Facial nerve (7th cranial nerve) |
| Smell | Molecules dissolved in fluid on mucous membranes in the nose | Sensitive ends of olfactory neurons in the mucous membranes | Olfactory nerve (1st cranial nerve) |

**Transduction, and the Coding of Stimulus Quantity and Quality**   The process by which a receptor cell produces an electrical change in response to a physical stimulus is called ***transduction***. That is, transduction is the process by which receptors in the eye respond to light, receptors in the ear respond to sound, receptors on

■ *How receptors respond to stimulus energy and code information about the amount and kind of energy present*

the tongue respond to chemicals dissolved there, and so on. While the details of this process are different for different senses, there are basic similarities across the senses. In every case the receptor cell is constructed in such a way that, in response to a stimulus appropriate to that sense, its membrane becomes more permeable to certain electrically charged particles, such as sodium or potassium ions. These particles then flow through the membrane, either from outside the cell to inside, or vice versa, and change the electrical charge across the membrane. This electrical change, called the ***receptor potential***, is analogous to the postsynaptic potential produced on neurons by the action of synaptic transmitters (described in Chapter 6). Receptor potentials in turn trigger events that lead to the production of action potentials (also described in Chapter 6) in the axons of sensory neurons.

For senses to be useful they must not only respond to a particular class of stimulus energy (such as sound or light), but they must also respond differently to variations in that energy. Every form of energy varies along at least two dimensions, a *quantitative* and a *qualitative* dimension. The quantitative dimension has to do with the amount or intensity of energy present. A sound or light can be weak or strong; molecules stimulating taste or smell can be diluted or highly concentrated. The qualitative dimension has to do with the precise kind of energy present. Lights of different wavelengths (which we perceive as different colors) are considered to be qualitatively different, as are sounds of different frequencies (which we perceive as different pitches), as are different chemicals (which we perceive as different smells or tastes). In transduction, information about the quantity and quality of the stimulus is preserved in the pattern of action potentials sent to the brain, a process referred to as ***coding***.

Coding of stimulus *quantity* results from the fact that stronger stimuli produce larger receptor potentials, which in turn produce faster rates of action potentials in sensory neurons. The brain interprets a fast rate of action potentials as a strong stimulus and a slow rate as a weak stimulus. Coding of stimulus *quality* occurs because different receptors within any given sensory tissue are tuned to respond best to somewhat different forms of energy. In the eye, for example, there are three different kinds of receptor cells involved in color vision, each most sensitive to a different range of wavelengths of light. In the ear, different receptors are most sensitive to different sound frequencies. And in the nose and tongue, different receptors are most sensitive to different molecules. Thus, in general, qualitative variations are coded as different *ratios* of activity in sensory neurons coming from different sets of receptors. For an illustration of qualitative and quantitative coding for the sense of taste, see Figure 8.2. You will see further illustrations, for hearing and vision, later in the chapter.

**Figure 8.2 *Quantitative and qualitative coding in the sense of taste***

*Shown here are the rates of action potentials in two different taste neurons when a weak or strong solution of sugar or salt is placed on the tongue. Notice that each neuron responds faster to a strong solution of a given substance than to a weak one (quantitative coding), but that Neuron A always responds faster than Neuron B when the stimulus is sugar, and the reverse is true when the stimulus is salt (qualitative coding). (Data are hypothetical, but are based on such findings as those of Nowlis & Frank, 1977.)*

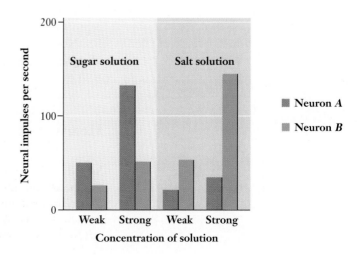

*An advantage of adaptation*
*Unless you have visited a printing plant, you can't imagine how bad inks can smell. This worker's placid expression suggests that sensory adaptation has rendered him oblivious to the odor—a condition that should greatly enhance "survival" in such an environment.*

**Sensory Adaptation** When you first put on your wristwatch, you feel the pressure on your skin, but later you don't. When you first turn on the lights, after sitting in the dark, the room seems very bright, but later not so bright. When you first wade into a lake, the water may seem terribly cold, but later only slightly cool. When you first enter a chemistry lab, the odor may seem overwhelming, but later you hardly notice it. The change in sensitivity that occurs when a sensory system is either stimulated or not stimulated for a length of time is called *sensory adaptation*. In general, in the absence of stimulation a sensory system becomes temporarily more sensitive (it will respond to weaker stimuli), and in the presence of stimulation it becomes temporarily less sensitive (it requires stronger stimuli to produce a response). Sensory adaptation is useful because it leads us to notice most the changes in, and to be relatively oblivious to the stable aspects of, our environment.

■ *How to tell whether sensory adaptation occurs in receptors or farther inward*

In many cases, sensory adaptation is mediated by the receptor cells themselves. If a stimulus remains for a period of time, the resultant receptor potential and rate of action potentials are at first great, but over time they are much reduced, resulting in a reduced sensation. In other cases, however, adaptation is mediated at least partly by changes farther inward, in the central nervous system. You can prove this yourself for the sense of smell (Matlin, 1988). If you place an odorous substance (such as an open bottle of nail polish remover or shaving lotion) on a desk in front of you, with one nostril plugged, you will adapt to it within about 5 minutes (it won't smell as strong). Then, if you unplug that nostril and quickly plug the other you will find that you are still adapted to the odor, even though it is now acting on receptors in the other nostril, different from those that it was acting on before. Thus, adaptation for smell must be due in part to changes in neurons in the brain that receive input from both nostrils. (You might wish to try a comparable experiment for vision. Keeping one eye covered, move from a dimly lit area into a bright area, preferably into sunlight, and sit there for about 15 minutes until the light no longer seems so bright. Then remove the cover and place it immediately over the other eye. Does the light suddenly get brighter? If adaptation is mediated by receptors in the eye, it should.)

Now, having reviewed some of the general issues and approaches in the study of sensory systems, let us look in more detail at three specific senses. We will begin with hearing.

## Hearing

**Sound** The term *sound* refers both to a type of physical stimulus and to the sensation produced by that stimulus, a fact that can cause semantic confusion as exemplified by the old riddle, "If a tree falls in the forest where there is no one to hear it, does it make a sound?" As a physical stimulus, sound is the vibration of air or some other medium produced by an object such as a tuning fork or one's vocal cords.

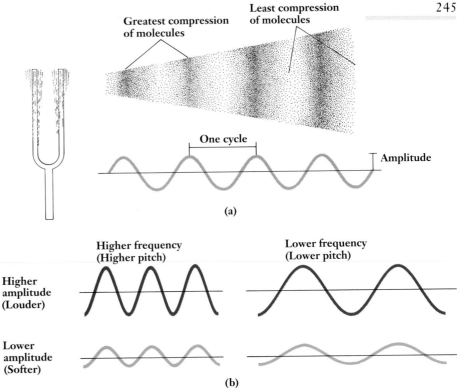

**Figure 8.3 *Characteristics of sound***

*The oscillating tuning fork (a) causes air molecules to vibrate in a manner that can be represented as a wave of pressure. Each wave contains an area where the air molecules are more compressed (the dark regions in the upper diagram) and an area where they are less compressed (the light regions) than normal. The peak pressure (the highest compression) of each wave defines the amplitude of the sound, and the number of waves that pass a given point per second defines the frequency. The higher the amplitude, the louder the sound; and the higher the frequency, the higher the pitch (b). (Adapted from Klinke, 1986.)*

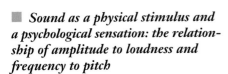

■ *Sound as a physical stimulus and a psychological sensation: the relationship of amplitude to loudness and frequency to pitch*

The vibration moves outward from the sound source in a manner that can be described as a wave (see Figure 8.3). The height of the wave indicates the total pressure exerted by the molecules of air (or another medium) as they move back and forth, which is referred to as the sound's **amplitude** or intensity and corresponds to what we hear as the sound's **loudness**. Sound amplitude is usually measured in logarithmic units of pressure called *decibels* (abbreviated *dB*). (See Table 8.2, which further defines decibels and contains the decibel ratings for a number of common sounds.)

**Table 8.2 *Sound-pressure amplitudes of various sounds, and conversion to decibels*** \*

| Example | $P$ (in sound-pressure units) | Log $P$ | Decibels |
|---|---|---|---|
| Softest detectable sound | 1 | 0 | 0 |
| Soft whisper | 10 | 1 | 20 |
| Quiet neighborhood | 100 | 2 | 40 |
| Average conversation | 1000 | 3 | 60 |
| Loud music from a radio | 10,000 | 4 | 80 |
| Heavy automobile traffic | 100,000 | 5 | 100 |
| Very loud thunder | 1,000,000 | 6 | 120 |
| Jet airplane taking off | 10,000,000 | 7 | 140 |
| Loudest rock band on record | 100,000,000 | 8 | 160 |
| Spacecraft launch (from 150 ft.) | 1,000,000,000 | 9 | 180 |

\*One sound-pressure unit ($P$) is defined as $2 \times 10^{-5}$ newtons/square meter (Klinke, 1986). When measured in sound-pressure units, the amplitude range of human hearing is enormous. A reason for converting to logarithmic units is to produce a smaller range of numbers. The logarithm (log) of a number is the power to which 10 must be raised to produce that number. For example, the log of 10,000 is 4, because $10^4 = 10,000$. A decibel (dB) is defined as $20 \log P$. Thus, 4 log units = 80 dB.

*Sources*: From *Human information processing*, 2nd ed. (p. 161) by P. H. Lindsay & D. A. Norman, 1977, New York: Academic Press. And from *Sensation and perception*, 2nd ed. (p. 271) by M. W. Matlin, 1988, Boston: Allyn and Bacon.

In addition to varying in amplitude, sound waves vary in *frequency*, which we hear as the sound's *pitch*. The frequency of a sound is the rate at which the molecules of air or another medium move back and forth. Frequency is measured in *hertz* (abbreviated *Hz*), which is the number of complete waves (or cycles) that occur at any given point per second. Sounds that are audible to humans have frequencies ranging from about 20 to 20,000 Hz. The simplest kind of sound is a *pure tone*, which is a constant-frequency wave of vibration that can be described as a sine wave (see Figure 8.3). Pure tones, which are useful in auditory experiments, can be produced in the laboratory, but they rarely occur in other contexts. Natural sound sources, including even musical instruments and tuning forks, vibrate at several frequencies at once and thus put out more complex waves than that shown in Figure 8.3. Natural sounds can be thought of as consisting of many different tones at once. To give you an idea of the relationship between frequency and pitch, the dominant (most audible) frequency of the lowest note on a piano is about 27 Hz, that of middle C is about 262 Hz, and that of the highest piano note is about 4186 Hz (Matlin, 1988).

**Basic Workings of the Ear**   Evolutionarily, hearing is a variation of touch. Touch is sensitivity to pressure on the skin, and hearing is sensitivity to pressure on a special sensory tissue in the ear. In some animals, such as moths, sound is sensed through modified touch receptors located on flexible patches of skin that vibrate in response to sound waves. In humans and other mammals the special patches of skin for hearing have migrated to a location inside the head, and special organs, the ears, have developed to magnify the pressure exerted by sound waves as they are transported inward. A diagram of the human ear is shown in Figure 8.4. To review its structures and their functions, we will begin from the outside and work inward.

The *outer ear* consists of the *pinna*, which is the flap of skin and cartilage forming the visible portion of the ear, and the *auditory canal*, which is the opening into the head that ends at the *eardrum* (or tympanic membrane). It can be thought of as an air-filled funnel for receiving sound waves and transporting them inward. The vibration of air outside the head (the physical sound) causes air in the auditory canal to vibrate, which in turn causes the tympanic membrane to vibrate.

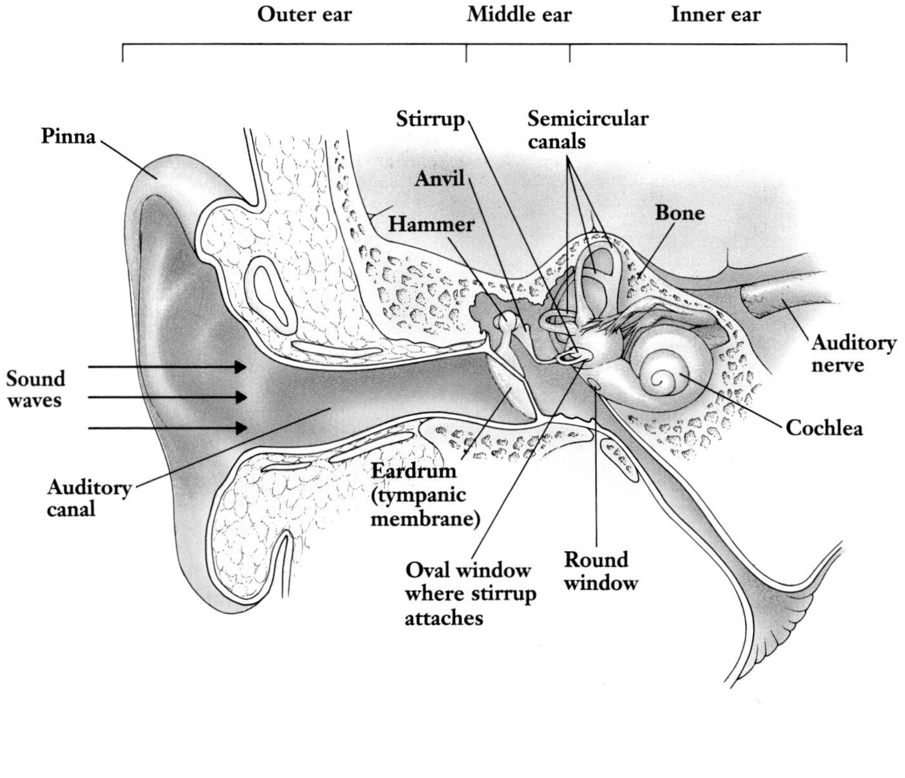

■ *How the outer ear funnels, the middle ear magnifies, and the inner ear transduces*

**Figure 8.4** *Parts of the human ear*

*Sound waves (vibrations of air) that enter the auditory canal cause the eardrum to vibrate, which causes the ossicles (hammer, anvil, and stirrup) to vibrate, which causes the oval window to vibrate, setting up waves of motion in the fluid inside the cochlea. The semicircular canals are involved in the sense of balance, not hearing.*

**Figure 8.5 *Transduction mechanism in the inner ear***
*This diagram depicts a longitudinal section of the cochlea (partially uncoiled), showing the outer and inner ducts. Sound waves in the fluid of the outer duct cause the basilar membrane to wave up and down. When the basilar membrane moves upward, its hairs bend against the tectorial membrane, initiating receptor potentials in the hair cells.*

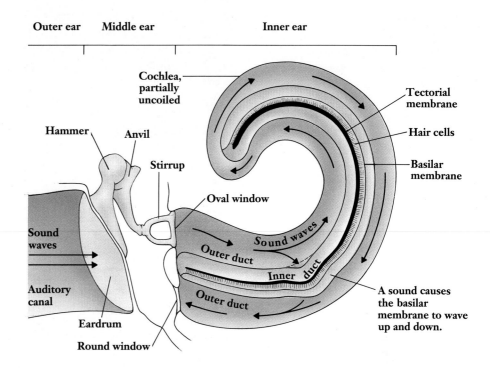

The **middle ear** is an air-filled cavity, separated from the outer ear by the eardrum. Its main structures are three tiny bones called **ossicles** (also called the *hammer*, *anvil*, and *stirrup*, because of their respective shapes), which are linked to the eardrum at one end and to the *oval window*, a membrane of the cochlea, at the other end. When sound causes the eardrum to vibrate, the ossicles vibrate and push against the oval window. Because the oval window has only about one-thirtieth the area of the tympanic membrane, the pressure (force per unit area) that is funneled to it by the ossicles is about thirty times greater than the pressure on the eardrum. Thus, the main function of the middle ear is to increase the amount of pressure that sound waves exert upon the inner ear.

The coiled **cochlea**, in the **inner ear**, is where the actual transduction process takes place. As depicted in the uncoiled view in Figure 8.5, the cochlea contains a fluid-filled *outer duct* that begins at the oval window, runs to the tip of the cochlea, and then runs back again to another membrane, the *round window*, located near the oval window. Sandwiched between the two parts of the outer duct is another fluid-filled tube, the *inner duct*. The membrane forming the floor of the inner duct is the **basilar membrane**, on which are located the receptor cells for hearing, called **hair cells**. There are four rows of hair cells (three outer rows and one inner row), each running the length of the basilar membrane. Each hair cell contains tiny hairs (called *cilia*) that protrude into the inner duct and whose ends abut against another membrane called the *tectorial membrane*. At its other end, each hair cell forms synapses with several **auditory neurons**, whose axons form the **auditory nerve**, which runs to the brain.

The process of transduction in the cochlea can be summarized as follows: The sound-induced vibration of the ossicles against the oval window initiates vibration in the fluid in the outer duct of the cochlea, which produces an up-and-down waving motion of the very flexible basilar membrane. The tectorial membrane above the basilar membrane is less flexible and doesn't move when the basilar membrane moves, so the hairs on the hair cells bend against the tectorial membrane each time the basilar membrane moves upward. This bending causes a physical change in the hair cell's membrane, which leads to an electrical change across the membrane (the receptor potential). This in turn causes each hair cell to release neurotransmitter molecules at its synapses upon auditory neurons, thereby increasing the rate of action potentials in those neurons (Hudspeth, 1983; Pickles, 1988).

*Warning: Noise can be dangerous*
*These electron micrographs show hair cells*
*on the basilar membrane of a guinea pig*
*(a) before and (b) after exposure to 24 hours*
*of sound loud enough to be comparable to a*
*rock concert. Note that on some cells the tiny*
*hairs are disarranged, and on others the*
*hairs are destroyed.*

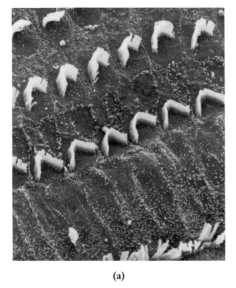

(a)

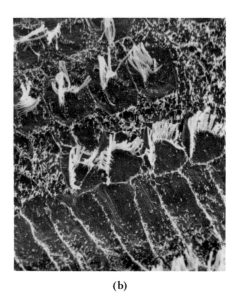

(b)

■ *Two kinds of deafness, and how a*
*new kind of hearing aid works*

With this knowledge of the ear it is possible to understand the physiological bases for two varieties of deafness. ***Conduction deafness*** occurs when the ossicles of the middle ear become rigid and cannot carry sounds inward from the tympanic membrane to the cochlea. People with this form of deafness can hear vibrations that reach the cochlea by routes other than the middle ear. A conventional hearing aid is helpful for such people, because it magnifies the sound pressure sufficiently to be conducted by other bones of the face into the cochlea.

***Sensorineural deafness*** occurs from damage to the cochlea, the hair cells, or the auditory neurons. Some degree of sensorineural hearing loss occurs in everyone as they get older, especially if they have been exposed over their lifetime to sustained loud sounds, which destroy hair cells (Kryter, 1985). People with complete sensorineural deafness are not helped by a conventional hearing aid, but many can potentially be helped by a ***cochlear implant***. This is a new form of hearing aid that transforms sounds into electrical signals, which are then conveyed by fine wires threaded through the cochlea to various sets of auditory neurons terminating within the cochlea (Loeb, 1985). In essence, the cochlear implant substitutes for the hair cells as a transducer and stimulates sets of auditory neurons directly by electrical means. It can be used when deafness is due to the destruction of hair cells, but not when the auditory nerve has been destroyed. Although still in the experimental stage of development, cochlear implants are currently used by hundreds of people worldwide, and in some cases they achieve sufficient sound resolution to understand speech (Blamey & others, 1987).

**The Coding of Sound Frequency** How do receptors on the basilar membrane code the differences in sound frequency that permit pitch detection? In the nineteenth century, Hermann von Helmholtz suggested that the basilar membrane may respond to sound in a way analogous to the strings of a harp. A harp's strings vibrate not only when plucked, but also when sound waves strike them, with different strings vibrating best to different frequencies. Helmholtz proposed that the basilar membrane may contain separate fibers that, like a harp's strings, resonate to different tonal frequencies and activate different neurons in the auditory nerve (Zwislocki, 1981).

■ *How sound travels across the membrane of the inner ear, how pitch is coded by place, and why lower tones mask higher tones*

Considerably later, in work begun in the 1920s that eventuated in a Nobel prize, Georg von Békésy showed that Helmholtz's general idea—that different frequencies activate different receptors—was correct, but that the details were wrong. Békésy developed a way to observe directly the action of the basilar membrane, and he discovered that it does not behave like a harp with separate strings, but rather like a bed sheet when someone shakes it at one end. Sound waves entering the cochlea set up *traveling waves* on the basilar membrane, which move from the proximal end (closest to the oval window) toward the distal end (the tip farthest away from the oval window). As each wave moves it gradually increases in amplitude up

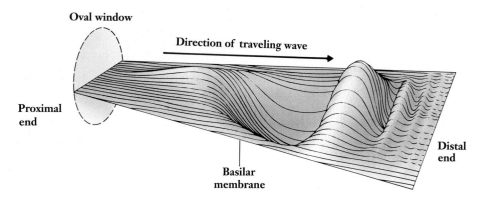

**Figure 8.6** *Diagram of a sound wave traveling on the basilar membrane*

*The wave shown here, peaking near the distal end of the membrane (far from the oval window), is from a relatively low-frequency sound. A wave from a higher-frequency sound would peak closer to the proximal end (near the oval window).*

to a certain maximum and then rapidly decreases and dies out, as illustrated in Figure 8.6. Of most importance, Békésy found that the position on the membrane at which the waves reach their peak depends on the frequency of the tone. High frequencies produce waves that travel only a short distance, peaking near the proximal end, and low frequencies produce waves that travel farther, peaking nearer the distal end. From this observation, Békésy hypothesized that rapid firing in neurons that come from the proximal end of the membrane, accompanied by little firing from other parts, is interpreted by the brain as a high-pitched sound; and rapid firing in neurons coming from a more distal portion is interpreted as a lower-pitched sound. Since then, other studies have confirmed the general validity of Békésy's hypothesis (Pickles, 1988).

One sensory phenomenon that is consistent with, and partly explained by, Békésy's traveling-wave theory is asymmetry in *auditory masking*, a phenomenon that is important in the production of music. If two tones occur simultaneously, the more intense tone tends to mask (prevent the hearing of) the less intense tone. Auditory masking is asymmetrical in that low-frequency tones mask high-frequency tones much more effectively than the reverse (Scharf, 1964). Thus, a bassoon can drown out a piccolo; but a piccolo will not drown out a bassoon, even if it is played at a much higher amplitude than the bassoon. To see how Békésy's theory helps explain this phenomenon, look at Figure 8.7. The wave produced by a low-frequency bassoon note encompasses the entire portion of the basilar membrane that is encompassed by the piccolo note (plus more). Thus, if the bassoon note is high enough in amplitude, it can interfere with the effect of the piccolo note; but the piccolo note, even at very high amplitude, cannot interfere with the effect that the bassoon note has on the more distal part of the membrane, because it never travels that far down the membrane.

Another observation that can be accounted for by Békésy's theory concerns the pattern of hearing loss that occurs as we get older. We lose our sensitivity to high frequencies to a much greater degree than to low frequencies. Thus, young children can hear frequencies as high as 30,000 Hz, and young adults can hear frequencies as high as 20,000 Hz, but a typical 60-year-old cannot hear frequencies above about 15,000 Hz (to see a graph of this, you may want to look ahead to Figure 8.28). Since this decline is greatest for people who live or work in noisy envi-

**Figure 8.7** *Why a low-frequency tone masks a high-frequency tone better than the reverse*

(a) *When a low-frequency tone (such as that from a bassoon) and a high-frequency tone (such as that from a piccolo) are played simultaneously, the bassoon can mask the piccolo because its action on the basilar membrane encompasses the entire portion on which the piccolo acts.* (b) *But the piccolo cannot mask the bassoon because, even when played at high amplitude, it does not affect the distal part of the membrane to which the bassoon's waves extend. (Adapted from Scharf, 1964.)*

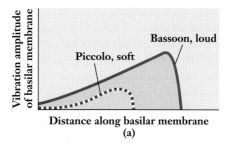
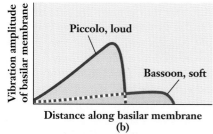

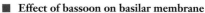

■ Effect of bassoon on basilar membrane     ■ Effect of piccolo on basilar membrane

*Unsafe sound*
*Pete Townshend (right), formerly the lead guitarist of The Who, can no longer play with the group because of severe damage to his hearing. Townshend has publicized his ailment to warn musicians and concert-goers of the dangers of loud music.*

ronments (Kryter, 1985), there is reason to believe that it is caused by the wearing out of hair cells with repeated use. But why should cells responsible for coding high frequencies wear out faster than those for coding low frequencies? The answer may lie in the fact that those responsible for coding high frequencies are acted upon by all sounds (as shown in Figure 8.7), while those responsible for coding low frequencies respond only to low-frequency sounds.

While Békésy's traveling-wave theory has been well validated, it is not the whole story. There is good evidence that for frequencies below about 4000 Hz (which includes the entire range of human speech), perceived pitch depends not just on which part of the basilar membrane is maximally active, but also on the *timing* of that activity (Pickles, 1988). The action potentials triggered in sets of auditory neurons tend to be locked in phase with sound waves, such that a separate burst of action potentials occurs each time a sound wave peaks; this contributes to the perception of pitch. It is interesting to note, in this regard, that the most sophisticated cochlear implants make use of both place and timing to produce some degree of pitch perception in people with sensorineural deafness (Pickles, 1988; Townshend & others, 1987). These devices break a sound signal into as many as a dozen separate channels based on frequency range, and the electrical output from each channel is carried by a wire to a different part of the basilar membrane. The best pitch perception (still not very good) occurs when the electrical signal sent to a given locus of the membrane is pulsed at a frequency similar to that of the sound wave that would normally peak at that location.

**The role of timing in the coding of frequency, and how the best cochlear implants produce perception of pitch**

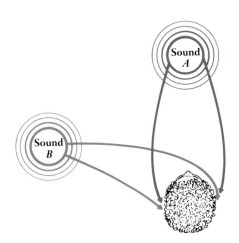

**Figure 8.8  Locating a sound**
*Waves coming from Sound B reach the left ear sooner than the right ear. The converse would be true for sound waves coming from the right. Neurons receiving input from the two ears are sensitive to this difference, providing the code for sound localization. Without moving the head, it is difficult to distinguish a sound directly in front (Sound A) from one directly behind the head, because in both cases the sound waves reach both ears simultaneously.*

**Further Processing by the Brain**    Based on information arriving through the auditory nerves, the experience of sound includes not only loudness and pitch, but also its *location in space* (see Figure 8.8), its *timbre* (the quality, based on the exact form of the sound wave, that distinguishes a natural sound from a pure tone), its time of *onset* and *offset*, and its *inflection* (the rise and fall of the dominant pitch). Most sounds, such as a spoken word, consist of a complex pattern of waves, of many frequencies at once, that changes continuously from the beginning of the sound to the end. All of the information that allows you to distinguish one such sound from another must be extracted by the brain from the pattern of action potentials in the auditory nerves. Studies based on single-cell recordings have shown that many neurons in the auditory cortex are highly specific in the pattern of sound to which they respond. Some respond only to a narrow range of frequencies, others only to certain combinations of frequencies, others only to rising or falling pitch, and still others only to brief clicks or bursts of sound (Pickles, 1988). In the end, activity in some combination of these cells must provide the basis for the auditory experience that occurs when you hear a canary singing or your professor enunciating the sweet word *psychology*.

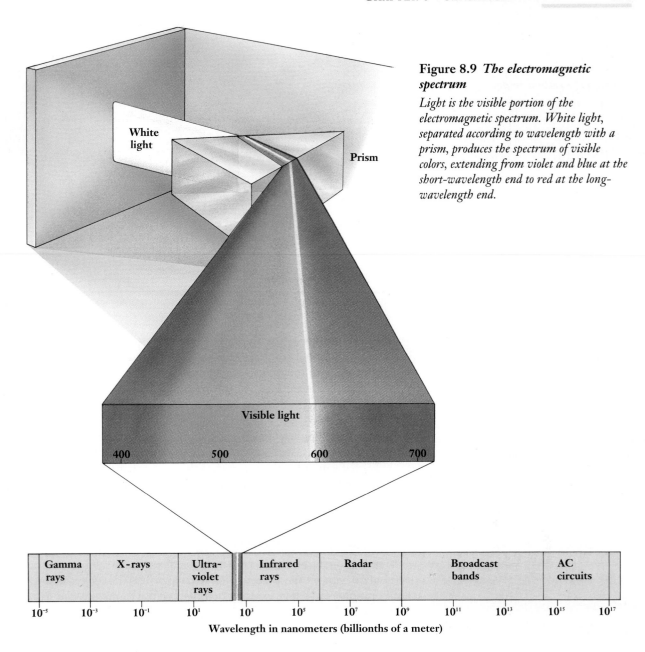

**Figure 8.9** *The electromagnetic spectrum*

*Light is the visible portion of the electromagnetic spectrum. White light, separated according to wavelength with a prism, produces the spectrum of visible colors, extending from violet and blue at the short-wavelength end to red at the long-wavelength end.*

White light

Prism

Visible light

400        500        600        700

| Gamma rays | X-rays | Ultra-violet rays | Infrared rays | Radar | Broadcast bands | AC circuits |

$10^{-5}$   $10^{-3}$   $10^{-1}$   $10^{1}$   $10^{3}$   $10^{5}$   $10^{7}$   $10^{9}$   $10^{11}$   $10^{13}$   $10^{15}$   $10^{17}$

**Wavelength in nanometers (billionths of a meter)**

## Vision

■ *Light as visible electromagnetic energy, and the relationship of wavelength to color*

**Light**   Unlike sound, light can travel through empty space, as it does in going from the sun or stars to the earth. Partly for that reason, scientists assume that it consists of particles, called *photons*. For our purposes, however, it is more useful to emphasize light's wavelike properties. The particles pulse in a wavelike way. Light waves are usually described in terms of their amplitude (or intensity) and their **wavelength** (the physical length of one complete cycle of the wave). The wavelengths of visible light range from about 400 to 700 nm (one nm, or nanometer, is a billionth of a meter). White light, such as that from the sun, consists of all visible wavelengths combined. When the wavelengths in white light are separated (with a prism, for example), the visual effect is an array of colors like that of the rainbow, because different wavelengths are seen as different colors (see Figure 8.9). [The term for the entire spectrum of energy that includes light is *electromagnetic energy.* Shorter waves of electromagnetic energy, below the visible range, include ultraviolet rays, x-rays, and gamma rays; and longer waves, above the visible range, include infrared rays, radar rays, and radio waves.]

**Figure 8.10** *Cross section of the eye, depicting the retinal image*
*The light rays that diverge from any given point on the surface of an object are brought back together (focused) at a distinct point on the retina, to create an image of the object on the retina. This drawing shows light rays diverging and being brought together for just two points on the leaf, but the same process is occurring for light rays coming from every point.*

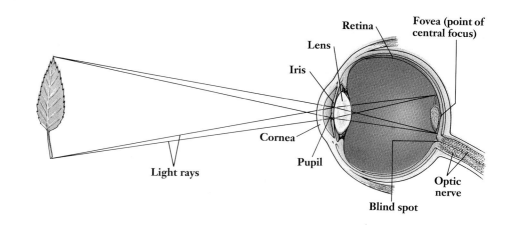

■ *How the cornea, iris, and lens help form images on the retina*

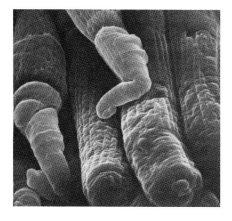

**Rods and cones**
*This electron micrograph shows that the photoreceptors are aptly named. Rods are responsible for vision in dim light, and cones for vision in bright light.*

■ *How cones and rods are distributed in different parts of the retina, and how they perform transduction*

**Basic Workings of the Eye**   The main parts of the eye are shown in Figure 8.10. The receptor cells for vision lie in the *retina*, a thin membrane of cells lining the rear interior of the fluid-filled eyeball. The rest of the eye is a device for focusing the light that is reflected from objects, in such a way as to form an image on the retina. The front of the eyeball is covered by the *cornea*, a transparent tissue that, because of its outward curvature, helps to focus the light that passes through it. Immediately behind the cornea is the pigmented, doughnut-shaped *iris*, which provides the color (usually brown or blue) of the eye. The iris is opaque, so the only light that can enter the interior of the eye is that which passes through the *pupil*. The pupil is not a structure, but only the hole in the center of the iris. The iris is a muscle, containing both circular and radial fibers, whose function is to control the amount of light that can pass through the pupil. When the circular fibers contract, the diameter of the pupil becomes smaller, letting in less light; and when the radial fibers (which are like spokes in a wheel) contract, the diameter becomes larger, letting in more light. Behind the iris is the *lens*, which adds to the focusing process already begun by the cornea. Unlike the cornea, the lens is adjustable—it becomes more spherical when focusing on objects close to the eye and flatter when focusing on those that are farther away. As people get older, the lens commonly loses some of its adjustability, which is the reason for wearing bifocals (glasses that contain two lenses, a lower one for close vision and an upper one for far vision). The focusing properties of the cornea and lens (plus glasses, for those who wear them) are such that light rays that diverge as they move toward the eye from any given point on a visual object are brought back together at a particular point on the retina, thereby forming an image of the object on the retina (see Figure 8.10).

The retina contains, among other things, millions of receptor cells, arranged mosaic-like in a single retinal layer. The receptor cells are of two types, *cones* and *rods*. (See Figure 8.11, which also shows two other layers of retinal cells, whose functions will be described later.) Cones are most concentrated in the *fovea*, which is the pinhead-sized area of the retina that is in the most direct line of sight (look again at Figure 8.10), and which is specialized for high visual *acuity* (the ability to distinguish minute details). The concentration of cones decreases sharply with increasing distance from the fovea. Rods, in contrast, exist everywhere in the retina except the fovea, and they are most concentrated in a ring about 20 degrees away from the fovea (see Figure 8.12). In all, there are about 6 million cones and 120 million rods in each human retina (Carlson, 1986).

The outer segment of the receptor cell, which is rod-shaped in the rod and cone-shaped in the cone (see Figure 8.11), contains a photochemical, which reacts to light. In the rod this photochemical is *rhodopsin*. When hit by light, the

**Figure 8.11 *Diagram of cells in the retina***

*Note that light must pass through the layers of cells (which are reasonably transparent) to reach the sensitive portions of rods and cones at the back of the retina.*

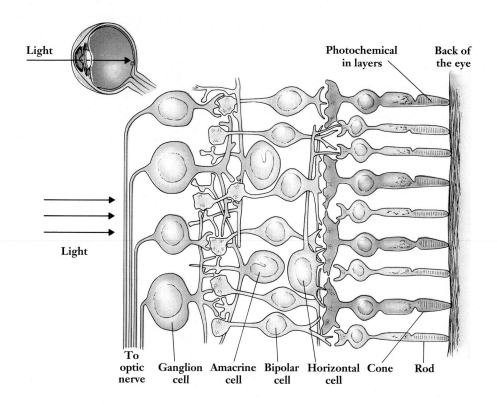

To optic nerve | Ganglion cell | Amacrine cell | Bipolar cell | Horizontal cell | Cone | Rod

rhodopsin molecules undergo a structural change, which triggers a series of chemical reactions in the rod's membrane, which in turn causes an electrical change across the membrane (Nathans, 1987; Schnapf & Baylor, 1987). The transduction process for cones is similar to that for rods, but (as you will see later) there are three different kinds of photochemicals for different cones. The electrical change in rods and cones in turn causes electrical responses in other cells in the retina.

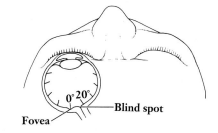

**Figure 8.12 *Distribution of cones and rods in the retina***

*Cones are most concentrated in the fovea, and rods are absent in the fovea and most concentrated in a ring 20 degrees away from it. There are no receptors at all in the blind spot.*

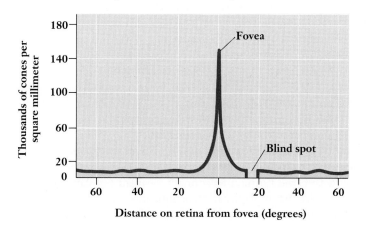

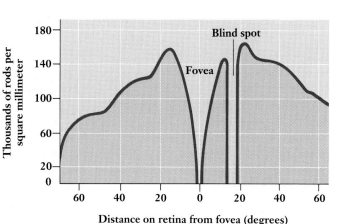

**Figure 8.13** *Demonstration of the blind spot*

*Close your left eye, and focus on the X with your right eye. Start with the pattern a little more than a foot from your eye and move it gradually closer, still focusing on the X. At about 10 inches, the bird will disappear. At that location, the image of the bird falls on the blind spot of the retina, shown in Figure 8.12. Yet you will probably still see the bars of the cage running across the area where the bird was located. They are perceptually filled in by extrapolation from the surrounding area.*

These lead to the production of action potentials in neurons that form the **optic nerve**, which runs to the brain. At the place on the retina where the axons of these neurons come together to form the optic nerve there is a **blind spot**, due to the absence of receptor cells (shown in Figure 8.12). We normally do not notice the blind spot, because our eyes are continuously moving and our perceptual system automatically fills it in, but you can demonstrate its existence by following the instructions in Figure 8.13.

■ *How cone vision and rod vision differ*

**The Duplex Nature of Human Vision**    Cones and rods provide the starting point for what can be thought of as two separate but interacting visual systems within the human eye. **Cone vision** (also called photopic vision or bright-light vision) is specialized for high acuity and for the perception of color. **Rod vision** (also called scotopic vision or dim-light vision) is specialized for sensitivity (the ability to see in very dim light). It lacks acuity (the edges of objects appear fuzzy) and the ability to distinguish colors. Rod vision is so sensitive that, based on calculations from laboratory studies, it should be possible on a clear night to see a single candle flame 30 miles away if no other lights are present (Galanter, 1962).

In very dim light, too dim to activate cones, you see only with rod vision; you can make out the general shapes of objects, but not their details or their colors. In such light you can see dim objects best when not looking directly at them—because, as noted before, there are no rods in the fovea (the direct line of sight). Sometime on a starry but moonless night, when you are out in the country where there are no streetlights, stay in the dark for a good 20 minutes (so that your eyes become fully adapted to the dark), and then find the dimmest star that you can see. The star will disappear when you look directly at it, but appear again when you look just a little bit away. You can see it best when looking 20 degrees away, which allows its light to strike the part of the retina where rods are most concentrated.

Part of the reason for the higher sensitivity of rods than cones lies in rhodopsin's high sensitivity to light, compared with the lower sensitivity of the photochemicals in cones (Schnapf & Baylor, 1987). Another part of the reason—which is also the reason for the reduced acuity of rod vision—lies in a difference between rods and cones in the way that their electrical activity is funneled to neurons in the optic nerve. To understand this difference, we must look at the pattern of neural connections in the retina.

■ *How the greater sensitivity but reduced acuity of rod vision compared with cone vision is promoted by differences in wiring within the retina*

As shown in Figure 8.11, both rods and cones synapse on short neurons called **bipolar cells**, which in turn synapse on larger neurons called **ganglion cells**. The ganglion cells have their cell bodies in the retina, and they have long axons, which leave the eye at the blind spot to form the optic nerve. Other neurons (horizontal cells and amacrine cells) within the retina interconnect adjacent bipolar and ganglion cells, creating a good deal of complexity in the connections within the retina. The net effect of these connections is that each ganglion cell receives input from a set of rods and/or cones, which are located adjacent to one another and define the ***receptive field*** of that cell. The receptive field of a ganglion cell (or of any other neuron in the visual system) is that portion of the retina from which that cell receives neural input. Because of a difference in the way that cones and rods feed into ganglion cells, there is a difference in receptive-field size between ganglion cells that receive input primarily or wholly from cones compared with those that receive input primarily or wholly from rods.

To see this difference and how it bears on acuity and sensitivity, look at Figure 8.14. As shown in the left-hand portion of the figure, each ganglion cell in the fovea receives input from a small number of cones, which means that its receptive field is small. Consequently, two spots of light very close to one another will act on separate ganglion cells, resulting in two distinct messages to the brain—a condition that permits them to be seen as separate spots (high acuity). The right-hand portion of the figure illustrates peripheral portions of the retina, where rods predominate. Here each ganglion cell receives input from a large number of receptor cells (thousands, in some cases), spread out over a relatively large area, which means that its receptive field is large. Two spots of light very close to one another will therefore act on the same ganglion cell, and thus lose their distinctiveness, causing them to blur into one spot in the person's perception (low acuity). For the same reason that acuity is decreased, however, sensitivity is increased. A small amount of electrical activity coming from each receptor cell, when stimulated by dim light, can add up to produce a relatively large amount of electrical activity in the ganglion cell. The funneling of the activity of many receptor cells to fewer sensory neurons is called ***convergence***; in general, in other sensory systems as well as vision, high convergence increases sensitivity at the expense of acuity.

**Figure 8.14** *Relationship of receptive-field size to visual acuity and sensitivity*

*Ganglion cells in the fovea receive input from a smaller number of receptor cells than do ganglion cells in the periphery, and they therefore have smaller receptive fields. This difference accounts for high acuity in the fovea and high sensitivity (but low acuity) in the periphery. Spots A and B of light in diagram (a) will activate two different ganglion cells, and hence maintain their distinctiveness (high acuity). The same two spots in diagram (b) will activate the same ganglion cell and lose their distinctiveness (low acuity), but each spot will add to the total activity of that cell (high sensitivity).*

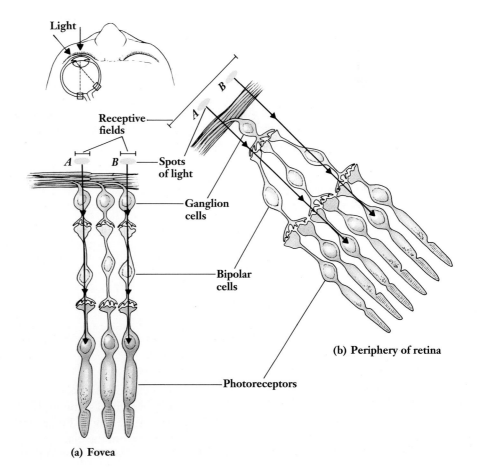

Light

Receptive fields

Spots of light

Ganglion cells

Bipolar cells

Photoreceptors

**(b) Periphery of retina**

**(a) Fovea**

■ *The chemical basis for light and dark adaptation, and why we see mostly with cones in bright light and with rods in dim light*

**Visual Adaptation**    The decreased visual sensitivity that occurs when you have been in bright light for a while is called *light adaptation*, and the increased sensitivity that occurs when you sit in the dark is called *dark adaptation*. These processes are mediated mostly by a change in the photochemicals of cones and rods. If you performed the experiment suggested earlier in this chapter, adapting one eye to the light while covering the other, you should have found an increase in brightness when you changed the cover to the other eye. That is because the cones and rods in the covered eye were still dark adapted. In bright light, the photochemical molecules tend to break down to two inactive substances, and in dim light or darkness they gradually reform. For rhodopsin, the process can be summarized as follows:

$$\text{rhodopsin} \underset{\text{dark}}{\overset{\text{light}}{\rightleftharpoons}} \text{opsin} + \text{retinal}$$

In a similar process, cone photochemicals also break down in the light, but not as completely as rhodopsin. Because the cone photochemicals are less broken down than the rod's rhodopsin, cones are more sensitive than rods in normal to bright light. Cones are also more sensitive than rods when you first go from normal light into a dark room. In addition to enabling you to see a little immediately, they are responsible for the improvement in your vision during the first 5 to 10 minutes—the period during which their chemicals regenerate. Further improvement after that, however, is due to rods, as rhodopsin continues to regenerate for another 15 to 20 minutes after cones have fully adapted. This two-part process of dark adaptation is depicted in Figure 8.15. This curve is typical only of those with normal vision. People who are completely color blind show the rods-only curve because they have no cone photochemicals (Grüsser & Grüsser-Cornehls, 1986), and people who have no rhodopsin (due to a temporary lack of vitamin A) show the cones-only curve (Hecht & Mandelbaum, 1938).

**Figure 8.15** *Dark-adaptation curves*

*The brown curve shows the minimal intensity of a spot of light that a person with normal vision can see after varying amounts of time in the dark. The lower the curve, the greater the sensitivity to light. For the first 8 minutes or so, the cones are more sensitive than the rods, but after that the rods are more sensitive. The two-part nature of the curve can be understood by comparing it to the dark-adaptation curve obtained for a person who has only rods (the green curve) and to that obtained if the light is presented in such a way that it strikes only the fovea, where only cones exist (the red curve). (From Grüsser & Grüsser-Cornehls, 1986.)*

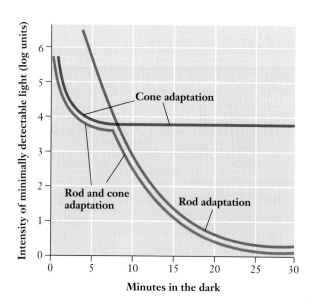

*Local adaptation* of specific portions of the retina occurs if the eyes focus for a period of time on a given stimulus. If you focus on the dot in the center of the pattern in the left-hand disk of Figure 8.16 for half a minute or so, those receptors that receive input from the black part of the pattern (which reflects little light) will become relatively dark adapted (more sensitive to light), and those that receive

**Figure 8.16** *Afterimage due to local adaptation*
*Focus on the white spot in the center of the pattern in the left-hand figure for about 30 seconds. Then shift your focus to the black spot in the right-hand figure. What you see is a negative afterimage, in which what was previously dark is now light, and vice versa.*

 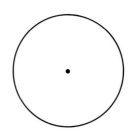

input from the white part of the figure will become relatively light adapted (less sensitive). Then, when you shift your eyes to the dot in the right-hand disk, the dark-adapted receptors will respond more to the solid white background than the light-adapted receptors will, so that what was light becomes dark, and vice versa.

**The Coding of Contrast and Contour**    The main purpose of vision, at least in humans, is not to detect the simple presence or absence of light, but rather to detect and identify objects. Objects are defined principally by their *contours* (their edges or borders). You can identify the pencil on your desk because of the contrast that exists at the contours separating it from the desk. It is not surprising, then, to discover that our visual system is designed to exaggerate contrast. That is, it registers a greater difference in brightness between adjacent visual stimuli than would be registered by a machine faithfully recording the actual physical difference in the light. If you look at a television screen that is turned off it appears a relatively light shade of gray. Yet when it is turned on the same screen can create the impression of black objects, even though no part of the screen can send less light to the eye when the screen is on than when it is off. The same intensity of light that formerly looked gray looks black when surrounded by higher-intensity light. This is an example of heightened contrast. Another example can be seen in Figure 8.17.

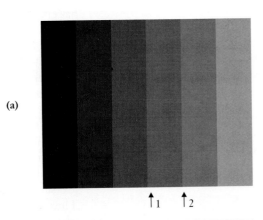

**Figure 8.17** *Enhancement of contrast*

*(a) Each solid gray band appears lighter near its boundary with a darker band, and darker near its boundary with a lighter band. Compare the perceived brightness just above arrow 1 with that just above arrow 2, for example. The graph underneath (b) shows how the perceived brightness changes across the figure, compared with the actual physical intensity of the reflected light. (Adapted from Matlin, 1988.)*

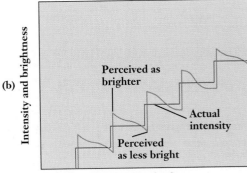

258

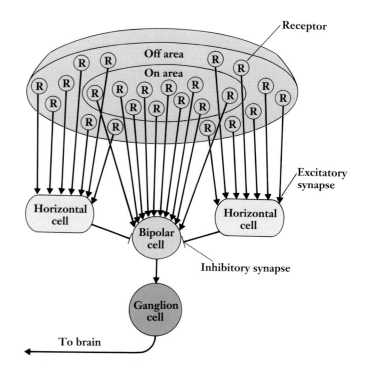

**Figure 8.18** *Neural connections that account for* on *and* off *receptive-field areas for bipolar and ganglion cells*

*Rods and/or cones in the* on *area directly excite a bipolar cell, and those in the* off *area excite horizontal cells, which in turn inhibit the bipolar cell. Activity in the bipolar cell is then transmitted to the ganglion cell. (Adapted from De Valois & De Valois, 1988.)*

**■ How connections from receptor cells to ganglion cells provide a basis for the coding of contrast**

A clue to the mechanism by which the nervous system enhances contrast came from work initiated by Stephen Kuffler (1953), who recorded the activity of individual ganglion cells (the cells whose axons form the optic nerve, as shown in Figure 8.11) in anesthetized cats while stimulating various parts of the retina with small spots of light. He found that any given ganglion cell produces a relatively steady baseline rate of action potentials when not stimulated, and that its activity could be either increased or decreased by stimulation in different parts of the cell's retinal receptive field. That is, he found that the receptive fields for most ganglion cells contain two portions, an *on* portion where light increases activity in the cell, and an *off* portion where light decreases activity. These fields are circular in shape, with the *on* and *off* regions arranged concentrically, such that a given receptive field has either an *on* or *off* center and an opposite surround. Figure 8.18 shows the pattern of connections from receptors to the ganglion cell that could create such receptive fields. An important consequence is that ganglion cells are very sensitive to contrast. An overall change in illumination, affecting *on* and *off* areas equally, has relatively little effect on receptor cells, because the inputs from the two areas tend to cancel each other out. When the edge of the visual stimulus lies within the receptive field, however, there may be differential stimulation of the *on* and *off* areas. Under these conditions of contrast, the cell either increases or decreases its electrical firing relative to its baseline rate.

The axons of ganglion cells form synapses on neurons in the visual portion of the thalamus, which in turn send their axons to the visual area of the cerebral cortex (see Figure 8.19). A few years after Kuffler's pioneering work, David Hubel and Thornton Wiesel (1962, 1979) performed similar studies with cats and monkeys, which led to their winning a Nobel prize in 1981. Rather than record from ganglion cells, they recorded the electrical activity of individual neurons in the visual cortex, while shining visual stimuli onto the animal's retina, to map out the neurons' receptive fields. Of greatest interest, they found that these cells are highly sensitive to contours, responding best not to circular spots of light or dark (as was the case for ganglion cells) but to light or dark bars and edges. They classified these cells as *simple*, *complex*, or *hypercomplex*, based on their different response characteristics.

**■ How the retinal receptive fields of simple cortical cells seem designed to code the slants of bars and edges**

*Simple cells* have retinal receptive fields that are oblong rather than circular, with *on* and *off* areas that run parallel to each other along the length of the oblong. In some simple cells, called *edge detectors*, one whole side of the field is an *on* area and the other side is an *off* area (see Figure 8.20). Edge detectors respond best

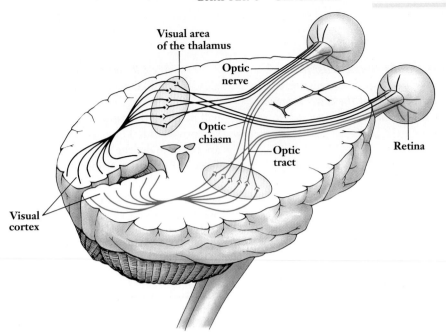

**Figure 8.19 *Pathway from the eyes to the visual cortex***

*Neurons in the optic nerves come together at the optic chiasm at the base of the brain and form the optic tracts, which run to nuclei in the thalamus, where they synapse on neurons that run to the visual cortex.*

when the edge between an area of light and dark is aligned precisely along the line separating the *on* and *off* portions of the receptive field. In other simple cells, called *bar detectors*, either an *on* or *off* area runs lengthwise down the middle of the oblong, with the opposite on either side (see Figure 8.20). Bar detectors respond best to narrow bars of light or dark appropriately placed in the receptive field. As shown in the figure, all simple cells respond best to edges or bars that are at a specific slant. Hubel and Wiesel found that as they went from column to column of simple cells in the visual cortex, a systematic change occurred in the orientation to which the cells were most responsive. For example, in one column all cells might be most responsive to a vertical bar, in the next column they might be most responsive to a bar rotated slightly clockwise, and so on.

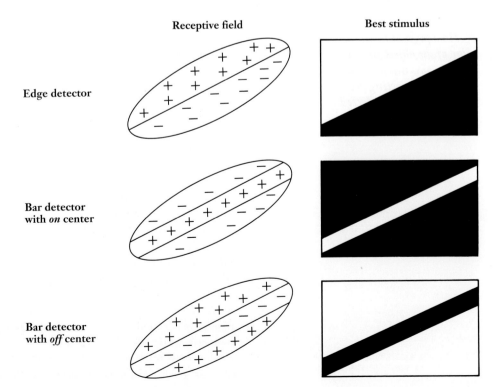

**Figure 8.20 *Retinal receptive fields for three simple cells of the visual cortex***

*In each case, the whole oval represents the area on the retina where a change in lighting can affect the rate of action potentials in the cortical cell. Areas with plus signs (on areas) are places where a spot of light increases activity in the cell, and areas with minus signs (off areas) are places where a spot of light decreases activity in the cell. The best stimulus for eliciting a high rate of response in the cell is shown to the right of each receptive field.*

■ *Beyond the simple cells: feature-detecting neurons whose responses are independent of the exact location of the image on the retina*

*Complex cells* are also most sensitive to edges or bars oriented at particular angles, but unlike simple cells their receptive fields are not divided into discrete *on* and *off* regions. A complex cell that is responsive to an edge at a particular angle will produce the same response to that stimulus no matter where it is placed in the receptive field. Thus, the important feature of complex cells is that their responses are to some degree independent of the exact retinal location of the stimulus. With these cells, unlike simple cells, the position of the stimulus on the retina can vary somewhat without varying the cell's response to the stimulus. It appears that these cells are the first step toward providing a visual perception of contour that is independent of exact retinal position. That is, electrical activity in these cells may underlie your ability to see the edge of an object as the same edge when you have moved your eyes (and hence have changed the location of the image of the edge on your retina) as it was before you moved your eyes.

*Hypercomplex cells*, as their name implies, have even more complex receptive fields than do complex cells. Some respond to edges or bars at a particular orientation placed anywhere in the receptive field, just like complex cells, but in addition are sensitive to the *length* of the edge or bar. Others respond equally to edges or bars at any of several different orientations. Still other cells respond best to specific geometric shapes, such as acute angles, that fall anywhere in their receptive field (which, for these cells, can be quite large).

Since Hubel and Wiesel's initial discovery of these three types of cells, additional research has led to new, more complex ways of categorizing visual cortical cells (De Valois & De Valois, 1988). But for our purposes the main point is that the arrangement of connections among neurons is such that, in progressing to higher stages in the visual processing system, one finds cells that respond to increasingly specific features of the stimulus. That is, their responses are determined less by the exact portion of the retina that is stimulated, and more by specific properties of the stimulus object itself, including not just its contours (as described above), but also its direction and rate of movement, its depth in space, and the wavelength of light that it reflects (perceived as color). All cells that respond to the specific properties of a visual stimulus—including the contour-sensitive cells just described—are called **feature detectors**.

■ *How pigments affect the perceived color of an object in white light, and how the mixing of pigments affects color by subtracting from the wavelengths that are reflected to the eye*

**Color Mixing**   As noted earlier, our experience of color depends on the wavelengths of light that reach our eyes, much as our experience of pitch depends on the frequencies of sound that reach our ears. The shortest visible waves are seen as violet, and as waves become longer the perceived color progresses through shades of blue, blue-green, green, green-yellow, yellow, orange, and red (look back at Figure 8.9). The colors of objects are determined by *pigments*, chemicals on their surface that absorb some wavelengths of light and thereby prevent them from being reflected. Different pigments allow different wavelengths to be reflected. A pigment that absorbs short and medium-length waves, for example, appears red, because only long (red-appearing) waves are reflected. Similarly, a pigment that allows only short waves to be reflected appears violet or blue, and one that allows only medium-length waves to be reflected appears yellow or green. A pigment that allows all wavelengths to be reflected about equally will appear white, gray, or black, depending on whether the relative amount of light reflected is high (white), moderate (gray), or low (black), and also depending on contrast effects (as described earlier).

Because pigments create the perception of color by *subtracting* (absorbing) some of the light waves that would otherwise be reflected to the eye, the mixing of pigments is called **subtractive color mixing**. As illustrated in Figure 8.21, if a blue pigment, which absorbs long waves, is mixed with a yellow pigment, which absorbs short waves, only medium-length waves will be reflected, and the mixture will be seen as green. When you were a child playing with watercolors you probably

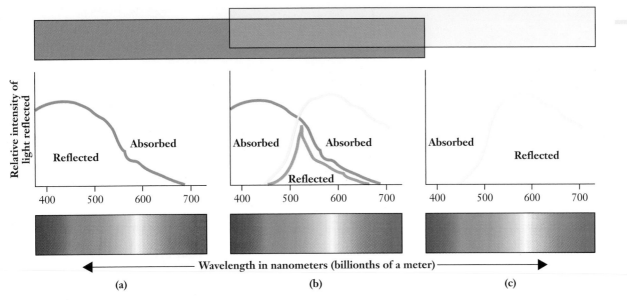

Relative intensity of light reflected

Reflected · Absorbed (a)

Absorbed · Reflected · Absorbed (b)

Absorbed · Reflected (c)

400 500 600 700

◄────── Wavelength in nanometers (billionths of a meter) ──────►

(a)　(b)　(c)

**Figure 8.21 *Subtractive color mixing***

*In this example, the blue pigment (a) absorbs most of the light that has wavelengths above 550 nm, and the yellow pigment (c) absorbs most of the light that has wavelengths below 500 nm. When the two pigments are mixed (b), the only light that is not strongly absorbed is that with wavelengths lying between 500 and 550 nm. This is the light that will be reflected, causing the mixture to appear green.*

 *How mixing lights of different wavelengths affects perceived color, consistent with two laws of additive color mixing*

proved the basic facts of subtractive color mixing many times. You may remember being disappointed when your attempt to produce a brilliant reddish-yellowish-greenish-blue, by mixing all of the paints together, resulted in something pretty close to black. In that experiment you subtracted out all of the wavelengths by mixing all of the pigments together.

The opposite of subtractive color mixing is ***additive color mixing***, which occurs when colored lights rather than pigments are mixed. This can be done by shining two or more beams of light, of different wavelengths, at the same spot on a white screen, which reflects them back together (see Figure 8.22). By the early eighteenth century, experiments had led to two general laws of additive color mixing. According to the ***three-primaries law***, it is possible to select three different wavelengths of light (called *primaries*) and, by mixing them in various proportions, match any color that the eye can see. The primaries can be any three wavelengths as long as one is taken from the long-wave end of the spectrum (red), one from the short-wave end (blue or violet), and one from the middle (green or green-yellow). According to the ***law of complementarity***, it is possible to find wavelengths that, when added together, produce the visual sensation of white. Such a pair are referred to as *complements* of each other.

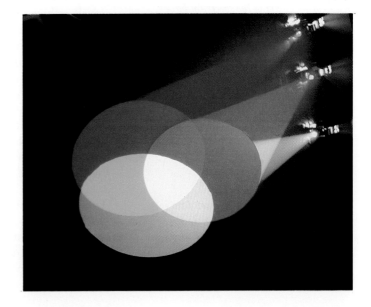

**Figure 8.22 *Additive color mixing***

*Additive color mixing occurs when lights of different wavelengths are mixed by shining them together on a surface that reflects all wavelengths. By varying the intensity of the three lights shown here it would be possible to match all of the colors that the eye can see.*

**Figure 8.23** *The standard chromaticity diagram*

*All of the facts of additive color mixing—related to both the three-primaries law and the law of complementarity—are summarized in this diagram. The three primaries here are lights of 460 nm (blue), 530 nm (green), and 650 nm (red). The proportions of red and green primaries that must be added to the blue primary to match any given color on the diagram are shown, respectively, on the horizontal and vertical axes. The proportion of blue can be calculated by subtracting the other two proportions from 100%. For example, if you wish to match the blue-green produced by a 490 nm light, the figure shows that your mixture must contain about 5% red primary, 30% green primary, and 65% blue primary (100% − 5% − 30% = 65%). As another example, the figure shows that the best white is produced by equal (33.3%) proportions of the three primaries.*

*The chromaticity diagram can also be used to find all possible pairs of complementary colors. Two colors are complementary if their additive mixture produces white. In the diagram, the possible colors produced by mixing any two wavelengths lie along the straight line connecting the points representing the two wavelengths on the diagram. Thus, the two ends of any straight line passing through the geometric center of the diagram (shown as white) represent complementary colors. Two such lines are drawn on the figure for purposes of illustration. Notice that wavelengths in the red to orange part of the spectrum have their complements in the green to blue-green part, and that wavelengths in the yellow part of the spectrum have their complements in the blue part.*

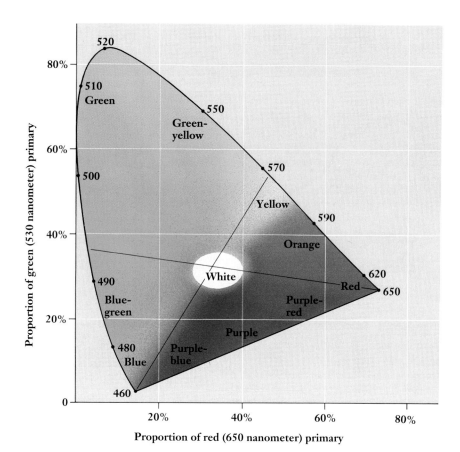

■ *How the three-primaries law is explained by the trichromatic theory, and how the latter is proven correct by the discovery of three cone types*

All of the facts associated with the laws of additive color mixing are taken into account in the *standard chromaticity diagram* (Figure 8.23). The colors in the periphery of the diagram are produced by single wavelengths and are called *saturated* colors. As you move from any point on the periphery toward the white center, the color comes more and more to resemble white; that is, it becomes increasingly *unsaturated* (white is regarded as fully unsaturated). For example, as you go along the line from the 650 nm point on the periphery to the center, you go from red to progressively whiter shades of pink (unsaturated red) to white. The figure's caption describes how the diagram can be used to determine (a) the color that will result from mixing the three standard primaries in any given proportion, and (b) which pairs of wavelengths are complements of each other.

It is important and rather exciting to realize that the facts of color mixing portrayed by the chromaticity diagram are *psychological* facts, not physical facts. The wavelengths of the three primaries do *not* become physically blended into one wavelength when added together to match the color produced by a fourth wavelength. A machine that detects wavelengths would have no difficulty distinguishing, say, a 550 nm light from the mixture of three primaries that would exactly match its greenish-yellow color. Similarly, when two complementary wavelengths are mixed to produce the sensation of white, they do not physically produce white light (which contains all the wavelengths). Such color matches, in which physically distinct stimuli look identical, must occur because of processes in the eye or in the nervous system farther inward. Indeed, the matches just described provided the insight that led, in the nineteenth century, to the development of two physiological theories of color vision—the trichromatic and opponent-process theories.

**The Trichromatic Theory of Color Vision** According to the *trichromatic theory*, color vision is mediated by three different types of receptors, each most sensitive to a different range of wavelengths. This idea was proposed first, in 1802, by Thomas Young, and 50 years later by Hermann Helmholtz, as an attempt to explain the three-primaries law of color vision. Young and Helmholtz reasoned that if every color that we see is the result of a unique proportion, or ratio, of activity among three types of receptors, then it would be possible to match any visible color by varying the relative intensities of three primary lights, each of which acts maximally on a different type of receptor. Young and Helmholtz developed their theory purely from behavioral data, on perceptual effects of color mixing, at a time when nothing was known about receptor cells in the retina. We now know from physiological studies that their theory was correct. There indeed are three types of cones in the human retina, each with a different photochemical that makes it most sensitive to the light within a particular band of wavelengths. In Figure 8.24 you can see an approximation of the actual sensitivity curves for each type of cone. The cones are labeled *blue*, *green*, or *red*, after the color that is experienced when that type of cone is more active than the other types. Notice that any given wavelength of light produces a unique ratio of activity in the three cone types. For example, a 550 nm light, which is seen as greenish-yellow, produces a slightly larger response in red cones than in green cones, and a very low response in blue cones. That same ratio of response in the three cone types could be produced by shining into the eye a mixture of red, green, and blue primaries, with the first two much more intense than the last.

**Figure 8.24** *How the three types of cones respond to different wavelengths of light*

*Any given wavelength produces a unique ratio of activity in the three cone types, and that ratio provides the initial code that permits us to see different wavelengths as different colors. For example, a 550 nm light, which is seen as greenish-yellow, produces a slightly larger response in red cones than in green cones, and a very low response in blue cones. Any combination of lights that would produce that same ratio of responses would be seen as greenish-yellow. (Data from Bowmaker & Dartnall, 1980.)*

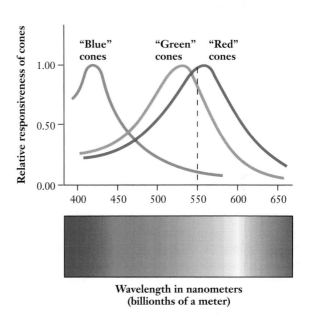

Wavelength in nanometers
(billionths of a meter)

■ *Why some people's vision obeys a two-primaries law rather than the three-primaries law, and why they are not good at picking cherries*

Some people, referred to as *dichromats*, have only two types of cones rather than three. All of the colors that they can see are due to different proportions of activity in their two types of cones, so their visual system obeys a *two-primaries law* of color mixing. That is, with these people it is possible to match any color that they can see by varying the proportion of just two different wavelengths rather than the usual three. The most common forms of dichromia involve the absence of either red or green cones (usually the green) due to a defect in the gene that normally produces the photochemical for that cone type (Nathans & others, 1986). Since the defective gene is recessive, and the genes for both the red and green photochemicals are located on the X chromosome, this trait is sex-linked and shows up much more often in men than in women (see Chapter 3).

People who lack either red or green cones are **red-green color blind**, meaning that they cannot distinguish colors ranging from green through the red end of the spectrum. If you look again at Figure 8.24, you will see why this would be the case.

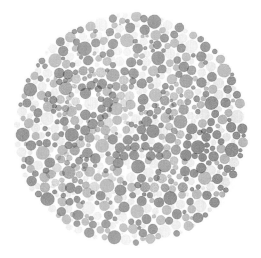

*Test for color blindness*
*In this test people with normal vision will see the number whereas those with red-green color blindness will see no number at all.*

The normal ability to distinguish colors in this range (from about 520 to 700 nm) is mediated almost entirely by differential activity in the red and green cones, because blue cones are almost completely inactive in this range. If either the red or green cones are missing, there will be only one type of cone responding in this range, and hence no physiological basis for distinguishing one wavelength from another. Many people with red-green color blindness don't know that they have this trait and may be puzzled by the fact that certain perceptual tasks that are very hard for them are easy for others. One man's red-green color blindness was first discovered when he proclaimed to his family how much he admired the perceptual skill of cherry pickers: "After all," he said, "the only thing that tells 'em it's a cherry is the fact that it's round and the leaves aren't. I just don't see how they find 'em in those trees!" (Coren & Ward, 1989).

**The Opponent-Process Theory of Color Vision**   While the trichromatic theory accounts nicely for the three-primaries law, and for certain types of color blindness, it does not explain the facts concerning complementary colors. To explain complementarity, Ewald Hering, another nineteenth-century scientist, developed the *opponent-process theory*. Hering was most impressed by the observation that complementary colors (blue and yellow, or green and red) seem to swallow each other up, erasing each other's color, when added together. For example, if you begin with blue light and gradually add more of its complement (yellow), the result is not "bluish-yellow," but an ever paler (more unsaturated) blue, which finally becomes white. (Look at the line from 460 to 570 nm in the chromaticity diagram, Figure 8.23. Note, too, how mixing complementary red and green lights similarly results in white.) To explain such facts, Hering proposed that color perception is mediated by physiological elements (which we now call cells) that can be either excited or inhibited depending on the wavelength of light, and that wavelengths that are complementary to each other have opposite effects on these mediators.

■ *How the law of complementarity is explained by the opponent-process theory, and how the latter is proven correct through recording the electrical activity of neurons that receive input from cones*

More specifically, Hering proposed that the ability to see blues and yellows is mediated by blue-yellow opponent cells, which are excited by wavelengths in the blue part of the spectrum and inhibited by those in the yellow part, or vice versa. In the same way, the ability to see greens and reds is mediated by green-red opponent cells, which are excited by wavelengths in the green part of the spectrum and inhibited by those in the red part, or vice versa. In addition, he proposed that the ability to distinguish bright from dim light, independent of wavelength, is mediated by a third set of cells (brightness detectors), which are excited by lights of any wavelength. This theory nicely accounts for the facts of complementary colors. A mixture of wavelengths from the blue and yellow parts of the spectrum, or from the green and red parts, would appear white (colorless but bright) because the two sets of wavelengths would have opposite effects on the opponent cells that promote color detection. Thus, they would cancel each other out, while at the same time acting in concert to excite the brightness detectors.

At one time the trichromatic and opponent-process theories were thought to be contradictory, but we now know that both are fundamentally correct. The retina contains three types of cones, and these code wavelength in accordance with Young and Helmholtz's trichromatic theory. But the cones feed into neurons farther inward through a pattern of connections that translates the trichromatic code into an opponent-process code, conforming to Hering's theory. By recording the activity in individual neurons while stimulating the eye with different wavelengths, scientists have found ganglion cells, and cells in the thalamus and the visual cortex, that behave in the manner predicted by Hering (De Valois & others, 1966; Jameson & Hurvich, 1989).

As you think back about the history of research and theories on color vision just presented, you will perhaps agree with me that it is a lovely illustration of the interplay of behavioral and physiological studies. The trichromatic and opponent-process theories were developed, in the nineteenth century, from behavioral evidence having to do with the perceptual effects of additive color mixing, before anything was known about the physiology of receptors and neurons. Later, both theories were confirmed physiologically, and today physiologists and psychologists are continuing to work out the finer details of the neural mechanisms through which they operate.

**A Final Comment on Feature Detection and Its Relationship to Perception**    In the preceding discussion you saw examples of research on the coding of contour and color in vision. Other research has centered on the coding of other properties of visual stimuli, such as their position in three-dimensional space and their movement. Feature detectors (neurons that respond uniquely to a specific characteristic of a visual stimulus) are spatially organized in the brain according to their function (Livingston & Hubel, 1988). Thus, different, localized sets of neurons in the visual cortex are specialized to carry the codes for contour, color, spatial position, movement, and so on. This segregation of functions explains why people who have had a stroke, damaging part of the cortex, sometimes lose the ability to see colors without losing the ability to see contours and movements, or lose the ability to see movements without losing the ability to see colors and contours (Kolb & Whishaw, 1985; Livingston & Hubel, 1988). Other neurons, which receive input from feature detectors, are involved in integrating individual features so that meaningful, unified objects and scenes can be perceived.

■ *Integrating features to see whole objects*

In a fascinating essay entitled "The Man Who Mistook His Wife for a Hat," Oliver Sacks (1970), a neurologist, described the plight of a brain-damaged patient who could see all of the elementary features of objects (their colors, contours, movements, and so on) and could recognize abstract geometric shapes (such as cubes and spheres), but who could not recognize the more complex objects that make up the everyday visual world. When Sacks showed the man a rose and asked him to identify it, his response was, "About six inches in length. A convoluted red form with a linear green attachment. It lacks the simple symmetry of the Platonic solids, although it may have a higher symmetry of its own. . . ." After a period of such reasoning about its parts, he finally guessed, uncertainly, that it might be some kind of flower. Then Sacks asked him to smell it. "Beautiful!" he exclaimed. "An early rose. What a heavenly smell!" He could tell a rose by smell but not by sight, even though he could see every one of its features and could put some of them together, such as the greenness and the longness of the stem. How is it that in those of us with normal vision all of the features of a rose come effortlessly together, so that we see immediately that it is a rose, without consciously noticing the more abstract elements of which it is composed? That is the kind of question to which we do not yet know the answer physiologically. It will be addressed in a nonphysiological fashion in the next chapter.

# Pain

From the beauty of a rose we move to the sensation you might get from its thorns. Pain is a body sense. When you hear, see, or touch something, you experience the sensation as coming from the external world; but when you feel pain, you experience it as coming from your own body. If you cut yourself with a knife, your feeling of pain is a sense not of the knife (that comes from your vision and touch), but of your own bodily state. Pain, somewhat akin to hunger and thirst, is not only a sense but a drive. A person in pain is motivated both to reduce the pain and to avoid future behaviors like the one that produced it (such as careless handling of knives and rose bushes).

The value of pain—the reason, presumably, that it was selected for in evolution—is dramatically illustrated by those rare, unlucky people who are born with a genetic disorder that makes them insensitive to pain (Melzack & Wall, 1982). They can experience all of the other sensations, including touch and temperature, and they can even report increasing intensities of these feelings; but pain itself, with its motivating qualities, is missing. Children with this disorder are not motivated to remove their hand from a hot stove, or to refrain from chewing on their tongue as they eat, or to change their body position (as most of us do from minute to minute) to relieve the strain on muscles and joints. Even if they are constantly watched throughout their childhood, and even if they learn intellectually to avoid certain activities, people with this disorder usually die young from the tissue deterioration or infections that result from their wounds.

**Transduction and Input to the Central Nervous System**    Anatomically, pain is closely related to the other cutaneous (skin) senses, touch and temperature. For all of these senses, the receptors are the sensory neurons themselves, which have receptive endings in the skin and long axons that enter the central nervous system by way of a spinal nerve or (in the case of neurons coming from the head) a cranial nerve. Pain neurons are thinner than other neurons from the skin, and their sensitive terminals, referred to as *free nerve endings*, are not surrounded by special capsules, or end organs, as are the endings of touch and temperature receptors (see Figure 8.25). Free nerve endings can be found in all body tissues from which pain is sensed, not just the skin but also the pulp of the teeth (from which comes the dreaded toothache), muscles (giving us the pain of cramps and muscle aches), membranes around bones and joints (from which we experience arthritis), and various visceral organs (giving us stomachaches and other inner pains).

Two different types of peripheral neurons are involved in pain. One type are very thin, unmyelinated, slow-conducting neurons called *C fibers*, and the other are

**Figure 8.25  *Pain receptors in the skin***

*The pain receptors are the sensitive endings of sensory neurons, called* free nerve endings, *because unlike touch receptors they are not enclosed in an end organ. Slow pain is carried by the very thin C fibers, fast pain by the thicker A-delta fibers, and the sense of touch by still thicker (and faster) A fibers.*

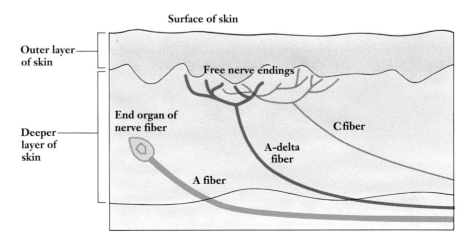

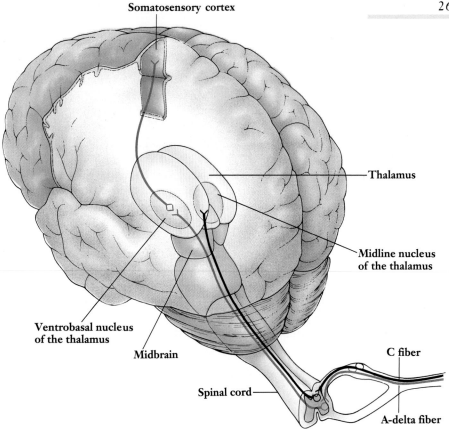

**Figure 8.26** *Pain pathways*
*The red line shows input from an A-delta fiber to a nucleus in the ventrobasal complex of the thalamus, and from there to the somatosensory cortex. The black line shows input from a C fiber to a midline nucleus in the thalamus, which sends projections (not shown) to various areas of the cerebral cortex and limbic system.*

Labels: Somatosensory cortex; Thalamus; Midline nucleus of the thalamus; Ventrobasal nucleus of the thalamus; Midbrain; Spinal cord; C fiber; A-delta fiber

■ *How two different sets of peripheral neurons respond differently to pain-inducing stimuli*

■ *How the two different sets of peripheral neurons feed into different tracts in the brain and mediate different aspects of the pain experience*

thicker, myelinated, faster-conducting neurons called *A-delta fibers* (again see Figure 8.25). When your skin is bruised or burned you feel two different waves of pain—an initial *fast*, sharp, highly localized pain followed by a *slow*, dull, more diffuse, often burning pain. The fast pain is believed to be mediated by A-delta fibers, and the slow by C fibers (Martin, 1985). The terminals of A-delta fibers are activated by strong physical pressure or temperature extremes, and those of C fibers are believed to be activated by the chemical changes that occur in the tissue surrounding them when the tissue is physically damaged (Kelly, 1985). Which chemical changes cause C fibers to become active is unknown, but one likely candidate is the increase in potassium ions. Potassium is normally highly concentrated inside cells, and when cells are damaged it leaks out into the extracellular fluid. The injection of potassium into a localized area of the skin produces pain in that area, and it also increases the rate of action potentials in C fibers (Kelly, 1985).

Another, longer-lasting effect of a skin wound or burn is that the area around the damaged tissue may become highly sensitive for a period of hours or days after the injury. A slight touch to the damaged area, which previously would have been barely felt, may now be extremely painful. This change is believed to be caused at least partly by the increased sensitivity of A-delta fibers when they are damaged (Melzack & Wall, 1982). These neurons, which normally can be activated only by very strong stimuli, can apparently be activated by weak stimuli when damaged.

**Central Pain Pathways** The two systems of pain—fast and slow—maintain their distinctiveness in the central nervous system as well as peripherally, sending their input to different parts of the thalamus (see Figure 8.26). The A-delta fibers synapse on cells in the spinal cord that lead to an area of the thalamus called the *ventrobasal complex*. This area also receives neurons that mediate the sense of touch, and it sends its output to the somatosensory area of the cerebral cortex—the same area that receives input from all of the skin and muscle senses. The somatosensory cortex has localized areas that receive touch and pain input from specific portions of the body (as was shown in Figure 6.16). This point-to-point organization provides a basis for our ability to localize the place on the skin from which either touch or pain originates.

The C fibers, in contrast, synapse on neurons in the spinal cord that lead to a set of *midline nuclei* in the thalamus, which in turn send their output to many higher brain areas, including the frontal lobe of the cerebral cortex. Surgical studies aimed at relieving pain in late-stage cancer patients have shown that lesions placed in the midline nuclei successfully relieve (at least for a period of time) deep, chronic pain without abolishing the patient's sense of touch or the fast, acute pain that is mediated by A-delta fibers (Mark & others, 1963). The connections from the midline nuclei to the frontal lobe of the cortex are especially important for the motivating aspects of pain. Patients who have had the front portion of the frontal lobe severed from the rest of the brain (an operation called a prefrontal lobotomy, which was once used as treatment for certain mental disorders and occasionally for severe chronic pain) report that they still "feel pain," and can even estimate its magnitude, but state that it no longer bothers them.

**Neural and Chemical Mechanisms for Inhibiting Pain**    In 1965, Ronald Melzack and Patrick Wall (1965, 1982) proposed a theory about pain and its inhibition called the **gate-control theory**. In essence, the theory holds that pain will be experienced only if the input from peripheral pain neurons passes through a "gate" located at the point that the pain-carrying neurons enter the spinal cord and lower brainstem. Research has since proven the theory to be correct and identified an important neural pathway involved in control of the gate. Neurons whose cell bodies are in a portion of the midbrain called the *periaqueductal gray* (abbreviated *PAG*) have axons that descend to terminate on inhibitory neurons in the lower brainstem and spinal cord. When the PAG neurons are active they excite the inhibitory neurons, which in turn inhibit transmission from the peripheral neurons to neurons that would normally carry pain messages to the thalamus and cortex (see Figure 8.27).

Electrical stimulation of the PAG has a powerful analgesic (pain-reducing) effect—so powerful, in fact, that abdominal surgery can be performed without drugs in animals that are receiving such stimulation (Reynolds, 1969). Electrical stimulation of this area has also been shown to reduce or abolish pain in people who suffer from pain that cannot be relieved by other means (Hosobuchi & others, 1979). Several lines of evidence show that these effects occur by way of the axons that run down from the PAG into the lower brainstem and spinal cord, shown in Figure 8.27 (Liebeskind & Paul, 1977). The PAG is also believed to be the main site at which opiate drugs (derivatives of opium), such as *morphine*, have their pain-relieving effects. Morphine easily passes into the brain and is taken up at special binding sites on neurons in various parts of the brain, including the PAG. Research with animals has shown that morphine increases neural activity in the PAG, and that even a tiny amount of the drug, too little to have an effect if injected elsewhere, relieves pain if injected directly into the PAG (Basbaum & Fields, 1984).

Of course, the PAG and its pain-inhibiting system did not evolve to respond specifically to morphine or other substances foreign to the body. Its basic function is to mediate the body's *own* capacity to reduce pain. We now know that certain chemicals produced within the body act like morphine to relieve pain. These chemicals are collectively called **endorphins**, a term that is short for *endogenous morphine-like substances* (*endogenous* means created within the body). Some endorphins are produced in the brain or spinal cord and serve as neurotransmitters. Others are secreted from the pituitary and adrenal glands, as hormones, into the blood, and have a variety of effects both peripherally and in the central nervous system (Henry, 1986). Endorphins are believed to inhibit pain by acting both in the PAG and at the point that pain-carrying neurons enter the spinal cord and lower brainstem (again see Figure 8.27).

■ *How activity in neurons coming from a specific part of the midbrain closes a gate to pain, and how morphine and endorphins inhibit pain*

**Figure 8.27  *Pain-inhibiting system***
*As illustrated here, activity in the midbrain's PAG blocks pain input by direct, inhibitory action on the connections from C fibers to pain neurons in the spinal cord and lower brainstem.*

**Natural Sources of Pain Reduction: Stress, Belief, and the Role of Endorphins**
During his search for the source of the Nile, the famous explorer David Livingston was attacked by a lion. He survived the incident and later wrote that although the lion shook him "as a terrier does a rat" and crushed his shoulder, he had felt "no sense of pain nor feeling of terror, though quite conscious of all that was happening" (Livingston, 1857). Other people have had similar experiences. For example, soldiers severely wounded in battle often do not notice their wounds until the battle is over. We are apparently endowed with a mechanism that prevents us from feeling pain at times when, for survival purposes, it is best to ignore our wounds. An animal or person faced with a predator or similar threat cannot afford to nurse a wound or favor it by limping; all resources must be used to fight or flee. There is now good evidence that *stress-induced analgesia*, as this phenomenon is called, occurs in response to many forms of stressful stimulation and is at least partly dependent on endorphins. Endorphins are secreted along with various other hormones by the pituitary and adrenal glands as part of the body's general response to stressful events (Terman & others, 1984).

*Evidence that stress-induced and placebo-induced analgesia are at least partly mediated by endorphins*

In one study of stress-induced analgesia, rats that were subjected to a series of electric shocks to their feet (the source of stress) became relatively insensitive to pain for several minutes afterward, as indicated by their lack of response to normally painful heat that was applied to their tails (Lewis & others, 1980). Rats that had been treated with a drug that blocks the action of endorphins, or with one that blocks its stress-induced release, did not show this stress-induced analgesia, indicating that the effect must have been mediated by endorphins. In similar experiments, the mere presence of a cat produced analgesia in rats (Lester & Fanselow, 1985), and the presence of a dominant mouse, that had previously defeated the test mouse in a fight, produced analgesia in mice (Miczek & others, 1986). In both of these cases the analgesic effect was shown to depend on endorphins.

In humans, dramatic reduction in pain can also, at times, be produced by the power of *belief* or faith. Some religious groups engage in practices that most of us would regard as torture, yet the participants appear to feel no pain. One group in India, for example, practices a hook-hanging ritual. A man who has been chosen to represent the power of the gods is secured to a rope by two steel hooks that pierce the skin and muscles on his back. He hangs from this rope, swinging back and forth, while he blesses the children and the crops of the village. He is honored to have been chosen, and apparently feels little or no pain (Melzack & Wall, 1982). A less dramatic example in our culture, where faith is more often placed in science and medicine, is the *placebo effect* on pain. In many cases a pill or injection that contains no active substance (the placebo) can reduce pain in a person who believes that the drug is a painkiller.

*The power of faith*
*Ancient sand paintings and ancient belief systems can help people deal with modern-day stressors. Joint problems are a frequent response to stress, and Native American healers have had tremendous success in relieving such pain.*

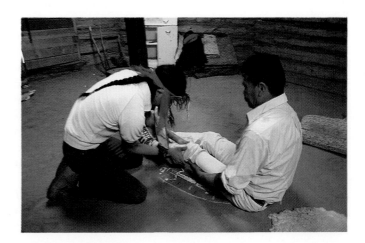

The placebo effect is at least partly mediated by endorphins. In one experiment, people who had undergone a tooth extraction reported less pain if given a placebo than if not, and this difference was abolished in subjects who were treated with a drug that inhibits the action of endorphins (Levine & others, 1979). Other experiments have shown that various cognitive techniques for relieving pain, such as meditating on the idea that the pain is disconnected from the rest of the body, also work at least partly through endorphins (Bandura & others, 1987). Might the man hanging from a hook in India also be secreting high endorphins? There is still much to be learned about the brain's ability to control pain, but the discovery of the endorphin system has provided a tremendous boost to that endeavor.

## Psychophysics

As pointed out early in this chapter, psychophysics is the study of the relationship between the physical characteristics of a stimulus and the sensory experience that it produces. The sensory experience is typically assessed by asking subjects to make some judgment about the stimulus, such as saying whether it is present or absent, or whether it is the same as or different from another stimulus. A number of experiments already alluded to in this chapter were psychophysical, including the experiments on color mixing that led to the three-primaries law and the law of complementarity. Lights were shown in varying combinations, and people were asked to judge whether their color looked the same as or different from that of other lights.

This section describes psychophysical studies of (a) the detection of weak stimuli, (b) the detection of small differences in intensity between different stimuli, and (c) the relationship between the physical intensity of a stimulus and the intensity of the sensory experience it produces. As you will see (with b and c), psychophysics is more mathematical than are most other areas of psychology. That is one of the reasons why some psychologists find it exciting. Psychophysics is just the right cup of tea for those psychologists who like a degree of precision in their science, are drawn by the elegance of mathematics, and are fascinated by the idea that certain psychological phenomena can be described meaningfully with algebraic equations.

**The Absolute Threshold, and Why It Is Not Absolute**  How sensitive are our senses? What is the faintest sound that we can hear or the faintest light that we can see? Psychophysicists refer to the faintest detectable stimulus, of any given type, as the *absolute threshold* for that type of stimulus. The absolute threshold within any sensory system—let's take hearing as our example—depends on a number of variables. It depends on who is tested (some people have more sensitive hearing than others), the precise kind of stimulus used as the signal (we are more sensitive to sounds at some frequencies than at others), the precise conditions in which the test is conducted (such as the amount of background noise), and the exact way in which the threshold is defined (for example, it might be defined as the weakest stimulus permitting 50 percent correct detection, or the weakest stimulus permitting 75 percent correct detection).

You can see the influence of two of these variables by looking at Figure 8.28, which shows an *audiogram* for a typical 60-year-old and a typical 20-year-old. An audiogram is a graph depicting a person's absolute thresholds for hearing tones of various frequencies. Notice that the 60-year-old has a higher absolute threshold than the 20-year-old at every frequency. That is, the tone must be more intense to be heard by the older person. The figure also shows how the absolute threshold varies with frequency. Both individuals are most sensitive (have the lowest thresholds) to tones in the range of 1000 to 3000 Hz. As the frequency becomes lower or higher than this, sensitivity decreases (the absolute threshold increases).

**Yuck! too sour**

*The sharp taste of a lemon may seem inordinately sour to a very young child and wonderfully refreshing to an adult. And because of a decline in taste-bud responsiveness, the acid flavor may be only a faint memory by old age.*

■ **Some variables that influence the absolute threshold**

**Figure 8.28** *Audiogram for a typical 60-year-old and a typical 20-year-old*

*The audiogram is a curve depicting the minimal intensity that the person can hear (the absolute threshold) for each tone frequency. Notice that the younger person has a lower threshold than the older person for each frequency, especially for high frequencies. For example, the graph shows that for a 5000-Hz tone the 60-year-old's absolute threshold is about 30 dB and the 20-year-old's is about 10 dB. Notice also that both have a lower threshold in the range of 1000 to 3000 Hz than at other frequencies.*

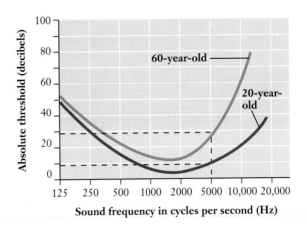

To determine a person's absolute threshold for a particular kind of stimulus (such as a 5000-Hz tone), a psychophysicist presents the stimulus many times, at various low intensities, each time asking the person if he or she detects it. The procedure sometimes also includes control trials in which the stimulus is not presented. When the stimulus is near the threshold level, it is sometimes detected and sometimes not, and sometimes the person believes the stimulus is present when it really isn't. Presumably, various random events—including outside sources of noise and occurrences within the person's nervous system—may either mask the signal or mimic it. Thus, the absolute threshold is not truly "absolute," but rather is arrived at arbitrarily by statistical averaging. For a given study, it may be defined as that intensity of the stimulus that is detected on some specified percentage of the trials in which it is present (see Figure 8.29).

**Figure 8.29** *The absolute threshold is statistically derived*

*If a stimulus—say, a 5000-Hz tone—is presented many times at each of several weak intensities, the proportion of times that the person correctly detects it increases as the intensity increases. Arbitrarily, the intensity at which correct detection occurs in 50 percent of the trials —in this case, 10 dB—is taken as the absolute threshold. (Data are hypothetical.)*

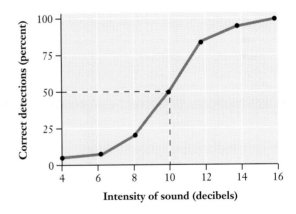

■ *How the measure of absolute threshold is affected by a liberal or conservative response bias, and how the bias can be assessed by a signal-detection experiment*

**Signal Detection as a Decision-Making Task**   A problem arising from the arbitrary nature of absolute thresholds is that reported stimulus detection depends not just on sensory ability, but also on *response bias*, the tendency to favor a particular response when uncertain about whether the stimulus is present or not. Some subjects might adopt a conservative response bias, saying yes only when certain that it is present; others might adopt a liberal response bias, saying yes when uncertain. Subjects who expect the stimulus to be present on most or all of the trials are more inclined to say yes on a given trial than those who expect that it will rarely be present. Also, those who are strongly motivated to detect the stimulus, even at the cost of sometimes saying that it is present when it isn't, will say yes more often than those who are less concerned about detecting it and more concerned about falsely saying that it is present.

Differences in subjective expectation and motivation take on great significance in signal-detection tasks in real-life settings. Consider, for example, a radiologist scanning x-ray images for faint signs of cancer. The likelihood of putting a particular set of x-rays in the possible-cancer pile versus the clean-bill-of-health pile may depend on (a) the radiologist's prior beliefs about the likelihood that the patient would have cancer, and (b) the balance between the radiologist's motivation, on the one hand, to detect cancer whenever it is present, and, on the other hand, to avoid unduly frightening or inconveniencing patients when it is not present. Some radiologists are more liberal in their willingness to say "cancer may be present here," and others are more conservative.

To compare people's actual sensory ability, psychophysicists have developed ways to specify the degree to which a person responds according to a liberal or conservative bias and to correct for that bias. To do this, they include trials in which the stimulus is not present as well as trials in which it is, and separate the subject's responses into four categories: (1) *hits* (the stimulus is present and the subject reports sensing it); (2) *misses* (the stimulus is present and the subject reports not sensing it); (3) *false alarms* (the stimulus is absent and the subject reports sensing it); and (4) *correct rejections* (the stimulus is absent and the subject reports not sensing it). A liberal bias would increase the number of hits and false alarms and decrease the number of misses and correct rejections; and a conservative bias would have the opposite effect (see Figure 8.30). By comparing the proportion of hits to false alarms, psychophysicists can derive a measure of sensitivity that is independent of response bias, called $d'$ (*d prime*) (Green, 1964). The greater the ratio of hits to false alarms, the greater is the person's sensitivity to the stimulus. In real-life signal-detection tasks—such as radiologists looking at x-ray images, or airport guards scanning luggage with metal detectors—the hit and false-alarm rate, and hence the person's response bias and actual sensitivity to the signal, can be determined by periodic testing with planted stimuli, some of which are known to contain the signal and some of which are known not to contain it.

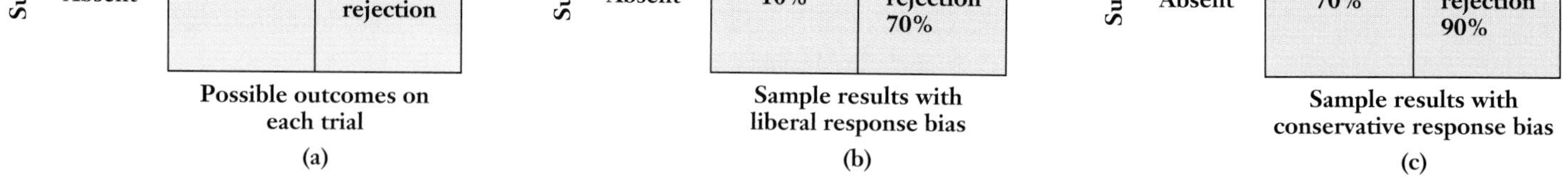

**Figure 8.30** *Signal-detection outcomes*
*Part (a) shows the definition of hits, misses, false alarms, and correct rejections. Parts (b) and (c) show hypothetical results for a person adopting a liberal or conservative response bias, with a signal near the absolute threshold. Notice that the liberal bias increases hits but also increases false alarms.*

The Difference Threshold and Weber's Law    Whereas the absolute threshold is the minimal intensity of a stimulus that a person can detect, the ***difference threshold*** is the minimal difference that must exist between two stimuli for the person to detect them as different. To determine a difference threshold for sound intensity, a person would be presented with a standard tone, always of the same intensity, and a comparison tone that is sometimes the same intensity as the standard tone and sometimes a different intensity, and asked to report whether it is the same or different. Like the absolute threshold, the difference threshold is a statistical concept. It is commonly defined as the amount of difference between the standard and comparison stimuli required for correct detection of the difference in 50 percent of the trials (though in some situations, where guessing would produce 50 percent correct detection, 75 percent is used as the criterion). Another name for the difference threshold is the *just-noticeable difference*, abbreviated *jnd*.

The first scientist to study jnd's systematically was Ernst Weber, a German physiologist of the early nineteenth century. The question that interested Weber was this: What is the relationship between the jnd and the intensity (or magnitude) of the standard stimulus? That is, if the standard stimulus is increased in intensity, what happens to the jnd? Does it stay the same, or does it change in some systematic way? In one series of experiments he applied this question to people's ability to judge differences between weights. In each trial he asked the subjects to pick up each of two weights (the standard weight and a comparison weight), one at a time, and judge which was heavier. Weber found that the jnd varied in direct proportion to the weight of the standard. Specifically, he found that for any standard weight that he used (within a certain range), the jnd was approximately 1/30 of the standard weight (Gescheider, 1976). Thus, a typical subject could just barely discriminate between a 15-gram and 15.5-gram weight, or between a 90-gram and 93-gram weight. In the first case the jnd was 0.5 gram, and in the second it was 3 grams, but in both cases it was 1/30 of the standard weight. In other experiments, Weber studied people's ability to discriminate between the lengths of two lines, one presented after the other, and again he found a constant proportionality between the standard stimulus and the difference threshold. For this task, however, the constant fraction was 1/100 rather than 1/30. Thus, a typical subject could just barely discriminate between a 100- and a 101-millimeter line, or between a 1000- and a 1010-millimeter line.

Based on these and similar experiments, Weber formulated a general law, now called *Weber's law*, stating that *the jnd for stimulus magnitude is a constant proportion of the magnitude of the standard stimulus.* The law can be formulated as

$$jnd = kM$$

in which $M$ is the intensity or magnitude of the stimulus used as the standard and $k$ is a proportionality constant referred to as the *Weber fraction*, which is different for different sensory tasks (1/30 for weight judgment and 1/100 for length judgment in the examples above). Since Weber's time, psychophysical experiments have confirmed Weber's law for many different types of stimuli. The law holds rather well over a reasonably wide portion of the possible range of intensities or magnitudes for most types of stimuli, but breaks down at the very low (near the absolute threshold) and high ends of the range.

**Relating Sensory Magnitude to Physical Magnitude: Psychophysical Scaling**
When a physical stimulus increases, our sensory experience of it also increases. When a sound becomes more intense, we hear it as louder; when a light becomes more intense, we see it as brighter; and so on. Is it possible to specify mathematically the relationship between the magnitude of a stimulus and the magnitude of the sensory experience produced by it? Gustav Fechner, another nineteenth-century German, used a purely theoretical approach to answering that question, based on Weber's law. The jnd is measured in physical units (such as grams, or sound-pressure units), yet it reflects a sensory phenomenon, the just-noticeable difference between two sensations. Fechner reasoned that the jnd could serve as a

■ *How Weber derived a law from data on just-noticeable differences (jnd's), and how the law can be used to predict jnd's*

■ *How Fechner arrived at a law relating sensory magnitude to the logarithm of stimulus magnitude, based upon Weber's law*

unit for relating physical and sensory magnitudes. His important assumption was that every jnd along a sensory dimension is equivalent to every other jnd along that dimension in the amount it adds to the sensory magnitude, and that jnd's can be added together. In other words, he assumed that a sound that is 100 jnd's above threshold would sound twice as loud as one that is 50 jnd's above threshold, or one-tenth as loud as one that is 1000 jnd's above threshold.

While assuming that jnd's are subjectively equal, Fechner knew from Weber's work that they are not physically equal. As you just saw, the jnd is directly proportional to the magnitude of the original stimulus. Thus, Fechner assumed that the amount of physical change needed to create a constant sensory change is directly proportional to the magnitude of the stimulus, and he showed mathematically that this can be expressed as a logarithmic relationship. From this, Fechner derived a general law, now called **Fechner's law**, stating that *the magnitude of the sensory experience of a stimulus is directly proportional to the logarithm of the physical magnitude of the stimulus.* As a formula, this could be written as

$$S = c \log M$$

where $S$ is the magnitude of the sensory experience, $c$ is a proportionality constant, and $M$ is the magnitude of the physical stimulus. An important feature of a logarithmic transformation is that it shrinks high numbers more than it does low numbers. Thus, Fechner's law accounts for the fact that, at the high end of a stimulus-magnitude scale, large changes are needed to produce as much effect on the sensation as is achieved by much smaller changes at the low end of the scale. For example, turning on one more light bulb adds a lot to the sensed brightness of a room in which only one bulb was on before, but it adds little if ten were on before. (Perhaps you are wondering just how Fechner could show, mathematically, that the assumption of constant proportionality, derived from Weber's law, implies a logarithmic relationship. If so, you can find the answer in the Statistical Appendix at the back of the book.)

Although Fechner believed his law to be valid on theoretical grounds, he did not believe that there was any experimental way to test it. He wrote (in 1860), "A real measure of sensation would demand that we be able to call a given sensation twice, thrice, or so-and-so as many times as intense as another—but who would say such a thing?" (quoted by Stevens, 1975). This belief, that people would not be able to report the magnitudes of their sensations in a consistent way, went relatively unchallenged until the early 1950s, when S. S. Stevens, a Harvard psychologist, began a series of experiments in which he asked people to do exactly what Fechner thought they could not do—report the magnitudes of their sensations in such a way that one could be called twice, thrice, or so-and-so as many times as intense as another.

Stevens's technique, called the **method of magnitude estimation**, was to ask subjects to assign numbers to the magnitudes of their sensations. For example, he would present a standard stimulus and call that a "10," and then he would present a comparison stimulus and ask the subject to give it a number that best approximates the magnitude of the new sensation compared to that of the standard. Thus, a sensation that appears to be twice that of the standard would be called "20," one that seems half that of the standard would be called "5," and so on. Stevens found that people had little difficulty carrying out these instructions, and that there was remarkable consistency from test to test in magnitude estimates for a given set of stimuli.

If Fechner's law were correct, Stevens should have found that his subjects' magnitude estimations were directly proportional to the logarithms of the stimulus intensities he used. He found, however, that the logarithmic relationship was only

■ *How Stevens tested Fechner's law and discovered the power law, relating sensory magnitude to stimulus magnitude raised by a constant power*

roughly accurate for most senses, and very inaccurate for some senses, and that for every sense the results could be described better by a different mathematical relationship—a power relationship. Based on this, Stevens proposed a ***power law*** as an alternative to Fechner's logarithmic law. According to Stevens's power law, *the intensity of a sensation is directly proportional to the intensity of the physical stimulus raised by a constant power.* The law can be formulated as

$$S = cM^p$$

where $S$ is the reported magnitude of the sensory experience, $M$ is the physical magnitude of the stimulus, $p$ is the power (or exponent) to which $M$ must be raised (which differs from one sensory dimension to another), and $c$ is a constant that depends on the size of the measurement units used.

How does Stevens's law compare to Fechner's? If you transform each side of the above equation logarithmically, the equation becomes:

$$\log S = \log c + p \log M$$

Thus, whereas Fechner's law holds that the sensory magnitude is directly proportional to the logarithm of the physical magnitude, Stevens's law maintains that the *logarithm* of the sensory magnitude is directly proportional to the logarithm of the physical magnitude.

Stevens and his colleagues performed dozens of experiments, involving magnitude estimations for many different kinds of stimuli. They almost always found that the results could be quite well represented by a power equation. For each kind of stimulus they could determine a unique exponent ($p$) to which the physical magnitude had to be raised to approximate the experienced magnitude. Table 8.3 shows the exponents that they compiled for several different kinds of stimuli. Notice that for most tasks shown in the table the exponent is less than 1, but for one

**Table 8.3** *Power-law exponents for various stimuli*

| Type of stimulus | Measured exponent ($p$)* |
| --- | --- |
| Brightness of a spot of light in the dark | 0.33 |
| Loudness of a 3000-cps tone | 0.67 |
| Smell of heptane | 0.60 |
| Taste of saccharine | 0.80 |
| Length of a line | 1.00 |
| Pain of an electric shock on the fingers | 3.50 |

*The exponent ($p$) is the power to which the stimulus magnitude must be raised to approximate the sensory magnitude.

Source: From *Psychophysics: Introduction to its perceptual, neural, and social prospects* (p. 13) by S. S. Stevens, 1975, New York: Wiley.

task (estimating the length of a line) it is exactly 1, and for another (estimating the pain of an electric shock) it is greater than 1. In cases where $p$ is less than 1, equal physical changes produce smaller sensory changes at the high end of the scale than at the low end, as was also true with Fechner's logarithmic law. When $p$ is greater than 1, however, the opposite relationship holds. Thus, adding a certain amount of electric shock to a relatively strong shock produces a greater increase in pain than does adding the same amount to a relatively weak shock. Finally, when $p$ is equal to 1, equal physical changes produce the same amount of sensory change whether one is starting with a strong or a weak stimulus. All of these relationships are graphically portrayed in Figure 8.31a. In Figure 8.31b, you can see that the results for each magnitude-estimation task fit a straight line when graphed on log-log coordinates—that is the proof of a power law. If Fechner's law had been correct, a straight line would have resulted from converting just the physical scale (the horizontal axis) to logarithms, without converting the sensory scale (the vertical axis) to logarithms.

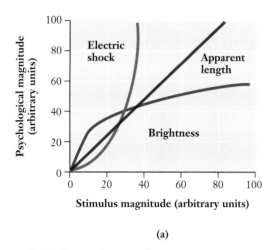

(a)

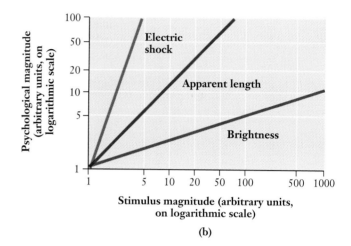

(b)

**Figure 8.31** *Stevens's power law illustrated for three sensory dimensions*
*Graph (a) shows how subjects' estimates of the sensory magnitude that they experienced increased as the stimulus magnitude increased, separately for the pain of an electric shock, the length of a line, and the brightness of a spot of light. Notice that the curvature is upward or downward depending on whether the exponent (p) is greater or less than 1. Graph (b) depicts the same data after both scales have been converted to logarithms. Now all of the lines are straight. By definition, a power law specifies a relationship in which the logarithm of one variable is linearly related to the logarithm of the other. (Adapted from Stevens, 1962.)*

■ *Speculation as to why our senses may have been selected in evolution to operate according to a power law*

Why do our senses obey a power law for so many different kinds of stimuli? Is it just coincidence, or is there some advantage that would lead each sense, in the course of evolution, to operate in accordance with a power law? Stevens (1975) thought a good deal about that question, and the answer he suggested goes something like this:

Our world of stimuli is constantly changing. As we move closer to or farther from the sources of stimulation, or as day turns to dusk, the overall intensity of the energy reaching us from specific objects in the environment changes greatly. If we are to recognize the same scenes, sounds, and smells under such varying conditions, then we must extract those features of each stimulus constellation that remain constant. One such constancy is the ratio of the magnitudes of the stimulus elements with respect to each other.

As you move toward or away from a sound source, the ratio of the amplitudes of the various tones in the sound remains relatively constant, even though the overall amplitude increases or decreases greatly. Similarly, the ratio of light reflected from a darker compared to a lighter portion of a visual scene remains nearly constant as the overall intensity fades at dusk. A power law, and only a power law, has the property that equal physical ratios are converted to equal sensory ratios. (You can find the proof of this statement in the Statistical Appendix.) For example, in the case of the power function for brightness, with an exponent of 0.33, every eightfold change in light intensity results in a twofold change in apparent brightness, no matter where on the intensity continuum we start from. Thus, if the light illuminating a visual scene decreases in physical intensity to one-eighth of what it was before, each part of the visual scene will appear half as bright as before, and the ratio of brightness among the parts will remain constant. The elegant feature of the power law, with $p$ less than 1, is that it compresses large physical changes down to smaller sensory changes, as does the logarithmic law; but, unlike the logarithmic law, it does this while preserving the constancy of stimulus ratios. Since the physical world preserves ratios, it is best that our sensory systems do, too.

# Concluding Thoughts

Broad themes can easily get lost in a chapter that is full of details, such as the one that you have just read. It is useful, in thinking back about the chapter, to highlight some themes that ran through it, and to reorganize some of the details around them. Here are four such themes:

**1.  The survival functions of sensory processes**  Our sensory systems, like every other part of us, evolved through natural selection based on their usefulness in promoting our ancestors' survival. They are not unbiased recorders of physical energies, but biological tools designed to pick out from the sea of energy around us the information that is potentially most useful. We are sensitive to some kinds of energies and not others, and, within the kinds to which we are sensitive, our senses extract and enhance some relationships and not others.

Here are some examples, described in the chapter, of how specific sensory processes might be understood in terms of their survival advantages: (a) Sensory adaptation (the decrease in sensitivity to prolonged, constant stimuli) helps us to ignore stimuli that remain unchanged and to attend most to changes in stimuli. (b) In vision, the heightening of contrast exaggerates the sensory effect of edges, so we see objects as standing out more sharply from their background than we would if our vision measured light intensities in an unbiased way. (c) Pain is a sensory system for warning us when our actions are damaging our tissues, and for motivating us to avoid such actions. But at times the necessity to respond to another threat overrides the advantage of favoring our wounds, and hence we also evolved mechanisms for inhibiting pain. (d) The fact that our senses obey a power law in converting stimulus magnitude to sensory magnitude may have come about because the power law preserves the constancy of ratios, helping us recognize a pattern in sound or light as the same pattern when the overall intensity increases or decreases.

Had this chapter been about sensation in a species that inhabits a more confined niche than humans do, you would have read about sensory analyzers that respond specifically to prey, predators, or other important parts of that niche. For instance, the frog's retina contains "bug detectors," neurons that respond only to small, moving spots and trigger tongue movements in the spot's direction; it also contains wavelength-sensitive receptors ideally designed to distinguish a blue pond from green grass and lily pads (Muntz, 1964).

**2.  Developing theories to explain behavior, and confirming the theories physiologically**  In every field within their science, psychologists develop theories or models to explain what might happen inside the individual to produce or mediate certain behavioral phenomena studied by that field. It is particularly exciting when the models are confirmed by discoveries about the nuts-and-bolts workings of the nervous system. There is no other area of psychology in which that excitement has occurred as often as in the study of sensation. Here are examples of the sequence from behavioral theory to physiological discovery, which you read about in this chapter: (a) Helmholtz developed a theory to explain the fact that pitch perception is related to sound-wave frequencies, and Békésy later confirmed that theory (in modified form) through direct observations of the basilar membrane. (b) Young and Helmholtz developed the trichromatic theory to explain the three-primaries law of color mixing, and research later confirmed that theory in the discovery of three cone types. (c) Hering developed the opponent-process theory to explain the law of complementarity in color mixing, and research later confirmed that theory in the discovery of neurons that respond to wavelengths in opponent-process fashion. (d) Melzack and Wall developed the gate-control theory to explain the body's ability to shut off pain, and other researchers confirmed that theory (and elaborated on its details) in the discovery of a neural pathway that descends from the brain and inhibits pain input at its point of entry into the central nervous system.

**3. The problem of objective assessment of subjective experience** A problem running through all of psychology is that of assessing what is in people's minds through objective, behavioral means. In the study of sensation that problem can be confronted in a more straightforward way than in other areas of psychology, because sensations are the aspects of mental life that are most reliably related to measurable aspects of the physical world. Psychophysics is the subfield that assesses these relationships most directly. Psychophysicists have developed means to assess the absolute threshold, the difference threshold, and the relative magnitude of one sensory experience compared to another, and they have tied these to measures of the physical stimulus. Psychologists in other fields sometimes borrow the methods of psychophysics to study subjective judgments that are far removed from raw sensations (Gescheider, 1976). The signal-detection procedure for assessing response bias has been applied in such tasks as the detection of guilt or innocence based on the kind of evidence that a jurist might hear; and Stevens's method of magnitude estimation has been used for such tasks as estimating the relative amount of pleasure that would be gained from winning various amounts of money.

**4. Processes common to the various sensory systems** This final theme most explicitly addresses the topic of this chapter, the mechanisms of sensation. For every sensory system there are certain basic questions that can be asked about its physiological workings: (a) What are the receptors, and how do they function to transduce some form of environmental energy in such a way as to change the rate of action potentials in sensory neurons? (b) How does the transduction process code the differing amounts and qualities of physical stimulation that we experience as different sensations? (c) How do neural mechanisms within the central nervous system modify sensory information as it goes from one way station to another, in ways that correspond with our sensory experiences? These are questions that you might use to guide your review of the physiology of hearing, vision, and pain.

## Further Reading

**David H. Hubel & Thorsten N. Wiesel** (1979). "Brain mechanisms of vision." *Scientific American, 241* (3), 150–162.
*These Nobel laureates summarize their research and that of others concerning the response characteristics of neurons in the visual cortex, the pattern of connections that may lead to those response characteristics, and their possible roles in visual perception.*

**Margaret S. Livingston** (1988). "Art, illusion and the visual system." *Scientific American, 258* (1), 78–85.
*Based on her joint research with Hubel, this author explains how our physiological knowledge of the separate neural coding of color, form, and spatial location can account for a number of surprising visual effects.*

**Ronald Melzack & Patrick D. Wall** (1982). *The challenge of pain.* New York: Basic Books.
*This classic book on the psychology and physiology of pain, by the men who developed the gate-control theory, is not a bit painful to read. In fact, it is delightful. Keep in mind, though, that the rapid rate of discoveries in this area has made the book's physiological account somewhat out of date.*

**Robert F. Schmidt** (Ed.) (1986). *Fundamentals of sensory physiology* (3rd ed.). New York: Springer-Verlag.

*This brief textbook provides a concise, no-nonsense account of the physiological bases for vision, hearing, taste, smell, pain, touch, body position, balance, and the sensory qualities of thirst and hunger. Each chapter is written by a different expert whose area of research pertains to the sensory system described.*

**S. S. Stevens** (1975). *Psychophysics: Introduction to its perceptual, neural, and social prospects.* New York: Wiley.

*This brilliant, slender book describes the research leading to the power law and the implications of that law. It is quite readable by the beginning student who is not intimidated by exponents or algebraic equations. Stevens also shows how the power law applies to higher-order judgments, beyond sensory judgments, such as those about the seriousness of crimes.*

**Jozef J. Zwislocki** (1981). "Sound analysis in the ear: A history of discoveries." *American Scientist, 69,* 184–192.

*This is a concise account of the history that led to our modern understanding of the ear's ability to code sound frequencies.*

## Looking Ahead

Sensation can be thought of as the first step in the processing of information that we receive from the environment. It is the step that we have the best understanding of physiologically. But think of all that we subsequently do with the information that we receive from our senses. We form meaningful *perceptions* from it, which guide our behavior. We form *memories* from it, which allow us to recall events long after they have happened. We use those perceptions and memories to *think* in rational and not-so-rational ways about our experiences and to make plans for future action. These things that we do with sensory experiences constitute a core part of the subject matter of psychology. They also constitute the topics of the next three chapters: perception, memory, and the human intellect.

# PART 4 COGNITIVE MECHANISMS OF BEHAVIOR

### PERCEPTION

### MEMORY

### THE HUMAN INTELLECT

*Our behavior is governed by our knowledge. We respond not so much to physical reality as to our understanding of it. This unit is about the processes by which we understand the world and use that understanding to guide our actions. It consists of three chapters. The first examines the basic processes of perception—how we recognize objects and scenes in our environment. The second deals with memory— how we store and organize information gained from experience. The third is concerned with the measurement and description of intelligence, and with the mental processes of reasoning and language.*

# CHAPTER 9

**Perceiving Patterns and Recognizing Objects**

**Attention: The Selectivity of Perception**

**Perceiving Objects in Relation to Space: Depth, Size, and Motion Perception**

# PERCEPTION

Perception is the step beyond sensation in the taking in of environmental information. Whereas *sensation* refers to the registration and coding of the various energies that impinge on the sense organs, **perception** refers to the ability to recognize or in some way make sense of that input. To do this, perceptual processes must integrate and organize the sensory input, extracting the useful information that resides not in the individual stimulus elements but in the arrangement of those elements in space and time.

Perception is as much a product of the nervous system as is sensation, and, in theory, should be explainable in terms of the activity of neurons. But perception is much harder to study physiologically than is sensation. The processes are more complicated, involving many more neurons and more complex interactions, and they occur entirely within the brain, which is less accessible to physiological study than are the sense organs. Whereas scientists can offer rather complete physiological accounts of many sensory processes, they have only scratched the surface in their attempts so far to explain perception physiologically.

Thus, the transition from the chapter on sensation to the chapter on perception also corresponds with the transition from a primarily physiological approach to a primarily cognitive one. The cognitive approach involves the construction of hypothetical models, which describe perception, memory, and other mental processes in terms of the manipulation of information, without reference to physiological mechanisms. You will see examples of such models in all three chapters of this unit.

All of the senses are involved in perception, and they often work together, as when you both see and smell the food on your plate, or see and hear a singing bird. This chapter, however, concentrates mostly on visual perception, which has long dominated the field of perceptual psychology. Auditory perception ranks a rather distant second in the amount it has been studied, and research on it has been concerned mostly with perception of speech, a topic touched on in this chapter and again in Chapters 11 and 12.

This chapter is divided into three main sections, dealing respectively with the following three questions: (1) How do we perceive patterns and recognize objects in the sensory information that enters our eyes? (2) How do we select, from the vast array of stimuli that confront us, those stimuli that are useful to the task at hand, and ignore those that are irrelevant? That is, how do we pay attention to some stimuli and not others? (3) How do we perceive the spatial characteristics of objects and judge their distance, size, and motion in the three-dimensional world? These questions are interrelated, and the same general models and points of view that will inform our thinking about one question can inform our thinking about the other questions as well.

# Perceiving Patterns and Recognizing Objects

As I look at the top of my desk, what strikes my retinas is a continuous field of light, varying from point to point in amplitude and wavelength. But I see the scene neither as a continuous field nor as a collection of points of light. Rather, I see discrete objects: a word processor, a pencil, a stapler, and a pile of books. If you were to look at the same scene, you would list its objects in pretty much the same way. How do we perceive discrete objects in the stimulus array that strikes our eyes? That is the basic question of this section.

*The difference between bottom-up and top-down perceptual processes*

How do I see the pencil on my desk? Most modern attempts to answer this question emphasize an interaction between two categories of processes, referred to as bottom-up and top-down. ***Bottom-up processes*** begin with the individual stimulus features recorded by the senses, bringing them together to form a perception of the whole. The pencil on my desk contains a point, a yellow color, and two parallel lines that form most of its contour. Bottom-up processes must somehow bring those features together, allowing me to see the pencil as a whole.

But how does my perceptual system know which features to bring together? Why are the parallel lines combined with the yellow color and the point rather than, say, with the blue blotter on which the pencil rests? Scientists who have tried to build computers that can recognize objects have found that bottom-up processes cannot work alone (see Watt, 1988). The computer must be provided with information that helps it decide which features to combine. For example, to recognize a pencil the computer must be programmed already with some knowledge about what pencils look like, and with rules for distinguishing objects in general from their background. The perceptual processes that make use of such knowledge are called ***top-down processes***.

My perception of the pencil requires an interplay of bottom-up and top-down processes. A simplified model might go something like this (see also Figure 9.1): (1) Bottom-up processes register a set of elementary features in the stimulus array before me—a set of lines, angles, colors, and so forth. (2) Top-down processes bring my knowledge of objects and my expectations about what is likely to be present to bear on a preliminary analysis of the features, and form the hypothesis that there is a pencil before me. (3) Bottom-up processes, receiving input about the pencil hypothesis, integrate the features in such a way that the hypothesis can be tested. (For example, bottom-up processes combine the parallel lines, the point, and the yellow color.) (4) Top-down processes analyze the input and confirm the hypothesis. Amazingly, this occurs almost instantaneously, with little or no conscious effort on my part. Although the two categories of perceptual processes work together, they are discussed separately in the following paragraphs, beginning with top-down processes.

**Figure 9.1** *Model of bottom-up and top-down perceptual processes*

*Bottom-up processes are those that detect and organize the features of the sensory stimulus, and top-down are those that use preexisting knowledge and expectancies to direct attention toward relevant features and to recognize an object.*

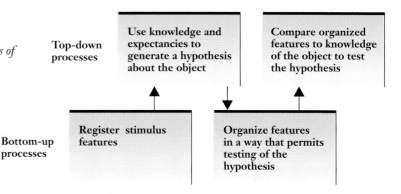

### Holistic Perception and Top-Down Analysis of Stimulus Input

My *conscious* perception of the pencil begins with my seeing the whole pencil. The earlier registration and bringing together of features must occur at a level of my mind's activity that precedes conscious experience. Consciously, it seems easier for me to identify the whole object as a pencil than to identify its features (its parallel lines, point, and yellow color). Thus, conscious perception is holistic. ***Holistic perception*** refers to the primacy of the whole over the parts—the tendency to perceive whole patterns, objects, and scenes, and to ignore the smaller parts of which they are composed. The holistic perception of an object or scene in turn contributes, top-down, to identifying the individual parts of the object or scene. I can find the point on the object in front of me more easily if I recognize it as a pencil than if I don't.

Historically, the idea of holistic perception has come largely from the Gestalt school of psychology. Therefore, I will begin this section with a description of the Gestalt point of view and some of the principles of perceptual grouping that the Gestaltists proposed. Then I will turn to evidence that perception of the whole contributes, in top-down fashion, to perception of the elements.

**Gestalt Principles of Perceptual Grouping** The ***Gestalt*** movement arose in Germany during the early twentieth century in response to the then-dominant structuralist school (as described in Chapter 1). The structuralists were interested in the basic elements of sensory experience, and believed that more complex perceptions could be understood as combinations of these elements. For example, Edward Titchener and his students were concerned with counting the number of separate degrees of brightness and hue that people could discriminate while looking at visual stimuli. The Gestaltists, on the other hand, argued that perception is not a matter of combining separate elements, but a matter of responding immediately to large, whole patterns. One of the leaders of the Gestalt movement, Max Wertheimer (1923/1938), argued against the structuralists, as follows: "I stand at the window and see a house, trees, sky. Now on theoretical grounds I could try to count and say: 'here they are . . . 327 brightnesses and hues.' Do *I have* '327'? No, I see sky, house, trees. . . ."

*Principle of similarity*

*Some sets of individuals in this crowd stand out as perceptual units because of the similarity in their clothing.*

The Gestalt point of view is most identified by the statement, *The whole is different from the sum of its parts.* The whole is different because it contains not only the parts, but contains them organized in a certain way; the meaningful information that is perceived lies in the organization. The German word *gestalt* translates roughly to "organized whole," and the Gestaltists believed that this

■ *Six principles of grouping that, according to Gestalt psychologists, lead us to see whole patterns rather than separate parts*

Proximity

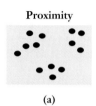

(a)

Similarity

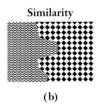

(b)

gestalt, not the individual sensory elements, is the proper unit of study. To them, the structuralist approach was like trying to account for the beauty of the Mona Lisa by carefully weighing the amount of paint used to produce each part of the masterpiece.

The Gestaltists proposed that the nervous system is innately predisposed to group incoming sensory elements according to certain rules or *principles of grouping*. These principles (from Wertheimer, 1923, and Koffka, 1935) include the following:

■ *Proximity* We tend to see stimulus elements that are near each other as part of the same object, and those that are separated as part of different objects. This helps us segregate a large set of elements into a smaller set of objects (see Figure 9.2a).

■ *Similarity* We tend to see stimulus elements that physically resemble each other as part of the same object, and those that don't resemble each other as part of different objects. This helps us distinguish between two adjacent or overlapping objects, based on a change in their texture elements. (Texture elements are repeated visual features or patterns that cover the surface of a given object, as illustrated in Figure 9.2b.)

■ *Closure* We tend to see forms as completely enclosed by a border and to ignore gaps in the border. This helps us perceive complete forms even when they are partly occluded by other objects (see Figure 9.2c).

Closure

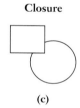

(c)

Good continuation

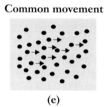

(d)

Common movement

(e)

Good form

(f)

**Figure 9.2  *Gestalt principles of grouping***
(a) Proximity—*we see three sets of dots rather than thirteen individual dots.*
(b) Similarity—*because we group similar texture elements together, we see two separate forms here.* (c) Closure—*we assume that the boundary of the circle is complete, continuing behind the square.*
(d) Good continuation—*we see two lines here, a–b and c–d, rather than four lines or other possible combinations such as a–c or b–d.* (e) Common movement—*if the set of dots with arrows were moving, we would see the dots as a single object.* (f) Good form—*because of its symmetry, the left-hand figure is more likely to be seen as one complete figure than the middle figure. The middle figure is more likely to be seen as two separate good forms, as shown in the right-hand figure.*

■ *Good continuation* When lines intersect, we tend to group the line segments in such a way as to form continuous lines with minimal change in direction. This helps us decide which lines belong to which object when two or more objects overlap (see Figure 9.2d).

■ *Common movement* When a set of stimulus elements move in the same direction and at the same rate, we tend to see them as part of a single object. This helps us distinguish moving objects from the background, and helps explain why it is easier to see a camouflaged animal when it moves than when it is motionless (see Figure 9.2e).

■ *Good form* This principle is less specific than the others. Essentially, it states that the perceptual system strives to produce percepts that are elegant—simple, uncluttered, symmetrical, and regular (Koffka, 1935). This principle encompasses the other principles listed above, but also includes more complex ways by which the perceptual system organizes stimuli into their most elegant arrangement. (Figures 9.2f and 9.7 both illustrate this.)

In addition to the six principles of grouping just listed, the Gestaltists called attention to our automatic tendency to divide any visual scene into *figure* (the object that attracts attention) and *ground* (background). As an example, look at Figure 9.3. The illustration could be described as two unfamiliar figures, one white and one black, whose borders coincide; but you probably do not see it that way. Most people automatically see it as just one white figure against a black background. According to the Gestaltists, the division into figure and ground is not arbitrary, but

**Figure 9.3  *Figure and ground***

*Because the white form is completely surrounded by the black form, we tend to see the white form as the figure and the black form as the ground.*

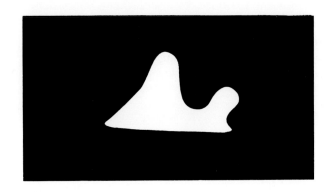

■ *How reversible figures illustrate the mind's strong tendency to divide a scene into figure and ground—even when there are no good cues for deciding which is which*

is directed by certain stimulus characteristics. In the example in Figure 9.3, the most important characteristic is probably *circumscription*: Other things being equal, we see the more circumscribed form (the one that is surrounded by the other) as figure and the circumscribing form (the one that surrounds the other) as ground.

The figure-ground relationship is not always completely determined by the stimulus, however. With some effort, you can imagine that the illustration in Figure 9.3 is a black square with an oddly shaped hole cut out of it, sitting on a white background, thereby reversing the figure-ground relation. When cues in the scene are sparse or ambiguous, the mind can choose which shape to see as figure and which as ground. Figure 9.4 illustrates the same phenomenon more dramatically. In this example of a *reversible figure* you may see alternately either a white vase against a dark ground or two dark profiles against a white ground. The important thing to notice is that you see one or the other, not both simultaneously. In line with the Gestalt figure-ground principle, the same part of the figure cannot simultaneously be both figure and ground, and thus at any instant you see either the vase or the faces, but not both at once.

**Figure 9.4  *Reversible figure***

*Because there are no strong cues as to which is figure and which is ground, this may be seen either as a white vase against a dark ground or as two dark profiles against a white ground. If you stare at it, your perception may alternate between the two.*

**Perceptual Set and Effects of Context on Object Recognition**    If you had been mentally prepared to see a vase when you first looked at Figure 9.4—for example, if you had just been talking about vases—you would most likely have seen the figure as a vase. Conversely, if you had been prepared to see people's profiles, that is what you would have seen. When the available stimuli offer a choice, what we see is affected by what we expect to see, that is, by our *perceptual set*. The idea of perceptual set leads us from the Gestaltists' principles of grouping to the general role that context and mental concepts play in perception.

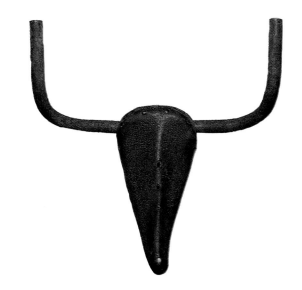

**Death's head (Flayed head)**

*This sculpture by Pablo Picasso (1944) illustrates the effect of context on perception. The objects the artist used to create the sculpture are easily recognized in another setting, but it takes a moment to recognize them here.*

### ■ How context affects the top-down processes involved in object recognition

Typically, our perceptual set for what we will see in any given part of a scene is influenced by our global understanding of the whole scene, and this helps us recognize parts that otherwise we might not. For example, look at the set of features in Figure 9.5b. By themselves, they are unrecognizable curves and angles that might be interpreted in any of a number of possible ways. When seen as features of a face, however, as in Figure 9.5a, they are unmistakably nose, eye, ear, and mouth. Notice, in Figure 9.5c, how much additional detail is required for the same features to be recognized out of context. In everyday life, practically every scene you look at contains elements that would be hard to recognize out of context. For example, when you look at a tree, you can find leaves or twigs that, because of their angle or distance from you, would be unrecognizable if seen away from the tree. Likewise, you probably recognize your psychology professor more easily in the classroom than you would at a shopping mall, and more easily at a shopping mall than you would at a roller derby.

**Figure 9.5  *Role of context in feature recognition***
*Very little detail is needed to recognize the nose, eye, ear, and mouth in the context of a face, but out of context more detail is needed. (From Palmer, 1975b.)*

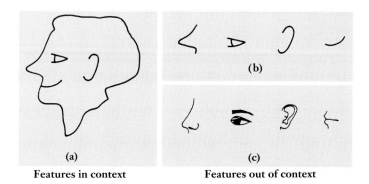

**Features in context**            **Features out of context**

Many experiments have confirmed that people can indeed identify objects more rapidly or accurately when viewing them in an appropriate scene than when viewing them out of context. In one such experiment, Stephen Palmer (1975a) showed subjects slides of common scenes, such as the kitchen scene in the left-hand part of Figure 9.6, and then, immediately after each scene, briefly showed them a slide of a specific object to identify, such as one of those depicted in the right-hand part of the figure. The subjects were much better at identifying objects that were appropriate to the scene they had just viewed than objects that were not appropriate to it, even though the subjects knew that the objects might not be related to the scene. Thus, after seeing the kitchen, they were more likely to identify correctly a loaf of bread than a mailbox or a drum. Misperceptions often fit the

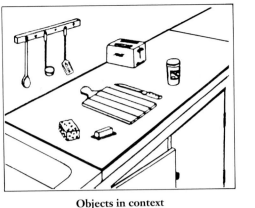

**Objects in context**        **Isolated objects**

**Figure 9.6** *Experiment on context and object recognition*

*Subjects first saw a contextual scene, such as that on the left, and then briefly saw an isolated object, such as one of those on the right (a loaf of bread, mailbox, or drum), and were required to name the object. Their accuracy was best when the object was appropriate to the scene (loaf of bread, in this case). (From Palmer, 1975a.)*

■ *Two illusions in which perception of the whole leads the perceptual system to manufacture a missing part*

**Figure 9.7** *Illusory contour*

*In response to this stimulus, the perceptual system creates a white triangle, the borders of which appear to continue across the white space, such that the triangle seems whiter than the white space. (Adapted from Kanizsa, 1976.)*

context in some way. Thus, the mailbox was commonly seen as a loaf of bread if it followed the kitchen scene, but not if it followed an outdoor scene.

**Illusions Deriving from Top-Down Analysis**   Many perceptual illusions derive from the context in which the illusory elements appear, and thus illustrate top-down analysis. Most impressive are illusions in which context not only affects perceived characteristics of an object (such as its size), but causes us to see or hear something that isn't present in the stimulus at all. As an example, look at the *illusory contour* illustration in Figure 9.7. You probably see a solid white triangle sitting atop three black discs and a black triangular frame. The contour of the white triangle appears to continue across the white space between the other objects. This is not simply a misperception caused by a fleeting glance. The longer you look at the whole stimulus, the more convinced you may become that the contour (border) between the white triangle and the white background is really there; the triangle seems *whiter* than the background. But if you try to look at the contour isolated from the rest of the stimulus, by cupping your fingers around it to form a peephole, you will see that the contour isn't really there. The white triangle and its border are illusions.

There is debate about the exact cause of the illusion in Figure 9.7 (see Pomerantz & Kubovy, 1986), but most researchers agree that it stems somehow from the perceptual system's attempt to make sense of the whole scene. The illusion is sometimes explained in terms of the Gestalt principle of good form. From that perspective, the white triangle emerges because its presence allows us to interpret the whole scene in a more elegant (simpler and more complete) way than would otherwise be possible. Without the white triangle we would see three incomplete discs, each with a segment removed, and three unconnected black angles. With the white triangle we see, more elegantly, three complete discs and a black triangular frame, which are all partially occluded by the white triangle. To see the white triangle as a unified object on top of the other objects, we must separate it from the white background of the page, and to do that our perceptual system creates the illusory contour and the illusion that the triangle is whiter than the page.

Context can create illusions in auditory as well as visual perception. A well-studied example is *phonemic restoration*. Phonemes are the individual vowel and consonant sounds that make up words, and phonemic restoration refers to the finding that people hear phonemes that have been deleted from words or sentences as if they were still there. Richard Warren (1970) first demonstrated this illusion in an experiment in which he removed an *s* sound and spliced in a coughing sound of equal duration in the following tape-recorded sentence at the place marked by an asterisk: *The state governors met with their respective legi\*latures convening in the capital city.* People listening to the doctored tape could hear the cough, but it did not seem to coincide with any specific portion of the sentence or block out any sound in the sentence. Even when they listened repeatedly, with instructions to determine what sound was missing, people were unable to detect that any sound was missing. After they were told which sound was missing, they still claimed to hear it each time they listened to the tape.

The context that provides the basis for phonemic restoration is the arrangement of the other phonemes and the meaningful words and phrases they produce. The restored sound is always one that turns a partial word into a whole word that is consistent in meaning with the rest of the sentence. Interestingly, even words that occur after the missing phoneme can influence which phoneme is heard. For example, people heard the stimulus sound *eel (again, the * represents a coughlike sound) to be either *peel*, *heel*, or *wheel*, depending on whether it occurred in the phrase, *The *eel was on the orange*, *The *eel was on the shoe*, or *The *eel was on the axle* (Warren, 1984).

Illusory contours and phonemic restoration are particularly powerful demonstrations of top-down processing. They show that our conception of the whole affects not only what parts of a stimulus array we notice, or what characteristics we ascribe to the parts, or how we label them, but in certain conditions can cause us to see or hear parts that aren't present in the stimulus at all.

### Feature Detection and Bottom-Up Analysis of Stimulus Input

Although perception of the whole influences the way we perceive the parts, the opposite is also true. In fact, logically, at some level, we must base our perception of a whole at least partly on perception of its parts and their relative locations, even though we may not be consciously aware of doing so. To illustrate this point, think about your ability to read a word. When you read that last sentence you immediately and effortlessly perceived the last word in the sentence to be *word*. How did you do it? Top-down analysis, based on the context of the rest of the sentence, certainly played a role. It would have taken you longer to read a word there that didn't make sense. But top-down processes cannot be the whole story. The actual stimulus on the page had to play some role. If the stimulus had looked like this—poem—you would not have read it as *word*.

▨ *Perception from the bottom up: features → components → object*

Printed words consist of individual letters, and each letter consists of a set of straight or curved lines arranged in a certain way. As a skilled reader, when you perceived *word*, you probably did not consciously notice its individual letters, and certainly not the individual lines within letters. Yet, at least some of these must have registered in your sensory system and contributed to your perception. In this example we can refer to the characteristics of the individual lines as features. Your perceptual system must have picked up at least some of the features, in order to pick up at least some of the letters, in order to perceive the word. These processes, which can be diagrammed as *features → letters → word*, are the bottom-up processes involved in reading. For a skilled reader these processes are automatic and unconscious, but they still must occur. More generally, all visual objects can be thought of as defined by a particular arrangement of components (analogous to letters), which in turn are defined by more primitive features. Thus, more generally, object perception can be diagrammed, bottom-up, as *features → components → object*. Research from a bottom-up perspective has focused on (a) the detection and integration of features, (b) the role of component recognition in object recognition, and (c) the role that learning plays in directing attention toward the most distinguishing features and components. Let us look at examples of each of these.

▨ *The difference between parallel and serial processing, and their roles in Treisman's feature-integration theory*

**Detection and Integration of Features**   The work of Anne Treisman nicely illustrates contemporary research on the bottommost part of bottom-up perceptual processes. Treisman has developed a *feature-integration theory*, which states that to see an object our perceptual apparatus must first pick up certain *primitive features* (such as the slant and curvature of individual lines) from the stimulus information, and then integrate those features into larger parts (Treisman, 1986; Treisman & Gormican, 1988). These processes, according to Treisman, occur in two fundamentally different steps. The first step, *detection of features*, occurs automatically

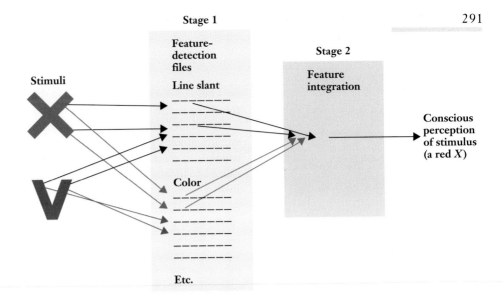

**Figure 9.8** *Treisman's theory of feature detection and integration*

*According to Treisman, stimulus features are detected and integrated in two separate stages of information processing. Stage 1 corresponds with feature-detector neurons (discussed in Chapter 8), which operate in parallel (simultaneously) on all stimuli that reach the eyes. The parallel processing of Stage 1 is illustrated here by showing that all of the features of both the X and V are detected at once (in different feature-detection files). Integration of features occurs at Stage 2, which operates serially on information from one localized area of the visual field at a time. Serial processing is illustrated here by showing that only the information from one stimulus, the X, is being processed. An instant later, Stage 2 could operate on the V, but it cannot operate on the X and V at once.*

■ *How pop-out phenomena and mistakes in joining features support Treisman's view that feature detection occurs through parallel processing and feature integration occurs through serial processing*

and involves ***parallel processing***. Parallel processing means that this step operates simultaneously on all parts of the stimulus array. That is, according to Treisman, we pick up at once the primitive features of all objects that are in our field of vision. This step involves the feature-detector neurons described in Chapter 8. The second step is the *integration of features*, which is less automatic and leads eventually to our conscious perception of whole, spatially organized patterns and objects. This step involves ***serial processing***, which occurs sequentially at one spatial location at a time, rather than simultaneously over the entire array. To visualize Treisman's theory, and to see the distinction between parallel and serial processing, look at Figure 9.8.

To understand the evidence on which Treisman's theory is based, look at the array of stimuli in Figure 9.9a. Notice that it takes no effort to find the single slanted line. You don't have to scan the whole array in serial fashion to find it; it just "pops out" at you. According to Treisman, this is because line slant is one of the primitive features that is processed automatically, through parallel processing. Now look at Figure 9.9b and find the single set of crossed lines among the vertical and horizontal lines. In this case the target does not pop out; you have to scan through the items in serial fashion to find it (though you can still find it quite quickly).

In controlled experiments, Treisman measured the time it took for people to locate specific target stimuli in arrays like those of Figure 9.9 but with varying

**Figure 9.9** *Stimuli that pop out or do not pop out*

*These stimulus arrays are similar to those used by Treisman and Gormican (1988). In (a) the single slanted line pops out; you notice it even if you aren't looking for it. This is evidence of* parallel *processing (all stimuli are automatically processed at once). In (b) the single set of crossed lines does not pop out; you have to look for it to notice it. This is evidence of* serial *processing (the stimuli are processed one at a time).*

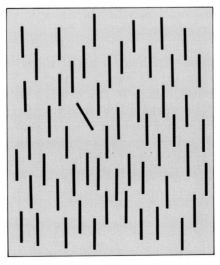

(a)                    (b)

numbers of distractors (defined as the nontarget stimuli). As long as the target differed from the distractors in one or more of Treisman's list of primitive features—slant, curvature, length, brightness, or color—people could detect a target equally quickly no matter how many distractors were present. This lack of effect of number of distractors is indicative of parallel processing. In contrast, the time required to locate targets defined by the joining of two or more primitive features, as in Figure 9.9b, increased in direct proportion to the number of distractors. This increase is indicative of serial processing, the necessity to attend to each item separately until the target is found.

Treisman also found that when people saw simple stimuli flashed briefly on a screen, they could easily say which primitive features were present, but sometimes misperceived which features went together, a phenomenon that she calls *illusory conjunctions*. For example, when shown a straight red line and a green curved one, all subjects knew that they had seen a straight line and a curved line, and a red color and a green color, but were sometimes mistaken about which color belonged to which line. Such findings led Treisman to conclude that the first step (parallel processing) registers features independently of their spatial location, and that different features that coincide in space (such as the color and curvature of a given line) are joined perceptually only at the second step (serial processing), which requires separate attention to each location.

You might reasonably ask whether Treisman is dealing with sensation or perception. The answer is that her work lies at the arbitrary border between the two. She is struggling with the question of how elementary sensory features are brought together in a way that makes possible the extraction of information needed to interpret the stimulus in a meaningful way. It is also significant that her theoretical work combines what is known at the physiological level (for example, about feature detectors) with the more metaphorical approach of cognitive psychology for processes that are not yet understood physiologically (for example, feature integration). Her results have helped stimulate new physiological research aimed at identifying neural systems that integrate features.

**Recognizing Objects Based on Components**   While Treisman has been concerned with the initial pickup and integration of primitive stimulus features, other theorists, including Irving Biederman (1987), have been studying the later stages in the perception of whole, natural objects. From a bottom-up perspective, the integration of spatially congruent features, postulated by Treisman's theory, leads to further integration of spatially adjacent sets of features into components, which in turn leads to perception of the whole object. Biederman's *recognition-by-components theory* addresses the components that form the most immediate basis for perceiving natural objects.

Biederman believes that our ability to recognize natural, three-dimensional objects is analogous to our ability to recognize printed words. There are only twenty-six different letters in the English alphabet, but these can be used to form hundreds of thousands of different words. Likewise, Biederman suggests that any object can be thought of as a particular arrangement of a small set of relatively simple geometric forms, such as blocks, cylinders, spheres, and cones. On the basis of certain fundamental properties of three-dimensional geometry, Biederman has suggested a list of thirty-six such forms, which he calls *geons*, some of which appear in Figure 9.10. By smoothing the edges and ignoring the details, all

*How a finite set of geometric forms (geons) can provide the basis for perception of an infinite set of objects*

**Figure 9.10** *Some geons*

*From principles of geometry, Biederman developed a list of thirty-six simple, three-dimensional forms or geons, which, he suggests, provide the basic perceptual components of more complex forms. Six sample geons are shown here. (Adapted from Biederman, 1987.)*

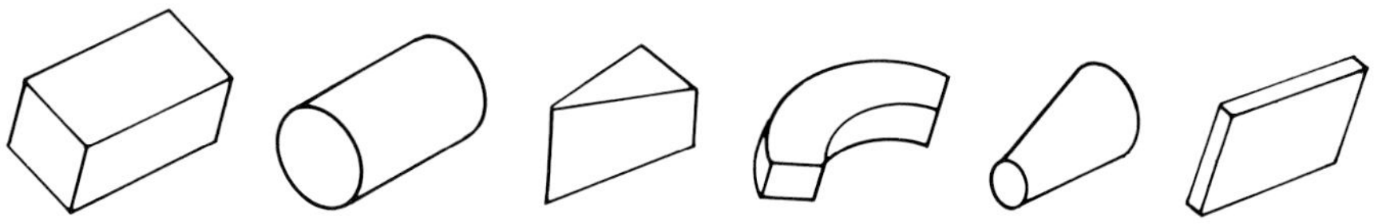

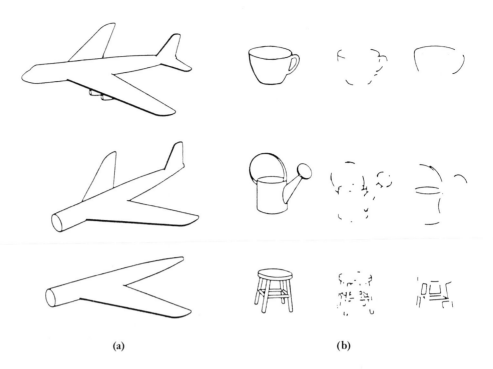

**Figure 9.11** *Support for Biederman's recognition-by-components theory*

*Part (a) shows an airplane consisting of nine, four, or two components (geons). Even with just a few components present it is recognizable. Part (b) shows a set of line drawings of objects degraded in two different ways. The degradation in the middle column preserves the connections between adjacent components, and that in the right-hand column does not. When people saw the degraded figures alone, they recognized those in the middle column but not those in the right-hand column. (Adapted from Biederman, 1987.)*

(a)                    (b)

■ *Evidence that some, but often not all, of an object's geons must be distinguishable to recognize the object*

■ *How an effect of brain damage supports Biederman's theory*

objects, according to this theory, can be seen as a set of geons organized in a certain way. You may already be familiar with this general idea from experience with learn-to-draw books that recommend sketching objects as sets of three-dimensional geometric shapes before fleshing out the details. According to Biederman, perception of an object depends on recognizing at least some of its geons and their arrangement relative to one another.

Evidence for Biederman's theory comes from experiments in which he asked people to identify objects that were flashed briefly on a screen (Biederman, 1987). In these experiments, he found that the speed and accuracy of recognition depended very much on the intactness and arrangement of individual geons within the object, and very little upon details within the geons themselves or upon the outline of the object as a whole. Figure 9.11 illustrates some of the stimuli that he used. The airplane in Figure 9.11a was recognized as an airplane even when most of its geons were removed (changing its overall outline), as long as the geons still present were intact and properly arranged. The various objects in Figure 9.11b were recognized when the lines were degraded in such a way as to preserve recognizability of individual geons and their connections to one another (middle column), but not when the same amount of line degradation occurred in such a way as to obscure the geons and their connections (right-hand column).

Biederman's theory is also supported by the presence of rare individuals who, because of damage to a specific part of the brain (in the occipital lobe of the cortex), suffer from a disorder called *visual-object agnosia*. The term *agnosia* (from the Greek *a*, meaning "not," and *gnosis*, meaning "perception") refers to any perceptual deficit, and visual-object agnosia refers to cases in which the person can perceive simple geometric forms (Biederman's geons), but not more complex objects (Kolb & Whishaw, 1990). I already mentioned one such individual in Chapter 8—the man who, when shown a rose, could describe its stem as "a long green attachment" and its petals as "convoluted red forms," but could not combine them to see the rose. Another patient with this disorder described a bicycle as a pole and two wheels, but could not identify it as a bicycle or guess its function (Hécaen & Albert, 1978). Apparently, the combining of components into recognizable whole objects is a separate step from the perception of components, and is carried out by a unique set of neurons in the cortex.

**Learning Which Parts to Attend To**    How do we make finer distinctions among objects than those that are based on the overall arrangement of geons? For example, how do we tell one kind of airplane from another? Most perceptual psychologists agree that these finer distinctions don't come automatically, but must be learned through experience in which, for one reason or another, the distinction is important (see Biederman, 1988). Some years ago, Eleanor Gibson, a well-known perceptual and developmental psychologist at Cornell University, developed a *distinctive-feature theory* of that learning process (Gibson, 1969). In essence, her theory is that we learn to notice the ***distinctive features*** of objects—defined as those features that best distinguish an object from others with which it might be confused—and to ignore the nondistinctive features. Consider, for example, the task of identifying a particular letter of the alphabet. Usually, in such a situation, we already know that the item we are looking at is a letter, so there is no need to distinguish it from all possible items, only from other letters. Thus, Gibson proposed that we learn to recognize letters efficiently by attending to those features that distinguish letters from other possible letters. In fact, she proposed a list of such features for each letter of the alphabet, and found experimental evidence that skilled readers indeed do attend most to the distinctive features.

According to Gibson, the kinds of features that we learn to notice for any particular object depend on the kind of distinction that we need to make. Consider the problem (suggested by Gibson) of identifying goats. One level of identification involves distinguishing goats, as a category, from other barnyard animals such as pigs or sheep. That is the level with which most of us are concerned when we identify goats, and so we learn to pay attention to the properties that are common to all goats but not to other animals. We notice, for example, the beardlike tuft of hair on the chin and use that as one of the distinctive features—a feature that is exaggerated in cartoon drawings of goats to make for easy recognition. But a specialist in goats, someone who tends them or sells them, must not only distinguish goats from other animals, or one breed from another, but must also distinguish individual goats within a breed. This is a difficult task for someone who is unfamiliar with goats, but easy for the goat expert because he or she has learned to notice the features that differ from goat to goat, such as the specific placement of spots of color, or more subtle features like the amount of separation between the eyes.

People often are not conscious of the features that they use in making such distinctions, which explains why someone can be an expert identifier without necessarily being able to teach others how to perform the same task. I remember, years ago, working on a maple sugar farm in Vermont and being faced with the problem of identifying sugar maples without their leaves in late winter. The old hands teased me about tapping the wrong kinds of maples (they said I also tapped oaks, pines, and telephone poles, but they exaggerated). Yet, none of them—and I think they really tried—was able to tell me how he or she distinguished sugar maples from other varieties. After several frustrated attempts, one expert concluded, "Well, you know, it just looks more *sugary* than other trees." Obviously he knew at some level of his mind what to look at, because he never made a mistake, but not at a level that was connected to his speaking ability.

In a more formal study, Irving Biederman and Margaret Shiffrar (1987) found that expert chicken sexers—people who could classify a newly hatched chick as male or female by glancing quickly at the cloaca (the bird's genital opening)—typically could not explain just how the cloaca of the male and the female differed. They said that this was the kind of skill that one learned gradually through months or even years of practice. The standard way to learn the task was to work for a long time with an expert, who would say whether the trainee was right or wrong on a given trial. Yet, Biederman and Shiffrar discovered that the actual features that experts used to make the classification could be easily described, and that a person

*How perceptual skill depends on knowing—either consciously or unconsciously—which features to attend to*

*Learning to look*

*For these birdwatchers, field guides may be as useful as field glasses. By highlighting the features that distinguish each species from the most similar other species, the guides help hobbyists identify species quickly and accurately. Field guides can also facilitate the identification of trees, even in winter.*

who could describe them could, with just 15 seconds of instruction, train people who had no previous experience to make the discrimination as accurately as the experts (Biederman, 1988). (It is nice to know that in one realm, at least, 15 seconds with a good teacher can be worth months of real-world experience.)

## Attention: The Selectivity of Perception

■ *The general meaning of* attention, *and its more specific meaning for perceptual psychologists*

In the discussion of the role of learning in object recognition, we have already eased ourselves into the problem of attention. *Attention*, in the most general sense of the term, refers to any focusing of mental activity along a specific track, whether that track consists purely of inner memories and knowledge (I am attending now to my knowledge of the meaning of *attention*) or is based on external stimuli (as when a chicken sexer attends to just the right features of the cloaca to distinguish male from female hatchling). Here we will use the term purely in the latter sense, as many perceptual psychologists do. We can define *attention* as the process or set of processes by which the mind chooses from among the various stimuli that strike the senses at any given moment, allowing only some of those stimuli to enter into higher stages of information processing.

As I sit on my porch composing this paragraph, I can stop and attend to the chirping of a single bird. As I listen, I am vaguely aware of my neighbors arguing through the open window next door, of traffic on the street, and even of other birds chirping nearby, but these do not enter my consciousness in a clear and detailed way, as does the song to which I am attending. Everything that I am not attending to is part of the background. If I wish, however, I can shift my attention from the bird to any of the other sounds. I can choose to listen to the neighbors' argument, and when I do that, the bird becomes part of the background. I can do the same with sight as I do with hearing—shift my focus, say, from sight of the bird, to the twig that it is standing on, to anything else in my field of view.

■ *Two sides to the coin of attention—selecting some stimuli while monitoring others*

There are two sides to our attentive ability. The one just emphasized is the ability to focus on one source of information while ignoring others. The other is the ability to monitor in some way those stimuli to which we are *not* attending—those that do not reach consciousness or do so only dimly—and use them as a basis for shifting attention. As I watch and listen to the bird, my attention can be disrupted and drawn away by important events that would otherwise be part of the background. Why do some stimuli but not others draw my attention? Simple intensity certainly plays a role. I cannot help but notice the motorcycle roaring down the street. In other cases, though, the ability of a stimulus to draw attention has more to do with its significance than intensity. I notice a mosquito about to land on my hand even though its sound and sight are slight. If one of the arguing neighbors were to use my name, I might notice that, even though I hadn't noticed any of their specific words before. Keep these two aspects of attention in mind as we turn first to some experiments on attention and then to theories about the selective process.

**Studies of Selective Listening**   Most research on selective listening has focused on the so-called *cocktail-party phenomenon*, the ability to listen to and understand one person's voice while ignoring other voices nearby. (This ability is useful not only at parties, but also in such places as air-traffic control towers, where messages come in from many different speakers at once.) In the laboratory this ability is usually studied by playing two spoken, tape-recorded messages at once and asking the subject to *shadow* one message—that is, to repeat immediately each of its words as they are heard—while ignoring the other message.

Early experiments (reviewed by Hawkins & Presson, 1986) showed that successful shadowing depends primarily on physical differences between the two voices and differences in their spatial location. Shadowing is very poor if the two messages are read by the same voice and played through speakers that are near each other. It improves greatly if the messages are read by different voices (especially if one is a woman's and the other is a man's), or if the voices are altered electronically to make them different in pitch. It also improves greatly if the messages come through speakers located in different parts of the room, or if they are played through separate earphones, one into each ear—a procedure called *dichotic listening*. Differences having to do with the meaning of words in the two messages have much less impact. When the two messages are read by the same voice, shadowing a passage of English prose is only slightly easier if the distracting message consists of nonsense words, or is in a foreign language, than if it is another passage of English prose.

■ *Evidence that selective listening to a voice depends mainly on its physical qualities; and that physical qualities, but not meanings, are usually noticed in an unattended voice, though some meanings may register unconsciously*

When people are attending to one spoken message, what kinds of information, if any, do they notice in the other message? Early dichotic-listening studies showed that subjects usually could report such physical characteristics of the unattended message as the gender of the speaker or variation in tone, but usually were unaware of any of the message's meaning or even whether the speaker switched to a foreign language (Cherry, 1953; Cherry & Taylor, 1954). Subsequent experiments, however, showed that some degree of meaning can be picked up from the unattended message. In one experiment, subjects who failed to identify most words in the unattended message, including one that had been repeated thirty-five times, nevertheless noticed their own names in that message on about one-third of all occasions that it was presented (Moray, 1959). In another experiment, subjects shadowed sentences containing words with two possible meanings, such as *They threw stones at the bank* (MacKay, 1973). At the same time, the other ear was presented with a word that resolved the ambiguity (*river* or *money* in this example). After the shadowing task, the subjects were asked to choose from a pair of sentences the one that was most like the shadowed sentences. Thus, in our example, the choice was between *They threw stones at the savings and loan association* and *They threw stones toward the side of the river*. Although the subjects could not report the nonshadowed word, they usually chose the sentence that was consistent with the meaning of that word. Thus, the unattended word apparently influenced their interpretation of the shadowed message, even though they were unaware of hearing that word.

**Selective listening**

*Cocktail parties are not the only setting at which the ability to attend to one voice and ignore others is valuable.*

**Studies of Selective Viewing**    On the face of it, selective viewing would seem to be a simpler problem than selective listening; we can control what we see just by moving our eyes, whereas we have no easy control over what we hear. But we can also attend selectively to different, nearby parts of a visual scene without moving our eyes.

An experiment by Irvin Rock and Daniel Gutman (1981) offers evidence for selective viewing without eye movement. The researchers presented, in rapid succession, a series of slides to viewers whose eyes were fixed on a spot at the center of the screen. Each slide contained two overlapping forms, one green and one red, and subjects were instructed to attend to just one color (some to green, others to red). (See Figure 9.12.) Most of the forms were nonsense shapes, but some were shaped like a familiar object, such as a house or a tree. After viewing the sequence, subjects were tested for their ability to recognize which forms had been shown, and the result was that they recognized most of the forms that had been presented in the attended color, but performed only at chance level on those that had been presented in the unattended color, regardless of whether the form was a nonsense shape or a familiar figure. Still, they did notice some of the physical characteristics of the unattended forms. For example, they were able to say if a form was unusually large or small, or was composed of a dotted line rather than solid. Thus, as was typical in selective-listening studies, people frequently picked up basic physical features but not the meaning of unattended visual stimuli.

An experiment by Robert Becklen and Daniel Cervone (1983) shows an even more dramatic example of selective viewing. These researchers made two separate videotapes of the same three men moving around a room, throwing a basketball to each other. In one tape the men wore black shirts and in the other they wore white shirts. Then, with the aid of a mirror, the researchers showed the two tapes fully overlapping on the same screen, creating an effect such as would occur if a television set were showing two channels at once. A casual viewer would see six individuals moving around, throwing basketballs, with one individual or a ball sometimes passing ghostlike through another. In the experiment, subjects were asked to attend just to the black-shirted players and to press a button each time one of them passed the ball, a task that they performed quite accurately. Midway through the 1-minute film an event occurred that, to a casual observer, was very noticeable. A woman carrying a large white umbrella sauntered across the playing area, spending a total of 5.5 seconds on screen, walking right through some of the players and the ball they were throwing (see Figure 9.13). Remarkably, when questioned immedi-

*Evidence that people effectively screen out irrelevant visual stimuli that overlap relevant visual stimuli*

**Figure 9.12  Overlapping forms used in an experiment on attention**

*To assess the degree to which vision can be selective, Rock and Gutman (1981) asked subjects to pay attention either to just the red or just the green shapes in a series of slides such as this, and then tested their recognition for both shapes in each slide. (From Rock, 1984.)*

**Figure 9.13  Overlapping videos**

*Becklen and Cervone found that subjects attending to the black shirted players did not notice the woman with the umbrella crossing the screen. (Adapted from Becklen and Cervone, 1983.)*

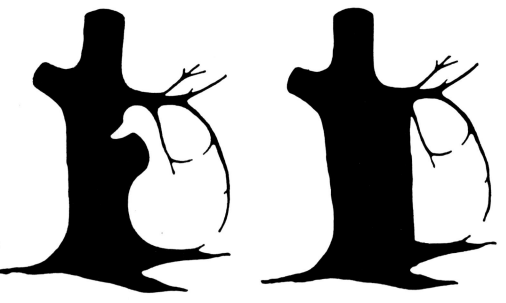

**Figure 9.14** *Tree with and without a duck*

*When subjects were presented with the stimulus on the left (in three 1-second flashes on a screen), they were aware of seeing a tree but not a duck. Yet, when subsequently asked to draw a nature scene, they were more likely to draw a scene having to do with ducks than were those who had been presented with the stimulus on the right. (From Eagle & others, 1966.)*

■ *Evidence that unconscious processing for meaning may occur in vision, as it does in audition*

■ *Evidence that practice in a particular task or set of tasks allows one to attend to more information at once*

ately afterward, only eighteen of the eighty-five subjects in the experiment had any memory of seeing a woman carrying an umbrella. Apparently, people who are focused intensely on a visual task are quite effective at screening out irrelevant information.

As is true for auditory stimuli, however, there is some evidence that the meaning of an unattended visual stimulus can be registered in some way and affect the person's behavior, even when the person does not consciously notice the stimulus. In one experiment suggesting this, Morris Eagle and his colleagues (1966) presented students briefly with either of the two visual stimuli shown in Figure 9.14. If you look carefully, you will see that the left-hand stimulus contains the outline of a duck, formed by the tree trunk and its branches. The researchers found that subjects who saw the stimulus for a brief period did not consciously notice the duck, yet, when they were asked subsequently to draw a nature scene, those who had seen the stimulus containing a duck were more likely to draw a scene having to do with ducks than were those who had seen the stimulus on the right.

**Effects of Practice on the Ability to Divide Attention**   While research on selective listening and viewing typically emphasizes the narrowness of attention, some researchers—most notably, Ulrich Neisser and his colleagues—have been more impressed by people's ability to divide their attention and to deal concurrently with a great deal of information, at a high level. In everyday life we frequently engage in more than one complex perceptual task at a time. For example, to drive a car safely you must keep track simultaneously of other traffic, the road, pedestrians, your speedometer, your own car's movement, and so on; and yet, if you are an experienced driver, you can do all that *and* carry on an intelligent conversation or watch along the road for a particular house number. The first of the additional tasks (carrying on the conversation) is probably easier than the second, because it involves a different sensory system and different cognitive processes from those involved in watching traffic and pedestrians. A good deal of research has shown that the more different two tasks are, the easier it is to carry them out simultaneously (Allport & others, 1972). Thus, it is much easier to watch for a signal on a screen and listen to a story than to watch two screens for different kinds of signals, or to listen to two stories.

Neisser (1976) has argued that the ability to perceive and respond to a large amount of information—whether in the same sense modality or different modalities—is best thought of as a *skill*, which, like any skill, improves with practice. He believes that there is no fixed limit to attentional capacity. Backing up this view, Neisser and his colleagues have shown that practice improves people's ability to divide attention. In one study (described in Becklen & Cervone, 1983), they found

**Headed for a fall**
*People differ in their ability to attend selectively to multiple stimuli. Although practice certainly helps develop the skill, some people may stretch it to the point of serious risk.*

■ **Evidence that the effect of practice on the ability to process many stimuli at once may be due to automatization**

that subjects who had a lot of practice at viewing overlapping videos (like that depicted in Figure 9.13) were more likely than less practiced subjects to notice events that were irrelevant to the task at hand—including the woman with the umbrella in a replication of Becklen and Cervone's study. Apparently, once the task was well learned, and thus easier, people could devote more attention to other aspects of the incoming stimulation. In other experiments, Neisser and his colleagues studied the ability of college students to perform simultaneously two cognitively similar attention-demanding tasks, both involving verbal ability (Spelke & others, 1976; Hirst & others, 1980). One was to read an unfamiliar story or encyclopedia article, and the other was to write down words or sentences dictated by the experimenter. At first the requirement of taking dictation interfered greatly with reading, but after many hours of practice subjects could do both at once with no loss of reading speed or comprehension, compared to control trials in which they read without taking dictation.

**Automatization of Perception**   Theorists who, contrary to Neisser, maintain that there are fixed limits to attentional capacity argue that practice does not increase the amount of information to which a person can attend, but rather increases the amount of information that he or she can analyze automatically, without attention. That is, they argue that with practice an increasing amount of the stimulus input is analyzed and responded to at a stage of information processing that precedes consciousness.

Walter Schneider and his colleagues (1984) have studied the automatization of perception in work that can be best understood by relating it to Treisman's work on feature detection. Treisman, you may recall, found that stimuli that are distinguished from others in certain primitive features, such as line orientation or color, can be detected at a glance, without a controlled search through the whole set of stimuli (shown in Figure 9.9). Schneider and his colleagues found that, with extended and consistent practice, stimulus differences that are more complex than those described by Treisman begin to pop out in a similar way. In their experiments, slides containing from one to four letters each were presented in rapid succession, and the subject's task was to press one button if any of a certain set of previously memorized target letters was present on the slide, and a different button if not. Accuracy and speed in the task were at first influenced by the number of distractor letters on the slide, but not after subjects had a great deal of practice with a given set of target letters. After much practice, subjects were able to notice immediately whether a target was present, regardless of how many other letters also appeared on the slide. Their ability at that time was like that of a skilled reader of medical x-rays, who at a glance sees the subtle but telltale signs of a malignancy; or a skilled driver, who with no conscious effort notices the slight swerving of one of the many cars in view; or a skilled maple sugarer, who cannot describe the difference between sugar maples and other trees but registers automatically that difference in deciding which trees to tap.

To say that a perceptual skill has become automatic is to say that certain information will be picked up whether or not the person is consciously trying to pick it up. This has its drawbacks as well as its advantages. Schneider and his colleagues (1984) found that once subjects could automatically distinguish target letters from distractors, they had unusual difficulty with new tasks in which previous targets were now among the distractors. Their attention continued to be drawn automatically to the previous targets, which slowed them down in finding the new targets. Similarly, if you are a skilled driver and are riding in the front passenger seat of a car, looking forward out the window, perhaps you can't help noticing that the car ahead of you is slowing down, and can't help pushing your foot down on an imaginary brake (the response, as well as the perception, is automatic), even though you are trying to be a relaxed, trusting passenger. In other words, perception can become not only automatic but obligatory; even with conscious effort we have difficulty ignoring stimuli that we have learned to respond to automatically.

One often-cited example of the obligatory nature of automatic perception is the **Stroop interference effect**, named after J. Ridley Stroop (1935), who was the first to describe it. Stroop showed people cards that contained words or other shapes printed in colored ink and asked them to name, as rapidly as possible, the ink color on each card. In some cases the word on a card was the name of the color of the ink in which it was printed (for example, the word *red* printed in red ink); in others it was the name of a different color (for example, the word *blue* printed in red ink); and in still others it was not a color name. The main result was that people were much slower at naming the ink color when the card contained the word for a different color than in any of the other cases. Even after considerable practice at trying to ignore the words and attend only to the ink color, the inhibitory effect persisted. To demonstrate this effect yourself, follow the instructions in Figure 9.15. Apparently, when primed to report color names, people find it almost impos-

▮ *Evidence that automatic processing can sometimes interfere with conscious processing*

**Figure 9.15 *The Stroop interference effect***

*Time yourself (or a friend) on each of the following tasks: (1) Name the colors in each box in column (a). (2) Name the ink colors used to print the words in columns (b), (c), and (d). (Time each of these separately.) Column (c) will take the longest, because the color words interfere with naming the ink colors—that is the Stroop interference effect. Column (d) may also take somewhat longer than either (a) or (b), because the noncolor words interfere somewhat with naming the ink colors. Column (b) should be quickest, because there the words facilitate naming the ink colors.*

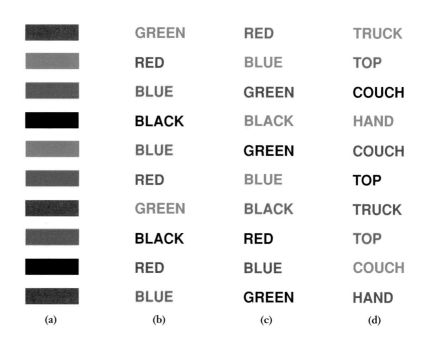

sible *not* to read color names that appear before their eyes, and the reading inhibits the response of naming the ink color when the two are different. As you would expect, children who have not yet learned to read are not susceptible to the Stroop effect, and children who are just learning to read are only slightly susceptible to it (Gibson, 1971). In fact, the Stroop effect is sometimes used as an index of the extent to which reading has become automatic for a child.

**Theories of Attention**   Suppose you were trying to design a machine that could select among sensory inputs in ways that were consistent with the research on attention that you have just been reading about. What would be the machine's main components, and what would each component do? That is the question that perceptual psychologists tackle when they develop theories, or models, of attention.

In Figure 9.16, I have diagrammed a simple model of attention that contains the most common components that perceptual psychologists have included in their more complex models (see Johnston & Dark, 1986; Kahneman & Treisman, 1984; and Schneider & Shiffrin, 1977). Notice that the model contains two main information-processing compartments. The first, called *automatic*, or *preattentive*, *processing*, receives input from the senses and performs some preliminary analysis of it. In most models, this compartment is assumed to be unselective and essentially unlimited in capacity, acting in parallel on all incoming information at once. The second compartment, called *controlled*, or *attentive*, *processing*, is assumed to be selective, limited in capacity, and to act serially only on a small portion of the available information. Attentive processing usually is assumed to be conscious, whereas preattentive processing is unconscious. The *selector*, which determines what enters the attentive compartment, is depicted between the two compartments.

> ■ *What different models of attention have in common, and how they differ*

**Figure 9.16** *A generalized model of attention*

*All sensory input is processed, in parallel, in the preattentive compartment, and then some of it is selected to enter the attentive compartment for further processing. The arrow going from the attentive compartment to the selector indicates top-down control of the selection criteria.*

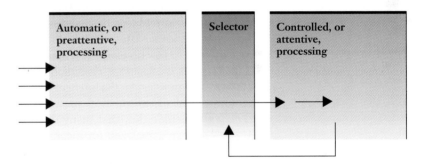

Given these common components, various theories have differed in their description of (a) the amount or kind of processing that can occur preattentively, (b) the nature of the selector, and (c) the sources of influence that can modify the selector (so that it selects different kinds of information at different times). One of the first such theories, developed by Donald Broadbent (1958), proposed that the preattentive compartment analyzes only the physical features of sensory stimuli, and that the selection of material into attention is based entirely on physical features. The selector in that *filter theory* was thought of as analogous to a filter (or sieve), which completely blocks passage of most particles but allows through those particles that have a particular physical definition. The nature of the filter—that is, which physical features it bases its distinction on—is varied by mechanisms in the attentive compartment that choose the stimulus track to be attended (say, a particular person's voice as defined by properties such as pitch range). This theory accounts for people's ability to hear or to see selectively based on physical distinctions, and to close out meanings in the unattended message, but does not account for the finding that sometimes meaning in unattended messages comes through.

To account for the registration of meaning from unattended messages, Anne Treisman (1969) modified Broadbent's original theory. She proposed that the selector is analogous not to a filter but to an electrical attenuator. It does not completely block unattended information, but rather attenuates its flow; that is, it weakens the input as if turning down the volume. This *attenuation theory* accounts for people's experience that unattended information is not completely absent from consciousness, but rather is less distinct and more quickly forgotten than is information to which one is attending. Because unattended information enters the second compartment, though in weakened form, it can potentially be analyzed for meaning. If the receiving mechanism in the second compartment is highly sensitive to certain stimuli (such as the person's own name), or has been prepared to receive certain stimuli (because of the meaning of previous input), those stimuli will be picked up and analyzed for meaning even though they have been attenuated. Once picked up, these stimuli can cause the person to switch attention from one input source to another.

Broadbent's and Treisman's theories are sometimes called ***early-selection theories***, because they both propose that the selection occurs early in the processing of stimulus input, before it is analyzed for meaning. ***Late-selection theories***, in contrast, propose that the preattentive compartment analyzes stimulus input at least to some degree for meaning as well as for physical characteristics, and that the meaning contributes to the determination of whether the information will be selected into the attentive compartment. Richard Shiffrin and Walter Schneider (1977), for example, developed a late-selection theory based on their experiments on the automatization of perception, discussed earlier. Through experience, the preattentive compartment becomes able to process stimuli for meaning, so that many familiar stimuli can be processed at a time without conscious attention. All studies showing that stimuli can be analyzed for meaning without consciousness can be taken as evidence for late-selection theories (see Duncan, 1980; Marcel, 1983).

How do early-selection theories, such as Treisman's, explain unconscious analysis of meaning? Essentially, they do this by distinguishing between attention and consciousness (Kahneman & Treisman, 1984). These theories suggest that a great deal of information passes into the attentive compartment and is analyzed for meaning, but that many degrees of consciousness are possible and only some of what is analyzed for meaning becomes conscious in a way that allows it to be remembered from one moment to the next. In these theories, selection into the attentive compartment is based on physical features, and all further processing occurs within that compartment. Such theories must include some way of accounting for further selection within the attentive compartment, such that some of the material there becomes sharply conscious and the rest doesn't.

Notice that the same bottom-up and top-down processes that were discussed previously in relation to object recognition are involved in attention. In fact, theories of attention are part and parcel of theories of object recognition. Stimuli in the environment are registered by the senses and are processed bottom-up. But information that is already in the mind works, top-down, to select from the registered stimuli those elements of information that are needed to form a conscious perception in line with the mind's conceptions or needs. As you might have guessed, Treisman's theory of attention is closely tied to her theory of pattern recognition. Stages 1 and 2 in her pattern-recognition theory (shown in Figure 9.9) correspond to the preattentive and attentive compartments of the attention model of Figure 9.16. In Treisman's view, only primitive stimulus features are analyzed preattentively, and pattern recognition occurs in the attentive compartment.

*The difference between early-selection and late-selection theories*

*Seeing the light*

*How do we judge the size of the people and the objects in this photograph? In this section you will learn how we can see a three-dimensional world in a two-dimensional representation.*

■ *How the unconscious-inference theory explains perception as analysis of cues*

## Perceiving Objects in Relation to Space: Depth, Size, and Motion Perception

Object recognition and attention are closely related not only to each other, but also to the topics to which we turn now—the perception of the depth, size, and movement of objects in space. Our visual world is one of three-dimensional space. It is not flat and static, but is filled with objects that (a) exist at differing depths (different distances from our eyes), (b) have definite sizes (take up certain amounts of space), and (c) may move from one position in space to another. How do we perceive the depth, size, and motion of objects?

Traditionally, psychologists interested in these issues have thought of the stimulus world as providing *cues* that the mind then uses, detective-like, to draw inferences about the depths, sizes, and movements of objects in view. What are the cues that allow the mind to infer that one object is closer than another? Or larger than another? Or moving while the other is stationary? The perspective that begins with these questions is called the ***unconscious-inference theory of perception***. This theory assumes that the preattentive (unconscious) compartment of the mind (a) analyzes cues that come from the sensory input; (b) builds up (infers) from those cues a perception that has qualities of depth, size, and movement; and (c) sends that perception on to the conscious (attentive) mind. Since the unconscious-inference theory has guided most research on depth, size, and motion perception, it also guides most of the discussion here. However, discussion at the end of the chapter contrasts this theory to a different broad perspective, the ***direct-perception theory***, which maintains that the mind need not act as a detective to infer the qualities of the perceptual world, because those qualities are all richly represented in the stimulus input and are simply picked up and registered by the senses, such that no inference is necessary.

### Perceiving Depth

If you stop reading for a moment and raise your eyes from this page you can see clearly all three dimensions of space. You see (1) an up-down dimension (an object can be above or below another), (2) a side-to-side dimension (an object can be to the right or left of another), and (3) a dimension of depth (an object can be farther away or closer than another in your line of sight). It is relatively easy to understand how you see the first two of these dimensions because they are preserved on the two-dimensional surface of the retina (see Figure 8.10). But how can you see the third dimension? What information on your two-dimensional retinas permits you to see depth? This question has long fascinated philosophers and psychologists, and over the years an impressive number of potential cues for depth perception have been described and studied.

**Binocular Cues**   Depth perception works best when you use both eyes. You can prove that with a simple demonstration. Pick up two pencils and hold them in front of you, one in each hand, with their points toward each other. Now, with one eye closed, move the pencils toward each other to make the points touch at their tips. Chances are, you will miss by a little bit on your first attempt, and your subsequent adjustments will have something of a trial-and-error quality. Now repeat the task with both eyes open. Is it easier? Do you find that now you can see which adjustments to make to bring the points together and that you no longer need trial and error?

Research shows that two types of cues contribute to the binocular advantage. The less important of the two is *convergence*, the inward turning of the eyes that occurs when you look at an object that is close to you. The closer an object is, the more the two eyes must converge in order to look at it. To experience this cue consciously, try focusing both eyes on your finger as you hold it a few inches in front of your nose. In theory, the perceptual system could judge the distance of an object from the degree to which the eyes converge when looking at it. In practice, however, convergence is a poor cue for distance. Experiments in which convergence is the only cue available indicate that it is useful for objects that are very close to the eyes (within a few inches), but not for other objects (see Hochberg, 1971).

The other, far more important cue requiring two eyes is **binocular disparity**. Because the eyes are about 6 centimeters apart, they view an object from slightly different directions, thus providing slightly different (disparate) views of it. To see how these different views can contribute to depth perception, hold a closed book vertically in front of you, with its binding toward you, as shown in Figure 9.17. Notice that with both eyes open you can see not only the binding but also both the front and back covers of the book. You see the front cover with your right eye and the back cover with your left eye. (You can prove this by closing one eye and then the other.) If you move the book farther away, you will find that the two eyes' views become less different (less disparate) than they were when the book was closer. The binding, which is the part of the view that the two eyes share, now takes up relatively more space and the covers take up relatively less space in either eye's view than they did before. Thus, the degree of disparity between the two eyes' views can serve as a cue to judge an object's distance from the eyes—the less the disparity, the greater the distance.

The ability to see depth when binocular disparity is the only depth cue available—called *stereopsis*—was first demonstrated in the early nineteenth century by Charles Wheatstone (see Hochberg, 1971). Wheatstone wondered what would happen if he drew two slightly different pictures of the same object or scene, one as seen by the left eye and one as seen by the right, and then viewed them simultaneously, each with the appropriate eye. To permit such viewing, he invented a device called a *stereoscope*. The effect was dramatic. When viewed through the stereoscope, the two pictures were fused perceptually into a single image containing

■ *How binocular disparity can serve as a cue for depth, and evidence that this cue can make a pair of flat pictures look three-dimensional*

**Entertainment in depth**

*As you enter the movie theater, you receive a pair of cardboard frames with one red lens and one green. The glasses permit each eye to see a slightly different image, creating a strong impression of three-dimensionality.*

depth. Stereoscopes were a great fad during the late nineteenth century. People could see scenes such as Buckingham Palace or the Grand Canyon in full depth by placing cards that contained two photographs of the same scene, shot simultaneously from slightly different angles, into their stereoscope (The Viewmaster, a child's toy, is a type of a stereoscope in common use today.) Three-dimensional motion pictures or comic books employ the same general principle. Each frame of the film or comic strip contains double images superimposed on one another, each in a different color, and the viewer wears colored glasses that allow only one image to enter each eye.

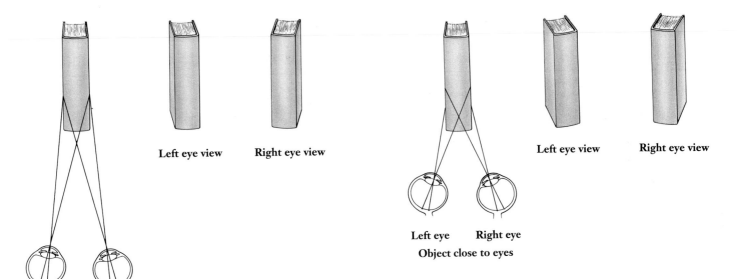

Left eye view    Right eye view

Left eye view    Right eye view

Left eye    Right eye
Object close to eyes

Left eye    Right eye
Object distant from eyes

**Figure 9.17 *Demonstration of binocular disparity***

*If you hold a book in front of you and view it first with one eye and then the other, you will see two different views with each eye, as shown here. You will also notice that the book shifts its position relative to background objects as you shift from one eye to the other. The farther away the book, the less difference you see with two eyes. The brain fuses the two images into a three-dimensional perception.*

■ *How motion parallax can serve as a cue for depth, and how it is similar to binocular disparity*

**Monocular Cues**    Although depth perception is better with two eyes, it is by no means absent with one. One important cue that does not depend on two eyes is *motion parallax*, which refers to the changed view one has of a scene or object when one's head moves sideways to the scene or object. You can demonstrate the role of this cue in depth perception in a way very similar to the demonstration for binocular disparity. Hold the book up with the binding toward you again (as in Figure 9.17) and view it now with just one eye as you rock your head back and forth. As your head moves, you gain different views of the book, seeing first one cover and then the other. If you now move the book farther away, the same head movement produces a less-changed view. Thus, the degree of change in either eye's view at one moment compared to the next, as the head moves in space, can serve as a cue for assessing the object's distance from the eyes—the smaller the change, the greater the distance.

As you can see from this demonstration, motion parallax is very similar to binocular disparity. In fact, binocular disparity is sometimes called *binocular parallax*. The word *parallax* refers to the apparent change in an object or scene that occurs when it is viewed from a new vantagepoint. In motion parallax the changed vantagepoint comes from the movement of the head, and in binocular parallax (or disparity) it comes from the separation of the two eyes. Motion parallax also accounts for a phenomenon that you have probably noticed many times while staring out the side window of a moving train or car: Objects that are farther away cross your field of view more slowly than do those that are nearby. Signs or utility poles next to the road race past you, while trees off in the distance pass leisurely by. At the farthest extreme, the sun (which, for perceptual purposes, is infinitely distant) doesn't move past you at all, but seems to float through the sky at the same speed and direction as you and the train or car. Again, the closer the scene or object, the more sharply your view of it changes as your head moves sideways to it.

**Figure 9.18** *Pictorial cues for depth*
*Occlusion, relative image size for familiar objects, linear perspective, texture gradient, and position relative to the horizon all serve as depth cues in this picture.*

■ *Five pictorial cues for depth*

Motion parallax depends on the geometry of true three-dimensionality and cannot be used to depict depth in two-dimensional pictures. All of the remaining monocular depth cues, however, can provide a sense of depth in pictures as well as in the real three-dimensional world, and thus are called ***pictorial cues***. You can identify the most important of these by examining Figure 9.18 and thinking of all the reasons why you see the man as standing in the foreground and the house as more distant.

  ■ *Occlusion* The man partially occludes (cuts off) the view of the house, which indicates that the man is closer to us than is the house. Near objects occlude more distant ones.

  ■ *Relative image size for familiar objects* The image of the man (both in the picture and on the viewer's retina) is taller than that of the house. Because we know that people are not taller than houses, we take the man's larger image as a sign that he must be closer to us than is the house.

  ■ *Linear perspective* The lines marking the sides of the driveway converge as they go from the man to the house, indicating that the house is farther away. Parallel lines appear to converge as they become more distant.

  ■ *Texture gradient* Texture elements of the picture, such as the stones on the driveway and the grass blades on the lawn, become gradually smaller, more densely packed, and less defined moving from the man to the house.

  ■ *Position relative to the horizon* The house is closer to the horizon than is the man. In outdoor scenes, objects nearer the horizon are usually seen as farther away than are those that are displaced from the horizon either up or down (see also Figure 9.19).

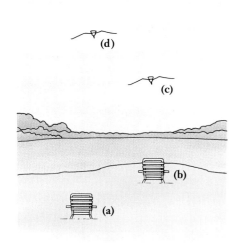

**Figure 9.19** *Proximity to the horizon as a depth cue*
*In this picture, (b) and (c) are seen as farther away than (a) and (d), respectively, because they are closer to the horizon.*

## Perceiving Size

**The Relationship of Size Perception to Depth Perception**   The ability to judge the size of an object is tied intimately to the ability to judge its distance. As Figure 9.20 illustrates, the size of the retinal image of an object is inversely proportional to the object's distance from the retina. Thus, if an object is moved twice as far away, it produces a retinal image half the height and width it did before. But you don't see the object as smaller, just farther away. The ability to see an object as un-

**Figure 9.20** *Relationship of retinal image size to object size and distance*

*If object B is twice as tall as object A, and is twice as far away, the two objects will produce the same-height retinal image (upper figure). If object C is the same height as object A, but is twice as far away, it will produce a retinal image half as tall as that produced by A (compare the lower figure to the upper).*

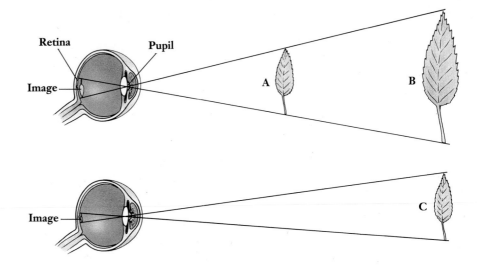

■ *How the ability to assess size accurately depends on perception of an object's distance from the eyes*

changed in size, despite change in the image size as it moves farther away or closer, is called *size constancy*. For familiar objects, such as a pencil or your father, previous knowledge of the object's size probably contributes to size constancy. But size constancy also occurs for unfamiliar objects if cues for distance are available.

Psychologists have shown that people cannot judge the size of unfamiliar objects without cues about distance. In one such experiment, subjects were asked to judge the relative sizes of objects that were placed at different distances down each of two hallways (Holway & Boring, 1941). As long as some depth cues were available, the judgments were quite accurate. The researchers then eliminated all such cues by requiring the subjects to view each object with one eye (eliminating binocular cues), through a peephole (eliminating motion parallax), and with the hallway completely darkened except for the object being viewed (eliminating pictorial cues). Under these conditions the subjects could no longer judge size accurately. With no depth cues, an object that was twice as tall and wide, but also twice as far away, as a second object appeared to be the same size as the second object.

*A size-distance illusion*

*We know that these young women must be approximately the same size, so what explains this illusion? The room is distorted; some walls and both windows are trapezoidal in shape. When we view this scene through a peephole (or the camera's eye), we automatically assume that the setting is normal, that the occupants are the same distance away, and therefore that their size is different.*

Müller-Lyer illusion

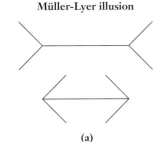

(a)

Ponzo illusion

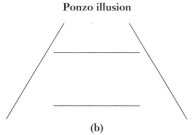

(b)

**Figure 9.21** *The Müller-Lyer and Ponzo illusions*

*In each case, one horizontal bar looks longer than the other, although they are actually the same length.*

■ *How unconscious assessment of depth may provide the basis for three size illusions*

**Preattentive Depth Processing as an Explanation for Size Illusions**   Visual illusions are misperceptions that occur under conditions in which certain cues that would be present when viewing most normal, real-world scenes are missing. Perceptual psychologists usually study illusions not for their own sake (though they are interesting), but because such study can help isolate from the many cues available in normal scenes those that are most critical in producing a particular perceptual effect. Here we will examine some research on size illusions that has taught perceptual psychologists about the normal information-processing steps involved in size perception.

Figure 9.21 illustrates two classic size illusions: the **Müller-Lyer illusion** (first described by F. C. Müller-Lyer in the mid-nineteenth century) and the **Ponzo illusion** (first described by Mario Ponzo in 1913). In each illusion two horizontal bars appear to be different in length, but if you measure them you will discover that they are identical. A more ancient example of a size illusion, which intrigued the ancient Greeks and Romans, is the **moon illusion**. Have you ever noticed how huge the moon looks when it is near the earth's horizon, just above the trees or buildings in the distance? Sometimes people even mistake it for the sun. The moon looks much smaller when it is closer to the zenith (straight up). This difference is truly an illusion. Objectively, the moon is the same size, and the same distance from us, whether it is located at the horizon or zenith. If you view the horizon moon through a peephole, so that you see it in isolation from other objects such as trees and buildings, the illusion disappears; it looks no larger than it does at the zenith.

The most common explanation of size illusions is the *depth-processing theory* (see Rock, 1984). This theory—consistent with everything said so far about the relation between size and distance—maintains that one object in each illusion appears larger than the other because of distance cues that, at some early stage of perceptual processing, make it appear farther away. If one object is judged to be farther away, but produces the same-sized retinal image, then it is judged to be larger than the other. This theory applies most readily to the Ponzo illusion, in which the two converging lines provide the depth cue of linear perspective, causing (according to the theory) the upper bar to be judged as farther away and hence larger than the lower one. The photograph in Figure 9.22 makes this point clear.

**Figure 9.22** *Depth-processing explanation of the Ponzo illusion*

*If this were a real, three-dimensional scene, not a photograph, the red object in the background would not only look larger but would* be *larger than that in the foreground. (Adapted from Gregory, 1968.)*

**Figure 9.23  *Depth-processing explanation of the Müller-Lyer illusion***

*Compare these sawhorses to the Müller-Lyer drawings in Figure 9.21. If these were real sawhorses, viewed from above in the three-dimensional world, the upside-down one would be longer than the rightside-up one.*

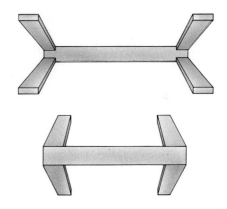

The application of the depth-processing theory to the Müller-Lyer and moon illusions is a bit more subtle. The assumption in this application is that people see the figures as three-dimensional objects, something like sawhorses viewed from above. The object with wings extending outward (top drawing in Figure 9.21a) may be seen as an upside-down sawhorse, with legs toward the viewer, and the one with inward wings (bottom drawing) may be seen as a rightside-up sawhorse, with its horizontal bar closer to the observer. If real sawhorses were viewed this way, the horizontal bar of the upside-down one would be farther from the observer than that of the rightside-up one, and if it produced the same-sized retinal image it would in fact be longer (see Figure 9.23). Regarding the moon illusion, recall that objects near the horizon are commonly seen as farther away than those that are displaced from the horizon (look back at Figure 9.19). With respect to most objects, such as trees, mountains, birds, and clouds, those nearer the horizon usually *are* farther away, so perhaps the perceptual system assumes that the moon is farther away at the horizon than at the zenith, and hence judges the horizon moon as larger. This theory of the moon illusion was first proposed by the Greek astronomer Ptolomy in the second century. Experiments by Lloyd Kaufman and Irvin Rock (1962), illustrated and described in Figure 9.24, have supported this theory more recently.

The depth-processing theory seems to offer an elegant, unitary explanation of the three illusions just described, but perhaps you have already thought of a problem with the explanation. Most people, when they look at the Müller-Lyer figures, do *not* see them as three-dimensional objects, but rather as flat, arrowlike objects; yet, they still see the illusion. Similarly, when people see the large-appearing horizon moon and are asked whether it seems farther away or closer than usual, they

**Figure 9.24  *Depth-processing explanation of the moon illusion***

*The upper curve shows the true positions of the moon as it pursues its circular orbit around the earth. If people unconsciously perceive the moon as moving across a sky shaped like a flattened dome (lower curve), the same-sized retinal image will appear smaller at the zenith than at the horizon, as indicated by the darker discs (compare this to the size-depth relation shown in Figure 9.20). As a separate test of whether people see the sky as a flattened dome consistent with the illusion, Kaufman and Rock asked subjects to direct a pointer midway between the horizon and the zenith. Line B shows the average direction in which they pointed. Notice that line B points to the midpoint appropriate for the flattened-dome view of the sky, and not that appropriate for the half-sphere view, which is indicated by line A. (Adapted from Kaufman & Rock, 1962.)*

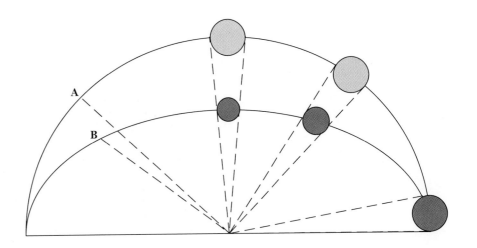

usually say closer. Even with the Ponzo illusion, many people do not notice depth in the figure; they do not see the top bar as farther away than the bottom one, but they still see the illusion.

To preserve the depth-processing explanation, theorists (for example, Gregory, 1968) have argued that depth may be assessed by two different mechanisms —one operating automatically and unconsciously, in the preattentive-processing compartment, and the other operating consciously, in the attentive compartment. Perhaps the cues just described lead to an unconscious perception that one object is farther away. But when asked to make a conscious judgment of distance, people may use other information, such as their knowledge that the Ponzo and Müller-Lyer illusions are two-dimensional drawings, or the large apparent size of the horizon moon in the moon illusion, and this may lead to a conscious assessment of distance that is different from the unconscious assessment.

If this explanation turns out to be true, it tells us something interesting about the sequence of steps by which size and depth judgments are made. It tells us that at least in some situations depth is assessed unconsciously before the conscious assessment of size is made; and then depth is assessed again consciously after the assessment of size is made. When cues are ambiguous, the second size assessment can be at odds with the first. Thus, the sequence for perceptual assessments about the horizon moon may be as follows: (1) Unconscious, preattentive processes judge that the moon is farther away than usual (because objects near the horizon are usually farthest away). (2) Unconscious processes judge that the moon is larger than usual (because if it is farther away but produces the same-sized retinal image, it must be larger). (3) The judgment that the moon looks larger than usual enters consciousness and leads to the conscious judgment that it must be closer than usual (because we know that the moon doesn't really change size, so its large apparent size must be due to closeness).

**Assimilation as Another Explanation for Size Illusions**    Not all researchers agree with the depth-processing explanation of size illusions, and few accept it as the only explanation. Of various alternatives offered, one that has drawn considerable research interest is the *assimilation theory*, which maintains that the visual system tends to incorporate nearby elements into an object's boundaries when assessing its size (Rock, 1984). This explanation applies most readily to the ***frame illusion***, in which a frame surrounding an enclosed area makes the enclosed area seem larger (see Figure 9.25), but it may also partly explain the three illusions discussed above.

Regarding the Müller-Lyer illusion, you could imagine that at some unconscious level the perceptual system compromises between two alternative sets of boundaries in assessing the length of each bar; one set consists of the actual ends of the bar, and the other consists of the tips of the attached wings. When the wings extend outward the compromise increases the apparent length of the bar, and

**Figure 9.25  *The frame illusion***

*The shaded area is actually the same size in each of these drawings, but to most people it appears larger with an outside frame (b) and smaller with an inside frame (c). The shaded area also appears larger when any cues are added that would tend to draw the eyes from its border outward (d), and smaller when any cues are added that would tend to draw the eyes from its border inward (e). According to the assimilation theory of size illusions, stimuli near an object's boundary tend to be assimilated into the perception of the boundary, moving it outward or inward, depending on where the stimuli are located.*

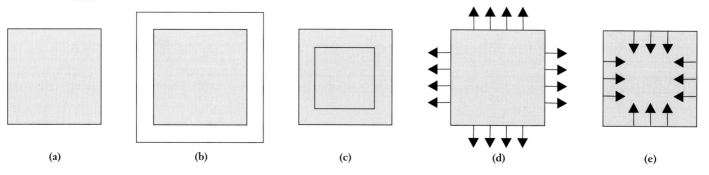

(a)            (b)            (c)            (d)            (e)

**How the assimilation theory may partly explain the Müller-Lyer, Ponzo, and moon illusions**

when they move inward it decreases the apparent length. Experiments that support this explanation show that size illusions can occur to some degree in figures that are analogous to the Müller-Lyer figure but lack any suggestion of depth, as illustrated in Figure 9.26. The Ponzo illusion may also be partly explained in terms of assimilation—the bar whose ends are closer to the two outside lines may seem larger because the outside lines are assimilated into its perception, and the other bar may seem smaller because the outside lines are too far away to be assimilated (Rock, 1984). Similarly, for the moon illusion, the perceived horizon moon may assimilate into it other objects that appear near the moon at the horizon, whereas the perceived zenith moon has no objects near it that can be assimilated.

**Figure 9.26 Müller-Lyer type illusions without depth cues**

*In (b) the ends of each bar and tips of each wing are represented by dots, and in (c) the figure is simplified still further by replacing the wings with an x, either outside or inside the dots. In neither (b) nor (c) are there cues for depth, yet the illusion remains to some degree. In (b) and (c) most people see the two dots representing the ends of the bars as farther apart in the top figure than in the bottom figure. Such findings suggest that the illusion may be caused partly by a tendency for the nearby elements to be assimilated into the length that is being judged. (Adapted from Coren, 1986.)*

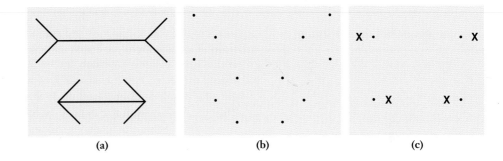

(a)          (b)          (c)

## Perceiving Motion

As mentioned in Chapter 8, movement-detector neurons have been found in the visual cortex, which respond to images that move across the retina in a particular direction and velocity. But the problem of movement perception is more complex than one of sensitivity to images moving across the retina. To convince yourself of this, imagine two different scenes. In the first, you are watching a car moving down the street. You keep your eyes fixed on the car, so its image remains stationary in the center of each fovea, yet you see the car as moving. All other objects in the scene, such as the lampposts that the car drives past, are moving across each retina as your eyes move to follow the car, yet you see them as stationary. In the second scene, you are sitting in the park admiring the flowers when a dog and squirrel dash across your line of sight. In this case, the objects that produce stationary retinal images are seen as stationary, and those that produce moving images are seen as moving. If you happen to have been moving your eyes at the same time, say from one flower to another, *all* of the objects would produce images that move across the retina, at differing speeds; yet you would still see the flowers as stationary and the dog and squirrel as moving. Given that either stationary or moving objects can produce images that move across the retina, how does the perceptual system decide what is moving?

**Why motion perception is not a trivial problem for the perceptual system to solve**

In theory, there are two possible solutions to the problem just described. One possibility is that the perceptual system keeps track of eye movements and factors them into an equation to assess objects' movement. If the eyes are moving at a certain rate and direction, and the image is moving across the retina at a certain rate and direction, then the object must be moving at a certain rate and direction. The other possibility is that the perceptual system establishes among the objects in any given scene a stable frame of reference and uses that, regardless of eye movements, to assess the movement of other objects. There is evidence that both of these solutions are correct, since illusory movement can result from faulty information about eye movements or a faulty frame of reference (see Rock, 1984). But here I will pursue only the second of the two, which under normal conditions is probably the more important.

**Importance of a Frame of Reference**   Movement, by its very definition, is a relativistic concept. Objects are said to have moved if they change their position, over time, with respect to other objects that provide the frame of reference. The earth moves relative to other parts of the universe, but our perceptual system is unaware of this and most commonly takes the earth and fixed objects on it as the frame of reference. In some cases, such as when you are in a train or airplane and not looking out the window, the frame of reference is not the earth, but rather objects fixed to the inside of the compartment in which you are traveling. The person sleeping in the seat beside you is in such cases seen as stationary, while the person walking down the aisle is seen as moving.

The importance of a frame of reference is demonstrated by movement illusions that occur when there is scant or ambiguous information about which elements should be taken as the frame of reference. If you are in a stationary train looking out the window at the side of another train right next to yours, and that train starts to move, you may experience your train as moving. That is because your visual system has established the other train as the frame of reference. Another, more romantic example is the *moon-cloud illusion*, which you have experienced if you have ever gazed up at the sky on a cloudy evening and seen the moon sailing across gaps in the clouds. In reality the motion of the moon with respect to the earth is too slow to detect, so its apparent movement from one cloud to the next is an illusion. Clouds, on the other hand, do drift across the sky at a perceptible rate. When you gaze up in the evening, with nothing but the clouds and the moon in your view, your perceptual system sometimes takes the clouds as the frame of reference and interprets the relative change in position of clouds and moon as movement of the moon. More systematic evidence of the importance of a frame of reference in motion perception can be found in experiments in which people view small spots of light or other illuminated objects in an otherwise completely dark room, and are asked to judge which element or elements are moving. Figure 9.27 illustrates and describes some typical results.

*Evidence from illusions that the perceptual system establishes a stable frame of reference, and judges movement relative to that frame*

**Figure 9.27 *Perceived motion of spots in a dark room***

(a) *A single, slowly moving spot in an otherwise completely dark room may be seen as stationary, since it may be taken as the frame of reference.* (b) *When two dots are visible and one is moving slowly, either dot may be seen as moving while the other is seen as the (stationary) frame of reference.* (c) *When an illuminated moving frame surrounds a dot, movement of the frame is seen as movement of the dot, because the frame is taken as the frame of reference. This is analogous to the moon-cloud illusion.*

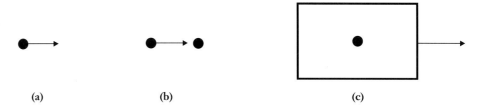

(a)                    (b)                    (c)

**Movement Within Movement: More Than One Frame of Reference**   If a bicycle with a reflector attached near the rim of one wheel were to cross your field of view, the reflector would move in a series of smooth hops, as shown in Figure 9.28a, a path that mathematicians refer to as a *cycloid curve*. If it were nighttime and the reflector were the only visible part of the bicycle, you would in fact see it moving in a cycloid curve and you might wonder what that strangely hopping object could be. But if you were to watch the same reflector during the day, you would not see it hop at all. Even if you consciously tried to see it moving in a cycloid path you would have difficulty doing so. Rather, you would see it as moving in a continuous circle around the center of the wheel, while the whole wheel was going forward. That is, you would see two different movements at once, each with a different frame of reference. The frame of reference for the forward movement would be the larger environment consisting of the road and stable elements along it, and that for the revolving movement would be the center of the wheel. The same applies to all instances in which elements within an object move relative to one another while the whole object moves relative to a larger frame.

■ *How wheels and people can be identified by the relative movement of their parts*

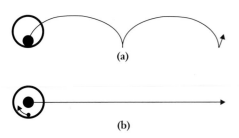

**Figure 9.28 *Perceived motion of spots on a rolling wheel***

*Part (a) depicts the cycloid curve that is seen when only one spot is visible on the rim of a rolling wheel. Part (b) depicts what is typically seen when an additional spot is added to the center of the wheel. Now there is no cycloid curve. Rather, the whole wheel is seen as moving forward, while the spot on the rim turns around the center in a circle. (Adapted from Cutting & Proffitt, 1982.)*

Our perceptual system is remarkably adept at seeing movement within movement, and can use that information to identify objects. People can often identify a wheel rolling forward on the basis of just two spots of light, one located at the wheel's center and the other located anywhere else on the wheel (see Figure 9.28b) (Cutting & Proffitt, 1982). Wheels, of course, have rather simple movement patterns compared to those of people and animals. Think, for example, of all of the movements within movements that you can observe while watching a person walk. The foot is moving with respect to the lower leg, the lower leg with respect to the upper leg, and so on. Every joint provides a separate frame of reference from which to observe a movement.

Gunner Johansson and his colleagues in Sweden have performed experiments in which small lights are attached to people's bodies, and they are then filmed while walking or undergoing other natural movements. Typically, twelve lights are used, each attached to a different major joint, and the film is made in such a way that only the lights can be seen (see Figure 9.29). When observers see a single still frame of such a film they have no idea what they are looking at, but as soon as the lights begin to move they recognize the object as a person undergoing a particular action. Just ¹/₁₀ second of viewing time, enough to go through two frames of the film, is sufficient for most viewers to see the lights as a human being walking (Johansson, 1975). Other experiments have shown that viewers can usually even judge the sex of the person in the film, based just on the way the tiny lights move as the person walks or jumps (Cutting & others, 1978; Runeson & Frykholm, 1986). Our ability to perceive subtle differences in movement patterns plays a more important role than we normally realize in identifying people and other animate objects.

**Figure 9.29 *Lights that are perceived as a person only when the person moves***

*In (a) lights are attached to the person's major joints. In the dark, the lights do not form a recognizable object when the person stands still (b), but are immediately recognized as a person when he or she begins to move. (From Michaels & Carello, 1981.)*

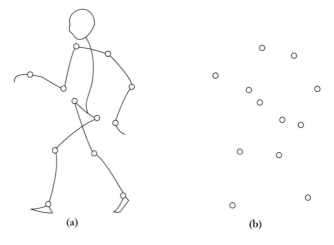

(a)                                             (b)

### Two Perspectives on the Use of Relational Information: Unconscious Inference and Direct Perception

■ *The difference between the unconscious-inference and direct-perception theories*

An overriding point of the discussion so far is that the perceptual system uses information about *relationships* among different parts of a scene to perceive the distance, size, and movement of any given part. Thus, perception of the *distance* of an object depends on cues such as whether the object occludes or is occluded by other objects; perception of *size* depends on perception of distance; and perception of *movement* depends on establishing some portion of the scene as a frame of reference. Now we will examine two broad, theoretical perspectives concerning the source and use of such relational information. One perspective, the *unconscious-inference theory*, maintains that perception involves a great deal of problem solving, though at an unconscious level. The sensory input provides clues that must be brought together and used, by the mind, along with information already stored there (memories), to figure out, or *infer*, the distance, size, and movement of objects. The other perspective, the *direct-perception theory*, emphasizes the richness of the stimulus input and minimizes the role of mental activity. From this perspective, all of the relevant information is directly available in the stimulus input, and perception is more a matter of translation than problem solving. Just as the wavelength of light is picked up and translated directly into color, somewhat more complex stimulus information is picked up and translated directly into depth, size, and motion. Let us look a little more closely now at each of these two perspectives.

**The Unconscious-Inference Theory**   Historically, the unconscious-inference theory has roots in empiricist philosophy, which emphasized associative learning as the basis for knowledge (see Chapter 5). The empiricists believed that infants at first experience the world as disordered sensations, and only through learning do they become able to arrange them into useful perceptions. One of these empiricists was Bishop George Berkeley, who argued in 1709 that infants must learn to use visual cues for depth perception. More specifically, Berkeley proposed that direct information about depth is acquired through such actions as reaching out and touching objects or crawling forward and bumping into them, and that the child gradually learns to use visual depth cues by associating them with this direct information.

The unconscious-inference theory was most explicitly developed, however, during the second half of the nineteenth century by Hermann von Helmholtz (the same man whose work on visual and auditory coding was discussed in Chapter 8). Like Berkeley, Helmholtz assumed that a good deal of learning must underlie people's perceptual abilities, but he was not as concerned with the learning process as with how people use the relevant information. Helmholtz believed that the mind must somehow take into account various items of information, and, through logical steps much like working out an algebraic equation, calculate the various characteristics of objects. For example, to perceive the size of an object, the mind must multiply the size of the retinal image by the perceived distance of the object, which must first have been calculated from available depth cues. Of course, Helmholtz realized that people do not consciously perform such calculations; thus, he coined the term *unconscious inference*.

*How the unconscious-inference theory leads to a focus on top-down and bottom-up mental processes, as well as to an interest in illusions*

Helmholtz's notion of unconscious inference is one of the key ideas that underlies modern cognitive psychology. When cognitive psychologists develop theories about the steps that the mind or brain goes through to perceive and reason, they do not assume that the person has to be conscious of those steps or of the conclusions that are reached. Computers can perform difficult calculations, too, and nobody assumes that computers are conscious. The unconscious-inference perspective underlies much of the discussion of form perception and object recognition in the first half of this chapter. Recall the discussion about the interaction of bottom-up and top-down processes in form perception. Such interaction is implicit in the unconscious-inference theory: Sensory information enters and is pieced together (bottom-up) through inferential processes that make use of the larger context and learned concepts (top-down). This perspective also informed the discussions of perceptual illusions that have occurred in several places in the chapter. Illusions represent errors in the inferential process, and by identifying the conditions that lead to such errors we learn about the mental steps that must occur in normal, accurate perception.

**The Direct-Perception Theory**   Whereas the unconscious-inference theory has roots in empiricist philosophy, the direct-perception theory has at least some of its roots in nativist philosophy. Nativists such as Immanuel Kant (1724–1804)

*What in the world makes landing possible?*

*James Gibson's ecological theory grew out of his attempts to answer such a question. Assigned the task of training pilots during World War II, he found that none of the traditional approaches to perception enabled him to understand the aspects of depth perception that permit a pilot to land a plane. And so he created a theory that takes into account the entire environment that surrounds the active perceiver.*

■ *How the direct-perception theory relates to an evolutionary perspective, and why it is also called the ecological theory*

looked to innate (inborn) characteristics of the mind as the root of knowledge. Kant, contrary to Berkeley, argued that the mind has an innate conception of three-dimensional space and can see depth without having to learn to do so, an idea that finds support in modern research with infants (as discussed in Chapter 12). During the early twentieth century, the nativist tradition was carried on by the Gestalt psychologists. As you saw earlier in this chapter, the Gestaltists believed that the mind responds innately and automatically to the organized patterns of sensory input and does not have to build these patterns from separate analysis of the elements. The Gestaltists had a different view about the workings of the brain from that of most other thinkers. They did not focus on the role of individual neurons or pathways, but instead hypothesized that there is a natural resonance between patterns of stimuli in the external world and patterns of activity in the brain, and that the global pattern of brain activity provides the basis for perception.

Though its roots lie partly in nativist philosophy and Gestalt psychology, the modern direct-perception theory was developed most explicitly by the late James Gibson in work that he began in the 1940s. Gibson—who was the husband of Eleanor Gibson, cited earlier in this chapter—was influenced in his thinking by a modern understanding of biological evolution. We evolved through natural selection based on survival in the real, three-dimensional world, and that process eventuated in a perceptual system that is extremely efficient in picking up the kinds of information that are needed to survive in that world. An exquisite ability to perceive the distance, size, and motion of objects is essential to capture prey, avoid predators, and engage in other survival-promoting actions. Such perceptions are too important to be left to an inferential process, which would take time and effort and could result in errors. Evolution created a more efficient system attuned to the kinds of information that directly signal depth, size, and motion. Gibson (1966, 1979) referred to his theory as an *ecological theory* to emphasize the intrinsic, inseparable relationship between the perceptual system and the physical and biological environments in which it evolved.

Whereas the unconscious-inference theory emphasizes the paucity of information in the stimuli that strike the sensory receptors, and the necessity of the mind to supplement that information with memories and calculations, the direct-perception theory emphasizes the richness of the stimulus information. According to Gibson, psychologists and philosophers have focused too much on mental processes and not enough on the stimulus array itself and the kinds of information it provides. Thus, Gibson shifted the emphasis from the study of the perceiver to the study of the external stimulus information that must be perceived. Like the unconscious-inference theory, the direct-perception theory emphasizes the use of information about relationships; but whereas the former theory assumes that the relationships emerge from mental calculations, the latter assumes that they exist directly in the sensory stimuli. Gibson referred to the relational aspects of sensory stimuli as *higher-order stimuli,* and argued that the perceptual system evolved to respond to these, not to the simpler, stimulus elements.

From the direct-perception perspective no distinction between bottom-up and top-down processing is required. The translation of sensory input to perception occurs instantly, and it is arbitrary whether we think of it as top-down or bottom-up. This perspective also minimizes the value of studying illusions, pointing out that these are almost completely limited to two-dimensional pictures or other artificial scenes that lack the rich information that is almost always available in the real, three-dimensional world. Gibson and others (for example, Neisser, 1976) have argued that perceptual psychologists have paid too much attention to the scant information in pictures and not enough to the higher-order information in real, three-dimensional scenes. Pictures are a recent invention in the time span of evolution; our perceptual system evolved to see not pictures but real scenes, and when viewing the latter it is rarely deceived.

**The Two Theories Applied to Visual Constancies**    To illustrate these two broad perspectives more concretely, let's see how each would explain various *visual constancies*—those characteristics of objects that look constant despite continuous changes in the retinal image.

A visual constancy that we have already discussed is *size constancy.* Look at Figure 9.30, which shows a cylinder as it would appear first at position *A,* close to the viewer, and then at position *B,* farther away. The cylinder appears to be the same size at each position, despite the change in the size of the retinal image that it produces. You already know how the unconscious-inference theory accounts for this constancy: The mind uses depth cues, such as the linear perspective and texture

> ■ *Why the direct-perception theory leads to a focus on the arrangement of stimuli in the environment rather than on mental processes and illusions*

> ■ *How constancy of size, shape, position, and motion are explained by each of the two theories*

**Figure 9.30 Size constancy explained by two theories**

*This illustration shows the same cylinder as it would appear close to the viewer and farther away. According to the unconscious-inference theory, we use linear perspective to assess the distance of the object at both positions, and use that assessment, along with the retinal image size, to judge the stimulus as the same size in either position. According to Gibson's direct-perception theory, on the other hand, no such calculations are necessary. The size is seen directly in the higher-order stimulus, which includes the texture elements (bricks) of the adjacent wall. The cylinder is exactly ten bricks tall at either position.*

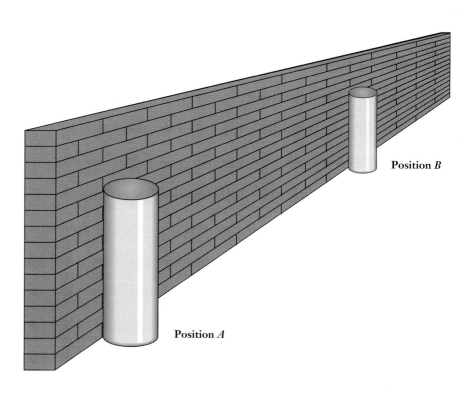

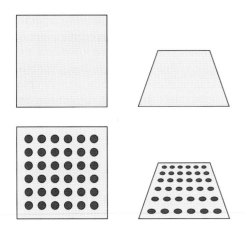

**Figure 9.31** *Shape constancy explained by two theories*

*You cannot tell if the upper, right-hand object is a trapezoid or a tilted square because there are no texture elements or other depth cues. You can tell that the bottom, right-hand object is a tilted square because of the texture elements (shown here as dots). According to the unconscious-inference theory, we use the change in size and placement of texture elements as depth cues to judge the degree of tilt, and then use that to judge the true shape of the object. According to the direct-perception theory, on the other hand, we can see that this is a square without calculating depth, because each side spans the same number of texture elements.*

gradient provided by the brick wall, to judge how far away the cylinder is. It then uses the distance information to calculate the cylinder's size. How can the direct-perception theory account for this constancy without recourse to mental calculation?

If Gibson is correct, it is a mistake to think of the cylinder and the bricks as separate stimuli that must be taken into account separately; they are part of the same higher-order stimulus. Nearly all natural scenes have texture elements within them, and we know innately that texture elements on a continuous surface are constant in size. The visual system automatically picks up the object in relation to the texture elements surrounding it. Thus, we perceive the cylinder at position *B* as the same size as it is at position *A* because, in terms of the number of texture elements spanned, it *is* the same size (in both positions the cylinder is exactly ten bricks tall). Notice that in this account, size constancy is explained in terms of a constancy that actually exists in the stimulus. According to Gibson, the visual system evolved in such a way as to ignore the size of the retinal image, and automatically perceives an object's size in relation to other parts of the scene, especially texture elements.

Another constancy, closely related to size constancy, is *shape constancy*. As an object is rotated in three-dimensional space, the shape of its retinal image changes dramatically, yet we continue to see the object's true shape. For example, a square sheet produces a trapezoidal retinal image when viewed at a slant (see Figure 9.31), yet we see it as a square, not a trapezoid. According to the unconscious-inference theory, depth cues are used to assess shape in much the same way as they are used to assess size. The mind calculates the distance of various parts of the object from the eyes, and uses those calculations, along with the shape of the retinal image, to calculate the shape that the image would take if the object were viewed from any other angle (Rock, 1984). In this way, all retinal images that could be produced by the same object result in equivalent perceptions.

Gibson's explanation of shape constancy, in contrast, involves no mental calculations. He argues that the visual system is designed not to pick up just the borders of objects, but rather it is attuned to surfaces, and surfaces normally have texture. According to Gibson, the surface in Figure 9.31 is seen as a square because,

*A textured world*

*Texture elements—provided here by the plants in the field—allow us automatically to perceive the shapes and slants of surfaces and to make the junctions between surfaces, according to Gibson.*

regardless of its slant, it remains a surface whose sides each have an equal number of texture units (represented by the dots in the figure). By defining a square in terms of a scale of texture units, the perceptual system makes its own job much easier; it is not necessary to calculate the relative depth of each side in order to see it as a square. Of course, the texture elements would be misleading if they varied in real size in a gradual way over the surface of the object, but this rarely happens in the real world. The changes that do occur are abrupt, and the perceptual system interprets them as borders between differently textured surfaces (as was shown in Figure 9.2b).

Two other, closely related constancies are *position constancy* and *motion constancy*. The former refers to the ability to see a stable object as stable, not moving, even while its image moves on the retinas as the eyes or head move; and the latter refers to the ability to see an object as moving at a constant velocity even though the rate at which its image moves across each retina decreases as the object becomes more distant. According to the unconscious-inference theory, both of these constancies result from calculations based on (a) the rate at which the eyes are moving, (b) the rate at which the image moves across the retina, and (c) the perceived distance of the object from the eyes. Imagine how difficult such calculations must be, especially when the rates and distances are constantly changing over time as the person moves about in three-dimensional space. Gibson, again, doubts that such calculations are necessary. His explanation is much simpler, along the lines developed a few pages back in the discussion of frames of reference for motion perception. He suggested that the perceptual system responds not to the absolute movements of separate images on the retina, but rather to relative movements within the entire scene. Thus, elements that are stable with respect to one another are automatically seen as the stable, unmoving frame, and elements that change position with respect to the frame are seen as moving. Rate of movement is judged not from an absolute scale but in relation to other elements in the scene. As an object moves farther into the distance, it still passes by a fixed number of texture elements per second.

■ *The complementary value of the two theories*

**Evaluating the Two Perspectives**   Usually when we find two broad, seemingly opposite theories, each with a long history and a rather large following, we can assume that both have merit. This is certainly true of the two perspectives that have just been discussed. Although psychologists who adopt the extreme of either view may argue, the majority of psychologists take a middle ground and see the two as more complementary than competitive, as two sides of the truth. Consistent with the direct-perception theory, the information needed to see depth, size, and motion does lie in relationships that exist in the stimulus input, and these relationships are perceived quickly, efficiently, and effortlessly. Yet, it is also true that perception is a function of the brain. Whether we think of the brain's role as direct pickup or unconscious inference, the brain somehow extracts the relevant relationships from the stimulus information, and the unconscious-inference theory calls our attention to that process.

Much of the attraction of the direct-perception theory lies in its assumption that the brain does not have to perform complex calculations to perceive the relevant stimulus relationships. But what does it mean to say that the brain directly "picks up" or is "attuned to" the correct relationships? How does the tuner work? Surely there must be a complex neural system involved. Any attempt to specify how neurons can pick up the relational information might lead to a model that is as complex—and perhaps not much different from—a model that specifies how neurons pick up elementary stimuli, integrate them, and perform the relevant calculations. By any account, the brain is an extraordinarily complex machine, vastly more sophisticated than our best computers, so it is not outlandish to assume that it can perform with split-second timing the complex calculations that are required of it by the unconscious-inference theory.

The greatest value of the two perspectives lies in the research they have stimulated. While the unconscious-inference theory leads psychologists to develop and test hypotheses about the sequence of mental steps involved in various aspects of perception, the direct-perception theory leads them to focus more on the actual stimulus information that is available to the perceptual system. Whereas the first perspective leads to experiments involving simple, artificial stimuli, including those that produce illusions, the second continuously reminds us that when viewing objects in the real world the perceptual apparatus may use varieties of information (higher-order stimuli) that are absent in such simple stimuli. Through emphasizing the kinds of information available in natural scenes, the direct-perception perspective leads to experiments involving new varieties of stimulus relationships and thus a better understanding of perception as it occurs in the natural environment.

## Concluding Thoughts

In concluding, it would be worthwhile to think some more about the three themes that served as organizing principles for the three main sections of this chapter:

1. **The distinction between top-down and bottom-up processes**  The first section, on pattern perception and object recognition, was organized around a broad distinction between top-down and bottom-up mental processes. This distinction is common in theories of perception, and reflects the idea that any perceptual act requires some kind of matching of stimulus input with knowledge already in the mind. The processes that bring in the stimulus information are bottom-up, and those that bring preexisting knowledge to the interpretation are top-down. As you review the chapter, remind yourself of the experiments and demonstrations that support this broad distinction and have led to more specific ideas about the ways in which each class of processes operates.

At the same time, however, if you really think about the top-down, bottom-up distinction, you may conclude correctly that it is often fuzzy. I presented the Gestalt principles of grouping in the section on top-down processes; but are those principles really top-down in their application? If you think of them as items of general knowledge brought to bear upon the analysis of stimuli, they are top-down. But if you think of them as automatic consequences of the way the mind registers and integrates stimulus input, they are bottom-up. As another example, I discussed the selective use of distinctive stimulus features in skilled, learned acts of recognition in the section on bottom-up processes. But is the selection of distinctive features really bottom-up? If you think of such skills as involving modification of the stimulus-input channels, such that certain features automatically are accented at the expense of others, then it is bottom-up. But if you think of such skills as learned knowledge brought to bear upon the stimulus input to recognize it, it is top-down. Thus, depending on your point of view, you can often think of the same phenomenon as a demonstration of either bottom-up or top-down processing.

2. **The distinction between preattentive and attentive processing**  The second section, on attention, centered on the idea that all (or at least much) stimulus input is analyzed to some degree, but only some of that input is analyzed in such a way as to contribute to the ongoing flow of conscious thought. This idea has led theorists to distinguish between two general compartments of the mind: a preattentive compartment, which can operate automatically, in parallel, on a vast amount of stimulus input at once; and an attentive compartment, which operates in a more con-

trolled way, in series, on a limited amount of input selected from the preattentive compartment. As you review the chapter, remind yourself of the experiments and demonstrations that have supported this broad distinction, and have led to specific ideas about the kinds of processes that occur in each compartment.

But again, as with the top-down, bottom-up distinction, it is not hard to find limitations in this distinction. To the degree that the distinction is based on consciousness, we have the problem that there are no sharp divisions between what is conscious and what is not, nor good research procedures for distinguishing between the two. To the degree that the distinction is based on the amount of information that can be analyzed in a certain way at once, there is again no sharp divide. For example, consider the effect of practice on the ability to process more than one source of information at a time in a sophisticated way. We can explain that effect either as an increase in the capacity of the attentive compartment or as a pushing of previously attentive steps down into the preattentive compartment, and clear criteria do not exist for deciding which explanation is best.

Because of problems like this, some perceptual psychologists have abandoned the two-compartment model and have developed far more complex models involving networks of many different compartments (or modules) that serve different and sometimes overlapping functions. As Kahneman and Treisman (1984) have put it, these new models liken the mind more to an organization—say, to General Motors or the Central Intelligence Agency—than to a series of boxes. How many individuals or bureaus in the CIA have to know something before the organization as a whole is said to know it? Likewise, how many parts of the mind have to recognize something before the person as a whole is said to have recognized it? The answer is arbitrary. There are different degrees and ways of knowing or recognizing.

**3. Two perspectives on the use of relational stimulus information**  The third section, on the use of stimulus relationships to perceive depth, size, and motion, concluded by contrasting two perspectives on the use of such relationships. One—the unconscious-inference theory—emphasizes the role of mental processes. Talk of top-down, bottom-up, attentive, and preattentive processing is all very relevant to this perspective. In the attempt to understand such processes, researchers in this tradition think of individual stimulus elements as providing cues that the mind actively uses to construct its perceptions of the outside world. To isolate and describe the mental steps involved, and the cues needed for each step to operate, these researchers perform experiments in which stimulus input is restricted in various ways, producing illusions or ambiguous perceptions. This approach coincides with the general approach in other areas of psychology—and in other sciences, too—of trying to understand how normal processes work by testing them in artificial conditions, where individual variables contributing to the processes can be separated and controlled. For example, if you want to describe the mathematics of gravity, you will test gravity in a place where there is no air to interfere with falling objects, even though you know that in the real world falling objects are affected both by gravity and air. The same logic applies in trying to describe the cues and processes involved in various perceptual tasks, by assessing perceptions with some normal cues present and others absent.

Yet, one may miss something by testing people only in restricted conditions. Maybe the experiment carves up the stimulus world in the wrong way, so that the important cues are not present in any of the experimental conditions, and the perceptions are artifacts of the laboratory rather than part of the story of normal perception. If the cues used in real-world perception lie in the broader arrangements of stimuli, then separation of stimuli in laboratory experiments does not separate out the normal cues, but obliterates them. That was James Gibson's main point, and it provides the starting place for the direct-perception theory. By shifting the focus from the perceiver to the perceived, this theory led to the concept of higher-order stimuli, which lie in the patterns of what had previously been considered separable stimulus cues. It is interesting to note, however, that researchers working from the direct-perception perspective, after developing ideas about higher-order stimuli, typically test those ideas under restricted environmental conditions, such as those provided by a person with spots of light moving in a completely darkened room. The next step will be to wonder about the mental processes involved in making use of such higher-order cues; then the distinction between the two perspectives will have vanished.

## Further Reading

**Irvin Rock** (1984). *Perception*. New York: Scientific American Books.

*This book, written for the nonspecialist by a leading perceptual researcher, is an excellent introduction to visual perception, emphasizing the unconscious-inference perspective. It is richly illustrated and has chapters on visual constancies, spatial vision, pattern perception, motion perception, illusions, and perception in relation to art.*

**Claire F. Michaels & Claudia Carello** (1981). *Direct perception*. Englewood Cliffs, NJ: Prentice Hall.

*This slender, philosophically oriented book is an excellent introduction to the direct-perception theory. It shows how the theory is tied both to evolutionary biology and to a broad perspective on science that emphasizes the value of studying whole systems before (or without) dissecting the parts. The perceiving animal and the perceived environment, according to these authors, are two parts of a single system.*

## Looking Ahead

Perception is the first step of cognition. The way we initially see or hear something influences the way we subsequently remember and think about it. Memory and thought are topics of the next two chapters, and some of the themes that have just been discussed will be continued there. For example, the ideas of bottom-up and top-down processes, applied in this chapter to the problem of constructing perceptions from stimuli, will be applied in the next chapter to the problem of reconstructing memories of past experiences from stored information. The problem of how material is selected into the attentive-processing compartment, discussed in this chapter in relation to external stimuli, will be enlarged in the next chapter to include selection from the memory stores. And the general approach of trying to understand mental processes in terms of a flow of information, from one processing stage to another, will be more fully developed. You will see in the next chapter an attempt to depict the whole mind as boxes and arrows that represent stores of information and movement of it from one store to another.

# CHAPTER 10

**An Information-Processing Model of Memory**

**Sensory Memory: The Preattentive Store**

**Short-term Memory and Encoding into Long-term Memory**

**Representation and Organization in Long-term Memory**

**Problems of Retrieval from Long-term Memory**

**Neuropsychological Evidence for Multiple Memory Systems**

# MEMORY

So many times, while working on this book, I have lamented my seeming lack of memory. I can't remember who did that experiment. I forgot to bring home the articles I need for this section. I've looked up that word a thousand times but still don't remember how to spell it; now where did I put the dictionary?

Like digestion, memory is one of those abilities that we tend to take for granted except when it fails us. Usually we are more aware of forgetting than we are of remembering. But stop and think for a moment about the awesomeness of human memory. Every waking moment is full of memories. Every thought, every learned response, every act of recognition is based on memory. In a very real sense, memory *is* the mind. Memory refers to our storehouse of information and to the processes that allow us to recall and use that information when we need it.

This is the second of a trio of chapters on cognitive processes. The first, on perception, dealt with how information enters the mind from the environment; and this one, on memory, deals with how that information is held by the mind and accessed for future use. The chapter begins by describing a model of memory that cognitive psychologists use as a framework for talking about essentially all of mental activity, and then proceeds to discuss such issues as memory encoding, organization, and retrieval. Memory is the core topic of cognitive psychology, and in this chapter you will get a flavor of the way that cognitive psychologists think and conduct research.

## An Information-Processing Model of Memory

Memory is too large and multifaceted a topic to study or talk about all in one piece. Progress has been made by breaking memory into various components that can be described and studied separately. But any such breakdown implies a theory about memory—a theory that memory consists of the proposed components, that these can be studied relatively independently, and that the larger picture can be understood in terms of the interaction of the components.

Theories in cognitive psychology are commonly called *models* and are often presented visually in diagrams that represent the interaction of cognitive components as boxes and arrows. Such models do not attempt to explain how each task is accomplished at the level of neural activity, but rather attempt to describe functionally what the task is. The model that guides the discussion in this chapter, depicted in Figure 10.1, has been so influential that it has come to be called the ***modal model of the mind***, where *modal* means "standard." Versions of this model were first proposed in the 1960s (by Waugh & Norman, 1965, and Atkinson & Shiffrin, 1968), and ever since it has served as a general framework for thinking and

**Figure 10.1** *The modal model of the mind*

*This model, described fully in the text, is called the* modal model *because it has become the standard (modal) framework that cognitive psychologists use for thinking and talking about the human mind.*

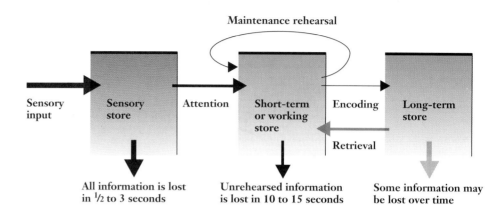

talking about the mind. This model serves as a structure for organizing this chapter, but keep in mind that it is only a model. Like any general model in psychology, it is simply one way of trying to make sense of the data from many behavioral studies. And like any model, it can place blinders on thought and research if it is taken literally rather than as a metaphor. Not all of the data are consistent with the model, and eventually a new model, which makes sense of more data, may become the modal model for future cognitive psychologists.

The current modal model portrays the mind as containing three *memory stores* (sensory, short-term, and long-term), conceived of as places where information is held. Each store is characterized by its *function* (the role it plays in the overall workings of the mind), its *capacity* (the amount of information it can hold at any given instant), and its *duration* (the length of time over which it can hold an item of information). In relation to the model, the term *memory* has two different meanings. It refers both to the mind's ability to hold information in a given store and to any individual item of information in that store. In addition to the stores, the model specifies a set of *control processes* that govern the processing of information within stores and the movement of information from one store to another. The following paragraphs describe each store and some of the control processes. Later in the chapter you will read of evidence that supports, extends, and in some cases partly contradicts these descriptions.

**Sensory Memory**    When lightning flashes on a dark night you can still *see* the flash and the objects it illuminates for a split second beyond its actual duration. Somewhat similarly, when a companion says, "You're not listening to me," you can still *hear* those words, and a few words of the previous sentence, for 2 or 3 seconds after their enunciation. Thus, you can answer (falsely), "I was too listening, you said . . ."—and then you can repeat your annoyed companion's last few words even though in truth you hadn't been listening when the words were uttered. These observations demonstrate that some trace of sensory input remains in your information-processing system for a brief period—less than 1 second for sights and up to 3 seconds for sounds—even when you are not paying attention to the input. This trace, and the ability to hold it, are called *sensory memory*, and the *sensory store* is the hypothetical place in the mind where the trace is held.

■ *The function, capacity, and duration of sensory memory*

The function of the sensory store is to hold all information that enters the senses for a brief period while it is processed for basic physical characteristics. Thus, this store is of very high capacity (can hold many items of information at once) but very short duration (information in it fades quickly). This store is also called the *preattentive store*, and it coincides with the preattentive-processing stage of information discussed in Chapter 9 (refer back to Figure 9.16). Processes involved in pattern recognition may act on information held in this store, and the process of attention acts upon it to select those items that will move on to the next store.

**The passing moment**
*The flow of thought through short-term memory is not unlike the scenery flowing by the window of a moving train.*

■ *The function, capacity, and duration of short-term memory*

**Short-term Memory**  The next store, the **short-term store**, is also called the *attentive store*, and it coincides with the attentive-processing stage of information processing introduced in Chapter 9 (see Figure 9.16). Information in this store, and the mind's ability to hold it there, are referred to both as **short-term memory** and as **working memory**. The latter term captures this store's function as the main workplace of the mind. Among other things, working memory is conceived of as the seat of conscious thought—the place where all conscious perceiving, feeling, comparing, computing, and reasoning takes place. As depicted by the arrows in Figure 10.1, information can enter this store from both the sensory store (representing the present environment) and the long-term store (representing knowledge gained from previous experiences). Both sources of input contribute to the continuous flow of thought that constitutes short-term or working memory. *Flow* is an apt metaphor here. The capacity of the short-term store is very small—only a few items of information can be perceived consciously or thought about at once. Yet, the total amount of information that moves through the short-term store over a period of minutes or hours can be enormous, just as the amount of water flowing through a narrow channel over time can be enormous.

It may seem strange to conceive of thought as occurring within a memory store. But in order to think, you must have information to think about, and that information must be remembered while you are thinking about it. Cognitive psychologists frequently draw an analogy between the mind's short-term store and the central processing unit of a computer. Information can be punched directly into the computer's central processing unit from a keyboard (analogous to input from the mind's sensory store); or it can be entered from a floppy disk or other long-term storage device (analogous to input from the mind's long-term store). The real work of the computer—the computations and manipulations of the information—occurs within the computer's central processing unit.

■ *The function, capacity, and duration of long-term memory*

**Long-term Memory**  Once an item has passed from the sensory store into the short-term store, it may or may not pass on to the **long-term store** and be encoded as **long-term memory**. Long-term memory corresponds most closely to most people's everyday notion of memory. It is the stored representation of all that a person knows. As such, its capacity must be enormous, essentially unlimited. Long-term memory contains the information that enables a person to recognize or recall the taste of an almond, the sound of a banjo, the face of a grade-school friend, the names of the foods eaten at last night's dinner, the words of a favorite sonnet, and the spelling of the word *sonnet*. Usually we are not aware of the millions of items of information in our long-term store. According to the model, the items lie dormant (or relatively so) like books on a library shelf or signals on a computer disk until they are called into the short-term store and put to use.

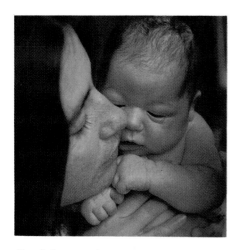

**Special memories**

*The first sight of her newborn may create miraculous memories for the mother, but no less miraculous is the newborn's own memory capacity. Research suggests that infants are born with environmentally based information in long-term memory that includes the sound of their mother's voice, and that they quickly learn how their mother smells.*

■ *The functions of attention, encoding, and retrieval according to the modal model*

The duration of the long-term store is just that—long term. You can learn a fact in the second grade and recall it on your sixtieth birthday. But you can't recall on your sixtieth birthday *every* fact that you knew in second grade or even every fact that you knew just a week before that birthday. One of the most interesting questions about long-term memory has to do with this problem of recall. When a person can't recall something that used to be in his or her long-term store, has the information been lost *from* the store (like a book stolen from the library), or has it been lost *in* the store (like a book that has been misshelved or whose call number can't be located)? This is a question to which we will return.

**Control Processes**   As noted earlier, control processes manipulate information within a store or move it from one store to another. Those that move information from one store to another, depicted as arrows in Figure 10.1, are attention, encoding, and retrieval. (Don't confuse *control processes* with *controlled processing*, which in Chapter 9 was contrasted with automatic processing. Control processes include all mental processes for controlling information, whether those processes are "controlled" or automatic.)

*Attention*   This process, which was discussed fully in Chapter 9, controls the flow of information from the sensory store into the short-term store. If you look back at Figure 9.16, you can equate preattentive processing with the sensory store and attentive processing with the short-term store, and you can visualize attention as the process that determines what information will flow from the first into the second. Information that is not selected by the attention process quickly fades and is lost from the information-processing system.

*Encoding*   This process controls movement from the short-term store into the long-term store. When you deliberately memorize a poem, or a list of names, you are consciously encoding it into long-term memory. Whatever rehearsal strategies you use, ranging from simple repetition to elaborate mnemonic schemes, are part of the encoding process. But most encoding is not deliberate; rather, it occurs incidentally, as a side effect of the special interest that you devote to certain items of information. One hypothesis, discussed later in the chapter, is that the likelihood of encoding information into the long-term store is related to the depth of thought that occurs concerning that information while it is in the short-term store. The deeper the thought, the greater the probability that the information thought about will be encoded.

*Retrieval*   This process controls the flow of information from the long-term store into the short-term store. Retrieval is what we commonly call remembering. Like both attention and encoding, retrieval can be either deliberate or automatic. Sometimes we actively search our long-term store for a particular piece of information. More often, however, information seems to float automatically into the short-term store from the long-term store. One image or thought in short-term memory seems to call forth the next in a stream that is sometimes logical, sometimes fanciful.

Other control processes have to do with the manipulation of information within a memory store. *Pattern recognition*, discussed in Chapter 9, can be thought of as a control process. To the extent that it occurs automatically, preattentively, we can think of this process as the comparing of information in the sensory store with that in the long-term store to find matches. When matches occur, and are relevant to the flow of thought, the process of attention can then pull the matched information into the short-term store. On the other hand, to the extent that pattern recognition requires focused attention, it can be thought of as occurring in the short-term store. Control processes involved in *problem solving*—a topic covered in Chapter 11—are thought of as taking place in the short-term store.

**Beyond the Basic Model: Dealing with Different Kinds of Information**  Many cognitive psychologists believe that the mind processes and stores different kinds of information differently, and some have suggested ways to expand or replace the modal model to take such differences into account (see Sherry & Schacter, 1987). For some years, Endel Tulving (1985) has argued for distinguishing among three general classes of information that, he claims, serve different purposes and are stored differently in the mind. The three classes are as follows:

- ***Procedural information***  This is the information that enables a person to perform a learned skill or habitual response, such as riding a bicycle or typing. We are not conscious of such information—we can't explain how we ride a bicycle, we just do it—so the notion of a conscious short-term store to which such information must be recalled for use is misleading. To account for the storage and use of procedural information, we must either assume that a compartment exists within the short-term store that is *not* manifested in the person's consciousness, or we must develop an entirely separate model for procedural memory.

- ***Semantic information***  This is a person's general knowledge of the world. It includes knowledge of word meanings (which is one definition of the term *semantics*), but also other general knowledge. Your knowledge that robins have red breasts, that Napoleon Bonaparte was a French emperor, and that apples and oranges are fruits are part of your semantic knowledge. As you will see later in this chapter, cognitive psychologists have developed special models to account for the manner by which semantic information is organized in long-term memory.

- ***Episodic information***  This is a person's knowledge of his or her own past experiences. Your memory of what you did and how you felt on your sixteenth birthday, or of what you ate for dinner last night, or of any other specific episode in your life is episodic information. To recall such information, you place yourself mentally back to a certain time and place in your past, which is different from what you do to recall semantic information. As Tulving has put it, to recall episodic information is to remember *when*, whereas to recall semantic information is to remember *that*. Semantic and episodic information are sometimes referred to collectively as ***declarative information***, a term emphasizing that these are the types of information that we can put into words, or declare (Richardson-Klavehn & Bjork, 1988).

To illustrate these three types of information further, think of the kinds of memories that you might take away from your first experience of playing some

*How procedural, semantic, and episodic information differ from one another*

**Where do we go from here?**
*For this hardy traveler, the answer to that question probably depended on the mobilization of three kinds of information: procedural information on how to ride his bike, semantic information about the place he was visiting and its language, and episodic information about previous events of the trip.*

game—say, horseshoes. First, you might carry away an improved ability to pitch the shoes, which would still be present the next time you play and result in a higher score. This illustrates procedural information. Second, you might carry away some facts about the game, such as how many points you earn for a ringer, which would become part of your stateable knowledge about horseshoes, even though you might forget where or when you learned it. This illustrates semantic information, the kind that might go into an essay entitled, "Facts About Horseshoes." Third, you might carry away some information that is tied in your memory to that specific episode or event in your life, such as with whom you played, how you felt, and whether or not the game was interrupted by rain. This illustrates episodic information, the kind that might go into an essay entitled, "The First Time I Played Horseshoes."

This tripartite division is just one way of distinguishing among different kinds of information. Information can also be divided according to the sensory route by which it enters (visual information, auditory information, and so on), by whether or not it takes the form of words (verbal information versus nonverbal information), or by any of a number of other means. As the chapter progresses, you will see how such distinctions have been important in memory research.

Having outlined the model, let's go through it more slowly, store by store, discussing research on the ways that information is held in each store or passed from one to another.

## Sensory Memory: The Preattentive Store

Usually we are unaware of the brief sensory impressions (our sensory memories) that outlast the physical stimuli acting on our sense organs. In fact, the existence of sensory memory was not generally recognized by psychologists until 1960, when George Sperling published a series of experiments demonstrating it. His work nicely shows how cognitive psychologists draw inferences about inner processes from observable behavior.

**Sperling's Discovery**   Sperling (1960) began with what would seem to be a simple question not about memory but about visual perception: How much can be seen in a single, brief glance? To answer the question, he presented subjects with arrays of letters such as the following:

X M R J<br>
P N K F<br>
F Z D B

He flashed each array for $1/20$ second and asked the subject to name as many of the letters as possible. He found that no matter how many letters were in the array, the most that people could name was four or five. Why? Sperling could imagine two possible answers. One possibility, which we might call the *capacity hypothesis*, is that the visual system can only register up to four or five letters in a single glance. This was the most common interpretation of such findings before Sperling's time. The second possibility, which we might call the *duration hypothesis*, is that the limitation is not on the ability to pick up the information but on the ability to retain the information long enough to report it. Subjects often claimed that they could see all of the letters in the array, but that the letters faded before they could name all of them. According to the duration hypothesis, all of the letters are held very briefly as a sensory trace (they can still be seen for a brief time after they are flashed), but only about four or five can be transferred into short-term memory for conscious identification and verbal reporting before they fade.

■ *How Sperling showed that the
ability to name items in a briefly
flashed stimulus is limited not by
visual pickup but by duration in
memory; how this led to postulation
of a sensory memory store; and how
Sperling timed the duration of visual
sensory memories*

To test the two hypotheses, Sperling developed a variation of his method, called *partial report*, in which subjects were asked to name only one row of letters in each array, chosen after the physical stimulus was terminated. In this variation, each flash of an array of letters was followed immediately by a tone signaling which row to report. A high pitch indicated the top row; a medium pitch, the middle row; and a low pitch, the bottom row. Sperling reasoned that, if the duration hypothesis is correct, subjects should usually report all four letters correctly in the partial-report test. The sensory trace of all of the letters would still be present when the tone was sounded, and the tone would tell the subject which letters in the trace to transfer into short-term memory and report, before they faded. On the other hand, if the capacity hypothesis is correct, subjects should do no better proportionately in this condition than in the *full-report* condition (in which the task was to report the whole array). They would not be able to report letters that their visual system had failed to register. Thus, if they could see only four or five (about 40 percent) of the twelve letters that were flashed, they should, on average, be able to report only about 40 percent of them correctly in either test condition.

The results, as you might have guessed, supported the duration hypothesis. Subjects usually identified correctly all four letters in the partial-report condition. Thus, their visual system must have registered all of the letters, and the limitation on full report must have resided in their inability to transfer more than a few of the letters into short-term memory. This is the finding that led to the idea that the sensory trace should be treated as a form of memory, preceding short-term memory. The tone could only have been effective if all letters in the array were stored briefly somewhere in the subjects' information-processing systems. But where? At the time of Sperling's work, psychologists considered short-term memory to be the first memory store. But if all of the letters were in the short-term store (the conscious store), then subjects should have been able to report them all in the full-report condition. To solve that problem, Sperling proposed that prior to entering short-term memory, information must be held briefly in another brief memory store, which we now call the sensory-memory store.

There appears to be a separate sensory-memory store for each different sensory system (vision, hearing, touch, smell, and taste), each with different characteristics, but only those for vision and hearing have been studied extensively.

**Visual Sensory Memory (the Icon)**    Visual sensory memory is also called ***iconic memory***, and the brief trace for a specific visual stimulus is called the *icon*. How long after a stimulus is ended does the icon last? To answer that question, Sperling (1960) performed another series of partial-report experiments, in which he varied the delay between the disappearance of the array of twelve letters and the presentation of the signal tone. The results are shown in Figure 10.2. As you can see, the

**Figure 10.2  *Duration of iconic memory***

*Sperling measured the duration of iconic (visual sensory) memory by varying the delay between seeing a briefly flashed array of letters (three rows with four letters per row) and hearing a signal indicating which row to report. Percent correct is the percentage of letters that the subject correctly named (out of four in the partial-report condition and twelve in the full-report condition). Notice that by the end of 1 second the percent correct in the partial-report condition was no better than that in the full-report condition, implying that by that time, the icon had fully vanished, so the signal was of no help. (Adapted from Sperling, 1960.)*

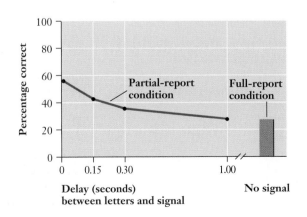

*Why don't we see this way?*

*If you're wondering why multiple representations of the icon don't distort your view of the visual world, the answer is that each new image from instant to instant blocks out the previous image.*

**Figure 10.3** *Sample stimuli used to show the picturelike nature of iconic memory*

*This pair of dot patterns (left-hand and middle figures) form a visible syllable (VOH) when superimposed (right-hand figure). They also do so when flashed in rapid succession (less than 0.3 second apart) so that their icons are fused in sensory memory. (From Eriksen & Collins, 1967.)*

■ *Evidence that auditory sensory memories last longer than visual sensory memories, and that their form can be modified before they are consciously experienced*

percent of correct answers dropped sharply as the delay increased from 0 to 0.3 second, and by 1 second was as low as that which had occurred in the full-report condition. From this, Sperling concluded that the icon fades quickly during the first $^1/_3$ second and completely vanishes by the end of 1 second. Other experiments have shown that the rate of fading depends on the level of illumination of the stimulus; icons from dim stimuli fade more quickly than those from brighter ones.

Seeing the icon is like seeing the original stimulus: The information is still in its original sensory form. This was nicely demonstrated by Charles Eriksen and James Collins (1967), who found that superimposing two icons produces an effect comparable to that of superimposing two pictures. They used pairs of dot patterns that appeared random when shown separately but formed a three-letter syllable when superimposed (see Figure 10.3). When Eriksen and Collins flashed such a pair successively, with a very brief delay between the two patterns, most subjects saw the syllable, just as they did when the two patterns were flashed simultaneously. As the delay was increased (up to 0.3 second), the likelihood of the subjects seeing the syllable dropped sharply.

**Auditory Sensory Memory (the Echo)** Auditory sensory memory is called *echoic memory*, and the brief trace for a specific sound is called the *echo*. Partial-report experiments analogous to Sperling's have demonstrated the existence of echoic memories and timed their duration. In such experiments, subjects hear spoken words played simultaneously through different loudspeakers (analogous to the different rows of letters in Sperling's experiments), and then see a signal telling them to report what they have heard from a specific speaker (partial-report condition) or from all speakers (full-report condition). Such experiments have shown that echoes do not fade as fast as icons. The partial-report signal is useful even if it is *initiated* as much as 2 or 3 seconds after the sounds have ended (Darwin & others, 1972).

Why should an echo last longer than an icon? A possible functional answer to that lies in the observation that hearing, by its very nature, is a process that requires the accumulation of information over time. The elements of an auditory stimulus follow one another in time, while those of a visual stimulus can strike the eye all at once. To understand a spoken word or sentence, for example, we must accumulate over time a series of separate sounds; and a long echoic memory may help us do that.

Recall the experiment on phonemic restoration (by Warren, 1984) described in Chapter 9, showing that the way people hear a word can depend on words that follow it. Subjects who were presented the sound *eel (where * was a cough) heard it as *peel* when the subsequent words were *was on the orange*, and as *heel* when the subsequent words were *was on the shoe*. Their experience was not of inferring the first consonant, but of actually hearing it. For that to happen, the sound *eel must have remained in sensory memory while the rest of the phrase was spoken, and must have been modified there before entering consciousness (short-term memory). This suggests that echoic memory is not an entirely passive store; some modification of sensory information apparently can occur within echoic memory in order to produce meaningful patterns.

## Short-term Memory and Encoding into Long-term Memory

Short-term (or working) memory, as conceptualized in the modal model, is the store in which conscious thought occurs (a topic to be discussed in Chapter 11). Information enters this store from the sensory store only if attention is paid to it. Here our concern is limited to the issues of how information is retained in the short-term store once it enters, and how rehearsal or thought about the information in this store helps encode it into the long-term store. Thus, we are concerned here with the mental processes that in everyday language are called memorizing.

### Rote Rehearsal

**Rote rehearsal** refers to a type of memorizing in which items of information are repeated to keep them in short-term memory or to encode them into long-term memory. This is the kind of memorizing that has been studied most often in experimental research, ever since the days of Hermann Ebbinghaus in the late nineteenth century. Ebbinghaus was one of the pioneering Germans who helped found psychology as an experimental science (discussed in Chapter 1). He is most famous for a long series of experiments on rote memory, in which he used himself as his only subject (Ebbinghaus, 1885/1913).

**Ebbinghaus's Pioneering Work** Ebbinghaus was well aware that the more meaningful and familiar an item of information is, the easier it is to remember. Since he wanted to study memory in a way that would be least affected by previous familiarity, he chose to use three-letter *nonsense syllables* as his memory items. His idea was that these would be approximately equal to each other in their degree of familiarity or unfamiliarity, and thus could serve as standard units in a memory experiment. He began by creating all of the possible consonant-vowel-consonant syllables (such as *RUP*, *GOX*, *PIM*) that did not form words in his native language (German), writing each on a separate card. Then, in each experiment, he chose a different random set of these cards as items to be memorized. His memorizing procedure was to turn over the cards one at a time and read each syllable aloud, at a rate controlled by the ticking of a metronome. He deliberately avoided memory strategies other than simply pronouncing the syllables, since his goal was to learn about the pure effects of rote rehearsal. Immediately after completing one reading of the set, he started again, always going through the cards in the same order. When he could anticipate correctly each syllable before turning over the card, he considered the set to have been memorized. Figure 10.4 shows the number of readings that it took him, on average, to memorize sets of various sizes. Notice that he could memorize seven or fewer syllables in a single reading, but that as the sets became larger the number of readings required increased dramatically.

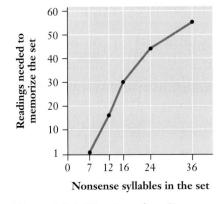

**Figure 10.4 *Number of readings needed to memorize lists of various lengths***

*These results are from one of Ebbinghaus's classic experiments with himself as subject. Notice that he could repeat a list of seven nonsense syllables after just one reading, but needed many more readings to repeat longer lists. This is explained today by saying that a list of seven items can be held in short-term memory, but longer lists must be encoded into long-term memory to be repeated. (Data from Ebbinghaus, 1885/1913.)*

■ *How Ebbinghaus's study of rote rehearsal supports a distinction between short-term and long-term memory*

Although Ebbinghaus did not himself distinguish explicitly between short-term and long-term memory, his results can be examined in light of that distinction. In this light, Ebbinghaus's ability to remember seven syllables in a test conducted immediately after one reading is evidence that seven syllables was the capacity of his short-term memory. Having read a list of seven syllables once, all seven would still be in the short-term store and he could repeat them again without looking at the cards. To memorize more than seven, he would have to encode at least some of them into long-term memory, which requires more than a single reading. Consistent with this interpretation, in other experiments in which he allowed a period of time without rehearsal to intervene between his reading of the list and the test, Ebbinghaus needed many more than one reading to memorize a list of seven syllables. During the nonrehearsal period, according to the model, the syllables would have faded from short-term memory so only those that had been encoded into long-term memory could be recalled.

**The Span and Duration of Short-term Memory**   The number of items that a person can retain in the short-term store at any given time is called the *span of short-term memory*. Ebbinghaus's span for nonsense syllables was apparently about seven, which is about the span that most people have for simple, easily repeated items, whether they are nonsense syllables, single letters, single digits, or unrelated words. Telephone numbers are usually seven digits long, and for most people it takes almost full concentration to hold new ones in mind from the time they hear them to the time they dial them.

*Working memory*

*A seven-digit phone number can sometimes exceed one's short-term memory span. This sales executive's short-term memory may already be holding so much information about the person she's calling that there is no room to store the person's number.*

The span of short-term memory is closely linked to the length of time (duration) that any single item will remain in the short-term store without being repeated. Following each repetition of an item, its trace in short-term memory fades quickly, and the item would be lost completely if not given new life by another repetition. The span of your short-term memory, therefore, is determined by the rate at which you can move mentally from item to item, repeating each as you go, and by the rate that each fades when not repeated. As you try to remember larger sets, it becomes harder to get through them all and back to the first before it disappears. Thus, keeping a list of items in short-term memory is like the job of a circus performer who keeps a set of plates spinning on the ends of sticks. As the number of plates increases, the performer must work more frantically to get back to each to renew its spinning before it falls from the stick.

Lloyd and Margaret Peterson (1959) developed a way to measure the rate at which items disappear from the short-term store when they are not rehearsed. The

■ *How the Petersons measured the rate of disappearance of unrehearsed short-term memories*

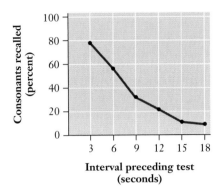

**Figure 10.5 *The duration of unrehearsed short-term memories***

*In this experiment, the delay between reading three consonants and then recalling them was filled with a distraction task (mental arithmetic). Subjects' recall declined sharply as the delay increased, and was barely above chance level by the end of 15 seconds. (From Peterson & Peterson, 1959.)*

Petersons read meaningless sets of three consonants (such as Q M B) to their subjects, which the subjects were to recall after intervals varying from 3 to 18 seconds. Normally this would be a very easy task; people would just repeat the three letters to themselves until the interval was over. But the Petersons prevented rehearsal by adding a *distraction task*. Specifically, they required subjects to spend the interval counting backward by threes from a three-digit number. Under these conditions the three consonants were lost very quickly. Even after 3 seconds, the subjects' performance was less than perfect, and at 18 seconds the subjects seldom recalled any of the consonants (see Figure 10.5). This experiment not only shows how rapidly items fade when they are not rehearsed, but also confirms the assumption that concurrent tasks (mental arithmetic and repeating the syllables) compete with one another for the limited capacity of the short-term store. Think back to our frantic plate spinner. How much more difficult his task would be if, at the same time, he also had to build a tower of cups and saucers.

**Primacy and Recency Effects in Serial List-Learning**   One line of evidence for a short-term versus long-term memory distinction, in the original development of the modal model, came from list-learning experiments demonstrating two *serial-position effects* (Atkinson & Shiffrin, 1968). If subjects are presented a series of items to be remembered one at a time and then (immediately afterwards) must repeat the items in any order (a procedure called *free recall*), they usually recall more items from the beginning and end of the series than they do those from the middle (see Figure 10.6). The enhanced recall for items at the beginning of the list is called the *primacy effect*, and that for items at the end of the list is called the *recency effect*.

In light of the model, these two effects can be explained as follows: Final items are recalled well because they are still in the short-term store when the test begins, and are simply "read off" without the necessity of retrieval from long-term storage. Early items are recalled well because they are rehearsed more than later ones,

**Figure 10.6 *Primacy and recency effects, and evidence that the latter depends on short-term memory***

*In this experiment, subjects rehearsed a list of fifteen words, one word at a time, and then wrote down as many words as they could remember in a free-recall test. In one condition (purple curve), the free-recall test was conducted immediately after the subject rehearsed the last word. In that condition, both the primacy and recency effects were observed. In other conditions, subjects spent either 10 or 30 seconds doing mental arithmetic before the free-recall test, and in those conditions the recency effect was lost but the primacy effect remained. (Adapted from Glanzer & Cunitz, 1966.)*

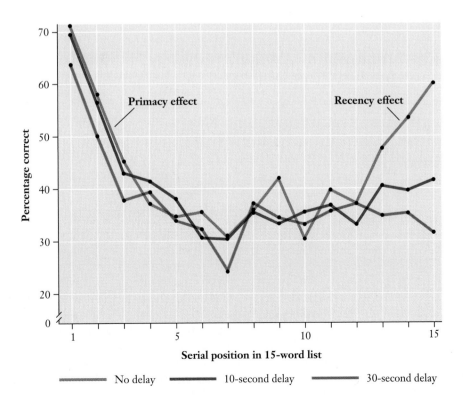
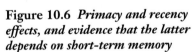

and therefore are more likely to be encoded into long-term memory from which they can be retrieved during the test. Early items are rehearsed more because they are the only items available to be rehearsed when they are first presented, whereas rehearsal of later items is split with that of earlier ones. Items in the middle of the list are not recalled as well because they occurred too late to be rehearsed as fully as early items and too early to still be in short-term memory at the time of the test. This two-part explanation, which attributes the recency effect to short-term memory and the primacy effect to long-term memory, finds support in a number of experiments.

If the recency effect results from short-term memory, then a distraction task that causes subjects to lose material from short-term memory should abolish that effect. Experiments have shown that this indeed happens. For example, Murray Glanzer and Anita Cunitz (1966) engaged subjects in mentally solving arithmetic problems for a short time before the free-recall test, and found that whereas the recency effect disappeared, the primacy effect did not. After distraction, subjects recalled items at the end of the list no better than items in the middle.

By similar reasoning, if the primacy effect is caused by more frequent rehearsal of early items, then any manipulation that equalizes the rehearsal of early and later items should abolish the primacy effect. Richard Atkinson and Richard Shiffrin (1971) performed an experiment that demonstrated this. They instructed subjects to recite aloud each item exactly three times when it was presented, and not to go back and rehearse earlier items in the list. As predicted, this strategy abolished the primacy but not the recency effect.

Although the short-term versus long-term distinction accounts nicely for the recency and primacy effects in list-learning experiments, it does not account for superficially similar effects that can be found in quite different memory tests (see Baddeley, 1986). For example, one study showed, not surprisingly, that at the end of their season rugby players could remember games played near the end of the season better than games played earlier (Baddeley & Hitch, 1977). This could be called a recency effect, but it clearly involves a different mechanism from the recency effect in list-learning studies. A distraction task just before the recall test for rugby games would not have wiped out this recency effect. In keeping with the model, this recency effect would have to be explained in terms of interference or decay in long-term storage, or problems of retrieval from long-term into short-term storage (which are topics that are discussed later).

### Beyond Rote Rehearsal

**Distinction Between Maintenance Rehearsal and Encoding Rehearsal**    In the experiments described so far, no explicit distinction was drawn between the processes involved in holding an item in the short-term store and encoding it into the long-term store. Early versions of the modal model assumed that the longer an item is held, by any means, as short-term memory, the greater the likelihood is that it will be encoded into the long-term store (Waugh & Norman, 1965; Atkinson & Shiffrin, 1968). However, a number of experiments conducted during the 1970s proved that at least under some conditions this assumption is false.

In one such experiment, Fergus Craik and Michael Watkins (1973) required subjects to keep a single, key word in mind while listening to a string of other words; then some subjects wrote down the key word before going on to the next key word and other subjects did not. To vary the amount of rehearsal time, subjects heard word strings of different lengths before writing (or not writing) each key word. Since initially the subjects were led to believe that they were being tested on short-term memory (on their ability to hold each key word in mind only until the next one was presented), there was no motivation for them to try to encode the words into long-term memory. At the end of the session, however, in a surprise

*Evidence from list-learning experiments that the recency effect involves short-term memory and the primacy effect involves long-term memory*

*Evidence that increasing the duration that information is maintained in short-term memory does not necessarily increase the likelihood of encoding it into long-term memory*

test, they were asked to recall as many of the key words as possible. To ensure that the key words would be erased from the short-term store, researchers had subjects first perform a distractor task involving mental arithmetic. Figure 10.7 shows the main results. As you can see, the length of the interval during which a key word was held in short-term memory bore no systematic relation to its likelihood of recall in the long-term test. In contrast, the requirement of writing down a key word *did* increase its likelihood of recall in that test.

**Figure 10.7** *Words recalled from long-term memory after varying periods in short-term memory*
*Subjects held each key word in mind while other words were read and then either reported the key word in writing or didn't report it. As shown here, the likelihood of recall in a subsequent test of long-term memory was not affected by the period that the word had been held in short-term memory, but was affected by reporting. The period measure (on the horizontal axis) is the number of other words (presented at a constant rate) between hearing the key word and either reporting it or going on to the next key word. (Data from Craik & Watkins, 1973.)*

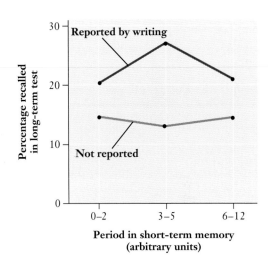

From this and similar experiments (for example, Rundus, 1977), researchers developed the idea that it is important to distinguish between **maintenance rehearsal**, the process by which a person holds information in short-term memory for a period of time, and **encoding rehearsal**, the process by which a person encodes information into the long-term store. The activities that are effective for maintenance are not necessarily effective for encoding.

**The Value of Elaboration**  Most of what we learn and remember in our everyday lives does not come from consciously trying to memorize. Rather, we remember things that capture our interest and stimulate our thought. The more deeply we think about something, the more likely we are to remember it later. To think deeply about an item is to do more than simply repeat it; it is to tie that item to a structure of information already existing in long-term memory. This process is called **elaboration**, or *elaborative rehearsal*, by psychologists who study its effect on memory. The immediate goal of elaboration is not to memorize but to *understand*; yet, the attempt to understand is perhaps the most effective of all ways to memorize most material.

■ *Evidence from both the classroom and the laboratory that the more deeply a person thinks about an item of information, the more likely it will be encoded into long-term memory*

In a study of fifth graders, John Bransford and his colleagues (1982) found that students who received high marks in school were far more likely to use elaborative rehearsal than were those who received lower marks. The researchers gave the children written passages to study for a later test and asked them to explain what they did as they studied each passage. For example, one passage described two different kinds of boomerangs, a returning kind and a nonreturning kind, each used for different purposes. Academically successful students often reported that they rehearsed the material by asking themselves questions about it. They might wonder what a nonreturning boomerang looked like, or why it would be called a boomerang if it didn't return, which caused them to think deeply about what a boomerang really was and about the information in the passage. Less successful students, in contrast, usually studied the passages simply by rereading them.

Programs aimed at helping students learn more in their classes and get higher grades (not necessarily the same thing) often focus on elaborative techniques. One program used in many college learning centers, which in controlled studies has proven successful in raising grades, involves teaching students to write down questions about every textbook section that they read, as they read it, and about every set of lecture notes they take, as they take the notes (Heiman, 1987). The process of generating questions about the material produces deeper thinking about it, which in turn leads to better memory and better performance on tests.

If I could offer a bit of advice about how to study this or any other textbook, it would be the following:

- Don't highlight or copy out passages as you read, but rather *question the text.*

- Constantly ask yourself such questions as: Do I understand the idea that the author is trying to convey here? Do I agree with it? Does it have relevance to my own life experiences? Has the author given evidence supporting it? Does the evidence seem reasonable? How is this idea relevant to the larger issues of the chapter?

- As you ask such questions, jot down notes in the margins that bear on your answers, such as, "This idea seems similar to . . . ," or "I don't understand what he means by . . . ."

Through this active process, you will encode the material in a far richer and more lasting way than you could possibly encode it by simple rereading. You will also, in the process, generate questions that you might ask other students or your instructor.

Even under standard laboratory conditions, in which items to be remembered are sets of unrelated words, elaboration improves encoding into long-term memory. In one of many experiments demonstrating this, Fergus Craik and Endel Tulving (1975) showed subjects a long series of printed words, one at a time, and for each word asked a question that required a different form of thought about the word. In some cases the question was simply about the printing of the word ("Is it in capital letters?"). In other cases the question asked about the word's sound ("Does it rhyme with train?"). In still others, the question referred to the word's meaning ("Would it fit in the sentence, *The girl placed the _____ on the table*"?). As you can see by looking at Figure 10.8, subjects remembered far more words if they had been asked questions that focused on meaning than they did in the other conditions. Other experiments have shown that even better memory occurs when people are asked to relate each word's meaning to their own experiences or characteristics ("Does the word describe you?") (Rogers & others, 1977).

Before leaving the topic of elaborative rehearsal, I should mention that the psychologists who most actively brought this topic to the attention of memory researchers (Fergus Craik and Robert Lockhart, 1972) did so originally as an argument against the modal model and for an alternative conception of memory called the *levels-of-processing theory.* This theory was designed to eliminate the notion of separate storage compartments, and to present memory entirely in terms of active mental processes. More specifically, according to the levels-of-processing theory there is no sharp distinction between short-term and long-term memory. Rather, how long or how well you remember something varies by degree, depending on the depth at which you processed that material (thought about it) when you learned it. Material processed at the deepest level, which involves extensive elaboration, might be remembered for a lifetime (perhaps your sweetheart's words when proposing to you). Material processed at the shallowest level, through simple repetition, might be lost as soon as you stopped repeating it (such as a telephone number that you expect to dial only once). In between these extremes are intermediate ways of processing that allow you to remember material just for the time you need it (such as where you parked your car this morning).

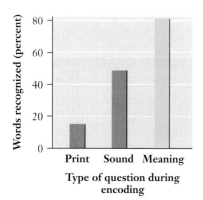

**Figure 10.8** *The method of elaboration used influences the likelihood of encoding into long-term memory*

*When subjects were shown a long sequence of words, and were asked questions that required them to focus on the way the word was printed, or how it sounded, or what it meant, the type of question dramatically affected the subjects' later ability to recognize the word as one that had appeared in the sequence. (Adapted from Craik & Tulving, 1975.)*

*A difference in depth of processing*
Flash cards and counting frames are both traditional ways to learn number facts. On the basis of what you have read, which method do you think is likely to be more effective?

■ *How chunking can be used to increase the amount of information that can be maintained in short-term memory*

Although the levels-of-processing theory has much to recommend it, most memory researchers use it as a supplement to, rather than a replacement for, the modal model. Most still find it useful to distinguish rather sharply between memories that are currently receiving conscious attention (short-term memories) and those that have been placed in a more passive store from which they can later be retrieved (long-term memories). When incorporated into the model, research on levels of processing is used as evidence that information can be encoded into the long-term store in a variety of ways, and that the means of encoding affects either the retention of the information in the long-term store or its retrievability from that store at a later time.

**The Value of Chunking Information into Larger Units**    In discussions of memory it is common to speak of "items" of information. For example, I noted earlier that most people can keep about seven "items" in the short-term store at a time through rote rehearsal. But what is an item? Perhaps the best definition of an item is something that the person treats mentally as a separate, discrete entity. One way to increase the efficiency of memory is to organize information mentally in such a way as to decrease the total number of items and to increase the amount of information in each item—a process known as *chunking* (Miller, 1956).

Chunking is especially helpful if the information can be organized in such a way as to match items that already exist in long-term memory, and thus are already endowed with meaning. As a simple illustration, suppose you were given the following list to hold in short-term memory or to encode into long-term memory: *M D P H D U S S R T W A*. Your task would be a lot easier if you saw this as a set of four common abbreviations—M.D., Ph.D., U.S.S.R., TWA—than if you saw it as a set of twelve randomly chosen letters. You could make the task still easier if you then chunked these abbreviations into a single little story: "The M.D. and the Ph.D. eloped to the U.S.S.R. on TWA." In developing such a story, you would not only be chunking, but also elaborating—making the information more meaningful by adding some new information of your own to it. Even if given a list of truly randomly chosen letters, you could probably find ways to chunk at least some of them into words, abbreviations, or pronounceable syllables, thereby making your memory task easier.

Chunking can enable a person with normal memory capacity to perform what seem to be miraculous memory feats. A dramatic case is that of a young man who, after many weeks of practice, increased his digit span (capacity to repeat a list of digits after hearing them just once) from the usual six or seven digits to approximately eighty (Ericsson & others, 1980). He was a cross-country runner, and his strategy was to chunk sets of digits into running times as they were read to him, and to elaborate on each chunk to give it additional meaning. Thus, 3–4–9–2 became "3 minutes 49.2 seconds, near record-mile time." Sequences that did not work well as running times became ages ("89.3, a very old man") or dates ("1944, near the end of World War II"). This strategy increased his digit span by about three- or four-fold, and to increase it still further he learned to combine these chunks into still larger ones (the three chunks just cited might become "3:49.2 by an 89.3-year-old in 1944"). In this way he gradually built up to the point where he could repeat strings of eighty randomly chosen digits that had been read to him just once. Yet, after all this, when given letters instead of digits to recall, his span fell back to six or seven. His training had not increased his general short-term memory capacity, but had enabled him to use it very efficiently for a certain kind of material.

Chunking helps explain why people who have had a good deal of experience with a certain kind of information are better at keeping in mind a new set of items of that kind than are people with less experience. For example, master chess players can reproduce the arrangement of pieces on a chess board after looking at it for just a few seconds (de Groot, 1965). This is because there are logical ways in which games of chess normally progress, and therefore logical relations among the pieces, which the expert can chunk together and remember as formations rather than as separate pieces. Because master players have those logical formations already stored in long-term memory, they can immediately organize the board into those meaningful chunks. If the pieces are arranged randomly rather than in ways that could occur in a real game, masters are no better than novices at remembering their location (Chase & Simon, 1973).

**Mnemonic Devices**  Mnemonic devices are mental tricks used to help encode material into long-term memory. Most can be understood as variations of chunking and elaboration.

■ *Why master chess players can remember the arrangement of chess pieces after a single, brief look, whereas novices can't*

*An ancient mnemonic device*

*These drawings from a sixteenth-century manual for Dominican friars illustrate a method for memorizing a list of ideas by converting them to a concrete, organized visual image. The friars were instructed to associate each idea with one of the objects in the right-hand drawing and then to mentally place the object somewhere along the familiar route shown in the left-hand drawing (the abbey and its outbuildings). Then, to recall the list, they only had to imagine themselves walking the route and seeing the objects—each object would remind them of the associated idea.*

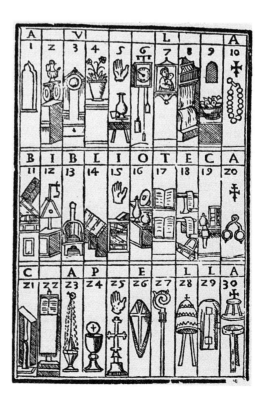

Beginning music students find it easier to remember the notes of the treble clef as *Every Good Boy Does Fine* than as the senseless string of letters *E G B D F*. Similarly, physiology students can recall the seven physiological systems (skeletal, circulatory, respiratory, digestive, muscular, nervous, and reproductive) by matching their first letters to the consonants in SACRED MANOR. Both devices involve chunking—in the first example, the five notes are chunked into one meaningful sentence, and in the second the seven systems are chunked into two meaningful words.

Techniques centering on elaborative rehearsal capitalize on the human tendency to remember things that make sense—even if the sense is fictional. There is no apparent logic to the fact that stone formations hanging down in a cave are called *stalactites* while those pointing up are called *stalagmites*. But you can make up a logic: A stalactite has a *c* in it, so it grows from the *ceiling*; a stalagmite has a *g*, so it grows from the *ground*. Memory of a person's name can be improved by thinking of a logical relation between the name and some characteristic of the person. Thus, Mr. Longfellow's name might be remembered by noting that he is tall and thin, or, if he is actually short and stout, by recalling that he is definitely not a long fellow. I suspect that my name has become easier for students to remember in recent years, as my hair has become increasingly gray.

Some mnemonic devices make use of *mental imagery*, the act of picturing in one's mind the actual items to be remembered. This process may be useful partly because mental imagery involves elaboration and chunking (see Bower, 1970). You have to think about an item in order to form an image of it, and an image can chunk separate items into one. Mental imagery may also be useful because it provides a visual code to supplement the verbal code in which the information was first represented. By encoding the material in two ways, you may increase the chance of its later retrieval.

The *keyword method* is a useful example of a mnemonic device employing mental imagery. Developed by Richard Atkinson (1975) and his colleagues, this two-step method is designed to facilitate the learning of foreign-language vocabulary. First, the student thinks of some easily visualized English word (the keyword) that sounds like some portion of the target foreign word; then the student forms a visual image of that word interacting with the translated meaning of the foreign word. For example, suppose you want to remember that the Spanish word for duck is *pato* (pronounced "pot-o"). First, you might choose the English word *pot* as the keyword; second, you might imagine a duck with a pot over its head (see Figure 10.9). Later, in a vocabulary test on translating from Spanish to English, you would associate *pato* with *pot* (because of the similarity in sound), and *pot* with *duck* (because of your mental image). In a test on translating from English to Spanish, this would be reversed—*duck* would remind you of *pot*, which would remind you of *pato*. The technique takes some effort to use, but research suggests that the effort may be worthwhile. In one experiment, students who studied a Spanish vocabulary list by the keyword method got 88 percent correct on a subsequent test, contrasted to 28 percent correct for those who studied for the same length of time by the more common method of rote rehearsal (Raugh & Atkinson, 1975).

Unlike the keyword method, which really seems to have practical value, some mnemonic systems described in popular memory-improvement books seem to require far more effort than they're worth. I once went to quite a bit of trouble to learn a system that was aimed at helping me remember long number sequences by recoding them into letters and then turning the letters into words. However, I found little use for it because I really don't need to remember many numbers, and I soon forgot the system. My own most useful mnemonic device is one I carry in my shirt pocket—a list I make each evening of the things I need to do the next day (though sometimes I forget to look at it).

**Pato—pot—duck**

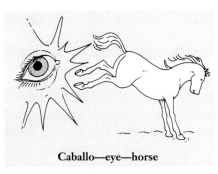

**Caballo—eye—horse**

**Figure 10.9 *How mental images can be used to learn foreign vocabulary***

*The Spanish word* pato, *meaning "duck," might be remembered by associating it with the English word* pot, *and then creating a mental picture associating* pot *with* duck. *The Spanish word* caballo *(pronounced* cob-eye-o*), meaning "horse," might be remembered by associating it with the English word* eye, *and then creating a mental picture associating* eye *with* horse. *(Adapted from Atkinson, 1975.)*

# Representation and Organization in Long-term Memory

We have been discussing the encoding of information into long-term memory. Now we turn to a different question: Once information is encoded into long-term memory, how is it stored? To a cognitive psychologist, this question breaks down into two subsidiary questions: How is information *represented* in long-term memory, and how is information *organized* in long-term memory?

## The Problem of Representation

Representation refers to the abstract relationship between a memory and the original experience on which the memory is based. How does the information held in long-term memory for a specific experience compare with the original sensory information from which the memory was formed? In the following sections we will examine this question as applied first to verbal memories, then to visual memories, and then to the representation of concepts.

**Representation of Verbal Information: The Structure-Meaning Issue**   Much of what we learn is verbal, that is, it comes to us through spoken and written words. The words contain the meaning, which we extract to understand the message. When we form long-term memories for such messages, what do we normally remember? Do we remember the original words, or do we remember the meaning without the original words? Everyday experience, as well as laboratory evidence, suggests that the latter is most often the case. I doubt if you can tell me the exact words I used to define short-term memory earlier in this chapter, but you can probably convey quite well the meaning.

Some years ago, Jacqueline Sachs (1967) asked people to listen to prose passages and then tested their ability to recognize whether new sentences were identical to sentences in the passage or changed in some way. She found that people accurately recognized changes in meaning but not changes in wording that left the meaning unchanged. For example, when the original sentence was *He sent a letter about it to Galileo*, most people identified *Galileo sent a letter about it* as different from the original, but did not identify *A letter about it was sent to Galileo* as different. The only condition in which subjects recognized changes in wording as accurately as changes in meaning was when the original sentence occurred at the end of the passage, so that it was still in short-term memory when the test occurred. This experiment and many others suggest that we usually encode the meaning of a statement but not its structure (specific chain of words) into long-term memory.

A more elaborate experiment showing that we remember the meaning more than the structure of verbal statements was performed by John Bransford and Jeffrey Franks (1971). Starting with one-sentence stories, each of which contained four basic facts, these researchers constructed sets of shorter sentences. For example, one of their four-fact story sentences was *The ants in the kitchen ate the sweet jelly which was on the table*. Each shorter sentence contained anywhere from one to three of these facts. For the story just given, a one-fact sentence might be *The jelly was sweet*, and a two-fact sentence might be *The ants in the kitchen ate the jelly*. These shorter sentences served as the acquisition sentences in the experiment.

During the experiment, subjects heard the acquisition sentences in a random order, such that those derived from different stories were interspersed with one another. Thus, a subject might hear *The ants in the kitchen ate the jelly* and then facts from other stories. Although no single acquisition sentence contained all of the facts of any of the original stories, the whole set of sentences taken together contained all of the facts of each story. In the next phase of the experiment, the sub-

■ *Evidence that people usually remember the meaning but not the wording of verbal statements*

**It's an actual fact—**

DANDRUFF and Listerine simply do not get along together. And, peculiarly, the real importance of this fact was discovered by dandruff sufferers themselves who persisted in writing in to the makers of Listerine, urging that this use be advertised.

Hundreds of letters, from women as well as men, are on file, making claims for Listerine much stronger even than the manufacturers of

Listerine would care to make. So if you are troubled with dandruff, you'll be glad to know that regular applications of Listerine, doused on clear and massaged in will actually do the trick.

It's really wonderful how it invigorates, cleanses and refreshes the scalp. And how it brings out that luster and softness that women want—and men like. Try it yourself and see. *Lambert Pharmacal Company, St. Louis, U S A.*

**DANDRUFF** *and Listerine simply do not get along together*

*Truth in advertising?*

*For nearly half a century, advertisers have been using "psychology" on consumers, and ads like this have capitalized on the fact that we jump to meaning rather than attending to specific wording. As you read the ad, ask yourself what the prospective buyer may have stored in memory.*

■ *Evidence that people remember the wording of statements that are high in interactional content*

jects heard various test sentences, some of which were identical to the one-, two-, or three-fact acquisition sentences and some of which were novel combinations of the facts from a given story.

The results of the experiment were striking. The more facts a test sentence contained, the more confident the subjects were that they had heard it before, whether or not they really had. Thus, they were more confident that they had heard *The ants in the kitchen ate the jelly* than *The jelly was sweet.* They were most confident that they had heard the four-fact sentences, though these had never been presented during the acquisition phase. Thus, for our example, they were most confident of having heard the sentence *The ants in the kitchen ate the sweet jelly which was on the table.*

How can we explain this strange finding? Why were the subjects consistently more likely to believe that they had heard the whole stories, which they had not heard, than the simpler sentences, which they *had* heard? Bransford and Franks interpreted their finding in terms of the mind's search for meaning. When presented with a random series of statements, the mind tries to put them together in a way that makes sense, that tells a coherent story. It is the story, not the individual statements, that becomes fixed in long-term memory. Because the four-fact sentences matched best the full meaning of the stories stored in memory, the subjects were most confident of having heard them.

From a functionalist perspective, it makes sense that people would normally store the meaning, not the structure, of verbal statements in long-term memory. What we need to remember is the potentially useful information, that which helps us deal more effectively with the world around us. It really doesn't matter if we remember *Close cover before striking* as *Close cover before lighting.* Either phrase is equally useful to prevent us from burning ourselves.

On the other hand, there are times when we do remember statements verbatim (word for word). We may memorize poems whose sounds we enjoy, and actors memorize thousands of lines when their jobs require it. Even when not deliberately trying to memorize, we may remember verbatim specific statements in which the wording was especially important to the original appreciation of the statement. Perhaps you can remember Rhett Butler's last line in the movie *Gone with the Wind* in exactly his words, because the same literal meaning stated differently would not have had the same impact.

In a study of memories from a natural conversation, Janice Keenan and her colleagues (1977) gave a surprise test to a group of psychology professors and graduate students 30 hours after they had held an informal luncheon seminar. They asked the subjects to select sentences that were identical to what had been uttered at the meeting from sets of sentences that had the same meaning but differed in wording. The main finding was that people quite accurately identified verbatim those sentences that were high in *interactional content*, that is, those in which speakers attempted to convey something about themselves or others present rather than simply factual information about the topic of the seminar. Such statements typically contained some degree of humor, sarcasm, or personal criticism, and their full meaning depended not just on the literal interpretation but on the exact words chosen. Rhett Butler could have said, simply, "I don't care" as he walked away from Scarlett. But he chose instead to say, "Frankly, my dear, I don't give a damn," and that is what we remember.

**Representation of Visual-Spatial Information: The Image Issue** If you remember what Rhett Butler said, do you remember what he looked like? Did he have a beard? Many people say that they try to answer such questions by calling up a visual image of the person and inspecting that image to see, for example, if there is a beard on the face.

Visual images appear to play an important role in much of our thinking, especially that about the spatial layout of things. I can never remember which way is west when I am facing south unless I picture myself standing on a map of the United States. Then I can see immediately that the West Coast is on my right. At a slightly higher level of thought, Einstein claimed that the concept of relativity came to him through visualizing what would happen if he chased a beam of light and caught up to it (Kosslyn, 1987). When you try to decide if a serving bowl you saw at the store would fit into a particular space in your cupboard, do you use a visual image? For a long time, psychologists avoided the concept of visual imagery because it seemed to imply the scientifically absurd notion of a picture actually existing in the head. But the study of such imagery has gained new respectability, in part because of neurological evidence (to be discussed in Chapter 11) that separate parts of the brain are involved in visual and verbal thought.

There are two general theories about the nature of long-term memories for visual scenes. One, called the **propositional theory**, is that such memories are stored in essentially the same way as verbal memories, as sets of **propositions**, which are defined as the smallest meaningful, separate units of information that can be stored in memory (Anderson, 1985). For example, if you look at the picture in Figure 10.10, you might store such propositions as: *It is a speedboat. It has an outboard motor at the stern, a small cabin with one porthole in the middle, and an anchor on the bow.* You would not necessarily store the propositions in those words, or in any words at all, but you could translate the propositions directly into words, just as if you had learned about the boat from a verbal description instead of a picture.

The other theory, called the **analogue theory**, is that we store visual information in a way that preserves the spatial gradients of the original scene and in that sense is functionally equivalent to a picture. Of course, no one would claim that the memory really *is* a picture in the head, or that it preserves all of the information that a picture would preserve. Rather, the claim is that the memory is stored in a form that we must inspect mentally *as if it were a picture* to extract the information from it. To grasp more fully the distinction between propositional and analogue representation of information, think of the difference between a digital clock, which gives you the time in terms of propositions (such as 1:32 P.M.), and the more traditional analogue clock, which indicates time by the movement of its hands. With the digital clock you read the time directly, whereas with the analogue clock you must infer the time from the spatial arrangement of the hands. When we recall a visually acquired memory, is our task more like looking at a digital clock or an analogue clock?

How can researchers test these theories to decide which is more valid? Some argue that the theories can't be tested, but others say that the theories lead to different predictions about how people should behave when asked questions about visually learned information. If the analogue theory is correct, people should behave in ways that are similar to looking at a picture when asked such questions; but if the propositional theory is correct, they should behave more as if they are looking up items in the dictionary. In one experiment, Stephen Kosslyn (1973) demonstrated that at least when people are instructed to form visual images, they do answer such questions as if looking at a picture.

Kosslyn showed people drawings, including that in Figure 10.10, and later asked them to visualize each drawing from memory. He asked them to focus, in their memory, on either the left or the right end of the drawing and then, as quickly as possible, to indicate (by pushing one of two buttons) whether or not a particular named component was present in the drawing. For example, referring to the boat drawing, he would say "motor" or "porthole" or "anchor" while the person was focusing at either the left or the right end of the boat in memory. He found that the farther away the named object was from the place of focus, the

*Difference between the propositional and analogue theories of visually acquired memories*

**Figure 10.10** *Sample stimulus used in a mental-imagery experiment*

*Subjects saw line drawings such as this, and later, when answering questions based on their memory of the drawing, showed reaction times suggesting that they were scanning a mental image. (From Kosslyn, 1980.)*

*How Kosslyn demonstrated that people examine visual images as if they were looking at pictures*

**Figure 10.11** *Evidence for mental rotation of visual images*
Cooper and Shepard presented subjects with letters that were sometimes mirror-reversed and were rotated at varying degrees from
upright. The task was to identify as quickly as possible whether the
letter was mirror-reversed or not. As shown here, the time required
to respond depended on the degree of rotation. The researchers interpreted this as evidence that subjects mentally rotate the image to an
upright position to compare it with an image stored in memory. The
farther they had to turn it, the longer it took them to respond.
(Adapted from Cooper & Shepard, 1973.)

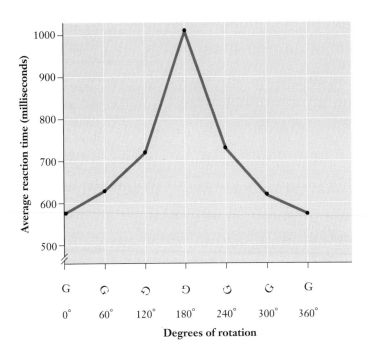

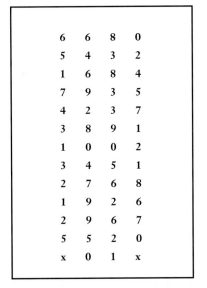

**Figure 10.12** *Array of numbers that
the mnemonist S. could recall as a
visual image*

With his remarkable visual memory, S.
could summon a visual image of this array
and read off the numbers in any direction.
(From Luria, 1968.)

longer it took subjects to push the button. It was as if they had to scan across the mental image to find the named property before responding. This, to Kosslyn, was evidence that the subjects' memory of the drawing indeed was organized spatially, like a picture.

Other evidence for the analogue theory comes from studies suggesting that people rotate visual mental images, much as they would rotate actual pictures or objects, to answer certain kinds of questions (see Figure 10.11 and its caption). It is hard to imagine how such rotation could be accomplished if each element were stored as a discrete proposition.

Occasionally we hear of people who have phenomenal visual memories. One such person was S., studied by the Russian psychologist A. R. Luria (1968), who automatically turned almost any sort of stimulus into a visual image. If given a table of digits to remember—such as that in Figure 10.12—he would study it for 2 or 3 minutes and then, months or even years later, be able to recall it as a picture and read off the items. As evidence that his memory was like a picture, he could recite the numbers equally well in any order that was consistent with the spatial layout of the original table—forward, backward, or along the rows, columns, or diagonals. This is very different from the performance of the young man mentioned earlier who learned to memorize a long string of digits by grouping them into meaningful chunks; that strategy would not permit reciting the digits in any but the originally encoded order.

Except for enabling him to earn a living as a performing mnemonist, S.'s phenomenal picture memory did not help him much in everyday life. In fact, his memory seemed to interfere with his ability to think deeply about anything, since each thought would bring forth irrelevant arrays of visually imaged trivia. S. struggled with the problem of how to forget, and he hit upon an interesting solution—he would write things down. While most of us write things down that we want to remember, S. wrote things down that he wanted to forget! He reasoned that if he wrote an item down, his mind would no longer sense a need to hold it in memory and would allow it to slip away, since he could always look it up from the written record. Strange as it may seem, this technique apparently worked.

**The difference between the feature and prototype theories of how concepts are represented mentally**

**Representation of Concepts**   To understand a sentence such as *The ants ate the jelly,* or to recognize the object in Figure 10.10 as a boat, a person must already have in long-term memory a mental representation of certain *concepts*—the concepts *ant, eat, jelly,* and *boat.* Concepts provide the basis for categorizing objects and events and can be considered the units of a person's general understanding of the world. Cognitive psychologists commonly use the term **schema** to refer to the mental representation of a concept. Whatever you have in long-term memory that allows you to classify some objects as boats and others as not boats is your schema for *boat.* How can schemas be best described? Traditionally, there have been two broad categories of answers to that question, which correspond at least roughly with the distinction between the propositional and analogue theories discussed above.

According to the propositional theory, more often called the **feature theory** in this context, schemas are best understood as sets of *defining features,* which can be stated as propositions. For example, the concept *bird* might be defined by a set of features that includes the following: animate, feathery, stands on two legs, flies, sings. A basic problem with this theory is that it is very difficult to create a list of features that uniquely and fully defines the category. Penguins don't fly or sing, and a plucked bird (even a dead plucked bird) is still recognized as a bird. Conversely, other objects can be found that would not be called birds and that have one or more of any list of bird features we could generate.

According to the analogue theory, called the **prototype theory** in this context, a schema is not a list of discrete features, but rather is a holistic, picturelike representation of a typical or average member of the category. If you close your eyes and imagine what to you is a typical bird, that may be your *prototype* for the bird concept. When you recognize birds, you may do so by matching them to your prototype. You recognize more quickly and accurately those that are more similar to the prototype than you do those that are less similar. Likewise, when you use the word *bird* in a sentence without qualifying the word, your meaning is best represented not by all birds but by your bird prototype.

**How Rosch's experiments tend to support the prototype theory of schemas**

The work of Eleanor Rosch (see Lakoff, 1987) is the best-known research used to support the prototype theory. In one experiment, Rosch (1973) asked people to rate various members of categories according to how typical each was of its category, and she found great consistency from person to person. For example, for the category *bird,* nearly everyone rated *robin* and *bluebird* as very typical and *chicken* and *penguin* as not very typical. In later experiments, Rosch (1975, 1977) used these ratings to see if they corresponded to other behaviors that would presumably reflect people's concepts. When she asked people to say whether specific pictured objects were or were not members of a certain category (such as *bird*), she found that they were quicker to say yes if it was a typical member (such as *robin*) than an atypical member (such as *chicken*). When she asked people to use category labels in a sentence, she found that most people made up sentences that were sensible for typical members of the category but not for atypical members. For example, given the label *bird,* a person might say, *The bird sat twittering on the twig of a tree,* which works well if *bird* means something like a robin or bluebird, but not if it means something like a chicken or penguin.

The debate between feature and prototype theorists quickly enters into issues that are difficult if not impossible to resolve. Feature theorists point out that although people may take longer to say that chickens are birds, they can do so; so their schemas must incorporate the whole category, not just typical members. Moreover, feature theories can be modified in ways to account for Rosch's findings. One might posit that not all members of the category to which the concept refers need to have all of the features that define the concept. Typicality by this view is an index of the number of features that a given object has from the total set that makes up the concept (Smith & others, 1974). Theories have also been developed that incorporate characteristics of both feature and prototype theories to account, on the one hand, for people's ability to categorize according to defining principles and, on the other hand, for Rosch's findings regarding typicality (Greenberg & Kuczaj, 1982).

**Schemas and scripts are culture-specific representations of typical scenes and events**

The term *schema* was used originally by the British psychologist Frederick Bartlett (1932) to refer not to concepts for specific objects such as birds, but to more complex concepts that may vary from culture to culture and have to do with the way that objects or events are organized in a person's experience. For example, in our culture people might share a relatively common schema of a living room, perhaps including a couch, an easy chair, and a rocking chair, all oriented around a television set, with a coffee table in front of the couch. When we enter a new living room, we recognize it as a living room and assess its unique features by comparing it with our already existing schema. Schemas that involve the organization of events in time, rather than the organization of objects in space, are commonly called **scripts** by today's cognitive psychologists (Schank & Abelson, 1977). The typical birthday party is a good example of a script in our culture: There are games, followed by the presentation of the cake, the blowing out of the candles, the singing of "Happy Birthday," the eating of the cake, the opening of the presents, and then more games. As you will see later, schemas and scripts do not just help us recognize familiar objects, scenes, or events that we encounter; they also affect the way that we remember those that we have previously encountered. We tend to distort our specific memories in directions that fit our schemas and scripts.

## Organization of Knowledge

To be retrievable, information must be organized. In a dictionary, information is retrievable because the entries are organized alphabetically. There it is easy to find every word that starts with *A*, but hard to find every word that is the name of a fruit. In a supermarket, items are organized in a different way: There it is easy to find the fruits, but hard to find all the items that start with *A*. We can draw an analogy here to the way we search for things in long-term memory. If I ask you to name things that start with *A*, you can easily read off a long string of such items from your memory. If I ask you to name different fruits, you can do that just as easily. Similarly, if I ask you to name things that are red, or that rhyme with cat, or that happened yesterday, or that taste sweet, you can use any of these categories to probe your memory and come up quickly with a number of items. In fact, it is difficult to think of any way of categorizing things that you cannot use to retrieve groups of items very quickly from long-term memory. The most remarkable thing about human long-term memory is not the enormous number of items it contains, but the incredible sophistication of its organization.

What might a filing system look like that allows such flexibility in retrieval? To date, no one has proposed a complete answer to that question. But a good number of partial answers have been proposed, often based on ways that computer memories can be organized. The most well known is a model proposed some years ago by Allan Collins and M. Ross Quillian (1969). Before examining this model, let us first explore an earlier approach to the problem of memory organization.

**The Traditional Associationist View** In Chapter 5 the principle of association by contiguity was presented, the idea that if two events occur at the same time (contiguously) their memories will be linked together in the mind. This idea, usually traced back to Aristotle, served for centuries as the leading principle for understanding memory organization. It is interesting now to think about how this principle might apply to procedural, episodic, and semantic information (distinguished early in this chapter).

*■ Why association by contiguity seems to be useful for understanding the organization of procedural and episodic memories, but not semantic memories*

Association by contiguity is useful in understanding the organization of procedural and episodic memories. Procedural memories, you may recall, are nonverbal memories for habits or skills. Habits such as a rat's pressing a lever in response to a green light, or my pressing my car's brake pedal in response to a red one, can be thought of as sequences of stimuli and responses, and the connections may have been learned because of their previous contiguity. Episodic memories are conscious memories of our own previous experiences, which are linked in time; again, the principle of association by contiguity is useful in understanding them. Your ability to recall as a cluster the events that occurred in a given episode of your life—such as everything that happened to you at breakfast yesterday—may reside in associations formed by the contiguity of those experiences.

But association by contiguity does not work as well in explaining the organization of semantic memories. Semantic memories form our store of general knowledge about the world, the store that presumably we enter when asked to think of things that are red or whose names start with *A*. This store seems to be organized not by contiguity but by *similarity*. Items that are similar seem to be linked together mentally whether or not we have ever experienced them contiguously (one after the other or together). Aristotle himself recognized that ideas are organized in terms of similarity as well as contiguity, and proposed **association by similarity** as a second basic principle. (He proposed a third principle, too, association by contrast, but that is really just an extension of similarity.)

*■ How association by similarity can be applied to semantic memories, and why this principle implies more complex organization than does association by contiguity*

Aristotle's second principle is far more difficult to understand in terms of how it could come about than the first. Contiguity represents association along just one dimension—a dimension of time at which the items were experienced. But similarity can occur on any dimension. Things can be similar in color, size, what they are used for, features of their names, and so on ad infinitum. To say that you can recall one red thing after another because of the principle of association by similarity is no explanation at all. How did your mind ever group all red things together and at the same time preserve each item's groupings along other dimensions?

One early psychologist who thought a good deal about the principle of association by similarity was William James (1890). He didn't explain it, but he did help draw attention to its importance. James suggested that the learning of new information always occurs through contiguity, but that subsequent reorganization is based on similarity. For example, you first learn what a canary is through experiencing its various properties (its yellow color, its song, the word used to label it, and so on) contiguously. Because of association by contiguity, any one of these properties can later call into memory the others, which taken together constitute your concept (schema) of a canary. But those properties also tie the canary concept mentally to other concepts in your mind, and that is the basis for association by similarity.

Each property of the canary can link the canary concept to other concepts that share that property. The yellow color ties it to other yellow objects, the song to other things that sing, the name to other things whose names start with *C*, and so on. Thus, properties of objects, learned through contiguity, become the links by which the mind organizes information according to similarity. James believed that the ability to organize information along many dimensions of similarity is the basic difference between the human mind and that of other animals. He expressed this idea poetically in the following contrast between dogs and humans (James, 1890): "Thoughts [in dogs] will not be found to call up their similars, but only their habitual successors. Sunsets will not suggest heroes' deaths, but supper-time. This is why man is the only metaphysical animal."

*■ The reason for thinking that, for efficiency, long-term memory would be organized hierarchically*

**A Hierarchical Model of Semantic Memory**    An idea that is ignored in the traditional, associationist way of thinking about the mind is that concepts may be hierarchically organized. Mental concepts refer to categories, and one category can be embedded within another in hierarchical fashion. For example, *canary* is embedded within the larger category *bird*, which is embedded within the still larger category *animal*. Computer programmers know that such hierarchies can represent very efficiently a large amount of information with a minimum of computer memory needed to hold it or retrieve it. One advantage is that information that applies to all members of a large category needs to be entered only once, tied to the large category's title, and does not have to then be separately entered for each of the subcategories. Collins and Quillian (1969, 1972) developed a model of human semantic memory designed to capture the advantages of hierarchical organization.

As illustrated in Figure 10.13, Collins and Quillian proposed that there are three kinds of components in semantic memory—units, properties, and pointers. *Units* are the categories themselves, which are hierarchically arranged; *properties* are the characteristics that describe each unit; and *pointers* are the associative bonds between units and other units, or between units and properties. As you can see in the figure, there are two different kinds of pointers: (1) *category pointers*, which show that one unit is a subset of a larger unit; and (2) *property pointers*, which link units to properties that describe that unit. If you follow the category pointers from the unit *canary* in the figure, you can see that a canary is a bird and that a bird is an animal. If you follow its property pointers, you can see that a canary is yellow and can sing. To specify properties of canaries that are common to birds in general, you must first follow the category pointer up to *bird* and then follow its property pointers. In this way you can find that a canary has feathers, has wings, and can fly.

■ *Collins and Quillian's hierarchical model of semantic memory, and how they tested it experimentally*

**Figure 10.13** *Example of organization of semantic memory according to Collins and Quillian's hierarchical model*

*In this diagram, category pointers (red) link subordinate categories with higher categories, and property pointers (purple) link categories with properties. Notice that an advantage of this organization is that properties common to a group of subordinate categories need be entered only once, at the node representing their common higher category. (From Collins & Quillian, 1969.)*

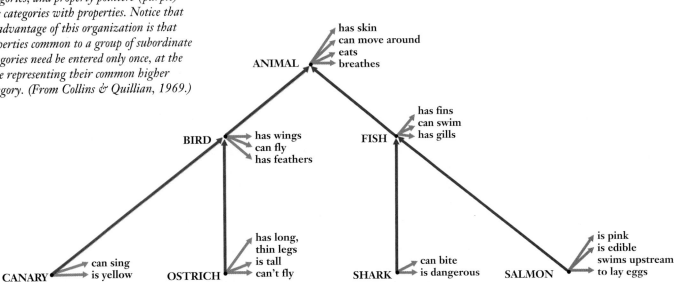

Another advantage of a hierarchical organization, aside from its efficiency in representing a large amount of information, is that it allows a person to make reasonable inferences that are not based on direct experience. Suppose you are asked, "Can a bird breathe?" Perhaps you have never seen a bird breathe, but if your memory is organized as shown in Figure 10.13, you can answer the question by following the category pointers all the way up to *animal* and then following the property pointers out from there. Since a bird is an animal, and animals can breathe, you can infer that birds can breathe.

How can one test a model such as Collins and Quillian's? Any model of the mind can be tested only if it makes specific predictions about how people should behave. A prediction of this model is that the more pointers you must traverse to answer a question, the longer it should take to answer the question. To test their

**Figure 10.14** *Average reaction times required to verify statements related to Collins and Quillian's hierarchy*

*The statements shown in the diagram are only samples of the statements used. Some were about properties of specific animals, and some were about categories to which an animal belonged. The critical variable (shown on the horizontal axis) was whether the answer to the statement required traversing 0, 1, or 2 category pointers according to the model depicted in Figure 10.13. (Adapted from Collins & Quillian, 1969.)*

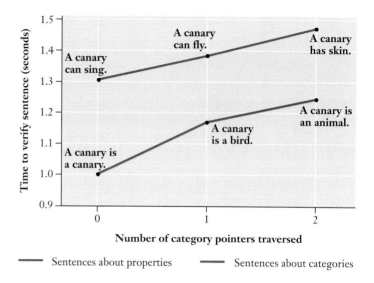

model, Collins and Quillian used a *sentence-verification task* in which they asked people to say "true" or "false" as quickly as possible after hearing sentences such as *A canary can sing* or *A canary can breathe*. Notice that, according to the model, people should be able to verify the first of these sentences more quickly than the second, because the first requires traversing only one pointer while the second requires traversing three. In general, Collins and Quillian's findings were consistent with their model (see Figure 10.14), though other experimenters since then have obtained mixed results (see Chang, 1986).

Collins and Quillian's model is not the final word on long-term memory organization, but it typifies the approach of contemporary cognitive psychology. The emphasis is on models that (a) can be represented in computer-like language, and (b) make specific, testable predictions about human behavior. To produce such explicit models, cognitive psychologists must focus on just a part of long-term memory rather than tackle the whole problem at once. Thus, Collins and Quillian's model deals only with our memories for certain kinds of categories and certain kinds of properties of those categories. It does not encompass more abstract categories such as *justice* and does not deal with all the properties of the categories that it does encompass. The model shows how we can quickly link canaries with other things that breathe, but does not show how we can also link them with things that have nothing to do with the taxonomy of animals, such as things that are yellow, or things whose names start with *C*. Are there separate hierarchical structures based on different kinds of properties? The model is at most a small beginning toward understanding our incredibly sophisticated and flexible memory filing system.

**How arranging information into a hierarchy can improve long-term memory for it**

**Improving Long-term Memory Through Hierarchical Encoding**   Whether or not long-term memories are naturally encoded in a hierarchical fashion, there is no doubt that the deliberate use of a hierarchical structure in encoding can improve such memories. In an experiment demonstrating this, Andrea Halpern (1986) gave people a chart listing fifty-four well-known song titles to be memorized. In some cases the chart was organized in the logical, hierarchical manner depicted in Figure 10.15, with songs arranged according to categories and subcategories. In other cases a similar chart was used, but organized randomly, with no systematic relation among categories, subcategories, and song titles. When tested later for their memory of the song titles, subjects who had studied the organized chart accurately recalled many more titles than those who had studied the disorganized chart. During the test they would first recall a category name and then the songs that had been listed under that name.

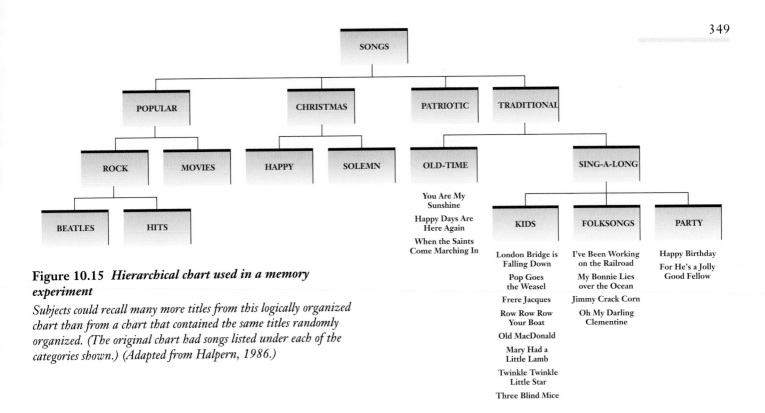

**Figure 10.15** *Hierarchical chart used in a memory experiment*
*Subjects could recall many more titles from this logically organized chart than from a chart that contained the same titles randomly organized. (The original chart had songs listed under each of the categories shown.) (Adapted from Halpern, 1986.)*

Of course, there is a practical lesson here (which you might add to the ideas about mnemonic aids discussed earlier): If you have to memorize a lot of material for an exam, organize it first in some meaningful, hierarchical way, with simple key word headings for each category and subcategory. In the exam you will be able to recall the headings and that, in turn, will help you recall the material under each heading. This is the tried-and-true principle underlying what many generations of students have known as the crib sheet—the list of key terms that summarizes the organizational structure of the material on which the students will be tested. (Of course, carrying crib notes on a piece of paper into the test room is cheating, but carrying the same information hierarchically organized in your head is not.)

## Problems of Retrieval from Long-term Memory

According to the modal model, long-term memories can affect behavior only if they are retrieved into the short-term store. Because studies of long-term memory (like any studies in psychology) rely on behavioral observations, all studies of long-term memory are studies of retrieval. All of the research on long-term memory that we have discussed so far—studies of encoding strategies, of representation, and of organization—were based on subjects' ability or lack of ability to retrieve the relevant information, or on the amount of time it took them to do so. Thus, the issue of retrieval has been implicit throughout our discussion of long-term memory. Now, however, we turn more explicitly to this issue, addressing three questions: (1) What causes forgetting (loss of retrievability over time) from long-term memory? (2) In what ways are our memories for specific events affected by information other than that encoded from the original event? (3) Does hypnosis affect retrievability?

### Why Do We Forget?

There can be no doubt that in general our ability to retrieve items from long-term memory decreases with time after original encoding, unless the items have been retrieved frequently in the interim. But the rate of decrease varies tremendously,

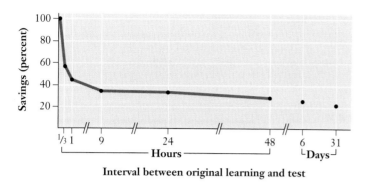

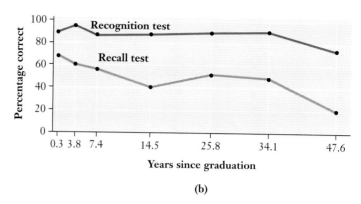

(a)

(b)

**Figure 10.16  *Forgetting curves for* (a) *nonsense syllables and* (b) *high-school classmates***

*Graph (a) depicts the results of a classic experiment in which Hermann Ebbinghaus tested his own memory for lists of nonsense syllables (thirteen syllables per list) at various intervals after original learning. The measure of memory (percent saved) was the number of repetitions required to relearn the list as a percentage of the number required for original learning.*

*Graph (b) depicts the results of a more recent experiment in which memories for names and faces of high-school classmates were tested in people who had graduated from 3 months to nearly 50 years before testing. In the* recognition *test, subjects had to match each name to one out of a set of yearbook portraits. In the* recall *test, they were shown yearbook portraits and had to recall the names without any other cues. [Graph (a) is based on data from Ebbinghaus, 1885/1913; graph (b) is adapted from Bahrick & others, 1975.]*

■ *The difference between retroactive and proactive interference, and the conditions under which these effects are most likely to occur*

depending on the depth at which the information was encoded originally, and also depending on the manner in which the test is conducted. In Figure 10.16 you can see two very different *forgetting curves*. The first is from Ebbinghaus's classic research with lists of nonsense syllables. As you can see, most forgetting occurred within the first hour; then the rate of loss became increasingly gradual, with little difference between tests conducted 1 day or 1 month thereafter. The second is from a study by H. P. Bahrick and his colleagues (1975) on people's memories for names and faces of their former high-school classmates—information that would have been learned more solidly than Ebbinghaus's nonsense syllables. As you can see, in this study people who had graduated 34 years earlier were as good as recent graduates at matching names to faces in a recognition (multiple-choice) test. On the other hand, a different test (recalling classmates' names from pictures with no other cues) revealed a considerable loss in memory over time since graduation.

What causes forgetting? An early theory, the *law of disuse*, held that memories simply fade away or decay gradually over time when they are not used (Thorndike, 1913). This theory is not well accepted today. The extreme form of the disuse theory, that *all* memories fade away when not used, seems to be disproved by data such as that shown in Figure 10.16b. A milder form of the theory, that *some* memories are lost from disuse, may be untestable because it is impossible to prove that loss of retrievability is not caused by something else. Alternatives to the disuse theory are *interference theories*, which maintain that other memories may interfere with the ability to retrieve any given memory, and *retrieval-cue theories*, which maintain that the ability to retrieve information depends on the availability of appropriate cues (reminders).

**Retroactive and Proactive Interference**   One early bit of evidence against the law of disuse came from an experiment conducted by John Jenkins and Karl Dallenbach (1924). These researchers found that subjects who memorized lists of nonsense syllables late at night and then slept during the interval before testing remembered more syllables than those who memorized the same lists in the morning and spent the retention interval engaged in normal waking activities. This result suggested that memory loss is caused by interference from other learning and mental activity that occurs when awake, and not by the simple passage of time.

Subsequent research has demonstrated two types of interference. *Retroactive interference* is the type that might have produced the greater forgetting by subjects who were awake compared to those who had slept in Jenkins and Dallenbach's experiment. This is interference that stems from material that is learned *after* the test material was learned. *Proactive interference*, on the other hand, is interference that stems from material learned *before* the test material was learned. Both kinds are commonly studied in the laboratory by giving subjects lists of words or nonsense syllables to memorize. If two lists are learned, the inhibiting effect the second

**Table 10.1** *Experimental designs used to assess retroactive and proactive interference*

| | Task 1 | Task 2 | Test |
|---|---|---|---|
| **Retroactive interference** | | | |
| Interference group | Learn *A* | Learn *B* | Test on *A* |
| Control group | Learn *A* | — | Test on *A* |
| **Proactive interference** | | | |
| Interference group | Learn *A* | Learn *B* | Test on *B* |
| Control group | — | Learn *B* | Test on *B* |

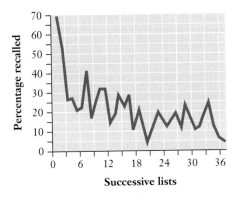

**Figure 10.17** *Proactive interference*

*Subjects learned a new list every 2 days and were tested before each new session on only the most recently learned list. As the experiment progressed, performance deteriorated, indicating proactive interference. (Adapted from Keppel & others, 1968.)*

***An artful solution***

*Classroom teachers, especially those who work with different groups of students each period, encounter serious interference effects in trying to learn their students' names. In the one-to-one situation in which art teachers work, name tags on each desk effectively solve this problem.*

list has on a person's memory of the first list is retroactive interference; the inhibiting effect the first list has on a person's memory of the second list is proactive interference (see Table 10.1).

A particularly striking example of proactive interference is shown in Figure 10.17. Subjects who learned thirty-six successive word lists, each separated by a 2-day interval, showed progressively poorer memory of the most recently learned list as the experiment continued. In the last test they remembered only about 5 percent of the words, compared to 70 percent in the first test. Proactive interference does not affect either the rate at which a new list is learned or the immediate memory for the list, but it leads to more rapid forgetting. The steep rate of forgetting shown by Ebbinghaus (look again at Figure 10.16a) is probably due to proactive interference, although he apparently was not aware of that phenomenon. Ebbinghaus learned hundreds of lists of nonsense syllables over the course of his experiments, so each new list would have been interfered with by the previous ones.

What causes retroactive and proactive interference? These phenomena are far from understood, and it is possible that the correct answer varies for different instances. According to one theory, proposed some years ago by John Ceraso (1967) and based on list-learning experiments, both forms of inhibition occur because the separately learned lists lose their distinctiveness with time and tend to merge, in memory, forming one large pool of information rather than two or more smaller ones. It is harder to search through a large pool of information and find an appropriate item than it is to search through a smaller pool.

Ceraso's and others' theories predict that interference should be greatest when the different learning tasks involve similar items (similar items are more likely to merge into one pool than are dissimilar items). Many experiments have confirmed this prediction (see Wickens, 1972). Lists of nonsense syllables interfere with other lists of nonsense syllables, but not with lists of words; and lists of words drawn from the same category (say, *animals*) interfere with each other but not with those drawn from a different category (say, *household furniture*). I once heard a story about an absent-minded ichthyology professor (fish specialist) who refused to learn the names of his students. Asked why, he responded, "Every time I learn a student's name I forget the name of a fish." Had he studied cognitive psychology he would have known that learning the names of one group of students might have interfered with his memory for names of another group of students, but not with his memory for names of fish (that is, unless students and fish were similar entities in his mind).

Laboratory studies of interference are sometimes criticized for the unnatural memory items they employ. Rarely in everyday life do we memorize lists. Can interference be demonstrated in more natural conditions? Yes. An excellent example has to do with your memory for where you have parked your car. Parking each day at your place of work or study is the kind of situation that should lead to interfer-

**A master of musical memory**

*The eminent conductor Arturo Toscanini was known during his lifetime for extraordinary feats of memory. He is said to have known every note of every instrument of 250 symphonic scores, 100 operas, and many other works. One famous story describes him briefly visualizing the music for an entire concert, and then reassuring an agitated second bassoonist that he would not be using a broken bottom key during the concert.*

◾ **The idea that cues that were prominent during original encoding are most useful as retrieval cues, and Mäntylä's evidence supporting that idea**

ence, since repeated instances of parking in the same lot fall within the same category of event. Alan Baddeley (1986) and his colleagues surreptitiously kept track of where scientists working at a research institute and visitors to the institute parked, and then surprised these people with a test asking them to recall where they had parked on specific days. As would be predicted by interference theory, colleagues who parked every day at the institute had poor memories of where they had parked several days earlier, whereas visitors who had parked there only once had excellent memories, even when they were tested a month later. In addition, visitors who had parked twice at the institute showed poorer memories for either of their parking places than did those who had parked at the institute only once. Their poorer memory for the first parking place demonstrates retroactive interference, and their poorer memory for the second parking place demonstrates proactive interference.

**Importance of Retrieval Cues**   In the study of long-term memory for classmates (in Figure 10.16b), the amount and rate of apparent forgetting depended very much on the way the question was asked. During the *recall test*, in which subjects had to identify classmates' names upon seeing their pictures without other cues, subjects experienced considerable forgetting. But during the *recognition test*, in which they had to match names and pictures that were presented together, subjects showed no evidence of forgetting at all over a 34-year period. This difference between recall and recognition is no surprise to students, who are familiar with both types of tests in their schoolwork. If you learned all the U.S. state capitals some time ago, you may not be able to answer the question, "What is the capital of Vermont?" But you are very likely to answer correctly if the same question is put in multiple-choice form: "Is the capital of Vermont Brattleboro, Rutland, Montpelier, Cabot, or Springfield?" Even without the list of choices, you might have found the answer in your memory if some other cues had been provided, such as, "It starts with *M*," or "It's a French name." Observations such as these suggest that forgetting often occurs not because the information vanishes from long-term memory, but because, with time, the information becomes harder to access, so more retrieval cues are needed.

What kinds of cues are most helpful? One generalization that has emerged from research on this question is the *encoding-specificity principle*, which maintains that cues that were prominent during the original encoding of a long-term memory will be most valuable for its retrieval (Tulving, 1974). This principle also coincides with the role of elaboration in encoding, discussed earlier in this chapter. To elaborate on a memory item is to associate it with many cues that can be used later for retrieval. Thus, if you had originally encoded Montpelier as the capital of Vermont by noticing that the syllable *mont* appears in both the capital name and the state name, and then recalling that *mont* is French for *mountain*, that Vermont is known as the Green Mountain state, and that many of the early settlers were French, you would have provided yourself with many possible retrieval cues, any one of which might have reminded you of the name of the capital the next time you saw the word *Vermont*.

Timo Mäntylä (1986) has shown that people have extraordinary recall ability if they make up their own retrieval cues at the time of encoding and are given those cues at the time of testing. Mäntylä presented a set of 500 nouns to subjects, one by one, all in one very long experimental session. He did not ask the subjects to memorize the nouns, but rather asked them to write down either one or three words that they regarded as properties of the object named by each noun. For example, for the word *barn* they might write *large, wooden, red*. He then surprised the subjects with a test of their ability to recall all 500 nouns. As cues, he gave them either their own self-generated properties or those produced by a different subject in the same experiment. Subjects who received three self-generated properties for each word were able to recall correctly more than 90 percent of the 500 nouns. When

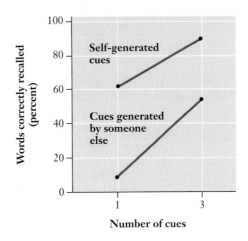

**Figure 10.18** *Value of self-generated retrieval cues*
*Subjects generated either 1 or 3 one-word properties related to each of 500 nouns. Later they were tested for their ability to recall each noun, using either their own self-generated properties or another subject's self-generated properties as retrieval cues. (Data from Mäntylä, 1986.)*

only one property was available, or the properties had been generated by someone else, recall was much poorer (see Figure 10.18).

**Roles of Environmental Context and Bodily State in Retrieval** Recall is facilitated not only by cues that are properties of the learned material, but also by cues from the setting in which learning took place. Have you ever returned to a former school, or a street where you once lived, and found that the sights and sounds, even the odors, evoked memories of people you knew or things you did—memories you thought you had forgotten? The increment in memory that occurs when the test environment is the same as the encoding environment is called ***context-dependent memory***. As an example involving an extreme variation in context, D. Godden and Alan Baddeley (1975) presented scuba divers with lists of words to learn either while under water or on land and later tested them either while under water or on land. Consistent with the hypothesis of context-dependent memory, those who learned the list while under water showed better recall if they were tested while under water, and those who learned the list on land showed better recall if they were tested on land. Other experiments (for example, Metzger & others, 1979) have shown that even a change from one classroom to another can have a small but significant effect on recall: Those who learn material in room *A* tend to recall it better in room *A* than in room *B*, and the opposite is true of those who learn the material in room *B*.

A phenomenon somewhat akin to context-dependent memory is ***state-dependent memory***, which refers to the increment in memory observed when a person's physiological condition or emotional state is the same in the test as it was during encoding. For example, James Eich (1980) found that subjects who learned a list of words while under the influence of marijuana recalled the words better if they were tested while under the influence of marijuana than if they were tested undrugged, while the opposite was true of those subjects who learned the words in the undrugged state.

Studies of context-dependent and state-dependent memory have shown that both are much more likely to occur when recall tests are used than when recognition tests are used (Godden & Baddeley, 1980; Eich, 1980). This finding supports the idea that both context and state aid memory by providing retrieval cues. Difficulty with retrieval is far more likely to be the limiting factor in a recall test than it is in a recognition test. In a recognition test the choices themselves typically provide all the cues that are needed, so correct response is less likely to be limited by ability to retrieve and more likely to be limited by whether or not the information exists in long-term memory. Thus, if you failed to identify Montpelier as the capital of Vermont in a recall test, this may be because of inadequate retrieval cues; but if you failed to identify it in a recognition test, it is more likely to be either because you never knew the fact or because the information had vanished from your long-term store. Neither context, nor physiological state, nor anything else can help you retrieve what you don't know.

■ *How context-dependent and state-dependent memories are demonstrated experimentally*

■ *Evidence that context and state have their facilitating effect by providing retrieval cues*

Several studies have explored the possibility that mood can provide a basis for state-dependent memory. In one study, which capitalized on the dramatic mood shifts shown by manic-depressive psychiatric patients, patients learned a set of word associations on one day and were tested 4 days later (Weingartner & others, 1977). Those patients whose mood had shifted in either direction between training and testing showed poorer recall than did those patients whose mood was the same (either elated or depressed) on the 2 days. In other experiments, nonclinical subjects have been induced through various means to take on a specific mood during learning and either the same or the opposite mood during testing. The findings have been mixed, some showing a degree of mood-dependent memory, others not (Bower, 1981; Blaney, 1986). To the extent that it occurs naturally, mood-dependent memory may help explain the tendency of moods to perpetuate themselves. If a sad mood calls forth memories from previous occasions when a person was sad, the sadness will be enhanced and prolonged.

### Memory Construction as a Source of Distortion

Remembering is not just a process of retrieving traces that were laid down during the original encoding; instead, it is an active, inferential process guided by a person's general knowledge about the world. When you hear a story or experience an event, your mind encodes into long-term memory only some parts of the available information. Later, when you try to recount the story or event, you retrieve the encoded fragments and fill in the gaps through your logic and knowledge, which tell you what must have happened even if you can't quite remember it. With repeated retelling, it becomes harder to distinguish what was present in the original encoding and what was added later on. Thus, memory of the story or experience is not a simple readout of the original information, but a *construction* built and rebuilt from various sources of information. Our ability to construct the past is adaptive, because it allows us to make sense of our incompletely encoded experiences. But the process can also lead to distortions.

■ *How Bartlett demonstrated that culture-specific schemas affect the way that people remember a story*

One of the first psychologists to call attention to the role that our general knowledge plays in our more specific memories was Frederick Bartlett, whose importance as an originator of the idea of culture-specific schemas was noted earlier. In one experiment, Bartlett (1932) asked British university students to listen to a Native American story entitled "The War of the Ghosts" and later asked them to retell the story from memory. He found that the story was often quite different in the retelling, and he noticed certain consistencies in the changes that occurred. Details not essential to the plot tended to drop out, and those that were essential were often exaggerated. Also, points in the story that were consistent with Native American beliefs but not with the students' beliefs were often changed to be more consistent with the latter. For example, the protagonist's obligation to certain spirits—an important part of the original story—tended to be transposed into an obligation to his parents. The changes were not deliberate; the students were trying to retell the story accurately, but they inevitably used their own ways of understanding things—their own schemas—to fill in the gaps in their memory.

■ *How Loftus demonstrated that information added after an event can affect people's apparent memory for the event, and how other researchers provided evidence challenging Loftus's interpretation*

The manner in which a person constructs memories can also be affected by information acquired after the original experience. In one experiment demonstrating this, Elizabeth Loftus and J. C. Palmer (1974) had subjects view a film depicting a traffic accident. Later, the researchers asked some of the subjects how fast the cars were going when they *hit* each other, and others how fast they were going when they *smashed into* each other. The question with the word *smashed* elicited higher estimates of speed than did the question with the word *hit*. Moreover, when the subjects returned a week later and were asked to remember the film and say if there was any broken glass in the accident, those who had heard the word *smashed* were more likely to remember seeing broken glass (though actually there was none in the film) than those who had heard the word *hit*. Loftus's findings have important implications for eyewitness testimony in court cases, in which lawyers on the two sides are trying to paint different pictures of what happened.

Loftus's research is also important because it has generated debate about the mutability of memories. Based on her experiments, Loftus believes that the new, misleading information actually replaces or distorts the original information so that the original information is no longer retrievable in its original form (Loftus & Loftus, 1980). But other researchers, including Michael McCloskey and Maria Zaragoza (1985), disagree, arguing that the new information merely supplements the original information and competes with it in subsequent tests. According to these researchers, misled subjects in Loftus's experiments must choose between their original memories and what they have been told by the experimenter, and in that case are likely to believe the experimenter and assume that their own memories are wrong. The new information has not caused their original memories to vanish or become distorted, but rather has led them to doubt those memories.

To test their hypothesis, McCloskey and Zaragoza (1985) conducted experiments similar to Loftus's, but modified the procedure so that misled subjects could be tested either with or without competition from the misleading information. All subjects saw a series of slides, then some of them heard misleading information about one of the slides, and then all of them were tested in one of two ways for their memory of the critical slide. In one test the misleading information was one of the response options and in the other test it wasn't. For example, in one experiment the critical slide contained a man holding a hammer, and the misled subjects were given information suggesting that he had been holding not a hammer but a screwdriver. Later, all subjects were given one of two different two-choice tests. Half had to choose between a hammer and a screwdriver as the tool that the man was holding, and the other half had to choose between a hammer and a wrench.

Notice that in this example one test required misled subjects to pit their original memory (hammer) against the misleading information (screwdriver). With that test, McCloskey and Zaragoza found that misled subjects performed more poorly than nonmisled subjects—they were more likely to choose the screwdriver. But the other test did not require subjects to pit the original information against the misleading information, since there had been no mention of a wrench prior to the test. With this test, the misled subjects performed just as well as the nonmisled subjects (see Table 10.2). Thus, the misleading information about the screwdriver apparently had not replaced the original information about the wrench, but had merely provided alternative information that competed with the original when it was one of the possible choices.

Still, suppose that McCloskey and Zaragoza's experiment had taken place over a longer period of time and that subjects retold the story in the slides many times

**Table 10.2** *Procedure and results of experiments demonstrating that misleading information competes with, but does not replace, the original memory*

| Group | Item on slide | Misleading information | Test | Results (percent correct) |
|---|---|---|---|---|
| Misled 1 | Hammer | Screwdriver | Hammer vs. screwdriver | 37 |
| Misled 2 | Hammer | Screwdriver | Hammer vs. wrench | 72 |
| Control 1 | Hammer | — | Hammer vs. screwdriver | 72 |
| Control 2 | Hammer | — | Hammer vs. wrench | 75 |

Note: Results are averages from six experiments. The items shown are only illustrative of the various items used.

*Source:* Data from "Misleading postevent information and memory for events: Arguments and evidence against memory impairment hypotheses" by M. McCloskey & M. Zaragoza, 1985, *Journal of Experimental Psychology: General, 114*, pp. 5 and 7.

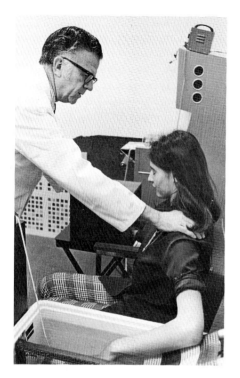

**Hypnotic induction**

*To induce hypnosis, researcher Ernest Hilgard instructs the subject to relax, to focus attention on his words, and to give up conscious control of her own thoughts.*

■ *Why hypnotized subjects' claims of vivid memories should not be taken at face value*

between the original viewing and the test. In that case, subjects might have lost their original memories for the slides and remembered only their previous retelling of the story. Then, in a test of hammer versus wrench, those whose retellings had the tool as a screwdriver (misled subjects) would do more poorly than those whose retellings had it as a hammer (nonmisled subjects). But I am speculating here; this experiment has yet to be performed.

### Effects of Hypnosis on Memory

Perhaps you have read fantastic claims about the power of hypnosis to bring back long-lost memories. Are they true? And just what is hypnosis?

*Hypnosis* has been defined (by Kihlstrom, 1985) as "a social interaction in which one person, designated the subject, responds to suggestions offered by another person, designated the hypnotist, for experiences involving alterations in perception, memory, and voluntary action." There is no completely objective way to describe the hypnotic state, but its two most essential ingredients are: (1) a giving up of considerable control over one's own thoughts and actions, turning that control over to the hypnotist; and (2) a condition of highly selective perception, focused on the hypnotist's voice or on objects or scenes suggested by the hypnotist. The state can be induced by a variety of techniques, most of which include instructions to relax and to fix attention on a specific sight or sound over a period of time. In general, people who easily become engrossed in imaginative activity in the nonhypnotized state are more easily hypnotized than are other people (Kihlstrom, 1985).

**Does Hypnosis Improve Retrieval?** On theoretical grounds, the claim that hypnosis can help a person to retrieve lost memories seems plausible. The focusing of attention might relieve a person from distracting, interfering thoughts, and the hypnotist's suggestion to relive the incident might help revive context-dependent or mood-dependent memories. But despite common belief and theoretical plausibility, there is little evidence that hypnosis really does facilitate retrieval.

Laboratory experiments, in which people learn specific material and then are tested with or without hypnosis, have consistently produced negative results (reviewed by Wagstaff, 1984, and Kihlstrom, 1985). Hypnosis often increases the likelihood of saying yes in recognition tests to items that had actually been present, but it also increases the likelihood of doing so to items that had not been present. Other experiments have shown that hypnotized subjects are more susceptible than nonhypnotized subjects to misleading information presented in the examiners' questions (Zelig & Beidelman, 1981). That is, hypnotized subjects are more likely to claim to remember whatever it is that the examiner seems to expect them to remember. This is not surprising because hypnosis, by definition, is a state of increased suggestibility. Another typical finding is that hypnotized subjects express more confidence in their memory than do nonhypnotized subjects, even though their memory is not objectively better.

Many police departments use hypnosis when interviewing witnesses in the belief that it improves the witnesses' recall. Might hypnosis be useful in the situations in which police use it, even though it doesn't improve memory in laboratory studies? This possibility was tested in a field experiment involving the Los Angeles Police Department and witnesses to actual crimes (Sloane, 1981). Half of the witnesses were interviewed by techniques that included hypnosis by police hypnotists, and the other half were interviewed only in a normal state of consciousness, and the information obtained from both groups was compared to objective facts turned up by subsequent police investigations. The results showed no effect of hypnosis at all, either on the amount of information recalled or its accuracy. Perhaps there are occasional cases in which hypnosis improves retrieval, but apparently as a rule it does not.

**Post-hypnotic Amnesia**   Hypnosis can, however, have another effect on memory. When deeply hypnotized subjects are told that upon awakening they will not remember what happened while under hypnosis, they often (though not always) reveal the specified lack of memory when later questioned, a phenomenon called ***post-hypnotic amnesia***. (The term *amnesia* means memory loss.) Their subjective experience is not one of pretending to forget, but of actual inability to remember. Post-hypnotic amnesia can be highly selective; subjects who are told to forget just one of several events that occurred during hypnosis will forget just that event. Such amnesia also can be combined with other post-hypnotic suggestions. For example, subjects may be told that they will not remember the hypnotist's words upon awakening, but will raise their hands when they hear a particular signal. Later, when the subjects are awake and find themselves raising their hands, they are unable to offer a reason for doing so.

An important feature of post-hypnotic amnesia is that it can always be reversed by a prearranged signal (Kihlstrom, 1985). If the subject is told, "You will forget everything that occurred under hypnosis until you hear this bell," the memories return when the bell is sounded. This shows that post-hypnotic amnesia does not involve actual loss of memories from the long-term store, but only a temporary interference with their retrievability. The memories must remain stored to be retrievable after the signal. Chapter 17 describes fugue states and states of multiple personality, which involve retrieval disruptions similar to post-hypnotic amnesia. Under certain conditions specific sets of memories apparently can be locked away for a period of time where they are unavailable, but can be unlocked and readily available at another time.

# Neuropsychological Evidence for Multiple Memory Systems

In presenting their original version of the three-store model that has guided our discussion in this chapter, Atkinson and Shiffrin (1968) wrote of research on brain-damaged patients as providing "perhaps the single most convincing demonstration of a dichotomy in the memory system." They were referring especially to studies of individuals who had suffered damage to a portion of the limbic system on both sides of the brain, and the dichotomy was that between short-term and long-term memory.

The psychological study of people with brain damage, aimed both at learning how to help them and at learning more about the human mind in general, is called ***neuropsychology***. The usual strategy in this field is to identify which mental abilities are lost and which are preserved in a group of people who have suffered damage to one or another part of the brain. If one ability is lost and another is not, this shows that the preserved ability can operate relatively independently of the lost ability. Thus, neuropsychology complements other approaches in cognitive psychology in the attempt to break the mind down into separate, interacting components. In these final paragraphs, we will look at neuropsychological evidence relevant to some distinctions already discussed, namely the distinctions between (a) short-term and long-term memory, (b) procedural and declarative memory, and (c) episodic and semantic memory.

**Separation of Long-term and Short-term Memory**   One of the most famous patients in the history of neuropsychology is a man known by the initials H. M., who was first studied extensively by Brenda Milner (1965, 1970) and then by many other researchers. At the age of 27, H. M. underwent surgery in which a portion of the temporal lobe of the cortex and underlying parts of the limbic system on each side of his brain were removed as treatment for severe epilepsy. The surgery was

*Evidence that a portion of the limbic system is critical for encoding long-term memories, but not for other memory processes*

**Brenda Milner**

*The Canadian neuropsychologist is best known for her long-term studies of memory loss in a surgical patient (H. M.). The work of Milner and her colleagues has left little doubt that structures in the temporal lobe are directly associated with memory in humans.*

■ **Evidence that rote rehearsal of auditory information may depend on brain areas closely associated with those for hearing**

effective against the epilepsy, but left H. M. with a severe, specific impairment in memory: He could still remember things that had occurred before the operation; his performance on IQ tests remained high (with some decline after many years); he could carry on conversations, read, solve problems, and keep information in mind as long as his attention remained focused on the task at hand; but he could not form new long-term memories. The minute his attention was distracted he would lose the information that he had just been thinking about.

To hold information in his mind for a period of time, H. M. sometimes used elaborate mnemonic schemes. In one test, for example, he successfully kept the number *584* in mind for 15 minutes, and when asked how he did this, he replied, "It's easy. You just remember 8. You see, 5, 8, and 4 add to 17. You remember 8; subtract from 17 and it leaves 9. Divide 9 by half and you get 5 and 4, and there you are—584. Easy." Yet, a few minutes later, after his attention had shifted to something else, he could not remember the number or the mnemonic scheme he had used, or even that he had been given a number to remember (Milner, 1970).

Of course, H. M.'s memory impairment had an enormous impact on his life. When his family moved after the operation he was never able to find his way to his new residence, and would give his old address when he was asked where he lived. He needed to be accompanied wherever he went and needed constant reminders of what he was doing. He was aware of his memory deficit, and once described it in the following way (in Milner, 1970): "Right now, I'm wondering, have I done or said anything amiss? You see, at this moment everything looks clear to me, but what happened just before? That's what worries me. It's like waking from a dream. I just don't remember."

H. M. is interesting to cognitive psychologists because he seems to demonstrate a very specific inability. In terms of the modal model, think of what H. M. can and cannot do. He can (a) bring new information into the short-term store through the process of attention, (b) bring long-term memories (acquired before his surgery) into the short-term store through the process of retrieval, and (c) hold information in the short-term store and think rationally about it. The only memory function that he is missing is the ability to encode new information into long-term memory. In fact, as you will see later, even this deficit needs qualification, since he can encode certain kinds of long-term memories, though not the kind that he can put into words.

The syndrome manifested by H. M. and by others with similar brain damage is called ***temporal lobe amnesia***. *Amnesia* refers to any memory loss, especially that caused by brain damage, and temporal lobe amnesia is loss stemming from destruction of limbic system structures that lie under the temporal lobe of the cortex. Many long-term alcoholics develop a similar pattern of memory loss, referred to as *Korsakoff's syndrome*, due to brain damage caused by the combination of alcohol and poor nutrition (specifically, lack of vitamin $B_1$) (Parkin, 1987).

Researchers disagree about exactly what part of the brain must be damaged for these syndromes to occur, though most agree that the area critical for the temporal lobe syndrome includes the hippocampus and perhaps part of the amygdala (see Figure 10.19), and that the area critical for Korsakoff's syndrome includes a neural tract that carries information from these limbic structures (Squire, 1987). These structures are not the place where long-term memories are stored, since their destruction does not result in loss of already-formed long-term memories. Rather, these structures appear to be important in the transference of new information from short-term into long-term memory.

A few patients have been found who have memory deficits opposite to that of temporal lobe amnesia or Korsakoff's syndrome (see Weiskrantz, 1989). These are people who, usually following a stroke (brain damage caused by a ruptured blood vessel), have impaired short-term but normal long-term memory. One such patient, known as K. M., could repeat only one or two digits after hearing them once,

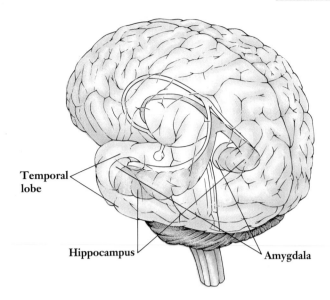

**Figure 10.19** *Brain area involved in temporal lobe amnesia*
*As shown here, the hippocampus lies under the temporal lobe of the cerebral cortex. Destruction of this structure in both sides of the brain produces a profound inability to encode new long-term memories.*

Temporal lobe

Hippocampus

Amygdala

compared to the six to eight that most people can repeat (Shallice & Warrington, 1970). A test using the procedure developed by Peterson and Peterson (the one described in Figure 10.5) revealed that items vanished from K. M.'s short-term memory immediately when he stopped rehearsing them, rather than lingering for 10 to 15 seconds as they do in most people. Yet, by rehearsing items one at a time, K. M. could transfer them into long-term memory as effectively as a person could without brain damage. Remarkably, this patient continued to function very well in his everyday life, suggesting that his loss was rather specific for rote rehearsal and had little effect on the flow of information that accompanies normal thought. The deficit also seemed to be specific for verbal material. He had no difficulty in short-term memory tests for information presented in pictures rather than words.

Although researchers are not certain about the location of the damage that produced K. M.'s deficit, there is reason to believe that the critical region is close to the auditory sensory area in the temporal lobe of the cortex (Weiskrantz, 1989). This suggests that auditory rote rehearsal (the mental repetition of words or other sounds) may involve a process that is related to, and neurologically associated with, processes involved in auditory perception. Other patients have been found who have selective short-term memory deficits for information in pictures, and typically they have damage in cortical areas close to the visual sensory area (Warrington & Weiskrantz, 1973). Chapter 11 pursues further the idea that there are separate brain structures for processing verbal and pictorial information.

**Separation of Procedural and Declarative Memory** The experiments that demonstrated H. M.'s memory loss involved tests in which he had to answer verbal questions. Thus, they were specific to *declarative memories*—memories that can be put into words. H. M. has also been tested nonverbally for his ability to learn and retain various skills or procedures, and these tests have quite regularly revealed no memory deficit.

For example, in one experiment, H. M. showed normal improvement from day to day in tracing patterns that could be seen only in their mirror image (a common test of motor-skill learning), even though he could not consciously remember, from one day to the next, ever having done the task before (Milner, 1965). In another experiment, his ability to solve the Tower of Hanoi puzzle (a common test of logic, in which a subject rearranges rings on pegs in accordance with certain rules) improved from test to test, and remained improved when he was retested a year later (Cohen, 1984). Similar results have occurred in studies of other patients with temporal lobe amnesia (Squire, 1987). Apparently, procedural memories are encoded by a route that does not require the limbic structures that are needed to encode declarative memories.

*■ How further studies of temporal lobe amnesia patients support the idea that there are separate systems for encoding declarative and procedural memories*

**How studies of monkeys have
led to a distinction between a habit
system and a cognitive memory
system paralleling that between
procedural and declarative systems
in humans**

Studies of monkeys, conducted by Mortimer Mishkin and his colleagues, complement these observations with human patients. Mishkin makes a distinction between a *habit system* and a *cognitive memory system*, which seems to parallel the distinction between a procedural memory system and a declarative memory system in people (Mishkin & Appenzeller, 1987). To test the habit system, Mishkin uses straightforward operant-conditioning procedures in which monkeys are rewarded for consistently making a particular response to particular stimuli. For example, a monkey might receive a peanut each time it picks up the square object and ignores the round one in a two-object choice, and demonstrate habit memory through its increased likelihood, from trial to trial, or day to day, of picking the square. In contrast, to test the cognitive-memory system, Mishkin combines operant conditioning with the requirement that the animal remember a new piece of information over a period of time on every trial. More specifically, one test he uses is *delayed nonmatching to sample*, in which on each trial the animal sees a specific object that it has never seen before (maybe a plastic square) and then, sometime later, is shown that object again along with a new object, and must choose the new object to receive a reward.

Of greatest interest, Mishkin and his colleagues have found that destruction of the hippocampus and amygdala in monkeys—the same structures that are involved in the temporal lobe syndrome in humans—completely abolishes their ability in cognitive-memory tests, but has essentially no effect on their performance in habit tests. The animals can still be operantly conditioned, and they retain the effects of conditioning from one day to another. In addition, they can still perform nonmatching-to-sample tasks if the delay between seeing the new object and the test is only a few seconds (within the span of short-term memory), but they cannot perform it if the delay is a minute or more. Based on this and other research, Mishkin suggests that cognitive encoding involves the limbic structures, whereas habit encoding involves a more primitive neural system, most likely in the basal ganglia—structures buried deeply in the brain and known to be important in the control of deliberate movements (described in Chapter 6).

**Evidence that some amnesic
patients can encode memories about
the world but not about their own
experiences**

**Separation of Episodic and Semantic Memory**   Other research with amnesic patients supports the idea that separate neural mechanisms may be involved in encoding semantic and episodic information into long-term memory (Schacter, 1987). For example, in one experiment patients with amnesia stemming from a variety of brain injuries (in areas not specified by the researchers) heard a series of fictitious statements, such as, "Bob Hope's father was a fireman." When tested a few minutes later, many of the patients could answer questions based on the content of the fictitious statements, indicating that they had incorporated the information into their semantic memory (their general store of knowledge), but could not recall where or when they had learned the information, indicating lack of episodic memory (Schacter & others, 1984). Thus, if asked what Bob Hope's father did for a living, they said that he was a fireman; but if asked how they knew he was a fireman, they said they did not know. In another study, an amnesic patient learned to program a microcomputer over a series of training sessions, and could explain in words how to do it; yet, when asked if he had ever worked with a microcomputer before, he persistently failed to remember having done so (Glisky & others, 1986).

How can a person encode information about the world without encoding whatever is needed to relate that information to an episode in his or her own life? Tulving (1985) has argued that episodic memory is an evolutionarily new addition to our cognitive machinery, which may be relatively unique to human beings. This evolutionary add-on, which gives us each a sense of our own past, and thus a sense of ourselves as individuals, may be more fragile—more destructible by brain damage—than the more primitive semantic system or the still more primitive procedural system.

## Concluding Thoughts

**1. The modal model as a functional representation of the mind** The modal model served throughout this chapter as the organizing structure for our thinking about memory and about the mind in general. You have read of three memory stores, of control processes related to the stores, and of research aimed at characterizing the stores and processes. Your review and thought about all of this will be most effective, I think, if you adopt a functionalist perspective. From that perspective, each store and process represents not a different part (or structure) of the mind, but instead represents a different job that the mind performs in its overall task of acquiring and using information. What is the main job (the main function) of (a) sensory memory, (b) short-term memory, (c) long-term memory, (d) encoding, and (e) retrieval?

Once you are clear on the main function, think about the properties of each store and process in relation to its function. How does the large capacity and short duration of sensory memory suit it to the job of preattentive processing? How might the capacity of short-term memory set limits on a person's thinking, and how can chunking help a person overcome those limits? Of what value might it be that elaborative rehearsal is far more effective than rote rehearsal in encoding information into long-term memory? How does our tendency to encode just the meaning of some verbal statements, and the meaning plus structure of others, suit the needs of everyday life? Why is a hierarchical structure efficient for holding lots of information in semantic long-term memory? In everyday life, why is it useful that cues present during encoding (including context and state) tend to be effective retrieval cues? What are the separate functions of procedural, semantic, and episodic memory systems?

**2. The modal model as an example of a schema** To the degree that you and I have incorporated the modal model into our own minds, it has become our schema for understanding memory. Remember what Bartlett said about schemas: Schemas allow us to organize and make sense of the world around us, but they can also distort our perceptions and thoughts. The model is a valuable schema for organizing research and thought about an extraordinarily complicated topic, but it can also cause us to distort that topic. To some degree, I may have distorted the field of memory research in writing this chapter, because I have written it with the model strongly in mind. To some degree, you may have distorted the research and findings even further to fit the model as you understand it. To some degree, cognitive psychology as a whole may have distorted the knowledge of memory by directing research toward aspects of memory that are most consistent with the model while ignoring other aspects that are equally important. The creative thinkers in this science, as in any other, are those who are not bound by current models or schemas, who find new ways to look at the topic, and who in that way open up new lines of research. Current research distinguishing between episodic and semantic memory is one example of work that goes beyond the model and may eventuate in a new schema of the human mind.

**3. Standard laboratory and ecological approaches to memory** A considerable amount of debate has arisen in cognitive psychology over the relative value of tightly controlled laboratory studies and more loosely controlled studies of memory in nonlaboratory contexts (see Neisser, 1978, and Banaji & Crowder, 1989). The laboratory approach to cognition stems directly from the work of the nineteenth-century German founders of experimental psychology, including Ebbinghaus and Wundt, who wished to isolate the separate processes of the mind and study them in relative independence of one another. Ebbinghaus invented the nonsense syllable in his effort to study memory independent of meaning, and that tradition has been continued by studies that use nonsense syllables, or random strings of digits, or unrelated words as memory items. As described in Chapter 1, Wundt invented the reaction-time measure as a way of assessing the complexity of mental processes, and that tradition has been continued in experiments such as Collins and Quillian's, which you read about in this chapter.

The contrasting approach, often called the ecological approach, emphasizes the value of studying memory in everyday life. Ecological theorists such as Ulrich Neisser argue that the standard laboratory procedures do not just isolate variables but often obliterate those that are most important to normal memory functions. They point out that the purpose of memory is not to retain nonsense syllables or unrelated strings of words, but rather to retain knowledge, which implies meaning. Memories are useful precisely because they are meaningful; from this perspective, it is useless to study memory independent of meaning. The relation of memory to meaning was the main idea behind Bartlett's pioneering research on the role of schemas in people's memories for events in their lives or for stories they heard. Other studies described in this chapter that fall within the ecological purview are those of memories for school lessons, for the names and faces of former classmates, and for parking places.

But the two approaches are not incompatible with each other. The role of meaning in memory, emphasized by the ecological theorists, can be studied in the laboratory. In fact, many of the experiments described in this chapter were of this type, including studies of (a) the effects of different forms of elaborative rehearsal on encoding, (b) the value of structuring the material to be remembered into a meaningful hierarchy, (c) the value of generating meaningful retrieval cues at the time of encoding, and (d) the effect that information provided after an original event can have on the constructed memory for that event.

Perhaps the theme of integrating ecological and laboratory approaches is becoming familiar to you. Chapter 5 described an ecological approach to learning, which originated with field studies but eventuated in laboratory experiments on species-specific and domain-specific learning processes. Chapter 9 outlined an ecological perspective in perception, which began with an assumption that the entire array of stimuli, not the bits and pieces, must be considered to understand perception, but eventuated in new ways of breaking down the array of information and of studying that breakdown in the laboratory. In general, the ecological approach is that which continuously raises questions about psychological processes in relation to the real-life contexts in which they operate. Once the questions are identified in field studies, they often can be pursued best in the more controlled conditions of the laboratory.

## Further Reading

**Roberta Klatzky** (1984). *Memory and awareness: An information-processing perspective.* New York: Freeman.

*In this brief book, Klatzky brings a modern information-processing perspective to bear on the age-old question of the nature of human awareness. She identifies three different kinds of awareness and discusses them in relation to memory stores and processes.*

**Ulrich Neisser** (Ed.) (1982). *Memory observed: Remembering in natural contexts.* San Francisco: Freeman.

*This book, edited by one of the leading advocates of an ecological perspective on memory, includes many interesting accounts of the strengths and failings of memory in people's actual lives. In one chapter, Neisser analyzes John Dean's memory for meetings with President Nixon, as expressed in Dean's testimony to the Senate Watergate Investigating Committee in 1973, matched against actual tape recordings of the meetings that subsequently became available. There is ample evidence here concerning the use of schemas to construct (often mistakenly) specific details.*

**Ronald A. Finke** (1989). *Principles of mental imagery.* Cambridge, MA: MIT Press.

*This is an interesting, nicely integrated summary of experimental research on the mental representation of visual-spatial information and the processes of encoding and retrieving such information.*

## Looking Ahead

In studying the topic of memory, we have entered the gate to the human intellect. Memories provide the basis for ideas, reasons, decisions, plans, and verbal utterances. Thinking and speaking are the abilities that appear to distinguish humans most from the other animals, and these are the central topics of the next two chapters, which deal with the human intellect and its development.

# CHAPTER 11

**Conceptions of Intelligence**

**Logical Reasoning and Problem Solving**

**Language and Its Relationship to Thought**

# THE HUMAN INTELLECT

When we compare ourselves with other species, we find that we are not the most graceful, nor the strongest, nor the swiftest, nor the fiercest, nor the gentlest, nor the most long-lived, nor the most resistant to the poisons accumulating in our atmosphere. We take our pride in our intellect. We fancy ourselves to be the most intelligent of animals; and, at least by our own definitions of intelligence, our fancy is apparently correct. We are the animals that know and reason; that classify and name the other animals; that try to understand all things, including even ourselves. We are also the animals that tell each other what we know, passing it along such that each generation starts off with more knowledge, if not more wisdom, than did the previous one.

This chapter, the last of the trilogy on cognition, is about those aspects of the human mind that most distinguish us from other animals. The first section is about four psychological approaches to describing and understanding the human intellect as a whole; the second is about mental processes involved in reasoning and problem solving; and the third is about language and its relationship to thought.

## Conceptions of Intelligence

People sometimes argue about the true meaning of intelligence, but such arguments are usually pointless. *Intelligence* is just a word, and, like any word, different people may use it to refer to different concepts. To find out how psychologists and educators who specialize in intelligence define it, Mark Snyderman and Stanley Rothman (1987) asked more than 1000 such specialists to check off, on a list of human abilities, those they considered to be important elements of intelligence. Nearly all of these individuals checked off abstract reasoning, problem solving, and capacity to acquire knowledge; more than half checked memory, adaptation to one's environment, mental speed, linguistic competence, mathematical competence, general knowledge, and creativity; and about one-fourth of the group checked sensory acuity, goal directedness, and achievement motivation. Thus, some experts conceived of intelligence as specific to higher-order reasoning and knowing, while others conceived of it as a broad set of characteristics that help people deal with their environment.

A question that arises immediately when thinking about possible meanings of intelligence is: To what extent are various mental abilities interrelated or dependent on one another? More specifically, do good problem solvers also have good memories? Do people who have a large store of general knowledge also have keen senses or fast reaction times? Do people with excellent language abilities also have excellent abilities for solving spatial puzzles or understanding maps? To the extent that the answer to such questions is yes, we might think of intelligence as a single, general ability that cuts across all sorts of mental tasks. To the extent that the answer is no, we must either choose which specific ability to call intelligence, or we must think of intelligence as a collection of separate abilities.

The following sections examine intelligence from four different psychological perspectives: (1) the *psychometric perspective*, which attempts to understand intelligence through the analysis of patterns of scores on mental tests; (2) the *information-processing perspective*, which attempts to describe the steps involved in carrying out mental tasks; (3) the *neuropsychological perspective*, which attempts to relate specific mental abilities to specific areas of the brain; and (4) the *ecological perspective*, which attempts to relate intelligence to the environmental context within which it occurs. The question of whether intelligence is best considered as one entity or a collection is a theme that will run through each of these sections.

## The Psychometric Approach to Intelligence

**Psychometrics** means psychological measurement. More fully, it refers to the measurement of psychological differences among people and to the statistical analysis of those differences as a way of learning about the structure of the human mind. Psychometrics encompasses the field of personality measurement (discussed in Chapter 16) as well as that of intellectual measurement, but it began historically with the latter.

**Galton and the Idea of Innate Mental Quickness and Acuity**   One of the first to attempt to measure intelligence systematically was the English scientist Sir Francis Galton (1822–1911). Galton's interest in intelligence grew out of his interest in heredity. He greatly admired the ideas about heredity and evolution developed by his cousin, Charles Darwin, and wanted to extend them into the realm of human mental ability. In 1869, Galton published a book showing that people who were famous for their intellectual achievements often had similarly famous relatives; and he argued, both in that book and later, that such similarity stemmed more from their shared biological heredity than from their shared environments (see Chapter 3). Subsequently, Galton began a research program aimed at identifying and measuring the biological differences that might allow some people to achieve much more than others. He viewed this not only as an academically interesting project that would advance understanding of the mind, but also as a practical endeavor. One of his goals was to develop a test that could screen people for their intellectual potential, so that public funds for education could be used for those with high potential and not "wasted" on those with low potential (Galton, 1865).

Galton carried out this research in his Anthropometric Laboratory (*anthropometric* means human measurement), which he set up first in 1884 at the International Health Exhibition in London and later moved to a science museum. For a small fee, visitors could step into his laboratory, have various measures taken, and receive a report of the results. Most of the measures were of basic motor and sensory abilities, such as reacting quickly to signals or detecting slight differences between two sounds, lengths, or weights. Based on his assumption that intelligence is an inherited property of the nervous system, Galton (1885) hypothesized that it should be manifested in these simple measures. In other words, Galton hoped to show that the biological underpinning for intellectual differences among people lay in their neural quickness and acuity—the speed and accuracy with which they could respond to environmental stimuli (see Eysenck, 1987).

As part of this research, Galton invented a statistical procedure to assess the degree of relationship between different measures, which was subsequently refined by Karl Pearson (1920) to produce the correlational method still used today (discussed in Chapter 2). Galton hoped to demonstrate with this procedure that his

*Francis Galton*

*A member of an intellectually gifted family, Galton's genius was wide ranging. In addition to his studies of individual differences and his development of the statistical concept of correlation, Galton invented a variety of mechanical devices, including a data-storage system and a periscope that enabled him to see over the heads of taller people.*

■ *How Galton's emphasis on heredity led him to believe that intelligence would be reflected in simple sensory and motor abilities, and how he subsequently searched for a measure*

various measures of the mind were related to one another, such that a high score on one measure would predict high scores on the others. To his disappointment, Galton found only weak correlations. Research by other psychologists using Galton's measures proved even more disappointing. For example, an analysis of scores collected from 300 students at Columbia University and Barnard College showed no significant relationship between reaction time or sensory acuity and academic grades (Wissler, 1901). Thus, Galton's measures seemed to be only moderately related to each other and unrelated to academic achievement, and for that reason most researchers in the field of intelligence lost interest in them (Fancher, 1985). As you will see later, however, some psychologists have recently revived Galton's approach, claiming that some sensory and reaction-time measures correlate quite strongly with intellectual achievement.

■ *How Binet's view of intelligence differed from Galton's, and how he went on to develop a test that measured a collection of abilities that are important for schoolwork*

**Binet and the Idea of Intelligence as a Collection of Abilities**   Modern intelligence tests have their ancestry not in Galton's measures of sensory acuity and reaction time, but rather in a test called the *Binet-Simon Intelligence Scale*, which was developed in France in 1905 by Alfred Binet and his assistant Theophile Simon. From the outset, Binet's view of intelligence was quite different from Galton's. He argued against Galton's idea that intelligence is closely related to sensory acuity, citing as one line of evidence the example of Helen Keller, who had been blind and deaf since her early childhood but who was universally regarded as highly intelligent (Binet & Simon, 1916). Binet believed that intelligence is best understood as a collection of various higher-order mental abilities that might be only loosely related to one another (Binet & Henri, 1896). He also differed from Galton on the heredity question, arguing that intelligence is nurtured through interaction with the environment and that an important function of schooling is to increase intelligence. In fact, the purpose of Binet and Simon's test—developed at the request of the French Ministry of Education—was to identify children who were not profiting as much as they should from their schooling, so that they might be given special education.

Binet and Simon's test was oriented explicitly toward the skills involved in schoolwork. It consisted of questions and problems designed to test memory, vocabulary, common knowledge, use of numbers, understanding of time, ability to combine ideas, and so forth. The problems were selected through a procedure that involved pretesting them with schoolchildren of various ages and comparing the results with teachers' ratings of each child's classroom behavior (see Binet & Simon, 1916). Items were kept in the test if children who were rated high by their teachers did better than those who were rated low; otherwise, they were dropped. Binet was aware of the circularity of this process: The test was supposed to measure intelligence better than existing measures, but to develop the test it was necessary to compare results with an existing measure (teachers' ratings). Yet, once developed, the test would presumably have advantages over teachers' ratings. Among other things, it would allow for comparison of children who had had different teachers or no formal schooling at all.

In 1908, Binet and Simon revised their test and introduced the concept of *mental age* to the scoring system (actually, they called it mental *level*, but others called it mental age and the latter term stuck). With this scoring system, a child received an intelligence score corresponding to the age group with which his or her performance best matched. Thus, a child of any age who performed as well as an average 10-year-old would be assigned a mental age of 10. For better or worse, this system probably did much to popularize the test. Mental age indicated directly whether a child was advanced or behind, and played on the pride and anxiety of parents and teachers. Within a few years, English translations of the Binet-Simon Scale were available, and testing caught on in England and North America even more than it did in France.

**Alfred Binet**
*Although he had a lasting influence on the appraisal of individual intelligence, Binet was not particularly appreciated by his contemporaries. He never obtained a university professorship, and his work with Theophile Simon was not publicly honored until 60 years after his death.*

■ *The original meaning of IQ, and the meaning of IQ in Wechsler's tests and in other standard IQ tests today*

**The Evolution of Intelligence Tests After Binet**   The first intelligence test commonly used in North America was the *Stanford-Binet Scale*, a modification of Binet and Simon's test that was developed in 1916 at Stanford University under the direction of Lewis Terman. By this time another refinement had been added to the scoring system: the *intelligence quotient*, or *IQ*, determined by dividing a child's mental age (MA) by his or her actual chronological age (CA) and multiplying by 100. Thus, IQ = (MA/CA) × 100. If a child's mental age as measured by the test was 11.5 and his or her chronological age was 10, then the child's IQ would be (11.5/10) × 100 = 115. An IQ of 100 would mean that a child was average for his or her age, and scores above or below 100 would mean that the child was above or below average.

Terman himself was particularly interested in the fate of highly intelligent children and used the Stanford-Binet Scale to identify a sample of children with IQs above 140 within the California school system. He followed this group throughout their lives and found that, on average, their early high IQs predicted adult success (Terman, 1954). They were more likely than others to do well in school, go to college, publish important writings, patent inventions, and earn high incomes. However, they also tended to be from privileged backgrounds to begin with, and it is hard to know to what degree their success was related to their IQ or to other attributes that accompany privilege. Another interesting finding from Terman's study was that, contrary to the stereotype of the frail, neurotic bookworm, the high-IQ group tended to be above average in all indices of health and emotional adjustment.

The Stanford-Binet Scale has been revised over the years and is still used quite widely, though the most common individually administered intelligence tests today are variations of a different test that was developed by David Wechsler in the 1930s. Wechsler's original purpose was to design an intelligence test for adults, because the Stanford-Binet Scale was designed for children; but later he modified his own adult test to produce a version for children also (Aiken, 1987). The descendents of Wechsler's tests most used today are the *Wechsler Adult Intelligence Scale, Revised (WAIS-R)* and the *Wechsler Intelligence Scale for Children, Revised (WISC-R)*.

By the time Wechsler was developing his intelligence test for adults, the term *IQ* was so ingrained in public consciousness that he retained it in the scoring system even though its original meaning had to be abandoned. (It would be senseless to say that a 20-year-old who scores as well as an average 60-year-old has an IQ of 300.) The scoring system for the WAIS-R is based on results obtained from large samples of adults in nine different age groups, ranging from 16 to 75. Those whose performance is average for their age group receive an IQ score of 100, and those whose performance is above or below average receive a score above or below 100 assigned in such a way that the overall distribution of scores looks like that shown in Figure 11.1. Table 11.1 summarizes the various subtests of the WAIS-R. The WISC-R is similar to the WAIS-R, but contains simpler problems.

The Stanford-Binet and Wechsler scales must be administered one-on-one by a trained tester. To permit mass testing, many group-administered intelligence tests have been developed over the years. They usually are given in multiple-choice format and may serve purposes more specific than just the broad assessment of intelligence. For example, the mathematics and verbal *Scholastic Aptitude Tests (SATs)* are often considered to be intelligence tests, and their results correlate quite strongly with scores on individually administered intelligence tests (Brody, 1985).

Psychometricians who develop and revise intelligence tests are very much concerned with the issues of reliability and validity (discussed more fully in Chapter 2). *Reliability* refers to the consistency of measurement. A test is reliable if it produces consistently about the same score when given repeatedly (usually in different forms) to the same person. Many studies have shown that modern, standard intelli-

**Stanford-Binet test materials**
*These materials are from the 1986 version of the test. In earlier versions, results consisted of a single, overall IQ score. In the current revision, separate scores are obtained for verbal reasoning, abstract/ visual reasoning, quantitative reasoning, and short-term memory.*

■ *The issues of reliability and validity as applied to intelligence tests, and why the latter is the more problematic of the two*

**Figure 11.1** *Standardized scoring of Wechsler IQ tests*

*The scoring system for Wechsler IQ tests is based on the assumption that intelligence is distributed in the population according to a normal distribution (represented by the bell-shaped curve). Thus, scores are assigned in such a way as to produce a normal distribution. More specifically, based on previous experience with the test, scores are assigned in such a way that a specific percentage of people within any given age group will score within each range of scores, as shown here. Notice that with this system about 68 percent of IQ scores are between 85 and 115, and about 95 percent are between 70 and 130. (For more on normal distributions and the method for standardizing test scores, see the Statistical Appendix.)*

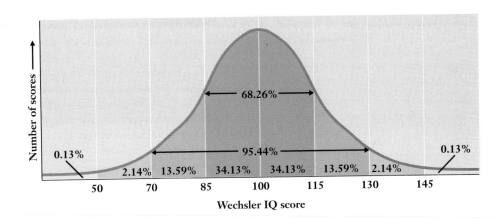

gence tests are reasonably reliable. Test-retest correlations for either the Stanford-Binet or Wechsler tests typically fall in the range of 0.80 to 0.95 (Jensen, 1980). Moreover, the Stanford-Binet and Wechsler tests are apparently similar in what they measure, since correlations between the two fall in the range of 0.75 to 0.90 (Wechsler, 1981).

**Table 11.1** *The eleven subtests of the WAIS-R*

**Verbal subtests**

*Information*  General-information questions.

*Digit span*  The task is to recite a series of digits immediately after hearing them. The series is increased on each trial until the person fails twice in succession. A second phase is like the first except the digits are recited backwards. The purpose is to test short-term memory.

*Vocabulary*  Words to be defined.

*Arithmetic*  Arithmetic problems to be solved.

*Comprehension*  Questions requiring rather detailed explanations are asked. The purpose is to test practical knowledge, social judgment, and ability to organize information.

*Similarities*  Questions are asked that take the form, "In what way are *A* and *B* alike?" The purpose is to measure inductive-reasoning ability.

**Performance subtests**

*Picture completion*  Pictures with missing parts are presented and the task is to find the missing part. The purpose is to test visual alertness and attention to details.

*Picture arrangement*  The task is to arrange sets of pictures in a way that tells a story (similar to a comic strip). The purpose is to test sequencing ability and planning.

*Block design*  The task is to arrange sets of red and white blocks in such a way as to match a specific design. The purpose is to test ability to analyze visual patterns.

*Object assembly*  The task is to put puzzle pieces together to form a picture. The purpose is to test ability to visualize a final form from its parts.

*Digit symbol*  A key is provided relating symbols to single-digit numbers, and the task is to use the key in translating a series of single-digit numbers into symbols. The purpose is to test attentiveness, quickness, and persistence in a simple perceptual-motor task.

Note: The verbal subtests contribute to the *verbal IQ*, and the performance subtests contribute to the *performance IQ*. The average of the two is used as the basis for the overall IQ.

*Source:* Adapted from *Assessment of intellectual functioning* (pp. 125–130) by L. R. Aiken, 1987, Boston: Allyn & Bacon.

*Validity* has to do with whether a test measures what it is supposed to measure. Validity is a more vexing problem than reliability, since any agreement about the validity of an intelligence test must be premised on agreement about the meaning of intelligence. If intelligence is defined as the ability to get high grades in school, then most standard intelligence tests are reasonably valid. Studies relating Stanford-Binet or Wechsler IQ scores to school grades typically produce correlation coefficients in the range of 0.30 to 0.70 (Jensen, 1980). More controversial, and not firmly settled one way or the other by evidence to date, is the issue of whether the test scores also correlate with abilities manifested outside of school. (You will see some evidence for lack of correlation later, in the discussion of the ecological approach to intelligence.)

**Factor Analysis as a Way to Learn About the Structure of Intelligence**   Having glimpsed some of the history and practical rationale behind intelligence testing, let us return to the theoretical issue of whether intelligence is a single entity or a collection of abilities. Galton believed it to be a single entity, perhaps best described as mental speed, which cuts across all intellectual tasks and should also show up in simple tests of reaction time and sensory acuity. Binet believed that intelligence is a collection of different abilities; yet, ironically, he founded the tradition of summarizing a person's intelligence with a single number.

Think for a moment about the implications of summarizing intelligence with a single number. Your IQ score may be 118; maybe mine is 105; and perhaps our friend Joe's is 98. You could line the three of us up: You're first, I'm second, and Joe is third. But isn't that oversimplifying things? Is it really possible to take something as complex as the human intellect and capture it with a single number? By analogy, think what it would be like to try to describe a person's physique with a single number. What number would you use—height? weight? arm length? girth of neck? some average of these plus others? No single measure nor any one-number average makes sense. To get a picture of what someone's body looks like, you would need a set of numbers measuring different parts of the body. Isn't the structure of intelligence at least as complex as that of the body?

Galton's approach to testing his idea that intelligence is a single entity was to look for correlations among different mental tests. If people who do well on one test also tend to do well on all other tests, then intelligence can be defined as the mental ability that cuts across the various tests. Galton's results were discouraging, but that may have been because both his tests and his statistical methods for analyzing correlations were crude. Charles Spearman (1904, 1927), an English psychologist and mathematician who was impressed by Galton's ideas, developed a more sophisticated battery of mental tests and a new statistical procedure, called *factor analysis*, for analyzing sets of correlations. Factor analysis is still today the principal psychometric method for studying the structure of intelligence.

To get an idea of how factor analysis has been used in studying intelligence, imagine that a set of six different mental tests had been given to a large number of individuals and that the correlation coefficient between each pair of tests had been calculated (using the correlational method described in Chapter 2). Imagine further that the results were as shown in Figure 11.2. Notice that each test correlates positively with each other test, meaning that people who tended to score high on one test also tended to score high on the others. According to the rationale developed by Spearman, such correlation implies that the tests measure some common, underlying mental ability, or *factor*. To Spearman, factor analysis was essentially a means of determining the degree to which different tests measure that single factor. Spearman referred to the common factor as **g**, for ***general intelligence***.

Notice, however, that none of the tests in Figure 11.2 correlates perfectly with any other (all correlations are less than 1.00). Spearman took that kind of result as

■ *How correlations among test scores led Spearman to posit a general intelligence* (g)

**Figure 11.2  *Hypothetical correlations among scores on six tests***

*Each correlation coefficient in the matrix is the correlation between the two tests indicated by its row and column. Thus, 0.35 is the correlation between Test 1 and Test 2. In this example, the correlations among Tests 1, 3, and 5 (in gold) and among Tests 2, 4, and 6 (in purple) are higher than any of the other correlations. This pattern can be interpreted to mean that Tests 1, 3, and 5 measure one kind of ability (maybe verbal), and Tests 2, 4, and 6 measure a different kind of ability (maybe visual-spatial).*

| Tests | 2 | 3 | 4 | 5 | 6 |
|---|---|---|---|---|---|
| 1 | 0.35 | 0.62 | 0.40 | 0.59 | 0.45 |
| 2 | – | 0.41 | 0.55 | 0.39 | 0.64 |
| 3 | – | – | 0.28 | 0.63 | 0.30 |
| 4 | – | – | – | 0.34 | 0.60 |
| 5 | – | – | – | – | 0.38 |

evidence that no test is a perfect measure of $g$, and that each test score is also affected by a more specific ability that he called $s$. Spearman believed that $s$ varies from test to test and might stem from the person's previous experience with the specific information or method of thinking called for by a particular test. Thus, Spearman's theory of intelligence can be illustrated as shown in Figure 11.3. The mind contains a single general ability ($g$) that affects scores on all sorts of mental tests, and a large set of specific abilities ($s_1, s_2, s_3, \ldots$) that affect scores on different tests differently. One of Spearman's goals was to develop a test that was the best possible measure of $g$.

**Figure 11.3  *Spearman's theory of intelligence***

*To explain why people who score high on one kind of mental test also tend to score high on other kinds of mental tests, Spearman hypothesized that people differ in general intelligence (g). To explain why the correlation among tests is not perfect, he hypothesized that each test score is also affected by a person's specific ability (s) related to that particular test. Thus, according to Spearman, a person's score on each of six different tests is affected by his or her amount of general intelligence plus his or her specific ability for that test.*

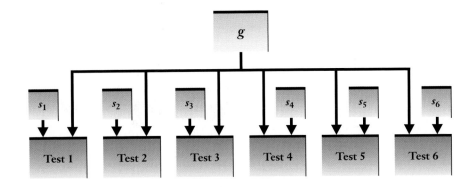

■ *How correlations among test scores led Thurstone to posit the existence of separate primary mental abilities*

Later, the American psychologist Louis Thurstone, who had a conception of intelligence more akin to Binet's than to Galton's or Spearman's, developed a different procedure for factor analysis, producing a different model for explaining the intercorrelations among tests. The goal of Thurstone's technique was to find clusters of tests that correlated more strongly with each other than with tests outside of the cluster (Thurstone, 1938, 1947). For example, using the hypothetical correlations shown in Figure 11.2, Thurstone's method would detect the fact that Tests 1, 3, and 5 correlate more strongly with each other than with other tests, as do Tests 2, 4, and 6. From such a pattern, Thurstone would conclude that one subset of tests is a good measure of one mental ability (call it $A$) and another is a good measure of another ability (call it $B$). Thurstone assumed that the different abilities that are best measured by different sets of tests are independent of one another, and he called them *primary mental abilities*.

**Figure 11.4 *Thurstone's theory of intelligence***

*To explain why the correlations among some mental tests are greater than those among others (such as the pattern in Figure 11.2), Thurstone hypothesized that the human mind contains a small set of different primary mental abilities. Tests that correlate most strongly with one another are measures of the same primary ability. To explain why tests in different clusters also correlate (to a smaller degree) with one another, Thurstone hypothesized that no test is a pure measure of any given ability, but is also to some degree affected by other abilities. In this example, Primary Ability A might be verbal comprehension, and Primary Ability B might be spatial visualization.*

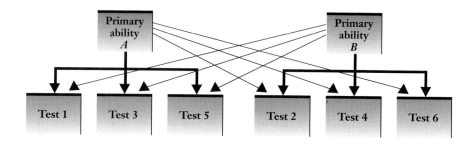

Thus, Thurstone's model of the mind was as depicted in Figure 11.4. At the top is not one general intelligence, but rather a set of primary abilities. Each primary ability affects scores on some tests more than on others. Based on an analysis of correlations among fifty-six different mental tests, Thurstone (1938) identified what he considered to be seven distinct primary abilities: verbal comprehension, verbal fluency, number (computation), spatial visualization, associative memory, perceptual speed, and reasoning.

Following Thurstone, many psychologists performed similar studies using new batteries of tests and new factor analytic procedures, generating new theories of the structure of intelligence. Most of the more recent theories combine Spearman's idea of *g* with Thurstone's idea of separate abilities. In these theories, the mind is depicted as a hierarchy; *g* is at the top, and underneath are various secondary abilities that are affected by *g* but that can also vary independently of one another. In Figure 11.5 you can see how this hierarchical approach could be applied to explain the pattern of correlations in Figure 11.2.

Different hierarchical models of intelligence differ primarily in the number of abilities (intelligences) they identify at the second level and in the way those abilities are described. One model, developed by Philip E. Vernon (1961), identifies two such abilities: a *practical-mechanical intelligence*, which contributes most to solving the kinds of problems encountered in everyday life; and a *verbal-educational intelligence*, which pertains to verbal ability and abstract thinking and contributes most to academic work. The scoring system for Wechsler IQ tests, which provides separate scores for performance and verbal abilities as well as an overall IQ score, is based on a model similar to Vernon's (look back at Table 11.1).

Another model, developed by Raymond Cattell (1971, 1987), also identifies two second-level abilities, but describes them differently from the way Vernon's model does. Cattell describes the second-level abilities as *fluid intelligence*, which is the raw ability to manipulate information, and *crystallized intelligence*, which is the mental ability derived from experience. According to Cattell, fluid intelligence peaks during a person's teenage years, whereas crystallized intelligence can increase throughout life if the person remains mentally active.

■ *How Spearman's and Thurstone's views are combined in hierarchical theories of intelligence, such as Vernon's and Cattell's*

**Figure 11.5 *Hierarchical model of intelligence***

*Most modern psychometric theories of intelligence incorporate the basic elements of both Thurstone's and Spearman's positions. In these theories, different sets of tests are differentially affected by different mental abilities, but the mental abilities are not entirely independent of one another. They are all affected by a general intelligence (g).*

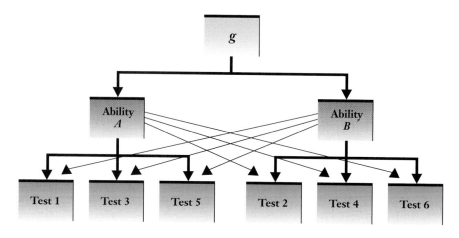

### Models of mental ability

*What constitutes intelligence? Is it separate abilities or a single entity? As you think about these questions, ask yourself what may underlie the brilliant leadership of someone like Nelson Mandela, shown during a 1990 visit to North America. And what may be the basis for the creative inventions of people like U.S. astronauts Kathryn D. Sullivan (left) and Sally L. Ride, shown displaying a device they created that holds them while they are sleeping?*

■ *How the information-processing approach attempts to understand intelligence in terms of components rather than kinds*

### The Information-Processing Approach to Intelligence

As you have seen, psychometricians attempt to understand the structure of intelligence by analyzing patterns of correlations among different tests given to a large number of people. With this method they identify different kinds of intelligence and determine the degree to which the kinds are independent of one another or are influenced by a common factor (*g*). The *information-processing approach*, to which we now turn, is in some ways a complement to the psychometric approach (Sternberg, 1985b). Its overall goal is to describe the specific mental steps or processes that give rise to any given instance of intelligent behavior. Thus, rather than describing the mind in terms of *kinds* of intelligence, this approach attempts to describe it in terms of *components* of intelligence, where each information-processing step represents a different component. From this perspective, differences among people in their test performance, or in their pattern of performance among different kinds of tests, may arise because of individual differences in the capacity, speed, or manner of functioning of one or another component.

To understand more concretely what is meant by a component, you might turn back to Figure 10.1, which depicts an information-processing model of the whole mind. In that model, conscious reasoning occurs in the store called short-term, or working, memory. Short-term memory is of limited capacity in the sense that it can hold only a certain amount of information at any given time (you can only think about a limited number of items at once). Information enters the short-term store by way of the senses (through the sensory memory store) and by way of retrieval from long-term memory, which is one's store of previously acquired knowledge. According to this model, to solve a problem on an intelligence test you must be able to register and recognize the stimulus information relevant to the problem, hold that information in short-term memory, retrieve from long-term memory previously acquired information relevant to the problem, and then combine all of the relevant information to arrive at a solution. Any limitation on your ability to perform one or another of these mental steps could reduce your chance of solving the problem correctly.

**The Search for Elementary Cognitive Correlates of Intelligence**   One research strategy that links the information-processing and psychometric traditions is that of correlating people's scores on standard IQ tests with their performance on  simple tests designed to measure specific information-processing components. As an example of this strategy, Earl Hunt (1985) tested a group of college students for their speed at judging whether a series of printed letters (such as CARD or CARG) is or is not an English word. All of the students made nearly all of those identifications correctly; but students with high verbal IQs made them a few milliseconds faster, on average, than did those with lower verbal IQs. From this and similar evidence, Hunt proposed that one component of general verbal intelligence is the ability to retrieve verbal information quickly from long-term memory and match it with incoming sensory stimulation. This speed might increase verbal IQ by allowing the person both to acquire more verbal information (such as from reading) and to use that information more efficiently in thinking.

Other researchers have shown surprisingly strong correlations between even simpler reaction-time scores and IQ—results that would be dear to Galton's heart were he alive today. In one such test, for example, a subject must hold a finger on a button until one of a set of stimulus windows lights up, and then must move the finger as quickly as possible to that window. Using this test, Arthur Jensen (1987) and his colleagues found moderately strong correlations (coefficients from 0.3 to 0.5) between reaction speed and general IQ when subjects had a relatively large number of choices (eight or more windows), but weak correlations when subjects had only a few choices. Based on these results, Jensen proposed that the correlation stems not from the ability to move the muscles rapidly, but from the ability to judge quickly which stimulus has lit up and to direct the movement toward that stimulus.

Based on such work, Jensen and others have revived the Galtonian notion of mental quickness (see Vernon, 1987). They suggest that general intelligence may be strongly linked to what they call *speed of information processing*. Their view is strengthened by the further finding that the correlation between reaction time and IQ is equally strong when untimed IQ tests are used as when timed IQ tests are used  (Vernon & Kantor, 1986), so the correlation is not simply a result of the fact that many standard IQ tests require the test taker to react quickly.

■ *How some research in the information-processing tradition has revived Galton's idea of mental quickness as the basis for general intelligence*

*High-speed information processing*
*Regardless of whether mental quickness is the basis for general intelligence, it is certainly important in many human endeavors. These air-traffic controllers must routinely make important decisions under extreme time pressure.*

Philip A. Vernon (1987) (not the same man as Philip E. Vernon, mentioned earlier) has suggested that speed of information processing may contribute to intelligence by allowing people to make optimal use of their limited-capacity short-term memories. Information fades quickly from short-term memory when it is not being acted upon, so the faster a person can process information, the more items he or she can bring together to make a mental calculation or to arrive at a reasoned decision. Perhaps you recall the analogy suggested in Chapter 10 between holding material in short-term memory and a circus performer's task of spinning pie plates on sticks. The faster the performer could move from one stick to another, the more plates he or she could spin before one of them fell. Similarly, in performing a task such as mental long division, the faster you can move from one calculating step to the next, the more likely you are to complete the task before you lose track of what you had accomplished in the previous steps.

■ *The problem of cause and effect in the cognitive-correlates approach*

Researchers who take the cognitive-correlates approach usually interpret the correlations as indicating a causal relation between the elementary process and general intelligence. Thus, Jensen, Vernon, and others suggest that speed of mental processing is an underlying cause of high general intelligence. But, as was emphasized in Chapter 2, correlations do not by themselves identify cause and effect. Perhaps the causal relationship is the other way around. Maybe a more intelligent person can do better on a reaction-time test because he or she figures out a better strategy for paying close attention to the stimuli and making a quick decision, thereby bringing higher-order reasoning to bear on what seems to be a very simple task. One cognitive psychologist who has suggested this possibility is Robert Sternberg (Marr & Sternberg, 1987).

■ *Sternberg's idea that some mental components regulate other mental components, and that the regulators are the main source of general intelligence*

**Sternberg's Theory of Intelligence: Regulating the Components**     Sternberg (1986b) has described intelligence as "mental self-government." By this he means that intelligence is the ability to regulate and coordinate the various lower-level processes (components) of the mind in ways that increase the chance of solving problems. Sternberg (1985a) ascribes this regulating ability to a special set of mental processes that he calls *metacomponents*. The prefix *meta-* in this context means beyond, or transcending. In Sternberg's theory, the metacomponents transcend the other components. They can be thought of as the executive officers of the mind, dealing with the overall goals and strategies of behavior and exerting their effects by controlling the lower components. Metacomponents define the problem, decide whether or not it is worth solving, select the lower components needed to solve it, control the order in which those components are activated, monitor the progress toward solution, and decide when the problem is solved.

Sternberg divides the lower components into two groups. One group consists of *knowledge-acquisition components*, which are most directly involved in learning (and which we will not discuss here). The other group consists of *performance components*, defined as the information-processing steps that act most directly on information when solving a problem or choosing a course of action. Performance components are involved in encoding stimulus information, retrieving information from long-term memory, comparing different sources of information, and producing behavioral responses. These are the processes most commonly studied by cognitive psychologists. In fact, many of the performance components are part of the general model of the mind presented in Chapter 10 (see Figure 10.1).

In a series of experiments, Sternberg and his colleagues mapped the steps through which people solve various logical-reasoning problems similar to those commonly found in IQ tests. The results led Sternberg to hypothesize that logical reasoning involves several distinct performance components, which are brought into play in different sequences for different kinds of problems. The flowchart in Figure 11.6 shows Sternberg's mapping of this sequence for the type of problem called an *analogy problem* (Sternberg & Gardner, 1983). Among the components shown on the chart are (a) *encoding*, which means reading or hearing the words of the problem and forming a mental representation of their meaning; (b) *inference*, which means making a guess about the general rule that provides the basis for solving the problem; (c) *application*, which means using the general rule to imagine a possible solution to the problem; and (d) *comparison*, which means contrasting the imagined solution with the possible answers given in the problem statement to see if they are similar.

Sternberg (1985a) developed a way to measure the amount of time that people devote to the separate steps in solving problems such as that depicted in Figure 11.6, and he found that people who perform well typically spend more time on the encoding steps and less time on other steps than do people who perform poorly. If you think about it, this is not a terribly surprising result. Encoding the available information before jumping to subsequent steps is important in solving any problem. How many times have you lost points on a test because you didn't read the question carefully or take the time to figure out exactly what was being asked before starting to work out the answer? In Sternberg's theory of intelligence, deciding

**Figure 11.6** *Steps in solving an analogy problem*

*This chart depicts the sequence of steps involved in solving analogy problems, according to Sternberg. To make the steps clear, a specific problem is used, but the chart is meant to characterize the steps in solving any problem of the general form, A is to B as C is to _____ (choose either $D_1$ or $D_2$). Each of the steps in the chart is a performance component in Sternberg's broader theory, but the choice to use these steps and the decision as to how much time to devote to each is a task of the metacomponents. (Adapted from Sternberg & Gardner, 1983.)*

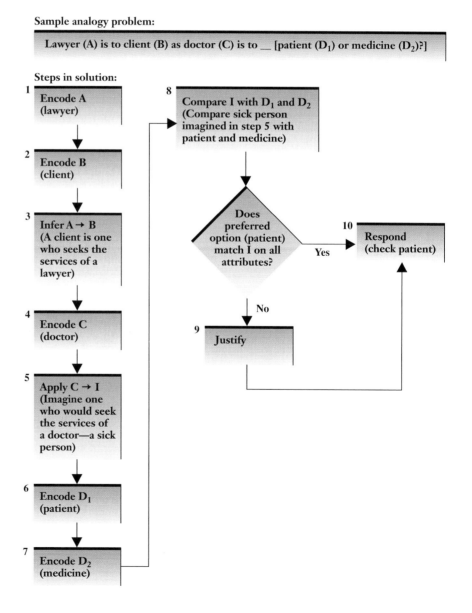

Sample analogy problem:

Lawyer (A) is to client (B) as doctor (C) is to __ [patient ($D_1$) or medicine ($D_2$)?]

Steps in solution:

1 Encode A (lawyer)

2 Encode B (client)

3 Infer A → B (A client is one who seeks the services of a lawyer)

4 Encode C (doctor)

5 Apply C → I (Imagine one who would seek the services of a doctor—a sick person)

6 Encode $D_1$ (patient)

7 Encode $D_2$ (medicine)

8 Compare I with $D_1$ and $D_2$ (Compare sick person imagined in step 5 with patient and medicine)

Does preferred option (patient) match I on all attributes?

Yes → 10 Respond (check patient)

No → 9 Justify

how much time to devote to each step in solving a problem is an important task of the metacomponents.

Sternberg (1985a, 1985b) has compared his information-processing theory of intelligence with the hierarchical theories of intelligence developed within the psychometric tradition. Like most of the psychometricians, he believes that a general intelligence, *g*, accounts for the correlations among scores on different tests. He explains *g* primarily—though not entirely—in terms of the metacomponents. People who are good at directing their mental resources toward a problem and developing a general strategy for solving it (the tasks of the metacomponents) are likely to do well on a wide variety of tests, ranging from simple reaction-time tests to those involving complex calculations. Sternberg (1986a) believes that people can increase the effectiveness of their metacomponents through deliberate practice, and in that way increase their intelligence.

**At the bar**

*The preparation of a legal brief brings into play many of the intellectual abilities that Robert Sternberg calls metacomponents, including defining the legal problem, choosing strategies to solve it, and selecting the lower-level skills needed to bring the case to a successful conclusion.*

### The Neuropsychological Approach to Intelligence

At the height of his career, the Russian composer V. G. Shebalin suffered a stroke (a rupturing of blood vessels in the brain) that damaged a portion of his left cerebral cortex. From then on, he had great difficulty expressing himself in words or understanding what others were saying, but he continued to create great music. His *Fifth Symphony*, composed after his stroke, was described by the composer Dmitri Shostakovich as "a brilliant creative work, filled with highest emotions, optimistic and full of life" (see Gardner, 1974).

As illustrated by the case of Shebalin, brain damage often leaves a person deficient in some areas of intellectual functioning yet still fully capable, or nearly so, in others. The study of such persons as a way to understand the role of specific brain areas in mental functioning is called **neuropsychology** (also discussed in Chapter 10). Neuropsychology is an approach to the human intellect that is complementary to, and often closely integrated with, the psychometric and information-processing approaches. While psychometricians attempt to understand the structure of the intellect through analyzing patterns of test scores, and information-processing theorists attempt to understand it in terms of hypothetical mental components, neuropsychologists attempt to understand it in terms of physical areas of the brain.

■ *How studies of people with brain damage led to the view that the left hemisphere is specialized for language and the right hemisphere is specialized for spatial understanding*

The most obvious physical division of the brain is that between the left and right hemispheres. By the end of the nineteenth century, it was well established

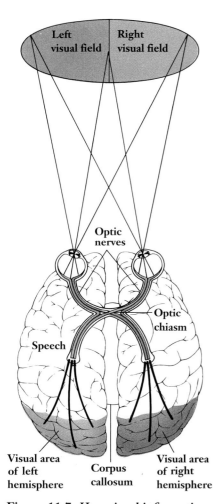

**Figure 11.7** *How visual information can be sent to one hemisphere or the other in a person whose corpus callosum has been cut*

*Neurons of the optic nerves either cross or don't cross at the optic chiasm, as shown above, in such a way that those that receive input from the left visual field go to the right half of the brain, and vice versa. Thus, it is possible to present visual information to just one hemisphere in split-brain patients by having the patient focus on a dot on a screen and then quickly flashing the stimulus to one side or the other of the dot.*

■ *How it is possible to test each hemisphere separately in split-brain patients, and how such tests confirm the view that the left hemisphere controls speech and the right hemisphere has superior spatial ability*

that people who suffer injuries to the left hemisphere of the brain are far more likely to lose their verbal abilities than are people with comparable injuries to the right hemisphere. Those with left-hemisphere damage are often unable to speak coherently or to understand what others are saying, even though their basic sensory and motor capacities remain intact. For decades, this observation was interpreted by the medical world to mean that the left hemisphere is "dominant" and that the right hemisphere is less important.

By the 1960s, however, evidence began to mount that the right hemisphere has special intellectual functions as well. In a study of soldiers who had suffered brain injuries in World War II, the Russian psychologist Alexander Luria (1966, 1970) found that people with right-hemisphere damage are often severely impaired in such tasks as recognizing faces, reading maps, or drawing geometric shapes. At about the same time, Brenda Milner (1974) and her colleagues in Montreal began studying the cognitive abilities of patients who had surgery to one side of the brain or the other as treatment for epilepsy. They found cases in which right-hemisphere surgery resulted in specific deficits in the ability to recognize or remember pictures. Thus, the idea grew that the right hemisphere is specialized for understanding spatial relationships and the left is specialized for language.

**The Split-Brain Syndrome**    The most dramatic evidence for separate abilities of the two hemispheres appeared when Roger Sperry and Michael Gazzaniga began in the 1960s to study people who, as a last-resort treatment for epilepsy, had undergone an operation in which the **corpus callosum** had been cut. The corpus callosum is a massive bundle of neurons connecting the right and left halves of the upper parts of the brain, including the cerebral cortex and the underlying limbic system (described in Chapter 6). Earlier, more casual observations had revealed no remarkable deficits in people who had had the operation. The operation was generally successful in reducing or eliminating epileptic seizures, and, after a period of recovery, there was usually no drop in measured IQ, in ability to carry on conversations, or even in ability to coordinate the two sides of the body in skilled tasks. But Sperry and Gazzaniga showed that under special test conditions in which information was provided just to one hemisphere or the other, these people behaved in some ways as if they had two separate minds with separate abilities.

The split-brain studies take advantage of the crossed sensory and motor connections of the brain. As was described in Chapter 6, the right hemisphere most directly controls movement in, and receives sensory information from, the left half of the body; and the reverse is true for the left hemisphere. Connections from the eyes to the brain are such that input from the *right visual field* (the right-hand half of a person's field of view) goes first to the left hemisphere, and that from the *left visual field* goes first to the right hemisphere (see Figure 11.7). In the normal brain, information that goes first to one hemisphere subsequently travels to the other through the corpus callosum. But after the split-brain operation, such neural communication from one hemisphere to the other no longer occurs. Thus, with the testing apparatus shown in Figure 11.8, and with split-brain patients as subjects, it is possible to (a) send visual information to just one hemisphere by presenting the stimulus in the opposite half of the visual field, (b) send tactile information to just one hemisphere by having the subject feel an object with the opposite hand, and (c) obtain a response from just one hemisphere by having the subject point to an object with the opposite hand.

In a typical experiment, pictures of common objects would be flashed in either the right or the left visual field. When flashed in the right field (to the left hemisphere), the split-brain patient could describe it as well as you or I might; but when flashed in the left field (to the right hemisphere), the patient would either claim that nothing had been flashed or would make a random guess. Then the re-

**Figure 11.8  *Testing apparatus for split-brain subjects***

*With this apparatus, it is possible to flash a stimulus to either visual field (or both at once) and to ask the person to identify objects by touch with either hand. This man will be able to locate the pencil with his left hand, even though he is unable to say, vocally, what word appeared on the screen. (Adapted from Gazzaniga, 1967.)*

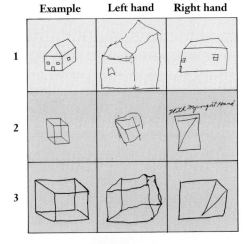

| Example | Left hand | Right hand |
|---|---|---|
| 1 | | |
| 2 | | |
| 3 | | |

**Figure 11.9  *Evidence for right-hemisphere superiority in spatial representation***

*Although the split-brain patient who produced these drawings was right-handed, he could copy geometric figures much better with his left hand (controlled by his right hemisphere) than with his right hand. (From Gazzaniga, 1967.)*

searchers would ask the same person to reach under a barrier with one hand or the other and identify, by touch, the object that had been flashed. The fascinating result was that the person could reliably identify with the left hand (but not with the right) the same object that he or she had just vocally denied having seen (Gazzaniga, 1967). Thus, if the object flashed to the right hemisphere was a pencil, the subject's left hand would pick out the pencil from a set of objects even while the subject's voice was continuing to say that nothing had been flashed. In other tests, Sperry and Gazzaniga found that split-brain patients were much better at solving spatial puzzles or drawing geometric diagrams with their left hand than their right, indicating right-hemisphere superiority in spatial tasks (see Figure 11.9).

Researchers have found large individual differences among split-brain patients in the degree to which the right hemisphere can comprehend speech. Some show essentially no right-hemisphere comprehension. They cannot participate in experiments such as that just described, because their right hemispheres don't understand such instructions as, "Pick up the object that you saw on the screen." At the other extreme, some patients have right-hemisphere comprehension that is nearly as good as their left (though their right hemisphere is still unable to facilitate speech); and a few patients show a reversal, with the right hemisphere superior to the left in language comprehension and production. Other tests, on people without the corpus callosum cut, indicate that about 4 percent of right-handed individuals and 15 percent of left-handed individuals have their speech centers located in the right rather than left hemisphere (Rasmussen & Milner, 1977).

Perhaps you are wondering how people who have had the split-brain operation get along in the world as well as they do. What keeps their two hemispheres from going off in opposite directions, creating conflict between the two halves of the body? In some instances, especially shortly after the surgery, conflict does occur. One man described a situation in which, while dressing in the morning, his right hand was trying to pull his pants on while his left hand was trying to pull them back off (Gazzaniga, 1970); apparently his right hemisphere wanted to go back to bed. But such conflicts are rare, and when they do occur the left hemisphere (right hand) usually wins.

The patient's ability to coordinate the two hemispheres probably involves several mechanisms. First, only the upper parts of the brain are divided when the corpus callosum is cut. Motor centers that control whole-body movements such as walking lie in the lower, undivided parts, and some sensory information may also pass from one hemisphere to the other by way of those lower routes (Springer &

Deutsch, 1989). In addition, under normal conditions, when the eyes can move around and things can be felt with both hands, the two hemispheres can receive the same or similar information through their separate channels. Finally, the hemispheres apparently learn to communicate indirectly with each other by observing the behavior that each other produces, a process that Gazzaniga (1967) labeled *cross-cuing*. For example, the right hemisphere may perceive something pleasant and precipitate a smile, and the left may feel the smile and say, "I'm happy."

■ *How studies of brain-intact individuals suggest that the right hemisphere is involved in music recognition, facial recognition, and nonverbal communication*

**Studying Hemisphere Differences in Brain-Intact Individuals**   In the normal brain with an intact corpus callosum, the two hemispheres interact constantly by way of neural messages sent through the 200 million axons that make up the corpus callosum. Because of these connections, each hemisphere receives input from and sends output to both sides of the body. Nevertheless, shortly after Sperry and Gazzaniga began their split-brain studies, Doreen Kimura in Montreal guessed that it might be possible to observe right-left brain differences in normal, brain-intact individuals. Even though all stimuli reach both hemispheres in the intact brain, those presented to one side of the body reach the opposite side of the brain more quickly, and perhaps more strongly, than they reach the same side. Based on this assumption, Kimura (1964) used headphones to present either spoken sentences or melodies to either the right or the left ear of normal, brain-intact subjects. She found that her subjects could recognize sentences slightly more easily if they were played into the right ear, and could recognize melodies slightly more easily if they were played into the left. Since then, hundreds of other experiments have been performed in which stimuli have been presented selectively to the right or the left ear, or the right or the left visual field, of people who have undamaged brains. As would be expected, the results of such studies are never as dramatic as those of studies conducted with split-brain patients, but in general they yield a similar pattern of results. People usually recognize verbal material better when it is presented to the right ear or right visual field, and recognize melodies or visual patterns better when they are presented to the left ear or left visual field.

**Figure 11.10** *Composite faces task*
*Which of the two right-hand faces (b or c) looks most like face (a)? In reality, face (a) is a normal photograph, and faces (b) and (c) are artificial constructions made by pairing one or the other side of face (a) with its own mirror image. Most people see face (c) as most like (a). Notice that face (c) is constructed from the side of face (a) that lies in the left field of view and would be most strongly processed by the right hemisphere.*

In some cases, hemispheric differences can be demonstrated even without special testing equipment. Look at Figure 11.10 and say quickly which of the two right-hand portraits (b or c) most closely matches the portrait on the left (a). Bryan Kolb and his colleagues (1983) found that most people chose (c) when asked that

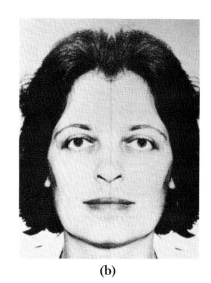
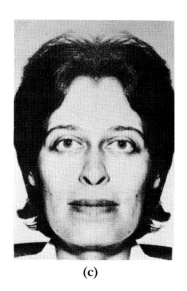

(a)                          (b)                          (c)

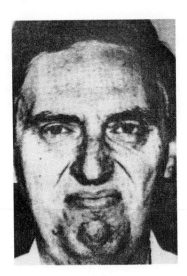

**Figure 11.11** *Asymmetry of emotional expression*
*People commonly express emotions most strongly on the left side of their face (controlled by the right hemisphere), as illustrated by this man's expression of disgust. (From Sackheim & Gur, 1978.)*

■ *The idea that the left hemisphere processes information in a discrete, propositional manner and the right hemisphere processes it in a graded, holistic manner*

question. If you look closely at the portraits you will see that (c) corresponds to the left half of portrait (a) (the half that more strongly enters your right hemisphere when you are looking at it), and (b) corresponds to the right half. Other studies of brain-intact as well as brain-damaged individuals have shown that emotional expressions are controlled primarily by the right hemisphere (see Figure 11.11).

**Characterizing the Hemisphere Differences: Two Modes of Thinking?** You have just read of evidence that the two hemispheres differ in some of their functions. One seems to be specialized for language and the other for a variety of non-linguistic functions including spatial analysis, emotional perception and expression, and at least some aspects of music recognition. Is there a more basic way to characterize the functions of the two hemispheres? Chapter 9 presented feature versus Gestalt theories of perception, and Chapter 10 discussed propositional versus analogue theories of visual memory. In each case, a dichotomy was drawn between a piece-by-piece, discrete mode of representing information, on the one hand, and a holistic, graded mode on the other. Many observers, both within and outside the field of psychology, have suggested that both sides of the dichotomy may be correct—feature and propositional theories may apply to left-brain functions, and Gestalt and analogue theories may apply to right-brain functions. Human intelligence, from that perspective, is an amalgam of two different styles of perceiving, remembering, and thinking, each with its separate advantages.

Particularly useful in characterizing the two hemispheres are experiments in which the same or similar stimuli are presented to each hemisphere and different ways of responding are observed. In one such experiment, Stephen Kosslyn and his colleagues flashed stimuli of the sort shown in Figure 11.12 to either the right or the left visual field of normal (brain-intact) college students (Kosslyn, 1987; Kosslyn & others, 1989). In some cases the task was to judge, as quickly as possible, whether a dot was on or off the outline of a blob, and in others it was to judge whether the dot was nearer or farther than 2 millimeters from the outline of the blob. The main finding was that the on-off judgment was made more quickly when the stimulus was presented in the right visual field (going more strongly to the left hemisphere), but the near-far judgment was made more quickly when it was presented in the left visual field. In this case both tasks involved analysis of visual material, but the first task (performed best by the left hemisphere) involved a discrete, categorical decision most consistent with a propositional mode of analysis (on or off the line), whereas the second involved a graded decision most consistent with an analogue mode of analysis (distance from the line).

**Figure 11.12** *Sample stimuli used to contrast categorical and graded perception*
*Stimuli such as the four shown here were flashed in either the left or right visual field, and subjects were asked to respond with either a categorical judgment (Is the dot on or off the line?) or a graded (distance) judgment (Is the dot more than 2 millimeters from the line?). The result was that subjects were quicker at the categorical task when the stimulus was in the right field (to left hemisphere) and quicker at the graded task when it was in the left field (to right hemisphere). (From Kosslyn, 1987.)*

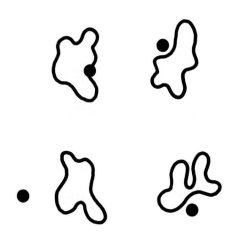

*How Gardner used case histories of special people to identify separate intelligences*

**Figure 11.13** *Drawing produced by a child who is deficient in other intellectual areas*

*This remarkable drawing was produced by a 5-year-old girl, Nadia, afflicted with an inherited condition (autism) that includes severe retardation in development of speech and social interaction. Her artistic skill emerged from her own efforts, without any training. (From Gardner, 1985.)*

**Gardner's Case-History Approach and His Multiple Intelligences Theory**
Partly from neuropsychological evidence, Howard Gardner (1985) developed a theory of intelligence that he calls the *multiple intelligences theory*. It is based principally on case histories of people in whom one or more mental abilities flourish in the relative absence of other mental abilities. Some of his cases are those of people, like the composer Shebalin, who lost some abilities but not others due to brain damage in adulthood. Another group that interests Gardner are those rare individuals referred to as *idiots savants*, who are born with a condition that leaves them mentally retarded in many intellectual realms, but who—often with no special training—develop normal or even superior ability in one area such as math or art. In Figure 11.13 you can see an example of the remarkable artistic skill of one such individual. Less rare are *prodigies*, who show normal or above-normal abilities in most areas, but extraordinary ability in one area, sometimes despite environmental forces that seem to work against the development of the ability. Still another source of evidence used by Gardner is the difference in the age at which various abilities emerge in the developing child. For example, language and musical ability show their greatest spurt of development during the preschool years, but mathematical ability rarely begins to surge before the age of 10 or 11.

On the basis of such evidence, Gardner has argued against the concept of a general intelligence that cuts across all mental tasks, and has resurrected the Thurstonian notion of separate intelligences that may vary independently of one another. From his work so far, Gardner has tentatively identified a set of seven such intelligences, which are described briefly in Table 11.2. Notice that three of these (linguistic, logical-mathematical, and spatial) fall within the category of abilities usually tested in standard IQ tests, but the other four (musical, bodily-kinesthetic, interpersonal, and intrapersonal) involve skills that usually have not been considered as part of intelligence in the psychometric tradition. Some psychologists believe that Gardner has stretched the meaning of intelligence too far, and that this last set of abilities should be called *talents* rather than intelligences. Gardner (1985) counters that he would be glad to call them talents if people would also refer to linguistic, spatial, and logical abilities as talents. Part of his message is that psychologists have overemphasized certain abilities that can be tested easily with paper and pencil or puzzles—glorifying them with the term *intelligence*—at the expense of other abilities that, to the world at large, are just as important. Each of the abilities that Gardner refers to as an intelligence requires complex brain

**Table 11.2** *The seven intelligences of Gardner's multiple intelligences theory*

| Type of intelligence | Description |
|---|---|
| 1. *Linguistic* | Verbal ability in general, but especially the ability to understand subtle shades of meaning |
| 2. *Logical-mathematical* | Reasoning |
| 3. *Spatial* | The ability to perceive and draw spatial relationships |
| 4. *Musical* | Singing, playing an instrument, composing music |
| 5. *Bodily-kinesthetic* | The ability to control one's muscle movements in graceful and skillful ways, as in dance, athletics, and tool use |
| 6. *Interpersonal* | Social skills, including the ability to understand and respond appropriately to others' nonverbal messages |
| 7. *Intrapersonal* | The ability to understand oneself, including one's own emotions and wishes, and to use that understanding effectively in guiding behavior |

mechanisms, is valued by human beings everywhere (though cultures vary with regard to which they value most), and is more or less uniquely developed in humans as compared to other species.

### An educational experiment

*At the Key School in Indianapolis, Indiana, the daily schedule includes a heavy dose of activities based on Howard Gardner's theory of multiple intelligences. Performing music they composed themselves is believed to develop musical intelligence, and building architectural models is believed to develop spatial intelligence. The school also covers a rigorous standard curriculum.*

■ **Evidence that intelligence in the work environment may not be reflected by scores on tests**

### The Ecological Approach to Intelligence

Most definitions of intelligence include the idea that its function is to help a person adapt to his or her environment. Yet, psychologists most often study intelligence using tests, tasks, and environmental settings that are quite different from those that most people deal with in everyday life. The only real-life environment that closely resembles the setting for an intelligence test is that of a school. This may help explain the relatively strong correlation commonly found between IQ and school performance, and the low or absent correlation commonly found between IQ and ability in other occupations (Ceci & Liker, 1986). The *ecological approach* to intelligence focuses on the relationship between intelligence and the environmental context within which it normally operates. How does intelligence manifest itself on the streets of the inner city, in solving problems at the factory, in raising children and running a household, or in the hunting life of Eskimos living above the Arctic Circle?

One strategy of the ecological approach is to observe people solving problems in their usual employment settings and to ask questions or conduct tests designed to understand how they solve their problems. Sylvia Scribner (1986) and her colleagues used this approach to study such groups as dairy workers, bartenders, salespeople, and waitresses as they went about their jobs. They found that people in such settings regularly solve complex problems, frequently doing so in more efficient and flexible ways than would be predicted by their scores on standard tests. For example, Scribner found that wholesale-delivery drivers who had to calculate the prices of different numbers of quarts of milk would vary their strategy depending on the number of quarts ordered. Thus, when milk was selling for 68¢ per quart, or $10.88 per case (16 quarts), and a customer ordered 17 quarts, the driver quickly converted the problem into an addition problem (1 case at $10.88, plus 1 quart at 68¢), which could easily be solved mentally. By this strategy, the driver saved the time and effort required to solve what would otherwise be a rather difficult multiplication problem (17 multiplied by 68¢). Interestingly, Scribner found no relation between drivers' abilities to solve these pricing problems quickly and correctly and their high-school math grades or their performance on a conventional arithmetic test that she gave them.

■ *Evidence that people from different cultures (a) approach intelligence tests quite differently, and (b) may develop different mental capacities depending on their environment and lifestyle*

Another strategy of the ecological approach is to compare standard test results of people from different cultures to see how culture affects mental development. One general conclusion from such research is that the basic way in which people approach intelligence tests—their understanding of what is expected of them—is culturally dependent. In non-Western cultures, people often find it absurd or presumptuous to respond to questions that do not pertain to their concrete experience (Scribner, 1977; Cole & Means, 1981). Thus, the logic question, "If John is taller than Carl, and Carl is taller than Henry, is John taller than Henry?" is likely to elicit the polite response, "I'm sorry, but I have never met these men." Yet, the same person has no difficulty solving similar logic problems that present themselves in the course of everyday experience.

**Another cultural context**

*The ecological approach emphasizes the importance of the context in which intelligent behavior occurs. Micronesians' skill at navigating long distances using information from the stars and from ocean currents is a kind of intelligence that is well adapted to their environment.*

As further illustration of cultural effects, Michael Cole and his colleagues (1971) described a situation in which researchers were trying to test a group of Kpelle people in Nigeria for their ability to sort pictures of common objects into separate categories. For various reasons, Western researchers consider it more intelligent to sort according to taxonomic category (such as putting all animals in one group and plants in another) than according to function (such as putting things that people eat into one group and things that people don't eat into another); and, in the West, intelligent people usually do sort by taxonomy. But the Kpelle, no matter what instructions they were given, consistently sorted by function rather than by taxonomy until, in frustration, the researchers asked them to sort the way that stupid people do—then they sorted by taxonomy! In other words, they had the mental capacity to sort by taxonomy, but in their culture this was not considered to be the intelligent way to organize things.

Still other cross-cultural studies have demonstrated that the specific abilities tested by the specific subtests of standard IQ tests may be affected by cultural variation. One interesting generalization derived from these studies is that people who survive by hunting and fishing commonly perform better on visual-spatial tests (such as the block design and object-assembly tests described in Table 11.1) than do people who survive by other means such as farming (Berry, 1971). The implication is that hunting and fishing require people to travel long distances, keeping track of landmarks and making maps of where they have been, which strengthens their visual-spatial intelligence. The Eskimos living north of the Arctic Circle seem to have particularly well developed abilities in this area (McShane & Berry, 1988). The Eskimos' environment provides very few cues telling them which way is home, so to find their way back from an excursion they must constantly construct mental maps based on the turns they make and the estimated distances between turns. Even Galton once remarked on the amazing spatial memories of Eskimo explorers (Werner, 1948). He had heard from a captain in the British Admiralty of an Eskimo who had explored 6000 miles of coastline just once in his kayak and had subsequently drawn from memory a map of the coast that was later found to be extraordinarily accurate.

## Logical Reasoning and Problem Solving

Thus far we have been concerned with the broad problem of describing the human intellect as a whole. You have read of psychometric, information-processing, neuropsychological, and ecological approaches to that task. We now shift our focus from the attempt to describe the mind as a whole to the attempt to understand how people actually solve particular kinds of problems that entail logical reasoning.

Perhaps because it is the main part of their own job description, philosophers have always placed reasoning at the pinnacle of human activity and been most interested in understanding it. Descartes's famous "I think, therefore I am" could have been "I move things, therefore I am"; or "I feel emotions, therefore I am"; but it wasn't. Psychology, in its more than 100 years of existence, has gone back and forth on the issue. When psychology first emerged from philosophy as a distinct discipline, reasoning was at the top of the list of phenomena to be studied by the new science. But two trends of the early twentieth century led psychologists away from it. One was behaviorism, which argued that observable action, not unobservable thought, is the proper subject matter for psychology; and the other was Freud's psychoanalytic approach, which emphasized the role of instinct and emotion and argued that what we call reason is often mere rationalization for, rather than the real cause of, what we do. With the rise of cognitive psychology during the second half of the twentieth century, however, the study of reasoning has been revived and become again an important part of psychology.

**How the psychological approach to understanding reasoning differs from the philosophical approach to understanding it**

Logicians (philosophers interested in reason or logic) look at reasoning differently from the way psychologists do. Logicians are most interested in the ideal case, that is, in the laws that describe reasoning as it is most efficiently and effectively performed. Cognitive psychologists, on the other hand, are more interested in reasoning as it is *typically* performed; hence, their theories are messier than those of the logicians.

To see what people actually do when they reason, psychologists must somehow make objective the processes that go on in the mind. There are several ways to try to do this. One approach is to ask people to think aloud, although with this means researchers can only observe those aspects of reasoning that the subject can put into words. A second approach is to examine the kinds of errors that people typically make and use them to draw inferences about the reasoning process. A third approach, which is perhaps the most common, is to give people problems that vary in systematic ways to see what kinds of changes make the problem easier or harder to solve. You will see examples of the last two of these approaches in the following subsections, dealing respectively with elements of logic and strategies for solving problems.

*■ The difference between deductive and inductive reasoning, and why the latter is also called hypothesis construction*

Drawing by Sidney Harris.

### Elements of Logic

**Deductive and Inductive Reasoning**   Logicians have long distinguished between two general classes of logical reasoning. One class, called **deductive reasoning**, or *deduction*, is reasoning from the general to the specific. In a deductive-reasoning task, you are asked to accept the truth of one or more general premises or axioms and to assert, based on that acceptance, whether a specific conclusion is true, false, or indeterminate. If you ever studied plane geometry, you would have consciously engaged in deductive reasoning as you tried to prove or disprove various correlates based on axioms that you were told were true. You have also almost certainly seen deductive-reasoning problems in the form of **syllogisms**—problems that contain a major premise and a minor premise, which the reasoner must combine in order to test a specific conclusion. Here is an example:

All chefs are violinists (*major premise*).

John is a chef (*minor premise*).

Is John a violinist?

Notice that in this problem you are asked to accept the truth of the two premises whether or not they fit with your real-world experience. The internal consistency of the argument is the point at issue. Syllogisms commonly appear on intelligence tests and are often used in experiments on deductive reasoning.

The other class of reasoning, called **inductive reasoning**, or *induction*, is in one sense the opposite of deduction. Induction is reasoning from the specific to the general, rather than the other way around. A person is presented with specific items or observations and is asked to infer the general rule that they exemplify. Inductive reasoning can also be called *hypothesis construction*, because the inferred rule is usually just one of many possible rules that are consistent with the observations. In evaluating a proposed solution to an inductive problem, one must ask whether or not the proposal is consistent with all of the observed data. As an example of an inductive task, consider the following series completion problem:

$$1 \quad 2 \quad 4 \underline{\quad\quad} \underline{\quad\quad}$$

What numbers did you place in the two blanks? You might have constructed the hypothesis that each number in this series is double the previous number, which would have led you to complete the series with 8 and 16. But suppose I now inform you that the first blank should be filled with a 7. With that, you would know that your original hypothesis was incorrect and you might generate a new hypothesis—that each number is the sum of the previous two numbers plus 1. With this hypothesis, you would place a 12 in the final blank. Notice that the more information you are given, the more certain you can be that your hypothesis is correct, as long as all of the numbers are consistent with it. But you can never be absolutely certain. No matter how many numbers you have seen, the next number might prove your hypothesis wrong. The interesting point about inductive reasoning is that a conclusion can never be proven correct with absolute certainty, but it can be proven wrong with absolute certainty. Scientists engage in inductive reasoning all the time as they try to infer general rules of nature from their observations of specific events or objects in the world.

**Visual Imagery in Deductive Reasoning**   Psychological research on deduction commonly uses syllogisms such as the one about chefs and violinists presented above. Such research has shown that (a) most people throughout the world who are not used to the game of syllogisms perform poorly unless the premises coincide with their concrete experiences, and (b) even highly educated people who are familiar with the game do much better if the premises coincide with their experi-

**Figure 11.14** *An image that can be used to solve a specific set of syllogisms*

*A person attempting to solve syllogisms based on the major premise* All chefs are violinists *might represent the premise with a mental image (or a drawing) that looks like this. The image can then be inspected to answer such questions as,* If John is not a chef, is he a violinist?

■ *Evidence that people use visual imagery to solve syllogisms*

ences than if they don't (Johnson-Laird, 1985). If people used abstract, logical rules of the sort described by logicians to solve syllogisms, it should not matter whether the major premise fits with common experience (*All chefs are humans*), doesn't fit with common experience (*All chefs are violinists*), or is a bit of nonsense (*All quilagogs are boomjams*). All that should matter is the general form of the problem and the relationship expressed by the words, "All          are          ."

Philip Johnson-Laird (1985) proposed the interesting hypothesis that people who succeed at syllogisms typically do so by turning the major premise into a visual image and then inspecting the image to "see" the consequences. To illustrate this hypothesis, consider the following four syllogisms, all based on the same major premise but with different minor premises:

All chefs are violinists (*major premise*).

1. John is a chef (*minor premise*). Is he a violinist?
2. John is a violinist (*minor premise*). Is he a chef?
3. John is not a chef (*minor premise*). Is he a violinist?
4. John is not a violinist (*minor premise*). Is he a chef?

One way to solve all of these syllogisms—consistent with Johnson-Laird's hypothesis—would be to visualize a room full of men, some of whom are holding violins (they are the violinists) and some of whom are wearing chef's hats (they are the chefs). Since the major premise says that all chefs are violinists, you will have to put violins in the hands of all the chefs; but since the major premise does *not* say that all violinists are chefs, you should include the possibility that some are not chefs by including some violinists without chef's hats. In addition, of course, there may be some people who are neither chefs nor violinists. The resulting picture might look like the one in Figure 11.14.

Now, to answer the four questions, all you have to do is examine the picture. The answer to question 1 must be yes, because everyone wearing a chef's hat is also holding a violin. The answer to question 2 must be indeterminate, because some of the men with violins are wearing chef's hats and some are not. The answer to question 3 must also be indeterminate, because some of the men without chef's hats have violins and some do not. And the answer to question 4 must be no, because none of the men without violins has a chef's hat.

If Johnson-Laird's hypothesis is right, the main constraint in solving such problems lies in generating the correct initial picture and holding it in mind while answering the questions. Consistent with Johnson-Laird's hypothesis, psychometric research has demonstrated that the ability to solve syllogisms correlates much more strongly with visual-spatial ability than with verbal ability as measured by standard intelligence tests (Frandsen & Holder, 1969; Guyote & Sternberg, 1981). Also, other researchers have found that people do much better with syllogisms if the major premise is easy to visualize than if it isn't. For example, in one experiment, Catherine Clement and Rachel Falmagne (1986) presented college students with syllogisms such as the following two:

■ If the man wants plain doughnuts, then he walks to the bakery across the intersection (*major premise*). The man walked to the bakery across the intersection (*minor premise*). Did he want plain doughnuts?

■ If the woman reorganizes the company structure, then she makes a profit for the year (*major premise*). The woman made a profit for the year (*minor premise*). Did she reorganize the company structure?

Notice that these syllogisms are identical in form and similar in linguistic complexity and the degree to which the premises seem sensible. But most people can more easily form a mental picture of someone crossing an intersection than of someone

**All *A*'s are *B*'s**

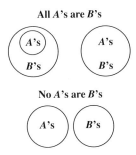

**No *A*'s are *B*'s**

## Figure 11.15  Euler circles

*Euler circles provide a means to turn the major premise of any syllogism into a concrete visual representation. One first converts the items of the premise (such as chefs and violinists) into A's and B's, and then represents the set of all possible A's and B's with circles that express the stipulated relationship. Notice that there are two possible representations consistent with the premise, All A's are B's. In one, A's are a subset of B's, and, in the other, A's and B's are identical sets. There is only one way to represent the premise, No A's are B's. Here the two sets do not overlap.*

■ *Evidence that people tend to ignore prior probabilities and information that is less readily available, and tend to anchor their initial judgments too firmly in inductive reasoning*

reorganizing the company structure. Consistent with Johnson-Laird's hypothesis, Clement and Falmagne found that syllogisms whose premises had been rated as easy to visualize were solved correctly by a higher percentage of students than those whose premises had been rated as hard to visualize. (Incidentally, the correct answer to both of these syllogisms is indeterminate.)

Perhaps the best solvers of syllogisms—those whose ability does not depend on the syllogism's specific content—are people who have mastered a little trick that allows them to turn any syllogistic premise into a picture. One version of this trick, illustrated in Figure 11.15, involves *Euler circles*, named after Leonard Euler, who used them in teaching logic to a German princess (Johnson-Laird, 1983). But, of course, the main point here goes beyond the game of solving syllogisms on tests. Johnson-Laird and others believe that many important scientific and philosophical innovations have come about because the innovator discovered a new way to visualize the problem. As mentioned in Chapter 10, Einstein claimed that he first developed the idea of relativity by imagining himself chasing a beam of light and catching up to it, and in that image he could see some of the consequences. Many other scientific innovators (for example, Feynman, 1985) have made similar claims about the value of visual imagery.

### Identifying Biases in Inductive Reasoning: Tversky and Kahneman's Research

As a second, quite different sample of psychological research on logical reasoning, we turn now to some of the work of Amos Tversky and Daniel Kahneman. These psychologists have studied inductive reasoning using problems that are similar to the kinds of judgments people make in everyday life. Their aim has been to identify the kinds of information people either use or ignore when attempting to make educated guesses based on limited information. Here is a sample problem (modified from Tversky & Kahneman, 1974):

> Steve is meek, tidy, has a passion for detail, is helpful to people, but has little real interest in people or real-world issues. Is Steve more likely to be a librarian or a salesperson?

What answer did you give? More important, what information did you take into account in making your choice? Did you compare the description of Steve's personality with your beliefs about the personalities of typical librarians and typical salespeople? If so, you used the kind of information that Tversky and Kahneman call *representativeness*, which refers to the extent to which the item to be classified (Steve, in this case) has characteristics that are typical or representative of the possible classes into which the item might be placed (librarian or salesperson, in this case). Another kind of information that you might have used is *prior probabilities*. Prior probabilities, in this case, refers to the likelihood that any randomly chosen man would be a librarian or a salesperson. Most people know that there are many more salespeople than there are librarians, so this information—if they thought to consider it—would tend to tip the judgment toward salesperson. A person might reasonably conclude that even though Steve's personality is more like that of a typical librarian than a typical salesperson, there are many more salespeople than librarians in this culture, so he is more likely to be a salesperson.

Tversky and Kahneman (1974) found that people often ignore prior probabilities in answering such questions, even if those probabilities are made explicit in the statement of the problem. In one experiment, they asked people to estimate the likelihood that a particular individual was either an engineer or a lawyer. Subjects in one condition were told that the individual had been randomly selected from a set of seventy engineers and thirty lawyers, and those in another condition were told that the set consisted of thirty engineers and seventy lawyers. When subjects

*A problem in inference*

*These people are on a company picnic. Some are stockbrokers and some are salespeople. If you were asked to guess, for each individual, whether that person is a stockbroker or a salesperson, what information would you take into account? If you knew that 70 percent of them are stockbrokers and 30 percent are salespeople, how would that affect your judgment?*

were asked to make the judgment with no other information, they used the 70:30 ratios effectively: In the first condition they said that there was a 70 percent likelihood that the person was an engineer, and in the second they said that this likelihood was 30 percent. But when a personality description was added, most people ignored the prior probabilities, even when the personality description provided no useful information. For example, a man described as "30 years old, married with no children, and high in ability and motivation" was judged as 50 percent likely to be an engineer regardless of whether the stated proportion of engineers in the set was 70 percent or 30 percent.

Two other sources of bias identified by Tversky and Kahneman are availability and anchoring. *Availability* refers to reliance on information that is prominent to the senses or to memory at the time, at the expense of other information that is less prominent but still available to the person who thinks about it. For example, when asked to estimate the percentage of people who die from various causes, most people overestimate causes that have recently been emphasized in the media (such as traffic accidents, fires, or murders) and underestimate less publicized but still well-known causes (such as heart disease). *Anchoring* refers to overreliance on initial guesses and failure to make sufficient adjustments when new information is added. For example, if you believe initially that most people from University *X* are unfriendly, and later you meet some people from University *X*, most of whom are friendly, you will adjust your hypothesis; but according to Tversky and Kahneman, you probably will not make as great an adjustment as you logically should.

Tversky and Kahneman's work is interesting because it helps identify and systematize some of the errors that people commonly make in inferential reasoning. One question that has emerged is whether people can become better reasoners if they are made aware of the common biases and taught to use normally ignored sources of information. Research suggests that such teaching does help (Nisbett & others, 1987), though it is uncertain to what degree the benefits extend outside of the laboratory or classroom to the judgments made in everyday life. In fact, it is uncertain to what extent the biases identified by Tversky and Kahneman actually exist in the judgments made in everyday life. For example, people might have answered the question about Steve in a particular way, ignoring prior probabilities, because they thought the psychologists were testing their ability to judge personality. One of the lessons of the ecological approach, remember, is that people often respond differently to tests than they do to similar problems faced in real life.

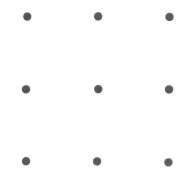

**Figure 11.16   *The nine dot problem***

*Your task is to draw four straight lines, no more and no less, that connect all nine dots shown above. You must draw the four lines without ever lifting your pencil from the page or retracing any line.*

## Some Strategies for Solving Problems

A *problem* exists whenever you are trying to reach some goal and the way to get there is not obvious. Any problem—whether it is a puzzle, a mathematical equation to be solved, or a real-life problem such as improving your relationship with your family—has an *initial state* (the disarranged puzzle pieces, the unsolved equation, or the present state of your family relationships); a *goal state* to be achieved; and a set of possible moves or *operations* for achieving the goal. To solve a problem you must (a) understand the problem, (b) identify the operations that could lead to a solution, (c) carry out the operations, (d) check the results, and (e) return to some earlier point in this chain if the results are not correct. The first two steps (understanding the problem and identifying a possible solution) are the most critical for solving many problems. It is here that the processes collectively called *insight* or *creative ingenuity* are often called for.

How do people find a possible solution to a problem that at first seems unsolvable? A fair amount of research and thought have been directed at this question, and the following paragraphs describe four general ideas that have emerged (based on Chi & Glaser, 1985, and Sternberg, 1986a).

**Breaking out of a Mental Set**   Some problems are difficult because their solutions depend on breaking a well-established habit of perception or thought, referred to as a ***mental set***. Two problems that have been used often to illustrate mental sets are the *nine dot problem* and the *candle problem*, described respectively in Figures 11.16 and 11.17. You might look at these problems and try to solve them before reading further. When you have solved the problems or spent as much time on them as you wish, turn to Figure 11.24 at the end of the chapter for solutions.

**Figure 11.17   *The candle problem***

*Using only the objects depicted at right—a candle, a book of matches, and a box of tacks—your task is to attach the candle to the bulletin board in such a way that it can be lit and will burn properly.*

■ *Why most people fail to solve the nine dot and candle problems, and why a lighthearted mood may help*

If you solved one or both problems, congratulations; if you didn't, join the crowd. Most people fail to solve the nine dot problem because they approach it with a mental set that assumes that each straight line must begin and end on a dot. Perhaps this set comes partly from connect-the-dots drawings done in childhood. Most people fail to solve the candle problem because they see the box as nothing but a container for the tacks; it never occurs to them that it could also serve as a shelf and candle holder. Karl Duncker (1945), who invented the candle problem and performed the first experiments with it, referred to this specific type of mental set as *functional fixedness*, defined as the inability to see an object as having a function other than its usual one. The candle problem is easier for most people if the box and tacks are presented separately rather than with the tacks inside the box (Adamson, 1952). Apparently, it is easier to see alternative functions for an object if it is not currently being used for its more common function.

What allows people sometimes, but not other times, to overcome a mental set? Earlier in this century, Gestalt psychologists argued that problems such as those just described are a bit like reversible figures (such as the one shown in Figure 9.4), and that finding a solution is a matter of *perceptual reorganization*. You look at the problem from different angles, turn away from it and look back again, try a few different manipulations of the objects, and then suddenly you see it differently from the way you did before and the solution becomes obvious. Although this view does not offer much specific advice on what you can do to achieve insight, it does suggest that any procedures that would allow your thought and perceptual processes to run more freely might help. Consistent with this view, researchers have found that conditions that increase subjects' anxiety, such as the presence of a judge, tend to decrease their likelihood of solving insight problems, whereas conditions that promote a degree of lightheartedness tend to increase their likelihood. As an illustration of the latter, Alice Isen and her colleagues (1987) found that college students were more than three times as likely to solve the candle problem if it was presented to them after watching 5 minutes of a comedy film than if it was presented after watching a neutral film (say, one about math) or in the usual laboratory condition, with no film.

**Finding a Useful Analogy**   Of course, insight is not *simply* a matter of overcoming a prior mental set. If it were, empty-headed people would be the best problem solvers. To solve an insight problem, you must not only set aside an approach that doesn't work, but you must find a new one that does. The new approach, like the one that doesn't work, must be based in some way on past experience. As William James (1890) pointed out long ago, problem solving is often a matter of finding a useful analogy (similarity) between the new situation and some other situation with which you are more familiar. A creative genius, according to James, is a person who finds useful analogies where others would not think to look for them. For example, Charles Darwin solved the problem of the mechanism of evolution (with the concept of natural selection) in part because he could see the similarity between selective breeding by horticulturalists and factors that limit breeding in nature.

A useful analogy in solving the candle problem is one between the tack box and a shelf, both of which are objects that can be attached to a wall and can provide a horizontal surface on which to mount a candle. Your reasoning in solving that problem might go something like this: *I know that I could set the candle upright on the wall if I had a shelf. Is there anything in the picture that is like a shelf? Aha, the box—it has a flat surface and can be attached to the wall with tacks so the surface sticks out horizontally!* Thus, you may have solved the problem in a less mysterious way than that implied by the Gestalt psychologists' notion of perceptual reorganization. You might have solved it through a deliberate search for a useful analogy.

**Representing the Information More Efficiently and Looking for Shortcuts**
Many problems are difficult because of the sheer amount of information that must be taken into account; efficient representation of the information is often the key to solving them. You already saw one example of this in the use of Euler circles to represent the information in a syllogism. One reason why experts in any given domain are better than novices is that they have learned to distinguish relevant from irrelevant information and to visualize the former in chunks, that is, in larger units

*How the deliberate search for an analogy can help a person solve a problem that at first seems unsolvable*

made up of organized sets of smaller units (discussed in Chapter 10). Experts in such areas as chess, electronics, and architecture have all been found to be more able than novices to represent the arrangement of pieces (chess pieces, portions of electrical circuits, or parts of a building) in meaningful chunks that can be manipulated mentally into alternative arrangements without overtaxing the capacity of short-term memory (Chi & Glaser, 1985).

**Knocking off a novice?**
*Age holds no advantage when your chess opponent is an expert, because an expert of any age can represent mentally the possible arrangements of chess pieces more efficiently than can a novice.*

■ *How a problem sometimes can be simplified by stating it differently*

Sometimes the key to solving a problem is restating it in a way that leads you to organize the information more efficiently. Look at the *stick-configuration problem* in Figure 11.18 and see if you can solve it before reading on. The original problem statement, "Your task is to find all possible ways to remove exactly five sticks . . . ," leads many people to focus on the sticks and to remove different sets of five sticks in trial-and-error fashion in the hope of hitting upon a solution. The difficulty with this approach is that more than 6000 combinations of five sticks exist in the seventeen sticks available, so most people give up or lose track of which combinations they have already tried long before solving the problem (Fischler & Firschein, 1987). Success is more likely if you think in terms of squares rather than sticks. Thus, you might restate the problem, "Find three squares, out of the six available, which, if preserved, would allow for the removal of exactly five sticks." There are only twenty combinations of three squares out of six, so it would not be too taxing to try all combinations until you've found the solution. Focusing on squares reduces the number of trials needed for a trial-and-error solution by a factor of 1/300. But focusing on squares can also lead to a more elegant solution, involving deductive reasoning rather than trial and error. A square has four sides, so the only way that twelve sticks (the number remaining after five are removed) can form three squares with no sticks left is if they share no sides in common. Inspection of the figure reveals immediately that there are only two combinations of three squares that have that characteristic: (1) upper left, middle right, lower left; and (2) upper right, middle left, lower right.

The stick-configuration problem provides a nice example for distinguishing between two general classes of rules for solving problems—algorithms and heuristics. An **algorithm** is any rule that, if followed correctly, will eventually solve the problem. For many problems, an algorithm may simply specify that the problem

■ *The difference between an algorithm and a heuristic, and why the former approach is better suited to computers than to humans if the number of possible moves is great*

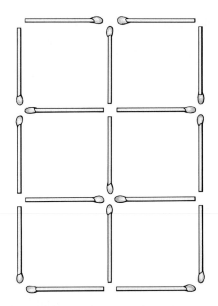

**Figure 11.18** *Stick-configuration problem*

*Your task is to find all possible ways to remove exactly five sticks from this pattern such that only three squares are left, with no sticks left over.*

■ *The value of subgoals and clear definitions, tempered with a caution*

solver produce the entire set of available moves (as defined by the problem), one at a time, until the correct solution occurs. Algorithmic reasoning might in such cases be called the brute-force approach to problem solving; it succeeds primarily by sheer resistance to exhaustion. Computers use such algorithms well because they can perform simple manipulations very rapidly, have perfect memories, and don't run out of patience. An algorithmic approach to the stick-configuration problem is to remove every possible combination of five sticks out of the seventeen available—about 6000 trials in all—and to make a notation of which trials leave just three squares. A computer could solve this problem almost instantly with such an algorithm, whereas a human might spend hours trying to solve it this way before flinging the sticks aside in frustration.

A *heuristic* is any rule that allows one to reduce the number of operations that are tried in solving a problem. In colloquial terms, a heuristic is a shortcut. In the stick-configuration problem, one heuristic would be to focus on squares rather than sticks and to try to find three squares in the configuration whose boundaries are made up of twelve different sticks. In general, human problem solvers are successful to the extent that they are able to come up with useful heuristics. Computers can use heuristics, too, if they are programmed to do so, but they are not yet good at inventing their own. They also have less need for them.

**Establishing Subgoals and Turning Ill-Defined Problems into Well-Defined Ones**   In games such as chess that involve a sequence of moves, and in most of the long-range problems presented by real life, it is not possible to map out a solution from beginning to end before making the first move. Rather, one must work toward the goal one step at a time. Each move in chess elicits a countermove, which must be taken into account in choosing the next move. Similarly, each step you take to reach your chosen career has some effect, not fully predictable, which you must take into account when you decide on the next step. In chess and in life, plans must usually center on shorter-term subgoals that bring one closer to the ultimate goal of capturing the king or obtaining a desired life position. Experiments have shown that people who succeed in solving problems involving a series of choices typically establish explicit subgoals, well chosen to bring them closer to their final goal (Chi & Glaser, 1985).

An important distinction between problems commonly studied in the laboratory and those confronted in real life is the extent to which they are well or ill defined. A *well-defined problem* is one in which the initial state, goal, and permissible operations for reaching the goal are all clearly stated; an *ill-defined problem* is one in which one or more of these is not clear. Suppose you want to be happier. That is a problem worth tackling; everyone, we assume, wants to be happier. But it is an ill-defined problem; it is hard to know where to begin to solve it. Counselors and therapists who are hired to help people solve such problems often emphasize the importance of restating the problem in more explicit, well-defined terms. What would bring happiness—more friends? more money? a more fulfilling job? more time to relax? Once that can be established, the problem has become more well defined, and some subgoals can be established with steps laid out to achieve them.

A difficulty with subgoals, or with any attempt to turn a general goal into a more explicit one, however, is that one may lose sight of the original purpose. Fixation on the subgoal itself can become a mental set that may blind a person to alternative routes to the larger goal. A chess player who focuses solely on trying to maneuver the bishop into a better position may overlook a shortcut to checkmate that was opened up by the opponent's last move. A person who focuses on more money as a path to happiness may forget the original aim (happiness) and devote his or her life to obtaining money for its own sake, overlooking other means to happiness that arise along the way. A good problem solver establishes subgoals, but keeps them subordinated to their original purpose.

# Language and Its Relationship to Thought

We take pride in ourselves as the thinking animal; but if a being from outer space were to characterize us compared to other earthly creatures, we might instead be classed as the linguistic animal. Other species can learn and use what they have learned to solve problems (discussed in Chapter 5), and they share with us an excellent capacity for nonverbal communication (discussed in Chapter 4). But only humans have a very flexible, abstract, symbol-based mode of communication—*verbal language* (hereafter just called *language*)—that permits the conveyance of every conceivable kind of information. Language allows us to tell each other not just about the here and now, but also about the past, future, far away, and hypothetical. We are effective problem solvers largely because we know so much, and we know so much because we learn not only from our own experiences in the world, but also from others' experiences, which are conveyed to us through language. Language allows humans to transmit knowledge from generation to generation, and thus provides the vehicle for human cultures.

Those of us in Western culture tend to think of the human mind as a property of the individual. You have your mind, I have mine. But think about that for a minute. Think about how much overlap there is between your mind and mine, and how dependent both of our minds are on the culture in which we live. Were it not for that overlap, I could not be writing to you and you could not make sense of what I am writing. We share knowledge and general ways of thinking because we are part of the same broad culture. What kind of mind would either you or I have if we each grew up on separate desert islands completely isolated from any other human beings?

Cognitive psychologists are interested in language for two reasons. First, language itself is a cognitive ability. The ability to produce and understand linguistic statements is a fundamental capacity of the human mind, and as such it falls within the purview of cognitive psychology. Second, language is interwoven with other cognitive abilities. The words that we acquire from our culture may affect the way we perceive, remember, and think. In the following sections we will first examine language as a cognitive system and then discuss its relationship to thought.

## *Language as a Cognitive System*

**Some Universal Characteristics of Human Language**    Linguists estimate that there are about 3000 distinct languages in the world today, all different enough that the speakers of one cannot understand those of another, yet all similar in many basic ways (Foss & Hakes, 1978). This similarity allows us to speak of *human language* in the singular.

Every language makes use of a system of *symbols*, defined as entities that stand for (refer to) other entities (the referents of the symbols). In all languages except for the sign languages used by the deaf, these symbols take the form of pronounceable sounds called **morphemes**. A morpheme is the smallest meaningful unit of a language, that is, the smallest unit that stands for some object, event, characteristic, or relationship. Often it is a word, but it can also be a prefix or suffix that is used in a consistent way to modify a word. Thus, in English, *dog* is both a word and a morpheme, *-s* is a morpheme but not a word, and *dogs* is a word consisting of two morphemes (*dog* and *-s*). The word *antidisestablishmentarianism* contains six morphemes (anti-dis-establish-ment-arian-ism), each of which has a separate entry in an English dictionary.

In any language we can distinguish two general classes of morphemes. One class, **content words**, includes nouns, verbs, adjectives, and adverbs—the morphemes that carry the main meaning of a sentence. The other class, **grammatical morphemes**, includes (in English) articles (*a, the*), conjunctions (such as *and, but*), prepositions (such as *in, of* ), and some prefixes and suffixes (such as *-ing, -ed* ). These serve primarily to fill out the grammatical structure of the sentence, though they also contribute to meaning.

Morphemes in any language are both arbitrary and discrete. To say that a morpheme is *arbitrary* is to say that there need be no similarity between its physical structure and that of the object or concept for which it stands. Nothing about the English morpheme *dog*, or the French morpheme *chien*, naturally links it to the four-legged, barking creature that it represents. Because of this arbitrariness, new morphemes can be invented whenever they are needed to stand for newly discovered objects or ideas or to express newly important shades of meaning. This gives great flexibility to language. In theory, it is possible in any language to express essentially any idea of which the human mind can conceive. To say that a morpheme is *discrete* is to say that it cannot be changed in a graded way to change its meaning. For example, you cannot say that one thing is bigger than another by changing the morpheme *big*. Rather, you must add a morpheme to it (such as *-er*) or replace it with a different morpheme (such as *huge*).

Arbitrariness and discreteness distinguish language symbols from the types of signals used in nonverbal communication. As described in Chapter 4, nonverbal signals typically develop from and bear physical resemblance to the behavioral acts that they are designed to communicate, such as fleeing or fighting. Moreover, nonverbal signals can be presented in a graded manner. One expresses *more* surprise, anger, or whatever nonverbally by presenting the signal more vigorously or with greater amplitude of movement. In everyday speech, you might communicate that one thing is bigger than another by saying, "This one is big but that one is **big**," but the vocal emphasis placed on the second *big* is a nonverbal addition. In speech, we commonly mix nonverbal with verbal communication to get our point across (which is one reason why speaking is usually easier than writing).

■ *The arbitrary and discrete nature of morphemes, and how this differentiates verbal language from nonverbal communication*

### Nonverbal supplements to verbal language
*Many of the cues that give meaning to a conversation are nonverbal. Through gestures and tone of voice, people add graded, nonverbal modifiers to their morphemes.*

■ *The hierarchical, rule-based nature of language*

In addition to commonalities in their symbol systems, all languages share the same basic hierarchical structure. A sentence in any language can be broken down into at least four levels, organized hierarchically (see Figure 11.19). At the top level is the sentence itself, which can be broken down into phrases, which can be broken down into words or morphemes, which can be broken down into elementary vowel and consonant sounds called *phonemes*. The power of this organization lies in the fact that a relatively few different phonemes (there are anywhere from fifteen to eighty of these in any given language) can be arranged in different ways to produce an enormous number of different possible words, which can be arranged in different ways to produce a limitless number of possible phrases and sentences.

Sentence

Phrases

Words or morphemes

Phonemes

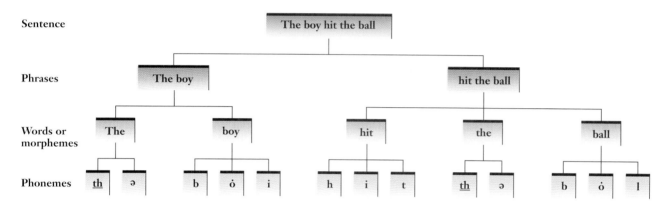

**Figure 11.19** *The hierarchical structure of language*
*Every spoken language contains these four levels to its organization.*

Every language is also characterized by rules that specify permissible ways that units at one level can be arranged to produce the next higher level. Collectively, these rules are referred to as the *grammar* of the language. Grammar includes rules of *morphology*, which specify how sounds can be arranged to produce morphemes and words, and rules of *syntax*, which specify how words can be arranged to produce phrases and sentences. These rules differ from language to language, but every language has them.

**Chomsky's Approach to Grammar, and Its Impact on Psychology**   People often think of grammar as something that they learned (or tried to learn) in elementary school (also known as *grammar* school, perhaps for this very reason). But grammar is learned tacitly long before formal schooling begins. The fact that 4-year-olds can carry on meaningful conversations with adults, producing and understanding new and unique sentences, implies that 4-year-olds have already acquired the essential grammar of their native language. Four-year-olds can't name or describe the rules of grammar (nor can most adults), yet they have somehow incorporated these rules mentally and use them tacitly to understand and produce grammatical sentences (discussed further in Chapter 12).

People's tacit knowledge of grammar is demonstrated in their ability to distinguish acceptable from unacceptable sentences. Nearly every English speaker can tell that *The mouse crawled under the barn* is a grammatical sentence, while *The crawled barn mouse the under* is not, though only a few can explain exactly why. The ability to distinguish grammatical from non-grammatical sentences is not based simply on meaning. As the linguist Noam Chomsky (1957) has pointed out, English speakers can recognize *Colorless green ideas sleep furiously* as grammatically correct though absurd.

■ *How Chomsky emphasized the rule-based nature of language and helped inspire psychologists to study it as a cognitive system*

Noam Chomsky is an important figure in cognitive psychology, even though his own field is not psychology but linguistics. In 1957, he published a slender, enormously influential book entitled *Syntactic Structures*, the goal of which was to outline a model of grammar that could be applied in describing any language. He

**Noam Chomsky**

*In his 1957 book,* Syntactic Structures, *Chomsky called attention to the idea that producing a verbal statement is a creative act guided by implicit mental rules. This work, and the revolution in psycholinguistics that it spawned, have enriched research and theory in cognitive psychology.*

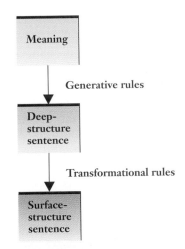

**Figure 11.20** *Chomsky's model of sentence production*

*According to Chomsky, one first uses generative rules to turn the intended meaning into a deep-structure version of the sentence, and then uses transformational rules to produce the surface-structure version.*

argued that such a model must have roots in the basic workings of the human mind, and in expressing that idea he explicitly linked the study of grammar to the field of psychology. At the same time, he attacked the then-dominant behavioral approach in psychology, arguing that any reasonable description of how people use language must go beyond behavioral observations to the mental rules underlying that behavior. Whereas behaviorists tended to emphasize the chainlike nature of sentences (one word following the next), Chomsky emphasized the hierarchical nature of sentences. Chomsky argued that a person must have some representation of the whole sentence in mind before uttering it, and then the person must apply grammatical rules to that representation in order to produce the utterance. Similarly, he argued that when listening to a sentence a person must hear it as a whole (not a chain of separate words) and apply grammatical rules to understand it.

To get an idea of the arguments that Chomsky employed, consider this sentence: *The boy who likes Mary hit the ball.* How do you know from the sentence that the boy, not Mary, hit the ball? *Mary* comes right before *hit the ball*, so a simple analysis in terms of adjacent pairs of words would tell you that Mary hit the ball. Apparently, you are able to view the sentence as more than a sequence of individual words or word pairs and use its whole structure to understand its meaning. Some rule you know about English syntax tells you that in this case *Mary* does not belong with *hit*, but rather is part of a set of words modifying *boy*. The rule tells you that the core sentence is *The boy hit the ball*, and that *who likes Mary* has been inserted to clarify which boy.

Chomsky's main concern was to find an efficient way to specify as efficiently as possible the relationship between the specific wording of a sentence, referred to as the **surface structure**, and the meaning that the speaker wishes to convey or that the listener understands. He pointed out that sentences with very different surface structures can have similar or identical meanings. For example, *The boy hit the ball* and *The ball was hit by the boy* have similar meanings even though their surface structures are very different. Conversely, he also pointed out that sentences with similar surface structures can have very different meanings. For example, *The boy is eager to please* and *The boy is easy to please* are very different in meaning. In this example, the change in one adjective switches the whole sentence around, such that the boy is the pleaser in one case and is the one who is pleased in the other.

As a framework for relating surface structure to meaning, Chomsky proposed that sentences are understood not directly in terms of their surface structure, but rather in terms of an underlying **deep structure** that is not articulated, but exists only in the mind of the speaker or listener. The deep structure of a sentence is an abstract, mental representation of the meaning of the sentence organized in the simplest possible grammatical form consistent with that meaning. To produce a sentence, according to Chomsky (1968), a person begins with a mental representation of the idea to be conveyed, then uses a set of grammatical rules called *generative rules* to generate the deep-structure representation of that sentence, and then uses another set of grammatical rules called *transformational rules* to transform the deep-structure sentence into one of the many possible surface-structure forms that it might take (see Figure 11.20). Conversely, to understand a sentence, a person uses the same set of rules in reverse, first producing a deep-structure representation and then extracting the meaning from it. Chomsky's theory is called the **generative-transformational theory**, named after the two sets of rules.

Whether or not Chomsky's theory provides the most efficient framework for understanding the relationship between the surface structures and meanings of sentences, it helped inspire many psychologists to study language as a cognitive system. Whereas Chomsky's approach is theoretical, asking how an idealized language user *might* generate and understand sentences, the approach of psychologists is empirical, asking how people actually *do* generate and understand sentences, and conducting research to try to find out.

**Slips of the Tongue as an Approach to Understanding Speech Production**
When you utter a sentence, you are rarely aware of any steps or rules by which you perform that act. It seems as if you have an idea to communicate, you open your mouth, and, *voilà*, out come the words. Yet, complex rule-abiding processes must mediate between the initial idea and its expression in words, and psycholinguists (psychologists who study language) have developed a variety of means to try to understand these processes. One means, which I will focus on here, is that of analyzing the kinds of errors that people commonly make in speech production.

Of particular interest is the class of errors called **spoonerisms**, named after William Spooner, an English clergyman and Oxford don who was famous for uttering them. A spoonerism is an error in which two elements in a sentence (phonemes, syllables, or morphemes) are mistakenly interchanged in position. Two of the most amusing spoonerisms attributed to Spooner himself were: (1) "*Work* is the curse of the *drink*ing class," uttered when he meant to say, "*Drink* is the curse of the *work*ing class"; and (2) "Our *queer* old *dean*," when he meant to say, "Our *dear* old *queen*." These examples may or may not have actually been uttered by Spooner (some suspect that his legend is largely a creation of his students), but research shows that truly accidental spoonerisms are quite common (Fromkin, 1973, 1980). Analyses of accidental spoonerisms show that they do not occur willy-nilly, but follow certain laws (Garrett, 1975, 1982).

Consistent with the idea that grammatical rules are firmly entrenched in the mind, slips of the tongue are far more likely to violate the meaning of a sentence than its grammar. Thus, when whole words or morphemes swap places in spoonerism, those that swap are usually in the same grammatical category. Nouns switch with nouns, verbs with verbs, adjectives with adjectives, and so on—in a way that preserves the grammatical structure. Thus, the intended sentence *The red pen is on the table* might come out as *The red table is on the pen*, but it won't come out as *The red on is pen the table*. Sometimes the switching of two words in a spoonerism requires an additional adjustment to keep the sentence grammatical, and in most cases that adjustment is in fact made. For example, the intended phrase *an aunt with money* might become *a money with aunt*. Here the article *an* changed to *a* to accommodate the switch from a noun starting with a vowel to one starting with a consonant.

Another generalization about spoonerisms is that swaps involving whole content words (nouns, verbs, adjectives, and adverbs) may occur across different phrases of a sentence; but swaps involving phonemes occur only within a phrase. Thus, *The red pen is on the table* might come out as *The red table is on the pen* (content words swapped across phrases) or *The ped ren is on the table* (phonemes swapped within the same phrase), but is not likely to come out as *The red ten is on the pable* (phonemes swapped across phrases).

From such findings, Merrill Garrett (1975, 1982) has hypothesized that content words and phonemes must be selected at two different stages of sentence production. At the *functional* stage, a rough form of the whole sentence is held in mind and worked on at once. This is where content words, represented abstractly without their sounds, are selected and might accidentally switch places. At a subsequent stage, the *positional* stage, the sentence is refined one phrase at a time. This is where grammatical morphemes and phonemes are added into the sentence, phrase by phrase, and where phonemes might accidentally switch places. Thus, the distinction between the functional and positional stages accounts for the observation that spoonerisms involving content words can occur over the whole sentence, whereas those involving phonemes can occur only within the same phrase.

In Figure 11.21 you can see a depiction of Garrett's complete model of sentence generation, which contains four stages in all. Notice that according to this model the sequence in producing a sentence is from the large and general to the small and specific. First, the whole meaning is represented in a nonverbal form

■ *How the analysis of spoonerisms contributed to a theory of the mental steps through which a sentence is produced*

**Figure 11.21  *Garrett's model of speech production***

*According to Garrett, a sentence is built mentally through a series of four stages or levels before it is uttered. The processes shown to the right of each arrow operate on what has already been built to produce the next level down. (Adapted from Smyth & others, 1987.)*

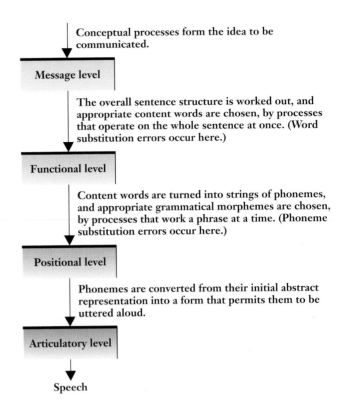

Conceptual processes form the idea to be communicated.

**Message level**

The overall sentence structure is worked out, and appropriate content words are chosen, by processes that operate on the whole sentence at once. (Word substitution errors occur here.)

**Functional level**

Content words are turned into strings of phonemes, and appropriate grammatical morphemes are chosen, by processes that work a phrase at a time. (Phoneme substitution errors occur here.)

**Positional level**

Phonemes are converted from their initial abstract representation into a form that permits them to be uttered aloud.

**Articulatory level**

Speech

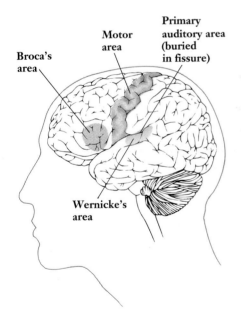

Primary auditory area (buried in fissure)

Motor area

Broca's area

Wernicke's area

**Figure 11.22  *Left-hemisphere language areas***

*Damage to Broca's area leads to loss of ability to generate grammatically complex sentences, but not to loss of ability to supply appropriate content words. Damage to Wernicke's area has the opposite effect.*

(message level); then the overall sentence structure is roughed out (functional level); then the phonemes and grammatical morphemes are added in, phrase by phrase (positional level); and, finally, the sentence is further refined in a way that permits it to be uttered aloud (articulatory level). In this model, building a sentence is analogous to building a house. First comes the overall plan; then the framework; then the walls, floor, and roof; and finally the veneer (siding, roof shingles, and wallpaper) that you see when the product is complete. As you will see soon, this model is also supported by neuropsychological evidence.

**Neuropsychological Approach to Language**  The human brain contains specialized neural systems for language, located in most people in the left hemisphere of the cerebral cortex. Any loss in language ability resulting from brain damage is called **aphasia**, and the study of people who have suffered such loss has contributed not only to our knowledge of the specific brain areas involved in language, but also to the development of cognitive models of speech production and comprehension.

In the mid-nineteenth century, Paul Broca (1861) discovered that people who have suffered damage to a specific portion of the left frontal lobe continue to understand language quite well but have great difficulty producing it. Their speech is labored and *telegraphic* in form, meaning that the minimum number of words is used to convey the message. Their speech consists almost entirely of content words, devoid of grammatical morphemes. If you ask a person with this disorder what he or she did today, the person might answer, "Buy bread store." This variety of aphasia is now called **Broca's aphasia**, and the area of the brain where damage produces it is called **Broca's area** (shown in Figure 11.22).

Not long after Broca's discovery, Carl Wernicke (1874) discovered that people with lesions in a specific portion of the temporal lobe of the left hemisphere suffer a form of aphasia quite different from that described by Broca. Unlike Broca's aphasics, these patients are deficient in language comprehension as well as production; and their production loss is almost the opposite of that of Broca's aphasics.

■ *The difference between Broca's and Wernicke's aphasias, and how the difference has led to a neuropsychological model of language*

Their speech is rich in grammatical morphemes and superficially quite fluent, but it is deficient in content words and often contains nonsense words. Here is an example from one such patient, trying to describe a simple picture (Schwartz, 1987): "Nothing the keesereez the, these are davereez and these and this one and these are living. This one's right in and these are . . . uh . . . and that's nothing, that's nothing. . . ." The most apparent deficiency is that the person can't come up with the correct names of objects or actions, leading to a heavy use of pronouns and sometimes nonsense words as substitutes. The speech retains its grammatical structure but loses its meaning. This pattern of disorder is called **Wernicke's aphasia**, and the brain area where damage produces it is often called **Wernicke's area** (see Figure 11.22).

On the basis of the most obvious deficits observed in the two aphasias, Wernicke hypothesized that the brain area now called Broca's area is most important for producing speech (because the speech of Broca's aphasics is so labored) and that the area now called Wernicke's area is most important for comprehending speech (because Wernicke's aphasics have much more difficulty understanding than do Broca's aphasics). According to this view, the poor language production of Wernicke's aphasics is secondary to their poor comprehension—you can't produce good speech if you don't understand what you are saying. For a century, Wernicke's distinction provided a core around which increasingly elaborate models of the brain's involvement in language were built (see Geschwind, 1972).

Recently, however, a somewhat different conception of the distinction between Broca's and Wernicke's areas has emerged. According to this view, Broca's area is most critical for syntax, including the choice and analysis of grammatical morphemes; and Wernicke's area is most critical for relating content words to their meaning (Schwartz, 1987). In this view, the tasks of each area cut across both comprehension and production. Evidence includes the finding that Broca's aphasics suffer deficits in comprehension as well as production. Although they can understand speech quite well when the meaning can be inferred from the context and content words alone, they commonly misunderstand sentences in which analysis of the syntax is critical (Zurif, 1980). For example, a Broca's aphasic who hears *The girl that the boy is chasing is tall* is much more likely than a brain-intact subject to be confused about who is chasing whom.

Figure 11.23 shows a simplified model of this new view of the involvement of Broca's and Wernicke's areas in speech comprehension and production. As you examine the speaking side of the model, notice the similarity between it and Garrett's model, which you saw earlier in Figure 11.21. The task of choosing content words, assigned to Wernicke's area in the neural model, is the same as one of the tasks leading to the functional level of a sentence in Garrett's model. Similarly, the task of choosing grammatical morphemes, assigned to Broca's area in the neural model, is the same as one of the tasks leading to the positional level in Garrett's model.

**Figure 11.23** *A neuropsychological model of speech comprehension and production*

*In comprehension, speech information is transported from the auditory area to Wernicke's area for analysis of meaning of content words, and to Broca's area for analysis of syntax. In speech production, content words are chosen by neural systems in Wernicke's area, grammatical refinements are added by neural systems in Broca's area, and then the information is sent to the motor cortex, which sets up the muscle movements for utterance.*

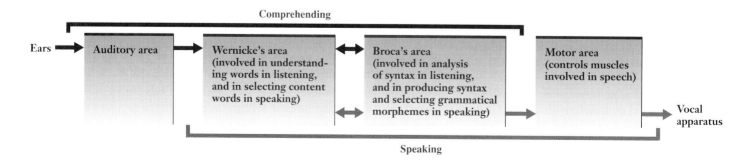

It is exciting when different approaches in cognitive psychology—such as those of examining slips of the tongue in brain-intact people and examining deficits caused by brain damage in different areas—lead to a similar model. But before ending this discussion, I should note that there is still considerable disagreement among neuropsychologists about how to interpret different patterns of aphasia. Some researchers favor the view outlined in Figure 11.23, but some favor other models. Research on aphasia is complicated, because no two aphasic patients are alike either in the exact area of brain damage they have suffered or the exact pattern of language loss they show. Most lesions are due to strokes (caused by ruptured blood vessels), which affect broad regions of the brain, not just Wernicke's or Broca's areas. Different researchers have found different ways to make sense of the innumerable patterns of aphasia that result.

### The Relation of Language to Thought

In the history of psychology, a wide range of views have been expressed about the relationship between language and thought. One extreme view was that of behaviorist John B. Watson (1924), who wrote, "What the psychologists have hitherto called thought is nothing but talking to ourselves." Watson believed that we learn to talk in much the same way as we learn other muscular skills (such as riding a bicycle), and that when we subsequently make the same muscular movements in a more hidden form (to ourselves rather than aloud), we call it thought. In a heroic experiment testing that hypothesis, a physician, Scott Smith, took a drug that temporarily paralyzed his muscles (he was on an artificial respirator during this period) and reported that the paralysis did not interfere with his ability to understand what was going on around him, nor with his ability to perform mental arithmetic or to reason in other ways (Smith & others, 1947). Thus, the extreme view that thought depends on the muscle movements of speech was proven wrong.

A more moderate theory of the dependence of thought on language was developed by the Soviet psychologist Lev Vygotsky in the 1930s. Vygotsky (1934/1962) argued that thought and language are separate processes in very young children, but that as they do become proficient in language children gradually internalize it, using language increasingly for their private thought as well as communication. At an early stage in this process, children's use of words for thought may require movement of speech muscles (you can see young children's lips move as they think), but with time children can use the words purely mentally, often in an abbreviated form such that they are no longer recognized as words. Such thought, which uses symbols that were acquired originally in the form of words, is called *verbal thought*. According to Vygotsky, in the process of developing verbal thought the basic ideas of the culture—reflected in the culture's words—are incorporated into the minds of the individual members of the culture.

Vygotsky's theory is discussed in more detail in Chapter 12, along with the contrasting position of Jean Piaget, a Swiss developmental psychologist who argued that language plays very little role in the development of thought. Our focus for now will be on an idea closely related to Vygotsky's theory, but more often attributed to an American linguist, Benjamin Whorf—the idea of linguistic relativity.

**Linguistic Relativity** Benjamin Whorf was a specialist in Native American languages. He found that some of these languages differ greatly from each other and from European languages in the way that they categorize various aspects of the physical world. For instance, some have many words for different types of snow, and others have only one. Some divide the spectrum of colors into just two or three categories, and others divide it into as many as twelve. In some languages verbs are clearly marked according to tense (present, past, and future), and in others they are

**It's all relative**

*This hunter, clearing a path to open water, has many different words for the various kinds of snow around him. An important question in the study of the relationship between language and thought is whether the differences among the languages of people affect their perception of snow—or of any other phenomenon.*

■ *Evidence that language does not affect color perception*

not. Whorf (1956) came to believe that such differences affect the way that people whose native languages are different perceive and think about snow, color, time, and the like. He proposed from this the hypothesis of ***linguistic relativity***: People who have different native languages perceive the world differently and think differently from each other because of their different languages.

Although Whorf had linguistic evidence that different languages categorize the world differently, he lacked the psychological evidence needed to support his theory. That is, he lacked evidence that people in different cultures, speaking different languages, actually perceive and think differently in ways that coincide with their language differences. Since Whorf's time, however, a number of studies have been conducted with an aim of supplying that evidence.

Much of the research on linguistic relativity has centered on the relationship between color perception and color labeling. In English (and also in French, Spanish, and many other languages), we have simple, one-word labels for those colors that we perceive as focal (or pure) colors—blue, green, yellow, and red. We perceive and describe other colors (that lie between the focal colors on the physical wavelength spectrum) as if they were mixtures of focal colors, such as bluish-green and greenish-yellow. Do we see the colors in this way because of the words we use to describe them? That is, do we see blue and green as pure colors because, as children, we heard them labeled with single words (*blue* and *green*), and see bluish-green as a mixture because we heard it labeled as a mixture (*bluish-green*)? A number of studies have been performed to find out if people who speak languages in which the colors are labeled differently see colors differently from the way we do. The general conclusion, contrary to linguistic relativity, is that people everywhere see colors in the same way (Kay & Kempton, 1984).

Eleanor Rosch (1973) conducted a set of studies of this type with native speakers of Dani, a New Guinea language that divides the color spectrum into just two categories. One category, *mili*, includes black, green, and blue (colors considered to be dark and cool); the other, *mola*, includes white, yellow, and red (considered to be light and warm). Rosch's evidence that Dani speakers see colors as Westerners do, even though they label them differently, includes the following findings: (a) When asked to select from a set of colors the best or most typical examples of *mili* or *mola*, they almost invariably chose one of our focal colors. Thus, for *mili*, different individuals chose black, green, or blue, but they did not choose bluish-green. (b) When taught new words for colors, they learned words for focal colors more easily than for nonfocal colors. (c) In a color-memory test, in which they had to pick a color that best matched one that they had previously been shown, Dani speakers performed better with focal than with nonfocal colors (as do English-speaking subjects). Rosch concluded that color perception is determined by universal characteristics of the visual system, not by language.

In focusing on color, Rosch and others put the linguistic-relativity hypothesis to a very stringent test, though it is a test that Whorf himself invited because of his emphasis on the linguistic relativity of perceptions of the physical world. Intuitively, the hypothesis seems more applicable to concepts and thoughts that are more abstract, less directly tied to physical stimuli. We turn now to some findings that are consistent with the linguistic-relativity hypothesis.

**Linguistic Relativity of Counterfactual Reasoning** Alfred Bloom (1981) has conducted an extensive set of studies designed to compare a specific type of reasoning in Chinese-speaking citizens of Taiwan and Hong Kong with the same in English-speaking citizens of the United States. According to Bloom, the idea for this research came when he was trying to assess the political attitudes of Chinese-speaking people in Hong Kong by asking them questions such as, "If the Hong Kong government were to pass a law requiring people to make weekly reports of their activities to the police, how would you react?" His attempts in this survey were frustrated because people seemed either unwilling to accept such questions or unable to understand them. A typical response was, "But the government hasn't made such a law."

Following up on this, Bloom found that the Chinese language lacks any easy way to produce *counterfactual arguments*, that is, arguments that begin with a statement that is known to be false. He also discovered that the Chinese rarely make such statements. For example, in a content analysis of a Chinese daily newspaper in Taiwan, he found only one instance of a counterfactual argument during a 3-week period, and that turned out to be a translation from a speech by the American diplomat Henry Kissinger. In everyday conversation, English-speaking people regularly produce counterfactual arguments, such as, "If Mary had studied, she would have done well on the test." According to Bloom, Chinese speakers are far more likely to express the same idea in a way that sticks closer to the facts, with statements such as, "Mary didn't study, and therefore she did poorly on the test."

To test systematically whether Chinese speakers would follow a counterfactual argument, Bloom prepared a story to be read in Chinese by college students in Taiwan and Hong Kong and in English by college students in the United States. The story began by introducing an eighteenth-century philosopher named Bier, followed by the statement, "Bier could not read Chinese, but if he had been able to read Chinese, he would have discovered . . . ." The story then went on to describe what Bier would have discovered and how his discovery would have influenced the course of history. When students were tested on the story afterward, nearly all of the American students showed they understood that the point of the story was that Bier had *not* affected history in the ways described, whereas nearly all of the Chinese students interpreted the story as stating that Bier did have those effects on history. According to Bloom, the difference was not due simply to a translation problem; the story was clear enough in Chinese. Rather, the Chinese students' thought processes were not oriented toward counterfactual arguments.

In another study, Bloom presented a counterfactual syllogism to a large group of Taiwanese and American subjects: "If all circles were large and this small triangle (△) were a circle, would it be large?" He found that only 25 percent of the Taiwanese, compared to 83 percent of the Americans, answered yes. In sum, Bloom's evidence is at least consistent with the linguistic-relativity hypothesis: The Chinese language is structured so that counterfactual arguments are difficult to produce; as a result, Chinese speakers rarely produce such arguments; and, as a result of that, they have difficulty understanding such arguments when they hear or read them.

But there is a problem with this interpretation of Bloom's findings. The study is correlational, and thus cannot directly prove a causal relationship. People in Taiwan or Hong Kong have grown up in a culture that differs from American culture in many ways—not just in language—and the difference in thinking could come from sources other than language. Perhaps other aspects of Chinese culture discourage (or do not encourage) counterfactual thinking. This idea was even suggested by some of the respondents in Bloom's initial study of political thought, who branded the counterfactual questions as "typically Western" or as a kind of make-believe game that should be avoided in serious political discussions.

**Studies of Bilingual Speakers as Evidence for Linguistic Relativity**  Another approach to the issue of linguistic relativity is to study bilingual individuals who have lived in two cultures with different languages and are fluent in both languages. Many bilingual speakers claim that they think differently in the two languages, and several studies have supported this claim.

Susan Ervin-Tripp (1964) studied women who had grown up in Japan, had married American servicemen, and had moved to the United States. These women continued to speak Japanese with their Japanese friends but spoke English with their families and co-workers. Ervin-Tripp tested the women psychologically in

■ *Evidence that one's language may predispose one for or against a specific style of reasoning*

■ *Evidence that bilingual speakers may think differently about the same subject when thinking in different languages, and that some mental schemas are specific to one language or another*

both Japanese and English. She found that the women often responded differently to the same questions depending on which language they were using, and that the differences typically coincided with known differences between Japanese and American cultural patterns. For example, in a sentence-completion test, a woman tested in Japanese completed the stem *When my wishes conflict with my family . . . ,* with the words (in Japanese) *. . . it is a time of great unhappiness.* When the same stem was presented in English, she responded (in English) *. . . I do what I want.* Ervin-Tripp suggests that for these women, Japanese words were tied to Japanese cultural values and ideas and English words were tied to American values and ideas. The Japanese and English words for *family* may have had the same dictionary meaning to the women, but the two words evoked quite different sets of thoughts and feelings.

More recently, Curt Hoffman and his colleagues (1986) have found that bilingual speakers may develop different impressions of a person depending on which language they are using when forming an impression. In their experiment, Chinese students at the University of Alberta, in Canada, read descriptions of hypothetical individuals in either English or Chinese and then wrote essays about their impressions of the person described—using English when the original description was in English and Chinese when the original description was in Chinese. Two of the original descriptions were of individuals who could easily be labeled by an English word but not by a Chinese word, and two were the reverse. For example, one description was designed to fit what in English is called an artistic character—a person with artistic ability, a temperamental disposition, a tendency toward fantasy, and an unconventional lifestyle. A converse example was a description designed to fit what in Chinese is called a *shi gu* individual—a person who has much worldly experience, a strong family orientation, and well-defined interpersonal skills. The labels were not used in the descriptions, but the descriptions were written so as to be consistent with those labels.

As predicted by the linguistic-relativity hypothesis, the students formed a firmer, more consistent impression of the artistic character when reading and thinking in English, and a firmer, more consistent impression of the *shi gu* character when reading and thinking in Chinese. Based on these results, Hoffman and his colleagues suggest that bilingual speakers have two different sets of schemas (mental representations of concepts), each tied to a different language. When the person thinks in one language, one set of schemas is evoked; when he or she thinks in the other language, the other set is evoked.

**Sexism and the Generic *Man*** If language shapes thought, then one way to change thought is to change language. This reasoning lies behind a concerted effort presently underway to rid English of constructions that tend to characterize males as more human than females. One such construction is use of the word *man* to stand for two different concepts: (1) human beings in general, the generic *man*; and (2) human males in particular. Many writers have argued that because these two concepts have the same label, they become fused into the same mental schema, leading English-speaking people to think of males as more typical examples of human beings than are females. This form of labeling is no accident. Historically, and still among many people today, men have been considered quite explicitly to be the primary humans and women have been considered to be secondary.

To test the degree to which *man*, used in the generic sense, elicits a mental perception of humans in general versus males in particular, Joseph Schneider and Sally Hacker (1973) performed an experiment involving hypothetical titles for chapters of a sociology textbook. One set of titles used the generic *man* construction: *Social Man, Urban Man, Economic Man,* and so on. Another set avoided that construction, with titles such as: *Society, Urban Life,* and *Economic Behavior.* The researchers gave one set of titles to one group of students and the other set to an-

***Shy and not so shy***
*Kiko Kawashima, who recently married a son of the Japanese Emperor Akihito, is fluently bilingual, having spent the first 6 years of her life in the United States. When she speaks Japanese, she is described as indirect and modest. When speaking English, she assumes a bolder personality, adding candor and humor.*

■ *Evidence that the two traditional meanings of the word* man *are not distinct in people's minds*

**What a difference a decade makes**

*When Richard Scarry's* Best Word Book Ever *was first published, few people thought about the effect of books on children's developing sense of their gender. Studies of children's literature in the early 1970s changed all that, and publishers began to replace stereotyped images and language with material that provides equal treatment, as these pages from the 1963 (left) and 1980 (right) editions of the book show.*

other group, and asked each student to find pictures from newspapers and magazines that would be suitable for illustrating each chapter. The striking result was that about 65 percent of pictures brought back by students in the *man* group depicted males only (the rest contained either both genders or females only), compared to about 50 percent male-only pictures brought back by the other group. These percentages were about the same for female as for male students. From this, the authors argue that the two meanings of *man* are in fact not distinct in people's minds. The students in this experiment surely knew, at one level of knowing, that *man* in those titles meant human beings in general; but their actual behavior suggested a mental compromise between that meaning and the male-only meaning.

**Figure 11.24 *Solutions to the nine dot and candle problems***

*These are the solutions to the problems in Figures 11.16 and 11.17.*

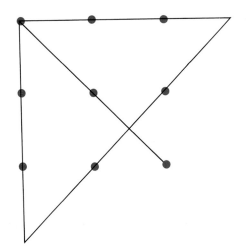

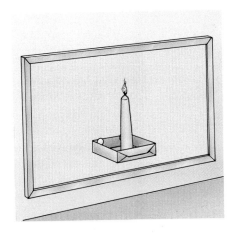

## Concluding Thoughts

The title of this chapter could have been the title of the book. Every approach in psychology contributes to an understanding of the human intellect, and all of the psychological processes that have been examined in previous chapters—learning, motivation, emotion, sensation, perception, and memory—are intertwined with reasoning and language in forming the human intellect. Here we have been concerned with the top of that structure—those aspects of the mind that most distinguish humans from other animals. As you review the chapter, you may want to pay particular attention to the following themes:

1. **The issue of multiple intelligences** One way to review the various theories of intelligence is to compare them on the question of whether intelligence is one characteristic or many. Galton thought of intelligence as a single entity, best described as quickness and acuity of the nervous system, that improves all realms of mental functioning. Binet thought of intelligence as a collection of school-related skills, such as vocabulary, arithmetic ability, and good memory. Spearman thought of intelligence as a single, hypothetical factor, $g$, that accounts for the statistical correlation found among different mental tests. Thurstone thought of intelligence as seven separate factors that account for the observation that tests can be grouped into seven clusters according to their patterns of intercorrelation.

Vernon, Cattell, and most other modern psychometric theorists think of intelligence as a hierarchy that has, at the top, a single $g$ that affects two or more basic abilities that are partly independent of one another. Sternberg, from the information-processing perspective, also subscribes to a hierarchical theory; he thinks of intelligence as a hierarchy of mental components that are brought into play differently for different kinds of tests. Neuropsychological research has led some theorists to think of intelligence as an amalgam of two modes of thought: a discrete, propositional, left-hemisphere mode; and a holistic, graded, right-hemisphere mode. Based on case histories in which one ability flourishes in the relative absence of others, Gardner has resurrected Thurstone's idea of independent intelligences, at the same time broadening the concept of intelligence to include a wider range of abilities.

2. **The concrete nature of human reasoning** Both logicians and psychologists have often distinguished between two forms of reasoning—concrete and formal. Concrete reasoning is described as reasoning in terms of entities with which a person is familiar from direct experience. It is presumably based heavily on memory of what has happened in the past when specific conditions were present. Formal reasoning is described as that which involves abstract principles of logic, independent of familiarity with the specific entities about which a person is reasoning, as in solving algebraic equations. Research on how people actually reason, however, blurs this distinction and emphasizes concrete processes. That would be a good theme to keep in mind as you review the subsection on the ecological approach to intelligence and the entire section on reasoning and problem solving. Ecological research suggests that people everywhere seem far more intelligent when reasoning about things with which they are familiar than when reasoning about other things. Studies of logic suggest that people who are best at solving syllogisms and similar formal problems typically convert them to concrete images, such as Euler circles, before solving them. Other studies of problem solving suggest that people who reason well in new realms often do so by finding analogies between the new realm and one with which they have had concrete experience. In that way, the unfamiliar becomes familiar.

3. **Two ways that language is important in cognitive psychology** Language is studied by cognitive psychologists both as a human ability unto itself and as a vehi-

cle for thought. In this chapter you saw samples of research pertaining to both of these ways of examining language. Chomsky's basic ideas, Garrett's model based on slips of the tongue, and the neuropsychological model based on Broca's and Wernicke's aphasias all have to do with the attempt to understand language as a human ability. The research on linguistic relativity has to do with the role of language in thought. Language is an increasingly important topic in psychology, and you will read considerably more about it, from a developmental perspective, in the next chapter.

## Further Reading

**Robert J. Sternberg** (Ed.) (1985). *Human abilities: An information-processing approach*. New York: Freeman.

*This book, which will be a challenge (but a rewarding one) for the beginning student, has chapters on verbal ability, mathematical ability, mental imagery, deductive reasoning, inductive reasoning, and problem solving, each written by a different expert in the field. Particularly interesting is Sternberg's own chapter, in which he discusses the concept of general intelligence from both a psychometric and an information-processing perspective.*

**Howard Gardner** (1985). *Frames of mind: The theory of multiple intelligences*. New York: Basic Books.

*Gardner combines scientific ingenuity with true literary talent. This book, in which he presents his multiple intelligences theory, is a joy to read.*

**Sally Springer & Georg Deutsch** (1989). *Left brain, right brain* (3rd ed.). New York: Freeman.

*Research on right- and left-hemisphere differences, including the split-brain studies, is always interesting. This book provides a well-documented account of such research in a form that can be understood by the beginning student.*

**John R. Hayes** (1989). *The complete problem solver* (2nd ed.). Hillsdale, NJ: Erlbaum.

*This is one of several excellent how-to books that have been written on problem solving. It brings psychological research to bear on the task of helping the reader increase his or her own problem-solving abilities. An especially useful chapter for college students is "Writing as Problem Solving."*

## Looking Ahead

In this chapter you have read about several ways—psychometric, information-processing, and neuropsychological—of dissecting the abilities of the adult mind. Still another route to understanding mental abilities is to watch them as they are built—that is, to observe how they grow in the developing child toward adult form. The next chapter is about cognitive development; it deals with many of the same issues that were raised in this chapter, but now from a developmental perspective. What can we learn about human thought and language by studying their development in children?

# PART 5  GROWTH OF THE MIND AND PERSON

COGNITIVE DEVELOPMENT

SOCIAL DEVELOPMENT

*One way to understand any structure is to watch it being built. This is the approach taken by developmental psychologists, who study the changes through which human behavior becomes increasingly complex and sophisticated from infancy into adulthood. This unit consists of two chapters on developmental psychology. The first is about the development of perception, language, and thought; and the second is about the development of social relationships and the roles that these relationships play in promoting other aspects of development.*

# CHAPTER 12

Some Basic Issues in the Study
of Development

Development of Perception and
Knowledge in Infancy

Development of Language

Development of Logical Thought

# Cognitive development

Nothing comes from nothing. Everything has a history, and the human mind is no exception. Actually, the human mind has more than one history. It has an *evolutionary history* (discussed in Chapter 3), which extends back through the millions of generations of our ancestors. It has a *cultural history*, the history of ideas and ways of thinking shared by people whose lives are intertwined. And it has a *developmental history*, the history that for each person begins at conception and continues for the 4 score years or so of the average person's life; this is our topic of discussion here. Developmental history is not independent of the other two histories. The way we develop is affected by our genes (the embodiment of evolutionary history), by our social environment (the embodiment of cultural history), and by physical aspects of our environment as well.

*Developmental psychology* charts changes in people's abilities and styles of behaving as they get older and tries to understand the factors that produce or affect those changes. Traditionally, this enterprise has been most often directed toward children, especially young children. Changes early in life are more rapid and therefore easier to study than those that occur later on. In addition, early changes may be especially important because they provide a foundation on which subsequent development occurs. On the other hand, development continues throughout life, and in recent years adult development has been the focus of an increased amount of research (some of which is discussed in Chapter 13).

Our main concern in this chapter is with the development of mental abilities in infancy and childhood. After a brief introductory section listing some issues that are basic to all of developmental psychology, we will turn to sections dealing with (a) the development of perception and knowledge in infancy, (b) the development of language, and (c) the development of logical thought.

## Some Basic Issues in the Study of Development

Before becoming immersed in more specific issues, let's consider some of the broad questions that guide the work of developmental psychologists—questions that apply both to this chapter and to Chapter 13.

**The Question of Orderliness of Change**  Most research in developmental psychology assumes that some degree of consistency exists in development from person to person. Most developmentalists seek changes that occur in a consistent order in most individuals and that are at least roughly linked to age. Such orderliness, when found, contributes to an understanding of *normative development*, the typical sequence of developmental changes found for a given group of people. For

■ *Three fundamental questions about developmental change: How orderly is it? Is it stagelike or continuous? What are its causes?*

example, the typical sequence of motor abilities involved in the development of walking might include lifting up the head and chest from a prone position, crawling, and so on. A normative chart would list the average age at which each ability first occurs.

Developmental psychologists are inclined to look for orderliness partly because it can provide a basis for generating theories about the nature of the more advanced (later-developing) ability. Thus, if all children must learn certain other motor skills before they can walk, then those same skills (or the basic abilities underlying them) may be part and parcel of the act of walking. Similarly, if all children can solve problems of type *A* before they can solve problems of type *B*, then whatever mental processes are required to solve the former problems may also be required to solve the latter. (Examples of this kind of reasoning by developmental psychologists appear in both this chapter and Chapter 13—in such diverse realms as young children's abilities to find hidden objects and adolescents' abilities to reason about moral issues.)

On the other hand, development is not always as orderly as many developmental psychologists, for the sake of elegance in their theories, might like it to be. Some developmentalists emphasize ***individual development***—the differences among individuals in developmental paths. They argue that those who emphasize normative development may often "see" more orderliness than actually exists, partly because of the research method most often employed.

**The sands of time**

*Age makes a difference in human behavior, and the research of developmental psychologists focuses on such change. Whether they are studying motor skills, creativity, or some other aspect of cognitive or social life, developmentalists are concerned with consistencies and differences across the life span.*

Two basic methods are used to compare people at different ages. The easiest and most commonly used is the ***cross-sectional method***, which tests various groups of people of different ages. Thus, in a cross-sectional study of reasoning ability, the same test might be given to a group of 5-year-olds, a group of 8-year-olds, and a group of 12-year-olds. The average score or typical mode of behaving in each age group might then be taken as the norm for that age. This method says nothing about individual development, because it does not track the sequence of changes that occur in any given individual. To study individual development a researcher must follow a single set of individuals over a period of their lives, assessing each individual at different ages to see how he or she has changed. This method, called the ***longitudinal method***, is not used as often as the cross-sectional method, because it requires that both the researchers and the subjects remain involved with the study over many months or years.

**The Question of Whether Change Is Stagelike or Continuous**   "Oh, it's just a stage he's going through" is one of the most common (and optimistic) laments of parents. Used this way, *stage* refers to the parents' belief that the child's present way of behaving will change. Developmental psychologists also talk about stages.

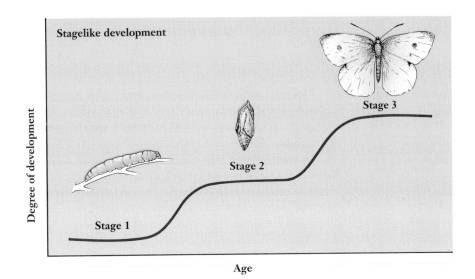

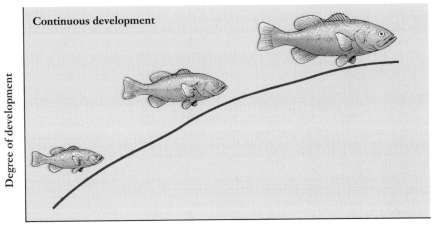

**Figure 12.1** *Stagelike compared to continuous development*

*According to some theories, the human mind develops in a stagelike way, analogous to the changes in the different life stages of a butterfly. According to other theories, its development is gradual and continuous, analogous to the fish's increased size from year to year.*

In many realms of development, two contrasting classes of theories can be found: *stage theories*, which hold that development is discontinuous with plateaus (the stages) separated by periods of rapid change (transition periods); and ***continuous theories***, which hold that change is gradual and continuous. (See Figure 12.1.)

Stage theories vary in the range of behavioral changes they are meant to describe. Some describe a very narrow realm. For example, later in the chapter you will read about a stage theory developed by Robert Siegler concerning the progression of ability to solve a specific class of problem involving judgments about balance. Others describe a very broad realm. At this extreme is the theory developed by Jean Piaget, the famous Swiss developmentalist, designed to describe changes in the mind as a whole. As you will see, Piaget argued that mental development proceeds through a sequence of stages, each marked by a new way of thinking that applies to all intellectual endeavors.

**The Question of Sources of Change: Nature, Nurture, and the Person's Own Actions**  From what does change arise? The nature-nurture issue, a theme of Chapter 3, arises again now as we think about development. Traditionally, some developmental psychologists have emphasized the role of biological maturation in development (the nature side) and others have emphasized the role of learning (the nurture side). From a *maturationist perspective*, developmental change occurs because of genetically programmed growth, especially growth in the brain, that permits the individual to think in new ways or engage in new kinds of behaviors. From a *learning perspective*, on the other hand, change occurs because of the acquisition of new habits and knowledge from experience in the world.

Today, few developmental psychologists can be classed as belonging to one or the other of these camps. Most call themselves *interactionists*, emphasizing their concern with the way that biological maturation and environmental experience combine to produce developmental change. As Chapters 3 and 4 emphasize, genes never work in a vacuum, but instead require a certain environment for their effects to occur. And as I emphasize in Chapter 5's discussion of ecological views of learning, the capacity to learn specific kinds of information depends on genetically controlled, biological preparation to learn that information. Most developmental psychologists today are acutely aware of the strong interdependence of genetic and environmental effects. Thus, rather than ask, "Is this developmental change due to biological maturation or to experience?" they are more likely to ask, "What kind of biological preparation and what kind of experience are needed for this change to occur?"

In an ultimate sense, development emerges from the interaction of genes and environment. But in a more immediate and observable sense it is not genes that interact with the environment but the *person*. The person at any point in time can be described as a structure that has certain behavioral characteristics built into it. Genes and environment have played critical roles in building this structure, but the structure now must also be considered an active force in its own development. Even before birth, the fetus kicking and squirming in the womb is exercising its muscles in ways that help prepare it for life outside the womb. And children in their self-motivated play are constantly developing skills that will help them in later life. Some developmental psychologists—most notably Piaget—have been most interested in understanding how the child's own, self-motivated activities at one stage of life promote growth to the next stage. Piaget was among the first developmental psychologists to call himself an interactionist; he saw mental development as arising from the child's active interactions with the environment. You will read much more about Piaget's views as we progress through the chapter.

## Development of Perception and Knowledge in Infancy

*Infancy*, roughly the first 18 to 24 months of life, is the time of most rapid developmental change—important change that lays the foundation for further development. Since infants (at least early in infancy) can't talk, psychologists can't ask them to describe what they perceive or know. But psychologists can observe infants' actions, and in carefully designed experiments they can draw inferences about infants' perceptual abilities and knowledge from their actions.

### Perceptual Development

On the day they are born, infants can respond to sensory stimuli. They look toward moving, blinking, or high-contrast visual stimuli; turn toward sounds; turn toward anything that touches their face; turn away from unpleasant odors; and suck a nipple more readily for a sweet liquid than for a sour one. Although all of the senses are functional at birth, most of them are not yet fully developed. This is especially true of vision, which is by far the most studied sense and is the focus of our attention here.

**Visual Acuity**   A common technique for measuring infants' visual acuity (ability to see detail) makes use of their natural preference for patterned rather than unpatterned stimuli (see Maurer & Maurer, 1988). In these studies, the patterns are black-and-white stripes and the unpatterned stimuli are patches of gray that reflect the same amount of light as the stripes. When a striped patch and a gray patch are

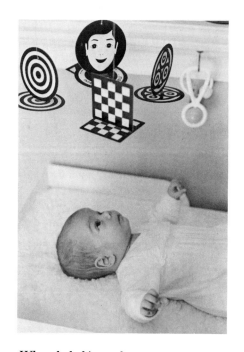

**What do babies see?**

*In the early 1960s, the research of Robert Fantz and others undermined a commonly held belief that newborns see nothing but a blur of light and dark. Infants' visual acuity and their interest in looking at patterns are now so well established that parents can buy mobiles and other toys based on Fantz's test stimuli.*

**How researchers measure visual acuity and its change in infancy**

**How infants' preference for novelty was used to determine the age at which they saw adjoining lines as a single, whole object**

placed side by side, each 1 foot away from the infant's eyes, 1-day-old infants spend more time looking at the stripes than at the gray patch only if the stripes are at least $\frac{1}{10}$ of an inch thick, suggesting that these infants cannot distinguish narrower stripes from gray. The same procedure reveals that 2-month-old infants can see stripes that are $\frac{1}{20}$ of an inch thick and that 8-month-old infants can see stripes that are $\frac{1}{80}$ of an inch thick. For comparison, both 6-year-olds and adults can typically see stripes that are about $\frac{1}{300}$ of an inch thick. Improvement in visual acuity during infancy is at least partly due to continued maturation of the cones, the receptor cells in the fovea that are most important for seeing detail (Youdelis & Hendrickson, 1986).

**Pattern Recognition**    Young infants not only prefer patterns over more homogeneous stimuli, but they also prefer new patterns over ones that they have already seen. Leslie Cohen and Barbara Younger (1984) used this preference for novelty in an experiment concerned with infants' abilities to integrate separate features of a pattern into a larger whole, which is a key aspect of all visual perception (discussed in Chapter 9). As stimuli, the researchers used simple two-line patterns such as those shown at the bottom of Figure 12.2. Which of the two right-hand stimuli (*B* or *C*) in this figure looks most like stimulus *A*? If seen as whole objects, as adults see them, *B* looks most like *A*; *B* is the same angle as *A* but turned to a different orientation. If seen as individual lines, *C* looks most like *A*; the separate lines of *C* are identical in shape and orientation to those of *A*. Cohen and Younger first presented stimulus *A* to the infants until the infants were bored with it. Then they presented stimulus *B* or *C* and recorded how long the infants looked at it. Since infants prefer novelty, the amount of time they spent looking at the new stimulus (*B* or *C*) could be taken as a measure of the extent to which they saw it as different from the original stimulus (*A*). The results (shown in Figure 12.2) indicate that 6-week-old infants saw *B* as the most different, but 14-week-old infants (like adults) saw *C* as the most different. From this finding, Cohen and Younger argued that the tendency to see two adjoining lines as a single object (an angle or corner) may not be present at birth, but may emerge sometime after the first 6 weeks of life.

**Figure 12.2  *Development toward seeing two lines as a single object***

*These graphs show the average amount of time that infants spent looking at each of three different two-line stimuli (A, B, and C) after having been exposed to one of them (A) until they were bored with it. Notice that the 6-week-olds showed most interest in stimulus B, which differed from the original in the orientation of its individual lines, whereas the 14-week-olds showed most interest in stimulus C, which differed from the original in its overall shape. This finding suggests that the younger infants perceived the individual lines rather than the stimulus as a whole, and that the older infants perceived the stimulus as a whole. (The stimuli shown here are samples. Some infants saw other sets of stimuli, which bore the same relationship to each other as those shown here.) (Adapted from Cohen & Younger, 1984.)*

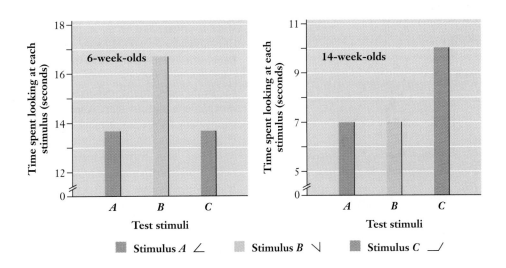

Other experiments have confirmed these results and have shown that increasingly sophisticated abilities to integrate features into whole objects continue to develop during the first year or more of infancy (see Aslin & Smith, 1988). This change is due partly to the continued maturation of neurons in the eyes and brain and partly to the child's growing knowledge gained from experience.

**■ Why older infants are fascinated by butterflies and younger infants are not**

**Figure 12.3  Visual cliff**
*Although his mother is calling, this child will not venture over the deep side of the visual cliff.*

**■ Evidence that self-produced locomotion promotes fear of a visual cliff**

Researchers such as Jerome Kagan have focused on the relationship between infants' choices of what to look at and the development of their ability to recognize objects. Kagan (1972, 1984) suggests that infants are most interested in objects that are only somewhat different from those with which they have become familiar, a phenomenon that he calls the *discrepancy principle*. According to Kagan, infants actively build mental concepts, or *schemas* (a term for mental concepts introduced in Chapter 10), of specific categories of objects and are most interested in objects that help them expand their existing schemas. In one study, for example, 8-month-olds showed much more interest in pictures of babies' faces than in pictures of butterflies, whereas the reverse was true for infants who were only a few months older (Reznick & Kagan, 1982). Kagan argues that 8-month-olds have formed a face schema mostly from seeing adults, so babies' faces are interesting to them because the faces are different enough to enhance that schema. Eight-month-old infants do not yet have a schema for butterflies or other small, flying animals. To the older infant, babies' faces are old hat and butterflies are interesting because they are sufficiently discrepant from a schema for small, flying animals that is now being developed.

**The Role of Self-Produced Locomotion in the Response to a Visual Cliff**   In a now-classic series of experiments, Eleanor Gibson and Richard Walk (1960) showed that infants who had learned to crawl could use their vision to avoid crawling off a visual cliff. The cliff consisted partly of a glass-topped table with a board across its center. On one side of the board (the shallow side) a checkerboard-patterned material was placed directly underneath the glass, and on the other side (the deep side) the same material was placed well below the glass (see Figure 12.3). Infants who were placed on the center board would readily crawl off onto the shallow side, but would studiously avoid the deep side. Even if their mothers called to them from the deep side they would not crawl in that direction and often cried in apparent frustration.

Gibson and Walk's experiments showed that infants avoided the cliff by the time they could crawl. Subsequently, other experiments showed that even infants who were too young to crawl could see the visual cliff, but only infants who had sufficient experience with crawling or another form of self-produced locomotion were motivated to avoid it. In one study, noncrawling infants from 2 to 6 months old showed a greater *decrease* in heart rate when they were placed face-down on the deep side of the cliff than when they were placed on the shallow side, which is taken to be a sign of interest rather than fear (Campos & others, 1970, 1978). In the same experiment, experienced crawlers showed an *increase* in heart rate on the deep side, a sign of fear. Another experiment showed that this difference was not simply due to age; infants who were the same age behaved differently on the visual cliff depending on how long they had been crawling (Bertenthal & others, 1984).

How does crawling lead babies to change their interpretation of the visual cliff? The intuitive answer, which most people would give, is that infants learn to fear drop-offs through experience with falling—for example, by crawling off the edge of a bed and falling on the floor. But another experiment showed that this does not seem to be the explanation, at least not the only one. Six-month-olds who had not yet learned to crawl were given a total of 40 hours of practice using a walker, which allowed them to move around on their own but prevented them from falling. When subsequently placed on the deep side of the visual cliff, these infants, like infants who could crawl, showed an increased heart rate (Bertenthal & others, 1984).

Apparently, self-produced locomotion promotes the fear and avoidance of cliffs even in infants who have had no experience with falling. Just how this link occurs is not clear, but it seems likely to be predisposed by evolution. From the viewpoint of survival, the emergence of a fear of cliffs at around the same time that the infant becomes mobile and can potentially fall from one is certainly advantageous. Thus, we might conclude tentatively that natural selection has provided humans with (a) a tendency to fear cliffs, and (b) a timing mechanism that causes the cliff-fearing tendency to be released as a result of experience with self-produced locomotion.

### Early Knowledge

**Infant Behavior Interpreted as Exploration**   In discussing perception we have been considering the early development of knowledge. To perceive an object is to match the sensory experience of the object with an inner representation (schema) of the object category; so, perception requires knowledge. Similarly, the ability to avoid cliffs or to move around objects in the environment implies knowledge about the general properties of three-dimensional space. Research on infants' selective attention to moderately unfamiliar objects and research on the role of movement in spatial perception indicate that children's active choices and movements are important to their growth of knowledge.

Other experiments have shown that infants are especially interested in the relationship between stimuli and their own self-produced movements. Two-month-old babies show more interest and delight in a mobile that moves in response to their own bodily movement than they do in an electrically propelled mobile whose movement they do not control (Watson, 1972). In another experiment, Hanus Papousek (1969) trained 4-month-olds to make a particular movement to turn on a small array of lights. The infants learned quickly, but once they became proficient they lost interest and responded only occasionally. However, when Papousek changed the conditions so that a different movement was needed to turn on the lights, the infants regained interest and made another burst of responses. The renewed interest must have been generated by the new relationship between response and stimulus, because the stimulus itself was unchanged. Apparently, the babies were interested not so much in the lights per se as in their own ability to control them.

**Piaget's View of Infant Cognitive Development**   No developmental psychologist has emphasized the relationship between action and knowledge more than Jean Piaget. Piaget (1936) proposed that infants not only gain knowledge through actions, but that to them, knowledge *is* action. He argued that early in infancy children have no mental symbols, so their only way to think about things is to act on them, that is, to scan them with their eyes, suck on them, grasp them, and so on. He referred to infancy as the ***sensorimotor stage*** of intellectual development, because intelligence at that stage consists of motor actions toward objects and the immediate sensory feedback that stems from those actions. Earliest actions are purely reflexive, but the infant is sensitive to their consequences and repeats those whose consequences are interesting. An important concept in Piaget's theory of infant cognition is that of *circular actions*, which are actions that the infant keeps repeating because of their consequences.

Piaget distinguished among three kinds of circular actions that emerge successively as the infant gets older. First are *primary circular actions*, which are repeated actions that involve only the infant's own body. Thus, a 2-month-old boy might get his thumb into his mouth, suck on it for a moment, let it fall out, and then move the thumb around until he gets it back in again, becoming increasingly adept at controlling this particular movement with each repetition. Beginning at about 4 months, *secondary circular actions* emerge, which are repeated actions on an external object. At this stage, an infant might swing an arm and hit a mobile hanging above him or her in the crib, enjoy the resulting movement, and then repeat the action again, becoming increasingly more skilled at the task. At about 1 year, *tertiary*

*Evidence that infants are motivated to learn to control their environment*

*Three kinds of circular actions, and Piaget's view of their role in the development of schemes*

**Jean Piaget**
*Because of his interest in the influence of the environment on children's cognitive development, Piaget's observations of children took place in natural settings. Here he is shown during a visit to a nursery school.*

◼ *Piaget's evidence for the gradual development of knowledge of object permanence, and Baillargeon's evidence that this knowledge may be present much earlier than Piaget believed*

(third-order) *circular actions* become prominent, which are actions repeated successively on different external objects. Now an infant who has just learned the action of twisting a knob may go around twisting all the knobs that he or she can reach—knobs on the radio, TV, and stove, and perhaps the knoblike nose on your face—observing the interesting and different effect that each produces.

What are infants accomplishing by all this activity? According to Piaget, they are building mental *schemes*. Piaget's term *scheme* does not mean quite the same thing as *schema*, the term used earlier in connection with Kagan's view of the growing mind. A schema is a schematic mental form of a perceptual concept, a sort of mental cartoon that depicts the main features of members of the category to which the schema refers. Piaget's *scheme*, on the other hand, is more closely related to action. It can be thought of as a mental blueprint that provides an organized pattern for action. Through repeated circular actions on the same or similar objects, the infant builds a mental scheme for that pattern of actions and assimilates (incorporates) various objects into that scheme. Thus, younger infants have a sucking scheme into which they assimilate their mother's breast, their own thumb, a pacifier, and so on. Older infants who go around twisting knobs are actively incorporating various objects into their newly developed twisting schemes.

Piaget believed that these early action schemes are truly the initial forms of thought. As the schemes develop, children become increasingly able to activate them mentally in the absence of the actual object, without producing overt movements; this, to Piaget, is the beginning of purely inner thought (thought without movement). As you will see later in the chapter, Piaget believed that development throughout childhood entails stages in which schemes become increasingly abstract, that is, less tied to actual actions and more tied to potential (possible or hypothetical) actions.

### Development of Object Permanence and the Ability to Find Hidden Objects

Using primarily his own three children as subjects, Piaget (1936) pioneered techniques for understanding infants' minds by observing how they respond to particular problems such as finding hidden objects. The ability to find objects depends not only on well-developed perceptual capacities—including the ability to recognize the object once it is found—but also on the ability to keep the object in mind when it is not in view. To be motivated to search for a hidden object, the child must understand that the object still exists even when it's out of view. Piaget referred to this understanding as **object permanence**. According to Piaget, object permanence is an extremely important part of mental development, because it represents the child's first ability to think of an object that is not immediately present.

On the basis of evidence from problems listed below, Piaget believed that object permanence develops gradually during the first 18 months of life. The problems are simple games, which you might have fun playing with an infant the next time you meet one of the appropriate age.

*The simple hiding problem* Attract the infant's attention with an interesting object, such as a ring of keys. Place the keys under a napkin or behind a barrier while the infant continues to stare at the keys and your movement. In experiments like this, Piaget found that infants up to about 4 months old completely forgot about the object as soon as it was hidden. They made no attempt to retrieve it and didn't even continue looking in its direction. "Out of sight, out of mind" seems to be the rule at this stage. By about 5 months of age the infants would look in the direction of the hidden object for a moment after it disappeared, but not until they were 6 to 8 months old would they pull away the napkin or reach under it to retrieve the hidden object.

*The changed hiding-place problem* The 8-month-old can solve the simple hiding problem but is still likely to fail when the task is made a little more difficult by hiding the object first at one place, for a series of trials, and then at a different place. Place two napkins in front of the infant and, using the procedure described above, hide the object at least twice under napkin *A*. The 8-month-old will delightedly retrieve it each time. On the next trial hide it under napkin *B* and make the child wait at least 3 seconds before he or she can reach for it (you can hold the infant's hands). Notice that the infant—despite watching the object disappear under napkin *B*, and despite the fact that the object makes a conspicuous lump under *B*—pulls away napkin *A*, not *B*, and acts surprised when the object doesn't appear. From this demonstration, Piaget concluded that the 8-month-old's emerging concept of object permanence is still quite fragile; when pitted against a learned motor habit, the habit wins out. The child's understanding of objects is still tightly bound to past actions.

*The invisible displacement problem* By about age 1 year, most children solve the changed hiding-place problem but fail this third problem. This time, before you hide the object under the napkin, close your hand around the object so the infant cannot see it. The infant sees the object disappear in your hand, sees you reach under the napkin, and sees your hand emerge with no object in it. Under these conditions, the 1-year-old is likely not to look under the napkin, but instead to persist in trying to find the object somewhere in your hand. Apparently, at this stage infants understand that objects exist at a particular location when not in view, and that objects can be moved from one place to another when in view; but they do not understand that objects can be moved from one place to another when not in view. Not until about age 18 months do infants succeed at this problem, which in Piaget's view is the time when they have developed a rather complete ability to conceive of objects in their absence. At this point, in Piaget's theory, the child emerges from the sensorimotor stage and enters the next stage of mental development, when true mental thinking can occur.

It is remarkable that these simple tasks, pioneered by Piaget with just three infants, have since provided the basis for dozens of experiments performed with hundreds of infants, and that in general Piaget's results have stood the test of time. Study after study has shown that infants do succeed in the tasks described above in the order that Piaget's children did. However, the typical age for each milestone is often determined to be somewhat younger than Piaget found, depending on how the test is conducted (see Figure 12.4).

**Figure 12.4 *Improvement in finding hidden objects***
*This graph shows the percentage of infants at various ages who passed each of three kinds of hiding problems. The problems were as described in the text, except objects were hidden under cups rather than under napkins. (Adapted from Wishart & Bower, 1984.)*

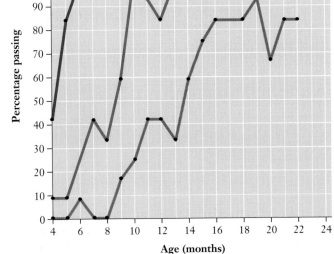

Simple hiding task
Changed hiding-place task
Invisible displacement task

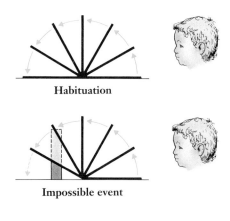

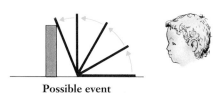

**Figure 12.5** *Evidence for knowledge of object permanence in very young infants*

Baillargeon (1987) first showed infants a screen rotating back and forth over a 180° arc until they were bored with it (habituation). Then she showed them the same rotating screen with an object behind it, such that the object was obscured from view each time the screen rotated upward. In the impossible event (using mirrors to create an illusion), the screen continued to rotate over the entire arc, as if the object behind it magically disappeared and then reappeared on each rotation. In the possible event, the screen stopped in each rotation at the place where it would bump into the object. Infants as young as 3½ months old looked longer at the impossible than at the possible event, suggesting that they were more surprised by it. (Adapted from Baillargeon, 1987.)

Using other kinds of tests, some researchers have disputed Piaget's claim that young infants cannot imagine the presence of objects that are not in view. For example, in one series of experiments Renée Baillargeon (1987) found that infants as young as 4 months old behaved as if they were more surprised when a rotating screen seemed to pass through and obliterate an object hidden behind it than when the screen seemed to stop at the point where it would bump into the object (see Figure 12.5). Developmental psychologists are increasingly coming to believe that a given concept may be understood at different levels by infants at different ages. Perhaps 4-month-olds have a primitive perceptual understanding that objects continue to exist when not in view, but must still acquire through experience a new level of that understanding before they can use it to guide their movements in finding hidden objects (Baillargeon & others, 1985). This is similar to the observation discussed previously that very young infants can see depth on the visual cliff but require further experience before they understand depth in a way that guides their movements.

# Development of Language

At the same time that infants are interacting with and learning about the physical world, they are also interacting with people and beginning to learn language. Of all of the things that people can do, none seem more complex than the ability to understand and speak a language. Thousands of words and countless subtle grammatical rules for modifying and combining words must be learned. Yet, nearly all people master their native language by the time they grow up; in fact, most people are well en route to this mastery by the time they are 3 or 4 years old. Before they can do such things as tie their shoes or understand that two plus two equals four, children have pretty much learned their native language. How can this occur? Most developmentalists agree that it requires a combination of innate mechanisms that predispose children for such learning, coupled with an environment that provides adequate models and an opportunity to practice. In this section, we will look first at the normal course of language development; then at ideas about both the innate and environmental prerequisites for language; and finally, to contrast it with the way humans learn language, at attempts to teach language to chimpanzees.

## *The Course of Language Development*

**Early Perception of Speech Sounds**  Infants seem to treat speech as something special as soon as they are born and maybe even when they are still in the womb. When allowed to choose between tape-recorded sounds by sucking in different ways on a nipple, 3-day-old infants chose to listen to human speech rather than to other sounds such as instrumental music (Butterfield & Siperstein, 1974), and chose their own mother's voice over that of another woman's (DeCasper & Fifer, 1980). The mother's voice is audible in the womb, so young humans may begin to recognize and prefer that sound even before they are born. Anthony DeCasper and Melanie Spence (1986) found that infants whose mothers had recited a particular prose passage each day during the last 6 weeks of pregnancy preferred listening to that passage over another one when they were tested shortly after birth.

Young infants are not only attuned to the overall patterns and rhythms of speech, but they can also distinguish the individual vowel and consonant sounds that are the *phonemes* of speech. Some experiments on infants' abilities to distinguish sounds use the following technique: The infant sucks on a pacifier that is wired to trigger the playing of a particular sound each time a sucking response occurs. When the infant becomes bored with a sound, as indicated by a reduced rate of sucking, the sound is changed (maybe from *pa* to *ba*). If the rate of sucking increases immediately thereafter, the assumption is that the infant hears the new sound as different from the previous one.

Experiments using this technique indicate that infants between about 1 and 6 months of age can hear the difference between any two sounds that constitute different phonemes in any of the world's languages, but that after 6 months they begin to *lose* the ability to hear subtle differences that are not important to their native language (see Kuhl, 1987). Thus, children growing up in an English-speaking culture lose the ability to distinguish among different /t/ sounds, which belong to the same phoneme category in English but not in Hindi (Werker & Tees, 1984). Similarly, children growing up in a Japanese culture lose the ability to distinguish between the English /l/ and /r/, which belong to the same phoneme category in Japanese (Eimas, 1975).

**Cooing and Babbling**   Normal infants produce two distinct categories of vocal sounds. One category, of course, is crying, which can occur immediately after birth and continues throughout life as a nonverbal means of emotional expression and a signal for help. The other category includes (a) *cooing*, which usually begins in the second month and consists of repeated, drawn-out vowels (*oooh-oooh, eeeh-eeeh*); and (b) *babbling*, which begins in the third or fourth month and consists of consonant-vowel sounds such as *paa-paa-paa* or *tooda-tooda*. Cooing and babbling occur most often when the infant is happy, and they seem to be forms of play that have evolved to exercise the infant's vocal apparatus in preparation for speech.

The onset and general form of cooing and babbling appear to be determined genetically. Deaf infants begin to coo and babble at the same age, with the same variety of sound patterns, as do hearing infants (Lenneberg, 1969); and cross-cultural studies have provided no evidence that the sounds produced by hearing infants during this play are influenced by the language that they hear (Locke, 1983). For example, infants in English-speaking homes are as likely as those in Hebrew-speaking homes to babble the guttural Hebrew /ch/, even though that sound is not part of English speech.

Although their age of onset and vocal form are not much influenced by the language environment, cooing and babbling appear to be social behaviors right from the beginning. Cooing is usually accompanied by smiling and is most likely to be elicited by a nodding human face or a model of one (Lenneberg, 1969). Older infants babble more to familiar people than to unfamiliar ones, and by about 7 months of age "conversations" commonly occur between babbling infants and their adult caregivers; the adult answers each babbled sequence as if it were a verbal statement, and the infant is silent and attentive during that response (Snow, 1984).

*■ Evidence that development in phoneme perception involves loss in the ability to make distinctions unimportant to the infant's native language*

***Early communication***
*Well before they can produce language, infants are capable of clear, if crude, communication. It is easy to understand from this child's emphatic gesture that he has finished eating.*

Such interactions may help infants learn such rules as conversational turn-taking even before they have learned any words.

■ *When is a word really a word?*

**First Words**   I can use examples from my own son's development to illustrate a general principle of early word acquisition. When Scott was about 10 months old, my wife and I noticed that some of his babblelike sounds were not random, but occurred reliably in specific contexts. He would say *ticka-ticka-ticka* while tickling things, *gooda-gooda-gooda* while playfully eating babyfood, and *hewo* into the receiver of our telephone when we let him play with it. We excitedly recorded these as our son's "first words." But now I have to ask: Were they really words? A word is a *symbol* (see Chapter 11). A symbol is something that *refers* to something outside of itself—some object, action, event, characteristic, or abstract idea. Was Scott referring to anything when he made those sounds? Did he have any understanding of the meaning of *tickle*, *good*, or *hello*, or were the sounds simply part of his action of tickling things, eating, and playing with the telephone, which he had learned by imitating my wife and me? There is no way to answer this question with certainty, but systematic observations have shown that babies very commonly produce word-like sounds as components of other actions before they begin to produce them in a clearly referential way (Greenfield & Smith, 1976). Some developmental psychologists refer to these earliest wordlike sounds as *performatives* to distinguish them from words that serve true symbolizing functions. A performative can be defined as a sound that the child has learned to produce in a particular context (such as playing with the telephone) without knowing the word's meaning.

*First words*

*Naming objects is an important step in the mastery of language, and it is also a source of great delight to infants and their caregivers. Here 1-year-old Genevieve uses her favorite word,* light.

No sharp dividing line exists between performatives and true words. The vocalization that we recorded as our son's sixth "word" was *ba*. At first he would say *ba* only after he had already been given the bottle, and it may well have been a performative. He would say *ba-ba-ba-ba* as soon as he got the bottle, as part of the joyous act of taking it into his hands, and occasionally would repeat the sound again between bouts of sucking. After several weeks of using the sound in this way, he began to use it in different contexts. For example, one time he pointed to his bottle on the kitchen shelf and happily said *ba*. Now, at what may have been the first glimmering of true referential use of a word, he seemed to be using the word to label the object he saw. It is significant, too, that in his first use of *ba* as a label he was not hungry or asking for the bottle—he refused it when it was subsequently offered—but rather was simply pointing it out. A general rule, based on observations of many babies, is that early words are usually used first to name things that are present, and only later to ask for things (Bloom & Lahey, 1978).

**Mapping the World into Words**    New words come slowly at first. But then, usually by 18 to 24 months of age, the rate begins to accelerate. By the third birthday and for several years thereafter, the typical child is learning words at a phenomenal rate—an average of something like one or two every waking hour (Miller, 1981). Relatively few of these are explicitly taught to the child; most must come from inferences that the child makes on the basis of hearing words as others use them. When a child hears a new word used in a particular situation, how does he or she know what aspect of the situation the word refers to?

Eve Clark (1987) has suggested that the task is made easier by a natural bias that the child has, which Clark refers to as the *principle of lexical contrast*. According to this principle, young children assume that every word has a different meaning from every other word—that is, that there are no synonyms. Thus, when they hear a new word that seems to label something in their immediate environment, they look for something for which they don't already have a word. In one experiment supporting this principle, 3- and 4-year-olds were presented with toy animals for which they already had names (a pig, a sheep, and a cow) plus one for which they did not have a name (a tapir). When they heard the novel word *gombe* in the presence of these objects, all of the children applied it to the novel animal (Clark, 1987). Other evidence for the principle comes from observing that children often resist others' attempts to teach them new names for objects for which they already have a name. For example, they will reply, "That not plane, that a jet-plane," or "It not a animal, it a dog" (Clark, 1987).

Another problem young children face, in addition to hooking up new words with their immediate referents, is that of deciding how to *extend* the word to new referents. Common nouns such as *ball* or *dog* refer not just to one object but to categories of objects, and a full understanding of the word requires that the child be able to apply it to all members of the category without applying it to nonmembers. Of course, children often make mistakes in this process. One kind of mistake is *overextension*, which is to use the word more broadly than its adult meaning would justify. Thus, *ball* might be used for a while for anything that is round or spherical, and *dog* might be used for all four-legged animals. My son overextended the word *dooda*, which was the name of a song on his favorite record. The only visible feature that distinguished the *dooda* record from the others in his set was its purple color, so he assumed that *dooda* must mean purple. For several months he referred to all purple things as *dooda*.

On the basis of studying overextensions recorded in baby diaries (parents' records of children's word uses), Clark (1973) proposed that young children implicitly define new words in terms of one or a few of the features of the objects that they have learned to label. Thus, a child who hears *ball* in association with a specific object assumes that the most prominent feature of the object—its roundness—is the defining characteristic, and thus applies the word to all round objects.

Other research, however, has shown that children also often *underextend* new words, using them more narrowly than do adults. Underextensions are harder to observe than overextensions; they are not naturally recorded by parents in baby diaries. If a child sees an apple and calls it a *ball*, that is recorded; but if a child sees a new kind of ball and doesn't call it anything, that is not recorded. (Recording this would be meaningless, anyway, because failure to name something doesn't mean that the child cannot name it.) To detect underextensions, researchers must specifically ask children to sort objects according to their names; in this situation, underextensions are quite common (Anglin, 1977).

When underextensions occur, the assumption can be made that the child at first learned to associate the word with just one specific object, using the word as if it were a proper noun, and later learned gradually to generalize the word to other objects that resemble the original referent. Thus, a child might at first assume that

■ *How children's avoidance of synonyms may help them in early word learning*

■ *Evidence that infants overextend some words and underextend others, and implications of this for theories of early word meaning*

the term *ball* stands only for the specific red beachball that was present when the word was first uttered, and only later learn that it also stands for other objects that in at least one way (roundness) resemble that beachball. Because overextensions and underextensions are both common, theorists today assume that young children understand some new words in terms of features and understand other new words in terms of overall similarity to the original referent.

**Putting Words Together and Acquiring Grammatical Rules** One of the most reliable characteristics of early utterances is that they are constrained in length. All infants go through a stage in which each of their statements is just one word long. Yet, these one-word statements may express multiword ideas, which parents can often interpret from the context and accompanying gestures (Greenfield & Smith, 1976). Thus, the statement *Ball* may mean "This is a ball," or "Billy is kicking the ball," or "Give me the ball." Only after several months of such one-word statements do children (typically at about 18 to 24 months old) begin to put two words together. From that point on, the average length of utterances increases gradually (Brown, 1973).

When children do begin to put words together, they commonly use only content words (mostly nouns and verbs, with some adjectives and adverbs), avoiding the less essential noncontent words such as articles (*a*, *the*) or prepositions (*in*, *under*). They usually put the content words in the grammatically correct sequence for simple, active sentences. For an English-speaking child, this means that subjects are placed before verbs, and verbs before objects. A child at the two-word stage will say, "Billy kick" to mean that Billy is kicking the ball, and "Kick Billy" to mean that someone is kicking Billy; and when finally ready to say, "Billy kick ball" will usually do so with the three words in the correct order. The ability to understand and use passive sentences, in which the object of the action precedes the actor—such as, *The ball was kicked by Billy*—comes later, typically at about age 5 (Bever, 1970).

When young children first acquire a new grammatical rule such as adding *-ed* to the end of a verb to create the past tense, they almost invariably overgeneralize the rule at first. That is, they use it in a more consistent fashion than do adult users of the language (see Rumelhart & McClelland, 1987). The 3-year-old who says "kicked," "played," and "laughed," also says "goed," "thinked," and "swimmed." Similarly, children who have just learned to add *-s* to pluralize nouns will talk about many *mouses*, *sheeps*, and *childs*. This overgeneralization is interesting, because it confirms that children know the rule. If they followed the rule only when adults did, one could argue that their usage involved simple imitation, not application of the rule. Further evidence that their grammar is based on rules and not on memorized sequences comes from the observation that young children can use the correct rules with made-up words as well as with words that they have heard before (see Figure 12.6).

Young children somehow discover the grammatical rules of their language by hearing examples of rule-based language around them. Children are not taught the rules explicitly; nobody sits a 2-year-old down and tries to explain how to create infinitives, possessives, or past-tense verbs. Although some parents occasionally correct their children's grammar, even this is rare (Brown & Hanlon, 1970), and long-term experiments in preschools have shown that a deliberate program of correcting grammar has negligible effects on rule acquisition (de Villiers & de Villiers, 1979). Through their own devices, children must actively (and probably unconsciously) infer grammar rules from examples of rule-based language taking place around them.

*Evidence that young children use grammatical rules and do not just mimic constructions that they hear*

This is a wug.

Now there is another one.
There are two of them.
There are two _____.

**Figure 12.6 One wug and two_____?**
*With this test, Jean Berko found that young children who had just begun to use the rule of forming plurals by adding -s would use the rule correctly even for words they had never heard before. (From Berko, 1958.)*

### Internal and External Supports for Language Development

Armed with some knowledge about the course of language development, let us now consider some ideas about the factors that promote language development. The ideas fall into two broad categories—*nativist theories* and *learning theories*.

**Nativist Theories** Nativist theories emphasize the role of innate, biological equipment. There is no doubt that we enter the world in many ways pre-equipped for language. We are born with (a) anatomical structures in our throat (the larynx and pharynx) that enable us to produce a broader range of sounds than any other mammal, (b) a preference to listen to speech and an ability to distinguish among all of the basic speech sounds, (c) mechanisms that cause us to go through a period of cooing and babbling, and (d) brain areas that are apparently biologically specialized for language (Broca's and Wernicke's areas, discussed in Chapter 11). Some nativist theorists, most notably the linguist Noam Chomsky (1965), go further and argue that we are also born predisposed to learn language in certain ways. Chomsky argues that linguistic rules are too complex for young children to learn through their general intelligence alone, and that children must be aided by an inborn understanding of aspects of language that are common to all languages (referred to as universal grammar) and by inborn guidelines that help them acquire the unique rules of their culture's language. Chomsky refers to these innate language-learning aids as the **language-acquisition device**, usually called by its acronym **LAD**.

One approach to learning about the LAD is to compare language development in different language cultures to find underlying regularities. This approach has been pursued most vigorously by Dan Slobin (1973, 1985). One regularity discovered by Slobin is that grammatical rules having to do with word order are almost always learned earlier than rules that involve modifying a word through adding a suffix or prefix. For example, children learn to mark the difference between subjects and objects of sentences sooner if the difference is marked by word order (as it is in English) than if it is marked by adding suffixes to the nouns (as in various other languages). From this, Slobin suggests that one innate guideline in acquiring syntax is *Pay attention to the order of words*. Another of Slobin's candidates for the status of innate guideline is *Pay attention to the ends of words*. His evidence for this comes from finding that grammatical constructions involving suffixes or postpositions (terms placed after the term being modified) are learned more quickly than those involving prefixes or prepositions (terms placed before the term being modified). As an example, terms that specify location are placed before the locative noun in English (*in* the drawer, *under* the table, etc.) but are placed after the locative noun in Hungarian, and Slobin has found that Hungarian children learn these expressions earlier than do English-speaking children.

A more recently explored means to learn about innate underpinnings for language acquisition is to study new languages that sometimes develop when people with different native languages colonize the same region. The first generation of such colonists communicate by a primitive, grammarless use of words taken from their various native languages, referred to as a **pidgin language**. Subsequently, the pidgin develops into a true language, with a full range of grammatical rules, at which point it is called a **creole language** (not to be confused with Creole—a language spoken in Haiti and by some southern Louisianans—which is just one example of a creole language). Derek Bickerton (1984) has studied creole languages from around the world and has arrived at two quite startling and controversial conclusions. First, creole languages appear to be fully developed, in one generation, by the children of the original colonists who developed the pidgin.

■ *How Chomsky's nativist view of language acquisition is supported by cross-language comparisons and the study of creole languages*

Apparently, the children impose grammatical rules on the pidgin they hear and use those rules consistently in their own speech—powerful evidence, in Bickerton's view, that children's minds are innately predisposed for grammar. Second, Bickerton concluded that creole languages that have developed in different parts of the world (from different combinations of parent languages) are all similar to one another in their grammatical structure, more so than are long-standing languages. Bickerton takes this to be evidence for innate grammar. Other languages have evolved away from the grammatical constructions that are most natural to the human mind, but creole languages have not had sufficient history to undergo this transformation.

*How a case study supports the idea that syntax, but not semantics, is learned more easily before adolescence than later*

Implicit in Bickerton's theory is the idea that children have a greater capacity for language learning and inventiveness than do adults. This idea, proposed explicitly by other nativist theorists (for example, Lenneberg, 1969), is often referred to as the *critical-period hypothesis*. One opportunity to test this hypothesis arose some years ago when a girl, referred to in psychological writings as Genie, was rescued at age 13 from the inhuman, completely language-deprived conditions in which she had been raised. All her life, Genie had been confined by her deranged parents to a small bedroom, isolated from the rest of the world and from all speech sounds; they had never spoken to her or in her presence. After her rescue, she was placed in a foster home where she was exposed to English in much the way that infants normally are, though supplemented by extra tutorial help; her progress was monitored by a language specialist, Susan Curtiss (1977).

In this new environment, Genie eventually developed quite good semantics (understanding of word meanings) but not good syntax (grammar). She acquired a large vocabulary and could produce meaningful, intelligent statements; but by age 20 she still had not acquired basic rules of English grammar that are normally acquired by age 4. Her syntactic development lagged way behind other indices of her intelligence. She would say such things as, "I hear music ice cream truck," and after hearing a sentence such as, "The boy hit the girl," she would be unsure about who had hit whom. This finding fits with observations of other children who have been deprived (though less severely) of early language opportunity, and it stands in marked contrast to observations of children who are retarded for genetic rather than environmental reasons, who generally show *less* deficit in syntax than in other areas of cognition (Curtiss, 1981). Thus, the cases of Genie and others support the view that people may be biologically primed to acquire the syntax of their native language during childhood and less able to do so later on.

*The operant-conditioning theory of language acquisition, and why it is not well accepted today*

**Learning and Social Learning Theories**   In 1957, in a book entitled *Verbal Behavior*, B. F. Skinner presented a strong version of the view that language is not especially different from other forms of behavior. He argued that language, like other behaviors, is operant behavior, acquired through operant conditioning. As described in Chapter 5, operant behavior is behavior that is used as a tool to operate on the environment in such a way as to achieve a reinforcing stimulus (more commonly called a reward). Clearly, we do use speech as a tool. We say "Help!" when we want help; "Please pass the butter" when we want butter; and "It's a nice day, isn't it?" when we want a similar social nicety in return. And these utterances indeed are influenced by their consequences. If you no longer received butter for saying, "Please pass the butter," and if you received nothing but frowns and scoffs for saying, "It's a nice day," you would stop saying those things and try some other means to get the things you wanted. But Skinner went further, arguing that speech is operant behavior from the very beginning and is shaped through reinforcement provided mainly by the parents. A hungry baby babbling in the crib happens by chance to utter *ba*. Interpreting this to mean "bottle," the parent brings the bottle, which reinforces *ba*, making it more likely to occur again the next time the baby is hungry. With time, however, the parent becomes less responsive to *ba*, but responds again to the chance variation *bot*; and so on until the baby is saying the English word *bottle* to request the bottle. Similarly, with the older child, more complex constructions evolve through reinforcement.

Few developmental psychologists today accept Skinner's explanation of language acquisition. One of the most glaring problems with his theory is the implication that language learning begins with the child's utterances, which must be presented aloud to be shaped by the parents. Developmentalists who study language have found that children usually learn to *understand* new words and grammatical constructions before they begin to produce them; and, in fact, children who are born with defective speech mechanisms, and thus can't produce utterances at all, nevertheless develop normal language comprehension (Lenneberg, 1962). In addition, it is hard to imagine how children could become competent in all of the rules of grammar simply through reinforcement. Do parents really, in any consistent way, reinforce children for use of proper grammar? Research on naturally occurring parent-child conversations has suggested that parents reinforce their children on the basis of the truth of their utterances, but rarely on the basis of their grammar (Brown & Hanlon, 1970). For example, when a child said, truthfully but ungrammatically, "Mama isn't boy, he a girl," the parent responded, "That's right"; but when the same child said, grammatically but falsely, "Walt Disney comes on Tuesday," the parent said, "No, he does not."

Psychologists who adopt the perspective called *social learning theory* take a broader view than Skinner did about how learning occurs. They maintain that children learn from others even without rewards, and that this applies to language as well as to other behaviors. Such theorists emphasize the social nature of human beings and the rich linguistic environment that the social world provides. Humans have a strong desire to learn about, and communicate with, each other, which leads parents and children alike to pay close attention to each other's gestures and utterances and to modify their own to get their point across. Whereas Chomsky assumes that infants must learn language by extracting principles from complex adult conversation, researchers from the social learning perspective point out that adults speak much more simply and clearly to young children than they do to other adults (Snow, 1984). There may be a LAD, but equally important from the social learning perspective is the **LASS**—the *language-acquisitions support system*—provided by the social world into which the infant is born (Bruner, 1983).

Research in the social learning tradition has shown that when adults speak to young children they often simplify their speech in ways that seem ideally designed to help the children learn word meanings and simple grammatical constructions. Typically, the simplification includes a reduction in sentence length; a focus on the here-and-now rather than on the past, future, or far away; and a tendency to repeat salient words, often accompanied by nonverbal cues to help convey their meaning (Snow, 1984). For example, a 6-month-old playing with a ball might be told, "Oh, you have a *ball*. A nice *ball*. What a pretty *ball*." Such speech is often referred to as *motherese*, though it is not just mothers who speak this way to infants. Fathers do, too, and even 4-year-olds do when they speak to their still-younger siblings. There is at least some evidence that this simplification helps promote language development. In a longitudinal study, David Furrow and his colleagues (1979) found that children whose mothers spoke the simplest forms of motherese to them during their second year exhibited more well-developed speech in their third year than did children whose mothers had not simplified their speech to the same degree.

However, other researchers have argued that motherese, at least as we know it, is not universal; yet, language acquisition is. Bambi Schieffelin and Elinor Ochs (1983) studied the Kalikuli people of the New Guinea rain forest, who believe that there is no reason to speak to infants who cannot yet speak themselves. In other ways, however, the early language environment of Kalikuli infants may be even richer than that of infants in our culture. Although not spoken to directly, the in-

■ *Evidence that adults' special ways of speaking to young children may assist them in language acquisition*

**Taking account of the listener**

*Most adults automatically simplify their speech when talking to the very young, and children do this, too. Like adults, older children modify the rate at which they speak to younger children, simplify their vocabulary and grammar, and, add broad gestures to reinforce meaning.*

fants go everywhere with their mothers and are constantly surrounded by the speech of adults and children. Once Kalikuli children do begin to speak, adults help them not so much by simplifying their own speech as by explicitly pointing out the proper way to say things. Apparently, a great deal of variability can occur in the LASS without loss of children's ability to learn language. Children's active efforts at acquiring language can be assisted by any of a variety of props that parents and others provide in their special speech to children.

### Teaching Language to Chimpanzees

■ *A brief history of the attempt to talk with chimpanzees*

It is often argued that language is a *uniquely human* ability. How uniquely human is it? Do animals fail to acquire anything like human language because they lack the natural endowment, or do they fail because their environment doesn't provide the right conditions? Most experiments attempting to teach language to animals have used chimpanzees as subjects, because they are the species most closely related to us. Years ago, a husband-and-wife team raised a chimp named Gua in their home, treating her and speaking to her very much the way they did their own child (Kellogg & Kellogg, 1933). They found that until age 3 or so, Gua's nonlinguistic development was comparable to the child's. She passed a number of developmental tests designed for preschool children, but did not learn language (Kellogg, 1968). She responded to simple commands better than a dog would, but did not understand more complex speech and did not produce any words. Similar experiments produced equally discouraging results. The supreme accomplishment was that of Vicki, a chimp raised by another husband-and-wife team (Hayes & Hayes, 1951). After diligent training, Vicki could mouth barely recognizable renditions of four words: *Papa, Mama, cup,* and *up.*

The picture changed during the 1960s, when Allan and Beatrice Gardner (1978), reasoning that chimps' vocal cords are inadequate for speech, began teaching a chimpanzee named Washoe to communicate in American Sign Language (ASL), the standard language used by the deaf (see Figure 12.7). Although it is produced with the fingers rather than the voice, ASL has all the basic characteristics of any natural language, including rules of syntax. Chimpanzees have flexible fingers and are expert mimics, so if they can learn language at all, ASL seems like an ideal

**Figure 12.7** *A signing chimpanzee*
*This chimpanzee, following the tradition of Washoe, has been trained to use American Sign Language. Here the trainer is signing, "What's this?" and the chimpanzee is signing, "Baby."*

**Figure 12.8** *Kanzi using the lexigram keyboard*

*Each symbol is a different word. When the chimpanzee (Kanzi, in this case) depresses a key, it is illuminated, both on the keyboard and on a larger screen that the trainer can see.*

choice. For training, Washoe was surrounded constantly by people who spoke a modified version of ASL to each other and to her. She also received more direct training in the form of operant conditioning and molding of her hands to form appropriate signs. Following Washoe, researchers trained other chimpanzees and a lowland gorilla named Koko to communicate in ASL or in other visual languages (Patterson, 1980; Premack & Premack, 1972). In one of the most extensive series of studies, Sue Savage-Rumbaugh and her colleagues taught several chimps a language in which geometric figures on a keyboard, called *lexigrams*, were used as words (see Figure 12.8) (Savage-Rumbaugh & Rumbaugh, 1980).

To what extent have these animals learned language? The answer keeps changing. From the time that the Gardners published their first findings until about 1979, many people believed that the chimpanzees were saying all kinds of wonderful things. Some even suggested that one might soon answer questions such as, "What is it like to be a chimpanzee?" Edited films of their languagelike behavior appeared on *Nova* and other television programs, and the world was impressed. But in 1979 Herbert Terrace and his colleagues at Columbia University began to raise hard questions about the animals' accomplishments. Terrace's group argued that signing by their chimpanzee, whose training in ASL was similar to Washoe's, could not properly be called language. The chimp showed no evidence of syntax and seemed to use signs almost entirely as operant responses—that is, as tools to gain immediate rewards—rather than as symbols to refer to objects or events in the environment. Terrace had named his chimp Neam Chimpsky (nicknamed Nim) to poke gentle fun at the linguist Noam Chomsky, a leading advocate of the view that only humans can learn language. But in the end, ironically, Terrace used Chimpsky to argue that Chomsky was more right than wrong. He challenged other researchers to prove that their chimps had rules of syntax and were really using signs as symbols. Such proof was not immediately forthcoming—at least not in a form that convinced the skeptics. Interest in chimp language began to fade.

Then, around 1984, interest was stirred again, principally by papers from Savage-Rumbaugh's laboratory in Atlanta. Savage-Rumbaugh took Terrace's criticisms seriously, and through painstaking experiments showed that her chimpanzees had acquired at least some rudiments of true symbolic usage, although she admitted their lack of syntax. Most interesting were her reports of accomplishments of a young pygmy chimpanzee named Kanzi, who seemed to be learning language in a way that no previous chimp had. Pygmy chimpanzees (*Pan paniscus*) are a different species from common chimpanzees (*Pan trolodytes*), and there is reason to believe that they are better communicators in their natural environment and therefore better candidates for learning a humanlike language (Susman, 1984). Washoe, Nim, and the others were common chimpanzees.

**Language Learning in Common Chimpanzees Compared to Human Children**
We will return to Kanzi shortly. First, it would be useful to contrast language learning in children with the linguistic accomplishments of common chimpanzees (based on Brown, 1986; Savage-Rumbaugh, 1984; Savage-Rumbaugh & others, 1983; Terrace, 1985; and Terrace & others, 1980):

■ *Four differences between language learning in chimpanzees and in human children*

■ *Motivation and ease of language learning* Children learn language eagerly and easily while interacting with adults who haven't given a shred of thought to how to teach it. We cannot even prevent children from learning language unless we lock them in closets. Chimps, in contrast, do not acquire language without deliberate training. They usually need constant prodding and rewards or they lose interest. The most skilled language users among common chimpanzees have received daily training for a half-dozen years or more, usually by a battery of skilled trainers, and yet their highest linguistic accomplishments do not approach those of a 3-year-old child.

■ *Functions of language* Children use language primarily to communicate their thoughts and experiences to other people. A 3-year-old who out of the blue says to her mother, "Yesterday, Mrs. Webster showed me the hugest and most beautiful apple," is not asking for anything. She is simply sharing an experience. Chimpanzees rarely if ever use language to share experiences, and never comment spontaneously on past experiences. They appear to use language almost completely as operant responses for immediate rewards. When they talk about apples, they usually say in one way or another, "Gimme apple." On the other hand, after extensive training they can use words to refer to objects that are not immediately present. For example, they can specify which of several absent foods they want before going to another room and selecting the specified food (Savage-Rumbaugh, 1984). This, argues Savage-Rumbaugh, is evidence that their words are true symbols.

■ *Length of utterance* Most chimpanzee statements remain at one or two words long, and the longer statements that do occasionally occur are highly redundant strings of words. For example, Nim's longest statement was translated as, "Give orange me give eat orange me eat orange give me eat orange give me you" (quoted by Brown, 1986). In contrast, children's utterances grow systematically in length as they gain in language competence, and when they produce long sentences the additional words usually provide additional meaning.

■ *Syntax* To date, there is little evidence that chimpanzees use syntax in creating or understanding sentences. In certain kinds of tests they can show sensitivity to word order, but they do not generalize the rules to new situations, and no chimp has acquired or invented a rule for distinguishing plural from singular nouns, for marking the tense of verbs, or for marking words by grammatical class.

■ *How recent findings with a pygmy chimp suggest that this species may be more capable than common chimps of humanlike language*

**Kanzi, the Pygmy Chimp**   Kanzi seems to have learned language differently from common chimpanzees. Raised in Savage-Rumbaugh's lab, he picked up the meaning of about thirty lexigrams just by watching his mother undergo training at the keyboard system shown in Figure 12.8. When he was finally allowed to use the keyboard himself, he was not rewarded for producing lexigrams, nor was he guided to particular lexigrams as other chimps had been. Rather, like a child he was provided with constant human companionship and was free but not forced to communicate using either the stationary keyboard or a portable one that he could carry around. Unlike other chimps, Kanzi seemed to use lexigrams for purposes other than to get rewards (Savage-Rumbaugh & others, 1985, 1986; Savage-Rumbaugh, 1987). For example, he would use the lexigram for apple *after* being given an apple, not just to ask for one. He would also routinely announce his intentions before acting. For example, before taking a trip to the treehouse he would press the lexigram for *treehouse*. In addition, Kanzi routinely combined lexigrams with his own system of gestures to produce rather complex statements. Thus, if he wanted to get caretaker *A* to chase caretaker *B*, he would press the lexigram for *chase* and then push caretaker *A*'s hand in the direction of caretaker *B*.

Still, however, obvious differences remain between Kanzi's language learning and that of a child. Kanzi received much more careful linguistic attention from caretakers than a child receives. Though rewards were not used deliberately in training, still (from my reading of the reports) Kanzi's language seems primarily oriented toward getting his caretakers to do what he wants them to do—to accompany him to the treehouse, to play games of chase, and so on. Children, of course, use language for such purposes, but they also use it to talk about things that are not part of their ongoing activity—about past and imaginary events, for example. Another difference is that Kanzi, like other chimpanzees, shows no consistent use of syntactic rules.

The attempts to teach language to chimpanzees are interesting for a variety of reasons: They teach us something about the cognitive abilities of an intelligent animal that is closely related to us and rapidly becoming extinct; they have resulted in ideas about ways of teaching language to severely retarded and linguistically handicapped human beings; and they have stimulated thinking about the nature of language. What are the criteria by which we decide whether a chimpanzee or any other creature (including a young child) has or has not acquired language? If we say it is referential use of symbols, then we would probably conclude that some chimpanzees have acquired language, but barely. If we say it is syntax, then we would probably conclude that they haven't. It will be fun to see what future chimps will say (Kanzi, incidentally, has a younger sister who is picking up language at a rapid rate), but my guess is that we will remain alone on earth as the only animals who can carry on a really interesting conversation.

# Development of Logical Thought

As children grow, their thinking becomes ever more logical, ever more effective in solving problems. How can these changes be characterized, and what are the processes through which they develop? In considering that question, we will first examine Piaget's research and theory on the growth of logical thought, and then we will turn to two other perspectives on the same issue—the information-processing and sociocultural perspectives.

## Piaget's Studies of Reasoning in Children

If asked who has had the greatest influence on the study of cognitive development, most psychologists would name Jean Piaget. In his long career at the University of Geneva (from the 1920s until his death in 1980), Piaget wrote more than fifty books and hundreds of articles on children's reasoning. He referred to himself as a *genetic epistemologist* (Piaget, 1970). *Epistemology* is the study of the structure of human knowledge, and the term *genetic* as used here refers to the origin and development of something. Thus, genetic epistemology is the study of the origin and development of the structure of knowledge that comprises the human mind. Piaget's goal was to understand how the adult mind—particularly the adult ability to reason objectively about the world—develops out of the more primitive abilities of the child. His basic approach was to ask children to solve specific problems and to explain the reasons for the solutions they offered.

In the following sections I will first describe some of the reasoning tasks that Piaget studied and then turn to his theory. Earlier in the chapter you read of the hiding tasks that Piaget used with infants; now we will examine some tasks he used with older children. As we discuss each task, think about how it tests an ability that is important for everyday adult reasoning.

■ *How Piaget tested children for egocentrism, conservation, cause-effect understanding, and hypothetico-deductive reasoning; and his general findings for different age groups*

**Egocentrism**    A little boy walks into the kitchen, stares into a bowl of what looks like butterscotch pudding, and starts the following loud "conversation" with his mother, who is upstairs, out of sight:

> **Child:** *Mommy, what's this?*
> **Mother:** *What?*
> **Child:** *What's this?*
> **Mother:** *What's what?*
> **Child** (holding up the bowl): *What's <u>this</u>?*
> **Mother:** *I don't know what you're talking about. What's what?*
> **Child** (plunging his hands into the bowl): *Never mind.*

This breakdown in communication is an example of the kind of observation that led Piaget to suggest that young children, up to the ages of about 5 to 7, are *egocentric*. By egocentric, he did not mean "selfish," but rather meant that young children are unable to take the perspective of another person, are unable to realize that others don't necessarily see or know what they see or know. The little boy apparently doesn't realize that his mother can't see what he sees. Piaget's evidence for egocentrism came partly from listening to children's conversations (Piaget, 1923) and partly from testing their judgments of what others see. In his classic *three-mountains experiment*, children were allowed to view the table-top scene depicted in Figure 12.9 from each side, and then, while on one side, were asked to choose a picture showing what the scene would look like to someone on another side. Most 4- and 5-year-olds did not choose the correct picture, but instead chose the picture that looked like the scene from their own side of the table (Piaget & others, 1948).

**Figure 12.9 *Piaget's three-mountains task***

*The child, sitting in position 1, is asked which depiction (1, 2, or 3) shows what a person on the opposite side of the table would see. Young children typically choose 1, a result that Piaget took as evidence of egocentrism.*

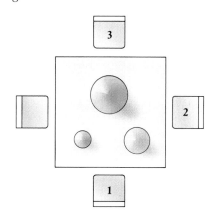

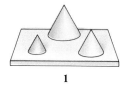
1

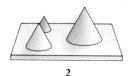
2

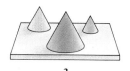
3

**Conservation** A little girl climbs to the top of a table and announces gleefully that now she is bigger than her father. Is she joking, or does she really believe it? If Piaget is right, she really believes it. He argued that young children have an immature concept of quantities such as number, length, width, weight, and volume. In particular, they do not understand principles of *conservation*, which specify that changes in the superficial appearance of objects do not change certain measures of the object. For example, if one object is smaller than another, it remains smaller no matter how far it is lifted off the ground.

***A nonconserver***

*Sarah, here aged 5³/4, cannot yet pass Piaget's test of conservation. Even though she knows the short glasses contain the same amount of milk and carefully watches the milk being poured into the tall glass, she still points to the tall glass when asked, "Which has more?"*

Piaget's most famous conservation experiments concern the principle that changing the shape of a substance does not change the amount of that substance (see Figure 12.10 for this and some other conservation tasks). In a typical experiment, two identical balls of clay are presented, and the child states correctly that they each contain the same amount of clay. Then, while the child watches, one ball is rolled into a sausage shape and the child is asked if it now contains the same

**Figure 12.10** *Tests of children's understanding of conservation*
*Children usually succeed on conservation of number and length tests before they succeed on conservation of substance tests.*

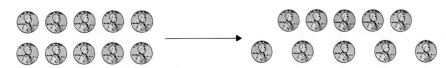

In conservation of number tests, two equivalent rows of coins are placed side by side and the child says that there is the same number in each row. Then one row is spread apart and the child is again asked if there is the same number in each.

In conservation of length tests, two same-length sticks are placed side by side and the child says that they are the same length. Then one is moved and the child is again asked if they are the same length.

In conservation of substance tests, two identical amounts of clay are rolled into similar-appearing balls and the child says that they both have the same amount of clay. Then one ball is rolled out and the child is again asked if they have the same amount.

amount of clay as the other. Children under the age of 6 or 7 usually answer that the sausage has more clay than the ball, because it is longer. In another version of the experiment, children are shown two identical glasses filled to the same level with water, and then—after the child correctly says that the amount of water is the same in each—the water in one is poured into a thinner, taller glass. Even though they see the water being poured, and admit that no new water has been added, children younger than about age 7 report that the taller glass contains more water. The child fails to understand that the amount of a substance cannot change if nothing is added to or subtracted from it.

**Cause-Effect Relationships** An important premise of adult reasoning is that events don't just happen; something has to make them happen. If the light in your room goes on, you know that someone must have pushed the light switch. You also know that there must be some sort of physical connection between the switch and the light to mediate this effect. Very young children, even infants, will push switches to turn lights on and off, showing great delight in their ability to control the environment. But does this imply that they have an adult's understanding of causality? According to Piaget (1926, 1927), it does not.

One line of evidence for this came from experiments in which Piaget asked children to complete sentence stems ending in *because*. He found that children younger than age 7 or 8 tended to complete these sentences in a way that represented the order in which events happened, not a causal relationship. For example, if given the stem *The girl fell off her bicycle because . . .* , a child might complete it with *. . . she broke her arm*. In other experiments, Piaget asked children about cause-effect mechanisms and found that young children couldn't answer and usually didn't see the relevance of the questions. When asked whether a bicycle would still work if the chain were removed, children younger than age 7 or 8 commonly said yes; and those who said no were equally likely to say so when Piaget asked about an inessential part such as the fender. At this age, according to Piaget, children are

practitioners, not scientists. They can make things like bicycles work, but they do not think about mechanisms. Six-year-olds who ask how a car goes are satisfied with the answer that when you press the gas pedal the car moves. Nine- or ten-year-olds, in contrast, want to know *why* pressing the pedal makes the car go—what the connection is between the pedal and the wheels.

**Hypothetico-Deductive Reasoning**  A biologist interested in the growth of tumor cells first thinks of all the factors known to produce cell growth, and then systematically tests each of the factors and their combinations on batches of tumor cells. A detective seeking the murder weapon first thinks of all the weapons that could have created the observed wound, and then searches for clues to confirm or deny each possibility. According to Piaget, this ability to generate and systematically test hypotheses first surfaces in the child from about age 11 to 13. In one experiment, Piaget gave children four flasks containing colorless liquids and a fifth flask containing an indicator liquid that would produce a color when combined with specific other chemicals (Inhelder & Piaget, 1958). After explaining that a combination of one or more of the four liquids with the indicator would yield a yellow color, he asked the children to try to produce that color. Children under about age 11 usually failed, because their trials were unsystematic. Older children succeeded by trying each combination in a logical, exhaustive sequence until they produced the yellow color.

A 9-year-old may be a tinker, an empirical scientist who can make discoveries about mechanisms by observing them, but according to Piaget it takes a 13-year-old to be a theorist. According to Piaget, the primary difference between the 9- and the 13-year-old is that the younger child can think only of that which *is*, whereas the older one can think of that which *is possible*. The mind of the younger child is bound by the concrete here-and-now, but no such barriers occur in the mind of the adolescent. By thinking of that which is possible, the older child can think of the logical possibilities before trying them, can test them systematically, and can draw generalized conclusions on the basis of observed results.

### Piaget's Theory of Mental Development

In the discussion of infancy, you read that Piaget believed that the roots of knowledge lie in action. At first, infants understand objects only in terms of their reflexive responses to them. As they gain more control of their movements, they develop schemes of voluntary action toward objects, such as a sucking scheme toward a pacifier or a grasping and shaking scheme toward a rattle. These schemes, which can be thought of as the mental blueprints controlling the actions, are the infants' only way of knowing the world. According to Piaget, as a child grows older new kinds of schemes develop that are less tied to actual physical movements or to the immediate environment and are more related to abstract ideas about possible movements in possible environments. Thus, Piaget believed that the mind develops through a succession of stages, each distinguished from the previous one by a new kind of scheme that permits a more sophisticated form of thought.

**Four Stages of Cognitive Development** Piaget divided the life span into four stages, each characterized by a new kind of scheme that has been built through the child's experiences in the stage that precedes it. A person cannot enter one stage without having gone through the previous one, and thus the sequence of the stages is invariant, though there can be considerable variation in the rate at which the person goes through them.

1. *Sensorimotor stage* (*birth to about 2 years old*) This stage (as described earlier) is the period before the child has any well-developed mental symbols, so thought is limited primarily to the infant's actual actions on objects that are present. The major task in this stage is to internalize schemes of action so they can begin to occur purely mentally without actual muscle movement. As schemes are increasingly internalized, infants develop the ability to think of objects that are not present and to act in purposeful ways toward goals that are not present. The development of language reflects a similar change. Earliest words are part of the infant's action toward objects that are present, but gradually the child comes to use words also to symbolize absent objects.

2. *Preoperational stage* (*about 2 to 7 years old*) As children become mentally free from strict control by the here-and-now, they enter the preoperational stage, which is characterized by a well-developed ability to symbolize the static qualities of objects and events. Now the child has no difficulty thinking about absent objects, and delights in developing new symbols to represent them. Put a saucepan into the hands of a preschooler and it is magically transformed into a ray gun or guitar—the saucepan becomes a symbol in the child's play.

   Yet, according to Piaget, severe limitations remain on the ways in which preoperational children can think. The schemes of this stage are named in a negative way—they are *pre*operational. Preoperational children can fully appreciate the stable, identifying features of objects, but cannot yet think *operationally*, which is to say that they cannot think logically about certain kinds of actions (operations) that can be performed on objects. For example, if you roll

**Piaget's theory of four stages in the development of schemes**

**The sensorimotor stage**

*According to Piaget's theory, this intent 11-month-old is expanding her understanding of the world by learning about the basic properties of objects. As she plays with the hollow blocks, she is probably assimilating a "fits inside" scheme into an existing "stacking" scheme.*

### The preoperational stage

*This preschooler, mixing a plastic salad, is engaged in the kind of pretend activity that helps children learn to make mental transformations. During their progression through the preoperational stage, children's symbolic substitutions become increasingly sophisticated.*

a ball of clay into a sausage shape, preoperational children notice the characteristics of the ball and the sausage, but do not understand fully the operation through which the ball was changed into the sausage. They are not aware that the shapes contain the same amount of clay if none was added or subtracted, and thus they fail in Piaget's test of conservation. Their answers to questions are based on superficial appearance and intuition, not logic about the nature of change. Although (or perhaps because) preoperational children do not fully understand change, they actively and continuously produce changes in the environment—pushing, pulling, squeezing, and in other ways manipulating objects to see what happens. Through this process they gradually develop schemes that include an understanding of change, and this development brings them into the next stage.

3. **Concrete-operational stage** (*about 7 to 12 years old*) According to Piaget, true logic begins when children can think about and understand **operations**. As defined by Piaget, an operation is a *reversible action*, that is, an action that can be undone by another action. Rolling a clay ball into a sausage is an operation because it can be reversed by rolling it back into the ball. Turning a light on by pushing a switch up is an operation because it can be reversed by pushing the switch back down. Children in the preoperational stage can perform such operations, but cannot yet represent them mentally. When they can, they are said to have *concrete-operational schemes*, and a whole battery of new reasoning abilities emerges. Such schemes are mental representations of the operations that can be performed on specific (concrete) objects in the world.

### The concrete-operational stage

*According to Piaget, thought is increasingly logical during middle childhood, but it still depends on the presence of real objects. Puzzles, like the one these 9- to 12-year-olds are solving, offer concrete opportunities for thinking through alternatives and tracing the steps to a solution.*

According to Piaget, the power of operational schemes lies in their reversibility. Because concrete-operational children can imagine rolling the clay sausage back into the same ball that it was before, they know that the sausage must consist of the same clay, in the same amount, as did the ball. Thus, they are prepared to understand, at least as applied to clay, the principle of conservation of amount. Similarly, reversibility permits an understanding of physical causation. The child who can imagine that pushing a light switch back down will restore the whole physical set-up to its previous state has the basis for understanding the cause-effect relationship between the switch and the light. Reversibility also provides the basis for transcending egocentrism. Consider, again, Piaget's three-mountains task. Moving to the other side of the table is an operation that transforms the view in a manner that can be reversed by moving back to the original side. Because concrete-operational children can perform that operation mentally, they understand that the same scene can look different to people viewing it from different sides. The reversibility of operational schemes allows a person to manipulate knowledge mentally without losing track of its original form, which to Piaget is a prerequisite for all logical reasoning.

Although concrete-operational children have come a long way in the direction of logic, their cognitive development is not yet complete. Piaget used the term *concrete* to describe the schemes of this stage because he believed that they are still tied closely to the child's actual experiences, either past or present, in the real world. The child can think about the kinds of things that he or she has experienced, but not about hypothetical things.

4. **Formal-operational stage** (*about 12 years old through adulthood*)  The last stage in Piaget's theory, the formal-operational stage, begins near the onset of adolescence. Now schemes are independent of specific, concrete experiences. Formal-operational adolescents can reason about abstract concepts and hypothetical ideas. They can apply operational thinking to actions that are not reversible in actual experience but are in theory. You cannot really unbeat an egg, but if you are a formal-operational reasoner, you can understand the theoretical principle that an egg can be unbeaten and restored to its original form. Thus, you can answer correctly conservation questions about a beaten egg as well as about a rolled-out piece of clay: "Is the amount of egg more, less, or the same after it has been beaten as before?" Formal-operational schemes allow adolescents to think of hypothetical possibilities and to plan logical courses of action in realms that they have never previously explored concretely. Formal mathematics and theoretical science become possible in this period, whereas only arithmetic and empirical (fact-based) science were possible before.

*The formal-operational stage*

*These young people are part of a recent campaign to fight drug and alcohol abuse. The idealism that attracts adolescents to social and political movements depends in part on their ability to imagine hypothetical possibilities, which is part of formal-operational thought.*

Whereas the concrete-operational child can attend only to the substance of an argument, the formal-operational adolescent can attend also to the *form* of the argument. Consider the following syllogism: *If all animals can fly, and if all rhinoceroses are animals, then all rhinoceroses can fly.* Concrete-operational reasoners will test this statement against their personal experience with rhinoceroses and conclude at once that it is false. Formal-operational reasoners, realizing that this is a question about logic, not about rhinoceroses, will accept the empirically false initial premise as a given, note the internal validity of the argument, and conclude that the statement is true.

*How the mind in Piaget's theory is more like a spider's web than a brick wall: The meaning of assimilation and accommodation*

**How Schemes Develop: Assimilation and Accommodation**    You have just read Piaget's theory of stages in the growth of mental schemes. How do these changes occur? According to Piaget, the child's own activities and thoughts within each stage serve constantly to stretch and expand the schemes that predominate at that stage, resulting eventually in a revolutionary change and hence transition into the next stage. This growth of schemes involves two complementary processes: assimilation and accommodation.

*Assimilation* is the process by which experiences are incorporated into existing schemes. It is basically an act of recognition. If you encounter a new object and can match it to an existing scheme, you have assimilated that object into the scheme. For example, if right now you were to see an Australian terrier, you would in some way recognize it even if you had never seen one before, because it would fit at least roughly with one or more of your schemes for small dogs. Just how you assimilated this new object, however, would depend on the kinds of schemes you have available. If you are a dog lover, you might assimilate the terrier as a friendly pet, a companion for play; otherwise, you might assimilate it as a noisy, biting creature to be avoided. Piaget was a biologist by training, and he considered the assimilation of experiences by the mind to be analogous to the assimilation of food by the body. Two people may eat the same food, but the food will be assimilated into the tissues differently depending on the inner structures that are involved in digestion and building the body. Just as nondigestible foods will not result in body growth, new experiences that are too different from existing schemes will not result in mental growth. A hand calculator given to a very young child will not contribute to the child's arithmetic skills, but the child may assimilate the calculator into another scheme. An infant would probably suck on it and a toddler might pound with it. Each child would have assimilated the calculator into his or her scheme that best matched that object.

The complement of assimilation is *accommodation*, defined as the change that occurs in an existing scheme or set of schemes as a result of having assimilated a particular event or object. Few stimuli fit perfectly with existing schemes, and as a result the existing mental structure must modify itself somewhat. The modification is accommodation. The mind is not like a brick wall, which only grows bigger as each new brick (unit of knowledge) is added; it is more like a spider's web, which changes its entire shape somewhat as each new thread is added. The web accommodates to the thread while the thread is assimilated into the web. The addition of new information to the mind changes somewhat the structure of schemes that are already present. Consider an infant who in play discovers that a cup placed on top of an open box will fall inside the box. Perhaps the child already had a scheme for stacking objects, which included the notion that one object placed on top of another will remain on top. But now that scheme must be modified to accommodate this new experience; it must now include the notion that if one object is hollow and open-topped, another object placed upon it may fall inside. At the same time, other schemes that include the notion that two objects cannot occupy the same place at the same time may also undergo accommodation; mental growth has occurred. In Piaget's view, children are most fascinated by those experiences that can be assimilated into existing schemes but not too easily, so that accommodation is required. This natural tendency leads children to direct their own play in ways that maximize their mental growth.

**Criticisms of Piaget's Theory**   To accept anyone's findings and theories as dogma runs counter to the nature of science: Findings are to be replicated, theories challenged. Piaget—like Freud, Skinner, and others who have attempted to build strong, explicit, wide-ranging theories in psychology—has been challenged on many counts. Here are some of the most common criticisms of his work:

■ *Three major criticisms of Piaget's theory of cognitive development*

■ *Lack of clear evidence for qualitatively different stages* The most dramatic and interesting claim of Piaget's theory is that children develop through stages in which they think in qualitatively different ways from the ways they think in other stages. If that claim is true, mental development should be characterized by periods of rapid change, when whole new constellations of abilities emerge more or less at once, followed by periods of relative stability (refer back to Figure 12.1). But the bulk of evidence seems to contradict this prediction. For example, the ability to solve conservation problems does not appear suddenly, but rather develops gradually over a period of several years. Most children can solve conservation-of-number tasks by age 5 but can't solve conservation-of-substance tasks until about age 8 (Gross, 1985).

Similarly, success or failure in seeing from another person's perspective in tests of egocentrism depends on the specific task. Piaget's three-mountains problem is hard; it is hard to visualize what the three-dimensional scene would look like from the other side, so children may give up and say that it looks the same from there as it does from their own side. Most children don't solve this problem until about age 8. But even 3-year-olds commonly solve a similar problem in which they view a card with a picture of a cat on one side and a dog on the other (Masangkay & others, 1974). When viewing the dog, they say correctly that a person on the other side of the card sees the cat.

Piaget was aware that children succeed at some tasks sooner than they do at other tasks in any given problem area—he even gave this phenomenon a name: *horizontal décalage*. He understood that the stage transitions are not sharp in the sense that all new abilities that depend on the new kind of schemes emerge at once. But Piaget's critics argue that the changes occur over such a long span—that each stage blurs so completely into the next—that the stage concept loses any real meaning. Research on adult problem solving (discussed in Chapter 11) further challenges Piaget's idea of qualitatively different ways of thinking. This research suggests that so-called formal reasoning is not qualitatively different from concrete reasoning. People who are good at solving abstract problems usually do so by thinking of analogies to more familiar problems, or by turning the problem statement into a familiar visual image, thereby converting what seems to be a formal task into a concrete one.

■ *Vagueness about the process of change, and problems with the tie between schemes and action* Some critics argue that Piaget's theory of the process of change is too vague, too general, too distanced from the behavioral data. What really is a scheme? What information must a scheme have in order, say, to permit a child to succeed in the conservation-of-clay problem? What exactly changes when assimilation and accommodation occur? Theorists in the information-processing tradition (to be described below) believe that theories of mental development should be much more explicit than Piaget's in their links to the actual behavioral improvements that they are designed to explain.

Piaget's emphasis on the relation of schemes to action also creates a problem. When Piaget speaks of action as the basis for mental development, he seems to mean that quite literally. The child acquires new knowledge by physically manipulating things in the physical environment. Yet, babies born without arms and legs, or with an inability to move them, develop normal cognition despite their relative lack of ability to act physically on the environment (Jordan, 1972). Also, as Kagan (1984) has pointed out, the theory doesn't explain how a 2-year-old can understand terms such as *you, is, like,* and *why* that refer to abstract concepts unrelated to specific actions.

■ *Underestimation of the role of the social environment* Piaget tends to see the child as a lone scientist discovering anew the basic laws of nature through experiments on the physical world. As you will see, theorists in the sociocultural tradition argue that mental development occurs largely through interaction with other people, not through solo interaction with nature.

Despite the criticisms, Piaget's work is greatly admired by most developmental psychologists today. He pioneered new ways of learning about children's thought, and he boldly set forth theories that stimulated others to conduct new research and develop new theories about the mind's growth. Perhaps the most admired of Piaget's contributions today is his great emphasis on the idea that children actively promote their own mental development. Given the opportunity, children select from their environments those stimuli and problems that are sufficiently challenging to their present ways of thinking—that is, whose assimilation requires just enough accommodation—to help advance their thought to new levels. This comes not from a conscious concern about educating themselves, but from a natural tendency to be interested in that which is challenging but not too challenging.

### The Information-Processing Perspective

■ *How the information-processing perspective on cognitive development differs from Piaget's*

Cognitive developmentalists who adopt the information-processing perspective treat the mind not as a single, global entity, as did Piaget, but rather as a set of interacting components. Their general goal is to relate specific changes in children's problem-solving abilities to specific changes in one or another of the mind's components. They do this by trying to describe explicitly the logical requirements of the task, on the one hand, and the change that has occurred in the child's mind, on the other.

As described in Chapters 10 and 11, the information-processing approach to cognition begins with the assumption that the mind is a system, analogous to a computer, for analyzing (processing) information from the environment. One way to divide the mind in information-processing terms is to think of it as containing a set of (a) *memory stores,* which hold on to information for either a short or prolonged period; (b) *control processes,* which move information from one store to another or manipulate it within a given store; and (c) *processing rules,* which are acquired from experience, for dealing with specific kinds of information or solving specific kinds of problems. Cognitive development might stem from changes in any or all of these components.

**Increased Capacity of Short-term Memory**   The standard information-processing model (shown in Figure 10.1) distinguishes among three memory stores: (1) a transient *sensory store* that holds sensory memory briefly while attentional mechanisms operate to bring some of it into the next store; (2) a *short-term store,* also called working memory, that holds information that is presently being thought about; and (3) a *long-term store,* which is the repository of all of one's knowledge that is not at the moment being thought about. Our concern here is with the short-term store, because that is where conscious thought occurs, and because limitations on the short-term store seem to provide an important constraint on one's ability to solve problems. To solve a problem, a person must be able to hold and manipulate in short-term memory all of the relevant information.

***The growth of memory***
*Research suggests that experience affects the development of children's memory strategies. In many cultures, a crucial experience is formal schooling, where children must often memorize material on which they will be tested.*

■ *How a continuous increase in the capacity of short-term memory could, in theory, produce stagelike development in problem-solving ability*

■ *Evidence that the developmental increase in short-term memory capacity could result more from experience than maturation*

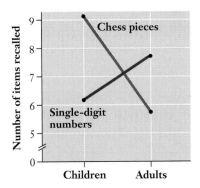

**Figure 12.11** *Short-term memory in 10-year-old chess experts compared to adult novices*

*When tested for short-term memory for the location of chess pieces on a chess board, the 10-year-old experts performed better than adults who were novices at chess. When the same groups were tested for short-term memory for single-digit numbers, the adults performed better than the children. (Adapted from Chi, 1978.)*

Some years ago, a mathematically oriented psychologist, Juan Pascual-Leone (1970), proposed that the most fundamental change underlying cognitive development is a gradual, maturational increase in the capacity of short-term memory, which he referred to as *M space* (mental space). Pascual-Leone and others working with this theory showed mathematically how the stages posited by Piaget could be accounted for by a gradual (not stagelike) change in *M* space (Case & others, 1982). Certain kinds of intellectual tasks require a particular amount of *M* space (just as certain computer programs require a particular amount of computer memory), and children will be able to perform such tasks only when they have matured to the point where they have enough *M* space. Pascual-Leone and his colleagues devised ways to estimate the amount of *M* space required for various Piagetian tasks, and they suggested that the tasks used to mark the onset of Piaget's concrete-operational stage all require about the same amount.

In line with Pascual-Leone's theory, measures of short-term memory capacity do increase with age throughout childhood. When asked to repeat after a brief delay a string of digits or letters that was presented just once, a typical 5-year-old can repeat about four, an 11-year-old can repeat about six, and an adult can repeat seven or eight (Chi, 1978). However, researchers disagree about the underlying cause of the improvement. Robbie Case and Pascual-Leone believe that the improvement is due to a maturational change in the brain that is independent of experience, but they supply no direct evidence for this. Equally plausible is the idea that memory improves because children acquire better strategies for keeping items in mind, or because they become more familiar with the memory items.

One bit of evidence for the latter view comes from an experiment by Michelene Chi (1978) that compared memory abilities of 10-year-old chess experts with those of adults who were novices at chess. The children outperformed the adults in memory for the locations of chess pieces on a chess board that they had briefly examined, and the adults outperformed the children in memory tests unrelated to chess (see Figure 12.11). Presumably, the children developed their superior chess memories through their greater experience with the game, which allowed them to acquire efficient ways to represent chess pieces mentally. By the same token, the adults might have acquired their superior memory in other realms through their greater experience in those realms.

**Improved Control Processes**   One important control process for solving problems is *selective attention*, the ability to focus on the relevant information and screen out the irrelevant. Several experiments have demonstrated that this ability improves with age. In one, children had to judge whether pairs of objects were the same or different in shape, color, or size, and it was found that sixth graders were better than second graders at focusing on the right dimension of comparison (Pick & others, 1972). For example, when their job was to answer questions based on shape, the sixth graders were less distracted than the second graders by differences or similarities in the objects' color or size.

Other important control processes that improve with age include strategies for keeping information in short-term memory and encoding it into long-term memory. In memory tests, even the simple act of rote rehearsal is less likely to occur in younger children than in older children. In one experiment, John Flavell and his colleagues (1966) observed lip movements as a sign of rehearsal during a memory task in children aged 5 to 10. Older children showed more lip movements and better performance on the memory test than younger children, and within each age group those who moved their lips showed better memory than those who didn't. Not surprisingly, other studies have shown that the use of more sophisticated memory strategies, such as chunking and elaborative rehearsal (discussed in Chapter 10), also increases with age (see Kail, 1984).

**Acquiring Specific Rules to Solve Specific Classes of Problems**   In contrast to Piaget's view that wide varieties of problems can be solved through the application of general principles of logic when the appropriate stage has been reached, information-processing theorists argue that specific rules must be learned for solving specific categories of problems. Consider, for example, the task of judging which side of a balance beam will tilt down when different numbers of weights are placed at varying distances on the two sides of the fulcrum (see Figure 12.12). This was one of the tasks that Piaget commonly used to test formal-operational thinking. More recently, from an information-processing perspective, Robert Siegler (1983) has described performance on this task in terms of rules that are specific just to this kind of problem.

**Figure 12.12   Sample balance-beam problems used by Siegler**

*Children and adolescents were told that each ring was the same weight and that the pegs were spaced equally distant apart from each other on each side of the fulcrum. The task was to predict which side would tilt down when the beam was released. (Adapted from Siegler, 1983.)*

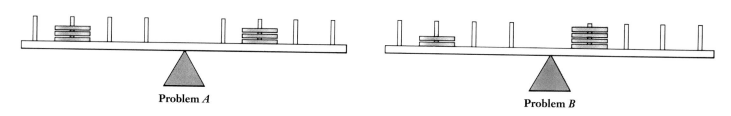

Problem *A*                    Problem *B*

■ *A stage theory that is much narrower than Piaget's: A sequence of rules for trying to solve balance-beam problems*

The ultimate rule for solving balance-beam problems is to multiply the amount of weight on each side by its distance from the fulcrum; the side for which this product is greater is the side that will go down. Siegler found that even among adults only a small minority understood this rule, and that most people responded in accordance with more primitive rules that could be ranked in a sequence directed toward the ultimate rule. More specifically, Siegler found that people performed in accordance with one of four rules. In rule 1, the most primitive, weight alone is taken into account; the person predicts that the end with the most weight will go down. In rule 2, weight alone is used unless the weights are the same, in which case distance is also taken into account. In rule 3, both weight and distance are taken into account, but when these conflict—when weight is greater on one side and distance greater on the other (as in problem B of Figure 12.12)—the person just guesses at which end will go down. Finally, in rule 4, the ultimate rule, judgment is based on weight multiplied by distance. Based on their performance on problem sets that would be solved either correctly or incorrectly by a given rule, nearly everyone whom Siegler tested showed consistent rule use from problem to problem. The errors were not random; rather, they were predictable based on use of one of the four rules. Developmentally, Siegler found that most 5-year-olds behaved according to rule 1; that most 9-year-olds behaved according to rule 2; and that most people ages 13 and up behaved according to either rule 2 or 3, in about equal numbers (Siegler, 1983).

In other experiments, Siegler (1983) allowed children to gain feedback on each trial by releasing the beam (so it could tip freely on its fulcrum) after their response to show them which end would go down. He found that the effect of feedback depended on the type of problem for which it was given. Children who behaved according to rule 1 profited from feedback on problems that disconfirmed rule 1 and confirmed rule 2 (such as problem *A* in Figure 12.12), but did not profit from feedback on problems that disconfirmed both rules 1 and 2 (such as problem *B* in Figure 12.12). From such data, Siegler suggests that children who are at one level of rule use may be prepared to take into account information needed to acquire the next rule in the sequence, but they cannot deal with information that would require them to skip the next rule and go directly to a more advanced one.

Notice that Siegler's account differs from Piaget's not only in its explicitness regarding the mental change, but also in its narrowness regarding the kinds of behaviors that change together. Moving to a higher rule to solve a balance-beam problem would not necessarily move the child to a higher level on conservation problems. Information-processing theorists have a less holistic view of mental development than did Piaget. You can become an expert in certain areas of reasoning and remain a novice in others.

### The Sociocultural Perspective

As its label implies, the sociocultural perspective on cognitive development emphasizes the role of culture and social interaction. The person most often credited with originating this perspective is Lev Vygotsky, a Soviet scholar who died in 1934 at age 38, after devoting just 10 years to formal research and writing in psychology. Vygotsky was well aware of Piaget's research and theory, and agreed with much of it. He agreed that cognitive development can be described in terms of the child's internalization of experiences, and that the main force of development is the child's active interaction with the environment. But he disagreed with Piaget's conception of the relevant environment. Whereas Piaget emphasized the child's interaction with the physical world, Vygotsky emphasized the child's interaction with the social world. Vygotsky argued that children learn even about the physical world through verbal descriptions from other people and through involvement in activities that are guided and interpreted by other people.

In keeping with the philosophy of Karl Marx, Vygotsky viewed the human mind as a product of cultural history. Thus, from his view, one can speak of the mind of a culture—for example, the "American mind" or the "Russian mind." Vygotsky's main question was how children acquire the mind of their culture through their specific interactions with parents, teachers, and other representatives of the culture. He proposed that the child is innately social, eager to communicate with and learn from others, and that adults are equally eager to communicate with and teach the child. He disagreed most strongly with Piaget's view that the child is egocentric, and argued that the child is *most* interested in the thoughts and perspectives of other people. The child's mind grows through interaction with other minds, and the main vehicle of that interaction is language.

**Vygotsky's Theory of the Role of Language in the Development of Thought**
In his book *Thought and Language*, Vygotsky (1934/1962) argued that the human mind exceeds that of other animals primarily because in humans the functions of thought and language come together. Other animals, particularly chimpanzees, can think (they can solve problems by means other than trial and error) and can communicate (through nonverbal means), but their systems for thinking and com-

*How Vygotsky's perspective on cognitive development differs from Piaget's*

*How Vygotsky challenged Piaget's concept of egocentrism, reinterpreted the phenomenon of egocentric speech, and outlined a theory of mental development centering on the internalization of language*

municating remain separate. Nonverbal communication expresses emotions, not thoughts; and when animals think, they do not use their nonverbal signals as aids in their thinking. According to Vygotsky, communication and thought are initially as separate in the human infant as in nonhuman animals, but through development they begin to interact. The child's language becomes increasingly rational (directed by thought) and the child's thought becomes increasingly verbal (making more use of words as mental symbols). This combining of thought and communication is what produces the real distinction between humans and other animals, according to Vygotsky. Without society, children would learn no language and their minds would develop little beyond those of other animals.

Vygotsky directly challenged Piaget's claim that children's speech is not fully communicative until they are about 7 years old. Much of Piaget's evidence had come from listening to children's "conversations" in a kindergarten and noting that each child seemed oblivious to what the other was saying. While working on their separate projects, one child might say, "I'll make it green" (not indicating what he or she would make green), and another might respond, "Horses like sugar and oats." Piaget (1923) referred to such noncommunicative speech as *egocentric speech* and argued that it is just another manifestation of the child's basic egocentrism. Vygotsky did not deny the existence of such speech, but had a very different interpretation of it.

Vygotsky (1934/1962) argued that children use speech in a truly communicative way from the beginning; but at about age 4 they begin to use speech *also* in talking to themselves as an aid in their own thinking, which is what Piaget had observed and labeled egocentric. At first, according to Vygotsky, egocentric speech occurs primarily in a conversational format, because it is not yet fully separated from communicative speech. When Vygotsky observed young children in various settings, he found that they were most likely to use egocentric speech in exactly the kind of situation in which Piaget had observed it—one in which children were physically together but working on separate projects. When children were just sitting and talking, or working on the same project, their speech was far more communicative (and, thus, less egocentric).

According to Vygotsky, egocentric speech declines at around age 7 not because of a decline in egocentrism, but because by then speech is internalized enough that the child can think in words without saying them aloud. Egocentric speech has become *inner speech* (Vygotsky's term) or *verbal thought*. With experience, inner speech becomes increasingly abbreviated such that in older children and adults words are no longer pronounced to the self but are purely mental symbols. According to Vygotsky, this new form of thought is far more powerful than the form of thought the child had before. In internalizing words, children internalize a far richer set of symbols than they could develop on their own. Words are symbols that were developed over the course of history, involving hundreds of generations of human use of language.

Vygotsky agreed with Piaget that a qualitative change in thinking occurs at about age 6 or 7; but whereas Piaget attributed the change to concrete operational schemes, Vygotsky attributed it to the internalization of speech. It is interesting to note that as early as the 1950s, before Vygotsky's ideas were known in the West, some North American psychologists had argued that improved problem solving between ages 5 and 7 may come from the child's increased ability to frame problems in words and to use words in working out a solution. In some experiments, 5- and 6-year-olds were found to perform as well as older children on certain problems when asked to say aloud what they were doing as they worked on the problem, but not otherwise (Kendler, 1972). Consistent with Vygotsky's theory, one interpretation of this finding is that these children were at a transition stage where they could use speech out loud to guide their actions but had not yet fully internalized it as verbal thought.

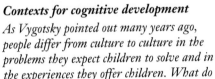

*Contexts for cognitive development*

*As Vygotsky pointed out many years ago, people differ from culture to culture in the problems they expect children to solve and in the experiences they offer children. What do you think these tasks might contribute to cognitive development?*

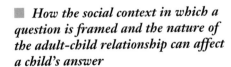
■ *How the social context in which a question is framed and the nature of the adult-child relationship can affect a child's answer*

**The Social Context of Thought and Its Implication in Tests of Logic**   As Katherine Nelson (1986) has pointed out, children spend much of their time involved in social routines, and much of their knowledge of both the social and physical world is embedded in their understanding of those routines. In our culture such routines might include helping a parent clean the house, going shopping with a parent, eating at fast-food restaurants, going to birthday parties, and so on. In another culture they might include helping to weave blankets or accompanying a parent on hunting trips. Each routine has a certain temporal sequence, and the child develops very early a mental representation of each sequence, referred to as a *script* (Schank & Abelson, 1977). Scripts (introduced in Chapter 10) are like Piaget's schemes in that they are internal representations of the child's activities, but unlike schemes they represent activities that (a) have a prolonged temporal sequence, and (b) are usually structured more by the child's social world than by the child himself or herself. Research has shown that even 3-year-olds are able to describe their routine activities quite accurately, indicating that they have acquired the common scripts of their culture (Nelson, 1986).

Other research has shown that children often appear far more logical when they are questioned in ways that allow them to bring their well-learned scripts to bear on the problem than when they are questioned in other ways. In one such experiment, inner-city children performed much better on a Piagetian conservation task when asked to think of what a "slick trickster" might do to fool someone about the amount of a substance than when the problem was presented to them in the more typical Piagetian manner (White & Glick, as described by Nelson, 1986). Apparently, these children did not understand conservation in the context of their scripts involving dialogue with a teacherlike experimenter, but did understand it in the context of more familiar street scripts, where a smooth operator might play the kind of trick that the experimenter was playing.

An important general point of the sociocultural perspective is that to understand intellectual development we must think about more than the logic inherent in the test problems and the logical capacities of the child. We must also think about the social context within which the child's knowledge is embedded. The ultimate function of the mind is not necessarily to be logical, but instead it is to find ways to get along in the social world to which each person must adapt in order to survive. The child acquires logical capacities in the context of that larger purpose, and, from the sociocultural perspective, logic must be understood in relation to that purpose.

## Concluding Thoughts

In concluding this chapter, it might be interesting to think about two different but not mutually exclusive philosophical perspectives on the developing child. One perspective emphasizes the role of the child's own activities and the other emphasizes the role of the social environment.

**1. Development as a product of the child's own activities** Children actively promote their own development. They arrive in the world not as blank tablets to be written on by experience, but as active beings who produce their own experiences. They come with reflexes, some of which develop through maturation and exercise into voluntary behaviors such as walking and manipulating objects. They come also with a natural tendency to be bored by what is too familiar and to look for what is new—a tendency that makes almost every moment a time of learning. You have seen how researchers have capitalized on infants' preference for the new, in experiments aimed at learning about infants' perceptual abilities.

Infants also enter the world with a special interest in language and a biological preparation to go through a period of vocal play that moves them along a path toward the utterance of words. Language—maybe the most cognitively complex body of information that anyone learns in a lifetime—is acquired by young children through their spontaneous interactions with people around them, regardless of whether or not anyone tries to teach it to them. Children who grow up hearing grammarless pidgin languages apparently even invent their own grammar, turning the pidgin into a real language. Piaget's theory of cognitive development centers on the active role of the child. Assimilation—the incorporation of new information into the mind—is, according to Piaget, a process that is necessarily governed by the child. Children direct their attention at any given time to those elements of the environment for which their minds are prepared, and they incorporate the information in whatever way they can understand it at the time.

**2. The dependence of development on the social environment** Although children are active beings who promote their own development, they are at the same time absolutely dependent on the environment into which they are born. All of their innate behavioral drives and abilities are useless without a responsive environment. They need solid surfaces against which to exercise their muscles if they are going to walk; and they need other people with whom to exercise their vocal play if they are going to talk. Infants and children may select what to assimilate from the cafeteria of information around them, but adults provide the cafeteria. Whereas Piaget emphasized the importance of children's own activities, Vygotsky and the sociocultural tradition emphasize the role of the social environment.

In a commentary on Piaget's theory of how children learn about cause-and-effect relationships through manipulating objects in their physical world, Vygotsky (1934/1962) raised the question of whether they would ever learn to understand this concept were it not part of the body of knowledge of their social world, represented in the language that they learn. He pointed out, as had Piaget himself, that children learn the word *because*, and begin to use it in their speech, before they fully understand its meaning. To Piaget the use of the word is incidental to cognitive development; it only reflects the child's understanding or misunderstanding. But to Vygotsky the use of the word is critical to cognitive development. Through using the word *because* in a communicative, social context, the child is forced to think about the word's meaning, and in that way the child acquires a higher way of thinking than would be possible without the benefit of language and the culturally accumulated knowledge represented in its words.

## Further Reading

**Daphne Maurer & Charles Maurer** (1988). *The world of the newborn.* New York: Basic Books.

*This is an excellent description of the abilities of very young infants and the research methods used to learn about them. It is written for the nonspecialist, but is based on research and is well documented. Topics include life in the womb, the process of birth, sensory abilities, motor abilities, and early acquisition of knowledge.*

**Jerome Bruner** (1983). *Child's talk: Learning to use language.* New York: Norton.

*In this slender book, Bruner introduces the concept of the LASS (language-acquisition support system) to complement Chomsky's LAD (language-acquisition device). The book emphasizes the social nature of the child and the communicative role of language. In Bruner's view, the child's desire to understand and be understood, complemented by the same on the part of his or her adult caregivers, is the driving force behind language acquisition.*

**John Flavell** (1985). *Cognitive development* (2nd ed.). Englewood Cliffs, NJ: Prentice Hall.

*This is a brief, clearly written text on cognitive development from infancy through adolescence. The author emphasizes the work and ideas of Piaget and research that has followed Piaget's tradition.*

**Jean Piaget** (1929). *The child's conception of the world.* London: Routledge & Kegan Paul.

*Many of Piaget's books are difficult to read, but this one, written early in his career, is an exception. In the introduction he spells out his method of learning about children's minds through interviewing them about their ideas. The data for this book are children's thoughts on such issues as where the names of things come from, how the sun and moon originated, where rain comes from, and what it means to think. The ideas expressed here provided a basis for much of Piaget's subsequent research.*

**Lev S. Vygotsky** (1934/1962). *Thought and language.* (E. Haufmann & G. Vaker, Eds. and Trans.). Cambridge, MA: MIT Press.

*This book was first published in the Soviet Union in 1934, shortly after Vygotsky's untimely death from tuberculosis at age 38, but was not translated into English until 1962. It is a collection of papers in which Vygotsky set forth his theory that the internalization of language is critical to the development of thought. One chapter is devoted to a critique of Piaget's theory, especially his concept of egocentrism.*

## Looking Ahead

This chapter has been about the development of perception, language, and thought; but you have already seen evidence that such development depends upon the child's social experiences. The next chapter deals specifically with the effects of the social world on the developing individual and is especially concerned with the development of social relationships, responsibility, and personal identity. It also deals with the whole life span, from infancy through old age.

# CHAPTER 13

Perspectives on Social
Development

Infancy: Attachment to Caregivers

Childhood: Becoming Socialized

Adolescence: Finding Oneself

Adulthood: Caring and Working

# SOCIAL DEVELOPMENT

Each of us is born into a social world to which we must adapt. Throughout life we are involved in relationships with other people. During *infancy* we are dependent physically and emotionally on adult caregivers. During *childhood* we learn to get along with other children and to abide by the rules and norms of society. During *adolescence* we begin to explore romantic relationships, and we may also work out a more conscious set of values and life plans. During *adulthood* we play caring roles for family and others, and work at jobs or careers that are an integral part of the social fabric. **Social development** refers to the development of a person's capacity for social relationships and to the effects that these relationships have on further development. In this chapter, after a brief overview of some theories of social development, we will examine the nature and development of social relationships in each phase of life, from infancy through old age.

## Perspectives on Social Development

Theories of social development can be divided roughly into three broad classes. The first class emphasizes the role of mental conflict that is created by the interaction between biologically based drives and the social environment. The second emphasizes the role that cognitive development plays in the person's ways of thinking about and acting in the social environment. The third emphasizes the role of the social environment itself in shaping each person's social behavior.

### Theories Emphasizing Drives and Mental Conflicts

One way to think about social development is to consider that each new person who enters the world is motivated by inborn drives that in some ways conflict with the needs and pressures of society. The most important pioneer in this way of thinking was Sigmund Freud (1856–1939). In Freud's view, each child is born with sexual and aggressive drives and wishes that provide the underlying energy for all of life, and development is a matter of learning to channel those drives in socially acceptable ways. The most important aspects of this learning occur within the first 5 to 6 years, in the child's interactions with parents. Such events as weaning from the breast and toilet training involve conflict between the child's and parents' wishes, and the manner in which such conflicts are resolved can have lifelong effects on the developing person's basic style of interacting with the world. Freud's *psychoanalytic theory* of personality, including its developmental aspect, is fully described in Chapter 16. You will find there that Freud divided the life span into five stages, three of which occur within the first 5 or 6 years of life and are critical to

■ *How Erikson's psychoanalytic theory of development differs from Freud's*

the formation of one's basic personality. In the present chapter we will focus not on Freud's stages, but on those proposed by Erik Erikson.

**Erikson's Theory of Life Stages**  Erikson (1902–   ) was trained in psychoanalysis by Anna Freud, Sigmund Freud's daughter, and has always considered himself to be a Freudian. Yet, Erikson's own theory—although it emphasizes inner drives and conflicts—differs greatly from Freud's. It does not center on sexual and aggressive drives, but instead on a set of *social drives*, which are people's needs to develop various kinds of relationships with others and to establish themselves as useful members of society. Erikson believes that these needs are biologically based and are not simply derived from social experience. The inborn social needs are what make the human being a fundamentally social animal.

Whereas Freud thought that nearly everything important to development happens during the first 5 or 6 years, Erikson (1963) argued that development continues throughout life. He divided the life span into eight stages—referred to as *psychosocial stages* to distinguish them from Freud's psychosexual stages—each of which is associated with a different problem or crisis to be resolved. A new dimension of personality is added at each stage (described in Table 13.1).

**Table 13.1** *Erikson's stages of psychosocial development*

**Stage 1: Basic trust versus mistrust (birth to 1 year)**

The baby enters the world completely at the mercy of others. If the first caregiver (usually the mother) meets the baby's needs dependably, the baby learns to trust that person, and this generalizes into a trust of others and the self.

**Stage 2: Autonomy versus shame and doubt (1 to 3 years)**

As they gain voluntary control of their actions—learning to walk, talk, feed themselves, and so on—young children become increasingly willful, and this runs counter to their parents' desires to control them. The resulting battle of wills is resolved in the direction of *autonomy* if the child acquires a positive sense of self-control. It is resolved in the direction of *shame and doubt* if the child acquires a sense that whatever he or she does is inadequate or bad.

**Stage 3: Initiative versus guilt (3 to 5 years)**

Having gained control of their own actions, children now begin to plan their actions in advance, which leads to a crisis about ability to plan. A positive resolution entails a sense of *initiative* (the ability to plan and initiate new actions), and a negative resolution entails a sense of *guilt* about one's plans and a sense of inability to guide one's own future.

**Stage 4: Industry versus inferiority (5 to 12 years)**

Children become increasingly involved with tasks such as school assignments, chores at home, and self-chosen games and hobbies. The lesson to be learned now is "the pleasure of work completion by steady attention and persevering diligence" (Erikson, 1963), which will promote a sense of competence, or *industry*. Unsuccessful resolution leaves the child with a sense of *inferiority*.

**Stage 5: Identity versus identity confusion (adolescence)**

Identity is the sense of who one is and where one is going in life (Erikson, 1959). Adolescents must lose their identity and establish a new one appropriate for adult life. Successful resolution leaves the person with a *positive identity*, and thus able to function in ways that are beneficial to self and society; unsuccessful resolution leaves the person with either *identity confusion* (lack of a stable identity) or a *negative identity* (one that is unhealthy or antisocial).

**Stage 6: Intimacy versus isolation (young adulthood)**

Intimacy is "the capacity to commit to concrete affiliation and partnership and to develop the ethical strength to abide by such commitments, even though they may call for significant sacrifices and compromises" (Erikson, 1963). Young adulthood is a time for learning to share oneself with another person. A person who fails at this will go through life with a sense of isolation, even if surrounded by other people.

**Stage 7: Generativity versus stagnation (middle adulthood)**

The crisis of this longest stage, from about 25 to 65 years of age, has to do with *generativity*, a sense of contributing to the next generation, which may be met through caring for children, teaching, or work that benefits the community at large. Those who fail at this will fall into *stagnation*, a sense of boredom and meaninglessness.

**Stage 8: Integrity versus despair (late adulthood to death)**

If the person has successfully resolved the previous conflicts, he or she will have a sense of completeness, or *integrity*. The key trait of the integrated person is *wisdom*, an ability to look at life in a more detached way and see broad truths and offer counsel to those still in earlier stages. At the other extreme, failure to resolve the earlier crises may lead to *despair*, a sense of helplessness and bitterness that comes from feeling that life has been incomplete and will end incomplete.

***Erik H. Erikson***

*Erikson is an intellectual nonconformist whose formal academic training ended with high school. His novel views have had a major impact on the study of children's development, and his clear and graceful literary style has made his books accessible to the general public.*

■ ***How cognitive theories link social development to improved reasoning ability***

As you study Table 13.1, notice that the personality dimension for each stage can be described as a continuum between two opposite poles. One pole is positive, strengthening the person and fostering further healthy development, and the other pole is negative, weakening the person and making further healthy development more difficult. Most often, the person resolves the conflict somewhere between the two extremes. For example, an infant usually emerges from the first stage somewhere between the extremes of *basic trust* and *basic mistrust*, neither completely trusting nor completely mistrusting. Notice also how each stage builds directly on the stage preceding it. To a considerable degree, successful resolution of the conflict at one stage is a prerequisite for successful resolution of the conflict at the next. However, Erikson does not believe that all is lost if a person fails to resolve a given crisis in the healthy direction. Given an appropriate social environment, it is possible to reverse the outcomes of previous stages, though such reversals are difficult.

Erikson's theory is important in developmental psychology today partly because of his emphasis on the idea that development continues throughout the life span. His ideas have helped inspire research on adolescent and adult development, as you will see later in this chapter.

### Theories Emphasizing Cognitive Growth

Whereas psychoanalytic theories emphasize the role of instinctive drives and conflicts in the person's development, *cognitive theories* emphasize the role of conscious reasoning. The most explicitly cognitive theories of social development are those influenced by the work of Jean Piaget, whose theory of cognitive development is discussed in Chapter 12. Piaget (1932) argued that changes in children's social behavior and sense of morality are to a considerable degree secondary to changes in their capacity for logical thought.

For example, Piaget argued that a more advanced morality accompanies the shift from the preoperational to the concrete-operational stage of reasoning (which, as discussed in Chapter 12, occurs at about age 7). A child in the preoperational stage, bound by egocentrism (the inability to take another person's perspective) and unable to think in operational terms, cannot fully appreciate the nature of rules. Rules are designed to serve the various needs of different people, so a full understanding of rules requires that a child be able to take into account the perspectives of other people. Also, to understand rules a child must understand something about how they are created. The making of a rule is an example of an operation—it is a reversible transformation (see Chapter 12). Rules can be made and unmade, and they can be changed in various ways as long as people agree to change them. When children transcend egocentrism and understand the nature of operations, they become capable of a more mature understanding of rules. Prior to that, according to Piaget, they behave largely in accordance with direct reward and punishment, coupled with a sense of obligation to follow authority. Later in the chapter, you will read about Lawrence Kohlberg's theory of moral development, which is an elaborate extension of Piaget's theory of moral development.

### Theories Emphasizing the Social Environment

Chapter 16 presents *social learning theories* of personality (such as the one developed by Albert Bandura), which center on the idea that people learn to behave in particular ways in particular social contexts. Applied to development, such theories tend to downplay the importance of inborn drives while accenting the importance of learning. Learning occurs through direct rewards and punishments received for behaving in particular ways in particular contexts, and through observing how others behave in those contexts. Thus, children learn to act one way in church and another way on the playground, in accordance with the social expectations pertaining to each setting.

Social learning theories overlap considerably with cognitive theories. In fact, Bandura (1986) now calls his own theory a *social cognitive theory*. The social environment provides the models and opportunities for experience, but people actively select from the available choices and interpret their experiences, incorporating them into their own growing understanding of the world and ways to behave within it.

**Bronfenbrenner's Social Ecology Theory** In recent years, psychologists who emphasize the importance of the social environment in development have paid increasing attention to the differences among the social environments provided by different cultures. One of the leaders of this movement is Urie Bronfenbrenner (1979, 1986), who has developed a theory that he calls a *social ecology theory*. In biology, the term *ecology* refers to the entire network of interactions among different plants and animals and the environments to which they must adapt. In Bronfenbrenner's usage, **social ecology** refers to the entire network of other people and the social setting to which the developing person must adapt psychologically, which varies from culture to culture.

Bronfenbrenner finds it useful to depict a person's social ecology as a set of concentric rings, illustrated in Figure 13.1. He gave technical names to the rings, but I have chosen to substitute the more descriptive labels shown in the figure. At the center is the child himself or herself. Surrounding the child is the *immediate environment*, consisting of the people and things with which the child is in contact at any given moment. The next level, the *relationships among immediate environments*, refers to the relationships that exist among those parts of the world that serve as the child's immediate environment at different times. For example, home and school are two immediate environments of a child. According to Bronfenbrenner (1986), the relationship between home and school is as important to the child's development as are the separate qualities of home and school. Thus, a child's ability to learn at school depends not only on how he or she is taught there, but also on the parents' attitudes toward the school, which in turn affect the child's attitudes. The next ring in Bronfenbrenner's theory is the *social context*, which refers to aspects of society that affect the child even though the child does not come into direct contact with them. The parents' places of work, the school board, the local government, the producers of television programming, and so on, all influence the child through their effects on his or her immediate environment.

■ *How the social ecology theory of development extends the concept of environmental influence to include the larger culture as well as the immediate environment*

**Figure 13.1** *Bronfenbrenner's theory of the contexts of development*

*Urie Bronfenbrenner conceives of the child as developing within a set of social contexts, which can be arranged (as they are here) according to the degree to which they pertain specifically to the child or to the broader society and culture of which the child is a part. (Adapted from Bronfenbrenner, 1979.)*

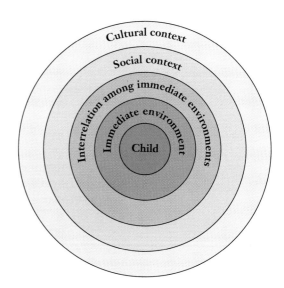

**Social ecology in action**
*Mainstream classroom practices commonly promote competition, and this can reduce the academic achievement of children reared in cultures where cooperation is highly valued. Awareness of the school/ culture relationship has led some teachers of Native American children to encourage group activities in their classrooms.*

The outside ring in Bronfenbrenner's theory is the *cultural context*, which is the entire set of beliefs, values, and accepted ways of behaving that characterize the historically connected group of people of which the child and his or her family are a part. As illustration of the importance of the cultural context, consider the act of *scarification*—the deliberate production of scars on the face or body of a boy or girl through knife cuts or burning. In our culture, such an act would be considered to be child abuse; it would be interpreted that way not only by neighbors and the law, but by the child, too, and hence the scars would be more than physical. But in a culture where this act is part of a long-established puberty ritual, it is considered by everyone, including the child, to be a sign of love, respect, and acceptance into a new stage of life. In such a society, a child who was *not* scarified at the appropriate time would feel neglected and abused.

**The Concept of a Social Clock**    Although it is not a formal theory, the idea of a *social clock,* described by Bernice Neugarten, is a useful tool for thinking about social development (Neugarten, 1979; Hagestad & Neugarten, 1985). Every culture has its expectations of what people normally do at various ages. People internalize that clock and judge their own lives accordingly. "How am I doing for my age?" asks the 10-year-old, the 20-year-old, the 40-year-old, and the 70-year-old. In our society, the social clock for children is timed to a considerable degree by school, and that for adults is timed to a considerable degree by societal expectations concerning family and career.

It is interesting to look back at Erikson's eight stages with the social clock in mind. Notice that the onset of Stage 4, *industry*, coincides with the age at which children in our society start school; Stage 5, *identity*, coincides with the age at which people in our society are trying to decide on a career; Stage 6, *intimacy*, with the age at which people are expected to get engaged or married; Stage 7, *generativity*, with the age at which people are expected to be raising children or working hard at their careers; and Stage 8, *integrity*, with retirement and the expectation of a more contemplative style of life. Do the stages stem from a biologically ingrained set of human needs, which must play themselves out in that order, or do they stem from the traditional expectations of our society, which have come down to us through cultural history? If Erikson had been raised in a non-Western, agrarian (agriculture-based) society, in which people live in extended families and children begin to work alongside their elders in the fields at a very early age, would he have come up with the same eight stages? This is the kind of question that the social-clock concept begs us to ask.

As we progress through the rest of the chapter, studying social development from infancy through old age, you will read about ideas from each of the above perspectives, though they will not always be pointed out explicitly. The greatest emphasis will be on developmental effects of variations in the social environment.

■ *How the concept of a social clock provides a possible explanation of Erikson's eight stages that is less biologically based than Erikson's own explanation*

# Infancy: Attachment to Caregivers

In 1950, John Bowlby, a British psychiatrist trained in the psychoanalytic theories of Freud and Erikson, undertook a massive study of the effects of children's separation from their parents on their development. World War II had left many thousands of European children orphaned, and Bowlby found that these children were left with serious, long-lasting emotional scars that went beyond whatever physical suffering they had endured. To explain these observations, Bowlby (1958, 1982) outlined a theory of development that centered on the importance of the young child's relationship to one or more specific, dependable adult caregivers who are sensitive to the child's emotional as well as physical needs. Bowlby used the term *attachment* to refer to the long-lasting emotional bonds that infants develop toward their principal caregivers (usually the mother). In his view, the quality of infant attachment has important psychological consequences that remain throughout life.

The discussion to follow centers on questions having to do with infants' relationships with their caregivers. Aside from basic physical needs such as nutrition, what do infants require from their caregivers if they are to develop in healthy ways? How do infants express their attachment to caregivers, and how can attachment be measured in psychological research? What parental behaviors promote attachment, and what are the consequences of secure or insecure attachment for later development? These are the questions that have motivated the research to be described below.

■ *Three lines of evidence that physical contact with caregivers is important for normal development in infancy*

**The Importance of Physical Contact**   During the 1940s, another psychiatrist, René Spitz, studied the developmental fate of infants in orphanages in the United States and Canada. He found that, despite adequate food and cleanliness, about one-third of such infants died before their first birthday and many others were severely retarded both physically and psychologically. Spitz concluded that the infants withered away from the lack of handling and emotional stimulation that characterized the orphanages (Gardner, 1972).

Partly inspired by Spitz's observations, Harry Harlow began a program of research during the 1950s using rhesus monkeys as subjects. He studied the development of monkeys that were reared without normal maternal care, and his research led him to conclude that close physical contact is one critical aspect of maternal care in monkeys. In one experiment, Harlow (1959) separated infant monkeys from their mothers and raised them in individual cages. Each infant was provided with two inanimate surrogate (substitute) mothers—one made of bare wire and the other covered with soft terry cloth (see Figure 13.2). The infants could feed themselves by sucking milk from a nipple that for half of them was attached to the wire surrogate and for the other half was attached to the cloth surrogate. Harlow's purpose was to determine if the infants would become attached to either of these surrogate mothers, as they would to a real mother, and to determine which characteristic—the milk-providing nipple or the soft cloth exterior—would be more effective in inducing attachment.

The results of two tests of attachment are summarized in Figure 13.3. Regardless of which surrogate contained the nutritive nipple, all infants treated the cloth-covered surrogate, not the wire one, as they would a mother. They clung to it, ran to it when threatened by a strange object, were braver in exploring an unfamiliar room when it was present, and pressed a lever repeatedly to look at it through a window. Harlow concluded that *contact comfort*, not feeding, is the more important variable in the formation of an infant monkey's attachment to its mother.

More recently, Tiffany Field and her colleagues (1986) found that touch has a remarkable effect on physical growth in premature infants. In their experiment,

**Figure 13.2 *Harlow's motherless monkeys***

*Harlow found that infant monkeys that were isolated from other monkeys and raised with two surrogate (substitute) mothers, one wire and one cloth, treated the cloth surrogate in many ways as they would their real mother. The monkey in the right-hand photo received its nourishment from a bottle attached to the wire surrogate, but treated the cloth surrogate as its mother in all other respects.*

**Figure 13.3 *Evidence of infant monkeys' preference for the cloth surrogate***

*These graphs show (a) the average number of hours that Harlow's monkeys spent on each of the surrogate mothers, and (b) the percentage of time that they ran to each when they were frightened by a strange object. Notice that the preference for the cloth surrogate was as strong for the monkeys that were fed on the wire surrogate as for those fed on the cloth surrogate. (Adapted from Harlow, 1959.)*

one group of premature infants was treated in the usual hospital way—kept in incubators and not handled except for routine physical care. The other group was also treated in this way, but in addition these infants were massaged by hand 45 minutes a day for 10 days. Although the amount of food consumed by the two groups was identical, the massaged infants gained almost 50 percent more weight, were more alert and active, showed more mature motor coordination, and left the hospital an average of 6 days earlier than did the unmassaged infants (for a savings of $3000 per infant in hospital expenses).

Humans and monkeys are not the only species whose infants require stimulation by touch. Mammals of many species spend enormous amounts of time licking their young, and experiments with rats have shown that young rats whose mothers are prevented from licking them do not grow properly, an effect mediated at least partly by reduced production of growth hormone (Schanberg & Field, 1987). Apparently, during the evolution of mammals, physical contact from the caregiver became a signal to the body that says, "You are cared for; it is OK to grow."

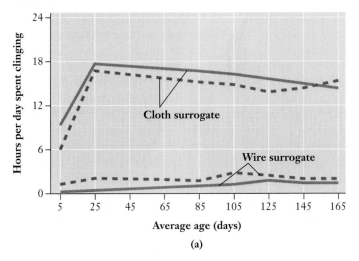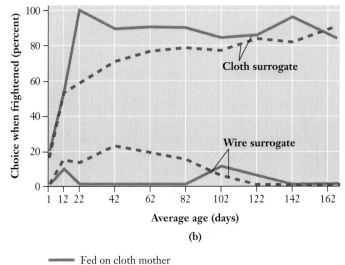

(a)  (b)

- - - Fed on wire mother ——— Fed on cloth mother

**Cross-Cultural Differences in Infant Care**   Large differences exist from culture to culture in many aspects of infant care. Compared to others, Western culture stands out for the relative lack of physical contact between infants and parents or other caregivers. For example, our culture apparently is unique in the expectation that infants and young children should sleep alone. One survey of ninety nonindustrialized cultures for which information was available revealed that in every one, infants normally slept in the same room with their mother or another closely related adult, usually in the same bed (Barry & Paxson, 1971).

*How !Kung infant-care practices differ from ours, and why caution is needed in interpreting the differences*

Melvin Konner (1972, 1982), a biologically oriented anthropologist, has argued that infant-adult relationships in hunter-gatherer societies are especially worth studying because these societies approximate a style of life believed to have been most common in our evolutionary history. Konner himself has studied the !Kung people of Africa's Kalahari Desert (the *!K* in *!Kung* stands for a clicklike sound that is different from our *K*). According to Konner's observations, !Kung infants spend most of their first year in direct contact with their mothers' bodies. During the day the mother carries the infant constantly in a sling at her side, pausing from her other activities to nurse whenever the infant shows an interest, which occurs on average every 15 minutes! At night the mother sleeps with her infant at her side. Nursing typically continues until the child is about 3 years old. The entire !Kung tribe are indulgent toward infants; when not being held by the mother, an infant is passed around among others who cuddle, fondle, kiss, and enjoy the baby. According to Konner, the !Kung never leave an infant to cry alone, and usually they detect the distress and begin to comfort the infant before crying even begins.

Books on infant care in our culture (for example, Spock & Rothenberg, 1985) commonly advise parents to refrain from always comforting infants when they cry (beyond the age of 3 to 6 months), on the grounds that constant comfort will spoil them. Yet, if Konner is correct, the !Kung *do* always comfort their infants, and the infants do not grow into spoiled or overly dependent children. In a comparative study, !Kung children over 4 years old showed more exploratory behavior and less dependence on their mothers or other adults than did British children of the same age (Blurton-Jones & Konner, 1973). By the time they are teenagers, !Kung children must do their share of providing food and other necessities in an environment that is full of danger (including the threat of attack by wild animals) and hardship (such as prolonged periods of drought). If their child-rearing practices had led to spoiling, the !Kung would not have survived in their harsh environment. On the other hand, one might argue that the rigors of !Kung life help offset the chance that !Kung child-rearing practices will lead to spoiling the child.

Of course, !Kung society is very different from our own, and few people would argue that it is possible or even desirable to transport !Kung child-rearing practices, whole cloth, into our culture. The !Kung, like most non-Western people, live in large extended families or kinship groups, and mothers receive lots of support in caring for infants. Yet, as Konner points out, such cross-cultural studies are valuable because they broaden our perspective and lead to a richer understanding of some aspects of infants' behavior. In any cross-cultural comparison, it is important to keep the entire cultural context of the compared practices in mind.

*A possible evolutionary explanation for the timing of infants' strong preferences to be near their primary caregivers*

**The Initial Manifestations of Infants' Attachment Behaviors**   Infants' attachments to their primary caregivers usually become apparent at about 7 or 8 months of age. Before then, babies do not respond to strangers much differently from the way they respond to their primary caregivers. But after that age, they are increasingly likely to cry or show other signs of fear when left alone or with strangers and to show signs of pleasure when reunited with their mothers or other familiar caregivers. This change has been observed in children in many different cultures, suggesting that it has a rather strong biological basis (see Kagan, 1976). From an evolutionary perspective, the emergence of these attachment-related behaviors at about the same time that infants begin to crawl may be no coincidence. Without the drive to be near the caregiver, the infant might crawl (or later walk) blithely away and get lost, but with it the infant tends to move within viewing range of the caregiver and to cry, hence drawing attention, if out of that range.

From a cognitive perspective, the emergence of attachment behaviors may be linked to the infant's growing understanding of the environment, especially the ability to distinguish the familiar and safe from the unfamiliar and potentially dangerous. Supporting this view are experiments showing that the degree of anxiety that infants manifest depends on the context in which the test occurs. Infants exhibit more separation and stranger anxiety in unfamiliar rooms than in familiar rooms, and they show more fear of strangers who behave in ways very different from their mothers than of strangers who behave in familiar ways (Skarin, 1977; Sroufe, 1977).

**The Strange-Situation Test** To study attachment objectively, one must somehow measure it. The most commonly used measure is the ***strange-situation test,*** developed by Mary Ainsworth, in which the infant is observed in an unfamiliar room while the mother (or other familiar caregiver) and a stranger move in and out of the room in a preplanned way (see Figure 13.4). With this test, Ainsworth and her colleagues (1978) found that most infants exhibit a pattern of responses classified as *securely attached.* They are confident and explore the room when the mother is present, become mildly upset and explore less when left alone or with a stranger, and eagerly seek contact with the mother when she returns. Infants classified as not securely attached differ from this pattern in a variety of ways. Some are upset when the mother is present; some do not seek contact with the mother when she returns; and a few even resist the mother's approach.

**Mary Ainsworth**
*Ainsworth's pioneering studies have explored the qualitative differences in the emotional bonds between infants and their caregivers.*

■ **How secure and insecure attachment patterns are assessed in the strange-situation test**

  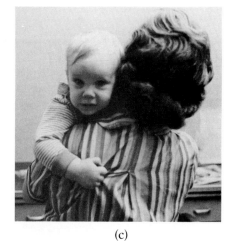
(a) (b) (c)

**Figure 13.4 *The strange-situation test***
*In this test of attachment, the mother (or other person to whom the infant is attached) moves in and out of an unfamiliar room, leaving the infant either with a stranger or alone. Here we see one infant, Brian, at different stages in the test: In (a) he plays confidently when his mother is present, in (b) he cries when she leaves, and in (c) he clings to her when she returns.*

Not everyone believes that the strange-situation test is an ideal measure of attachment. Jerome Kagan (1984), for example, has argued that it relies too much on the infant's reaction to novelty and may be a measure of temperamental differences in fear rather than of strength of attachment to the mother. But those who defend the measure point to studies showing little or no correlation between attachment classification by this test and measures of temperament (Bates, 1987; Belsky & Rovine, 1987). They also point to studies showing that secure attachment with this test correlates with measures of positive parent-child interaction in the home (discussed on the next page).

■ *Evidence that secure attachment follows sensitive care in early infancy, and that it is a favorable indicator for healthy further development*

**Figure 13.5**  *Interactional synchrony*
*Researchers have found that interactions such as this during the first 1 to 3 months of life correlate with secure attachment measured several months later.*

■ *Evidence that lack of opportunity for attachment in infancy can be made up for with sensitive and loving care later on*

**Precursors and Consequences of Secure Attachment**   In a longitudinal study of twenty-six infant-mother pairs, Ainsworth and her colleagues found that infants whose mothers were the most prompt and consistent in comforting them when they cried showed (a) the greatest decrease in crying as they grew older, and (b) the most secure attachment to their mother in the strange situation when tested later in infancy (Bell & Ainsworth, 1972; Ainsworth, 1979). Since then, other studies have shown positive correlations between the promptness and sensitivity of maternal responses to young infants' signals and later measures of secure attachment (Sroufe & Fleeson, 1986; Isabella & others, 1989). (See Figure 13.5.)

In other research, children who were securely attached as infants were found later in childhood to be more confident, more independent, better at solving problems, and emotionally healthier than children who were not securely attached in infancy (Ainsworth, 1979; Lewis & others, 1984; Pastor, 1981). These findings do not necessarily prove that better later performance is due to early attachment. Mothers who are highly responsive to their infants (and thus promote secure attachment) are probably also attentive mothers later on, and it could be that this *later* mothering is the main cause of their children's healthy adjustments. Also, to the extent that infants' innate temperaments contribute to attachment, the same temperaments that promote secure attachment may also promote successful adaptation later in life. Yet, whether or not it determines later abilities, secure attachment in infancy is certainly a favorable developmental sign.

What about the other side of the coin? What happens when infants are deprived of the opportunity to become attached? To answer this question, Barbara Tizard studied children who had spent their infancies in British orphanages whose policy prevented staff members from forming close personal relationships with the children (Tizard & Rees, 1974; Tizard & Hodges, 1978). Although the infants were handled fairly frequently, handlers changed constantly, thereby preventing attachment. Tizard studied children who were adopted from these institutions into caring families after the age of 2. She found that many of the children had serious emotional problems at first, but that eventually most of them overcame their problems and developed loving ties with their adoptive parents and siblings. By the time they started school, most of these children were well adjusted, though as a group they continued to show somewhat higher than average amounts of attention seeking and other behavioral problems, according to teachers' ratings. Tizard's study and others like it support the view that human development is characterized by flexibility and resilience (see Clarke & Clarke, 1976). Effects of deprivation at one time in development can often be counteracted at another time if the environment provides the opportunity.

**Multiple Caregivers and Multiple Attachments**   Unlike geese, which become imprinted on only one mother or mother-substitute (described in Chapter 5), human infants can become attached to more than one person—including the father, older siblings, grandparents, and other caregivers (see Ainsworth, 1982). Typically, the infant's attachment is stronger to the mother than to the father, but this may be because even today mothers in every society are more involved in their infants' care than are fathers (Lamb, 1986).

In many families, both parents work outside the home and infants spend their days with other caregivers. Does this affect the infant's attachment to his or her parents? At present, no firm answer exists to this question. Some studies have found no effect of full-time day-care on the security of infants' attachments to their mothers (Kagan & others, 1978; Fox, 1977), whereas other studies have found that infants in full-time day-care are less securely attached to their mothers (Vaughn & others, 1980; Barglow & others, 1987) or fathers (Belsky & Rovine, 1988) than are their counterparts who are not in day-care. Comparison of studies suggests that day-care begun very early (before 12 months of age), or poor-quality day-care, may decrease the security of attachment to the mother, whereas high-quality day-care begun after the first year probably does not. But even this conclusion is still controversial. As Sandra Scarr (1984) has pointed out in a thoughtful book on this topic, the effects of day-care versus mother-care probably depend upon the individual characteristics of the child and family as well as upon the quality of day-care available.

*Having a good day*

*Researchers may argue about the long-term effects of day-care on children's social and emotional development, but there is little disagreement that high-quality settings like the one shown here offer the best opportunity for growth. Such centers offer toddlers a safe environment, with opportunities for exploration, and responsive, consistent, nurturing care.*

■ *Evidence that security blankets really produce a sense of security in blanket-attached children, and one hypothesis about the origin of such attachments*

**Attachments to Inanimate Objects**   As any follower of Linus in the Peanuts comic strip knows, young children sometimes form powerful attachments to a particular soft, inanimate object, such as a special blanket or teddy bear. If you try to substitute a nice new blanket for the old raggedy one, you are in for a big fight (not unlike what would happen if you tried to substitute a nice new mother for the old one). In an experiment using a technique similar to the strange-situation test, blanket-attached infants were calmed in an unfamiliar environment by their blankets just as much as either they or other infants were by their own mothers (Passman & Weisberg, 1975). With the blanket present, the children explored the room; without it, they cried or showed other signs of fear.

It is not clear why some infants become so strongly attached to an inanimate object, but one hypothesis is that it has to do with their sleeping alone. The attachment object is almost invariably something that the child has slept with since infancy. To relieve their fear of being alone at night, infants may—like Harlow's monkeys—attach themselves to the softest, most comforting substitute available, which is most commonly a blanket. Unlike Harlow's monkeys, these infants are in contact with their real mothers and other caregivers during the day, so the attachment to the inanimate object is in addition to other attachments. Consistent with this hypothesis, K. Michael Honig and Brenda Townes (1976) found much less attachment to blankets or other inanimate objects among Korean infants, all of whom slept in the same room with their mothers or grandmothers during the first year, than among North American infants, most of whom slept alone.

# Childhood: Becoming Socialized

Childhood, which for the purposes of this discussion begins at age 2 or 3 and ends at puberty, is the period of life when various social forces act most deliberately to shape the growing person into one who will abide by the rules and norms of society. In the following sections, we will examine the roles of parents, play, and school in the socializing process, as well as some of the ways that such forces act differently on boys and girls, directing them along different developmental paths.

## *Parenting Styles*

Parents influence the social development of their children through many means. To the extent that they have the resources to decide where to live, where to send their children to school, where to go on trips, and so on, parents influence their children by selecting the environments to which they are exposed. Parents are also models from whom children learn by observation (discussed in Chapter 5). Through that means, everything that a parent does that is observable to the child can influence the child's development. Parents also communicate in various ways their expectations of their children, which can influence the children's expectations of themselves and hence their development. But most research on parental influence has focused on parents' styles of *discipline*. Discipline refers to the direct and immediate ways by which parents respond to their children's misbehavior or perceived future misbehavior.

**Hoffman's Theory of Discipline**   Martin Hoffman (1983) has proposed that discipline techniques commonly used by parents can be divided into three categories. One category is *power assertion*, which is the use or threatened use of punishments and rewards (more often the former than the latter) to control a child's behavior. The second category is *love withdrawal*, which occurs when parents—often unwittingly—express disapproval of the *child*, not just of the child's specific wrong action. This may take the form of verbal statements such as, "You are worthless," or nonverbal actions such as behaving in a cold and rejecting way toward the child. Like many other psychologists, Hoffman disapproves of too much power assertion or love withdrawal. He argues that power assertion focuses attention on the punishments and rewards themselves rather than on ethical reasons why an action is wrong or right. Thus, the child may continue to perform wrong actions in situations in which there is little chance of being caught, or may perform good actions only in situations in which someone is sure to notice and provide a reward (see Brody & Shaffer, 1982). Moreover, both punishment and love withdrawal elicit negative emotions in the child (anger in the case of punishment, anxiety in the case of love withdrawal), which may weaken the parent-child relationship and promote further misbehavior.

Hoffman's third category of discipline is ***induction***, a form of verbal reasoning in which the parent induces the child to think about his or her actions and the consequences they may have for other people. This technique, which Hoffman strongly favors, makes use of and nourishes the child's capacity for empathy (feeling what another person feels). For example, a parent may say to a little child, "When you hit Billy, it hurts him and makes him cry"; or to a somewhat older child, "When you tease Susan and call her names, it makes her feel that nobody likes her." When using this technique in its purest form, the parent does not order the child to behave in a certain way; nor does the parent place sanctions on the child. Rather, the parent simply draws attention to certain natural consequences of the child's action that he or she may not have thought about. Thus, the *child* decides whether or not to continue the previous behavior. This allows the child to attribute a change in

*Hoffman's three categories of discipline and why he favors the category called* induction behavior to his or her own moral standards ("I don't want to hurt someone") rather than to an external and not always present source of reward or punishment.

Although Hoffman favors induction, he believes that sometimes power assertion is necessary to get a child to stop engaging in a seriously wrong action. In such cases, he argues, induction mixed with power assertion helps reduce the potentially negative consequences of the latter technique. If the child understands that the parents have a moral reason behind their punitive action, that it is not arbitrary or motivated by spite or loss of love, then the child is less likely to react with anger or anxiety and more likely to think about and possibly internalize the parents' moral reasoning.

**Correlations Between Discipline Style and Children's Behavior**    Theory is one thing and evidence is another. Is there evidence supporting the just-described ideas about the harmful effects of unadulterated power assertion and the beneficial effects of induction? Many studies, mostly of middle-class, North American families, have shown correlations between parental styles of discipline and children's behavior that are at least consistent with these ideas. For example, in one study, seventh graders were assessed through ratings by teachers and peers for their tendency to behave morally, and the children's parents were assessed through interviews for the extent to which they used power-assertive and inductive discipline techniques (Hoffman & Saltzstein, 1967). The measures of moral behavior correlated positively with parental use of induction and negatively with use of power assertion.

In another study, Diana Baumrind (1967, 1971a) assessed the behavior of young children by observing them at nursery school and in their homes, and assessed the discipline styles of their parents through interviews and home observations. She found that most parents could be classed into one of the following three groups: (1) *authoritarian*, who valued obedience for its own sake and used a high degree of power assertion to control their children; (2) *authoritative*, who were less concerned with control for its own sake but still very concerned that their children behave properly, and who preferred inductive discipline when possible but did not avoid power assertion when necessary to gain compliance; and (3) *permissive*, who were most tolerant of their children's disruptive actions and least likely to use discipline at all.

■ *How Baumrind classified parents' discipline styles into three types and found evidence favoring one of them*

Drawing by Koren, ©1988 The New Yorker Magazine, Inc.

"Sam, neither your father nor I consider your response appropriate."

Baumrind's main finding was that children of authoritative parents showed the most positive qualities. Among other things, they were friendlier, more cooperative, and less likely to disrupt others' activities than children who were in the other groups. A follow-up study of the same children showed that the advantages for those with authoritative parents were still present at age 9 (Baumrind, 1986). From the perspective of Hoffman's theory, the authoritarian parents may have used too much power assertion, the permissive parents may have used too little of any discipline techniques, and the authoritative parents may have balanced a principally inductive discipline style with just enough power assertion to ensure attention to the message. Another possible interpretation of the difference between the permissive and authoritative groups, however, is that the children of permissive parents fared worse not so much from lack of parental discipline as from the reduced expectations that their parents seemed to have of them (Baumrind, 1971a).

Some evidence for the importance of expectations and dialogue, independent of discipline, was found in the behavior of a small group of parents that comprised a fourth style, which Baumrind (1971b) labeled as *harmonious*. These parents were like permissive parents in their absence of power assertion and apparent lack of concern about controlling their children, but they seemed to have great respect for their children's own ideas and capacities for self-control. Their interactions with their children involved a great deal of two-way communication, which seemed to have the effect that the children developed their own internalized values very early, such that direct parental control was rarely necessary. Although there were too few families in this group for statistical significance, these children seemed to be as sociable and competent as those in the authoritative group.

**Some limitations of the findings correlating children's behavior with parental styles**

Hoffman's, Baumrind's, and others' studies correlating parenting styles with children's behavior are certainly interesting in relation to the question of how to be a good parent. But we should be cautious in interpreting them. First, the correlations that are found, while statistically significant, are not terribly strong. Many exceptions occur; children from authoritarian homes are often well adjusted, and children from authoritative homes are often not. A second limitation lies in the problem of inferring causality from correlational data (see Chapter 2). Researchers in this area tend to assume that a correlation between parental style and behavioral traits in children represents a cause-effect relationship in which the parental style is the cause of the children's traits. But in doing so they may be underestimating the extent to which children influence their parents (Bell & Harper, 1977). There may be lots of reasons, completely independent of parenting style, why some children misbehave more than others—and those who misbehave may elicit more power assertion from their parents than those who routinely are good. A third problem lies in the cultural relativity of the findings—what is true of middle-class, North American families may not be true of other groups.

Hoffman and Herbert Saltzstein (1967) noted that the correlation between power assertion and poor social development found for middle-class families did not hold up for economically less well-off families in their study; and Baumrind (1973) made a similar observation regarding the relatively few Black families in her study. By now there is ample evidence that parenting styles must be understood in the context of the culture in which they occur (Bronfenbrenner, 1986). In North America, authoritarian parenting is more common among the relatively poor than among the relatively well-to-do, a fact that sociologists ascribe to the differing realities of life for the two groups. In extensive interviews of people from various walks of life, Melvin Kohn (1977) found that parents faced with financial insecurity were especially concerned that their children develop qualities that would lead to secure employment. Thus, they valued conformity and respect for rules, on the one hand, and ability to resist exploitation, on the other; and a power-assertive style of parenting seemed to make sense in that context. Moreover, children who see power assertion as the standard parental style in their neighborhood, and who understand it as an expression of parental concern, not rejection, may respond to it quite differently than do middle-class children.

### Theories About the Developmental Functions of Play

Children are active forces in their own social development. They socialize themselves through their play and friendships. A considerable amount of research has been conducted on changes that occur in play and friendships as children grow older (see Damon, 1983). Here, however, we will focus our discussion on broad theories of the value of social play in children's development.

Play, almost by definition, is what children do when their other needs are met and they are free to choose their own activities. It apparently occurs, in roughly similar forms, in children in every culture (Schwartzman, 1978). One of the first to write about the developmental functions of play was the philosopher Karl Groos (1898, 1901), who argued that play stems from instinctive drives that evolved because they serve educative functions. According to Groos, play is the main vehicle by which young mammals in general, and young humans in particular, acquire the skills they will need as adults. For example, lion cubs that are playfully fighting and chasing are acquiring the skills they will need in serious fights and predatory chases later on.

In keeping with Groos's general approach, human play can be categorized in accordance with the skills that are exercised. There is *rough-and-tumble play*, which promotes physical coordination and ability to fight and run; *constructive play* (building or making things), which exercises manual skills and planning ability; *sociodramatic play* (adopting roles and acting out make-believe situations), in which social roles and skill in carrying them out are developed; and *formal games with rules* (such as board games and athletic competitions), in which children acquire an understanding of rules, which are essential for social order. Although the general forms of play appear to be universal, the specific contents of play depend upon the culture (see Johnson & others, 1987). The son of a hunter plays at hunting; my son played with computers.

**Theories of play that center on (a) its general educative function, (b) its value in working through emotional crises, (c) its value in development of moral reasoning, and (d) its value in understanding rules and social roles**

**Let's pretend**

*Make-believe play is an important activity for preschoolers. Pretend games not only give them a chance to act out social roles, but also offer opportunities to express fears and to learn to play cooperatively.*

Sigmund Freud and other psychoanalytic theorists developed a different way of thinking about play. They proposed that play is a vehicle by which children resolve emotional problems or fulfill wishes that cannot be satisfied in reality. Thus, from Freud's perspective, a boy who for deep unconscious reasons wishes his father were dead might play at hunting gorillas—each imaginary gorilla shot is a symbol of the father. In Erik Erikson's (1963) more moderate psychoanalytic theory, play mirrors the life stages that children go through, helping them master the crises and conflicts of each stage. Consistent with the psychoanalytic perspective are reports that children who have gone through an emotional crisis may focus their play on issues closely related to that crisis. According to one such report, a group of nursery-school children who had unfortunately witnessed a man fall 20 feet to the ground and suffer serious injury were very disturbed by the incident and played for months afterward at such themes as falling, injury, hospitals, and death (Brown & others, 1971).

Whereas psychoanalytic theories emphasize the role of play in overcoming emotional crises, cognitive theories emphasize its role in the development of new ways of thinking. In his book, *The Moral Judgment of the Child*, Piaget (1932) argued that social play helps the child gain a more advanced understanding of rules and morality. Parents—at least the Genevan parents of the 1920s and 1930s that Piaget knew—establish rules for their children in black-and-white terms, with little room for discussion. In contrast, during unsupervised play with peers there is no all-powerful authority figure to settle disputes, so children learn to argue out their disputes, to present reasons, and in that way can develop an understanding of right and wrong based at least partly on reason rather than on authority.

The Soviet psychologist Lev Vygotsky was another cognitive theorist who wrote about social play. As described in Chapter 12, Vygotsky argued that social interaction is central to all aspects of mental development, so it is not surprising that he ascribed great importance to social play. Vygotsky (1933/1978) argued that, contrary to popular opinion, social play is not free and spontaneous, but is always governed by rules that define the range of permissible actions that each participant can produce. In real life, young children behave spontaneously—they cry when they are hurt, laugh when they are happy, and say, "I want that" when they really want something. But in social play they must suppress their spontaneous urges and behave in accordance with the rules of the game or the role that they have agreed upon. Consider, for example, children playing "house," in which one child is the mommy, another is the baby, and another is the pet dog. To play this game, each child must keep in mind a conscious conception of what it means to be a mommy, a baby, or a dog, and must govern his or her actions in accordance with that conception. Thus, Vygotsky argued, social play fosters children's ability to behave according to a conscious understanding of roles and rules, which is a critical part of socialization. As children grow older, this ability is transferred to nonplay situations: At school they take the role of student, at work the role of worker.

Consistent with Vygotsky's view, Catherine Garvey (1974, 1977) has found that young children put great effort into planning and enforcing rules in their sociodramatic play. Children who break the rules—who start acting like themselves rather than the role they have agreed to play—are sharply reminded by the others of what they are supposed to be doing: "Dogs don't sit at the table; you have to get under the table." Other recent research supports Vygotsky's view of the benefits of such play. Positive correlations have been found between the amount of sociodramatic play that children engage in and ratings of their social competence (Connolly & Doyle, 1984), and encouragement of sociodramatic play in nursery school has been found to improve social competence (see Johnson & others, 1987).

### School as a Socializing Force

*How schools are social communities that influence children's attitudes and behaviors in ways other than through the formal curriculum*

Children in Western cultures spend much of their lives in school. While the main function of schools may be to teach the three R's and various academic and vocational subjects, schools are also important for their socializing role. The formal curriculum typically includes lessons in the values and ideals of the larger community. Thus, children may study principles of democracy in civics classes or the problem of drugs in health classes. Perhaps even more important than the formal curriculum is the *implicit curriculum* of school—the requirement to follow the school's rules (written or unwritten), to get along with the various people there, and to behave in accordance with the expectations of teachers and other students.

A long-standing debate in education concerns the extent to which teachers should exercise firm authority or should give students relative freedom. Those who argue for the former believe that teacher-imposed structure is essential to the acquisition of both basic knowledge and the kind of self-discipline needed to persist at tedious or difficult tasks that are required for success in jobs and careers. Those who argue for the latter believe that imposed structure reduces children's natural curiosity and spontaneity and imparts social values that run counter to the democratic ideals of personal choice and individual responsibility. Related to this debate are studies comparing children in so-called *open classrooms*—classrooms where children have a somewhat greater opportunity to choose their own activities—with children in traditional classrooms. A review of all such studies conducted prior to 1979 indicated that children in open classrooms are, on average, more curious, creative, cooperative, and favorably inclined toward school than are those in traditional classrooms, and that they perform neither better nor worse on standard tests of academic learning (Horwitz, 1979).

More radical than open classrooms are experiments in schooling that allow children complete freedom in matters pertaining to their education. Such experiments are worth considering here because they raise basic questions about children's social and intellectual capacities, and about the environmental conditions that foster children's capacities for self-direction. Two such schools of historical significance are the Yasnaya Polyana School for peasant children, founded by the Russian writer Leo Tolstoy (1861/1967), and Summerhill, an English boarding school run for half a century by A. S. Neill (1960). A more recent example is the Sudbury Valley School, a day school for people of kindergarten through high-school age, which has been operating for more than 20 years in Massachusetts, and which I have had the opportunity to observe for a number of years.

Sudbury Valley School is almost the antithesis of traditional schools. As a social structure, it is a participatory democracy (see Greenberg, 1987a & b). All school rules and other important decisions (including the hiring and firing of staff) are made by a one-person, one-vote procedure, and infractions of rules are tried through a judicial system that involves school members of all ages. Thus, students constantly participate in democratic processes and make moral decisions regarding the rights, privileges, and needs of individual members of the community. As an educational institution, the school provides books, labs, knowledgeable staff members, and apprenticeships outside the school, but does not require students to use them. Students must initiate and direct their own learning, asking staff or other students for help when they want it. There are no required classes, no tests, no grades, and no evaluation of students (except informally if requested by a student).

■ *How one school fulfills its educative function not through a formal curriculum, but by providing a community that fosters self-respect and self-directed learning*

**Sharing an interest**

*These three members of the Sudbury Valley School appear to be equally intent on completing their project correctly. Free age mixing is one of the key elements of the educational philosophy of this nontraditonal school.*

Sudbury Valley School is so out of line with traditional schools that many people, on first hearing about it, assume that its graduates would not succeed in adult life. But a follow-up study of the graduates indicates that as a group they have done remarkably well, even by the most traditional standards of what it means to "do well" (Gray & Chanoff, 1986). They have had no particular difficulty getting into and graduating from good colleges, and they have made their mark in a wide range of careers. On interviews and questionnaires, most of the students contend that their unique schooling has made them more self-disciplined and socially responsible than they otherwise would be. The success of these students cannot be attributed to a selective admissions policy, because the school admits essentially all students who apply and whose families can pay the school's very low tuition.

No one is required to study at Sudbury Valley School, yet most students learn what they need for a successful adult life. What forces operate at this school to promote learning? Observations at the school suggest the following as a partial list (Greenberg, 1987a & b; Gray & Chanoff, 1984):

1. The school is permeated by an atmosphere of trust and respect for each individual child. Respect from others seems to promote high self-respect, which in turn leads even young children to make responsible choices.

2. Because students are not segregated by age into separate classrooms, but can mix freely with all school members, the school provides students with a wide variety of models. Students often become attached for a period of time to a particular older student or adult and learn much of what that person knows. Also, older students may acquire confidence and a sense of maturity through their interactions with younger students.

3. The school permits children to pursue fully their own interests and express their curiosity. Teaching at the school usually occurs through trying to answer students' questions or directing them to other sources to find the answers. Thus, at any given time students are learning primarily what they are eager to learn, and because the questions are their own, they are much more likely to find the answers meaningful and to remember them.

4. Children at the school (all of whom live at home and commute to school) are aware of the expectations of the larger society beyond the school and are concerned about how they will fit into that society. This concern is reinforced by the single requirement for graduation—successful defense before the school community of the thesis "I am ready to take part as a responsible person in the adult world."

Of course, Sudbury Valley School is not the only type of school that has proven successful. Other schools that have different philosophies, but at which people believe strongly in what they are doing, have also proven exciting and educationally effective for those involved. I have discussed Sudbury Valley School because it is a school that I know well; because it illustrates some long-standing ideas about the role of social context in children's behavior and development; and because it demonstrates that a great deal of variation from traditional schooling can occur without jeopardizing children's chances for success. Research suggests that children could benefit from more choices in schools, more attempts to develop school environments that take into account children's capacities for self-direction and responsibility. It is disgraceful that children, especially those from families who can't afford a choice, are so often required to attend schools that are unsafe and that foster cynicism rather than social and intellectual growth.

### Gender as a Factor in Socialization

Life is not the same for boys and girls. That is true not just in our culture, but in every culture that has been studied (Maccoby & Jacklin, 1987). To some degree,

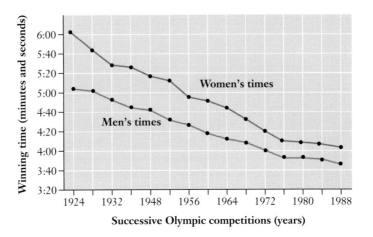

**Figure 13.6** *Example of a gender difference changing over time*

*In many realms, differences between males and females depend at least partly on the culture's expectations, which can change over history. Shown here are the winning times for the 400-meter freestyle swim in Olympic competition over a 64-year period. Notice the decreasing difference between men's and women's times. Janet Evans, the 1988 women's gold medalist, swam faster that year than did the fastest man in 1968 or any previous year. (Data from the 1989 World Almanac.)*

■ *How differential treatment at home and school may direct boys and girls along different routes*

**Eleanor E. Maccoby**

*In her long and distinguished career, Maccoby has immeasurably increased our understanding of the processes by which children acquire the habits, values, goals, and knowledge of their societies.*

differences may be biological in origin, mediated by hormones (see Chapters 4 and 7). But hormones don't explain why the differences themselves vary from culture to culture, as shown by Margaret Mead (1935) and many other anthropologists, or why in Western culture the differences have changed over the course of history (for an example of one such change, see Figure 13.6).

The emphasis here on social rather than biological forces is highlighted by use of the term *gender* rather than *sex*. Although most dictionaries present the two as synonyms, psychologists tend to use *sex* to refer to the clear-cut biological bases for categorizing people as male or female (principally the difference in sex organs), and *gender* to refer to the entire set of differences commonly attributed to males and females, which may be partly or wholly socially determined (Deaux, 1985). You were born one sex or the other, but from the moment of birth—from the moment that someone announced, "It's a girl!" or "It's a boy!"—you also had a gender. Immediately, in the minds of all who heard the announcement, you were tied through a web of mental associations to all kinds of "girlish" or "boyish" traits, activities, and material belongings.

**Differential Treatment by Adults**   Parents and other adults view and handle even very young infants differently depending on their gender. Fathers who were asked to rate their infants on the day after birth were more likely to rate the newborn as soft, small, and beautiful if it was a girl, and as firm, strong, and well coordinated if it was a boy (Rubin & others, 1974). Consistent with this difference in perception, fathers have been found consistently to play more gently with infant girls than with infant boys (Maccoby & Jacklin, 1974). Mothers, too, tend to handle baby boys and baby girls differently, though the difference is more subtle. In one study, mothers were asked to hold a 6-month-old female infant, who in some cases was dressed as a girl and introduced as Beth, and in other cases was dressed as a boy and introduced as Adam (Culp & others, 1983). The mothers talked to Beth more than they did to Adam, and gave Adam more direct gazes unaccompanied by talk. Parents also furnish infants' rooms differently depending on gender. Boys are more likely to have toy vehicles, toy animals, and live animals, and girls are more likely to have dolls and lace fabrics (Rheingold & Cook, 1975). Such differences in treatment cannot be due to differences stemming from the infants themselves, since objective studies show that girls and boys younger than 18 months do not differ perceptibly in size, physical strength, temperament (Plomin & DeFries, 1985), or preferences for various toys (Rheingold & Cook, 1975; Maccoby & Jacklin, 1974).

As children grow older, differential treatment continues. In general, boys are allowed to explore farther from home and are encouraged to be more independent, whereas girls are encouraged more to take part in domestic activities (Huston & others, 1986). Both at home and in nursery schools, adults express more approval for behaving in ways that are regarded as gender appropriate (such as girls playing with dolls or boys playing with trucks) and more disapproval for behaving in ways regarded as gender inappropriate (Fagot, 1977; Archer & Lloyd, 1985).

**Mastering the machine**

*As computers have become increasingly common in North American classrooms, there has been considerable disagreement about their impact. Some critics fear that their presence will accentuate gender differences if boys are encouraged to become competent users of the machines and girls are not.*

■ *How boys' and girls' groups differ and how peer pressure can augment the differences between the genders*

School is supposed to be the great homogenizer, and in our society boys and girls attend the same classrooms and usually study the same subjects. But a number of studies have shown that teachers often expect different results from boys and girls and that such expectations may become self-fulfilling prophesies. In one study, observations in many classrooms revealed that second-grade teachers spent more time with boys on math and more time with girls on reading (Leinhardt & others, 1979), which may help explain why, on average, boys become better than girls at math and girls become better than boys at reading (Good & Findley, 1985). Other studies have shown that teachers criticize boys and girls differently for poor academic performance, especially in math (Dweck & Bush, 1976; Dweck & others, 1978). Criticism of boys more often contains the implication that poor performance comes from not trying hard enough, whereas that of girls is more muted and has the implication that poor performance is due to lack of ability, which is beyond the girls' control. Carol Dweck and her colleagues suggest that this difference may help explain why girls tend to be less confident than boys in their own abilities. When asked to describe their academic abilities, girls usually underestimate theirs, especially in math, and boys usually overestimate theirs (Eccles, 1985).

**Peer Groups as Forces for Gender Differentiation**   The fact that boys and girls commonly play separately and differently is, I am sure, not news to you. Even in nursery school boys interact more with boys, girls more with girls (Maccoby & Jacklin, 1987), and the tendency toward separation becomes greater with each passing year until about sixth grade (Thorne, 1986). Some social scientists have argued that boys' and girls' peer groups are so different that they should be viewed as separate subcultures, each with its own values, directing its members along different developmental lines (Maltz & Borker, 1982). The *world of boys* has been characterized as consisting of relatively large, hierarchically organized groups in which individuals or coalitions attempt to prove their superiority or dominance through competitive games, teasing, and boasting. In contrast, the *world of girls* has been characterized as consisting of smaller, more intimate groups, based more on an ideology of cooperation and equality. In their speech, girls are more likely than boys to use the pronoun *we* rather than *I*, less likely to interrupt one another, less likely to contradict one another directly, and more likely to acknowledge what the other has said before offering a different view (Maltz & Borker, 1982).

Differences between girls' and boys' groups cannot be explained simply on the basis of the characteristics of girls and boys as individuals. Peer pressure exaggerates whatever differences may exist to begin with. Even 3- and 4-year-olds are less likely to play with toys deemed not appropriate to their gender if a peer is present than if they are playing alone (Serbin & others, 1979). Other studies have shown that children's play is more gender-differentiated in large groups, such as during recess or lunch hour on the school playground, than in smaller neighborhood groups (Maccoby & Jacklin, 1987; Thorne, 1986). Some psychologists have expressed concern that play is not only gender segregated, but segregated in ways that may be harmful to development—preventing boys from exercising the tender side of their nature or girls from exercising more self-assertion.

Based on systematic observations on elementary-school playgrounds, Barrie Thorne (1986) outlined the following asymmetries between boys' and girls' play:

1. Boys control more space than do girls. Girls typically play close to the building, whereas boys' play areas extend to the far reaches of the school's grounds.

2. Gender separation is maintained mostly by ridiculing those who cross gender lines, but this process is not symmetrical. Boys are much more likely to be teased and taunted by both boys and girls for playing with girls than are girls for playing with boys. Indeed, some girls, so-called tomboys who enjoy sports, become fully accepted into boys' groups and still retain their popularity with girls. A boy who prefers to play with girls is not treated so benignly. The im-

plication is that it is worse for a boy to like or to be like girls than it is for a girl to like or to be like boys.

3. Boy-girl interactions are sexualized at a surprisingly young age. Children commonly tease each other about "going with" or "loving" someone, and games between boys and girls often involve mock sexual themes, such as "kiss and chase." Again, though, the sexualization is not symmetrical. Girls are more sexualized than boys. Boys are more likely than girls to describe members of the other gender in sexual terms, and girls are more likely than boys to center their own play on romantic themes.

**Causes of Gender Segregation** The tendency for boys and girls to segregate themselves probably emerges from a combination of forces. Adults' differential expectations and treatment of boys and girls may play a role. Models—such as in television ads and children's books—that exaggerate differences between males and females may also play a role by molding children's conceptions of gender toward extremes. The simple act of *labeling* boys and girls as different groups can also promote gender segregation, presumably by reinforcing the group distinction. The amount of gender segregation on school playgrounds has been reported to decline when teachers consciously avoid calling attention to gender in the classroom—for example, when they avoid such activities as lining boys and girls up separately or using such phrases as, "I see the girls are ready and the boys aren't" (see Maccoby & Jacklin, 1987).

But gender segregation probably cannot be understood simply as a result of adult influences. It is actively maintained by children themselves. From an evolutionary perspective, gender is not an arbitrary concept, but is closely related to sex, which in turn is closely related to reproduction. Children may have a biologically based need to establish in their own minds and in the minds of others around them a sense of their own *gender identity*, that is, a clear sense of belonging to one gender or the other. To do so, they may pay special attention to the cultural definitions of male and female and exaggerate the differences in their own minds and activities (Kohlberg, 1966).

Gender segregation may also come about partly from differences in behavioral styles that are independent of a conscious concept of gender. If boys like roughhousing and sports more than girls do, they will do those things mostly with boys; and if girls like intimate dialogue more than boys do, they will engage in such dialogue mostly with girls. Girls typically begin to avoid boys at an earlier age than boys avoid girls (LaFreniere & others, 1984), and there is evidence that this difference may have to do with a difference in mode of communication.

Carolyn Jacklin and Eleanor Maccoby (1978) placed pairs of unacquainted 33-month-old children in the same room, with their mothers present, and recorded their behavior as each pair was given one interesting toy after another. As Figure 13.7 shows, same-gender pairs interacted with each other much more than did mixed pairs. In mixed pairs, the girl tended to withdraw after a brief period and stand near her mother while the boy continued to play with the toy. This occurred despite the fact that the children were dressed in similar clothing and were not referred to by name or other gender-identifying terms, and despite the fact that boys in this setting were not noticeably rougher than girls. Closer analysis of the children's behavior suggested that the girls may have withdrawn because they found themselves unable to exert an equal share of influence in the interaction when the partner was a boy (Maccoby & Jacklin, 1987). Boys were less likely to respond to girls' requests and suggestions than were either boys or girls to respond to boys' requests and suggestions. Consistent with this finding, other studies of preschoolers have shown that girls are more likely than boys to produce and respond to polite suggestions, and that boys are more likely to produce and respond to direct commands (Serbin & others, 1984; Maccoby & Jacklin, 1987).

*How gender segregation may be promoted by (a) adult influences, (b) children's own thinking, and (c) gender differences in communicative style*

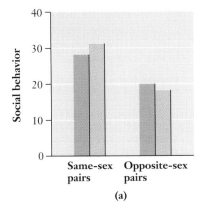

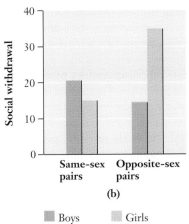

■ Boys   ■ Girls

**Figure 13.7** *Effects of gender on social interactions between 33-month-olds*

(a) *Jacklin and Maccoby found that the total amount of social behavior exhibited by 33-month-old children, paired together in a play room, was greater for same-gender pairs than it was for opposite-gender pairs.* (b) *This difference was accounted for mostly by the strong tendency for girls to withdraw from interaction with male partners. (Adapted from Jacklin & Maccoby, 1978.)*

# Adolescence: Finding Oneself

Adolescence is the transition period from childhood to adulthood. It begins with the first signs of puberty (the physical changes leading to reproductive capacity), and it ends when the person is viewed by himself or herself, and by others, as a full member of the adult community. In traditional societies, in which adult roles are clearly defined and have been learned through the child's direct involvement with the adult world, the transition to adulthood may coincide quite closely with the physical changes of puberty and may be officially marked by puberty rites or other celebrations. But in our society the transition has no clear-cut end. The law grants different adult privileges at different ages—in my home state you can drive a car at 16, vote at 18, and purchase alcohol at 21. More important, the age at which people begin careers or families in our society—often seen as marks of entry into adulthood—varies greatly. It is not uncommon to hear people in their late twenties, especially those in graduate school, refer to themselves as "kids," a tacit acknowledgment of their sense that they are still adolescents.

Erikson (1963, 1968) defined adolescence as the period during which a person finds an adult identity. The aspects of finding an identity that I will focus on here are (a) becoming more independent of parents, (b) adapting to increased sexuality, (c) establishing a set of adult goals, and (d) establishing a moral philosophy to carry into adulthood.

## Relationships in Adolescence

**Breaking Away, or Establishing New Relationships with Parents**    "I said, 'Have a nice day' to my teenage daughter as she left the house, and she responded, 'Will you *please* stop telling me what to do!'" This joke, long popular among parents of adolescents, could be matched by the following, told by an adolescent: "Yesterday, I tried to really communicate with my mother. I told her how important it is that she trust me and not try to govern everything I do. She responded, 'Oh, sweetie, I'm so glad we have the kind of relationship in which you can be honest and tell me how you really feel. Now please, if you are going out, wear your warmest coat and be back by 10:30.'"

Adolescence is often characterized as a time of rebellion against parents. But the rebellion, if we call it that, is rarely out-and-out rejection. Surveys taken at various times and places over the past several decades have shown consistently that most adolescents admire their parents, accept their parents' religious and political convictions, and claim to be more or less at peace with them (Adelson, 1986). Rather, the typical rebellion is aimed specifically at the more immediate forms of control that parents hold over the child's behavior. At the same time that adolescents are asking to be treated more like adults, parents may fear new dangers that can accompany this period of life—such as those associated with sex, alcohol, drugs, and automobiles—and try to tighten controls instead of loosen them. So adolescence is often marked by conflicts centering on parental authority. Surveys show that such conflicts are usually most prominent early in adolescence and decline later on (Collins, 1988).

One approach to understanding family relationships is to ask family members to discuss such issues as where to go for a vacation, and then analyze the conversations to find consistent patterns of communication between each pair. Laurence Steinberg (1981) used this approach with boys and their parents and found that as boys went through puberty, their relationships with their mother and father changed in certain consistent ways. The first half of puberty was marked by increased mother-son conflict, as each interrupted the other more and neither deferred to the other. Later, by the time most pubertal changes had occurred,

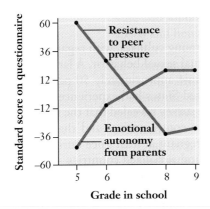

**Figure 13.8** *Changes in perceived dependence on parents and peers during adolescence*

*Based on responses to questionnaire items, the sense of emotional autonomy from parents (including feeling independent from parents and no longer idealizing them) increased, and resistance to peer pressure decreased, from fifth through eighth grade. The latter change was assessed with questions that asked the young person to choose between two hypothetical courses of action, one suggested by the youngster's best friends and the other representing what the youngster really thinks he or she should do. (Adapted from Steinberg & Silverberg, 1986.)*

*Gay pride*

*Gay and Lesbian You[ ] of social and support g[ ] lesbian communities. [ ] empowerment, comfo[ ] women of all ages, rac[ ]*

■ *How cliques and crowds help break down the gender barrier, according to a study conducted in an urban setting*

mother-son conflict declined, primarily because by then mothers commonly deferred to their sons. In other words, at least in those types of interactions, sons gained power while mothers lost power. Father-son interactions did not change in this way. If anything, sons became *more* deferential to their fathers as they matured physically. In a similar study with girls and their mothers, John Hill (1988) and his colleagues found a different pattern of change. As girls matured during puberty, they became more assertive with both of their parents. Mothers also became more assertive, and they did not back off in late puberty the way they did with sons, so mother-daughter discussions became increasingly intense. Fathers, on the other hand, became less assertive as their daughters matured and were more likely to defer to them. Thus, taking both Steinberg's and Hill's studies into account, as adolescents matured physically they tended to gain power in relation to the opposite-sex parent but not the same-sex parent.

**Importance of the Peer Group** As young people gain a feeling of independence from their parents, they look increasingly to their peers, both for clues as to how to behave and for emotional support. A number of studies, such as that described in Figure 13.8, suggest that conformity to peers increases during the same years that the sense of dependence on parents decreases. Other studies indicate that both boys and girls begin to spend much more time talking with peers than they did before, often in close and caring ways (Kelly & Hansen, 1987), though, as noted earlier, girls have a head start in this. When asked to describe the meaning of their friendships, adolescents of both genders talk about the sharing of thoughts, feelings, and secrets, whereas younger children are more likely to talk about the sharing of play and material things (Damon, 1983; Oden, 1988).

Adolescent peer groups play an important role in breaking down the gender barriers that were erected in childhood. This is one of the main conclusions of a classic study conducted by Dexter Dunphy (1963) in Sydney, Australia. By gaining the confidence of a large number of adolescents, Dunphy was able to chart the membership of many peer groups and study them both by direct observation and questionnaires given to group members. He found two varieties of such groups, which he labeled *cliques* and *crowds*. A clique was a close-knit group, ranging from three to nine individuals, who saw themselves as best friends, and who spent great amounts of time together throughout the week. A crowd was a larger group consisting of several cliques, which would get together for parties or other planned occasions, usually on weekends.

Younger adolescents' cliques were exclusively one sex or the other, but their crowds usually consisted of a mix of girls' and boys' cliques. The clique leaders were usually those individuals who were the earliest to begin dating, and crowds were often made up of the cliques to which dating couples belonged. In the crowd, boys and girls could interact in a setting made more secure by the presence of their best same-sex friends. Between crowd gatherings, the members of cliques would spend hours analyzing the events of the last gathering and encouraging each other toward further interaction with members of the opposite sex. In later adolescence, as more individuals began to date regularly, single-sex cliques tended to break apart, and new, more loosely associated groups, consisting usually of two or more pairs of dating couples, would take their place.

Dunphy's study shows one route—perhaps most common in middle-class, urban settings—by which adolescents break down the gender barrier and begin dating. Once dating has begun there is much to be learned. Girls and boys—who have to some degree been members of different worlds—must overcome awkward stages of fear and embarrassment, adjust their styles of communication, and somehow match their idealized images of a romantic relationship with the realities of the person they are getting to know. This process may be further confounded by ambiguities and fears surrounding sexuality.

**Roots of the Self-concept: From Physical to Psychological**    The earliest understanding of self that can be clearly documented is the infant's understanding that he or she has a physical body that is similar to, yet recognizably different from, that of other human beings. This must be an important discovery, because it concretely proves to the child that he or she is a particular human being. It helps the child understand both his or her connection to the rest of humanity and his or her uniqueness. Research based on children's reactions to their images in mirrors indicates that recognition of the physical self is usually present by about age 15 months (Lewis & Brooks-Gunn, 1979).

Beyond infancy, further development of the self-concept has been studied primarily by asking people to describe themselves (Damon, 1983). Preschoolers describe themselves almost exclusively in physical terms. Thus, an articulate 4-year-old might say of herself, "I have curly hair, I can run fast, and I have blue sneakers." By about ages 6 to 8, children begin to describe themselves to some degree in psychological as well as physical terms, and development thereafter involves a continuous increase in both the frequency and sophistication of psychological descriptions. The earliest such descriptions tend to refer to transitory states, such as, "I feel sad," but as they grow older children increasingly describe themselves in terms of more stable psychological characteristics, that is, in terms of their *personality*. At first, personality descriptions center mostly on social characteristics such as, "I am shy," "I am kind," "I feel best when I'm with my close friends." Descriptions of this sort peak in early adolescence. In later adolescence and adulthood, self-descriptions are increasingly likely to include something about personal beliefs and purely inner traits. Thus, a young man might describe himself as "a devout Christian," or "a person who values my independence," or "a person who worries too much about the little details of daily life."

In sum, the self-concept seems to center first on the *physical self*, then on the *social self* (which others can see and comment on), and finally on an *inner self*, consisting of values and traits that may not be apparent to others. At each step in this development, the earlier understanding of self is not lost but is incorporated into the newer understanding. Thus, on looking at her physical self in the mirror, a young adolescent may think not just about the fact of her "curly hair," but also about the social impact this has on others and the psychological impact it has on herself. And the older adolescent may add a deep concern about the importance of overcoming vanity, while still, like the 2-year-old, admiring her image in the mirror (but only when nobody is looking). We are complex creatures, indeed, and development of the self-concept is a process of understanding ever more of our own complexity.

**Research on Identity Formation**    A considerable amount of research has centered on Erikson's idea that adolescence is the period in which an *identity crisis* must be met and solved (refer back to Table 13.1). Such research has often used a method of assessing identity formation that was developed by James Marcia (1966, 1980). Marcia defined identity in terms of two dimensions that are especially important in Erikson's concept of identity—*occupational commitment* (commitment to a specific career or other long-term activity) and *ideological commitment* (commitment to a definable set of religious, ethical, or political values). Using an interview technique to assess the strength of these commitments and the amount of personal struggle or questioning involved in choosing them, Marcia developed a system for classifying people in terms of their identity status (see Figure 13.9).

One consistent finding from research using Marcia's system is that, at least for middle-class males in our society, the prime time for experiencing an identity crisis is between the ages of 18 and 21 (Waterman, 1982). It is probably no coincidence that these years coincide with the first 3 years of college for most of the individuals studied. College is a time when young people think actively about their careers, and when they challenge previously accepted values. Another consistent finding is

*How self-descriptions typically change as one progresses from early childhood into adulthood*

*How the differ: young males and j sexual relationshi problems*

*How Erikson's concept of an identity crisis has been defined for the purpose of research, and some findings that have emerged from such research*

*Evidence that s discovered, not che*

**Figure 13.9** *Four categories of identity formation*

*James Marcia developed a procedure to categorize young people into four groups depending on the strength of their career and ideological commitments, and on the degree of questioning or mental struggle involved in establishing those commitments. Notice that the* moratorium *group is currently in an identity crisis and the* achieved *group has already gone through it. The other two groups have not experienced such a crisis.*

| | | Strength of commitments | |
| --- | --- | --- | --- |
| | | High | Low |
| Degree of struggle | High | **Achieved:** Have already gone through an identity crisis. | **Moratorium:** Are currently in an identity crisis. |
| | Low | **Foreclosure:** Have inherited commitments (from parents). Experienced no crisis. | **Diffusion:** Lack commitments and are not concerned about them. |

Historic note: Until his life's destiny was further clarified, Robin Hood spent several years robbing from the rich and giving to the porcupines.

that not everyone experiences an identity crisis by Marcia's definition (Marcia, 1980; Waterman, 1982). Many people go into adult life apparently content to pursue goals and values established for them by others, without a period of questioning (Marcia's *foreclosure* category). Others appear to be unconcerned about a career and appear to avoid ideology (Marcia's *diffusion* category). As Marcia (1980) has suggested, both healthy and unhealthy sides exist to the noncrisis styles. Foreclosed individuals may be viewed as steadfast, committed, and cooperative, or as rigid, dogmatic, and conforming. Identity-diffused individuals may be viewed as carefree and independent, or as careless and directionless.

Studies relating Marcia's identity-statuses to other measures of personality and behavior among college students have shown that those who either are experiencing a crisis or have already experienced it (the *moratorium* and *achieved* categories of Figure 13.9) tend to rank higher in self-esteem, sense of independence, and capacity for intimacy than do those in the other two states (see Marcia, 1980). On the other hand, in one study students in the foreclosure category seemed to be the most well adjusted by a number of measures. They studied diligently, kept regular hours, seemed happy, were less riled by upsetting circumstances, and were most likely to describe their homes as loving and affectionate (Donovan, 1975).

Identity formation may not be the same for women as it is for men. Carol Gilligan (1982) has argued that Erikson's concept of identity (and, by implication, Marcia's measurement of it) is biased toward males. Even though most women in our society have jobs or careers, and are as likely as men to have ideological values, they are less likely to define themselves in those terms. They are more likely to define themselves in terms of personal relationships and responsibilities. Gilligan suggests that Erikson's fifth life stage (the identity crisis) is more strongly intertwined with the sixth stage (the crisis of intimacy) for women than it is for men. Using Marcia's or similar measures, fewer correlations are found between identity achievement and positive self-perception for women than for men (Waterman, 1982). Interestingly, in one study young women who grew up in homes with no father were more likely than other young women to be in Marcia's achieved category (St. Clair & Day, 1979). Perhaps the model of their own working mother, or the lack of stable family relationships, led them to focus more on personal achievement and less on relationships.

## Moral Reasoning

Even young children show a concern for others. Preschool children (ages 3 to 5) who were paired with their younger brothers and sisters in the strange-situation test were observed trying to comfort their younger siblings (Stewart & Marvin, 1984). Infants less than 2 years of age have been observed to hug, kiss, or give toys or food to persons who were showing signs of sadness, apparently to cheer them up

***The importance of empathy***

*Although most research on moral reasoning focuses on thinking processes, such thought does not take place in an emotional vacuum. It depends in part on the capacity to feel what other people are feeling, even if that means sharing another's distress.*

■ *How Kohlberg's stages can be viewed as a progression toward an increasingly broad social perspective*

(Radke-Yarrow & others, 1983). Martin Hoffman (1975, 1987) has argued that the origins of morality lie in an innate capacity for *empathy*, that is, a capacity to feel what another person is feeling. Because we can feel the sadness or pain of another person, we strive to help that person overcome that sadness and pain. As you recall, Hoffman's theory of discipline emphasizes the parent's role in calling forth the child's empathy when the child has hurt or failed to help another person.

Another line of thought about the origin of morality emphasizes logical reasoning more than feeling. Piaget pioneered this line of thought in his discussion of the shift in style of moral reasoning in middle childhood. But the psychologist who carried this approach out most fully, extending it into adolescence and adulthood, is Lawrence Kohlberg.

**Kohlberg's Theory: Stages of Moral Reasoning**   Kohlberg's basic approach—in research that he began in the 1950s and has been carried on by others since his death in 1987—is to present people with dilemmas that embody conflicting claims for justice, ask them what the story's protagonist should do and why, and analyze their answers for evidence of different types of moral reasoning. Consider his best-known dilemma (slightly modified from Colby & others, 1983):

> In Europe a woman was near death from a special kind of cancer. A druggist in her town had recently discovered a drug that doctors thought might save her, but he was charging $2000 for a small dose—ten times what the drug cost him to make. The sick woman's husband, Heinz, went to everyone he knew to borrow the money, trying every legal means to obtain it, but he could only get about $1000, which was half of what he needed to buy the drug. He told the druggist that his wife was dying, and asked him to sell it cheaper or allow him to pay the rest later. But the druggist said, "No, I discovered the drug and I'm going to make money from it." Heinz became desperate and considered breaking into the drugstore to steal the drug for his wife. Should Heinz steal the drug? Why or why not?

Before proceeding further, you might find it interesting to think about how you would respond to this dilemma. Why do you think Heinz should or shouldn't steal the drug? Give as complete a response as possible. Or, better yet, raise the dilemma with a friend or two to see how they explain their answers. This will give you a feeling for the reasoning processes by which people form or defend moral judgments. Kohlberg was interested in the method of thinking rather than the actual moral decision in these dilemmas. Kohlberg developed a system for classifying people's reasoning into five different categories, which he believed represent successive stages in the development of moral reasoning. The stages, along with examples of responses to the Heinz dilemma that illustrate each, are described in Table 13.2 (based on Kohlberg, 1984; Rest, 1986).

As you study the table, notice that each stage takes into account a broader portion of the social world than does the previous one. The sequence begins with thought of oneself alone (Stage 1), and then progresses to encompass other individuals directly involved in the questioned action (Stage 2), others who will hear about and evaluate the action (Stage 3), society at large (Stage 4), and, finally, universal principles concerning all of humankind (Stage 5). According to Kohlberg, the stages represent a true developmental progression in the sense that to reach any given stage a person must first pass through the preceding ones. Thinking within one stage, and discovering the limitations of that way of thinking, provides the motivating force for progression to the next. Kohlberg did not claim that everyone goes through the entire sequence; in fact, his research suggested that few go beyond Stage 4 and many don't go past Stage 2 or Stage 3. Nor did he link his stages to specific ages, though he believed that adolescence and young adulthood is the time when advancement into the higher stages is most likely to occur. The higher stages require formal-operational thinking (ability to think abstractly and hypothetically), which Kohlberg, like Piaget (discussed in Chapter 12), saw as

**Figure 13.10** *Results of a longitudinal study of moral reasoning*

*This graph, based on a longitudinal study of males from a relatively high socioeconomic background, shows the percentage of subjects at each age who were reasoning at each of Kohlberg's stages. Notice the rise and fall in Stage 3 and the consistent rise in Stage 4 reasoning over the adolescent and young adult years. Very little Stage 5 reasoning was found, but it also increased with age. (Adapted from Colby & others, 1983.)*

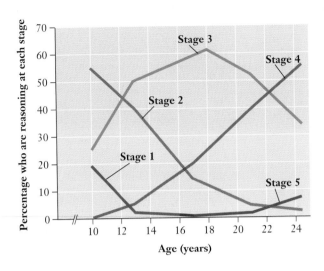

■ *Some often-raised criticisms of Kohlberg's theory*

Chapter 12), saw as emerging in adolescence. Figure 13.10 illustrates the results of one long-term study supporting Kohlberg's theory about the sequence of stages.

Kohlberg's theory has not gone without criticism. Some researchers have challenged his claim for an invariant sequence to the stages, citing evidence based on his own methods that people sometimes go from a higher-numbered stage to a lower one as they grow older (Liebert, 1984). Others have argued that the theory does not adequately explain why a person progresses from stage to stage; it places too much emphasis on the role of thought alone and not enough on social learning (Gibbs & Schnell, 1985).

**Table 13.2** *Kohlberg's stages of moral reasoning*

**Stage 1:  Obedience and punishment orientation**

Reasoners in this stage focus on direct consequences to themselves. An action is bad if it will result in punishment, not bad if it will not. *Pro* (reason for stealing the drug): "If he lets his wife die, he will get in trouble." *Con* (reason for not stealing the drug): "He shouldn't steal it because he'll be caught and sent to jail."

**Stage 2:  Self-interested exchanges**

Reasoners here understand that different people have different self-interests, which sometimes come into conflict. To get what you want you have to make a bargain, giving up something in return. *Pro*: "It won't bother him much to serve a little jail term, if he still has his wife when he gets out." *Con*: "His wife will probably die anyway before he gets out of jail, so it won't do him much good."

**Stage 3:  Interpersonal accord and conformity**

Reasoners here try to live up to the expectations of others who are important to them. An action is good if it will improve a person's relationships with significant others, bad if it will harm those relationships. *Pro*: "Your family will think you're an inhuman husband if you don't." *Con*: "Everyone will think you are a criminal. You won't be able to face anyone again."

**Stage 4:  Law-and-order morality**

Reasoners here argue that, to maintain social order, each person should resist personal pressures and feel duty-bound to follow the laws and conventions of the larger society. *Pro*: "It's a husband's duty to save his wife." *Con*: "It's always wrong to steal. What if everyone stole? Then there would be no law."

**Stage 5:  Human-rights and social-welfare morality**

Reasoners here still have a strong respect for laws, but balance that with ethical principles that may transcend specific laws. Laws that fail to promote the general welfare or that violate basic ethical principles can be changed, reinterpreted, or in some cases deliberately flouted as a form of protest. The goal is justice within the law. *Pro*: "The law isn't really set up for these circumstances. Taking the drug in this situation isn't really right, but it's justified." *Con*: "You can't completely blame Heinz for stealing in this case, but he shouldn't get carried away by his own emotions and forget the long-range point of view. He has to consider the value of respect for law and the value of all of the lives involved."

Note: Under each stage description are examples of pro and con responses on the Heinz dilemma (based on examples in Kohlberg, 1984, and Rest, 1986). Earlier versions of the theory included a sixth stage, which emphasized universal ethical principles almost to the exclusion of other considerations. Stage 6 has been dropped in current versions, however, because of failure to find people who reason in accordance with it.

A third criticism often raised is that moral reasoning as measured by Kohlberg's method may have little to do with actual moral behavor (see Damon, 1983). Logically, it is certainly possible to be a high-caliber moral philosopher, great at coming up with reasons for one choice or the other in hypothetical dilemmas, without being a moral person. Kohlberg himself argued that the fit between moral reasoning and moral behavior is far from perfect, but he provided evidence that ranking on his moral reasoning test does correlate moderately well with a number of measures of moral behavior (see Blasi, 1980). For example, in one study students who ranked high on the moral reasoning measure were less likely to cheat on a test than students who ranked lower (Kohlberg, 1975). In another study, people who ranked high were more likely than others to refuse an experimenter's demand that they give what appeared to be painful electric shocks to another person (Kohlberg & Candee, 1984).

Still another common criticism is that Kohlberg's theory may fail to represent all possible moral perspectives. More specifically, critics argue that it is biased toward a Western tradition of codified laws and abstract principles of justice, and that it has no stage or category that adequately captures non-Western traditions in which moral thought is embedded in an understanding of personal relationships and communal needs (Simpson, 1974; Snarey, 1985). Non-Westerners tested by Kohlberg's method—including Tibetan monks and village leaders in Kenya and New Guinea who were selected for their ethical leadership—rarely scored beyond Stage 3 (Snarey, 1985). Non-Westerners are less inclined than Westerners to believe that a person can decide what is right or wrong without more knowledge of the individuals involved—how each person would feel, what specific effects it would have on their family, and so on. This concern with individual relationships and feelings tends to land them in Stage 3 in Kohlberg's system, but that stage does not do justice to the sophisticated, communalistic moral philosophy that may underlie their answers.

Carol Gilligan (1982, 1987) has made a similar point about differences between men and women in our society. Kohlberg's original studies were of males only, and later studies sometimes, but not always, revealed lower average scores for females than for males (for both sides of this issue, see Bussey & Maughan, 1982, and Walker, 1984). According to Gilligan, women often get placed at Stage 3 in Kohlberg's system for essentially the same reason that Tibetan monks do—they frame their answers more in terms of personal relationships than in terms of laws or abstract principles.

*Gilligan's view that justice and caring are two different moral voices, and that males and females differ in the relative strength of each*

**Gilligan's "Two Voices" Approach to Moral Reasoning**   As an alternative to Kohlberg's approach, Gilligan (1987) studies moral reasoning by asking adolescents and young adults to describe, in extended interviews, moral dilemmas that they have actually faced in their own lives. She finds "two voices" in the transcripts of these descriptions—one she calls *justice* and the other *caring*. Whereas the justice voice speaks of principles of right and wrong, the caring voice speaks of specific people's feelings and the consequences that an action will have for them. For example, when a 12-year-old girl discussed her decision to confront a camp director about an unfair rule, the justice voice described why the rule was unfair, and the caring voice described how the rule was upsetting her younger brother and how the camp director might feel if his rule were challenged (Gilligan & others, 1990).

In studies comparing the two genders for the extent to which each voice was present in such interviews, Gilligan (1987) found that the justice voice was stronger in boys and men and the caring voice was stronger in girls and women. Other researchers, however, using somewhat different methods of measuring the two voices, have failed to find consistent gender differences (Ford & Lowery, 1986; Walker & others, 1987). Researchers agree that the caring voice becomes relatively stronger and the justice voice relatively weaker when the dilemma is personal and real rather than hypothetical, but at present there is no agreement on whether there are average gender differences in the strengths of the two voices.

## Adulthood: Caring and Working

Freud (1935) defined emotional maturity as the capacity to love and work. Love and work are also the main themes of Erikson's early- and mid-adult stages (Stages 6 and 7 in Table 13.1) and in fact are central to nearly all research and theory on adult development. In two long-term studies of men, George Vaillant and Eva Milofsky (1980) found evidence supporting Erikson's idea that some degree of success in developing an intimate love relationship must occur before a man can feel fully committed to a career or to helping the broader society. Based on another extensive study of men, Daniel Levinson (1978, 1986) proposed a theory that men go through a predictable sequence of crises in their attempts to find meaning in their work and family relationships. Various other theorists have written about women's attempts to balance their concern for family with their desire to pursue a career (for example, Neugarten, 1984). These are representative of the types of issues on which developmental psychologists studying adulthood have focused.

Whereas some developmentalists, including Levinson (1986) and Vaillant (1977), believe that adult development follows an inevitable sequence, others, including Bernice Neugarten (1979, 1984), do not. In the first part of this chapter, I mentioned Neugarten's concept of a social clock, the social expectations about what people should be doing at particular times in life. She believes that our society is now entering an era of relative "clocklessness" for adults. To paraphrase Neugarten (1979), we are becoming accustomed to such images as the 28-year-old college president (male or female), the 50-year-old grandmother who has just completed medical school, and the 65-year-old father of a preschooler who takes care of the child while his wife works. Adult lives follow lots of different patterns.

### Family

**Marriage** In the children's fairy tale, the prince (who used to be a frog) and princess fall in love, marry, and live happily ever after. Reality is not always like that. Why do some marriages work and others don't? Why do some couples seem to grow happier together with each passing year, and others fall into stale, bored routine or bitter strife?

Among the not-surprising ingredients of successful marriages that have been identified by interviews and observations of happily married couples are the following: (a) The partners *like* one another and think of the other not just as husband or wife but as best friend (Lauer & Lauer, 1985). (b) They have a shared view of the responsibilities of husband and wife (Bahr & others, 1983; Bowen & Orthner, 1983). (c) They are strongly committed to the marriage and are each willing to go more than half way to carry the relationship through hard times (Lauer & Lauer, 1985). (d) They argue in constructive ways rather than unconstructive ways (Gottman & Krokoff, 1989). (e) They are able to understand each other's thoughts and feelings, even when not explicitly expressed (Gottman, 1979).

The last point, which has to do with nonverbal communication between husband and wife, is especially worth pursuing. John Gottman and his colleagues have for many years been studying patterns of communication in couples who rate themselves as either highly satisfied or dissatisfied with their marriage. One interesting finding is a strong positive correlation between marital satisfaction and the

**Resetting the social clock**

*Bernice Neugarten believes that social expectations about what people should be doing at particular stages of life are becoming increasingly flexible. One indicator of such change is the growing number of middle-aged and older college students.*

■ *Evidence that one important factor in marital success is the husband's ability to understand the wife's nonverbal signals*

husband's ability to understand his wife's nonverbal signals. In one study, Gottman (1979) analyzed videotapes of married couples engaged in conversations about marital problems. He found that in unhappy marriages the wife responded to the unspoken emotional needs of her husband but the husband did not respond to the unspoken needs of his wife; in happy marriages, by contrast, the two were equal in understanding and responding to each other's needs.

**Cultural connections**

*Research on successful marriage may misrepresent the lives of couples in traditional societies. Contrast the two couples shown here and think about what might constitute success for people living outside of modern industrial societies.*

In another study, Gottman and Albert Porterfield (1981) asked each partner to try to communicate to his or her spouse a particular meaning using words that could be interpreted in more than one way. For example, the words, "I'm cold, aren't you?" might be used to communicate any of three possible messages: (1) I wonder if you are cold. (2) Please warm me up with physical affection. (3) Please turn the thermostat up. Each person's attempt to communicate such messages was videotaped and then was "read" both by that person's spouse and by a stranger (another married man or woman). The most significant finding was that in unhappy marriages the husband was actually worse, on average, at reading his wife's signals than was the stranger, whereas in happy marriages the husband was better at reading them than was the stranger. No such relationship was found for wives' reading of husbands' messages—they were apparently equally good at it whether or not the marriage was happy.

Gottman's work brings us back to a theme developed earlier in the chapter. Remember those 33-month-old girl-boy pairs in Jacklin and Maccoby's experiment who couldn't play well together because the boy didn't respond to the girl's signals for change, which were more subtle than the boy's? The same thing can happen at 33 *years* old. Clearly, one of the prerequisites of a good marriage is that two people of different genders—who grew up in somewhat different worlds, in which there were different patterns of communication—must learn to understand one another. Perhaps because the social world of girls places more emphasis on intimacy than does that of boys, the young man commonly lags behind his partner in accomplishing this task. Yet, if Gottman is right, he must succeed if the marriage is going to be a happy one.

■ *Some effects that parenthood has on adults' activities and social relationships*

**Sharing responsibilities**

*The strains associated with parenting can be greatly reduced if everyone pitches in to help. An additional benefit of such sharing is the breakdown of gender stereotypes.*

■ *Evidence that job satisfaction increases with age, and some possible reasons why*

**Parenthood**   When more than 2000 married men and women were asked what event was most important in making them feel that they were really an adult, the most common response for both genders was, "Becoming a parent" (Hoffman & Manis, 1979). With parenthood comes responsibility for the life of another human being. Based on studies in several different cultures, David Gutmann (1975) has argued that certain universal changes occur in men and women when they become parents, which he calls the *parental imperative*. According to Gutmann, men become less reckless, more authoritative, and more preoccupied with making a living for their family; and women become more nurturant, more gentle, and more preoccupied with direct care of the child. In our society, parenthood leads a couple into new ties with the larger community. Parents are naturally more concerned than nonparents about such issues as schools, parks, and safety on the streets; they vote more often than nonparents (Adelson & Hall, 1987); and they are more likely to join a church or synagogue. Parenthood promotes new friendships with other couples who have children and a drifting away from old friends who don't. It also strengthens the couple's ties with their own parents, the child's grandparents, who now may be looked to for guidance, emotional support, and help with child-care.

The obligations associated with parenting can be a strain on the marriage itself. Several studies have shown that couples' satisfaction with their marriage tends to decrease during the childrearing years and increase again when the children leave home (see Bee, 1987). With children there is less opportunity for husband and wife to be alone—less dialogue, intimacy, and sex. Many couples experience what seems like a second honeymoon when their children leave home and they have the opportunity to rediscover each other, perhaps with a bit less passion but with more wisdom and tenderness.

### Employment

**The Career Cycle**   There is a certain regularity to careers in our society, more so for men than for women. The early to mid-twenties is typically a time of career exploration—taking initial steps and perhaps changing careers if the first choice is unsatisfying. In Levinson's theory of adult development, this is a time of creating and charting a path toward one's *Dream*, which Levinson capitalizes and defines as one's idealized vision of what he or she is working toward—becoming plant manager, president of a company, famous journalist, or whatever (Levinson, 1978). The next 15 to 20 years, in Levinson's theory, is a time of working toward the Dream, accompanied perhaps by a modification of it to coincide with reality, or in some cases by a complete change in Dream midway through. By age 45, people (omitting those who started late) in most careers have advanced about as far as they will up the career ladder. For those who have not achieved the Dream, or who were distracted from pursuing it, or who achieved it and found it less rewarding than they had imagined, this can be an occasion for midlife crisis. Beyond age 45, people are less likely to see themselves as climbing the ladder and may adopt a more relaxed attitude toward their career, enjoying the day-to-day work for its own sake and the social relationships associated with it.

Large-scale statistical studies show that most people—in most lines of work, both blue collar and white collar—experience a continuous increase in job satisfaction as they grow older, at least from age 20 through 60 (Rhodes, 1983). Older people not only *say* that they like their jobs better, but they demonstrate it through such evidence as fewer avoidable absences from work (Rhodes, 1983). Increased satisfaction during the first couple of work decades may result from changing jobs until a more satisfying one is found, advancement to more interesting positions within a given job, and acquisition of greater skill and competence. The continued rise in satisfaction after that may be due to the increased job security that accompanies seniority and the more relaxed attitude that comes when the person is no longer trying to climb the ladder.

■ *Evidence that career advancement and life satisfaction may not be correlated, but that job loss can be psychologically damaging*

**Relationship of Employment to Life Satisfaction**   Surprisingly, given the great weight that our society attaches to careers, remarkably little evidence exists that career advancement beyond a certain minimum increases people's general satisfaction with life (Bee, 1987). In one study at a large corporation, middle-aged men who had progressed furthest up the corporate ladder expressed more satisfaction with their jobs than did their less successful age-mates, but did not express more satisfaction with their lives overall (Bray & Howard, 1983). The men who had not risen seemed on average to have a different set of priorities from those of men who had risen—they were less aggressive, less selfish, more nurturant, more family oriented, and more religious.

On the other hand, actual loss of a job can have devastating effects on life satisfaction that are not simply due to loss of income. In one study, based on a series of interviews of eighty-two families in which the husband had lost his job due to general layoffs, job loss was found to produce anxiety, depression, and self-blame in most men (Liem & Liem, 1988; Liem, 1987). This occurred for both white-collar and blue-collar workers, and it occurred regardless of whether the family had extra economic resources to carry them through the period of unemployment. The men talked about their sense of not fulfilling the expectations that they, their family, or others had of themselves; of loss of the personal friendships that they had at work; and of loss of the pleasures and sense of achievement associated with the work itself. Wives also suffered when the husbands were unemployed, even in cases in which the wives were employed. According to Ramsay Liem (1987), the husband's emotional state—not the wife's reaction to his loss of job—was the main source of tension in the marriage. Husbands often vented their frustration on their wives, thereby alienating the one person who could provide them the most comfort and support during a hard time.

*The daughter track*

*Most women, whether employed or not, accept the social identity of caregiver. For Charlas Rhodes, 51, shown here with her 71-year-old mother, Arena Whytus, this has meant leaving a job, moving to another city, and setting up a new home so that her mother would not have to be placed in a nursing home. Although she gets little sleep and has virtually no social life, Rhodes says she has no regrets and feels herself blessed by the opportunity to care for her mother.*

■ *Evidence that out-of-home work typically reduces the stress experienced by women*

Although in the past most studies of the psychological effects of employment or unemployment have been of men, recently there have been some studies of women. Women today are far more likely than men to hold two jobs—one outside the home and the other inside the home. In families in which the husband and wife work an equal number of hours outside the home, the wife still usually does most of the child-care, grocery shopping, cooking, and house cleaning (Maret & Finlay, 1984). What are the effects of combining out-of-home and at-home work on women's psychological and physical well-being? A review of research on that topic concluded, somewhat surprisingly, that work outside the home most often reduces rather than increases the stress experienced by women (Baruch & others, 1987).

The job at the office or plant, hectic as it may sometimes be, is usually more ordered and predictable than the job at home, and provides relief. Also, in a world where the role of housewife is afforded little esteem, where social relationships most often originate at the out-of-home workplace, and where "money talks," the out-of-home job gives a woman respect, friends, and power that she may not have had before. Only in cases in which a low-prestige job is added on top of a particularly heavy family load has out-of-home work been shown statistically to increase the stress experienced by women (Baruch & others, 1987).

### Growing Old

Beyond age 65 or 70, most people are retired from their jobs and are finished with the direct care of children. What happens then? Based on current projections of life expectancy, and taking into account the greater longevity of college graduates compared to the rest of the population, the majority of you who are reading this book will live past your eightieth birthday. You may actually live more years in postretirement than you did in childhood. If your health and pension are good, your postretirement will allow you greater freedom than you ever had before.

■ *Some possible reasons why women live longer than men*

Women in the United States live an average of 7 years longer than men (U.S. Bureau of the Census, 1986). Some people have attempted to explain this difference by arguing that women's occupations are less stressful than men's, but that explanation is contradicted by evidence that the advantage for women persists regardless of occupation. In fact, in the Soviet Union, which has a longer history of equivalent occupations for men and women than does the United States, women live on average 10 years longer than men (Siegel, 1980). Part of the difference undoubtedly stems from the fact that women take better care of their health than do men. They smoke less, drink less, drive more carefully, have better diets (especially in old age), and consult doctors more readily when something is wrong (Botwinick, 1984). The difference in smoking may be especially important. Smoking dramatically increases the risk of heart disease (the single leading killer today) and lung cancer, both of which occur at higher rates in men than in women (Hammond & Horn, 1984). To the degree that the gender gap in longevity is due to smoking, we should find it narrowing over the next couple of decades, as fewer men and more women smoke today than in times past.

Some people fear old age. There is no denying that aging entails loss. We lose gradually our youthful looks and some of our physical strength, agility, sensory acuity, and mental quickness. We lose some of our social roles (especially those related to employment) and some of our authority (as people take us less seriously).

*The joys of aging*
*For many people, interacting with grandchildren is one of the pleasures of old age. Contrary to the stereotype of aged people as lonely and isolated, most live within visiting distance of relatives and see a good deal of them.*

We lose loved ones who die before us, and of course with each year we lose one more year from our own life expectancy. Yet, if you ask the elderly, old age is not as bad as it seems to the young. In one study, in which younger adults were asked to project themselves into the future and rate their expected life satisfaction in late adulthood, their ratings were much lower than the life-satisfaction scores obtained from people who had already reached that age (Borges & Dutton, 1976). Researchers have found that ratings of life satisfaction and self-esteem are on average as high in old age as at any other time in adulthood (Costa & others, 1987; Bengston & others, 1985). Priorities and expectations change as we age to match realities, and along with losses there are gains. With greater free time and fewer responsibilities comes the opportunity to spend more time at hobbies, community service, travel, reading, contemplation, and enjoying friends and relatives.

*Early evidence for, and later evidence against, the idea that disengagement is for most people a natural and healthy aspect of aging*

**Disengagement Versus Activity Theories of Old Age**    One long-standing idea about old age is that it is a time of gradual disengagement from the world. The psychoanalytic theorist Carl Jung (1969) believed that past middle age there is a gradual shift in personality from *extroversion*, defined as orientation to the outer world, to *introversion*, defined as orientation to the inner, subjective world. Erikson's theory that the last stage of life is a time of mental integration of past experiences (see Table 13.1) also implies at least some degree of disengagement from the present world. Based on a longitudinal study of elderly residents of Kansas City, Elaine Cumming and William Henry (1961) concluded that disengagement is a natural and healthy part of aging. They found that with time older people became less concerned with others and the world around them and more concerned with thoughts about such issues as their own past life and their afterlife.

However, other researchers challenged Cumming and Henry's interpretation. Nobody disagreed with the finding that older people often do become disengaged, but they challenged the idea that disengagement is the person's own choice. The counter idea was that society's failure to provide meaningful roles and activities for older people, coupled with physical changes such as deafness and lameness, forces many older people into reduced worldly involvement. Many studies following Cumming and Henry's showed that the most active and engaged older people, not the most disengaged, are generally the most satisfied with their current lives (see Botwinick, 1984). The consensus today is that, for most people, continued active involvement is the key to a happy old age. On the other hand, what is true of the majority is not necessarily true of everyone. Researchers have consistently found that some older people are very content to withdraw from the social world. These are typically the same people who, as younger adults, preferred a more contemplative, less active lifestyle, which in their later years they can finally pursue in a way that they never could before (Maddox & Campbell, 1985).

*Evidence that even a small measure of control over one's environment can increase happiness and longevity in old age*

**Importance of Control Over One's Environment**    It is useful to distinguish between two groups of older adults, referred to by Neugarten (1974) as the *young-old* and the *old-old*. The young-old, which includes the vast majority of older people, are those whose health allows them to be self-sufficient. Most of the young-old live in their own homes, cook their own meals, and choose their own activities each day. The old-old are those who cannot fully take care of themselves and are cared for by their adult children or in nursing homes or other institutions. Research on the old-old indicates that their happiness and even their ability to stay alive depend to a considerable degree on their retention of some control over their lives despite their dependent status. In one experiment conducted in convalescent homes, residents who were given some degree of control—such as the ability to choose what they ate and how the furniture in their room was arranged—showed an improved mood and a higher survival rate compared to other residents of the same homes (Rodin, 1986).

■ *Evidence that having someone with whom to share thoughts and feelings is important to happiness and health in old age*

**Importance of a Confidant**   In an experiment that was concerned primarily with memory abilities in old age, researchers visited a nursing home and interviewed the residents four times during a 6-week period (Langer & others, 1979). In one condition, the interviewers simply asked a lot of questions about the resident's daily activities and past experiences. In the other condition, called *reciprocal self-disclosure*, the interviewers also told the interviewees about themselves, disclosing details about their own activities and experiences. This simple intervention had a remarkable effect. The reciprocal self-disclosure group not only showed greater improvement in memory on the formal tests used in the experiment, but also, according to the ratings of nurses who did not know which residents were in which group, showed improved mood, alertness, and sociability compared to the other group.

These results are consistent with other evidence that one of the principal requirements for a happy and healthy old age is someone to confide in. For most elderly people who are not in nursing homes, the spouse is the main confidant, and loss of a spouse can be tragic to the surviving person if he or she has no other confidant. Death of a spouse has repeatedly been shown to produce depression, anxiety, and reduced satisfaction with life (Lieberman & Borman, 1981). Death rates from practically all causes—including heart disease, stroke, hypertension, cancer, accidents, suicide, pneumonia, diabetes, and tuberculosis—are dramatically higher among widowed or divorced older people than among those of the same age who are still living with a spouse (Lynch, 1977). All these effects occur for both genders, but are greater for men than for women.

Why do women seem to cope better with the loss of a spouse than do men? The statistical finding may partly result from a selection effect. Men are much more likely than women to remarry following the death of a spouse (partly because there are so many more older women than older men). Those men who remarry are not counted among the widowers, and those who don't remarry may have been the ones who were at greater risk of death to begin with. But selection aside, there is reason to believe that older women adapt to the single life better than do older men. Women know better how to take care of themselves, and they keep closer social ties to relatives and friends than do men.

**Approaching Death**   The one certainty of life is that it ends in death. Surveys have shown that fear of death typically peaks in a person's fifties, which is when adults first begin to find a significant number of their age-mates dying from such causes as heart attack and cancer (Riley, 1970; Karp, 1988). Older people have less fear of death. They are more likely to accept it as inevitable; and death in old age, when a person has lived a full life, seems less unfair than it did earlier on.

Various theories have been proposed regarding the stages or mental tasks involved in preparing for death. Based on her own experience with caring for dying patients, Elisabeth Kübler-Ross (1969) proposed that people go through five stages when they hear that they are incurably ill and will soon die: (1) *denial*—"The diagnosis can't be right," or "I'll lick it"; (2) *anger*—"Why me?"; (3) *bargaining*—"If I do this, can I live a little longer?"; (4) *depression*—"All is lost"; and (5) *acceptance*—"I am prepared to die." Another theory is that preparation for death consists of reviewing one's life and trying to make sense of it (Butler, 1975).

As useful as such theories may be in understanding individual cases, research shows that there is no universal approach to death. Each person does it differently. One person may review his or her life, another may not. One person may go through one or several of Kübler-Ross's stages but not all of them, and others may go through them in different sequences (Kastenbaum, 1985). The people who I have seen die all did it in pretty much the way they did other things in life. When my mother discovered that she would soon die—at the too-young age of 62—it was very important to her to have her four sons around, not so we could comfort her as much as so she could tell us some of the things she had learned about life that we might want to know. She spent her time talking about what, from her present perspective, seemed important and what seemed not. She reviewed her life not to justify it, but to tell us why some things she did worked out and others didn't. She had been a teacher all her life, and she died one.

## Concluding Thoughts

There are many ways to think about the course of human life. Biographers, who write about specific individuals, usually focus on those aspects of their subjects' lives that made them unique. A unique temperament, set of family expectations, hometown, set of friends, and set of meaningful chance experiences might all be described as part of the stew that produced a particular scientist, artist, or diplomat. Developmental psychologists, in contrast, are usually more interested in the life course of people in general than that of a particular individual, which means that they usually study the regularities rather than the differences in development. In concluding this chapter (and this two-chapter unit on development), it would be worthwhile to think in general terms about the possible sources of regularity from person to person in development. In theory, such regularity can stem from the following three sources:

**1. Biological maturation as a source of regularity** Psychoanalytic theories, and theories originating in ethology or sociobiology, tend to emphasize this source of regularity. The body changes in certain obvious and predictable ways as a person progresses through infancy, childhood, adolescence, young and mid-adulthood, and old age—and those changes certainly influence behavior. The degree to which more subtle biological changes in drive and temperament may also occur and contribute to the regularity in behavioral development is more debatable. Erikson's theory of the eight stages of life is a good example of an attempt to link psychological development to biologically based capacities and drives (though he does not ignore the role of experience).

**2. Logical inevitability as a source of regularity** Cognitive theories of development tend to emphasize this source of regularity. *Logical inevitability*, as the term is used here, refers to the idea that the understanding of certain concepts necessarily depends on the prior understanding of one or more simpler concepts. Thus, the simpler concepts and the behaviors they produce will always precede the more complex concepts and the behaviors they produce. Kohlberg's theory of the development of moral reasoning is a good example of this idea. Kohlberg argued that people progress through the stages in a specific order because each stage logically builds on the ones before it. According to Kohlberg, it is not possible to reason at Stage 3, for example, without being able to reason at Stage 2, because Stage 3 logically encompasses Stage 2. Presumably any kind of being, including a creature from outer space that is capable of moral thought, or a computer programmed to learn ways of thinking morally, would have to go through the stages in that order.

**3. Social constraints and expectations as a source of regularity** The third source of regularity is the one imposed by the social environment. Bronfenbrenner's social ecology theory and Neugarten's concept of a social clock both emphasize this source. People who develop in the same culture, in which laws, customs, and social expectations are based on a shared set of assumptions about what people can or should do at certain ages, will as a result share a similar life course. In our culture, people usually learn algebra at about age 14 not because of biological or logical inevitability, but because that is the age at which they are required to study it in school. Similarly, laws and social expectations affect the age at which people in our culture get jobs, become independent of their parents, start families of their own, and retire from their jobs.

One way to review this chapter (and the previous one, too) would be to look back at each theory or finding that had to do with predictable change over the life course or some portion of it and to think about it in relation to the three just-described sources of regularity. How might biological maturation, logical inevitability, and/or social constraints account for the developmental change described?

## Further Reading

**Erik H. Erikson** (1968). *Identity: Youth and crisis.* New York: Norton.
*For students who wish to learn about Erikson's psychoanalytic view of development, this brief book is perhaps the best place to begin. In the first half of the book, Erikson describes his clinical approach to understanding the life cycle and his overall view of the various life stages, centering the latter on the role of each stage in the development of one's personal identity. In the second half, Erikson discusses the identity crisis of adolescence and young adulthood, illustrating it with the case history of the psychologist William James.*

**Jean Piaget** (1932/1965). *The moral judgment of the child.* New York: Free Press.
*For the beginning student, this is perhaps the most readable and interesting of Piaget's books. It is also the only book in which Piaget places great emphasis on the role of social relationships in development. Especially interesting is his description of the manner by which children's unsupervised play in games such as marbles leads them to a higher understanding of rules and democratic processes.*

**William Damon** (1983). *Social and personality development: Infancy through adolescence.* New York: Norton.
*This is an excellent general text on the topic of its title. It focuses on children's understanding of themselves and social relationships, and the processes through which these change as they grow older.*

**Kevin MacDonald** (1988). *Social and personality development: An evolutionary synthesis.* New York: Plenum.
*This is an ambitious attempt to integrate many of the standard theories and classic findings in developmental psychology into a broad, biologically based conception of human development. It weaves together many of the ideas that you read about in this chapter with ethological and sociobiological ideas that were presented in Chapter 4. You may or may not agree with the result, but it will certainly give you something to think about.*

## Looking Ahead

One theme of the chapter that you have just read is that psychological development is in part a product of the social setting within which the person develops. We turn now to a two-chapter unit on social psychology, which focuses even more explicitly on the social environment. It deals with the mechanisms or processes through which people perceive, understand, and are influenced by each other.

# PART 6 THE PERSON IN A WORLD OF PEOPLE

SOCIAL COGNITION

SOCIAL INFLUENCES ON BEHAVIOR

*We are social beings through and through. We are motivated to understand others; we are concerned about what others think of us; and our understanding of ourselves is strongly affected by our perception of what others think of us. This two-chapter unit is on social psychology—the attempt to understand human thought and behavior in relation to the social contexts in which they occur. The first chapter is about the mental processes involved in understanding others, ourselves, and the social world in general. The second is about some of the ways by which the presence or activities of other people, real or imagined, influence our behavior.*

# CHAPTER 14

Perceiving Others

Perceiving and Presenting the Self

Meanings of Friendship and Love

Attitudes

# SOCIAL COGNITION

As Aristotle pointed out 23 centuries ago, we are by nature social animals. We are born completely dependent on other humans and we remain dependent on them in countless ways throughout life. We need others for our emotional as well as economic well-being. If alone too much, we feel lonely; and loneliness is a drive, not unlike hunger, that impels us to behave in such ways as to remove the aversive state. We are motivated not only to be with others, but to be approved of by them, and that motive plays an enormous role in the ways we think and act.

*Social psychology*, which will occupy us for this chapter and the next, is the area of psychology most directly concerned with the influence that other people have on an individual's thought and behavior. Gordon Allport (1968) once defined social psychology as "an attempt to understand and explain how the thought, feeling, and behavior of individuals are influenced by the actual, imagined, or implied presence of others." Notice that this definition includes the study of *thought* and *feeling* as well as behavior, and that these are viewed as functions of the *imagined* or *implied* presence of others as well as their actual presence.

Consistent with Allport's definition, most social psychologists assume that the social environment must be described in terms of how it is perceived and understood by the person. *Social cognition*, which is our topic for this chapter, is the study of the mental processes that are involved in people's interpretations of, and reactions to, their social world. The chapter is divided into four parts. The first is concerned with the processes involved in perceiving other people. The second is about the processes of perceiving oneself and projecting an image of oneself to other people. The third part deals with the cognitive components underlying friendship and love. And the fourth part addresses the formation of attitudes and their relation to behavior.

## Perceiving Others

We are amazingly quick to form impressions of other people, often based on little information. When we see a painting or photograph of a person we may use the two-dimensional cues there to size up the whole person—we may assign the person a past, a personality, a set of feelings. Artists and photographers play on our tendency to do that. Similarly, when we hear a description of a single utterance or action produced by a total stranger, we tend to build a mental picture of the whole person from that shred of information. And when we have actually met someone, no matter how briefly, we are inclined to say, "I *know* that person," and to half believe that we do. Let us examine some processes and biases involved in forming first impressions.

## Basic Processes of Person Perception

**The Person Schema as a Mental Representation of the Whole Person**   Nearly 50 years ago, Solomon Asch (1946) outlined a perspective on person perception that was closely tied to the Gestalt view of perception. The basic premise of the Gestalt view is that we naturally see objects as wholes, not as separate parts (see Chapter 9). When only a portion of an object is present, we automatically fill in the gaps to create, in our minds, a representation of the whole object. In applying this notion to person perception, Asch argued that we use whatever information we have about a person to build a mental picture of the whole person—not just the physical aspects, but his or her personality as well.

In modern cognitive terminology, the organized set of information or beliefs that we have about any entity or event is called a schema (discussed in Chapter 10), and the organized set of information or beliefs that we have about a person is called a ***person schema***. A schema can be either sketchy or detailed. Suppose you know that you are about to meet a person, but you don't know anything about the person. Immediately you activate your schema of a person in general, which contains those qualities that are common to most people. As you get more information, you begin to fill in the details of that schema, making it more distinct, more representative of a specific person rather than of a person in general. Global ideas in the initial schema, such as *two arms* and *some degree of friendliness*, are replaced, often very quickly, by more specific ideas, such as *long arms with delicate fingers* and *quiet but friendly once you get to know her*. This way of organizing information is extraordinarily efficient. It makes use, at every moment, of information that you already have about a person to enable you to understand and incorporate new information.

**Making Attributions from Behaviors**   Using a specific behavior to form an impression of a person's personality involves making an inference about the cause of the behavior—an inference that the behavior was caused by some relatively stable, inner characteristic of the person, such as friendliness if the action was a friendly one, or carelessness if it was a careless one. Another term for such an inference is ***attribution***. In its most general sense, an attribution is any claim about the cause of something; in the field of social cognition, it is any claim about the cause of a person's behavior.

The study of how people make attributions was initiated by Fritz Heider, who, like Asch, was one of the pioneers in the field of social cognition. Heider (1958) suggested that all people are, in a sense, "naive psychologists." He suggested that everyone tries to understand the causes of others' behavior and that they do this by intuitively attributing the behavior to stable, inner characteristics of the people who are producing the behavior. For example, if you see a man smile, you may attribute the smile to his friendliness or to his guile, depending on other information that you have about him and the circumstances under which the smile occurred. What you carry away from the encounter is not so much a memory that the man smiled as a memory that he was friendly or deceitful; and that memory is added to your schema of that person.

Heider also noted that under some circumstances people attribute behavior not to internal characteristics of the behaving person, but to characteristics of the environment. If you saw a man running and screaming in fear, and then saw that a tiger was chasing him, you would probably not conclude that he is a particularly fearful person, but rather would attribute his fear to the situation—almost anyone would be afraid of a loose tiger. To use behavioral observations to build a picture of a person, one must first judge whether the behavior implies anything unique about the person, or is the sort of action that almost anyone would perform under the circumstances.

***What is your impression of this man?***
*Can you guess what kinds of feelings he's expressing? Before you make a firm attribution, turn the page.*

■ *Heider's view that people intuitively tend to attribute other people's actions to characteristics of their personality*

■ *Kelley's model of the logic that should lead a person to make internal (personality) attributions in some cases and external (situational) attributions in others*

Following up on Heider's ideas about attributions, Harold Kelley (1967, 1973) developed a model of the logic that people might use to judge whether a particular behavior should be attributed to some characteristic of the person or to something about the immediate environment. To illustrate the common sense of Kelley's model before describing it more formally, let me apply it to a specific example. Suppose you observe Susan getting angry while she is caught in a traffic jam. In theory, you might attribute her anger to her *personality* (say, her irritability), to the *situation* (being caught in a traffic jam), to some *extraneous factor* distinct from the traffic jam or her personality (perhaps she had just had a bad day at work), or to some combination of these. According to Kelley, before making the attribution you would ideally want to know the answer to the following three questions: (1) Does Susan regularly get angry when caught in traffic jams? (2) Are most other people who are caught in the traffic jam angry? (3) Does Susan get angry in many other situations (besides traffic jams)? If the answer to the first question is no (she doesn't usually get angry in traffic jams), then you will most likely attribute her anger on this occasion to an extraneous factor. However, if the answer to the first question is yes, then you will most likely attribute Susan's anger to the traffic jam, her personality, or to a combination of both, depending on the answer to the next two questions.

Assuming a yes to the first question (Susan regularly gets angry in traffic jams), you will most likely attribute her anger (a) to the *traffic jam* if the answer to the second question is also yes (most people in the traffic jam are angry) and that to the third question is no (Susan does not get angry in many other situations); (b) to her *personality* if the answer to the second question is no (most people in the traffic jam are not angry) and that to the third question is yes (Susan gets angry in many other situations); and (c) to the *combination* of Susan's personality and the traffic jam if the answers to the second and third questions are both no (Susan isn't angered by most situations, but unlike most people she is easily angered by the traffic jam—her anger represents her characteristic response to a specific situation).

Putting this in more formal terms, Kelley assumed that when people make attributions they ideally take into account three factors, which correspond to the three questions above: (1) *consistency* across time (How consistently does this person show this behavior in this situation?); (2) *consensus* across people (How similar is this person to others in reacting to this situation?); and (3) *distinctiveness* across situations (How different is this person's reaction in this situation from his or her reaction in other situations?). Then the following relationships apply in making attributions (simplified somewhat from Kelley, 1967):

- Low consistency → attribution to extraneous factors (such as chance)
- High consistency coupled with high consensus and/or high distinctiveness → attribution to the situation
- High consistency coupled with low consensus and/or low distinctiveness → attribution to personality
- High consistency coupled with low consensus and high distinctiveness → attribution to the person-situation combination

Stated in these abstract terms, Kelley's model seems difficult to follow. But if you translate each of the above statements into a specific statement about Susan and the traffic jam, you will be able to see how each statement coincides with common sense. The model is based on the assumption that adequate information is available, that people use that information logically, and that the goal in making attributions is to develop a means of predicting how others are likely to behave in the future. A number of experiments have shown that when people are provided with the required information about consistency, consensus, and distinctiveness, and they consciously attempt to be logical in their attributions, they usually do make attributions in accordance with Kelley's model (McArthur, 1972). But in real life, people rarely have all of the required information, or the time to use it; they take various intuitive shortcuts in making attributions. As you will see soon, certain systematic biases or errors are common in that process.

**Using a Schema to Interpret New Information About a Person**   Person perception, like perception in general, involves both bottom-up and top-down processing of information. As discussed for perception in general in Chapter 9, bottom-up processing refers to the detection and integration of parts of an object to build a conception of the whole object, and top-down processing refers to the use of one's current conception of the whole to identify or interpret the parts. Also discussed there is the observation that various illusions or perceptual errors can arise from top-down processing. The same is true in person perception. One's current schema of a person, whether or not it is accurate, can guide the detection and interpretation of new information about that person in a way that seems to confirm the current schema.

For example, suppose you have been led to believe that a particular person, Harry, has a tendency toward sadism, and later you learn that Harry is training to join the police force. Because you already see Harry as a cruel person, you are likely to attribute his career choice not to courage, respect for social order, or other positive qualities, but to his cruelty. Images of police brutality may come to mind, and these may even serve as further evidence of Harry's basic cruelty: "It figures that Harry would become a cop. It gives him the opportunity to beat up on poor people and minorities. He must be even more sadistic than I thought." On the other hand, suppose you had initially been led to believe that Harry is a warm and caring person. Now if you hear that he is training to join the police you are likely to think of heartwarming images of police officers rescuing kittens and babies, helping children cross the street, and gently talking young delinquents out of their wayward ways: "It figures that Harry would become a police officer. He wants to serve humanity and is willing to risk his life to do so. What a fine man!" Thus, the very same information can be used as evidence for Harry's cruelty or his kindness, depending on the initial schema.

To demonstrate that this kind of effect can really occur, Kelley (1950) conducted an experiment involving perception of a guest lecturer by students in a course at MIT. Before the guest arrived, half of the students received a written biographical sketch of him that included the statement, "People who know him consider him to be a very warm person, industrious, critical, practical, and determined," and the other half received the same sketch except that the words "very warm" were replaced by the words "rather cold." Then the guest appeared and led a 20-minute discussion, and afterwards all students were asked to fill out a form evaluating his performance. The main results were that students who had received the sketch containing the description "very warm" were more likely to take part in the discussion and to rate the guest and his performance positively than were students who had received the sketch containing the description "rather cold." Thus, the two groups responded differently to the same lecture and made different attributions about the lecturer's performance depending on the initial schema set up for them.

*How one's preexisting schema for a person can affect, and in some cases distort, one's perceptions of the person*

*A context for interpretation*

*Now that you know the situation, the meaning of the runner's expression—his joyful exultation—is quite clear. As naive psychologists, we constantly try to make sense of other people's feelings, attributing them to inner qualities of the person unless special circumstances draw our attention to the environment.*

## Biases in Person Perception

We come into contact with so many people that we do not have time to deliberate carefully in forming our impression of each person. To save time and mental energy we use shortcuts in our reasoning, which may be efficient, but which are not always logical and can distort, or *bias*, our perceptions in certain systematic ways.

Such biases are important to understand, because they are part of the psychological basis for prejudice and discrimination. What follows are some of the biases in person perception that have been identified and studied by social psychologists.

**Disproportionate Influence of Early Information: The Primacy Effect**   The *primacy effect* is the tendency for information received early to carry more weight than information received later in one's final assessment of a person. The existence of this tendency suggests that people use early information to develop a schema of the person and then use that schema to interpret (and possibly distort) subsequent information. In an early demonstration of the primacy effect, Asch (1946) showed that people who hear someone described first as *intelligent* and *industrious*, then as *impulsive* and *critical*, and finally as *stubborn* and *envious* develop a more positive final impression of the person than do those who hear the same descriptors in the reverse order. Apparently, hearing the positive adjectives first leads people to interpret the subsequent neutral and negative adjectives in a positive light—being impulsive, critical, and stubborn could be understood as aspects of being intelligent and industrious. Conversely, hearing the negative adjectives first may cast a negative light on the other adjectives—being critical, impulsive, and industrious could be understood as aspects of being envious and stubborn.

Asch's demonstration is somewhat artificial and could be explained as resulting from subjects' intuitive assumption that someone describing another person would list the most prominent traits first. But experiments using other methods have generally confirmed the primacy effect. For example, in one experiment subjects were given two paragraphs about a young man named Jim. Paragraph *A* described him in activities that would lead to an inference that Jim was quite sociable, and Paragraph *B* described him in activities that would lead to an inference that he was a loner. The result was that subjects who read the paragraphs in the order *A–B* were most likely to describe Jim in the end as sociable, and those who had read them in the reverse order were most likely to describe him as a loner (Luchins, 1957).

**Undue Influence of Surface Characteristics**   Some aspects of a person's appearance are noticeable immediately, even before the person has said or done anything. You can immediately see a person's facial features and clothing, and these may influence your initial schema and hence the way you interpret subsequent information. Consistent with all those children's stories in which the good people (the princesses and princes) are beautiful and the bad people (the witches and ogres) are ugly, many experiments have shown that people intuitively assume that physically attractive people are more intelligent, competent, sociable, and moral than less attractive people (Dion, 1986; Patzer, 1985). In one experiment, fifth-grade teachers were given report cards and photographs of children whom they did not otherwise know and were asked to rate each child's intelligence and achievement. The result was that teachers rated physically attractive children as brighter and more successful than unattractive children with identical report cards (Clifford & Walster, 1973). In a similar experiment, adults were more likely to attribute a child's misbehavior to environmental circumstances if the child was physically attractive, and to the child's personality if the child was not physically attractive (Dion, 1972).

Another surface characteristic that can affect judgments is the degree to which a person's facial features resemble those of a baby (see Figure 14.1). In a series of experiments conducted in both the United States and Korea, Leslie McArthur and Diane Berry (1987; Berry & McArthur, 1985) have found that baby-faced adults are perceived as more naive, honest, helpless, kind, and warm than are mature-faced adults of the same age, even though the perceivers could tell that the baby-faced person was not really younger. In an experiment suggesting that this bias could influence the outcome of judicial proceedings, Berry and McArthur (1988)

■ *Evidence that early information weighs more strongly than later information in forming an impression of a person*

**Figure 14.1  *The look of naiveté***

*Adults whose faces are babyish (top) are commonly seen as more naive, honest, helpless, kind, and warm than are mature-faced adults (bottom). The characteristics of a baby face include a round head, large forehead, large eyes, short nose, and small chin.*

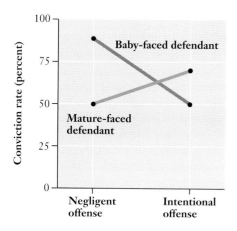

**Figure 14.2** *Evidence that a face can influence a verdict*

*Despite the fact that identical evidence was presented, a baby-faced defendant was more likely to be judged by subjects in this experiment as guilty of a crime of negligence than a crime of intent, whereas the opposite was true of a mature-faced defendant. (Adapted from Berry & McArthur, 1988.)*

▪ *How stereotypes are a kind of schema, and evidence that they can bias our perceptions of individuals*

▪ *A theory about the roles of automatic and controlled mental processes in prejudice, and evidence supporting the theory*

gave college students written descriptions of evidence against a young man who had been charged with either a crime of negligence (forgetting to warn a customer of the dangers of a product) or intent (deliberately deceiving a customer into believing that a product wasn't dangerous). A photograph of the defendant, who was either baby-faced or mature-faced, was attached to the description. As predicted, the students were more likely to find baby-faced defendants guilty of negligence than intent, and the reverse was true for mature-faced defendants (see Figure 14.2). Apparently, it was hard to imagine that such a naive-looking man would deliberately deceive a customer, but it was easy to imagine that he would make a mistake.

**Stereotypes: Their Effects on Automatic and Controlled Perception**  We all carry around in our heads schemas not just for individual persons, and persons in general, but also for particular groups of persons. You may have schemas for men, women, Asians, Californians, Blacks, Catholics, and college professors. Such schemas are called *stereotypes*. The first person to use the term *stereotype* in this way was the journalist Walter Lippmann (1922), who defined it as "the picture in the head" that a person may have of a particular group or category of people. Lippmann pointed out that stereotypes distort our perceptions of individuals and can provide a basis for prejudice and discrimination. Plenty of evidence, from social psychology labs as well as elsewhere, bears Lippmann out. For example, consistent with the prevalent stereotype in our culture that women are less competent than men at various tasks, experiments have shown that both men and women are more likely to attribute successful performance to luck if the performer is a woman and to ability if the performer is a man (see Deaux, 1984). As another example, consistent with a stereotype that Black men are violent, White viewers who saw one man lightly shove another during a heated discussion were more likely to interpret the shove as an act of aggression if the shover was Black and as playfulness or dramatization if he was White (Duncan, 1976).

Patricia Devine (1989) at the University of Wisconsin has developed a theory of stereotypes that distinguishes between the roles they play in *automatic* and *controlled* processing of stimulus information. As described in Chapter 9, automatic processing refers to the rapid, unconscious, uncontrollable initial stages of perception, and controlled processing refers to the more deliberate, time-consuming later processes that involve conscious awareness. According to Devine's model, essentially everyone in a given culture knows the stereotypes prevalent in that culture, and that knowledge inevitably comes into play in the automatic processing of information about a person. But not everyone consciously subscribes to the stereotypes. In Devine's terminology, *unprejudiced* people are those who consciously reject stereotypes, and *prejudiced* people are those who consciously accept them. Thus, in Devine's model, both unprejudiced and prejudiced people automatically bring a stereotype into play when first seeing or hearing about a person who belongs to a particular group, but unprejudiced people censor the stereotype when they become aware that it is influencing their perception.

In experiments testing her model, Devine used a questionnaire to identify groups of White college students who were either relatively prejudiced or unprejudiced toward Blacks. She found that both groups were equally knowledgeable of the culture's stereotype of Blacks, but that when they were asked to describe their own attitudes (under anonymous conditions) the prejudiced group tended to agree with the stereotype and the unprejudiced group disagreed. Then, to test the most important prediction of her model—that both groups would be equally affected by the stereotype when they weren't conscious of it—Devine (1989) performed an experiment in which the stereotypes were mentally activated without awareness.

To do this she involved the subjects in a perceptual task that seemed as if it had nothing to do with stereotypes. Both prejudiced and unprejudiced subjects were asked to look at a spot at the center of a screen and to identify the location of words that were flashed at various off-center positions. The words were flashed too quickly to be read consciously and remembered, but, in line with other experiments on unconscious perception (discussed in Chapter 9), Devine assumed that the words would nevertheless be perceived at an unconscious level and affect the conscious interpretation of later information. For subjects in the *stereotype-activation* condition, the words were designed to call forth the stereotype of a Black person. They included such words as *Negro, black, ghetto, Africa, blues,* and *basketball.* For subjects in the *nonactivation condition,* words were used that are not especially associated with Black people. Neither set contained words that directly have to do with hostility, which was the element of the Black stereotype that was to be tested in this study.

Immediately after the perceptual task, subjects heard a description of some behaviors that had been performed by a man named Donald, and they were asked to form an impression of his character. Among Donald's behaviors were some that might or might not be interpreted as hostile, such as refusing to pay his rent until his apartment was painted. No mention was made of Donald's race, but Devine assumed that those who had been exposed to the Black-associated words in the perceptual task would unconsciously have in mind the stereotype of a Black man as they heard the paragraph and would interpret ambiguous information about Donald in terms of that stereotype. The result, consistent with Devine's prediction, was that subjects in the stereotype-activation condition rated Donald higher in hostility and unfriendliness than did those in the nonactivation condition; this was equally true for unprejudiced and prejudiced subjects.

**A ballet teacher and her student**

*If it took you a moment to decide which woman in this photograph is the teacher (at right), your response illustrates the power of stereotypes. The view that older people are not capable of vigorous, disciplined physical activity is widespread in our culture and expresses a form of prejudice called* ageism.

An implication of Devine's work is that overcoming prejudice is like resisting any well-learned habit. If Devine is correct, we unconsciously react in ways that are ingrained by previous learning (in this case, the learned stereotype), and only by conscious effort can we stifle those reactions and substitute new ones. Beyond the scope of this theory, however, are the ways through which we may overcome even our unconsciously accepted stereotypes through direct experiences with members of the stereotyped group whose behaviors contradict the stereotype.

**Ingroup-Outgroup Biases**    Stereotyping is based on people's tendency to develop schemas for whole groups of individuals. Not surprisingly, the kinds of schemas that people develop for *ingroups*, defined as groups to which they themselves belong, differ in certain systematic ways from the kinds of schemas they develop for *outgroups*, defined as groups to which they themselves don't belong.

**Evidence that people perceive outgroup members to be more homogeneous and less virtuous than ingroup members**

People usually perceive members of an outgroup as relatively homogeneous (similar to each other) and members of an ingroup as relatively heterogeneous (different from each other). In one study demonstrating this, college students watched a small set of students from a particular college behave in a certain way and then were asked to estimate what percentage of other students from that college would behave in the same way. The estimated percentages were higher when the college was different from the subjects' own than when it was the same (Quattrone & Jones, 1980). In another study, men were found to perceive women as more similar to one another than men are to one another, and women were found to perceive the opposite (Park & Rothbart, 1982). Such findings probably stem at least partly from the fact that people know more individuals in their ingroups than in their outgroups and thus are more aware of the differences that exist among those in their own group. In addition, people may react negatively to the idea that they themselves are "just like" others of their group, and this may lead them to see their own group as more diverse than other groups.

People also typically view members of their ingroups more favorably than they view members of outgroups. This favoritism is often labeled **ethnocentrism**, though it occurs for all kinds of groups, not just ethnic groups. It can occur even when there is no realistic basis at all for assuming that two groups differ. For example, in one laboratory experiment, people who knew that they had been assigned to separate groups by a purely random process—a coin toss—nevertheless rated members of their own group more positively than they did those of the other group (Locksley & others, 1980).

Henri Tajfel (1982) has argued that this tendency to exaggerate the virtues of one's own group at the expense of others is part of a more general drive to build one's self-esteem. According to Tajfel, people define themselves partly in terms of the groups to which they belong, and thus they bias their perceptions of those groups in a positive direction, just as they bias their perceptions of themselves. Other research (examined in Chapter 15) emphasizes the role that competition among different groups plays in the development of positive ingroup and negative outgroup biases. In the real world, groups are more likely to hold negative attitudes toward one another if they are competing for jobs or other resources than if they see their interests as compatible.

**Blaming the Victim, and the Just-World Bias**   Another bias in person perception, called **blaming the victim**, is a tendency to seek out flaws in the behavior or character of people who have suffered some misfortune. Numerous studies have shown that victims of rape, robbery, terrorism, accidents, illnesses, and social injustice often suffer doubly: once from the misfortune itself, and then again from the subtle or not-so-subtle blame that they receive from others for "causing" or "allowing" the misfortune to happen (Lerner & Miller, 1978; McDuff, 1988; Ryan, 1971). The same behaviors or traits that were previously praised ("He is a friendly person") may now be seen as negative and as the cause of the person's suffering ("He is the kind of man who lets strangers into his home, so of course he was robbed").

In an early demonstration of blaming the victim, young women watched another woman receive what appeared to be painful electric shocks (though in reality there were no shocks and the "victim" was acting), and then they were asked to evaluate the victim's personality (Lerner & Simmons, 1966). Some subjects were led to believe that the victim would continue to receive shocks and would not be compensated (they were told that she had agreed to do so for the sake of the experiment and that now she must follow through), and others were led to believe that the shocks were now over and she would be amply rewarded with money. The result was that subjects in the first group evaluated the woman's character less favorably than did those in the second group.

**Is help deserved?**

*These Christmas shoppers, giving a Salvation Army fundraiser a wide berth, might answer no. Often people justify their indifference by assuming that the needy are unworthy of help, rather than by thinking about the causes of their suffering.*

■ *Evidence that people irrationally blame victims for their misfortune, and evidence for one possible explanation of this behavior*

**A victim of bias?**

Leonard Nimoy called his autobiography I Am Not Spock. *Do you think it likely that he has encountered the fundamental attribution error in many situations?*

■ *Evidence that the fundamental attribution error is at least sometimes truly an error, and evidence that in at least one sense it is truly fundamental*

Why does victim blaming occur? One hypothesis, suggested by Melvin Lerner (1970), is that victim blaming is part of a more general bias toward the belief that life is fair, called the ***just-world bias***. If life is fair, then people who suffer must for some reason deserve to suffer. But why should people assume that life is fair? One possibility is that the just-world bias (and victim blaming) stems from people's psychological need to defend themselves from the fear that bad things could happen to them: "If life is not fair, then no matter how I behave, or how good a person I am, something terrible could happen to me."

In a series of experiments supporting this self-defensive view of victim blaming, William Thornton and his colleagues presented college women with a story about a woman who was raped, and then asked the subjects to evaluate the degree to which the woman was at fault for what had happened to her. Subjects who could see themselves in a mirror as they heard the story, and subjects who showed the most distress while hearing it, were more likely to blame the victim than were those who could not see themselves or who showed less distress (Thornton, 1984; Thornton & others, 1986). According to Thornton, these results indicate that women who were most aware of themselves as they heard the story, and most afraid that the same thing could happen to them, were most likely to counter that fear by finding reasons in the other woman's own behavior for the rape. (Of course, Thornton's work does not explain why men are often more likely than women to blame a victim of rape.)

**The Fundamental Attribution Error**   In his original writings on the process of attribution, Heider (1958) argued that people commonly attribute another person's behavior too much to the person's inner characteristics and not enough to the environmental situation. That is, people tend to ignore the situation that might make a person act in a particular way at a particular time and are too quick to assume that the behavior represents something stable about the person. Later, Lee Ross (1977) referred to this bias as the ***fundamental attribution error***, and, for better or worse, that label has stuck.

In many situations it is hard to say for sure that attributing behavior to the person rather than to the situation is actually an error, but one situation in which it clearly is an error is that in which a performer is simply following a script and the subjects making the attributions know that the performer is following a script. In one experiment, male college students heard another student read a political statement that he had been assigned to read (Gilbert & Jones, 1986). Even when the assignment was made by the subjects themselves, so that they knew he had no choice about what to read, subjects rated the reader as liberal if the statement he read was liberal and as conservative if it was conservative.

According to a theory proposed by Daniel Gilbert (1989), which I will call the *automaticity theory*, the fundamental attribution error is not only an error, but is also truly fundamental in the sense that it represents a basic characteristic of the mind. Using the same distinction between automatic and controlled processing that I mentioned in relation to Devine's theory of stereotyping and prejudice, Gilbert suggests that attributions to internal characteristics occur automatically and that attributions to the situation are, by comparison, more controlled. Thus, if Gilbert is correct, your first, natural, automatic impulse upon seeing Susan get angry in a traffic jam is to assume that Susan is the kind of person who is easily angered. Only through conscious effort might you then counter your impulse by considering the role of the traffic jam and the possibility that she is not easily angered in other situations. In support of this theory, Gilbert and his colleagues have shown that the fundamental attribution error is greater for subjects whose conscious mental attention is occupied with other tasks (such as reciting lists of words) than for subjects who can devote their full attention to the attributional process (see Gilbert, 1989).

■ *Evidence that the fundamental attribution error may be partly a product of Western culture*

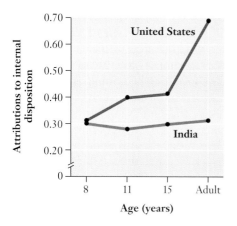

**Figure 14.3** *Cultural differences in making attributions*
*When asked to explain a particular behavior produced by a particular person, the proportion of attributions to internal disposition (personality or attitude) was greater among people in the United States than it was among Hindus in India, and this difference was greater for adults than for children. (Data from Miller, 1984. The proportions were determined by dividing the number of internal attributions by the total number of internal plus external attributions for each group, ignoring attributions that were neither clearly internal nor external.)*

■ *Two theories to explain why people are more likely to make internal attributions about others' behavior than about their own, and evidence for each*

Another theory of the fundamental attribution error, not necessarily incompatible with the automaticity theory, is that it is at least partly learned from the larger culture (Jellison & Green, 1981). According to this view, which I will call the *cultural-norm theory*, Western philosophies and religions emphasize the idea that people are in charge of their own destinies, so people growing up in Western cultures learn to attribute behavior to characteristics of the person more than to the environment. If this is true, then people growing up in a culture such as India's—in which philosophies and religions place greater emphasis on the role of fate or environmental circumstances in controlling one's destiny—might not show the fundamental attribution error. To test this theory, Joan Miller (1984) asked middle-class children and adults in the United States and in India's Hindu community to think of an action by someone they knew, and then to explain why that person had acted in that way. Consistent with the cultural-norm theory, the Indians made fewer attributions to personality and more to the situation than did the Americans. This difference was greater for adults—who would presumably have incorporated the cultural norms more strongly—than it was for children (see Figure 14.3).

**The Actor-Observer Discrepancy**   The fundamental attribution error is less likely to occur when people make attributions about their own behavior than when they make attributions about someone else's. This difference is referred to as the **actor-observer discrepancy** (Nisbett & others, 1973). Stated differently, the actor-observer discrepancy refers to the observation that the person who performs an action (the actor) commonly attributes the action to the situation—"I am whistling because it is a beautiful day," or "I read those statements because I was asked to read them." In contrast, another person who sees the same action (the observer) is more likely to attribute it to the actor's internal characteristics—"She is whistling because she is a happy-go-lucky person," or "He read those statements because he is a political liberal."

What causes the actor-observer discrepancy? One theory, which I will call the *knowledge-across-situations theory*, is that the discrepancy arises because people have seen themselves in many more situations than they have seen others, and this has sensitized them to the variations in their own behavior from setting to setting. As described by Kelley's model of the logic of attributions, one's belief about the generality (opposite of distinctiveness) of a person's behavior across situations contributes to the kind of attribution one makes. High generality leads to an internal attribution, and low generality leads to an external attribution. According to the knowledge-across-situations theory, you know that your own behavior varies from setting to setting (low generality, or high distinctiveness), but you are less likely to know that about someone else's behavior. For example, you may assume that your psychology professor's calm demeanor in the classroom is indicative of his or her behavior everywhere, and thus attribute it to personality, but this may only be because you haven't seen your professor at home, in traffic court, or on the softball field. Consistent with this interpretation, people usually judge the behavior of their close friends as more flexible—more determined by the situation and less by unvarying personality traits—than that of people whom they don't know as well (Nisbett & others, 1973; Sande & others, 1988).

A second theory, which I will call the *visual-orientation theory*, is that the actor-observer discrepancy stems from a basic characteristic of visual perception: Our eyes point outward and are drawn toward other people. When we watch someone *else* perform an action, our eyes are fixed on that person, so we are most aware of the person and attribute causal properties to him or her. But when we perform an action ourselves, we see the surrounding environment, not ourselves, and attribute causal properties to that.

Support for the visual-orientation theory can be found in an experiment conducted by Michael Storms (1973) in which some male college students (the actors) engaged in 5-minute get-acquainted sessions while others (the observers) watched. After the session, each observer was asked to evaluate the degree to which the behavior of the actor who he had been assigned to watch was the result of the actor's personality or the unique situation (such as being in an experiment and meeting someone for the first time), and each actor was asked to make the same evaluation of his own behavior. Before making the ratings, subjects in the *videotape-reversed condition* were shown videotapes of the get-acquainted session that reversed the visual orientation of actor and observer: The actors saw themselves, and the observers saw the environment from the same visual perspective from which the actors had seen it during the original conversation. Subjects in the *videotape-unreversed condition* were shown videotapes that simply showed the scene as they had seen it originally: The observers saw the actor whom they had been observing, and actors saw the environment as they had seen it during the original session. A third group, in the *nonvideotape condition*, made their ratings solely on the basis of their memory of the original experience.

The researchers found that reversing the visual orientation also reversed the actor-observer discrepancy. In the videotape-reversed condition, actors made more attributions to their own personality and less to the situation, and observers made more attributions to the situation and less to the actor's personality, than in either of the other two conditions.

**The Self-Serving Bias**  The actor-observer discrepancy tends to break down when people make attributions about highly successful or beneficial behaviors. Not surprisingly, when making attributions about an action that turns out to be highly successful, people are, on average, more likely to make internal attributions if they have performed the action than if someone else has. This is part of the *self-serving bias*, which is the tendency to attribute one's own success to inner qualities about the self and one's own failures to external circumstances. In one of many studies demonstrating this bias, students who performed well on an examination attributed their high grades to their own hard work and ability, whereas those who performed poorly attributed their low grades to luck, the unfairness of the test, or other factors beyond their control (Bernstein & others, 1979).

The self-serving bias allows us all to think of ourselves as above average when logic dictates that only half of us actually can be so. The most common explanation of this bias is that it is an unconscious process designed to maintain self-esteem. Consistent with this interpretation, people who suffer from depression (whose self-esteem is shattered) do not demonstrate the self-serving bias (Peterson & Seligman, 1984), a finding discussed further in Chapter 17.

*■ An attributional bias that seems to promote self-esteem*

## Perceiving and Presenting the Self

In the discussions of the actor-observer and self-serving biases, we have examined some differences between people's perceptions of themselves and their perceptions of others. We now turn more directly to the topic of self-perception. How do people develop a concept of themselves, and how does this concept, coupled with concern for others' opinions, affect the way they behave in the social environment?

### The Self as a Social Product

Who are you? Before reading beyond this sentence, try to answer that question by writing ten or more brief statements that begin, *I am*_____. After you have writ-

**One true self**

*Some people seem more driven than others to present a public self. As you consider this collection of bumper stickers, ask yourself which way the influence flows. Are the labels emblematic of the person's influence on society, or of society's influence on the person?*

■ *Evidence that others' expectations can affect a person's behavior and self-concept, such that the expectations become self-fulfilling prophesies*

ten your list of self-statements, look at it to find ways that your self-understanding has derived from your social world. Some of your statements may refer to socially defined groups to which you belong: *I am a student . . . a Roman Catholic . . . an adult.* Others may refer to the nature of your interactions with other people or with society at large: *I am socially outgoing . . . a family-oriented person . . . a political activist.* Still other statements may refer to traits that you attribute to yourself either because other people have attributed them to you, or because you have seen that you stand out in those ways in comparison to other people: *I am short . . . rather good looking. . . good at math.*

You probably won't find any self-statement in your list that does *not* stem in one way or another from your social environment. Many years ago, in making this same point, the sociologist Charles Cooley (1902) coined the term the *looking-glass self* to refer to the idea that we learn about ourselves by looking at others around us. Our social world is the looking glass in which we see ourselves. We see ourselves in others' reactions to us, and we also use our perceptions of others' traits and abilities as the yardsticks with which we measure our own. Research on expectancy effects, social roles, and social comparison all support the idea of the looking-glass self; these are the topics to which we now turn.

**Effects of Others' Expectations**   In George Bernard Shaw's play *Pygmalion* (upon which the musical *My Fair Lady* was based), Eliza Doolittle, who has been transformed from an impoverished cockney flower girl to a lady of high society, says to the young man who has fallen in love with her, "You see, really and truly . . . the difference between a lady and a flower girl is not how she behaves but how she's treated. I shall always be a flower girl to Professor Higgins, because he always treats me as a flower girl, and always will; but I know I can be a lady to you, because you always treat me as a lady, and always will."

To some degree, a person is what others expect or assume that person to be. Others' beliefs affect the way they behave toward the person, which in turn affects the person's own behavior and self-concept. This idea has been supported by experiments in which one person (*A*) is deliberately misled about the characteristics of another person (*B*), with the result that *A*'s behavior toward *B* leads *B* to behave in accordance with the originally misleading expectation. For example, in one experiment young men were asked to engage in 10-minute phone conversations with young women whom they had not met. If the man was led to believe that the woman was especially attractive, bright, and warm, he opened the conversation in a brighter and warmer manner than if he was led to believe the opposite. The woman at the other end, not knowing about the way in which the man's view of her had been biased, responded to him according to the way he had spoken to her—brightly and warmly if she was believed to be that, more dully otherwise (Snyder & others, 1977). In another experiment, the same result occurred in reverse—the woman was misled about the man with whom she was speaking, and he responded in kind (Anderson & Bem, 1981). In these and similar experiments, an initially arbitrary designation, determined by a random procedure, became for a short period a self-fulling prophecy.

What might happen if a person were treated in accordance with an arbitrary set of expectations over a longer period of time? To find out, Robert Rosenthal and Lenore Jacobson (1968) led elementary-school teachers to believe that certain students would show a spurt in intellectual growth during the next few months, as indicated by a special test that all students had taken. In reality, the students labeled as *spurters* had been selected not on the basis of a test score, but at random. Yet, when they were tested 8 months later, the selected students showed significantly greater gains in IQ and academic performance than did their classmates.

What caused the "spurters" to spurt? Many studies since Rosenthal and Jacobson's have shown that teachers who expect some children to perform better than others in fact treat those children quite differently from the others. They are more likely to engage these children in conversations, praise them for work well done, give them adequate time to answer difficult questions, give them challenging assignments, and notice and reinforce their self-initiated efforts (Cooper & Good, 1983; Harris & Rosenthal, 1985). In response to these teachers' behaviors, the children apparently develop a better self-concept about their scholastic ability, which contributes to their working harder and doing better (see Jussim, 1986).

Other experiments have shown that explicitly attributing certain positive traits to schoolchildren can lead them to behave in ways consistent with those traits. In one experiment, some children were told repeatedly that they *were* neat and tidy (*attribution condition*); others were told that they *should be* neat and tidy (*persuasion condition*); and still others were given no special message about neatness and tidiness (*control condition*). The result was that those in the attribution condition showed significantly greater gains in neatness, as measured by the absence of littering, than did those in either of the other conditions (Miller & others, 1975). In a second experiment conducted along similar lines, telling students that they were good at math led to greater improvements in math scores than telling them that they should try to become good at math (see Figure 14.4). Apparently, when children are given a positive label, it can become part of their self-concept, and they try to live up to it.

**Figure 14.4** *Effect of attribution compared to persuasion*

(a) *Fifth graders who were repeatedly told that they were neat and tidy (attribution condition) showed greater gain in use of the waste basket than did those in the other conditions. (b) Second graders who were repeatedly told that they were good at math (attribution condition) showed greater improvement in math scores than did those in the other conditions. In each case, the students were tested three times: once right before (pretest), once immediately after (immediate posttest), and once a few weeks after (delayed posttest) the experimental conditions were in effect. (Adapted from Miller & others, 1975.)*

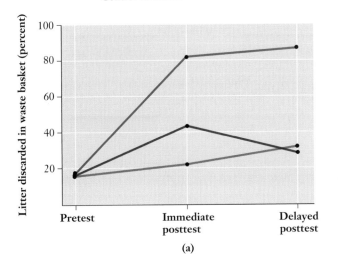

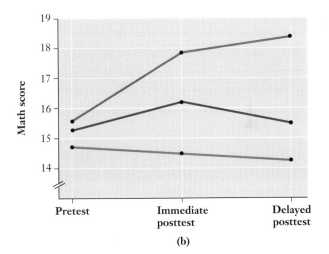

■ *How one's self-concept can vary from role to role, and why multiple self-concepts may be valuable*

**Social Roles and Multiple Selves** Long ago, William James (1890) argued that each person has not just one self, but many, each corresponding to his or her relationship with a different person or set of people. Psychologists who emphasize the relationship between self-concept and *social role* have expanded upon this idea. Each of us occupies a number of different roles in society, and we have a somewhat different concept of ourselves associated with each. I am a *father, husband, son, neighbor,* and *college professor* to different people. When I think of myself in each role, different sets of traits and abilities come to mind. My understanding of myself in each role is mediated partly by the larger society's stereotype of what fathers, husbands, sons, neighbors, and college professors are like, and partly by the more specific expectations of the individuals to whom I am those things.

**A role model**

*With a large proportion of women now in the work force, the stereotyped notion of* father *and* worker *as separate roles may be disappearing. Or perhaps we are simply developing new stereotypes.*

Research has shown that people typically describe themselves differently when one of their social roles is mentally activated than when another is. Such work has led to weblike models of the self-concept, in which some self-perceived traits are attached to specific roles, serving as nodes in the web, while others are attached to several or all roles, tying the nodes together (Rosenberg, 1988; Hoelter, 1985). For example, a person might see herself or himself as *authoritative* in the role of employer, *submissive* in the role of daughter or son, *companionable* in the role of wife or husband, and *caring* in all of these roles—so here the trait of being caring cuts across roles and is a source of consistency in the self-concept (see Figure 14.5).

You might expect that having multiple self-concepts, each associated with a different role, would be psychologically stressful, but research suggests the opposite (Linville, 1985, 1987; Dance & Kuiper, 1987). The sense of having multiple roles and a wide variety of traits seems to protect a person from depression when one role is lost or diminished in importance—as might happen in a divorce, or when children grow up and leave home, or when a job is lost. Moreover, the sense of having many roles and traits to draw on apparently adds to a person's confidence in his or her ability to handle new situations. The flexibility that characterizes people's self-attributions compared to their attributions about others (the actor-observer discrepancy) may stem at least partly from their belief that they have many different, even contradictory, personality traits that they can call on in different situations (Sande & others, 1988).

**Figure 14.5  *The multiple nature of the self-concept***

*The self-concept can be represented as a web with different nodes for different social roles. Some self-perceived traits may be tied to just one role (such as husband or employer), and others may be tied to several or all roles.*

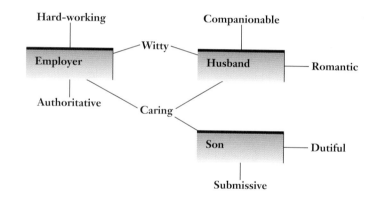

■ *How people actively build self-concepts by comparing themselves to others*

**Constructing Self-concepts Through Social Comparison**   Thus far I have emphasized the idea that self-concepts are to some degree imposed upon us by others' expectations and by the roles we occupy in society. But that idea, if left to stand by itself, would suggest that we are more passive than we actually are. We don't just accumulate self-concepts from the labels and expectations provided by others; we actively build them, using the labels and expectations, but molding them in our own unique way and adding to them some deductions of our own. To understand ourselves, to identify our unique characteristics and measure our abilities, we actively compare ourselves to other people, a process called **social comparison** (Festinger, 1954). In perception everything is relative to some frame of reference, and in self-perception the frame of reference is other people. To see oneself as short, wealthy, good at math, or not very musical is to see oneself as those things *compared to other people*. A direct consequence of social comparison is that the self-concept varies depending upon the **reference group**, the group with whom the comparison is made. If my reference group in evaluating my height consisted of basketball players, I would see myself as short; if they were jockeys, I would see myself as a giant.

**A borderline comparison**

*For many East Germans, the weeks following the opening of the East-West border, and preceding unification, turned into a giant shopping spree. As you read about social comparison theory, ask yourself whether they would have felt so deprived of material goods if they and the West Germans were not the same nationality.*

In studies of children's self-concepts, William McGuire and his colleagues found that children who were asked to describe themselves tended to focus on those traits that most distinguished them from others in their group (McGuire & McGuire, 1981, 1988; McGuire & Padawer-Singer, 1976). Thus, children in racially homogeneous classrooms rarely mentioned their race, but those in racially mixed classrooms quite commonly did, especially if their race was in the minority. Similarly, children who were unusually tall or short compared to others in their group were more likely than others to mention their height; and children whose siblings were the opposite gender from themselves were more likely to mention their gender than those whose siblings were the same gender as themselves (see Figure 14.6). Such findings are consistent with the view that people understand themselves by contrasting themselves with members of their reference group to find the ways in which they are unique.

**Figure 14.6** *Evidence that children define themselves in terms of differences from their reference group*

*As shown here, children were more likely to mention their gender when describing themselves if their gender was in the minority in their household than if it was in the majority. (Adapted from McGuire & McGuire, 1988.)*

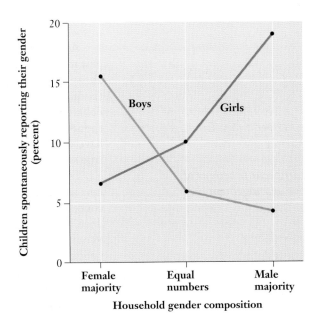

People compare themselves to others not simply to identify or describe themselves, but also to evaluate themselves, a process that can be charged with emotion. Since a person's relative standing in any comparison depends as much on the reference group as on his or her own characteristics or abilities, the choice of reference group can dramatically affect one's self-esteem. Many first-year college students who had received outstanding grades in high school feel crushed when their marks are only average compared to their new reference group, their highly selected college classmates. William James (1890), reflecting on extreme instances of these kinds of comparisons wrote: "So we have the paradox of the man shamed to death because he is only the second pugilist or second oarsman in the world. That he is able to beat the whole population of the globe minus one is nothing; he has 'pitted' himself to beat that one and as long as he doesn't do that nothing else counts."

### The Social Presentation of the Self

As conscious social beings, we know that other people form impressions of us just as we form impressions of them, and we care about those impressions. Other people's impressions affect the way they behave toward us, and that in turn affects our thoughts about ourselves. So, when we go out among other people we do not carry on our business just as we would alone. Instead, we control our behavior to influence what others will think. We present ourselves: Here I am, this is the way I want you to perceive me. Social psychologists use the term *impression management* to refer to the entire set of ways by which people either consciously or unconsciously attempt to influence others' impressions of them (Schlenker, 1980).

The sociologist Erving Goffman was an important pioneer in the study of impression management. In his book entitled *The Presentation of Self in Everyday Life* (1959), Goffman elaborated extensively on the analogy implied by Shakespeare's line, "All the world's a stage." Goffman portrayed us as actors, playing at different times on different stages to different audiences, always trying to convince our current audience that we are the character we are playing. The members of each of our audiences in this play of life are also actors, and they are trying to convince *us* that they are the characters they are playing. According to Goffman, as the play goes on we may see through each others' costumes, lines, and pantomimes, but we rarely let on that we do. An unspoken social rule—which is part of politeness or tact—is to act toward others as if they are the characters they are playing, as long as they are not too outrageous. To break this rule would be to upset the smoothness of social life and run the risk of having ourselves exposed as well.

Although the theater analogy is useful, it can also be misleading. It may suggest more duplicity, more conscious deception, than is warranted by what is known about impression management. There need not be a division in our minds between the images we are trying to project to others and our sincere, though sometimes deluded, beliefs about ourselves. If our true self-concept has multiple nodes, corresponding to different social roles, then we are not just acting out parts when we behave differently in different contexts, but are expressing different aspects of our true self as we understand that self to be.

Impression management may serve two separate but overlapping functions: It may serve to (1) control others' behavior toward us, and (2) validate our own self-concept by getting others to agree that we are who we think we are (Baumeister & Tice, 1986; Swann, 1987). The first function may or may not involve deception. We may project aspects of ourselves that we truly believe, or may consciously or unconsciously attempt to deceive others, in order to get other people to react to us in desired ways. The second function, however, cannot involve deception unless it is self-deception. To validate our self-concept through the eyes of others, we must project aspects of ourselves that we believe are true.

■ *Impression management viewed as theater, and a limitation of that perspective*

■ *Two different functions of impression management*

*Making an impression*

*To get elected, politicians must manage impressions—not necessarily to deceive, but rather to control others' voting behavior. For U.S. President George Bush and other successful political leaders, a central problem after election is how to act against the image that got them elected without upsetting their supporters or appearing duplicitous.*

■ *Evidence that an undeserved high reputation can promote self-handicapping*

**An Example of an Impression-Management Strategy: Self-Handicapping** Most research explicitly concerned with impression management has focused on the first of the two just-stated functions, especially on the means by which people try to look better than they really are. Among the characteristics that most of us want to project are those of *friendliness* (so others will like us), *honesty* (so others will trust us), and *competence* (so others will admire us). Few of us are above putting on a friendly smile for show, hiding our transgressions and weaknesses, or subtly exaggerating our virtues and abilities when we think we can get away with it. Perhaps because it is easiest to study in the laboratory, much research on impression management has centered on strategies by which people attempt to preserve or bolster a reputation of competence at specific tasks or endeavors. An example of such a strategy, which I will use here to illustrate impression-management research, is that of ***self-handicapping***.

Self-handicapping is the strategy of giving oneself an obvious handicap in a task in order to provide an excuse for anticipated poor performance (Berglas & Jones, 1978). It seems to be employed most often by people who have a high reputation that they are afraid they can't live up to. Fearing defeat to a young upstart in chess, the old master may surrender a few playing pieces at the beginning, so that a loss will be attributed to graciousness rather than to failing ability. Fearing a poor grade on a test, the student whom everyone calls brilliant may stay out all night before the test, flaunting the lack of study, to set up an excuse for the possibility of poor performance.

In a laboratory study showing that an undeserved high reputation can lead to self-handicapping, male college students were given a set of problems to solve, and then some were told they had done well and others were told they had done poorly (Tucker & others, 1981). Actually, the problems were unsolvable, so those who were told they had done well could only assume that they had been lucky. Then, on the pretext that this was a study of the effects of alcohol on thought, the students—all of whom were drinkers and of legal drinking age—were given a choice of how much alcohol they would like to drink before taking a second test with similar problems. The result was that those who were told they had done well chose to drink more alcohol than those who were told they had done poorly. Apparently, the first group did not want to risk the reputation that they had just established, so to invalidate the second test as a measure of their ability they chose to drink a lot. The second group, on the other hand, had little to lose and could possibly gain from a second test, so they did not want to invalidate the test; hence, they chose to drink little.

■ *Why people may be motivated to get others to think of them as they think of themselves, and how this can produce effects opposite to the expectancy effects described earlier*

**Asserting and Validating the Self-Concept**    We now turn to the second function of impression management, that of asserting and validating the self-concept. If the social environment is the looking glass in which we see ourselves, then we may want to project toward that glass an image that we believe to be true of ourselves, so we can see it and become more certain of its truth. The premise here is that people are motivated to maintain a relatively stable view of themselves, and to do so they must get others to accept that view. If I think of myself as a Rambo-like character, but I cannot convince you of it, my faith in that image will be shaken. I must eventually arrive at a self-image that you and others accept; then, to maintain that image, I must continue to play the part.

William Swann (1985, 1987) has argued that the drive to maintain a consistent self-image is separate from the drive to look good in others' eyes, and that it can even lead people who have a negative self-image to portray themselves to others in negative ways. As an illustration, Swann (1985) described the case of a battered child who, to maintain a self-image as deserving to be beaten, consistently avoided people who liked him, sought out those who disliked him, and responded to praise by increasing his negative behavior and self-derogation.

In a series of experiments, Swann found that when people discover that another person's concept of them is different from their own, they often respond by projecting their own self-concept more strongly. For example, in one experiment, people who perceived themselves to be dominant became all the more dominant if their conversation partner initially thought they were submissive, and people who perceived themselves to be submissive became all the more submissive if their partner initially thought they were dominant (Swann & Hill, 1982). Notice that this is the opposite of the expectancy effect described earlier in the chapter, in which people behaved in accordance with others' expectations. Swann's research suggests that conformity to another person's expectation occurs when the target person's self-concept is relatively neutral concerning the trait in question, and that the opposite—active resistance to another person's expectation—occurs when the person's self-concept emphasizes a trait that is opposite to the other's expectation (Swann & Ely, 1984).

■ *Evidence that some people are more concerned with, and more successful at, impression management than are others*

**Individual Differences in Impression Management: Self-Monitoring**    In some situations, the two goals of self-presentation described above conflict with one another. The goal of manipulating the beliefs or behavior of one's present audience would lead a person to behave differently with different audiences; and the goal of maintaining a consistent view of oneself would lead a person to behave relatively similarly with different audiences. Some years ago, Mark Snyder (1974) developed

*Who's having fun?*

*A strong concern about other people's impressions and the self-confidence needed to manipulate those impressions are key factors in self-monitoring. Do you think someone who has the first characteristic but not the second would enjoy this party?*

**Table 14.1  *Sample questions from the self-monitoring scale***

> 1. I can make impromptu speeches even on topics about which I have almost no information.  *(T)*\*
> 2. When I am uncertain how to act in a situation, I look to the behavior of others for cues.  *(T)*
> 3. I rarely need the advice of my friends to choose movies, books, or music.  *(F)*
> 4. Even if I am not enjoying myself, I often pretend to be having a good time.  *(T)*
> 5. I would not change my opinions (or the way I do things) in order to please someone else or win their favor.  *(F)*
> 6. I never have been good at games like charades or improvisational acting.  *(F)*

\*The *T* or *F* in parentheses is the response (True or False) that indicates high self-monitoring.
*Source:* From "Self-monitoring of expressive behavior" by M. Snyder, 1974, *Journal of Personality and Social Psychology, 30*, pp. 526–537.

a test for a personality characteristic that he labeled ***self-monitoring***, which seems to distinguish between people who favor one or the other of these two goals when they come into conflict. Snyder defines self-monitoring as sensitivity to other people's immediate reactions to oneself, combined with a desire and ability to control those reactions. *High self-monitors* are those people who will most dramatically modify their behavior to please their current audience, and *low self-monitors* are those who maintain greater consistency in behavior from one audience to another. Table 14.1 shows some sample questions from Snyder's self-monitoring scale.

In a series of studies, Snyder and his colleagues have found that people who score high on the self-monitoring scale differ from those who score low in the following ways: (a) High self-monitors are better actors than low self-monitors. For example, when asked to convey specific emotions while reading lines, highs conveyed the emotions better than lows (Snyder, 1974). (b) High self-monitors are more concerned with social norms and conformity than low self-monitors. For example, when taking a personality test, highs were more likely than lows to glance at a sheet indicating how others answered the questions before they answered the questions themselves (Snyder, 1974), and in discussions they were more likely to modify their opinions to be compatible with those of their audience (Snyder & Monson, 1975). (c) High self-monitors have a greater number of friends than low self-monitors, but their friendships are usually less intimate (Snyder & Smith, 1986). Consistent with this, highs tend to choose friends who are attractive or appear competent, or who share some specific activity with them, whereas lows tend to choose friends who share their values and attitudes (Jamiesen & others, 1987).

Other research suggests that high self-monitors, based on Snyder's test, actually have two separate characteristics. One is a strong concern about other people's impressions of them and the other is the self-confidence and acting ability needed to manipulate those impressions (Briggs & Cheek, 1986). People who have the first characteristic but not the second are not considered to be high self-monitors, but fall into the category commonly called shy (Buss, 1980). Because they care strongly about others' reactions and doubt their ability to obtain favorable reactions, they become anxious and tend to withdraw from social situations.

Self-monitoring, like any other personality measure, varies in degree. Most people score neither extremely high nor extremely low on the scale, but somewhere near the middle (Snyder, 1979). They are consistent enough to carry a sense of an integrated self from one situation to another, but at the same time adaptable enough to get along reasonably well with a wide variety of people in a wide variety of situations.

## Meanings of Friendship and Love

Beyond the perception of others and the self is the perception of relationships between others and the self, including those special relationships called friendship and love. Many approaches have been taken to understanding such relationships. In Chapter 4 close relationships are discussed in evolutionary, survival-promoting terms; and in Chapter 13 different kinds of close relationships are linked to different periods of development, from infancy through old age. Now, from a social cognitive perspective, we will take a brief look at friendship and love as represented in the individual's mind. What do people mean when they refer to someone as a friend, or when they speak of themselves as being in love?

**Friendship as a Set of Implicit Rules**   One way to define friendship is as a set of implicit, mental rules that guide the way people behave toward friends. To determine if there is universality to such rules, Michael Argyle and Monika Henderson (1984) interviewed people in England, Italy, Japan, and Hong Kong about the meaning of friendship. They found in all of these countries that close friends are expected to (a) support each other emotionally and be concerned if the other person isn't happy, (b) volunteer help in times of need, (c) trust and confide in each other, and (d) stand up for one another in the other person's absence. In each country people claimed that violation of any of these rules would signal that a friendship was falling apart or becoming less close.

Another approach to identifying rules of friendship is to observe how friends, compared to people who are not friends, interact in structured laboratory tasks. Taking this tack, Margaret Clark and her colleagues have found that friends usually interact according to principles of *communality*, whereas nonfriends usually interact according to principles of *exchange*. More specifically, when asked to cooperate in a task to achieve a reward, friends, or those who hoped to become friends, (a) kept track of their joint accomplishments but not their individual accomplishments toward completing the task (Clark, 1984); (b) divided their reward according to the perceived needs of each person rather than according to their individual contributions in performing the task (Clark & others, 1986); and (c) felt insulted by the suggestion that their favor toward the other person should be reciprocated (Clark & Waddell, 1985). By contrast, nonfriends kept track of their individual accomplishments, divided rewards according to each person's contribution, and expected immediate reciprocation for any favors performed for the other person.

Although principles of exchange do not characterize short-term interactions among friends, they may still be involved, in a less easily measured way, in the long-term maintenance of a friendship. Evidence can be found that friendships and marriages tend to fall apart if over the long run one party feels that he or she is benefiting much more or much less than the other (Clark & Reis, 1988). People don't like to see themselves either as exploiters or as exploited. Moreover, even very close friends and happily married couples may apply exchange rules to certain, confined aspects of their relationship. Many a happy marriage is kept happy partly because the partners take turns washing the dishes, doing the laundry, or giving each other backrubs.

**Romantic Love Compared to Friendship**   People usually think of love as friendship plus something more. More of what? Most psychologists who have studied this issue have focused specifically on *romantic love*, the kind that involves, among other things, sexual attraction. In early research on this, Zick Rubin (1970) asked college students who were involved in heterosexual love relationships to fill out questionnaires describing their feelings toward (a) their lover, and (b) their best same-sex friend. He found that the main distinctions between these two classes of

*Evidence that friends operate according to rules of communality rather than rules of exchange, at least in short-term tasks*

*Emotional intensity as a distinguishing feature of love compared to friendship, and evidence that the distinction may be greater for men than for women*

**Endless love**

*In Western society, romantic love can be found across the age span, although such relationships are often assumed to be an unimportant part of later life.*

■ *Evidence that romantic love may have different meanings in different cultures*

■ *How Sternberg's three components of love can describe a wide variety of relationships, and how the components differ in their time course of development*

relationships, aside from sexuality per se, had to do with emotional intensity. People admired and enjoyed the company of their lover and best friend about equally; but they felt more *intense caring* (desire to help), *emotional dependence* (perceived need to be with the other), and *exclusiveness* (sense that nobody else could substitute for this person) toward their lover than toward their best friend. Moreover, although this difference occurred for both genders, it was greater for men than for women. Women felt more emotionally involved with their same-sex friends than did men, so their feelings toward their same-sex friends and their lovers were more similar to each other than was the case for men. Since Rubin's original study, other researchers have compared the feelings of romantic love and nonromantic friendship in wider ranges of people, of various ages and backgrounds, married as well as unmarried, with results that are similar to Rubin's (Hatfield & Walster, 1978; Davis & Todd, 1982).

Extending the idea that love involves strong emotional attachment and perceived need for the beloved, Phillip Shaver and his colleagues (1988) have argued that adult romantic love is similar in form, and perhaps in underlying mechanisms, to infants' attachments to their parents. In both romantic love and infant attachment, (a) close physical contact and caressing are critical; (b) cooing and babytalk are common; (c) the person feels more safe, secure, and confident when the other is present; (d) the person is distressed when the other person leaves and excited when the other person returns; (e) a sense of fusion with the other person exists when all is going well; and (f) there is a feeling of exclusivity—a feeling that the other person could not be replaced by someone else. In a further extension of the analogy, these researchers have found that romantic attachments can be classed into secure and insecure categories along very much the same lines as infant attachments have been classed (described in Chapter 13).

A qualifying note to the emphasis on emotional intensity in romantic relationships, however, comes from cross-cultural research. Francis Hsu (1981) has argued that in China and other Asian countries people downplay the emotional aspects of love, and are more concerned with how the relationship will mesh with each person's larger network of relationships and responsibilities. Hsu sees this difference as consistent with a more general distinction between Asians' greater concern for extended family and social harmony and Westerners' greater concern for the individual's separate feelings. In keeping with this view, when students at the University of Miami were asked to describe an ideal love relationship, those who were from Asian backgrounds ascribed less importance than did others to physical attraction and emotional intensity, and gave more importance to practical issues, such as the ability to work together and solve mutual problems (Hendrick & Hendrick, 1986).

**Sternberg's Triangular Model of Love** Perhaps the most elegant and all-encompassing model of love developed so far is Robert Sternberg's (1986, 1988) *triangular model*. Sternberg statistically analyzed questionnaire data describing people's feelings in various kinds of love and friendship relationships. He found what seem to be three separate dimensions to those feelings, which make up the three sides of his triangular model. These are (1) *passion*, which includes sexual desire and other emotional feelings of need to be with the beloved (the *hot* side of love); (2) *intimacy*, which includes a sense of closeness, mutual understanding, and the sharing of thoughts and feelings (the *warm* side of love); and (c) *decision/commitment*, which is the person's conscious decision to promote and maintain the relationship (the *cold*, rational side of love).

In this model, passion is critical to romance, intimacy is critical to friendship, and decision/commitment is critical to the long-term maintenance of any relationship when the sailing is rough. One strength of the model is that it can describe not just one or two varieties of relationships, but an infinite variety, each differing from

**Figure 14.7** *Sternberg's typology of love*

*These types of relationships represent hypothetical extremes based on Sternberg's triangular theory. Most actual relationships will fit between these types, because the various components are not all or none, but exist as a matter of degree. (Adapted from Sternberg, 1986.)*

| Type of relationship | Passion | Intimacy | Decision/ commitment |
|---|---|---|---|
| Nonlove | Absent | Absent | Absent |
| Liking | Absent | Present | Absent |
| Infatuated love | Present | Absent | Absent |
| Empty love | Absent | Absent | Present |
| Romantic love | Present | Present | Absent |
| Companionate love | Absent | Present | Present |
| Fatuous love | Present | Absent | Present |
| Consummate love | Present | Present | Present |

▓ Present
░ Absent

others in the relative proportions of the three ingredients. To illustrate its range, Sternberg (1986) has used the model to describe eight *limiting types* of relationships, which can be derived from the eight possible combinations that occur if each dimension is either very high or very low. These are shown in Figure 14.7.

The triangular theory can also be used to describe the development of relationships over time (Sternberg, 1986). As depicted in Figure 14.8, passion is usually the fastest-rising of the three components, which fits with research showing that at the very beginning of a dating relationship physical attractiveness of the partner is the main determinant of a person's desire to continue the relationship (Walster & others, 1966; Hatfield & Sprecher, 1986). Intimacy develops more slowly; people may fall passionately in love in an instant, but it takes time to become friends. The third component, decision/commitment, may develop gradually, as the two partners' lives become more intertwined; or it may develop in quantum leaps, tied to such events as a decision to marry or to have children. Interviews of people who have had long and satisfying marriages suggest that this third component is at least as important as the first two in their relationship's success (for example, Lauer & Lauer, 1985). There are times in every relationship when the going is hard, when one partner or the other feels that he or she is carrying the full load, and commitment carries relationships through such times.

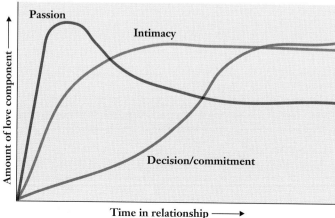

**Figure 14.8** *The growth of love*

*According to Sternberg's model, the three components of love typically develop at different rates, as illustrated here.*

# Attitudes

Thus far we have been discussing social cognition as applied to the perception of other individuals, the self, and close personal relationships. Now we turn to a broader application, one that ties the individual to the entire social world.

An *attitude* is any belief or opinion that has an evaluative component—a belief that something is good or bad, likable or unlikable, attractive or repulsive. The object of the attitude might be an event, an inanimate object, a person, a group of people, a political idea, a kind of behavior, or anything at all. Your attitudes range from your feelings about a specific brand of toothpaste to your feelings about democracy or religion. Attitudes are a key topic in social cognition, because they provide a link between the individual human mind and society at large. Attitudes arise from experience in the social environment, and they help guide behavior in that environment. The study of attitudes and how they are formed or changed also has a practical side. An enormous amount of effort in our society goes into the attempt to modify people's attitudes. All of advertising, political campaigning, and the democratic process itself (in which people speak freely in support of their views) can be thought of as attempts to change other people's attitudes.

## Functions and Origins of Attitudes

**Functions**   What is an attitude for? That is perhaps the most basic question one can ask about attitudes. Any answer to it carries implications about how attitudes are acquired and the relationship they have to behavior. In the 1950s, several theorists (Katz, 1960; Smith & others, 1956) proposed that attitudes can serve four classes of purposes, which can be summarized as follows:

■ *How attitudes can serve any or all of four different functions*

1. *Utilitarian function*   This is the most obvious function; it refers to the role that an attitude plays in guiding one's actual behavior with respect to the object of the attitude. The utilitarian function applies most readily to those attitudes that are acquired through direct experience with the object of the attitude. If you have a positive attitude toward strawberry ice cream, your next-door neighbors, and English classes, those attitudes are serving a utilitarian function if they actually lead you to seek out those things.

2. *Defensive function*   This refers to the role of attitudes in quieting one's own anxiety or boosting one's self-esteem. If a person who is cut from the hockey team develops a negative attitude toward hockey, this attitude may be serving the defensive function of protecting him or her from the feeling of loss or failure. Similarly, a negative attitude toward someone who is suffering might be a defense against the fear that the same thing could happen to oneself (as discussed in the section on blaming the victim).

3. *Social-adjustive function*   This refers to the role of attitudes in impression management. People sometimes adopt quickly the attitudes of a new group that they have joined, and in such cases the attitudes may serve principally the social-adjustive function of promoting the person's acceptance or esteem within the group. People may also adopt or maintain particular attitudes as a way of appearing unique or strong minded to others.

4. *Value-expressive function*   This refers to the role of attitudes in defining and asserting the self. This function is especially served by those attitudes—such as belief in democracy, or worship, or the value of hard work—that are so central to one's self-concept that they can be betrayed only at risk of betraying the self. Attitudes serving this function may arise from one's early training, or may be developed later through extended immersion in activities that support the attitude's development.

These attitude functions are not mutually exclusive. A single attitude may serve all four functions relatively equally, or it may serve almost entirely just one or another. My attitude toward strawberry ice cream is purely utilitarian, but if my parents had owned a strawberry ice-cream factory that attitude might serve any of the other functions as well. Notice that the last three functions are served by the *expression* of the attitude, either to the self or to others, regardless of whether the attitude plays a role in guiding one's behavior in relation to the attitude object.

For many years after the 1950s, social psychologists paid little attention to the functions of attitudes, but interest revived in the 1980s. In one study, Gregory Herek (1986) analyzed essays written by heterosexuals concerning their attitudes toward homosexuals and found that the essays could be categorized according to the degree to which they seemed to fill each of the above needs: Utilitarian attitudes were based on practical considerations and direct experience, which would lead the person either to approach or to avoid homosexuals; defensive attitudes were those that seemed grounded in the person's anxiety about his or her own sexuality; social-adjustive attitudes were those couched either explicitly or implicitly in terms of what other people think about homosexuals; and value-expressive attitudes were those based on fundamental principles that seemed dear to the author.

Other research has shown that people with different personality styles are differentially affected by persuasive messages or commercials that appeal to one or another of these functions (see Snyder & DeBono, 1987). As you might expect, people high in self-monitoring are most influenced by messages that emphasize how others feel on the issue (social-adjustive function), and people low in self-monitoring are most influenced by messages that appeal to their personal values (value-expressive function) or give practical information (utilitarian function).

**Role of a Reference Group in Attitude Change and Persistence: The Bennington College Study**   People who live with or interact with each other typically have similar attitudes. Children have similar attitudes to their parents, and people of all ages have similar attitudes to the peer groups with whom they most commonly interact (McGuire, 1985). It is not hard to think of possible reasons for this: People living with or communicating with each other are exposed to similar information; are subject to the same persuasive messages; may have come together partly because of preexisting similar attitudes; and may modify their own attitudes toward each other's for social-adjustive purposes. The process of social comparison, discussed earlier in relation to evaluating one's own traits and abilities, also applies in the attitude realm (Festinger, 1954). People tend to validate their own attitudes by comparing them to those of a reference group, consisting either of peers or of people occupying a higher rank (upward comparison), and are uncomfortable with attitudes that are out of step with the reference group. One of the most thorough, long-term studies of the role of a reference group in attitude change and persistence was initiated in 1934 by Theodore Newcomb (1943) at Bennington College in Vermont.

At the time of Newcomb's study, Bennington College had a politically liberal faculty, but drew most of its students from wealthy and hence politically conservative families. Most first-year students shared their parents' conservative views, but with each successive year at Bennington they became more liberal. In the 1936 presidential election, for example, 62 percent of the first-year students, 43 percent of the sophomores, and only 15 percent of the juniors and seniors favored Alf Landon, the conservative Republican, over the liberal Democrat, Franklin Roosevelt. By the time the first-year students became juniors and seniors, they too had become politically liberal.

What produced this change in attitude? The specific classroom lessons to which students were exposed may have played some role, but other social forces were also at work. People who occupied the most prestigious positions—the fac-

*How four years at a politically liberal college affected students' political attitudes, and how subsequent social relationships influenced the retention of those attitudes*

ulty, older students, leaders of various campus organizations—were politically liberal, and adopting their views helped one fit in with the community. In interviews, many women said that they adopted new attitudes at least partly to make friends and gain prestige. The relatively few who remained conservative throughout their 4 years at Bennington were far more likely than the others to be socially isolated, to feel that they were not really part of the college community.

What happened to these women's political attitudes after they left Bennington? Without the Bennington College community to support their new-found liberalism, did they slip back to their original conservatism? To answer this question, 20 years later Newcomb located and reinterviewed most of the graduates whom he had previously studied (Newcomb, 1963; Newcomb & others, 1967). Most of these women had remained liberal compared to others of comparable wealth and station in life, and the interviews suggested that they retained their liberalism at least partly because they continued to associate with people whose views were like theirs. Most of them had married liberal husbands, and those who had were more likely to remain liberal than those who hadn't. Those graduates who remained the staunchest liberals were also most likely to belong to organizations and social groups with liberal attitudes.

**Central and Peripheral Routes to Attitude Construction**   So far we have considered the functions of attitudes and the role of reference groups in their origin and persistence. Now we turn to a more cognitive question: How do people process information mentally in constructing an attitude? Most of the research on this has focused on people's responses to persuasive messages. Researchers have found it useful to distinguish between two general routes by which the mind can engage the information in a persuasive message—a ***central route***, which entails logical analysis of the message content, and a ***peripheral route***, which includes all other ways of using the information (Petty & Cacioppo, 1986).

The peripheral route includes simple association and respondent conditioning (discussed in Chapter 5), in which the mere pairing of an object or idea with a positive or negative event leads to a positive or negative attitude toward the object or idea. Presumably, this is the basis for all those television ads that pair a product (beer, car, shirt, or whatever) with beautiful people, happy scenes, and lovely music. Beyond simple association, the peripheral route may also involve certain *decision rules*, also called *heuristics*, which are shortcuts to a full, logical elaboration of information in the message (Chaiken, 1986). People use decision rules implicitly, unaware that they are doing so. Some examples of these rules include the following: (a) If there are a lot of numbers and big words in the message, then it must be well documented. (b) Famous or high-status people are more likely to be correct than unknown or low-status people. (c) If many other people believe this, then it must be true. (d) If the message is phrased in terms of values that I believe in, it is probably right.

People who use attitudes for different purposes may differ in the decision rules they use. For example, in one series of experiments, high self-monitors relied most heavily on rule (c) in the above list, consistent with a social-adjustive use of the attitude, and low self-monitors relied most heavily on rule (d), consistent with a value-expressive use of the attitude (Snyder & DeBono, 1987).

Research suggests that people tend to be *cognitive misers*, using the relatively effortless peripheral route to analyze most messages and reserving the more difficult, time-consuming central route for messages that have high personal relevance (Petty & Cacioppo, 1986). In one experiment supporting this view, Richard Petty and his colleagues (1981) presented college students with persuasive messages in favor of requiring students at their college to pass a set of comprehensive examinations as a requirement for graduation. Different students received different messages, which varied in (a) the *strength* of the arguments (a central

*How various alternatives to logical analysis make up a peripheral route to attitude construction, and evidence that people reserve the central route for issues that are personally important to them*

factor), (b) the alleged *source* of the arguments (a peripheral factor), and (c) the *personal relevance* of the message. The weak-argument message consisted of slightly relevant quotations, personal opinions, and anecdotal observations, and the strong-argument message contained well-structured statistical evidence that the proposed policy would improve the reputation of the university and its graduates. The source was varied by stating in some cases that the arguments had been prepared by high-school students, and in other cases that they had been prepared by the Carnegie Commission on Higher Education. Finally, the personal relevance was varied by stating in the high-relevance condition that the proposed policy would begin next year, so current students would be subject to it, and in the low-relevance condition that it would begin in 10 years. After hearing the message, students in each condition were asked to rate the extent to which they agreed or disagreed with the proposal.

Figure 14.9 illustrates the results. As you can see, in the high-relevance condition the quality of the arguments was most important. Students in that condition tended to be persuaded by strong arguments, and not persuaded by weak arguments, regardless of the alleged source. Thus, in that condition, students were processing the message by the central route. In the low-relevance condition, on the other hand, the quality of the arguments had much less impact, and the source of the arguments had much more impact. Apparently, when the policy was not going to affect them, students did not attend carefully to the arguments, but instead used the peripheral route, invoking the decision rule that experts (members of the Carnegie Commission) are more likely to be right than are nonexperts (high-school students). There is no real surprise here. The idea that people will think more logically about issues that directly affect them than about those that don't was a basic premise of philosophers who laid the foundations for democratic forms of government.

**Figure 14.9** *Effect of persuasive arguments on attitude under various experimental conditions*

*In this graph, movement above the horizontal axis indicates agreement with the persuasive message, and movement below the axis indicates disagreement with it. When the issue was of high personal relevance, the strength or weakness of the arguments had more impact than did the source of the arguments, but when the issue was of low personal relevance, the reverse was true. (Adapted from Petty & others, 1981.)*

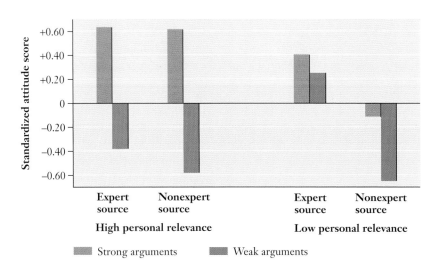

### Cognitive Dissonance as a Force for Attitude Consistency and Change

An attitude may enter the mind from the social environment, by either a peripheral or central route, but once it is there it joins the other attitudes, beliefs, and bits of knowledge that make up the person's whole mind. What happens if two of those elements are contradictory? Many years ago, Leon Festinger (1957) proposed that the awareness of contradiction or lack of harmony among two or more elements of one's mind creates a feeling of disturbance or discomfort, which he called ***cogni-***

*tive dissonance.* Festinger proposed, in his *cognitive dissonance theory,* that people are motivated to avoid or alleviate this discomforting state. In other words, he proposed that people are motivated to behave and think in ways that reduce disharmony (dissonance), or maintain harmony (consonance), among their various attitudes, beliefs, and bits of knowledge. Here we will consider some implications of this theory, as applied to the maintenance and change of attitudes.

**Avoiding Dissonant Information**   I once heard a person cut off a political discussion with the words, "I'm sorry, but I refuse to listen to something that I disagree with." People don't usually come right out and say that, but have you noticed how often they seem to behave that way? Given a choice of books or articles to read, lectures to attend, or documentaries to watch, people most often seem to choose those that they have reason to believe are consistent with their preexisting views. That observation, to the extent that it is true, is consistent with the theory of cognitive dissonance. One way to avoid dissonance is to avoid situations in which we might discover facts or ideas that run counter to our current views. People certainly don't always behave that way, but a considerable body of research indicates that they very often do (Frey, 1986; Chaiken & Stangor, 1987).

Paul Sweeney and Kathy Gruber (1984) conducted a study during the 1973 Senate Watergate hearings that provided a real-world illustration of this phenomenon. (The hearings uncovered illegal activities associated with then President Richard Nixon's reelection campaign against George McGovern.) By interviewing the same voters before, during, and after the hearings, Sweeney and Gruber discovered that (a) Nixon supporters avoided news about the hearings (but not other political news), and were as strongly supportive of Nixon after the hearings as they were before; (b) McGovern supporters eagerly sought out information about the hearings, and were as strongly opposed to Nixon afterward as they were before; and (c) previously undecided voters paid moderate attention to the hearings, and were the only group whose attitude toward Nixon was significantly influenced (in a negative direction) by the hearings. So, consistent with the dissonance theory, all but the undecideds approached the hearings in a way that seemed designed to protect or strengthen, rather than challenge, their previous view.

**Firming up an Attitude to Be Consistent with an Action**   We make most of our choices in life with less than absolute certainty. We vote for a candidate without certainty that he or she is best, buy one car even though some of the evidence favors another, or choose to major in psychology even though some other fields have their attractions. Any lingering doubts we may have after we have irrevocably made one choice or the other—after we have cast our ballot, made our down payment, or registered for courses and drop–add is past—would be dissonant with our knowledge of what we have done, and, according to the cognitive dissonance theory, we should be motivated to set them aside.

A number of studies have shown that people do tend to set their doubts aside after making a decision. Even in the absence of new information, people suddenly become more confident of their choice after acting on it than they were just before. For example, in one study, bettors at a horse race were more confident that their horse would win if they were asked immediately after they had placed their bet than if they were asked immediately before (Knox & Inkster, 1968). In another study, voters who were leaving the polling place spoke more positively about their favored candidate than did those who were entering it (Frenkel & Doob, 1976).

**Changing an Attitude to Justify an Action**   Sometimes people behave in ways that run counter to their attitude; then they are faced with the dissonant cognitions, "My attitude is *this,* but I did *that.*" They can't undo what they did, but they can relieve dissonance by modifying—maybe even reversing—their attitude. Be-

*How the cognitive dissonance theory explains people's seeking some information and avoiding other information*

*How the cognitive dissonance theory explains why people are more confident about a choice just after they have made it than just before*

**How the cognitive dissonance theory explains why people who behave contrary to their attitude are likely to change their attitude**

fore turning to research showing that people do often change their attitudes to be consistent with their actions, let me illustrate the idea with a passage written more than 200 years ago by the great inventor, statesman, and master of practical psychology, Benjamin Franklin. In this passage from his autobiography, Franklin (1949) describes how he changed the attitude of a political opponent who had tried to block his appointment to a high office:

> I did not like the opposition of this new member, who was a gentleman of fortune and education with talents that were likely to give him in time great influence. . . . I did not, however, aim at gaining his favour by paying any servile respect to him, but after some time took this other method. Having heard that he had in his library a certain very scarce and curious book, I wrote a note to him expressing my desire of perusing that book and requesting he do me the favour of lending it to me for a few days. He sent it immediately; and I returned it in about a week with another note expressing strongly my sense of the favour. When we next met in the House, he spoke to me (which he had never done before), and with great civility. And he ever afterwards manifested a readiness to serve me on all occasions, so that we became great friends, and our friendship continued to his death. This is another instance of the truth of an old maxim I had learned, which says, "He that has once done you a kindness will be more ready to do you another than he whom you yourself have obliged."

According to the cognitive dissonance theory, what might have happened in the former opponent's mind to change his attitude toward Franklin? He received Franklin's request to borrow the book, and, for reasons of which he may not have been fully aware, such as the simple habit of courtesy, he did not turn it down. But once he sent the book to Franklin he was thrown into a state of cognitive dissonance. One belief, *I do not like Ben Franklin*, was discordant with another, *I have just lent Franklin a very valuable book*. The second of these beliefs could not be denied, since that was objective fact, so dissonance could best be relieved by changing the first: *Ben Franklin isn't really a bad sort. At least I know he's honest. If he weren't honest, I certainly wouldn't have lent him the book.* Such thinking reduced or erased the dissonance, and also set the stage for new, friendlier behaviors toward Franklin in the future.

Notice that, according to this analysis, the man changed his attitude toward Franklin because he saw the decision to lend the book as his own choice and he saw no good reason why he should have made that choice if he didn't like Franklin. If Franklin had paid him or threatened him to get him to lend the book, the lending of it would not have created dissonance with the belief that he disliked Franklin. He would say, "I lent the book to Franklin only because he paid me," or " . . . only because he threatened me." Since either of these would have been sufficient justification, no dissonance would have resulted, and no attitude change would have been necessary.

The effect that is illustrated by this analysis of Franklin's story is today called the ***insufficient-justification effect***. It can be defined as follows: If a person is induced to behave in a way that is contrary to his or her attitude, and lacks any obvious way to justify that behavior, the person will tend to modify his or her attitude to make it more consistent with the behavior. During the last few decades many dozens of experiments have demonstrated this effect and have helped identify the conditions under which it occurs.

**How researchers have identified four different conditions that increase the likelihood that the insufficient-justification effect will occur**

One requirement, for the insufficient-justification effect to occur, is that there must be no obvious high incentive for performing the counter-attitudinal action. In an early demonstration of this, Leon Festinger and James Carlsmith (1959) gave college students a boring task (loading spools into trays and turning pegs in a pegboard) and then offered to "hire" them to tell another student that the task was exciting and enjoyable. Some students were paid $1 for telling this lie and others were paid $20 for telling it. The result was that those in the $1 condition changed their own attitude toward believing that the task really was enjoyable, whereas those in the $20 condition continued to see it as boring. Presumably, subjects in the $1 condition could not justify their lie on the basis of the little they were paid, so they convinced themselves that they were not lying, that the task really was enjoyable. Those in the $20 condition, on the other hand, could justify their lie by saying to themselves, "I said the task was enjoyable when it was actually boring, but who wouldn't tell such a small lie for $20?"

Another essential condition for the insufficient-justification effect is that the person must believe that he or she freely chose to perform the counter-attitudinal action; otherwise, the action could be justified simply by saying, "They made me do it." In one experiment demonstrating the importance of free choice, students were asked to write essays strongly supporting a bill in the state legislature that most students opposed (Linder & others, 1967). Students in the *free-choice condition* were clearly told that they didn't have to write the essays, but were encouraged to do so (and none refused). Students in the *no-choice condition* were simply told to write the essays, as if by volunteering to be in an experiment they were now obliged to do what the experimenter directed them to do. After writing the essays, all students were asked to describe their own attitude toward the bill; only those in the free-choice condition showed a significant shift in the direction of favoring it compared to a control group who had not written counter-attitudinal essays.

A number of researchers have challenged the view that the insufficient-justification effect is due simply to cognitive dissonance. One alternative view is that the mental discomfort that leads to attitude change comes not from attitude inconsistency per se, but rather from the possibility that one's actions might have created some harm to oneself or others if the original attitude were correct. Consistent with this view, some studies have shown that performing a counter-attitudinal action did not produce attitude change if subjects were subsequently led to believe that their action actually had no effect (Scher & Cooper, 1989). Still other research suggests that the attitude change has more to do with impression management than with a drive for real cognitive consistency; people changed their attitude after a counter-attitudinal action only if they believed that others knew how they had acted (Baumeister & Tice, 1984). Thus, in some conditions at least, the attitude change may serve to convince others, not the self, that no discrepancy exists between one's attitude and behavior.

Taking all of this research into account, if as a modern-day Ben Franklin you wanted to change someone's attitude toward your own by inducing the person to behave in a way that is consistent with your view, you might maximize your success by (a) minimizing any obvious incentive for the behavior, (b) maximizing the appearance of free choice, (c) choosing a behavior that would seem to be harmful when viewed from the perspective of the old attitude, and (d) maximizing the public nature of the behavior, so the person would have to justify it to others as well as to himself or herself.

### Why Don't People Always Behave According to Their Attitudes?

Social scientists first became interested in attitudes mainly because they conceived of them as mental guides of behavior (see Allport, 1935). The premise, consistent with common sense, was that by knowing a person's attitudes you could predict how he or she would behave. Thus, someone with a positive attitude toward the environmental movement should be more likely to recycle newspapers than someone with a negative attitude toward it; or someone with a strong attitude favoring honesty should behave in a more honest way than someone with a weaker attitude favoring honesty. It may seem somewhat surprising that this common-sense assumption has often been challenged, both on theoretical grounds and on the basis of research.

■ *How Skinner and other behaviorists have accounted for attitude-behavior inconsistency*

■ *Two early studies that demonstrated attitude-behavior inconsistency*

**Everything's better the second time around**

*As a result of the ecology movement, what used to be waste is now seen as a useful resource. New attitudes have so changed people's behavior that many communities are having to invent ways of using recycled material.*

The strongest theoretical challenge came from strict behaviorists such as B. F. Skinner (1957), who argued that attitudes are simply *verbal habits* that play a role in what people say to each other but are irrelevant to other aspects of behavior. According to this view, people learn to say things like, "Honesty is the best policy," because they are rewarded for saying such things by their social group. But when confronted by an opportunity to reap a substantial reward by lying, their behavior is controlled by a new set of rewards and punishments that may lead to an action that is completely contrary to the attitude.

You have already seen some evidence that people don't always behave according to their attitudes. All of the insufficient-justification studies, just described, involved getting people to behave contrary to their attitudes. Those studies, taken by themselves, turn the attitude-behavior relationship backward from the common-sense assumption. There, attitudes didn't determine behavior, but rather behavior determined attitudes—people modified their attitudes to justify their actions.

One of the earliest studies to call attention to the lack of predictability of behavior from attitudes was conducted by Richard LaPiere (1934). During the early 1930s, when attitude surveys showed rampant prejudice against Asians in the United States, LaPiere traveled back and forth across the United States accompanied by a young Chinese couple. During their travels they checked into 67 different hotels, auto camps, and tourist homes, and entered 184 different restaurants and cafes. In only one of these establishments were they refused service, and in nearly all they were treated with at least a normal degree of courtesy. Yet, when the proprietors of these same establishments were surveyed by questionnaire as to whether they would house or serve Chinese customers, a resounding 92 percent responded no.

Another early demonstration of lack of attitude-behavior correlation occurred in a study of cheating in a college course (Corey, 1937). Early in the semester, students filled out a questionnaire measuring their attitudes toward cheating, and later they were provided with what appeared to be an easy opportunity to cheat while grading their own true-false tests. Actually, the tests had been previously graded by the instructor, so cheating could be assessed by subtracting the score determined by the instructor from that reported by the student. A good deal of cheating occurred, and no correlation at all was found between the attitude measure and actual cheating. Those who had expressed a very strong anticheating attitude were just as likely to cheat as were those who had expressed a weaker anticheating attitude. A strong correlation was found, however, between cheating and the student's true score on the test. The lower the true score, the more likely the student was to try to raise it by cheating.

By the end of the 1960s, based on studies like those just described, some psychologists had concluded that attitudes play almost no role in guiding behavior (for example, Wicker, 1969, 1971). But others responded with data showing that under some conditions a strong relationship between attitudes and behavior is found. The question soon turned from, "*Do* attitudes guide behavior?" to "*When* and *how* do they guide behavior?" We will now examine three categories of answers to the latter question.

**Attitudes Must Be Retrieved from Memory to Affect Behavior**   From an information-processing perspective, attitudes, like any other beliefs, are stored in memory and can influence a person's decision to behave in a certain way only if recalled at the time the decision is made. Behavior occurs in a continuous flow, and we rarely stop to think about all of our relevant attitudes before we act. Perhaps, in LaPiere's study, the hotel and restaurant proprietors who had a negative attitude toward Asians were simply not reminded of that attitude upon seeing a friendly, clean-cut Asian couple, and therefore the attitude did not manifest itself. Or perhaps, in Corey's study, the stress of seeing how badly they had done on the test so overwhelmed the students that they simply failed to recall their attitudes about cheating. This line of reasoning suggests that any cues that remind a person of his or her attitudes would increase the attitude-behavior correlation. Consistent with this view, a number of experiments have shown that if people are presented with a task that requires them to think about their attitude on an issue shortly before behaving, the correlation between the attitude and behavior increases markedly (for example, Snyder & Swann, 1976).

*How the presence of a mirror may remind people of their attitudes and increase attitude-behavior consistency*

Other experiments have indicated that the presence of a mirror can remind people of all aspects of their self-concepts, including their attitudes, and in that way promote attitude-behavior consistency (Wicklund & Frey, 1980). For example, in one experiment college students rated pornographic pictures and passages in a way that was much more consistent with their previously stated attitudes about pornography (measured a month earlier) if they could see themselves in a mirror during the rating than if they couldn't (Gibbons, 1978). In another experiment, trick-or-treaters who came to the experimenters' houses on Halloween were more likely to take extra candy when they believed that nobody was watching, if no mirror was present, than if a mirror happened to be placed behind the candy bowl (Beaman & others, 1979).

Russell Fazio (1986) has argued that the strongest attitude-behavior relationships occur when the attitude was formed through direct, repeated experience with the attitude object, because in those cases the object automatically reminds the person of the attitude. If you have a negative attitude toward bacon because on several occasions you ate it and got sick, then the sight and smell of bacon will automatically elicit your negative attitude and you won't eat it. On the other hand, if you have a negative attitude toward bacon because you read somewhere that it is high in nitrates, and you read somewhere else that nitrates are bad for you, your attitude will not be elicited automatically by bacon's sight and smell. In that case you will need some other cue, extrinsic to the bacon itself, to remind you of the attitude, or you will need to rely on a habit of checking your set of food-related attitudes before you eat anything. Only after repeated rehearsal of your intellectually derived attitude about bacon would the attitude automatically be brought forth when you saw or smelled it.

*How two other kinds of cognitions may inhibit people from behaving according to their attitudes*

**People May Perceive Barriers to Behaving According to Their Attitudes** The decision to behave in a certain way involves other cognitions as well as attitudes. In what he calls a *theory of planned behavior*, Icek Ajzen (1985, 1987) has proposed that the conscious intention to behave in a particular way depends on one's (a) *attitude*, defined as one's own desire to act in that way or not; (b) *subjective norm*, defined as one's beliefs about what others who are important at the moment would think about the action; and (c) *perceived control*, defined as one's sense of his or her ability to carry out the action (see Figure 14.10). Applying Ajzen's model to LaPiere's

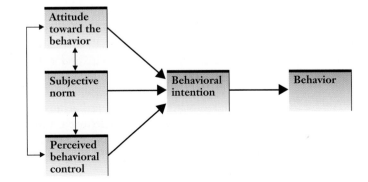

**Figure 14.10** *A theory of planned behavior*

*According to Ajzen's theory, the decision to behave in a certain way is a product of three categories of cognitions. (Adapted from Ajzen, 1987.)*

study, the proprietors may have wanted to turn the Chinese couple away (consistent with their attitude), but decided against it because they perceived that others who were present (including LaPiere and the Chinese couple themselves) would have disapproved (subjective norm), or because they perceived that they lacked any gracious means to carry out that action (low perceived control).

Research supporting Ajzen's model has shown that, depending on various factors, any of the three inputs to behavioral intention may predominate. For example, in a study of dieting and weight loss based on Ajzen's model, perceived control (confidence in the ability to stay on a diet) was a better predictor of weight loss than was either attitude (own desire to lose weight) or subjective norm (belief about whether others thought one should lose weight) (Schifter & Ajzen, 1985). In another study, students who were high on a personality measure of self-monitoring were most influenced by the subjective norm in determining how much time they devoted to their studies, whereas students who were low in self-monitoring were most influenced by their own attitude (Miller & Grush, 1986).

**Attitudes May Conflict with One Another**   An important limitation of many attitude-behavior studies is that they measure only one attitude, when in fact behavior can be affected by a whole set of attitudes, some of which may conflict with one another concerning the behavior in question. In LaPiere's study, the couple who approached the proprietors were not only Chinese, but were also clean-cut, friendly, articulate, married, and accompanied by a White sociology professor; so the proprietors' negative attitude toward Asians may have been outweighed by a positive attitude toward cleanliness, friendliness, articulateness, marriage, and White college professors. Similarly, in Corey's study, students' negative attitudes about cheating may have been outweighed by stronger negative attitudes about failing a test.

A number of studies have shown that if attitude questions are phrased in specific terms, identifying the conditions that would be present in the behavioral test, the attitude-behavior correlation increases greatly (Ajzen & Fishbein, 1980; Cooper & Croyle, 1984). Following this approach, if LaPiere's questionnaire had asked, "Would you accept a clean-cut, friendly, articulate Chinese couple accompanied by a White sociology professor as guests in your establishment?" he might have found a stronger correlation between the questionnaire response and the behavior measured.

Another approach to the problem of conflicting attitudes is to try to develop a fuller picture of a person's whole set of attitudes, and to see how that picture relates to specific behaviors. In experiments following this approach, Milton Rokeach focused on central attitudes, or *values*—such as the importance one ascribes to freedom, equality, or personal happiness—which he views as basic axioms that underlie one's decisions about appropriate ways to behave. Instead of asking people about their attitude on one specific issue, Rokeach asked them to rank order a set of values according to the importance they attach to them (see Table 14.2). This procedure forces respondents to pit commonly accepted values against one another, which should increase the likelihood of making accurate predictions of behavior in situations in which values conflict. In a series of studies, Rokeach found high correlations between the relative ranking of particular values on his questionnaire and quite specific, real-world behaviors. For example, he found that White college students who ranked equality especially high were more likely than other students to (a) make eye contact when speaking with a Black person, (b) join a political group supporting equal rights, and (c) participate in a rally for equal rights (Rokeach, 1980).

*How many attitudes, some conflicting with one another, may come into play in any specific behavioral situation*

*How Rokeach predicts people's actions by having them rank the importance of various central attitudes, or values*

**Table 14.2** *Values studied by Rokeach\**

| Values in rank order | |
| --- | --- |
| 1. A world at peace | 10. True friendship |
| 2. Family security | 11. A sense of accomplishment |
| 3. Freedom | 12. Inner harmony |
| 4. Equality | 13. A comfortable life |
| 5. Self-respect | 14. Mature love |
| 6. Happiness | 15. A world of beauty |
| 7. Wisdom | 16. Pleasure |
| 8. National security | 17. Social recognition |
| 9. Salvation | 18. An exciting life |

*The values are listed, top to bottom, in the order in which they were ranked by a cross-sectional sample of U.S. citizens.

*Source:* Adapted from "Change and stability in American value systems, 1968–1971" by M. Rokeach, in M. Rokeach (Ed.), *Understanding human values*, 1979, New York: Free Press.

■ *How political positions can be analyzed in terms of two sometimes conflicting values—freedom and equality*

Rokeach's research has helped inspire recent attempts to understand the complexities of political thought. For example, based partly on a model developed by Rokeach, Phillip Tetlock (1984) analyzed the political reasoning of members of the British House of Commons in terms of the relative weights that each individual placed on the sometimes conflicting values of freedom and equality. According to Tetlock's analysis, extreme liberals and extreme conservatives develop simple, straightforward policy arguments because they rely heavily on just one of those two values. For conservatives that value is freedom, and for liberals it is equality. Moderates, by contrast, develop more complex, multifaceted arguments because they weigh freedom and equality more equally. Thus, when debating a proposal for a more steeply graded income tax, conservatives oppose the proposal because it infringes on people's freedom to do what they want with their money, and liberals favor it because it promotes a more equitable distribution of wealth, whereas moderates neither clearly favor nor oppose it, but develop a more complex compromise view that takes both of those concerns into account.

As you can see, the study of attitudes is a huge area. It spans the distance from your reaction to bacon on your plate to your beliefs about how it should be distributed across society.

## Concluding Thoughts

**1. Automatic versus controlled processes in social cognition** In the terminology of modern cognitive psychology, automatic processes are those mental activities that occur without conscious attention, and controlled processes are those that require conscious attention. One way to review this chapter would be to go through it, section by section, thinking about the relative roles of automatic and controlled processes in each of the phenomena described. That distinction was discussed explicitly in relation to Devine's theory of stereotyping and prejudice, Gilbert's explanation of the fundamental attribution error, and the research on peripheral versus central routes of attitude change. But it can be found implicitly in many other parts of the chapter as well.

As a rule, the irrational biases in people's thinking—which have been the central focus of much of social-psychological research—can be attributed to automatic processes; and people's deliberate attempts to counteract such biases can be attributed to controlled processes. But many other phenomena described in the chapter might stem from either automatic or controlled processes (or a combination of the two), depending on the situation. Some examples of such phenomena are the use of social comparison to construct self-concepts and attitudes, the use of impression-management strategies to preserve or build a reputation, and the use of various behavioral and mental strategies to reduce cognitive dissonance.

**2. The value of a functionalist perspective** A theme that I have often emphasized in other chapters is that behavior usually serves some purpose for the behaving individual. This is as true of automatic and irrational behaviors as it is of controlled and rational behaviors; even self-harmful behaviors may stem from processes that originally came about (through evolution or learning or both) to serve some beneficial function. As social animals, one of our most basic needs is to be accepted and approved of by those other members of our species who constitute our close community. Our ability to survive and reproduce depends on that. We also seem to need to think well of ourselves, perhaps because such thoughts encourage our belief that we can surmount various obstacles to our survival.

Thus, another possible way to review this chapter is to go through it, section by section, thinking about possible ways in which each phenomenon described may be related to one or both of these twin needs—getting along with others and thinking well of ourselves. Such explanations will not work in every case, and in those cases you might think about other possible functions that the phenomenon might serve, or about how it could be a side effect of some aspect of our mental construction that is useful in a different context.

**3. Theory in social psychology** Social psychologists commonly divide their field into what they call theories. Some examples of these that were described in this chapter are attribution theory, social comparison theory, impression-management theory, and cognitive dissonance theory. The term *theory* has different meanings in different contexts, and in this context it obviously does not refer to a specific hypothesis that is to be proven correct or incorrect. All of the just-listed theories are clearly correct in the sense that they refer to phenomena that really occur. People certainly make attributions about others' behavior; people certainly compare themselves to others as a way of evaluating themselves and their attitudes; people certainly attempt to control the impressions that others develop of them; and people certainly are sometimes upset when they become aware of contradictions in their own cognitions.

The issue for social psychologists working on any of these theories is not whether or not the basic phenomenon named by the theory occurs, but rather is the extent to which that phenomenon adequately explains specific behaviors that could, in principle, stem from other causes. Thus, impression management obviously occurs, but it is not obvious that the specific category of behavior called self-handicapping is best explained in terms of impression management. Similarly, cognitive dissonance obviously occurs and affects behavior in some cases, but it is not obvious that this is the best explanation of the observation that people often change their attitude after performing a counter-attitudinal action. As you review each research study described in this chapter, think about how the findings might be explained by one or another broad social-psychological theory.

## Further Reading

**James S. Uleman & John A. Bargh** (Eds.) (1989). *Unintended thought.* New York: Guilford.

*This is a collection of articles about the role of automatic thought in social cognition. Some articles deal with basic mechanisms of automatic thought, others with the ways in which such thought affects daily life, and still others with the means by which people can regain control of their thinking. Though oriented toward the specialist, most of the articles are written clearly and simply enough to be read with interest by the beginning student.*

**Hans-Werner Bierhoff** (1989). *Person perception and attribution.* New York: Springer-Verlag.

*This brief text nicely summarizes social-psychological research and theory on the processes by which we perceive other people and make sense of their behavior.*

**Erving Goffman** (1959). *The presentation of self in everyday life.* Garden City, NY: Doubleday.

*This classic work, based on Goffman's insightful observations of people in everyday life, helped inspire research and theory in the area of impression management. It is fun to read.*

**Richard Petty & John Cacioppo** (1981). *Attitudes and persuasion: Classic and contemporary approaches.* Dubuque, IA: Wm. C. Brown.

*In this text, two experts concisely and clearly summarize the major theories of attitude formation and change and the evidence on which each theory is based.*

## Looking Ahead

Because we are concerned about what others think of us, other people greatly influence our behavior. The next chapter is about that influence. It deals with such topics as compliance, conformity, audience effects, and group decision making.

# CHAPTER 15

A Perspective: The Person in a
Field of Social Forces

Influence of Others' Requests

Influence of Others' Presence or
Examples

# SOCIAL INFLUENCES ON BEHAVIOR

As thinking, social beings, we are sensitive to the pressures of our social world. That is, we are sensitive to the real and imagined demands, requests, expectations, judgments, and examples that seem to flow constantly in our direction from other people. This chapter is about such pressures, called *social forces*. How can these forces best be described? In what ways, and through what mechanisms, do they influence our behavior? What conditions increase or decrease their impact? These questions will guide us as we progress through discussions of compliance, obedience, audience and coparticipant effects, conformity, group decision making, and intergroup conflict. But first, before turning to the more specific topics, let's consider the general concept of social forces.

## A Perspective: The Person in a Field of Social Forces

**The Legacy of Lewin**   The perspective of this chapter stems historically from the thought of Kurt Lewin, a pioneer of social psychology who left Germany in 1933 and moved to the United States. As a Jewish observer of the early stages of Nazism, and as an immigrant to a new country, Lewin was profoundly aware of the power that the social environment can have, for good or bad, on the thought and behavior of individual persons. Having been trained in Gestalt psychology in Germany, Lewin also came with a holistic view of the person and environment; he reacted against the stimulus-response perspective that characterized much of North American psychology at the time.

Lewin's own perspective, which he called *field theory*, was premised on the idea that each person exists in a field of forces that act simultaneously to push or pull the person in various directions (Lewin, 1951). Some of these forces stem from within—they are the person's own desires, goals, and abilities. Interacting with these are social forces that stem from the environment, but must be interpreted by the person in order to exert their influence. As an illustration of this interplay of forces, your decision about whether to spend this evening going to a party (Goal 1) or studying (Goal 2) might depend partly on your own beliefs about what would be most enjoyable or edifying (Force 1) and partly on your perceptions of what your friends (Force 2), family (Force 3), and professors (Force 4) want or expect you to do (see Figure 15.1 on page 528).

Of course, Lewin did not believe it was possible to produce a picture of all of the forces acting on any given person at any given time. Rather, he wanted to understand the various *kinds* of forces and the conditions that affect their strength so as to predict in a general way the effects that particular social changes would have on behavior. To do this he advocated the use of controlled experiments, in which

*■ How Lewin's field theory portrays the individual as existing in a field of psychological forces that affect his or her behavior*

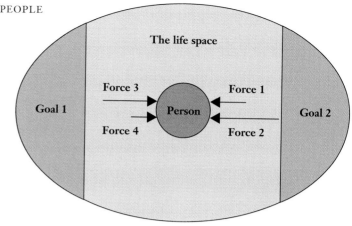

**Figure 15.1** *Lewinian diagram of the life space*
*Lewin viewed the person as subject to a field of forces that push him or her toward or away from various goals. In this simplified diagram, Goal 1 might be going to a party this evening and Goal 2 might be spending the evening studying; Force 1 might be the person's own wish; and Forces 2, 3, and 4 might be the person's perceptions of the desires of his or her friends, family, and professors, respectively.*

**Kurt Lewin**

*A pioneer in social psychology, Lewin was known for his ability to identify problems in the social environment and study them within a theoretical framework. Regarding the supposed distinction between "theoretical psychology" and "practical psychology," he was known to say, "There is nothing more practical than a good theory."*

■ *The three propositions of social impact theory, and why they must be understood in psychological, rather than physical, terms*

one social force could be studied at a time. You will encounter many examples of such experiments in this chapter.

**Social Impact Theory**   More recently, the concept of social force has been elaborated upon by Bibb Latané, in what he calls *social impact theory*. Latané (1981) defines *social impact* as "any of the great variety of changes in physiological state and subjective feelings, motives and emotions, cognitions and beliefs, values and behavior, that occur in an individual . . . as a result of the real, implied, or imagined presence or action of other individuals." In short, social impact is any detectable effect that occurs in a person as a result of social force. Social impact theory is concerned with variables that increase or decrease the impact of any social force. In this theory, the term *source* refers to a person who exerts a social force, and the term *target* refers to a person who experiences its impact. The theory specifies three general propositions about the effects of variation in the source and target:

1. The amount of impact of any social force is a multiplicative function of the *strength*, *immediacy*, and *number* of sources. To illustrate this proposition, Latané (1981) drew an analogy between social impact and the effect of light bulbs illuminating a solid surface. Impact (illumination) increases as the sources (light bulbs) increase in strength (wattage), immediacy (closeness to the surface), and number (see Figure 15.2a).

    Of course, with social forces the strength, immediacy, and number of sources must be defined psychologically. Unlike physical forces, social forces are not actual rays of energy traveling from source to target, but are hypothetical constructs referring to the target person's beliefs or perceptions. The *strength* of a source depends on the extent to which the target respects, admires, needs, or fears that source. You are not affected by people whom you do not care about. The *immediacy* of a source is in some cases measurable in physical distance from the target, in inches or miles, but in other cases it is not. If you live separately from your parents, they may become more immediate as sources of impact if you have just been reminded of them, even though they are still the same number of miles away. The *number* of sources is in some cases a simple count of the people who are physically present and exerting a specific influence on the target, but in other cases it is the number of people whom the target imagines or believes to be exerting an influence. If you believe that your parents want you to behave in a certain way, then they are sources of social force for you to behave in that way, whether or not your belief is correct.

2. The increased impact of each additional source diminishes as the number of sources becomes larger. This is analogous to the change in perceived brightness that comes from adding more light bulbs. Adding a single light bulb has a big effect if only one bulb had been lit before, but a small effect if ten bulbs had been lit before. Similarly, two people who want you to do something will have considerably more impact than one person, but eleven people will have barely more impact than ten.

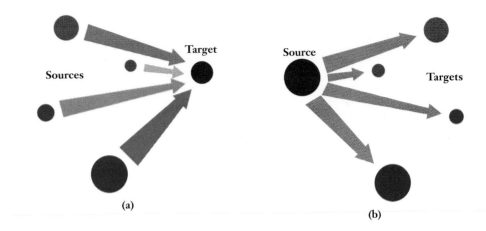

**Figure 15.2** *Multiplication and division of social impact*
(a) *According to the first proposition of social impact theory, the total impact of a social force on an individual increases as the strength, immediacy, and number of sources increases.* (b) *According to the third proposition of the theory, the total impact of a social force is divided among the targets, so the impact on any one target decreases as the number of targets increases. (From Latané, 1981.)*

■ *How the propositions of social impact theory are illustrated by experiments on stage fright*

3. The impact of a social force on a given target is inversely related to the number of targets. The assumption here is that impact is divided among targets, so, as the number of targets increases, the impact on any one target decreases (see Figure 15.2b). As an example, children scolded in a group will feel less impact of the scolding, per child, than will one child who receives the same scolding alone.

To illustrate the three propositions of social impact theory, Latané used the results of various experiments on stage fright. Consistent with the first proposition, stage fright increases as the status (strength) and the number of people in the audience increases (see Figure 15.3a). Consistent with the second proposition, the slope of the curve describing the increase in stage fright diminishes as the size of the audience gets larger (again see Figure 15.3a). And, consistent with the third proposition, stage fright decreases as the number of performers who share the stage in a group performance increases (see Figure 15.3b).

The propositions of social impact theory are not very surprising when applied to any specific kind of social force, such as that which produces stage fright. They are useful, however, because they nicely summarize a wide range of observations. Because these same propositions apply to all kinds of social forces, they bring some unity to the study of social influence. Regardless of the kind of influence—whether it is stage fright stemming from an audience, shame stemming from a scolding, sales pressure stemming from salespeople, or pressure to conform stemming from the perception that others are all behaving in a particular way—the amount of

**Figure 15.3** *Effects of audience status, audience size, and number of performers on stage fright*

*These results come from two different studies. The results in (a) are from an experiment in which subjects imagined themselves reciting a poem in front of various audiences and then adjusted the brightness of a light to match their anticipated anxiety. Those in (b) are from a study in which college students who performed either alone or in groups of various sizes in an actual talent show estimated—using Stevens's method of magnitude estimation, described in Chapter 8—the degree of anxiety they had felt while on stage. [Graph (a) is adapted from Latané, 1981; graph (b) is adapted from Jackson & Latané, 1981.]*

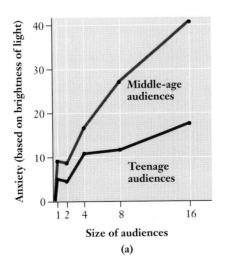
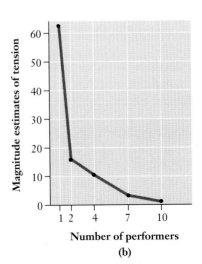

influence on the person increases as the strength, immediacy, and number of individuals perceived as exerting the influence increases, and decreases as the number of perceived other targets of that influence increases.

As you progress through the rest of the chapter you will find many examples of relationships that fit with social impact theory. But the focus will be more on questions that are not directly addressed by the theory—questions about the differing kinds of social influences that exist and the psychological mechanisms through which they operate.

## Influence of Others' Requests

One of the most obvious and potent forms of social influence is the direct request. Most people find it hard to look a requester in the eye and say no. In one experiment demonstrating this, researchers who did not look physically intimidating walked up to strangers in Grand Central Station in New York City and asked them to empty their pockets to prove that they had not just taken a dime from a phone booth (Moriarty, 1975b). Only 20 percent refused. It was as if people were primed to comply, and needed some special reason or excuse to say no. Lacking an excuse that would seem acceptable to the requester, people will very often do or give what they would rather not.

In polite society the tendency to comply usually serves us well. Most requests are reasonable, and we know that in the long run doing things for others pays off, as others in turn do things for us. But not all of society is polite. There are people in all sectors who, out of selfishness, or because their jobs demand it, or because they are working for causes in which they sincerely believe, will exploit our tendency to comply.

Social impact theory predicts that you should be more likely to comply to a request if (a) the person making the request is high rather than low in status, (b) the person making the request is right in front of you rather than far away (as in a request made by phone or mail), (c) more than one person is making the request, and (d) you stand alone rather than with others as the target of the request. Both experiments and everyday observations suggest that all of these hold true (Latané, 1981; Cialdini, 1987, 1988). You will see some evidence supporting these points later, in the discussion of a classic series of experiments on obedience to authority figures. But first let us examine some other general principles of compliance, gleaned in part from analyses of sales techniques.

### Some Principles of Compliance

Robert Cialdini (1984, 1987) is a social psychologist who has devoted more than lip service to the idea of combining real-world observations with laboratory studies. To learn about compliance from the real-world experts, he took training in how to sell encyclopedias, automobiles, and insurance; infiltrated advertising agencies and fundraising organizations; and talked to recruiters, public-relations specialists, and political lobbyists. He learned their techniques, extracted from them what seemed to be basic principles, and then showed those principles in operation under the more tightly controlled conditions made possible by experimental research. The following paragraphs describe a set of compliance principles, some of which are taken directly from Cialdini's work and others of which are alluded to by him but come more from the work of other social psychologists. As you read each principle, think about it from both the scientific viewpoint (what evidence supports it) and the practical viewpoint (in what real situations, beyond those mentioned, may this principle apply).

**The Peripheral Processing of Requests** Chapter 14 describes a distinction between central and peripheral processing of persuasive messages. Central processing is the use of logical reasoning, and peripheral processing is the use of habits or ingrained decision rules that involve little cognitive effort. We tend to reserve our limited central-processing capacity for decisions that are most important to us and to apply peripheral processing to less important decisions. If you ask, "How are you?" as you pass me on the street, I will normally through habit respond, "Fine," not bothering to think about whether I really am fine or whether you, at that moment, really want to know. Similarly, if you ask a small favor of me, I may grant it without bothering to think about its logic. My decision in that case may be based on the *form* of the request, such as whether it is politely made, rather than on an understanding of your reason for asking.

In an experiment demonstrating this principle, researchers approached people who were about to use the copy machine in a university library and asked their permission to go ahead of them to copy either five pages (small request) or twenty pages (large request) (Langer & others, 1978). Both types of requests were presented in one of the following three ways: (1) *No reason*—"Excuse me, I have five (twenty) pages. May I use the copy machine?" (2) *Logical reason*—"Excuse me, I have five (twenty) pages. May I use the copy machine, because I'm in a rush?" (3) *Pseudo reason*— "Excuse me, I have five (twenty) pages. May I use the copy machine, because I have to make some copies?" Notice that the pseudo reason contains the word *because*, which gives it the superficial appearance of a reason, but in fact contains no information that is not apparent in the request alone. Why would anyone want to use the copy machine other than "to make some copies"?

Figure 15.4 shows the results of the experiment. As you can see, the pseudo reason was as effective as the logical reason in increasing people's compliance when the request was small, but was as ineffective as no reason when the request was large. Apparently, with the large request people were motivated to think about the reason before complying, but with the small one they were satisfied just to hear the word *because*. The decision rule here seems to be: *If the request is small, and the person making the request seems to have a reason, comply. If the request is large, think about the reason before complying.* Other research suggests that people who are mentally preoccupied with other matters are more likely to comply automatically to a request than are those who are giving the requester their full attention (Cialdini, 1988).

**Cognitive Dissonance as a Compliance Principle** Chapter 14 contains an extensive discussion of the theory of cognitive dissonance. The basic idea of the theory is that people are discomforted by contradictions among their beliefs, or between their beliefs and actions, and thus are motivated to change their beliefs or actions to maintain consistency. According to Cialdini's analysis, a number of standard sales tricks make use of this principle.

The objective of one such trick, called the **four-walls technique**, is to get potential customers to say things that are consistent with the idea that owning the product would be a good thing. The customer's statements set up cognitive walls, which more or less box the customer into agreeing to the deal when it is finally proposed. This is the technique of door-to-door salespeople who begin as if conducting a survey, with questions such as the following (from Cialdini, 1987): (a) "Do you feel that a good education is important for your children?" (b) "Do you think that children who do their homework will get a better education?" (c) "Do you believe that a good set of reference books can help children do their homework?" (d) "Well, then, it sounds like you'll want to hear about this fine set of encyclopedias I have to offer at an excellent price. May I come in?" After expressing a favorable attitude toward education and reference books on the first three questions, most people find it hard to say no to the fourth.

■ *Evidence that people often use peripheral rather than central processing in deciding to comply, especially if the request is small*

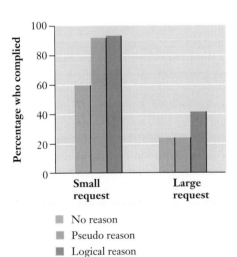

**Figure 15.4** *Evidence of peripheral processing of a small but not a large request*

*In the small-request condition (to allow someone to photocopy five pages ahead of them), subjects were as strongly influenced by a pseudo reason as by a logical reason. In the large-request condition (to allow someone to copy twenty pages ahead of them), a pseudo reason was no more effective than was no reason. (Data from Langer & others, 1978.)*

**How three sales tricks—the four-walls, low-ball, and foot-in-the-door—may be explained by the cognitive dissonance theory**

Perhaps the most underhanded sales trick involving cognitive dissonance is that called the **low-ball technique**, or *throwing the low ball*, reported to be used quite often in automobile dealerships. The salesperson works out a very attractive deal (the low ball) on a particular car, and the customer verbally agrees to the deal. Then the salesperson draws up the papers, takes them into the manager's office ostensibly for his or her signature, and comes out apologizing because the manager won't allow the car to be sold at such a low price. Meanwhile—while the salesperson is enjoying a cup of coffee in the manager's office—the customer has become more strongly committed to the car than before. Thinking that the purchase is all but made, the customer sets aside lingering doubts and mentally exaggerates the car's advantages to reduce cognitive dissonance; and this in turn prepares the customer to agree in the end to a higher price than he or she would have accepted before.

In controlled experiments, Cialdini and his colleagues (1978) showed that this technique is indeed effective in getting people to accept a less favorable deal than they would have accepted otherwise. Its basic principle is that people who think that they have just bought something exaggerate its worth, presumably to reduce whatever cognitive dissonance they have about buying it; then, when they discover that they haven't bought it after all, they are willing to pay a higher price for it than they were before.

One of the most common sales techniques that may operate through cognitive dissonance is the **foot-in-the-door technique**. Before defining this one, let me give you an example of it in which I was outwitted by a clever gang of driveway sealers. One day while I was raking leaves in front of my house, these men pulled up in their truck and asked if they could have a drink of water. I, of course, said yes; how could I say no to a request like that? Then they got out of the truck and one said, "Oh, if you have some lemonade or soda, that would even be better; we'd really appreciate that." Well, all right, I did have some lemonade. As I brought it to them, one of the men pointed to the cracks in my driveway and commented that they had just enough sealing material and time to do my driveway that afternoon, and they could give me a special deal. Normally, I would never have agreed to a bargain like that on the spot; but having given them the lemonade, it seemed almost impossible for me to say no. I ended up paying far more than I should have, and they did a very poor job. I had been taken in by what I now see clearly to be a novel twist on the foot-in-the-door sales technique.

The basis of the foot-in-the-door technique is that people are more likely to agree to a large request if they have already agreed to a small one. The driveway sealers got me twice on that: Their request for water primed me to agree to their request for lemonade, and their request for lemonade primed me to agree to their deal about sealing my driveway. Cialdini (1987) has argued that the foot-in-the-door technique works largely through the principle of cognitive dissonance. Having agreed, apparently of my own free will, to give the men lemonade, I must have justified that action to myself by thinking, *These are a pretty good bunch of guys*, and that thought was dissonant with any temptation I might have had a few moments later, when they proposed the sealing deal, to think, *These people may be cheating me.* So I pushed the latter thought out of my mind before it fully registered.

**Evidence that the foot-in-the-door technique can be used to increase a person's general tendency to support good causes**

In some cases, as in my example with the driveway sealers, the foot-in-the-door technique may work because compliance to the first request induces a sense of trust or commitment toward the person making the request; but in other cases it may work by inducing a sense of commitment toward a specific cause, or toward causes in general. An illustration of the latter can be found in one of the first experiments on the foot-in-the-door technique (Freedman & Fraser, 1966). A researcher approached homeowners in California, presenting each person with one of four different small requests having to do with a specific cause. For some the cause was safe driving and for others it was keeping California beautiful. Within

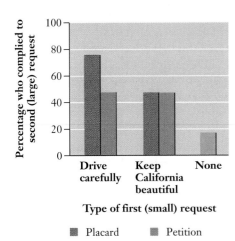

**Figure 15.5** *Results of a foot-in-the-door experiment*

*Shown here are the percentages of people who agreed to put a large "Drive carefully" sign on their front lawn, when asked 2 weeks after receiving one of four different smaller requests or no request. (Data from Freedman & Fraser, 1966.)*

■ *How the door-in-the-face technique may be explained by the reciprocity norm, and why it should backfire if a delay occurs between the first and second requests*

each of these groups, some homeowners were asked to support the cause by placing a small placard in their window and others were asked to support it by signing a petition. Nearly all of the homeowners complied. Then, two weeks later, a different researcher approached the same individuals, as well as a new group of homeowners, with a much larger request—to place a large, ugly sign saying "Drive carefully" on their front lawn.

Figure 15.5 shows the results. As you can see, the highest rate of compliance to the second request occurred when the first request had involved the same cause (driving safely) and type of action (putting up a placard) as the second. But the other groups who had received an initial request also complied more than did those who had not received one. Even if the first request involved a different cause (keeping California beautiful) and action (signing a petition) from the second, it increased compliance to the second request. As suggested by the experimenters, compliance to the first request may have solidified in people's minds the idea that they were public-spirited individuals who in general would do things for good causes—an idea that would be consistent with agreeing to the second request.

**The Reciprocity Principle and Downward Negotiation**  Anthropologists and sociologists have found that people all over the world abide by a *reciprocity norm* (Gouldner, 1960). That is, people everywhere feel obliged to return favors. This norm is so ingrained that people may even feel driven to reciprocate favors that they didn't want in the first place. Cialdini (1984) suggests that this is why such techniques as pinning a flower on the lapel of an unwary stranger before asking for a donation or giving a free bottle of furniture polish to a potential vacuum-cleaner customer are so effective. Having received the gift, it is hard for the victim to turn away without giving something in return.

Another common sales and solicitation method that according to Cialdini (1984) works partly through the reciprocity principle is that of starting with a very large request or high price and quickly negotiating down to a smaller one. This method is commonly called the *door-in-the-face technique*, because the first request usually elicits a clear no. I get hit by this method every year when a representative from the college I attended calls me, tells me about their new scholarship or building fund, and mentions an astronomically high figure as a suggested donation. As soon as I have gasped and explained that the suggested amount is way out of my range, the caller very politely suggests a much lower amount, which would also be valued. According to Cialdini, this method probably raises the likelihood of my agreeing to the second request for two reasons: (1) The caller's revised, much smaller request seems like a concession, an attempt to accommodate my personal needs, so I feel compelled to reciprocate through the only means available in that interaction—complying with the smaller request. (2) Contrasted with the first request, the second seems much lower than it would if it had stood alone.

The door-in-the-face method is the opposite of the foot-in-the-door method, and this suggests a possible problem. If people who comply with an initial low request feel *more* committed to the cause (the rationale of foot-in-the-door), then shouldn't people who refuse an initial high request feel *less* committed to the cause? Based on the cognitive dissonance principle, turning down the request to donate a huge amount of money to my alma mater should make me think of many reasons not to donate to the college, and this in turn should reduce the likelihood of my complying to the second request. Maybe that is why the caller moves so quickly to the smaller request—in doing so, he or she doesn't give me time to reduce cognitive dissonance through thinking of negative things about the college. Perhaps if more time elapsed between the first and second requests, the door-in-the-face method would boomerang, reducing the likelihood of complying to the second request.

That such a boomerang effect can indeed occur was shown in an experiment directly comparing the foot-in-the-door and door-in-the-face methods (Cann & others, 1975). Subjects in the *foot-in-the-door* condition received an initial small request (to answer a few questions on traffic safety), to which most complied. Subjects in the *door-in-the-face* condition received an initial large request (to record traffic flow at an intersection for 2 hours), to which most did not comply. In each of these conditions, half of the subjects received a moderately sized second request (to distribute pamphlets on traffic safety to fifteen people) immediately after the first request, and the other half received the same second request a week later. All four of these groups were compared, in rate of compliance to the second request, to a control group who received only the latter request.

As you can see in Figure 15.6, both techniques increased compliance in the immediate condition, but only the foot-in-the-door technique did so in the delayed condition. In the delayed condition, the door-in-the-face subjects behaved as would be predicted by the cognitive dissonance principle—they were *less* likely than the control group to agree to the second request. The delay apparently gave people time to think of reasons to justify their turning down the first request, which in turn prepared them to turn down the second request.

**Figure 15.6** *Results of an experiment comparing the foot-in-the-door and door-in-the-face techniques*

*Subjects in the foot-in-the-door condition received an initial small request (which most of them agreed to), and subjects in the door-in-the-face condition received an initial large request (which most of them refused). The control group received no initial request. Then, either immediately after the first request (no-delay condition) or 1 week later (delay condition), all subjects received a moderately sized second request. As shown here, the percentage of subjects who complied to the second request was dramatically affected by the delay in the door-in-the-face condition but not in the foot-in-the-door condition. (Data from Cann & others, 1975.)*

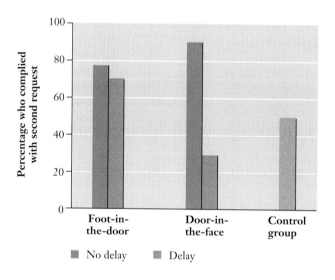

■ *How the reactance principle may explain the decreased attractiveness of an item that you are encouraged to choose and the increased attractiveness of one that seems unavailable*

**The Reactance Principle**   Balancing our tendency to comply is our tendency to assert our independence and freedom. When pressure to behave in a certain way is too blatant, too obvious a threat to our freedom, it can have the opposite of its intended effect, a phenomenon called ***psychological reactance*** (Brehm, 1966). In Massachusetts, where I live, most people believe in wearing automobile seat belts; but when the legislature passed a law requiring seat belt use a few years ago, the voters rebelled and forced the law's repeal through a referendum. Most would continue to wear seat belts, but they weren't going to let the state tell them that they *had* to (too bad, in my opinion, but that carries us beyond the point at hand).

In experiments demonstrating psychological reactance, subjects who believed that their right or opportunity to behave in a particular way was being restricted responded by removing or deliberately flouting the restriction (Brehm & Brehm, 1981; Wicklund, 1974). In one experiment, people who were subjected to obvious pressure to choose a particular pair of sunglasses subsequently rated those glasses as lower in value than did people who had not been pressured (Wicklund & others, 1970). The intuitive understanding of the reactance principle leads most people to

**A challenging situation**
*Not all rule flouting can be attributed to psychological reactance. These comfortable, easily available seats would probably be occupied regardless of the message on the sign.*

■ *The function and dysfunction of obedience*

■ *How Milgram demonstrated that a remarkably high percentage of people would follow a series of orders to hurt another person*

soften the way they make requests so as to preserve the appearance of choice. When a teacher says to the class, "Would you all please take out your pencils and answer the following questions," the class at some level knows that this isn't a question, or even a request, but a command—yet, the gentle phrasing helps prevent reactance by maintaining the superficial appearance of choice.

Clever salespeople may exploit the reactance principle not just by softening their sales pitch, but occasionally by acting as if they are trying to prevent you from making a particular purchase. They may act as if they would rather not sell you that particular item, implying, perhaps, that very few of them are left, thus threatening your freedom to own one. In an experiment conducted long ago, children who were given a choice of candies overwhelmingly picked the one that was placed farthest away and under a wire screen (Wright, 1937). Apparently, the ruse that the experimenter was trying to hide the piece of candy made that piece more attractive. With adults the attempt to hide the forbidden item must be less obvious, but the idea is the same. When a group of college students were led to believe that their cafeteria would be closing down for a while because of a fire, they rated its food more favorably than they had before the announcement (West, 1975).

### Obedience: Milgram's Experiments and Beyond

*Obedience* refers to those cases of compliance in which the person making the request is perceived as an authority figure or leader and the request is perceived as an order or command. Most often we think of obedience as a good thing. Obedience to parents, teachers, and country is part of everyone's social training. Running an army, an orchestra, a hospital, or any organization involving large numbers of people would be almost impossible if people did not routinely carry out the instructions given to them by their leaders or bosses. You can't argue about everything if anything is going to get accomplished.

But obedience also has its down side. The most tragic cases are those instances or epochs in which people obey a leader who is evil, unreasonable, or sadly mistaken. As the novelist and social critic C. P. Snow (1961) once wrote, "When you think of the long and gloomy history of [humankind], you will find more hideous crimes have been committed in the name of obedience than have ever been committed in the name of rebellion." A prime example of this gloomy history is the Holocaust of World War II, in which millions of Jews, gypsies, homosexuals, mentally ill people, and other men, women, and children deemed worthless by the Nazi government were systematically slaughtered. They were slaughtered through a chain of command, in which many of the slaughterers viewed themselves as simply following orders. Another example is the My Lai massacre of 1968, in which U.S. soldiers, obeying orders from their platoon leader, who in turn claimed to be obeying orders from higher up, murdered the defenseless women, children, babies, and old men of the village of My Lai in Vietnam. Some of the soldiers objected to the order, and some wept as they carried it out, but none rebelled (Kelman & Hamilton, 1989).

This gloomy side of obedience led the late Stanley Milgram to carry out a series of experiments at Yale University in the early 1960s that are now perhaps the most well known of all experiments in social psychology.

**Milgram's Basic Procedure and Finding** Let us suppose that you are a volunteer who has answered Milgram's ad to participate in a psychological experiment. You enter the laboratory and meet the experimenter and another person who is introduced to you as a volunteer subject like yourself. The experimenter, a stern and impassive 31-year-old man, explains that this is going to be a study of the effects of punishment on learning, and that one of you is going to play the role of teacher

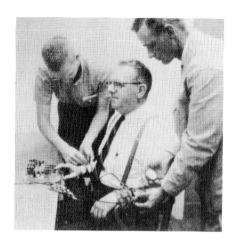

**Figure 15.7** *The victim in Milgram's obedience experiments*

*While being strapped into the chair where he would ostensibly receive an electric shock each time he gave a wrong answer in a memory test, this pleasant, middle-aged man mentioned that he had a heart condition.*

and the other that of learner. You draw slips of paper to see who will play which, and you find that your slip says "teacher." The other subject, an affable 47-year-old man, will be the learner. You watch while his arms are strapped into a chair and electrodes are taped to his wrist (see Figure 15.7). The experimenter explains that the straps will prevent excessive movement while the learner is shocked, and he comments that electrode paste has been applied to the skin "to avoid blisters and burns." While he is being strapped in, the learner expresses some apprehension, saying that he is concerned because he has a heart condition. The experimenter explains, "Although the shocks can be extremely painful, they cause no permanent tissue damage."

After observing this part of the procedure, you—the teacher—are taken to an adjoining room, from which you can communicate with the learner through an intercom. Your job is to read off the questions of a verbal-memory test and to give the learner an electric shock whenever he gives a wrong answer. The shock generator in front of you is an impressive instrument with thirty switches, each labeled with a voltage designation, from 15 up to 450 volts. In addition, verbal descriptions are written on the box for successive sets of switches, ranging from "Slight shock" up to "Danger, severe shock," followed by two switches labeled "XXX."

As the experiment progresses, the learner makes frequent mistakes, and at each mistake you give him a stronger shock than you had given before. The learner receives the early shocks silently, but when you get to 75 volts he responds with an audible "unghh," and at stronger shocks his protests become more extreme. At 150 volts he cries out, "Experimenter, get me out of here! I won't be in the experiment any more! I refuse to go on!" At 180 volts he hollers, "I can't stand the pain!" By 270 volts his response to each shock is an agonized scream, and at 300 volts he shouts in desperation that he will no longer provide answers in the memory test. The experimenter instructs you to continue anyway, treating each nonresponse as a wrong answer. At 315 and 330 volts the learner screams violently, and then, most frightening of all, from 345 volts on, the learner makes no sound at all. He does not respond to your questions, and he does not react to the shock.

What do you do in this situation? At various points you look to the experimenter and ask if he should check on the learner or if the experiment should be terminated. You may even plead with the experimenter to let you quit giving shocks. At each of these junctures the experimenter responds firmly with well-rehearsed prompts. First he says, "Please continue." If you still protest, he responds, "The experiment requires that you continue." This is followed, if necessary, by, "It is absolutely essential that you continue," and "You have no other choice; you must go on." These prompts are always used in sequence. If you still refuse to go on after the last one, the experiment is discontinued.

In reality—as you, sitting comfortably and reading this book, have probably figured out—the learner receives no shocks. He is a confederate of the experimenter, trained to play his role. But you, as a subject in the experiment, do not know that. You believe that the learner is suffering, and at some point you begin to think that his life may be in danger. What do you do? If you are like most people, believe it or not, you will go on with the experiment to the very end, eventually giving the learner the strongest shock on the board—450 volts, "XXX." In a typical rendition of this experiment, 65 percent (twenty-six out of forty) of the subjects continued to the very end of the series. They did not find it easy to do this. Many pleaded with the experimenter to let them stop, and almost all of them showed signs of great tension, such as sweating and nervous tics, but they went on.

Why didn't they quit? There was no reason to fear retribution for halting the experiment. The experimenter, although stern, did not look like a physically aggressive man. He did not make any threats. The $5 pay they received for participating was so small as to be irrelevant; at any rate, all subjects had been told that the $5 was theirs just for showing up. So why didn't they quit?

■ *Why Milgram's finding calls for explanation in terms of the social situation rather than in terms of unique personality characteristics of the subjects*

**Explaining the Finding**   Upon first hearing about the results of Milgram's experiment, most people are tempted to suggest that the volunteers must have been in some way abnormal to do such a thing as give painful, perhaps deadly shocks to a middle-aged man with a heart condition. But that answer—which, incidentally, is in line with the fundamental attribution error described in Chapter 14 (the tendency to attribute behavior too much to internal characteristics of the person and not enough to the environmental situation)—doesn't hold up. The volunteers were in fact perfectly normal individuals, and the experiment has been replicated dozens of times, with many different groups of subjects, with essentially the same results each time. Milgram (1974) himself found the same results for women as for men, and among men he found the same results for college students, professionals, and workers of a wide range of ages and backgrounds. Others have repeated the experiment outside of the United States, and the consistency from group to group has been far more striking than the differences (Miller, 1986). No category of person has been found to be immune from the tendency to obey at a high rate in the Milgram experiment.

Another temptation is to assume that the experiments show that people in general are sadistic. But nobody who has seen Milgram's film of subjects actually giving the shocks would conclude that. The subjects experienced no pleasure in what they were doing, and they were obviously upset by their belief that the learner was in pain.

How, then, can the results be explained? Here are some of the factors that Milgram (1974) and other social psychologists (see Miller, 1986) have deemed important:

■ *Evidence that obedience in Milgram's experiments was a product of (a) the subjects' preexisting beliefs, (b) the experimenter's self-assurance, (c) the experimenter's immediacy, and (d) the sequential nature of the task*

■ *Preexisting beliefs about authority and the value of science*   The subject comes to the laboratory as a product of a social world that effectively, and usually for beneficent reasons, trains people to obey legitimate authorities. An experimenter, especially one at such a reputable institution as Yale University, must surely be a legitimate authority in the context of the laboratory. In addition, the subject arrives with a degree of faith in the value of scientific research, which Milgram referred to as an *overarching ideology*, analogous to the overarching political or religious ideologies that motivate people to make much greater voluntary sacrifices when, for example, they join an army. Thus, the person enters the laboratory highly prepared to do what the experimenter asks, and believing that to do so is a good thing.

Consistent with the idea that subjects' prior beliefs about the legitimacy of the experiment were important, Milgram found that when he moved the experiment from Yale to a downtown office building, under the auspices of a fictitious organization, Research Associates of Bridgeport, the percentage who were fully obedient dropped somewhat—from 65 percent to 48 percent.

■ *The experimenter's self-assurance and acceptance of responsibility*   To obey, in a situation such as the one set up by Milgram, is to assume that the person giving orders knows what he or she is doing and is responsible, and that your role is essentially that of a cog in a wheel. The preexisting beliefs mentioned above helped prepare subjects to accept the cog's role, but the experimenter's unruffled self-confidence during what would seem to be a time of crisis no doubt helped subjects continue accepting that role as the experiment progressed. To reassure themselves, they often asked the experimenter questions like, "Who is responsible if that man is hurt?" and the experimenter routinely answered that he was responsible for anything that might happen. The importance of the subjects' attribution of responsibility to the experimenter was shown directly in an experiment conducted by another researcher (Tilker, 1970), patterned after Milgram's, in which obedience dropped sharply when subjects were told beforehand that they should assume responsibility for the learner's well-being.

**Figure 15.8** *Giving a shock while in close proximity to the victim*

*In one of Milgram's experiments, subjects were required to hold the victim's arm on the shock plate each time a shock was given. Fewer obeyed in this condition than when the victim received shocks in another room.*

■ *How Milgram's research has been criticized on ethical grounds and grounds of scientific validity, and how the research has been defended*

■ *The immediacy of the experimenter and the distance of the learner* If you think of Milgram's subjects in relation to social impact theory, you can picture them as caught between two conflicting social forces. On one side was the experimenter demanding that the experiment be continued, and on the other was the learner asking that it be stopped. Not only did the experimenter have the greater initial authority (higher strength), but he was also physically closer and perceptually more salient (higher immediacy). He was standing in the same room with the subject while the learner was in another room, out of sight. To test the importance of immediacy, Milgram (1974) varied the placement of the experimenter or the learner in some replications of the experiment. In one variation, the experimenter left the room when the experiment began and communicated with the subject by telephone, using the same verbal prompts as in the original study; in this case, only 23 percent obeyed to the end, compared to 65 percent in the original condition. In another variation, the experimenter remained in the room with the subject, but the learner was also brought into that room; in this case, 40 percent obeyed to the end. In still another variation, the subject was required to hold the learner's arm on the shock plate while the shock was administered (see Figure 15.8), with the result that 30 percent obeyed to the end. Thus, any change that moved the experimenter farther away from the subject, or the learner closer, tended to tip the balance away from obedience.

■ *The sequential nature of the task* If you think about it, Milgram's subjects had no compelling reason to quit at the very beginning of the experiment. After all, the first few shocks were very weak, and subjects had no way to know how many errors the learner would make or how strong the shocks would become before the experiment ended. Although Milgram did not use this term, we might think of his method as a very effective version of the foot-in-the-door technique. Having complied to earlier, smaller requests (giving weaker shocks), subjects found it hard to refuse new, larger requests (giving stronger shocks). The technique was especially effective in this case, because each shock was only a little stronger than the previous one. At no point were subjects asked to do something radically different from what they had already done. To refuse to give the next shock would be to admit that it was probably also wrong to have given the previous shocks—a thought that would be dissonant with subjects' knowledge that they indeed had given those shocks.

**The Ethics and Validity of Milgram's Experiments**  Because of their dramatic results, Milgram's experiments immediately attracted much attention and criticism from psychologists and other scholars. Some critics focused on ethics (for example, Baumrind, 1964). They were disturbed by such statements as the following, which appeared in Milgram's (1963) initial report: "I observed a mature and initially poised businessman enter the laboratory smiling and confident. Within 20 minutes he was reduced to a twitching, stuttering wreck, who was rapidly approaching a point of nervous collapse." Was the study of sufficient scientific merit to warrant inflicting such stress on subjects, leading some to believe that they might have killed a man? To this day disagreement persists concerning that question, but it is worth noting that most of the subjects in the experiment did not regret their participation later on. In response to a questionnaire that Milgram sent to all subjects a year after their participation, 84 percent said they were either glad or very glad that they had participated, another 15 percent were neutral, and less than 2 percent said they were either sorry or very sorry that they had (Milgram, 1964).

Milgram took great care to protect his subjects from psychological damage. Before leaving the lab, subjects were fully informed of the real nature and purpose of the experiment; they were informed that most people in this situation obey the orders to the end; they were reminded of how reluctant they had been to give shocks; and they were reintroduced to the learner, who offered further reassurance that he was fine and felt very well disposed toward them. A year later, psychiatric interviews were held with forty of the former subjects, and no evidence of harm was found (Errera, 1972). Still, the question of whether the results justified even the temporary psychological anguish that these people experienced is a valid one for which no easy answer exists.

Other critics challenged Milgram's view that experiments of this type can help elucidate such real atrocities as the Nazi Holocaust. Some (for example, Orne & Holland, 1968) argued that Milgram's subjects must have believed, at some level of their consciousness, that they could not really be hurting the learner, because no sane experimenter would allow that to happen. From that perspective, the subjects' real conflict may have been between the belief that they weren't really hurting the learner and the possibility that they were. Unlike subjects in Milgram's study, Nazis who were gassing people could have had no doubt about the effects of their actions. They had far less cause to believe that they were following a benevolent authority, and far more to believe that they were following a dangerous one. Their motive could not have been based on a belief that the authority was actually kindly disposed toward the victims of the order; it was more likely based either on their fear of the authority, who might gas them or their families, or on their own acceptance of the evil cause. Milgram's study offers no shortcut to understanding the Holocaust or the many other atrocities involving obedience that have occurred both before that and since. To understand them we must understand the historical context in which they occurred—the fears, prejudices, economic conditions, and propaganda of the time.

Accepting its limitations, I personally am persuaded that Milgram's work was worthwhile for two reasons. First, science aside, the experiments provide a moral allegory for our time. People all over the world have heard of the research, and hearing about it has given many pause to think about obedience in ways that they might not have before. Precisely because the experiments involved a less complicated situation than such events as the Holocaust or the My Lai massacre, and because no real harm was done, they are easier to grasp and think about; and even just the knowledge of them may help people resist the temptation, in real situations, to assume that they are not responsible for their actions if they are made in response to someone else's request or command. Second, from a scientific position, Milgram's studies are part of a larger body of research that has helped identify some of the principles of compliance and obedience. Whereas specifics will vary from one setting to another, certain underlying principles may hold across a wide variety of settings. Preexisting beliefs about the importance of obedience, the authority's confident manner, the immediacy of the authority, and the sequential nature of tasks may contribute to real atrocities in much the same way that they contributed to obedience in Milgram's studies, even though the motives and specific conditions are very different.

■ *Evidence that the presence of others who question an order can decrease the likelihood of obedience*

**Other Obedience Studies: The Role of Social Support for Rebellion** Another important factor in most of Milgram's experiments is that subjects were alone in their predicament. In one variation, however, the task of teacher was divided between the subject and another person (who was actually another confederate of the experimenter); at some point the confederate refused to continue and the experimenter asked the real subject to take over the whole job. In this condition, only 10 percent of real subjects obeyed to the end (Milgram, 1974). Conversely, in another variation, in which the confederate continued to the end, 93 percent of real subjects did, too. In an unfamiliar and stressful situation, having a model to follow can have a potent effect. But Milgram's experiment has never been run with more than one real subject at a time (Brown, 1986). What would happen if the other presumed subject was not a stooge, instructed to rebel or obey, but was a second real

**The ultimate rebellion**

*Notable exceptions to rules of conformity are whistle blowers, people whose concerns about social and political policies may motivate them to risk their careers by revealing corruption or mismanagement at their place of work. This woman, who worked in quality control at a nuclear plant, was fired for blowing the whistle on defects in the plant and subsequent cover-ups.*

subject, hearing the experimenter's orders and genuinely trying to decide how to respond? Other research suggests that in many cases the two subjects would hear each other's protests, begin to share their concern through dialogue, and join forces in rebelling.

Of special interest here are two separate but similar experiments performed in hospitals. In both, hospital nurses on regular duty were telephoned by a man who identified himself as a doctor and asked them to administer immediately a particular drug, to a particular patient, at a dose that the nurses knew to be two or three times the maximum recommended. In the first experiment, the nurses were called at a time when they were likely to be alone on the ward, and the result was that 95 percent would have given the drug had they not been stopped by the experimenter's accomplice who was secretly watching them (Hofling & others, 1966). In the second experiment, the nurses were called at a time when other medical professionals were present, and in this case only 11 percent would have given the drug (Rank & Jacobson, 1977). In the second experiment, most nurses immediately said something about the unusual order to another nurse or doctor, who encouraged them in their belief that it was strange, which in turn led them to check with other hospital authorities. Although other differences between the two experiments could have contributed to the different results, the immediate availability of other medical professionals with whom to consult seemed to be a major factor.

## Influence of Others' Presence or Examples

You have seen that the way a person responds to an order can vary depending on the presence of other people and their reactions to the order. Now let us look more broadly at some ways in which the presence of others and the examples they set can affect a person's behavior. We will begin with a discussion of the effects that an audience or coparticipants can have on a person's behavior, and then we will turn to research on conformity, group discussion, and intergroup conflict.

### Audience and Coparticipant Effects

**Performing in Front of Others: Social Facilitation and Inhibition**    The first published experiment in social psychology (according to Hendrick, 1977) was conducted by Norman Triplett near the end of the nineteenth century. Triplett (1898) had observed that bicycle racers usually perform better when they race with each other than when they race alone against the clock. To test the generality of this phenomenon, he asked children to wind fishing reels as rapidly as possible; he found that they wound the reels faster when they worked in pairs than when each worked alone.

Triplett's experiment did not distinguish between the competitive effect that might be engendered when two individuals perform the same task together and the energizing effect that might come from the mere presence of another individual. However, subsequent experiments showed that improvement often occurs even when others are present just to watch. In one experiment, for example, college students who had achieved skill at a particular motor task (following a moving target with a hand-held pointer) subsequently performed it more accurately when observed by a group of graduate students than when tested alone (Travis, 1925). Similar effects were also demonstrated with nonhuman animals, including even insects. For example, in one experiment individual ants built tunnels faster when one or two other ants were present than when they were alone (Chen, 1937). The tendency to perform a task better in front of others than when alone was soon accepted as a general law of behavior, and was given a name—*social facilitation*.

**A victim of pressure?**

*Figure skater Debi Thomas, who was widely publicized as invincible at the 1988 winter Olympics, slipped several times during the final competition and finished a close third. As the last skater of the evening, did bad ice disrupt her performance, or was it inhibited by the extraordinarily high state of arousal and self-consciousness created by the event and the preceding expectations?*

Although many experiments confirmed the phenomenon of social facilitation, other experiments showed the opposite effect—*social inhibition*, a decline in performance when observers are present. For example, students who were asked to develop arguments opposing the views of certain classical philosophers developed better arguments when they worked alone than when they worked in the presence of either coperformers or observers (Allport, 1920). The presence of observers also reduced performance in solving math problems (Moore, 1917), learning a finger maze (Husband, 1931), and memorizing lists of nonsense syllables (Pressin, 1933). In animal studies, too, the presence of others inhibited the learning of new responses (Rasmussen, 1939).

Why the contradiction? Why did social facilitation occur in some experiments and social inhibition in others? Surprisingly, not until the 1960s was a coherent theory developed to answer this question. Robert Zajonc (1965), who developed the theory, noticed in reviewing the experiments that social facilitation usually occurred with relatively simple or well-learned tasks (such as winding fishing reels or, for ants, digging tunnels), and that social inhibition usually occurred for tasks that were more complex or involved learning something new (such as constructing logical arguments or learning a route through a maze). From this observation, Zajonc proposed the following generalization: *The presence of others facilitates performance of dominant (well-learned, simple, or instinctive) responses, and inhibits performance of nondominant (new, complex, or unnatural) responses.*

Zajonc went on, in his theory of social facilitation and inhibition, to explain both effects by linking them to a more general phenomenon—the effect of high arousal or drive on performance. As discussed in Chapter 7, high arousal—no matter how it is produced—typically improves performance on simple or well-learned tasks and worsens performance on complex or poorly learned tasks in both humans and other animals. Thus, according to Zajonc, the primary effect of the presence of others is to increase arousal or drive, after which easy responses become easier and hard responses become harder (see Figure 15.9). Evidence for the theory comes from studies showing that (a) the presence of observers does often increase arousal in a person performing a task (Zajonc, 1980), and (b) either facilitation or inhibition can occur in the same task, depending on the performer's skill. As an example of the latter, in one experiment expert pool players performed better when they were watched conspicuously by a group of four observers than when they thought they were not being observed, and the opposite was true for novice pool players (Michaels & others, 1982).

The presence of others may enhance arousal through various means. Zajonc (1965) suggested that humans and other animals are innately aroused by other members of their species. But other theorists, focusing on humans, have placed greater emphasis on learned effects such as evaluation anxiety. The role of evaluation anxiety has been demonstrated in experiments showing that both social facilitation and inhibition decline if the audience is blindfolded or not paying attention (Cottrell & others, 1968), and that both increase if the audience is high in status or expertise and is there explicitly for the purpose of evaluation (Geen, 1980). Another proposal is that an audience can be a source of distraction and in that way can increase arousal even in the absence of evaluation anxiety. In support of this view, researchers have found that nonsocial distractors (such as noises) can also have either facilitating or inhibiting effects on performance, depending on the kind of task (Baron, 1986).

Recently, a remarkable audience effect has been uncovered in the world of professional sports, which may or may not be explainable through an extension of Zajonc's theory. In examining the records of World Series baseball games over a 59-year period, Roy Baumeister and Andrew Steinhilber (1984) discovered that, contrary to the usual home-field advantage, the home team usually *lost* the final and decisive championship game. More specifically, whereas home teams won 60

■ *How Zajonc's theory explains why social facilitation occurs for some tasks and social inhibition occurs for others*

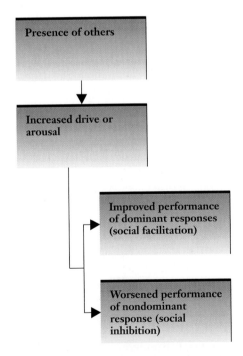

**Figure 15.9** *Zajonc's theory of social facilitation and inhibition*

*This theory relates social facilitation and inhibition to a more general effect of high arousal or drive on dominant (habitual) and nondominant (nonhabitual) responses.*

■ *How home-team collapse in championship games might be explained by Zajonc's theory or by an alternative theory centering on self-consciousness*

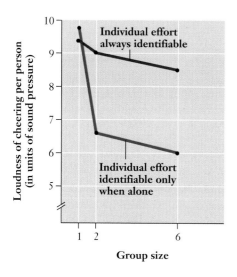

**Figure 15.10** *Effects of accountability and group size on effort*

*The task was to cheer as loudly as possible. As shown here, social loafing (reduced effort when working in groups) occurred when subjects believed that their individual effort was identifiable only when alone; it did not occur when they believed that their individual effort was always identifiable. (Data from Williams & others, 1981.)*

■ *Evidence that social loafing depends on lack of individual accountability*

percent of the first two games in the World Series, they won only 41 percent of final, decisive games and only 39 percent of final games if the series was not decided until the seventh game. Turning to another sport, these researchers found an almost identical set of statistics for semifinal and championship series in professional basketball in North America. What could be causing teams to collapse when playing decisive championship games at home?

*Collapse* is the right word for it: The home teams' losses were apparently due to their own worsened play rather than to improved play on the part of the visiting teams. As evidence for that, Baumeister and Steinhilber found that home baseball teams made about twice as many fielding errors in final games as in earlier games, whereas visiting teams made about the same number as in earlier games. One possible explanation, consistent with Zajonc's arousal theory, is that the potentially decisive championship game, coupled with the strong desire to perform well in front of the home audience, leads to a level of arousal that is so great that it inhibits performance even in these highly skilled professionals. The optimal level of arousal for a task in which a person is highly skilled is higher than that for a task in which the person is less skilled; but for any task it may be possible to reach a state of arousal that is higher than optimal (look back at Figure 7.17).

Baumeister and Steinhilber themselves favor a different explanation. They suggest that the combination of a potentially decisive game and a supportive audience increases the players' self-consciousness (rather than general arousal), so their attention is focused more on themselves than on external stimuli associated with the game. Because of self-consciousness, the responses that are normally automatic to them become less automatic, and thus the players are more likely to make errors. Their situation may become a bit like that of the centipede who, when asked, "Which leg do you move first when you start to walk," found itself no longer able to walk. A considerable amount of research supports this general explanation of "choking" under pressure (Baumeister & Showers, 1986).

**Slacking off with Others: Social Loafing**    Social facilitation and inhibition occur when each individual's performance can be evaluated. In contrast, when individuals work together in such a way that their efforts are pooled and indistinguishable, a different phenomenon sometimes occurs—*social loafing*, which is defined as a reduction in effort when working in a group. Social loafing has been demonstrated in such diverse tasks as pulling a rope (Dashiell, 1935), cheering (Latané & others, 1979), and creative problem solving (Harkins & Szymanski, 1989).

In an experiment showing an inverse relationship between social loafing and individual accountability, college students were asked to shout as loudly as they could, alone and in groups of two or six (Williams & others, 1981). In one condition they believed that only the whole group's sound could be measured when they shouted in groups, and in another they were fitted with recording microphones and told that their individual contributions to the group sound would be measured. Figure 15.10 shows the results. As you can see, in the first condition individual effort dropped off considerably as group size increased, whereas in the second condition it did not. Of course, social loafing need not always occur. When people work together for highly desired ends and group spirit is high, they may each put in their full effort even in the absence of individual accountability (Hackman, 1986).

**Watching While Others Watch: The Unresponsive Bystander**    In a normally quiet neighborhood in New York City in 1964, a young woman named Catherine Genovese was brutally attacked for a period of 30 minutes outside her apartment building. Her screams drew the attention of at least thirty-eight people, who watched through their apartment windows while she was repeatedly stabbed and finally murdered. Not one of the bystanders came to her aid or even called the police. The incident stirred a national outcry: What has become of people? Are we so

**Is help on the way?**
*Research suggests that this disabled motorist would be more likely to receive help if fewer motorists were on the road. The interesting question is: Why?*

inured to horror that we simply watch it without lifting a finger? This incident, and others like it, also stirred many social psychologists to investigate what is now called the **unresponsive-bystander phenomenon.**

Most people who hear of such an incident try to explain it in terms of personality characteristics of the bystanders—they are uncaring, numb, New Yorkers, or whatever. But—to repeat what must by now be a familiar refrain—social psychologists are more likely to explain such an incident in terms of the social context in which the incident occurred. What social forces may have been operating on the observers to reduce their likelihood of helping? In the years since Genovese's death, social psychologists have staged hundreds of emergencies—in laboratories, subway cars, on the street—to identify conditions that affect the likelihood that bystanders will help. Such studies have shown that under some conditions people rush to help, and under others they do not. We will examine here just one of the variables found to be important—the presence or absence of other bystanders.

Many experiments have shown that a person who witnesses an emergency when alone is more likely to come to the victim's aid than is a person who witnesses an emergency in the presence of others (Latané & Nida, 1981). For example, in one experiment, college students who were filling out a questionnaire were interrupted by the sound of the researcher, behind a screen, falling and crying out, "Oh . . . my foot . . . I . . . can't move it; oh . . . my ankle . . . I can't get this thing off me" (Latané & Rodin, 1969). In some cases the student was alone, and in other cases two students sat together filling out questionnaires. The remarkable result was that 70 percent of those who were alone tried to come to the aid of the researcher, and only 20 percent of those who were in pairs did so. What a strange finding. Apparently—at least in some cases—a person is better off having an accident with just one potential helper present than with two! Why? Researchers have suggested three interrelated explanations, each of which has received experimental support (Latané & Nida, 1981; Dovidio, 1984):

■ *Three possible explanations of the inhibiting effect of other bystanders on any one bystander's likelihood of helping*

- *Informational influence of others' inaction* If you are the only witness to an emergency, you decide if it is a real emergency, and whether you should try to help or not, on the basis of information that comes to you from the victim. But if other bystanders are present, you take your cue not just from the victim, but also from the other bystanders. You wait just a bit to see what they are going to do, and quite likely you find that they do nothing (because they are waiting to see what you are going to do). Observing the others doing nothing may lead you to redefine the situation. If the others aren't acting, maybe this is not a real emergency, or, if it is an emergency, maybe there is nothing that can be done. This explanation is supported by experiments showing that if other bystanders indicate, by voice or facial expressions, that they *do* interpret the situation as an emergency, their inhibiting effect is reduced or abolished (Bickman, 1972).

■ *Normative influence of others' inaction, and evaluation anxiety* If you are alone, your attention is focused on the victim and how you can help. But if others are present, your attention is split between the victim and your concern about how others may evaluate you. Since the others aren't acting, you would be violating what seems to be a norm if you were to spring into action, and you might look foolish to the other bystanders. Thus, evaluation anxiety inhibits your ability to develop a plan of action, or your willingness to carry it out, or both. Notice that according to this explanation, the unresponsive-bystander phenomenon is a special case of social inhibition. Evidence for this explanation comes from studies showing that if the bystanders know each other well—which would presumably reduce their anxiety about each others' evaluation, or lead them to realize that all share a norm of helping—then each others' presence has less of an inhibitory effect (Rutkowski & others, 1983; Schwartz & Gottlieb, 1980).

■ *Diffusion of responsibility* If you are alone when an emergency occurs, you feel a full measure of responsibility to help, because nobody else is available to help. But if others are present, the responsibility is divided—each person feels less responsible than he or she would alone. Depending on the situation, the reduced responsibility may be below the threshold needed to induce action in any of the bystanders present. This explanation is supported by a study showing that solitary witnesses to an emergency were much more likely to report in a later interview that they had felt responsible than were people who had witnessed an emergency with others (Schwartz & Gottlieb, 1980). It is also supported by experiments showing that the presence of other bystanders does not inhibit an individual from helping if that individual is clearly in the best position to help (because of location or special ability) or had been previously singled out as the one who should help (Bickman, 1972; Moriarty, 1975a).

In sum, consistent with all three explanations, the presence of other bystanders is most likely to reduce the chance that any one of them will respond if (a) none of the bystanders acts in a manner suggesting that someone should do something, (b) the bystanders don't know each other and have no idea what the others would think about their action, and (c) no particular bystander is obviously better able to help than is any of the others.

**Caught up in the Crowd: Deindividuation**    People sometimes do things in crowds or mobs that they wouldn't do individually—sometimes horrible things. At My Lai, for example, once the slaughter began, some of the soldiers went beyond their orders and got caught up in a frenzied spree of rape and torture before murdering their victims (Kelman & Hamilton, 1989). Many years ago, the French sociologist Gustave LeBon (1896) argued that people in a crowd may lose their sense of personal responsibility and behave as if governed by a primitive, irrational, hedonistic mind that seems to belong more to the group as a whole than to any one individual. Psychologists today refer to this state of reduced personal responsibility as *deindividuation*. It seems to be brought on by a combination of (a) *reduced accountability* that comes from being a relatively anonymous member of a crowd (which links this phenomenon to social loafing and the unresponsive-bystander phenomenon), and (b) *shifted attention* away from the self and toward the highly arousing external stimulation associated with the mob's actions (Diener, 1977; Prentice-Dunn & Rogers, 1983).

The role of anonymity in crowd-induced deindividuation is supported by a study of *suicide baitings*, incidents in which crowds gather to egg on a person who is threatening suicide (such as shouting "jump" to a distraught person perched on the ledge of a tall building). Based on news reports, the study showed that suicide baiting occurs most often in large cities, at night, when a large crowd has gathered

■ *Evidence that reduced accountability and highly arousing external stimulation can promote behaviors that violate social norms or one's personal standards*

**Potential for violence?**

*In the excitement of sporting events, crowds sometimes lose control—a phenomenon that researchers studying deindividuation have tried to explain. Although this crowd of soccer fans did not riot, the ingredients for such violence are present: anonymity (due to the size of the crowd and their similar costumes) and highly arousing external stimulation.*

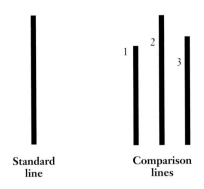

Standard
line

Comparison
lines

**Figure 15.11 *Sample stimuli used by Asch to study conformity***

*The task on each trial was to select the comparison line that was identical in length to the standard. On critical trials, the confederates unanimously made a specific wrong choice (either 1 or 3, in this example). (Adapted from Asch, 1956.)*

(Mann, 1981)—all of which are factors that would promote anonymity. Other evidence for the role of anonymity comes from anthropological studies showing that in general the more brutal a group's customs are, the more likely they are to wear uniforms or paint their faces (Watson, 1973). By wearing uniforms or war paint they erase their personal identities and merge themselves with the group. It is not Billy who murders the villagers—it is the army that does, and the uniform helps Billy and those who know him make that distinction.

A number of researchers have attempted to produce states approximating deindividuation in the laboratory. In one experiment showing the role of anonymity, groups of students were asked to take part in giving electric shocks to another student (who was actually a confederate of the researcher). The students themselves could choose the shock intensity, and the main result was that they chose to give stronger shocks if they wore hooded costumes and were not identified by name than if they wore their normal clothes and name tags (Zimbardo, 1970). In another experiment showing the role of intense stimulation, students who had just completed a set of invigorating group activities while rock music blared in the background chose to give stronger shocks than did students who hadn't been exposed to these conditions (Prentice-Dunn & Spivey, 1986). A self-report questionnaire in the latter experiment also revealed that students in the deindividuating condition experienced reduced self-awareness, a greater sense of being part of the group, more euphoria, and more alteration of their normal thought patterns than did those in the control condition.

Research has shown that deindividuation can heighten other forms of non-normative behaviors, not just aggression. In one experiment, college women participated more actively in a discussion of pornographic literature, and enjoyed the discussion more, if they wore baggy lab coats without individual identification than if they wore their own clothes and a name tag (Singer & others, 1965).

## Conformity

Have you ever been in a situation in which something seemed obvious to you, but others around you all held a different opinion—the same different opinion—from yours? If so, what effect did their unanimity have on you? Did you (a) honestly change your opinion to match theirs, either because you assumed that they must be right or because their opinion led you to re-examine the issue and see it differently? Or did you (b) pretend to agree, to get along or to avoid seeming odd or like a troublemaker, even though you continued to hold your original view privately? Or did you (c)—like the fabled child who announced that the Emperor was wearing no clothes—continue to assert your original opinion publicly as well as privately, despite what everyone else said? During the 1950s, Solomon Asch performed a series of experiments in which people were placed in the kind of dilemma just described, in a starker way than most of us experience in everyday life.

**Asch's Experiments: Basic Procedure and Finding**   Asch's original purpose in the experiments to be described here was to show *absence* of conformity (Asch, 1952). He expected to demonstrate that people will not be swayed from opinions that are based on direct perceptual experience, even though they may be swayed from more subjectively based opinions. But the experiments surprised Asch and changed the direction of his research. They revealed far more conformity than he had predicted.

Asch's (1956) basic procedure was as follows: A college student was brought into the lab and seated with six to eight other students who also appeared to be subjects, and then the group was told that their task was to judge the lengths of lines. On each trial they were shown one standard line and three comparison lines, and they were asked to judge which comparison line was identical in length to the standard (see Figure 15.11). As a perceptual task, this was almost absurdly easy; in

**Figure 15.12  *A perplexed subject in Asch's experiment***

*It is not hard to tell who the real subject is in this photograph taken on a critical trial in one of Asch's experiments.*

■ *How Asch demonstrated that a tendency to conform could lead people to disclaim the evidence of their own eyes*

■ *How Asch distinguished between normative and informational influence in his conformity experiments*

previous tests, subjects performing the task alone almost never made mistakes. But, of course, this was not really a perceptual task; it was a test of conformity. Unbeknownst to the real subject, the others in the group were confederates of the experimenter who had been instructed to give a specific *wrong* answer on certain critical trials. Choices were stated out loud by the group members, one at a time in the order of seating, and seating had been arranged so that the real subject was always the next to last to respond (see Figure 15.12). The question of interest was this: On critical trials, would subjects be swayed by the confederates' wrong answers, or would they respond as they would had they been alone?

Of more than 100 total subjects tested under the conditions just described, 75 percent were swayed by the confederates on at least one of the twelve critical trials in the experiment. Some of the subjects conformed on every trial, others on only one or two. Taking all of the data together, subjects conformed in an average of 37 percent of the critical trials. That is, on about one-third of trials on which the confederates gave a wrong answer, the subject also gave a wrong answer, usually the same wrong answer as the confederates had given. In other experiments, Asch (1951) varied the size of the group; he found that conformity rose sharply as the number of confederates answering prior to the subject increased from one to three, and that it leveled off after that. A unanimous group of three was as effective in inducing conformity as was a unanimous group of seven or even fifteen.

**Conforming to Be Right, or to Be Liked?**    Why did Asch's subjects yield to the majority? When Asch questioned them after the experiment, very few said that they had actually seen the lines as the confederates had seemed to see them. But many indicated that they had been led to doubt their own perceptual ability. They made such comments as (from Asch, 1956): "I thought that maybe because I wore glasses there was some defect"; "At first I thought I had the wrong instructions, then that something was wrong with my eyes and my head"; and "There's a greater probability of eight being right [than one]." Such statements suggest that the subjects yielded because they really believed that the majority was right. This kind of influence is called *informational*—the group's response is taken as information to be considered in trying to arrive at a correct answer to the question.

On the other hand, as Asch suggested, maybe these comments were largely rationalizations. Maybe the real reason for conformity had more to do with a desire to be liked or accepted by the others than with a desire to be right. Perhaps the subjects found it more stressful to seem different from the others than to give an answer that they believed to be incorrect. To test this possibility, Asch (1956) repeated the experiment under conditions in which the confederates responded out loud as before, but subjects responded privately in writing. To accomplish this, Asch arranged to have the real subjects arrive "late" to the experiment; then he told them that no more subjects were needed, but that they might participate in a different way by listening to the subjects (all of whom were actually confederates) and then writing down, rather than repeating aloud, what they believed to be the correct answer. In this condition, the amount of conformity dropped to about one-third of that in the earlier experiments. Thus, whereas some subjects in the original experiments may have conformed to be correct, most conformity was apparently motivated by the desire to be liked or accepted by the group—it disappeared when that was no longer an issue. This kind of influence is called *normative*—people are motivated to behave consistently with group norms regardless of their private beliefs.

In experiments similar to Asch's, Jennifer Campbell and her colleagues (1986, 1989) have found that the relative amount of informational compared to normative influence of unanimous confederates depends on the difficulty of the task (Campbell & others, 1986; Campbell & Fairey, 1989). When the discrimination task was difficult, subjects in their studies conformed primarily because they believed that the confederates were likely to be correct (informational influence). But when the task was easy, conformity was motivated primarily by concern for what others would think of them (normative influence). Conformity in these different conditions was affected differently by the group size. With a difficult task, where the subject was looking to the other(s) for information, a single confederate was as effective in inducing conformity as was a unanimous group of three. With an easy task, where concern for getting along was the more important motive, a single confederate was much less effective than was a unanimous group of three (Campbell & Fairey, 1989).

**Influence of a Minority**   Thus far we have examined conformity only in tests in which a single subject was faced by a group of others who *unanimously* favored a response that was objectively incorrect. What would happen if the others were not unanimous? Asch (1956) found that if a single confederate disagreed with the others, regardless of how many others there were (from two to fourteen), the amount of conformity on his line-judging task dropped dramatically—to about one-fourth of that in the unanimous condition. This effect occurred even if the dissenting confederate gave a wrong answer, as long as it differed from the others' answers. Any response that dissented from the majority apparently encouraged subjects to resist the majority's influence and to give the correct answer.

In experiments patterned after Asch's, the French psychologist Serge Moscovici and his colleagues (1969) turned Asch's question around and asked: What effect can an incorrect *minority* have on the responses of a majority? Their experiments involved groups containing four real subjects and two confederates. In each critical trial, the group was shown a sky-blue patch and its members were asked to name the color. When the two confederates consistently, in trial after trial, called the blue patch green, the effect was to induce actual subjects to call it green on an average of 8 percent of the trials. In contrast, when the confederates were not consistent but called the patch green on two-thirds of the trials and blue on the other third, actual subjects called it green in only 1 percent of the trials; and in control groups where there were no confederates, subjects almost never called it green. From this and other experiments, Moscovici has argued that a minority can influence significantly the judgments of a majority if the minority is unwavering in its opinion (Moscovici, 1976; Moscovici & Mugny, 1983).

According to Moscovici, the effect of a minority is different from the effect of a majority. A majority can exert influence through normative means (through the person's fear of appearing different), in which case the person's public opinion changes but the private opinion does not; but a minority can exert influence only through informational means. That is, a minority can have an effect only if it succeeds in getting the others to look at the stimulus (or issue) differently and to change their private opinions. Where debate is permitted, this can occur through the force of the arguments. However, in the stark conditions of the just-described experiment, it can occur only through the consistent and confident style by which the minority members express their judgments.

*Evidence that the motive for conformity is different for difficult tasks than for easy tasks*

*Evidence that even a single defection from the majority opinion dramatically reduces the likelihood of others' conforming*

*Evidence that a consistent minority can sway at least some members of the majority, and that it does so through informational, not normative, influence*

**Standing up against the majority**
*In politics, minorities need good organization as well as unwavering opinion to carry the day. Under the leadership of Phyllis Schlafly (shown here at a rally), Stop ERA was able to defeat a constitutional amendment supported by a majority of the American public.*

■ *How Lewin explained meat-buying habits in terms of a perceived group norm, and how he showed that group discussion could change those habits by changing the perceived norm*

Other experiments, using difficult tasks in which subjects had to determine which of several pictures contained a particular embedded figure, have demonstrated directly this difference between majority and minority influence (Nemeth & Wachtler, 1983). A consistent *majority* was able to pressure real subjects into agreeing to either objectively right or objectively wrong answers. Thus, they had a beneficial effect (increasing the number of correct answers given by the real subjects) when they were correct and a deleterious effect (decreasing the number of correct answers given by the real subjects) when they were incorrect. A consistent *minority*, on the other hand, failed to pressure real subjects into agreeing to objectively wrong answers, but did cause the real subjects to study the problems more carefully and to find the correct answers more often. Thus, they had a beneficial effect (increasing the number of correct answers given by real subjects) whether or not they themselves were correct.

## Group Discussion and Decision Making

All of the conformity experiments just described were conducted under artificial conditions in which the judgment to be made was all or none and no discussion was permitted. We turn now to some studies conducted under more natural conditions in which the judgments were more complex or subjective and in which people could argue out their disagreements.

**Group Discussion as a Way of Changing a Norm: Lewin's Experiment**   A useful place to begin our examination of group discussion is with a classic experiment conducted by Kurt Lewin (1947) during World War II. Among the many practical problems occasioned by the war was a shortage of meat. Because of the shortage, the U.S. government wished to persuade people to buy visceral meats such as heart, kidney, and sweetbread (thymus), which had previously been wasted. Nutritionists had shown that these are highly nutritious, and anthropologists had shown that they are often regarded as delicacies in other cultures. But in the United States during the 1940s, despite a barrage of government propaganda, most people refused to buy and eat these cuts. What could be done to change people's meat-buying behavior? Lewin saw in this question an opportunity to test his idea that social norms are extremely important in governing the way that people behave, as well as his idea that group discussion can change behavior by changing people's perceptions of such norms.

Lewin hypothesized that the refusal to buy and eat visceral meats was motivated by the consumers' sense that to do so would be considered abnormal. An individual might become convinced privately that it's all right to prepare sweetbread for the family, but would be inhibited through fear of deviating from the norm. What would the neighbors think? This line of reasoning led Lewin to conclude that people would buy visceral meats if they could be persuaded that others would not think worse of them for doing so, and he hypothesized that group discussion would be an effective way to accomplish this.

To test his hypothesis, he compared two different approaches—lecture and group discussion—for persuading female Red Cross volunteers to begin preparing visceral meats at home. Some volunteers attended a lecture at which the advantages of using visceral meats were explained clearly, and others attended a group discussion at which the same information was presented in a setting in which they were encouraged to present their own views. As expected, early in the discussion the volunteers were reluctant to express an interest in trying visceral meats, but after one or two broke the ice many others were emboldened to say that they, too, were convinced that the use of such meats would be good for their pocketbooks, their family's health, and their country's security. By the end of the discussion, all of the participants indicated, by a show of hands, that they would be willing to serve such meats at home. A follow-up survey several weeks later showed that about 30 percent of the people in the discussion group had actually bought and prepared visceral meats, whereas only 3 percent in the lecture group had done so.

According to Lewin's analysis, the discussion succeeded and the lecture failed because only the discussion had permitted a shift in perceived norms to occur. Sitting at the lecture, people had no way to know what others in the audience were thinking. The discussion, on the other hand, allowed them to learn that others also favored the idea of using visceral meats, so the idea no longer seemed so abnormal. Thus, to state the case more generally, when people favor a form of behavior but don't carry through with it for fear of what others would think, a discussion that clarifies what others think may lead to changed behavior.

**Group Polarization of Attitudes**   Some years ago, a graduate student at MIT, James Stoner (1961), reported a surprising effect of group discussion. Stoner had asked subjects to respond to a number of fictitious dilemmas. In these stories, an individual is trying to decide whether or not to embark on a particular, risky course of action. The subjects' task was to advise that person on the decision. For example, in one story a young chemist is trying to decide if he should work on a very difficult research problem that might lead to nothing—in which case 5 years of his career would be wasted—or might lead to an important discovery. Should he embark on this project if the chance that he will succeed is 90 percent? 70 percent? 50 percent? 30 percent? 10 percent? The subjects' task was to indicate the lowest probability of success that would be acceptable to make the risky course of action reasonable for the chemist. Stoner's subjects first responded individually to such problems and then met in groups of six for group decisions. Surprisingly, the group decisions usually differed from the average of the individual decisions in the direction of greater risk. That is, groups advised action at lower probabilities of success on most problems than did individuals working alone—a finding that came to be called the *risky shift* (Myers, 1982).

The earliest indication that the risky shift was only the tip of a larger iceberg came from the observation that some risk problems, constructed like the one just described, regularly produced a *cautious shift* rather than a risky one. For example, in one such problem a man is trying to decide whether to marry a certain woman with whom he has had an alternately happy and unhappy courtship (Brown, 1986). On this problem, groups routinely advocated greater caution than did individuals—that is, groups required a greater likelihood of success (defined here as a happy marriage) than did individuals before they would advise the man to marry.

What was the basic difference between problems leading to a risky shift versus a cautious shift? The difference seemed to be that, in general, the problems leading to a risky shift elicited relatively risky choices even before group discussion, whereas those leading to a cautious shift elicited relatively cautious choices before group discussion (Myers, 1982). Thus, on problems such as that faced by the chemist, most people initially favored high risk, then group discussion led them to favor even higher risk; and on problems such as that faced by the suitor, most initially favored low risk, then group discussion led them to favor even lower risk.

Such findings led finally to the conclusion that the risky and cautious shifts are part of a more general phenomenon, now called **group polarization**. The general rule of group polarization can be stated as follows: *If people have a tendency toward a particular view on some issue, and then they get together to discuss the issue with others who have the same tendency, they will eventually adopt a more extreme view in the same direction as their initial tendency.*

Group polarization has since been demonstrated using a wide variety of problems or issues for discussion. For example, in one experiment, mock juries evaluated traffic-violation cases that had been set up to produce either high or low initial judgments of guilt. After group discussion, jurors rated the high-guilt cases at even

*How the risky shift was eventually explained as part of a general tendency for group discussion to lead like-minded individuals to a more extreme view than they held initially*

higher levels of guilt, and the low-guilt cases at even lower levels, than they had be-fore group discussion (Myers & Kaplan, 1976). In other experiments, researchers divided people into groups based on their different initial views on such issues as race or national defense, and found that group discussions (held separately by each group) widened the gap between groups. Thus, group discussion caused racial preju-dice to increase in initially prejudiced groups and to decrease in initially unpreju-diced groups (Myers & Bishop, 1970). It caused advocacy of a strong military to increase in groups initially favoring a strong military and to decrease in groups ini-tially favoring a weaker military (Minix, 1976; Semmel, 1976). (See Figure 15.13.)

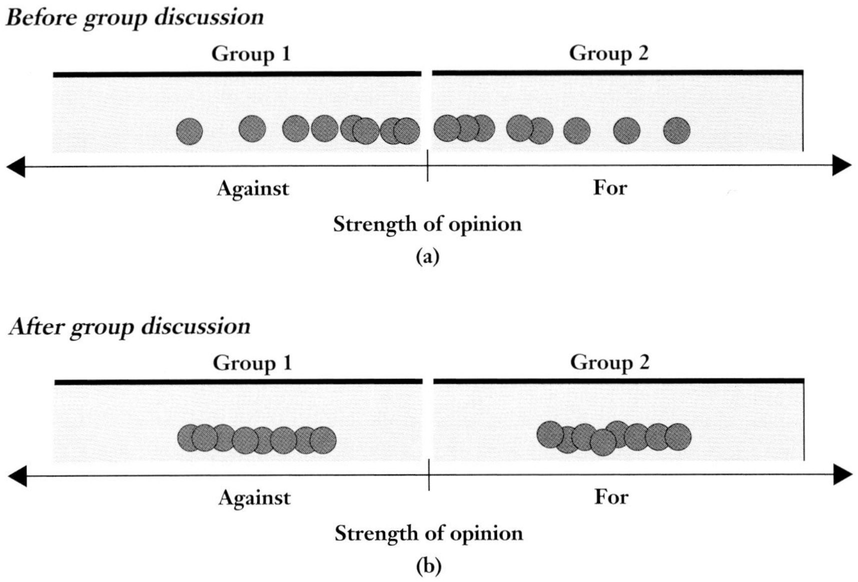

**Figure 15.13 Schematic illustration of group polarization**

*Each circle represents the opinion of one individual. When the individuals are divided into two groups based on the direction of their initial position (a), and then discuss the issue with other members of their group, the majority move toward a more extreme position than they held before (b).*

*Before group discussion*

Group 1          Group 2

← Against        For →

Strength of opinion
(a)

*After group discussion*

Group 1          Group 2

← Against        For →

Strength of opinion
(b)

To the degree that group polarization occurs in everyday life, it can have im-portant consequences. For example, when students whose political views are barely right of center get together to form a young-conservatives club, their views should shift farther toward the right; and the opposite should occur in a young-liberals club. Prisoners who enter jail with little respect for the law and spend their time talking with other prisoners who share that view should leave prison with even less respect for the law than they had before. Professors who believe that students are getting lazier each year should become even more convinced of that after having lunch with other professors who agree with their initial view. Everyday observa-tions suggest that such shifts indeed do occur.

■ **Three hypotheses about the under-lying cause of group polarization: one based on the desire to be right, and two based on the desire to be liked**

What causes group polarization? According to one set of views, called *infor-mational hypotheses*, group polarization stems from the actual arguments and evidence that individuals hear in the group discussion (Vinokur & Burnstein, 1974). People are more likely to put forth arguments in the direction that they favor than in the opposite direction, so when like-minded people get together they hear many arguments in one direction and relatively few in the other. Thus, they leave the discussion with a stronger opinion in the original direction than they had when they entered it. According to *normative hypotheses*, on the other hand, the key information that emerges in group discussion is not the actual argument, but is in-formation about where others in the group stand on the issue. Whereas informa-tional hypotheses focus on people's attempts to arrive at a correct solution to the problem, normative hypotheses focus on people's attempts to be accepted or admired by the other group members.

**Save the forest**

*Any group who initially share an opinion are likely to hold that opinion even more strongly after they have met and discussed it than they did before.*

Two different normative hypotheses have been proposed to explain group polarization. One, which I will call the *one-upmanship hypothesis*, maintains that when people discover that the group as a whole favors the same general position that they favor, each person tries to come across as a more vigorous supporter of that position than the others, resulting in movement toward an increasingly extreme position. This theory originated partly from evidence that people indeed do admire points of view that are more extreme but in the same direction as their own (Levinger & Schneider, 1969; Myers, 1982). Thus, by adopting more extreme positions, individual group members might increase the degree to which they are admired by other members of the group.

The other normative hypothesis, which I will call the *group-stereotyping hypothesis*, maintains that group polarization stems from people's tendency to conform to what they perceive to be the group's opinion, coupled with a systematic bias in that perception. According to this hypothesis, people tend to stereotype groups, including those to which they belong, by mentally exaggerating the group's point of view. Thus, according to this hypothesis, group members perceive their group as a whole as having a more extreme position than it actually has, and because they want to be like others in their group they shift their own view toward that more extreme position. Consistent with this hypothesis, experiments have shown that people who hear a set of arguments slightly favoring a particular position tend to exaggerate the extent to which the arguments favor that position if they believe that the individuals presenting the argument are part of a group (Mackie, 1986).

Many experiments have shown that all three of these hypotheses have some degree of validity. That is, group polarization seems to stem from a combination of shared information, one-upmanship, and the tendency for each group member to exaggerate the average position of the group as a whole (Isenberg, 1986; Kaplan, 1987; Mackie, 1986). As you might expect, shared information tends to be most important when the topic is one that potentially can be settled on the basis of facts, whereas normative processes tend to be most important when the topic is subjective, involving personal preferences or values (Kaplan, 1987).

**Conditions That Lead to Good or Bad Group Decisions**    Group polarization may or may not be a bad thing, depending on the particular circumstances. If it arises from sharing the best available evidence and logic, leading to a better group decision, it is good. If it arises from collective ignorance, selective withholding of arguments on the less-favored side, false perceptions of others' views, and the participants' attempts to look good to each other, it is bad, especially if the resulting decision is one that will affect people's lives. Now let us examine the conditions that lead to either good or bad group decisions.

■ *How Janis explained some White House policy blunders with his groupthink theory*

In a book entitled *Groupthink*, Irving Janis (1982) analyzed some of what he considers to be the most important policy blunders or fiascoes developed in the United States White House in recent decades. Among them are the decisions to invade Cuba in 1961 (the Bay of Pigs invasion), the escalation of the Vietnam War during the late 1960s, and the Watergate burglary cover-up in the early 1970s. Janis argues that each of these decisions came about because a tightly knit clique of presidential advisors, whose principal concerns were group unity and pleasing their leader (Presidents Kennedy, Johnson, and Nixon, respectively), failed to examine critically the choice that their leader seemed to favor and instead devoted their energy toward defending that choice and suppressing criticisms of it. To refer to this way of thinking, Janis (1982) coined the term **groupthink**, which he defined as "a mode of thinking that people engage in when they are deeply involved in a cohesive ingroup, when the members' striving for unanimity overrides their motivation to realistically appraise alternative courses of action."

552

**The Challenger incident**
*The flawed decision making that Irving Janis calls* groupthink *has been implicated in the 1986 explosion of the U.S. space shuttle Challenger. In striving for unanimity in the decision to launch, managers ignored engineers' warnings about the dangers posed by subfreezing temperatures.*

■ *Experimental evidence supporting some elements of the groupthink theory*

As an example counter to groupthink, Janis (1982) also described the procedure that President Kennedy used to decide how to respond to the Soviet Union's shipment of missiles to Cuba in 1962. Most of the advisors on that decision were the same men who had supported the ill-fated Bay of Pigs invasion 18 months earlier, but this time Kennedy—who had apparently learned from his earlier mistake—insisted that the advisors truly examine all of the evidence and argue out all possible responses. He brought in outsiders to present their views; he held back his own view; and he assigned his brother, Robert Kennedy (who was then attorney general), the role of devil's advocate to be sure that all arguments would be challenged. The result was far from a unanimous, smooth decision, but in the end the majority favored a strategy of blockading Cuba that turned out to be successful.

A number of experiments, conducted both before and after Janis developed his groupthink model, have examined the effects of group composition and leadership on groups' abilities to solve problems. In one such experiment, actual bomber crews—each consisting of a pilot, a navigator, and gunner who were used to working together—were given problems to solve individually or as a group. As individuals the navigators were best at solving the problems, but working in a group they were relatively ineffective because both they and the gunners paid too much attention to the pilots, who occupied highest status in the crew (Torrance, 1954). In other experiments, better or more solutions were produced by (a) groups in which leaders had been instructed not to advocate a view themselves, but to encourage group members to present their own views and challenge each other (Maier & Solem, 1952; Leana, 1985); (b) groups that focused on the problems rather than on developing group cohesion (Callaway & Esser, 1984); and (c) groups of people who scored toward the high end of a personality measure of dominance, and thus were not intimidated about disagreeing with each other (Callaway & others, 1985). (All of these groups were compared to appropriate control groups.)

### Group Versus Group

A sad fact about groups is that they often battle, in one way or another, with other groups, and they often stir individuals to feelings of prejudice and acts of discrimination and even violence. The history of humankind can be read as a record of intergroup conflict. Why are groups so often at odds with one another?

Obviously, this question cannot be answered completely in the remaining pages of this chapter. Some people, addressing the question from an ethological perspective, have argued that humans have an inborn tendency acquired through evolution to be chauvinistic about the groups to which they belong and distrustful of other groups (discussed in Chapter 4). Others have argued, from a social-cognitive perspective, that the process of labeling and categorizing people into groups leads to stereotyping, then to exaggeration of differences between groups, and hence to distrust (discussed in Chapter 14). Another idea is that people mentally elevate their own group, and denigrate other groups, to raise their own self-esteem (also discussed in Chapter 14). Group polarization and other aspects of groupthink may also play a role: Through discussion with others in their own group, people may magnify whatever preexisting negative attitudes they share about another group and may encourage each other in harmful activities against that group.

Still another approach to understanding intergroup conflict centers on the structure of rewards that may lead one group's self-interests to be at odds with those of another. That approach, sometimes called the *realistic-conflict theory* (Campbell, 1965), is the one to which we will pay most attention here.

**The Robbers Cave Experiment**   Early support for the realistic-conflict theory came from a famous experiment conducted by Muzafer Sherif and his colleagues (1961, 1966). The goal of the experiment—conducted with 11- and 12-year-old boys at a 3-week camping program in Oklahoma's Robbers Cave Park (an area once used as a hideout by Jesse James)—was to identify conditions that would create and reduce hostility between groups. To establish two groups, the researchers assigned the boys to two separate cabins, at a considerable distance from each other, and provided the boys in each cabin with tasks designed to build group cohesiveness, such as setting up camping equipment and improving the swimming area. In the course of a few days, with little adult intervention, each cabin of boys acquired the characteristics of a distinct social group. Each group had its own leaders, its own rules and norms of behavior, and its own name—the Eagles and the Rattlers.

When the groups were well established, the researchers proposed a series of competitions between them—an idea that the boys eagerly accepted. They would compete for valued prizes in such games as baseball, touch football, and tug-of-war. In line with Sherif's predictions, the series of competitions had the following three effects: (1) It promoted *ingroup solidarity.* As they worked on plans to defeat the other group, the boys forgot their internal squabbles and differences, and their loyalty to their own group became stronger. (2) It promoted *negative outgroup stereotyping.* Even though the boys had all come from the same background (White, Protestant, and middle class), and had been assigned to the groups on a purely random basis, they began to see members of the other group as very different from themselves, and as very similar to each other in negative ways. For example, the Eagles began to see the Rattlers as dirty and rough, and to distinguish themselves from that group they adopted a "goodness" norm and a "holier than thou" attitude. (3) Most important, it promoted *hostile intergroup actions.* Initial good sportsmanship in the competitions collapsed. The boys began to call their rivals names, accuse them of cheating, and cheat in retaliation. After being defeated in one game, the Eagles burned one of the Rattlers' banners, which led to an escalating series of raids and other hostilities. What at first was a peaceful camping experience turned gradually into something verging on intertribal warfare.

In the final phase of the experiment, the researchers tried to reduce hostility between the two groups, which was a much harder task than that of provoking it. In two previous experiments, similar to the one at Robbers Cave, Sherif had tried a

■ *How Sherif and his colleagues demonstrated that a competitive reward structure promotes intergroup hostility and a cooperative reward structure promotes intergroup friendship*

number of procedures to reduce hostility, all of which had failed. *Peace meetings* between leaders had failed because those who agreed to meet lost status within their own group for conceding to the enemy. *Individual competitions* (similar to the Olympic games) had failed because the boys turned them into between-group competitions by keeping track of total victories by members of each group (just as we find, unfortunately, with the international Olympics). *Sunday sermons* on brotherly love and forgiveness had failed because, while claiming to agree with the messages, the boys simply did not apply them to their actions.

At Robbers Cave, Sherif tried two new strategies. The first was *joint participation in pleasant activities.* Hoping that mutual enjoyment of noncompetitive activities would lead them to forget their hostility, Sherif arranged for the two groups to eat their meals together and share in other enjoyable activities such as watching movies and shooting off firecrackers. This didn't work either. It merely provided opportunities for further hostilities. For example, meals were transformed into what the boys called "garbage wars."

The second new strategy, however, was successful. This involved the establishment of *superordinate goals,* defined as goals that were highly desirable and could be achieved best through cooperation between the two groups. The researchers created one such goal by staging a breakdown in the camp's water supply. In response to this crisis, boys in both groups volunteered to explore the 1-mile-long water line to find the break, and on their own initiative worked out a strategy to divide their efforts in doing so. Two other staged events also elicited cooperation: The boys worked out a system to share their prize money to rent a movie, which they had been led to believe that the camp could not afford; and they helped start the camp's stalled food truck by pulling together on a rope tied to it. By the end of this series, hostilities had nearly ceased, and the two groups were arranging friendly encounters on their own initiative, including a campfire meeting at which they took turns presenting skits and singing songs. On their way home, one group treated the other to milkshakes with money left from its prizes.

A general term for the condition that led to intergroup hostility in Sherif's experiment is **negative goal interdependence,** which is defined as a condition in which each individual or group can achieve a goal only by preventing another individual or group from achieving a goal. During the competitive phase of their camping experience, the Eagles and Rattlers could win prizes only by beating the other group and thereby preventing them from winning prizes. A general term for the condition that led to intergroup friendship is **positive goal interdependence**—a condition in which each individual or group can achieve a goal best by helping another individual or group achieve a goal. During the cooperative phase, the Eagles and Rattlers shared the same goals (such as finding the water leak), which they could achieve best by working together. Using these terms, the main conclusions from the Robbers Cave study can be stated as follows: (a) Negative goal interdependence produced not only competition but also a general state of intergroup hostility; and (b) positive goal interdependence produced not only cooperation but also a general state of intergroup friendship. The hostility and friendship had consequences that went well beyond the specific competitive and cooperative goals that had been established by the researchers. They affected all aspects of the interactions between the two groups.

**Other Studies Involving Negative or Positive Goal Interdependence**   The basic principles illustrated in the Robbers Cave study—that hostility emerges from negative goal interdependence, and friendship from positive goal interdependence—are not unique to young boys at summer camp. The following are some other illustrations of these principles.

Robert Blake and Jane Mouton (1961, 1979) conducted a series of experiments

■ *How the effects of perceived negative or positive goal interdependence have been demonstrated (a) with business executives, (b) in school classrooms, and (c) in surveys of people's attitudes toward minority groups*

**Fun for all**

*At work and at play, positive goal interdependence has been found to be extremely effective in breaking down barriers between groups.*

with business executives that were conceptual replications of the Robbers Cave experiment. Business executives don't engage in garbage wars, but they do engage in subtler, sometimes more invidious forms of intergroup aggression. In their experiments, Blake and Mouton would bring together twenty to thirty executives for a 2-week period to discuss interpersonal and intergroup relations, and would divide them into two groups to work separately on various problems. Once a group spirit had emerged in each group, a series of competitions would be suggested, in which each group would develop its own solution to a business-related problem, and the two solutions would be compared to see which was better. The result was that a win-lose orientation usually emerged in which each group was as pleased if the other group did badly as if their own group did well; and the executives began to view members of the other group in negative, stereotyped terms. As in Sherif's study, hostility and stereotyping were reduced or abolished when the groups worked on self-chosen problems together, with a goal of achieving the best possible solution rather than deciding which group was better.

A second illustration involves a study conducted in interracial classrooms. In the early 1970s, the city of Austin, Texas, was required by a court order to desegregate its schools. To help find ways to reduce or prevent racial conflict within classrooms—where White, Black, and Mexican-American students were to be brought together for the first time—the school board hired Elliot Aronson, a social psychologist. As part of this project, Aronson and his colleagues (1978) developed and tried out a method of instruction they called the *jigsaw classroom*. The essence of this method was to divide children in each classroom into groups of five or six, cutting across racial lines, and to establish positive goal interdependence both within and among groups, so that children of different races would have to cooperate with each other to achieve their desired ends.

For example, for a fifth-grade lesson about Joseph Pulitzer, a biography of Pulitzer was written in six parts and a different part was given to each of the six members of a group. First the children studied their own parts; then they met with children from other groups who had been given the same part, to share and consolidate what they had learned; then they returned to their own group to teach their part to, and learn the other parts from, the other group members. At the end, each child was tested on the whole biography. Thus, to do well on the test, the children were forced to cooperate with each other. They had to ask the right questions to learn what the others knew, and, in turn, they had to share their own knowledge with the others. Grading was not competitive; everyone could get an *A* if everyone learned the lesson. Controlled comparisons showed that children in the jigsaw classrooms liked each other (including those of different races) better, developed higher self-esteem, and on average learned more than did children in other classrooms in the same schools.

Aside from controlled experiments, a number of surveys of people's attitudes toward minority groups have also found that intergroup hostility is related to negative goal interdependence or the perception of such. In one survey, anti-Black sentiment among U.S. Whites was strongly correlated with the perception that economic gain by Blacks necessitated economic loss by Whites (Vanneman & Pettigrew, 1972). In another survey, conducted in Jerusalem, negative attitudes and hostile behavior toward ultra-Orthodox Jews (a minority group) on the part of other Jewish groups was closely correlated with the perception that government programs supporting the former were at odds with the self-interests of the latter (Struch & Schwartz, 1989).

**Evidence That Groups Are More Competitive Than Individuals**  As shown by the studies just described, competitive conditions tend to promote intergroup hostility, and cooperative conditions tend to promote intergroup friendship. In addi-

■ *How experiments using a prisoner's-dilemma game have demonstrated that groups are more likely than individuals to interpret an ambiguous reward structure as competitive*

tion, however—and this takes us beyond the realistic-conflict theory—groups are generally more likely than individuals to *interpret* a given situation as competitive, where the situation could in theory be seen as either competitive or cooperative. This conclusion is supported by a variety of different kinds of evidence (Tajfel & Turner, 1979), but I will focus here on that coming from a particular class of laboratory game called ***prisoner's-dilemma games.***

Prisoner's-dilemma games were based originally on a hypothetical dilemma in which two prisoners accused of a crime must decide separately whether to cooperate ("stay mum") or exploit one another ("squeal" about the other prisoner's involvement in the crime). Each prisoner's sentence is affected by the combination of the prisoner's own decision to cooperate or not and that of the other prisoner. When the games are played in social psychology labs, the consequences are not prison sentences, but monetary rewards. To see how such a game works, look at Figure 15.14, which shows the payoff matrix for one such game. On each trial, each player can choose to make either a cooperative response (say, by pushing a green button) or a competitive response (say, by pushing a red button). Neither knows how the other has played until they have both responded, and the payoff to each player depends on the combination of the two responses, as illustrated in the figure. In all prisoner's-dilemma games, the payoff matrix has the following characteristics: (a) The *highest total payoff* to the two players combined occurs if they both cooperate (30¢ + 30¢ = 60¢ in the example); (b) the *lowest total payoff* occurs if they both compete (20¢ + 20¢ = 40¢ in the example); (c) the *highest individual payoff* to a single player occurs if that individual competes while the other cooperates (40¢ in the example); and (d) the *lowest individual payoff* occurs if that individual cooperates while the other competes (10¢ in the example).

**Figure 15.14** *Sample payoff matrix for a prisoner's-dilemma game*

*Shown here is one of the reward structures used in experiments in which groups were found to be more competitive than individuals. As in any prisoner's-dilemma game, this reward structure is such that the highest total reward to the two players (or two groups of players) occurs if both choose to cooperate, but the highest reward to any one player (or group) occurs if that player (or group) chooses to compete at the same time that the other chooses to cooperate. Because the game is played repeatedly and payoffs come after each play, players can earn a significant amount of money.*

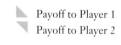
Payoff to Player 1
Payoff to Player 2

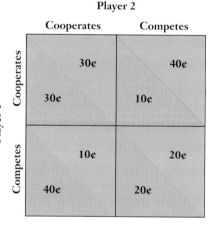

Notice that the structure of rewards in a prisoner's-dilemma game is such that if the players' mutual goal is to beat the system, then the logical move is to cooperate on every play. By doing this the players will earn, together, the most money that the game permits. On the other hand, if their goal is to beat each other, the logical move for each individual is to compete. By competing they are assured of either a tie or a win on every move, depending on what the other does, whereas cooperation produces either a tie or a loss.

The point I've been leading up to is this: People play prisoner's-dilemma games very differently when they are part of a group that is playing with another group than when they play as individuals. They are much more likely to interpret and play the game competitively in groups than as individuals, even though the logical moves are the same in both conditions. For example, in one experiment, students playing in teams of two chose to compete on about 70 percent of their plays, whereas those playing as individuals competed on fewer than 30 percent of their plays (McCallum & others, 1985). Later experiments showed a similar disparity between three-person teams and individuals, and that the disparity existed only if the members of each team actually functioned as a group—that is, only if they decided together which response to make on each play (Insko & others, 1987, 1988).

Why do groups behave more competitively than individuals in prisoner's-dilemma games? One possibility, suggested by Chester Insko and his colleagues (1987), is that individuals secretly wish to act competitively to demonstrate their superiority, but are inhibited from doing so when they are alone because they fear that such a mode of play would not be socially acceptable. In groups they overcome the inhibition because, in hinting at their wish, they find that their groupmates share that wish, which makes it socially acceptable (at least among their group). Notice that this interpretation is essentially the same as Lewin's explanation for the effect of group discussion on people's meat buying. People overcome their inhibitions about behaving in a particular way by discovering in group discussion that to do so would not be unacceptable to the others present. Another possible explanation suggested by these authors is that people have learned from previous experience to associate groups with competition. Because of such learning, when they play prisoner's dilemma in groups they automatically assume that the game calls for competition, but when they play alone they do not make this assumption.

**Mutual conciliation**

*The recognition of shared economic and political interests repeatedly brings world leaders together to try to reduce international tension. Research on group behavior highlights some of the factors that contribute to intergroup competition and offers clues on ways that nations can learn to work together.*

Regardless of its explanation, the tendency for groups to interpret an ambiguous reward structure as competitive—combined with the tendency for competition to engender ingroup chauvinism, outgroup negative stereotyping, and between-group hostility—may contribute to the intergroup problems that exist in the world. Perhaps to eliminate such problems we will have to eliminate not only clear-cut cases of negative goal interdependence, but ambiguous cases as well, and highlight conditions of unambiguously positive goal interdependence. As the world gets smaller, and as nations realize increasingly the importance of cooperation to achieve superordinate goals, world peace could become a reality. Just as the boys at Robbers Cave cooperated to stop the leak in their water line, so may we cooperate to stop the leak in our ozone layer—and the pollution of our oceans, and the international drug trade, and. . . . These are goals that can only be solved if nations work together.

## Concluding Thoughts

**1. The desire to be accepted by others as an underpinning of much of social influence** In surveying the corpus of research and theory on social influence, one cannot help but be struck by the frequent recurrence of a single, simple idea: Human beings have a remarkably strong desire to be approved of by other human beings who are nearby. That was a theme of the discussion of impression management in Chapter 14 and it has continued as a theme through much of this chapter.

Why do we find it hard to refuse a direct request? Why do we find it hard not to reciprocate a favor, even one that we did not want in the first place? Why did Milgram's subjects find it hard to tell the experimenter that he was asking them to do a terrible thing and they would not go on? Why do people become aroused—leading to social inhibition or facilitation—when they know that their performance is being evaluated, even if the evaluator is a stranger and the evaluation doesn't count for anything? Why do people work harder at experimental tasks when they believe that their individual performance can be monitored and loaf when they believe it can't? Why did subjects in Asch's experiment deny the clear evidence of their own two eyes when it ran counter to what others were saying? Why did the opinions of peers (expressed in group discussion) in Lewin's experiment have a greater impact on people's meat-buying behavior than the sound logic and expert advice presented by the lecturer? Why do group polarization and groupthink occur?

I don't want to oversimplify. The desire to be accepted is surely not the *whole* answer to these questions, but it seems to be an important part of it. As you review each of the phenomena and experiments described in the chapter, you might ask yourself: To what extent (if at all) can this be explained by people's desire to be accepted by others, and what additional explanatory principles seem to be needed?

**2. Normative versus informational influences on behavior** A dichotomy between normative and informational sources of social influence was presented in three distinct places in the chapter. You read of normative versus informational theories of (a) the effect that other bystanders have on any one bystander's willingness to help a person in distress, (b) the tendency to conform in Asch's and similar experiments, and (c) the polarizing effect that group discussion has on people's opinions or attitudes. In reviewing these topics, think again about the basic difference between the two kinds of influences. Normative influences have to do with people's concern to be like or better than what they perceive to be the norm for their group, and informational influences have to do with people's use of other people's responses as information to be included in solving a problem. Normative influences have to do with people's desire to be accepted or liked, and informational influences have to do with people's desire to be right. You might also think about how this dichotomy could be applied to some of the other phenomena described in this chapter. For example, can any of the proposed explanations of Milgram's obedience findings be placed in the normative or informational categories?

**3. Some other explanatory concepts** In addition to the desires to be accepted and to be right, some other explanatory concepts mentioned in the chapter could also be described in the terminology of desires. One is the desire to be consistent, which is the basis of the theory of cognitive dissonance, discussed in Chapter 14 and used in this chapter to help explain the effectiveness of three sales tricks (the four-walls, low-ball, and foot-in-the-door techniques). Another is the desire to be free, called the reactance principle when it is used by social psychologists to explain people's reactions against forces that seem to be limiting their options in some way. Still another is the desire to belong to a superior group, which may underlie the phenomenon of ethnocentrism described in Chapter 14 and some of the group-versus-group effects described in the present chapter. Finally, the desire to win tangible rewards such as money was presented in this chapter as an underlying explanation for people's tendency to compete under conditions of negative goal interdependence and to cooperate under conditions of positive goal interdependence.

## Further Reading

**Robert Cialdini** (1984). *Influence: How and why people agree to things.* New York: Morrow.

*Cialdini has combined field observations of sales techniques with laboratory research to identify basic principles of social influence. In this fun-to-read book, oriented toward the nonspecialist, he spells out these principles and provides numerous examples. After reading it you will never be quite as susceptible to sales pressure as you were before.*

**Stanley Milgram** (1974). *Obedience to authority: An experimental view.* New York: Harper & Row.

*This is a fascinating, firsthand account of one of the most famous series of experiments in social psychology. Milgram describes here his reasons for initiating the research, his findings in many variations of the basic experiment, and his interpretations of and reactions to the findings.*

**Irving Janis** (1982). *Groupthink: Psychological studies of policy decisions and fiascoes* (2nd ed.). Boston: Houghton Mifflin.

*In this interesting book, Janis describes his theory of the causes and symptoms of groupthink and applies it to an analysis of a number of unsuccessful policies (and two successful policies) developed by advisors to U.S. presidents.*

**Roger Brown** (1986). *Social psychology: The second edition.* New York: Free Press.

*This is a thought-provoking, beautifully written introduction to many of the main ideas and ways of thinking in social psychology. Especially relevant to the topic of social influence are Brown's insightful, chapter-length discussions of obedience and rebellion, group polarization, ethnocentrism, and conflict resolution. Although it is ranked as one of the more sophisticated introductions to social psychology, the interested beginning student should have little difficulty reading it (and may have great difficulty putting it down).*

## Looking Ahead

As you have seen, social psychologists attempt to account for human behavior in terms of the social environment within which the behavior occurs. Their goal usually is to identify general principles that characterize most people's responses to specific social situations, and they are relatively unconcerned with individual differences among people. In the next chapter, on theories of personality, we turn to the opposite approach—the attempt to account for behavior in terms of the inner characteristics of the person, which can differ from one person to the next.

# PART 7  PERSONALITY AND DISORDERS

**THEORIES OF PERSONALITY**

**MENTAL DISORDERS**

**TREATMENT**

*We do not all approach life in the same way. We differ in our emotions, motives, and styles of thinking and behaving, and these differences give each of us a unique personality. Although most of these differences are healthy and add spice to our lives, some differences create problems for the differing individual and are classed as mental disorders. This final unit has three chapters. The first is about broad theories that psychologists have developed to account for the differences among us. The second is about problems of identifying mental disorders and understanding their origins. And the third is about methods that psychologists and psychiatrists have developed to help people overcome or live with their problems or disorders.*

# CHAPTER 16

**Freud's Psychodynamic Theory**

**Post-Freudian Psychodynamic Theories**

**Humanistic Theories**

**Social Learning Theories**

**Trait Theories and Psychometric Research**

# THEORIES OF PERSONALITY

■ *What personality theories attempt to accomplish*

■ *How personality theories can be categorized according to the kinds of evidence on which they are based*

*Personality* is a word that was used a lot in my junior high school. A girl attempting to explain her latest infatuation would say, "It's not his looks, it's not his athletic ability, it's certainly not his intelligence—it's his *personality* that I like." All listening would nod their heads, knowing what she was talking about.

**Personality**, as the term is used in psychology, means pretty much the same thing as it did in junior high. It refers to a person's general style of interacting with the world, especially with other people—to such things as whether a person is withdrawn or outgoing, excitable or placid, tidy or messy, generous or stingy. It refers especially to the ways in which individuals differ from each other in such characteristics. A basic assumption underlying the personality concept is that people do differ from one another in their general style of behavior, in ways that are at least relatively consistent across time and place.

A **personality theory** is a formal attempt to describe and explain the ways in which people differ in their general style of behavior. Whereas other theories in psychology have to do with specific aspects of thought and behavior, personality theories are about the whole person. They are among the broadest, most sweeping theories in psychology, and are perhaps best thought of as philosophies of the person. Most personality theories include an opinion about each of the following four elements: (1) the motivating forces, or drives, that underlie behavior; (2) the mental structures, or components of the mind, that interpret the environment and make decisions that guide behavior; (3) the ways in which personalities can differ from one another, either in motivating force or mental structure; and (4) the ways in which such differences develop from birth to adulthood. Thus, a complete theory of personality is a theory of motivation, cognition, individual differences, and development—all rolled into one.

One useful way to categorize theories of personality is in accordance with the types of evidence used in their construction. *Clinically based theories* are those developed primarily by psychotherapists, who use their intimate knowledge of their clients as a basis for developing a theory of personality. The psychodynamic and humanistic theories, which make up more than half the discussion in this chapter, are clinically based. *Laboratory-based theories* are those developed primarily by research psychologists who study such traditional issues as learning, cognition, and social influence through experimental means, and who then extrapolate from such research to develop a theory of personality. The social learning theories in this chapter are laboratory based. Finally, *psychometrically based theories* are those developed by researchers whose main tools are paper-and-pencil questionnaires and statistical procedures for compiling and analyzing the results. The trait theories in this chapter are psychometrically based.

Now, let's examine the issue of personality more deeply—though perhaps no more passionately—than we did in junior high school. As you study each theory, think about the principal explanatory concepts that it invokes, the evidence upon which it is based, and the question of whether or not it is useful in understanding the behavior of people you know. Personality theories are useful to the degree that they help us make sense of the real-life behavior of individuals or help us predict how they will behave in the future. Theories are harmful to the degree that they sidetrack our thinking by causing us to focus too heavily on one set of motives or mental structures while ignoring others that may be more important.

## Freud's Psychodynamic Theory

Before you began studying psychology, your image of a typical psychologist might have been a caricature of Sigmund Freud, stroking his beard and mumbling, "I wonder what he really meant by that." Freud more or less founded psychotherapy and the clinical approach to the development of personality theories. As a young physician in late nineteenth-century Vienna, Freud came to believe that many of his patients' complaints were rooted not in organic disease but in mental conflicts of which they themselves were unaware. Based on this insight, he developed an approach to psychotherapy and a theory of personality, both of which he referred to as *psychoanalysis*. Our focus here is on the theory of personality; the approach to psychotherapy is discussed in Chapter 18.

Psychoanalytic theory includes a model of the mind that emphasizes the idea of unconscious mental forces in conflict with one another. Its view of development emphasizes the importance of early childhood experiences. The theory is also referred to as a *psychodynamic theory*, because of its emphasis on mental forces (the word *dynamic* refers to energy or force).

### Freud's Model of the Mind

**The Ideas of Unconscious Motivation**    The most basic idea in Freud's theory is that the main causes of behavior lie deeply buried in the unconscious mind, that is, in the part of the mind that affects the individual's conscious thought and action but is not itself open to conscious inspection. The reasons people give one another and themselves to explain their behavior are not the true motivating causes of their behavior. To illustrate this idea, Freud often drew an analogy between everyday behavior and the phenomenon of post-hypnotic suggestion.

In a demonstration of post-hypnotic suggestion, a person is hypnotized and then given an instruction such as, "When you awake, you will not remember what happened during hypnosis. However, 10 minutes from now you will walk to the back of the room, pick up the umbrella lying there, and open it." Then the subject is awakened and appears to behave in a perfectly normal, self-directed way until the prearranged moment arrives, at which point he or she is overcome by an irresistible impulse to perform the commanded action. The person consciously senses the impulse and consciously performs the behavior, but has no conscious memory of the origin of the impulse (the hypnotist's command). If asked why he or she is opening the umbrella, the subject may come up with a plausible though clearly false reason, such as, "I thought I should test it, because it may rain later." According to Freud (1912/1932), this illustrates artificially the relationship between unconscious and conscious reasons that underlie everyday actions. The real reasons lie in our unconscious minds, and the conscious reasons that we give are cover-ups, plausible but false rationalizations designed to justify our actions to ourselves and others. They are not false in the sense of conscious lies, however; consciously, we believe them to be true.

*A Freudian skip*
*Many of us played the childish game of stepping over sidewalk cracks. In developing his theory, Freud tried to explain the private parts of personality—from puzzling superstitions to people's deepest passions.*

■ *How the concept of unconscious motivation can be illustrated by the phenomenon of post-hypnotic suggestion*

***Oh, my racing heart!***
*Freud described a number of mechanisms by which drives become redirected into other forms of behavior. If monster truck racing had existed in his day, he might have interpreted it as a relatively undisguised manifestation of both sex and aggression.*

■ *How Freud used people's free associations, dreams, and "mistakes" as routes to learning about their unconscious minds*

**Sex and Aggression as Motivating Forces**    The usual source of unconscious motivation in Freud's theory is not hypnotists' commands. Rather, the source is inner, unconscious, instinctive drives. Freud was particularly interested in the sex drive, which he interpreted broadly as the main pleasure-seeking and life-seeking drive. The most direct ways of expressing this drive (and thereby obtaining pleasure) often run counter to the dictates of society. Therefore, the instinctive force, called *libido*, that underlies this drive becomes redirected and provides the mental energy that motivates a wide range of thoughts and actions that at the surface do not appear to be sexual. Freud was also interested in the drive of aggression, which, like the sex drive, must be controlled if people are to live peaceably in society, and which therefore becomes redirected and energizes other forms of behavior. Thus, in Freud's view, much of human behavior consists of disguised forms of sex and aggression. The unconscious mind disguises the behavior to protect the conscious mind from knowledge that would be repugnant to it.

**Routes to the Unconscious: Free Association, Dreams, and Mistakes**    Freud believed that to understand his patients' actions and problems he had to learn about the content of their unconscious minds. But how could he do that if by definition the unconscious consists of those things that the patient cannot talk about? He could do it by *analyzing* certain aspects of their speech and other observable behavior. This is where the term *psychoanalysis* comes from. His technique was to treat the patient's behavior as clues to the unconscious. In detective-like fashion he collected clues and tried to piece them together in a way that made sense, that told a coherent story about the unconscious causes of the person's conscious thought and behavior.

What sorts of clues would be most useful? Since the conscious mind always attempts to act in ways that are consistent with conventional logic, Freud reasoned that those elements of thought and behavior that are *least* logical would provide the best clues to the unconscious. They would represent elements of the unconscious mind that have leaked out relatively unmodified by consciousness.

To encourage a flow of such clues, Freud developed the technique of *free association*. He instructed patients to sit back (or lie down on a couch), relax, free their minds from the constraints of conventional logic, and report every image and idea that entered their awareness, no matter how absurd it might seem. As an exercise you might try this technique on yourself, recording your session on tape or writing down each idea that comes to you. When you go over the material that you produce, you may be fascinated by the contents; perhaps you will feel that you can infer from it certain wishes, fears, or other ideas that you would not otherwise admit to yourself.

Freud also used the technique of asking patients to describe their dreams to him. According to Freud's theory, a dream is the purest exercise of free association. During sleep, conventional logic is largely absent, and the forces that normally hold down unconscious ideas are weakened. Still, even in dreams the unconscious is partially disguised. Freud distinguished between the latent content and manifest content of a dream. The *latent content* is the underlying, unconscious meaning of the dream, and the *manifest content* is the dream as it is consciously experienced and remembered by the dreamer. The analyst's task in interpreting a dream is the same as that in interpreting any other form of free association—to see through the disguises and uncover the latent content from the manifest content. The disguises in dreams come in many forms. Some are unique to a particular person, but some are universal (which, according to Freud, makes the analyst's job much easier). These universal disguises have become known as *Freudian symbols*, some of which are described in the following quote from Freud (1900/1953) himself (also see Figure 16.1):

**Figure 16.1** *Freudian symbols in a work of art painted 4 centuries before Freud*

*This is a detail from* The Garden of Earthly Delights, *painted in the late fifteenth century by the Dutch artist Hieronymus Bosch. It is believed to represent Bosch's conception of decadence or Hell. Notice the dreamlike (nightmarish) quality and the numerous Freudian symbols.*

The Emperor and Empress (or King and Queen) as a rule really represent the dreamer's parents; and a Prince or Princess represents the dreamer himself or herself . . . . All elongated objects, such as sticks, tree-trunks and umbrellas (the opening of these last being comparable to an erection) may stand for the male organ—as well as all long, sharp weapons, such as knives, daggers, and pikes . . . . Boxes, cases, chests, cupboards, and ovens represent the uterus, and also hollow objects, ships, and vessels of all kinds. Rooms in dreams are usually women; if the various ways in and out of them are represented, this interpretation is scarcely open to doubt. In this connection interest in whether the room is open or locked is easily intelligible. There is no need to name explicitly the key that unlocks the room.

Still another route to the unconscious for Freud was to analyze mistakes, especially slips of the tongue, that occur in everyday behavior. In Freud's view, mistakes are never simply random accidents, but are expressions of unconscious wishes. In one of his most popular books, *The Psychopathology of Everyday Life*, Freud (1901/1960) backed up this claim with numerous examples of such errors, along with his interpretation. For example, he reported an incident in which a young woman, complaining about the disadvantages of being a woman, stated, "A woman must be pretty if she is to please the men. A man is much better off. As long as he has his *five straight limbs* he needs no more." According to Freud, this slip involved a fusion of two separate clichés, *four straight limbs* and *five senses*, which would not have occurred had it not expressed an idea that was on the woman's mind (either unconscious or conscious) that she consciously would have preferred to have concealed. In another context the same statement could have been a deliberate, slightly off-color joke; but Freud claims that in this case it was an honest slip of the tongue, as evidenced by the woman's embarrassment upon realizing what she had said.

Just as he believed that slips of the tongue are meaningful, Freud also believed that instances of forgetting are meaningful. For example, when a person forgets a previously well known word or phrase, the unconscious motive is to protect the conscious mind from some idea associated with that word or phrase. To illustrate this point, Freud (1901/1960) described a wonderful incident in which a young man he met on vacation was unable to recall the Latin word *aliquis* while trying to quote a line from Virgil's *Aeneid*. As a challenge, the young man, aware of Freud's theories, asked Freud to explain why he had been unable to think of that particular word. Taking up the challenge, Freud said that he could answer the question only if the man would undergo the procedure of free association and say aloud, uncensored, every idea that came to his mind after first saying the word *aliquis*. In the ensuing chain of associations, *aliquis* brought forth the idea of *liquid*, which brought forth the idea of *blood*, which brought forth a number of other ideas, including two saints—St. Januarius and St. Augustine—the first of whom was involved in the "miracle of the blood" and both of whom have names that are associated with months of the calendar. Putting together the ideas of month, blood, and certain other notions that had come from the man's associations, Freud announced that he had solved the mystery. He asked the young man if it were not true that a lady friend of his had recently failed to show her monthly menstrual period! Amazed, the young man confessed that this was true and that indeed he had reason to fear she might be pregnant. According to Freud, the man's unconscious mind had caused him to forget the word *aliquis* to protect his conscious mind from being reminded of a possibility that he greatly feared.

**Divisions of the Mind: Id, Ego, Superego**   To explain the kinds of conflicts that seemed to reside in the minds of his patients and others he knew, Freud (1933/1964) postulated that the mind consists of three often conflicting components: the id, the ego, and the superego.

■ *How Freud divided the mind into three main components that are often in conflict with one another*

The *id* provides the basic source of energy in Freud's theory. It is the entire set of drives with which a person is born, and its only goal is the gratification of those drives. It operates in strict accordance with the *pleasure principle*: Find pleasure (through the gratification of drives) and avoid pain. It has no concern for right or wrong, no respect for constraints imposed by the environment, and, for that matter, no appreciation of reality. If the id generates a wish for which there is no available object of gratification, it can satisfy itself simply through imagination. This kind of thinking, in which reality and fantasy are not differentiated, is referred to by Freud as the *primary process*. The closest we come to experiencing such thought consciously is in dreams, in which primary-process thought emerges into consciousness in least-disguised form.

The *ego* develops in infancy as an outgrowth of the id. It is the part of the mind that permits a person to function reasonably in the environment. It operates according to the *reality principle*: A wish can be gratified only if a means for gratification is available in the environment. The ego includes, among other things, a person's understanding of reality and capacity for logic. Freud referred to the ego's mode of thinking, which involves conscious perception of the environment and logical thought, as the *secondary process*. In accordance with the reality principle, the ego prevents the individual from being satisfied completely by fantasies. Your ego tells you that if you want to become a famous psychologist, you must study and work hard in the real world, not simply daydream about being a famous psychologist. The ego is also the great arbiter of the mind. It works out compromises among the demands of the id, superego, and external reality.

The *superego* develops in early childhood as another outgrowth of the id. It is the internalized representation of society's moral rules, which the child acquires primarily through interaction with his or her parents. Its purpose is to oppose the gratification of drives when the means to gratification would violate morality. Its main weapon toward that end is its ability to create the feeling of guilt, which is highly unpleasant and thus to be avoided by both the pleasure-seeking id and the peace-seeking ego. Perhaps you could become a famous psychologist by fabricating data—pretending you had done experiments that you really hadn't. Your id would approve of that, and so would your ego if it thought you could get away with it. But at the mere thought of such an act your superego would create such a strong sense of guilt that your ego, constantly striving for tranquility, would shut the thought off before it was acted upon.

Look at Figure 16.2 to see the relationship between each of these three components and the unconscious-conscious distinction discussed earlier. Notice that the id is entirely unconscious and that the other two divisions are each partly conscious and partly unconscious. The superego includes a person's conscious understanding of moral premises, but also includes deep-seated, unconscious, less rational moral forces. The ego includes a person's conscious knowledge of the world, but also includes *repressed memories*, that is, memories that are so anxiety provoking that they have been pushed into the unconscious and can't be recalled through normal retrieval procedures. In addition, the processes by which the ego interacts with the id and superego are unconscious.

**Figure 16.2  *Freud's divisions of the mind***
*The conscious mind is depicted here as the visible tip of an iceberg, and the unconscious mind as the much larger mass that is submerged. Notice that the id is entirely unconscious and that the ego and superego are partly conscious and partly unconscious. (Adapted from Freud, 1933/1964.)*

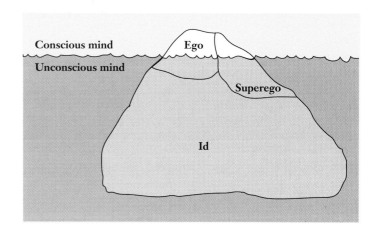

■ *How the ego is affected by three sources of anxiety, and how various defense mechanisms serve to reduce the ego's conscious experience of anxiety*

**Anxiety and the Ego's Defense Mechanisms**   In Freud's model, the ego has the most direct control of conscious thought and behavior. It attempts to exert that control in such a way as to meet the demands of three different forces that act on it: the real world, the id, and the superego. These forces exert their demands through the production of *anxiety*, defined by Freud (1926/1964) as the unpleasant feeling that accompanies the ego's sense of impending danger. The real world contains real dangers, such as a snake about to bite or a threatened loss of job and income. The id contains dangers in the form of its strong drives and desires, which, if not controlled, could cause a person to behave in self-destructive ways (such as jumping off a cliff to experience the pleasure of flight). The superego poses the danger of crippling the ego with guilt if it recognizes an action as violating a moral stricture. Freud gave separate names to the anxieties stemming from each of these three sources: *Reality anxiety* is the ego's fear of threats in the real world, *neurotic anxiety* is the ego's fear of the id's irrational wishes, and *moral anxiety* is the ego's fear of the guilt that the superego can produce.

How does the ego reduce the anxiety generated from these sources? It may do so in some cases through realistic problem solving. For example, it may reduce the threat of job loss by causing the person to look for a more secure job. In other cases, however, the ego may reduce anxiety through means of self-deception, which are referred to as ***defense mechanisms***. The theory of defense mechanisms was most thoroughly developed by Anna Freud (1936/1946), Sigmund's daughter, who herself became a psychoanalyst. Following are some of the most important defense mechanisms:

- **Repression** Repression is the most fundamental defense mechanism. It is the process by which the ego keeps anxiety-provoking wishes or memories out of the conscious mind. Repression holds the id's fearsome wishes down in the unconscious id, preventing them from entering and threatening the ego. A person who is afraid of his or her own sexual wishes may repress them so they do not enter consciousness. Repression also pushes anxiety-provoking memories out of consciousness, into the unconscious portion of the ego. For example, at age 5 a young friend of mine witnessed a person with a knife attack his father. A day later, when his father tried to talk to him about the incident, the boy appeared to have no memory of it at all; he didn't know what his father was talking about. Given the circumstances, it seems unlikely that he was pretending not to remember. The thought that his father (who was his only parent) might be killed was apparently so threatening that he had repressed the entire incident.

  According to Freud, some degree of repression is essential to normal functioning, but too much is harmful. In Freud's theory, a person has only a certain allotment of mental energy, so if too much is bound up in the active process of repression there will be little left for other activities. People who are highly repressed have so little energy left that they behave in stilted, wooden, nonspontaneous ways. Also, repression of the id's wishes reduces the opportunity to gratify those wishes consciously, and hence reduces a person's experience of pleasure. With little energy and little pleasure, the repressed person is at risk of becoming depressed.

  Repression provides the underlying basis for most of the other defense mechanisms. Freud visualized repression as a damming up of a pool of mental energy. In this metaphor, just as water will leak through any crack in a dam, repressed wishes and memories will leak through the walls of repression, into the conscious part of the ego, wherever the barrier is not perfect. When such material leaks through, however, the ego can still defend itself by distorting the ideas in ways that make them less threatening. All of the remaining defense mechanisms are means for such distortion.

**Defense!!!**

*The rerouting of aggression into sports —an example of Freud's construct sublimation—offers rewards to players and fans alike. Although Freud based his notion of defenses on observations of disordered behavior, he recognized their adaptive functions in everyday life.*

- **Displacement** *and* **sublimation** Displacement occurs when a drive that was directed toward one activity by the id is redirected by the ego toward a safer activity that is symbolically equivalent to the original. For example, a child long past infancy may still have a strong desire, in the id, to suck at the mother's breast—a desire that is now threatening and repressed, because it violates the superego's assessment of what is proper and the ego's assessment of what is possible. When this desire enters the ego it may be displaced, say, toward sucking a lollipop—an action that is both realistic and acceptable to the superego. In some cases, displacement may direct the id's energies toward activities that are particularly valued by society, such as artistic, scientific, or humanitarian endeavors. These displacements, which are most in line with the ideals of the superego, are referred to as *sublimations*. In a book on the life of Leonardo da Vinci, Freud (1910/1947) suggested that da Vinci's fascination with painting Madonnas was a sublimation of his desire for his mother, which had been frustrated at an early age due to being separated from her. As another example, a highly aggressive person may perform valuable service in a competitive profession as sublimation of the drive to beat others.

- **Reaction formation** This is the turning of a frightening wish into its safer opposite. For example, a young woman who unconsciously hates her mother and wishes her dead may consciously experience these feelings as intense love for her mother and strong concern for her safety.

*Projection*  This occurs when a person consciously experiences his or her own unconscious emotion or wish as though it were someone else's. Thus, a person with intense, unconscious anger may project that anger onto her friend—that is, she may feel that it is her friend, not she, who is angry.

*Rationalization*  This is the use of conscious reasoning to explain away anxiety-provoking thoughts or feelings. For example, a man who cannot face his own sadistic tendencies may rationalize the beatings he gives his children by convincing himself that children need to be beaten and that he is only carrying out his fatherly duty. Freud's theory encourages us to be wary of conscious logic, since it may often serve to mask true feelings and wishes.

### Freud's View of Personality Development

Personality, as defined earlier, refers to the more or less consistent differences among people in their behavioral styles. In Freud's theory, personality has to do with the characteristic ways that individuals channel their inborn mental energy, especially their libido. These characteristics emerge from an interaction between the child's wish-fulfilling behaviors and the way that others, especially parents, react to those behaviors early in childhood. Freud divided personality development into a series of five stages, now referred to as **psychosexual stages**: the *oral, anal, phallic, latency,* and *genital* stages (see Hall, 1979). The most important are the first three, which occur within the first 5 years of life. Freud believed that by the end of the phallic stage a person's basic personality is fixed. Behavior continues to change after age 5 as a result of such factors as bodily maturation and new learning, but those changes simply represent new ways of expressing one's personality, not changes in the personality itself.

The names of the first three stages refer to different parts of the body that Freud considered to be *erogenous zones*—the areas where sexual pleasure is experienced. Thus, each of these stages is associated with a particular type of sexual pleasure and a particular orientation toward the world for gaining pleasure. As a person passes through each stage, some portion of the total libido may become *fixated* at that stage. **Fixation** at any stage means that to some degree the person will, throughout life, attempt to achieve pleasure in ways that are symbolically equivalent to the ways that pleasure was achieved at that stage in childhood. Fixation can occur because of either too little gratification at a given stage (the person goes through life trying to find what was missed) or too much gratification (the person has no motivation to move beyond that stage). Let us examine briefly each stage, looking at the contribution it can make to adult personality.

During the *oral stage*—roughly the first year of life—pleasure comes from taking things into the mouth and sucking on them, especially the mother's breast. The infant at this stage is a relatively passive receiver of pleasure, which is given by another person more or less at the infant's demand. Fixation at this stage can have a number of possible consequences for adult personality. At the most direct, behavioral level it may lead to continued oral activities, such as gum chewing, smoking, or overeating. More important, the oral drive can be displaced toward symbolic ways of taking in. Orally fixated individuals may go through life trying to take in such things as knowledge, love, or money—often in demanding ways, expecting others to feed them whatever it is that they want.

During the *anal stage*—roughly the second year—the focus of pleasure is the anus, which is stimulated most directly through the passing of feces. The most significant activity now is toilet training, in which the child is for the first time subjected to parental demands. The demands produce mental conflict in the child. On the one hand, the child wishes to gain immediate pleasure by expelling feces whenever there is an urge to do so. On the other hand, the child wishes to gain the

■ *How experiences in the first three stages in Freud's theory of personality development predispose the person to particular behavioral styles later on*

**Too much pleasure?**

*Freud believed that gratification as well as deprivation can cause fixation at a developmental stage. If he could have seen this infant's unrestrained enjoyment, he might have predicted future resistance to toilet training.*

parental praise that would come from holding feces in and expelling it only when placed on the toilet. Fixation at the anal stage implies continued conflict between the drive to hold in feces and the drive to expel it. Through displacement, the holding in may take the form of stinginess, excessive neatness, and rigidity of behavior; and the expelling may take the form of generosity, messiness, and creativity or looseness of behavior. Some anally fixated people are at one end of this spectrum, others are at the other end, and still others are at different ends in different realms of their life (one may keep a messy kitchen but a neat notebook).

During the *phallic stage*—from about age 3 to 5—the penis becomes the important source of pleasure for the boy, and the lack of a penis becomes the important issue in the girl's development. The boy's discovery of the pleasure of masturbation is mixed with his love of his mother (who has satisfied all of his needs so far). His id becomes filled with sexual fantasies directed toward his mother, and this in turn leads the boy to fear and hate his father, the main rival for his mother's attention. Freud referred to this set of wishes and emotions as the **oedipal crisis**, named after the tragic hero of Sophocles' play *Oedipus Rex* (who unknowingly killed his father and married his mother). In Freud's theory, the boy finally resolves the oedipal crisis by identifying with his father, that is, by thinking of himself in some sense as his father. In this way he no longer hates and fears his father, and he can indirectly (through his father) satisfy his sexual desire for his mother. If a satisfying identification with the father is not formed, the boy will fail to resolve completely the oedipal crisis. Fixated at the phallic stage, he may be compelled to go through life trying to prove that he is a man, constantly putting on a show of toughness and repressing the gentler side of his nature.

The girl's phallic stage centers on her discovery that boys have a penis and she doesn't. Her sense of deprivation, referred to as *penis envy* (not one of Freud's more popular concepts today), causes her to turn against her mother, who also lacks a penis and whom the girl blames for her own lack, and to develop a sexual longing for her father, who possesses the organ that she would like to have. In the end, the girl resolves her oedipal crisis (sometimes referred to as the *electra crisis*, named after Oedipus's sister) by identifying with her mother and in that way symbolically possessing her father through her mother. Fixation at the phallic stage for a woman implies failure to form a successful identification with the mother, and therefore failure to overcome penis envy. The fixated woman will go through life feeling inferior to men. Consequently, she may attempt to satisfy her needs through men (especially older men, who are father figures), using seductive and flirtatious behaviors to keep their attention. Or she may attempt to dominate men, symbolically castrating them, to overcome her sense of inferiority.

In both sexes, fixation at the phallic stage also implies failure to overcome the incestuous desire for the opposite-sex parent; therefore, sexuality in such individuals is tinged with the fear and guilt associated with incest. Both the male and female may appear superficially to be highly sexual, but deep down they are afraid of sex.

The remaining two stages occupy the bulk of life, during which the already-formed personality plays itself out in various kinds of interaction with the world. The *latency stage*—from age 5 or 6 to the onset of puberty—is a time of repressed sexuality, during which libido is displaced into such midchildhood activities as hobbies, athletics, school learning, and making friends. At puberty, sexuality reappears in a new form, oriented in a more realistic way toward other people and less toward the person's own body, marking the onset of the *genital stage*, which lasts to the end of life. Libido is now invested in activities that lead to the *generation* of new life, such as falling in love, marrying, raising children, and caring for other people. (The term *genital* is misleading as the name for this stage, since now, unlike in the phallic stage, sexuality goes beyond sensations in the genitals. It is too bad that Freud's translators didn't call it the *generative stage*, since that fits better with

Freud's meaning.) Of course, the way a person meets the tasks of the genital stage depends on how crises were met and resolved in the first three stages. If too much libido is fixated at earlier stages, there can be little left for the adult tasks. As Freud (1935/1960) once put it, the healthy adult finds pleasure in love and work, which are the central generative tasks. The unhealthy adult doesn't, because energy is tied up in infantile wishes and fears.

### Personality Research Based on Freud's Theory

You have now seen a sketch of Freud's theory of personality and its development. The most important points are that (a) behavior is motivated by unconscious drives, (b) defense mechanisms block and rechannel these drives before they are manifested in conscious thought and behavior, and (c) through a series of developmental stages people acquire characteristic ways of channeling their drives. Many of Freud's followers have argued that such ideas can be tested only through the in-depth study of individual cases using Freud's technique of psychoanalysis. They insist that laboratory studies oversimplify the real issues of personality and fail to provide a context in which unconscious motives can reveal themselves. However, a number of researchers have tried, with mixed success, to test Freud's ideas using laboratory or other statistically based procedures (see Erdelyi, 1985, and Fisher & Greenberg, 1985). Here is a brief sampling of research that tends to support Freud's views.

**Evidence for Defense Mechanisms**   Perhaps the most testable of Freud's ideas are those concerning defense mechanisms. Many years ago, when the theory of defenses was still quite new, Robert Sears (1936) performed a study supporting the validity of projection as a defense mechanism. Recall that projection is a process by which people attribute to others characteristics that exist in themselves but that they have repressed. Sears asked members of college fraternity houses to rate first themselves and then each of their housemates, confidentially, on a set of personality dimensions that included *stinginess–generosity*, *obstinacy–agreeableness*, and *orderliness–disorderliness*—where extreme scores in either direction could be viewed as part of an anal personality complex.

*Evidence that people who have repressed knowledge about their own traits may project those traits onto others*

On the basis of these ratings, he identified individuals who were rated at one extreme or the other on a given trait by their housemates, but who rated themselves either neutrally or in the other direction. These people apparently lacked conscious insight about one or more of their own traits. In keeping with the view that projection occurs in such cases, he found that these same young men rated their housemates unusually high on the same traits that they failed to see in themselves. Fraternity members who were rated high on a trait and had insight (that is, who also rated themselves high) did not show this tendency to rate others high on the trait.

*Evidence for repression as a personality characteristic*

More recently, Gary Schwartz and his colleagues have performed a series of studies on repression. They used a questionnaire to identify people who seemed to repress their emotional experiences, and then conducted further tests to see how those people (referred to as *repressors*) differed from other subjects. When asked to complete sentences that contained sexual or aggressive themes, repressors claimed not to feel stressed, yet by a physiological measure (an index of sweating) they manifested more stress than did other subjects (Weinberger & others, 1979). In another test, repressors recalled fewer childhood emotional experiences than did other subjects (Davis & Schwartz, 1987). It would be interesting to know if these individuals also show other characteristics that, according to Freud, should accompany a repressed personality style. Do they have less mental energy for other activities? Are they more vulnerable than other people to depression?

**Figure 16.3** *What do you see here?*
*The rationale behind the Rorschach test is that people project some of their unconscious wishes and memories into their perceptions of the inkblots.*

**Projective Tests as Research Tools**   In addition to the procedures that Freud used to probe the unconscious mind (free association, dream analysis, and analysis of mistakes), psychologists today have a new set of tools called ***projective tests***. Projective testing is really a variant of free association. The person being tested is shown an ambiguous visual stimulus and is asked to say quickly, without logical explanation, what it looks like or what ideas it brings to mind. Taking a projective test is a bit like responding to a work of abstract art. When you and a friend look at an abstract painting, you may see quite different things in the painting. The difference does not lie in the painting, but rather represents a difference between you and your friend; thus, when you interpret the painting you are saying something about yourself. In psychoanalytic terms, you are projecting some aspect of yourself upon the painting. Because you are consciously talking about the painting, not yourself, material that your defense mechanisms would not allow you to admit about yourself can flow more freely into your description. The two most commonly used projective tests are the *Rorschach*, in which the visual stimuli are symmetrical inkblots and the task is to say what the inkblot looks like (see Figure 16.3), and the *Thematic Apperception Test (TAT)*, in which the stimuli are pictures of ambiguous scenes including one or more persons and the task is to tell a story about what might be happening in the picture (see Figure 16.4).

Projective tests are used both in therapy with individual patients and in research studies comparing different groups of people. When used in therapy, the patient's responses are interpreted in relation to all of the other bits of information that the analyst has about the patient—as one more piece of the jigsaw puzzle that must be put together to form a complete picture of the patient's unconscious mind (discussed in Chapter 18). When used in research, each person's responses are used as a basis for statistical comparison between groups.

**Figure 16.4** *What is going on here?*
*The assumption behind the TAT is that people project material from their unconscious minds into the stories that they tell when they are shown pictures such as this and are asked to describe what is happening.*

■ *How projective tests were used in a study comparing the personalities of comedians and clowns with those of noncomic actors*

A study by Seymour and Rhoda Fisher (1981) provides an example of the use of projective tests in research. The Fishers compared thirty-five professional comics (comedians and clowns) with thirty-five noncomic actors to see if the two groups differed in personality in any consistent way. As part of the study, the subjects were given Rorschach and TAT tests, and scorers who did not know which responses came from which group scored the responses for the presence of certain themes. The researchers found that themes having to do with evil were more common for comics than for the other actors. Comics were likely to see such things as monsters and devils in the inkblots. At the same time, however, they were also more likely to depreciate the significance of the evil, using such phrases as "a monster, but it's really nice," or "two devils, funny devils, not to be taken seriously." Partly from this evidence, the researchers concluded that comics as a group are especially sensitive to evil and that many of them may have developed their comic ability as a way of coping with their perceptions of evil.

### Critique of Freud's Theory

Freud's theory has been described by both admirers and critics as creative (which is not always praise), insightful (also, incite-full to some), and even fantastic (a word with two meanings). Freud called himself a scientist, but psychologists engaged in scientific research have always been among his harshest critics. Many have argued that Freud's true genius was not that of a scientist, but closer to that of a novelist. He gleaned insights from his patients and worked them into fascinating dramas, the main characters of which lay deep in the patient's mind. To appreciate this more fully, read one or more of his case histories, such as *The "Rat Man"* (described in Chapter 18) or *The Psychotic Doctor Schreber*.

#### Spellbound

*Freud's work has inspired paintings, novels, plays, and films. In this scene from the Alfred Hitchcock film* Spellbound, *Ingrid Bergman, a psychoanalyst, is treating Gregory Peck, a patient whose emotional confusion was created by repressed memories of his brother's accidental death.*

■ *How Freud's work has affected Western culture and the science of psychology*

For better or worse (I personally think better, all in all), Freud's work has had an enormous impact on twentieth-century Western society. As a measure of that, notice how many of Freud's terms and ideas have become part of everyday conversation. We often hear people describe their or others' behavior with such terms as *projection, repression, id, superego, oral fixation,* or *anal retentiveness*. If you take an art or literature course, you may hear your instructor apply Freudian terms to the process of creation, alluding perhaps to libidinal desires welling up from the artist's unconscious to be spilled out on canvas.

Freud's work, whether you think it is scientific or not, has also had important effects on the science of psychology. By bringing home to psychology the importance of irrational, unconscious, emotion-laden forces in human behavior, Freud helped direct the discipline away from the comparatively sterile attempt of the late nineteenth century to analyze the mind purely in terms of conscious thought. Also, by portraying even young infants as mentally active beings, and by emphasizing (probably overemphasizing) the role of early experience in personality development, Freud sparked interest in developmental psychology, especially the study of young children and their interactions with parents. Finally, as described in Chapters 17 and 18, Freud's ideas are still very important in modern thought about mental disorders and their treatment.

Despite—or perhaps because of—its enormous impact, Freud's work has always been criticized from within the ranks of psychology for its unscientific nature. The most common criticisms can be summarized as follows:

> *Limitations of the data*   The data on which Freud built his theory came mostly from (a) his analysis of his patients, most of whom were neurotic, upper-class citizens of Vienna; and (b) his own self-analysis. Thus, his theory was built on the concerns and problems of a narrow portion of humanity and may not be applicable to all people everywhere. For example, people struggling daily to put food on the table may be less concerned about subtle aspects of their sex life than are people who have a more leisurely existence. Another limitation is that the data consisted largely of free associations, dreams, and childhood memories presented in a therapy context in which the patients knew that certain themes—those relevant to Freud's formulations—would be of greatest interest. Freud did not take notes during these sessions, and so another problem for anyone wishing to evaluate the evidence is the necessity to rely on Freud's own memory and accurate reporting when he described the cases supporting his ideas.

> *Influence of personal biases*   The theorist's personal biases inevitably come into play in any theory in psychology, and this is especially a problem when the data upon which the theory is built are not publicly available. Among other biases, Freud was subject to the male chauvinism of his time. For example, his theory that women feel inferior to men because of penis envy placed the blame for that feeling on an unchangeable fact of anatomy rather than on the social environment.

> *Vague terms and untestable concepts*   Good science is different from good poetry. In poetry, a word or phrase may be valued precisely because it can be interpreted in more than one way, and thus can trigger many ideas in the reader's mind and mean different things to different people. But scientists must take pains to state clearly and literally what they mean. Terms have to be defined such that all readers will get the same meaning. This is a problem in Freud's writing. For example, when Freud attributes an enormous amount of human behavior to the sex drive, it makes a difference how he defines that drive. Does he literally mean the drive to copulate, or is he using it to refer to the drive for any bodily pleasure? The theory loses much of its plausibility if the former is true, and much of its punch if the latter is true. By playing it both ways, Freud keeps some measure of plausibility while retaining the punch—good literature, but bad science.

Partly because of the vagueness of terms and concepts, it is hard to imagine how some of Freud's central ideas could be tested scientifically. Take, for instance, his concept that all children experience an oedipal wish—to have sex with the opposite-sex parent. How could you ever prove that concept right or wrong, if you added to it (as Freud did) that the wish may be entirely unconscious and expressed only in masked ways? If you begin with the assumption that Freud is right, you can easily explain almost anything that a child does as an expression of the oedipal wish. For example, every instance in which a child crawls into bed with a parent could be interpreted as oedipal behavior. But if you begin with the assumption that Freud was not right, you could find a dozen other plausible ways of explaining the same behavior; for example, the child might be seeking warmth or security.

■ *How Freud has been criticized for the subjectiveness of his evidence and the vagueness of his terms and concepts*

*A distinguished gathering*

*In 1909, Freud and several disciples journeyed to Clark University in Massachusetts, where he gave a series of lectures on psychoanalysis. The invitation was arranged by psychologist G. Stanley Hall, seated between Freud (left) and Jung (right) in the front row.*

## Post-Freudian Psychodynamic Theories

Beginning early in his career, Freud attracted a number of followers, who were inspired by his work and joined him to form an international society of psychoanalysts. Among these were some who developed ideas that ran counter to Freud's, which eventually led them to part company with Freud and establish alternative personality theories and approaches to psychotherapy.

The first to propose an alternative theory was Alfred Adler (1870–1937). Adler lived in Vienna and was a close associate of Freud's from 1902 to 1911, but then split with Freud and developed a theory called *individual psychology*. Another was Carl Jung (1875–1961), a Swiss psychoanalyst who exchanged hundreds of letters with Freud between 1906 and 1913, but then split with him and developed a theory called *analytical psychology*. Both Adler and Jung separated from Freud largely on the grounds that Freud placed too much emphasis on the sex drive and not enough on other aspects of human nature.

A third early theorist to contradict Freud was Karen Horney (1885–1952), who began a psychoanalytic practice in Berlin in 1918. As one of the first female psychoanalysts, Horney opposed some of Freud's male-centered ideas, including the view that women suffer from penis envy. A fourth, who came considerably later, is Erik Erikson (1902–    ). Erikson studied under Anna Freud (Sigmund's daughter) in Vienna and then went on to enjoy a long career in the United States as a researcher and child psychoanalyst. His theory of the stages of personality development are discussed in Chapter 13.

Although each of these theories (and others that could be listed) differ in important ways from Freud's, they retain certain core elements of Freud's theory. These elements—which lead them to be classed with Freud's as psychodynamic theories—include the ideas that (a) unconscious mental forces are important in determining a person's conscious thought and behavior; (b) these unconscious forces work largely through the production of anxiety, which a person strives to reduce through his or her modes of thought and action (personality style); and (c) early childhood experiences are especially important in shaping one's personality.

In addition to sharing characteristics acquired from Freud's theory, most post-Freudian psychodynamic theories share certain other characteristics, which tend to differentiate them as a group from Freud's theory. Among these are their strong

■ *Three ways in which post-Freudian psychodynamic theories are similar to Freud's, and three ways in which they differ from his* emphases on the importance of (a) social needs, (b) self-esteem, and (c) psychological wholeness. Although Freud did not ignore these issues (especially the second and third), they were not as explicit in his theory as they were in the psychodynamic theories that came after his. The following subsections illustrate these characteristics, one at a time, with ideas from the theories of Adler, Jung, Horney, and Erikson.

**The Importance of Social Needs** Freud viewed people as basically asocial, forced into society more by necessity than desire, and interacting principally in terms of sex, aggression, and displaced forms of these. In contrast, most post-Freudian theorists have viewed people as inherently social beings whose needs for others extend well beyond sex and aggression. These needs are generally seen as belonging to the ego rather than to the id, and therefore are referred to as *ego-social needs*. Among them are the needs for the security and favorable evaluation that others can provide, and the need to sense that one is contributing to others.

Different theories emphasize different ego-social needs. To take one example, Horney's theory focuses on *security* as an inborn human need that can be filled only by other people. A central concept in her theory is that of *basic anxiety*, which she defined as "the feeling a child has of being isolated and helpless in a potentially hostile world" (Horney, 1945). In her theory, parents strongly influence a child's lifelong personality through the ways in which they make the child feel secure (or fail to do so). If a child finds security in relating to parents, the child will continue to find security in other relationships throughout life. If a child fails to find security in relating to parents, the child will grow up feeling insecure and distrustful of others (Horney, 1937). Depending on other conditions, this insecurity and distrust may manifest itself through avoiding others, submitting to others (in an ingratiating way that denies one's own self-worth), or dominating others (gaining power over them).

Erikson's theory identifies a variety of ego-social needs and proposes that different ones are most important at different stages of development. Thus, infants need security, children need support and encouragement for their independence and skillfulness, adolescents need models to help them form adult identities, young adults need intimacy, and older adults need to care for others. At each stage, the manner in which these needs are met influence the personality that enters the next stage. (A more complete summary of Erikson's theory can be found in Table 13.1 in Chapter 13.)

**The Importance of Self-esteem** The need for self-esteem can be thought of as one of the social needs, since a person's sense of self-esteem depends very much on feedback from other people (an idea discussed in Chapter 14). This need was especially emphasized by Alfred Adler (1930), who argued that all people begin life with a feeling of inferiority that stems from the helpless and dependent nature of early childhood. In Adler's theory, the way that people learn to cope with or to overcome this feeling provides the basis for their lifelong personality. Some people are so overwhelmed by their sense of inferiority that they develop an *inferiority complex*, meaning that they go through life feeling inadequate and dependent. Others develop a *superiority complex*, which is really a mask for their sense of inferiority, in which the attempt to overcome inferiority centers on trying to prove that they are better than other people around them. The psychologically healthy person has neither of these complexes, but rather has a mature sense of his or her own abilities and worth (high self-esteem) and can direct those abilities toward socially useful achievements.

Self-esteem is also an important idea in Horney's theory. Horney (1950) proposed that people have two self-images—an *ideal self* and a *real self*—and that people strive to make the latter more like the former. People whose ideal self is unrealistic, too discrepant from their real self, will go through life with low self-

■ *How the ego-social need of security is important in Horney's theory, and how various ego-social needs are important in Erikson's*

**Karen Horney**

*One of the first psychoanalysts to offer a rebuttal to Freud's ideas about women, Horney argued that psychoanalysis must consider facts about women's social circumstances as well as their anatomy.*

■ *How Adler's concept of overcoming inferiority and Horney's concept of a discrepancy between the ideal and real selves illustrate the role of self-esteem in personality development*

esteem and suffer from the *tyranny of the should*, the constant feeling that they *should* be doing things differently or better than they currently are. Psychologically healthy individuals, on the other hand, have a close enough fit between their ideal and real selves to feel good about themselves and their activities.

**The Importance of Psychological Wholeness**    In Freud's theory, the mind contains separate, often conflicting components, and the ego must work out compromises among them. Theorists since Freud have often viewed the ego as not just an arbiter but an integrator, a device to produce cohesion and harmony among the mind's potentially conflicting forces. This idea is most prominent in Carl Jung's theory of personality.

*How Jung's theory emphasizes the importance of integrating the various opposing aspects of the person into a harmonious whole*

Jung's (1968) very complex theory includes the idea that the mind contains various forces, which, for optimal mental health, must be brought into balance by an integrating force called the *self* (a concept roughly analogous to Freud's *ego*). Many of these forces are polar opposites of one another. Thus, each person has a *persona* (a mask, or outer person, presented to others) and a *shadow* (a dark, deep, passionate inner person containing the capacity for evil). Each person also has an *anima* (the female side of the person) and an *animus* (the male side). In addition, each person has two opposing orientations to the world: *introversion* (orientation toward the inner world of thoughts and feelings) and *extroversion* (orientation toward the external world of things and people). These forces, when integrated, do not have to conflict; they can complement one another to produce a sense of wholeness and an enhanced ability to deal with the various kinds of challenges that the world has to offer. Thus, in Jung's view, a psychologically healthy person is one who can accept and use constructively all sides of his or her human nature rather than allow any one side to dominate at the expense of its opposite.

**Criticisms of Post-Freudian Psychodynamic Theories**    The criticisms most commonly raised about the post-Freudian theories are similar to those raised about Freud's theory. All psychodynamic theories are based primarily on clinical evidence, subjectively interpreted by the theorist. Thus, all of them may be heavily influenced by the theorist's personal biases, and little objective data is available to those who wish to examine the evidence critically. All psychodynamic theories place great emphasis on the role of anxiety in personality processes, which may simply reflect the fact that those who seek psychotherapy—and thus become test cases for the therapist's theory—are people who suffer especially from anxiety. Any theory based mainly on people's psychological problems may be inadequate as a complete theory of personality.

## Humanistic Theories

In the emphasis of post-Freudian psychodynamic theories on social needs and conscious (ego) processes, you saw a movement away from Freud's pessimistic view that the person is driven by sexual and aggressive instincts that are necessarily at odds with the goals of society. The culmination of this movement—toward a more cheerful view—resides in the personality theories labeled *humanistic*.

In their founding of an official organization and a journal (the *Journal of Humanistic Psychology*, first published in 1961), the early leaders of the humanistic movement—including Carl Rogers, Abraham Maslow, Charlotte Buhler, Rollo May, Victor Frankl, and Thomas Szasz—declared themselves to be a "Third Force" in the science of psychology. The other two forces, seen as the dominant schools of thought at the time, were behaviorism and Freudian psychoanalysis. Rogers, Maslow, and the others argued that both of those forces missed the essential characteristics of being human, and thus tended to dehumanize the person. Behaviorism focused on simple learning processes that occur in lower animals as well as people, and Freud's theory focused on the animal instincts of sex and aggression. The goal of humanistic psychology was to emphasize the uniquely human aspects of the person.

### Basic Tenets of Humanistic Psychology

*How humanistic theories are characterized by their emphasis on phenomenology, their resistance to reductionism, and their concept of a natural drive toward self-actualization*

Three themes that seem to unite humanistic theories are the following (see Tageson, 1982):

1. *Phenomenological approach* The term **phenomenology** refers to the study of subjective mental experiences. Humanistic theorists argue that people do not simply react to the physical reality of the world around them, but instead behave according to their mental interpretation of that reality, that is, according to their *phenomenological reality*. For example, if you are approached on a deserted street by a stranger, you behave in accordance with your interpretation of what the stranger is doing, which may or may not coincide with what the stranger is actually doing. An especially important part of phenomenological reality is the *self-concept* (an idea that was also important in post-Freudian psychodynamic theories), defined as the set of beliefs that people have about themselves. Regardless of whether it is accurate or not, a person's self-concept helps determine how the person will behave. For example, a person who believes, rightly or wrongly, that he or she is socially incompetent will avoid social experiences.

   The emphasis on phenomenological reality stems directly from the humanists' view that people (unlike animals) control their own actions through conscious decision making. Over time, each person acquires a unique set of beliefs, which collectively constitute his or her self-concept and understanding of the world, and which provide the foundation for decisions about how to behave. To know the person you must learn about those beliefs.

2. *Holistic view of the person* Humanistic psychology is partly a reaction against the reductionism of other approaches. *Reductionism* is the attempt to understand an entity by reducing it to a set of basic elements. The early behaviorists' attempt to understand the flow of behavior by breaking it down into separate, reflexive, stimulus-response connections is one form of reductionism. Freud's attempt to break down the structure of personality into id, ego, and superego—each with its various components and energies—is another. Whereas most humanistic psychologists do not deny the value of reductionism for understanding specific mental processes such as sensation or memory, they argue that reductionism should be avoided in a personality theory, because a person is a unified whole that is more than the sum of its parts. A person is not just memory plus emotion plus reason, or learning plus instinct, or id plus ego plus superego. Rather, a person is a single, unified entity that works toward goals that apply to the whole person, rather than to any specific part of the person.

   The argument for a holistic approach can perhaps be made clearer by considering what would happen if you suddenly lost some particular aspect of your functioning. Suppose you suddenly became blind. At one moment you would be a person who could see, and the next you would be a person who couldn't. But that would be only the beginning. Over time you would change in ways that would allow you to continue to exist and grow mentally without vision. You would replace old hobbies and old ways of interacting with people with new ones. You would learn to use your other senses more efficiently than before, and you would strengthen certain aspects of your memory to compensate for loss of ability to use visual cues. In a less dramatic way, everything that happens to you as you go through each day of life reverberates through your entire system, and to understand those happenings you must be considered as a whole, not as a collection of separate parts.

3. *The actualizing tendency*  Whereas psychodynamic theories emphasize the tendency to protect the self against anxiety and return to a more quiescent state, humanistic theories emphasize the positive tendency of the person to grow psychologically. The overriding, holistic purpose of individuals is to *actualize* their potentials—that is, to become what they are capable of becoming. What this means specifically will vary from person to person and from time to time in one's life. But for each individual, the goals of this process must come from within the person, and the route can be chosen only by the person himself or herself. If the environment places obstacles in the way of actualization, one's whole system becomes oriented toward overcoming those obstacles.

### Self-actualization

*At the Sudbury Valley School, which exemplifies Carl Rogers's view that learning should be self-directed, students are free to choose their own activities. They can climb trees at any time of day, or do anything else that doesn't interfere with other people's rights. Research suggests that the graduates of this school have been unusually successful in careers calling for a high degree of creativity.*

Rogers (1963, 1977) often compared psychological actualization in humans to physical growth in plants. A tree growing on a cliff by the sea must battle against the wind and saltwater, and it does not grow as well as it would in a better setting; yet, its inner potential continues to operate and it grows as best as it can under the circumstances. Nobody can tell the tree how to grow—its growth potential lies within itself.

Humanistic theorists do not ignore the importance of the environment. Full growth, full actualization, requires a fertile environment. But the direction of actualization and the ways of using the environment must come from within the organism. In the course of evolution, organisms have acquired the capacity to use the environment in ways that maximize growth. In humans, some of these ways are experienced phenomenologically as free, conscious choices. This inner ability to make choices that promote positive psychological development is the actualizing tendency. To grow best, individuals must be permitted to make those choices, and must trust themselves to do so.

With these basic tenets in mind, let us look at the specific ideas of two of the founders of humanistic psychology—Carl Rogers and Abraham Maslow.

### Rogers's Theory

Rogers (1902–1987) was born in Illinois, raised in a devoutly Protestant family, studied theology, earned a Ph.D. in clinical psychology, and enjoyed a long career as a psychotherapist, university professor, writer, and founder of various self-improvement groups. His theory of personality is often referred to as *self theory*, because its central construct is the person's sense of self. Rogers (1959) claimed that at first he avoided this construct because it seemed unscientific, but was forced to consider it after listening to his clients in therapy sessions. Person after person would say, "I feel I am not being my real self"; "I wouldn't want anyone to know the real me"; "I wonder who I am." From such statements, Rogers gradually came to believe that a concept of self is an important part of a person's phenomenological world, and that the most general goal that people have when they enter therapy is "to become their real selves."

*▣ What it means not to be oneself, according to Rogers, and how the ability to be oneself is affected by childhood experiences*

**Incongruence and Conditions of Worth**   But how, you might ask, can one *not* be oneself? If we look at this question in terms of physical reality, then of course the notion of not being yourself is ridiculous. By definition, whatever you are is you. But if people *feel* that they are not always themselves, then the phenomenological meaning of self must be different from the physical meaning. Rogers concluded that when people sense that they are not themselves, they are sensing an *incongruence* (discrepancy) between their self-concept and their actual thoughts or behavior.

What is the source of this incongruence? According to Rogers, it arises from *conditions of worth* that distort the self-concept and make it incompatible with normal human experience. Conditions of worth stem originally from judgments made by other people. For example, a little girl who is told that she is bad when she is feeling angry may come to exclude anger from her self-concept. Yet, being human, she can't avoid feeling angry at times, and when she feels this she is made anxious because of incongruence with her self-concept. To reduce that anxiety, and to maintain her self-concept, she may deny or distort her experience of anger, but in doing so she thwarts her opportunity for psychological growth. Anger, like any other emotion, is part and parcel of the actualizing tendency, and one must accept all aspects of that tendency if healthy growth is to occur.

*▣ Why Rogers believed that therapists, parents, and educators should not evaluate or direct their clients or children*

**Rogers's Views of Therapy, Parenting, and Education**   In Rogers's view the main goal of psychotherapy is to allow clients to lose some of their dependence on other people's judgments (their conditions of worth) so that their self-concept and behavior can be more consistent with their actualizing tendency. The therapist accomplishes this by listening to and accepting everything that the client says without judging it. By accepting, empathizing with, and reflecting back all of the client's thoughts and feelings, the therapist helps the client accept those aspects of the self that were previously denied.

Ideal parents, according to Rogers, are those who affirm and accept all of a child's experiences and do not impose conditions of worth. Parents may have to control a child's behavior, but in doing so they can still show that they accept the child's feelings and experiences. If the angry little girl begins to destroy valuable objects, the parents should not say, "Stop being angry." Instead, they should say something like, "I understand that you are angry. That's okay. I get angry, too. But you're going to have to express it in a different way—I'm not going to let you break these things."

Regarding education, Rogers (1969) argued that the drive to learn is an inherent aspect of the actualizing tendency, and that learning occurs best when it is self-motivated, self-directed, and involves the whole person (emotions and intellect). Rogers suggested that the term *facilitator* (short for facilitator of education) be substituted for *teacher*, and proposed that facilitators should provide an atmosphere conducive to learning, but should not direct or coerce the child's learning.

■ *Some evidence supporting Rogers's view of the conditions that promote creativity*

A central aspect of self-actualization is creativity. In a paper on that topic, Rogers (1954) predicted that creativity would be maximized by child-rearing practices that included (a) unconditional love and acceptance (no conditions of worth), and (b) freedom to explore ideas and modes of expression without external criticism or evaluation. Years later, David Harrington and his colleagues (1987) tested this prediction by examining data they had collected over an 11-year period concerning more than 100 children and their parents. Using questionnaires and direct observations to rate parenting style, and using teachers' ratings and other means to rate creativity, they found a strong positive correlation between a Rogerian parenting style in the preschool years and creativity in adolescence. Another source of support for Rogers's theory comes from a study suggesting that graduates of the Sudbury Valley School (described in Chapter 13), which operates in ways consistent with Rogers's theory, have been particularly successful in music, art, and other fields that require high creativity (Gray & Chanoff, 1986).

### Maslow's Theory

Abraham Maslow (1908–1970) was born in New York City of immigrant parents, received a Ph.D. in psychology studying dominance behavior in monkeys, left animal research to study human needs, and became one of the leaders of humanistic psychology. Unlike all of the other personality theorists discussed so far, Maslow was not a psychotherapist. Yet, his method was basically the clinical one of attempting to understand people through getting to know them well. Unlike the therapists, Maslow focused on psychologically healthy people.

**The Hierarchy of Needs**   Maslow (1970) argued that to become a self-actualizing person, one must satisfy five sets of needs that can be arranged in a hierarchy (see Figure 16.5). From bottom to top, they are (1) *physiological needs*, which include the minimal essentials for life, such as food and water; (2) *safety needs*, which have to do with protection from possible threats in the environment; (3) *belongingness and love needs*, the needs to establish bonds with other people; (4) *esteem needs*, the needs for competence, self-respect, and respect from others; and, finally, (5) *self-actualization needs*, the needs for self-expression, creativity, and, in Maslow's words, "a sense of connectedness with the broader universe." Maslow argued that a person can focus on higher needs only if lower ones are already relatively satisfied.

Notice that Maslow's deficiency needs (all levels below self-actualization) correspond closely with needs that play central roles in psychodynamic theories. Freud's theory centers on needs at Maslow's lowest level (assuming that sex and aggression are physiological needs, which is where Freud would have put them); Horney's theory of basic anxiety centers on Maslow's second and third levels (needs for safety and love); and Adler's theory of overcoming inferiority centers on Maslow's fourth level (esteem needs). Thus, Maslow's theory incorporates the needs of these previous theories and then adds to them the self-actualizing needs.

Also worth noting is that Maslow's view of the prerequisites for creativity is different (almost opposite) from Freud's. According to Freud, people create because they *can't* satisfy a more basic need (usually the sexual need), and therefore they direct the energy from that need through sublimation into art, poetry, or whatever is their chosen means of expression. According to Maslow, on the other hand, people can be truly creative only if they have satisfied their more basic needs enough to be relatively free of them. Maslow's idea runs counter to the concept of the starving artist, the idea that great art is based on suffering. It also seems contradictory to Fisher and Fisher's evidence, described earlier, that comedians and clowns (who are undeniably creative) have an unusually high need to protect themselves from evil—a need that would presumably be placed at Maslow's level 2.

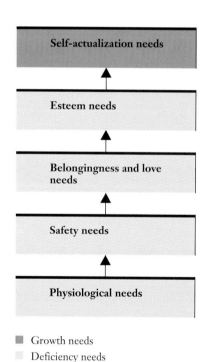

■ Growth needs
■ Deficiency needs

**Figure 16.5** *Maslow's hierarchy of human needs*

*According to Maslow, needs at the lower portion of the hierarchy must be at least relatively satisfied before people can satisfy needs higher up. The most psychologically healthy people are those whose deficiency needs are sufficiently satisfied that they can focus on self-actualization.*

*Abraham Maslow*
*A leader of the humanistic movement in psychology, Maslow has come to represent the group's views about human values and personal fulfillment.*

**How Maslow's hierarchy of needs combines the needs emphasized by psychodynamic theories and adds to them**

But Maslow qualifies his theory by adding that lower needs do not have to be fully satisfied—only *relatively* satisfied—to focus on higher needs; and that any one form of behavior might be motivated by more than one level of need at once. To a self-actualizing comedian, for example, humor might put food on the table (level 1), defend against threats (level 2), serve as a vehicle for bonding with other people (level 3), bring praise and self-esteem (level 4), and, at the same time, be an aesthetic form of self-expression that brings the humorist into contact with an elevated form of consciousness (level 5). Given its ability to accommodate to just about any relationship between lower needs and self-actualization, it is hard to see how Maslow's theory could be proven wrong; thus, it is not the kind of theory that can be tested scientifically. Still, many people find it useful as a general framework for thinking about human motives.

**How Maslow studied the characteristics of self-actualizers, and how his study can be criticized on scientific grounds**

**Characteristics of Self-Actualizing Individuals** One of Maslow's goals was to paint a picture of the healthy, self-actualizing human being. To do this he studied biographies and public documents about the lives of famous people such as Abraham Lincoln, Albert Einstein, Eleanor Roosevelt, and Albert Schweitzer, who seemed to have functioned at the highest level. Using interviews and informal observations he also studied friends and students whom he judged to be self-actualizing. From these studies, he drew up a list—shown in Table 16.1 (on page 584)—of the characteristics that all such people seemed to have in common.

*A peak experience*
*As they ecstatically celebrate their triumph over the Lobuche Peak in Nepal, these climbers exemplify the exploration, curiosity, and self-development that are basic to the human personality as seen by the humanists.*

**Table 16.1** *Maslow's list of characteristics of self-actualizing individuals*

According to Maslow, self-actualizers:

- perceive reality accurately;
- accept themselves, others, and nature;
- are spontaneous and unpretentious;
- are problem centered rather than self centered;
- value solitude;
- are self-directed;
- react with awe at the mysteries of life;
- have peak experiences accompanied by a sense of union with the universe;

- identify with all of humanity;
- seek fewer friendships than do others, but take them more seriously;
- have democratic values;
- have a strong ethical sense;
- have a philosophical, unhostile sense of humor;
- are creative;
- resist enculturation.

*Source:* Adapted from *Motivation and personality* by A. H. Maslow, 1970, New York: Farrar, Straus & Giroux.

Maslow's method in producing this list was not very scientific. Since himself was the judge both of whom to include in the study and of their characteristics, it can be argued that he simply chose as subjects people who had certain characteristics of which he approved, and then studied those people and found that they indeed *did* have those characteristics—a circular process. Maslow (1970) argued that his method was not circular. He claimed that his criterion for choosing subjects was their proven ability to make full use of their talents and potentials, and that he was surprised to discover that they were also similar in so many other ways. But a more objective, systematic validation of Maslow's list is still wanting. At present it can be read as an inspiring statement of Maslow's personal values or as a set of hypotheses for possible future study, not as scientific evidence for a core set of characteristics of the most psychologically healthy people.

### Critique of Humanistic Theories

Humanistic psychology, like Freud's theory before it, has had a strong effect on the culture at large. It is associated with what has come to be called the *human-potential movement*, which refers to the entire collection of ways—including group encounters, meditation, and physical exercises—in which people consciously attempt to actualize their potentials. It has affected thinking about parenting and has helped inspire experiments in education, and it has also provided the basis for effective means of psychotherapy (discussed in Chapter 18). The main criticisms of humanistic psychology can be summarized as follows:

■ *Three common criticisms of humanistic theories*

*Concepts difficult to test scientifically* Like clinically based theories in general, scientific support for humanistic theories is relatively weak. How can researchers test a concept such as self-actualization unless it is defined in such a way as to be objectively identifiable? Also, it is especially hard to know how to generate valid data for a theory that emphasizes phenomenology. How can anyone know for sure when people's statements about themselves represent what they really think about themselves? People may actually have a wide variety of self-concepts (as discussed in Chapter 14), each pertaining to a different social role or setting. The self-concept expressed in therapy may not be the same as the one expressed in other situations, and it may be strongly influenced by the client's perception of what the therapist expects to hear.

*Paucity of explanatory power* To say that higher human actions are motivated by an actualizing tendency is to say little unless one can spell out the conditions under which the tendency arises. Maslow's idea that lower needs must be partly met doesn't help much, for the reasons that I already discussed. Rogers's ideas about the conditions of child rearing conducive to self-actualization are more testable, and have generated some research that tends to support his view, but more is needed.

- *Overly romantic view of human nature* Humanistic theorists often seem to assume that everything good about a person stems from within the person, and that everything bad stems from external social forces (such as conditions of worth) that act on the person. This is the opposite of Freud's view that the instincts of the id tend to lead us to behave in unacceptable ways and that morality (the superego) is imposed by society. The truth probably lies somewhere in between. Evolutionary theory and observations of people everywhere suggest that selfishness is as much a part of human nature as is cooperativeness, and that society must operate to restrain people's selfishness and facilitate their cooperativeness.

## Social Learning Theories

*Social learning theories* of personality (also called *cognitive-social theories* or even *cognitive social learning theories*) stem from the long tradition in psychology of laboratory research on learning, cognition, and social influence—the types of research described in previous chapters of this text. Social learning theories' emphasis on the role of social experiences links them to the ego-social tradition in post-Freudian psychodynamic theories; and their emphasis on the importance of conscious, learned beliefs links them to the phenomenological aspect of humanistic theories.

If there is a principal founder of the social learning approach to personality, it is Julian Rotter (1916–    ). While still in high school, Rotter became fascinated by the writings of Alfred Adler, especially Adler's idea that people's beliefs about their own abilities contribute to their actual efforts and achievements (Rotter, 1982). He went on to earn a Ph.D. in clinical psychology; enjoyed a long career conducting basic research on learning, cognition, and the relationship of these to personality; and wrote the first book on the social learning approach to personality (entitled *Social Learning and Clinical Psychology*, 1954). Two other important pioneers of this approach are Albert Bandura (1925–    ) and Walter Mischel (1930–    ), who also earned doctoral degrees in clinical psychology and went on to do university-based research. The careers of these three men are intertwined: Rotter was one of Mischel's main advisors in graduate school, and for a long time Mischel and Bandura worked together at Stanford University.

### Basic Tenets of Social Learning Theories

**■ How social learning theories are characterized by their emphasis on objective behavioral data, social learning, cognitive constructs, and the situational specificity of traits**

The identifying characteristics of the social learning approach to personality can be summarized as follows (based on Rotter, 1954, and Bandura, 1977, 1986):

1. *Importance of objective behavioral data* Social learning theorists do not trust the intuitive judgments of the clinically based psychodynamic and humanistic approaches. They also tend to distrust the questionnaire data of the psychometrically based trait approaches (to be described in the next section), unless the questionnaires have been well validated through direct behavioral observation. They argue that a useful personality theory must predict people's actual behavior, objectively measured, not just what people *say* about themselves in the clinician's office or on questionnaires.

**Color my world**

*The social learning perspective points up the importance of mainstream activities and attachments in preventing personality deterioration in the elderly.*

2. *Learning in the social environment* As implied by the label *social learning*, this approach centers on the assumption that personality characteristics are learned, and that such learning comes from interacting with the social environment. Because each person must adapt to a different set of social conditions, each person acquires a different set of characteristic ways of behaving that make up his or her personality. Social rewards—such as praise or acceptance—are emphasized as the reinforcers of such learning. The importance of learning by observing others is also stressed. As discussed in Chapter 5, Bandura was a pioneer in the study of observational learning, or modeling.

3. *Cognitive constructs as personality variables* Unlike the early behaviorists, who viewed learning as the forming of specific stimulus-response connections, social learning theorists see learning as the forming of mental representations of objects, events, and relationships (see Chapter 5). From this perspective, people approach life like scientists (though less systematically). They actively seek out information about their world, construct hypotheses based on that information, and use the hypotheses to guide their actions. These hypotheses, or cognitive constructs, include *goals and values* (beliefs about appropriate purposes or ends of behavior), *expectancies* (beliefs about what will happen if one acts in a certain way), and *cognitive categories* (mental constructs for categorizing people, objects, and actions, which provide a basis for generalizing from one situation to another).

   From this perspective, personality can be defined as the entire set of one's cognitive constructs. Because everyone has a unique set of these, everyone has a unique personality; and because people continue to learn throughout life, modifying their constructs, personality is never completely fixed. Bandura (1986) has referred to the ongoing interaction between internal (especially cognitive) and external (environmental) variables as *reciprocal determinism*. The person acts on the environment, and the environment on the person, in a continuous, lifelong process.

4. *Situational specificity of personality variables* Learning always occurs within an environmental context (referred to here as the situation). Therefore, learned cognitive constructs, which provide the basis for personality, are more or less tied to situations. For example, if you learned to be aggressive on the athletic field, this learning may not generalize to other situations. Thus, from the social learning perspective, people cannot be described adequately in terms of global traits applicable to all situations, but can be described more adequately in terms that include both the trait and the context in which it is manifested. Thus, one person might be aggressive on the athletic field but timid in the classroom; outgoing on the stage but socially withdrawn at parties; or scrupulously honest with neighbors but dishonest on income taxes.

### Two Cognitive Constructs: Locus of Control and Self-efficacy

To provide a more concrete sense of the social learning approach, let us look at two cognitive constructs that have been studied extensively by social learning theorists—locus of control and self-efficacy.

**Rotter's Concept of Locus of Control**   Rotter (1954) argued that people consciously direct their behavior toward goals in the environment, and that people's choices of goals and approaches toward achieving them depend on their beliefs about those goals. Some beliefs have to do with the value of each goal. Due to their different social learning experiences, people assign different priorities to goals. For example, one person may place a high value on grades in school, whereas another may rank grades as relatively less important. Other things being equal, the former will work harder for school grades than the latter. A second set of beliefs, more relevant to the present discussion, are those concerning the relationship between actions and goals, which Rotter referred to as *expectancies.*

People differ in the degree to which they expect that the receipt of goals will be determined by their own efforts or by factors outside of their control. A person who believes that grades in school are determined primarily by luck, or by the whim of the instructor, will not work hard for high grades even if he or she strongly desires them. In a series of laboratory experiments, Rotter and his colleagues (1961) found that people made use of cues as to whether rewards in various laboratory tasks or games were based on skill or on chance in their determination of whether or not to work hard at the task.

Consistent with the emphasis of social learning theories on the situation, Rotter (1966) argued that expectancies about the control of rewards are often situation specific. That is, people learn that in some situations they can control what rewards they receive and in other situations they cannot. But in many situations the degree to which rewards depend on a person's own efforts is not obvious. Rotter suggested that in these situations people behave according to a generalized disposition (a personality trait), acquired from their past experiences, to believe that rewards are or are not usually controllable by their own efforts. He referred to this disposition as **locus of control**, and developed a questionnaire designed to measure it.

Table 16.2 shows some sample questions from Rotter's locus-of-control questionnaire. People whose answers reflect a belief that individuals control their own rewards (and, by extension, their own fate) are said to have an *internal* locus of control, and those whose answers reflect a belief that rewards (and fate) are controlled by factors outside the self are said to have an *external* locus of control.

Since its development, hundreds of studies have shown consistent, though usually not very high, correlations between scores on Rotter's locus-of-control scale and actual behavior in various situations. People who score toward the internal end of the scale are, on average, more likely than those who score toward the external end to try to control their own fate. They are more likely to take preventive health care measures (see Phares, 1978); more likely to seek out information on how to protect themselves during a tornado warning (Sims & Baumann, 1972); more likely to resist group pressures to conform in laboratory tests of conformity (Crowne & Liverant, 1963); and more likely to prefer games of skill over games of chance (Schneider, 1972).

*How a sense of control or lack of control over rewards can be situation specific to some degree, but can also be due to a personality dimension that spans situations*

*How Rotter's questionnaire measures locus of control, and how research evidence has tended to validate the measure*

**Table 16.2  *Sample questions from Rotter's locus-of-control scale*** *

The task on each item is to decide which alternative (*a* or *b*) seems more true. The actual test consists of twenty-three items similar to those shown here.

Item: a. In the long run, people get the respect they deserve in this world.
b. Unfortunately, an individual's work often passes unrecognized, no matter how hard he or she tries.

Item: a. I have often found that what is going to happen will happen.
b. Trusting to fate has never turned out as well for me as making a decision to take a definite course of action.

Item: a. In the case of the well-prepared student, there is rarely if ever such a thing as an unfair test.
b. Many times exam questions tend to be so unrelated to course work that studying is really useless.

*For the items shown here, *internal* locus of control is indicated by choosing *a* for the first and third items and *b* for the second item.

*Source:* From "Generalized expectancies for internal versus external locus of control of reinforcement" by J. B. Rotter, 1966, *Psychological Monographs: General and Applied, 80* (Whole no. 609), p. 11.

**Where is the locus of control?**

*Based on what you have read, do you think these people are likely to score at the internal or external end of the locus-of-control scale?*

■ *How self-efficacy differs from locus of control, and evidence that self-efficacy is correlated with performance on various tasks*

■ *The cause-and-effect problem concerning self-efficacy, and evidence that self-efficacy does play a causal role*

Although you might expect that people who score in the external direction would have a relaxed, devil-may-care attitude toward life, research shows that in fact they generally feel more anxiety and stress than do those who score in the internal direction (Phares, 1978, 1984). This correlation can be interpreted in a number of possible ways. One possibility is that the feeling of inability to control one's own fate raises anxiety directly (it is scary to believe that what happens to you depends on luck), and the sense of control reduces anxiety. A second possibility is that people who have an internal sense of control work harder and thus are more successful in life, and success reduces anxiety. Still a third possibility is that both reduced anxiety and internal locus of control are a consequence of success in life; that is, success may both give people a sense of control and reduce their anxiety. In accordance with the principle of reciprocal determinism, all three of these interpretations could be correct.

**Bandura's Concept of Self-efficacy**    Much of Bandura's recent research centers on people's beliefs about their own ability to perform specific tasks, which he refers to as *self-efficacy*. Thus, people who feel confident that they can perform a certain task are said to have high self-efficacy about the task, and people who feel that they cannot perform the task are said to have low self-efficacy about it. Self-efficacy is sometimes confused with locus of control, but Bandura (1982, 1986) considers the two concepts to be distinct. Whereas self-efficacy refers to the person's sense of his or her own ability to perform a task, locus of control refers to the person's sense of whether or not that ability will pay off. Although self-efficacy and an internal locus of control usually go together, they do not always. Thus, if you believe that you are very skilled at math, but you believe that the skill is worthless because it is unrecognized by your math professor or others in society, then you have high self-efficacy but an external locus of control in that area. Conversely, if you believe that skill at math would bring you great reward, but that you don't have that skill, then you have low self-efficacy and an internal locus of control in that area.

Bandura and his colleagues have shown in many experiments that methods aimed at improving subjects' performances on tasks are effective to the degree that they convince people that they *can* perform the task better—that is, to the degree that they raise self-efficacy. For example, in one study, various treatments were used to help people overcome their fear of snakes. The result was that those subjects who claimed after treatment that they now *expected* that they would be able to pick up and handle a large snake were indeed most likely to succeed at the task (Bandura & others, 1977). Similar results have been found for such diverse tasks as arithmetic problems (Schunk & Hanson, 1985) and physical exertion on an exercise machine (Bandura & Cervone, 1983).

An implication of Bandura's theory is that educational and child-rearing methods that highlight the person's abilities or successes will lead to greater success than methods that highlight inabilities or failures. But this implication is based on the assumption that self-efficacy helps *cause* improved performance and is not simply a by-product of it. Bandura believes this assumption to be true, but others have pointed out that most of the experiments purporting to show causal effects of self-efficacy can be interpreted in alternative ways (Brody, 1988). For example, in the snake-handling study, treatment may have resulted primarily in decreased fear of snakes, which in turn may have had two separate consequences: (1) increased real ability to handle them, and (2) increased confidence in ability to handle them. By that analysis, the increased ability was not caused by the increased self-efficacy; instead, both were caused by the decreased fear. (To carry this analysis one awful step further, perhaps "The Little Engine That Could"—in that classic children's story about self-efficacy—made it up the mountain *not* because it kept saying, "I think I can, I think I can," but rather because it was strong enough and had enough fuel; and perhaps it said, "I think I can" because it could tell that it was strong enough and had enough fuel. Self-efficacy may predict behavior accurately without helping to cause it.)

On the other hand, some experiments do provide evidence that self-efficacy can play a causal role. Perhaps the most compelling are those in which subjects who have been led to believe that they can solve problems that are actually unsolvable (and therefore have developed high self-efficacy concerning them) persist longer at trying to solve them than do subjects who have not been deceived in this way (Bandura, 1982; Schunk, 1984). Such studies provide a plausible chain through which self-efficacy may affect success on solvable problems: High self-efficacy → increased effort or persistence → success. (The Little Engine That Could succeeded because it tried harder than the other engines. The moral is safe for yet another generation!)

### Critique of Social Learning Theories

The social learning perspective has been extraordinarily valuable for its emphasis on the situational specificity of personality characteristics, for its emphasis on the role of conscious beliefs in people's behavior, and for its use of experimental methods to test hypotheses about personality. The objective recording of behavior under controlled conditions in laboratory research produces data that are less contaminated by the theorist's biases than are the clinically based data of other approaches. But the laboratory also restricts the kinds of issues that social learning theorists address. The two most common criticisms of the social learning approach are both linked to limitations of the laboratory method:

*Lack of holism* Some psychologists argue that social learning theories are not really personality theories, but rather are theories of specific learning and cognitive processes. A theory of self-efficacy or of locus of control may be very useful, but it is not the same thing as a theory of the person. The laboratory may not be a good place to develop a picture of the whole person. The essence of laboratory research is to focus on one variable (or a small number of variables) at a time—that is, on pieces of the person—and to control for or balance out all other variables (including other pieces of the person). Clinically based theorists argue that you can't build a picture of a person by putting together the pieces discovered in the laboratory; you have to start with the person as a whole, and the only way to do that is by getting to know individual people very well, which can be done best through the hours of dialogue that occur in a clinical setting.

*Overemphasis on cognition, and underemphasis on drives and emotions* In focusing on cognitive constructs or beliefs, the social learning approach tends to ignore drives and emotions as personality variables. This limitation, too, may stem at least partly from the laboratory method. Drives and emotions may be unconscious (not verbally stateable by subjects) and not easily detected in short-term laboratory experiments. Also, the laboratory itself tends to produce a certain uniformity of drive and emotion. People do not approach the laboratory as a place to enjoy a sexual adventure, or to blow off steam—rather, they approach it with the idea that they are volunteering for psychological research and that their job is to do as well as possible whatever task the researcher asks them to do.

Thus, differences that occur among subjects in the laboratory are unlikely to be due to differences in drives and emotions, and are most likely to be due to differences in their skill at the task, or their beliefs about their skill (self-efficacy), or their beliefs about the way in which rewards are controlled in the task (locus of control)—the very factors that social learning theorists emphasize. But real life is not simply a matter of performing tasks that are put before

*How two limitations of the social learning approach to personality may stem from its basis in laboratory research*

us. We choose our tasks and create our problems in the context of a rich web of drives, emotions, and environmental stimuli that are reduced or controlled in the laboratory. Clinicians who spend long periods talking with people about their lives and problems are less likely than laboratory researchers to ignore such issues.

## Trait Theories and Psychometric Research

Each of the personality theories described so far includes ways of describing differences among people. Thus Freud differentiated people according to how they channel sexual energy (such as in oral fixation or anal retentiveness); Horney according to their ways of dealing with the inborn sense of insecurity; Maslow according to their position on a hierarchy of needs that they are trying to fulfill (with self-actualizers at the top); and Rotter according to their beliefs about the link between behavior and rewards (locus of control). In each of the theories discussed so far, the way of describing individual differences is secondary to the theory's explanation of behavior in general. Each of those theories can be described first and foremost as a theory of human motives or goals, with individual differences accounted for within the context of the motives or goals emphasized by the theory (sex for Freud, security for Horney, self-actualization for Maslow, and rewards for task completion for Rotter). Trait theories, by contrast, take the description of individual differences as their main purpose.

A ***trait theory*** can be defined as a formal system for describing and measuring the ways in which personalities differ. Whereas the theories discussed up until now were developed through either the clinical or laboratory method, trait theories are developed principally through the psychometric method. Psychometrics (introduced in relation to intelligence testing in Chapter 11) refers to the systematic attempt to measure psychological characteristics, usually with written questionnaires or tests. Whereas other theorists derive their explanations of individual differences from their ideas about motivation, trait theorists take the study of individual differences as their primary task. They attempt to discover the most basic dimensions along which people differ, using quantitative methods that (at least in principle) are unbiased by prior theoretical considerations.

### Basics of the Trait Approach

As background to the discussion of specific theories to follow, let us here consider the meaning of *trait* (a concept used implicitly thus far in the chapter) and discuss the general approach of trait theorists to studying traits.

**The Trait Concept**    A ***trait*** can be defined as a relatively stable predisposition to behave in a certain way. It is considered to be part of the person, not part of the environment. People carry their traits with them from one environment to another, though the actual manifestation of a trait in the form of behavior depends on an interaction between the trait and the environment. For example, aggressiveness as a trait might be defined as one's inner predisposition to fight (for simplicity, I am defining aggressiveness narrowly here). That predisposition is presumed to stay with the person as he or she goes from one environment to another, although the actual behavior of fighting depends upon an interaction between that predisposition and provocations that exist in the environment. Aggressiveness in a person is analogous to "meltability" in margarine: Margarine melts only when subjected to heat, but some brands take less heat to melt than do others, and that difference lies in the margarine, not the environment.

***How trait theories differ from other personality theories in their approach to identifying individual differences***

■ *How traits differ from states*

It is useful also to distinguish the term *trait* from *state*. Chapter 7 is about states (of motivation and emotion), which, like traits, are defined as inner entities that can be inferred from overt behavior. The conceptual difference between a trait and a state has to do with the relative permanence of the former and the changeable nature of the latter. A trait is the enduring quality that influences the likelihood of entering temporarily a particular state. Thus, the trait of aggressiveness might influence the likelihood that a person will enter the state of anger. In the margarine analogy, the trait of meltability influences the likelihood that the margarine will enter the state of being melted.

Another important point about traits is that they are not characteristics that people have or lack in all-or-none fashion, but rather are dimensions along which people differ in degree. If we had a means of measuring aggressiveness in a large number of people, our results might approximate the kind of curve referred to as a normal distribution (illustrated in Figure 3.12), in which the majority of people are near the middle of the range and relatively few are at the extremes.

■ *How surface traits are inferred from behavior, and how source traits are inferred from surface traits*

**Surface Traits and Source Traits**   Traits cannot be observed directly, but must be inferred from observable behaviors, including responses that people make to items on psychological tests or questionnaires. One way to depict the relationship between behaviors and traits is shown in Figure 16.6. Notice that the depiction is hierarchical. At the bottom are specific, observable behaviors. At the next level up are *surface traits*, each of which is linked directly to a different class of observable behaviors. For instance, a person who argues a lot might be said to have the surface trait of high argumentativeness. At the highest level, linking more than one surface trait, are *source traits*, the most basic personality dimensions, which are taken to be the source of the more observable surface traits. To identify a source trait, one must first identify a number of surface traits that seem to go together. For instance, if the highly argumentative person also gets into a lot of physical fights, a source trait of aggressiveness might underlie the two kinds of behaviors. In contrast, if the argumentative person is one who also reads a lot, asks lots of questions, and rarely gets into physical fights, we might conclude that the source trait is not aggressiveness but intellectuality, with argument being the person's way of testing ideas.

The goal of most trait theorists, as you will see below, is to identify a single set of trait dimensions that can be used to describe all people. To achieve this goal, trait theorists use statistical means to identify source traits that account for the greatest variation among people, and develop ways to measure those traits through written questionnaires.

**Figure 16.6** *Hierarchical relationship among behaviors, surface traits, and a source trait*

In trait theories, surface traits are inferred from people's behaviors and source traits are inferred by identifying surface traits that correlate with one another. (Adapted from Eysenck, 1982.)

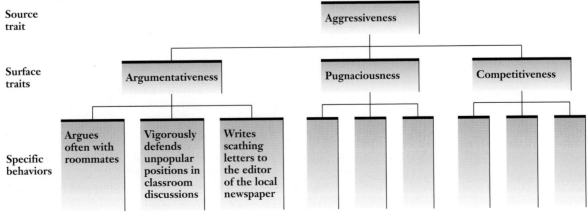

*How Cattell used ratings on many different surface traits to identify a set of sixteen source traits*

**Table 16.3** *Cattell's sixteen source traits or personality factors\**

| |
|---|
| A. Sociable–unsociable |
| B. Intelligent–unintelligent |
| C. Emotionally stable–unstable |
| E. Dominant–submissive |
| F. Cheerful–brooding |
| G. Conscientious–undependable |
| H. Bold–timid |
| I. Sensitive–insensitive |
| L. Suspicious–trusting |
| M. Imaginative–practical |
| N. Shrewd–naive |
| O. Guilt proclivity–guilt rejection |
| $Q_1$. Radicalism–conservatism |
| $Q_2$. Self-sufficiency–group adherence |
| $Q_3$. Self-disciplined–uncontrolled will |
| $Q_4$. Tense–relaxed |

*\*In this table, descriptive terms have been substituted for the technical terms that Cattell himself coined for each trait. For each factor a high score on the 16 PF Questionnaire indicates tendency toward the left-hand term, and a low score indicates tendency toward the right-hand term.*

*Source: Adapted from Personality and mood by questionnaire (pp. 53–54) by R. B. Cattell, 1973, San Francisco: Jossey-Bass.*

## A Sampling of Trait Theories

Fundamentally, a trait theory is simply a statement of the source traits that account for the greatest statistically measured variation among people. Different theories differ in the number of source traits they identify and the description of those traits. Here are three examples:

**Cattell's Sixteen-Dimensional Theory**   Raymond Cattell (1905–      ), a British-born psychologist who has spent most of his research career in the United States, is one of the pioneers of the attempt to describe personality in terms of measurable traits. His undergraduate degree was in chemistry, and his goal in psychology was to develop a sort of chemistry of personality. Just as an infinite number of different molecules can be described in terms of a finite number of atoms, Cattell wished to develop a system by which an infinite number of different personalities could be described in terms of a finite number of trait dimensions. To do this, he needed to discover the source traits that most efficiently describe the differences among people, and develop a way of measuring them.

How can a researcher discover source traits? Cattell prided himself in making no prior assumptions about what these might be—he wanted to find them through objective, statistical means. In essence, his approach was to collect massive amounts of data concerning as many surface traits as possible in a large sample of people, and then to use statistical means to determine which surface traits correlated most strongly with one another and were thus indicative of a common source trait. He began with data about the lives of the people he was studying, which he called *L-data* (life data). Ideally, L-data would have come from objective observations of people's actual behavior, but in practice the data consisted mostly of ratings of each person on a long list of surface traits, made by individuals who knew that person well. The result was, for each person, a score on each of many different surface traits, such as talkativeness, patience, jealousy, and so on. The list used for these ratings was produced by condensing the 18,000 or so adjectives describing personality that can be found in an unabridged dictionary down to about 170 that seemed logically to be different from one another.

Cattell then subjected the L-data to factor analysis (described in Chapter 11) to determine which surface traits were most strongly correlated with one another. His assumption was that if a set of surface traits are highly intercorrelated, then they must be influenced by the same source trait. By finding clusters of surface traits that correlated strongly with one another within the cluster, but not across clusters, Cattell identified a preliminary set of source traits and gave each a name. His next step was to develop and administer questionnaires, on which people responded to questions about their own characteristics. The data from these he called *Q-data* (questionnaire data). He then subjected the Q-data to factor analysis to see if they would generate the same set of factors that had been obtained from the L-data. If this occurred, he could assume that the questionnaire was measuring the same source traits as had been revealed in the L-data, and thus that the traits measured by the questionnaire were valid in the sense of being related to the person's ways of behaving in daily life.

The upshot of this research, which spanned many years and involved dozens of separate studies, was the identification of sixteen different source traits and the development of a questionnaire called the *16 PF Questionnaire* to measure them (Cattell, 1950, 1973). (*PF* stands for *personality factors*, which was Cattell's term for source traits.) The questionnaire consists of nearly 200 statements about specific aspects of behavior, such as "I like to go to parties." To each statement, the respondent must select one of three possible answers—yes, occasionally, or no. The sixteen source traits that the questionnaire is designed to measure are listed in Table 16.3. Today, the 16 PF Questionnaire is used both as a clinical tool for assessing personality characteristics of clients in psychotherapy and as a research tool in studies of personality. As an example of the latter, see Figure 16.7.

**Figure 16.7** *Personality profiles of scientists and clergy members*

*Shown here are the average ratings on each of the source traits, or factors, in Cattell's 16 PF Questionnaire for a group of well-known scientists and a group of clergy members. The sixteen trait dimensions, indicated along the horizontal axis, are as described in Table 16.3. By comparing the two curves, you can find differences between the average personalities of the two groups. For example, the researchers are lower in sociability (Factor A) and higher in radicalism (Factor $Q_1$) than are the clergy members. (Adapted from Cattell, 1965.)*

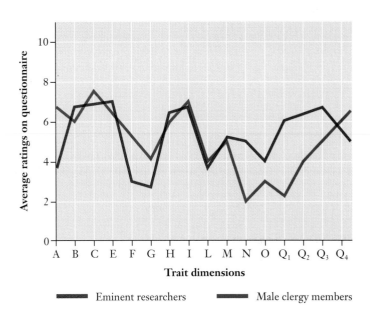

**Eysenck's Two-Dimensional Theory**   Hans Eysenck (1916–   ) is a German-born, British psychologist whose basic approach to developing a trait theory was quite similar to Cattell's. In his early studies, Eysenck (1952) gathered large amounts of data, including objective information about life histories and data from psychological tests, from men who were seen at a military hospital, and subjected the data to factor analysis. Eysenck used factor analysis somewhat differently than did Cattell, and his method resulted in a factor structure containing far fewer factors or source traits than Cattell's. In fact, his early studies revealed just two source-trait dimensions that seemed to account quite well for most of the consistent individual differences in the original data.

One dimension, which he labeled *introversion–extroversion* (using the terms that were initially coined by Jung), seemed to be related to a person's tendency to avoid or seek excitement in the external environment. The surface traits associated with introversion included the tendencies to seek quiet, to be introspective, and to be relatively nonsociable; and the opposite were associated with extroversion. The second dimension, which he labeled *neuroticism–stability*, seemed to be related to a person's propensity to become emotionally upset. The surface traits associated with neuroticism included moodiness, anxiety, suggestibility, and low willpower; and the opposite were associated with stability.

Eysenck developed a questionnaire, called the *Eysenck Personality Inventory*, to measure people's position on these source traits. With this system, people can be classified into four main groups, depending on their position on each of the two dimensions: introverted–neurotic, introverted–stable, extroverted–neurotic, and extroverted–stable. Figure 16.8 (on page 594) illustrates Eysenck's two-dimensional system for classifying people and notes some of the surface traits of those who fall in different parts of the grid. (In later work, Eysenck identified a third dimension, having to do with concern or lack of concern for others' needs, turning his two-dimensional theory into a three-dimensional one.)

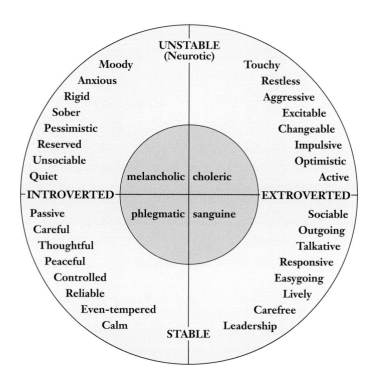

**Figure 16.8** *Eysenck's depiction of personality types*
*The four quadrants of this circle represent the four possible combinations of introversion–extroversion and neuroticism–stability in Eysenck's theory. Some of the surface traits associated with each of these combinations are listed in the outer ring. The terms in the inner circle refer to an ancient Greek typology that divided people into four types that are similar to Eysenck's types: melancholic (moody and withdrawn), choleric (irritable and outgoing), sanguine (stable and outgoing), and phlegmatic (stable and withdrawn). (Adapted from Eysenck, 1982.)*

■ *How Eysenck explains the difference between introverts and extroverts in terms of a basic property of the nervous system, and how research has supported his explanation*

Eysenck believes that differences among people in the basic traits depicted by this theory are determined by inherited physiological characteristics of the nervous system (Eysenck & Eysenck, 1985). For example, he believes that differences in introversion–extroversion stem from differences in the arousability of the central nervous system from sensory input. Eysenck proposed that everyone seeks a moderate degree of arousal, which is optimal for psychological functioning. He proposed further that introverts have easily aroused central nervous systems, so they avoid excess stimulation to prevent arousal from exceeding the optimal level, and that extroverts have nervous systems that are not easily aroused, so they seek excess stimulation to reach the optimal level (see Figure 16.9). Put differently, an extrovert might need a roller-coaster ride or a rock concert to achieve the same arousal that an introvert can get from a bicycle ride or a sonata.

Supporting this theory is evidence that introverts (as identified by Eysenck's personality inventory) do react more strongly than do extroverts to various stimuli. They (a) show greater disruption in performance on a learning task when loud noise is present (Geen, 1984); (b) manifest a greater skin-conductance response (a sign of arousal) to a sudden noise (Smith & others, 1984); (c) salivate more profusely when lemon juice is squirted into their mouth (Eysenck & Eysenck, 1967); and (d) are less tolerant of painful electric shock (Bartol & Costello, 1976).

**Figure 16.9.** *Illustration of Eysenck's theory of the physiological basis for introversion and extroversion*
*Eysenck postulates that all people seek approximately the same level of nervous system arousal (shown here by the gray band). He further postulates that introverts have nervous systems that are more easily aroused by environmental stimulation than do extroverts (shown here by the more sharply rising line for introverts compared to extroverts). The result (shown by the vertical dashed lines) is that introverts seek a lower level of environmental stimulation than do extroverts.*

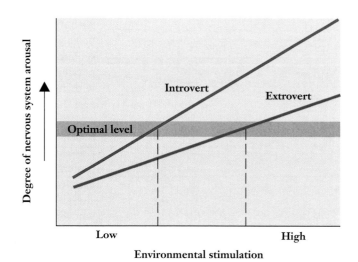

**The Big Five Theory**   Many trait researchers today find that Cattell's theory, with sixteen different dimensions, is too complex and contains redundant factors, and that Eysenck's theory is too simple, failing to capture important differences among personalities. In recent years, a large number of factor-analytic studies have been conducted using more sophisticated versions of the methods pioneered by Cattell and Eysenck, and the results have been described by researchers in this area as remarkably consistent. To quote one pair of researchers (Digman & Inouye, 1986): "A series of research studies of personality traits has led to a finding consistent enough to approach the status of a law. The finding is this: If a large number of rating scales is used and if the scope of the scales is very broad [that is, if they cover a large number of behaviors or surface traits] the domain of personality descriptors is almost completely accounted for by five robust factors."

The five factors, often referred to by trait researchers as the *Big Five*, have turned up repeatedly in studies conducted in various countries, in several different languages, and with children as well as adults; they are described in Table 16.4 (based on Digman & Inouye, 1986; McCrae & Costa, 1985, 1987). Notice that two of the dimensions are the same as Eysenck's original two (*extroversion* and *neuroticism*). The other three are *agreeableness, conscientiousness*, and *openness to experiences*. The contention of several groups of trait researchers today is that if you want to choose a convenient number of trait terms that will most efficiently summarize the measurable personality differences among people, these are the terms to choose. Nearly all of the hundreds of different adjectives commonly used to describe personalities correlate quite strongly, in factor-analytic studies, with one of these five dimensions.

**Table 16.4**   *The "Big Five" personality factors\**

> *Extroversion–introversion:* Sociable–retiring; fun loving–sober; talkative–quiet; spontaneous–inhibited.
>
> *Neuroticism–placidity:* Worrying–calm; vulnerable–hardy; self-pitying–self-satisfied; impatient–patient.
>
> *Agreeableness–antagonism:* Courteous–rude; selfless–selfish; trusting–suspicious; flexible–stubborn.
>
> *Conscientiousness–undirectedness:* Careful–careless; reliable–undependable; fair–unfair; ambitious–aimless.
>
> *Openness–nonopenness:* Imaginative–unimaginative; independent–conforming; curious–uncurious; daring–unadventurous.

\*Under each source trait are listed some of the surface traits whose intercorrelation provided the basis for inferring that source trait.

*Source:* Adapted from "Updating Norman's 'adequate taxonomy': Intelligence and personality dimensions in natural language and in questionnaires" by R. R. McCrae & P. T. Costa, 1985, *Journal of Personality and Social Psychology, 49*, p. 85.

## *Questions About the Consistency of Traits Across Situations, Time, and Generations*

You now have a general understanding of the ways in which trait theorists identify and measure personality traits. Now let us turn to some fundamental questions about traits: Are they consistent in a given person from situation to situation? Are they consistent over time? Are they passed on genetically from one generation to the next?

**Are Traits Consistent Across Situations? The Challenge from Social Learning Theory**    A basic premise of trait theory is that traits are inner characteristics of the person, and are carried with the person from one environmental context (situation) to another. The strongest challenge to this premise has come from social learning theorists, especially Walter Mischel (1968, 1984). Recall that a basic position of social learning theory is that people learn to behave in particular ways in particular situations, so the same person's behavioral style may vary greatly from one setting to another. Mischel has argued forcefully that trait theorists make the same error that people in general make when they try to explain other people's behavior. They overemphasize the role of personality characteristics and underemphasize the role of environmental provocation—an error that is referred to by social psychologists as the *fundamental attribution error* (discussed in Chapter 14). Mischel argues that real evidence for cross-situational consistency of traits would have to come from observations of people's actual behavior in a variety of situations, not from questionnaires or clinical inferences.

*Are traits consistent across situations?*

*Do people usually show the same traits in different contexts of their lives, as this woman seems to? After 20 years of controversy, researchers still disagree. Some emphasize sameness across situations; others focus on differences due to situation.*

■ *How Mischel argued that traits are situation specific, and how trait theorists defended the idea that traits are properties of the person that cut across situations*

In his initial argument against the trait concept, Mischel (1968) referred to a classic study of morality conducted by Hugh Hartshorne and Mark May (1928), in which thousands of schoolchildren were provided with opportunities to be dishonest, in a wide variety of situations, under conditions in which they did not know that their dishonesty could be detected. The tests included such forms of dishonesty as lying to parents, falsifying school records, cheating on a test at school, and stealing money at a club meeting. Of greatest importance to Mischel's argument, Hartshorne and May found that correlations within any given situation were quite high, but correlations across situations were very low. That is, children who were dishonest in one situation (say, cheating on a test) were quite likely to be dishonest again in a similar situation (cheating on another test), but were not much more likely than average to be dishonest in a different situation (say, stealing money).

Later, Mischel and Philip Peake (1982) performed a similar study, though smaller in scope, in which they assessed repeatedly, by direct observation, nineteen different forms of behavior presumed to be related to a trait of conscientiousness in a group of students at Carleton College in Minnesota. Included were measures of regularity of class attendance, promptness in completing assignments, bed neatness, and neatness of class notes. Like Hartshorne and May, they found high consistency within any of these measures, but low consistency across different measures. From such evidence, Mischel argued that to describe people meaningfully you have to speak in terms that relate behavior to the situation—such as *honest on tests*, or *conscientious about keeping room clean*—not in such global terms as *honest* or *conscientious*, which would be at the level of source traits.

Trait theorists have not taken Mischel's arguments lying down. They have responded, among other ways, by re-examining data from the studies that Mischel referred to and arguing that even those studies can be interpreted as support for the trait concept. Regarding Hartshorne and May's study, to say that people differ with respect to the situations in which they are most likely to manifest dishonesty is not the same thing as saying that they do not differ in overall dishonesty. Hartshorne and May themselves noted that, despite the situational differences, large differences occurred among individual children in average dishonesty score when all situations were combined, much larger than could be accounted for by chance. Similarly, when two separate averages were calculated for each child—by dividing the different situations randomly into two sets—a high correlation was found between the two averages (Epstein, 1979). That is, children who were unusually likely to be dishonest in one combined set of situations were also unusually likely to be dishonest in the other.

Concerning Mischel and Peake's study, Douglas Jackson and Sampo Paunomen (1985) have argued that the study merely shows that conscientiousness—defined as Mischel and Peake defined it, to encompass such diverse activities as studing many hours and keeping one's bed neat—is not a meaningful source trait. (Conscientiousness is a source trait in the Big Five theory, but it is not defined as Mischel and Peake defined it.) These investigators reanalyzed Mischel and Peake's original data, using factor analysis, and found that the measures clustered into several groups, each of which might be construed as a separate trait. For example, different measures of *neatness* (bed neatness, desk neatness, and neatness of class notes) correlated highly with one another, as did different measures of *academic diligence* (class-assignment punctuality, time spent studying, percentage of studies completed, and study-session attendance). The lack of correlation between between neatness and academic diligence simply means that these are different traits and should not be lumped together.

Today, more than two decades after Mischel inaugurated the debate, the two sides seem to agree on the facts, but disagree—because of their different goals—about which facts are most important (see Epstein & O'Brien, 1985; Mischel, 1984; Shoda & others, 1989). Clearly, traits can be found that have a statistically significant degree of cross-situational generality, especially if generality is assessed by comparing one large set of situations with another large set. This fact is most important to trait theorists, whose goal is to develop convenient ways to describe overall differences among people—the types of differences that may not matter much on one specific action, but may matter considerably in the long and broad course of a person's whole life. It is also clear, however, that traits have a considerable degree of situational specificity, and this fact is most important to social learning theorists, whose goal is to understand how people will behave in specific situations.

**Are Traits Consistent Across Time? Evidence from Longitudinal Studies** If you ever have the opportunity to attend a twenty-fifth-anniversary reunion of your high-school class, don't miss it; it is a remarkable experience. Before you stands a person who claims to be your old friend Marty, whom you haven't seen for 25 years. The last time you saw Marty he was a skinny kid with lots of hair, wearing floppy sneakers and a sweatshirt. What you notice first are the differences: This

*How the trait-situation debate may boil down to a difference between the goals of different researchers*

Marty is not skinny, has very little hair, and isn't wearing sneakers. But it doesn't take long to break through that. Within about 10 minutes you have the almost eerie knowledge that you are talking with the same person you used to pitch pennies with behind the school. The voice is the same, the sparkle in the eyes, the quiet sense of humor, the way of walking. And when it is Marty's turn to stand up and speak to the reunion group, he, who always was the most nervous about speaking before the class, is still most reluctant to do so. There's no doubt about it—this Marty, who now has two kids older than he was when you last saw him, is the same Marty you always knew. They didn't send a substitute.

But that is all impression. Is he really the same? Perhaps Marty is in some sense *your* construction, and it is your construction that has not changed over the years. Maybe if they put an imposter there and called him Marty, and gave him some shared memories to talk about, you would still see him as the same old Marty. Or maybe it's just the situation. This, after all, is a high-school reunion, held in your old school gymnasium, which hasn't changed a bit, and maybe you've all been transported back in your minds and are coming across much more like your old selves than you normally would. Maybe you're all trying to be the same kids you were 25 years ago, if only so people will recognize you. Clearly, if we really want to answer the question of how consistent personality is over long periods, we've got to be a bit more scientific.

By now, a good many studies have been conducted in which people fill out personality questionnaires, or are rated by family or friends on a long list of characteristics, at widely separated times in their lives. In general, the results suggest a high degree of stability of central personality traits throughout adulthood. Among the most stable traits, interestingly, are those having to do with extroversion–introversion and neuroticism–placidity—the same two dimensions that Eysenck highlighted in his theory (Conley, 1984). In one such study, women were rated for numerous personality traits at age 30 by one set of observers and at age 70 by a different set, with the finding that the degree of extroversion and neuroticism was especially consistent over this 40-year period (Mussen & others, 1980).

In another study, a large number of men filled out a personality inventory at various times over a 30-year period, with the finding that the 30-year test-retest correlation was highest on the items that measured degree of extroversion—a whopping 0.74 (Leon & others, 1979). (Keep in mind that +1.00 is a perfect correlation and that test-retest reliability on most personality tests is well below perfect even when one test is taken immediately after the other.) In still another study, self-ratings, ratings by others, life-history information, and scores on personality questionnaires were collected from several hundred men and women at three widely separated times, when the subjects were about 24, 42, and 68 years old. All of these data were then factor analyzed in such a way as to identify source traits that were most consistent over time, and the three that emerged as most consistent were the degree of extroversion, neuroticism, and impulse control (Conley, 1985).

In sum, the evidence is strong that in certain basic ways of relating to the world you are going to be pretty much the same person 20 or 40 years from now as you are today. If you are outgoing and sociable now, you will probably be so then. If you prefer a quiet evening at home now, you will prefer it then. If you are emotionally excitable now, you will be emotionally excitable then. That, of course, does not mean that you will not change in many important ways, nor that you have no control over your future. But to a large extent those changes will have to do with ways in which you work with your basic traits, not with the traits themselves. One introvert is happy in middle age because his job, as a scientist, offers ample opportunity for solitude and reflection, and another is miserable because he persists at trying to succeed in politics.

*How research has shown that certain traits, especially the two identified by Eysenck, are remarkably stable over the course of adult life*

***Some families make spectacles of themselves***

*And some do not. This family of avid readers seems to represent the introversion end of Eysenck's introversion–extroversion personality trait dimension.*

■ *How the twin and adoption methods, described in Chapter 3, have been used to assess the heritability of intelligence traits*

**How Heritable Are Traits?**  Many trait theorists, including Cattell and Eysenck, have argued that differences among individuals in central personality traits are strongly influenced by genes. That contention has been supported by many studies, using the same basic methods as described in Chapter 3 in connection with studies of the heritability of intelligence. The most common approach has been to administer personality questionnaires, such as Cattell's 16 PF inventory or Eysenck's inventory, to pairs of genetically identical twins and fraternal twins (the latter are no more similar genetically than are ordinary siblings). The usual finding is that identical twins are much more similar than are fraternal twins on every personality dimension measured, enough so as to lead to an average heritability estimate of about 0.50 for most traits (meaning that about 50 percent of the variability among individuals is due to genetic differences and the remainder is due to a combination of environmental differences and measurement error) (Goldsmith, 1983; Rushton & others, 1986).

*Inherited jeans?*

*The similarity in costume is certainly not genetic, but trait theorists would argue that the similarity in personality is due to genes.*

Such findings have frequently been criticized on the grounds that parents and others may treat identical twins more similarly than they do fraternal twins, and similar treatment rather than genes may lead to their greater similarity in personality. To get around that possibility, researchers at the University of Minnesota, led by David Lykken, have given personality tests to twins who were separated in infancy and raised in different homes, as well as to twins raised in the same home (Tellegen & others, 1988). Their results are consistent with the previous studies: The identical twins were more similar to one another than were the fraternal twins on essentially every trait, regardless of whether they had been raised in the same or different homes, again leading to heritability scores averaging close to 0.50.

Lykken and his colleagues were surprised to find high heritability even for traits that at face value would seem to be heavily affected by learning. For example, the score on *traditionalism*—a measure of conservative values and respect for discipline and authority—was quite strongly affected by heredity. This must mean that people who are born with a certain set of genetic predispositions are more likely to pick up traditional values from their environment than are those born with a different set of predispositions.

Another finding from the Minnesota study that has surprised many psychologists is the remarkably little effect that being raised in the same home had on the personality measures. Twin pairs were about equally similar to one another on most traits whether or not they were raised in the same family. The Minnesota group concluded that the environmental differences that contribute to people's differing personalities must be nearly as great for people who live in the same family as for those who live in different families. Sandra Scarr and her colleagues (1981) earlier came to a similar conclusion through a different route. They compared nontwin, adopted children with both their biological and adoptive siblings, and found much greater personality similarities to the former than the latter. In fact, for most personality measures, they found that children were no more similar to their adoptive siblings than any two randomly compared children were to each other.

We must be cautious in interpreting the results of heritability studies involving adopted children (twin or nontwin), such as those just described (see Chapter 3). Adoption agencies require certain standards of adoptive families, so the range of environmental differences among adoptive homes does not represent the full range of differences that can exist from one home to another in the population at large. When specific comparisons are made between people from very different homes (such as homes with alcoholic versus nonalcoholic parents), or from entirely different cultures, the extent of environmental contribution to personality differences is much greater than in the studies discussed here.

### Critique of Trait Theories

Trait theories, and the psychometric approach associated with them, are explicit attempts to bring statistical methods to the study of personality. As you have seen, repeated studies have produced similar results regarding such issues as the identification of a common set of source traits (the Big Five), consistency of traits over the life span, and genetic heritability of traits. Yet, this approach is not without its critics. Some of the main criticisms are as follows:

■ *The problem of measurement validity*  Although trait theorists pride themselves on their statistical procedures, their data come almost exclusively from questionnaires. A common criticism of this approach is that people's descriptions of themselves or others on questionnaires may not reflect actual behavior. People may not be very good judges of their own or their friends' behaviors. Correlations among different questionnaire items, which provide the basis for factor analysis, may stem from the respondents' learned, and perhaps mistaken, views about what behaviors go together—that is, from their learned stereotypes about personality rather than from accurate self-observations (Shweder, 1982). Although some studies have shown significant correlations between trait scores and objectively measured behaviors—as you saw in the case of correlations between introversion–extroversion scores and responses to various stimuli—more such studies are needed, with other trait scores, to see if they truly measure the behavioral tendencies they are supposed to measure.

■ *Traits and trait structures as oversimplifications*  Human beings may be too complex to sum up meaningfully through scores on two, five, or even sixteen trait dimensions. Trait theories are based implicitly on the assumption that a finite set of source traits exists, each of which controls a different set of observable behavioral characteristics, and this assumption may be false. Moreover, by averaging the responses to many different questionnaire items to produce each trait score, trait theorists may ignore important differences in the meaning that any given score may have for different people. For example, two people who both score moderately high on introversion may do so for quite different reasons—one, perhaps, hates to give public lectures but enjoys parties, and the

■ *How trait theories have been criticized on the grounds of measurement validity, oversimplification, and their tendency to overemphasize biological determinants*

opposite may be true for another. This is the main point that Mischel and other social learning theorists make in their argument that the proper unit of personality is not the trait (something solely within the person) but the trait-situation interaction.

*Overemphasis on biological determinants* The very concept of traits, as internal constructs, tends to promote the assumption that they are biologically determined. Both Cattell and Eysenck assumed that trait differences are due largely to genetic differences among people. As you have seen, trait scores on psychometric tests are to a considerable extent influenced by heredity. But the degree of that influence may be partly an artifact of the way that traits are measured. Any given trait score is based on answers to a large number of questions, which cut across a large set of environmental situations. Important learned differences among people may have to do with the environmental contexts in which they display such tendencies, but trait scores, by cutting across contexts, are insensitive to those differences. Thus, personality tests may measure those aspects of personality that are most susceptible to genetic influence, ignoring those that are most susceptible to environmental influence, thereby exaggerating the degree to which personality as a whole is genetically determined. At least one careful study showed far less heritability of personality traits, and much greater influence of the family, when traits were measured by objective behavioral observations, in specific contexts, rather than through questionnaires (Plomin & Foch, 1980).

**Table 16.5** *Summary of some personality theories*

| Theory | Motivation | Mental structure | Individual differences | Developmental source of individual differences |
|---|---|---|---|---|
| Freud's psychodynamic theory | Instinctive drives (especially sex and aggression) | Id (instincts), ego (realistic logic), and superego (morality) | Different ways of channeling the energy of instinctive drives | Interaction between inborn drives and responses of society (especially parents) in early childhood |
| Adler's psychodynamic theory | Socially acquired drives (especially that for personal achievement) | Beliefs about one's own abilities (organized by the ego) | Differences in feeling of inferiority or superiority | Interaction between the child's achievement attempts and the responses of society (especially parents) |
| Rogers's humanistic theory | Self-actualization (self-expression) | The self-concept (beliefs about the self) | Different conditions of worth associated with the self-concept | Value judgments made by parents and other authority figures |
| Rotter's social learning theory | To obtain rewards by completing tasks | Beliefs about the value of rewards and their dependence on behaviors | Different beliefs about one's ability to control rewards (locus of control) | Learning, based on rewards provided by the social environment, throughout life |
| Eysenck's trait theory | To find environments and tasks consistent with one's traits | Traits (hypothetical inner constructs inferred from observed behaviors) | People differ in degree on basic traits, such as introversion versus extroversion | Basic traits are inherited, but people learn ways of coping that are suitable to their traits and environments |

# Concluding Thoughts

One way to review this chapter would be to expand (either mentally or on paper) the chart presented in Table 16.5. For each personality theory (or class of theory) described in the chapter, you might elaborate on (a) the drives, or motives, that it emphasizes; (b) the mental constructs that it identifies; (c) the kinds of differences among individuals that it focuses on; and (d) its explanation of the developmental origins of such differences. In addition, another way to review the chapter would be to think about each theory or class of theory in relation to the following two questions:

**1. What is the purpose of each personality theory?** Each personality theory can be viewed as an effort by the theorist to solve a particular kind of intellectual or practical problem, and the differences among the theories make sense in that light. Freud was a pioneer in the field of psychotherapy. In his private practice, he spent many hours with patients whose suffering did not stem from organic disease, poverty, or other externally observable causes, but instead seemed to stem from irrational forces in their minds. Freud's main purpose was to try to understand those forces. His theory, with its emphasis on instinctive drives and unconscious ways of directing them, makes most sense in relation to that purpose. Clinically based theories following Freud's were designed in part to correct for what seemed to be the excessive weight that Freud attached to instinctive, unconscious drives, and to account for the problems in social relationships and self-esteem that many people seeking psychotherapy presented. Thus, post-Freudian psychodynamic theorists began to emphasize social drives, the self-concept, and conscious thought patterns, and humanistic theorists went even further in those emphases.

The social learning theories and trait theories are not as tightly tied to clinical issues as are the other theories. Social learning theorists are primarily laboratory-based psychologists who share with other laboratory psychologists the general goal of predicting how people will behave in particular situations. They recognize that individuals often behave differently from one another in any given situation, and their goal is to understand such differences in terms of people's previous experiences. Thus, their explanatory principles usually center on learning and on cognitions associated with learning (such as expectancies). Trait theorists, in contrast, are less interested in predicting specific behaviors and more interested in identifying fundamental differences among individuals that cut across situations and are relatively impervious to effects of learning. Thus, trait theories can be understood as attempts to identify the most stable and heritable ways in which people differ from one another.

**2. On what kind of evidence is each theory based?** Related to their differing goals, personality theories also differ in the kinds of evidence used to support them. Psychodynamic and humanistic theories are based principally on the theorist's intimate knowledge of clients in therapy, or on extensive case histories collected through interviews, biographies, or other means. Social learning theories are based primarily on laboratory research, conducted under objective conditions, usually with subjects the researcher does not know personally. Trait theories are based primarily on the statistical analysis of questionnaires, on which people have rated their own characteristics or have been rated by friends or family members who know them well. As you review the theories and the critiques of each, think about the ways in which each theory's source of evidence accounts for both its strengths and weaknesses.

## Further Reading

**Sigmund Freud** (1901; reprinted 1960). *The psychopathology of everyday life* (J. Strachey, Ed.; A. Tyson, Trans.). New York: Norton.
*This is one of Freud's most popular and fun-to-read books. It is full of anecdotes having to do with forgetting, slips of the tongue, and bungled actions. In each anecdote, Freud argues that an apparent mistake was really an expression of an unconscious wish.*

**C. William Tageson** (1982). *Humanistic psychology: A synthesis.* Homewood, IL: Dorsey.
*This is a very readable account of the major philosophical themes of humanistic psychology and their relationship to the more specific ideas developed by individual theorists.*

**Nancy Cantor & John F. Kihlstrom** (1987). *Personality and social intelligence.* Englewood Cliffs, NJ: Prentice Hall.
*These authors use recent research in the field of social cognition to develop a cognitive social learning theory of personality. The cornerstone of their theory is social intelligence, which they define as "the concepts, memories, and rules—in short, the knowledge—that individuals bring to bear in solving personal life tasks."*

**Hans J. Eysenck & Michael W. Eysenck** (1985). *Personality and individual differences: A natural science approach.* New York: Plenum.
*Hans Eysenck is one of the pioneers in the development of trait theories, and this book is an excellent place to learn about the overall goals and methods of trait theorists. The first half of the book is about the problem of describing personality (identifying traits), and the second half is about the problem of explaining personality (identifying the causes of traits).*

**Nathan Brody** (1988). *Personality: In search of individuality.* New York: Academic Press.
*This is another excellent book on trait theories. Brody shows how the trait approach has withstood the challenge from social learning theorists (concerning situational specificity of traits), and how the debate has been resolved in a way that legitimizes the study of traits as characteristics that cut across situations. The book also contains chapters on the genetic and physiological bases for traits.*

## Looking Ahead

All of the personality theories that you have read about in this chapter were developed at least partly as a way of understanding people's psychological problems. The remaining two chapters focus directly on such problems. Chapter 17 deals with the issues of defining, categorizing, and explaining mental disorders—issues that are similar to those met by trait theorists in defining, categorizing, and explaining traits in general. Chapter 18 deals with the treatment of mental disorders, and there you will see how various theories of personality that you have read about here relate directly to different approaches to psychotherapy.

# CHAPTER 17

Basic Issues and Problems

Anxiety Disorders

Somatoform and Dissociative
Disorders

Psychoactive Substance-Use
Disorders

Mood Disorders

Schizophrenia

# MENTAL DISORDERS

An important theme running through this book is that psychological processes are usually adaptive; that is, they usually promote survival and well-being. Drives and emotions motivate survival-enhancing actions; perceptions provide useful information to guide such actions; and thoughts produce effective plans for actions. But sometimes, for any of a variety of reasons, these processes break down: Drives become too strong, too weak, or misdirected; emotions become overwhelming; perceptions become inaccurate; thoughts become confused; and behavior becomes ineffective. All of us experience such disturbances occasionally to some degree, and accept them as a normal part of life. But sometimes these disturbances are so strong, prolonged, or recurrent that they seriously interfere with a person's ability to live a satisfying life. Then the person is said to have a ***mental disorder***.

This chapter has sections on each of six major classes of mental disorders—anxiety disorders, somatoform disorders, dissociative disorders, psychoactive substance-use disorders, mood disorders, and schizophrenic disorders. But before we address these, let's examine some of the basic issues and problems concerning the definition and identification of mental disorders.

## Basic Issues and Problems

### What Is a Mental Disorder?

*Mental disorder* is a fuzzy concept, impossible to define in a precise way. This should come as no surprise. Most concepts, if you think about them, are fuzzy. Try to define precisely, for example, such an everyday concept as a *chair*. Some things are clearly chairs, and others, like the rock you sometimes sit on in the park, are only "sort of" chairs. Every attempt to define *mental disorder* raises controversy. The most frequently used definition, developed by the American Psychiatric Association for its diagnostic manual, treats mental disorders as analogous to medical diseases, and borrows from medicine the terms *symptom* and *syndrome*. A ***symptom*** is any characteristic of a person's actions, thoughts, or feelings that could be a potential indicator of a mental disorder; and a ***syndrome*** is the entire pattern of symptoms manifested by a given individual. According to the American Psychiatric Association (1987), a syndrome may be taken as evidence of a mental disorder if, and only if, it satisfies the following criteria:

1. It must involve *distress* (painful feelings) and/or *impairment of functioning* (interference with ability to work, play, or get along with people); and it must be *clinically significant*, meaning that the distress or impairment must be serious enough to warrant professional treatment.

*How the concept of mental disorder is defined in the official diagnostic manual of the American Psychiatric Association*

**Mental distress or mental disorder?**

*Feelings of sadness, pessimism, and low self-esteem are evident here, but is the source of the distress the situation or something inside the person? This question is central to defining the concept* mental disorder.

■ *Why the determination of mental disorder always entails human judgment*

2. The source of distress or impairment must be located within the person, that is, in the person's biology, mental structure (ways of perceiving, thinking, or feeling), or learned habits, and not just in the person's immediate environment. The distress or impairment must not be simply a normal response to a specific event in the person's life, such as the death of a loved one. Although it may be triggered by such an event, it must go well beyond the usual reaction to such events.

3. The disturbance must not be explainable purely as an effect of poverty, prejudice, or other social forces that prevent a person from behaving adaptively, nor as a deliberate decision to act in a way contrary to the norms of society. Thus, a person who voluntarily undergoes starvation to protest a government policy is not considered to have a mental disorder.

Although this definition is useful as a guide for identifying mental disorder, it raises many questions. Just how "distressing" or "impairing" must a syndrome be to be considered "clinically significant"? What if it is distressing or impairing to other people, but not to the person whose behavior is presumably disordered? Since all of behavior involves an interaction between the person and environment, how can we tell when the source of impairment is really within the person, rather than just in the environment? How unusual must a response to a stressful situation be to be considered out of the range of normal? In the case of someone living in poverty or experiencing discrimination, how can we tell if the person's actions are normal responses to those conditions or represent something more? How can we distinguish deliberate acts of deviance from acts that result from mental disorder? Who has the right to decide if a person is mentally disordered: the person himself or herself, the person's family, a psychiatrist or psychologist, a court of law? These are all tough questions that can never be answered strictly scientifically. The answers always represent human judgments, and they are always tinged by the social values of those doing the judging.

## Perspectives on Mental Disorders

Mental disorders can be viewed from a variety of perspectives. Let us look at four such perspectives, each of which involves a different way of describing disorders and thinking about their causes.

**The Biological/Medical Perspective**    This perspective, sometimes referred to as the *medical model*, begins with the assumption that mental disorders are, or are like, physical diseases. The ancient Greeks, especially Hippocrates, are often credited as originators of this perspective. Hippocrates looked in the body's fluids for physical causes of people's disturbed emotions and behavior. The medical model was revived in Europe near the end of the Middle Ages. By the nineteenth century, it was the dominant perspective in Europe and North America, and it remains so today.

Adherents to this perspective are most likely to speak of mental disorders as *illnesses* that have distinct *etiologies* (causes) and *prognoses* (expected outcomes), and to refer to persons receiving treatment as *patients*. The medical model is accepted most widely today among *psychiatrists*—mental health professionals who have undergone a standard medical training and received an M.D. degree before specializing in mental problems. *Clinical psychologists*—who typically have a Ph.D. from a clinical psychology program—are somewhat less likely to accept the medical model. (Distinctions among various mental health professionals are described further in Chapter 18.)

■ *How the medical model has influenced the vocabulary used in talking about mental disorders*

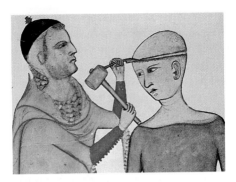

**Madness as possession**

*This twelfth-century painting probably depicts trephination (piercing the skull to permit evil spirits to escape). With the revival of the medical model in the late Middle Ages, people gave up the use of trephination and other brutal treatments that had been based on the belief that abnormal behavior indicates possession.*

■ *How Freud's theory accounts for mental disorders in terms of processes occurring in the unconscious mind*

■ *How the cognitive-behavioral perspective accounts for mental disorders in terms of learned actions and thoughts*

■ *How the sociocultural perspective accounts for cross-cultural differences in mental disorders*

Actually, there are two versions of the medical model. One is the literal version, which holds that mental disorders really *are* physical diseases—diseases of the brain or other physiological systems (such as the endocrine system) that act on the brain. The other, more figurative version, holds that mental disorders are *analogous* to physical diseases. From this view, disordered thoughts or emotions stem from disturbances that are not identifiable in concrete, anatomical terms, but are nevertheless considered to be located within the individual. This view bests fits with the diagnostic manual of the American Psychiatric Association.

**Freud's Psychodynamic Perspective**    Freud's psychodynamic perspective, also called *psychoanalysis*, falls within the figurative mode of the medical-model tradition. As discussed in Chapter 16, Freud described the mind in terms of divisions that are often in conflict with one another. The id (center of instincts), ego (center of reason, compromise, and self-protection), and superego (center of morality) are not physical parts of the brain, but are functional parts of the mind. They are products of the brain, to be sure, but are not something that one would expect to find in the anatomy.

In Freud's view, mental disorders occur when conflicts among these parts of the mind get out of hand, resulting in anxiety and in various mental manipulations (defense mechanisms), controlled by the ego, for relieving anxiety. The anxiety and resultant defenses can produce severe distortions of reality, obsessive thoughts or actions, physical paralysis of body parts, or other effects that impair the person's chance of surviving or finding happiness. The therapist's task is to discover through psychoanalysis what is going on in the person's unconscious mind and to make the person aware of those conflicts so that the ego's conscious reasoning processes can play a greater role in resolving them.

**The Cognitive-Behavioral Perspective**    The *behavioral perspective* in clinical psychology grew from the attempt to apply the findings of research on basic learning processes—particularly classical and operant conditioning—to the understanding and treatment of psychological problems. Similarly, the *cognitive perspective* grew from the attempt to apply the findings of research on cognitive processes to the understanding and treatment of psychological problems. Today, these perspectives have merged to form what is often called the *cognitive-behavioral perspective*.

Clinical psychologists who adopt this perspective usually refer to the people they treat as *clients* who have *problems*, rather than as patients who have illnesses. The clients' problems are seen as originating not in the client himself or herself, but in the client's past or present environment. From this perspective, so-called mental disorders are described as learned, maladaptive ways of acting and thinking that have been acquired through the person's interaction with the environment. Thus, irrational fears may have been learned through classical conditioning; such maladaptive behaviors as excessive drinking may have been learned through operant conditioning, and maladaptive thought patterns, such as "Nobody likes me," or "Anything I do will fail," may have been learned from demanding parents or through other social interactions. Various procedures for replacing such undesired habits with desired habits have been developed, and these are described in Chapter 18.

**The Sociocultural Perspective**    The *sociocultural perspective* on mental disorders combines insights from social psychology, sociology, and anthropology. From this perspective, mental disorders must be understood in terms of their relationship to the values, norms, and psychological pressures that characterize a given cultural group. Three interrelated points that are often made from this perspective can be summarized as follows:

1. *Striking differences exist among different cultures in the prevalence of particular symptoms and syndromes.* Most striking are so-called *culture-bound syndromes* that are almost completely limited to specific cultural groups. For example, a syndrome called *koro*, marked by an incapacitating fear that the penis will withdraw into the abdomen and cause death, is relatively common among men in Southeast Asia, but almost nonexistent elsewhere (Kline, 1963). An example closer to home is *anorexia nervosa*, marked by an extraordinary preoccupation with thinness and a refusal to eat, sometimes to the point of death by starvation. This syndrome occurs almost exclusively among young, middle- to upper-class women in North America and to a lesser degree in other Western or Westernized societies (American Psychiatric Association, 1987). Even disorders that are prevalent throughout the world—such as major depression and schizophrenia—often entail different constellations of symptoms in different cultures (Kleinman, 1988).

2. *Cultures differ in their manner of labeling and reacting to particular syndromes.* Among most contemporary North Americans, hearing the voice of one's dead husband or wife is considered abnormal—a hallucination, possibly a symptom of serious mental disorder. In contrast, in some Native American tribes this experience is common and is considered to be a natural part of grieving (Kleinman, 1988). Until recently, homosexuality was considered to be a mental disorder in many Western cultures, though in various other parts of the world it was seen as quite normal. As cultures change, conceptions of mental disorder also change. In 1973, the American Psychiatric Association officially dropped homosexuality from its list of mental disorders—a change that came in part because of research showing that homosexuality is compatible with personal well-being and ability to function well in society, and in part from a change in the sociopolitical climate that made homosexuality more acceptable (Rothblum & others, 1986).

3. *The way a culture labels and reacts to a specific syndrome affects the way the person feels about himself or herself, and affects the ultimate adjustment that the person makes.* According to a specific theory within the sociocultural perspective, called **labeling theory**, the act of naming a disorder affects the way the disorder will be expressed and the likelihood of recovery (Scheff, 1984). Giving a name to a person's disorder ties that person—in the minds of others and in the labeled person's own mind—to the culture's stereotype of what it means to have the disorder, and the stereotype can influence the way the person subsequently behaves. As one example, people in non-Western cultures who manifest a syndrome that would be diagnosed in the West as schizophrenia seem to recover more often, or more completely, than do people who are diagnosed with schizophrenia in our culture (Lin & Kleinman, 1988). According to the labeling theory, they show better recovery because they do not suffer from the stigma and negative expectations that accompany the schizophrenia label in our society (Waxler, 1984).

**A Framework for Thinking About Multiple Causation**    The four just-described perspectives emphasize different ways of thinking about the causes of mental disorders; but theorists of all perspectives recognize that any given disorder has multiple causes. A general framework for thinking about causes breaks them down into the following three categories:

■ *How the causes of mental disorders can be categorized into three types*

1. **Predisposing causes** are those that are in place well before the onset of the disorder and have to do with the person's susceptibility to the disorder. Genetically inherited characteristics are most often mentioned in this category. But learned beliefs and habitual patterns of reacting to or thinking about stressful situations may also be included here, as may the sociocultural environment

from which one acquires such beliefs and habits. A young woman reared in upper-class, Western society is more likely to have acquired beliefs and values that predispose her to anorexia nervosa than is a young woman from a rural community in China.

2. *Precipitating causes* are the immediate events in a person's life that bring on the disorder. Any loss, such as the death of a loved one or the loss of a job; any real or perceived threat to one's well-being, such as physical disease; any new responsibilities, such as might occur as a result of marriage or job promotion; or any large change at all in the day-to-day course of life can, in the sufficiently predisposed person, bring on the mood or behavioral change that leads to diagnosis of a mental disorder. Precipitating causes are often talked about under the rubric of *stress*, a term that sometimes refers to the life event itself and sometimes to the worry, anxiety, sense of hopelessness, or other negative experiences that accompany the life event. When the predisposition is very high, a seemingly trivial event can be sufficiently stressful to bring on a mental disorder. When the predisposition is very low, even an extraordinarily high degree of loss, threat, or life change may fail to bring on a mental disorder (see Figure 17.1).

3. *Maintaining causes* are those consequences of a disorder that help keep it going once it begins. In some cases, a person may experience rewards, such as extra attention, for behaving in an otherwise maladaptive way, and this may help maintain the behavior. In other cases, negative consequences of the disorder may add to the person's stress, and this may help maintain the disorder. For example, a sufferer of depression may withdraw from friends, and lack of friends may prolong the depression. Expectations associated with a particular disorder may also play a maintaining role. Thus, in a culture where schizophrenia is deemed to be incurable, a person given that diagnosis may simply give up trying to change his or her behavior for the better.

### Categorization and Diagnosis of Mental Disorders

We humans are inveterate categorizers. Rarely do we see an unfamiliar object as completely new and unique; instead, we see it as a member of some familiar category—a chair, a rose, a piece of quartz. Our world is more predictable and describable when we can relate each new object and event to a familiar category. This same response applies in the realm of mental disorders. Beginning long before the era of modern psychology and psychiatry, humans everywhere have had systems for categorizing and labeling the psychological miseries that people experience. In keeping with the medical model that has long dominated in Western culture, the process of assigning a category label to a person's mental disorder is referred to as *diagnosis*.

Categorizing and diagnosing are essential ingredients of any scientific study of mental disorders. Without a system to identify people whose disorders are similar to each other, the accumulation of knowledge about causes, effective treatments, and eventual outcomes would be impossible. But such a system can be scientifically useful only to the degree that it is reliable and valid.

The *reliability* of a diagnostic system refers to the degree to which different diagnosticians, all trained in use of the system, reach the same conclusion when they independently diagnose the same individuals. If you have ever gone to two different doctors with a physical complaint and been given two different, nonsynonymous labels for your disease, then you know that even in the realm of physical disorders diagnosis is by no means completely reliable. The *validity* of a diagnostic system is an index of the extent to which the categories it identifies are clinically meaningful. Do two people with the same diagnosed disorder suffer in similar

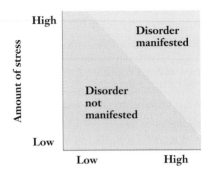

**Figure 17.1** *Hypothetical relationship between predisposition and stress in initiating a mental disorder*

*According to the model depicted here, the amount of stress needed to bring on a mental disorder decreases as the predisposition for the disorder increases.*

■ *Why the scientific study of mental disorders requires a system of categorization and diagnosis that is reliable and valid*

ways? Does the label help predict the future course of the disorder? Does it help in deciding on a meaningful treatment? To the degree that questions like these can be answered yes, the diagnostic system is valid. (The general concepts of reliability and validity are discussed in Chapter 2.)

From the late nineteenth into the mid-twentieth century, various ways of categorizing and labeling mental disorders emerged. One commonly used system divided mental disorders into neuroses and psychoses. *Neuroses* were disorders in which the person is not out of touch with reality and anxiety is the underlying problem. *Psychoses* were disorders involving marked distortions in perception or thought such that the person is in important ways out of touch with reality. Within these broad categories, certain terms for more specific disorders also became common, such as *phobia* as a type of neurosis and *schizophrenia* as a type of psychosis. But in general there was no agreed-upon way of defining these or other classes of disorders, and thus no agreed-upon diagnostic system.

**DSM-III-R: A Standard Diagnostic Guide**   In 1952, to promote more effective communication in the rapidly growing mental health field, the American Psychiatric Association developed the first version of what was meant to be a standardized system for labeling and diagnosing mental disorders. It was called the *Diagnostic and Statistical Manual of Mental Disorders*, mercifully abbreviated *DSM*. This system was revised in 1968 to form DSM-II; again in 1980 to form DSM-III; and again in a minor way in 1987 to form ***DSM-III-R*** (third edition, revised).

The first two editions of the DSM were quite slim. Diagnostic categories were defined briefly, in general terms, leaving a great deal up to the judgment of the individual diagnostician. Those editions also based many of their classes on tenuous assumptions about the inner causes of disorders, taken largely from Freud's theory. For example, some disorders within the general category called neuroses were defined in terms of unconscious anxiety and defenses against that anxiety, even though anxiety was not present as an observable symptom. The result was that studies aimed at assessing the reliability of diagnosis with those systems consistently revealed very little reliability. For some categories, in fact, reliability was barely greater than would be expected if labels had been assigned randomly (Matarazzo, 1983; Spitzer & Fleiss, 1974).

■ *How the developers of DSM-III attempted to increase its reliability*

The overriding goal of the group that created DSM-III was to define disorders in an objective way so as to increase diagnostic reliability. Categories based on unobserved, hypothetical causes were dropped, and new categories were defined as much as possible on the basis of the actual symptoms reported by the client or observed by the clinician. The terms *neurosis* and *psychosis* were dropped as category labels, though they were retained in their adjectival form to refer to symptoms: A ***neurotic symptom*** is one that clearly involves anxiety, and a ***psychotic symptom*** is one that involves gross distortion in perception or thought. The syndrome associated with any given disorder in DSM-III (or DSM-III-R) might include both neurotic and psychotic symptoms, as well as symptoms that are neither neurotic nor psychotic (such as despondency).

Table 17.1 overviews the major classes of disorders in DSM-III-R. Notice that the only major class identified by cause is that called *organic mental syndromes and disorders*, defined by the presence of known damage to the brain. The other disorders are defined principally in terms of the most prominent symptoms. Within each major category, an attempt is made to set out objective criteria that must be satisfied before diagnosis of any specific disorder can be made. In addition, a standard interview format has been developed to help the clinician gather the information needed from a client to make a DSM-III-R diagnosis (Spitzer & others, 1987).

Unlike the reliability studies using DSM and DSM-II, those using DSM-III and DSM-III-R have shown high levels of reliability for most diagnostic categories—comparable in some cases to the levels achieved in diagnosing physical diseases (Matarazzo, 1983; Grove, 1987). While the consensus today is that DSM-III-R is reasonably reliable when used carefully, questions about the validity of many of the categories remain to be answered (McReynolds, 1989). Unlike reliability, there is no standard method to assess validity. To the degree that a diagnosis helps predict other, unassessed aspects of a disorder, or helps in deciding on a useful treatment, or leads to discoveries about common causes, the diagnosis is valid. William Coryell and Mark Zimmerman (1987) explored one approach to assessing validity by comparing diagnoses based on DSM-III-R with descriptions of each person's mood and behavior given by close relatives of the diagnosed person. In general, they found that the picture of the clients' symptoms that emerged from such interviews was consistent with that of the DSM-III diagnosis, which they took as evidence for one kind of diagnostic validity.

The question of validity lies at the heart of research on mental disorders. The basic procedure in nearly all such research is to study people who have a given diagnosis and to discover in what other ways they resemble each other and differ from those who do not have that diagnosis. You will find examples of such research for specific disorders in subsequent sections of this chapter.

**Table 17.1  *Summary of DSM-III-R categories of mental disorders***

**Anxiety disorders*** Disorders in which fear or anxiety is a prominent symptom, including *phobias, panic disorder, generalized anxiety disorder, obsessive-compulsive disorder,* and *post-traumatic stress disorder.*

**Somatoform disorders*** Disorders involving physical (somatic) symptoms that originate from unconscious psychological processes, including *conversion disorder, somatoform pain disorder, somatization disorder,* and *hypochondriasis.*

**Dissociative disorders*** Disorders in which a part of one's experiences is separated (dissociated) from one's conscious memory or identity, including *psychogenic amnesia, fugue states,* and *multiple personality disorder.*

**Psychoactive substance-use disorders*** Disorders characterized by dependence on or abuse of a drug such as alcohol, nicotine, cocaine, or an opiate. The disorder here is the intense desire for the drug and the disruption of behavior and thought that accompanies that desire.

**Mood disorders*** Disorders marked by depression or mania, including *major depression, dysthymia, bipolar disorder,* and *cyclothymia.*

**Schizophrenia*** A long-term psychotic disorder marked by delusions, hallucinations, formal thought disturbances, and flattened or inappropriate affect.

**Delusional disorder** A disorder involving persistent delusions (usually of persecution), *not* accompanied by other disruptions of thought or mood that would lead to a diagnosis of schizophrenia.

**Sexual disorders** Disorders of sexual functioning that are presumed to be psychological in origin.

**Sleep disorders** Disorders of sleep, including *insomnia* (too little sleep) and *hypersomnia* (too much sleep), and disorders involving sleepwalking, sleep terror, or fear of dreams.

**Disorders usually first evident in infancy, childhood, or adolescence** A diverse group of disorders that always, or almost always, first appear before adulthood, including *attention deficit disorder,* various eating disorders (such as *anorexia nervosa*), and various disorders of thought and language.

**Organic mental syndromes and disorders** A diverse group of disorders that stem from known damage to the brain or alteration of the brain's chemical environment, including disorders due to strokes, physical trauma to the brain, degenerative brain diseases (such as *Alzheimer's disease*), and the direct action of drugs on the brain.

**Personality disorders** Disorders involving inflexible, maladaptive personality traits, including *antisocial personality disorder* (a history of antisocial acts and violation of others' rights, with no sense of guilt), *histrionic personality disorder* (excessively emotional, overly dramatic, attention seeking), and *narcissistic personality disorder* (unwarranted sense of self-importance and demand for constant attention or admiration).

*Notes:* (1) The first six categories (marked by asterisks) are described in more detail in the text. (2) Because personality disorders involve a person's long-standing style of thinking and acting rather than a change in the person, they are categorized in DSM-III-R on a separate dimension or axis (Axis II) from the other categories (which are part of Axis I). (3) DSM-III-R categories omitted from this table include: (a) *psychotic disorders not classified elsewhere,* defined as disorders that involve loss of touch with reality but cannot be classified as schizophrenia or delusional disorder; (b) *factitious disorders,* defined as made-up or self-induced syndromes designed to attract attention or care; (c) *disorders of impulse control not elsewhere classified,* which includes pathological gambling, kleptomania, and pyromania; and (d) *adjustment disorder,* defined as a maladaptive reaction to an identifiable source of stress.

**Figure 17.2 *One-month prevalence of various mental disorders***

*Shown here are the percentages of adult men and women who were diagnosed by DSM-III criteria as having various mental disorders within the previous 1-month period in a survey conducted in five metropolitan areas of the United States. Only those disorders for which the 1-month prevalence was greater than 0.3 percent are shown in this graph. Taking all disorders together, 14 percent of men and 16.6 percent of women had at least one disorder. (Data from Regier & others, 1988.)*

**Prevalence of Mental Disorders**　Shortly after the development of DSM-III (and before DSM-III-R), the National Institute of Mental Health initiated a massive survey to assess the prevalence of mental disorders in various locations in the United States. The data were collected by trained interviewers and analyzed by computers programmed to make diagnoses on DSM-III criteria. This study is still in progress, but data from some locations have already been analyzed. The results indicate that more than 30 percent of U.S. citizens age 18 and over have at some point in their lives suffered from at least one disorder diagnosable in DSM-III, and that approximately 15 percent had manifested such a disorder within a 1-month period prior to the time of the survey (Robins & others, 1984; Regier & others, 1988). Figure 17.2 shows the 1-month prevalence found for the most common disorders, separately for men and women. You may wish to look back at this figure as you read about the various disorders later in the chapter.

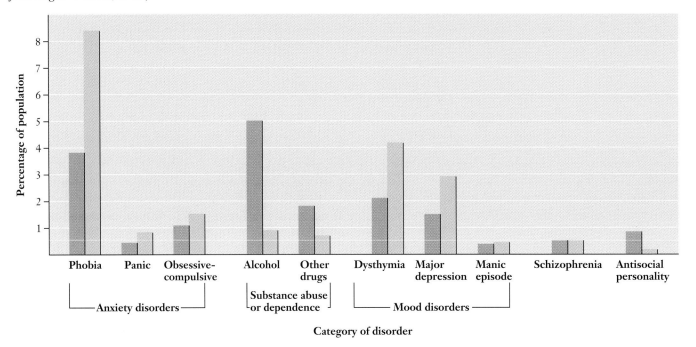

- Males, 18 years and older
- Females, 18 years and older

**■ *How gender differences in the prevalence of specific mental disorders can be accounted for within the sociocultural perspective***

**What Accounts for Apparent Gender Differences in Prevalence?**　Figure 17.2 reveals a pattern of gender differences that has also been found in other studies. Little difference between males and females is found in the overall prevalence when all disorders are combined, but large differences are found for specific categories. In particular, women are more likely than men to be diagnosed with anxiety or mood disorders, and men are more likely than women to be diagnosed with alcohol or drug-use disorders. In theory, such differences might arise directly from biological differences between men and women, or they might arise from the different roles and expectations that society ascribes to men and women. Within the sociocultural category of causes, the following, more specific explanations have been offered:

- *Differences in tendency to report or suppress psychological distress*　The diagnosis of anxiety and mood disorders necessarily depends to a great extent on self-report. Men, who are supposed to be the "stronger" sex, may be less inclined to admit their mental distress in interviews or questionnaires. Supporting this

*A substantial difference*

*Men outnumber women with respect to a diagnosis of alcoholism, and this may reflect both a difference in actual prevalence and a difference in the way the disorder is manifested.*

view, experiments have shown that when men and women are subjected to the same stressful situation, such as a school examination, men report less anxiety than do women even though they show physiological signs of distress that are as great as, or greater than, those shown by women (Polefrone & Manuck, 1987). Men might also use alcohol and illegal drugs to suppress their mental distress, or might express it in the form of anger rather than fear or sadness. Anger is the one negative emotion that in our society is more acceptable in men than in women (Hyde, 1986), and it is the only common negative emotion that does not correspond directly to a major category in DSM-III or DSM-III-R. A person who expresses severe distress in terms of fear or sadness may receive a diagnosis (of anxiety or mood disorder), but a person who expresses it in terms of anger probably will not.

*Bias in diagnosis* Diagnosticians may, to some degree, find certain disorders more often in one gender or the other because they *expect* to find them there. To test this possibility, Maureen Ford and Thomas Widiger (1989) mailed a fictitious case history to several hundred clinical psychologists throughout the United States and asked them to make diagnoses using DSM-III criteria. For some the case was constructed to resemble the criteria for *antisocial personality*, a disorder found more often in men than women; and for others it was constructed to resemble the criteria for *histrionic personality*, a disorder found more often in women. (You can find a brief description of each of these disorders under Personality Disorders in Table 17.1.) Each of these case types was written in a separate, otherwise identical form applying to a male patient or a female patient. As you can see in Figure 17.3, the diagnoses were strongly af-

**Figure 17.3** *Evidence of a gender bias in diagnosis*

*In this study, fictitious case histories were more likely to be diagnosed as antisocial personality if they described a fictitious male patient, and as histrionic personality if they described a fictitious female patient, regardless of which disorder the case history was designed to resemble. (Data from Ford & Widiger, 1989.)*

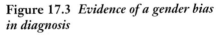

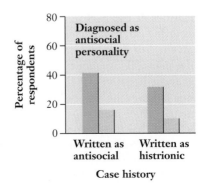
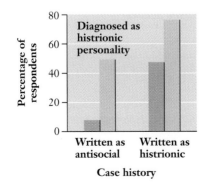

Male case
Female case

**Double trouble**

*The sociocultural perspective underscores the risk of mental disorders in women and other groups who chronically lack control over their lives and who often face economic and other forms of discrimination.*

fected by gender. Given the exact same case histories, the male patient was far more likely than the female to receive a diagnosis of antisocial personality, and the female was far more likely than the male to receive a diagnosis of histrionic personality.

Might a similar bias have operated in the survey of the prevalence of disorders, shown in Figure 17.2? That question is hard to answer. On the one hand, the interviewers were trained to ask questions and record data using a standard format, and diagnoses were then made from those data by a computer program, which presumably had no gender bias programmed into it. On the other hand, there is no way to rule out the possibility that interviewers unconsciously interpreted and recorded responses differently depending on the gender of the person they were interviewing.

Some critics have argued that DSM-III contains inherent gender biases within the definitions of some of its disorders. For example, they argue that the diagnostic system is such that staying home during the day—an event more common among women than among men due to social roles in our society—can be counted as a symptom of depression. Thus, if a woman whose job is caring for the home and children, and a man whose job is outside of the home, are the same in all other respects, the woman is more likely to receive a diagnosis of depression. (For both sides of the inherent-bias argument, see Kaplan, 1983, and Williams & Spitzer, 1983.)

*Differences in stressfulness of male and female roles*   A third approach has been to assume that to some degree gender differences in mental disorders are real, and to search for possible causes in the different social roles of men and women. Some psychologists (for example, Barnett & Baruch, 1987) have argued that the traditional role of wife and mother in our society is more conducive to anxiety and depression than is the role of husband and father. The wife and mother spends more time in isolation from other adults, performing jobs that are accorded little prestige by society at large. Moreover, she is often made to feel responsible for events over which she has little real control, such as her children's illnesses, accidents, or poor school performance. It is argued that the combination of high demands, low real control, and low prestige is the ideal mix for creating both anxiety and depression. Consistent with this view, taking a job outside of the home (even when it is added to the at-home job) has been found to reduce psychological distress in women (Baruch & others, 1987). In addition, analysis of data collected between 1950 and 1980 suggests that over the course of those years, as employment for men and women became somewhat more similar, the gender gap in anxiety and mood disorders decreased (Kessler & McRae, 1981).

■ *Evidence that labeling a person as mentally disordered affects the way the person is perceived and the way he or she behaves*

**A Danger in Labeling**   Diagnosing and labeling may be essential for the scientific study of mental disorders, but labels can be harmful. Controlled experiments have shown that a label implying mental disorder can blind clinicians and others to qualities of the person that are not captured by the label, can reduce the esteem accorded to the person by others, and can reduce the labeled person's self-esteem. For example, in one experiment psychotherapists who watched a videotape of a man talking about his personal problems rated the man's level of adjustment far more negatively if they were led to believe that he was a mental patient than if they believed he was not a patient (Langer & Abelson, 1974). In another experiment, former mental patients performed more poorly in a social interaction if they believed that the person with whom they were interacting knew about their former patient status than if they believed that the person was unaware of that status (Farina & others, 1971). Chapter 18 describes further evidence for harmful effects of labels, based on the personal experiences of hospitalized mental patients and of individuals who have feigned that status for research purposes.

What can be done to diminish the blinding effect of labels? As a partial solution to the problem (but certainly not a complete one), the American Psychiatric Association (1987) now suggests that clinicians apply diagnostic labels only to people's disorders, not to people themselves. For example, a client or patient might be referred to as *a person who has schizophrenia*, or *who suffers from alcoholism*, but should not be referred to as *a schizophrenic* or *an alcoholic*. The distinction might at first seem subtle, but if you think about it you may agree that it is not so subtle in psychological impact. If we say, "John has schizophrenia," we tend to be reminded that John is first and foremost a person, with qualities like those of other people, and that his having schizophrenia is just one of many things we could say about him. On the other hand, if we say, "John is a schizophrenic," there is a tendency to think that everything about him is summed up by that label. As I talk about specific disorders in the remainder of this chapter and the next, I will attempt to follow this advice even though it produces some awkward wording at times. I also urge you to add, in your mind, yet another step of linguistic complexity. When I refer to "a person who has schizophrenia," you should read this statement as "a person who *has been diagnosed by someone* as having schizophrenia," keeping in mind that diagnostic systems are never completely reliable.

**Medical Students' Disease**   In describing the potentially harmful effects of labels, I have been talking about the power of suggestion. Another problem involving the power of suggestion is *medical students' disease*. This disease, which could also be called *introductory psychology students' disease*, is characterized by a strong tendency to relate personally to, and to find in oneself, the symptoms of any disease or disorder described in a textbook. The disease, which really does strike many students, was described in the nineteenth century by the humorist Jerome K. Jerome (1889/1982) in an essay about his own discomfort upon reading a textbook of medical diagnoses. After describing his discoveries that he must have typhoid fever, St. Vitus's Dance, and a multitude of other diseases, he wrote, "The only malady I concluded I had *not* got was housemaid's knee . . . I had walked into that reading-room a happy, healthy man. I crawled out a decrepit wreck." As you read the following pages, brace yourself against medical students' disease. Everyone has at least some of the symptoms, to some degree, of essentially every disorder that can be found in this chapter, DSM-III-R, or any other compendium.

## Anxiety Disorders

The rabbit crouches, frozen in the grass, minimizing its chance of being detected. Its sensory systems are at maximum alertness, all tuned to the approaching dog; its muscles are tense, ready to leap away at the first sign that it has been detected; its heart races, and its adrenal glands spew out hormones, preparing for extended flight if necessary. Here we see fear operating adaptively, as it was designed to operate by evolution.

We humans differ from the rabbit on two counts: Our biological evolution added a massive, thinking cerebral cortex atop the more primitive structures that organize fear; and our cultural evolution led us to develop a habitat far different from that of our ancestors. Our pattern of fear is not unlike the rabbit's, but it can be triggered by an enormously greater variety of both real and imagined stimuli, and in many of those situations the fear is not adaptive. It is not adaptive when the job candidate freezes at an interview; or when the student's mind is overwhelmed by fear of failure while taking an examination; or when a person's ability to imagine the worst possible consequence of every action leads to an inability to act at all, or to a life confined to familiar paths.

*Anxiety disorders* are those in which fear or anxiety is the most prominent symptom. Although *fear* and *anxiety* can be used as synonyms, the former term is more often used when the feared stimulus is quite specific, and the latter is more often used when it is vague or not identifiable. DSM-III-R recognizes five subclasses of anxiety disorders, each of which is discussed briefly below. The treatment of these and other disorders is discussed in Chapter 18; but it is worth noting here that, as a group, anxiety disorders are the easiest disorders to treat and have the best long-term prognoses (chances of recovery).

■ *How the five categories of anxiety disorders differ from one another, and how each might be explained from one or more perspectives*

**Generalized Anxiety Disorder**   Generalized anxiety is called *generalized* because it is not focused on any one specific threat; instead, it attaches itself to various threats, both real and imagined, or may take a free-floating form in which it is not attached to any consciously recognized threat. Other symptoms include more or less continuous muscle tension, irritability, difficulty sleeping, and (sometimes) gastrointestinal upsets that result from overactivity of the autonomic nervous system. Although very few people experience generalized anxiety at the high level required for the diagnosis of *generalized anxiety disorder*, many people experience it at lower levels, a fact attested to by the huge number who take tranquilizers or drink alcohol on a regular basis to "calm their nerves."

To some degree, generalized anxiety seems to be a price of our industrial and postindustrial way of life. The world changes more rapidly now than in times past. Change implies uncertainty, and uncertainty provokes anxiety. In a world of changing values and expectations, how do we judge right from wrong, good from bad, safe from unsafe? Of the many unpredictable paths that seem open at any point in life, how do we decide which to take? Will today's skills meet tomorrow's demands? The threats implied by such questions may be experienced by many people only dimly, in a way that leads not to conscious articulation of specific dangers, but to generalized anxiety. And, unlike the predator that scares the rabbit one minute and is gone the next, these threats are constantly with us.

Many reasons for differences among people in amount of generalized anxiety can be found. Some research indicates that varying degrees of biological predisposition for the condition may be inherited and may reside at least partly in the sensitivity of the autonomic nervous system (Eysenck, 1975). Other research suggests that a learned belief in one's own incompetence or inefficacy (inability to cope with demands and threats) may predispose a person for generalized anxiety or help maintain that state when it occurs (Beck & Emery, 1985). Any major change in the person's life, or any unexpected, uncontrollable negative event, can trigger off a state of generalized anxiety in a person who is sufficiently predisposed (Blazer & others, 1987).

The decision as to how much generalized anxiety one must experience before it is diagnosed as a disorder is arbitrary. Perhaps because generalized anxiety is so common in the population, the authors of DSM-III-R chose to define it as a disorder only when the state is prolonged (at least 6 months), is of a degree that seriously impairs day-to-day functioning, and is not compounded by the presence of some other DSM-III-R disorder. By those criteria, generalized anxiety disorder is rarely diagnosed (American Psychiatric Association, 1987).

**Phobias**   In contrast to generalized anxiety, a *phobia* is a fear that is very clearly related to a particular category of object or event. In the most common cases, referred to as *simple phobias*, the fear is of something specific, such as a particular type of animal (such as snakes), substance (such as blood), or situation (such as height, or being closed in). In other cases, referred to as *social phobias*, the basic fear is of being scrutinized or evaluated by other people; included here are fears of public speaking, of eating in public places, or of meeting new people. Usually a phobia sufferer is aware of the irrationality of the fear, but that awareness doesn't help. The person knows full well that the neighbor's kitten won't claw anyone to death, that a person can't drown in ankle-deep water, or that the crowd of 10-year-olds at the corner won't attack. People with phobias suffer doubly: They suffer from the fear itself, and also from their knowledge of how irrational they are to have such a fear.

Probably everyone has some irrational fears, and, as in all other anxiety disorders, the difference between the normal condition and the disorder is an arbitrary one of degree, not kind. Simple phobias are usually of things that many people fear to some extent, such as snakes, spiders, blood, darkness, or heights; and social phobias may simply be extreme forms of shyness. In line with this view, simple phobias usually originate in early to middle childhood, when fears of such things as animals and darkness are most common among people in general, and social phobias usually originate in adolescence, which is the time when normal shyness is most likely to be a problem (Marks, 1987).

Simple phobias are much more often diagnosed in females than in males, whereas social phobias are diagnosed about equally often in the two genders; these facts, too, are consistent with the idea that phobias are on a continuum with normal fears. Men and boys in our society are much less likely than are women and girls to admit to fears of such things as spiders and darkness, but are about equally likely to admit to shyness. The gender difference in simple phobias could stem from the fact that boys in our society are more strongly encouraged than are girls to overcome their childhood fears, or to hide them if they don't overcome them (Fodor, 1982).

As in the case of most other mental disorders, little is known about how phobias usually arise. Freud believed that the consciously feared object is merely a symbol for a more deep-seated unconscious fear. For example, in one of his famous cases, Freud (1909a/1963) attributed the fear of horses in a 5-year-old boy named Hans to the child's oedipal crisis. According to Freud's analysis, horses stood in Hans's unconscious for his father, the real source of fear during the oedipal crisis. Freud's theory of phobias is difficult to test and not widely adhered to today.

Behaviorists, from John B. Watson (1924) on, have argued that phobias are acquired by classical conditioning, through experiences in which the now-feared stimulus had been paired with some unconditionally fearful stimulus. A problem with this interpretation is that most people with phobias cannot recall any specific experiences with the feared stimulus or situation that could have provided the basis for such learning (McNally & Steketee, 1985; Murray & Foote, 1979). It also does not explain such findings as this: In Burlington, Vermont, where there are no dangerous snakes, the single most common simple phobia is of snakes (Agras & others, 1969). If phobias are acquired by conditioning, why aren't phobias of such things as automobiles or (in Burlington) icy sidewalks more common? Another theory, first proposed by Martin Seligman (1971), is that people are genetically prepared from past evolution to fear certain classes of objects or events (discussed in Chapter 5). This idea is helpful in understanding why phobias of snakes, darkness, and height are more common than are those of automobiles and electric outlets, but it does not explain why some people acquire phobias and others don't.

**Obsessive-Compulsive Disorder** An *obsession* is a disturbing thought that intrudes repeatedly on a person's consciousness even though the person recognizes it as irrational. A *compulsion* is a repetitive action that is usually performed in response to an obsession. Most people experience moderate forms of these, especially in childhood. I remember a period in sixth grade when, while reading in school, the thought would repeatedly enter my mind that reading could make my eyes fall out. The only way I could banish this thought and go on reading was to close my eyelids down hard—a compulsive act that I fancied might push my eyes solidly back into their sockets. Of course, I knew that both the thought and the action were ir-

*A dreadful view*

*Phobia comes from a Greek word meaning "flight," or "fear." If you experience such feelings when viewing this scene, you have some sense of what a person with a height phobia feels when looking out a one-story window.*

**Magnificent obsession**

*An obsession is a disorder only if it is harmful to the self or others. If it is not harmful, it may sometimes bring a measure of fame.*

rational, yet the thought kept intruding, and the only way I could abolish it for a while was to perform the action. Like most normal obsessions and compulsions, this one did not really disrupt my life, and it simply faded with time.

People who are diagnosed with **obsessive-compulsive disorder** are those for whom such thoughts and actions don't fade, but worsen and seriously interfere with daily life. An obsessive-compulsive disorder is similar to a phobia in that it involves a specific, irrational fear. The main difference is that the fear now is of something that exists only as a thought and can be reduced only by performing some ritual, whereas in a phobia the fear is of something that exists in the real environment and can be avoided by staying away from that thing. People with obsessive-compulsive disorder, like those with phobias, suffer also from their own knowledge of the irrationality of what they are doing, and much of their lives are governed by their attempts to hide their strange behaviors from other people.

Analysis of the obsessions experienced by people with this disorder, compared to normal obsessions experienced by people who don't have the disorder, has revealed no systematic differences in content, only in intensity (Rachman & De Silva, 1978). The most common obsessions concern death, disease, or disfigurement, and the most common compulsions involve checking or cleaning. People with checking compulsions may spend hours each day repeatedly checking doors to be sure they are locked, the stove to be sure it is turned off, automobile wheels to be sure they are on tight, and so on (Rachman, 1985). People with cleaning compulsions may wash their hands every few minutes, scrub everything they eat, and sterilize their dishes and clothes in response to their obsessions about disease-producing germs and dirt. In other cases, compulsions can be found that bear no logical relation to the obsession that triggers them. For example, one woman who was obsessed by the thought that her husband would die in an automobile accident could in fantasy protect him and relieve her anxiety by dressing and undressing in a specific pattern twenty times every day (Marks, 1987).

Speculation about the causes of obsessive-compulsive disorder is similar to that about phobias. Freud believed that conscious obsessions are masks for unconscious wishes, which may often be opposite in content to the obsession. For example, in one case he interpreted a man's obsessive fear that his father would die as a mask for his unconscious *wish* that his father would die (Freud, 1909b/1963). Behavioral theorists point out that compulsive actions, regardless of how they are started, are reinforced each time they occur by the sharp reduction in anxiety that follows them (Foa & others, 1985). Cognitive theorists have supplied evidence that this disorder occurs most often in people who already have a general tendency to think in rigid ways and to expect the worst in new situations (Steketee & Foa, 1985). Biologically oriented theorists point to recent success in treating the disorder with drugs; to evidence that the disorder often follows damage to a specific area of the brain (the basal ganglia); and to studies showing a unique pattern of metabolic activity in the brains of those with the disorder (Rapaport, 1989).

**Panic Disorder**   Panic is a feeling of helpless terror, such as one might experience if cornered by a predator with no way out. For people who suffer from **panic disorder**, this sense of terror comes at unpredictable times, unprovoked by any specific threat in the environment. Because the panic is unrelated to any specific situation or idea, the panic victim, unlike the victim of a phobia or obsessive-compulsion, cannot avoid it by avoiding specific situations or engaging in compulsive rituals. The attacks themselves usually last several minutes, and are usually accompanied by high physiological arousal (including rapid heart rate and shortness of breath) and a fear of losing control, that is, of behaving in some frantic, desperate way (Barlow & Craske, 1988). Between attacks the victim may experience almost constant anxiety about having another attack. The victim especially fears having an attack in a public place, where embarrassment or humiliation might follow if he or she loses control in front of others. About 90 percent of panic-attack victims develop *agoraphobia*, defined as an intense fear of public places, sometime after their first panic attack (Breier & others, 1986).

Because panic attacks seem to come on spontaneously, most hypotheses about their cause have been biological in nature. One line of research has shown that people with this disorder often have high levels of lactic acid in their blood, and injection of lactic acid can bring on panic attacks in people who are prone to them (Klein & Rabkin, 1981). Other research has shown that certain drugs usually used to treat depression are often effective in preventing the recurrence of panic attacks (Marks, 1987). Consistent with the latter finding, people with panic disorder often suffer at some point in their lives from serious depression, suggesting that a common biochemical predisposition may be involved in these two otherwise quite different disorders (Breier & others, 1986).

On the environmental side, the panic victim commonly experiences the first attack shortly after some stressful event has occurred in his or her life, such as the loss of a loved one, change of job, or pregnancy (Breier & others, 1986). And, from a cognitive perspective, the manner in which the panic victim interprets the physiological changes within his or her body can increase or decrease the sense of panic (Clark, 1988). Thus, a person who learns to interpret each attack as a temporary physiological condition experiences less fear during and between attacks than does a person who interprets each attack as a sign of mental derangement or impending doom.

**Post-traumatic Stress Disorder** Unlike the other anxiety disorders, ***post-traumatic stress disorder*** is directly and explicitly tied to a traumatic incident or set of incidents that the affected person has experienced. It is most common in torture victims, concentration camp survivors, people who have been violently assaulted, people who have survived a horrible accident, and soldiers who have experienced the horrors of battle. The disorder may begin immediately after the traumatic experience or later, sometimes many months later. It typically involves painful and uncontrollable reliving of the traumatic events, both in nightmares and daytime thoughts. Other common symptoms are sleeplessness, guilt (perhaps for surviving while others didn't), depression (perhaps stemming from the sense of injustice in the world and the lack of control one has over one's fate), and general irritability. In an effort to relieve such symptoms, post-traumatic victims may turn to alcohol or street drugs, which often compounds the problem.

Post-traumatic stress seems to be particularly likely to occur if a person cannot make sense of the trauma that he or she has experienced. This observation has been used by some to explain why U.S. veterans of the Vietnam War have experienced this disorder at a much higher rate than did U.S. veterans of World War II. Whereas U.S. citizens felt a sense of national unity about their purpose in World War II, they felt ambiguity and in many cases hostility concerning their purpose in Vietnam. According to one study, 20 percent of Vietnam veterans were still—15 years after their period of service—suffering from post-traumatic stress disorder by DSM-III criteria (Card, 1987).

## Somatoform and Dissociative Disorders

Prior to DSM-III, somatoform and dissociative disorders were classed with anxiety disorders even though they do not necessarily involve anxiety as an observable symptom. In keeping with its goal of classifying disorders in terms of observable symptoms, DSM-III broke with tradition and placed these disorders in separate classes of their own.

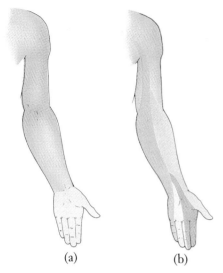

(a)          (b)

**Figure 17.4  *A conversion disorder***

*The experience of no sensation in the hand, but continued sensation in all other parts of the arm, called* glove anesthesia, *shown in (a), cannot result from nerve damage, because no nerves innervate the hand without innervating part of the arm. The actual areas of sensory loss that would occur if specific nerves were damaged are shown in (b). Thus, whenever glove anesthesia occurs, it is most likely a conversion disorder.*

■ *Why somatoform disorders are especially difficult to diagnose*

■ *How somatoform disorders are explained from an (a) psycho-dynamic, (b) behavioral, and (c) sociocultural perspective*

### Somatoform Disorders

Somatoform literally means "bodily form," and ***somatoform disorders*** are those in which the person experiences bodily ailments in the absence of any physical disease that could cause them. Four varieties of somatoform disorders are described in DSM-III-R: (1) *conversion disorder*, in which the person temporarily loses some bodily function, perhaps (in the most dramatic cases) becoming blind, deaf, or partially paralyzed; (2) *somatoform pain disorder*, which is similar to conversion disorder except that the complaint is of pain in some part of the body rather than loss of a bodily function; (3) *somatization disorder*, which is characterized by a long history of dramatic complaints about many different medical conditions, most of which are vague and unverifiable, such as dizziness, heart palpitations, and nausea; and (4) *hypochondriasis*, which is characterized by a long-term, unwarranted preoccupation with physical health and the belief that every slight ailment is a symptom of some grave disease. Little reliable information exists about the prevalence of somatoform disorders. This is partly because people with such disorders usually go to physicians (who are not trained in psychiatric diagnosis) rather than to clinical psychologists or psychiatrists, and partly because the diagnoses are inherently difficult to make.

How can a diagnostician tell if a patient's physical complaint represents a somatoform mental disorder or an actual physical disease? Occasionally, the mental origin can be inferred because the complained-of symptom could not logically come from a physical disease (see Figure 17.4 for an example). In other cases, it can be inferred because the problem came on suddenly after a psychologically stressful event, or disappeared suddenly after the resolution of a psychological problem. But in most cases no clear way exists for deciding to what degree the complaint stems from real bodily problems or from psychological causes. Many errors of diagnosis have been made in both directions. Sometimes needless surgery or other medical treatment occurs because a somatoform disorder is mistaken for a physical disease, and other times needed medical treatment is withheld because a physical disease is mistakenly considered to be purely psychological. In one study of patients who were originally diagnosed as having a conversion disorder, about half were later found to have a physical disease that could have been the basis for their complaint (Slater, 1975).

In the past, somatoform disorders (especially conversion disorders) were referred to as *hysteria*, which is the Greek word for uterus. This label came originally from the ancient Greek view that such disorders occur only in women and arise from a "wandering uterus," which could invade and inflict pain, paralysis, or insensitivity in various parts of the woman's body. For centuries, hysteria was diagnosed much more often in women than in men. Even today, somatoform disorders are diagnosed more often in women than in men, but at least some studies suggest that their actual occurrence is equally high in the two genders (Lipowski, 1988; Slavney & Teitelbaum, 1985).

Why do somatoform disorders occur? Why should a person feel pains or experience diseases that do not exist? One possibility is that these symptoms are simply side effects of mental distress. Maybe the neural mechanisms for experiencing psychological and bodily misery are so intertwined that activity in one tends to trigger activity in the other. Another possibility is that the symptoms are more than side effects. Perhaps they are designed quite specifically, though unconsciously, to help solve some real or imagined problem.

This second possibility was proposed most explicitly by Sigmund Freud, who believed that every action produced by either the conscious or unconscious mind has a purpose. If the unconscious mind makes a person feel sick or paralyzes a leg, then it must do so for some reason that is known only to the unconscious mind. Eventually, as he developed his specific psychodynamic theory, Freud concluded that the unconscious purpose is always to reduce anxiety related to an unresolved childhood sexual conflict. For example, a man who is afraid of sex because of his failure to resolve the oedipal conflict might, when confronted by sexual opportunities in adulthood, become ill or partly paralyzed to make it seem to himself and others that sexual activity would be impossible. From a more liberalized psychodynamic view, however, somatoform disorders might serve to resolve all sorts of problems, not just sexual ones. Consider the following case of conversion disorder (quoted from Rosenhan & Seligman, 1984):

> Baer, a burly, young construction worker, is paralyzed from the waist down. Since the problem does not seem to have a neurological basis, he is sent from Neurology to Psychiatry, where the following dialogue takes place:
>
> **Doctor:** *Do you know anyone else who is paralyzed?*
>
> **Baer:** (after thinking for a period of time and showing no emotion) *Yeah, come to think of it, Tom, a good friend of mine, is . . . Broke his neck.*
>
> **Doctor:** *How did it happen?*
>
> **Baer:** *It was really sad, and you know, I guess I was pretty much at fault . . . We were at a party about a month ago . . . I thought he should live a little, try some LSD . . . We downed a couple of tabs, and within a few minutes he was flying, seeing all sorts of weird things. He ran out of the apartment . . . Next thing I know, he jumped off the bridge . . . He was still alive when the rescue squad got him down from the high tension lines. They say he'll never walk, or anything, again.*
>
> **Doctor:** *Baer, tell me again when your problem started.*
>
> **Baer:** *Out of nowhere. I was at work, driving my forklift down at the station. As I crossed the tracks under the high tension lines, suddenly I was all dead down there . . . Oh, my God! Don't you see what I have done!*

A psychodynamic interpretation of this incident might go as follows: Baer felt guilty about his involvement in the event that led to his friend's paralysis. Later, when seeing the high tension lines on which his friend had become paralyzed, his guilt was elevated to an unbearable level and his unconscious mind responded by rendering him paralyzed—an act that relieved his guilt by placing him in the role of victim rather than perpetrator. Later, in conversation with the psychiatrist, the relationship between his own paralysis and his friend's became clear to him, and when that occurred his own paralysis could no longer function as a defense mechanism. Shortly thereafter he regained the use of his legs, and, one hopes, eventually found some less crippling way to deal with his feelings of guilt.

Some cases of conversion disorder seem to be aimed explicitly at threats in the real world or toward material gain. For example, a considerable number of pilots in World War II developed blindness conversions that prevented them from continuing dangerous missions, and often the blindness they experienced was specific to their duties: Night flyers lost the ability to see in dim light but not in daylight, and day flyers developed the opposite symptoms (Ironside & Batchelor, 1945). In other cases, conversions have occurred when the affected person stood to gain a large sum from insurance or a lawsuit if incapacitated (Ford, 1983). It is hard to tell when such cases represent true conversion or conscious faking. In fact, no sharp line may exist between conversion disorders and faking. A person may consciously want a particular illness to occur, and this may lead to the first imagined symptoms, which the person may or may not consciously abet. Imagine a man whose lawyer and relatives are saying, "Are you *sure* your neck doesn't hurt? You know, if it does, you can collect $20,000." When he discovers first a slight twinge of pain, which later becomes so strong that he has to miss work, is he (a) a liar, (b) a person whose vivid imagination has led to a conversion disorder, or (c) a legitimate victim of slowly developing whiplash? He himself may not know.

***Traumatic blindness***

*Chhean Im is one of many Cambodian women whose acute vision problems have been tied to seeing atrocities committed by, and to being tortured by, the Khmer Rouge. Because of cultural differences and problems with diagnosis, Western psychologists have just begun to develop ways of treating the disorder.*

From a behavioral perspective, a long-standing pattern of complaints about physical problems, such as those that characterize somatization and conversion disorders, might be acquired through reinforcement in the form of attention or relief from responsibilities, and might be maintained because of continued reinforcement of that type. Consistent with this view is the finding that these disorders in adulthood are often associated with a childhood history of attention to illnesses, either real or imagined, by the child's overprotective parents (Lipowski, 1988; Barksy & others, 1986).

From a sociocultural perspective, the incidence of somatoform disorders and the form they take are affected by cultural beliefs. Few people in North America or Europe today believe that a person can be stricken suddenly blind, deaf, or paralyzed; so those forms of somatoform disorders are rarer now than they used to be. Moreover, as disorders purely of mood or emotion become more legitimized by a culture, the incidence of somatoform disorders tends to go down and that of anxiety and mood disorders tends to go up. Based on cross-cultural and historical research, Arthur Kleinman (1988) has argued that somatization and depression may be two ways of feeling and expressing the same underlying problem. According to Kleinman, a sense of hopelessness is usually experienced as depression in Western cultures today, but in the past was more often experienced as physical aches and pains, as it still is in China and many other parts of the world.

### Dissociative Disorders

**Dissociation** refers to a process by which a period of a person's life, ranging from a few minutes to years, is separated off mentally such that it cannot be recalled or can be recalled only under special conditions. Dissociation can be produced in many people through hypnosis. Given an appropriate post-hypnotic suggestion, the hypnotized person may not be able to recall any events that occurred during the hypnotic period, or may be able to recall them only when a prearranged signal occurs (Hilgard, 1977). Dissociative disorders are believed by many who study them to involve states that are similar to hypnosis (for example, Bliss, 1986).

Varieties of **dissociative disorders** are distinguished in DSM-III-R according to their complexity. In the simplest type, called *psychogenic amnesia*, memory loss is the only prominent symptom. The amnesia may be selective for a specific traumatic experience, or it may be more global and include loss of memory for all facts about the self, including one's own name and place of residence. A second level of complexity occurs in those rare cases diagnosed as *psychogenic fugue*. (*Fugue* here refers to a hypnotic-like state, and *psychogenic* means that it stems from psychological causes.) Here the person not only loses memory of his or her previous identity, but wanders away from home and develops a new identity that is quite separate from the earlier one. When the fugue ends, perhaps days or months later, the person regains his or her original identity, with all of its associated memories, and at the same time loses memory of everything that happened during the fugue. The most complex and intriguing variety of dissociative disorder is ***multiple personality disorder***, which is what I will focus on for the rest of this discussion.

Let us assume that you are a clinical psychologist or psychiatrist interviewing a new client. Before you sits a demure, exhausted-looking young woman who speaks in earnest tones about her complete devotion to her husband and child and about the headaches that she has been experiencing lately. Then, at a difficult moment in the conversation, she closes her eyes, and when she opens them you see before you a new person. She sits differently, talks differently, and the expression on her face is that of a different person. No longer demure and exhausted, she is vivacious and talkative. She looks you in the eye and speaks with confidence, calling you "Doc." This woman has no headaches, and she claims to have no children or husband either. "I can't be bothered with that. Life is too short," she says, and gives you a wink. This woman calls herself by a different name from the other one. She knows the other, though, and speaks of her with a combination of contempt and pity as a person who has never learned how to live. She knows the husband and child, too, and doesn't like them at all. In later sessions, as you get to know both of these women better, you find that although the second woman knows about the first, the first woman knows nothing of the second. The first talks about "losing time" (discovering that time has passed without her knowing what happened); about finding herself in strange places such as hotel rooms; and about finding dresses that had mysteriously appeared in her closet—garish ones that she would never buy herself.

The account just described is based on the book *The Three Faces of Eve*, written by two psychiatrists, Corbett Thigpen and Hervey Cleckley (1957), about a case of multiple personality that they had treated. The first personality is referred to as Eve White, the second as Eve Black. Later, a third, more mature and stable personality emerges, referred to as Jane. Still later, after the book was completed, new personalities continued to emerge—twenty-two in all over a period of nearly 20 years (McKeller, 1979). Eventually, after many years of therapy, the woman overcame the disorder and since 1974 has been one person—the integrated person whom she considers to be her real self (Sizemore, 1989).

Multiple personality disorder is defined in DSM-III-R as a disorder in which two or more distinct personalities or self-identities are manifested by the same person at different times. The switch from one identity to another apparently occurs automatically, usually in response to some environmental provocation. At the time of Thigpen and Cleckley's book, this disorder was believed to be extraordinarily rare. In fact, prior to 1970 only about 100 cases could be found in the psychiatric literature (Boor, 1982), but since then the number of reported cases has mushroomed. One specialist reports having known of 500 cases by 1979 and of over 5000 by 1985 (Braun, 1985).

In most reported cases, the personality change is not as obvious as that described for Eve, and individuals often go through years of psychotherapy before their multiple personalities are discovered. Skeptics have suggested that the popularization of this disorder over the past 2 decades has led patients to simulate its symptoms in therapy (either consciously or unconsciously) and has led therapists to see it where it doesn't exist (Spanos & others, 1985). Another suggestion is that multiple personalities are inadvertently created by the hypnotic procedures that therapists commonly use to identify them. In other words, a patient who has been hypnotized and asked to produce an alternative personality may unconsciously oblige the therapist and produce one, at the same time accepting the idea that this personality was always there and is just now being uncovered. Perhaps that occurs in many cases, but considerable evidence now exists that multiple personality is a legitimate disorder in a substantial number of people.

*Evidence that multiple personality exists as a real disorder and that it stems from childhood abuse coupled, perhaps, with an inborn ability to dissociate*

One of the most carefully documented studies of multiple personality was conducted by Philip Coons and his colleagues (1988) in Indiana. Over a 13-year period they identified fifty cases at their clinic that satisfied DSM-III criteria, and they studied them through interviews and by searching out confirmatory evidence outside of the clinic. Their findings included the following: (a) Of the fifty cases, forty-six were women. (b) In all but two cases the individuals had been physically and/or sexually abused repeatedly and severely in childhood, most often by their parents. Of the two who were not abused as children, one was a woman whose disorder originated in her early twenties at a time when she was repeatedly being beaten by her husband, and the other was a man whose mother had been diagnosed with schizophrenia. (c) Except for the one woman just mentioned, each patient had apparently begun a pattern of dissociation sometime before the age of 10. These findings are consistent with the results of other, less formal clinical studies (Bliss, 1986; Braun, 1985).

Most clinicians who study or treat multiple personality think of it as a disorder that begins in early childhood as a way of dealing with repeated abuse. To meet the abuse, the child may learn to go into a hypnotic-like trance that reduces pain or emotional feelings during the abuse and helps shut out the memory of it when it stops. With time these trances may become more elaborate, taking the form of distinct personalities. For example, a child being tortured might construct a personality who "enjoys" the torture, or a tough personality who "can take it." Having learned to produce new personalities to deal with these extreme conditions, the individual may use these same personalities or may develop new ones to deal with the more normal problems of life. Of course, not everyone who is abused repeatedly in childhood develops multiple personalities. Another prerequisite may be an inborn, biologically based capacity to dissociate. Consistent with this view, multiple personality patients are extremely easy to hypnotize compared to those who suffer from other mental disorders or no disorder (Bliss, 1986).

## Psychoactive Substance-Use Disorders

A psychoactive substance is a drug that acts on the brain and affects a person's emotions, perceptions, or thoughts. A *psychoactive substance-use disorder* involves the abuse of or dependence upon such a drug. *Drug abuse* implies persistent use of the drug in a way that is harmful to the self or society. *Drug dependence* (which in DSM-III-R is a synonym for *addiction*) implies that the person feels compelled—for physiological or psychological reasons (or both)—to take the drug on a regular basis and feels severe distress without it. A person who repeatedly drives while drunk, or who continues to drink even though he or she knows that alcohol is exacerbating a stomach ulcer, or who periodically misses work because of a drinking spree, is said to abuse alcohol. A person who feels that he or she cannot get through the day without drinking is said to be dependent on alcohol. In DSM-III-R, separate abuse and dependence disorders are listed for alcohol, cocaine, opiates (such as heroin), and a variety of other drugs.

It would be hard to overestimate the problems that drugs cause for individuals and society. The most abused drug, today as well as in the past, is alcohol. In the United States, alcohol is reported to be involved in about 55 percent of automobile fatalities, 50 percent of homicides, 30 percent of suicides, 65 percent of drownings, 50 percent of deaths by falling, 52 percent of fires leading to death, 60 percent of child-abuse cases, and 85 percent of home violence (FitzGerald, 1988; National Institute of Alcohol Abuse and Alcoholism, 1987). In addition to the effects of the legal drug alcohol, illegal drugs—especially cocaine and heroin—wreak havoc in the form of murders, robberies, and wasted lives. During the 1980s, cocaine use increased dramatically in North America, and cocaine-related problems were made even worse by the introduction of a particularly potent, smokeable form of cocaine called crack. Crack has been described by many users as creating almost immediate psychological dependence because it produces an enormous, short-lasting high (euphoria) followed by a crash (sense of depression and deprivation) that leaves the person craving the next high.

The following paragraphs examine the causes of substance-use disorders from the biological, cognitive-behavioral, and sociocultural perspectives. The focus is on alcohol abuse and dependence, because that disorder is most common and has been most fully studied.

**The Biological Perspective**    Psychoactive drugs alter mood, thought, or behavior by altering the biology of the brain. Here are three classes of such alterations:

■ *How the effects of psychoactive drugs can be divided into three categories, and how each category can be illustrated by the effects of alcohol*

1. ***Intoxicating effects*** are the short-term effects for which the drug is usually taken, and they may last for minutes or hours after a single dose. (For a summary of such effects and their physiological mechanisms for many drugs, see Table 6.1 in Chapter 6.) Alcohol's intoxicating effects include, at low to moderate doses, relief from anxiety and, in some people, a sense of euphoria. Alcohol also slows down all brain functions, causing slowed thinking, poor judgment, slurred speech, uncoordinated movements, and even coma or death, depending on the dose.

2. ***Withdrawal effects*** occur after the drug is removed from the system. Usually such effects occur only after a long period of continuous or frequent drug use. These effects apparently result from adaptation to the drug such that the brain functions in some ways more normally with the drug than without it. (For a more complete discussion, see Chapter 6.) In a person who is physiologically addicted to alcohol, withdrawal effects begin to occur within 8 to 20 hours after alcohol has been cleared from the body. These symptoms—referred to as *delirium tremens* (or *DTs*)—are those of an extraordinarily overactive brain. They include hallucinations; feelings of panic; muscle tremors ("the shakes"); sweating, high heart rate, and other signs of autonomic arousal; and sometimes brain seizures, which can result in death. The death rate from DTs that are not treated medically is estimated to be somewhere between 15 and 50 percent (Light, 1986).

3. ***Permanent effects*** are irreversible forms of brain damage that can result from frequent drug use, or that can occur in a developing fetus if the mother uses the drug during pregnancy. One permanent effect of long-term, heavy alcohol use is *alcohol amnesic disorder* (also called *Korsakoff's syndrome*), which entails severe memory impairment and difficulties with motor coordination associated with damage to certain areas of the brain's limbic system. Another permanent effect of alcohol is *fetal alcohol syndrome*, a condition of mental retardation and physical abnormalities in a child stemming from a mother's consumption of large amounts of alcohol during pregnancy.

■ *Evidence that the predisposition for alcoholism is influenced by genes*

People differ in their likelihood of becoming dependent on alcohol, and a considerable amount of research suggests that those differences are partly genetic in origin. In a study conducted in Denmark, boys with a severely alcoholic biological parent (usually the father) were found to be about four times as likely as boys with

**Alcoholics Anonymous**

*In A.A. groups, people meet as equals to share their experiences and strengths and to help one another recover from alcohol misuse. The core of the recovery program is a series of twelve steps, the most basic of which is admitting that one is an alcoholic.*

no alcoholic parent to develop alcoholism themselves, even if they were raised from early infancy on by nonalcoholic adoptive parents (Goodwin, 1976, 1979). In the same study, girls who had an alcoholic parent were not at heightened risk for the disorder. Other studies have also suggested that risk for alcoholism may be more heritable in males than females. On the basis of such findings, some researchers have proposed a distinction between two types of alcoholism: *Type 1*, or *milieu limited*, which can occur in both genders and is predisposed more by the environment (the "milieu") than by heredity; and *Type 2*, or *male limited*, which is rarer, more severe, occurs only in males, and is strongly predisposed by heredity (Cloniger & others, 1981).

Recently, a team of researchers led by Kenneth Blum and Ernest Noble (1990) have found direct evidence for a genetic difference between people (mostly men) who had died from alcoholism and an otherwise comparable group who had died from other causes and had not suffered from alcoholism. Seventy-seven percent of the alcoholic group had, on their chromosome 11, a specific gene that was found in only 28 percent of the nonalcoholic group. Other evidence suggests that this same gene (called the *dopamine $D_2$ receptor gene*) augments the effectiveness of neurotransmission in areas of the brain where dopamine is the transmitter substance. As described in Chapter 7, dopamine is a transmitter in brain pathways that mediate the sense of pleasure or euphoria. Thus, one possible interpretation is that people who have this gene derive more pleasure from alcohol than do other people, which causes them to seek alcohol more than do other people once they have experienced its effects, which in turn increases their likelihood of becoming addicted. If this hypothesis is correct, we might expect that people who have this gene would also be predisposed to abuse other pleasure-producing drugs—an idea that has yet to be tested.

**The Behavioral and Cognitive Perspectives**   Consuming alcohol or taking any drug is a learned, voluntary action. Behaviorists have long described addictive behavior in terms of operant conditioning. From this view, the short-term pleasure or relief from pain resulting from the drug is a powerful reinforcer for continued drug use. This view is quite consistent with the biological work, discussed above, suggesting that people who are most likely to become addicted to a drug are those who are biologically predisposed to experience the most pleasure from it. Classical conditioning may also come into play. As described in Chapter 5, cues associated with an environment in which a drug is frequently taken can become conditioned stimuli for physiological responses that tend to counteract the drug effect (Siegel, 1988). This phenomenon has been used to explain why a person who has been drug free and has felt no craving for it during a long stay in a treatment center may suddenly experience an intense craving upon returning to the environment in which he or she had habitually taken the drug. Cues in that environment may trigger conditioned physiological responses that are opposite to those produced by the drug. The responses feel like withdrawal symptoms and thus induce the craving.

From a cognitive perspective, the act of taking a drug requires a decision to take it, and that decision is based in part on a person's beliefs or expectancies concerning the drug and its effects. In a longitudinal study, researchers found that they could predict which nondrinking teenagers would become alcohol abusers on the basis of their beliefs about alcohol (Roehling & others, 1987). Those who believed that alcohol has valued effects—such as making a person more sociable, powerful, or sexually vital—were more likely to be alcohol abusers 1 or 2 years later than were those who did not have such beliefs. Other studies have shown that an important step in the development of alcoholism occurs when a person begins to use alcohol not just socially but as a way of coping with negative emotions (Cooper & others, 1988). Once the person thinks of alcohol as a general way of quieting negative emotions, its use increases and the person is well on the path to alcohol abuse

*■ How one gene may predispose a person to alcoholism by increasing the pleasure that alcohol produces*

*■ How behavioral theorists describe addiction in terms of conditioning, and how cognitive theorists describe it in terms of learned expectancies*

**Figure 17.5** *A cognitive model of alcoholism*

*In this model, positive alcohol expectancies plus a tendency to avoid confronting one's own strong emotions are predisposing causes of alcohol abuse or dependence. (Adapted from Cooper & others, 1988.)*

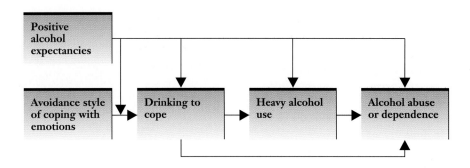

or dependence. Based on such research, M. Lynne Cooper and her colleagues (1988) have proposed a cognitive model of alcoholism in which the predisposing causes are (a) positive expectancies about the effects of alcohol, and (b) a learned fear of negative emotions or a tendency to avoid such emotions (see Figure 17.5).

**The Sociocultural Perspective** If the likelihood of abusing alcohol or other drugs is related to a person's beliefs about the substance, then where do these beliefs come from? They come from family, friends, and the entire social environment to which the person is exposed. Research has shown that most young people who abuse alcohol or other drugs were first encouraged to do so by their peers, and that the ability to resist such peer pressure is directly related to the strength and cohesiveness of family ties (Oetting & Beauvais, 1988; Zucker & Gomberg, 1986). Other research has shown large cultural and subcultural differences in alcohol abuse that correspond to cultural traditions. In the United States, the lowest rates of alcoholism occur among ethnic Jews, Chinese, Japanese, Italians, and Greeks, all of whom have traditions of strong negative sanctions for heavy drinking or drunkenness (Vaillant, 1983; Peele, 1988). Among such groups alcohol may be used for religious purposes or as a beverage to accompany a meal, but drinking to get drunk is not accepted. In contrast, the Irish come from a long tradition of accepting and sometimes even romanticizing drunkenness, and the rate of alcoholism among Irish Americans is very high (Vaillant, 1983; Peele, 1988). Cultural beliefs probably also contribute to the fivefold difference between men and women in prevalence of alcoholism; in practically every culture, drunkenness is seen as less acceptable in women than in men.

- *Evidence that cultural traditions dramatically affect the prevalence of alcoholism*

## Mood Disorders

*Mood* refers to a prolonged emotional state that colors many if not all aspects of a person's thought and behavior. It is useful (though somewhat oversimplified) to think of a single dimension of mood, running from depression at one end to elation at the other. Because we have all tasted both ends, we have an idea of what they are like. Both are normal experiences, but at times either of them can become too intense or prolonged and can promote harmful, even life-threatening actions. Severe depression can prevent a person from working, lead a person to withdraw from friends, or even provoke suicide. Severe elation, called *mania*, can lead to outrageous behaviors that turn other people away, or to dangerous acts that stem from a false sense of security and bravado. DSM-III-R identifies two main categories of **mood disorders**: These are **depressive disorders**, characterized by prolonged or extreme depression; and **bipolar disorders**, characterized by alternating episodes of depression and mania.

**Table 17.2  Typical thoughts of a person with an anxiety disorder compared to those of a person with a depressive disorder**

### Anxious person

What if I get sick and become an invalid?

Something will happen to someone I care about.

Something might happen that will ruin my appearance.

I am going to have a heart attack.

### Depressed person

I'm worthless.

I'm a social failure.

I have become physically unattractive.

Life isn't worth living.

*Source:* Adapted from "Differentiating anxiety and depression: A test of the cognitive content-specificity hypothesis" by A. T. Beck, G. Brown, J. I. Eidelson, R. A. Steer, & J. H. Riskind, 1987, *Journal of Abnormal Psychology, 96,* p. 181.

## Depression

To get an idea of depressive thinking, look at Table 17.2, which contrasts the thoughts of a person diagnosed as depressed to those of a person diagnosed as anxious (Beck & others, 1987). Whereas the anxious person worries about what might happen in the future, the depressed person feels that all is already lost. He or she feels worthless, deserted, hopeless. Such thoughts are captured in the following quotation from Norman Endler (1982), a highly respected psychologist who is describing his own bout with depression:

> I honestly felt subhuman, lower than the lowest vermin . . . I could not understand why anyone would want to associate with me, let alone love me . . . I was positive that I was a fraud and a phony . . . I couldn't understand how I had written the books and journal articles that I had and how they had been accepted for publication. I must have conned a lot of people.

In DSM-III-R, the principal symptom of depression is loss of interest and pleasure in life, compounded usually by a sense of self-blame, worthlessness, and thoughts of death. Other symptoms may include increased or decreased sleep, increased or decreased appetite, and either agitated or retarded motor symptoms. Agitated symptoms include repetitive, aimless movements such as hand wringing or pacing; and retarded symptoms include slowed speech and slowed body movements. To warrant diagnosis of a depressive disorder, such symptoms must be either very severe or very prolonged, and must not be attributable directly to a specific life experience. Two main classes of depressive disorders are distinguished in DSM-III-R. One, called *major depression*, is characterized by very severe symptoms that last essentially without remission for at least 2 weeks. The other, called *dysthymia*, is characterized by less severe symptoms that last over at least a 2-year period. Quite often, bouts of major depression are superimposed on a more chronic state of dysthymia, in which case the person is said to have *double depression*.

## Depression

*As illustrated in this painting by Edvard Munch, the world looks bleak to a depressed person.*

As was shown in Figure 17.2, both major depression and dysthymia are quite prevalent, and both are diagnosed more often in women than in men.

**A Biological Theory: Reduced Action of Monoamines**   Research using the standard methods of studying twins and adoptees has shown that the predisposition for depression is strongly affected by heredity (Wender & others, 1986; Bertelsen, 1979). Other biological research has centered on the possibility that depression is mediated by a biochemical imbalance in the brain. Research conducted during the 1950s found that severe depression could often be treated successfully with drugs, and later work showed that such drugs increase the action of a group of neurotransmitters in the brain referred to as monoamines. Other research has shown that drugs that reduce the level of monoamines or inhibit their action can produce feelings of depression in people who were not initially depressed. Such findings led to the *monoamine theory of depression*, which holds that depression results from too little activity at brain synapses where monoamines are the neurotransmitters (Schildkraut, 1965).

*Reasons for thinking that depression may stem from reduced activity of certain neurotransmitters in the brain, and why that theory has been hard to prove*

At the cellular level, antidepressant drugs (drugs used to treat depression) increase the action of monoamine neurotransmitters by (a) blocking the action of an enzyme in axon terminals that normally breaks down monoamines, which increases the amount available for neurotransmission; (b) blocking the reuptake of monoamine molecules back into the axon terminals from synaptic gaps, and in that way prolonging their action in synapses; and (c) increasing the sensitivity of receptor sites for monoamine neurotransmitter molecules on postsynaptic membranes, such that a given amount of neurotransmitter has a larger effect than it otherwise would have. The third mechanism is believed to be most important for the long-term clinical effects of most antidepressant drugs (Ashton, 1987). (To review the parts of the synapse, you may want to refer back to Figure 6.5.)

The three main monoamine transmitters in the brain are norepinephrine, dopamine, and serotonin, all of which are known from animal research to be involved in neural mechanisms underlying motivation and arousal. Dopamine and norepinephrine are especially important in motivational and pleasure-enhancing mechanisms (discussed in Chapter 7), and serotonin is especially important in mechanisms that promote calmness, sleep, and relief from pain. Thus, a decline in norepinephrine or dopamine could be responsible for the loss of motivation and pleasure that accompanies any severe depression, and a decline in serotonin could be responsible for the sleeplessness, irritability, and restless movements that occur specifically in agitated depression (Willner, 1985). Although the monoamine theory was proposed nearly 30 years ago, its validity is still uncertain. Research in this area is made difficult by the fact that all drugs that induce or relieve depression have multiple effects on the brain, influencing the action of all three monoamines and other neurotransmitters as well. Moreover, the finding that depression can be influenced by drugs that affect monoamines does not necessarily imply that naturally occurring mood changes are caused by changed levels of monoamines.

**A Behavioral Theory: Learned Helplessness**   Another line of research has related the onset of depression to stressful experiences in people's lives. In one study of this sort, Andrew Billings and his colleagues (1983) interviewed more than 400 men and women who were beginning treatment for depression, and an equal number who had not been diagnosed as depressed, about their experiences over the previous year. They found the following: (a) Compared to the nondepressed group, the depressed group had experienced about twice as many losses, such as death of a loved one, loss of a job, decline in income, or divorce. (b) The depressed group had been subjected to relatively more sources of prolonged psychological pressure, including medical conditions, frequent family arguments, work pressures, and ambiguity about the expectations of employers or bosses.

*Evidence from surveys of people and experiments with animals that depression may stem from stressful events that one cannot control*

(c) The depressed group had relatively fewer emotionally supportive friends or relatives. These findings did not simply represent a report bias on the part of the depressed individuals; they were confirmed in separate interviews of nondepressed family members (usually spouses).

One theory that is consistent with the findings above is that depression is a psychological giving up of the attempt to control one's own fate, brought on by repeated negative experiences over which one has no control. This theory, called the *learned helplessness theory of depression*, was originally proposed by Martin Seligman based on experiments with dogs (Seligman & others, 1968). Seligman found that dogs that had previously received a series of inescapable electric shocks failed, when tested later in a different apparatus, to learn to escape shocks by jumping over a hurdle. These dogs passively accepted the shocks without looking for a means of escape. In contrast, dogs that had either received no previous shocks or had received shocks that they could turn off by pressing against a panel had no difficulty learning to jump over the hurdle.

The learned helplessness theory is not necessarily incompatible with the monoamine theory, as was shown in experiments conducted by Jay Weiss and his colleagues (1976) with rats. In Weiss's experiments, the rats in the helpless condition received inescapable electric shocks, other rats received shocks that could be escaped by turning a wheel, and still other rats received no shocks. Conditions were controlled such that rats in the helpless condition received the same number and patterning of shocks as did those in the escape condition. The researchers then measured the amount of norepinephrine in the brains of these animals and found that this monoamine was lowest in rats that had been in the helpless condition. Apparently, the experience of helplessness had caused these rats to produce less norepinephrine. From this work, Weiss suggested that being in a helpless situation may produce depression through the following chain: helpless situation → reduced norepinephrine → depressed mood and behavior.

The finding just described is important because it demonstrates a reciprocal relationship between psychological experience and physiology. In any theory relating one or another mental disorder to an altered level of a neurotransmitter, we must include the possibility that the alteration in transmitter may stem from experiences that are essentially psychological in nature, not just from biological factors such as genes or drugs.

**A Cognitive Theory: The Attribution of Helplessness**    Although stressful events can increase a person's chance of becoming depressed, not everyone who undergoes such experiences becomes depressed. In the study by Billings and his colleagues, some of the nondepressed subjects had experienced losses and pressures that were objectively more severe than the average of those for the depressed group. Observations of this sort provide the starting point for cognitive theories of depression, which hold that depression stems not so much from the objective events themselves as from the way they are interpreted.

One of the first to emphasize the role of cognition in depression was Aaron Beck (1967), a psychiatrist who observed that his depressed clients held consistently pessimistic views of themselves, their world, and the future, and that they seemed to maintain these views by distorting their experiences in negative ways. They would mentally exaggerate bad experiences and minimize or overlook good ones. Beck developed a mode of therapy (discussed in Chapter 18) that centers on training depressed people to assess their experiences more optimistically.

Following Beck, Lyn Abramson and Martin Seligman developed a more specific cognitive theory of depression, sometimes called the *attributional helplessness theory of depression* (Seligman & others, 1979; Abramson & others, 1988).

*Evidence that the effects of uncontrollable stressful events on mood and behavior might be mediated partly by reduced levels of a particular neurotransmitter in the brain*

*How the learned helplessness theory was modified from a behavioral theory into a cognitive theory*

This theory is a revision of Seligman's earlier learned helplessness theory. It shares with that theory the idea that depression involves a sense of helplessness, but adds to it the idea that in humans the sense of helplessness comes not just from the objective events that happen, but from the *attributions* that people make about those events. As described in Chapter 14, an attribution is an inference about the cause of something. According to the attributional helplessness theory, people differ in their *attributional style*, and that is what determines who will or will not become depressed as a result of particular experience. More specifically, the theory holds that people who are prone to depression consistently attribute their negative experiences to causes that are *internal* (that is, that are within themselves rather than outside of themselves), *stable* (won't change), and *global* (will affect a wide range of activities and experiences). As an illustration, consider the following attributions that different students might make about why they received a poor grade on a test:

- "I received a poor grade because this test happened to be an unfair one." This attribution is *external* because it has to do with the fairness of the test rather than with some quality within the student. It is *unstable* because it does not contain an implication that all tests will be unfair. And it is *specific* (not global) because it contains no implication about other areas of endeavor. The attribution does not assume that the whole world is unfair, only that this particular test was unfair. This student will not, according to the theory, feel depressed as a result of the poor grade.

- "I received a poor grade because I didn't study hard enough. Next time I'll work harder and do better." In this case, the attribution is *internal* because the student takes responsibility for the failure; but, like the first student's attribution, it is *unstable* and *specific*. The student limits the assessment of not working hard just to this one instance, and does not see it as a general quality of his or her academic performance, nor as applicable to other realms of endeavor. This student, too, should not feel depressed.

- "I received a poor grade because I am incompetent." Here, the attribution is *internal* (the student's own incompetence), *stable* (incompetence is a stable trait, not something that comes and goes), and *global* (incompetence is the sort of trait that would affect not just test taking, but all realms of life). This is the student who, according to the theory, is most likely to feel depressed as a result of the poor grade.

*Evidence that a certain attributional style correlates with depression, and the problem with interpreting that correlation in terms of cause and effect*

Seligman and his colleagues have developed a questionnaire designed to assess people's routine ways of explaining their experiences. Consistent with the theory, the tendency of people to make internal, stable, and global attributions for their negative experiences, as measured by the questionnaire, correlates strongly with the degree to which they are depressed, as assessed by other measures (Seligman & others, 1988). But such research does not necessarily show that the attributional style is a cause of depression; the negative style of thinking could simply be one of the symptoms of depression. To show that this style of thinking is a cause of depression, researchers must demonstrate that the style exists before the person actually becomes depressed and that it plays a role in generating the depressed state. Although some research suggests that this is the case (Metalsky & others, 1987), strong evidence is still lacking.

**Depression Breeds Depression** Most of us, when we experience a depressed mood, are able to relieve that mood through our own thoughts and actions. After a certain period of gloom, we grab our bootstraps and pull ourselves up, using such

■ *How depression can be depicted as a vicious triangle, and how different approaches to treating it correspond with the triangle's corners*

tried-and-true means as positive thinking, talking with friends, or undertaking activities that we especially enjoy. But severely depressed people—those who qualify for a diagnosis of major depression—typically don't do those things. Their patterns of thought and action continue to work against their recovery, rather than for it. Figure 17.6 depicts what might be called the *vicious triangle of severe depression*, in which a person's mood, thought, and action interact in such a way as to keep him or her in a depressed state. Depressed mood promotes negative thinking and withdrawal from enjoyable activities; negative thinking promotes withdrawal from enjoyable activities and depressed mood; and withdrawal from enjoyable activities promotes depressed mood and negative thinking. Each corner of the triangle supports the others.

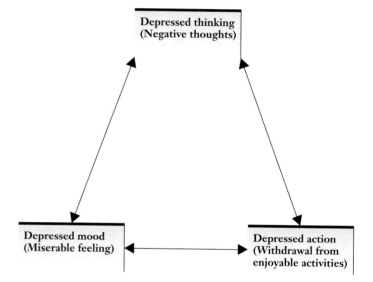

**Figure 17.6  *The vicious triangle of severe depression***
*Mood, thought, and behavior feed on one another to maintain the depressed state.*

Each corner of the triangle also corresponds to a different therapeutic approach to breaking the triangle of depression (described more fully in Chapter 18). Drug therapy attempts to alleviate mood directly, which in turn should increase positive thinking and actions. Behavioral therapy attempts to get the person to act in ways that bring more pleasure, which in turn should improve mood and promote positive thoughts. Cognitive therapy attempts to change the person's way of thinking in a positive direction, which in turn should improve behavior and mood.

### Bipolar Disorders

Major depression and dysthymia are sometimes called *unipolar disorders*, because they are characterized by mood changes only in one direction—downward from normal. In bipolar disorders (commonly called *manic-depression*), mood sometimes swings downward, creating a *depressive episode*, and other times upward, creating a *manic episode*. Such episodes may last anywhere from a few days to several months, and periods of normal mood may occur in between. DSM-III-R identifies two main varieties of bipolar disorders, which differ in degree. **Bipolar disorder** (used in the singular) refers to the more severe variety, and **cyclothymia** refers to the less severe variety, in which the mood changes are not as great. The manual also acknowledges the possibility of disorders characterized only by recurrent mania without depression, but notes that they are very rare.

The manic episodes in bipolar disorders typically involve inordinate feelings of power, confidence, and energy, as illustrated by the following quotation from a woman describing her own disorder (Fieve, 1975):

When I start going into a high, I no longer feel like an ordinary housewife. Instead, I feel organized and accomplished, and I begin to feel I am my most creative self. I can write poetry easily. I can compose melodies without effort. I can paint . . . I have countless ideas about how the environmental problem could inspire a crusade for the health and betterment of everyone . . . I don't seem to need much sleep . . . I feel sexy and men stare at me. Maybe I'll have an affair, or perhaps several. I feel capable of speaking and doing good in politics.

■ *Evidence that heightened creativity can accompany mild manic episodes*

The feeling of enhanced ability and creativity during mild to moderate manic episodes is probably not entirely an illusion. A number of studies have found a disproportionately high incidence of cyclothymia among eminently creative artists and writers and have shown that those individuals produced their best work during manic episodes (Andreasen, 1978; Hershman & Lieb, 1988). In another study, people with cyclothymia, selected only on the basis of their clinical diagnosis, were found to be more creative in their regular work and home life than were a control group with no diagnosed mental disorder (Richards & others, 1988). In the same study, however, people with the more serious bipolar disorder were not more creative than those in the control group. Apparently, the disorganization of thought and action that accompanied their more extreme bouts of mania offset any creative advantage that they may have enjoyed.

On the negative side, mania can result in actions that are highly disruptive to the lives of affected individuals and their families. Extreme mania may be accompanied by bizarre thoughts and dangerous behaviors, such as jumping off a building in the false belief that one can fly; and even milder states may be accompanied by spending sprees, absence from work, or sexual escapades that the affected person later regrets.

Research with twins and adoptees to assess heritability has shown that the predisposition for bipolar disorder is strongly influenced by genes (for example, Bertelsen, 1979). To date, neither the environmental nor biological factors that may induce the mood swings in bipolar disorders have been identified. Although some evidence exists that stressful life events may help bring on manic and depressive episodes in people who are predisposed for a bipolar disorder (Ambelas, 1987), the evidence for such effects is not nearly as strong as it is for unipolar depression. As described in Chapter 18, bipolar disorder can often be controlled with the drug lithium, but how lithium produces this effect is as yet unknown.

■ *How SAD differs from bipolar disorder and cyclothymia*

A few people have been identified who regularly undergo severe depression during the fall and winter months, followed by mild mania in the spring—a disorder called *SAD* (*seasonally affective disorder*). The mood changes in SAD are apparently controlled by seasonal changes in the availability of sunlight, as the disorder can be treated by exposure to very bright fluorescent lighting during the evening hours in the fall and winter (Wehr & others, 1986). This is a different disorder from either bipolar disorder or cyclothymia; people with the latter disorders rarely show seasonal regularity to their mood changes.

## Schizophrenia

John sits alone in his dismal room, surrounded by plastic garbage bags that he has hoarded during his late-night excursions onto the street. He is unkempt and scrawny. He lost his job months ago. He has no appetite and hasn't eaten a real meal in weeks. He is afraid to go out during the day because he sees in every passing face a spy who is trying to learn, by reading his mind, the secret that will destroy him. He hears voices telling him that he must stay away from the spies, and he also hears his own thoughts as if they were broadcast aloud for all to hear. He sits still, trying to keep calm, trying to reduce the volume of his thoughts. He suffers from *schizophrenia*.

## Characteristics and Variations of the Disorder

Schizophrenia is a serious and relatively prevalent disorder. It is found in about 0.5 percent of the adult population at any given time (see Figure 17.2) and in about 1 percent of people at some time in their lives (Robins & others, 1984). It accounts for a higher percentage of the inpatient population of mental hospitals than any other diagnostic category. It usually appears first in late adolescence or early adulthood, though it can appear much later. Sometimes people make a full recovery from schizophrenia, sometimes they make a partial recovery, and sometimes the disorder takes a deteriorating course throughout the person's life.

■ *How schizophrenia is characterized in terms of cognitive and perceptual, behavioral, and emotional symptoms*

No two sufferers of schizophrenia have quite the same symptoms. But to receive the DSM-III-R diagnosis of schizophrenia, the symptoms must include: (a) cognitive or perceptual distortion, such that the person is in some ways seriously out of touch with reality; and (b) deterioration from a former level of functioning, usually including a sharp decline in ability to work and care for oneself. In addition, most cases are marked by social withdrawal. The person may be physically withdrawn from others, as is John, or psychologically withdrawn, as are those living within a family but not communicating with its members in a socially connected way. Disturbances in affect (emotion) are also common. Some cases involve *flattened affect*, in which emotional expressions are muted or absent, facial muscles are immobile, and speech is slow, labored, and monotonous. Flattened affect may also be accompanied by loss of basic drives such as hunger, or loss of the pleasure that normally comes from fulfilling such drives. Other cases involve *inappropriate affect*, in which emotions are expressed but in ways that are inconsistent with what the person is saying or thinking. For example, a person with inappropriate affect may laugh uproariously while describing an extremely sad experience.

The label *schizophrenia* was first used by the Swiss psychiatrist Eugen Bleuler (1911/1950), whose writings are still an important source of information and insight about the disorder. The term comes from the Greek words *schizo*, which means split, and *phrenum*, which means mind, so it literally means "split mind." Bleuler believed, as do many theorists today, that schizophrenia entails a split among such mental processes as attention, perception, emotion, motivation, and thought, such that these processes operate in relative isolation of one another, leading to bizarre and disorganized thoughts and actions. Bleuler's term has caused many nonpsychologists to confuse schizophrenia with multiple personality. The mind of a person with schizophrenia is *not* split in the sense that occurs in multiple personality; dissociation does not occur.

■ *How the distortions in thought and perception that characterize schizophrenia can be categorized into three varieties*

**Delusions, Hallucinations, and Formal Thought Disturbances**   The symptoms of schizophrenia that most distinguish it from other disorders are those involving distortions in perception and thought, most of which can be placed in one of the following three categories:

1. *Delusions*  These are false beliefs held in the face of compelling evidence to the contrary. Common types of delusions in schizophrenia are (a) *delusions of persecution*, which are a person's beliefs that others are plotting against him or her; (b) *delusions of grandeur*, beliefs in one's own extraordinary importance (for example, that one is the "Queen of England"); and (c) *delusions of being controlled*, such as believing one's movements are being controlled by invisible wires or radio waves in puppet-like fashion. Often several delusions may occur together in a single delusional scenario.

2. *Hallucinations*  These are false sensory perceptions—seeing or hearing things that aren't there. The most common hallucinations are auditory, usually in the form of hearing voices. Hallucinations and delusions typically work together to support one another. For example, a man who has a delusion of persecution may repeatedly hear the voice of his persecutor insulting or threatening him.

**Art by persons diagnosed with schizophrenia**

*These untitled drawings by Adolf Wölfi (left) and Adolph Nesper (right) typify the unusual personal symbolism and eerie rhythmical forms that characterize these patients' work. As you examine each drawing, ask yourself whether it expresses illness or recovery.*

Another symptom that may involve both hallucination and delusion is *thought broadcasting*, in which the person "hears" his or her own thoughts as if they were spoken aloud and has the delusion that others can hear them, too.

3. **Formal thought disturbances** These are breakdowns in the form or pattern of logical thinking. In some instances, the mind jumps wildly from one idea to another in a manner not guided by logic but by such factors as simple word associations—a pattern referred to as *overinclusion*. A classic example is this greeting to Bleuler (1911/1950) from one of his patients: "I wish you a happy, joyful, healthy, blessed and fruitful year, and many good wine-years to come as well as a healthy and good apple-year, and sauerkraut and cabbage and squash and seed year." Notice that once the patient's mind hooked onto fruit (in "fruitful year") it entered into a chain of associations involving fruit and vegetables that had little to do with the original intent of the statement. Another variety of formal thought disturbance is known as *paralogic*, in which reasoning is superficially based on rules of logic, but in fact is flawed in ways that are obvious to others. Paralogic may help support a delusion, as in the case of a woman who supported her claim to be the Virgin Mary as follows: "The Virgin Mary is a virgin. I am a virgin. Therefore, I am the Virgin Mary" (Arieti, 1966).

Perceptual and thought disturbances are not always as dramatic as the examples just given, which is part of the reason why the diagnosis of schizophrenia is by no means perfectly reliable. We all hold certain beliefs that may seem like delusions to others; we all sometimes fall prey to poor logic as we attempt to support our beliefs; and we all sometimes think we hear sounds that are not physically present. As in the case of the other disorders discussed in this chapter, there is no sharp division here between normal and abnormal, but instead a continuous gradation.

**Types of Schizophrenia** Ever since Bleuler's classic work, people who study schizophrenia have attempted to divide it into distinct types based on the predominant symptoms. DSM-III-R, using a system similar to that first developed by Bleuler, identifies four main types: (1) *paranoid type*, characterized mainly by delu-

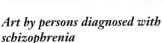

■ *How DSM-III-R divides schizophrenia into four types; and how another system divides it into two types*

**Figure 17.7** *A person in a catatonic stupor*

*People with schizophrenia withdraw from their environment in various ways. One of the most extreme forms of withdrawal is the catatonic stupor, in which the person may remain motionless for hours on end in an uncomfortable position.*

sions of persecution and grandeur; (2) *catatonic type*, characterized mainly by nonreaction to the environment (see Figure 17.7); (3) *disorganized type*, characterized mainly by formal thought disorders, incoherence of speech, and either inappropriate or flattened affect; and (4) *undifferentiated type*, a sort of catch-all category for cases that do not meet the criteria of the other categories. These types are not discretely separate from one another, and probably do not represent truly different disorders, but are convenient labels to indicate which symptoms are most prominent in particular individuals.

Within the last 15 years or so, many researchers and clinicians have found a different system of categorization to be more useful than the one just described (Crow, 1980; Andreasen & Olsen, 1982; Green & Walker, 1986). In this system, schizophrenia is broken down into two types: **Type I schizophrenia**, also called *positive-symptom schizophrenia*, is characterized mainly by excesses in perception, thought, and behavior. Its predominant symptoms are hallucinations, delusions, bizarre associations, and the acting out of bizarre behaviors. **Type II schizophrenia**, also called *negative-symptom schizophrenia*, is characterized mainly by deficits in perception, thought, and behavior. Its predominant symptoms are poverty of speech (slow, labored, unspontaneous speech), flattened affect, reduced drive, difficulty with muscle movements, and thought disorder characterized more by lack of thought than by bizarre associations.

In support of this typology, cases that fall most clearly within these different categories seem to be associated with different kinds of disturbances in the brain and with different long-term outcomes (see Table 17.3). On the other hand, most people with schizophrenia have both positive and negative symptoms that manifest themselves at different times. The two categories of symptoms can occur in different individuals in all possible proportions (Lenzenweger & others, 1989), so the distinction between the two types is not clear cut. One view is that Type I simply represents the less serious cases, and Type II the more serious cases, of what is fundamentally the same disorder (Gottesman & others, 1987).

**Table 17.3** *Differences between Type I and Type II schizophrenia*

| Characteristics | Type I | Type II |
|---|---|---|
| Clinical symptoms | Positive (delusions, hallucinations, bizarre actions) | Negative (flattened affect, poverty of thought and speech) |
| Responses to stimuli | Overresponsive; highly distractible | Underresponsive |
| Response to antipsychotic drugs | Reduction or loss of positive symptoms | Little effect on negative symptoms |
| Prognosis | Good chance of partial or complete recovery | Poor chance of recovery |

**Defective Attention and Concentration**    How might we make sense of the various symptoms that characterize schizophrenia? Bleuler (1924/1951) suggested that a unifying characteristic of the disorder is that people who suffer from it seem "incapable of holding a particular thought in the proper channel." Many people with schizophrenia describe their own early symptoms in terms of defective attention and concentration (Freedman & Chapman, 1973), as exemplified by the following quotations: "Every face in the windows of a passing streetcar would be engraved in my mind . . . A hodge-podge of unrelated stimuli were distracting me from things that should have had my undivided attention" (MacDonald, 1960). "Nothing settles in my mind—not even for a second . . . Too many things come into my head at once and I lose control . . . My mind is not right if I walk or speak. It is better to stay still and not say a word" (Chapman, 1966). Laboratory studies have confirmed that people with schizophrenia perform especially poorly on tasks involving selective attention and concentration. For example, they show greater deterioration in ability to repeat a passage of prose, or to hold a set of numbers in mind, when distracting sounds are added than do people diagnosed with other disorders or with no disorder (Wielgus & Harvey, 1988; Green & Walker, 1986).

One possible unifying—though oversimplified—way to understand the symptoms of schizophrenia goes something like this: The basic underlying defect is an inability to filter out relevant from irrelevant stimuli (poor attention), or relevant from irrelevant memories and ideas (poor concentration). Without these filtering mechanisms, delusions, hallucinations, and formal thought disorders can arise from the jumble of sensory impressions and ideas that are mixed together in the mind. The negative symptoms (the general slowing of behavior and withdrawal from the world) might, by this account, arise as an attempt to reduce the confusing jumble of stimuli and ideas that bombard the mind and to achieve some measure of mental calm. This explanation is almost certainly not the whole story; but, based both on the self-reports of people who have suffered from the disorder and on laboratory evidence, it seems to be an important part of it.

**The Relationship Between Normal Mental Imagery and Hallucinations** Consistent with the hypothesis that schizophrenia entails a breakdown in attention and concentration is the more specific hypothesis that hallucinations might result from an inability to distinguish vividly imagined sounds or scenes from those that actually exist in the external world. Some years ago, Sanford Mintz and Murray Alpert (1972) pointed out that, among people who do not have schizophrenia, about 50 percent can form very realistic auditory images and 10 percent can form very realistic visual images. When asked to imagine that they are listening to a specific popular song, or that they are looking at a specific, well-known scene, about 50 percent of people report that they can hear the song as if it were really there, and about 10 percent report that they can see the scene as if it were really there. These experiences are not hallucinations, because even though the imagined song or scene is very vivid, the subject knows that it is not really there. What is most interesting is that these percentages, taken from people without schizophrenia, match closely the percentages of people with schizophrenia who experience auditory and visual hallucinations: About 50 percent experience auditory hallucinations and 10 percent experience visual hallucinations. Perhaps hallucinations arise when a person who has a normal capacity for vivid auditory or visual imagery develops, in addition—as a fundamental characteristic of schizophrenia—an inability to distinguish vividly imagined sounds or sights from real ones.

To test this possibility, Mintz and Alpert (1972) asked individuals who had been diagnosed with schizophrenia, but who were not currently in an active phase of their disorder (that is, were not currently experiencing hallucinations or other positive symptoms), to imagine that they were listening to the song "White Christmas." Nearly all of those subjects who had previously experienced auditory hallucinations reported that they could imagine the song very vividly, whereas almost none of those who did not have auditory hallucinations as part of their syndrome reported that they could. Thus, auditory hallucination during the active phase of schizophrenia seems to correspond with a normal capacity for high auditory imagery at other times.

Mintz and Alpert's study is interesting because it illustrates a relationship between a specific symptom of schizophrenia (auditory hallucination) and a normal cognitive ability (vivid auditory imagination). In general, the cognitive approach to schizophrenia is to try to understand its symptoms in terms of specific deficits in otherwise normal cognitive processes. When such an understanding is achieved, the symptoms seem much less bizarre than they did before.

*How a defect in selective attention might account for both positive and negative symptoms of schizophrenia*

*Evidence supporting the view that hallucinations result from the coupling of schizophrenia with a preexisting capacity for vivid mental imagery*

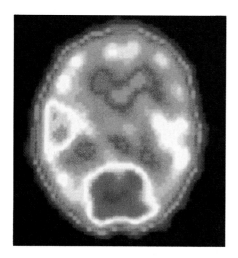

**A picture of brain abnormality**

*This PET scan of the brain of a person diagnosed with schizophrenia shows abnormally low levels of activity in the frontal lobes (the large areas of green). Since these areas underlie attentional mechanisms, the pattern is consistent with the idea that schizophrenia reflects a defect in attention.*

■ **Evidence that the positive symptoms of schizophrenia may be mediated by excessive activity at brain synapses where dopamine is the neurotransmitter**

## Potential Causes

**Biological Contributions**   Studies of twins and adoptees on the role of heredity in the incidence of schizophrenia are discussed extensively in Chapter 3. Such studies show that genes play an important role in a person's susceptibility to schizophrenia, but are not the only important variable. Perhaps the clearest evidence for the latter comes from cases of genetically identical twins who are discordant for the disorder—that is, cases in which one twin develops schizophrenia and the other does not (see Table 3.2).

Beyond heredity, but still in the realm of biological causes, lies evidence that prenatal factors and birth traumas may also be predisposing causes of schizophrenia. Birth records of discordant identical twins reveal that in most cases the twin who eventually developed schizophrenia was born second and had a lower birth weight than the other twin, indicative of having a less favorable position in the uterus (Wahl, 1976). Other studies have shown that people with schizophrenia are more likely than other people to have had a difficult birth, involving possible oxygen deprivation or other trauma to the brain (Spohn & Patterson, 1980; DeLisi & others, 1988). In some cases, viral infections before or shortly after birth may also play a role, though that idea is quite controversial (Torrey, 1988).

Another biological approach has been to try to identify specific abnormalities in the brain that correspond with schizophrenia. The longest-standing theory from this approach is the ***dopamine theory of schizophrenia***, which maintains that the symptoms of schizophrenia arise from overactivity at synapses where dopamine is the neurotransmitter. The evidence is based mainly on the effects of drugs. Antipsychotic drugs, which are effective in reducing positive schizophrenic symptoms, are known to decrease the activity of dopamine at synapses. They block the release of dopamine from presynaptic terminals, and also block postsynaptic receptor sites, thereby reducing the effectiveness of dopamine as a transmitter. These drugs also interfere with the action of various other neurotransmitters, but there is reason to believe that their action on dopamine is most important. (See Figure 17.8 for one such line of evidence.)

Further support for the dopamine theory lies in the finding that drugs such as cocaine and amphetamines, which are known to increase the action of dopamine in the brain, can greatly exacerbate the symptoms of schizophrenia in people with the disorder (Davis, 1974), and at higher doses can even induce such symptoms in peo-

**Figure 17.8  *Correlation between the clinical and chemical potency of antipsychotic drugs***

*Each dot in this graph represents a different antipsychotic drug. Its position on the horizontal axis depicts the average daily dose of the drug when used to treat schizophrenia, and its position on the vertical axis depicts the amount of the drug needed to block the release of dopamine from synaptic terminals in a standard laboratory test. The strong positive correlation between these two measures, shown here, is one line of evidence that the clinical effectiveness of these drugs operates through their dopamine-blocking action. (From Seeman & Lee, 1975.)*

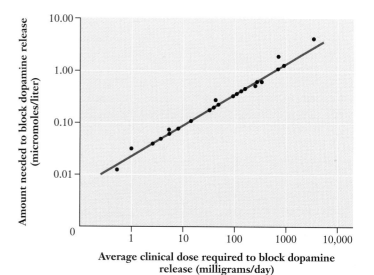

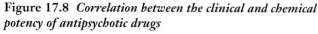

• Each dot stands for a different drug

ple who do not have the disorder (Griffith & others, 1972). Finally, the most direct but still controversial evidence is the finding of unusually high concentrations of dopamine and/or more dopamine receptors in the brains of recently deceased individuals who had been diagnosed with schizophrenia (MacKay & others, 1982; Lee & Seeman, 1980). In these studies, only brains from individuals who had not been treated with drugs were used, so the elevated dopamine and receptor levels were not a result of having taken antipsychotic drugs.

The dopamine theory seems to apply best to the positive symptoms of schizophrenia, because the drugs that alter dopamine have their largest effect on those symptoms. In line with the hypothesis that these symptoms may arise from a deficit in attention (discussed above), dopamine may be involved in the brain's attentional mechanism (Carlson, 1986). Thus, a simple model relating biochemistry to positive schizophrenic symptoms might go something like this: overactivity of dopamine in synapses → attention deficit → mixing of fantasy and reality → hallucinations, delusions, and formal thought disorders.

If the negative symptoms of schizophrenia are also secondary to disrupted attention, then they, too, should be alleviated by antipsychotic drugs; but usually they are not. Perhaps any alleviating effects that the drugs have on the negative symptoms are counteracted by the overall slowing of mental functions (and hence increase in such symptoms) that these drugs produce as side effects. There is also reason to believe, however, that the negative symptoms in the most serious and chronic cases of schizophrenia may arise from brain damage that goes well beyond a neurotransmitter dysfunction. Among the brain abnormalities often associated with such cases are reduced size of the cerebral cortex, reduced size of structures in the limbic system, and enlargement of the cerebral ventricles (fluid-filled spaces within the brain) (DeLisi & others, 1988; Mirsky & Duncan, 1986).

■ *How researchers are currently studying children who are genetically at risk for schizophrenia to identify the environmental conditions that influence the development of the disorder*

**The Role of Psychologically Stressful Experiences**   I have focused on the role of biological factors in schizophrenia because that is where most research evidence lies so far. But a number of longitudinal studies have been initiated in recent years aimed at identifying environmental experiences that may contribute to the development of the disorder (Asarnow, 1988). A general strategy of such studies is to identify a group of children who are genetically at risk for schizophrenia (one or more of their biological parents had the disorder), assess the home environment in which they are raised, and look for consistent relationships between that environment and the eventual occurrence or lack of occurrence of schizophrenia. It will be some time yet before these studies reach their conclusion, but already some significant findings have emerged. For example, a study in Finland compared children at risk for schizophrenia who were raised in adoptive homes that were rated as disturbed with those raised in adoptive homes rated as not disturbed. (In this study, a disturbed home was one that was high in conflict and anxiety, and low in stability of the roles of various family members.) Those in the disturbed homes showed more evidence of mental problems, including schizophrenic-like symptoms (though not diagnosed schizophrenia), than did those in the nondisturbed homes (Tienari & others, 1987).

Other studies show that children who are genetically at risk for schizophrenia often have difficulties with attention and concentration that are in the same direction as those of adults who have the disorder (Nuechterlein, 1983; Mirsky & Duncan, 1986). Thus, environments that would not be particularly stressful to most children might be quite stressful to children who are at risk. An environment with a lot of stimulation and change might be particularly difficult for children and adolescents who lack to some degree the normal ability to filter out extraneous stimuli. In theory, at least, the accumulation of such experiences, coupled with biological changes that occur in adolescence and early adulthood, might precipitate the disorder in those who are genetically predisposed.

# Concluding Thoughts

**1. The continuum between normality and abnormality** Although a diagnosis of a mental disorder is categorical (all or none), the symptoms on which diagnoses are made are not; they vary in degree throughout the population. Thus, any decision as to whether a particular person does or does not have a mental disorder is based on arbitrary criteria as to how severe or prolonged each symptom must be in order to call the syndrome a disorder.

As you review each disorder described in the chapter, think about its symptoms in relation to the kinds of moods, emotions, thoughts, and behaviors that all of us manifest to some degree. Doing so helps remove some of the mystique from the concept of mental disorder and helps us identify with people whose troubles are like ours, only stronger. Thinking of disorders in terms of extremes of normal processes has also helped scientists understand them better. For example, in this chapter you read about evidence relating (a) the symptoms of phobias and obsessive-compulsive disorders to normal fears, thoughts, and actions; (b) the symptoms of depression and bipolar disorders to normal despondency and elation; and (c) the hallucinations experienced in schizophrenia to a normal capacity for vivid mental imagery.

**2. The multiple causes of mental disorders** By this time in your study of psychology, you are no doubt used to the idea that human feelings, thoughts, and actions emerge from the interaction of many causes. This idea also applies to the feelings, thoughts, and actions that lead to the diagnosis of a mental disorder. The differences among us that are considered disorders—no less than the differences that are considered normal—are caused by differences in our genes and in our past and present environments.

One way to review this chapter would be to think about each disorder in relation to the three classes of causes—predisposing, precipitating, and maintaining—that were introduced near the beginning of the chapter. How might genes operate through the person's physiology to predispose him or her to the disorder? How might learned ways of thinking or acting predispose a person to the disorder? How might specific stressful events in life interact with the predisposition to precipitate the disorder? How might the disordered behavior itself, or people's reactions to it, help maintain the disorder once it begins? For each disorder, think about the relationship between the research or ideas described and possible answers to these questions.

**3. Perspectives on mental disorders** The various perspectives (biological, psychodynamic, behavioral, cognitive, and sociocultural) that were discussed in the chapter focus on different sets of causes of mental disorders. To a considerable degree, the perspectives exist because people who conduct research or therapy on mental disorders differ in their goals and training. Psychiatrists have medical degrees; they are trained to think in terms of diseases, and they are the only mental health professionals who can regularly prescribe drugs. Psychiatry also has a long tradition, stemming from Freud, of emphasis on unconscious mental processes. Thus, psychiatrists lean toward biological and psychodynamic perspectives. Clinical psychologists, in contrast, are trained heavily in psychology and very little in biology or medicine. They are well versed in research on learning and cognition; thus, their perspective is frequently behavioral and cognitive. Sociologists, anthropologists, and social psychologists who study mental disorders are trained to focus on the social and cultural context of behavior. Thus, they tend to take the sociocultural perspective, seeing the predisposing and maintaining causes of mental disorders as lying in social expectations of how people should behave.

## Further Reading

**Peter Tyrer & Derek Steinberg** (1987). *Models for mental disorder: Conceptual models in psychiatry.* Chichester, England: Wiley.
*This is a concise, easy-to-read introduction to the medical, psychodynamic, behavioral, and sociocultural perspectives on mental disorders.*

**Arthur Kleinman** (1988). *Rethinking psychiatry: From cultural category to personal experience.* New York: Free Press.
*Kleinman is a Western-trained psychiatrist who has practiced psychiatry extensively in rural China. In the preface he asks, rhetorically, "Can psychiatry be a science if it is limited to middle-class [W]hites in North America, the United Kingdom, and Western Europe?" Throughout the book he uses cross-cultural studies and his own clinical experiences to argue that a full understanding of mental disorders must take into account people's varying goals, values, expectations, and social relationships.*

**Robert Spitzer, Miriam Gibbon, Andrew Skodol, Janet Williams, & Michael First** (1989). *DSM-III-R casebook.* Washington, DC: American Psychiatric Press.
*This book, designed to help clinical students learn to use DSM-III-R, is free of jargon and can be read easily by the first-year psychology student. It consists of brief case descriptions of the problems suffered by real individuals, each followed by an explanation of how that case would be diagnosed. It is an excellent source from which to gain a more vivid understanding of mental disorders, even for the person who will never be required to diagnose one.*

**Dale Peterson** (Ed.) (1982). *A mad people's history of madness.* Pittsburgh: University of Pittsburgh Press.
*This is a fascinating collection of excerpts from autobiographies, written over the past 500 years, by people who either were, or were regarded as, seriously mentally disordered. They describe their suffering, people's reactions to them, and their own efforts toward recovery. Some of the excerpted books are well known and have helped shape reforms in the understanding and treatment of people with mental disorders.*

## Looking Ahead

I hope you didn't catch medical students' disease from this chapter, but in case you did, don't worry: The next chapter is on treatment. Of course, real mental disorders are serious problems, and effective means for treating them are among the most valuable contributions that psychology has made and is continuing to make to human welfare.

# CHAPTER 18

**Care as a Social Issue**

**Clinical Assessment**

**Psychotherapies**

**Biological Treatments**

# TREATMENT

The worst thing about having a Ph.D. in psychology is that when I go to a party and am introduced as a psychologist, people either become embarrassed and quiet, or they start telling me their problems. I have learned to explain immediately that I am not *that* kind of psychologist—not a clinical psychologist who treats people, but a teacher and a researcher who studies certain aspects of learning and motivation. Apparently, many people think that psychology *is* clinical psychology; but we've only come to it in this last chapter of the book. In this chapter you will read about (a) the social issue of care for the seriously disturbed; (b) methods of clinical assessment (how clinical psychologists and psychiatrists try to determine what is wrong); (c) four major forms of psychotherapy (psychodynamic, humanistic, cognitive, and behavioral); and (d) biological approaches to treatment (especially drugs).

## Care as a Social Issue

### *What to Do with the Seriously Disturbed?*

■ *How Western society's response to people with serious mental disorders has changed since the Middle Ages*

**A History of Caring (and Lack Thereof)**    Prior to the last 2 centuries or so, little thought was given to the idea that society has an obligation toward people with mental disorders. During the Middle Ages, and even into the seventeenth century, people with serious mental disorders—the kind called madness or lunacy (and today most commonly diagnosed as schizophrenia)—were often considered to be in league with the devil, and "treatment" commonly consisted of torture, hanging, burning at the stake, or sending them to sea in "ships of fools" to drown or be saved, depending upon divine Providence. By the eighteenth century, such "religious" views had waned somewhat and a more secular attitude began to prevail, which attributed mental disorders not to supernatural powers, but to the basic degeneracy and unworthiness of the disordered people themselves. Now the principal treatment for those who couldn't care for themselves was to put them in places out of the way of decent society—places that were called hospitals, but in reality were dark, damp, miserable dungeons, where inmates were frequently kept chained to the walls, alive but in a state that was perhaps worse than death (see Figure 18.1 on page 644).

Not until the beginning of the nineteenth century did humanitarian reform begin to occur in a significant way. The most well known leader of reform in Europe was Philippe Pinel (1745–1826), who, as director of a large mental hospital in Paris, removed the inmates' chains, transferred them to sunny and airy rooms, and gave them access to the hospital grounds for exercise. Pinel discovered that some inmates who had been thought to be permanently and hopelessly deranged actually

**Figure 18.1** *Life in a nineteenth-century mental hospital*

*One source of pressure for mental hospital reform in early nineteenth-century England were portraits, such as this, painted by George Cruikshank. The man shown here had been bound to the wall by foot-long chains for 12 years at the time of the portrait.*

recovered under these new conditions and could be released from the hospital. In the United States, the leading reformer was Dorothea Dix (1802–1887), a Boston schoolteacher who visited dozens of jails and almshouses where people with mental disorders were housed, and publicized the appalling conditions that she found. An important part of this *reform movement*, or *moral-treatment movement*, as it was variously called, was the building of large, state-supported asylums for the mentally disordered. The idea behind such institutions was high minded: to provide kindly care and protection for those unable to care for themselves. Unfortunately, public sympathy was rarely sustained at this high level, at least not in the tangible form of financial support. Almost invariably the asylums became overcrowded, understaffed, and reverted to conditions not unlike those that had appalled Pinel and Dix. As recently as the 1940s, the following report could be written about a state mental institution in Philadelphia (Deutsch, 1948):

> The male "incontinent ward" was like a scene out of Dante's Inferno. Three hundred nude men stood, squatted and sprawled in this bare room . . . Winter or summer, these creatures never were given any clothing at all . . . Many patients [in another ward] had to eat their meals with their hands . . . Four hundred patients were herded into a barn-like dayroom intended for only 80. There were only a few benches; most of the men had to stand all day or sit on the splintery floor . . . The hogs in a nearby pigpen were far better fed, in far greater comfort than these human beings.

By the mid-1950s, disenchantment with large state institutions led to a new kind of reform movement in the United States—a movement to *deinstitutionalize* people with mental disorders, to get them back into the community. This new movement was inspired partly by the development of effective antipsychotic drugs that enabled people with mental disorders to function more normally and to be less in need of constant care. It was also inspired by a general mood of optimism in the nation, a feeling that everyone could "make it" if given the chance. President John F. Kennedy gave the movement a boost in 1960, calling for a "bold new approach" to the treatment of mental disorders and encouraging the U.S. Congress to pass legislation to establish community-based mental health centers (Bassuk & Gerson, 1978). By the early 1970s, hundreds of such centers were in operation. Once again, the idea was high minded: Community mental health centers would free people from the need for long-term care in mental institutions. The centers would provide transitional homes for formerly institutionalized patients who were now to be integrated back into the community, and would offer outpatient care to enable them to continue living in the community. These centers would also work with people in the community to reduce the incidence of mental disorders, through such means as counseling and programs aimed at reducing sources of stress that were presumed to promote disorders.

Unfortunately, the dream of the community mental health movement, like the earlier dream of asylums, has remained mostly unrealized. The number of chronic patients in state mental institutions has been greatly reduced (see Figure 18.2), but it is debatable whether the quality of life for former patients has been improved. Today, they are often found in run-down rooming houses, shelters for the homeless, understaffed nursing homes, and, as in the days of Dorothea Dix, in jails (see Kiesler & Sibulkin, 1987). They have generally not been integrated into the community, but are living on the fringes of the community. We still have a long way to go in the direction of humanitarian care. The problem is not so much one of science as of compassion, of willingness to spend the money and energy needed to make any system—whether of asylums or community centers—work as it should.

**Continuing Problems with Mental Hospitals: Rosenhan's Study**   Mental hospitals today are not the same horrors they once were. Some are quite decent places, with excellent staff and successful programs of therapy and rehabilitation. Yet, in

■ *How Rosenhan studied life in mental hospitals, and what he found*

**Figure 18.2** *Change in the number of inpatients in, and annual admissions to, U.S. state mental hospitals from 1950 to 1980*

*The number of resident patients at any one time in state mental hospitals in the United States dropped sharply between 1955 and 1980. This change was due primarily to shorter hospital stays, as indicated by the fact that the number of admissions to such hospitals increased during the same period. (From Brown, 1985.)*

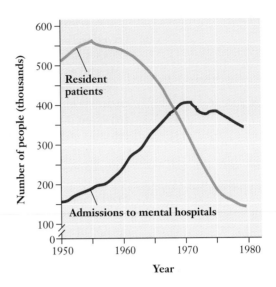

*Dorothea Dix*

*This Boston schoolteacher's crusade resulted in new asylums for the mentally ill and improved conditions in existing institutions.*

many such institutions, especially those that depend on government support, enormous problems persist. Studies show that many state mental hospitals are devoid of real attempts at therapy and often use drugs more as a means of keeping order than as part of a well-planned program of treatment (Okin, 1983).

To get a patient's-eye view of life in mental hospitals, David Rosenhan (1973), a psychologist at Stanford University, conducted a study in which he and seven other sane individuals feigned mental illness to gain admission to different psychiatric hospitals. After making an appointment, they appeared at the hospital admitting office and complained of a single symptom—hearing voices that said, "Empty, hollow, thud." They answered all other questions about their problems and history honestly. Once in the hospital, they behaved as normally as possible, and when asked about the voices they said that they no longer heard them. None of these pseudopatients was ever detected as an imposter by hospital staff, though real patients often did make this detection, saying things like, "You're not really mentally ill; you must be a reporter studying the hospital." Perhaps the main reason that they remained undetected is that the staff had very little contact with them; pseudopatients' total time with psychiatrists and psychologists averaged less than 7 minutes per day, including group meetings.

Even more striking than the small amount of interaction with staff was the dehumanizing nature of those interactions that did occur. When pseudopatients (or real patients) approached them to ask questions, staff members commonly averted their eyes and walked away, or replied in a way that was irrelevant to the question. In other ways as well, staff members communicated an attitude that patients were not to be taken seriously as thinking individuals. They talked about patients in front of them as if they were not there. A nurse unbuttoned her uniform to adjust her brassiere before a ward of male patients, not to be seductive, but because she felt no need to show normal social decorum in front of patients. Some attendants beat patients or abused them verbally, showing no qualms about doing so in front of other patients; but they stopped immediately when other staff members approached. As Rosenhan put it, "Staff are credible witnesses, patients are not." The pseudopatients' normal behaviors were frequently interpreted in terms of mental illness. For example, no staff member ever asked the pseudopatients why they were so often writing in notebooks (which they did to record their experiences), yet a subsequent inspection of the hospital records showed that their "writing behavior" was regularly described as part of their pathological symptomatology.

Rosenhan argues that the problems that he and the other pseudopatients observed were not due just to insufficient staffing or lack of funds. The twelve hospitals they studied included some that were well financed and well staffed. However, staff who could have spent time with patients preferred to stay inside the glassed-in "cage" that segregated them from the patients. According to Rosenhan, the more critical problem was the attitude that permeated the hospital staff, from the psychiatrists on down to the attendants. Staff members seemed unable to look through the label *mentally ill*, or through the bizarre symptoms that patients *sometimes* show, to see that patients are not always crazy and are usually capable of normal human interactions.

**Bright Spots**    Within the past 2 decades, a number of highly successful programs for helping seriously disordered individuals have been developed, both within and outside of mental hospitals (see Liberman, 1988).

In a remarkable study within the state mental hospital system in Illinois, Gordon Paul and Robert Lentz (1977) selected eighty-four very dysfunctional patients who had been hospitalized for an average of 17 years, each with a diagnosis of schizophrenia, and assigned them randomly to different treatments. One group was assigned to a ward in which they received *standard hospital treatment*, the kind they had already been receiving, emphasizing custodial care and drug therapy. A second group was assigned to *milieu therapy*, which involved close interaction between staff and patients, heightened respect for patients (who were referred to as residents), heightened expectations concerning the responsibilities of both staff and patients, a degree of democratic decision making on the ward, and reduction or elimination of antipsychotic drugs whenever possible.

A third group was assigned to *social learning therapy*, which contained most of the just-mentioned elements of milieu therapy and, in addition, entailed a highly directed effort to teach patients the social skills they would need to live outside the hospital. Patients in this group were engaged in organized, skill-learning activities during 85 percent of their waking hours. In contrast, those in the standard ward spent only 5 percent of their waking hours in classes, therapy sessions, or other organized activities. The staff-to-patient ratio and the proportion of professional to nonprofessional staff were the same in all three wards. The study continued for 5 years, by which time 97 percent of the patients in the social learning ward, 71 percent in the milieu ward, and 46 percent in the standard ward had been able to leave the hospital and live in the community for at least 18 months. By every other measure as well, the social learning ward was far more successful than the standard ward.

Paul and Lentz's study, as well as a number of other studies, proves that it is possible to do far more for seriously disturbed mental patients than is currently done. Why haven't such studies had a greater impact on practice? Successful programs operate in ways that are contrary to long-standing traditions and habits that are hard to break (see Kiesler & Sibulkin, 1987). Each new program must be spearheaded by a group of committed, energetic individuals who are willing to buck the system, have enough political savvy to get their program approved, and can find staff members who are enthusiastic about trying something new.

### Structure of the Mental Health System

Thus far, we have been discussing the care and treatment of the most seriously disordered individuals. But most people who seek mental health services have much milder problems. Before we turn to the discussions of assessment and therapy procedures that constitute the remainder of the chapter, let us look at the structure of the mental health system.

*How an experiment showed that people who had been long-term mental patients could profit from a therapeutic environment that was quite different from the usual*

**Places of Treatment** Roughly in descending order of seriousness of the disorders treated there, the main categories of places where mental health services are provided are as follows:

- *Mental hospitals* These provide custodial care for patients who cannot care for themselves or be cared for by family members at home. In addition, they provide brief hospitalization (typically 2 to 4 weeks) to stabilize individuals who are suffering from acute psychotic attacks. The number of people in mental hospitals has greatly declined over the past 3 or 4 decades.

**Not for therapy only**

*In this Havana psychiatric hospital, the tradition of therapeutic basket weaving has been turned into a commercially viable activity.*

- *General hospitals* During the same period in which the number of patients in mental hospitals has declined, the number of psychiatric inpatients in general hospitals has increased. In fact, today the majority of psychiatric inpatients are in general hospitals, sometimes in special psychiatric wards but more often not (Kiesler & Sibulkin, 1987). A general hospital is usually preferable to a mental hospital for patients whose stay will be short. Among other things, less stigma is associated with hospitalization there, and its location near the patient's home makes visiting easier for family members and friends.

- *Nursing homes* Many older chronic mental patients, who in former times would have been in mental hospitals, are now in nursing homes, which usually do not employ special treatment personnel for such people (Kiesler & Sibulkin, 1987). The conditions in these homes vary tremendously.

- *Halfway houses* These, usually located in residential areas of cities, are places where people who have been discharged from a hospital reside during their transition back to the community. The halfway house (or *group home*, as it is often called) provides a place to sleep, eat, and socialize; and it may also provide help in finding employment and a permanent place to live. Residents are expected to leave the house during the day to work, look for work, or go to school. Such houses are usually run by nonprofessionals who consult regularly with government-employed psychiatrists, psychologists, and social workers.

*Community mental health centers* These offer free or low-cost services, including psychotherapy, support groups, and telephone crisis hotlines. In addition, such centers often sponsor classes, initiate legislation, and engage in other activities aimed at preventing psychological problems in the community.

*Private offices* For people who can afford it, and whose problems do not require hospitalization, the private office of a psychiatrist, clinical psychologist, or social worker is usually the treatment place of choice.

**Providers of Treatment**   Psychotherapy and other mental health services are provided by an array of professionals with various kinds of training. The major classes of these professionals are the following:

*Psychiatrists* have a medical degree, obtained through standard medical school training, followed by special training and residency in psychiatry. They can work in any of the settings above, but most often choose hospitals and private practice. They are the only mental health specialists who can prescribe drugs.

*Clinical psychologists* have a doctoral degree in psychology with training in research and clinical practice. Many are employed by universities as teachers and researchers in addition to their clinical practice. As clinicians they may work in any of the settings described above.

*Counseling psychologists* have a doctoral degree from a counseling program. Their training is similar to that of clinical psychologists, but usually entails less emphasis on research and more on practice. They may work in any of the settings described above. In general, counseling psychologists are more likely than are psychiatrists or clinical psychologists to work with people who have problems of living that do not warrant a diagnosis of mental disorder.

*Counselors* have a master's degree from a counseling program. Though they may work in any of the settings above, they are more likely to work in a school or other institution, with people who are dealing with school- or job-related problems. They receive less training in research and psychological assessment procedures than do doctoral-level clinical or counseling psychologists.

*Psychiatric social workers* have a master's degree in social work, followed by advanced training and experience working with people who have psychological problems. They may be employed in any of the settings above, but are most often employed by public social work agencies, and commonly visit people in their homes to offer support and guidance.

*Psychiatric nurses* usually have a bachelor's or master's degree in nursing followed by advanced training in the care of mental patients. They usually work in hospitals and may conduct psychotherapy sessions as well as provide more typical nursing services.

**Consumers of Treatment**   There is no such thing as a typical patient or client of mental health services. Consumers range from those with serious psychotic symptoms, unable to care for themselves, to people who are functioning well but believe that psychotherapy may help them find more happiness or meaning in life. In between, the vast majority are people who are not incapacitated but have serious fears, worries, or other difficulties that may or may not be related to recent stressful events in their lives. A large-scale survey, conducted in three cities in the United States, revealed that in a 6-month period about 3 percent of all adults visited a mental health specialist, and that about 33 percent of those individuals had no diagnosable mental disorder by DSM-III criteria (described in Chapter 17) (Shapiro & others, 1984). By far the most common reasons for seeking help were feelings of anxiety and depression.

# Clinical Assessment

*Assessment* is the process by which a mental health professional gathers and compiles information about a patient or client for the purpose of developing a plan of treatment. One part of assessment, discussed in Chapter 17, is diagnosis—the classifying and labeling of the disorder according to some standard set of guidelines, such as those in DSM-III-R. But assessment includes more than diagnosis. In fact, some clinicians deliberately avoid classifying and labeling their clients' problems except where necessary for record-keeping purposes (such as when filing for insurance reimbursement). The more important goal is to understand the person as a unique individual, with a unique set of life circumstances, ways of thinking, and ways of behaving that must be taken into account in formulating a treatment plan. Assessment ideally occurs not only before treatment, but throughout it, to monitor changes and determine when treatment should be modified or discontinued. Assessment is far from an exact science. Despite clinicians' attempts to be objective, assessment is largely a matter of making educated guesses; it is subject to the biases and distortions that can affect anyone's judgments of another person.

Clinicians who have different theoretical orientations have different views as to what kinds of information are useful in assessment. To a psychodynamically oriented clinician, what the client *doesn't* say (and thus may be repressing) may be as important as what he or she *does* say. To a humanistic clinician, the client's conscious perceptions and beliefs (his or her phenomenological world) are important and to be taken seriously whether or not they are objectively accurate. To a cognitively oriented clinician, the person's habitual patterns of thinking are most important. And to a behaviorally oriented clinician, objective facts about the client's actual behaviors and the settings in which they occur are most important. As assessment aids, a variety of procedures and tools may be employed, some of which are described below.

*How interviews, objective questionnaires, personality tests, projective tests, behavioral monitoring, and neurological tests are used in assessing a client's condition*

**Assessment Interviews**   George Kelly (1958), a clinical psychologist whose ideas helped found the humanistic and cognitive traditions, once offered the following simple advice about clinical assessment: "If you want to know what is going on in a person's mind, ask him; he may tell you."

The *assessment interview* is by far the most common assessment procedure. It is basically a dialogue through which the clinician tries to learn about the client. The dialogue may be unstructured, leaving to the client the task of deciding what is important or unimportant; or it may be highly structured, consisting of an ordered set of questions asked by the clinician and answered by the client. It typically touches on the client's immediate symptoms, the environment in which the client lives and works, the client's past history, and other information that seems relevant to the client's problem. The client's nonverbal behaviors, such as long pauses, body tension, or emotional expressions may also be taken into account in interpreting his or her verbal responses.

**Objective Questionnaires**   To supplement interviews, *objective questionnaires* have been developed to help clients report their feelings, thoughts, and behaviors. Some of these are simply lists of adjectives or brief, descriptive statements; the client is asked to check off those that apply to himself or herself. Others use a multiple-choice format in which the client must for each item choose from among several possible statements the one that most applies to himself or herself. Some objective questionnaires cover a broad range of possible symptoms or characteristics, whereas others focus on a narrow range having to do with a particular class of disorder. An example of the latter is the *Beck Depression Inventory*, illustrated in

**Table 18.1** *Sample items from the Beck Depression Inventory*

The client's task on each item is to pick out the one statement that best describes how he or she has been feeling for the past week.

**Item (pessimism)**
I am not particularly pessimistic or discouraged about the future.
I feel discouraged about the future.
I feel I have nothing to look forward to.
I feel that I won't ever get over my troubles.
I feel that the future is hopeless and that things cannot improve.

**Item (sense of failure)**
I do not feel like a failure.
I feel I have failed more than the average person.
I feel I have accomplished very little that is worthwhile or that means anything.
As I look back on my life, all I can see is a lot of failures.
I feel I am a complete failure as a person (parent, husband, wife).

*Source:* From *Depression: Clinical, experimental, and theoretical aspects* (pp. 333–334) by A. T. Beck, 1967, New York: Harper & Row.

Table 18.1. Objective questionnaires offer a degree of standardization that is useful for clinical research or for any comparison of one client with others. In addition, they are less subject to bias than are face-to-face interviews in which the clinician's way of asking the questions may influence the client's answers.

**Psychometric Personality Tests: The MMPI as an Example** *Psychometric personality tests* are objective questionnaires that have been developed through psychometric methods (discussed in Chapter 16) to assess a wide range of personality characteristics. Two examples of such tests are Cattell's 16 PF Questionnaire and Eysenck's Personality Inventory (discussed in Chapter 16), both of which are sometimes used for clinical assessment. But by far the most commonly used psychometric personality test for clinical assessment is the *Minnesota Multiphasic Personality Inventory*, abbreviated **MMPI**.

The original purpose of the MMPI—developed at the University of Minnesota in the late 1930s—was to provide an objective means to diagnose mental disorders, uncontaminated by the biases of any particular clinician (Hathaway & McKinley, 1943). In developing the test, all potential questions were pretested on groups of patients (criterion groups) who had already been diagnosed as having a specific mental disorder, and also on a large control group who had no diagnosed disorder (the so-called Minnesota normals). Questions that were commonly answered differently by a patient group than by the controls were kept, and others were thrown out. The goal was to identify questions that would distinguish different patient groups from each other and from the control group. Recently, the test has been updated to form the **MMPI-2**, and the scoring system has been revised on the basis of results obtained from a large, representative sample of U.S. citizens (Butcher & others, 1990).

The new version contains 567 items, each of which is a statement about the self, to which the person must answer *true, false,* or *cannot say*. Most items contribute to a score on one or more of fifteen different *content scales* that are related to different categories of psychological problems. Included among these are anxiety, depression, anger, cynicism, type *A* (hard-driving) personality, social discomfort (shyness), and family problems. In most cases, the relationship between an item's content and the scale to which it contributes is quite obvious. Thus, the response *true* to the statement *The future seems hopeless to me* adds a point to the scale measuring depression.

In addition to the content scales, the test has scales designed to assess honesty and care in completing the test. The *L* scale assesses the extent to which the person taking the test is lying in an attempt to make a good impression. For example, the response *true* to the statement *I never get angry* adds a point to the *L* scale, because the test assumes that everyone gets angry at times. The *F* scale assesses either carelessness or lack of the required reading or thinking ability needed to fill out the questionnaire. Thus, the response *true* to the statement *Everything smells the same* will add a point to the *F* scale, based on the assumption that true inability to discriminate among different odors is practically nonexistent. A high score on one or more of these scales implies that the answers to other questions cannot be trusted and that the results should either be thrown out or interpreted with great caution.

Despite its frequent use, or perhaps because of it, the original version of the MMPI was often criticized. One critic referred to it as a "psychometric nightmare," impossible to interpret in any objective way (Rodgers, 1972). Others argued that the test was culturally biased, producing false signs of disorder in people whose backgrounds were different from those of the mostly White, middle-class Minnesotans with whom the test was originally developed (Gynther, 1972). For example, the response *true* to the statement *People say insulting and vulgar things about me* might be misleading if scored as a sign of paranoia in a member of a discriminated-against minority (Pervin, 1980). The work that went into forming MMPI-2 was largely designed to remedy such problems, though it is too early yet to assess the revision's success in these regards.

**Projective Tests**   Projective tests, specifically the Rorschach and TAT (Thematic Apperception Test), are described in Chapter 16. In the Rorschach test, the person is shown a series of inkblots and is asked to say what each looks like, and in the TAT the person is shown a series of pictures of people interacting and is asked to tell a short story about each picture (see Figures 16.3 and 16.4). Unlike the questionnaires and psychometric tests described above, in which lack of conscious thought invalidates responses, projective tests aim to bypass conscious thought and encourage the client to say things that might be clues to his or her unconscious wishes and beliefs. This method of assessment is most compatible with psychoanalytic approaches to therapy.

Clinicians have developed standard procedures for scoring projective tests, in which pre-established rules are used to code the content of the client's responses (Dana, 1985; Erberg, 1985). For example, standard scoring for the Rorschach includes methods to rate the degree of morbidity (tendency to see death and decay) and aggressiveness (tendency to see fights) in each response. But the validity of such systems is highly controversial. Many clinicians who use projective tests prefer to interpret them less formally, using their own experience coupled with other information they have about the client. In a sense, all of psychoanalysis is assessment, and the therapy process itself is much like projective testing. Everything that the client says and does—whether in response to inkblots or in response to requests to free associate or describe dreams—contributes to the picture that the therapist develops of the client's unconscious mind. When used this way, there is no statistical way to determine whether or not projective tests are valid.

**Behavioral Monitoring**   The term *behavioral monitoring* refers to any system for counting or recording actual instances of desired or undesired behaviors. In Paul and Lentz's experiment comparing treatments for hospitalized patients, staff members charted each patient's progress by keeping daily counts of their positive and negative actions (defined according to their symptoms). In a less formal way, ward nurses or other observers in any mental hospital keep a daily log of patients' activities to assess improvement or deterioration. Behavior therapists who work with noninstitutionalized clients emphasize *self-monitoring*, in which clients keep written records of their own actions that they are trying to increase or decrease. Thus, a person trying to eliminate a hand-washing compulsion might keep a record of each instance of hand washing, or a person with an eating disorder might keep a record of each food and the amount consumed. The very process of keeping records heightens awareness of the behavior, which in itself can sometimes solve the problem. In addition, the records and graphs can provide a strong incentive for change—everyone likes to see evidence of improvement.

**Neuropsychological Assessment**    If there is a reason to think that brain damage might underlie a patient's psychological difficulties, the patient may be sent to a neurologist or a neuropsychologist for a set of psychological tests designed to find clues to such damage. The most commonly used set of neuropsychological tests, the *Halstead-Reitan battery*, includes tests of motor control (such as moving the index finger rapidly up and down), perception (such as identifying objects by touch), and cognition (items from a standard IQ test are used) (Barth & Macciocchi, 1985). If these or other neuropsychological tests suggest brain damage, more direct approaches for detecting such damage may be used, such as an EEG, a CAT scan, or an MRI scan.

The *EEG* (*electroencephalogram*) is a measure of the pattern of electrical activity of the brain, taken through electrodes attached to the scalp (see Chapter 7); it can be analyzed for abnormal patterns that indicate possible brain damage. The *CAT scan* (*CAT* stands for *computerized axial tomography*) is a newer, much more costly method, in which multiple x-rays of the brain are taken from various angles and analyzed by a computer to produce pictures of individual sections of the brain, which can be inspected to find anatomical abnormalities. The *MRI scan* (*MRI* stands for *magnetic resonance imaging*) is a still newer and more costly technique, by which pictures of brain sections are constructed based on electromagnetic radiation produced by specific molecules in the brain when the brain is subjected to a strong magnetic field. If any of these tests indicates brain damage, the patient may be given special training to compensate for the deficits. The damage may also be treated with medicine or even with surgery if such treatment is warranted (for example, in the case of a potentially lethal tumor).

## Psychotherapies

*Psychotherapy* refers to any formal, theory-based, systematic treatment for mental problems or disorders that uses psychological rather than physiological means and is conducted by a trained therapist. Psychotherapy normally involves dialogue between the person in need and the therapist, and its aim is usually to restructure some aspect of the person's way of feeling, thinking, or behaving. If you have ever helped a child overcome a fear, encouraged a friend to give up a bad habit, or cheered up a despondent roommate, you have engaged in a process akin to psychotherapy, though less formal.

By one count, more than 400 supposedly different forms of psychotherapy have appeared over the years, each with a different name (Karasu, 1986). Here we will limit ourselves to the approaches most often taught in clinical psychology and psychiatric programs and most often practiced by those trained in such programs. We will also limit ourselves to *individual therapies*, those in which a therapist works with one person at a time. Many psychotherapists work with groups (in *group therapy*), couples (in *couple therapy* or *marriage counseling*), or families (in *family therapy*), but generally the principles behind their work are extensions of the individual ap-

**Couple therapy**
*This form of treatment is often chosen to solve interactional problems—for example, difficulties created by differences in the partners' values, expectations, or needs.*

proaches described below. The main addition in group therapies is that they allow more opportunity to practice social skills and get feedback from people other than the psychotherapist. The main addition in couple and family therapies is that they allow couples and families to express their interpersonal difficulties in front of one another on neutral ground and to practice new ways of communicating with one another. Moreover, the problem is seen as residing in the dynamics of the family system, rather than any one individual.

### Psychoanalysis and Other Psychodynamic Therapies

*Psychoanalysis* refers specifically to the approach developed by Sigmund Freud, and *psychodynamic therapy* refers generally to any therapy approach that is based on the premises that psychological problems are manifestations of inner mental conflicts and that conscious awareness of those conflicts is a key to recovery.

**Breuer's Treatment of Anna O.: A Precursor to Psychoanalysis**   In describing the origin of psychoanalysis, Sigmund Freud often credited an older friend and colleague of his, Joseph Breuer, and specifically referred to Breuer's treatment of a patient known as Anna O. In turn, Breuer gave credit to Anna O. herself, who often took the lead in telling him how he could help her (Erdelyi, 1985). Anna was a brilliant, upper-class Viennese woman who in 1880 at the age of 21, while nursing her dying father, developed a multitude of symptoms indicative of what was then called hysteria (and is now called conversion disorder, as described in Chapter 17). Among her symptoms, which would come and go, were an inability to drink fluids (hydrophobia), a squint in both eyes that rendered her unable to see, and paralysis of her right arm. Breuer, a neurologist, was called in to treat Anna, but because her symptoms had no apparent neurological basis he at first just visited her regularly to check on her and try to comfort her.

Often when Breuer arrived to visit Anna, he found her in a hypnotic-like trance, and in that state she often talked in an animated, uninhibited fashion about herself and her past experiences. As she talked she sometimes recalled experiences that she had previously forgotten (or had repressed, to use Freud's later term), and, of greatest interest, her recollection and recounting of those experiences brought relief from one or more of her symptoms. For example, at a time when she felt revolted by the thought of drinking any fluids and could quench her thirst only by eating fruits, Anna recalled a scene in which she had observed her governess's dog

■ *How the case of Anna O. led to the idea that unconscious memories and their associated unconscious emotions can cause neurotic symptoms*

drinking from a glass. The event had greatly disgusted her at the time, partly because of her already-existing contempt for both the dog and the governess, but out of politeness she had stifled her emotional reaction. After remembering this incident and re-experiencing her emotional reaction to it, she was immediately relieved of her dread of drinking. She asked for a glass of water and drank heartily for the first time in weeks.

To make Anna's treatment more efficient, Breuer began to use hypnosis (when she wasn't in one of her naturally occurring trances) to get her to talk freely about her past experiences. Under hypnosis, Anna traced the origin of her squint to an experience in which, while caring for her father, she had squinted to hold back tears so he would not see that she was crying. She traced the origin of her paralyzed arm to another experience in which, while sitting by her father's sickbed, she had a terrifying fantasy of a snake attacking him and found that she could not reach

**An experiment in hypnosis**

*The hypnotic technique with which Breuer treated Anna O. was earlier used by the French neurologist Jean Charcot, who showed that people suffering from "hysterical" loss of motor or sensory function could be made to see or walk. Charcot is shown here demonstrating hypnosis.*

out to protect him because her arm, slung over the back of the chair, had (in reality) gone to sleep and was temporarily paralyzed. Thus, by tracing each of her symptoms back to an initial triggering event and experiencing emotions related to that event, Anna overcame her symptoms one by one.

Why was the recollection of emotionally stressful events helpful? Anna herself referred to the technique as "chimney sweeping," an allusion to her idea that digging up and sweeping away unpleasant memories was helping her. Breuer called it the *cathartic technique. Catharsis* means purging (eliminating some foul substance), and in Breuer's view the technique purged the patient of the bottled-up effects of emotionally charged memories. Breuer suggested that when an emotional event occurs but the emotion is not consciously experienced, the unconscious memory of the event festers in the mind and can produce symptoms of the sort that Anna O. experienced (Breuer & Freud, 1895/1955). Only by reliving the event, and consciously feeling the emotion, can the patient's symptoms be alleviated.

**Freudian Psychoanalysis**    From Breuer's case of Anna O. and several other early cases (described by Breuer & Freud, 1895/1955), Freud learned that (a) memories that were once conscious can become unconscious, (b) emotionally charged unconscious memories can provide the basis for neurotic symptoms, and (c) these symptoms may disappear if the patient becomes conscious of the memories that underlie them and experiences consciously the emotions associated with the memories. These ideas provided the framework from which Freud began his work with neurotic patients and the ground upon which he based his theory and practice of psychoanalysis. Psychoanalysis as a theory of personality is described in Chapter 16. Here I will briefly summarize its main characteristics as an approach to psychotherapy:

■ *How Freudian psychoanalysis is characterized by (a) an emphasis on childhood experiences; (b) the use of free association, dreams, resistance, and transference; and (c) the view that insight leads to cure*

- ■ *Importance of childhood sexual experiences* The biggest difference between Freud's eventual psychoanalytic approach and the earlier one that emerged from Breuer's work with Anna O. concerns the role of infantile sexual conflicts (discussed in Chapter 16). In Freud's theory, all neuroses (emotional disorders) stem from an interaction between two categories of experiences. The first and most basic category consists of *predisposing experiences*, which occur in the first 5 to 6 years of life and relate to infantile sexual wishes and conflicts. The second category consists of *precipitating experiences*, which occur later and most immediately bring on the emotional breakdown. From this vantagepoint, all of the experiences identified in Breuer's treatment of Anna O. were in the precipitating category.

  Had Freud (after developing his full theory) been Anna O.'s therapist, he would have tried to uncover not only the events that immediately brought on her symptoms, but also her childhood memories and wishes that made those events so significant. *Why* was the sight of a dog drinking from a glass so traumatic? *Why* was it so important to hide her tears from her father? *Why* did she have the snake fantasy while watching over her ill father? These are questions that did not arise in Breuer's work, but would have been important to Freud. Freud would have framed his answers in terms of childhood sexual feelings, probably involving her father, that must have been rearoused during the period in which she was nursing him.

- ■ *Free association and dreams as clues to the unconscious* The term *analysis* in psychoanalysis comes from Freud's finding that patients rarely recall unconscious memories simply by talking (with or without hypnosis), as Anna O. did, so the psychoanalyst must infer them from clues in the patient's words and behavior. Freud's principal technique for obtaining such clues was free association, in which the patient would lie on a couch in a relaxed state and talk freely about whatever came to his or her mind in relation to certain symptoms or ideas. Freud also asked patients to describe their dreams. As explained in Chapter 17, he interpreted the seemingly illogical associations and ideas that came from these methods as symbolic expressions of the unconscious memories or wishes that were at the core of the person's psychological problems.

*The original therapeutic couch*

*This photograph of Freud's consulting room shows the couch on which patients reclined while he sat, out of their line of sight, listening to their free associations. Contemporary psychoanalysts have generally abandoned the couch in favor of a more egalitarian face-to-face encounter.*

*Role of resistance* Freud found that patients almost invariably resist the therapist's attempt to bring their unconscious memories or wishes into consciousness. This **resistance** may manifest itself in such forms as refusing to talk about certain topics, "forgetting" to come to therapy sessions, or arguing incessantly in a way that diverts the therapeutic process. Freud assumed that resistance stems from the more general defensive processes (described in Chapter 16) by which people protect themselves from becoming conscious of anxiety-provoking thoughts. Resistance provides clues that therapy is going in the right direction, toward critical unconscious material; but it can also slow down the course of therapy or even bring it to a halt. To avoid too much resistance, the therapist must present interpretations gradually, when the patient is ready to accept them. A difficulty with the concept of resistance, of course, is knowing when a patient's disagreements should be taken at face value and when they should be considered to be signs of resistance.

*Role of transference* In psychotherapy a patient expresses strong emotional feelings—sometimes love, sometimes anger—toward the therapist. Freud believed that the true object of such feelings is usually not the therapist but some other significant person in the patient's life whom the therapist symbolizes. Thus, **transference** is the phenomenon by which the patient's unconscious feelings about a significant person in his or her life are experienced consciously as feelings about the therapist. Freud considered transference to be an important part of psychoanalysis: It provides further clues about the patient's unconscious mind; and, even more important, it offers the analyst an opportunity to point out the patient's strong emotions and to comment on the possibility that they stand for unconscious feelings the patient has about some other person. As with resistance, a problem exists in interpreting transference. It is hard to know when emotions directed at the therapist are transferred from another relationship and when they represent the patient's true feelings about the therapist.

*Relationship between insight and cure* Psychoanalysis is essentially a process in which the analyst makes inferences about the patient's unconscious conflicts and relays that information to the patient. How does such knowledge help? In Freud's theory, it helps by making conscious the disturbing wishes and memories that are the source of the neurotic symptoms. Once conscious, they can be expressed and experienced directly, or, if they are unrealistic, the conscious ego can modify them into healthier pursuits. At the same time, the patient is

**Play therapy**

*In this extension of psychodynamic therapy, children use dolls and other toys to express and gain insight into their feelings.*

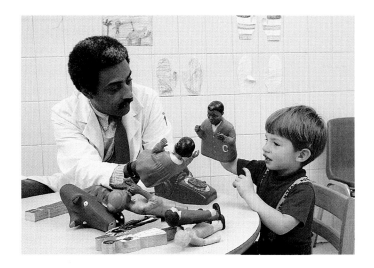

freed of the defenses that had kept that material repressed, and has more psychic energy for other activities. But for all of this to happen, the patient must truly accept the analyst's insights, viscerally as well as intellectually. The analyst cannot just tell the patient about his or her unconscious conflicts, but must lead the patient gradually in such a way that he or she actually experiences the emotions.

■ *How the case of the Rat Man exemplifies (a) Freud's concepts of precipitating and predisposing causes, and (b) Freud's use of free association, dream analysis, and transference*

**Case Example: Freud's Analysis of the Rat Man**   Following is a summary of one of Freud's most famous cases, which illustrates his procedure. A 29-year-old man, referred to in the case history as the Rat Man, came to Freud complaining of various fears, obsessions, and compulsions that had begun 6 years earlier and had prevented him from completing his university studies and going on to a career. One of his most revealing symptoms was an obsessive fantasy that a horrible "rat torture" would be applied to both his father and the woman whom the Rat Man was courting. In this torture, a pot of hungry rats was strapped against the victims' buttocks and would chew their way out through the only available opening. Freud used this fantasy, as well as many other clues, to interpret the Rat Man's problems. Let's first examine the interpretation and then some of the evidence upon which Freud based it.

According to Freud (1909/1963), the *precipitating cause* of the Rat Man's disorder was his conflict over whether or not to marry the woman he had been courting since the age of 20. Unable to decide consciously, his unconscious mind resolved the conflict by making him ill (producing his neurotic symptoms), and this kept him from completing his studies and starting a career (which were prerequisites for marriage). The *predisposing cause* was a more fundamental, unconscious oedipal conflict between his love and hatred of his father, originating in early childhood. These two causes were linked. The Rat Man's conflict about marrying the woman was a reenactment of his love-hate feelings about his father. To marry her would be an act of hatred toward his father, and not to marry her would be an act of love toward him.

The connection between these two conflicts had been cemented when the Rat Man's father died shortly after he had begun to court the woman in question. The Rat Man knew that his father had opposed the relationship, and unconsciously (and irrationally) believed that he had caused his father's death by continuing the relationship against his father's wishes. Yet, he also imagined unconsciously that his father was still alive and that he could murder his father once more by following through with the marriage. Among the many converging lines of evidence that led Freud to these conclusions were the following:

- At one point Freud asked the Rat Man to free associate to the concept *rats* (*ratten* in German), and the man immediately came up with *rates* (*raten* in German), meaning "installments" or "money." The Rat Man had previously mentioned that his father opposed his relationship with the woman because of her lack of money, and that his father had wanted him to marry a certain wealthy cousin. Thus, this part of the analysis suggested to Freud that the rat fantasy had to do with the father's opposition to the woman.

- At another point the Rat Man described an event that took place when he was about 4 years old, which he had learned of from his mother. His father was beginning to beat him for having bitten his nurse, but the boy had responded with such an outpouring of angry words that his father, shaken by the anger, stopped the beating and never beat him again. In Freud's analysis, this incident had great significance. Freud assumed that biting the nurse was a sexual act for the young boy and that the father's response of beating him contributed to the Rat Man's lifelong fear of his father's reactions to his sexual wishes. At the same time, the boy's power over his father—his anger had made the father stop the beating—helped stamp into the Rat Man the unconscious fear that he could kill his father through anger. From that time until his psychoanalysis, the Rat Man never consciously experienced anger toward his father. In addition, Freud saw direct symbolic links between this early childhood incident and the rat-torture obsession: Rats, biting into and destroying his woman friend and his father, symbolized another small, biting beast—the Rat Man himself—who had once bitten first his nurse (his love object at the time) and then, with angry words, his father.

Transference also entered into the analysis. The Rat Man reported a fantasy in which Freud wanted him to marry his (Freud's) daughter, and a dream in which Freud's daughter had two spots of dung on her face instead of eyes. Freud interpreted the dung as symbolic of money, and he interpreted the fantasy and dream as a symbolic reconstruction of the man's conflict, with Freud replacing the Rat Man's father in urging him to marry a wealthy relative. At another point—which Freud regarded as the major breakthrough—the Rat Man became irrationally angry at Freud, jumping up from the couch and shouting abusive words at him. Reflecting on this incident later, the Rat Man recalled that his sudden anger was accompanied by a fear that Freud would beat him and that he had jumped up to defend himself. By this time in the analysis, it took little convincing for the Rat Man to share Freud's view that this was a reenactment of the incident in which his father had beaten him and he had responded so angrily.

This transference experience finally brought the Rat man to conscious awareness of his previously unconscious fear and anger toward his father, which led, according to Freud, to recovery from his neurotic symptoms. In a sad footnote to the case, Freud (1923/1963) added that after a short period as a healthy man, the Rat Man was killed as an officer in World War I.

**Post-Freudian Variations**   Most psychodynamic therapists today do not practice classic psychoanalysis, as taught by Freud, but instead practice one of several derivatives or variations of that approach, which can be roughly categorized as follows (see Nietzel & Bernstein, 1987, or Kutash & Wolf, 1986):

*Psychoanalytic psychotherapies* adhere closely to Freud's theory of personality but modify his techniques. The most common modification is to reduce the number of sessions required for analysis, by using methods that are aimed at getting more quickly at unconscious material. Whereas classic psychoanalysis usually requires hundreds of sessions (2 or more years of two to five sessions per week), some psychoanalytic psychotherapies aim to accomplish the same task in as few as twenty to forty sessions. The couch is dispensed with and the client and analyst sit face-to-face; the analyst more actively directs the client's attention toward relevant memories and ideas; and sometimes techniques such as role playing are used to facilitate transference and speed the therapeutic process.

*Ego-oriented psychodynamic therapies* modify aspects of Freud's theory as well as method, without overthrowing the theory. In particular, less attention is paid to early childhood and the id's wishes, and more attention is paid to the client's adult life and the ego's defense mechanisms. These therapies aim to discover and expose ways in which defenses distort the client's experiences and relationships. By breaking down the defenses, even without uncovering their origins, the therapist helps the client develop a healthier range of responses.

*Non-Freudian psychodynamic therapies* are not based directly on Freud's theory at all, but rather on alternative psychodynamic theories—such as Adler's, Jung's, or Horney's (discussed in Chapter 16)—that emphasize mental conflicts different from those deemed important by Freud. In Adlerian therapy, for example, the client's feeling of inferiority, and conflicts engendered by that feeling, are considered to be especially important.

### Humanistic Therapy

As described in Chapter 16, the humanistic view of the person emphasizes the positive potential for growth—the so-called actualizing potential—presumed to lie within each person. However, for this potential to exert its effects, people must be conscious of their inner feelings and desires, and not deny or distort them. Thus, in this respect, humanistic therapy is similar to psychodynamic therapy: Both aim to make clients more aware of inner feelings and wishes. From the humanistic perspective, people often deny or distort their feelings and wishes because of judgments imposed from outside. The main goal of humanistic therapy is to help clients become aware of their own feelings and wishes, so that they can gain control of their own lives rather than operate in accordance with their perceptions of what others expect. In one version of humanistic therapy, called *Gestalt therapy*, the therapist uses the client's facial expressions, body posture, and other nonverbal cues to judge whether the client's statements are consistent with what the client truly feels or believes, and actively challenges the client each time inconsistency is detected (Perls & others, 1951). But by far the most common humanistic therapy is that developed by Carl Rogers, which rarely involves a direct challenge to the client's statements.

**Rogers's Client-Centered Therapy**   When a random sample of psychotherapists were asked in the early 1980s to name the person who most strongly influenced their work, Carl Rogers (1902–1987) was cited more often than anyone else (Smith, 1982). Rogers called his therapeutic approach ***client-centered therapy***, because it focuses on the thoughts, abilities, and cleverness of the client rather than those of the therapist. The client, not the therapist, figures out what is wrong, makes plans for improvement, and decides when improvement has occurred. The therapist in this case is not an analyst, not a detective trying to infer things about the client that the client doesn't know, but instead is more like a sounding board, a compassionate yet professional sounding board for the client's ideas and emotions. How these ideas and emotions sound and feel to the client, not to the therapist, is most important.

From Rogers's perspective, psychological problems originate when people learn from their parents or other authorities to deny their own feelings and to distrust their own ability to make decisions. As a result of such learning, they look to others as guides to how to feel and act, and at the same time rebel inside or feel resentful about living according to others' preferences. The client-centered therapist tries to provide a context within which clients can become aware of and accept their own feelings and learn to trust their own decision-making abilities. To do so, the therapist must manifest empathy, positive regard, and genuineness, as defined in the following list (Rogers, 1951):

*Carl Rogers*

*The inventor of client-centered therapy was a charismatic individual who personally embodied the empathy and genuineness that are the essence of his method of therapy.*

■ *How empathy, positive regard, and genuineness are important aspects of Rogers's humanistic approach to psychotherapy*

*Empathy* refers to the therapist's attempt to understand what the client is saying or feeling at any given moment. Such understanding must come from an *internal frame of reference*, in which the therapist sees things from the client's viewpoint, not from an external frame, in which the therapist makes judgments as an outside expert. As part of the attempt to achieve and show this understanding, the therapist frequently *reflects back* the ideas and feelings that the client expresses. A typical exchange might go like this:

> **Client:** *My mother is a mean, horrible witch!*
>
> **Therapist:** *I guess you're feeling a lot of anger toward your mother right now.*

To an outsider, the therapist's response here might seem silly, a statement of the obvious. But to the client and therapist fully immersed in the process, the response serves several purposes. First, it shows the client that the therapist is listening and trying to understand. Second, it reflects back to the client not the literal words that the client has said, but the feeling that seems to lie behind them—a feeling which the client may or may not have been fully aware of at the moment. Third, it offers the client a chance to correct the therapist if the therapist is wrong. By clarifying things to the therapist, the client clarifies them to himself or herself.

*Positive regard* implies a belief on the therapist's part that the client is worthy and capable. The client may not feel or act that way, but the therapist must see the client's inner worth and potential ability. Through experiencing the therapist's positive regard, clients begin to feel more positive about themselves, and this is essential if they are going to take charge of their own lives. Positive regard does not imply approval of everything that the client does, but does suggest faith in the client's *capacity* to make appropriate decisions. Consider the following hypothetical exchange:

> **Client:** *Last semester in college I cheated on every test.*
>
> **Therapist:** *I guess what you're saying is that last semester you did something against your values—you cheated on every test.*

Notice that the therapist here doesn't condone the client's cheating, but still says something positive. The therapist has inferred that the client is not proud of cheating, that the client's values are better than that, and those values are brought to the fore in the therapist's reaction.

*Genuineness* implies that the therapist cannot fake empathy and positive regard, but must really feel them. If the therapist's words and feelings don't match, the words will not be believable to the client. The capacity for genuine empathy and positive regard toward all clients might seem to be a rare quality, but Rogers suggests that it can be cultivated by opening up oneself, deliberately trying to stand in the client's shoes to see things as the client sees them.

The humanistic approach is often described as nonscientific, but Rogers himself had great respect for science and urged clinical psychologists to test their theories with objective data. Beginning in 1940, Rogers and his colleagues recorded and transcribed complete sets of therapy sessions and compared clients' statements in later sessions with earlier ones (Rogers, 1951; Rogers & Dymond, 1954). Consistent with humanistic theory, they found that as time in therapy increased, clients made more comments about their own feelings, wishes, responsibilities, and ability to control their fate, and fewer comments about outside forces that controlled them. Thus, statements such as, "My mother is a mean, horrible witch!" made in early sessions would later give way to statements such as, "I can see both good and bad qualities in my mother, and to some extent it is my own fear of being like her that has been a problem."

Of course, it is one thing to show changes in what clients *say* over the course of therapy, and another to demonstrate that these statements reflect real changes in their lives outside of therapy. The latter is harder to test objectively, and is an issue to which we will return later, for psychotherapy in general. Critics of the client-centered approach also argue that therapists may actually lead their clients far more than they think they do. Therapists do not just reflect the client's thoughts and feelings; they reflect selectively, and thus may condition the client to focus on things that the therapist deems important. This direction may be more subtle than that which occurs in other therapies, but is direction nonetheless.

■ *How Rogers's use of empathy, positive regard, and genuineness helped a man who had been diagnosed with schizophrenia*

**Case Example: Rogers's Treatment of a Silent and Bitter Young Man**   Rogers's greatest challenge as a therapist came when, as part of a research study, he conducted client-centered therapy with severely withdrawn inpatients in a state mental hospital (Rogers, 1967). One of these individuals was Jim, who was 28 years old and had been hospitalized for 2½ years with a diagnosis of schizophrenia. Prior to the sessions quoted from below, Rogers had met with Jim once a week for months, and most of that time had been spent in silence. According to Rogers, the two sessions excerpted from below were a turning point, because for the first time the young man began to express how he felt.

[At about 40 minutes into the session, marked mostly by silence.]

**Jim:** *I just ain't no good to nobody, never was and never will be.*

**Rogers:** *Feeling that now, hm? . . . Those really are lousy feelings. Just feel that you're no good at all, hm?*

**Jim:** *Yeah.* [Muttering in a low, discouraged voice.] *That's what this guy I went to town with just the other day told me.*

**Rogers:** *This guy that you went to town with really told you that you were no good? Is that what you're saying? Did I get that right?*

**Jim:** *M-hm.*

**Rogers:** *I guess the meaning of that, if I get it right, is that here's somebody that meant something to you and what does he think of you? Why, he's told you that he thinks you're no good at all. And that just really knocks the props out from under you.* [Jim weeps quietly.] *It just brings the tears.*

[Silence of 20 seconds.]

**Jim:** [Defiantly.] *I don't care though.*

**Rogers:** *You tell yourself you don't care at all, but somehow I guess some part of you cares because some part of you weeps over it.*

[This is followed by more silence, more weeping, and more reflection by Rogers on how it must hurt to feel that someone thinks you're no good. The next session begins again with lots of silence, punctuated by bitter statements in which Jim says that he wants to die. We pick up the conversation as Rogers breaks a long silence by asking whether the wish to die is related to the comment discussed in the previous session.]

**Rogers:** *Can't help but wonder whether it's still true that some things this friend said to you—are those still part of the thing that makes you feel so awful?*

**Jim:** *In general, yes.*

**Rogers:** *M-hm.*

[Silence of 47 seconds, interrupted by another comment from Rogers. Then:]

**Jim:** *I ain't no good to nobody, or I ain't no good for nothin', so what's the use of living?*

**Rogers:** *M-hm. I guess a part of that is—here I'm kind of guessing and you can set me straight, I guess a part of that is that you felt, "I tried to be good for something as far as he was concerned. I really tried. And now—If I'm no good to him, if he feels I'm no good, then that proves I'm just no good to anybody." Is that, uh—anywhere near it?*

**Jim:** *Oh, well, other people have told me that, too.*

**Rogers:** *Yeah, m-hm. I see. So you feel if, if you go by what others—what several others have said, then, you are no good. No good to anybody.*
[This is followed by more silence, interrupted by a few comments along the same track. Then:]

**Jim:** [Muttering in discouraged tone.] *That's why I want to go, 'cause I don't care what happens.*

**Rogers:** *M-hm, m-hm . . . You don't care what happens. And I guess I'd just like to say—I care about you. And I care what happens.*
[Silence of 30 seconds, and then Jim bursts into tears.]

**Rogers:** [Tenderly.] *Somehow that just—makes all the feelings pour out.* [Silence of 35 seconds.] *And you just weep and weep. And feel so badly.*

Commenting on the transaction above, Rogers (1967) wrote:

> Jim Brown, who sees himself as stubborn, bitter, mistreated, worthless, useless, hopeless, unloved, unlovable, *experiences* my caring. In that moment his defensive shell cracks wide open, and can never be quite the same. When someone *cares* for him, and when he feels and experiences this caring, he becomes a softer person whose years of stored up hurt come pouring out in anguished sobs. He is not the shell of hardness and bitterness, the stranger to tenderness. He is a person hurt beyond words, and aching for the love and caring which alone can make him human. This is evident in his sobs. It is evident too in his returning to my office [shortly after the session], partly for a cigarette, partly to say spontaneously that he will return.

After this session, according to Rogers, Jim gradually became more open, spontaneous, and optimistic at their meetings. After several months, he was able to leave the hospital and support himself with a job. Eight years later, on his own initiative, Jim called Rogers to tell him that he was still employed, had friends, was content with life, and that his feelings toward Rogers were still important, even though they had not been in touch during all that time (Meador & Rogers, 1973).

### Cognitive Therapy

**Cognitive therapy** begins with the assumption that people disturb themselves through their own thoughts. Maladaptive thoughts make reality seem worse than it is and in that way produce anxiety or depression. The goal of cognitive therapy is to identify maladaptive ways of thinking and replace them with adaptive ways that provide a base for more effective coping with the real world.

Cognitive therapy is similar to humanistic therapy in its focus on conscious mental experiences, but in other respects it is different. Whereas humanistic therapy is client centered, cognitive therapy is *problem centered*. That is, whereas humanistic therapists try to help their clients understand themselves better as whole persons, cognitive therapists focus more directly on their clients' specific problems. Compared to either humanistic or psychodynamic therapists, cognitive therapists adopt more of a let's-get-down-to-business attitude. The cognitive therapist-client relationship is similar to a teacher-student relationship in that the therapist helps the client identify and correct his or her faulty reasoning. Most cognitive therapists even assign homework to be completed between one session and the next. The two best-known pioneers of cognitive therapy are Albert Ellis and Aaron Beck.

**Ellis's Rational-Emotive Therapy**    After trying and becoming disenchanted by both psychodynamic and humanistic approaches to therapy, Albert Ellis began in 1955 to develop his own approach, which he labeled ***rational-emotive therapy*** (*RET*) (Ellis, 1986). The basic premise of RET is that people's irrational interpretations of their experiences, not the objective experiences themselves, cause their

■ *How cognitive therapy differs from Rogers's humanistic therapy*

■ *How Ellis explains people's emotions in terms of their beliefs*

negative emotions. Ellis gives humorous names to certain styles of irrational thinking. Thus, *musturbation* is the irrational belief that one *must* have some particular thing or *must* act in some particular way to be happy or worthwhile. If a client says, "I must get all *A*'s this semester in college," Ellis might respond, "You're musturbating again." *Awfulizing*, in Ellis's vocabulary, is the mental exaggeration of setbacks or inconveniences. A client who feels bad for a whole week because of a dent in his or her new car might be told, "Stop awfulizing." Ellis is notoriously direct in his approach to correcting what he sees as clients' irrational views, quite the opposite of Rogers.

The following dialogue between Ellis (1962) and a client not only illustrates Ellis's style, but also makes explicit his theory of the relationship between thoughts and emotions. The client has just complained that he was unhappy because some men with whom he played golf didn't like him.

**Ellis:** *You think you were unhappy because these men didn't like you?*

**Client:** *I certainly was!*

**Ellis:** *But you weren't unhappy for the reason you think you were.*

**Client:** *I wasn't? But I was!*

**Ellis:** *No, I insist: You only think you were unhappy for that reason.*

**Client:** *Well, why was I unhappy then?*

**Ellis:** *It's very simple—as simple as A, B, C, I might say. A in this case is the fact that these men didn't like you. Let's assume that you observed their attitude correctly and were not merely imagining they didn't like you.*

**Client:** *I assure you that they didn't. I could see that very clearly.*

**Ellis:** *Very well, let's assume they didn't like you and call that* A. *Now,* C *is your unhappiness—which we'll definitely have to assume is a fact, since you felt it.*

**Client:** *Damn right I did!*

**Ellis:** *All right, then:* A *is the fact that the men didn't like you, and* C *is your unhappiness. You see* A *and* C *and you assume that* A, *their not liking you, caused your unhappiness. But it didn't.*

**Client:** *It didn't? What did, then?*

**Ellis:** B *did.*

**Client:** *What's* B?

**Ellis:** B *is what you said to yourself while you were playing golf with those men.*

**Client:** *What I said to myself? But I didn't say anything.*

**Ellis:** *You did. You couldn't possibly be unhappy if you didn't. The only thing that could possibly make you unhappy that occurs from without is a brick falling on your head, or some such equivalent. But no brick fell. Obviously, therefore, you must have told yourself something to make you unhappy.*

In this dialogue, Ellis invokes his famous *ABC theory of emotions: A* is the *Activating event* in the environment, *B* is the *Belief* that is triggered off in the client's mind when the event occurs, and *C* is the *emotional Consequence* of that belief. Therapy proceeds by changing *B*, the belief. In this particular example, the man suffers because he believes irrationally that he must be liked by everyone (an example of musturbation), so if someone doesn't like him he is unhappy. The first step will be to convince the man that it is irrational to expect everyone to like him and that there is little or no harm in not being liked by everyone. The next step, after the man admits to the belief's irrationality, will be to help him get rid of the belief, so that it doesn't recur in his thinking. That takes hard work. Long-held beliefs do not simply disappear when they are seen to be irrational. They have become habits that occur automatically unless actively resisted. Ellis gives his clients homework designed to train them to catch and correct themselves each time the habitual thought pattern appears.

**Beck's Cognitive Therapy**    Aaron Beck began to develop a cognitive approach to the treatment of depression in 1960, after observing that his depressed clients routinely distorted their experiences in ways that helped them maintain negative views of themselves, their world, and their future. He observed that they would *minimize* positive experiences, *maximize* negative experiences, and *misattribute* negative experiences to their own deficiencies when they were not really at fault. In later work, Beck and his associates also identified patterns of thinking that promote anxiety (such as exaggerating the likelihood of accidents or diseases occurring), and they expanded their cognitive therapy to include clients with anxiety disorders (Beck & Emery, 1985). In therapy sessions, Beck's approach is gentler than is Ellis's. Instead of telling his clients directly about their irrational thoughts, he leads them, with a Socratic style of questioning, to discover and correct the thoughts themselves. He prefers this approach, because it is less threatening than the direct approach and because it helps show clients that they can correct their own thoughts and need not always depend on the therapist. Beck's approach is illustrated by the following case summary.

■ *How Beck's treatment of a depressed woman illustrates his approach to identifying and correcting maladaptive, automatic patterns of thought*

**Case Example: Beck's Treatment of a Depressed Young Woman**    The client in this case (from Beck & Young, 1985) was Irene, a 29-year-old, married woman with two young children who was diagnosed with major depression. She had not been employed outside her home since marriage, and her husband, who had been in and out of drug-treatment centers, was also unemployed. She was socially isolated and felt that people looked down on her because of her poor control over her children and her husband's drug record. She was treated for three sessions by Beck and then was treated for a longer period by another cognitive therapist.

During the first session, a number of her automatic (habitual) negative thoughts were identified, including: *Things won't get better. Nobody cares for me. I am stupid.* By the end of the session, she agreed to Beck's suggestion to try to invalidate the first of those thoughts by doing certain things for herself, before the next session, that might make life more fun. She agreed to take the children on an outing, visit her mother, go shopping, read a book, and find out about joining a tennis group—all things that she claimed she would like to do. Having completed that homework, she came to the second session feeling more hopeful. However, she began to feel depressed again when, during the session, she misunderstood a question that Beck asked her, which, she said, made her "look dumb." In response, Beck began to question her to help her to distinguish between the *fact* of what happened (not understanding a question) and her *belief* about it (looking dumb), and then to correct her belief:

> Beck: *OK, what is a <u>rational</u> answer [to why you didn't answer the question]? A realistic answer?*
>
> Irene: *I didn't hear the question right, that is why I didn't answer it right.*
>
> Beck: *OK, so that is the fact situation. And so, is the fact situation that you look dumb or you just didn't hear the question right?*
>
> Irene: *I didn't hear the question right.*
>
> Beck: *Or is it possible that I didn't say the question in such a way that it was clear?*
>
> Irene: *Possible.*
>
> Beck: *Very possible. I'm not perfect so it's very possible that I didn't express the question properly.*
>
> Irene: *But instead of saying you made a mistake, I would still say I made a mistake.*
>
> Beck: *We'll have to watch the video to see. Whichever. Does it mean if I didn't express the question, if I made the mistake, does it make me dumb?*
>
> Irene: *No.*
>
> Beck: *And if you made the mistake, does it make you dumb?*

**Irene:** *No, not really.*

**Beck:** *But you felt dumb?*

**Irene:** *But I did, yeah.*

**Beck:** *Do you still feel dumb?*

**Irene:** *No. Right now I feel glad. I'm feeling a little better that at least somebody is pointing all these things out to me because I have never seen this before. I never knew that I thought that I was that dumb.*

As homework between the second and third sessions, Beck gave Irene the assignment of catching, writing down, and correcting her own dysfunctional thoughts using the form shown in Figure 18.3. Subsequent sessions were aimed at eradicating each of her depressive thoughts, one by one, and reinforcing the steps she was taking to improve her life. Progress was rapid. She felt increasingly better about herself, as measured by the Beck Depression Inventory (illustrated in Table 18.1). During the next several months, she (a) joined a tennis league, (b) got a job as a waitress, (c) took and performed well in a college course in sociology, and (d) left her husband after trying and failing to get him to develop a better attitude toward her or to join her in couple therapy. By this time, according to Beck, she was cured of her depression, had created for herself a healthy environment, and no longer needed therapy.

**Figure 18.3** *Homework sheet for cognitive therapy*

*The purpose of this homework is to enable clients to become aware of and correct the automatic thoughts that contribute to their emotional difficulties. (Adapted from Beck & Young, 1985.)*

| DATE | SITUATION | EMOTION(S) | AUTOMATIC THOUGHT(S) | RATIONAL RESPONSE | OUTCOME |
|---|---|---|---|---|---|
| | Describe:<br>1. Actual event leading to unpleasant emotion, or<br><br>2. Stream of thoughts, daydream, or recollection, leading to unpleasant emotion. | 1. Specify sad/ anxious/ angry, etc.<br><br>2. Rate degree of emotion, 1–100. | 1. Write automatic thought(s) that preceded emotion(s).<br><br>2. Rate belief in automatic thought(s), 0–100%. | 1. Write rational response to automatic thought(s).<br><br>2. Rate belief in rational response, 0–100%. | 1. Rerate belief in automatic thought(s), 0–100%.<br><br>2. Specify and rate subsequent emotions, 0–100. |
| 7/15 | Store clerk didn't smile at me when I paid for purchase. | Sad – 60<br>Anxious – 40 | Nobody likes me – 70%<br><br>I look awful – 80% | Maybe the clerk was having a bad day or maybe she never smiles at customers – 70% | 1. 20%<br>30%<br><br>2. Pleasure – 25% |

**Explanation:** When you experience an unpleasant emotion, note the situation that seemed to stimulate the emotion. (If the emotion occurred while you were thinking, daydreaming, etc., please note this.) Then note the automatic thought associated with the emotion. Record the degree to which you believe this thought: 0% = not at all, 100% = completely. In rating degree of emotion: 1 = a trace, 100 = the most intense possible.

**Hanging in the balance**

*Confidence-building activities, such as the one shown here, are sometimes recommended by behavior therapists to help clients increase their feelings of self-worth and self-efficacy.*

■ *Some ways in which behavior and cognitive therapies have always been similar*

## Behavior Therapy

***Behavior therapy*** is the psychotherapy approach rooted in the laboratory research of such pioneers as Ivan Pavlov, John B. Watson, and B. F. Skinner, who formulated principles of classical and operant conditioning in terms of stimulus-response relationships (see Chapter 5).

In principle, and in line with their philosophical forebears, behavior therapists might prefer to ignore mental phenomena such as thoughts and emotions, and concentrate only on direct relationships between observable aspects of the environment (stimuli) and observable behaviors (responses); but in practice they cannot. After all, clients in behavior therapy, like those in any form of psychotherapy, complain about such mental phenomena as fears, anxiety, obsessive thoughts, and depressed feelings. To deal with these problems within the theoretical framework of behaviorism, behavior therapists have traditionally spoken of mental events as *covert responses* (hidden responses) that follow the same laws of conditioning as overt responses.

Contemporary behavior therapists, however, increasingly use language similar to that of cognitive therapists in describing mental events. In fact, behavior and cognitive therapies have to a considerable degree merged to form what is often called ***cognitive-behavior therapy***. This merging parallels a similar progression in academic research laboratories, where studies of learning have shifted from a stimulus-response emphasis to one that focuses on mental processes as mediators between stimuli and responses (see Chapter 5).

Behavior and cognitive therapies have always shared important characteristics. Both commonly claim to be "problem centered" more than "client centered." That is, they focus directly on helping the person overcome his or her specific problems rather than on treating the "whole person." Both usually characterize these problems as learned habits, and take the approach that what has been learned can be unlearned. Both place great importance on behavior monitoring and advocate changing techniques if earlier ones don't give positive results rather quickly. In the following sections we will look at some of the most common behavior therapy techniques, beginning with those most closely related to principles of respondent and operant conditioning.

**Fear of flying**

*Airline pilot Tom Bunn (left) and a friend encourage a man who has chosen flooding as a means of overcoming his fear of flying. Through an organization called SOAR, Bunn offers his services to individuals with airplane phobias.*

**Exposure Treatments to Eliminate Fears** Behavior therapy has proven especially successful in treating simple phobias, in which the fear is of something well defined such as high places or a specific type of animal (Marks, 1987). From a behavioral perspective, fear is a reflexive response, usually involving tightened muscles and a certain pattern of autonomic activity that can be triggered by various unconditioned or conditioned stimuli. An unconditioned stimulus for fear is one (such as a sudden loud noise) that elicits the response in an individual who has had no previous experience with the stimulus, and a conditioned stimulus for fear is one that elicits the response only because it was previously paired with an unconditioned stimulus for fear (see Chapter 5).

An important characteristic of the fear reflex is that repeated or prolonged exposure to the eliciting stimulus, in a setting where no real danger occurs, results in gradual loss of the reflex. If the eliciting stimulus is an unconditioned stimulus, this loss is called *habituation*. Thus, a sudden loud noise elicits an unconditioned fear response when first presented; but if this stimulus is repeated many times, and no harm occurs, the fear response is lost through habituation. If the eliciting stimulus is a conditioned stimulus, the loss in the reflex is called *extinction*. If a signal light elicits fear because the light was previously paired with some harmful occurrence (such as an electric shock), repeated exposure to the light without any harm causes gradual extinction of the reflex.

From this perspective, the most direct way to eliminate an unwanted fear would be simply to expose the client to the feared stimulus until the reflex is habituated or extinguished. Behavior therapists refer to this technique as *flooding* (because the person is "flooded" with the stimulus and the accompanying fear until the latter is lost). For example, a person who is afraid of dogs might be induced to sit in the same room with a dog until the fear is gone. In some cases, flooding is accomplished through imagination rather than actual exposure to the feared stimulus. The therapist teaches the client techniques for vivid imagining, and then the client imagines the feared object or event until it is no longer feared.

But flooding is not always possible or desirable. Some clients refuse to expose themselves to the feared situation, even in imagination, and others may panic and have to leave the feared situation or terminate the imagined scene. The experience of panic might even intensify the original fear. An alternative procedure, described long ago by John B. Watson (1924), is *counter-conditioning*, in which the person is trained through respondent conditioning to react to the feared stimulus with a response—such as pleasure, relaxation, or anger—that is incompatible with fear. To illustrate this procedure, Watson described a demonstration carried out by one of his associates, Mary Cover Jones, with a 3-year-old boy named Peter.

Peter was extremely frightened of rabbits, and Jones's goal was to counter-condition him to react to rabbits with pleasure rather than fear. Peter enjoyed his daily snack of milk and crackers, so Jones decided to make a live rabbit a conditioned stimulus for a pleasure response by pairing it with the snack. The most straightforward way would be to place the rabbit directly in front of Peter simultaneously with the snack; but if she had done that, the rabbit would probably have been a stronger stimulus than the snack, and Peter, rather than losing his fear of rabbits, might have developed an unfortunate fear of milk and crackers. So Jones used a more cautious approach. On the first day, she put the rabbit in a cage at the other end of a long room in which Peter ate his snack. Peter noticed the rabbit, but it did not disturb his enjoyment of the snack. Then, each day Jones moved the rabbit a little closer, until eventually she could put it on Peter's lap without his showing any fear. Figure 18.4 (on page 668) illustrates the interpretation of this as classical conditioning. Notice that the rabbit is used as the conditioned stimulus, and the snack as the unconditioned stimulus, for a response (pleasure) that is incompatible with fear.

*How flooding, counter-conditioning, and systematic desensitization can be used to eliminate fears*

*Professor Gallagher and his controversial technique of simultaneously confronting the fear of heights, snakes and the dark.*

**Figure 18.4 *Outline of the counter-conditioning procedure used by Mary Cover Jones***
*At first, the boy is afraid of the rabbit. During the conditioning phase, the rabbit is the conditioned stimulus, and the snack is the unconditioned stimulus, for a pleasurable response incompatible with fear. After conditioning, the boy responds with pleasure rather than fear to the rabbit.*

**Before conditioning**
  Rabbit → fear; snack → pleasure

**Conditioning**
  Rabbit:    Snack → pleasure
  Rabbit:    Snack → pleasure
  Rabbit:    Snack → pleasure
  Rabbit:    Snack → pleasure

**After conditioning**
  Rabbit → pleasure

A version of counter-conditioning most often used today is ***systematic desensitization***, originated by Joseph Wolpe (1958). In this technique, clients are first trained in muscle relaxation until they can relax easily in response to a cue from the therapist. Then they are asked to imagine a scene that would normally elicit some degree of anxiety, and they are given the cue to relax while imagining that scene. When that is accomplished with ease, they gradually move on through increasingly frightening scenes, again imagining each while relaxing. For example, a woman afraid of heights might be asked to relax first while imagining that she is looking out a second-floor window, then a third-floor window, and so on, until she can relax while imagining that she is looking down from the top of a skyscraper.

Notice the similarity between this procedure and Jones's counter-conditioning procedure. The feared scene, paired in imagination with the cue to relax, presumably becomes a conditioned stimulus for relaxation, which is incompatible with fear. Just as Jones started with the rabbit far away and gradually brought it closer, systematic desensitization starts with a mildly fearful imagined scene and gradually works up to more fearful ones. An assumption here is that the ability to relax while imagining the previously feared situation will generalize, so that the person will be able to relax in the presence of the actual situation.

■ *How flooding, counter-conditioning, and systematic desensitization may all operate through the same principle—exposure*

Many experiments have shown that the three just-described techniques are quite effective (Rachman & Wilson, 1980; Marks, 1987), but controversy exists over how or why they work. A prominent view today is that the most important ingredient in all behavioral treatments for fears is the *exposure* of the client to the feared stimulus, either in reality or imagination, so that habituation or extinction can occur. Flooding, counter-conditioning, and systematic desensitization are now often classed together under the term ***exposure treatments***, and experiments have shown that the longer and more intense the exposure, the more effective the treatment (see Foa & Kozak, 1986). From this perspective, counter-conditioning and systematic desensitization are effective not because they actually teach the individual to make a new response (such as a pleasure response or relaxation response) to the previously feared stimulus, but because they help induce the reluctant client to remain in the presence of the feared stimuli, without panicking, until habituation or extinction occurs.

■ *How the effect of catharsis in psychoanalysis might be interpreted from a behavioral perspective*

It is interesting to think back about the psychoanalytic treatment of fear-related conditions and apply this behavioral analysis. Why did Anna O. lose the paralysis in her arm when she recalled, under Breuer's hypnosis, the fearful memory of the fantasized snake attacking her father? Why did the Rat Man lose his neurotic obsessions after he recalled, on Freud's couch, the fearful incident of being beaten by his father? If we assume that fear responses can occur without conscious awareness (an assumption compatible with both psychoanalytic and behavioral theory), and that Anna O.'s and the Rat Man's symptoms were manifestations of learned, unconscious fears, then we might assume that Breuer's and Freud's treatments were effective for the same reason that systematic desensitization is effective. The client vividly imagines and re-experiences, in the safe conditions provided by the psychoanalyst, the stimuli associated with the original traumatic event, thereby permitting extinction of the conditioned fear response to those stimuli, and hence loss of symptoms. Too simple? Maybe. But Breuer himself noted that in the early stages of Anna O.'s disorder, her arm paralysis was brought on whenever she saw something (such as a tree branch) that looked like a snake (Breuer & Freud, 1895/1955)—a reaction that is akin to a conditioned response.

■ *How maladaptive habits can be interpreted in terms of operant conditioning and eliminated by use of aversive stimuli*

**Aversion Treatment to Eliminate Bad Habits** From the behavioral perspective, much of what we do can be understood as *habit*. A habit is a learned action that has become so ingrained that the person performs it unconsciously and may even feel compelled to perform it. Most habits are good; they permit us to do automatically things that are beneficial. Thus, stepping on the automobile brake in response to a red traffic light is a habit that saves many lives every day. But some habits—such as addictive drinking, compulsive gambling, or compulsive hand washing (in obsessive-compulsive disorder)—are harmful. Regardless of how such behaviors originated, they persist because they are followed immediately by pleasure or relief from discomfort. The person addicted to alcohol feels relief from withdrawal symptoms after a drink, the compulsive gambler experiences a thrill when placing a bet, and the obsessive-compulsive hand washer experiences relief from the fear of germs after washing his or her hands. Thus, such behaviors can be understood at least partly in terms of operant conditioning, the process by which responses that are followed either by positive reinforcement (something pleasant) or by negative reinforcement (removal of something unpleasant) are likely to occur again in the future (see Chapter 5).

*Aversion treatment*

*In an attempt to eliminate this man's tobacco addiction, the therapist is trying to make him sick. Do you think the client learned that smoking a cigarette is associated with nausea, or only that smoking two cigarettes is?*

A behavioral analysis suggests that the basic obstacle to getting rid of bad habits is that operant responses are controlled more by their immediate effects than by their long-term effects. A person might know that drinking alcohol in quantity destroys the liver and brain, that gambling is in the end a losing proposition, and that repeated hand washing wastes time and may eat away the skin; yet, the behaviors persist because such knowledge is less effective in controlling the behaviors than is the short-term pleasure or relief they bring. To eliminate such habits, the person must somehow change the reinforcement contingencies, and this is where aversion treatment comes in. Put simply, *aversion treatment* is the application of an aversive (painful or unpleasant) stimulus immediately after the unwanted response, or immediately after the person has experienced cues that would normally elicit the response. Thus, a woman who is a compulsive gambler might be given shocks to the fingers as she reaches out onto a simulated gambling table to place a bet; or a man addicted to alcohol might be given a drug to make him feel nauseated in the presence of alcohol. Such treatment can be understood in terms of either operant or classical conditioning (see Chapter 5). In operant conditioning terms, the aversive stimulus is punishment for behaving in the objectionable way or initiating such behavior. In classical conditioning terms, the aversive stimulus is an unconditioned stimulus for an avoidance reaction, which becomes conditioned to cues, such as the sight of the gambling table or alcohol, which previously elicited attraction.

Aversion treatment has always been controversial, partly because of the ethical problem of deliberately hurting a person (even when the person agrees to the procedure), and partly because of its mixed results. One limitation is that learned aversions often do not generalize beyond the original conditions. This limitation stems from the fact that conditioning depends more on cognition (the subject's knowledge of the conditions present) than the early behaviorists believed. Clients may experience the learned aversion only as long as they know that they are connected to the shock generator or that they have taken the drug that will induce nausea.

A well-documented case to illustrate this point involves the use of the drug *antabuse* to treat alcohol addiction. Antabuse reacts with alcohol in a person's body to induce severe nausea and headaches shortly after alcohol is consumed. In the early days of antabuse use, behavior therapists believed that people who drank alcohol after taking the drug would develop a conditioned aversion to alcohol, which they would retain even without further antabuse treatment. Unfortunately, however, experience has shown that most people suffering from long-term alcoholism avoid alcohol when on antabuse but go back to it quickly after they stop the antabuse treatments (Forrest, 1985). Today, antabuse is recognized as an effective treatment for alcoholism only if taken continuously, often for the rest of the person's life.

**Some Other Behavioral Techniques**   In addition to the exposure and aversion treatments described above, behavior therapists have developed an arsenal of other techniques for treating behavioral problems. Among them are the following:

*Token economies*   A token economy is essentially a monetary-exchange system adapted for use in a mental hospital or other institution where patients are confined. Its purpose is to provide a direct incentive for patients to do things that are deemed good for them or others. Thus, patients may receive tokens for such activities as making their bed, helping out in the kitchen, or helping other patients in specified ways, and they can cash in the tokens for desired privileges, such as movies or treats at the hospital commissary. This technique helps combat the lethargy, boredom, and dependence that are so common in mental hospitals (Ayllon & Azrin, 1968), and it was an important part of the successful social learning program in the study by Paul and Lentz (1977) described earlier.

*Contingency contracts*   A contingency contract is a formal, usually written agreement between two or more people in which certain specified services or rewards, provided by one party, are made contingent upon the actions of the

*A general limitation of aversion treatment, and an illustration of it in the treatment of alcohol addiction with antabuse*

**Assertiveness training**

*In this technique, widely used in business organizations, individuals learn the skills necessary for effective social interaction.*

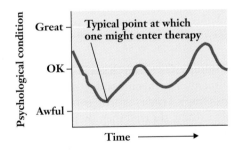

**Figure 18.5  The peaks and valleys of life**

*If a person enters psychotherapy while in a valley, he or she is likely to feel better after a time, even if the therapy is ineffective. For this reason, therapy groups must be compared with control groups to determine if therapy is effective.*

other. For example, a contingency contract between a therapist and a client may specify that the therapist will meet with the client each week only if the client completes the agreed-upon homework. As another example, a family therapist may help an embattled husband and wife work out a contract in which one party agrees to behave in certain ways toward the other (say, continue to live in the same house) only if the other behaves in certain ways (say, takes specific steps toward getting a job or overcoming a drug addiction). To be effective, a contingency contract must clearly spell out the behaviors expected and the consequences for meeting or not meeting those expectations.

*Assertiveness and social skills training* *Assertiveness* can be defined as the ability to express one's own desires and feelings and to maintain one's rights, in interactions with others, while at the same time respecting the others' rights. A high percentage of people in therapy are there partly because they lack the assertiveness or social skills necessary for effective and comfortable social interactions. Because of this lack, they may either avoid other people or go through life doing what others want them to do rather than what they themselves want to do. In either case, they are often lonely, because they have not made real emotional contact with others. Assertiveness and social skills training include all direct methods by which a therapist attempts to teach a client to be more assertive, effective, and comfortable in social interactions. At first the therapist may demonstrate social skills or methods of assertion, or may give the client phrases to memorize and practice—such as *Well, that's not a bad idea, but today I would really rather _____*. Later, *role-playing* sessions might be introduced, in which the person plays out, with the therapist or with other clients in a group, various scenes requiring assertion (such as asking for a raise, refusing a sexual advance, or explaining to parents that one's mail is private) or social skills (such as asking for or accepting a date).

*Modeling*  As a therapy technique, modeling is the process of teaching a person to do something by having him or her watch another person do it (discussed more generally in Chapter 5). Thus, as part of assertiveness training a therapist might model (demonstrate) ways to be assertive. In the realm of fear reduction, Albert Bandura and his colleagues (1982) have shown in many experiments that people can overcome snake or spider phobias by watching others handle the feared creature during several sessions, before being asked to approach or handle it themselves.

## Evaluating Psychotherapies

You have just read about four major varieties of psychotherapy. Do they work? That might seem like a strange question at this point. After all, didn't Freud cure the Rat Man, didn't Rogers help the silent young man, didn't Beck and his associates cure the depressed young woman, and haven't behavior therapists cured many people of their fears and bad habits? But case studies—even thousands of them—showing that people are better off at the end of therapy than at the beginning cannot tell us for sure that therapy works. Maybe they would have improved anyway, without therapy. An adage about the common cold goes something like this: "Treat a cold with the latest remedy and you'll get rid of it in 7 days; leave it untreated and it'll hang on for a week." Maybe psychological problems or disorders are like colds in this respect. Everyone has peaks and valleys in life, and people are most likely to start therapy while in one of the valleys. Thus, even if therapy has no effect, most people will feel better at some point after entering it than they did when they first began (see Figure 18.5). When that happens, there is a natural tendency for both the therapist and the client to believe that improvement was due to the treatment, which could be entirely an illusion.

■ *Why case studies do not prove that psychotherapy works, and why experiments are necessary*

The only way to know if psychotherapy really works is to perform controlled experiments, in which groups of people undergoing therapy are compared with otherwise similar control groups who are not undergoing therapy. Within the last 3 decades, hundreds of such experiments have been conducted, and reviews of them have led to the following general conclusions (Smith & others, 1980; Stiles & others, 1986):

1. Psychotherapy works: On average, people in treatment improve more than do those not in treatment.

2. No single type of psychotherapy stands out as clearly better than any other type when all studies are combined, though some types may be better for specific kinds of problems.

3. Various *nonspecific factors*, which are common to all recognized types of psychotherapy, seem to contribute heavily to therapy outcome.

In the following paragraphs, I will summarize some of the evidence behind these conclusions.

■ *How an experiment in Philadelphia demonstrated that behavior therapy and psychoanalytic psychotherapy were both effective*

**Example of a Therapy Outcome Study: The Philadelphia Experiment**   One of the best known and most highly esteemed experiments on therapy outcome was conducted at a psychiatric outpatient clinic in Philadelphia (Sloane & others, 1975). The subjects were ninety-four men and women, ages 18 to 45, who sought psychotherapy at the clinic. Most of these individuals suffered from anxiety disorders. They were assigned by a random procedure to one of three groups. One group received once-a-week sessions of *behavior therapy* for 4 months (including such procedures as systematic desensitization and assertiveness training) from one of three highly experienced behavior therapists. The second group received the same amount of *psychoanalytical psychotherapy* (including such procedures as probing into childhood memories, dream analysis, and interpretation of resistance) from one of three highly experienced psychoanalytically oriented therapists. The members of the third group, the *control group*, were placed on a waiting list and given no treatment during the 4-month period, but were called periodically to let them know that they would eventually be accepted for therapy.

To measure treatment effectiveness, all subjects, including those in the control group, were assessed both before and after the 4-month period by psychiatrists who were uninformed of the groups to which the subjects had been assigned. As illustrated in Figure 18.6, all three groups improved during the 4-month period, but the treatment groups improved significantly more than did the control group. Moreover, the two treatment groups did not differ significantly from each other in degree of improvement.

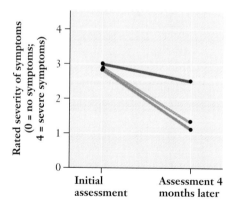

Behavior therapy
Psychoanalytic psychotherapy
Waiting list (no therapy)

**Figure 18.6  *Results of the Philadelphia experiment***

*Psychiatrists rated the severity of each subject's symptoms before and after a 4-month treatment period. As shown here, those in the two therapy groups improved more than did those who were placed on the waiting list. (Adapted from Sloane & others, 1975.)*

**An Analysis of the Combined Results of Therapy Outcome Experiments**   By the late 1970s, 475 separate outcome experiments had been conducted, each of which compared one or more types of psychotherapy with a control group that did not receive therapy. Most, like the Philadelphia study, showed therapy to be superior to no therapy. Many, unlike the Philadelphia study, showed one kind of therapy to be superior to another, though in different studies different therapies came out on top. To digest the results of all of those experiments and arrive at some general conclusions, Mary Lee Smith and her colleagues (1980) performed what is called a *meta-analysis* of the 475 studies. They reanalyzed the data from every study, converting the results into *standard effect-size units*, which could be compared across studies. (This was done by subtracting the outcome measure for the control group from that for the therapy group, and then dividing by the standard deviation of the scores, as explained further in the Statistical Appendix.) When they averaged all of these standardized scores, for all treatment groups in all stud-

■ *How an analysis of hundreds of therapy outcome experiments has shown that therapy works, that various therapies are about equally effective overall, and that different therapies may be most effective for different problems*

ies, the results indicated that about 80 percent of people in the psychotherapy groups showed greater improvement than did the average person in a control group.

When Smith and her colleagues computed the average effect-size separately for different types of psychotherapy, they found that every type produced significant improvement and that little if any difference existed in the average improvement for different types. In another analysis, however, they calculated the effect-sizes for each type of therapy separately for different kinds of outcome measures, and that analysis suggested that different therapies may be best for different kinds of problems. For example, as you can see in Table 18.2, fear and anxiety seem to be treated better by behavioral and cognitive therapies than by psychodynamic therapies, whereas the reverse seems true for achievement problems and addictions; and humanistic therapy seems best for raising self-esteem. These results must be interpreted cautiously, since the different experiments differed in many ways other than the types of therapy employed; but at least they provide interesting hypotheses to test in large-scale single experiments in the future.

**Table 18.2** *Average standard effect-size for different therapy types and outcome measurements**

| | Outcome measured | | | | |
|---|---|---|---|---|---|
| **Type of therapy** | *Fear or anxiety* | *Self-esteem* | *Addiction* | *Social behavior* | *Work or school achievement* |
| Psychodynamic | 0.78 | 0.66 | 1.05 | 0.94 | 1.24 |
| Humanistic | 0.61 | 0.99 | ** | 0.45 | 0.54 |
| Cognitive | 1.67 | 0.65 | 0.53 | ** | 0.28 |
| Cognitive-behavioral | 1.78 | 0.73 | ** | 1.23 | 0.60 |
| Behavioral | 1.12 | 0.23 | 0.75 | 0.42 | 0.45 |

*The effect size is the difference in outcome measure between the treatment group and the control group, divided by the standard deviation of outcome scores (see Statistical Appendix).
**Too few studies to warrant inclusion.
*Source:* Adapted from *The benefits of psychotherapy* (p. 97) by M. L. Smith, G. V. Glass, & T. I. Miller, 1980, Baltimore, MD: Johns Hopkins University Press.

■ *Evidence that the most important ingredients of psychotherapy may be the offering of support and hope*

**Role of Nonspecific Factors** If psychotherapy works, the next logical question is: Why does it work? As you know, each therapy has its own set of principles to explain its effects; but some people have argued that therapy works mostly because of so-called *nonspecific factors*, which cut across different therapies and are unrelated to the specific principles on which the therapy is based. Many such factors have been proposed, but they can be categorized under two general labels: support and hope (Stiles & others, 1986).

*Support* includes acceptance, empathy, encouragement, and guidance. By devoting time to the client, listening warmly and respectfully, and not being shocked at the client's statements or actions, any good psychotherapist communicates the attitude that the client is a worthwhile human being, and this may directly enhance the client's self-esteem and indirectly lead to other improvements as well. Moreover, almost any therapist, regardless of theoretical orientation, will start sessions by asking the client how things have gone since the last meeting; the anticipation of such reporting may encourage clients to work on self-improvement so they can give a better report. In addition, most therapists make at least some common-sense suggestions that have little to do with their theories, of the sort that anyone's wise friend or relative might make, but carrying more weight because they come from a recognized authority.

**Support offered here**

*The therapist's relaxed posture, active engagement, and position facing the client are all nonspecific factors that contribute to clients' feelings of self-worth.*

Many studies have demonstrated the value of support, as defined above. In a long-term study at the Menninger Clinic, Robert Wallerstein (1989) found that contemporary psychoanalysts, in fact, provided more support and less insight to their clients than would be expected from psychoanalytic theory, and that support even without insight seemed to produce stable therapeutic gains. In another study, the success rate of therapists was found to depend more on the degree to which their clients felt understood by them than on the therapist's theoretical orientation (Lafferty & others, 1989). And, in still another study, college professors who were not trained in psychology or methods of therapy, but who had reputations of good rapport with students, were as effective in helping depressed college students in twice-a-week therapy sessions as were highly trained and experienced clinical psychologists (Strupp & Hadley, 1979). Such results have led one well-known psychodynamic therapist, Hans Strupp (1989), to conclude that "the first and foremost task for the therapist is to create an accepting and empathic context, which in itself has great therapeutic value because for many people it is a novel and deeply gratifying experience to be accepted and listened to respectfully."

*Hope*, the second category of nonspecific factors, may come partly from the sense of support, but may also come from other aspects of the therapeutic environment. Most psychotherapists believe in what they do. They speak with authority and confidence about their methods, and they offer scientific-sounding theories or even data to back up their confidence. Thus, clients also come to believe that the therapy will work. Many studies have shown that people who believe that they will get better have an improved chance of getting better, even if the specific reason for the belief is false. This is the basis for the well-known ***placebo effect*** in studies of drugs. In these studies, patients given a pill that contains no active substance (the placebo) improve, compared to those given no pill, if the patient believes that the pill has curative powers. The term *placebo effect* is now used to refer to any improvement that comes from a person's belief in the treatment rather than from other therapeutic factors. The placebo effect is an element that all sought-after healing procedures have in common, whether provided by psychotherapists, medical doctors, faith healers, or folkhealers.

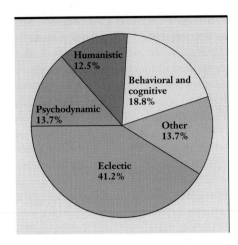

**Figure 18.7** *The theoretical orientations of a sample of psychotherapists*

*Shown here are the results of a survey in which 422 practicing clinical and counseling psychologists were asked to identify their theoretical orientation. (Data from Smith, 1982.)*

■ *Evidence that many psychotherapists have moved away from rigid adherence to specific schools*

How much of the improvement observed in psychotherapy is due to the person's belief in the process (hope)? That is hard to answer. In tests of drug treatments, the psychological factor of hope and the direct chemical effects of the drug are relatively easy to separate, but in psychotherapy—where the whole treatment is psychological—no clear distinction can be made between hope as a nonspecific side effect of psychotherapy and hope as a specific goal of psychotherapy. Some experiments on therapy outcome include a *placebo group* who receive pseudo-psychotherapy that is designed to provide the element of hope without providing the specific elements deemed important to the therapy being tested. For example, in one study systematic desensitization was compared to a made-up placebo treatment called *systematic ventilation*, in which people talked about their fears in systematic ways (Kirsch & others, 1983). In general, in such experiments the placebo group does better than do nontreated controls, but not as well as do those receiving the more standard form of psychotherapy being tested (see Barker & others, 1988). But it is hard to interpret such results; on the one hand, hope may not be raised as fully in placebo groups as in therapy groups, and on the other, placebo treatments may include elements that could produce therapeutic effects through means other than hope. For example, talking about fears in systematic ventilation could have therapeutic value.

**The Movement Toward Eclecticism**    As more is understood about the common elements of different psychotherapies, and as evidence accrues that different procedures may be most effective for different problems, many psychotherapists are moving away from strict allegiance to a single approach and becoming *eclectic* in orientation. By eclectic, they mean that they use techniques gleaned from various approaches, in accordance with the specific problems and characteristics of the client with whom they are working. In a survey conducted about a decade ago, 41 percent of psychotherapists identified themselves as eclectic (see Figure 18.7), and that percentage may well have increased since then (Beitman & others, 1989). To borrow a phrase from Bernard Beitman and his colleagues (1989), the "dogma eat dogma" environment that has traditionally characterized debate about psychotherapy is giving way to discussion based more on research and less on rigid adherence to specific theories. If the trend continues, schools of thought in psychotherapy may be replaced before long by catalogues of alternative methods and principles, all described in a common language, available to any practitioner, and complete with citations to research indicating the disorders or problems for which each technique has proved most useful.

## Biological Treatments

Biological treatments for mental disorders attempt to relieve the disorder by directly altering bodily processes. In the distant past, such treatments included drilling holes in the skull to let out bad spirits and blood-letting to drain diseased humors. Today, in decreasing order of extent of use, the three main types of biological treatments are drugs, electroconvulsive shock therapy, and psychosurgery.

### Drugs

A new era in the treatment of mental disorders began in the early 1950s when two French psychiatrists, Jean Delay and Pierre Deniker (1952) reported that they had reduced or abolished the psychotic symptoms of schizophrenia with a drug called *chlorpromazine*. Today, dozens of different drugs are available for treating mental disorders, the main categories of which are described below.

■ *The value and limitations of drugs used to treat schizophrenia, depression, bipolar disorder, and generalized anxiety*

**Antipsychotic Drugs**   Antipsychotic drugs are used to treat schizophrenia and other disorders in which psychotic symptoms predominate. Chlorpromazine (sold as Thorazine), belonging to a chemical class called *phenothiazines*, was the first such drug, but now many others exist as well. As described in Chapter 17, antipsychotic drugs seem to produce their effects by decreasing the activity of the neurotransmitter dopamine in the brain. Many well-designed experiments have shown that such drugs really do reduce or abolish the hallucinations, delusions, and bizarre actions that characterize the active phase of schizophrenia, and that they prevent or forestall the recurrence of such symptoms when they are taken continually (Ash-(Ashton, 1987; Linden, 1984). For the results and methods of one such study, see Figure 18.8. On the other hand, serious problems remain with such drugs, and many critics argue that they are used far more often than necessary. (Recall that Paul and Lentz were able to remove most patients in their study from drugs with their social learning program.)

**Figure 18.8** *Effects of antipsychotic drug treatment and counseling on rate of relapse among people with schizophrenia*

*In this experiment, 374 patients with schizophrenia were randomly assigned to treatment with either an antipsychotic drug (chlorpromazine) or a placebo, following a 2-month period during which all had received the drug. Within each of these two groups, half received regular counseling, which focused on their social and vocational roles, and half received no regular counseling. As shown here, the rate of relapse (defined as worsening of symptoms enough to be rehospitalized) was much less for those receiving the antipsychotic drug than for those receiving the placebo. Counseling produced a smaller, but still significant, beneficial effect, beginning after the sixth month. (Adapted from Hogarty & Goldberg, 1973.)*

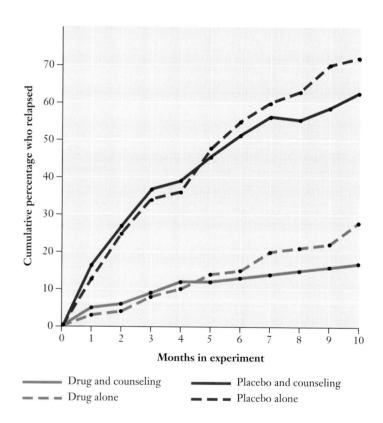

One problem is that although the drugs relieve the positive symptoms of schizophrenia (hallucinations, delusions, and bizarre behavior) in many patients, they usually do not relieve the negative symptoms (flattened affect, poverty of speech and thought, and lack of motivation) (Carpenter & others, 1985). Thus, although the drugs make it possible for people with schizophrenia to live out of the hospital, they do not restore the zest or pleasure that should come from doing so. Life becomes more normal but not necessarily happier. Moreover—and this is why many people with schizophrenia refuse to take them—the drugs can produce very unpleasant and potentially harmful side effects. Through direct action on the autonomic nervous system, they can produce dizziness, nausea, dry mouth, blurred vision, constipation, and (in men) sexual impotence. Through effects on motor control areas in the brain, they can produce symptoms akin to Parkinson's disease (shaking and difficulty in controlling voluntary movements) (Klein & others, 1980). In addition, about 40 percent of patients who take antipsychotic drugs for long periods of time eventually develop a serious and often irreversible motor disturbance called *tardive dyskinesia*, manifested as involuntary jerking of the tongue, face, and sometimes other muscles (Karon, 1989).

A more controversial problem is that antipsychotic drugs may in some cases reduce the chance of eventual full recovery from schizophrenia. Researchers have long known that one subgroup of people diagnosed with schizophrenia have an excellent chance of recovery without drugs. These are people whose symptoms (a) are almost entirely positive rather than negative, and (b) appeared suddenly rather than gradually. Treating such people with drugs is tempting, because the drugs immediately abolish the positive symptoms. In at least one experiment, however, patients in this good-prognosis category who were treated with drugs were significantly more likely to have a relapse several months later than were other patients in this category who were treated for the same period of time with a placebo (see Warner, 1985). Prolonged use of antipsychotic drugs causes the brain to make permanent biochemical adjustments that effectively increase its sensitivity to dopamine (Rupniak & others, 1984a & b), and this may be the mechanism by which the drugs can turn a temporary psychotic state into a more permanent problem. Increased sensitivity to dopamine is also probably the basis for tardive dyskinesia (Ashton, 1987).

**Antidepressant Drugs**  The drugs used most commonly to treat depression are members of a chemical class called *tricyclics*, of which *imipramine* (sold as Tofranil) and *amitriptyline* (sold as Elavil) are examples. In line with the monoamine theory of depression discussed in Chapter 17, these drugs are believed to reduce depression by increasing the availability of norepinephrine and other monoamine transmitters in synapses. In controlled experiments, about 70 percent of people on such drugs recovered from major depression over a period of several weeks, compared to about 30 percent of those who took a placebo (Ashton, 1987; Lickey & Gordon, 1983). Several experiments have revealed that antidepressant drugs are about as effective as psychotherapy in treating depression (DiMascio & others, 1979; Murphy & others, 1984; Greenberg & Fisher, 1989), and at least in some cases the two combined are better than either alone (see Figure 2.3 in Chapter 2). Antidepressants are not addictive, and their side effects—which can include fatigue, dry mouth, and blurred vision—are not as bad as those of antipsychotic drugs but are still a problem for many people. In recent years, a so-called new generation of antidepressants has emerged; these drugs have fewer side effects and appear to be as effective as tricyclics (Ashton, 1987).

**Lithium for Bipolar Disorder**  Lithium is a mineral element that, taken regularly in pill form, has long been the preferred treatment for bipolar disorder. Lithium helps control both the manic and the depressive phases of the disorder, but it is especially effective against the manic phases (Klein & others, 1980). To date, no one knows just how lithium works, but consistent with the monoamine theory of mood disorder, the most prevalent view is that it stabilizes the level of monoamines in the brain, or it stabilizes the brain's sensitivity to monoamines (Ashton, 1987). The main problem with lithium is that it produces serious side effects at high doses, including dehydration, and an overdose can cause death.

**Antianxiety Drugs**  By far the most commonly prescribed psychoactive drugs are those used to treat anxiety, commonly referred to as *tranquilizers*. At one time, barbiturates such as phenobarbital were often prescribed as tranquilizers, and many people became seriously addicted to them. During the 1960s, barbiturates were replaced by a new, safer group of antianxiety drugs belonging to a chemical class called *benzodiazepines*, including *chlordiazepoxide* (sold as Librium) and *diazepam* (sold as Valium). According to some estimates, by 1975 more than 10 percent of adults in the United States and western Europe were taking these drugs on a regular basis (Lickey & Gordon, 1983; Lipman, 1989). Since then their use has declined, partly because of growing recognition that they are not as safe as they were once thought to be.

Benzodiazepines are most effective against generalized anxiety and are usually not effective against phobias, obsessive-compulsive disorder, and panic disorder (Lipman, 1989). Most people who take the drugs have subclinical levels of generalized anxiety (less than would be necessary for a DSM-III-R diagnosis), and most prescriptions are written by general practitioners and internists rather than psychiatrists. Biochemically, the drugs appear to produce their tranquilizing effects by augmenting the action of the neurotransmitter *GABA* (*gamma-aminobutyric acid*) in the brain (Sullivan & others, 1984). GABA is an inhibitory transmitter, so its increased action decreases the excitability of neurons where it acts.

Side effects of benzodiazepines at high doses include drowsiness and a decline in motor coordination. More important, the drugs have an additive effect when combined with alcohol, so that an amount of alcohol that would normally be safe can produce a coma or death in people taking a benzodiazepine. If you're taking such a drug, don't drink! In addition, antianxiety drugs are now known to be at least moderately addictive, and very unpleasant withdrawal symptoms—sleeplessness, sweating, anxiety, and even panic—occur in those who stop taking them after having taken high doses for a long time (Petursson & Lader, 1986). These symptoms subside within about 2 weeks, but they drive many people back to the pills before the end of that period.

### Other Biologically Based Treatments

**Electroconvulsive Shock Therapy**   *Electroconvulsive shock therapy*, or *ECT*, is used primarily in cases of severe depression that do not respond to psychotherapy or antidepressant drugs. To members of the general public, this treatment often seems barbaric, a remnant of the days when victims of mental disorders were tortured to exorcise the demons; indeed, it once was a rather brutal treatment. The brain seizure induced by the shock would cause violent contractions of the body's muscles, sometimes breaking bones. But today ECT is administered in a way that is painless and quite safe (and not at all like that depicted in movies such as *One Flew over the Cuckoo's Nest*). Before receiving the shock, the patient is anesthetized so no pain will be felt, and is given a drug that blocks muscle activity so no damaging muscle contractions will occur. Then an electric current is passed through the patient's skull, and this sets up a seizure in the brain that lasts a minute or so. In some cases, called *unilateral ECT*, the current is applied just to one side of the brain (usually the right, nonlanguage side); in others, called *bilateral ECT*, it is applied across the whole brain. Usually such treatments are given in a series, one every 2 or 3 days for about 2 weeks.

Overall, about 70 percent of people suffering from major depression, who were not helped by other treatments, experience remission from depression with ECT (Weiner & Coffey, 1988). In some cases, the remission is permanent; in others, depression recurs after a period of several months or more, and then another series of treatments may be given. Nobody knows how ECT produces its antidepressant effect. In animals, such shocks cause a massive, immediate release of monoamines and other neurotransmitters, followed by longer-lasting changes in transmitter production and in the sensitivity of postsynaptic receptors; and most theories of the effects of ECT focus on one or another of those long-term changes (Sackeim, 1988).

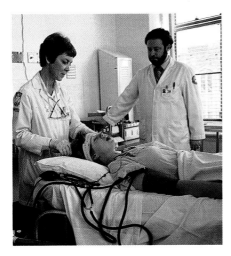

*Electroconvulsive therapy*
*Unilateral ECT is the treatment of choice for severe depression that does not respond to drug therapy. Although modern technology has rendered the treatment painless and physically safe, controversy remains over the question of whether it produces any lasting brain dysfunctions.*

■ **Evidence that ECT is effective in treating severe depression, and the reason why it is now often given just to the brain's right hemisphere**

Bilateral ECT often causes loss of memories for events that occurred shortly before the treatment, and a series of treatments can cause some degree of memory loss for earlier events as well. This problem is greatly reduced by use of right-hemisphere unilateral ECT. In controlled experiments, right-hemisphere treatment is usually as effective against depression as bilateral treatment (Weiner & Coffey, 1988). It produces little if any loss of conscious, verbal memories, though there may be some loss of pictorial memories as measured by people's ability to recognize geometric designs that they had seen before the shocks (Sachs & Gelenberg, 1988). Unilateral left-hemisphere treatment, in contrast, reduces verbal memories more than pictorial memories and is less effective in relieving depression. Such findings are consistent with other evidence (discussed in Chapter 11) that the right hemisphere is most involved in visual recognition and emotion, whereas the left is most involved in verbal processes.

■ *Why prefrontal lobotomies are no longer performed, and why less drastic forms of psychosurgery are occasionally performed*

**Psychosurgery** The most controversial treatment for mental disorders is *psychosurgery*, the surgical cutting or production of lesions in portions of the brain to relieve a mental disorder. From the late 1930s into the early 1950s, tens of thousands of men and women were subjected to an operation called *prefrontal lobotomy*, in which the front portions of the brain's frontal lobes were surgically separated from the rest of the brain. Individuals with severe cases of schizophrenia, bipolar disorder, depression, obsessive-compulsive disorder, and pathological violence were subjected to the operation. The prefrontal lobotomy was so highly regarded that in 1949 the Portuguese neurologist who developed the technique, Egas Moniz, was awarded the Nobel Prize. By the mid-1950s, however, prefrontal lobotomies had gone out of style, partly because newly developed drug treatments offered an alternative, and partly because of mounting evidence that, although lobotomy relieved people of their incapacitating emotions, it left them incapacitated in new ways (Valenstein, 1986). The anterior portions of the prefrontal lobes are a critical part of the brain's circuit for integrating plans with action (see Chapter 6), and lobotomized patients showed lifelong deficits in the ability to make plans and behave according to them.

Beginning in about 1960, a new, more refined version of psychosurgery came into use, and it continues to be used in rare cases today. The new procedure involves destruction of small areas of the brain by applying radio-frequency current through fine wire electrodes implanted temporarily into the brain. In the most common such operation, called a *cingulotomy*, the cingulum (a small structure in the limbic system known to be important in emotionality) is partly destroyed. Follow-up studies of patients who have undergone these electrode operations—including two studies by U.S. government commissions to determine if the procedure should be banned—have led to the following general conclusions (reported in Valenstein, 1980): (a) After the operations, patients do not seem to be worse off than they were before; there is no obvious neurological, behavioral, or cognitive harm. (b) Cingulotomies have successfully relieved severe, chronic depression in some patients who had failed to respond to any other treatment. (c) Psychosurgical lesions in another limbic area (the amygdala) have successfully relieved repeated episodes of uncontrollable violence in some patients, especially those whose violent outbursts were initiated by abnormal neural activity. (d) Psychosurgery has not been successful in relieving thought disorders and flattened affect in people with schizophrenia.

For the foreseeable future, psychosurgery will probably continue to be used sparingly, as a treatment of last resort for a few people who are very severely and chronically incapacitated by strong emotions that have proven untreatable by any other means.

## Concluding Thoughts

**1. Self-knowledge and self-acceptance as goals of psychodynamic and humanistic therapies**  The psychodynamic and humanistic approaches to treatment focus less on the person's specific symptoms or problems and more on the person as a whole than do the other approaches. A psychoanalyst or other psychodynamic therapist who is asked to describe the purpose of therapy might well respond with the Socratic dictum: *Know thyself.* The goal of such therapies is to enable clients to learn about aspects of themselves that were previously unconscious, so that they can think and behave in ways that are more rational and integrated than they did before. Most humanistic therapists would agree with the Socratic dictum, but they would add, and place greater emphasis on, a second dictum: *Accept thyself.* Humanistic therapists argue that people often learn to dislike or deny important aspects of themselves, because of real or imagined criticism from other people. The task for the humanistic therapist is to help clients regain their self-esteem, so they can regain control of their lives. As you review the discussions of psychodynamic and humanistic therapies, think about the specific ideas and techniques in relation to their broad purposes.

**2. Biological, behavioral, and cognitive therapies as derivatives of basic approaches to psychological research**  Biological, behavioral, and cognitive therapies focus more closely on clients' specific symptoms than do psychodynamic and humanistic therapies. These three approaches differ from each other, however, in that they emphasize different levels of causation of behavior. In that respect, they mirror the approaches taken by research psychologists who focus on (a) physiological mechanisms, (b) the role of environmental stimuli and learned habits, and (c) the role of cognitive mediators of behavior.

Biological treatments are founded on the knowledge that everything psychological is a product of the nervous system. Drugs, electroconvulsive therapy, and psychosurgery all involve attempts to help a person overcome psychological problems or disorders by altering the nervous system in some way. Behavioral treatments are founded on the knowledge that people acquire, through conditioning, habitual and sometimes maladaptive ways of responding to stimuli in the world around them. The goal of behavior therapy is to eliminate the maladaptive responses and replace them with useful responses. Cognitive treatments are founded on the knowledge that people interpret and think about stimuli in their environment, and that those interpretations and thoughts affect the way they feel and behave. The goal of cognitive therapy is to eliminate maladaptive ways of thinking and replace them with useful ways of thinking. As you review these approaches to therapy, think about their specific ideas and techniques in relation to their broad purposes.

**3. Psychotherapy and science**  Two questions can be asked about the relationship between psychotherapy and science: (a) Is psychotherapy a science? (b) Has science shown that psychotherapy works? These are fundamentally different questions.

The first question concerns the degree to which the techniques used in psychotherapy are based on scientific principles and can be described objectively. Most psychotherapists would respond that their practice is a blend of science and art—that it is based on theories that stem from scientific research, but that it also involves a great deal of intuition, not unlike the sort of intuition that is critical to any prolonged interaction between two human beings. Each client is a distinct individual with distinct problems and needs, who does not necessarily fit snugly with the statistically derived principles that have emerged from scientific research. One way to compare the various psychotherapy approaches is on the degree to which they emphasize empathy and intuition compared to the rigorous application of laboratory-derived principles. Rogers's humanistic therapy lies at one end of this spectrum and behavioral therapy lies at the other.

The second question concerns the use of scientific methods to evaluate psychotherapy. The history of psychotherapy has often been marked by feuds among advocates of one approach or another, each arguing that theirs is the only valid way. As increasingly well controlled outcome studies have been conducted, the feuds have died down somewhat. Evidence has mounted that all of the well-established psychotherapies work about equally well, on a statistical basis, though some may be more effective than others in treating certain kinds of problems. Such findings have led to increased recognition of the importance of the nonspecific factors shared by the various approaches. They have also helped inspire a movement toward eclecticism, in which psychotherapists draw from each tradition those methods that seem most appropriate to the client's specific needs.

## Further Reading

**Jeffrey Zeig** (Ed.) (1987). *The evolution of psychotherapy*. New York: Brunner/Mazel.
*This interesting volume is the result of a conference at which twenty-six well-known psychotherapists—representing psychodynamic, humanistic, cognitive, behavioral, family, and group approaches—each described the basic rationale of their approach and responded to questions from other participants.*

**Danny Wedding & Raymond Corsini** (Eds.) (1989). *Case studies in psychotherapy*. Itasca, IL: Peacock.
*This is a collection of twelve case histories. In each, a well-known psychotherapist describes the problems experienced by a particular client and the method through which the client was helped. Various versions of psychodynamic, humanistic, and cognitive-behavioral therapies are represented here.*

**Aaron T. Beck** (1976). *Cognitive therapy and the emotional disorders*. New York: International Universities Press.
*The most notable development in psychotherapy in the past 2 decades has been the increased use of cognitive psychotherapeutic techniques. In this book, one of the leading founders of cognitive therapy describes the main principles of that approach and presents examples of its application in treating depression, generalized anxiety, phobias, and somatoform disorders.*

## Looking Ahead

That's it; there isn't any more. I hope you have enjoyed the book and have found it to be a useful survey of the vast field of psychology. Perhaps the book has helped you decide which areas of psychology you would like to study further, either through additional courses or through your own reading. As you look over the offerings of the Psychology Department at your college or university, you will probably find that the courses map quite readily onto the various parts of this book. I hope you pursue the areas that interest you most.

# STATISTICAL APPENDIX

**Organizing and Summarizing a Set of Scores**

**Converting Scores for Purposes of Comparison**

**Calculating a Correlation Coefficient**

**Supplement on Psychophysical Scaling**

Statistical procedures are tools for dealing with data. Some people find them fascinating for their own sake, just as some become intrigued by the beauty of a saw or a hammer. But most of us, most of the time, care about statistics only to the extent that they help us answer questions. Statistics become interesting when we want to know our batting average, or the chance that our favorite candidate will be elected, or how much money we'll have left after taxes. In psychology, statistics are interesting when they are used to analyze data in ways that help answer important psychological questions.

Some of the basics of statistics are described in Chapter 2. The main purpose of the first three sections of this appendix is to supplement that discussion and make it more concrete by providing some examples of statistical calculations. The second section (Converting Scores for Purposes of Comparison) also contains information that is relevant to the discussions of IQ measurement in Chapter 11 and meta-analysis in Chapter 18. The final section of this appendix (Supplement on Psychophysical Scaling) supplements the discussion of Fechner's and Stevens's work in the section on psychophysics in Chapter 8.

## Organizing and Summarizing a Set of Scores

This section describes some basic elements of descriptive statistics: the construction of frequency distributions, the measurement of central tendency, and the measurement of variability.

**Ranking the Scores and Depicting a Frequency Distribution**   Suppose you gave a group of people a psychological test of introversion–extroversion, structured such that a low score indicates introversion (a tendency to withdraw from the social environment) and a high score indicates extroversion (a tendency to be socially outgoing). Suppose further that the possible range of scores is from 0 to 99, that you gave the test to twenty people, and that you obtained the scores shown in the left-hand column of Table A.1. As presented in that column, the scores are hard to describe in a meaningful way; they are just a list of numbers. As a first step toward making some sense of them, you might rearrange the scores in *rank order*, from lowest to highest, as shown in the right-hand column of the table. Notice how the ranking facilitates your ability to describe the set of numbers. You can now see that the scores range from a low of 17 to a high of 91 and that the two middle scores are 49 and 50.

**Table A.1** *Twenty scores unranked and ranked*

| Scores in the order they were collected | The same scores ranked |
|---|---|
| 58 | 17 |
| 45 | 23 |
| 23 | 31 |
| 71 | 36 |
| 49 | 37 |
| 36 | 41 |
| 61 | 43 |
| 41 | 45 |
| 37 | 45 |
| 75 | 49 |
| 91 | 50 |
| 54 | 54 |
| 43 | 57 |
| 17 | 58 |
| 63 | 61 |
| 73 | 63 |
| 31 | 71 |
| 50 | 73 |
| 45 | 75 |
| 57 | 91 |

**Table A.2**  *Frequency distribution formed from scores in Table A.1*

| Interval | Frequency |
|----------|-----------|
| 0– 9 | 0 |
| 10–19 | 1 |
| 20–29 | 1 |
| 30–39 | 3 |
| 40–49 | 5 |
| 50–59 | 4 |
| 60–69 | 2 |
| 70–79 | 3 |
| 80–89 | 0 |
| 90–99 | 1 |

A second useful step in summarizing the data is to divide the entire range of possible scores into equal intervals and determine how many scores fall in each interval. Table A.2 presents the results of this process, using intervals of 10. A table of this sort, showing the number of scores that occurred in each interval of possible scores, is called a ***frequency distribution***. Frequency distributions can also be represented graphically, as shown in Figure A.1. Here, each bar along the horizontal axis represents a different interval, and the height of the bar represents the frequency (number of scores) that occurred in that interval.

As you examine Figure A.1, notice that the scores are not evenly distributed across the various intervals. Rather, most of them fall in the middle intervals (centering around 50), and they taper off toward the extremes. This pattern would have been hard to see in the original, unorganized set of numbers.

**Figure A.1**  *A frequency distribution depicted by a bar graph*

*This graph depicts the frequency distribution shown in Table A.2. Each bar represents a different interval of possible scores, and the height of each bar represents the number of scores that occurred in that interval.*

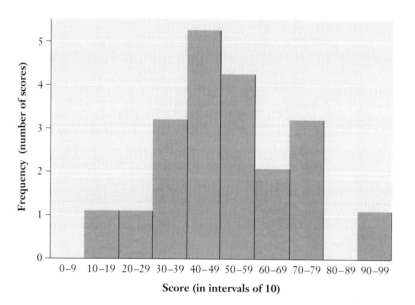

**Shapes of Frequency Distributions**   The frequency distribution in Figure A.1 roughly approximates a shape that is referred to as a ***normal distribution*** or *normal curve*. A perfect normal distribution (which can be expressed by a mathematical equation) is illustrated in Figure A.2a. Notice that the maximum frequency lies in the center of the range of scores and that the frequency tapers off—first gradually, then more rapidly, and then gradually again—symmetrically on the two sides, forming a bell-shaped curve. Many measures in nature are distributed in accordance with a normal distribution. Height (for people of a given age and sex) is one example. A variety of different factors (different genes and nutritional factors) go into determining a person's height. In most cases, these different factors—some promoting tallness and some shortness—average themselves out, so that most people are roughly average in height (accounting for the peak frequency in the middle of the distribution). A small proportion of people, however, will have just the right combination of factors to be much taller or much shorter than average (accounting for the tails at the high and low ends of the distribution). In general, when a measure is determined by several independent factors, the frequency distribution for that measure at least approximates the normal curve. The results of most psychological tests also form a normal distribution if the test is given to a sufficiently large group of people.

But not all measures are distributed in accordance with the normal curve. Consider, for example, the set of scores that would be obtained on a test of English

**Normal, unimodal distribution**

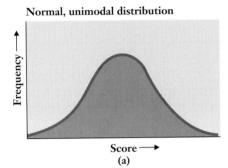

**Bimodal distribution**

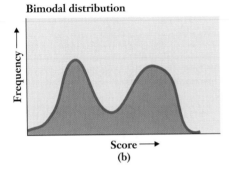

**Positively skewed, unimodal distribution**

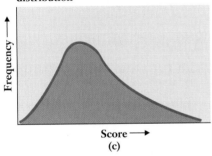

**Negatively skewed, unimodal distribution**

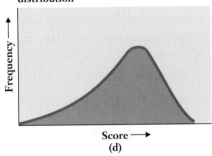

**Figure A.2** *Four differently shaped frequency distributions*
*You can imagine that each of these curves was formed from a set of bars similar to those in Figure A.1, but the bars would be narrower and more numerous (the intervals would be smaller) and the data sets would be much larger.*

vocabulary if some of the people tested were native speakers of English and others were not. You would expect in this case to find two separate groupings of scores. The native speakers would score high and the others would score low, with relatively few scores in between. A distribution of this sort, illustrated in Figure A.2b, is referred to as a *bimodal distribution*. The **mode** is the most frequently occurring score or range of scores in a frequency distribution; thus, a bimodal distribution is one that has two separate areas of peak frequencies. The normal curve is a *unimodal distribution*, because it has only one peak in frequency.

Some distributions are unimodal, like the normal distribution, but are not symmetrical. Consider, for example, the shape of a frequency distribution of annual incomes for any randomly selected group of people. Most of the incomes might center around, let's say, $20,000. Some would be higher and some lower, but the spread of higher incomes would be much greater than that of lower incomes. No income can be less than $0, but no limit exists to the high ones. Thus, the frequency distribution might look like that shown in Figure A.2c. A distribution of this sort, in which the spread of scores above the mode is greater than that below, is referred to as a *positively skewed distribution*. The long tail of the distribution extends in the direction of high scores.

As an opposite example, consider the distribution of scores on a relatively easy examination. If the highest possible score is 100 points and most people score around 85, the highest score can only be 15 points above the mode, but the lowest score can be as much as 85 points below it. A typical distribution obtained from such a test is shown in Figure A.2d. A distribution of this sort, in which the long tail extends toward low scores, is called a *negatively skewed distribution*.

**Measures of Central Tendency**    Perhaps the most useful way to summarize a set of scores is to identify a number that represents the center of the distribution. Two different centers can be determined—the median and the mean (both described in Chapter 2). The **median** is the middle score in a set of ranked scores. Thus, in a ranked set of nine scores, the fifth score in the ranking (counting in either direction) is the median. If the data set consists of an even number of scores, determining the median is slightly more complicated because two middle scores exist rather than one. In this case, the median is simply the midpoint between the two middle scores. If you look back at the list of twenty ranked scores in Table A.1, you will see that the two middle scores are 49 and 50; the median in this case is 49.5. The **mean** (also called the *arithmetic average*) is found simply by adding up all of the scores and dividing by the total number of scores. Thus, to calculate the mean of the twenty introversion–extroversion scores in Table A.1, simply add them (the sum is 1020) and divide by 20, obtaining 51.0 as the mean.

Notice that the mean and median of the set of introversion–extroversion scores are quite close to one another. In a perfect normal distribution, these two measures of central tendency are identical. For a skewed distribution, on the other hand, they can be quite different. Consider, for example, the set of incomes shown in Table A.3 (on page A-4). The median is $19,500, and all but one of the other incomes are rather close to the median. But the set contains one income of $900,000, which is wildly different from the others. The size of this income does not affect the median. Whether the highest income were $19,501 (just above the median) or a trillion dollars, it still counts as just one income in the ranking that determines the median. But this income has a dramatic effect on the mean. As shown in the table, the mean of these incomes is $116,911. Because the mean is most affected by extreme scores, it will always be higher than the median in a positively skewed distribution and lower than the median in a negatively skewed distribution. In a positively skewed distribution, the most extreme scores are high scores (which raise the mean above the median), and in a negatively skewed distribution they are low scores (which lower the mean below the median).

**Table A.3** *Sample incomes, illustrating how the mean can differ greatly from the median*

| Rank | Income |
|------|--------|
| 1 | $15,000 |
| 2 | 16,400 |
| 3 | 16,500 |
| 4 | 17,700 |
| 5 | (19,500) |
| 6 | 21,200 |
| 7 | 22,300 |
| 8 | 23,600 |
| 9 | 900,000 |
| | Total: $1,052,200 |

**Mean = $1,052,200 ÷ 9 = $116,911**
**Median = $19,500**

Which is more useful, the mean or the median? The answer depends on one's purpose, but in general the mean is preferred when scores are at least roughly normally distributed, and the median is preferred when scores are highly skewed. In Table A.3 the median is certainly a better representation of the set of incomes than is the mean, because it is typical of almost all of the incomes listed. In contrast, the mean is typical of none of the incomes; it is much lower than the highest income and much higher than all the rest. This, of course, is an extreme example, but it illustrates the sort of biasing effect that skewed data can have on a mean. Still, for certain purposes, the mean might be the preferred measure even if the data are highly skewed. For example, if you wanted to determine the revenue that could be gained by a 5 percent local income tax, the mean income (or the total income) would be more useful than the median.

**Measures of Variability**    The mean or median tells us about the central value of a set of numbers, but not about how widely they are spread out around the center. Look at the two frequency distributions depicted in Figure A.3. They are both normal and have the same mean, but they differ greatly in their degree of spread or variability. In one case the scores are clustered near the mean (low variability), and in the other they are spread farther apart (high variability). How might we measure the variability of scores in a distribution?

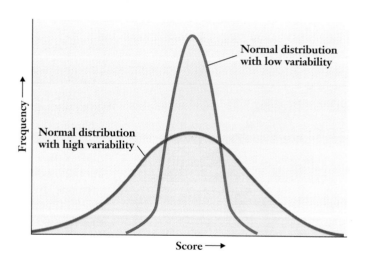

**Figure A.3** *Two normal distributions*
*These normal distributions, superimposed on one another, have identical means but different degrees of variability.*

One possibility would be to use the *range*—that is, simply the difference between the highest and lowest scores in the distribution—as a measure of variability. For the scores listed in Table A.1, the range is 91 – 17 = 74 points. A problem with the range, however, is that it depends on just two scores, the highest and lowest. A better measure of variability would take into account the extent to which all of the scores in the distribution differ from each other.

One measure of variability that takes all of the scores into account is the *variance*. The variance is calculated by the following four steps: (1) Determine the mean of the set of scores. (2) Determine the difference between each score and the mean; this difference is called the *deviation*. (3) Square each deviation (multiply it by itself). (4) Calculate the mean of the squared deviations (by adding them up and dividing by the total number of scores). The result—the mean of the squared deviations—is the variance. This method is illustrated for two different sets of scores in Table A.4. Notice that the two sets each have the same mean (50), but most of the scores in the first set are much closer to the mean than are those in the second set. The result is that the variance of the first set (25.5) is much smaller than that of the second set (729).

**Table A.4** *Calculation of the variance and standard deviation for two sets of scores that have identical means*

| First set of scores | | | | Second set of scores | | |
|---|---|---|---|---|---|---|
| Score | Deviation (Score − 50) | Squared deviation | | Score | Deviation (Score − 50) | Squared deviation |
| 42 | −8 | 64 | | 9 | −41 | 1681 |
| 44 | −6 | 36 | | 19 | −31 | 961 |
| 47 | −3 | 9 | | 31 | −19 | 361 |
| 49 | −1 | 1 | | 47 | −3 | 9 |
| 52 | +2 | 4 | | 56 | +6 | 36 |
| 54 | +4 | 16 | | 70 | +20 | 400 |
| 55 | +5 | 25 | | 78 | +28 | 784 |
| 57 | +7 | 49 | | 90 | +40 | 1600 |

First set: Total = 400, Mean = 400/8 = 50; Total = 204, Mean = 204/8 = 25.5
Variance = Mean squared deviation = 25.5
Standard deviation = $\sqrt{\text{Variance}}$ = $\sqrt{25.5}$ = 5.0

Second set: Total = 400, Mean = 400/8 = 50; Total = 5832, Mean = 5832/8 = 729
Variance = Mean squared deviation = 729
Standard deviation = $\sqrt{\text{Variance}}$ = $\sqrt{729}$ = 27.0

Because the variance is based on the squares of the deviations, the units of variance are not the same as those of the original measure. If the original measure is points on a test, then the variance is in units of squared points on the test (whatever on earth that might mean). To bring the units back to their original form, all we need to do is take the square root of the variance. The square root of the variance is the ***standard deviation***, which is the measure of variability that is most commonly used. Thus, for the first set of scores in Table A.4, the standard deviation = $\sqrt{25.5}$ = 5.0; for the second set, the standard deviation = $\sqrt{729}$ = 27.0.

## Converting Scores for Purposes of Comparison

Are you taller than you are heavy? That sounds like a silly question, and it is. Height and weight are two entirely different measures, and comparing them is like the proverbial comparison of apples and oranges. But suppose I worded the question this way: Relative to other people of your gender and age group, do you rank higher in height or in weight? Now that is an answerable question. Similarly, consider this question: Are you better at mathematical or at verbal tasks? This, too, is meaningful only if your mathematical and verbal skills are judged relative to those of other people. Compared to other people, do you rank higher in mathematical or in verbal skills? To compare different kinds of scores with each other, we must convert each score into a form that expresses directly its relationship to the whole distribution of scores from which it came.

**Percentile Rank**   The most straightforward way to see how one person compares to others on a given measure is to determine the person's ***percentile rank*** for that measure. The percentile rank of a given score is simply the percentage of scores that are equal to that score or lower, out of the whole set of scores obtained on a given measure. For example, in the distribution of scores in Table A.1, the score of 37 is at the 25th percentile, because five of the twenty scores are at 37 or lower ($^5/_{20}$ = $^1/_4$ = 25%). As another example in the same distribution, the score of 73 is at the 90th percentile because eighteen of the twenty scores are 73 or lower ($^{18}/_{20}$ = $^9/_{10}$ = 90%). If you had available the heights and weights of a large number of people of your age and gender, you could answer the question about your height compared to your weight by determining your percentile rank on each. If you were at the 39th percentile in height and the 25th percentile in weight, then, relative to others in your group, you would be taller than you were heavy. Similarly, if you were at the 94th percentile on a test of math skills and the 72nd percentile on a test of verbal skills, then, relative to the group who took both tests, your math skills would be better than your verbal skills.

**Standardized Scores**   Another way to convert scores for purposes of comparison is to *standardize* them. A ***standardized score*** is one that is expressed in terms of the number of standard deviations that the original score is from the mean of original scores. The simplest form of a standardized score is called a ***z score***. To convert any score to a z score, you first determine its deviation from the mean (subtract the mean from it), and then divide the deviation by the standard deviation of the distribution. Thus,

$$z = \frac{\text{score} - \text{mean}}{\text{standard deviation}}$$

For example, suppose you wanted to calculate the z score that would correspond to the test score of 54 in the first set of scores in Table A.4. The mean of the distribution is 50, so the deviation is $54 - 50 = +4$. The standard deviation is 5.0. Thus, $z = {}^4/_5 = +0.80$. Similarly, the z score for a score of 42 in that distribution would be ${}^{(42-50)}/_5 = -{}^8/_5 = -1.60$. Remember, the z score is simply the number of standard deviations that the original score is away from the mean. A positive z score indicates that the original score is above the mean, and a negative z score indicates that it is below the mean. A z score of +0.80 is 0.80 standard deviations above the mean, and a z score of –1.60 is 1.60 standard deviations below the mean.

Other forms of standardized scores are based directly on z scores. For example, Scholastic Aptitude Test (SAT) scores were originally (in 1941) determined by calculating each person's z score, then multiplying the z score by 100 and adding the result to 500 (DuBois, 1972). That is,

$$\text{SAT score} = 500 + 100(z)$$

Thus, a person who was directly at the mean on the test ($z = 0$) would have an SAT score of 500; a person who was 1 standard deviation above the mean ($z = +1$) would have an SAT score of 600; a person who was 2 standard deviations above the mean would have 700; and a person who was 3 standard deviations above the mean would have 800. (Very few people would score beyond 3 standard deviations from the mean, so 800 was set as the highest possible score.) Going the other way, a person who was 1 standard deviation below the mean ($z = -1$) would have an SAT score of 400, and so on.

Today, SAT scores are still based on the original standardization made in 1941. The test has been updated by means designed to keep the difficulty the same, but the scoring system has not been restandardized. Thus, a person today who scores 500 has performed average compared to people who took the test in 1941, not average compared to people taking the test today. Since 1941, average SAT scores have drifted downward; in 1990, the average scores were 424 for the verbal portion and 476 for the math portion. This means that the average person who took the SAT test in 1990 performed 0.76 standard deviations below the 1941 average on the verbal portion and 0.24 standard deviations below the 1941 average on the math portion. The decline is caused at least in part by the broader range of people taking the test now than in 1941, when only a relatively elite group applied to college. In addition, the greater decline on the verbal portion than on the math portion may be partly due to television and other cultural changes that have led young people today to read less than did young people in 1941 (Eckland, 1982).

Wechsler IQ scores (discussed in Chapter 11) are also based on z scores. They were standardized—separately for each age group—by calculating each person's z score on the test, multiplying that by 15, and adding the product to 100. Thus,

$$IQ = 100 + 15(z)$$

This process guarantees that a person who scores at the exact mean achieved by people in the standardization group will have an IQ score of 100, that a person who scores 1 standard deviation above that mean will have a score of 115, that a person who scores 2 standard deviations above that mean will have a score of 130, and so on.

**Relationship of Standardized Scores to Percentile Ranks**   If a distribution of scores precisely matches a normal distribution, one can determine percentile rank from the standardized score, or vice versa. As you recall, in a normal distribution the highest frequency of scores occurs in intervals close to the mean, and the frequency declines with each successive interval away from the mean in either direction. As illustrated in Figure A.4, a precise relationship exists between any given z score and the percentage of scores that fall between that score and the mean.

**Figure A.4  Relationship between z score and percentile rank for a normal distribution**

Because the percentage of scores that fall between any given z score and the mean is a fixed value for data that fit a normal distribution, it is possible to calculate what percentage of individuals would score less than or equal to any given z score. In this diagram, the percentages above each arrow indicate the percentile rank for z scores of –3, –2, –1, 0, +1, +2, and +3. Each percentage is the sum of the percentages within the portions of the curve that lie under the arrow.

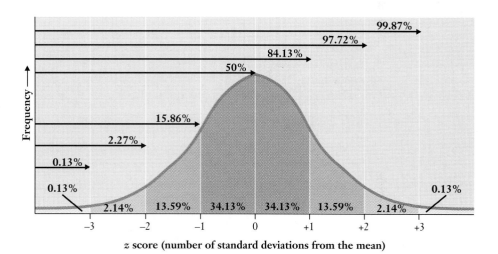

As you can see in the figure, slightly more than 34.1% of all scores in a normal distribution will be between a z score of +1 and the mean. Since another 50% will fall below the mean, a total of slightly more than 84.1% of the scores in a normal distribution will be below a z score of +1. By using similar logic and examining the figure, you should be able to see why z scores of –3, –2, –1, 0, +1, +2, and +3, respectively, correspond to percentile ranks of about 0.1, 2.3, 15.9, 50, 84.1, 97.7, and 99.9, respectively. Detailed tables have been made that permit the conversion of any possible z score in a perfect normal distribution to a percentile rank.

## Calculating a Correlation Coefficient

The basic meaning of the term *correlation* and how to interpret a correlation coefficient are described in Chapter 2. As explained there, the correlation coefficient is a mathematical means of describing the strength and direction of the relationship between two variables that have been measured mathematically. The sign (+ or –) of the correlation coefficient indicates the direction (positive or negative) of the relationship; and the absolute value of the correlation coefficient (from 0 to 1.00, irrespective of sign) indicates the strength of the correlation. To review the difference between a positive and negative correlation, and between a weak or strong correlation, look back at Figure 2.4 and the accompanying text. Here, as a supplement to the discussion in Chapter 2, is the mathematical means for calculating the most common type of correlation coefficient, called the *product-moment correlation coefficient.*

To continue the example described in Chapter 2, suppose you collected both the IQ score and GPA (grade point average) for each of ten different high-school students and obtained the results shown in the "IQ score" and "GPA" columns of Table A.5. As a first step in determining the direction and strength of correlation between the two sets of scores, you might graph each pair of points in a *scatter plot,* as shown in Figure A.5 (compare this figure to Figure 2.4). The scatter plot makes it clear that, in general, the students with higher IQs tended to have higher GPAs, so you know that the correlation coefficient will be positive. However, the relationship between IQ and GPA is by no means perfect (the plot does not form a straight line), so you know that the correlation coefficient will be less than 1.00.

The first step in calculating a correlation coefficient is to convert each score to a z score, using the method described in the section on standardizing scores. Each z score, remember, is the number of standard deviations that the original score is away from the mean of the original scores. The standard deviation for the ten IQ scores in Table A.5 is 11.88, so the z scores for IQ (shown in the column marked $z_{IQ}$) were calculated by subtracting the mean IQ score (103) from each IQ and dividing by 11.88. The standard deviation for the ten GPA scores in Table A.5 is 0.76, so the z scores for GPA (shown in the column marked $z_{GPA}$) were calculated by subtracting the mean GPA (2.5) from each GPA and dividing by 0.76.

To complete the calculation of the correlation coefficient, you multiply each pair of z scores together, obtaining what are called the *z-score cross-products,* and then determine the mean of those cross-products. The product-moment correlation coefficient, *r*, is, by definition, the mean of the z-score cross-products. In Table A.5, the z-score cross-products are shown in the right-hand column, and the mean of them is shown at the bottom of that column. As you can see, the correlation coefficient in this case is +0.69—a rather strong positive correlation.

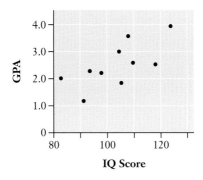

**Figure A.5** *Scatter plots relating GPA to IQ*

*Each point represents the IQ and the GPA for one of the ten students whose scores are shown in Table A.5. (For further explanation, refer to Figure 2.4 in Chapter 2.)*

**Table A.5** *Calculation of a correlation coefficient* **(r)**

| Students (ranked by IQ) | IQ score | GPA | $z_{IQ}$ | $z_{GPA}$ | Cross-products $(z_{IQ}) \times (z_{GPA})$ |
|---|---|---|---|---|---|
| 1 | 82 | 2.0 | −1.77 | −0.66 | 1.17 |
| 2 | 91 | 1.2 | −1.01 | −1.71 | 1.73 |
| 3 | 93 | 2.3 | −0.84 | −0.26 | 0.22 |
| 4 | 97 | 2.2 | −0.51 | −0.39 | 0.20 |
| 5 | 104 | 3.0 | +0.08 | +0.66 | 0.05 |
| 6 | 105 | 1.8 | +0.17 | −0.92 | −0.16 |
| 7 | 108 | 3.5 | +0.42 | +1.32 | 0.55 |
| 8 | 109 | 2.6 | +0.51 | +0.13 | 0.07 |
| 9 | 118 | 2.5 | +1.26 | 0.00 | 0.00 |
| 10 | 123 | 3.9 | +1.68 | +1.84 | 3.09 |
| | Sum = 1030 | Sum = 25.0 | | | Sum = 6.92 |
| | **Mean = 103** | **Mean = 2.5** | | | **Mean = 0.69 = r** |
| | **SD = 11.88** | **SD = 0.76** | | | |

# Supplement on Psychophysical Scaling

This section should *not* be read as a supplement to Chapter 2. It concerns two issues discussed in the section on psychophysical scaling in Chapter 8.

**Derivation of Fechner's Law from Weber's Law**   In Chapter 8, I described Ernst Weber's law, according to which the just-noticeable difference (jnd) between a comparison stimulus and a standard stimulus is directly proportional to the physical magnitude of the standard stimulus ($M$). As a formula, this is

$$\text{jnd} = kM$$

I then noted that Gustav Fechner used Weber's law to derive a law of psychophysical scaling, according to which the magnitude of a sensory experience ($S$) is directly proportional to the logarithm of the physical magnitude of the stimulus ($M$). As a formula, this is

$$S = c \log M$$

Here I will use the numbers shown in Table A.6 to demonstrate the logic of Fechner's derivation of his law from Weber's. The logic begins with the assumption that every jnd is subjectively equal to every other jnd. Thus, the sensory scale in the left-hand column of the table is a jnd scale, and each step in that scale produces an equal change in the magnitude of sensory experience ($S$). The example is for loudness of a 2000 Hz sound, for which the Weber fraction ($k$) is $1/10$ and the minimal intensity that can be heard is 1 sound-pressure unit. With these assumptions, Weber's law predicts that the intensity that will be 1 jnd above the minimum will be 1.10 units ($1 + 1/10$th of $1 = 1.10$). Similarly, the intensity that will be 2 jnd's above threshold will be 1.21 units ($1.10 + 1/10$th of $1.10 = 1.21$).

**Table A.6** *Demonstration that a jnd sensory scale is linearly related to the logarithm of the physical stimulus (log **M**)*

| S in jnd units | M in sound-pressure units if k = 1/10 | Log M |
|---|---|---|
| 0 | 1.00 | 0 |
| 1 | 1.10 | 0.041 |
| 2 | 1.21 | 0.082 |
| 3 | 1.33 | 0.123 |
| 4 | 1.46 | 0.164 |
| 5 | 1.61 | 0.205 |

Continuing in this way, it is possible to derive the physical intensity of the stimulus that would be any given number of jnd's above threshold. The results, for 5 jnd's, are shown in the middle column of the table. Notice that each successive jnd step involves a greater increase in the physical intensity than did the step before. For example, going from 0 to 1 jnd above threshold requires an addition of 0.10 physical units, whereas going from 4 to 5 jnd's requires an addition of 0.15 physical units ($1.61 - 1.46 = 0.15$). Thus, the relationship between the first and second columns is not linear. The third column of the table shows the logarithms (to base 10) of the numbers in the middle column. (If you have a calculator, you can check them yourself. The logarithm of 1 is 0, that of 1.1 is 0.041, and so on.) Notice that now, after the logarithmic transformation, the numbers do form a linear relationship with the numbers in the first column. Each jnd step corresponds with an increase of approximately 0.041 log units. Thus, in line with Fechner's law, each constant step in sensory magnitude corresponds with a constant step in the logarithm of the physical intensity of the stimulus.

**Illustration Showing That Stevens's Power Law Preserves Sensory Ratios**   At the end of Chapter 8, I described Stevens's power law, which states that the magnitude of a sensory experience ($S$) is directly proportional to the physical magnitude of the stimulus ($M$) raised by a constant power ($p$). As a formula, this is

$$S = cM^p$$

I then pointed out (as had Stevens) that our sensory systems may have evolved to operate according to a power law because such a law preserves constant sensory ratios as the overall physical intensity of stimulation waxes or wanes. For example, as a sound becomes closer (and therefore more intense), we hear its various pitches as maintaining the same ratios of intensity to each other as before, and thus we hear it as the same sound. As another example, as light fades in the evening, the relative brightness of one object compared to another in the visual scene remains constant. To make this more concrete, I mentioned in Chapter 8 that, according to Stevens's power law, every eightfold change in light intensity causes a twofold change in apparent brightness, no matter where on the intensity continuum we start from. Following are calculations proving that point.

For brightness estimations, $p = 1/3$ (as shown in Table 8.4). Let $S_1$ be the sensory magnitude for a stimulus whose physical magnitude is $M$, and let $S_2$ be the sensory magnitude for a stimulus that is physically eight times as intense as $S_1$ (that is, whose physical magnitude is $8M$). In accordance with the power law,

$$S_1 = cM^{1/3} \text{ and } S_2 = c(8M)^{1/3}$$

The ratio of $S_2/S_1$ can now be calculated as follows:

$$\frac{S_2}{S_1} = \frac{c(8M)^{1/3}}{cM^{1/3}} = \frac{(8M)^{1/3}}{M^{1/3}} = (8M/M)^{1/3} = 8^{1/3} = 2$$

Thus, regardless of the value of the original stimulus magnitude ($M$), an eightfold increase in that magnitude will produce a doubling of the sensory magnitude, or an eightfold decrease will produce a halving of the sensory magnitude. So, if the physical intensity of each part of a visual scene decreases to one-eighth what it was before, the sensory intensity experienced from each part of the scene will be cut in half and each part of the scene will maintain the same ratio of intensity to each other part as it had before.

# GLOSSARY

**absolute threshold** In psychophysics, the faintest (lowest-intensity) stimulus of a given sensation (such as sound or light) that an individual can detect. For contrast, see *difference threshold*. (p. 270)

**accommodation** In Piaget's theory of cognitive development, the change that occurs in an existing mental scheme or set of schemes as a result of the assimilation of the experience of a new event or object. See also *assimilation*. (p. 438)

**action potentials** Neural impulses; the all-or-nothing electrical bursts that begin at one end of the axon of a neuron and move along the axon to the other end. (p. 168)

**actor-observer discrepancy** The observation that a person who performs an action (the actor) is likely to attribute the action to the environmental situation, whereas the person who observes the same action (the observer) is likely to attribute it to the actor's inner characteristics (personality). See also *attribution, fundamental attribution error*. (p. 500)

**adapt** To change to suit new conditions of the environment. (p. 85)

**adaptation** See *adapt, sensory adaptation*.

**additive color mixing** The mixing of colored lights (lights containing limited ranges of wavelengths) by superimposing them to reflect off the same surface. It is called *additive* because each light adds to the total set of wavelengths that are reflected to the eye. For contrast, see *subtractive color mixing*. (p. 261)

**adoptive method** A method for studying the heritability of a characteristic, in which the similarity of adoptive relatives is compared with that of biological (birth) relatives. See *heritability*. (p. 68)

**algorithm** A rule specifying a set of steps that, if followed correctly, is guaranteed to solve a particular class of problem. For contrast, see *heuristic*. (p. 393)

**alleles** Different genes that can occupy the same locus on a pair of chromosomes and thus can potentially pair with one another. (p. 52)

**altruism** In sociobiology, a type of helping behavior in which an individual increases the survival chance or reproductive capacity of another individual while *decreasing* its own survival chance or reproductive capacity. For contrast, see *cooperation*. (p. 112)

**amplitude** The amount of physical energy or force exerted by a physical stimulus at any given moment; for sound, this physical measure is related to the psychological experience of loudness. (p. 245)

**analogue theory of visual memory** The theory that memories for visual scenes are functionally equivalent to pictures, that is, that such memories preserve the spatial gradients of the original scene in such a way that its recall is an experience similar to looking at a picture. For contrast, see *propositional theory of visual memory*. (p. 342)

**analogy** In ethology and comparative psychology, any similarity among species that is not due to common ancestry, but rather has evolved independently in the species because of some similarity in their habitat or lifestyle. For contrast, see *homology*. (p. 94)

**antithesis principle** In Darwin's theory of the origin of nonverbal signals, the idea that, as a result of natural selection or learning or both, opposite emotions or behavioral intentions will be expressed by opposite movements or postures. (p. 98)

**anxiety disorders** The class of mental disorders in which fear or anxiety is the most prominent symptom. It includes *generalized anxiety disorder, obsessive-compulsive disorder, panic disorder, phobias*, and *post-traumatic stress disorder*. (p. 616)

**aphasia** Any loss in language ability due to brain damage. See also *Broca's aphasia, Wernicke's aphasia*. (p. 399)

**arousal response** A pattern of measurable physiological changes (including tense muscles, increased heart rate, and secretion of certain hormones) that helps prepare the body for the possible expenditure of a large amount of energy. (p. 226)

**artificial selection** The deliberate selective breeding of animals or plants by humans for the purpose of modifying the genetic makeup of future generations. See *selective breeding*. For contrast, see *natural selection*. (p. 82)

**assertiveness training** In behavior therapy, a direct method of training people to express their own desires and feelings and to maintain their own rights in interactions with others, while at the same time respecting the others' rights. (p. 671)

**assessment** In clinical practice, the process by which a mental health professional gathers and compiles information about a client for the purpose of describing the person's problems or disorder and developing a plan of treatment. (p. 649)

**assessment interview** A dialogue through which a mental health professional learns about a client. (p. 649)

**assimilation** In Piaget's theory of cognitive development, the process by which experiences are incorporated into the mind, or, more specifically, into mental schemes. See also *accommodation*. (p. 438)

**association areas** Areas of the cerebral cortex that receive input from the primary or secondary sensory areas for more than one sensory modality (such as vision and hearing) and are involved in associating this input with stored memories, in the processes of perception, thought, and decision making. (p. 181)

**association by contiguity** See *law of association by contiguity*.

**association by similarity** See *law of association by similarity*.

**attachment** The long-lasting emotional bonds that infants develop toward their principal caregivers. More broadly, the long-lasting emotional bonds that any individual develops toward any other individual or object. (p. 454)

**attention** In perception, the process or set of processes by which the mind chooses from among the various stimuli that strike the senses at any given moment, allowing only some of those stimuli to enter into higher stages of information processing. In the modal model of the mind, the process that controls the flow of information from the sensory store to the short-term store. (p. 295) More broadly, any focusing of mental activity along a specific track, whether that track consists purely of inner memories and knowledge or is based on external stimuli. (p. 326)

**attitude** Any belief or opinion that has an evaluative component—a belief that something is good or bad, likable or unlikable, attractive or repulsive. (p. 513)

**attribution** In social cognition, any inference about the cause of a person's behavioral action or set of actions. More generally, any inference about the cause of any observed action or event. (p. 492)

**attributional helplessness theory of depression** The theory that depression stems from the sense of helplessness that occurs when a person with a particular, pessimistic attributional style is confronted with a series of negative experiences. (p. 630)

**auditory masking** The phenomenon by which one sound (usually a lower-frequency sound) tends to prevent the hearing of another sound (usually a higher-frequency sound). (p. 249)

**auditory nerve** The cranial nerve that contains the sensory neurons for hearing and the vestibular sense (important for balance). (p. 247)

**auditory neurons** The sensory neurons for hearing, which run from the cochlea of the inner ear, through the auditory nerve, into the brain. (p. 247)

**authoritarian parents** In Baumrind's typology, parents whose discipline style is characterized by one-way communication (from parent to child), emphasis on obedience for its own sake, and use of power-assertive methods to control children's behavior. See also *authoritative parents, permissive parents*. (p. 461)

**authoritative parents** In Baumrind's typology, parents whose discipline style is characterized by two-way communication and reasoning, coupled with concern that the child behave properly and with willingness to use power-assertive methods to gain compliance when necessary. See also *authoritarian parents, permissive parents*. (p. 461)

**autonomic motor system** The set of motor neurons that act upon visceral muscles and glands. (p. 173)

**autosomes** All of the chromosomes other than the sex chromosomes; that is, all of the chromosomes that are possessed in equal number by males and females. (p. 49)

**aversion treatment** In behavior therapy, a method for eliminating an undesired habit by applying some painful or unpleasant stimulus immediately after the unwanted response occurs or immediately after the person has experienced stimuli that would normally elicit the response. (p. 670)

**avoidance response** A response that occurs *before* the onset of an aversive (unpleasant) stimulus, preventing that stimulus from occurring for some period of time. (p. 140)

**axon** A thin, often very long, tubelike extension from a neuron that is specialized to carry neural impulses (action potentials) to other cells. (p. 166)

**axon terminal** A swelling at the end of an axon that is designed to release a chemical substance (neurotransmitter) onto another neuron, muscle cell, or gland. (p. 166)

---

**basal ganglia** The large masses of gray matter in the brain that lie on each side of the thalamus; they are especially important for the initiation and coordination of deliberate movements. (p. 179)

**basilar membrane** A flexible membrane in the cochlea of the inner ear; the wavelike movement of this structure in response to sound stimulates the receptor cells for hearing. See also *hair cells*. (p. 247)

**behavior** The observable actions of an individual person or animal. (p. 3)

**behavior therapy** The psychotherapy approach based on the philosophy of behaviorism and rooted in basic behavioral research on learning. In this approach, psychological problems are considered to stem from learned habits, and learning techniques are used to treat them. (p. 666)

**behavioral genetics** The study of the effects of genes on behavior. (p. 47)

**behavioral monitoring** Any assessment procedure that involves counting or recording actual instances of desired or undesired behaviors. (p. 651)

**behaviorism** A school of psychological thought that holds that the proper subject of study is observable behavior, not the mind, and that behavior should be understood in terms of its relationship to observable events in the environment rather than in terms of hypothetical events within the individual. (pp. 13, 121)

**bias** A technical term referring to nonrandom (directed) effects on research results, caused by some factor or factors that are extraneous to the research hypothesis. For contrast, see *error*. (p. 36)

**biased sample** A subset of the population under study that is not representative of the population as a whole. (p. 39)

**binocular disparity** The cue for depth perception that stems from the separate (disparate) views that the two eyes have of any given visual object or scene; the farther away the object is, the more similar are the two views of it. (p. 304)

**biofeedback training** A variety of operant conditioning in which a signal, such as tone or light, is made to come on whenever a certain desirable physiological change occurs, and the person is instructed to try to keep the signal on for increasing periods of time. It is used as treatment for such problems as headaches and high blood pressure. (p. 134) *bipolar cells* The class of neurons in the retina that receive input from the receptor cells (rods and cones) and form synapses on ganglion cells (which form the optic nerve). (p. 254)

*bipolar disorder* A mood disorder characterized by episodes of extreme depression alternating with episodes of extreme mania. See *depression, mania.* (p. 632)

*blaming the victim* The tendency to seek out flaws in the behavior or character of people who have suffered some misfortune. (p. 498)

*blend* The simultaneous, nonverbal expression of two or more emotions by mixing the muscle movements or postures that express one emotion with those that express the other. (p. 100)

*blind* In scientific research, the condition in which those who collect the data are deliberately kept uninformed about aspects of the study's design (such as which subjects have had which treatment) that could lead them either unconsciously or consciously to bias the results. See also *bias, observer-expectancy effect.* (p. 38)

*blind spot* The place in the retina of the eye where the axons of visual sensory neurons come together to form the optic nerve. Because the blind spot lacks receptor cells, light that strikes it is not seen. (p. 254)

*blood-brain barrier* The tight capillary walls and the surrounding glial cells that prevent many chemical substances from entering the brain from the blood. (p. 190)

*bottom-up processes* In theories of perception, mental processes that begin with the individual stimulus features recorded by the senses and bring them together to form a perception of the larger object or scene. For contrast, see *top-down processes.* (p. 284)

*brainstem* The primitive, stalklike portion of the brain that can be thought of as an extension of the spinal cord into the head; it consists of the medulla, pons, and midbrain. (p. 177)

*Broca's aphasia* A specific syndrome of loss in language ability that occurs due to damage in a particular part of the brain called *Broca's area*; it is characterized by telegraphic speech in which the meaning is usually clear but the small words and word endings that serve grammatical purposes are missing. For contrast, see *Wernicke's aphasia.* (p. 399)

*Broca's area* A specific area in the temporal lobe of the human cerebral cortex (usually in the left hemisphere) that is involved in language; damage there produces Broca's aphasia. (p. 399)

*cell body* The widest part of a neuron, which contains the cell nucleus and other basic machinery common to all cells. (p. 166)

*cell membrane* The thin, porous outer covering of a neuron or other cell, which separates the cell's intracellular fluid from extracellular fluid. (p. 168)

*central drive system* According to the central-state theory of drives, a set of neurons in the brain that, when active, most directly promotes a specific motivational state, or drive. (p. 200)

*central nervous system* The brain and spinal cord. (p. 166)

*central route to attitude construction* The logical analysis of available information for the purpose of developing or modifying an attitude. For contrast, see *peripheral route to attitude construction.* (p. 515)

*central-state theory of drives* The theory that the most direct physiological bases for motivational states, or drives, lie in neural activity in the brain. According to most versions of this theory, different drives correspond to activity in different, localizable sets of neurons. See also *central drive system.* (p. 200)

*cerebellum* The relatively large, conspicuous, convoluted portion of the brain attached to the rear side of the brainstem; it is especially important for the coordination of rapid movements. (p. 179)

*cerebral cortex* The outermost, evolutionarily newest, and (in humans) by far the largest portion of the brain; it is divisible into two hemispheres (right and left), and each hemisphere is divisible into four lobes, the occipital, temporal, parietal, and frontal. (p. 180)

*chromosomes* The structures within the cell nucleus that contain the genetic material (DNA). (p. 49)

*chunking* A strategy for improving the ability to remember a set of items by grouping them mentally to form fewer items. (p. 337)

*circadian rhythm* Any cyclic physiological or behavioral change in a person or other living thing that has a period of about one day even in the absence of external cues signaling the time of day. (p. 221)

*classical conditioning* A training procedure or learning experience in which a neutral stimulus (the conditioned stimulus) comes to elicit a reflexive response through its being paired with another stimulus (usually an unconditioned stimulus) that already elicits that reflexive response; originally studied by Pavlov. See also *conditioned response, conditioned stimulus, unconditioned response, unconditioned stimulus.* (p. 124)

*client-centered therapy* The humanistic approach to psychotherapy developed by Rogers, in which the therapist refrains from offering advice or leading the course of therapy, but rather listens to the client with empathy and respect and reflects the client's thoughts and feelings back to him or her. (p. 659)

*clinical psychologist* A mental health professional who has a doctoral degree in psychology with special training in research and clinical practice. A clinical psychologist may conduct psychotherapy, but usually may not prescribe drugs. For contrast, see *psychiatrist.* (p. 648)

*closure principle* See *Gestalt principles of grouping.*

*cochlea* A coiled structure in the inner ear in which the receptor cells for hearing are located. (p. 247)

*cochlear implant* A type of hearing aid used, experimentally, to treat sensorineural deafness; it transforms sounds into electrical impulses and directly stimulates the tips of auditory neurons within the cochlea. (p. 248)

*coding* In sensation, the process by which information about the quality and quantity of a stimulus is preserved in the pattern of action potentials sent through sensory neurons to the central nervous system. (p. 243)

*cognitive-behavior therapy* The psychotherapy approach that stems from a union of cognitive and behavioral theory; it usually characterizes psychological problems as learned habits of thought and action, and its approach to treatment is to help people change those habits. See also *behavior therapy, cognitive therapy.* (p. 666) *cognitive dissonance* The discomfort associated with the awareness of disagreement or lack of harmony between two or more of one's own cognitions (beliefs or bits of knowledge). (p. 516)

*cognitive dissonance theory* Festinger's theory that many human actions and attitude changes can be understood as attempts to relieve cognitive dissonance. (p. 517)

*cognitive map* The mental representation of the spatial layout of a familiar environment, inferred from the individual's ability to move in that environment as if guided by a map. (p. 150)

*cognitive psychology* The study of the ability to acquire, organize, remember, and use knowledge to guide behavior; it involves the construction of hypothetical mental processes to explain observable behavior. (pp. 16, 143, 283)

*cognitive therapy* An approach to psychotherapy that begins with the assumption that people disturb themselves through their own thoughts and that they can overcome their problems through changing the way they think about their experiences. (p. 662)

*common movement principle* See *Gestalt principles of grouping*.

*compliance* Behaving in accordance with another person's request or expectation. (p. 530)

*concept* A rule or other form of mental information for categorizing stimuli into groups. (p. 144)

*concordance* In behavioral genetics research, an index of heritability that is found by identifying a set of individuals who have a particular trait or disorder and then determining the percentage of some specific class of their relatives (such as identical twins) who have the same trait or disorder. (p. 75)

*concrete-operational stage* In Piaget's theory of cognitive development, the third stage (about 7 to 12 years old), in which the child can think logically about reversible actions (operations), but only when applied to objects with which the child has had direct (concrete) experience. See also *operations*. (p. 436)

*conditioned reflex* In classical conditioning, a reflex that occurs only because of previous conditions in the individual's experience; a learned reflex. For contrast, see *unconditioned reflex*. (p. 124)

*conditioned response* In classical conditioning, a reflexive response that is elicited by a stimulus (the conditioned stimulus) because of the previous pairing of that stimulus with another stimulus (the unconditioned stimulus) that already elicits a reflexive response. For contrast, see *unconditioned response*. (p. 124)

*conditioned stimulus* In classical conditioning, a stimulus that comes to elicit a reflexive response (the conditioned response) because of its previous pairing with another stimulus (the unconditioned stimulus) that already elicits a reflexive response. For contrast, see *unconditioned stimulus*. (p. 124)

*conduction deafness* Deafness that occurs when the ossicles of the middle ear become rigid and cannot carry sounds inward from the tympanic membrane to the cochlea. (p. 248)

*cones* The class of receptor cells for vision that are located in and near the fovea of the retina, operate in moderate-to-bright light, and are most important for the perception of color and fine detail. For contrast, see *rods*. (p. 252)

*cone vision* The high-acuity color vision that occurs in moderate-to-bright light and is mediated by cones in the retina; also called photopic or bright-light vision. See *cones*. For contrast, see *rod vision*. (p. 254)

*conformity* The tendency to behave as others behave. (p. 545)

*content words* Words, including nouns, verbs, adjectives, and adverbs, that are most essential to the meaning of a sentence. For contrast, see *grammatical morphemes*. (pp. 394–395)

*context-dependent memory* The improved ability to retrieve information from memory that occurs when an individual is in the same environment as that in which the memory was originally encoded. (p. 353)

*contingency contract* In behavior therapy, a formal, usually written agreement in which certain specified services or rewards, provided by one party, are made contingent upon the actions of the other party. (p. 670)

*continuous measure* In psychology, a measure of behavior or personality in which all possible gradations can occur within an observed range. (p. 61)

*continuous reinforcement* In operant conditioning, the condition in which the response always produces a reinforcer. See *reinforcer*. For contrast, see *partial reinforcement*. (p. 135)

*continuous theories of development* In developmental psychology, theories that maintain that psychological development is a gradual, continuous process. For contrast, see *stage theories of development*. (p. 413)

*control processes* In the modal model of the mind, the mental processes that operate on information in the memory stores and move information from one store to another. See *attention, encoding, retrieval*. (p. 324)

*convergence* In a sensory system, the funneling of the activity of many receptor cells upon fewer sensory neurons; high convergence increases sensitivity at the expense of acuity. More generally, in the nervous system, any case in which a single neuron receives synaptic input from more than one other neuron. (p. 255)

*cooperation* In sociobiology, a type of helping behavior in which interaction among two or more individuals increases the survival chance or reproductive capacity of each individual involved in the interaction. For contrast, see *altruism*. (p. 112)

*cornea* The curved, transparent tissue at the front of the eyeball, which helps to focus light rays as they first enter the eye. (p. 252)

*corpus callosum* A massive bundle of axons connecting the right and left hemispheres of the higher parts of the brain, including the cerebral cortex. (pp. 182, 378)

*correlates of structure* Darwin's term for changes in a species that occur as nonadaptive side effects of other, adaptive changes. (p. 88)

*correlation coefficient* A numerical measure of the strength and direction of the relationship between two variables. (pp. 34, A-7)

*correlational study* Any scientific study in which the researcher observes or measures (without directly manipulating) two or more variables to find relationships between them. Such studies can identify lawful relationships, but cannot determine whether change in one variable is the cause of change in another. (p. 30)

*counter-conditioning* A behavior therapy technique for eliminating an undesired conditioned response (such as a conditioned fear response) by pairing the conditioned stimulus for the undesired response with an unconditioned stimulus for a new response (such as pleasure) that is incompatible with the undesired response. (p. 667)

*cranial nerve* A nerve that extends directly from the brain. See *nerves*. For contrast, see *spinal nerve*. (p. 173)

*creole language* A new language, with grammatical rules, that develops from a pidgin language in colonies established by people who had different native languages. See *pidgin language*. (p. 425)

*critical period* A relatively restricted time period in an individual's development during which a particular form of learning can best occur. See *imprinting*. (p. 158)

*cross-sectional method* In developmental psychology, the procedure for studying the effects of age, in which people of different ages are compared with one another. For contrast, see *longitudinal method*. (p. 412)

*crossed-extension reflex* The reflexive extension (stiffening) of one limb that occurs when the corresponding limb on the other side of the body is undergoing a flexion reflex. See *flexion reflex*. (p. 176)

*crossing over* During meiosis, the random interchange of DNA sections between chromosomes within each set of four. (p. 50)

*cyclothymia* A mood disorder similar to bipolar disorder but involving less extreme depression and mania. See *bipolar disorder*. (p. 632)

*dark adaptation* The increased visual sensitivity that occurs when the eyes are exposed for a period of time to dimmer light than was present before the adaptation period. For contrast, see *light adaptation*. (p. 256)

*declarative information* That information stored in memory that can be expressed in words (declared); a collective term for *semantic* and *episodic information*. (p. 327)

*deductive reasoning* Logical reasoning from the general to the specific; the reasoner begins by accepting the truth of one or more general premises or axioms and uses them to assert whether a specific conclusion is true, false, or indeterminate. For contrast, see *inductive reasoning*. (p. 386)

*deep structure* In Chomsky's theory of language, the abstract, mental representation of the meaning of a sentence, organized in the simplest possible grammatical form consistent with that meaning. For contrast, see *surface structure*. (p. 397)

*defense mechanisms* In psychoanalytic theory, self-deceptive means by which the mind defends itself against anxiety. See *displacement, projection, rationalization, reaction formation, repression*. (p. 568)

*deindividuation* The reduced sense of personal responsibility that can occur when in a crowd or when distracted by highly arousing external stimulation, which can lead a person to perform actions that run counter to his or her personal beliefs or morals. (p. 544)

*delusion* A false belief that is maintained despite compelling evidence to the contrary. (p. 634)

*dendrites* The thin, tubelike extensions of a neuron that typically branch repeatedly near the neuron's cell body and are specialized for receiving signals from other neurons. (p. 166)

*dependence* See *drug dependence*.

*dependent variable* In any experiment, the variable that is believed to be dependent upon (affected by) another variable (the independent variable). In psychology, it is usually some measure of behavior. (p. 28)

*depression* A subjective sense of sadness, defeat, worthlessness, self-hatred, and hopelessness. (p. 628)

*depressive disorders* The class of mood disorders characterized by prolonged or frequent bouts of depression. (p. 627)

*deprivation experiment* An experiment in which animals are raised in ways that deprive them of some of their usual experiences in order to determine what experiences are essential (or not) for a particular species-specific behavior to develop. (p. 91)

*descriptive statistics* Mathematical methods for summarizing sets of data. (p. 33)

*descriptive study* Any study in which the researcher describes the behavior of an individual or set of individuals without systematically investigating relationships between specific variables. (p. 30)

*developmental psychology* The branch of psychology that charts changes in people's abilities and styles of behaving as they get older and tries to understand the factors that produce or influence those changes. (p. 411)

*difference threshold* In psychophysics, the minimal difference that must exist between two otherwise similar stimuli for an individual to detect them as different; also called the *just-noticeable difference* (*jnd*). (p. 272)

*direct-perception theory* The theory that perceptual mechanisms register directly the critical stimulus relationships that are present in the external environment, such that perception is not dependent upon mental inference. For contrast, see *unconscious-inference theory of perception*. (pp. 303, 315).

*discrimination training* The procedure, in both classical and operant conditioning, by which generalization between two stimuli is diminished or abolished by reinforcing the response to one stimulus and extinguishing the response to the other. See *extinction, generalization, reinforcement*. (pp. 127, 138)

*discriminative stimulus* In operant conditioning, a stimulus that serves as a signal that a particular response will produce a particular reinforcer. (p. 138)

*displacement* The defense mechanism by which a drive is diverted from one goal to another that is more realistic or acceptable. Also called *sublimation* in cases where the goal toward which the drive is diverted is highly valued by society. (p. 569)

*dissociation* A process by which some portion of a person's experiences are cut off mentally from the rest of his or her experiences, such that they cannot be recalled or can only be recalled under special conditions. (p. 622)

*dissociative disorders* The class of mental disorders that are characterized by dissociation. It includes *multiple personality disorder, psychogenic amnesia*, and *psychogenic fugue*. (p. 622)

*distinctive features* In Eleanor Gibson's theory of perceptual learning, those stimulus features of an object (or class of objects) that best distinguish it from other objects (or classes) with which it might be confused. (p. 294)

**dizygotic twins**  See *fraternal twins*.

**dominance hierarchy**  The ranking of individuals within a colony or group according to the degree to which others refrain from challenging that individual when their interests conflict. (p. 111)

**dominant gene**  A gene that will produce its observable effects in either the *homozygous* or the *heterozygous* condition. (p. 52)

**door-in-the-face technique**  A technique for gaining compliance in which one first asks for a large contribution or favor before asking for a smaller one. Hearing the first request, and refusing it, predisposes the person to comply to the second. (p. 533)

**dopamine theory of schizophrenia**  The theory that the symptoms of schizophrenia arise from overactivity at synapses in the brain where dopamine is the neurotransmitter. (p. 638)

**double blind experiment**  An experiment in which both the observer and the subjects are blind with respect to the subjects' treatment conditions. See also *blind*. (p. 38)

**Down syndrome**  A chromosomal disorder, usually involving an entire extra chromosome 21, which is typified by a specific set of physical problems and by low-normal or retarded intellectual functioning; also called *trisomy-21*. (p. 60)

**drive**  See *motivational state*.

**drug abuse**  The persistent taking of a drug in a way that is harmful to the self or that causes one to behave in a way that is harmful or threatening to others. (p. 624)

**drug dependence**  The condition, which may or may not stem from physiological withdrawal symptoms, in which a person feels compelled to take a particular drug on a regular basis; also called *drug addiction*. (p. 624)

**drug tolerance**  The phenomenon by which a drug produces successively smaller physiological and behavioral effects, at any given dose, if it is taken repeatedly. (p. 190)

**DSM-III-R**  The commonly used abbreviation for the *Diagnostic and Statistical Manual of Mental Disorders, Third Edition, Revised*, published by the American Psychiatric Association, which defines a wide variety of mental disorders and establishes criteria for diagnosing each. (p. 610)

**dualism**  Descartes's theory that two distinct systems—the material body and the immaterial soul—are involved in the control of behavior; also called *interactionism*. For contrast, see *materialism*. (p. 4)

**dysthymia**  A mental disorder characterized by feelings of depression that are less severe than those in major depression, but which last for at least a 2-year period. See also *major depression*. (p. 628)

***

**early-selection theories**  Theories of attention, such as Broadbent's *filter theory* and Treisman's *attenuation theory*, according to which the selective process of attention occurs relatively early in the mind's analysis of sensory information, before the information has been analyzed for meaning. For contrast, see *late-selection theories*. (p. 302)

**echoic memory**  Sensory memory for the sense of hearing. (p. 330)

**ecological perspective (or approach)**  In research on learning, the view that different learning mechanisms have developed through natural selection to serve different survival needs, and that these mechanisms are best understood in relation to daily life in the natu-

ral environment. (p. 153) More generally, the view that behavioral or mental capacities are best understood by considering how they serve the individual's needs in the environment. (p. 383)

**EEG**  See *electroencephalogram*.

**ego**  In Freud's three-part division of the mind, the source of logical thought and realistic compromise among the various forces that act within the mind; the division of the mind that enables the person to function in the real world. See also *id, superego*. (p. 567)

**elaborative rehearsal**  The process of thinking about an item of information in such a way as to tie the item mentally to other information in memory, which helps to encode the item into long-term memory. For contrast, see *rote rehearsal*. (p. 335)

**electroconvulsive shock therapy (ECT)**  A procedure for treating severe depression, in which the person is anesthetized and given a muscle relaxant, and then an electric current is passed through the patient's skull in such a way as to set up a seizure either in one hemisphere of the brain (unilateral ECT) or in both hemispheres (bilateral ECT). (p. 678)

**electroencephalogram (EEG)**  A record of the electrical activity of the brain that can be obtained by amplifying the weak electrical signals picked up by recording electrodes pasted to the person's scalp. It is usually described in terms of wave patterns. (p. 217)

**emotion**  A subjective feeling, the intensity of which is typically related to the degree of physiological arousal that accompanies it. (p. 229)

**empiricism**  The idea that all human knowledge and thought ultimately comes from sensory experience; the philosophical approach to understanding the mind that is based on that idea. For contrast, see *nativism*. (p. 6)

**encoding**  In the modal model of the mind, the mental process by which long-term memories are formed. See also *long-term memory*. (p. 326)

**encoding rehearsal**  Any active mental process by which a person strives to encode information into long-term memory. For contrast, see *maintenance rehearsal*. (p. 335)

**endocrine glands**  Glands that are specialized to secrete hormones into the circulatory system. (p. 187)

**endorphins**  Chemical substances produced in the body that act both as hormones and as neurotransmitters and are important for reducing the experience of pain. (p. 268)

**environmentality**  The proportion of the variability in a particular characteristic, in a particular group of individuals, that is due to environmental compared to genetic differences among the individuals. For contrast, see *heritability*. (p. 64)

**episodic information**  The class of information stored in memory that represents past events (episodes) in the person's own life. For contrast, see *procedural information, semantic information*. (p. 327)

**error**  A technical term referring to random variability in research results. For contrast, see *bias*. (p. 36)

**escape response**  An operant response that is reinforced by the removal of a negative reinforcer. See *negative reinforcer*. (p. 140)

**ethnocentrism**  The tendency for people to view and act toward their ingroups more favorably than they do toward their outgroups. (p. 498)

*ethology* The study of animal behavior in the natural environment, which uses evolutionary adaptation as its primary explanatory principle. (pp. 15, 89)

*excitatory synapse* A synapse at which the neurotransmitter increases the likelihood that an action potential will occur, or increases the rate at which they are already occurring, in the neuron on which it acts. For contrast, see *inhibitory synapse*. (p. 171)

*experiment* A research design for testing hypotheses about cause-effect relationships, in which the researcher manipulates one variable (the independent variable) in order to assess its effect on another variable (the dependent variable). (p. 28)

*exposure treatment* Any method of treating fears—including flooding counter-conditioning, and systematic desensitization— that involves exposing the client to the feared object or situation (either in reality or imagination) so that the process of extinction or habituation of the fear response can occur. (p. 668)

*extinction* In classical conditioning, the gradual disappearance of a conditioned reflex that results when a conditioned stimulus occurs repeatedly without the unconditioned stimulus. (p. 126) In operant conditioning, the decline in response rate that results when an operant response is no longer followed by a reinforcer. (p. 135) See *classical conditioning, operant conditioning*.

*extroversion* Psychological orientation toward the outer world, especially the world of people. For contrast, see *introversion*. (pp. 484, 593)

*eyebrow flash* A momentary raising of the eyebrows, lasting about ⅙ of a second, which is a nonverbal sign of either greeting or flirtation in cultures throughout the world. (p. 102)

*factor analysis* A statistical procedure for analyzing the correlations among various measurements (such as test scores) taken from a given set of individuals; it identifies hypothetical, underlying variables called *factors* that could account for the observed pattern of correlations and assesses the degree to which each factor is adequately measured by each of the measurements that was used in the analysis. (p. 370)

*feature detector* In vision, any neuron in the brain that responds to a specific property of a visual stimulus, such as its color, orientation, movement, or shape of its contour. More generally, any neuron in the brain that responds to a specific property (feature) of any sensory stimulus. (p. 260)

*feature theory of schemas* The theory that a schema (the mental representation of a concept) is best characterized as a set of separate, discrete propositions that define the category of object or event that the schema represents. For contrast, see *prototype theory of schemas*. (p. 344)

*Fechner's law* The idea that the magnitude of the sensory experience of a stimulus is directly proportional to the logarithm of the physical magnitude of the stimulus. For contrast, see *power law*. (p. 274)

*field study* Any scientific research study in which data are collected in a setting other than the laboratory. (p. 32)

*field theory* Lewin's broad social psychological theory that each person exists in a field of psychological forces—made up of the person's own desires, goals, and abilities and the person's perceptions of others' expectations or judgments—that act simultaneously to push or pull the person in various directions. (p. 527)

*figure* In perception, the portion of a visual scene that draws the perceiver's attention and is interpreted as an object rather than as the background. For contrast, see *ground*. (p. 286)

*fixation* In Freud's psychoanalytic theory, the failure of some portion of the mind to advance beyond a particular childhood stage of psychosexual development, so that the person goes through life attempting to achieve pleasure in ways that are symbolically equivalent to the ways that pleasure is normally achieved in that stage. See also *psychosexual stages*. (p. 570)

*fixed action pattern* Ethologists' term for a behavior that occurs in essentially identical fashion among most members of a species (though it may be limited to one sex or the other), is elicited by a specific environmental stimulus, and is typically more complex than a reflex. (p. 89)

*fixed-interval (FI) schedule* In operant conditioning, a schedule of reinforcement in which a fixed period of time must elapse after each reinforced response before another reinforcer can be obtained. (p. 136)

*fixed-ratio (FR) schedule* In operant conditioning, a schedule of reinforcement in which the response must be emitted a certain fixed number of times (more than once) before it produces a reinforcer. (p. 136)

*flexion reflex* The reflexive folding of a limb (leg or arm) toward the body, usually in response to a potentially damaging stimulus to the limb. (p. 176)

*flooding* A behavior therapy technique for treating phobias, in which the person is presented with the feared object or situation until the fear response is extinguished or habituated. (p. 667)

*foot-in-the-door technique* A technique for gaining compliance in which one first asks for some relatively small contribution or favor before asking for a larger one. Complying to the first request predisposes the person to comply to the second. (p. 532)

*formal-operational stage* In Piaget's theory of cognitive development, the fourth stage (about 12 years old through adulthood), in which the individual is capable of reasoning about abstract concepts and hypothetical ideas. (p. 437)

*formal thought disturbance* A breakdown in the form or pattern of logical thinking, which often characterizes schizophrenia. (p. 635)

*founder effect* The genetic difference between two populations of the same species that results when one of the populations was founded by a small group of individuals that migrated to a new area and happened to have some unusual genes; a form of *genetic drift*. (p. 87)

*four-walls technique* A sales trick in which the salesperson asks a set of leading questions that cause the potential customer to say things that would contradict (and cause cognitive dissonance with) a subsequent refusal to purchase the product that the salesperson is trying to sell. (p. 531)

*fovea* The pinhead-sized area of the retina of the eye in which the cones are concentrated and that is specialized for high visual activity. (p. 252)

**frame illusion** The illusion by which a frame around the outside of an object makes the object look larger, and a frame placed within the border of an object makes the object look smaller. (p. 310)

**fraternal twins** Two individuals who developed simultaneously in the same womb, but who originated from separate zygotes (fertilized eggs) and are therefore no more genetically similar to one another than are ordinary siblings; also called *dizygotic twins*. For contrast, see *identical twins*. (pp. 51–52)

**free association** 1. In psychoanalysis, the procedure in which a patient relaxes, frees his or her mind from the constraints of conscious logic, and reports every image and idea that enter his or her awareness. 2. Any procedure in which a person reports the first word or thought that enters his or her mind in response to a particular word, picture, or other stimulus. (p. 565)

**free nerve endings** The sensitive tips of sensory neurons, located in the skin and other peripheral tissues, that are *not* surrounded by specialized end organs and are involved in the sense of pain. (p. 266)

**frequency** For any form of energy that changes in a cyclic or wave-like way, the number of cycles or waves that occur during a standard unit of time. For sound, this physical measure is related to the psychological experience of pitch. (p. 246)

**frequency distribution** A table or graph depicting the number of individual scores, in a set of scores, that fall within each of a set of equal intervals. (p. A-2)

**frontal lobe** The frontmost lobe of the cerebral cortex, bounded in the rear by the parietal and temporal lobes; it contains the motor area and parts of the association areas involved in planning and making judgments. (p. 180)

**functionalism** A school of psychological thought, founded by William James and others, that focuses on understanding the functions, or adaptive purposes, of mental processes. For contrast, see *structuralism*. (p. 10)

**functionalist approach** In psychology, the general approach that emphasizes the functions of behavior or mental processes. Whereas *functionalism* was a discrete school of thought in the early history of psychology, the *functionalist approach* has been integrated into many areas of psychology. (p. 86)

**fundamental attribution error** The tendency to attribute a person's behavior too much to the person's inner characteristics (personality) and not enough to the environmental situation. See also *attribution*. (p. 499)

---

*g* See *general intelligence*.

**ganglion cells** The sensory neurons for vision; their cell bodies are located in the retina, and their axons run by way of the optic nerve into the brain. (p. 254)

**gate-control theory** Melzack and Wall's theory that pain will be experienced only if the input from peripheral pain neurons passes through a "gate" located at the point that the pain-carrying neurons enter the spinal cord or lower brainstem. (p. 268)

**gender** As used by psychologists, the entire set of characteristics, which may be partly or wholly socially determined, that identify a person as male or female; to be distinguished from *sex*, which refers to the clearly biological features that distinguish males and females. (p. 467)

**gender identity** A person's subjective sense of being male or female. (p. 469)

**gene** The portion of a DNA molecule containing the code for one specific type of protein molecule; the basic unit of heredity. (p. 48)

**general adaptation syndrome** A sequence of changes found by Selye to occur in animals that are exposed for prolonged periods to a highly stressful condition. It includes the *alarm stage* (characterized by an arousal response), the *stage of resistance* (characterized by relatively normal functioning despite the stressful stimulation), and the *stage of exhaustion* (characterized by damage to body tissues, resulting in illness or death). (p. 228)

**general intelligence** In Spearman's theory of intelligence (and in other theories based on Spearman's), the underlying mental ability that affects performance on a wide variety of mental tests and accounts for the statistical correlation among scores on such tests; also called *g*. (p. 370)

**generalization** In classical conditioning, the phenomenon by which a stimulus that resembles a conditioned stimulus will elicit the conditioned response even though it has never been paired with the unconditioned stimulus. In operant conditioning, the phenomenon by which a stimulus that resembles a discriminative stimulus will increase the rate at which the animal produces the operant response, even though the response has never been reinforced in the presence of that stimulus. (p. 127)

**generalized anxiety disorder** A mental disorder characterized by prolonged, severe anxiety that is not consistently associated in the person's mind with any particular object or event in the environment or any specific life experience. (p. 616)

**generative-transformational theory of language** Chomsky's theory that the ability to produce and understand language can be specified as a set of rules for generating deep-structure sentences (*generative rules*) and another set of rules for transforming deep-structure sentences into any of various surface structures (*transformational rules*). See also *deep structure, surface structure*. (p. 397)

**genetic drift** All forms of chance events, other than natural selection, that can cause different populations of a given species to be genetically different (to have different gene pools). See also *founder effect*. (p. 87)

**genotype** The set of genes inherited by the individual. See also *phenotype*. (p. 48)

**Gestalt principles of grouping** The rules, proposed by Gestalt psychologists, concerning that manner by which the perceptual system groups sensory elements together to produce organized perceptions of whole objects and scenes. They include the principles of (a) *proximity* (nearby elements are grouped together), (b) *similarity* (elements that resemble one another are grouped together), (c) *closure* (gaps in what would otherwise be a continuous border are ignored), (d) *good continuation* (when lines intersect, those segments that would form a continuous line with minimal change in direction are grouped together), (e) *common movement* (elements moving in the same direction and velocity are grouped together), and (f) *good form* (elements are grouped in such a way as to form percepts that are simple and symmetrical). (p. 286)

**Gestalt psychology** A school of psychological thought, founded in Germany, which emphasizes the idea that the mind must be understood in terms of organized wholes, not elementary parts. For contrast, see *structuralism*. (pp. 11, 285) *gland* Any bodily structure designed to secrete a chemical substance. See also *endocrine glands.* (p. 173)

*glial cells* Any of various non-neural cells in the nervous system, which help protect neurons from damage or in other ways facilitate neural functioning. (p. 168)

*good continuation principle* See *Gestalt principles of grouping.*

*good form principle* See *Gestalt principles of grouping.*

*grammar* The entire set of rules that specify the permissible ways that smaller units can be arranged to form morphemes, words, phrases, and sentences in a language. (p. 396)

*grammatical morphemes* The class of words, suffixes, and prefixes that serve primarily to fill out the grammatical structure of a sentence rather than to carry its main meaning. For contrast, see *content words.* (p. 395)

*ground* In perception, the portion of a visual scene that is interpreted as the background rather than as the object of attention. For contrast, see *figure.* (p. 286)

*group polarization* The tendency for a group of people who already share a particular opinion to hold that opinion more strongly—or in a more extreme form—after discussing the issue among themselves. (p. 549)

*groupthink* A mode of thinking in which members of a group are more concerned with group cohesiveness and unanimity than with realistic appraisal of the actions being considered. (p. 551)

*habituation* The decline in the magnitude or likelihood of a reflexive response that occurs when the stimulus is repeated several or many times in succession. (p. 123)

*hair cells* The receptor cells for hearing, which are arranged in rows along the basilar membrane of the cochlea in the inner ear. (p. 247)

*hallucination* A false sensory perception; the experience of seeing, hearing, or otherwise perceiving something and believing it to be present, when in fact it is not present. (p. 634)

*helping* In sociobiology, any behavior that increases the survival chance or reproductive capacity of another individual. See also *altruism, cooperation.* (p. 112)

*heritability* The proportion of the variability in a particular characteristic, in a particular group of individuals, that is due to genetic compared to environmental differences among the individuals. For contrast, see *environmentality.* (p. 62)

*heritability coefficient* A measure of heritability, which can vary from 0 (no heritability) to 1 (complete heritability); specifically, variance due to genes divided by total variance. See *heritability.* (p. 62)

*heterozygous* The condition in which a pair of genes occupying the same locus on a pair of chromosomes are different from one another. For contrast, see *homozygous.* (p. 52)

*heuristic* A shortcut in problem solving; a rule for reducing the number of mental operations (or information-processing steps) taken to solve a problem. For contrast, see *algorithm.* (p. 393)

*higher-order conditioning* A classical-conditioning procedure in which a stimulus becomes a conditioned stimulus through being paired with a previously conditioned stimulus, rather than through being paired with an unconditioned stimulus. (p. 128)

*holistic perception* The tendency, emphasized by Gestalt psychologists, to perceive whole patterns, objects, and scenes, and to ignore the smaller parts of which they are composed; the concept that wholes take precedent over parts in perceptual experience. (p. 285)

*homeostasis* The constancy in the body's internal environment that must be maintained through the expenditure of energy. (p. 199)

*homology* In ethology and comparative psychology, any similarity among species that exists because of the species' common ancestry. For contrast, see *analogy.* (p. 93)

*homozygous* The condition in which a pair of genes occupying the same locus on a pair of chromosomes are identical to one another. For contrast, see *heterozygous.* (p. 52)

*hormone* Any chemical substance that is secreted naturally by the body into the blood and can influence physiological processes at specific target tissues (such as the brain) and thereby influence behavior. (p. 187)

*humanistic personality theories* Theories of personality that emphasize (a) the person's subjective mental experiences, (b) a holistic view of the person, and (c) the person's inner drive toward higher psychological growth, or self-actualization. (pp. 578–580)

*hypothalamus* A small brain structure lying just below the thalamus, connected directly to the pituitary gland and to the limbic system, that is especially important for the regulation of motivation, emotion, and the internal physiological conditions of the body. (p. 180)

*iconic memory* Sensory memory for the sense of vision. (p. 329)

*id* In Freud's three-part division of the mind, the source of instincts and mental energy. See also *ego, superego.* (p. 565)

*identical twins* Two individuals who are genetically identical to one another because they originated from a single zygote (fertilized egg); also called *monozygotic twins.* For contrast, see *fraternal twins.* (p. 50)

*identity* A person's self-concept, especially as it relates to the person's view of his or her social roles and responsibilities. (p. 474)

*impression management* The entire set of ways by which people either consciously or unconsciously attempt to influence other people's impressions (perceptions and judgments) of them. (p. 506)

*imprinting* Ethologists' term for a relatively sudden and irreversible form of learning that can occur only during some critical period of the individual's development. See *critical period.* (p. 158)

*incentive* Any object or end that exists in the external environment and toward which behavior is directed. Also called a *reinforcer, reward,* or *goal.* (p. 198)

*independent variable* In an experiment, the condition that the researcher varies in order to assess its effect upon some other variable (the dependent variable). In psychology, it is usually some condition of the environment or of the organism's physiology that is hypothesized to affect the individual's behavior. (p. 28)

*individual development* The unique sequence of developmental changes, and age at which each change occurs, that differentiate one person's development from that of others. For contrast, see *normative development.* (p. 412)

*induction* In Hoffman's typology of discipline styles, a form of verbal reasoning in which a parent (or other caregiver) induces the child to think about his or her actions and the consequences they have for other people. (p. 460)

*inductive reasoning* Logical reasoning from the specific to the general; the reasoner begins with a set of specific observations or facts and uses them to infer a more general rule to account for those observations or facts; also called *hypothesis construction.* For contrast, see *deductive reasoning.* (p. 386)

*inferential statistics* Mathematical methods for helping researchers determine how confident they can be in drawing general conclusions (inferences) from specific sets of data. (p. 33)

*information-processing approach (or perspective)* The general approach in psychological research and theory that begins with the premise that the mind is a device that acquires, stores, and analyzes information and uses information to control behavior. The goal of this approach is to explain behavior in terms of the steps in the decision-making process that lead the individual to respond in one way and not another under specific conditions. (pp. 373, 440)

*ingroup* A group to which an individual belongs or has the subjective sense of belonging. For contrast, see *outgroup.* (p. 497)

*inhibitory synapse* A synapse at which the neurotransmitter decreases the likelihood that an action potential will occur, or decreases the rate at which they are already occurring, in the neuron upon which it acts. For contrast, see *excitatory synapse.* (p. 171)

*inner ear* The portion of the ear lying farthest inward in the head; it contains the cochlea (for hearing) and the vestibular apparatus (for the sense of balance). (p. 247)

*insufficient-justification effect* A change in attitude that serves to justify an action that seems unjustified in the light of the previously held attitude. (p. 518)

*interneuron* A neuron that exists entirely within the brain or spinal cord and carries messages from one set of neurons to another. (p. 167)

*interview* A self-report method of data collection in which the individual being studied (or assessed) answers questions in an oral dialogue; often used for clinical assessment. (p. 31)

*intoxicating effects of a drug* The relatively short-term effects on mood and behavior that stem from the immediate physiological effects of a drug, and that subside as the amount of the drug in the body diminishes. (p. 625)

*introspection* The process of looking inward to examine one's own conscious experience; the method used by Titchener and other structuralists. (p. 9)

*introversion* Psychological orientation toward the inner, subjective world. For contrast, see *extroversion.* (pp. 484, 593)

*iris* The colored (usually brown or blue), doughnut-shaped, muscular structure in the eye, located behind the cornea and in front of the lens, that controls the size of the pupil and in that way controls the amount of light that can enter the eye's interior. (p. 252)

*James-Lange theory of emotion* The theory, developed independently by William James and Carl Lange, that emotions *are* one's sense of one's own bodily arousal. According to this theory, arousal causes the emotion, rather than the other way around. (p. 230)

*just-noticeable difference ( jnd)* See *difference threshold.*

*just-world bias* The tendency to believe that life is fair, which can lead people to assume that individuals who suffer misfortune deserve their misfortune. (p. 499)

*karyotype* The photographic representation of the chromosomes in a cell of an individual, organized in accordance with a standard numbering system. (p. 49)

*kin selection theory of altruism* The sociobiological theory that apparent acts of altruism have come about through natural selection because such actions are disproportionately directed toward close genetic relatives and thus promote the survival of others who have the same genes. See also *altruism.* (p. 113)

*labeling theory* The theory that the act of labeling a person as having a mental disorder establishes—in the labeled person's mind and in other people's minds—a set of expectations that may prolong the disorder, affect the manner in which it is manifested, or even create a disorder where none existed before. (p. 608)

*laboratory study* Any research study in which the subjects are brought to a specially designated area (laboratory) that has been set up to facilitate the researcher's ability to control the environment or collect data. (p. 32)

*language-acquisition device (LAD)* Chomsky's term for the special, innate characteristics of the human mind that allow children to learn their native language; it includes innate knowledge of basic aspects of grammar that are common to all languages and an innate predisposition to attend to and remember the critical, unique aspects of the language. (p. 425)

*language-acquisition support system (LASS)* The term used by social learning theorists to refer to the simplification of language, and the use of gestures, that occur when parents or other language users speak to young children, which helps children learn language; developed as a complement to Chomsky's concept of the LAD (language-acquisition device). (p. 427)

*late-selection theories* Theories of attention that maintain that the selective process of attention occurs relatively late in the mind's analysis of sensory information, after the information has been analyzed for meaning. For contrast, see *early-selection theories.* (p. 302)

*latent learning* Learning that is not demonstrated in the subject's behavior at the time that the learning occurs, but can be inferred from its effect on the subject's behavior at some later time. (p. 151)

*law of association by contiguity* Aristotle's principle that if two environmental events (stimuli) occur at the same time or one right after the other (contiguously), those events will be linked together in the mind. (pp. 125, 345)

*law of association by similarity* Aristotle's principle that objects, events, or ideas that are similar to one another become linked (associated) in the person's mind (structure of memory), such that the thought of one tends to elicit the thought of the other. (p. 346)

*law of complementarity* The observation that certain pairs of limited-wavelength lights that produce different colors (such as red and green) alone will produce the perception of white (no color) when mixed. See also *additive color mixing*. (p. 261)

**law of effect** Thorndike's principle that responses that produce a satisfying effect in a particular situation become more likely to recur in that situation, and responses that produce a discomforting effect become less likely to recur in that situation. (p. 131)

**learned helplessness theory of depression** The theory that depression is a psychological giving up of the attempt to control one's own fate, brought on by repeated negative experiences over which the person has no control. (p. 630)

**learning** The process or set of processes through which sensory experience at one time can affect an individual's behavior at a future time. (p. 121)

**lens** In the eye, the transparent structure behind the iris that helps focus light that has passed through the pupil. (p. 252)

**lesion** Any localized area of damage in biological tissue, such as in the brain. (p. 201)

**libido** The instinctive force that underlies the sex drive; in Freud's psychoanalytic theory, the main life force. (p. 565)

**light adaptation** The decreased visual sensitivity that occurs when the eyes are exposed for a period of time to brighter light than was present before the adaptation period. For contrast, see *dark adaptation*. (p. 256)

**limbic system** An interconnected set of brain structures (including the amygdala and hippocampus) that form a circuit wrapped around the thalamus and basal ganglia, underneath the cerebral cortex. These structures are especially important for the regulation of emotion and motivation and are involved in the formation of long-term memories. (p. 179)

**linguistic relativity hypothesis** Whorf's theory that people who have different native languages perceive the world differently and think differently from each other because of their different languages. (p. 402)

**localization of function** The concept that different, localizable parts of the brain serve different, specifiable functions in the control of mental experience and behavior. (p. 7)

**locus** In genetics, a position on a chromosome that contains the DNA of a single gene. (p. 52)

**locus of control** According to Rotter, a person's perception of the typical source of control over rewards. *Internal locus of control* refers to the perception that people control their own rewards through their own behavior, and *external locus of control* refers to the perception that rewards are controlled by external circumstances or fate. (p. 587)

**longitudinal method** In developmental psychology, the procedure in which the same individuals are studied at different ages, so that each individual's ability or characteristic can be compared at one age with his or her ability or characteristic at another age. For contrast, see *cross-sectional method*. (p. 412)

**long-term memory** In the modal model of the mind, information that is retained in the mind for long periods (often throughout life). For contrasts, see *sensory memory, short-term memory*. (p. 325)

**long-term store** The third memory store in the modal model of the mind; the hypothetical place in the mind that retains information for long periods (often throughout life). (p. 325)

**loudness** That quality of the psychological experience (sensation) of a sound that is most directly related to the amplitude of the physical sound stimulus. (p. 245)

**low-ball technique** A sales trick in which the salesperson suggests a low price for the item being sold, and then, when the potential customer has agreed to buy it at that price, pretends to discover that the item cannot be sold for that price. The customer's earlier agreement to buy the item may cause him or her to exaggerate mentally the item's worth and therefore to be more likely than before to buy it at the higher price. (p. 532)

---

**maintaining causes of a mental disorder** Those consequences of a mental disorder—such as the way other people treat the person who has it—that help keep the disorder going once it begins. See also *precipitating* and *predisposing causes of a mental disorder*. (p. 609)

**maintenance rehearsal** Any active mental process by which a person strives to hold information in short-term memory for a period of time. For contrast, see *encoding rehearsal*. (p. 335)

**major depression** A mental disorder characterized by severe depression that lasts essentially without remission for at least two weeks. (p. 628)

**mania** A mood state typically characterized by extreme mental excitement, an unrealistic sense of euphoria, and an overestimation of one's own abilities. (p. 632)

**materialism** Hobbes's theory that nothing exists but matter and energy. For contrast, see *dualism*. (p. 6)

**mating bond** A prolonged association between two or more members of the same species for the purpose of reproduction, which entails some degree of exclusivity in copulation on the part of at least one of the individuals in the association. See also *monogamy, polyandry, polygyny*. (p. 105)

**mean** The arithmetic average of a set of scores, determined by adding the scores and dividing the sum by the number of scores. (pp. 33, A-3)

**median** The center score in a set of scores that have been rank-ordered. (pp. 33, A-3)

**medical model** In clinical psychology or psychiatry, the view that mental disorders either *are* or *are analogous to* physical diseases. (p. 606)

**medulla** The lowest portion of the brainstem, bounded at one end by the spinal cord and at the other by the pons, which is responsible, with the pons, for organizing reflexes more complex than spinal reflexes. (p. 177)

**meiosis** The form of cell division involved in producing egg or sperm cells, which results in cells that are genetically dissimilar and that each have half the number of chromosomes of the original cell. (p. 50)

**memory** 1. The mind's ability to retain information over time. 2. Information retained in the mind over time. (p. 324)

**memory span** See *span of short-term memory*.

**memory stores** In cognitive psychology, hypothetical constructs that are conceived of as places where information is held in the mind. See also *long-term store, sensory store, short-term store*. (p. 324)

**mental disorder** A disturbance in a person's emotions, drives, thought processes, or behavior that (a) involves serious and relatively prolonged distress and/or impairment in ability to function, (b) is not simply a normal response to some event or set of events in the person's environment, and (c) is not explainable as an effect of poverty, prejudice, or other social forces that prevent the person from behaving adaptively, nor as a deliberate decision to act in a way that is contrary to the norms of society. (p. 605)

**mental set** A habit of perception or thought, stemming from previous experience, that can either help or hinder a person in solving a new problem. (p. 390)

**metacomponents** In Sternberg's information-processing model of intelligence, the mental components (processes) that regulate and coordinate the activities of the various lower-level mental components in solving a problem or choosing a course of action. See also *performance components*. (p. 375)

**method of magnitude estimation** Stevens's psychophysical method in which people are asked to estimate the magnitude of a subjective experience (such as the perceived loudness of a sound), usually by assigning a number to it. (p. 274)

**midbrain** The upper portion of the brainstem, bounded at its lower end by the pons and at its upper end by the thalamus, which contains neural centers that organize basic movement patterns. (p. 177)

**middle ear** The air-filled cavity, separated from the outer ear by the eardrum; its main structures are three ossicles (tiny bones), which vibrate in response to sound waves and stimulate the inner ear. (p. 247)

**mind** 1. The entire set of an individual's sensations, perceptions, memories, thoughts, dreams, motives, emotional feelings, and other subjective experiences. (p. 3) 2. In cognitive psychology, the set of hypothesized information-processing steps that analyze stimulus information and organize behavioral responses. (pp. 17–18)

**mitosis** The form of cell division involved in normal body growth, which produces cells that are genetically identical to each other. (p. 50)

**MMPI-2** The *Minnesota Multiphasic Personality Inventory, Second Edition*. A psychometric personality test that is commonly used for clinical assessment. See *assessment, psychometric personality test*. (p. 650)

**modal model of the mind** In cognitive psychology, the information-processing model that divides the mind into three *memory stores* (sensory, short-term, and long-term) and a set of mental processes (called *control processes*) that operate on information within the stores and move information from one store to another. (p. 323)

**mode** The most frequently occurring score in a set of scores; in a frequency distribution, the interval that contains the highest frequency of scores. (p. A-3)

**modeling** The process of teaching a person what to do, or how to do it, by having the person watch another person (the model) engage in that behavior. (p. 671)

**modern synthesis** In evolutionary theory, the ideas that have resulted from combining Darwin's principle of natural selection with a modern understanding of genes. (p. 82)

**monoamine theory of depression** The theory that the feeling of depression stems from too little activity at synapses in the brain where monoamines (norepinephrine, dopamine, and sertonin) are the neurotransmitters. (p. 629)

**monogamy** A mating system in which one female and one male bond only with each other. See *mating bond*. For contrast, see *polyandry, polygyny*. (p. 105)

**monozygotic twins** See *identical twins*.

**mood disorders** A class of mental disorders characterized by prolonged or extreme disruptions in mood. It includes the *depressive disorders* and *bipolar disorders*. (p. 627)

**moon illusion** The illusion by which the moon appears larger when seen near the horizon and smaller when seen near the zenith, even though it is objectively the same size and distance from the viewer in either location. (p. 308)

**morphemes** The smallest meaningful units of a verbal language; words, prefixes, or suffixes that have discrete meanings. (p. 394)

**motion parallax** The cue for depth perception that stems from the changed view one has of a scene or object when one's head moves sideways to the scene or object; the farther away an object is, the smaller is the change in view. (p. 305)

**motivation** The entire constellation of factors, some inside the organism and some outside, that cause an organism to behave in a particular way at a particular time. See also *incentive, motivational state*. (p. 197)

**motivational state** An internal, reversible condition in an individual that orients the individual toward one or another type of goal (such as food or water). This condition is not observed directly but is inferred from the individual's behavior; also called a *drive*. (pp. 197–198)

**motor area** An area in the rear part of the frontal lobe of the cerebral cortex that is directly involved in the control of movements, especially finely coordinated movements of small muscles, such as in the fingers and vocal apparatus. (pp. 181, 183)

**motor neuron** A neuron that carries messages from the brain or spinal cord, through a nerve, to a muscle or gland. (p. 166)

**Müller-Lyer illusion** A visual size illusion in which a horizontal line looks longer if attached at each end to an outward-extending, V-shaped object, and looks shorter if attached at each end to an inward-extending, V-shaped object. (p. 308)

**multiple personality disorder** A mental disorder in which two or more distinct personalities or self-identities are manifested by the same person at different times. (p. 622)

**mutations** Errors that occasionally and unpredictably occur during DNA replication, producing a "replica" that is different from the original. Mutations are believed to be the original source of all genetic variability. (p. 82)

**myelin sheath** A casing of fatty cells wrapped tightly around the axon of some neurons. (p. 166)

---

**nativism** The idea that certain elementary ideas are innate to the human mind and do not need to be gained through experience; the philosophical approach to understanding the mind that is based on that idea. For contrast, see *empiricism*. (p. 6)

**natural selection** The selective breeding that results from the obstacles to reproduction that are imposed by the natural environment; it is the driving force of evolution. See *selective breeding*. For contrast, see *artificial selection*. (p. 82)

**naturalistic observation** Any data-collection procedure in which the researcher records subjects' ongoing behavior in a natural setting, without interfering with that behavior. (p. 31)

**nature** An individual's biological (genetic) endowment. For contrast, see *nurture*. (p. 47)

**nature-nurture debate** The long-standing controversy as to whether the differences among people are principally due to their genetic differences (nature) or differences in their past and present environment (nurture). (p. 47)

**negative contrast effect** In operant conditioning, the decline in response rate, when the size of a reinforcer (or reward) is reduced, to a rate below that which occurs for subjects that had been receiving the smaller reinforcer all along. For contrast, see *positive contrast effect*. (p. 148)

**negative goal interdependence** A condition that engenders competition because the structure of rewards is such that each individual (or group) can obtain a reward only by preventing another individual (or group) from obtaining a reward. For contrast, see *positive goal interdependence*. (p. 554)

**negative reinforcement** In operant conditioning, the condition in which a response results in *removal* of a negative reinforcer. See *negative reinforcer*. (p. 140)

**negative reinforcer** In operant conditioning, a stimulus (such as electric shock or loud noise) that is *removed* after a response, and whose removal increases the likelihood that the response will recur. (p. 140)

**nerves** Large bundles containing the axons of many neurons. Located in the peripheral nervous system, they connect the central nervous system with muscles, glands, and sensory organs. (p. 166)

**neurohormone** A chemical substance that is similar to a neurotransmitter in that it is secreted from the axon terminals of neurons, but is classed as a hormone because it is secreted into blood vessels rather than onto other neurons. (p. 188)

**neurons** Single cells in the nervous system that are specialized for carrying information rapidly from one place to another and/or integrating information from various sources; also called *nerve cells*. (pp. 165–166)

**neuropsychological assessment** Any assessment procedure designed to find clues to brain damage that might be underlying a psychological problem. (p. 652)

**neuropsychology** The study of how the nervous system organizes and controls behavior that is specifically human. Neuropsychologists study people who have suffered brain damage due to injury or disease, both to help those people and to learn about the psychological functions performed by specific parts of the brain. (pp. 16, 357, 377)

**neurosis** In diagnostic systems based on psychoanalytic theory, any mental disorder in which the person is not out of touch with reality and the symptoms can be understood as expressions of anxiety or defenses against anxiety. For contrast, see *psychosis*. (p. 610)

**neurotic symptom** Any symptom of possible mental disorder that can be clearly recognized as a manifestation of anxiety. For contrast, see *psychotic symptom*. (p. 610)

**neurotransmitter** A chemical substance released from the axon terminal of a neuron, at a synapse, which influences the activity of another neuron, a muscle cell, or a glandular cell; also called a *transmitter*. (p. 170)

**nonregulatory drive** Any motivational state (such as the sex drive) that serves some function *other than* that of preserving some constancy of the body's internal environment. For contrast, see *regulatory drive*. (p. 200)

**nonspecific factors** In psychotherapy, those aspects of the therapist's interaction with the client that are not derived from the specific principles on which the therapy is based, but which may play an important role in the therapy process. (p. 673)

**nonverbal communication** Communication through bodily postures, movements, and facial expressions, that is, through means other than words or symbols that stand for words. (p. 97)

**normal distribution** A bell-shaped frequency distribution in which the mean, median, and mode are identical and the frequency of scores tapers off symmetrically on both sides, as defined by a specific mathematical equation. See *frequency distribution*. (pp. 61, A-2)

**normative development** The typical sequence of developmental changes, and the typical ages at which each change occurs, that are found for a given group of people. For contrast, see *individual development*. (p. 411)

**nucleus** In neuroanatomy, a cluster of cell bodies of neurons within the central nervous system (not to be confused with the cell nucleus within each cell). (p. 175)

**nurture** The entire set of environmental conditions that affect an individual's development. See also *nature*, *nature-nurture debate*. (p. 47)

---

**obedience** Those cases of compliance in which the person making the request is perceived as an authority figure or leader and the request is perceived as an order or command. See *compliance*. (p. 535)

**object permanence** Piaget's term for the understanding that an object still exists even when it is out of view. (p. 418)

**objective questionnaire** In clinical assessment or in personality research, a questionnaire on which a client or research subject checks off adjectives or statements that describe his or her own behaviors, thoughts, or feelings. (p. 649)

**observational learning** Learning by watching others. See also *modeling*. (p. 151)

**observational method** Any data-collection procedure in which the researcher directly observes the behavior of interest rather than relying on subjects' self-descriptions. (p. 31)

**observer-expectancy effect** Any bias in research results that derives from the researcher's desire or expectation that a subject or set of subjects will behave in a certain way. See *bias*. (pp. 27, 38)

**obsessive-compulsive disorder** A mental disorder characterized by a repeated, disturbing, irrational thought (the *obsession*) that can only be terminated (temporarily) by performing some action (the *compulsion*). (p. 618)

**occipital lobe** The rearmost lobe of the cerebral cortex, bounded in front by the temporal and parietal lobes; it contains the visual area of the brain. (p. 180)

**oedipal crisis** In Freud's psychoanalytic theory, the mental conflict that occurs during the phallic stage of development, which stems from the child's feeling of sexual attraction to the opposite-sex parent and consequent fear or resentment of the same-sex parent. For the girl, this crisis is sometimes called the *electra crisis*. (p. 571)

**operant conditioning** A training or learning process by which the consequence of a behavioral response affects the likelihood that the individual will produce that response again; also called *instrumental conditioning*. (pp. 130, 132)

**operant response** Any behavioral response that produces some reliable effect on the environment, which influences the likelihood that the individual will produce that response again; also called *instrumental response*. (pp. 130, 132)

**operation** Piaget's term for a reversible action that can be performed either in reality or mentally upon some object or set of objects. For example, rolling a clay ball into a clay sausage is an operation, because the sausage can be rolled back again to form the ball. (p. 436)

**opponent-process theory of color vision** Designed by Hering to explain the law of complementarity, this theory holds that units (neurons) that mediate the perception of color are excited by one range of wavelengths and inhibited by another (complementary) range of wavelengths. According to the theory, such units cancel out the perception of color when two complementary wavelength ranges are superimposed. See also *law of complementarity*. (p. 264)

**optic nerve** The cranial nerve that contains the sensory neurons for vision, which run from the eye's retina into the brain. (p. 254)

**ossicles** Three tiny bones (the hammer, anvil, and stirrup) in the middle ear, which vibrate in response to sound waves and stimulate the inner ear. (p. 247)

**outer ear** The pinna (the visible, external portion of the ear) and the auditory canal (the air-filled opening that extends inward from the pinna to the middle ear). (p. 246)

**outgroup** A group to which an individual does not belong or has the subjective sense of not belonging. For contrast, see *ingroup*. (p. 497)

**overjustification effect** The phenomenon in which a person who initially performs a task for no reward (except the enjoyment of the task) becomes less likely to perform that task for no reward after a period during which he or she has been rewarded for performing it. (p. 149)

---

**panic disorder** A mental disorder characterized by the repeated occurrence of panic attacks at unpredictable times and with no clear relationship to environmental events. Each attack involves an intense feeling of terror, which usually lasts several minutes and is accompanied by signs of high physiological arousal. (p. 618)

**parallel processing** In perception, the early (unconscious) steps in the analysis of sensory information that act simultaneously on all (or at least many) of the stimulus elements that are available at any given moment. For contrast, see *serial processing*. (p. 291)

**parasympathetic division of the autonomic motor system** The set of motor neurons that act upon visceral muscles and glands and mediate many of the body's regenerative, growth-promoting, and energy-conserving functions. For contrast, see *sympathetic division of the autonomic motor system*. (p. 174)

**parental investment** The time, energy, and risk to survival involved in producing, feeding, and otherwise caring for each offspring. (p. 105)

**parietal lobe** The lobe of the cerebral cortex that lies in front of the occipital lobe, above the temporal lobe, and behind the frontal lobe; it contains the somatosensory area of the brain. (p. 180)

**partial reinforcement** In operant conditioning, any condition in which the response sometimes produces a reinforcer and sometimes does not. See *reinforcer*. For contrast, see *continuous reinforcement*. (p. 135)

**percentile rank** For any single score in a set of scores, the percentage of scores in the set that are equal to or lower than that score. (p. A-5)

**perception** The recognition, organization, and meaningful interpretation of sensory stimuli. For contrast, see *sensation*. (pp. 239, 283)

**perceptual set** An expectation, established from prior experience, that leads a person to interpret an ambiguous stimulus in one way and not another. (p. 287)

**performance components** In Sternberg's information-processing model of intelligence, the mental components (processes) that act most directly on information when solving a problem or choosing a course of action. See also *metacomponents*. (p. 375)

**peripheral nervous system** The entire set of cranial and spinal nerves, which connect the central nervous system (brain and spinal cord) to the body's sensory organs, muscles, and glands. (p. 166)

**peripheral route to attitude construction** Any method for modifying or developing an attitude that does not entail logical analysis of the available information. For contrast, see *central route to attitude construction*. (p. 515)

**permanent effects of a drug** Irreversible forms of bodily damage, including brain damage, that result from drug use. (p. 625)

**permissive parents** In Baumrind's typology, parents whose discipline style is characterized by lack of discipline, even in the face of their children's disruptive actions or misbehavior. See also *authoritarian parents, authoritative parents*. (p. 461)

**person schema** The organized set of mental information that one has about a particular person, set of people, or people in general. See also *schema*. (p. 492)

**personality** The relatively consistent patterns of thought, feeling, and behavior that characterize each person as a unique individual. (p. 563)

**personality theory** A formal attempt to describe and explain the ways in which people differ from one another in their characteristic patterns of thought, feeling, and behavior. (p. 563)

**phenomenology** The study of subjective mental experiences; a theme of humanistic theories of personality. (p. 579)

**phenotype** The observable properties of an individual's body and behavior. See also *genotype*. (p. 48) *phobia* Any mental disorder characterized by a strong, irrational fear of some particular category of object or event. (p. 616)

*phonemes* The various vowel and consonant sounds that provide the basis for a spoken language. (pp. 396, 420)

*physiological psychology* The study of the physiological mechanisms, in the brain and elsewhere, that mediate behavior and psychological experiences. (p. 16)

*pictorial cues for depth perception* The depth cues that operate not only when viewing real scenes, but can also operate when viewing pictures. They include occlusion, relative image size for familiar objects, linear perspective, texture gradient, and (for outdoor scenes) position relative to the horizon. (p. 306)

*pidgin language* A primitive system of communication that emerges when people with different native languages colonize the same region; it uses words from the various native languages and has no or minimal grammatical structure. See also *creole language*. (p. 425)

*pitch* The quality of the psychological experience (sensation) of a sound that is most related to the frequency of the physical sound stimulus. (p. 246)

*pituitary gland* An endocrine gland that is located directly beneath the hypothalamus and is controlled by neural activity in that structure. Its hormones control the activity of many other endocrine glands, and for that reason it is sometimes called the "master endocrine gland." (p. 188)

*PKU* Abbreviation for *phenylketonuria*, a genetic disorder caused by a recessive gene and characterized by the body's inability to break down phenylalanine (an amino acid found in most protein-containing foods). (p. 56)

*placebo* In drug studies, an inactive substance given to subjects assigned to the nondrug group. (p. 38)

*placebo effect* In psychological research, any effect on a subject's behavior or feelings that stems from the subject's expectations as to how he or she should behave or feel as a result of a particular treatment. (pp. 38, 674)

*polyandry* A mating system in which one female bonds with more than one male. See *mating bond*. For contrast, see *monogamy*, *polygyny*. (p. 105)

*polygenic characteristic* Any trait or characteristic for which the observed variation is affected by many genes. (p. 61)

*polygyny* A mating system in which one male bonds with more than one female. See *mating bond*. For contrast, see *monogamy*, *polyandry*. (p. 105)

*pons* The portion of the brainstem bounded at its lower end by the medulla and its upper end by the midbrain, which is responsible, with the medulla, for organizing reflexes more complex than spinal reflexes. (p. 177)

*Ponzo illusion* A visual size illusion in which two converging lines cause objects between the two lines to look larger near the converging ends of the lines and smaller near the diverging ends. (p. 308)

*positive contrast effect* In operant conditioning, the increase in response rate, when the size of the reinforcer (or reward) is increased, to a rate that increases above that which occurs for subjects that had

been receiving the larger reinforcer all along. For contrast, see *negative contrast effect*. (p. 148)

*positive goal interdependence* A condition that engenders cooperation because the structure of rewards is such that each individual (or group) can best obtain a reward through actions that simultaneously help another individual (or group) obtain a reward. For contrast, see *negative goal interdependence*. (p. 554)

*positive reinforcement* In operant conditioning, the condition in which a response results in a positive reinforcer. (p. 140)

*positive reinforcer* In operant conditioning, a stimulus (such as food or money) that is presented after a response and that increases the likelihood that the response will recur. (p. 140)

*post-hypnotic amnesia* The inability, after awakening from hypnosis, to remember specific items of information that were presented during hypnosis; it occurs in response to the hypnotist's suggestion during hypnosis that the information will not be remembered. (p. 357)

*post-traumatic stress disorder* A mental disorder that is directly and explicitly tied to a particular traumatic incident or set of incidents (such as torture) that the affected person has experienced. (p. 619)

*power law* In psychophysics, Stevens's idea that the intensity of a sensation is directly proportional to the intensity of the physical stimulus raised by a constant power. For contrast, see *Fechner's law*. (p. 275)

*precipitating causes of a mental disorder* The events that most immediately bring on a mental disorder in a person who is sufficiently predisposed for the disorder. See also *maintaining* and *predisposing causes of a mental disorder*. (p. 609)

*predisposing causes of a mental disorder* Those conditions that are in place well before the onset of a mental disorder and that make the person susceptible to the disorder. They may include genetic predispositions, early childhood experiences, and the sociocultural environment in which one develops. See also *maintaining* and *precipitating causes of a mental disorder*. (p. 608)

*preoperational stage* In Piaget's theory of cognitive development, the second stage (from about 2 to 6 years of age), in which the child can appreciate the stable, identifying features of objects and think about them when they are absent, but lacks the ability to think logically about reversible actions (operations) that can be performed on objects. See also *operations*. (p. 435)

*primacy effect* In list-learning experiments, the greater ability to recall items from the beginning of the list (those that were rehearsed first) than other items in the list. See also *recency effect*. (p. 333) In person perception, the tendency for information received early to carry more weight than information received later in one's final assessment of a person. (p. 495)

*primary process* In Freud's psychoanalytic theory, the kind of thinking that characterizes the id, in which reality and fantasy are not differentiated and the goal is to seek pleasure through the most direct routes. For contrast, see *secondary process*. (p. 567)

*primary reinforcer* In operant conditioning, a stimulus, such as food or water, that is innately reinforcing; also called an *unconditioned reinforcer*. See *reinforcer*. For contrast, see *secondary reinforcer*. (p. 139)

**primary sensory areas** Specialized areas of the cerebral cortex that receive input from sensory nerves and tracts by way of the relay nuclei in the thalamus. They include the visual area (in the occipital lobe), auditory area (in the temporal lobe), and somatosensory area (in the parietal lobe). (pp. 8, 181, 242)

**prisoner's-dilemma games** A class of laboratory game in which the tendency to compete can be pitted against the tendency to cooperate. In such games, the highest combined payoff to the two players occurs if both choose the cooperative response, but the highest individual payoff goes to a player who chooses the competitive response on a play in which the other chooses the cooperative response. (p. 556)

**proactive interference** The loss of memory for one set of information that results from the prior learning of another (usually similar) set of information. For contrast, see *retroactive interference*. (p. 350)

**procedural information** The class of information stored in memory that enables a person to perform specific learned skills or habitual responses. For contrast, see *episodic information, semantic information*. (p. 327)

**projection** The defense mechanism by which a person consciously experiences his or her own unconscious emotion or wish as though it belongs to someone else or to some part of the environment. (p. 570)

**projective tests** Psychological tests involving free association, in which the person being tested is presented with an ambiguous stimulus and is asked to say quickly, without logical explanation, what the stimulus looks like or what ideas it brings to mind. See also *free association, projection*. (pp. 573, 651)

**promiscuity** A mating system in which mating bonds are not formed and individuals of either sex may copulate with many different individuals over a short period of time. See *mating bond*. For contrast, see *monogamy, polyandry, polygyny*. (p. 105)

**propositions** The smallest, separate, meaningful units of information that are stored in memory. (p. 342)

**propositional theory of visual memory** The theory that memories for visual scenes are stored in essentially the same way as verbal memories are stored, as sets of discrete units of information (propositions). For contrast, see *analogue theory of visual memory*. (p. 342)

**prototype theory of schemas** The theory that a schema (the mental representation of a concept) is best characterized as a holistic, picturelike representation of a typical or average member of the category of object or event that the schema represents. For contrast, see *feature theory of schemas*. (p. 344)

**proximate explanations** Explanations of behavior that state the immediate environmental conditions or the mechanisms within the individual that cause the behavior to occur. For contrast, see *ultimate explanations*. (p. 86)

**proximity principle** See *Gestalt principles of grouping*.

**psychiatrist** A mental health professional who has a medical degree, obtained through standard medical-school training, followed by special training and residency in psychiatry. A psychiatrist may conduct psychotherapy and prescribe drugs. For contrast, see *clinical psychologist*. (p. 648)

**psychoactive substance-use disorder** The class of mental disorders characterized by drug abuse or dependence. (p. 624)

**psychoanalysis** 1. The theory of personality developed by Freud that emphasizes the roles of unconscious mental processes, early childhood experiences, and the drives of sex and aggression in personality formation; also called *psychoanalytic theory*. (pp. 12, 564) 2. Freud's therapy technique in which such methods as free association, dream analysis, and analysis of transference are used to learn about the person's unconscious mind; the goal is to make the unconscious conscious. (pp. 607, 653)

**psychodynamic theory of personality** Any theory that describes personality and its development in terms of inner mental forces that are often in conflict with one another and are shaped by experiences in early childhood. (p. 564)

**psychodynamic therapy** Any approach to psychotherapy that is based on the premise that psychological problems are manifestations of inner mental conflicts and that conscious awareness of those conflicts is a key to recovery. See also *psychoanalysis*. (p. 653)

**psychological reactance** The tendency to react against perceived restrictions on one's own freedom and to value more highly an object or form of behavior when threatened with the possible inability to obtain that object or to engage in that behavior. (p. 534)

**psychology** The science of behavior and the mind. (p. 3)

**psychometric personality test** An objective questionnaire that has been developed through systematic, statistically based methods (usually involving factor analysis) to assess a wide range of personality characteristics. See *MMPI-2*. (p. 650)

**psychometrics** The systematic measurement of psychological differences among people and the statistical analysis of those measures as a way of learning about the structure of the human mind. (p. 366)

**psychophysics** The scientific study of the relationship between physical characteristics of stimuli and the psychological (sensory) experiences that the stimuli produce. (pp. 241, 270)

**psychosexual stages** In Freud's psychoanalytic theory, the life stages—oral, anal, phallic, latency, and genital—through which personality is formed and expressed; in each stage, sexual energy centers around a different purpose. (p. 570)

**psychosis** In diagnostic symptoms based on psychoanalytic theory, any mental disorder involving marked distortions in perception or thought, such that the person is in important ways out of touch with reality. For contrast, see *neurosis*. (p. 610)

**psychotherapy** Any formal, theory-based, systematic treatment for mental problems or disorders that uses psychological means (such as dialogue or training) rather than physiological means (such as drugs) and is conducted by a trained therapist. (p. 652)

**psychotic symptom** Any symptom of possible mental disorder that entails gross distortions in perception or thought. For contrast, see *neurotic symptom*. (p. 610)

**punishment** In operant conditioning, the process through which the consequence of a response *decreases* the likelihood that the response will recur. For contrast, see *reinforcement*. (p. 141)

**questionnaire** A self-report method of data collection or clinical assessment method in which the individual being studied (or assessed) checks off items on a printed list, answers multiple-choice questions, or writes out answers to essay questions aimed at producing a self-description. (p. 31)

***

*rational-emotive therapy* A type of cognitive therapy developed by Albert Ellis, based on the idea that people's irrational interpretations of their experiences, not the experiences themselves, cause their negative emotions. (p. 662)

*rationalization* The defense mechanism by which a person uses conscious reasoning to justify or explain away his or her harmful or irrational behaviors or thoughts. (p. 570)

*reaction formation* The defense mechanism by which the mind turns a frightening wish into its safer opposite. (p. 569)

*recency effect* In list-learning experiments, the greater ability to recall items from the end of the list (those most recently rehearsed) than other items in the list. See also *primacy effect*. (p. 333)

*receptive field* For any neuron in the visual system, that portion of the retina that, when stimulated by light, results in a change in electrical activity in the neuron. More generally, a property of a neuron in any sensory system; it is the area of sensory tissue (or set of receptor cells) that, when stimulated by an appropriate stimulus, produces an electrical change in the neuron in question. (p. 255)

*receptor potential* The electrical change that occurs in a receptor cell (such as a rod or cone in the eye, or a hair cell in the inner ear) in response to the energy of a physical stimulus (such as light or sound). (p. 243)

*receptors* Specialized biological structures—which in some cases are separate cells and in other cases are the sensitive tips of sensory neurons—that respond to physical stimuli by producing electrical changes that can initiate neural impulses. (p. 242)

*recessive gene* A gene that will produce its observable effects only in the homozygous condition, that is, only when paired with a gene that is identical to it. (p. 52)

*reciprocity norm* The widespread sense of obligation that people have to return favors. (p. 533)

*reciprocity theory of altruism* The sociobiological theory that apparent acts of altruism have come about through natural selection because they are actually forms of long-term cooperation rather than true altruism. See also *altruism, cooperation*. (p. 113)

*red-green color blindness* Color blindness that is characterized by difficulty in distinguishing among the colors of the spectrum ranging from green through red; it is caused by the lack of one of the two cone types that are maximally sensitive to light in the long-wavelength end of the spectrum. (p. 263)

*reference group* A group of people with whom an individual compares himself or herself for the purpose of self-evaluation. See also *social comparison*. (p. 504)

*reflex* A simple, relatively automatic, stimulus-response sequence mediated by the nervous system. See *response, stimulus*. (pp. 6, 122, 176)

*reflexology* An approach to understanding human behavior, developed by physiologists in the nineteenth century, that was based on the premise that all behavior occurs through reflexes. (p. 6)

*regulatory drive* Any motivational state (such as hunger or thirst) that helps maintain some constancy of the body's internal environment that is necessary for survival. For contrast, see *nonregulatory drive*. (p. 200)

*reinforcement* 1. In classical conditioning, the pairing of a conditioned stimulus with an unconditioned stimulus, which increases the strength of the conditioned reflex on future trials. See *classical conditioning* (p. 127) 2. In operant conditioning, the presentation of a positive reinforcer or removal of a negative reinforcer when a response occurs, which increases the likelihood that the subject will repeat the response. See *negative reinforcer, positive reinforcer*. For contrast, see *punishment*. (p. 140)

*reinforcer* In operant conditioning, any stimulus change that occurs after a response and tends to *increase* the likelihood that the response will be repeated. See *negative reinforcer, positive reinforcer*. (p. 133)

*reliability* The capacity of a measurement system to produce similar results each time it is used with a particular subject or set of subjects under a particular set of conditions. (pp. 36, 368, 609)

*REM (rapid eye movement) sleep* The recurring stage of sleep during which the EEG resembles that of an alert person, rapid eye movements occur, the large muscles of the body are most relaxed, and true dreams are most likely to occur. It is sometimes called *emergent stage 1*. For contrast, see *slow-wave sleep*. (p. 219)

*repression* The defense mechanism by which the mind prevents anxiety-provoking ideas from becoming conscious. (p. 569)

*research hypothesis* The guess, or inference, that a researcher attempts to test in a scientific study. (p. 35)

*resistance* In psychotherapy, the client's conscious or unconscious attempts to block the course of therapy. Psychodynamic therapists interpret it as a defense against the anxiety that accompanies the discovery of previously unconscious memories or wishes in the course of therapy. (p. 656)

*response* Any well-defined behavioral action, especially one that is elicited by some form of environmental stimulation or provocation. (pp. 14, 122)

*resting potential* The constant electrical charge that exists across the membrane of an inactive neuron. (p. 168)

*retina* A thin membrane of cells that lines the rear interior of the eyeball; it contains the receptor cells for vision (rods and cones). (p. 252)

*retrieval* In the modal model of the mind, the mental process by which long-term memories are brought into the short-term (working) memory store where they become part of the flow of thought. See also *long-term memory, short-term memory*. (p. 326)

*retroactive interference* The loss of memory for one set of information that results from the subsequent learning of another (usually similar) set of information. For contrast, see *proactive interference*. (p. 350)

*reversible figure* A visual stimulus (usually a picture) in which any given part is seen sometimes as the *figure* and other times as the *ground*. (p. 287)

*rhodopsin* The photochemical in rods that undergoes structural changes in response to light and thereby initiates the transduction process for rod vision. (p. 252)

**rhythm generator** A neuron in the central nervous system that undergoes a continuous, repeating cycle of change in its electrical activity, controlled by chemical processes built into the neuron itself, and in that way helps control rhythmic behavioral or physiological processes. (p. 172)

**ritualization** An evolutionary process by which behaviors that originally served some noncommunicative function are modified so that they serve primarily a communicative role. (p. 97)

**rods** The class of receptor cells for vision that are located in the peripheral portions of the retina (away from the fovea) and are most important for seeing in very dim light. For contrast, see *cones*. (p. 252)

**rod vision** The low-acuity, high-sensitivity, noncolor vision that occurs in dim light and is mediated by rods in the retina of the eye. For contrast, see *cone vision*. (p. 254)

**rote rehearsal** The memorizing process in which items of information are repeated (either aloud of subvocally) to keep them in short-term memory or encode them into long-term memory. For contrast, see *elaborative rehearsal*. (p. 331)

---

**schema** The mental representation of a concept; the information stored in long-term memory that allows a person to identify a group of different events or items as members of the same category. (p. 344)

**schemes** Piaget's term for the mental entities that provide the basis for thought and that change in a stagelike way through development. They contain information about the actions that one can produce on objects, either in reality or symbolically in the mind. (p. 418)

**schizophrenia** A serious class of mental disorder that is characterized by disrupted perceptual and thought processes, often including hallucinations and delusions. (pp. 73, 633)

**science** An approach to answering questions that is based on the systematic collection and logical analysis of objectively observable data. (p. 3)

**script** A variety of schema that represents in memory the temporal organization of a category of event (such as the sequence of occurrences at a typical birthday party). (p. 345)

**secondary process** In Freud's psychoanalytic theory, the kind of thinking that characterizes the ego, which involves the person's logical thought and understanding of reality. For contrast, see *primary process*. (p. 567)

**secondary reinforcer** In operant conditioning, a stimulus that has acquired reinforcing capacity through previous training, usually through serving as a discriminative stimulus for some other reinforced response. See *reinforcer*. For contrast, see *primary reinforcer*. (p. 139)

**secondary sensory areas** Specialized areas of the cerebral cortex, each of which receives input from a single primary sensory area and presumably contains neural mechanisms that analyze that input and help extract useful information from it. See also *primary sensory areas*. (p. 181)

**selective breeding** The mating of those members of a strain of animals or plants that manifest a particular characteristic, which may or may not be done deliberately to affect the genetic makeup of fu-

ture generations of that strain; can be used to assess *heritability*. (p. 64)

**self-concept** One's entire set of beliefs about oneself. (p. 503)

**self-efficacy** A person's subjective sense of his or her own ability to perform a particular task or set of tasks. (p. 588)

**self-handicapping** An impression-management strategy in which a person gives himself or herself an obvious handicap in a task in order to provide an excuse for anticipated poor performance. (p. 507)

**self-monitoring** A personality characteristic defined as sensitivity to other people's immediate reactions to oneself, combined with a desire and ability to control those reactions. (p. 509)

**self-report method** A data-collection method in which the people being studied are asked to rate or describe their own behaviors or mental states. See also *interview, questionnaire*. (p. 31)

**self-serving bias** The tendency for people to attribute their successes to their own inner characteristics and their failures to external circumstances beyond their control. See also *attribution*. (p. 501)

**semantic information** The class of information stored in memory that represents the person's general knowledge of the world. For contrast, see *episodic information, procedural information*. (p. 327)

**sensation** The psychological experience associated with a sound, light, or other simple stimulus, and the initial information-processing steps by which sense organs and neural pathways take in stimulus information from the environment. For contrast, see *perception*. (p. 239)

**sensitivity** The capacity of a measurement system to detect fine differences among individuals in the characteristic being measured. (p. 36)

**sensorimotor stage** In Piaget's theory of cognitive development, the first stage (birth to about 2 years old), in which the child lacks well-developed mental symbols, so thought is limited primarily to the child's actual actions on objects and the sensory feedback that comes from those actions. (pp. 417, 435)

**sensorineural deafness** Deafness due to damage to the cochlea, the hair cells, or the auditory neurons. (p. 248)

**sensory adaptation** The temporary decrease in sensitivity to sensory stimulation that occurs when a sensory system is stimulated for a period of time, and the temporary increase in sensitivity that occurs when a sensory system is not stimulated for a period of time. See also *dark adaptation, light adaptation*. (p. 244)

**sensory areas of the cerebral cortex** See *primary sensory areas, secondary sensory areas*.

**sensory memory** In the modal model of the mind, the memory trace that preserves the original information in a sensory stimulus for a brief period (less than 1 second for sights and up to 3 seconds for sounds) following the termination of the stimulus; it is experienced as if one is still sensing the original stimulus. For contrasts, see *long-term memory, short-term memory*. (p. 324)

**sensory neuron** A neuron that carries messages from a sensory organ, through a nerve, into the brain or spinal cord. (pp. 167, 242)

**sensory physiological psychology** The scientific study of the relationship between physiological responses in sensory organs and the nervous system and the psychological (sensory) experiences that accompany those responses. (p. 241)

**sensory physiology** The scientific study of the relationship between environmental stimuli and the physiological responses they produce in sensory organs and the nervous system. (p. 241)

**sensory store** The first memory store in the modal model of the mind; the hypothetical place in the mind where information is retained in its original sensory form for a very brief period; also called the *preattentive store*. (p. 324)

**serial processing** The steps in the processing of sensory information that operate sequentially, an item at a time, on the available sensory information. For contrast, see *parallel processing*. (p. 291)

**sex chromosomes** Those chromosomes that provide the genetic basis for the difference between males and females of the species. See also *X chromosome, Y chromosome*. For contrast, see *autosomes*. (p. 49)

**sex-linked disorder** Any genetic disorder caused by a recessive gene located on the X chromosome; they are more likely to occur in men than in women. (p. 57)

**shaping** An operant-conditioning procedure in which successively closer approximations to the desired response are reinforced until the response finally occurs. See *reinforcement*. (p. 135)

**short-term memory** In the modal model of the mind, information that is retained in the mind as long as conscious thought is devoted to it, but which then fades relatively quickly (in a matter of seconds); also called *working memory*. For contrast, see *sensory memory, long-term memory*. (p. 325)

**short-term store** The second memory store in the modal model of the mind; the hypothetical place in the mind that retains information to which conscious attention is being devoted. (p. 325)

**sign stimulus** Ethologists' term for any stimulus (well-defined environmental event) that elicits a fixed action pattern. See *fixed action pattern*. (p. 89)

**similarity principle** See *Gestalt principles of grouping*.

**simple phobia** Any phobia in which the feared object is a well-defined category of object (such as snakes) or environmental situation (such as heights) *other than* other people. See also *phobia*. For contrast, see *social phobia*. (p. 616)

**size constancy** The perceptual ability to see an object as the same size despite change in image size as it moves farther away or closer. (p. 307)

**skeletal motor system** The set of motor neurons that act upon skeletal muscles. (p. 173)

**skeletal muscles** The muscles attached to bones, which produce externally observable movements of the body when contracted. For contrast, see *visceral muscles*. (p. 173)

**sleep thought** A mental experience during sleep that lacks the vivid sensory and motor hallucinations of a *true dream* and is typically experienced as similar to daytime thought. (p. 224)

**slow-wave sleep** Stages 2, 3, and 4 of sleep characterized by the prominent occurrence of slow (delta) waves in the EEG. For contrast, see *REM (rapid eye movement) sleep*. (p. 219)

**social clock** A culture's set of expectations concerning the appropriate activities of people at various ages or life stages, which in turn affect the life course of people within that culture. (p. 453)

**social cognition** The mental processes that are involved in people's perceptions of, and reactions to, other people and the social environment; also the study of those mental processes. (p. 491)

**social comparison** Any process in which an individual evaluates his or her own abilities, characteristics, ideas, or achievements by comparing them with those of other people. See also *reference group*. (p. 504)

**social development** The person's developing capacity for social relationships and the effects of those relationships on further development. (p. 449)

**social ecology** The entire network of other people, economic conditions, cultural institutions, and other social or cultural influences that can affect a person's behavior and development. (p. 452)

**social facilitation** The tendency to perform a task better in front of others than alone. For contrast, see *social inhibition*. (p. 540)

**social impact** Any change in a person's physiological condition that stems from the actual or imagined presence of one or more other individuals. (p. 528)

**social impact theory** Latané's social psychological theory concerning the amount of social impact that the actual or imagined presence of others will have on a person. (p. 528)

**social inhibition** The tendency to perform a task worse in front of others than alone. For contrast, see *social facilitation*. (p. 541)

**social learning theories of personality** Laboratory-based personality theories claiming that personality characteristics (a) are learned through interaction with the social environment; (b) are best understood as cognitive constructs (such as goals and expectancies); and (c) are relatively specific to the environmental situations in which they were learned, such that personality can change as one goes from one environment to another. Also called *cognitive theories* or *cognitive social learning theories*. (p. 585)

**social loafing** The reduction in effort expended on a task by a person when working with others compared to the effort that the same person would expend on the task when working alone. (p. 542)

**social phobia** Any phobia in which the basic fear is of being scrutinized or evaluated by other people. For contrast, see *simple phobia*. (p. 616)

**social psychology** The branch of psychology that attempts to understand how the behavior and subjective experiences of individuals are influenced by the actual or imagined presence of other people. (p. 491)

**social role** Any role or position in one's social network (such as the role of mother, employer, or student) that is associated with a set of expectations as to how a person in that role or position should behave. (p. 503)

**social skills training** In behavior therapy, a direct method for training people to interact more effectively with other people. See also *assertiveness training*. (p. 671)

**sociobiology** The study of social systems in animals from an evolutionary perspective. (p. 104)

**sociocultural approach (or perspective)** The general approach to psychological research and theory that emphasizes the role of culture and social interactions in the development and manifestation of behavioral or psychological characteristics. (pp. 443, 607)

**somatoform disorders** The class of mental disorders in which the person experiences bodily ailments in the absence of any physical disease that could cause them. It includes *conversion disorder*, *somatoform pain disorder*, and *somatization disorder*. (p. 620)

**somatosensation** The set of senses that derive from the whole body, such as from the skin, muscles, and tendons, as opposed to those senses that come from the special sensory organs of the head. (p. 173)

**source traits** In trait theories of personality, the relatively small set of basic traits (personality characteristics) that are inferred from statistical intercorrelations among various surface traits. See also *surface traits*, *trait*. (p. 591)

**span of short-term memory** The number of items of information (such as single, randomly chosen digits) that a person can retain in short-term memory at any given time through rote rehearsal; also called *memory span*. (p. 332)

**species-specific behavior** Any behavior pattern that is so characteristic of a given species of animal that it can be used to help identify that species. (p. 89)

**spinal nerve** A nerve that extends directly from the spinal cord. See *nerve*. For contrast, see *cranial nerve*. (p. 173)

**spinal reflex** A reflex that is organized by neurons within the spinal cord, and that therefore can be elicited even if the spinal cord is no longer connected to the brain. (p. 176)

**spontaneous recovery** In both classical and operant conditioning, the return—due to passage of time with no further testing or training—of a conditioned response that had previously undergone extinction. (p. 127)

**spoonerisms** Speech errors in which two elements of a sentence (phonemes, syllables, or morphemes) are accidentally interchanged in position. (p. 398)

**stage theories of development** In developmental psychology, theories that maintain that psychological development is discontinuous, with plateaus (periods of relative stability) separated by periods of rapid change. For contrast, see *continuous theories of development*. (p. 413)

**standard deviation** A measure of the variability in a set of scores, determined by taking the square root of the variance. (pp. 33, A-5)

**standardized score** A score that is expressed in terms of the number of standard deviations the original score is from the mean of the original scores. (p. A-6)

**state-dependent memory** The improved ability to retrieve information from memory that occurs when a person is in the same physiological condition (such as that induced by a drug) that he or she was in when the memory was originally encoded. (p. 353)

**statistical significance** A statistical statement of how small the likelihood is that an obtained result occurred by chance. By convention, research findings are said to be *statistically significant* if the probability is less than 5 percent that the data could have come out as they did if the research hypothesis were wrong. (p. 35)

**stereotypes** Mental concepts that people have for particular groups of people (such as races or ethnic groups) that exaggerate the differences between groups, minimize the differences among individual members of the same group, and may provide a basis for prejudice and discrimination. (p. 496)

**stimulus** A well-defined element of the environment that can potentially act on an individual's nervous system and thereby influence the individual's behavior. (pp. 14, 122)

**strange-situation test** A test of an infant's attachment to a particular familiar person, in which the infant's behavior is observed in an unfamiliar room while the familiar person and a stranger move in and out of the room in a preplanned way. (p. 457)

**stress** The process or set of processes through which some stimulus or change in the environment (the stressor) can produce long-term physiological or psychological debilitation in an individual. (p. 228)

**stress-induced analgesia** The reduced sensitivity to pain that occurs when one is subjected to highly arousing (stressful) conditions. (p. 269)

**Stroop interference effect** Named after J. Ridley Stroop, the effect by which a printed color word (such as the word *red*) interferes with a person's ability to name the color of ink in which the word is printed, if the ink color is not the color named by the word. (p. 300)

**structuralism** A school of psychological thought, founded principally by Titchener, whose goal was to identify the basic elements of the mind and to determine how those elements combine with one another to produce more complex thoughts. For contrast, see *functionalism*. (p. 9)

**sublimation** See *displacement*.

**subtractive color mixing** The mixing of pigments whereby each pigment absorbs a different set of wavelengths of light that would otherwise be reflected to the eye. For contrast, see *additive color mixing*. (p. 260)

**superego** In Freud's three-part division of the mind, the source of morality and guilt. See also *ego*, *id*. (p. 567)

**surface structure** In Chomsky's theory of language, the specific wording of an uttered or written sentence. For contrast, see *deep structure*. (p. 397)

**surface traits** Traits (personality characteristics) that are most directly inferred from a person's external behavior. See also *source traits*. (p. 591)

**syllogism** A type of deductive-reasoning problem that contains a major and a minor premise, from which the reasoner must test the truth, falsity, or indeterminacy of a specific conclusion. (p. 386)

**sympathetic division of the autonomic motor system** The set of motor neurons that act upon visceral muscles and glands and mediate many of the body's responses to stressful stimulation, preparing the body for possible "fight or flight." For contrast, see *parasympathetic division of the autonomic motor system*. (p. 174)

**symptom** In clinical psychology or psychiatry, any characteristic of a person's actions, thoughts, or feelings that could be a potential indicator of a mental disorder. (p. 605)

**synapse** The functional connection through which neural activity in the axon of one neuron influences the action of another neuron, a muscle cell, or a glandular cell, and the structures most directly associated with that connection. (p. 170)

**syndrome** In clinical psychology or psychiatry, the entire pattern of symptoms manifested in an individual's behavior and self-statements, which, collectively, may constitute evidence of a mental disorder. (p. 605)

*syntax* The set of grammatical rules for a given language that specify how words can be arranged to produce phrases and sentences. (p. 396)

*systematic desensitization* A behavior therapy technique for eliminating phobias or fears, in which the client is first trained to relax and then to imagine various versions of the feared object or scene, progressing from weak to stronger forms of it, while remaining relaxed. (p. 668)

*temporal lobe* The lobe of the cerebral cortex that lies in front of the occipital lobe and below the parietal and frontal lobes, which contains the auditory area of the brain. (p. 180)

*temporal lobe amnesia* The loss in memory abilities that occurs as a result of damage to structures in the limbic system that lie under the temporal lobe of the cerebral cortex. (p. 358)

*test* A stimulus or problem, or set of these, that a researcher or clinician presents to a subject or client for the purpose of collecting information about that individual's behavioral or psychological state or capacities. (p. 31)

*thalamus* the brain structure that sits directly atop the brainstem; it functions as a sensory relay station, connecting incoming sensory tracts to special sensory areas of the cerebral cortex. (p. 178)

*three-primaries law* The observation that one can choose three limited-wavelength lights (called *primaries*) and, by mixing them in differing proportions, match any color that the human eye can see. See also *additive color mixing*. (p. 261)

*token* In operant conditioning, a secondary reinforcer (such as money) that can be saved and turned in later for another reinforcer. See *secondary reinforcer*. (p. 139)

*token economy* An exchange system, adapted for use in a mental hospital or other institution, in which tokens are awarded for behaving in specific ways deemed desirable and the tokens can in turn be exchanged for goods or privileges. (p. 670)

*tolerance* See *drug tolerance*.

*top-down processes* In theories of perception, mental processes that bring preexisting knowledge or expectations about an object or scene to bear upon the perception of that object or scene. For contrast, see *bottom-up processes*. (p. 284)

*tract* A bundle of neural axons coursing together within the central nervous system; analogous to a *nerve* in the peripheral nervous system. (p. 175)

*trait* A hypothetical, relatively stable, inner characteristic that influences the way a person responds to various environmental situations. (p. 590)

*trait theories of personality* Theories of personality that are based on the idea that people can be described and differentiated in terms of hypothetical underlying personality dimensions, called *traits*, which can be measured by questionnaires or other quantitative means. (p. 590)

*transduction* The process by which a receptor cell (such as a rod or cone in the eye, or a hair cell in the inner ear) produces an electrical change in response to the energy of a physical stimulus (such as light or sound). (p. 242)

*transference* In psychotherapy (especially psychoanalysis), the phenomenon by which a client's unconscious feelings about a significant person in his or her life are experienced consciously as feelings about the therapist. (p. 656)

*transmitter* See *neurotransmitter*.

*trichromatic theory of color vision* Proposed independently by Young and Helmholtz to explain the three-primaries law of color vision, this theory holds that the human ability to perceive color is mediated by three different types of receptors, each of which is most sensitive to a different range of wavelengths. See also *three-primaries law*. (p. 262)

*true dream* A mental experience during sleep in which the person has the feeling of actually seeing or in other ways sensing various scenes and objects, and of actually moving and behaving in the dream environment. For contrast, see *sleep thought*. (p. 223)

*twin method* A method for studying the heritability of a characteristic, in which the similarity between identical twins is compared with that between fraternal twins. See *heritability*. (p. 68)

*Type A behavior* A pattern of behavior that is characteristic of people who are unusually impatient, tense, and easily riled by environmental disruptions. (p. 229)

*Type B behavior* A pattern of behavior that is characteristic of people who are relatively patient, relaxed, and not easily riled by environmental disruptions. (p. 229)

*Type I schizophrenia* The category of schizophrenia characterized principally by *positive symptoms* (excesses in perception, thought, and action) such as hallucinations, delusions, bizarre associations, and bizarre actions; also called *positive-symptom schizophrenia*. (p. 636)

*Type II schizophrenia* The category of schizophrenia characterized principally by *negative symptoms* (poverty of perception, thought, and action) such as flattened affect, slow and labored speech, reduced drive, and slow movements; also called *negative-symptom schizophrenia*. (p. 636)

*ultimate explanations* Explanations of behavior that state the role that the behavior plays or once played in survival and reproduction, that is, explanations of why the potential for the behavior was favored by natural selection. For contrast, see *proximate explanations*. (p. 86)

*unconditioned reflex* A reflex that does not depend upon previous conditions in the individual's experience; an unlearned reflex. For contrast, see *conditioned reflex*. (p. 124)

*unconditioned response* A reflexive response that does not depend upon previous conditioning, or learning. For contrast, see *conditioned response*. (p. 124)

*unconditioned stimulus* A stimulus that elicits a reflexive response without any previous training, or conditioning. For contrast, see *conditioned stimulus*. (p. 124)

*unconscious-inference theory of perception* The theory that perception is the end result of unconscious reasoning processes in which the mind uses sensory information as cues to infer the characteristics of objects or scenes that are being perceived. For contrast, see *direct-perception theory*. (pp. 303, 314)

**unresponsive-bystander phenomenon** The tendency for bystanders not to help the victim of an emergency if other bystanders are present. (p. 543)

**validity** The degree to which a measurement system actually measures the characteristic that it is supposed to measure. (pp. 37, 370)

**variable-interval (VI) schedule** In operant conditioning, a schedule of reinforcement in which an unpredictable amount of time, varying around some average, must elapse between the receipt of one reinforcer and the availability of another. (p. 137)

**variable-ratio (VR) schedule** In operant conditioning, a schedule of reinforcement in which the response must be emitted a certain *average* number of times before a reinforcer will appear, but the number needed on any given instance varies randomly around that average. (p. 136)

**variance** A measure of the variability of a set of scores, determined by obtaining the difference (deviation) between each score and the mean, squaring each deviation, and calculating the mean of the squared deviations. (p. A-4)

**vestigial characteristics** Inherited characteristics of anatomy or behavior that are no longer useful to the species, but were presumably useful at an earlier time in evolution. (p. 96)

**visceral muscles** Internal muscles, such as those of the heart, arteries, and gastrointestinal tract. For contrast, see *skeletal muscles*. (p. 173)

**visual constancies** Those characteristics of objects or scenes that remain constant in our visual perception of them despite changes in the retinal image. They include size constancy, shape constancy, and position constancy. (p. 316)

**wavelength** The physical length of one complete cycle of a wave; for light, this physical measure is related to the psychological (sensory) experience of color. (p. 251)

**Weber's fraction** In Weber's law, the proportionality constant that relates the difference threshold to the magnitude of the original stimulus. (p. 237)

**Weber's law** The idea that, within a given sensory modality (such as vision), the difference threshold (amount that the stimulus must be changed in magnitude to be perceived as different) is a constant proportion of the magnitude of the original stimulus. (p. 273)

**Wernicke's aphasia** A specific syndrome of loss of language ability that occurs due to damage in a particular part of the brain called *Wernicke's area*. Speech in a person with this disorder typically retains its grammatical structure, but loses its meaning due to the speaker's failure to provide meaningful content words (nouns, verbs, adjectives, and adverbs). For contrast, see *Broca's aphasia*. (p. 400)

**Wernicke's area** A specific area in the frontal lobe of the human cerebral cortex (usually in the left hemisphere) that is involved in language; brain damage there produces Wernicke's aphasia. (p. 400)

**withdrawal symptoms** The physiological, mental, and behavioral disturbances that can occur when a long-term user of a drug stops taking the drug. (pp. 190, 625)

**working memory** See *short-term memory*.

**X chromosome** The human sex chromosome that normally exists in duplicate in the female and in single (unpaired) fashion in the male. See also *sex chromosomes*. (p. 49)

**Y chromosome** The human sex chromosome that normally exists in single (unpaired) fashion in the male and is absent in the female. See also *sex chromosomes*. (p. 49)

**Yerkes-Dodson law** The idea that the optimal degree of arousal for performing a task depends on the nature of the task. High arousal is best for easy tasks and low arousal is best for difficult tasks. (p. 228)

**z score** The simplest form of a standardized score; it is the score minus the mean divided by the standard deviation. (p. A-6)

**zygote** The single cell that is formed when an egg and sperm cell unite; the first, single-cell form of a newly developing individual. (p. 50)

# REFERENCES

**Abramson, L. Y., Alloy, L. B., & Metalsky, G. I.** (1988). The cognitive diathesis-stress theories of depression: Toward an adequate evaluation of the theories' validities. In L. B. Alloy (Ed.), *Cognitive processes in depression*. New York: Guilford. (p. 630)

**Adams, D. B., Gold, A. R., & Burt, A. D.** (1978). Rise in female-initiated sexual activity at ovulation and its suppression by oral contraceptives. *The New England Journal of Medicine, 299*, 1145–1150. (p. 211)

**Adamson, R. E.** (1952). Functional fixedness as related to problem solving. *Journal of Experimental Psychology, 44*, 288–291. (p. 391)

**Adelson, J.** (1986). *Inventing adolescence: The political psychology of everyday schooling*. New Brunswick, NJ: Transaction. (p. 470)

**Adelson, J., & Hall, E.** (1987). Children and other political naïfs. In E. Hall (Ed.), *Growing and changing*. New York: Random House. (p. 481)

**Adkins-Regan, E.** (1981). Early organizational effects of hormones: An evolutionary perspective. In N. T. Adler (Ed.), *Neuroendocrinology of reproduction*. New York: Plenum. (p. 209)

**Adler, A.** (1930). Individual psychology. In C. Murchison (Ed.), *Psychologies of 1930*. Worcester, MA: Clark University Press. (p. 577)

**Agras, S., Sylvester, D., & Oliveau, D.** (1969). The epidemiology of common fears and phobias. *Comprehensive Psychiatry, 10*, 151–156. (p. 617)

**Aiken, L. R.** (1987). *Assessment of intellectual functioning*. Boston: Allyn & Bacon. (p. 368)

**Ainsworth, M. D. S.** (1979). Attachment as related to mother-infant interaction. *Advances in the Study of Behaviour, 9*, 2–52. (p. 458)

**Ainsworth, M. D. S.** (1982). Attachment: Retrospect and prospect. In C. M. Parkes & J. Sevenson-Hinde (Eds.), *The place of attachment in human behavior*. New York: Basic Books. (p. 458)

**Ainsworth, M. D. S., Blehar, M. C., Waters, E., & Wall, S.** (1978). *Patterns of attachment: A psychological study of the strange situation*. Hillsdale, NJ: Erlbaum. (p. 457)

**Ajzen, I.** (1985). From intentions to actions: A theory of planned behavior. In J. Kuhl & J. Beckmann (Eds.), *Action control: From cognition to behavior*. Heidelberg: Springer. (p. 521)

**Ajzen, I.** (1987). Attitudes, traits, and actions: Dispositional prediction of behavior in personality and social psychology. In L. Berkowitz (Ed.), *Advances in experimental social psychology* (Vol. 20). New York: Academic Press. (p. 521)

**Ajzen, I., & Fishbein, M.** (1980). *Understanding attitudes and predicting social behavior*. Englewood Cliffs, NJ: Prentice Hall. (p. 522)

**Akerstedt, T., & Fröberg, J. E.** (1977). Psychophysiological circadian rhythms in women during 72 hours of sleep deprivation. *Waking and Sleeping, 1*, 387–394. (p. 223)

**Alexander, R. D.** (1987). *The biology of moral systems*. New York: Aldine de Gruyter. (p. 114)

**Allison, T., & Cicchetti, D. V.** (1976). Sleep in mammals: Ecological and constitutional correlates. *Science, 194*, 732–734. (p. 220)

**Allport, D. A., Antonis, B., & Reynolds, P.** (1972). On the division of attention: A disproof of the single channel hypothesis. *Quarterly Journal of Experimental Psychology, 24*, 225–235. (p. 298)

**Allport, F. H.** (1920). The influence of the group upon association and thought. *Journal of Experimental Psychology, 3*, 159–182. (p. 541)

**Allport, G. W.** (1935). Attitudes. In C. Murchison (Ed.), *Handbook of social psychology*. Worcester, MA: Clark University Press. (p. 519)

**Allport, G. W.** (1968). The historical background of modern social psychology. In G. Lindzey & E. Aronson (Eds.), *The handbook of social psychology* (2nd ed., Vol. 1). Reading, MA: Addison-Wesley. (p. 491)

**American Psychiatric Association** (1987). *Diagnostic and statistical manual of mental disorders (third edition, revised)*. New York: Author. (pp. 605, 608, 615, 616)

**American Psychological Association** (1981). Ethical principles of psychologists. *American Psychologist, 36*, 633–638. (p. 41)

**American Psychological Association** (1982). *Ethical principles in the conduct of research with human participants*. Washington, DC: Author. (p. 41)

**Anderson, J. R.** (1985). *Cognitive psychology and its implications* (2nd ed.). New York: Freeman. (p. 342)

**Anderson, S., & Bem, S. L.** (1981). Sex typing and androgyny in dyadic interaction. *Journal of Personality and Social Psychology, 41*, 74–86. (p. 502)

**Andreasen, N. C.** (1978). Creativity and psychiatric illness. *Psychiatric Annals, 8*, 113–119. (p. 633)

**Andreasen, N. C., & Olsen, S. A.** (1982). Negative versus positive schizophrenia: Definition and validation. *Archives of General Psychiatry, 39,* 789–794. (p. 636)

**Anglin, J. M.** (1977). *Word, object, and conceptual development.* New York: Norton. (p. 423)

**Archer, J., & Lloyd, B.** (1985). *Sex and gender.* Cambridge: Cambridge University Press. (p. 467)

**Ardrey, R.** (1961). *African genesis.* New York: Atheneum. (p. 114)

**Ardrey, R.** (1966). *The territorial imperative.* New York: Atheneum. (p. 114)

**Argyle, M., & Henderson, M.** (1984). The rules of friendship. *Journal of Social and Personal Relationships, 1,* 211–237. (p. 510)

**Arieti, S.** (1966). Schizophrenic cognition. In P. Hook & J. Zubin (Eds.), *Psychopathology of schizophrenia.* New York: Grune & Stratton. (p. 635)

**Aronson, E., Blaney, N., Stephan, C., Sikes, J., & Snapp, M.** (1978). *The jigsaw classroom.* Beverly Hills, CA: Sage. (p. 555)

**Asanuma, H., & Sakata, H.** (1967). Functional organization of a cortical efferent system examined with focal depth stimulation in cats. *Journal of Neurophysiology, 30,* 35–54. (p. 183)

**Asarnow, J. R.** (1988). Children at risk for schizophrenia: Converging lines of evidence. *Schizophrenia Bulletin, 14,* 613–631. (pp. 77, 639)

**Asch, S. E.** (1946). Forming impressions of personality. *Journal of Abnormal and Social Psychology, 41,* 258–290. (pp. 492, 495)

**Asch, S. E.** (1951). Effects of group pressure upon the modification and distortion of judgment. In H. Guetzkow (Ed.), *Groups, leadership and men.* Pittsburgh: Carnegie Press. (p. 546)

**Asch, S. E.** (1952). *Social psychology.* Englewood Cliffs, NJ: Prentice Hall. (p. 545)

**Asch, S. E.** (1956). Studies of independence and conformity: I. A minority of one against a unanimous majority. *Psychological Monographs: General and Applied, 70* (9, Whole no. 416). (pp. 545, 546, 547)

**Aschoff, J.** (1969). Desynchronization and resynchronization of human circadian rhythms. *Aerospace Medicine, 40,* 844–849. (p. 221)

**Ash, M. G.** (1985). Gestalt psychology: Origins in Germany and reception in the United States. In C. E. Buxton (Ed.), *Points of view in the modern history of psychology.* New York: Academic Press. (p. 12)

**Ashton, H.** (1987). *Brain systems, disorders, and psychotropic drugs.* Oxford: Oxford University Press. (pp. 629, 676, 677)

**Aslin, R. N., & Smith, L. P.** (1988). Perceptual development. *Annual Review of Psychology, 39,* 435–473. (p. 415)

**Atkinson, R. C.** (1975). Mnemotechnics in second-language learning. *American Psychologist, 30,* 821–828. (p. 339)

**Atkinson, R. C., & Shiffrin, R. M.** (1968). Human memory: A proposed system and its control processes. In K. W. Spence & J. T. Spence (Eds.), *The psychology of learning and motivation: Advances in research and theory* (Vol. 2). New York: Academic Press. (pp. 323, 333, 334, 357)

**Atkinson, R. C., & Shiffrin, R. M.** (1971, August). The control of short-term memory. *Scientific American,* 82–90. (p. 334)

**Axelrod, R.** (1984). *The evolution of cooperation.* New York: Basic Books. (p. 113)

**Ayllon, T., & Azrin, N. H.** (1968). *The token economy: A motivational system for therapy and rehabilitation.* New York: Appleton-Century-Crofts. (p. 670)

**Baddeley, A.** (1986). *Working memory.* Oxford: Clarendon. (pp. 334, 352)

**Baddeley, A., & Hitch, G. J.** (1977). Recency reexamined. In S. Dornic (Ed.), *Attention and performance, VI.* Hillsdale, NJ: Erlbaum. (p. 334)

**Bahr, S. J., Chappell, C. B., & Leigh, G. K.** (1983). Age at marriage, role enactment, role consensus, and marital satisfaction. *Journal of Marriage and the Family, 45,* 795–803. (p. 479)

**Bahrick, H. P., Bahrick, P. O., & Wittlinger, R. P.** (1975). Fifty years of memory for names and faces. *Journal of Experimental Psychology: General, 104,* 54–75. (p. 350)

**Baillargeon, R.** (1987). Object permanence in 3½- and 4½-month-old infants. *Developmental Psychology, 23,* 655–664. (p. 420)

**Baillargeon, R., Spelke, E. S., & Wasserman, S.** (1985). Object permanence in five-month-old infants. *Cognition, 20,* 191–208. (p. 420)

**Banaji, M. R., & Crowder, R. G.** (1989). The bankruptcy of everyday memory. *American Psychologist, 44,* 1185–1193. (p. 361)

**Bancroft, J.** (1978). The relationship between hormones and sexual behavior in humans. In J. B. Hutchinson (Ed.), *Biological determinants of sexual behaviour.* New York: Wiley. (p. 212)

**Bandura, A.** (1969). *Principles of behavior modification.* New York: Holt, Rinehart & Winston. (p. 152)

**Bandura, A.** (1977). *Social learning theory.* Englewood Cliffs, NJ: Prentice Hall. (pp. 152, 585)

**Bandura, A.** (1982). Self-efficacy mechanisms in human agency. *American Psychologist, 37,* 122–147. (pp. 588, 589)

**Bandura, A.** (1986). *Social foundations of thought and action: A social cognitive theory.* Englewood Cliffs, NJ: Prentice Hall. (pp. 152, 452, 585, 586, 588)

**Bandura, A., Adams, N. E., & Beyer, J.** (1977). Cognitive processes mediating behavioral change. *Journal of Personality and Social Psychology, 35,* 125–139. (p. 588)

**Bandura, A., & Cervone, D.** (1983). Self-evaluative and self-efficacy mechanisms governing the motivational effects of goal systems. *Journal of Personality and Social Psychology, 45,* 1017–1028. (p. 588)

**Bandura, A., O'Leary, A., Taylor, C. B., Gauthier, J., & Gossard, D.** (1987). Perceived self-efficacy and pain control: Opioid and nonopiod mechanisms. *Journal of Personality and Social Psychology, 53,* 563–571. (p. 270)

**Bandura, A., Reese, L., & Adams, N. E.** (1982). Microanalysis of action and fear arousal as a function of differential levels of perceived self-efficacy. *Journal of Personality and Social Psychology, 43,* 5–21. (p. 671)

**Barash, D. P.** (1982). *Sociobiology and behavior* (2nd ed.). New York: Elsevier. (pp. 86, 108)

Barber, T. X. (1976). *Pitfalls in human research*. New York: Pergamon. (p. 43)

Barglow, P., Vaughn, B. E., & Molitor, N. (1987). Effects of maternal absence due to employment on the quality of infant-mother attachment in a low-risk sample. *Child Development, 58*, 945–954. (p. 458)

Barker, S. L., Funk, S. C., & Houston, B. K. (1988). Psychological treatment versus nonspecific factors: A meta-analysis of conditions that engender comparable expectations for improvement. *Clinical Psychology Review, 8*, 579–594. (p. 675)

Barlow, D. H., & Craske, M. G. (1988). The phenomenology of panic. In S. Rachman & J. D. Maser (Eds.), *Panic: Psychological perspectives*. Hillsdale, NJ: Erlbaum. (p. 618)

Barnett, R. C., & Baruch, G. K. (1987). Social roles, gender, and psychological distress. In R. C. Barnett, L. B. Biener, & G. K. Baruch (Eds.), *Gender and stress*. New York: Free Press. (p. 614)

Baron, R. S. (1986). Distraction-conflict theory: Progress and problems. In L. Berkowitz (Ed.), *Advances in experimental psychology, vol. 19*. New York: Academic Press. (p. 541)

Barry, H. III, & Paxson, L. (1971). Infancy and early childhood: Cross-cultural codes 2. *Ethnology, 10*, 466–508. (p. 456)

Barsky, A. J., Wyshak, G., & Klerman, G. L. (1986). Hypochondriasis: An evaluation of the DSM-III criteria in medical outpatients. *Archives of General Psychiatry, 43*, 493–500. (p. 622)

Barth, J. T., & Macciocchi, S. N. (1985). The Halstead-Reitan neurological test battery. In C. S. Newmark (Ed.), *Major psychological assessment instruments*. Boston: Allyn & Bacon. (p. 652)

Bartlett, F. C. (1932). *Remembering: A study in experimental and social psychology*. Cambridge: Cambridge University Press. (pp. 345, 354)

Bartol, C. R., & Costello, N. (1976). Extraversion as a function of temporal duration of electric shock: An exploratory study. *Perceptual and Motor Skills, 42*, 1174. (p. 594)

Baruch, G. K., Biener, L., & Barnett, R. C. (1987). Women and gender in research on work and family stress. *American Psychologist, 42*, 130–136. (pp. 482, 483, 614)

Basbaum, A. I., & Fields, H. L. (1984). Endogenous pain control systems: Brainstem spinal pathways and endorphin circuitry. *Annual Review of Neuroscience, 7*, 309–338. (p. 268)

Bassuk, E. L., & Gerson, S. (1978, February). Deinstitutionalization and mental health services. *Scientific American*, 46–53. (p. 644)

Bates, J. E. (1987). Temperament in infancy. In J. D. Osofsky (Ed.), *Handbook of infant development* (2nd ed.). New York: Wiley. (p. 457)

Baumeister, R. F., & Showers, C. J. (1986). A review of paradoxical performance effects: Choking under pressure in sports and mental tests. *European Journal of Social Psychology, 16*, 361–383. (p. 542)

Baumeister, R. F., & Steinhilber, A. (1984). Paradoxical effects of supportive audiences on performance under pressure: The home field disadvantage in sports championships. *Journal of Personality and Social Psychology, 47*, 85–93. (p. 541)

Baumeister, R. F., & Tice, D. M. (1984). Role of self-presentation and choice in cognitive dissonance under forced compliance: Necessary or sufficient causes? *Journal of Personality and Social Psychology, 46*, 5–13. (p. 519)

Baumeister, R. F., & Tice, D. M. (1986). Four selves, two motives, and a substitute process self-regulation model. In R. F. Baumeister (Ed.), *Public self and private self*. New York: Springer-Verlag. (p. 506)

Baumrind, D. (1964). Some thoughts on ethics of research: After reading Milgram's "Behavioral study of obedience." *American Psychologist, 19*, 421–423. (p. 538)

Baumrind, D. (1967). Child care practices anteceding three patterns of preschool behavior. *Genetic Psychology Monographs, 75*, 43–88. (p. 461)

Baumrind, D. (1971a). Current patterns of parental authority. *Developmental Psychology Monograph, 4*, 1–103. (pp. 30, 461, 462)

Baumrind, D. (1971b). Harmonious parents and their preschool children. *Developmental Psychology, 4*, 99–102. (p. 462)

Baumrind, D. (1973). The development of instrumental competence through socialization. In A. D. Pick (Ed.), *Minnesota symposium on child psychology* (Vol. 7). Minneapolis: University of Minnesota Press. (p. 462)

Baumrind, D. (1986). *Familial antecedents of social competence in middle childhood*. Unpublished monograph, Institute of Human Development, University of California, Berkeley. (p. 462)

Beaman, A. L., Klentz, B., Diener, E., & Svanum, S. (1979). Self-awareness and transgression in children: Two field studies. *Journal of Personality and Social Psychology, 37*, 1835–1846. (p. 521)

Beck, A. T. (1967). *Depression: Clinical, experimental, and theoretical aspects*. New York: Harper & Row. (p. 630)

Beck, A. T., Brown, G., Eidelson, J. I., Steer, R. A., & Riskind, J. H. (1987). Differentiating anxiety and depression: A test of the cognitive content-specificity hypothesis. *Journal of Abnormal Psychology, 96*, 179–183. (p. 628)

Beck, A. T., & Emery, G. (1985). *Anxiety disorders and phobias: A cognitive perspective*. New York: Basic Books. (pp. 616, 664)

Beck, A. T., & Young, J. E. (1985). Depression. In D. H. Barlow (Ed.), *Clinical handbook of psychological disorders: A step-by-step treatment manual*. New York: Guilford. (pp. 664, 665)

Becklen, R., & Cervone, D. (1983). Selective looking and the noticing of unexpected events. *Memory and Cognition, 11*, 601–608. (pp. 297, 298)

Bee, H. L. (1987). *The journey of adulthood*. New York: Macmillan. (pp. 481, 482)

Beitman, B. D., Goldfried, M. R., & Norcross, J. C. (1989). The movement toward integrating the psychotherapies: An overview. *American Journal of Psychiatry, 146*, 138–147. (p. 675)

Bell, A. P., Weinberg, M. S., & Hammersmith, S. K. (1981). *Sexual preference: Its development in men and women*. Bloomington, IN: Indiana University Press. (p. 473)

Bell, R. Q., & Harper, L. V. (1977). *Child effects on adults*. Hillsdale, NJ: Erlbaum. (p. 462)

Bell, S., & Ainsworth, M. (1972). Infant crying and maternal responsiveness. *Child Development, 43*, 1171–1190. (p. 458)

**Belsky, J., & Rovine, M.** (1987). Temperament and attachment security in the strange situation: An empirical rapprochement. *Child Development, 58,* 787–795. (p. 457)

**Belsky, J., & Rovine, M.** (1988). Nonmaternal care in the first year of life and the security of infant-parent attachment. *Child Development, 59,* 157–167. (p. 458)

**Bengston, V. L., Reedy, M. N., & Gordon, C.** (1985). Aging and self-conceptions. In J. E. Birren & K. W. Schaie (Eds.), *Handbook of the psychology of aging* (2nd ed.). New York: Van Nostrand Reinhold. (p. 484)

**Benson, H.** (1984). *Beyond the relaxation response.* New York: Berkley. (p. 229)

**Berghe, P. L. van den** (1983). Human inbreeding avoidance: Culture in nature. *The Behavioral and Brain Sciences, 6,* 91–123. (p. 117)

**Berglas, S., & Jones, E. E.** (1978). Drug choice as a self-handicapping strategy in response to noncontingent success. *Journal of Personality and Social Psychology, 36,* 405–417. (p. 507)

**Berko, J.** (1958). The child's learning of English morphology. *Word, 14,* 150–177. (p. 424)

**Bernstein, I. L., & Borson, S.** (1986). Learned food aversion: A component of anorexia syndromes. *Psychological Review, 93,* 462–472. (p. 153)

**Bernstein, W. M., Stephan, W. G., & Davis, M. H.** (1976). Explaining attributions for achievement: A path analytic approach. *Journal of Personality and Social Psychology, 37,* 1810–1821. (p. 501)

**Berry, D. S., & McArthur, L. Z.** (1985). Some components and consequences of a babyface. *Journal of Personality and Social Psychology, 48,* 312–323. (p. 495)

**Berry, D. S., & McArthur, L. Z.** (1988). What's in a face? Facial maturity and the attribution of legal responsibility. *Personality and Social Psychology Bulletin, 14,* 23–33. (pp. 495, 496)

**Berry, J. W.** (1971). Ecological and cultural factors in spatial perceptual development. *Canadian Journal of Behavioural Science, 3,* 324–336. (p. 384)

**Bertelsen, A.** (1979). A Danish twin study of manic-depressive disorders. In M. Schou & E. Strömgren (Eds.), *Origin, prevention, and treatment of affective disorders.* Orlando, FL: Academic Press. (pp. 629, 633)

**Bertenthal, B. I., Campos, J. J., & Barrett, K. C.** (1984). Self-produced locomotion: An organizer of emotional, cognitive, and social development in infancy. In R. N. Emde & R. J. Harmon (Eds.), *Continuities and discontinuities in development.* New York: Plenum. (p. 416)

**Bessman, S. P., Williamson, M. L., & Koch, R.** (1978). Diet, genetics, and mental retardation interaction between phenylketonuric heterozygous mother and fetus to produce nonspecific diminution of IQ: Evidence in support of the justification hypothesis. *Proceedings of the National Academy of Sciences, 78,* 1562–1566. (p. 56)

**Bever, T.** (1970). The cognitive basis for linguistic structures. In J. R. Hayes (Ed.), *Cognition and the development of language.* New York: Wiley. (p. 424)

**Bickerton, D.** (1984). The language bioprogram hypothesis. *The Behavioral and Brain Sciences, 7,* 173–221. (p. 425)

**Bickman, L.** (1972). Social influence and diffusion of responsibility in an emergency. *Journal of Experimental Social Psychology, 8,* 438–445. (pp. 543, 544)

**Biederman, I.** (1987). Recognition-by-components: A theory of human image understanding. *Psychological Review, 94,* 115–147. (pp. 292, 293)

**Biederman, I.** (1988). Aspects and extensions of a theory of human image understanding. In Z. W. Pylyshyn (Ed.), *Computational processes in human vision: An interdisciplinary perspective.* Norwood, NJ: Ablex. (pp. 294, 295)

**Biederman, I., & Shiffrar, M. M.** (1987). Sexing day-old chicks: A case study and expert systems analysis of a difficult perceptual-learning task. *Journal of Experimental Psychology: Learning, Memory, and Cognition, 13,* 640–645. (p. 294)

**Billings, A. G., Cronkite, R. C., & Moos, R. H.** (1983). Social-environmental factors in unipolar depression: Comparisons of depressed patients and nondepressed controls. *Journal of Abnormal Psychology, 92,* 119–133. (p. 629)

**Binet, A., & Henri, V.** (1896). La psychologie individuelle. *Année Psychologie, 11,* 163–169. (p. 367)

**Binet, A., & Simon, T.** (1916; reprinted 1973). *The development of intelligence in children.* New York: Arno Press. (p. 367)

**Bishop, J. A., & Cook, L. M.** (1975, January). Moths, melanism and clean air. *Scientific American,* 90–99. (p. 83)

**Bitterman, M. E.** (1975). The comparative analysis of learning. *Science, 188,* 699–709. (p. 149)

**Blake, R. R., & Mouton, J. S.** (1961). Reactions to intergroup competition under win-lose conditions. *Management Science, 7,* 420–435. (p. 554)

**Blake, R. R., & Mouton, J. S.** (1979). Intergroup problem solving in organizations: From theory to practice. In W. G. Austin & S. Worchel (Eds.), *The social psychology of intergroup relations.* Monterey, CA: Brooks/Cole. (p. 554)

**Blamey, P. J., Dowell, R. C., Brown, A. M., Clark, G. M., & Seligman, P. M.** (1987). Vowel and consonant recognition of cochlear implant patients using formant-estimating speech processors. *Journal of the Acoustical Society of America, 82,* 48–57. (p. 248)

**Blaney, P. H.** (1986). Affect and memory: A review. *Psychological Bulletin, 99,* 229–246. (p. 354)

**Blasi, A.** (1980). Bridging moral cognition and moral action: A critical review of the literature. *Psychological Bulletin, 88,* 1–45. (p. 478)

**Blazer, D., Hughes, D., & George, L. D.** (1987). Stressful life events and the onset of a generalized anxiety syndrome. *American Journal of Psychiatry, 144,* 1178–1183. (p. 616)

**Bleuler, E. P.** (1911; reprinted 1950). *Dementia praecox, or the group of schizophrenias* (J. Zinkin, Trans.). New York: International Universities Press. (pp. 634, 635)

**Bleuler, E. P.** (1924; reprinted 1951). *Textbook of psychiatry* (A. A. Brill, Trans.). New York: Dover. (p. 636)

**Bliss, E. L.** (1986). *Multiple personality, allied disorders, and hypnosis.* Oxford: Oxford University Press. (pp. 622, 623, 624)

**Bloom, A. H.** (1981). *The linguistic shaping of thought: A study of the impact of language on thinking in China and the West*. Hillsdale, NJ: Erlbaum. (p. 402)

**Bloom, F. E.** (1981, October). Neuropeptides. *Scientific American*, 148–169. (p. 172)

**Bloom, F. E., & Lazerson, A.** (1988). *Brain, mind, and behavior* (2nd ed.). New York: Freeman. (p. 175)

**Bloom, L. M., & Lahey, M.** (1978). *Language development and language disorders*. New York: Wiley. (p. 422)

**Blum, K., Noble, W. P., Sheridan, P. J., Montgomery, A., Ritchie, T., Jagadeeswaran, P., Nogami, H., Briggs, A. H., & Cohn, J. B.** (1990). Allelic association of human dopamine D$_2$ receptor gene in alcoholism. *Journal of the American Medical Association*, *263*, 2055–2060. (p. 626)

**Blumenthal, A. L.** (1985). Wilhelm Wundt: Psychology as the propaedeutic science. In C. E. Buxton (Ed.), *Points of view in the modern history of psychology*. New York: Academic Press. (pp. 8, 9, 17)

**Blurton-Jones, N. G.** (1967). An ethological study of some aspects of social behavior of children in nursery school. In D. Morris (Ed.), *Primate ethology*. Chicago: Aldine. (p. 104)

**Blurton-Jones, N. G., & Konner, M. J.** (1973). Sex differences in the behavior of Bushman and London two- to five-year-olds. In J. Crook & R. Michael (Eds.), *Comparative ecology and behavior of primates*. New York: Academic Press. (p. 456)

**Bolles, R. C.** (1970). Species-specific defense reactions and avoidance learning. *Psychological Review*, *77*, 32–48. (p. 157)

**Bolles, R. C.** (1984). Species-typical response predispositions. In P. Marler & H. Terrace (Eds.), *The biology of learning*. Berlin: Springer-Verlag. (p. 157)

**Boor, M.** (1982). The multiple personality epidemic. *Journal of Nervous and Mental Disease*, *170*, 302–304. (p. 623)

**Borbély, A.** (1986). *The secrets of sleep*. New York: Basic Books. (p. 222)

**Borges, M. A., & Dutton, L. J.** (1976). Attitudes toward aging. *The Gerontologist*, *16*, 220–224. (p. 484)

**Botwinick, J.** (1984). *Aging and behavior: A comprehensive integration of research findings* (3rd ed.). New York: Springer. (pp. 483, 484)

**Bouchard, T. J., & McGue, M.** (1981). Familial studies of intelligence: A review. *Science*, *212*, 1055–1059. (pp. 69, 70)

**Bowen, G. L., & Orthner, D. K.** (1983). Sex-role congruency and marital quality. *Journal of Marriage and the Family*, *45*, 223–230. (p. 479)

**Bower, G. H.** (1970). Imagery as a relational organizer in associative learning. *Journal of Verbal Learning and Verbal Behavior*, *9*, 529–533. (p. 339)

**Bower, G. H.** (1981). Mood and memory. *American Psychologist*, *36*, 129–148. (p. 354)

**Bowlby, J.** (1958). The nature of the child's tie to his mother. *International Journal of Psychoanalysis*, *39*, 35–373. (p. 454)

**Bowlby, J.** (1982). *Attachment and loss* (2nd ed.). New York: Basic Books. (p. 454)

**Bowmaker, J. K., & Dartnall, H. J. A.** (1980). Visual pigments of rods and cones in a human retina. *Journal of Physiology*, *298*, 501–511. (p. 263)

**Bransford, J. D., & Franks, J. J.** (1971). The abstraction of linguistic ideas. *Cognitive Psychology*, *2*, 331–350. (p. 340)

**Bransford, J. D., Stein, B. S., Vye, N. J., Franks, J. J., Auble, P. M., Mezynski, K. J., & Perfetto, G. A.** (1982). Different approaches in learning: An overview. *Journal of Experimental Psychology: General*, *111*, 390–398. (p. 335)

**Braun, B. G. (Ed.)** (1985). *Treatment of multiple personality disorder*. Washington, DC: American Psychiatric Press. (p. 623)

**Bray, D. W., & Howard, A.** (1983). The AT&T longitudinal studies of managers. In K. W. Schaie (Ed.), *Longitudinal studies of adult psychological development*. New York: Guilford. (p. 482)

**Bray, G. A., & Gallagher, T. F., Jr.** (1975). Manifestation of hypothalamic obesity in man: A comprehensive investigation of eight patients and a review of the literature. *Medicine*, *54*, 301–330. (p. 204)

**Bregman, E.** (1934). An attempt to modify emotional attitude of infants by the conditioned response technique. *Journal of Genetic Psychology*, *45*, 169–198. (p. 157)

**Brehm, J. W.** (1966). *A theory of psychological reactance*. New York: Academic Press. (p. 534)

**Brehm, S. S., & Brehm, J. W.** (1981). *Psychological reactance: A theory of freedom and control*. New York: Academic Press. (p. 534)

**Breier, A., Charney, D. S., & Heninger, G. R.** (1986). Agoraphobia with panic attacks. *Archives of General Psychiatry*, *43*, 1029–1036. (p. 619)

**Breuer, G.** (1982). *Sociobiology and the human dimension*. Cambridge: Cambridge University Press. (p. 116)

**Breuer, J., & Freud, S.** (1895; reprinted 1955). *Studies on hysteria*. In J. Strachey (Ed. & trans.), *The standard edition of the complete psychological works of Sigmund Freud*. London: Hogarth Press. (pp. 654, 669)

**Briggs, S. R., & Cheek, J. M.** (1986). The role of factor analysis in the development and evaluation of personality scales. *Journal of Personality*, *51*, 106–148. (p. 509)

**Brinkman, C.** (1984). Supplementary motor area of the monkey's cerebral cortex: Short- and long-term deficits after unilateral ablation and the effects of subsequent callosal section. *Journal of Neuroscience*, *4*, 918–929. (p. 184)

**Broadbent, D. E.** (1958). *Perception and communication*. London: Pergamon. (p. 301)

**Broadhurst, P. L., Fulker, D. W., & Wilcock, J.** (1974). Behavioral genetics. *Annual Review of Psychology*, *25*, 389–413. (p. 66)

**Broca, P.** (1861; reprinted 1965). Paul Broca on the speech centers (M. D. Boring, Trans.). In R. J. Herrnstein & E. G. Boring (Eds.), *A source book in the history of psychology*. Cambridge, MA: Harvard University Press. (pp. 7, 399)

**Brody, G. H., & Shaffer, D. R.** (1982). Contributions of parents and peers to children's moral socialization. *Developmental Review*, *2*, 31–75. (p. 460)

**Brody, N.** (1985). The validity of tests of intelligence. In B. B. Wolman (Ed.), *Handbook of intelligence: Theories, measurements, and applications.* New York: Wiley. (p. 368)

**Brody, N.** (1988). *Personality: In search of individuality.* New York: Academic Press. (p. 588)

**Bronfenbrenner, U.** (1975). Nature and nurture: A reinterpretation of the evidence. In A. Montague (Ed.), *Race and IQ.* New York: Oxford University Press. (p. 71)

**Bronfenbrenner, U.** (1979). *The ecology of human development.* Cambridge, MA: Harvard University Press. (p. 452)

**Bronfenbrenner, U.** (1986). Ecology of the family as a context for human development: Research perspectives. *Developmental Psychology, 22,* 723–742. (pp. 452, 462)

**Brown, N. S., Curry, N. E., & Tittnich, E.** (1971). How groups of children deal with common stress through play. In N. E. Curry & S. Arnaud (Eds.), *Play: The child strives toward self-realization.* Washington, DC: NAEYC. (p. 464)

**Brown, P.** (1985). *The transfer of care: Psychiatric deinstitutionalization and its aftermath.* London: Routledge & Kegan Paul. (p. 645)

**Brown, R.** (1973). *A first language.* Cambridge, MA: Harvard University Press. (p. 424)

**Brown, R.** (1986). *Social psychology: The second edition.* New York: Free Press. (pp. 429, 430, 539, 549)

**Brown, R., & Hanlon, C.** (1970). Derivational complexity and order of acquisition in child speech. In J. R. Hayes (Ed.), *Cognition and the development of language.* New York: Wiley. (pp. 424, 427)

**Bruner, J. S.** (1983). *Child's talk: Learning to use language.* New York: Norton. (p. 427)

**Burchfield, S. R. (Ed.)** (1985). *Stress: Psychological and physiological interactions.* Washington, DC: Hemisphere. (pp. 228, 229)

**Buss, A. H.** (1980). *Self-consciousness and social anxiety.* San Francisco: Freeman. (p. 509)

**Bussey, K., & Maughan, B.** (1982). Gender differences in moral reasoning. *Journal of Personality and Social Psychology, 42,* 701–706. (p. 478)

**Butcher, J. N., Graham, J. R., Williams, C. L., & Ben-Porath, Y. S.** (1990). *Development and use of the MMPI-2 content scales.* Minneapolis, MN: University of Minnesota Press. (p. 650)

**Butler, R. N.** (1975). *Why survive?* New York: Harper & Row. (p. 485)

**Butterfield, E. C., & Siperstein, G. N.** (1974). Influence of contingent auditory stimulation upon non-nutritional suckle. *Proceedings of third symposium on oral sensation and perception: The mouth of the infant.* Springfield, IL: Charles C. Thomas. (p. 420)

**Caggiula, A. R., & Hoebel, B. G.** (1966). "Copulation-reward site" in the posterior hypothalamus. *Science, 153,* 1284–1285. (p. 216)

**Caldwell, J., Croft, J. E., & Sever, P. S.** (1980). Tolerance to the amphetamines: An examination of possible mechanisms. In J. Caldwell (Ed.), *Amphetamines and related stimulants: Chemical, biological, clinical and social aspects.* Boca Raton, FL: CRC Press. (p. 194)

**Callaway, M. R., & Esser, J. K.** (1984). Groupthink: Effects of cohesiveness and problem-solving procedures on group decision making. *Social Behavior and Personality, 12,* 157–164. (p. 552)

**Callaway, M. R., Marriott, R. G., & Esser, J. K.** (1985). Effects of dominance on group decision making: Toward a stress-reduction explanation of groupthink. *Journal of Personality and Social Psychology, 49,* 949–952. (p. 552)

**Campbell, D. T.** (1965). Ethnocentric and other altruistic motives. In D. Levine (Ed.), *Nebraska symposium on motivation* (Vol. 13). Lincoln, NE: University of Nebraska Press. (p. 553)

**Campbell, J. D., & Fairey, P. J.** (1989). Informational and normative routes to conformity: The effect of faction size as a function of norm extremity and attention to the stimulus. *Journal of Personality and Social Psychology, 57,* 457–468. (p. 547)

**Campbell, J. D., Tesser, A., & Fairey, P. J.** (1986). Conformity and attention to the stimulus: Some temporal and contextual dynamics. *Journal of Personality and Social Psychology, 51,* 315–324. (p. 547)

**Campbell, K.** (1970). *Body and mind.* Notre Dame, IN: University of Notre Dame Press. (p. 5)

**Campos, J. J., Hiatt, S., Ramsay, D., Henderson, C., & Svejda, M.** (1978). The emergence of fear on the visual cliff. In M. Lewis & L. A. Rosenblum (Eds.), *The development of affect* (Vol. 1). New York: Plenum. (p. 416)

**Campos, J. J., Langer, A., & Krowitz, A.** (1970). Cardiac responses on the visual cliff in prelocomotor human infants. *Science, 170,* 196–197. (p. 416)

**Cann, A., Sherman, S. J., & Elkes, R.** (1975). Effects of initial request size and timing of a second request on compliance: The foot in the door and the door in the face. *Journal of Personality and Social Psychology, 32,* 774–782. (p. 534)

**Cannon, W. B.** (1932; reprinted 1963). *The wisdom of the body.* New York: Norton. (p. 199)

**Card, J. J.** (1987). Epidemiology of PTSD in a national cohort of Vietnam veterans. *Journal of Clinical Psychology, 43,* 6–27. (p. 619)

**Carlson, N. R.** (1986). *Physiology of behavior* (3rd ed.). Boston: Allyn & Bacon. (pp. 252, 639)

**Carpenter, W. T., Jr., Heinrichs, D. W., & Alphs, L. D.** (1985). Treatment of negative symptoms. *Schizophrenia Bulletin, 11,* 440–452. (p. 676)

**Carroll, M. A., Schneider, H. G., & Wesley, G. R.** (1985). *Ethics in the practice of psychology.* Englewood Cliffs, NJ: Prentice Hall. (p. 40)

**Case, R., Kurland, M., & Goldberg, J.** (1982). Operational efficiency and the growth of short-term memory span. *Journal of Experimental Child Psychology, 33,* 386–404. (p. 441)

**Cattell, R. B.** (1950). *Personality: A systematic, theoretical, and factual study.* New York: McGraw-Hill. (p. 592)

**Cattell, R. B.** (1965). *The scientific analysis of personality.* Baltimore, MD: Penguin. (p. 593)

**Cattell, R. B.** (1971). *Abilities: Their structure, growth, and action.* Boston: Houghton Mifflin. (p. 372)

**Cattell, R. B.** (1973). *Personality and mood by questionnaire.* San Francisco: Jossey-Bass. (p. 592)

**Cattell, R. B.** (1987). *Intelligence: Its structure, growth and action.* Amsterdam: North-Holland. (p. 372)

**Ceci, S. J., & Liker, J.** (1986). Academic and nonacademic intelligence: An experimental separation. In R. J. Sternberg & R. K. Wagner (Eds.), *Practical intelligence: Nature and origins of competence in the everyday world.* Cambridge: Cambridge University Press. (p. 383)

**Ceraso, J.** (1967, October). The interference theory of forgetting. *Scientific American,* 117–124. (p. 351)

**Chagnon, N. A.** (1979). Mate competition, favoring close kin, and village fissioning among the Yanomamö Indians. In N. A. Chagnon & W. Irons (Eds.), *Evolutionary biology and human social behavior: An anthropological perspective.* North Scituate, MA: Duxbury Press. (p. 117)

**Chagnon, N. A., & Irons, W.** (1979). *Evolutionary biology and human social behavior: An anthropological perspective.* North Scituate, MA: Duxbury Press. (p. 116)

**Chaiken, S.** (1986). The heuristic model of persuasion. In M. P. Zanna, J. M. Olson, & C. P. Herman (Eds.), *Consistency in social behavior: The Ontario symposium,* Vol. 2. Hillsdale, NJ: Erlbaum. (p. 515)

**Chaiken, S., & Stangor, C.** (1987). Attitudes and attitude change. *Annual Review of Psychology, 38,* 575–630. (p. 517)

**Chang, T. M.** (1986). Semantic memory: Facts and models. *Psychological Bulletin, 99,* 199–220. (p. 348)

**Chapman, J.** (1966). The early symptoms of schizophrenia. *British Journal of Psychiatry, 112,* 225–251. (p. 637)

**Chase, M. H., & Morales, F. R.** (1987). Sleep states and somatomotor activity. In G. Adelman (Ed.), *Encyclopedia of neuroscience.* Boston: Birkhäuser. (p. 226)

**Chase, W. G., & Simon, H. A.** (1973). Perception in chess. *Cognitive Psychology, 4,* 55–81. (p. 338)

**Chen, S. C.** (1937). Social modification of the activity of ants in nest-building. *Physiological Zoology, 10,* 420–436. (p. 540)

**Cherry, E. C.** (1953). Some experiments on the recognition of speech, with one and with two ears. *Journal of the Acoustical Society of America, 25,* 975–979. (p. 296)

**Cherry, E. C., & Taylor, W. K.** (1954). Some further experiments on the recognition of speech with one and two ears. *Journal of the Acoustical Society of America, 26,* 554–559. (p. 296)

**Chesler, P.** (1969). Maternal influence in learning by observation in kittens. *Science, 166,* 901–903. (p. 152)

**Chi, M. T. H.** (1978). Knowledge structures and memory development. In R. S. Siegler (Ed.), *Children's thinking: What develops?* Hillsdale, NJ: Erlbaum. (p. 441)

**Chi, M. T. H., & Glaser, R.** (1985). Problem-solving ability. In R. J. Sternberg (Ed.), *Human abilities: An information-processing approach.* New York: Freeman. (pp. 390, 392, 393)

**Chomsky, N.** (1957). *Syntactic structures.* The Hague: Mouton. (pp. 396, 397)

**Chomsky, N.** (1959). A review of B. F. Skinner's "Verbal Behavior." *Language, 35,* 26–58. (p. 18)

**Chomsky, N.** (1965). *Aspects of a theory of syntax.* Cambridge, MA: MIT Press. (p. 425)

**Chomsky, N.** (1968). *Language and mind.* New York: Harcourt Brace Jovanovich. (p. 397)

**Cialdini, R. B.** (1984). *Influence: How and why people agree to things.* New York: Morrow. (pp. 530, 533)

**Cialdini, R. B.** (1987). Compliance principles of compliance professionals: Psychologists of necessity. In M. Zanna, J. M. Olson, & C. P. Herman (Eds.), *Social influence: The Ontario symposium, Vol. 5.* Hillsdale, NJ: Erlbaum. (pp. 530, 531, 532)

**Cialdini, R. B.** (1988). *Influence: Science and practice* (2nd ed.). Glenview, IL: Scott, Foresman. (pp. 530, 531)

**Cialdini, R. B., Caccioppo, J. T., Bassett, R., & Miller, J. A.** (1978). The lowball procedure for producing compliance: Commitment then cost. *Journal of Personality and Social Psychology, 36,* 463–476. (p. 532)

**Cicchetti, D., & Beeghly, M.** (1988). *Down syndrome: A developmental perspective.* Cambridge: Cambridge University Press. (p. 60)

**Clark, A. S., Pfeifle, J. K., & Edwards, D. A.** (1981). Ventromedial hypothalamic damage and sexual proceptivity in female rats. *Physiology and Behavior, 27,* 597–602. (p. 209)

**Clark, D. M.** (1988). A cognitive model of panic attacks. In S. Rachman & J. D. Maser (Eds.), *Panic: Psychological perspectives.* Hillsdale, NJ: Erlbaum. (p. 619)

**Clark, E.** (1973). What's in a word? On the child's acquisition of semantics in his first language. In T. Moore (Ed.), *Cognitive development and the acquisition of language.* New York: Academic Press. (p. 423)

**Clark, E.** (1987). The principle of contrast: A constraint on language acquisition. In B. MacWhinney (Ed.), *Mechanisms of language acquisition.* Hillsdale, NJ: Erlbaum. (p. 423)

**Clark, M. S.** (1984). Record keeping in two types of relationships. *Journal of Personality and Social Psychology, 47,* 549–557. (p. 510)

**Clark, M. S., Mills, J., & Powell, M.** (1986). Keeping track of needs in communal and exchange relationships. *Journal of Personality and Social Psychology, 51,* 333–338. (p. 510)

**Clark, M. S., & Reis, H. T.** (1988). Interpersonal processes in close relationships. *Annual Review of Psychology, 39,* 609–672. (p. 510)

**Clark, M. S., & Waddell, B.** (1985). Perceptions of exploitation in communal and exchange relationships. *Journal of Social and Personal Relationships, 2,* 403–418. (p. 510)

**Clarke, A. M., & Clarke, A. D. B.** (1976). *Early experience: Myth and evidence.* London: Open Books Publishing. (p. 458)

**Clement, C. A., & Falmagne, R. J.** (1986). Logical reasoning, world knowledge, and mental imagery: Interconnections in cognitive processes. *Memory and Cognition, 14,* 299–307. (p. 387)

**Clifford, M. M., & Walster, E.** (1973). The effects of physical attractiveness on teacher expectation. *Sociology of Education, 46,* 248–258. (p. 495)

**Cloninger, C. R., Bohman, M., & Sigvardsson, S.** (1981). Inheritance of alcohol abuse: Cross fostering analysis of adopted men. *Archives of General Psychiatry, 38,* 861–868. (p. 626)

**Cohen, F. L.** (1984). *Clinical genetics in nursing practice.* Philadelphia: Lippincott. (p. 60)

**Cohen, L. B., & Younger, B. A.** (1984). Infant perception of angular relations. *Infant Behavior and Development, 7,* 37–47. (p. 415)

**Cohen, N. J.** (1984). Preserved learning capacity in amnesia: Evidence for multiple memory systems. In L. R. Squire & N. Butters (Eds.), *The neuropsychology of memory.* New York: Guilford. (p. 359)

**Colby, A., Kohlberg, L., Gibbs, J., & Lieberman, M.** (1983). A longitudinal study of moral judgment. *Monographs of the Society for Research in Child Development, 48* (Whole nos. 1 & 2). (pp. 476, 477)

**Cole, M., Gay, J., Glick, J., & Sharp, D. W.** (1971). *The cultural context of learning and thinking.* New York: Basic Books. (p. 384)

**Cole, M., & Means, B.** (1981). *Comparative studies of how people think.* Cambridge, MA: Harvard University Press. (p. 384)

**Collins, A. M., & Quillian, M. R.** (1969). Retrieval time from semantic memory. *Journal of Verbal Learning and Verbal Behavior, 8,* 240–247. (pp. 345, 347, 348)

**Collins, A. M., & Quillian, M. R.** (1972). How to make a language user. In E. Tulving & W. Donaldson (Eds.), *Organization of memory.* New York: Academic Press. (p. 347)

**Collins, W. A.** (1988). Research on the transition to adolescence: Continuity in the study of developmental processes. In M. R. Gunnar & W. A. Collins (Eds.), *Development during the transition to adolescence: Minnesota symposia on child psychology, vol. 21.* Hillsdale, NJ: Erlbaum. (p. 470)

**Conley, J. J.** (1984). The hierarchy of consistency: A review and model of longitudinal findings on adult individual differences in intelligence, personality, and self opinion. *Personality and Individual Differences, 5,* 11–26. (p. 598)

**Conley, J. J.** (1985). Longitudinal stability of personality traits: A multitrait-multimethod-multioccasion analysis. *Journal of Personality and Social Psychology, 49,* 1266–1282. (p. 598)

**Connolly, J. A., & Doyle, A.** (1984). Relation of social fantasy play to social competence in preschoolers. *Developmental Psychology, 20,* 797–806. (p. 464)

**Cook, L. M., Mani, G. S., & Varley, M. E.** (1986). Postindustrial melanism in the peppered moth. *Science, 231,* 611–613. (p. 83)

**Cooley, C. H.** (1902; reprinted 1964). *Human nature and the social order.* New York: Schocken Books. (p. 502)

**Coons, P. M., Bowman, E. S., & Milstein, V.** (1988). Multiple personality disorder: A clinical investigation of 50 cases. *Journal of Nervous and Mental Disease, 176,* 519–527. (p. 623)

**Cooper, H. M., & Good, T. L.** (1983). *Pygmalion grows up: Studies in the expectation communication process.* New York: Longman. (p. 503)

**Cooper, J., & Croyle, R. T.** (1984). Attitudes and attitude change. *Annual Review of Psychology, 35,* 395–426. (p. 522)

**Cooper, L. A., & Shepard, R. N.** (1973). Chronometric studies of the rotation of mental images. In W. G. Chase (Ed.), *Visual information processing.* New York: Academic Press. (p. 343)

**Cooper, M. L., Russell, M., & George, W. H.** (1988). Coping, expectancies, and alcohol abuse: A test of social learning foundations. *Journal of Abnormal Psychology, 97,* 218–230. (pp. 626, 627)

**Cooper, R. M., & Zubek, J. P.** (1958). Effects of enriched and restricted early environments on the learning ability of bright and dull rats. *Canadian Journal of Psychology, 12,* 159–164. (p. 66)

**Coren, S.** (1986). An efferent component in the visual perception of direction and extent. *Psychological Review, 93,* 391–410. (p. 311)

**Coren, S., & Ward, L. M.** (1989). *Sensation and perception* (3rd ed.). New York: Harcourt Brace Jovanovich. (p. 264)

**Corey, S. M.** (1937). Professed attitudes and actual behavior. *Journal of Educational Psychology, 28,* 271–280. (p. 520)

**Coryell, W., & Zimmerman, M.** (1987). Progress in the classification of functional psychoses. *American Journal of Psychiatry, 144,* 1471–1474. (p. 611)

**Costa, P. T., Zonderman, A. B., McCrae, R. R., Cornoni-Huntley, J., Locke, B. Z., & Barbano, H. E.** (1987). Longitudinal analyses of psychological well-being in a national sample: Stability of mean levels. *Journal of Gerontology, 42,* 50–55. (p. 484)

**Cottrell, N. B., Wack, D. L., Sekerak, G. J., & Rittle, R. H.** (1968). Social facilitation of dominant responses by the presence of an audience and the mere presence of others. *Journal of Personality and Social Psychology, 9,* 245–250. (p. 541)

**Cox, T.** (1984). Stress: A psychophysiological approach to cancer. In C. L. Cooper (Ed.), *Psychological stress and cancer.* Chichester, England: Wiley. (p. 229)

**Craik, F. I., & Lockhart, R. S.** (1972). Levels of processing: A framework for memory research. *Journal of Verbal Learning and Verbal Behavior, 11,* 671–684. (p. 336)

**Craik, F. I., & Tulving, E.** (1975). Depth of processing and the retention of words in episodic memory. *Journal of Experimental Psychology: General, 104,* 268–294. (p. 336)

**Craik, F. I., & Watkins, M. J.** (1973). The role of rehearsal in short-term memory. *Journal of Verbal Learning and Verbal Behavior, 12,* 599–607. (pp. 334–335)

**Crow, T. J.** (1980). Molecular pathology of schizophrenia: More than one process? *British Medical Journal, 280,* 66–68. (p. 636)

**Crowne, D. P., & Liverant, S.** (1963). Conformity under varying conditions of personal commitment. *Journal of Abnormal and Social Psychology, 66,* 547–555. (p. 587)

**Culp, R. E., Cook, A. S., & Housley, P. C.** (1983). A comparison of observed and reported adult-infant interactions: Effects of perceived sex. *Sex Roles, 9,* 475–479. (p. 467)

**Cumming, E., & Henry, W.** (1961). *Growing old: The process of disengagement.* New York: Basic Books. (p. 484)

**Curtiss, S.** (1977) *Genie: A psycholinguistic study of a modern-day "wild child."* New York: Academic Press. (p. 426)

**Curtiss, S.** (1981). Dissociations between language and cognition: Cases and implications. *Journal of Autism and Developmental Disorders, 11,* 15–30. (p. 426)

**Cutting, J. E., & Proffitt, D. R.** (1982). The minimum principle and the perception of absolute, common, and relative motions. *Cognitive Psychology, 14,* 211–246. (p. 313)

**Cutting, J. E., Proffitt, D. R., & Kozlowski, L. T.** (1978). A biomechanical invariant for gait perception. *Journal of Experimental Psychology: Human Perception and Performance, 4,* 357–372. (p. 313)

**Czeisler, C. A., Kronauer, R. E., Allen, J. S., Duffy, J. F., Jewett, M. E., Brown, E. N., & Ronda, J. M.** (1989). Bright light induction of strong (type O) resetting of the human circadian pacemaker. *Science, 244,* 1328–1333. (p. 222)

**Daly, M., & Wilson, M.** (1983). *Sex, evolution, and behavior* (2nd ed.). Boston: Willard Grant Press. (pp. 105, 106)

**Daly, M., & Wilson, M.** (1988). *Homicide.* New York: Aldine de Gruyter. (pp. 116, 117)

**Damon, W.** (1983). *Social and personality development.* New York: Norton. (pp. 463, 471, 474, 478)

**Dana, R. H.** (1985). Thematic apperception test (TAT). In C. S. Newmark (Ed.), *Major psychological assessment instruments.* Boston: Allyn & Bacon. (p. 651)

**Dance, K. A., & Kuiper, N. A.** (1987). Self-schemata, social roles, and a self-worth contingency model of depression. *Motivation and Emotion, 11,* 251–268. (p. 504)

**Darwin, C.** (1859; reprinted 1963). *The origin of species.* New York: Washington Square Press. (pp. 7, 81)

**Darwin, C.** (1872; reprinted 1965). *The expression of the emotions in man and animals.* Chicago: University of Chicago Press. (pp. 7, 97, 99, 101, 103)

**Darwin, C. T., Turvey, M. T., & Crowder, R. G.** (1972). An auditory analogue of the Sperling partial report procedure: Evidence for brief auditory storage. *Cognitive Psychology, 3,* 255–267. (p. 330)

**Dashiell, J. F.** (1935). Experimental studies of the influence of social situations on the behavior of individual human adults. In *A handbook of social psychology.* Worcester, MA: Clark University Press. (p. 542)

**Davidson, J. M.** (1980). Hormones and sexual behavior in the male. In D. T. Krieger & J. C. Hughes (Eds.), *Neuroendocrinology.* Sunderland, MA: Sinauer Associates. (p. 211)

**Davidson, J. M., Camargo, C. A., & Smith, E. R.** (1979). Effects of androgen on sexual behavior in hypogonadal men. *Journal of Clinical Endocrinology and Metabolism, 48,* 955–958. (p. 211)

**Davidson, J. M., & Myers, L. S.** (1988). Endocrine factors in sexual psychophysiology. In R. C. Rosen & J. G. Beck (Eds.), *Patterns of sexual arousal: Psychophysiological processes and clinical applications.* New York: Guilford. (p. 211)

**Davis, C. M.** (1928). Self selection of diet in newly weaned infants: An experimental study. *American Journal of Diseases of Children, 36,* 651–679. (p. 155)

**Davis, J. M.** (1974). A two-factor theory of schizophrenia. *Journal of Psychiatric Research, 11,* 25–30. (p. 638)

**Davis, K. E., & Todd, M.** (1982). Friendship and love relationships. In K. E. Davis & T. O. Mitchell (Eds.), *Advances in descriptive psychology* (Vol. 2). Greenwich, CT: JAI Press. (p. 511)

**Davis, P. J., & Schwartz, G. E.** (1987). Repression and the inaccessibility of affective memories. *Journal of Personality and Social Psychology, 52,* 155–162. (p. 572)

**Deaux, K.** (1984). From individual differences to social categories: Analysis of a decade's research on gender. *American Psychologist, 39,* 105–116. (p. 496)

**Deaux, K.** (1985). Sex and gender. *Annual Review of Psychology, 36,* 49–81. (p. 467)

**DeCasper, A. J., & Fifer, W. P.** (1980). Of human bonding: Newborns prefer their mothers' voices. *Science, 208,* 1174–1176. (p. 420)

**DeCasper, A. J., & Spence, M. J.** (1986). Prenatal maternal speech influences newborns' perception of speech sounds. *Infant Behavior and Development, 9,* 133–150. (p. 420)

**de Groot, A. D.** (1965). *Thought and choice in chess.* The Hague: Mouton. (p. 338)

**Delabar, J.-M., Goldgaber, D., Lamour, Y., Nicole, A., Huret, J.-L., & others.** (1987). ß amyloid gene duplication in Alzheimer's disease and karyotypically normal Down syndrome. *Science, 235,* 1390–1392. (p. 60)

**Delay, J., & Deniker, P.** (1952). Trente-huit cas de psychoses traitees par la cure prolongee et continue de 4560 RP. *Comptes Rendus Congrès des Médecins Aliénistes et Neurologistes de France et des Pays de Langue Française, 50,* 497–502. (p. 675)

**DeLisi, L. E., Dauphinais, I. D., & Gershon, E. S.** (1988). Perinatal complications and reduced size of brain limbic structures in familial schizophrenia. *Schizophrenia Bulletin, 14,* 185–191. (pp. 638, 639)

**Dement, W. C.** (1972). *Some must watch while some must sleep.* San Francisco: Freeman. (p. 223)

**Dement, W. C.** (1979). The relevance of sleep pathologies to the function of sleep. In R. Drucker-Colin, M. Shkurovich, & M. B. Sterman (Eds.), *The functions of sleep.* New York: Academic Press. (p. 222)

**Dement, W. C., & Kleitman, N.** (1957). Cyclic variations in EEG during sleep and their relation to eye movements, body motility, and dreaming. *Electroencephalography and Clinical Neuropsychology, 9,* 673–690. (p. 218)

**Descartes, R.** (1637; reprinted 1972). *Treatise of man* (T. S. Hall, Trans.). Cambridge, MA: Harvard University Press. (p. 5)

**Deutsch, A.** (1948). *The shame of the states.* New York: Harcourt, Brace. (p. 644)

**Deutsch, J. A.** (1963). Learning and self-stimulation of the brain. *Journal of Theoretical Biology, 4,* 193–214. (p. 216)

**De Valois, R. L., Abramov, I., & Jacobs, G. H.** (1966). Analysis of response patterns of LGN cells. *Journal of the Optical Society of America, 56,* 96–977. (p. 265)

**De Valois, R. L., & De Valois, K. K.** (1988). *Spatial vision.* Oxford: Oxford University Press. (pp. 258, 260) de Villiers, J. G., & de Villiers, P. A. (1979). *Language acquisition*. Cambridge, MA: Harvard University Press. (p. 424)

Devine, P. G. (1989). Stereotypes and prejudice: Their automatic and controlled components. *Journal of Personality and Social Psychology, 56*, 5–18. (p. 496)

Dewsbury, D. A. (!988). The comparative psychology of monogamy. In D. W. Leger (Ed.), *Comparative perspectives in modern psychology. Nebraska Symposium on Motivation, 1987*. Lincoln, NE: University of Nebraska Press. (pp. 107, 108, 116)

Dickinson, A. (1989). Expectancy theory in animal conditioning. In S. B. Klein & R. R. Mowrer (Eds.), *Contemporary learning theories: Pavlovian conditioning and the status of learning theory*. Hillsdale, NJ: Erlbaum. (pp. 147, 148)

Dickinson, A., & Dawson, G. R. (1987). The role of the instrumental contingency in motivational control of performance. *Quarterly Journal of Experimental Psychology, 39B*, 77–93. (p. 148)

Diener, E. (1977). Deindividuation: Causes and consequences. *Social Behavior and Personality, 5*, 143–155. (p. 544)

Digman, J. M., & Inouye, J. (1986). Further specification of the five robust factors of personality. *Journal of Personality and Social Psychology, 50*, 116–123. (p. 595)

DiMascio, A., Weissman, M. M., Prusoff, B. A., Neu, C., Zwilling, M., & Klerman, G. L. (1979). Differential symptom reduction by drugs and psychotherapy in acute depression. *Archives of General Psychiatry, 36*, 1450–1456. (pp. 29, 35, 40, 677)

Dion, K. K. (1972). Physical attractiveness and evaluation of children's transgressions. *Journal of Personality and Social Psychology, 24*, 207–213. (p. 495)

Dion, K. K. (1986). Stereotyping based on physical attractiveness: Issues and conceptual perspectives. In C. P. Herman, M. P. Zanna, & E. T. Higgins (Eds.), *Physical appearance, stigma, and social behavior: The Ontario symposium, vol. 3*. Hillsdale, NJ: Erlbaum. (p. 495)

Domjan, M., and Burkhard, B. (1986). *The principles of learning and behavior* (2nd ed.). Monterey, CA: Brooks/Cole. (pp. 145, 147)

Donovan, J. M. (1975). Identity status and interpersonal style. *Journal of Youth and Adolescence, 4*, 37–55. (p. 475)

Dovidio, J. F. (1984). Helping behavior and altruism: An empirical and conceptual overview. In L. Berkowitz (Ed.), *Advances in experimental social psychology* (Vol. 17). New York: Academic Press. (p. 543)

DuBois, P. H. (1972). College Board Scholastic Aptitude Test. In O. K. Buros (Ed.), *The seventh mental measurements yearbook* (2 vols.). Highland Park, NJ: Gryphon. (p. A-6)

Duggan, J. P., & Booth, D. A. (1986). Obesity, overeating, and rapid gastric emptying in rats with ventromedial hypothalamic lesions. *Science, 231*, 609–611. (p. 204)

Duncan, B. L. (1976). Differential social perception and attribution of intergroup violence: Testing the lower limits of stereotyping of blacks. *Journal of Personality and Social Psychology, 34*, 590–598. (p. 496)

Duncan, J. (1980). The locus of interference in the perception of simultaneous stimuli. *Psychological Review, 87*, 272–300. (p. 302)

Duncker, K. (1945). On problem-solving. *Psychological Monographs, 58* (Whole no. 270). (p. 390)

Dunphy, D. C. (1963). The social structure of urban adolescent peer groups. *Sociometry, 26*, 230–246. (p. 471)

Dweck, C. S., & Bush, E. S. (1976). Sex differences in learned helplessness: I. Differential debilitation with peer and adult evaluators. *Developmental Psychology, 12*, 147–156. (p. 468)

Dweck, C. S., Davidson, W., Nelson, S., & Enna, B. (1978). Sex differences in learned helplessness: II. The contingencies of evaluative feedback in the classroom. III. An experimental analysis. *Developmental Psychology, 14*, 268–276. (p. 468)

Eagle, M., Wolitzky, D. L., & Klein, G. S. (1966). Imagery: Effect of a concealed figure in a stimulus. *Science, 151*, 837–839. (p. 298)

Easton, T. A. (1972). On the normal use of reflexes. *American Scientist, 60*, 591–599. (p. 177)

Eaton, G. G. (1976, October). The social order of Japanese macaques. *Scientific American*, 96–106. (p. 112)

Ebbinghaus, H. (1885; reprinted 1913). *Memory: A contribution to experimental psychology* (H. A. Ruger & C. E. Bussenius, Trans.). New York: Teachers College Press. (pp. 331, 350)

Eccles, J. (1985). Sex differences in achievement patterns. In T. B. Sonderegger (Ed.), *Nebraska symposium on motivation 1984*. Lincoln, NE: University of Nebraska Press. (p. 468)

Eckland, B. K. (1982). College entrance examination trends. In G. R. Austin & G. Garber (Eds.), *The rise and fall of national test scores*. New York: Academic Press. (p. A-6)

Edelman, G. M. (1987). *Neural Darwinism*. New York: Basic Books. (pp. 182, 224)

Eibl-Eibesfeldt, I. (1961, December). The fighting behavior of animals. *Scientific American*, 112–121. (p. 91)

Eibl-Eibesfeldt, I. (1975). *Ethology: The biology of behavior* (2nd ed.). New York: Holt, Rinehart & Winston. (pp. 96, 102)

Eibl-Eibesfeldt, I. (1989). *Human ethology*. New York: Aldine de Gruyter. (pp. 98, 102, 116)

Eich, J. E. (1980). The cue-dependent nature of state-dependent retrieval. *Memory and Cognition, 8*, 157–173. (p. 353)

Eimas, P. D. (1975). Speech perception in early infancy. In L. B. Cohen & P. Salapafek (Eds.), *Infant perception*. New York: Academic Press. (p. 421)

Ekman, P. (1973). Cross-cultural studies of facial expression. In P. Ekman (Ed.), *Darwin and facial expression*. New York: Academic Press.

Ekman, P. (1985). *Telling lies*. New York: Norton. (p. 101)

Ekman, P., & Friesen, W. V. (1975). *Unmasking the face*. Englewood Cliffs, NJ: Prentice Hall. (pp. 99, 100)

Ekman, P., & Friesen, W. V. (1982). Measuring facial movements with the facial action coding system. In P. Ekman (Ed.), *Emotion in the human face*. Cambridge: Cambridge University Press. (pp. 99, 101)

Ekman, P., Levenson, R. W., & Friesen, W. V. (1983). Autonomic nervous system activity distinguishes among emotions. *Science*, *221*, 1208–1210. (pp. 234, 235)

Ellis, A. (1962). *Reason and emotion in psychotherapy*. New York: Lyle Stuart. (p. 663)

Ellis, A. (1986). Rational-emotive therapy. In I. L. Kutash & A. Wolf (Eds.), *Psychotherapist's casebook*. San Francisco: Jossey-Bass. (p. 662)

Ellis, L., & Ames, M. A. (1987). Neurohormonal functioning and sexual orientation: A theory of homosexuality-heterosexuality. *Psychological Bulletin*, *101*, 233–258. (p. 210)

Ellis, L., Ames, M. A., Peckham, W., & Burke, D. (1988). Sexual orientation of human offspring may be altered by severe maternal stress during pregnancy. *Journal of Sex Research*, *25*, 152–157. (p. 210)

Emlen, S. T. (1975, August). The stellar-orientation system of a migratory bird. *Scientific American*, 102–111. (pp. 92–93)

Endler, N. S. (1982). *Holiday of darkness: A psychologist's personal journey out of his depression*. New York: Wiley. (p. 628)

Epstein, S. (1979). The stability of behavior: I. On predicting most of the people much of the time. *Journal of Personality and Social Psychology*, *37*, 1097–1126. (p. 597)

Epstein, S., & O'Brien, E. J. (1985). The person-situational debate in historical and current perspective. *Psychological Bulletin*, *98*, 513–537. (p. 597)

Erberg, P. (1985). The Rorschach. In C. S. Newmark (Ed.), *Major psychological assessment instruments*. Boston: Allyn & Bacon. (p. 651)

Erckmann, W. J. (1983). The evolution of polyandry in shorebirds: An evolutionary hypothesis. In S. K. Wasser (Ed.), *Social behavior of female vertebrates*. New York: Academic Press. (p. 107)

Erdelyi, M. H. (1985). *Psychoanalysis: Freud's cognitive psychology*. New York: Freeman. (pp. 18, 572, 653)

Ericsson, K. A., Chase, W. G., & Faloon, S. (1980). Acquisition of a memory skill. *Science*, *208*, 1181–1182. (p. 338)

Eriksen, C. W., & Collins, J. F. (1967). Some temporal characteristics of visual pattern perception. *Journal of Experimental Psychology*, *74*, 476–484. (p. 330)

Erikson, E. H. (1963). *Childhood and society* (2nd ed.). New York: Norton. (pp. 450, 463, 470)

Erikson, E. H. (1968). *Identity: Youth and crisis*. New York: Norton. (p. 470)

Errera, P. (1972). Statement based on interviews with forty "worst cases" in the Milgram obedience experiments. In J. Katz (Ed.), *Experimentation with human beings: The authority of the investigator, subject, professions, and state in the human experimentation process*. New York: Russell Sage Foundation. (p. 539)

Ervin-Tripp, S. (1964). An analysis of the interaction of language, topic, and listener. *American Anthropologist*, *86* (6, Pt. 2), 86–102. (p. 403)

Essock-Vitale, S. M., & McGuire, M. T. (1980). Predictions derived from the theories of kin selection and reciprocation assessed by anthropological data. *Ethology and Sociobiology*, *1*, 233–243. (p. 117)

Etscorn, F., & Stephens, R. (1973). Establishment of conditioned taste aversions with a 24-hour CS-US interval. *Physiological Psychology*, *1*, 251–253. (p. 154)

Evarts, E. V. (1979, September). Brain mechanisms in movement. *Scientific American*, 164–179. (p. 183)

Eysenck, H. J. (1952). *The scientific study of personality*. London: Routledge & Kegan Paul. (p. 593)

Eysenck, H. J. (1973). *The inequality of man*. London: Temple Smith. (p. 69)

Eysenck, H. J. (1975). A genetic model of anxiety. In L. G. Sarason & C. D. Spielberger (Eds.), *Stress and anxiety: Vol. 2*. New York: Wiley. (p. 616)

Eysenck, H. J. (1982). Development of a theory. In H. J. Eysenck (Ed.), *Personality, genetics, and behavior: Selected papers*. New York: Praeger. (pp. 591, 594)

Eysenck, H. J. (1987). Speed of information processing, reaction time, and the theory of intelligence. In P. A. Vernon (Ed.), *Speed of information-processing and intelligence*. Norwood, NJ: Ablex. (p. 366)

Eysenck, H. J., & Eysenck, M. W. (1985). *Personality and individual differences: A natural science approach*. New York: Plenum. (p. 594)

Eysenck, S. B. G., & Eysenck, H. J. (1967). Salivary response to lemon juice as a measure of introversion. *Perceptual and Motor Skill*, *24*, 1047–1051. (p. 594)

Fagot, B. I. (1977). Consequences of moderate cross-gender behavior in pre-school children. *Child Development*, *48*, 902–907. (p. 467)

Fancher, R. E. (1985). *The intelligence men: Makers of the IQ controversy*. New York: Norton. (pp. 69, 367)

Farina, A., Gliha, D., Boudreau, L. A., Allen, J. G., & Sherman, M. (1971). Mental illness and the impact of believing others know about it. *Journal of Abnormal Psychology*, *77*, 1–5. (p. 614)

Farone, S. V., & Tsuang, M. T. (1985). Quantitative models of the genetic transmission of schizophrenia. *Psychological Bulletin*, *98*, 41–66. (p. 76)

Faust, I. M. (1984). Role of the fat cell in energy balance physiology. In A. J. Stunkard & E. Stellar (Eds.), *Eating and its disorders*. New York: Raven. (p. 207)

Fazio, R. H. (1986). How do attitudes guide behavior? In R. M. Sorrentino & E. T. Higgins (Eds.), *Handbook of motivation and cognition: Foundations of social behavior*. New York: Guilford. (p. 521)

Feder, H. H. (1984). Hormones and sexual behavior. *Annual Review of Psychology*, *35*, 165–200. (pp. 189, 209, 210, 211, 212)

Festinger, L. (1954). A theory of social comparison processes. *Human Relations*, *7*, 117–140. (pp. 504, 514)

Festinger, L. (1957). *A theory of cognitive dissonance*. Stanford: Stanford University Press. (p. 516)

Festinger, L., & Carlsmith, J. M. (1959). Cognitive consequences of forced compliance. *Journal of Abnormal and Social Psychology*, *58*, 203–210. (p. 518)

Feynman, R. P. *Surely you're joking, Mr. Feynman!* New York: Bantam Books. (p. 388)

**Field, T., Schanberg, S. M., Scafidi, F., Bauer, C. R., Vega-Lahr, N., Garcia, R., Nystrom, J., & Kuhn, C. M.** (1986). Effects of tactile/kinesthetic stimulation on preterm neonates. *Pediatrics, 77,* 654–658. (p. 454)

**Fieve, R. R.** (1975). *Mood swing.* New York: William Morrow. (p. 632)

**Fischler, M. A., & Firschein, O.** (1987). *Intelligence: The eye, the brain, and the computer.* Reading, MA: Addison-Wesley. (p. 392)

**Fisher, S., & Fisher, R. L.** (1981). *Pretend the world is funny and forever: A psychological analysis of comedians, clowns, and actors.* Hillsdale, NJ: Erlbaum. (p. 573)

**Fisher, S., & Greenberg, R. P.** (1985). *The scientific credibility of Freud's theories and therapy.* New York: Columbia University Press. (p. 572)

**FitzGerald, K. W.** (1988). *Alcoholism: The genetic inheritance.* Garden City, NY: Doubleday. (p. 624)

**Flaherty, C. F.** (1982). Incentive contrast: A review of behavioral changes following shifts in reward. *Animal Learning and Behavior, 10,* 409–440. (p. 149)

**Flaherty, C. F.** (1985). *Animal learning and cognition.* New York: Knopf. (p. 149)

**Flavell, J. H., Beach, D. H., & Chinsky, J. M.** (1966). Spontaneous verbal rehearsal in a memory task as a function of age. *Child Development, 37,* 283–299. (p. 442)

**Floody, O. R., Blinn, N. E., Lisk, R. D., & Vomachka, A. J.** (1987). Localization of hypothalamic sites for the estrogen-priming of sexual receptivity in female hamsters. *Behavioral Neuroscience, 101,* 309–314. (p. 211)

**Flourens, P. J. M.** (1824; reprinted 1965). *Pierre Jean Marie Flourens on the functions of the brain* (M. D. Boring, Trans.). In R. J. Herrnstein & E. G. Boring (Eds.), *A source book in the history of psychology.* Cambridge, MA: Harvard University Press. (p. 7)

**Flynn, J. P.** (1967). The neural basis of aggression in cats. In D. C. Glass (Ed.), *Neurophysiology and emotion.* New York: Rockefeller University Press and Russell Sage Foundation. (p. 235)

**Foa, E. B., & Kozak, M. J.** (1986). Emotional processing of fear: Exposure to corrective information. *Psychological Bulletin, 99,* 20–35. (p. 668)

**Foa, E. B., Steketee, G. S., & Ozarow, B. J.** (1985). In M. Mavissakalian, S. M. Turner, & L. Michelson (Eds.), *Obsessive-compulsive disorder.* New York: Plenum. (pp. 618, 619)

**Foch, T. T., & McClearn, G. E.** (1980). Genetics, body weight, and obesity. In A. J. Stunkard (Ed.), *Obesity.* Philadelphia: Saunders. (p. 207)

**Fodor, I. G.** (1982). Gender and phobia. In I. Al-Issa (Ed.), *Gender and psychopathology.* New York: Academic Press. (p. 617)

**Ford, C. S., & Beach, F. A.** (1951). *Patterns of sexual behavior.* New York: Harper & Row. (p. 473)

**Ford, C. V.** (1983). *The somatizing disorders: Illness as a way of life.* New York: Elsevier Biomedical. (p. 621)

**Ford, M. R., & Lowery, C. R.** (1986). Gender differences in moral reasoning: A comparison of the use of justice and care orientations. *Journal of Personality and Social Psychology, 50,* 777–783. (p. 478)

**Ford, M. R., & Widiger, T. A.** (1989). Sex bias in the diagnosis of histrionic and antisocial personality disorders. *Journal of Consulting and Clinical Psychology, 57,* 301–305. (p. 613)

**Forrest, G. G.** (1985). Antabuse treatment. In T. E. Bratter & G. G. Forrest (Eds.), *Alcoholism and substance abuse: Strategies for clinical intervention.* New York: Free Press. (p. 670)

**Foss, J. D., & Hakes, D. T.** (1978). *Psycholinguistics: An introduction to the psychology of language.* Englewood Cliffs, NJ: Prentice Hall. (p. 394)

**Foulkes, D.** (1985). *Dreaming: A cognitive-psychological analysis.* Hillsdale, NJ: Erlbaum. (pp. 223, 224)

**Fox, N.** (1977). Attachment of kibbutz infants to mother and metapelet. *Child Development, 48,* 1228–1239. (p. 458)

**Frandsen, A. N., & Holder, J. R.** (1969). Spatial visualization in solving complex verbal problems. *Journal of Psychology, 73,* 229–233. (p. 387)

**Franklin, B.** (1949). *The autobiography of Benjamin Franklin.* Berkeley, CA: University of California Press. (p. 518)

**Freedman, B., & Chapman, L. J.** (1973). Early subjective experience in schizophrenic episodes. *Journal of Abnormal Psychology, 82,* 46–54. (p. 636)

**Freedman, J. L., & Fraser, S. C.** (1966). Compliance without pressure: The foot-in-the-door technique. *Journal of Personality and Social Psychology, 4,* 195–202. (pp. 532, 533)

**Frenkel, O. J., & Doob, A. N.** (1976). Post-decision dissonance at the polling booth. *Canadian Journal of Behavioural Science, 8,* 347–350. (p. 517)

**Freud, A.** (1936; reprinted 1946). *The ego and the mechanisms of defense* (C. Baines, Trans.). New York: International Universities Press. (p. 569)

**Freud, S.** (1900; reprinted 1953). *The interpretation of dreams* (J. Strachey, Ed. & trans.). London: Hogarth Press. (p. 565)

**Freud, S.** (1901; reprinted 1960). *The psychopathology of everyday life* (A. Tyson, Trans., & J. Strachey, Ed.). New York: Norton. (pp. 566, 567)

**Freud, S.** (1909a; reprinted 1963). Analysis of a phobia in a five-year-old boy. In P. Rieff (Ed.), *The sexual enlightenment of children.* New York: Collier Books. (p. 617)

**Freud, S.** (1909b; reprinted 1963). Notes upon a case of obsessional neurosis. In P. Rieff (Ed.), *Three case histories.* New York: Collier Books. (pp. 618, 657)

**Freud, S.** (1910; reprinted 1947). *Leonardo da Vinci: A study in psychosexuality.* New York: Random House. (p. 569)

**Freud, S.** (1912; reprinted 1932). A note on the unconscious in psychoanalysis. In J. Rickman (Ed.), *A general selection from the works of Sigmund Freud.* London: Hogarth Press. (p. 564)

**Freud, S.** (1923; reprinted 1963). [Note appended to the 1963 reprint of "Notes upon a case of obsession neurosis."] In P. Rieff (Ed.), *Three case histories.* New York: Collier Books. (p. 658)

Freud, S. (1926; reprinted 1964). Inhibitions, symptoms, and anxiety. In J. Strachey (Trans. & ed.), *The standard edition of the complete works of Sigmund Freud* (Vol. 20). London: Hogarth Press. (p. 568)

Freud, S. (1933; reprinted 1964). *New introductory lectures on psychoanalysis.* In J. Strachey (Trans. & ed.), *The standard edition of the complete works of Sigmund Freud* (Vol. 20). London: Hogarth Press. (pp. 567, 568)

Freud, S. (1935; reprinted 1960). *A general introduction to psychoanalysis.* New York: Washington Square Press. (pp. 479, 572)

Frey, D. (1986). Recent research on selective exposure to information. *Advances in Experimental Social Psychology, 19,* 41–80. (p. 517)

Fromkin, V. A. (1973). *Speech errors as linguistic evidence.* The Hague: Mouton. (p. 398)

Fromkin, V. A. (1980). *Errors in linguistic performance: Slips of the tongue, ear, pen and hand.* New York: Academic Press. (p. 398)

Fuller, J. L., & Thompson, W. R. (1978). *Foundations of behavior genetics.* New York: Wiley. (p. 64)

Furrow, D., Nelson, K., & Benedict, H. (1979). Mother's speech to children and syntactic development: Some simple relationships. *Journal of Child Language, 6,* 423–442. (p. 427)

Futuyma, D. J. (1986). *Evolutionary biology* (2nd ed.). Sunderland. MA: Sinauer. (p. 82)

Galanter, E. (1962). Contemporary psychophysics. In R. Brown, E. Galanter, E. Hess, & G. Mandler (Eds.), *New directions in psychology.* New York: Holt, Rinehart & Winston. (p. 254)

Galef, B. G., Jr. (1985). Social learning in wild Norway rats. In T. D. Johnston & A. T. Pietrewicz (Eds.), *Issues in the ecological study of learning.* Hillsdale, NJ: Erlbaum. (p. 156)

Galef, B. G., Jr., & Clark, M. M. (1971). Social factors in the poison avoidance and feeding behavior of wild and domesticated rat pups. *Journal of Comparative and Physiological Psychology, 75,* 341–357. (p. 156)

Gallistel, C. R., & Beagley, G. (1971). Specificity of brain-stimulation reward in the rat. *Journal of Comparative and Physiological Psychology, 76,* 199–205. (p. 216)

Galton, F. (1865). Hereditary talent and character. *Macmillan's Magazine, 12,* 157–166, 318–327. (pp. 69, 366)

Galton, F. (1869; reprinted 1962). *Hereditary genius: An inquiry into its laws and consequences.* Cleveland: World Publishing. (pp. 67, 366)

Galton, F. (1876). The history of twins as a criterion of the relative powers of nature and nurture. *Royal Anthropological Institute of Great Britain and Ireland Journal, 6,* 391–406. (p. 68)

Galton, F. (1907). *Inquiries into human faculty and its development.* New York: Dutton. (p. 68)

Gantt, W. H. (1953). Principles of nervous breakdown—schizokinesis and autokinesis. *Annals of the New York Academy of Sciences, 56,* 143–163. (p. 127)

Gantt, W. H. (1975). Unpublished lecture on Pavlov given at The Ohio State University, April 25. (p. 123)

Garcia, J., McGowan, B. K., Ervin, F. R., & Koelling, R. A. (1968). Cues—their relative effectiveness as a function of the reinforcer. *Science, 160,* 794–795. (p. 154)

Garcia, J., McGowan, B. K., & Green, K. F. (1972). Biological constraints on conditioning. In A. H. Black & W. G. Prokasy (Eds.), *Classical conditioning II: Current research and theory.* New York: Appleton-Century-Crofts. (p. 153)

Gardner, H. (1974). *The shattered mind.* New York: Random House. (p. 377)

Gardner, H. (1985). *Frames of mind.* New York: Basic Books. (p. 382)

Gardner, L. I. (1972, July). Deprivation dwarfism. *Scientific American,* 76–82. (p. 454)

Gardner, R., & Gardner, B. T. (1978). Comparative psychology and language acquisition. In K. Salzinger & F. L. Denmark (Eds.), Psychology: The state of the art. *Annals of the New York Academy of Sciences, 309,* 37–76. (p. 428)

Garrett, M. F. (1975). The analysis of sentence production. In G. H. Bower (Ed.), *The psychology of learning and motivation* (Vol. 9). New York: Academic Press. (p. 398)

Garrett, M. F. (1982). Production of speech: Observations from normal and pathological language use. In A. W. Ellis (Ed.), *Normality and pathology in cognitive functions.* London: Academic Press. (p. 398)

Garvey, C. (1974). Some properties of social play. *Merrill-Palmer Quarterly, 20,* 163–180. (p. 464)

Garvey, C. (1977). *Play.* Cambridge, MA: Harvard University Press. (p. 464)

Gazzaniga, M. S. (1967, August). The split brain in man. *Scientific American,* 24–29. (pp. 379, 380)

Gazzaniga, M. S. (1970). *The bisected brain.* New York: Appleton-Century-Crofts. (p. 379)

Geen, R. G. (1980). The effects of being observed on performance. In P. B. Paulus (Ed.), *Psychology of group influence.* Hillsdale, NJ: Erlbaum. (p. 541)

Geen, R. G. (1984). Preferred stimulation levels in introverts and extraverts: Effects on arousal and performance. *Journal of Personality and Social Psychology, 45,* 1303–1312. (p. 594)

Geliebter, A., Westreich, S., Hashim, S. A., & Gage, D. (1987). Gastric balloon reduces food intake and body weight in obese rats. *Physiology and Behavior, 39,* 399–402. (p. 204)

Gescheider, G. A. (1976). *Psychophysics: Methods and theory.* Hillsdale, NJ: Erlbaum. (pp. 273, 278)

Geschwind, N. (1972, April). Language and the brain. *Scientific American,* 76–83. (p. 400)

Ghez, C. (1985a). Introduction to the motor systems. In E. R. Kandel & J. H. Schwartz (Eds.), *Principles of neural science* (2nd ed.). New York: Elsevier. (p. 185)

Ghez, C. (1985b). Voluntary movement. In E. R. Kandel & J. H. Schwartz (Eds.), *Principles of neural science* (2nd ed.). New York: Elsevier. (p. 184)

**Gibbons, F. X.** (1978). Sexual standards and reactions to pornography: Enhancing behavioral consistency through self-focused attention. *Journal of Personality and Social Psychology, 36,* 976–987. (p. 521)

**Gibbs, J. C., & Schnell, S. V.** (1985). Moral development "versus" socialization. *American Psychologist, 40,* 1071–1080. (p. 477)

**Gibson, E. J.** (1969). *Principles of perceptual learning and its development.* Englewood Cliffs, NJ: Prentice Hall. (p. 294)

**Gibson, E. J.** (1971). Perceptual learning and the theory of word perception. *Cognitive Psychology, 2,* 351–358. (p. 301)

**Gibson, E. J., & Walk, R. D.** (1960, April). The visual cliff. *Scientific American,* 64–71. (p. 416)

**Gibson, J. J.** (1966). *The senses considered as perceptual systems.* Boston: Houghton Mifflin. (p. 315)

**Gibson, J. J.** (1979). *The ecological approach to visual perception.* Boston: Houghton Mifflin. (p. 315)

**Gilbert, D. T.** (1989). Thinking lightly about others: Automatic components of the social inference process. In J. S. Uleman & J. A. Bargh (Eds.), *Unintended thought.* New York: Guilford. (p. 499)

**Gilbert, D. T., & Jones, E. E.** (1986). Perceiver-induced constraint: Interpretations of self-generated reality. *Journal of Personality and Social Psychology, 50,* 269–280. (p. 499)

**Gilligan, C.** (1982). *In a different voice: Psychological theory and women's development.* Cambridge, MA: Harvard University Press (pp. 475, 478)

**Gilligan, C.** (1987). Adolescent development reconsidered. In C. E. Irwin, Jr. (Ed.), *Adolescent social behavior and health.* San Francisco: Jossey-Bass. (p. 478)

**Gilligan, C., Brown, L. M., & Rogers, A. G.** (1990). Psyche embedded: A place for body, relationships, and culture in personality theory. In A. I. Rabin, R. A. Zucker, R. A. Emmons, & S. Frank (Eds.), *Studying persons and lives.* New York: Springer. (p. 478)

**Glanzer, M., & Cunitz, A. R.** (1966). Two storage mechanisms in free recall. *Journal of Verbal Learning and Verbal Behavior, 5,* 351–360. (pp. 333, 334)

**Glisky, E. L., Schacter, D. L., & Tulving, E.** (1986). Computer learning by memory-impaired patients: Acquisition and retention of complex knowledge. *Neuropsychologia, 24,* 313–328. (p. 360)

**Godden, D., & Baddeley, A. D.** (1975). Context-dependent memory in two natural environments. *British Journal of Psychology, 66,* 325–331. (p. 353)

**Godden, D., & Baddeley, A. D.** (1980). When does context influence recognition memory? *British Journal of Psychology, 71,* 99–104. (p. 353)

**Goffman, E.** (1959). *The presentation of self in everyday life.* Garden City, NY: Doubleday. (p. 506)

**Goldsmith, H. H.** (1983). Genetic influences on personality from infancy to adulthood. *Child Development, 54,* 331–355. (pp. 67, 599)

**Gonzalez, M. F., & Deutsch, J. A.** (1981). Vagotomy abolishes cues of satiety produced by gastric distension. *Science, 212,* 1283–1284. (p. 204)

**Good, T. L., & Findley, M. J.** (1985). Sex role expectations and achievement. In J. B. Dusek (Ed.), *Teacher expectations.* Hillsdale, NJ: Erlbaum. (p. 468)

**Goodall, J.** (1986). *The chimpanzees of Gombe.* Cambridge, MA: Harvard University Press. (pp. 108, 109, 110)

**Goodall, J.** (1988). *In the shadow of man* (rev. ed.). Boston: Houghton Mifflin. (p. 112)

**Goodwin, D. W.** (1976). *Is alcoholism hereditary?* New York: Oxford University Press. (p. 626)

**Goodwin, D. W.** (1979). Alcoholism and heredity. *Archives of General Psychiatry, 36,* 57–61. (p. 626)

**Gordon, S., & Gilgun, J. F.** (1987). *Adolescent sexuality.* In V. B. Van Hasselt & M. Hersen (Eds.), *Handbook of adolescent psychology.* New York: Pergamon. (p. 472)

**Gottesman, I. I., McGuffin, P., & Farmer, A. E.** (1987). Clinical genetics as clues to the "real" genetics of schizophrenia (a decade of modest gains while playing for time). *Schizophrenia Bulletin, 13,* 23–47. (p. 636)

**Gottesman, I. I., & Shields, J.** (1966). Schizophrenia in twins: 16 years' consecutive admissions to a psychiatric clinic. *British Journal of Psychiatry, 112,* 809–818. (p. 75)

**Gottesman, I. I., & Shields, J.** (1973). Genetic theorizing and schizophrenia. *British Journal of Psychiatry, 122,* 15–30. (p. 75)

**Gottesman, I. I., & Shields, J.** (1982). *Schizophrenia: The epigenetic puzzle.* Cambridge: Cambridge University Press. (p. 73)

**Gottlieb, G.** (1965). Imprinting in relation to parental and species identification by avian neonates. *Journal of Comparative and Physiological Psychology, 59,* 345–356. (p. 158)

**Gottman, J. M.** (1979). *Marital interaction: Experimental investigations.* New York: Academic Press. (pp. 479, 480)

**Gottman, J. M., & Krokoff, L. J.** (1989). Marital interaction and satisfaction: A longitudinal view. *Journal of Consulting and Clinical Psychology, 57,* 47–52. (p. 479)

**Gottman, J. M., & Porterfield, A. L.** (1981). Communicative competence in the nonverbal behavior of married couples. *Journal of Marriage and the Family, 43,* 817–834. (p. 480)

**Gould, J. L.** (1982). *Ethology: The mechanisms and evolution of behavior.* New York: Norton. (p. 15)

**Gould, S. J.** (1983). Hyena myths and realities. In S. J. Gould (Ed.), *Hen's teeth and horse's toes: Further reflections in natural history.* New York: Norton. (p. 88)

**Gould, S. J., & Eldredge, N.** (1977). Punctuated equilibria: The tempo and mode of evolution reconsidered. *Paleobiology, 3,* 115–151. (p. 83)

**Gouldner, A. W.** (1960). The norm of reciprocity: A preliminary statement. *American Sociological Review, 25,* 161–178. (p. 533)

**Gray, P., & Chanoff, D.** (1984). When play is learning: A school designed for self-directed education. *Phi Delta Kappan, 65,* 608–611. (p. 466)

**Gray, P., & Chanoff, D.** (1986). Democratic schooling: What happens to young people who have charge of their own education? *American Journal of Education, 94,* 182–213. (pp. 466, 582)

**Green, D. M.** (1964). Psychoacoustics and detection theory. In J. A. Swets (Ed.), *Signal detection and recognition by human observers.* New York: Wiley. (p. 272)

**Green, M., & Walker, E.** (1986). Attentional performance in positive- and negative-symptom schizophrenia. *The Journal of Nervous and Mental Disease, 174,* 208–213. (pp. 636, 637)

**Greenberg, D.** (1987a). *Free at last: The Sudbury Valley School.* Framingham, MA: Sudbury Valley School Press. (pp. 465, 466)

**Greenberg, D.** (1987b). *The Sudbury Valley School experience* (2nd ed.). Framingham, MA: Sudbury Valley School Press. (pp. 465, 466)

**Greenberg, J., & Kuczaj, S. A.** (1982). Towards a theory of substantive word-meaning acquisition. In S. A. Kuczaj (Ed.), *Language development, vol. 1: Syntax and semantics.* Hillsdale, NJ: Erlbaum. (p. 345)

**Greenberg, R. P., & Fisher, S.** (1989). Examining antidepressant effectiveness: Findings, ambiguities, and some vexing puzzles. In S. Fisher & R. P. Greenberg (Eds.), *The limits of biological treatments for psychological distress: Comparisons with psychotherapy and placebo.* Hillsdale, NJ: Erlbaum. (p. 677)

**Greenfield, P. M., & Smith, J. H.** (1976). *The structure of communication in early language development.* New York: Academic Press. (pp. 422, 424)

**Gregory, R. L.** (1968, November). Visual illusions. *Scientific American,* 66–76. (pp. 308, 310)

**Griffith, J. D., Cavanaugh, J., Held, N. N., & Oates, J. A.** (1972). Dextroamphetamine: Evaluation of psychotomimetic properties in man. *Archives of General Psychiatry, 26,* 97–100. (p. 639)

**Griffitt, W.** (1987). Females, males, and sexual responses. In K. Kelley (Ed.), *Females, males, and sexuality: Theories and research.* Albany, NY: State University of New York Press. (p. 213)

**Groos, K.** (1898). *The play of animals.* New York: Appleton. (p. 463)

**Groos, K.** (1901). *The play of man.* New York: Appleton. (p. 463)

**Gross, T. F.** (1985). *Cognitive development.* Monterey, CA: Brooks/Cole. (p. 439)

**Grossman, S. P.** (1979). The biology of motivation. *Annual Review of Psychology, 30,* 209–242. (p. 203)

**Grove, W. M.** (1987). The reliability of psychiatric diagnosis. In C. G. Last & M. Hersen (Eds.), *Issues in diagnostic research.* New York: Plenum. (p. 611)

**Grüsser, O. J., & Grüsser-Cornehls, U.** (1986). Physiology of vision. In R. F. Schmidt (Ed.), *Fundamentals of sensory physiology* (3rd ed.). New York: Springer-Verlag. (p. 256)

**Gusella, J. F., Wexler, N. S., Conneally, P. M., Naylor, S. L., Anderson, M. A., Tanzi, R. E., Watkins, P. C., Ottina, K., Wallace, M. R., Sakaguchi, A. Y., & others** (1983). A polymorphic DNA marker genetically linked to Huntington's disease. *Nature, 306,* 234–238. (p. 57)

**Guthrie, E. R.** (1952). *The psychology of learning.* New York: Harper & Row. (p. 147)

**Gutmann, D. L.** (1975). Parenthood. In N. Datan & L. H. Ginsberg (Eds.), *Life-span developmental psychology.* New York: Academic Press. (p. 481)

**Guyote, M. J., & Sternberg, R. J.** (1981). A transitive-chain theory of syllogistic reasoning. *Cognitive Psychology, 13,* 461–525. (p. 387)

**Gynther, M. D.** (1972). White norms and black MMPIs: A prescription for discrimination? *Psychological Bulletin, 78,* 386–402. (p. 651)

**Hackman, J. R.** (1986). The design of work teams. In J. Lorsch (Ed.), *Handbook of organizational behavior.* Englewood Cliffs, NJ: Prentice Hall. (p. 542)

**Hagestad, G. O., & Neugarten, B. L.** (1985). Age and the life course. In R. B. Binstock & E. Shanas (Eds.), *Handbook of aging and the social sciences* (2nd ed.). New York: Van Nostrand Reinhold. (p. 453)

**Hall, C. S.** (1979). *A primer of Freudian psychology.* New York: New American Library. (p. 570)

**Halpern, A. R.** (1986). Memory for tune titles after organized or unorganized presentation. *American Journal of Psychology, 99,* 57–70. (pp. 348, 349)

**Hamilton, W. D.** (1964). The genetical theory of social behaviour, I, II. *Journal of Theoretical Biology, 12,* 12–45. (p. 113)

**Hammond, E. C., & Horn, D.** (1984). Smoking and death rates—report on forty-four months of follow-up of 187,783 men. *Journal of the American Medical Association, 251,* 2840–2853. (p. 483)

**Haney, T. L., & Blumenthal, J. A.** (1985). Stress and the Type A behavior pattern. In S. R. Burchfield (Ed.), *Stress: Psychological and physiological interactions.* Washington, DC: Hemisphere. (p. 229)

**Harbin, T. J.** (1989). The relationship between the Type A behavior pattern and physiological responsivity: A quantitative review. *Psychophysiology, 26,* 110–118. (p. 229)

**Harkins, S. G., & Szymanski, K.** (1989). Social loafing and group evaluation. *Journal of Personality and Social Psychology, 56,* 934–941. (p. 542)

**Harlow, H. F.** (1959, June). Love in infant monkeys. *Scientific American,* 68–74. (pp. 454, 455)

**Harper, L. V., & Sanders, K. M.** (1975). The effect of adults' eating on young children's acceptance of unfamiliar foods. *Journal of Experimental Child Psychology, 20,* 206–214. (p. 156)

**Harrington, D. M., Block, J. H., & Block, J.** (1987). Testing aspects of Carl Rogers's theory of creative environments: Child-rearing antecedents of creative potential in young adolescents. *Journal of Personality and Social Psychology, 52,* 851–856. (p. 582)

**Harris, M. J., & Rosenthal, R.** (1985). Mediation of interpersonal expectancy effects: 31 meta-analyses. *Psychological Bulletin, 97,* 363–386. (p. 503)

**Hartshorne, H., & May, M.** (1928). *Studies in deceit.* New York: Macmillan. (p. 596)

**Hasler, A. D., & Larsen, J. A.** (1955, August). The homing salmon. *Scientific American,* 72–76. (p. 159)

**Hassett, J.** (1978). *A primer of psychophysiology.* San Francisco: Freeman. (p. 217)

**Hatfield, E., & Sprecher, S.** (1986). *Mirror, mirror . . . The importance of looks in everyday life.* Albany, NY: State University of New York Press. (p. 512)

**Hatfield, E., & Walster, G. W.** (1978). *A new look at love.* Lantham, MA: University Press of America. (p. 511)

**Hathaway, S. R., & McKinley, J. C.** (1943). *MMPI manual.* New York: Psychological Corporation. (p. 650)

**Hawkins, H. L., & Presson, J. C.** (1986). Auditory information processing. In K. R. Boff, L. Kaufman, & J. P. Thomas (Eds.), *Handbook of perception and human performance, Vol. II: Cognitive processes and performance.* New York: Wiley. (p. 296)

**Hay, D.** (1985). *Essentials of behaviour genetics.* Melbourne: Blackwell. (pp. 56, 57)

**Hayes, K. J., & Hayes, C. H.** (1951). The intellectual development of a home-raised chimpanzee. *Proceedings of the American Philosophical Society, 95,* 105–109. (p. 428)

**Hebb, D.** (1958). *A textbook of psychology.* Philadelphia: Saunders. (p. 62)

**Hécaen, H., & Albert, M. L.** (1978). *Human neuropsychology.* New York: Wiley. (p. 293)

**Hecht, S., & Mandelbaum, M.** (1938). Rod-cone dark adaptation and vitamin A. *Science, 88,* 219–221. (p. 256)

**Hefferline, R. F., Keenan, B., & Harford, R. A.** (1959). Escape and avoidance conditioning of human subjects without their observation of the response. *Science, 130,* 1338–1339. (p. 133)

**Heider, F.** (1958). *The psychology of interpersonal relations.* New York: Wiley. (p. 492)

**Heiman, M.** (1987). Learning to learn: A behavioral approach to improving thinking. In D. N. Perkins, J. Lockhead, & J. Bishop (Eds.), *Thinking: The second international conference.* Hillsdale, NJ: Erlbaum. (p. 336)

**Heimer, L., & Larsson, K.** (1967). Impairment of mating behavior in male rats following lesions in the preoptic-anterior hypothalamic continuum. *Brain Research, 3,* 248–263. (p. 209)

**Hendrick, C.** (1977). Social psychology as an experimental science. In C. Hendrick (Ed.), *Perspectives in social psychology.* Hillsdale, NJ: Erlbaum. (p. 540)

**Hendrick, C., & Hendrick, S.** (1986). A theory and method of love. *Journal of Personality and Social Psychology, 50,* 392–402. (p. 511)

**Hendricks, B., Marvel, M. K., & Barrington, B. L.** (1990). The dimensions of psychological research. *Teaching of Psychology, 17,* 76–82. (p. 28)

**Henry, J. L.** (1986). Role of circulating opioids in the modulation of pain. In D. D. Kelly (Ed.), *Stress-induced analgesia* (Vol. 467 of the *Annals of the New York Academy of Sciences*). New York: New York Academy of Sciences. (pp. 187, 268)

**Herek, G. M.** (1986). The instrumentality of attitudes: Toward a neofunctional theory. *Journal of Social Issues, 42,* 99–114. (p. 514)

**Herman, C. P.** (1980). Restrained eating. In A. J. Stunkard (Ed.), *Symposium on obesity: Basic mechanisms and treatment.* Philadelphia: Saunders. (p. 207)

**Herrnstein, R. J.** (1971). *IQ in the meritocracy.* Boston: Little, Brown. (p. 69)

**Herrnstein, R. J.** (1979). Acquisition, generalization, and discrimination reversal of a natural concept. *Journal of Experimental Psychology: Animal Behavior Processes, 5,* 116–129. (p. 144)

**Herrnstein, R. J.** (1984). Objects, categories, and discriminative stimuli. In H. L. Roitblat, T. G. Bever, & H. S. Terrace (Eds.), *Animal cognition.* Hillsdale, NJ: Erlbaum. (p. 144)

**Hershman, D. J., & Lieb, J.** (1988). *The key to genius.* Buffalo, NY: Prometheus. (p. 633)

**Hess, E. H.** (1958, March). "Imprinting" in animals. *Scientific American,* 81–90. (p. 158)

**Hess, E. H.** (1972, August). "Imprinting" in a natural laboratory. *Scientific American,* 24–31. (p. 158)

**Hilgard, E. R.** (1977). *Divided consciousness: Multiple controls in human action and thought.* New York: Wiley. (p. 622)

**Hill, J. P.** (1988). Adapting to menarche: Familial control and conflict. In M. R. Gunnar & W. A. Collins (Eds.), *Development during the transition to adolescence: Minnesota symposia on child psychology, vol. 21.* Hillsdale, NJ: Erlbaum. (p. 471)

**Hinson, R. E., Poulos, C. X., Thomas, W., & Cappell, H.** (1986). Pavlovian conditioning and addictive behavior: Relapse to oral self-administration of morphine. *Behavioral Neuroscience, 100,* 368–375. (p. 129)

**Hirst, W., Spelke, E. S., Reaves, C. C., Caharack, G., & Neisser, U.** (1980). Dividing attention without alternation or automaticity. *Journal of Experimental Psychology: General, 109,* 98–117. (p. 299)

**Hobson, J. A.** (1987). (1) Sleep, (2) Sleep, functional theories of, (3) Dreaming. All in G. Adelman (Ed.), *Encyclopedia of neuroscience.* Boston: Birkhäuser. (pp. 219, 220, 224)

**Hobson, J. A.** (1988). *The dreaming brain.* New York: Basic Books. (p. 224)

**Hochberg, J.** (1971). Perception II: Space and movement. In J. W. Kling & L. A. Riggs (Eds.), *Woodworth & Schlosberg's experimental psychology* (3rd ed.). New York: Holt, Rinehart & Winston. (p. 304)

**Hoebel, B. G., & Teitelbaum, P.** (1966). Weight regulation by normal and hypothalamic hyperphagic rats. *Journal of Comparative and Physiological Psychology, 61,* 189–193. (p. 205)

**Hoelter, J. W.** (1985). The structure of self-conception: Conceptualization and measurement. *Journal of Personality and Social Psychology, 49,* 1392–1407. (p. 504)

**Hoffman, C., Lau, I., & Johnson, D. R.** (1986). The linguistic relativity of person cognition: An English-Chinese comparison. *Journal of Personality and Social Psychology, 51,* 1097–1105. (p. 404)

**Hoffman, L. W., & Manis, J. D.** (1979). The value of children in the United States. *Journal of Marriage and the Family, 41,* 583–596. (p. 481)

**Hoffman, M. L.** (1975). Developmental synthesis of affect and cognition and its implications for altruistic motivation. *Developmental Psychology, 11,* 607–622. (p. 476)

**Hoffman, M. L.** (1983). Affective and cognitive processes in moral internalization. In E. T. Higgins, D. N. Ruble, & W. W. Hartup (Eds.), *Social cognition and social development*. Cambridge: Cambridge University Press. (p. 460)

**Hoffman, M. L.** (1987). The contribution of empathy to justice and moral judgment. In N. Eisenberg & J. Strayer (Eds.), *Empathy and its development*. Cambridge: Cambridge University Press. (p. 476)

**Hoffman, M. L., & Saltzstein, H. D.** (1967). Parent discipline and the child's moral development. *Journal of Personality and Social Psychology, 5*, 45–57. (p. 461)

**Hofling, C. K., Brotzman, E., Dalrymple, S., Graves, N., & Pierce, C. M.** (1966). An experimental study in nurse-physician relationships. *The Journal of Nervous and Mental Disease, 143*, 171–180. (p. 540)

**Hofstadter, R.** (1955). *Social Darwinism in American thought*. Boston: Beacon Press. (p. 114)

**Hogarty, G. E., & Goldberg, S. C.** (1973). Drug and sociotherapy in the aftercare of schizophrenic patients: One-year relapse rates. *Archives of General Psychiatry, 28*, 54–64. (p. 676)

**Hohmann, G. W.** (1966). Some effects of spinal cord lesions on experienced emotional feelings. *Psychophysiology, 3*, 143–156. (pp. 232, 233)

**Holway, A. F., & Boring, E. G.** (1941). Determinants of apparent visual size with distance variant. *American Journal of Psychology, 54*, 21–37. (p. 307)

**Honig, K. M., & Townes, B. D.** (1976). Infants' attachment to inanimate objects: A cross-cultural study. *American Academy of Child Psychiatry Journal, 15*, 49–61. (p. 459)

**Hooff, J. A. van** (1972). A comparative approach to the phylogeny of laughter and smiling. In R. A. Hinde (Ed.), *Nonverbal communication*. Cambridge: Cambridge University Press. (p. 103)

**Hooff, J. A. van** (1976). The comparison of facial expression in man and higher primates. In M. von Cranach (Ed.), *Methods of inference from animal to human behaviour*. Chicago: Aldine. (p. 103)

**Hook, E. B.** (1973). Behavioral implications of the human XYY genotype. *Science, 179*, 139–149. (p. 59)

**Horne, J. A.** (1979). Restitution and human sleep: A critical review. *Physiological Psychology, 7*, 115–125. (p. 222)

**Horne, J. A.** (1988). *Why we sleep: The functions of sleep in humans and other mammals*. Oxford: Oxford University Press. (p. 222)

**Horney, K.** (1937). *The neurotic personality of our time*. New York: Norton. (p. 577)

**Horney, K.** (1945). *Our inner conflicts*. New York: Norton. (p. 577)

**Horney, K.** (1950). *Neurosis and human growth: The struggle toward self-realization*. New York: Norton. (p. 577)

**Horwitz, R. A.** (1979). Psychological effects of the "open classroom." *Review of Educational Research, 49*, 71–86. (p. 465)

**Hosobuchi, Y., Rossier, J., Bloom, F. E., & Guillemin, R.** (1979). Stimulation of human periaqueductal gray for pain relief increases immunoreactive beta-endorphin in ventricular fluid. *Science, 203*, 279–281. (p. 268)

**Hothersall, D.** (1990). *History of psychology* (2nd ed.). New York: McGraw-Hill. (pp. 6, 13, 123, 125)

**Hrdy, S. B.** (1981). *The woman that never evolved*. Cambridge, MA: Harvard University Press. (pp. 108, 116)

**Hsu, F. L. K.** (1981). *Americans and Chinese: Passage to difference* (3rd ed.). Honolulu: University Press of Hawaii. (p. 511)

**Hubel, D. H., & Wiesel, T. N.** (1962). Receptive fields, binocular interaction, and functional architecture of the cat's visual cortex. *Journal of Physiology* (London), *160*, 106–154. (p. 258)

**Hubel, D. H., & Wiesel, T. N.** (1979, September). Brain mechanisms of vision. *Scientific American*, 150–162. (p. 258)

**Hudspeth, A. J.** (1983, January). The hair cells of the inner ear. *Scientific American*, 54–64. (p. 247)

**Huff, D.** (1954). *How to lie with statistics*. New York: Norton. (p. 39)

**Hunt, E.** (1985). Verbal ability. In R. J. Sternberg (Ed.), *Human abilities: An information-processing approach*. New York: Freeman. (p. 374)

**Husband, R. W.** (1931). Analysis of methods in human maze learning. *Journal of Genetic Psychology, 39*, 258–278. (p. 541)

**Huston, A. C., Carpenter, C. J., & Atwater, J. B.** (1986). Gender, adult structuring of activities, and social behavior in middle childhood. *Child Development, 57*, 1200–1209. (p. 467)

**Huxley, J. H., Mayr, E., Osmond, H., & Hoffer, A.** (1964). Schizophrenia as a genetic morphism. *Nature, 204*, 220–221. (p. 87)

**Hyde, J. S.** (1986). Gender differences in aggression. In J. S. Hyde & M. C. Linn (Eds.), *The psychology of gender*. Baltimore, MD: Johns Hopkins University Press. (p. 613)

**Inhelder, B., & Piaget, J.** (1958). *The growth of logical thinking from childhood to adolescence*. New York: Basic Books. (p. 434)

**Insko, C. A., Hoyle, R. H., Pinkley, R. L., Hong, G., Slim, R. M., Dalton, B., Lin, Y. W., Ruffin, P. P., Dardis, G. J., Bernthal, P. R., & Schopler, J.** (1988). Individual-group discontinuity: The role of a consensus rule. *Journal of Experimental Social Psychology, 24*, 505–519. (p. 557)

**Insko, C. A., Pinkley, R. L., Hoyle, R. H., Dalton, B., Hong, G., Slim, R. M., Landry, P., Holton, B., Ruffin, P. F., & Thibaut, J.** (1987). Individual versus group discontinuity: The role of intergroup contact. *Journal of Experimental Social Psychology, 23*, 250–267. (p. 557)

**Ironside, R., & Batchelor, I. R. C.** (1945). The ocular manifestation of hysteria in relation to flying. *British Journal of Ophthalmology, 29*, 88–98. (p. 621)

**Isabella, R. A., Belsky, J., & von Eye, A.** (1989). Origins of infant-mother attachment: An examination of interactional synchrony during the infant's first year. *Developmental Psychology, 25*, 12–21. (p. 458)

**Isen, A. M., Daubman, K. A., & Nowicki, G. P.** (1987). Positive affect facilitates creative problem solving. *Journal of Personality and Social Psychology, 52*, 1122–1131. (p. 391)

**Isenberg, D. J.** (1986). Group polarization: A critical review and meta-analysis. *Journal of Personality and Social Psychology, 50*, 1141–1151. (p. 551)

**Ito, M.** (1986). Neural systems controlling movement. *Trends in Neurosciences, 9*, 515–522. (pp. 177, 178)

**Jacklin, C. N., & Maccoby, E. E.** (1978). Social behavior at 33 months in same-sex and mixed-sex dyads. *Child Development, 49*, 557–569. (p. 469)

**Jackson, D. N., & Paunonen, S. V.** (1985). Construct validity and the predictability of behavior. *Journal of Personality and Social Psychology, 49*, 554–570. (p. 597)

**Jackson, J. M., & Latané, B.** (1981). All alone in front of all those people: Stage fright as a function of number and type of co-performers and audience. *Journal of Personality and Social Psychology, 40*, 73–85. (p. 529)

**Jacobs, P. A., Brunton, M., Melville, M. M., Brittain, R. P., & McClemont, W. F.** (1965). Aggressive behavior, mental subnormality and the XYY male. *Nature, 208*, 1351–1352. (p. 59)

**James, W.** (1884). Some omissions of introspective psychology. *Mind, 9* (January), 1–26. (p. 10)

**James, W.** (1890; reprinted 1950). *The principles of psychology.* New York: Dover. (pp. 9, 10, 23, 230, 346, 391, 503, 506)

**Jameson, D., & Hurvich, L. M.** (1989). Essay concerning color constancy. *Annual Review of Psychology, 40*, 1–22. (p. 265)

**Jamiesen, D. W., Lydon, J. E., & Zanna, M. P.** (1987). Attitude and activity preference similarity: Differential bases of interpersonal attraction for low and high self-monitors. *Journal of Personality and Social Psychology, 53*, 1052–1060. (p. 509)

**Janis, I.** (1982). *Groupthink: Psychological studies of policy decisions and fiascoes* (2nd ed.). Boston: Houghton Mifflin. (pp. 551, 552)

**Jellison, J. M., & Green, J.** (1981). A self-presentation approach to the fundamental attribution error: The norm of internality. *Journal of Personality and Social Psychology, 40*, 643–649. (p. 500)

**Jenkins, J. G., & Dallenbach, K. M.** (1924). Obliviscence during sleep and waking. *American Journal of Psychology, 35*, 605–612. (p. 350)

**Jensen, A. R.** (1969). How much can we boost IQ and scholastic achievement? *Harvard Educational Review, 39*, 1–123. (p. 71)

**Jensen, A. R.** (1980). *Bias in mental testing.* New York: Free Press. (pp. 34, 369, 370)

**Jensen, A. R.** (1987). Individual differences in the Hick paradigm. In P. A. Vernon (Ed.), *Speed of information-processing and intelligence.* Norwood, NJ: Ablex. (p. 374)

**Jerome, J. K.** (1889; reprinted 1982). *Three men in a boat (to say nothing of the dog).* London: Pavilion Books. (p. 615)

**Johansson, G.** (1975, June). Visual motion perception. *Scientific American*, 76–87. (p. 313)

**Johnson, J. E., Christie, J. F., & Yawkey, T. D.** (1987). *Play and early childhood development.* Glenview, IL: Scott, Foresman. (pp. 463, 464)

**Johnson-Laird, P. N.** (1983). *Mental models: Towards a cognitive science of language, inference, and consciousness.* Cambridge, MA: Harvard University Press. (p. 388)

**Johnson-Laird, P. N.** (1985). Deductive reasoning ability. In R. J. Sternberg (Ed.), *Human abilities: An information-processing approach.* New York: Freeman. (p. 387)

**Johnston, D. W.** (1985). Psychological interventions in cardiovascular disease. *Journal of Psychosomatic Research, 29*, 447–456. (p. 229)

**Johnston, T. D., & Pietrewicz, A. T. (Eds.)** (1985). *Issues in the ecological study of learning.* Hillsdale, NJ: Erlbaum. (p. 153)

**Johnston, W. A., & Dark, V. J.** (1986). Selective attention *Annual Review of Psychology, 37*, 43–75. (p. 301)

**Jones, E. F., Forrest, J. D., Goldman, N., Henshaw, S. K., Lincoln, R., Rosoff, J. I., Westoff, C. F., & Wulf, D.** (1985). Teenage pregnancy in developed countries: Determinants and policy implications. *Family Planning Perspectives, 17*, 53–63. (p. 472)

**Jordan, N.** (1972). Is there an Achilles' heel in Piaget's theorizing? *Human Development, 15*, 379–382. (p. 440)

**Jouvet, M.** (1967, February). The states of sleep. *Scientific American*, 62–70. (p. 226)

**Jouvet, M.** (1972). The role of monoamines and acetylcholine-containing neurons in the regulation of the sleep-waking cycle. *Ergebnisse der Physiologie, 64*, 166–307. (p. 226)

**Julien, R. M.** (1985). *A primer of drug action* (4th ed.). San Francisco: Freeman. (p. 192)

**Jung, C. G.** (1968). *Analytical psychology: Its theory and practice.* New York: Pantheon. (p. 578)

**Jung, C. G.** (1969). *The structure and dynamics of the psyche.* Princeton, NJ: Princeton University Press. (p. 484)

**Jussim, L.** (1986). Self-fulfilling prophecies: A theoretical and integrative review. *Psychological Review, 93*, 429–445. (p. 503)

**Kagan, J.** (1972, March). Do infants think? *Scientific American*, 74–82. (p. 416)

**Kagan, J.** (1976). Emergent themes in human development. *American Scientist, 64*, 186–196. (p. 456)

**Kagan, J.** (1984). *The nature of the child.* New York: Basic Books. (pp. 416, 440, 457)

**Kagan, J., Kearsley, R. B., & Zelazo, P. R.** (1978). *Infancy: Its place in human development.* Cambridge, MA: Harvard University Press. (p. 458)

**Kahneman, D., & Treisman, A.** (1984). Changing views of attention and automaticity. In R. Parasuraman & D. R. Davies (Eds.), *Varieties of attention.* New York: Academic Press. (pp. 301, 302)

**Kail, R.** (1984). *The development of memory in children* (2nd ed.). New York: Freeman. (p. 442)

**Kalat, J. W.** (1985). Taste-aversion learning in ecological perspective. In T. D. Johnston & A. T. Pietrewicz (Eds.), *Issues in the ecological study of learning.* Hillsdale, NJ: Erlbaum. (p. 154)

**Kamin, L. J.** (1969). Predictability, surprise, attention, and conditioning. In B. A. Campbell & R. M. Church (Eds.), *Punishment and aversive behavior.* New York: Appleton-Century-Crofts. (p. 147)

**Kamin, L. J.** (1974). *The science and politics of IQ.* New York: Wiley. (p. 71)

**Kanizsa, G.** (1976, April). Subjective contours. *Scientific American*, 48–52. (p. 289)

**Kaplan, M.** (1983). A woman's view of DSM-III. *American Psychologist, 38*, 786–792. (p. 614)

**Kaplan, M. F.** (1987). The influencing process in group decision making. In C. Hendrick (Ed.), *Review of personality and social psychology, vol. 8: Group processes*. Newbury Park, CA: Sage. (p. 551)

**Karasu, T. B.** (1986). The specificity versus nonspecificity dilemma: Toward identifying therapeutic change agents. *American Journal of Psychiatry, 143*, 687–695. (p. 652)

**Karon, B. P.** (1989). Psychotherapy versus medication for schizophrenia: Empirical comparisons. In S. Fisher & R. P. Greenberg (Eds.), *The limits of biological treatments for psychological distress: Comparisons with psychotherapy and placebo*. Hillsdale, NJ: Erlbaum. (p. 677)

**Karp, D.** (1988). A decade of reminders: Changing age consciousness between fifty and sixty years old. *The Gerontologist, 28*, 727–738. (p. 485)

**Kastenbaum, R.** (1985). Dying and death. In J. E. Birren & K. W. Schaie (Eds.), *Handbook of the psychology of aging* (2nd. ed.). New York: Van Nostrand Reinhold. (p. 485)

**Katz, D.** (1960). The functional approach to the study of attitudes. *Public Opinion Quarterly, 24*, 163–204. (p. 513)

**Kaufman, L., & Rock, I.** (1962, July). The moon illusion. *Scientific American*, 120–130. (p. 309)

**Kay, P., & Kempton, W.** (1984). What is the Sapir-Whorf hypothesis? *American Anthropologist, 86*, 65–79. (p. 402)

**Keenan, J. M., MacWhinney, B., & Mayhew, D.** (1977). Pragmatics in memory: A study of natural conversation. *Journal of Verbal Learning and Verbal Behavior, 16*, 549–560. (p. 341)

**Keesey, R. E., & Corbett, S. W.** (1984). Metabolic defense of the body weight set-point. In A. J. Stunkard & E. Stellar (Eds.), *Eating and its disorders*. New York: Raven. (p. 208)

**Keller, F. S., & Schoenfeld, W. N.** (1950). *Principles of psychology: A systematic text in the science of behavior*. New York: Appleton-Century-Crofts. (p. 139)

**Kelley, H. H.** (1950). The warm-cold variable in first impressions of persons. *Journal of Personality, 18*, 431–439. (p. 494)

**Kelley, H. H.** (1967). Attribution theory in social psychology. In D. Levine (Ed.), *Nebraska symposium on motivation, 1967*. Lincoln, NE: University of Nebraska Press. (p. 493)

**Kelley, H. H.** (1973). The process of causal attribution. *American Psychologist, 28*, 107–128. (p. 493)

**Kellogg, W. N.** (1968). Communication and language in the home-raised chimpanzee. *Science, 162*, 423–427. (p. 428)

**Kellogg, W. N., & Kellogg, L. A.** (1933). *The ape and the child*. New York: McGraw-Hill. (p. 428)

**Kelly, D. D.** (1985). Central representation of pain and analgesia. In E. R. Kandel & J. H. Schwartz (Eds.), *Principles of neural science* (2nd ed.). New York: Elsevier. (p. 267)

**Kelly, G. A.** (1958). The theory and technique of assessment. *Annual Review of Psychology, 9*, 323–352. (p. 649)

**Kelly, J. A., & Hansen, D. J.** (1987). Social interactions and adjustment. In V. B. Van Hasselt & M. Hersen (Eds.), *Handbook of adolescent psychology*. New York: Pergamon. (p. 471)

**Kelman, H. C., & Hamilton, V. L.** (1989). *Crimes of obedience: Toward a social psychology of authority and responsibility*. New Haven, CT: Yale University Press. (pp. 535, 544)

**Kendler, H. H.** (1987). *Historical foundations of modern psychology*. Philadelphia: Temple University Press. (pp. 8, 9)

**Kendler, T. S.** (1972). An ontogeny of mediational deficiency. *Child Development, 43*, 1–17. (p. 444)

**Kennedy, J. L., Giuffra, L. A., Moises, H. W., Cavalli-Sforza, L. L., & others.** (1988). Evidence against linkage of schizophrenia to markers on chromosome 5 in a northern Swedish pedigree. *Nature, 336*, 167–170. (p. 76)

**Keppel, G., Postman, L., & Zavortink, B.** (1968). Studies of learning to learn: VIII. The influence of massive amounts of training upon the learning and retention of paired-associate lists. *Journal of Verbal Learning and Verbal Behavior, 7*, 790–796. (p. 351)

**Kessler, R. C., & McRae, J. A., Jr.** (1981). Trends in the relationship between sex and psychological distress. *American Sociological Review, 46*, 443–452. (p. 614)

**Kettlewell, B.** (1973). *The evolution of melanism*. Oxford: Clarendon. (p. 83)

**Kety, S. S.** (1988). Schizophrenic illness in the families of schizophrenic adoptees: Findings from the Danish national sample. *Schizophrenia Bulletin, 14*, 217–222. (p. 75)

**Kety, S. S., Rosenthal, D., Wender, P. H., Schulsinger, F., & Jacobson, B.** (1976). Mental illness in the biological and adoptive families of adopted individuals who have become schizophrenic. *Behavior Genetics, 6*, 219–225. (p. 74)

**Kiesler, C. A., & Sibulkin, A. S.** (1987). *Mental hospitalization: Myths and facts about a national crisis*. Newbury Park, CA: Sage. (pp. 644, 646, 647)

**Kihlstrom, J. F.** (1985). Hypnosis. *Annual Reviews of Psychology, 36*, 385–418. (pp. 356, 357)

**Kimura, D.** (1964). Left-right differences in the perception of melodies. *Quarterly Journal of Experimental Psychology, 16*, 355–358. (p. 380)

**King, B. M., Smith, R. L., & Frohman, L. A.** (1984). Hyperinsulinemia in rats with ventromedial hypothalamic lesions: Role of hyperphagia. *Behavioral Neuroscience, 98*, 152–155. (p. 204)

**Kinsey, A. C., Pomeroy, W. B., & Martin, C. E.** (1948). *Sexual behavior in the human male*. Philadelphia: Saunders. (p. 473)

**Kinsey, A. C., Pomeroy, W. B., Martin, C. E., & Gebhard, P. H.** (1953). *Sexual behavior in the human female*. Philadelphia: Saunders. (pp. 213, 473)

**Kirsch, I., Tennen, H., Wickless, C., Saccone, A. J., & Cody, S.** (1983). The role of expectancy in fear reduction. *Behavior Therapy, 14*, 520–533. (p. 675)

**Kissin, B.** (1986). *Conscious and unconscious programs in the brain*. New York: Plenum. (p. 230)

**Kleiman, D. G.** (1977). Monogamy in mammals. *Quarterly Review of Biology, 52*, 39–69. (p. 107)

**Klein, D. F., Gittelman, R., Quitkin, F., & Rifkin, A.** (1980). *Diagnosis and drug treatment of psychiatric disorders: Adults and children* (2nd ed.). Baltimore, MD: Williams & Wilkins. (p. 677)

**Klein, D. F., & Rabkin, J. G.** (1981). *Anxiety: New research and changing concepts.* New York: Raven. (p. 619)

**Kleinman, A.** (1988). *Rethinking psychiatry: From cultural category to personal experience.* New York: Free Press. (pp. 608, 622)

**Kline, N. S.** (1963). Psychiatry in Indonesia. *American Journal of Psychiatry, 119,* 809–815. (p. 608)

**Klinke, R.** (1986). Physiology of hearing. In R. F. Schmidt (Ed.), *Fundamentals of sensory physiology.* New York: Springer-Verlag. (p. 245)

**Knox, R. E., & Inkster, J. A.** (1968). Postdecision dissonance at post time. *Journal of Personality and Social Psychology, 8,* 319–323. (p. 517)

**Koffka, K.** (1935). *Principles of Gestalt psychology.* New York: Harcourt Brace Jovanovich (p. 286)

**Kohlberg, L.** (1966). A cognitive-developmental analysis of children's sex-role concepts and attitudes. In E. E. Maccoby (Ed.), *The development of sex differences.* Stanford: Stanford University Press. (p. 469)

**Kohlberg, L.** (1975, June). The cognitive developmental approach to moral education. *Phi Delta Kappan,* 670–677. (p. 478)

**Kohlberg, L.** (1984). *The psychology of moral development.* San Francisco: Harper & Row. (pp. 476, 477)

**Kohlberg, L., & Candee, D.** (1984). The relationship of moral judgment to moral action. In W. M. Kurtines & J. L. Gewirz (Eds.), *Morality, moral behavior, and moral development.* New York: Wiley. (p. 478)

**Köhler, W.** (1917; reprinted 1973). *Intelligenzprüfungen an Anthropoiden* (3rd ed.). Berlin: Springer. (p. 11)

**Kohn, M. L.** (1977). *Class and conformity: A study in values* (2nd ed.). Chicago: University of Chicago Press. (p. 462)

**Kolb, B., Milner, B., & Taylor, L.** (1983). Perception of faces by patients with localized cortical excisions. *Canadian Journal of Psychology, 37,* 8–18. (p. 380)

**Kolb, B., & Whishaw, I. Q.** (1985). *Fundamentals of human neuropsychology* (2nd ed.). New York: Freeman. (p. 265)

**Kolb, B., & Whishaw, I. Q.** (1990). *Fundamentals of human neuropsychology* (3rd ed.). New York: Freeman. (pp. 180, 185, 293)

**Konner, M. J.** (1972). Aspects of the developmental ethology of a foraging people. In N. G. Blurton-Jones (Ed.), *Ethological studies of child behaviour.* Cambridge: Cambridge University Press. (p. 456)

**Konner, M. J.** (1982). *The tangled wing: Biological constraints on the human spirit.* New York: Harper & Row. (p. 456)

**Kornhuber, H. H.** (1974). Cerebral cortex, cerebellum and basal ganglia: An introduction to their motor functions. In F. O. Schmitt & F. G. Worden (Eds.), *The neurosciences: Third study program.* Cambridge, MA: MIT Press. (pp. 178, 179, 183)

**Kosslyn, S. M.** (1973). Scanning visual images: Some structural implications. *Perception and Psychophysics, 14,* 90–94. (p. 342)

**Kosslyn, S. M.** (1980). *Image and mind.* Cambridge, MA: Harvard University Press. (p. 342)

**Kosslyn, S. M.** (1987). Seeing and imaging in the cerebral hemispheres: A computational approach. *Psychological Review, 94,* 148–175. (pp. 342, 381)

**Kosslyn, S. M., Koenig, O., Barrett, A., Cave, C. B., Tang, J., & Gabrieli, J. D. E.** (1989). Evidence for two types of spatial representations: Hemispheric specialization for categorical and coordinate relations. *Journal of Experimental Psychology: Human Perception and Performance, 15,* 723–735. (p. 381)

**Kruuk, H. (1972).** *The spotted hyena.* Chicago: University of Chicago Press. (p. 88)

**Kryter, K. D.** (1985). *The effects of noise on man* (2nd ed.). Orlando, FL: Academic Press. (pp. 248, 250)

**Kübler-Ross, E.** (1969). *On death and dying.* New York: Macmillan. (p. 485)

**Kuffler, S. W.** (1953). Discharge patterns and functional organization of mammalian retina. *Journal of Neurophysiology, 16,* 37–68. (p. 258)

**Kuhl, P. K.** (1987). Perception of speech and sound in early infancy. In P. Salapatek & L. Cohen (Eds.), *Handbook of infant perception, Vol. 2: From perception to cognition.* New York: Academic Press. (p. 421)

**Kurland, J. A.** (1979). Paternity, mother's brother, and human sociality. In N. A. Chagnon & W. Irons (Eds.), *Evolutionary biology and human social behavior: An anthropological perspective.* North Scituate, MA: Duxbury Press. (p. 117)

**Kutash, I. L., & Wolf, A. (Eds.)** (1986). *Psychotherapist's casebook.* San Francisco: Jossey-Bass.

---

**Lack, D.** (1968). *Ecological adaptations for breeding in birds.* London: Methuen. (p. 107)

**Lafferty, P., Beutler, L. E., & Crago, M.** (1989). Differences between more and less effective psychotherapists: A study of select therapist variables. *Journal of Consulting and Clinical Psychology, 57,* 76–80. (p. 674)

**La Freniere, P., Strayer, F. F., & Gauthier, R.** (1984). The emergence of same-sex affiliative preferences among preschool peers: A developmental/ethological perspective. *Child Development, 55,* 1958–1965. (p. 469)

**Laird, J. D.** (1974). Self-attribution of emotion: The effects of expressive behavior on the quality of emotional experience. *Journal of Personality and Social Psychology, 29,* 475–486. (pp. 233, 234)

**Lakoff, G.** (1987). Cognitive models and prototype theory. In U. Neisser (Ed.), *Concepts and conceptual development: Ecological and intellectual factors in categorization.* Cambridge: Cambridge University Press. (p. 344)

**Lamb, M. E.** (1986). *The father's role: Applied perspectives.* New York: Wiley. (p. 458)

**Lander, E. S.** (1987, March 25). The new human genetics: Mapping inherited diseases. *Princeton Alumni Weekly,* 10–16. (p. 57)

Langer, E. J., & Abelson, R. P. (1974). A patient by any other name . . . : Clinician group differences in labeling bias. *Journal of Consulting and Clinical Psychology, 42*, 4–9. (p. 614)

Langer, E. J., Beck, P., Weinman, C., Rodin, J., & Spitzer, L. (1979). Environmental determinants of memory improvement in late adulthood. *Journal of Personality and Social Psychology, 37*, 2003–2013. (p. 485)

Langer, E. J., Blank, A., & Chanowitz, B. (1978). The mindlessness of ostensibly thoughtful action. *Journal of Personality and Social Psychology, 36*, 635–642. (p. 531)

LaPiere, R. T. (1934). Attitude and actions. *Social Forces, 13*, 230–237. (p. 520)

Latané, B. (1981). The psychology of social impact. *American Psychologist, 36*, 343–356. (pp. 528, 529, 530)

Latané, B., & Nida, S. (1981). Ten years of research on group size and helping. *Psychological Bulletin, 89*, 308–324. (p. 543)

Latané, B., & Rodin, J. (1969). A lady in distress: Inhibiting effects of friends and strangers on bystander intervention. *Journal of Experimental Social Psychology, 5*, 189–202. (p. 543)

Latané, B., Williams, K., & Harkins, S. (1979). Many hands make light the work: The causes and consequences of social loafing. *Journal of Personality and Social Psychology, 37*, 822–832. (p. 542)

Lauer, J., & Lauer, R. (1985, June). Marriages made to last. *Psychology Today*, 22–26. (pp. 479, 512)

Leana, C. R. (1985). A partial test of Janis' groupthink model: Effects of group cohesiveness and leader behavior on defective decision making. *Journal of Management, 11*, 5–17. (p. 552)

LeBon, G. (1896). *The crowd.* London: Ernest Benn. (p. 544)

Lee, T., & Seeman, P. (1980). Elevation of brain neuroleptic/dopamine receptors in schizophrenia. *American Journal of Psychiatry, 137*, 191–197. (p. 639)

Leinhardt, G., Seewald, A., & Engel, M. (1979). Learning what's taught: Sex differences in instruction. *Journal of Educational Psychology, 71*, 432–439. (p. 468)

Lenneberg, E. H. (1962). Understanding language without ability to speak: A case study. *Journal of Abnormal and Social Psychology, 65*, 419–425. (p. 427)

Lenneberg, E. H. (1969). *Biological foundations of language.* New York: Wiley. (pp. 421, 426)

Lenzenweger, M. F., Dworkin, R. H., & Wethington, E. (1989). Models of positive and negative symptoms in schizophrenia: An empirical evaluation of latent structures. *Journal of Abnormal Psychology, 98*, 62–70. (p. 636)

Leon, G. R., Gillum, B., Gillum, R., & Gouze, M. (1979). Personality stability and change over a 30-year period—middle to old age. *Journal of Consulting and Clinical Psychology, 47*, 517–524. (p. 598)

Leon, G. R., & Roth, L. (1977). Obesity: Psychological causes, correlations, and speculations. *Psychological Bulletin, 84*, 117–139. (p. 206)

Lepper, M. R., & Greene, D. (1978). Overjustification research and beyond: Toward a means-ends analysis of intrinsic and extrin-sic motivation. In M. R. Lepper & D. Greene (Eds.), *The hidden costs of reward: New perspectives on the psychology of human motivation.* New York: Wiley. (p. 149)

Lerner, M. J. (1970). The desire for justice and reactions to victims. In J. Macaulay & L. Berkowitz (Eds.), *Altruism and helping behavior.* New York: Academic Press. (p. 499)

Lerner, M. J., & Miller, D. T. (1978). Just world research and the attribution process: Looking back and looking ahead. *Psychological Bulletin, 85*, 1030–1051. (p. 498)

Lerner, M. J., & Simmons, C. H. (1966). The observer's reaction to the "innocent victim": Compassion or rejection? *Journal of Personality and Social Psychology, 4*, 203–210. (p. 498)

Lester, L. S., & Fanselow, M. S. (1985). Exposure to a cat produces opioid analgesia in rats. *Behavioral Neuroscience, 99*, 756–759. (p. 269)

Levine, J. D., Gordon, N. C., & Fields, H. L. (1979). The role of endorphins in placebo analgesia. *Advances in Pain Research and Therapy, 3*, 547–550. (p. 270)

Levinger, G., & Schneider, D. J. (1969). Test of the "risk is a value" hypothesis. *Journal of Personality and Social Psychology, 11*, 165–169. (p. 551)

Levinson, D. J. (1978). *The seasons of a man's life.* New York: Ballantine. (pp. 479, 481)

Levinson, D. J. (1986). The conception of adult development. *American Psychologist, 41*, 3–13. (p. 479)

Lewin, K. (1947). Frontiers in group dynamics: I. Concept, method and reality in social science: Social equilibria and social change. *Human Relations, 1*, 5–41. (p. 548)

Lewin, K. (1951). *Field theory in social science: Selected theoretical papers by Kurt Lewin* (D. Cartwright, Ed.). New York: Harper & Row. (p. 527)

Lewin, R. (1987). Brain grafts benefit Parkinson's patients. *Science, 126*, 149. (p. 192)

Lewis, J. W., Cannon, J. T., & Liebeskind, J. C. (1980). Opioid and nonopioid mechanisms of stress analgesia. *Science, 208*, 623–625. (p. 269)

Lewis, M., & Brooks-Gunn, J. (1979). *Social cognition and the acquisition of self.* New York: Plenum. (p. 474)

Lewis, M., Fiering, C., McGuffog, C., & Jaskir, J. (1984). Predicting psychopathology in six-year-olds from early social relations. *Child Development, 55*, 123–136. (p. 458)

Lewontin, R. (1970, March). Race and intelligence. *Bulletin of the Atomic Scientists*, 2–8. (p. 72)

Lewontin, R., & Gould, S. J. (1978). The spandrels San Marco and the Panglossian paradigm: A critique of the adaptationalist programme. *Proceedings of the Royal Society of London, 205*, 581–598. (p. 87)

Lewontin, R. C., Rose, S., & Kamin, L. J. (1984). *Not in our genes.* New York: Pantheon. (p. 69)

Liberman, R. P. (1988). *Psychiatric rehabilitation of chronic mental patients.* Washington, DC: American Psychiatric Press. (p. 646)

**Lickey, M. E., & Gordon, B.** (1983). *Drugs for mental illness: A revolution in psychiatry.* New York: Freeman. (pp. 677, 678)

**Lieberman, M. A., & Borman, L. D.** (1981). Who helps widows: The role of kith and kin. *National Reporter, 4,* 2–4. (p. 485)

**Liebert, R.** (1984). What develops in moral development? In W. Kurtines & J. Gewirtz (Eds.), *Morality, moral behavior, and moral development.* New York: Wiley. (p. 477)

**Liebeskind, J. C., & Paul, L. A.** (1977). Psychological and physiological mechanisms of pain. *Annual Review of Psychology, 28,* 41–60. (p. 268)

**Liem, R.** (1987). The psychological costs of unemployment: A comparison of findings and definitions. *Social Research, 54,* 319–353. (p. 482)

**Liem, R., & Liem, J. H.** (1988). Psychological effects of unemployment on workers and their families. *Journal of Social Issues, 44,* 87–105. (p. 482)

**Light, W. J. H.** (1986). *Neurobiology of alcohol abuse.* Springfield, IL: Charles C. Thomas. (p. 625)

**Lin, K., & Kleinman, A. M.** (1988). Psychopathology and clinical course of schizophrenia: A cross-cultural perspective. *Schizophrenia Bulletin, 14,* 555–567. (p. 608)

**Linden, R., Davis, J. M., & Rubinstein, J.** (1984). Antipsychotics in the maintenance treatment of schizophrenia. In H. C. Stancer, P. E. Garfinkel, & V. M. Rakoff (Eds.), *Guidelines for the use of psychotropic drugs: A clinical handbook.* New York: Spectrum. (p. 676)

**Linder, D. E., Cooper, J., & Jones, E. E.** (1967). Decision freedom as a determinant of the role of incentive magnitude in attitude change. *Journal of Personality and Social Psychology, 6,* 245–254. (p. 519)

**Lindsley, J. G.** (1983). Sleep patterns and functions. In A. Gale & J. A. Edward (Eds.), *Physiological correlates of human behavior (Vol. 1: Basic issues).* New York: Academic Press. (p. 226)

**Linville, P. W.** (1985). Self-complexity and affective extremity: Don't put all of your eggs in one cognitive basket. *Social Cognition, 3,* 94–120. (p. 504)

**Linville, P. W.** (1987). Self-complexity as a cognitive buffer against stress-related illness and depression. *Journal of Personality and Social Psychology, 52,* 663–676. (p. 504)

**Lipman, R. S.** (1989). Pharmacotherapy of the anxiety disorders. In S. Fisher & R. P. Greenberg (Eds.), *The limits of biological treatments for psychological distress: Comparisions with psychotherapy and placebo.* Hillsdale, NJ: Erlbaum. (p. 678)

**Lipowski, Z. J.** (1988). Somatization: The concept and its clinical application. *American Journal of Psychiatry, 145,* 1358–1368. (pp. 620, 622)

**Lippmann, W.** (1922; reprinted 1960). *Public opinion.* New York: Macmillan. (p. 496)

**Livingston, D. (1857).** *Missionary travels and researches in South Africa.* London: J. Murray. (p. 269)

**Livingston, M., & Hubel, D.** (1988). Segregation of form, color, movement, and depth: Anatomy, physiology, and perception. *Science, 240,* 740–749. (p. 265)

**Llinás, R. R.** (1988). The intrinsic electrophysiological properties of mammalian neurons: Insights into central nervous system function. *Science, 242,* 1654–1664. (p. 172)

**Locke, J. L.** (1983). *Phonological acquisition and change.* New York: Academic Press. (p. 421)

**Locksley, A., Ortiz, V., & Hepburn, C.** (1980). Social categorization and discriminatory behavior: Extinguishing the minimal intergroup discrimination effect. *Journal of Personality and Social Psychology, 39,* 773–783. (p. 498)

**Loeb, G. E.** (1986, February). The functional replacement of the ear. *Scientific American,* 104–111. (p. 248)

**Loehlin, J. C., Willerman, L., & Horn, J. M.** (1988). Human behavior genetics. *Annual Review of Psychology, 39,* 101–133. (pp. 60, 70, 71, 75)

**Loftus, E. F., & Loftus, G. R.** (1980). On the permanence of stored information in the human brain. *American Psychologist, 35,* 409–420. (p. 355)

**Loftus, E. F., & Palmer, J. C.** (1974). Reconstruction of automobile destruction: An example of the interaction between language and memory. *Journal of Verbal Learning and Verbal Behavior, 13,* 585–589. (p. 354)

**Logue, A. W.** (1988). A comparison of taste aversion learning in humans and other vertebrates: Evolutionary pressures in common. In R. C. Bolles & M. D. Beecher (Eds.), *Evolution and learning.* Hillsdale, NJ: Erlbaum. (p. 153)

**Lorenz, K.** (1935; reprinted 1970). Companions as factors in the bird's environment (R. Martin, Trans.). In K. Lorenz (Ed.), *Studies in animal and human behavior (Vol. 1).* Cambridge, MA: Harvard University Press. (p. 158)

**Lorenz, K. Z.** (1966). *On aggression.* New York: Harcourt, Brace & World. (pp. 100, 111)

**Lorenz, K. Z.** (1974). Analogy as a source of knowledge. *Science, 185,* 229–234. (pp. 94, 95)

**Lott, B.** (1987). Sexuality: A feminist perspective. In K. Kelley (Ed.), *Females, males, and sexuality: Theories and research.* Albany, NY: State University of New York Press. (p. 213)

**Luchins, A.** (1957). Primacy-recency in impression formation. In C. I. Hovland (Ed.), *The order of presentation in persuasion.* New Haven, CT: Yale University Press. (p. 495)

**Luria, A. R.** (1966). *Human brain and psychological processes.* New York: Harper & Row. (p. 378)

**Luria, A. R.** (1968). *The mind of a mnemonist.* London: Penguin. (p. 343)

**Luria, A. R.** (1970, March). The functional organization of the brain. *Scientific American,* 66–78. (p. 378)

**Lykken, D. T.** (1982). Research with twins: The concept of emergensis. *Psychophysiology, 19,* 361–373. (p. 71)

**Lynch, J. J.** (1977). *The broken heart: The medical consequences of loneliness.* New York: Basic Books. (p. 485)

**Maccoby, E. E., & Jacklin, C. N.** (1974). *The psychology of sex differences.* Stanford: Stanford University Press. (p. 467)

**Maccoby, E. E., & Jacklin, C. N.** (1987). Gender segregation in childhood. In H. W. Reese (Ed.), *Advances in child development and behavior, vol. 20.* New York: Academic Press. (pp. 466, 468, 469)

**MacDonald, N.** (1960). Living with schizophrenia. *Canadian Medical Association Journal, 82,* 218–221. (p. 636)

**MacKay, A. V. P., Iversen, L. I., Rossor, M., Spokes, P., Bird, E., Arregui, A., Creese, I., & Snyder, S. H.** (1982). Increased brain dopamine and dopamine receptors in schizophrenia. *Archives of General Psychiatry, 39,* 991–997. (p. 639)

**MacKay, D. G.** (1973). Aspects of the theory of comprehension, memory and attention. *Quarterly Journal of Experimental Psychology, 25,* 22–40. (p. 296)

**Mackie, D. M.** (1986). Social identification effects in group polarization. *Journal of Personality and Social Psychology, 50,* 720–728. (p. 551)

**Mackintosh, N. J., & Dickinson, A.** (1979). Instrumental (Type II) conditioning. In A. Dickinson & R. A. Boakes (Eds.), *Mechanisms of learning and motivation.* Hillsdale, NJ: Erlbaum. (p. 147)

**Maddox, G. L., & Campbell, R. T.** (1985). Scope, concepts, and methods in the study of aging. In R. H. Binstock & E. Shanas (Eds.), *Handbook of aging and the social sciences* (2nd ed.). New York: Van Nostrand Reinhold. (p. 484)

**Maier, N. R. F., & Solem, A. R.** (1952). The contribution of a discussion leader to the quality of group thinking: The effective use of minority opinions. *Human Relations, 5,* 277–288. (p. 552)

**Maltz, D. N., & Borker, R. A.** (1982). A cultural approach to male-female miscommunication. In J. J. Gumperz (Ed.), *Language and social identity.* Cambridge: Cambridge University Press. (p. 468)

**Mann, L.** (1981). The baiting crowd in episodes of threatened suicide. *Journal of Personality and Social Psychology, 41,* 703–709. (p. 545)

**Mäntylä, T.** (1986). Optimizing cue effectiveness: Recall of 500 and 600 incidentally learned words. *Journal of Experimental Psychology: Learning, Memory, and Cognition, 12,* 66–71. (pp. 352, 353)

**Marcel, A. J.** (1983). Conscious and unconscious perception: An approach to the relations between phenomenal experience and perceptual processes. *Cognitive Psychology, 15,* 238–300. (p. 302)

**Marcia, J. E.** (1966). Development and validation of ego identity status. *Journal of Personality and Social Psychology, 3,* 551–558. (p. 474)

**Marcia, J. E.** (1980). Identity in adolescence. In J. Adelson (Ed.), *Handbook of adolescent psychology.* New York: Wiley. (pp. 474, 475)

**Maret, E., & Finlay, B.** (1984). The distribution of household labor among women in dual-earner families. *Journal of Marriage and the Family, 46,* 357–364. (p. 482)

**Margules, D. L., & Olds, J.** (1962). Identical "feeding" and "rewarding" systems in the lateral hypothalamus of rats. *Science, 135,* 374–375. (p. 215)

**Mark, V. H., Ervin, F. R., & Yakovlev, P. L.** (1963). Stereotactic thalamotomy: III. The verification of anatomical lesion sites in the human thalamus. *Archives of Neurology, 8,* 528–538. (p. 268)

**Marks, I. M.** (1987). *Fears, phobias, and rituals: Panic, anxiety, and their disorders.* New York: Oxford University Press. (pp. 617, 618, 619, 667, 668)

**Marler, P.** (1970). A comparative approach to vocal learning: Song development in white-crowned sparrows. *Journal of Comparative and Physiological Psychology, 7,* 1–25. (p. 92)

**Marr, D. B., & Sternberg, R. J.** (1987). The role of mental speed in intelligence: A triarchic perspective. In P. A. Vernon (Ed.), *Speed of information-processing and intelligence.* Norwood, NJ: Ablex. (p. 375)

**Martin, J. H.** (1985). Receptor physiology and submodality coding in the somatic sensory system. In E. R. Kandel & J. H. Schwartz (Eds.), *Principles of neural science* (2nd ed.). New York: Elsevier. (p. 267)

**Masangkay, Z. S., McCluskey, K. A., McIntyre, C. W., Sims-Knight, J., Vaughn, B. E., & Flavell, J. H.** (1974). The early development of inferences about the visual percepts of others. *Child Development, 45,* 357–366. (p. 439)

**Maslow, A. H.** (1970). *Motivation and personality* (2nd ed.). New York: Harper & Row. (pp. 582, 584)

**Mason, J. R., & Reidinger, R. F.** (1982). Observational learning of food aversions in red-winged blackbirds (*Agelaius phoenicius*). *Auk, 99,* 548–554. (p. 156)

**Masters, W. H., & Johnson, V. E.** (1966). *Human sexual response.* Boston: Little, Brown. (p. 210)

**Matarazzo, J. D.** (1983). The reliability of psychiatric and psychological diagnosis. *Clinical Psychology Review, 3,* 103–145. (pp. 610, 611)

**Matlin, M. W.** (1988). *Sensation and perception* (2nd ed.). Boston: Allyn & Bacon. (pp. 244, 246, 257)

**Matthews, D., & Edwards, D. A.** (1977). Involvement of the ventromedial and anterior hypothalamic nuclei in the hormonal induction of receptivity in the female rat. *Physiology of Behavior, 19,* 319–326. (p. 211)

**Matthews, K. A., & Haynes, S. G.** (1986). Type A behavior pattern and coronary risk: Update and critical evaluation. *Journal of Epidemiology, 123,* 923–960. (p. 229)

**Maurer, D., & Maurer, C.** (1988). *The world of the newborn.* New York: Basic Books. (p. 414)

**Mayr, E., & Provine, W. B. (Eds.)** (1980). *The evolutionary synthesis: Perspectives on the unification of biology.* Cambridge, MA: Harvard University Press. (p. 82)

**McArthur, L. Z.** (1972). The how and what of why: Some determinants and consequences of causal attribution. *Journal of Personality and Social Psychology, 22,* 171–193. (p. 494)

**McArthur, L. Z., & Berry, D. S.** (1987). Cross-cultural agreement in perceptions of babyfaced adults. *Journal of Cross-Cultural Psychology, 18,* 165–192. (p. 495)

**McCabe, M. P., & Collins, J. K.** (1979). Sex roles and dating orientation. *Journal of Youth and Adolescence, 8,* 407–424. (p. 472)

**McCallum, D. M., Harring, K., Gilmore, R., Drenan, S., Chase, J. P., Insko, C. A., & Thibaut, J.** (1985). Competition and cooperation between groups and between individuals. *Journal of Experimental Social Psychology, 21,* 301–320. (p. 557)

**McCloskey, M., & Zaragoza, M.** (1985). Misleading postevent information and memory for events: Arguments and evidence against memory impairment hypotheses. *Journal of Experimental Psychology: General, 114,* 1–16. (p. 355)

**McCrae, R. R., & Costa, P. T.** (1985). Updating Norman's "adequate taxonomy": Intelligence and personality dimensions in natural language and in questionnaires. *Journal of Personality and Social Psychology, 49,* 710–721. (p. 595)

**McCrae, R. R., & Costa, P. T.** (1987). Validation of the five-factor model of personality across instruments and observers. *Journal of Personality and Social Psychology, 52,* 81–90. (p. 595)

**McDuff, D. R.** (1988). Presentation at the Annual Meeting of the American Psychiatric Association, as noted by Alison Bass in *Boston Globe,* May 5, p. 94. (p. 498)

**McEwen, B. S.** (1989). Endocrine effects on the brain and their relationship to behavior. In G. J. Siegel, B. W. Agranoff, R. W. Albers, & P. B. Molinoff (Eds.), *Basic neurochemistry: Molecular, cellular, and medical aspects* (4th ed.). New York: Raven Press. (pp. 189, 190)

**McEwen, B. S., DeKloet, E. R., & Rostene, W.** (1986). Adrenal steroid receptors and actions in the nervous system. *Physiological Review, 66,* 1121–1188. (p. 190)

**McGuire, W. J.** (1985). Attitudes and attitude change. In G. Lindzey & E. Aronson (Eds.), *Handbook of social psychology (Vol. 2)* (3rd ed.). New York: Random House. (p. 514)

**McGuire, W. J., & McGuire, C. V.** (1981). The spontaneous self-concept as affected by personal distinctiveness. In M. D. Lynch, A. Norem-Hebeisen, & K. Gergen (Eds.), *The self-concept.* New York: Ballinger. (p. 505)

**McGuire, W. J., & McGuire, C. V.** (1988). Content and process in the experience of self. In L. Berkowitz (Ed.), *Advances in experimental social psychology (vol. 21).* New York: Academic Press. (p. 505)

**McGuire, W. J., & Padawer-Singer, A.** (1976). Trait salience in the spontaneous self-concept. *Journal of Personality and Social Psychology, 33,* 743–754. (p. 505)

**McKellar, P.** (1979). *Mindsplit: The psychology of multiple personality and the dissociated self.* London: Dent & Sons. (p. 623)

**McKenna, R. J.** (1972). Some effects of anxiety level and food cues on the behavior of obese and normal subjects. *Journal of Personality and Social Psychology, 221,* 311–319. (p. 206)

**McKim, W. A.** (1986). *Drugs and behavior: An introduction to behavioral pharmacology.* Englewood Cliffs, NJ: Prentice Hall. (p. 194)

**McNally, R. J., & Steketee, G. S.** (1985). Etiology and maintenance of severe animal phobias. *Behavioral Research and Therapy, 23,* 431–435. (p. 617)

**McReynolds, P.** (1989). Diagnosis and clinical assessment: Current status and major issues. *Annual Reviews of Psychology, 40,* 83–108. (p. 611)

**McShane, D., & Berry, J. W.** (1988). Native North Americans: Indian and Inuit abilities. In S. H. Irvine & J. W. Berry (Eds.), *Human abilities in cultural context.* Cambridge: Cambridge University Press. (p. 385)

**Mead, M.** (1935). *Sex and temperament in three primitive societies.* New York: William Morrow. (p. 467)

**Meador, B. D., & Rogers, C. R.** (1973). Client-centered therapy. In R. Corsini (Ed.), *Current psychotherapies.* Itasca, IL: Peacock. (p. 662)

**Meddis, R.** (1977). *The sleep instinct.* London: Routledge & Kegan Paul. (p. 223)

**Meiselman, K. C.** (1978). *Incest: A psychological study of causes and effects with treatment recommendations.* San Francisco: Jossey-Bass. (p. 117)

**Melzack, R., & Wall, P. D.** (1965). Pain mechanisms: A new theory. *Science, 150,* 971–979. (p. 268)

**Melzack, R., & Wall, P. D.** (1982). *The challenge of pain.* New York: Basic Books. (pp. 266, 267, 268, 269)

**Mercer, D.** (1986). *Biofeedback and related therapies in clinical practice.* Rockville, MD: Aspen Systems. (p. 134)

**Metalsky, G. I., Halberstadt, L. J., & Abramson, L. Y.** (1987). Vulnerability to depressive mood reactions: Toward a more powerful test of the diathesis-stress and causal mediation components of the reformulated theory of depression. *Journal of Personality and Social Psychology, 52,* 386–393. (p. 631)

**Metzger, R. L., Boschee, P. F., Haugen, T., & Schnobrich, B. L.** (1979). The classroom as a learning context: Changing rooms affects performance. *Journal of Educational Psychology, 71,* 440–442. (p. 353)

**Michaels, C. F., & Carello, C.** (1981). *Direct perception.* Englewood Cliffs, NJ: Prentice Hall. (p. 313)

**Michaels, J. W., Blommel, J. M., Brocato, R. M., Linkous, R. A., & Rowe, J. S.** (1982). Social facilitation and inhibition in a natural setting. *Replications in Social Psychology, 2,* 21–24. (p. 541)

**Miczek, K. A., Thompson, M. L., & Shuster, L.** (1986). Analgesia following defeat in an aggressive encounter: Development of tolerance and changes in opioid receptors. In D. D. Kelly (Ed.), *Stress-induced analgesia* (Vol. 467 of the *Annals of the New York Academy of Sciences*). New York: New York Academy of Sciences. (p. 269)

**Mill, J. S.** (1848; reprinted 1978). *Principles of political economy.* Toronto: University of Toronto Press. (p. 69)

**Mill, J. S.** (1869; reprinted 1980). *The subjection of women.* Arlington Heights, IL: Harlan Davidson. (p. 69)

**Milgram, S.** (1963). Behavioral study of obedience. *Journal of Abnormal and Social Psychology, 67,* 371–378. (p. 538)

**Milgram, S.** (1964). Issues in the study of obedience: A reply to Baumrind. *American Psychologist, 19,* 848–852. (p. 538)

**Milgram, S.** (1974). *Obedience to authority: An experimental view.* New York: Harper & Row. (pp. 537, 538, 539)

**Miller, A. G.** (1986). *The obedience experiments: A case study of controversy in social science.* New York: Praeger. (p. 537)

**Miller, G. A.** (1981). *Language and speech.* San Francisco: Freeman. (p. 423)

**Miller, G. E.** (1956). The magic number seven plus or minus two: Some limits on our capacity for processing information. *Psychological Review, 63,* 81–97. (p. 337)

**Miller, J. G.** (1984). Culture and the development of everyday social explanation. *Journal of Personality and Social Psychology, 46,* 961–978. (p. 500)

**Miller, L. E., & Grush, J. E.** (1986). Individual differences in attitudinal versus normative determination of behavior. *Journal of Experimental Social Psychology, 22,* 190–202. (p. 522)

**Miller, N. E.** (1948). Studies of fear as an acquirable drive: I. Fear as motivation and fear-reduction as reinforcement in the learning of a new response. *Journal of Experimental Psychology, 38,* 89–101. (p. 141)

**Miller, N. E.** (1985). The value of behavioral research on animals. *American Psychologist, 40,* 423–440. (p. 41)

**Miller, R. L., Brickman, P., & Bolen, D.** (1975). Attribution versus persuasion as a means for modifying behavior. *Journal of Personality and Social Psychology, 31,* 430–441. (pp. 32, 503)

**Milner, B.** (1965). Memory disturbance after bilateral hippocampal lesions. In P. Milner & S. Glickman (Eds.), *Cognitive processes and the brain.* Princeton, NJ: Van Nostrand. (pp. 357, 359)

**Milner, B.** (1970). Memory and the medial temporal regions of the brain. In K. H. Pribram & D. E. Broadbent (Eds.), *Biology of memory.* New York: Academic Press. (pp. 357, 358)

**Milner, B.** (1974). Hemispheric specialization: Scope and limits. In F. O. Schmitt & F. G. Worden (Eds.), *The neurosciences: Third research program.* Cambridge, MA: MIT Press. (p. 378)

**Minix, D. A.** (1976). *The role of the small group in foreign policy decision making: A potential pathology in crisis decisions?* Paper presented to the Southern Political Science Association. (For description, see D. G. Myers, 1982.) (p. 550)

**Mintz, S., & Alpert, M.** (1972). Imagery vividness, reality testing, and schizophrenic hallucinations. *Journal of Abnormal Psychology, 79,* 310–316. (p. 637)

**Mirsky, A. F., & Duncan, C. C.** (1986). Etiology and expression of schizophrenia: Neurobiological and psychosocial factors. *Annual Review of Psychology, 37,* 291–319. (p. 639)

**Mischel, W.** (1968). *Personality and assessment.* New York: Wiley. (p. 596)

**Mischel, W.** (1984). Convergences and challenges in the search for consistency. *American Psychologist, 39,* 351–364. (pp. 596, 597)

**Mischel, W., & Peake, P. K.** (1982). Beyond déjà vu in the search for cross-situational consistency. *Psychological Review, 89,* 730–755. (p. 596)

**Mishkin, M., & Appenzeller, T.** (1987, June). The anatomy of memory. *Scientific American,* 80–87. (p. 360)

**Money, J., & Ehrhardt, A.** (1972). *Man and woman, boy and girl.* Baltimore: Johns Hopkins University Press. (p. 211)

**Moore, H. T.** (1917). Laboratory tests of anger, fear, and sex interests. *American Journal of Psychology, 28,* 390–395. (p. 541)

**Moray, N.** (1959). Attention in dichotic listening: Effective cues and the influence of instructions. *Quarterly Journal of Experimental Psychology, 11,* 56–60. (p. 296)

**Morgan, C. T.** (1943). *Physiological psychology.* New York: McGraw-Hill. (p. 202)

**Moriarty, T.** (1975a). Crime, commitment and the responsive bystander: Two field experiments. *Journal of Personality and Social Psychology, 31,* 370–376. (p. 544)

**Moriarty, T.** (1975b, April). A nation of willing victims. *Psychology Today,* 43–50. (p. 530)

**Morris, N. M., Udry, J. R., Khan-Dawood, F., & Dawood, M. Y.** (1987). Marital sex frequency and midcycle female testosterone. *Archives of Sexual Behavior, 16,* 27–37. (p. 212)

**Morris, R. G. M.** (1981). Spatial localization does not require the presence of local cues. *Learning and Motivation, 12,* 239–260. (p. 150)

**Moscovici, S.** (1976). *Social influence and social change.* New York: Academic Press. (p. 547)

**Moscovici, S., Lage, E., & Naffrechoux, M.** (1969). Influence of a consistent minority on the responses of a majority in a color perception task. *Sociometry, 32,* 365–380. (p. 547)

**Moscovici, S., & Mugny, G.** (1983). Minority influence. In P. B. Paulus (Ed.), *Basic group processes.* New York: Springer-Verlag. (p. 547)

**Mowrer, O. H.** (1947). On the dual nature of learning—a reinterpretation of "conditioning" and "problem-solving." *Harvard Educational Review, 17,* 102–148. (p. 140)

**Mowrer, O. H.** (1960). *Learning theory and behavior.* New York: Wiley. (p. 147)

**Mulcaster, R.** (1582; reprinted 1929). *The first part of the elementarie, which intreateth of right writing of our English tung.* In R. H. Quick, *Essays on educational reformers.* London: Longmans, Green. (p. 47)

**Müller, J.** (1838; reprinted 1842, 1965). *Elements of physiology* (Vol. 2) (W. Baly, Trans.). Excerpted in R. J. Herrnstein & E. G. Boring (Eds.), *A source book in the history of psychology.* Cambridge, MA: Harvard University Press. (p. 7)

**Muntz, W. R. A.** (1964, May). Vision in frogs. *Scientific American,* 110–119. (p. 277)

**Murdock, G. P.** (1981). *Atlas of world cultures.* Pittsburgh: University of Pittsburgh Press. (p. 116)

**Murphy, G. E., Simons, A. D., Wetzel, R. D., & Lustman, P. J.** (1984). Cognitive therapy and pharmacotherapy: Singly and together in the treatment of depression. *Archives of General Psychiatry, 41,* 33–41. (p. 677)

**Murray, E. J., & Foote, F.** (1979). The origin of fear of snakes. *Behavioral Research and Therapy, 17,* 489–493. (p. 617)

**Mussen, P., Eichorn, D. H., Honzik, M. P., Bieher, S. L., & Meredith, W.** (1980). Continuity and change in women's characteristics over four decades. *International Journal of Behavioral Development, 3,* 333–347. (p. 598)

**Myers, D. G.** (1982). Polarizing effects of social interaction. In H. Brandstatter, J. H. Davis, & G. Stocker-Kreichgauer (Eds.), *Group decision making.* New York: Academic Press. (pp. 549, 551)

**Myers, D. G., & Bishop, G. D.** (1970). Discussion effects on racial attitudes. *Science, 169,* 778–779. (p. 550)

**Myers, D. G., & Kaplan, M. F.** (1976). Group-induced polarization in simulated juries. *Personality and Social Psychology Bulletin, 2,* 63–66. (p. 550)

**Nathans, J.** (1987). Molecular biology of visual pigments. *Annual Review of Neuroscience, 10,* 163–194. (p. 253)

**Nathans, J., Piantanida, T. P., Eddy, R. L., Shows, T. P., & Hogness, D. S.** (1986). Molecular genetics of inherited variation in human color vision. *Science, 232,* 203–210. (pp. 57, 263)

**National Institute of Alcohol Abuse and Alcoholism** (1987). *Alcohol and health.* Rockville, MD: Author. (p. 624)

**Nauta, W. J. H., & Feirtag, M.** (1986). *Fundamental neuroanatomy.* New York: Freeman. (p. 167)

**Nemeth, C. J., & Wachtler, J.** (1983). Creative problem solving as a result of majority vs. minority influence. *European Journal of Social Psychology, 13,* 45–55. (p. 548)

**Newcomb, T. M.** (1943). *Personality and social change: Attitude formation in a student community.* New York: Dryden. (p. 514)

**Newcomb, T. M.** (1963). Persistence and repression of changed attitudes: Long-range studies. *Journal of Social Issues, 19,* 3–14. (p. 515)

**Newcomb, T. M., Koenig, K., Flacks, R., & Warwick, D.** (1967). *Persistence and change: Bennington College and its students after 25 years.* New York: Wiley. (p. 515)

**Neill, A. S.** (1960). *Summerhill.* New York: Hart Publishing. (p. 465)

**Neisser, U.** (1976). *Cognition and reality.* San Francisco: Freeman. (pp. 298, 316)

**Neisser, U.** (1978). Memory: What are the important questions? In M. M. Gruneberg, P. E. Morris, & R. N. Sykes (Eds.), *Practical aspects of memory.* London: Academic Press. (p. 361)

**Nelson, K.** (1986). Event knowledge and cognitive development. In K. Nelson (Ed.), *Event knowledge: Structure and function in development.* Hillsdale, NJ: Erlbaum. (p. 445)

**Netley, C.** (1983). Sex chromosome abnormalities and the development of verbal and nonverbal abilities. In C. L. Ludlow & J. A. Cooper (Eds.), *Genetic aspects of speech and language disorders.* New York: Academic Press. (p. 59)

**Neugarten, B. L.** (1974). Age groups in American society and the rise of the young-old. *Annals of the American Academy of Political and Social Sciences, 415,* 187–198. (p. 484)

**Neugarten, B. L.** (1979). Time, age, and the life cycle. *American Journal of Psychiatry, 136,* 887–894. (pp. 453, 479)

**Neugarten, B. L.** (1984). Interpretive social science and research on aging. In A. Rossi (Ed.), *Gender and the life course.* Chicago: Aldine. (p. 479)

**Newman, J., & Layton, B. D.** (1984). Overjustification: A self-perception perspective. *Personality and Social Psychology Bulletin, 10,* 419–425. (p. 149)

**Newsom, C., Favell, J. E., & Rincover, A.** (1983). Side effects of punishment. In S. Axelrod & J. Apsche (Eds.), *The effects of punishment on human behavior.* New York: Academic Press. (p. 142)

**Nietzel, M. T., & Bernstein, D. A.** (1987). *Introduction to clinical psychology* (2nd ed.). Englewood Cliffs, NJ: Prentice Hall. (p. 658)

**Niijima, A.** (1982). Glucose-sensitive afferent nerve fibers in the hepatic branch of the vagus nerve in the guinea pig. *Journal of Physiology, 332,* 315–323. (p. 204)

**Nisbett, R. E., Caputo, C., Legant, P., & Marecek, J.** (1973). Behavior as seen by the actor and as seen by the observer. *Journal of Personality and Social Psychology, 27,* 154–164. (p. 500)

**Nisbett, R. E., Fong, G. T., Lehman, D. R., & Cheng, P. W.** (1987). Teaching reasoning. *Science, 238,* 625–631. (p. 389)

**Novin, D., Robinson, B. A., Culbreth, L. A., & Tordoff, M. G.** (1983). Is there a role for the liver in the control of food intake? *American Journal of Clinical Nutrition, 9,* 233–246. (p. 204)

**Nowlis, G. H., & Frank, M.** (1977). Qualities in hamster taste: Behavioral and neural evidence. In J. LeMagnen & P. MacLeod (Eds.), *Olfaction and taste* (Vol. 6). Washington, DC: Information Retrieval. (p. 243)

**Nuechterlein, K. H.** (1983). Signal detection in vigilance tasks and behavioral attributes among offspring of schizophrenic mothers and among hyperactive children. *Journal of Abnormal Psychology, 92,* 4–28. (p. 639)

**Oden, S.** (1988). Alternative perspectives on children's peer relationships. In T. D. Yawkey & J. E. Johnson (Eds.), *Integrative processes and socialization: Early to middle childhood.* Hillsdale, NJ: Erlbaum. (p. 471)

**Oetting, E. R., & Beauvais, F.** (1988). Common elements in youth drug abuse: Peer clusters and other psychosocial factors. In S. Peele (Ed.), *Visions of addiction: Major contemporary perspectives on addiction and alcoholism.* Lexington, MA: Lexington Books. (p. 627)

**Offer, D., Ostrov, E., & Howard, K. I.** (1981). *The adolescent.* New York: Basic Books. (p. 472)

**Öhman, A.** (1986). Face the beast and fear the face: Animal and social fears as prototypes for evolutionary analysis of emotion. *Psychophysiology, 23,* 123–145. (p. 157)

**Öhman, A., Fredrikson, M., Hugdahl, K., & Rimmö, P. A.** (1976). The premise of equipotentiality in human classical conditioning: Conditioned electrodermal responses to potential phobic stimuli. *Journal of Experimental Psychology: General, 105,* 313–337. (p. 157)

**Okin, R. L.** (1983). On the future of state hospitals: Should there be one? *American Journal of Psychiatry, 140,* 577–581. (p. 645)

**Olds, J.** (1956, October). Pleasure centers in the brain. *Scientific American, 195,* 105–116. (p. 214)

**Olds, J., & Milner, P.** (1954). Positive reinforcement produced by electrical stimulation of the septal area and other regions of the rat brain. *Journal of Comparative and Physiological Psychology, 47,* 419–427. (p. 214)

**Olds, M. E., & Fobes, J. L.** (1981). The central basis of motivation: Intracranial self-stimulation studies. *Annual Review of Psychology, 32,* 523–574. (p. 216)

**Olton, D. S.** (1979). Mazes, maps, and memory. *American Psychologist, 34,* 583–596. (pp. 158–159)

**Orne, M. T., & Holland, C. G.** (1968). On the ecological validity of laboratory deception. *International Journal of Psychiatry, 6*, 282–293. (p. 539)

**Overmann, S. R.** (1976). Dietary self-selection by animals. *Psychological Bulletin, 83*, 218–235. (p. 154)

---

**Page, D., Mosher, R., Simpson, E. M., Fisher, E. M. C., Mardon, G., Pollack, J., McGillivray, B., Chapelle, A., & Brown, L.** (1987). The sex-determining region of the human Y chromosome encodes a finger protein. *Cell, 51*, 1091–1104. (p. 209)

**Palmer, S. E.** (1975a). The effects of contextual scenes on the identification of objects. *Memory and Cognition, 3*, 519–526. (pp. 288, 289)

**Palmer, S. E.** (1975b). Visual perception and world knowledge: Notes on a model of sensory-cognitive interaction. In D. A. Norman & D. E. Rumelhart (Eds.), *Explorations in cognition*. San Francisco: Freeman. (p. 288)

**Papousek, H.** (1969). Individual variability in learned responses in human infants. In R. J. Robinson (Ed.), *Brain and early behaviour*. New York: Academic Press. (p. 417)

**Park, B., & Rothbart, M.** (1982). Perception of out-group homogeneity and levels of social categorization: Memory for the subordinate attributes of in-group and out-group members. *Journal of Personality and Social Psychology, 42*, 1031–1068. (p. 498)

**Parkin, A. J.** (1987). *Memory and amnesia: An introduction*. Oxford: Blackwell. (p. 358)

**Parmelee, A. H., Wenner, W. H., Akiyama, Y., Schultz, M., & Stern, E.** (1967). Sleep states in premature infants. *Developmental Medicine and Child Neurology, 9*, 70–77. (p. 224)

**Partridge, L., & Halliday, T.** (1984). Mating patterns and mate choice. In J. R. Krebs & N. B. Davies (Eds.), *Behavioural ecology: An evolutionary approach*. Sunderland, MA: Sinauer. (p. 109)

**Pascual-Leone, J.** (1970). A mathematical model for the transition rule in Piaget's developmental stages. *Acta Psychologica, 32*, 301–345. (p. 441)

**Passingham, R. E., Perry, V. H., & Wilkinson, F.** (1983). The long-term effects of removal of sensorimotor cortex in infant and adult rhesus monkeys. *Brain, 106*, 675–705. (p. 183)

**Passman, R. H., & Weisberg, P.** (1975). Mothers and blankets as agents for promoting play and exploration by young children in a novel environment: The effect of social and nonsocial attachment objects. *Developmental Psychology, 11*, 170–177. (p. 459)

**Pastor, D. L.** (1981). The quality of mother-infant attachment and its relationship to toddlers' initial sociability with peers. *Developmental Psychology, 17*, 326–335. (p. 458)

**Patterson, F. G.** (1980). Innovative use of language by a gorilla: A case study. In K. Nelson (Ed.), *Children's language* (Vol. 2). New York: Gardner Press. (p. 429)

**Patzer, G. L.** (1985). *The physical attractiveness phenomena*. New York: Plenum. (p. 495)

**Paul, G. L., & Lentz, R. J.** (1977). *Psychosocial treatment of chronic mental patients: Milieu versus social-learning programs*. Cambridge, MA: Harvard University Press. (pp. 646, 670)

**Pavlov, I. P.** (1927; reprinted 1960). *Conditioned reflexes* (G. V. Anrep, Ed. & trans.). New York: Dover. (pp. 124, 125, 126, 127, 128, 129, 145)

**Pearson, K.** (1920). Notes on the history of correlation. *Biometrika, 13*, 25–45. (p. 366)

**Peele, S.** (1988). A moral vision of addiction: How people's values determine whether they become and remain addicts. In S. Peele (Ed.), *Visions of addiction: Major contemporary perspectives on addiction and alcoholism*. Lexington, MA: Lexington Books. (p. 627)

**Penfield, W., & Perot, P.** (1963). The brain's record of auditory and visual experience. *Brain, 86*, 595–696. (p. 224)

**Peris, F. S., Hefferline, R. F., & Goodman, P.** (1951). *Gestalt therapy*. New York: Julian. (p. 659)

**Pervin, L. A.** (1980). *Personality: Theory, assessment, and research* (3rd ed.). New York: Wiley. (p. 651)

**Peterson, C., & Seligman, E. P.** (1984). Causal explanations as a risk factor for depression: Theory and evidence. *Psychological Review, 91*, 347–374. (p. 501)

**Peterson, L. R., & Peterson, M. J.** (1959). Short-term retention of individual verbal items. *Journal of Experimental Psychology, 58*, 193–198. (pp. 332, 333, 359)

**Petty, R. E., & Cacioppo, J. T.** (1986). The elaboration likelihood model of persuasion. In L. Berkowitz (Ed.), *Advances in experimental social psychology* (Vol. 19). New York: Academic Press. (p. 515)

**Petty, R. E., Cacioppo, J. T., & Goldman, R.** (1981). Personal involvement as a determinant of argument-based persuasion. *Journal of Personality and Social Psychology, 41*, 847–855. (pp. 515, 516)

**Petursson, H., & Lader, M. H.** (1986). Benzodiazepine dependence. In J. Gabe & P. Williams (Eds.), *Tranquillisers: Social, psychological, and clinical perspectives*. London: Tavistock. (p. 678)

**Pfaff, D., & Modianos, D.** (1985). Neural mechanisms of female reproductive behavior. In N. Adler, D. Pfaff, & R. W. Goy (Eds.), *Handbook of behavioral neurobiology* (Vol. 7: Reproduction). New York: Plenum. (p. 211)

**Pfaff, D. W., & Sakuma, Y.** (1979). Deficit in the lordosis reflex of female rats caused by lesions in the ventromedial nucleus of the hypothalamus. *Journal of Physiology, 288*, 203–210. (p. 209)

**Pfungst, O.** (1911; reprinted 1965). *Clever Hans: The horse of Mr. von Osten* (C. L. Rahn, Trans.). New York: Holt, Rinehart & Winston. (pp. 25, 26)

**Phares, E. J.** (1978). Locus of control. In H. London & J. E. Exner (Eds.), *Dimensions of personality*. New York: Wiley. (pp. 587, 588)

**Phares, E. J.** (1984). *Introduction to personality*. Columbus, OH: Merrill. (p. 588)

**Piaget, J.** (1923). *The language and thought of the child* (M. Worden, Trans.). New York: Harcourt, Brace & World. (pp. 432, 444)

**Piaget, J.** (1926). *Judgment and reasoning in the child* (M. Worden, Trans.). New York: Harcourt, Brace & World. (p. 433)

**Piaget, J.** (1927). *The child's conception of physical causality* (M. Worden, Trans.). New York: Harcourt, Brace & World. (p. 433)

**Piaget, J.** (1932; reprinted 1965). *The moral judgment of the child.* New York: Free Press. (pp. 451, 464)

**Piaget, J.** (1936; reprinted 1963). *The origins of intelligence in the child.* New York: Norton. (pp. 417, 418)

**Piaget, J.** (1970). *Genetic epistemology* (E. Duckworth, Trans.). New York: Norton. (p. 431)

**Piaget, J., Inhelder, B., & Szeminska, A.** (1948; reprinted 1960). *The child's conception of geometry.* New York: Basic Books. (p. 432)

**Pick, A. D., Christy, M. D., & Frankel, G. W.** (1972). A developmental study of visual selective attention. *Journal of Experimental Child Psychology, 14,* 165–175. (p. 442)

**Pickles, J. O.** (1988). *An introduction to the physiology of hearing* (2nd ed.). New York: Academic Press. (pp. 247, 249, 250)

**Pierrel, R., & Sherman, J. G.** (1963, February). Train your rat the Barnabus way. *Brown Alumni Monthly,* 8–14. (p. 139)

**Plomin, R., & DeFries, J. C.** (1985). *Origins of individual differences in infancy.* New York: Academic Press. (p. 467)

**Plomin, R., DeFries, J. C., & McClearn, G. E.** (1990). *Behavioral genetics: A primer* (2nd ed.). New York: Freeman. (pp. 51, 58, 61, 71, 76)

**Plomin, R., & Foch, T. T.** (1980). A twin study of objectively assessed personality in childhood. *Journal of Personality and Social Psychology, 39,* 680–688. (p. 610)

**Polefrone, J., & Manuck, S.** (1987). Gender differences in cardiovascular and neuroendocrine response to stressors. In R. C. Barnett, L. Biener, & G. K. Baruch (Eds.), *Gender and stress.* New York: Free Press. (p. 613)

**Pomerantz, J. R., & Kubovy, M.** (1986). Theoretical approaches to perceptual organization: Simplicity and likelihood principles. In K. R. Boff, L. Kaufman, & J. P. Thomas (Eds.), *Handbook of perception and human performance, Vol. II: Cognitive processes and performance.* New York: Wiley. (p. 289)

**Powers, B., & Valenstein, E. S.** (1972). Sexual receptivity: Facilitation by medial preoptic lesions in female rats. *Science, 175,* 1003–1005. (p. 209)

**Powley, T. L.** (1977). The ventromedial hypothalamic syndrome, satiety, and a cephalic phase hypothesis. *Psychological Review, 84,* 89–126. (p. 205)

**Premack, A. J., & Premack, D.** (1972, October). Teaching language to an ape. *Scientific American.* 92–99. (p. 429)

**Prentice-Dunn, S., & Rogers, R. W.** (1983). Deindividuation in aggression. In R. G. Geen & E. I. Donnerstein (Eds.), *Aggression: Theoretical and empirical reviews (Vol. 2).* New York: Academic Press. (p. 544)

**Prentice-Dunn, S., & Spivey, C. B.** (1986). Extreme deindividuation in the laboratory: Its magnitude and subjective components. *Personality and Social Psychology Bulletin, 12,* 206–215. (p. 545)

**Pressin, J.** (1933). The comparative effects of social and mechanical stimulation on memorizing. *American Journal of Psychology, 45,* 263–270. (p. 541)

**Pucey, A. E.** (1980). Inbreeding avoidance in chimpanzees. *Animal Behaviour, 28,* 543–552. (p. 110)

**Quattrone, A., & Jones, E. E.** (1980). The perception of variability within in-groups and out-groups: Implications for the law of small numbers. *Journal of Personality and Social Psychology, 38,* 141–152. (p. 498)

**Racey, P. A., & Skinner, J. D.** (1979). Endocrine aspects of sexual mimicry in spotted hyenas *Crocuta crocuta. Journal of Zoology* (London), *187,* 315–326. (p. 88)

**Rachman, S. J.** (1985). An overview of clinical research issues in obsessional-compulsive disorders. In M. Mavissakalian, S. M. Turner, & L. Michelson (Eds.), *Obsessive-compulsive disorder.* New York: Plenum. (p. 618)

**Rachman, S. J., & DeSilva, P.** (1978). Abnormal and normal obsessions. *Behavioral Research and Therapy, 16,* 223–248. (p. 618)

**Rachman, S. J., & Wilson, G. T.** (1980). *The effects of psychological therapy* (2nd ed.). New York: Pergamon. (p. 668)

**Radke-Yarrow, M., Zahn-Waxler, C., & Capman, M.** (1983). Children's pro-social dispositions and behavior. In P. H. Mussen & E. M. Hetherington (Eds.), *Handbook of child psychology: Vol. 4: Socialization, personality, and social development* (4th ed.). New York: Wiley. (p. 476)

**Rank, S. G., & Jacobson, C. K.** (1977). Hospital nurses' compliance with medication overdose orders: A failure to replicate. *Journal of Health and Social Behavior, 18,* 188–193. (p. 540)

**Rapaport, J. L.** (1989, March). The biology of obsessions and compulsions. *Scientific American,* 83–89. (p. 618)

**Rasmussen, E. W.** (1939). Social facilitation. *Acta Psychologica, 4,* 275–294. (p. 541)

**Rasmussen, T., & Milner, B.** (1977). The role of early left brain injury in determining lateralization of cerebral speech functions. *Annals of the New York Academy of Sciences, 299,* 355–369. (p. 379)

**Raugh, M. R., & Atkinson, R. C.** (1975). A mnemonic method for learning a second-language vocabulary. *Journal of Educational Psychology, 67,* 1–16. (p. 339)

**Ravussin, E., Lillioja, S., Knowler, W. C., Christin, L., Freymond, D., Abbott, W. G. H., Boyce, V., Howard, B., & Bogardus, C.** (1988). Reduced rate of energy expenditure as a risk factor for body-weight gain. *The New England Journal of Medicine, 318,* 467–472. (p. 208)

**Razran, G. A.** (1939). A quantitative study of meaning by a conditioned salivary technique (semantic conditioning). *Science, 90,* 89–91. (p. 144)

**Redican, W. K.** (1982). An evolutionary perspective on human facial displays. In P. Ekman (Ed.), *Emotion in the human face.* Cambridge: Cambridge University Press. (pp. 98, 104)

**Regier, D. A., Boyd, J. H., Burke, J. D., Rae, D. S., Myers, J. K., Kramer, M., Robins, L. N., George, L. K., Karno, M., & Locke, B. Z.** (1988). One-month prevalence of mental disorders in the United States. *Archives of General Psychiatry, 45,* 977–986. (p. 612)

**Reisenzein, R.** (1983). The Schachter theory of emotion: Two decades later. *Psychological Bulletin, 94,* 239–264. (p. 233)

Rescorla, R. A. (1973). Effect of US habituation following conditioning. *Journal of Comparative and Physiological Psychology, 82,* 137–143. (p. 146)

Rescorla, R. A. (1987). A Pavlovian analysis of goal-directed behavior. *American Psychologist, 42,* 119–129. (pp. 147, 148)

Rescorla, R. A. (1988). Pavlovian conditioning: It's not what you think it is. *American Psychologist, 43,* 151–160. (pp. 146, 147)

Rescorla, R. A., & Wagner, A. R. (1972). A theory of Pavlovian conditioning. Variations in effectiveness of reinforcement and non-reinforcement. In A. Black & W. F. Prokasky, Jr. (Eds.), *Classical conditioning II.* New York: Appleton-Century-Crofts. (p. 147)

Rest, J. R. (1986). *Moral development: Advances in research and theory.* New York: Praeger. (pp. 476, 477)

Reynolds, D. V. (1969). Surgery in the rat during electrical analgesia induced by focal brain stimulation. *Science, 164,* 444–445. (p. 268)

Reznick, J. S., & Kagan, J. (1982). Category detection in infancy. In L. Lipsitt (Ed.), *Advances in infancy research* (Vol. 2). Norwood, NJ: Ablex. (p. 416)

Rheingold, H., & Cook, K. (1975). The contents of boys' and girls' rooms as an index of parents' behavior. *Child Development, 46,* 459–463. (p. 467)

Rhodes, S. R. (1983). Age-related differences in work attitudes and behavior: A review and conceptual analysis. *Psychological Bulletin, 93,* 328–367. (p. 481)

Richards, R., Kinney, D. K., Lunde, I., Benet, M., & Merzel, A. P. C. (1988). Creativity in manic-depressives, cyclothymes, their normal relatives, and control subjects. *Journal of Abnormal Psychology, 97,* 281–288. (p. 633)

Richardson-Klavehn, A., & Bjork, R. A. (1988). Measures of memory. *Annual Review of Psychology, 39,* 475–543. (p. 327)

Richter, C. P., & Eckert, J. F. (1938). Mineral metabolism of adrenalectomized rats studied by the appetite method. *Endocrinology, 22,* 214–224. (p. 199)

Riley, J. W., Jr. (1970). What people think about death. In O. B. Brim, Jr., H. E. Freeman, S. Levine, & N. A. Scotch (Eds.), *The dying patient.* New York: Russell Sage Foundation. (p. 485)

Roberts, S. B., Savage, J., Coward, W. A., Chew, B., & Lucas, A. (1988). Energy expenditure and intake in infants born to lean and overweight mothers. *The New England Journal of Medicine, 318,* 461–466. (p. 208)

Robins, L. N., Helzer, J. E., Weissman, M. M., Orvaschel, H., Gruenberg, E., Burke, J. D., & Regier, D. A. (1984). Lifetime prevalence of specific psychiatric disorders in three sites. *Archives of General Psychiatry, 41,* 949–958. (pp. 612, 634)

Robinson, D. N., & Uttal, W. R. (1983). *Foundations of psychobiology.* New York: Macmillan. (p. 165)

Rock, I. (1984). *Perception.* New York: Scientific American Books. (pp. 297, 308, 310, 311, 317)

Rock, I., & Gutman, D. (1981). The effect of inattention on form perception. *Journal of Experimental Psychology: Human Perception and Performance, 7,* 275–285. (p. 297)

Rodgers, D. A. (1972). Minnesota Multiphasic Personality Inventory. In O. K. Buros (Ed.), *The seventh mental measurements yearbook* (Vol. 1). Highland Park, NJ: Gryphon. (p. 651)

Rodin, J. (1981). Current status of the internal-external hypothesis for obesity. *American Psychologist, 36,* 361–372. (p. 207)

Rodin, J. (1986). Aging and health: Effects of the sense of control. *Science, 233,* 1271–1276. (p. 484)

Roehling, P. V., Smith, G. T., Goldman, M. S., & Christiansen, B. A. (1987). *Alcohol expectancies predict adolescent drinking: A three year longitudinal study.* Paper presented at the 95th Annual Convention of the American Psychological Association, New York. (p. 626)

Rogers, C. R. (1951). *Client-centered therapy: Its current practice, implications, and theory.* Boston: Houghton Mifflin. (pp. 659, 660)

Rogers, C. R. (1954). Toward a theory of creativity. *ETC: A Review of General Semantics, 11,* 249–260. (p. 582)

Rogers, C. R. (1959). A theory of therapy, personality, and interpersonal relationships, as developed in the client-centered framework. In S. Koch (Ed.), *Psychology: A study of a science* (Vol. 3). New York: McGraw-Hill. (p. 581)

Rogers, C. R. (1963). The actualizing tendency in relation to "motives" and to consciousness. In M. R. Jones (Ed.), *Nebraska symposium on motivation.* Lincoln, NE: University of Nebraska. (p. 580)

Rogers, C. R. (Ed.) (1967). *The therapeutic relationship and its impact: A study of psychotherapy with schizophrenics.* Madison, WI: University of Wisconsin Press. (pp. 661, 662)

Rogers, C. R. (1969). *Freedom to learn.* Columbus, OH: Merrill. (p. 581)

Rogers, C. R. (1977). *Carl Rogers on personal power.* New York: Delacorte Press. (p. 580)

Rogers, C. R., & Dymond, R. F. (1954). *Psychotherapy and personality change.* Chicago: University of Chicago Press. (p. 660)

Rogers, T. B., Kuiper, N. A., & Kirker, W. S. (1977). Self-reference and the encoding of personal information. *Journal of Personality and Social Psychology, 35,* 677–688. (p. 336)

Rokeach, M. (1980). Some unresolved issues in theories of beliefs, attitudes, and values. In M. M. Page (Ed.), *1979 Nebraska symposium on motivation.* Lincoln, NE: University of Nebraska Press. (p. 522)

Roland, P. E., Larsen, B., Larsen, N. A., & Skinhoj, E. (1980). Supplementary motor area and other cortical areas in organization of voluntary movements in man. *Journal of Neurophysiology, 43,* 118–136. (p. 184)

Rolls, E. T. (1982). Feeding and reward. In B. G. Hoebel & D. Novin (Eds.), *The neural basis of feeding and reward.* Brunswick, ME: Haer Institute. (p. 203)

Rosch, E. (1973). On the internal structure of perceptual and semantic categories. In T. E. Moore (Ed.), *Cognitive development and the acquisition of language.* New York: Academic Press. (pp. 344, 402)

Rosch, E. (1975). Cognitive representations of semantic categories. *Journal of Experimental Psychology: General, 104,* 192–223. (p. 344)

**Rosch, E.** (1977). Human categorization. In N. Warren (Ed.), *Advances in cross-cultural psychology* (Vol. 1). London: Academic Press. (p. 344)

**Rose, S.** (1973). *The conscious brain.* New York: Knopf. (p. 17)

**Rosen, J. J., Glass, D. H., & Ison, J. R.** (1967). Amobarbital sodium and instrumental performance changes following reward reduction. *Psychonomic Science, 9,* 129–130. (p. 149)

**Rosen, R. C., & Beck, J. G.** (1988). *Patterns of sexual arousal: Psychophysiological processes and clinical applications.* New York: Guilford. (p. 213)

**Rosenberg, S.** (1988). Self and others: Studies in social personality and autobiography. In L. Berkowitz (Ed.), *Advances in experimental social psychology* (Vol. 21). New York: Academic Press. (p. 504)

**Rosenhan, D. L.** (1973). On being sane in insane places. *Science, 179,* 250–258. (p. 645)

**Rosenhan, D. L., & Seligman, M. E. P.** (1984). *Abnormal psychology.* New York: Norton. (p. 621)

**Rosenthal, R.** (1965). Introduction to O. Pfungst, *Clever Hans: The horse of Mr. von Osten.* New York: Holt, Rinehart & Winston. (p. 27)

**Rosenthal, R.** (1976). *Experimenter effects in behavioral research* (enlarged ed.). New York: Irvington. (p. 27)

**Rosenthal, R., & Jacobson, L.** (1968). *Pygmalion in the classroom.* New York: Holt, Rinehart & Winston. (p. 502)

**Ross, L.** (1977). The intuitive psychologist and his shortcomings: Distortions in the attribution process. In L. Berkowitz (Ed.), *Advances in experimental social psychology.* New York: Academic Press. (p. 499)

**Roth, M.** (1957). Interaction of genetic and environmental factors in the causation of schizophrenia. In D. Richter (Ed.), *Schizophrenia: Somatic aspects.* New York: Pergamon. (p. 77)

**Rothblum, E. D., Solomon, L. J., & Albee, G. W.** (1986). A sociopolitical perspective of DSM-III. In T. Millon & G. L. Klerman (Eds.), *Contemporary directions in psychopathology: Toward the DSM-IV.* New York: Guilford. (p. 608)

**Rotter, J. B.** (1954; reprinted 1973, 1980). *Social learning and clinical psychology.* New York: Johnson Reprint Co. (pp. 585, 586)

**Rotter, J. B.** (1966). Generalized expectancies for internal versus external locus of control of reinforcement. *Psychological Monographs: General and Applied, 80* (Whole no. 609). (p. 587)

**Rotter, J. B.** (1982). Brief autobiography of the author. In J. B. Rotter (Ed.), *The development and application of social learning theory: Selected papers.* New York: Praeger. (p. 585)

**Rotter, J. B., Liverant, S., & Crowne, D. P.** (1961). The growth and extinction of expectancies in chance controlled and skilled tasks. *Journal of Psychology, 52,* 161–177. (p. 587)

**Routtenberg, A.** (1978, November). The reward system of the brain. *Scientific American, 239,* 154–164. (p. 215)

**Rozin, P., & Kalat, J.** (1971). Specific hungers and poison avoidance as adaptive specializations of learning. *Psychological Review, 78,* 459–486. (p. 154)

**Rubin, J. Z., Provenzano, F. J., & Luria, Z.** (1974). The eye of the beholder: Parents' views on the sex of newborns. *American Journal of Orthopsychiatry, 44,* 512–519. (p. 467)

**Rubin, Z.** (1970). Measurement of romantic love. *Journal of Personality and Social Psychology, 16,* 265–273. (p. 510)

**Rudy, J. W., Stadler-Morris, S., & Peter, A.** (1987). Ontogeny of spatial navigation behaviors in the rat: Dissociation of "proximal"- and "distal"-cue-based behaviors. *Behavioral Neuroscience, 101,* 62–73. (p. 150)

**Rumelhart, D. E., & McClelland, J. L.** (1987). Learning the past tense of English verbs: Implicit rules or parallel distributed processing. In B. MacWhinney (Ed.), *Mechanisms of language acquisition.* Hillsdale, NJ: Erlbaum. (p. 424)

**Rundus, D.** (1977). Maintenance rehearsal and single-level processing. *Journal of Verbal Learning and Verbal Behavior, 16,* 665–681. (p. 335)

**Runeson, S., & Frykholm, G.** (1986). Kinematic specification of gender and gender expression. In V. McCabe & G. J. Balzano (Eds.), *Event cognition: An ecological perspective.* Hillsdale, NJ: Erlbaum. (p. 313)

**Rupniak, N. M. J., Kilpatrick, G., Hall, M. D., Jenner, P., & Marsden, C. D.** (1984b). Differential alterations in striatal dopamine receptor sensitivity induced by repeated administration of clinically equivalent doses of haloperidol, sulpiride or clozapine in rats. *Psychopharmacology, 84,* 512–519. (p. 677)

**Rupniak, N. M. J., Mann, S., Hall, M. D., Fleminger, S., Kilpatrick, G., Jenner, P., & Marsden, C. D.** (1984a). Differential effects of continuous administration of haloperidol or sulpiride on striatal dopamine function in the rat. *Psychopharmacology, 84,* 503–511. (p. 677)

**Rushton, J. P., Fulker, D. W., Neale, M. C., Nias, D. K. B., & Eysenck, H. J.** (1986). Altruism and aggression: The heritability of individual differences. *Journal of Personality and Social Psychology, 50,* 1192–1198. (p. 599)

**Russek, M.** (1971). Hepatic receptors and the neurophysiological mechanisms controlling feeding behavior. In S. Ehrenpreis (Ed.), *Neurosciences research* (Vol. 4). New York: Academic Press. (p. 204)

**Rutkowski, G. K., Gruder, C. L., & Romer, D.** (1983). Group cohesiveness, social norms, and bystander intervention. *Journal of Personality and Social Psychology, 44,* 545–552. (p. 544)

**Ryan, W.** (1971). *Blaming the victim.* New York: Pantheon. (p. 498)

---

**Sachs, G. S., & Gelenberg, A. J.** (1988). Adverse effects of electroconvulsive therapy. In A. J. Frances & R. E. Hales (Eds.), *Review of psychiatry, Vol. 7.* Washington, DC: American Psychiatric Press. (p. 679)

**Sachs, J. S.** (1967). Recognition memory for syntactic and semantic aspects of connected discourse. *Perception & Psychophysics, 2,* 437–442. (p. 340)

**Sackeim, H. A.** (1988). Mechanisms of action of electroconvulsive therapy. In A. J. Frances & R. E. Hales (Eds.), *Review of psychiatry, Vol. 7.* Washington, DC: American Psychiatric Press. (p. 678)

**Sackheim, H. A., & Gur, R. C.** (1978). Lateral asymmetry in intensity of emotional expression. *Neuropsychologia, 16,* 473–482. (p. 381)

**Sacks, O.** (1970). *The man who mistook his wife for a hat, and other clinical tales.* New York: Harper & Row. (p. 265)

**St. Clair, S., & Day, H. D.** (1979). Ego identity status and values among high school females. *Journal of Youth and Adolescence, 8,* 317–326. (p. 475)

**St. George-Hyslop, P. H., Tanzi, R. E., Polinsky, R. J., Haines, J. L., Nee, L., & others** (1987). The genetic defect causing familial Alzheimer's disease maps on chromosome 21. *Science, 235,* 885–890. (p. 60)

**Sajwaj, T., Lipet, J., & Agras, S.** (1974). Lemon-juice therapy: The control of life-threatening rumination in a six-month-old infant. *Journal of Applied Behavior Analysis, 7,* 557–563. (p. 142)

**Sande, G. N., Goethals, G. R., & Radloff, C. E.** (1988). Perceiving one's own traits and others': The multifaceted self. *Journal of Personality and Social Psychology, 54,* 13–20. (pp. 500, 504)

**Savage-Rumbaugh, E. S.** (1984). Verbal behavior at a procedural level in the chimpanzee. *Journal of the Experimental Analysis of Behavior, 41,* 223–250. (pp. 429, 430)

**Savage-Rumbaugh, E. S.** (1987). Communication, symbolic communication, and language: Reply to Seidenberg and Petitto. *Journal of Experimental Psychology: General, 116,* 288–292. (p. 430)

**Savage-Rumbaugh, E. S., McDonald, K., Sevcik, R., & Hopkins, B.** (1985). Language acquisition and use by a pygmy chimpanzee. *American Journal of Primatology, 8,* 362. (p. 430)

**Savage-Rumbaugh, E. S., McDonald, K., Sevcik, R. A., Hopkins, B., & Rupert, E.** (1986). Spontaneous symbol acquisition and communicative use by pygmy chimpanzees. *Journal of Experimental Psychology: General, 115,* 211–235. (p. 430)

**Savage-Rumbaugh, E. S., Pate, J. L., Lawson, J. L., Smith, T., & Rosenbaum, S.** (1983). Can a chimpanzee make a statement? *Journal of Experimental Psychology: General, 112,* 457–492. (p. 429)

**Savage-Rumbaugh, E. S., & Rumbaugh, D. M.** (1980). Language analogue project II: Theory and tactics. In K. Nelson (Ed.), *Children's language* (Vol. 2). New York: Gardner Press. (p. 429)

**Scarr, S.** (1984). *Mother care/other care.* New York: Basic Books. (p. 459)

**Scarr, S., & Carter-Saltzman, L.** (1983). Genetics and intelligence. In J. L. Fuller & E. C. Simmel (Eds.), *Behavior genetics: Principles and applications.* Hillsdale, NJ: Erlbaum. (p. 72)

**Scarr, S., Weber, P. L., Weinberg, R. A., & Wittig, M. A.** (1981). Personality resemblance among adolescents and their parents in biologically related and adoptive families. *Journal of Personality and Social Psychology, 40,* 885–898. (p. 600)

**Scarr, S., & Weinberg, R. A.** (1976). IQ test performance of black children adopted by white families. *American Psychologist, 31,* 726–739. (p. 72)

**Schachter, S.** (1970). Some extraordinary facts about obese humans and rats. *American Psychologist, 26,* 129–144. (p. 206)

**Schachter, S.** (1971). *Emotion, obesity, and crime.* New York: Academic Press. (pp. 232, 233)

**Schacter, D. L.** (1987). Implicit memory: History and current status. *Journal of Experimental Psychology: Learning, Memory, and Cognition, 13,* 501–518. (p. 360)

**Schacter, D. L., Harbluk, J. L., & McLachlan, D. R.** (1984). Retrieval without recollection: An experimental analysis of source amnesia. *Journal of Verbal Learning and Verbal Behavior, 23,* 593–611. (p. 360)

**Schanberg, S. M., & Field, T. M.** (1987). Sensory deprivation stress and supplemental stimulation in the rat pup and preterm human neonate. *Child Development, 58,* 1431–1447. (p. 455)

**Schank, R. C., & Abelson, R. P.** (1977). *Scripts, plans, goals and understanding.* Hillsdale, NJ: Erlbaum. (pp. 345, 445)

**Scharf, B.** (1964). Partial masking. *Acustica, 14,* 16–23. (p. 249)

**Scheff, T. J.** (1984). *Being mentally ill: A sociological theory* (2nd ed.). New York: Aldine. (p. 608)

**Scher, S. J., & Cooper, J.** (1989). Motivational basis of dissonance: The singular role of behavioral consequences. *Journal of Personality and Social Psychology, 56,* 899–906. (p. 519)

**Schiefflin, B., & Ochs, E.** (1983). A cultural perspective on the transition from prelinguistic to linguistic communication. In R. Golinkoff (Ed.), *The transition from prelinguistic to linguistic communication.* Hillsdale, NJ: Erlbaum. (p. 427)

**Schiff, M., Duyme, M., Dumaret, A., Stewart, J., Tomkiewicz, S., & Feingold, J.** (1978). Intellectual status of working-class children adopted early into upper-middle-class families. *Science, 200,* 1503–1504. (p. 72)

**Schifter, D. E., & Ajzen, I.** (1985). Intention, perceived control, and weight loss: An application of the theory of planned behavior. *Journal of Personality and Social Psychology, 49,* 849–851. (p. 522)

**Schildkraut, J. J.** (1965). The catecholamine hypothesis of affective disorders: A review of supporting evidence. *American Journal of Psychiatry, 122,* 509–522. (p. 629)

**Schlenker, B. R.** (1980). *Impression management: The self-concept, social identity, and interpersonal relations.* Monterey, CA: Brooks/Cole. (p. 506)

**Schmidt, R. F.** (1986). Motor systems. In R. F. Schmidt (Ed.), *Fundamentals of neurophysiology* (3rd ed.). New York: Springer-Verlag. (pp. 178, 185)

**Schnapf, J. L., & Baylor, D. A.** (1987, April). How photoreceptor cells respond to light. *Scientific American,* 40–47. (pp. 253, 254)

**Schneider, J. M.** (1972). Relationship between locus of control and activity preferences: Effects of masculinity, activity, and skill. *Journal of Consulting and Clinical Psychology, 38,* 225–230. (p. 587)

**Schneider, J. W., & Hacker, S. L.** (1973). Sex role imagery and use of the generic "man" in introductory texts: A case of the sociology of sociology. *The American Sociologist, 8,* 12–18. (p. 404)

**Schneider, W., Dumais, S. T., & Shiffrin, R. M.** (1984). Automatic and control processing and attention. In R. Parasuraman & D. R. Davies (Eds.), *Varieties of attention.* New York: Academic Press. (pp. 299, 300)

**Schneider, W., & Shiffrin, R. M.** (1977). Controlled and automatic human information processing: I. Detection, search, and attention. *Psychological Review, 84,* 1–66. (p. 301)

**Schunk, D. H.** (1984). Self-efficacy perspective on achievement behavior. *Educational Psychologist, 19,* 48–58. (p. 589)

**Schunk, D. H., & Hanson, A. R.** (1985). Peer models: Influence on children's self-efficacy and achievement. *Journal of Educational Psychology, 77,* 313–322. (p. 588)

**Schwartz, M. F.** (1987). Patterns of speech production deficit within and across aphasia syndromes: Application of a psycholinguistic model. In M. Coltheart, G. Sartori, & R. Job (Eds.), *The cognitive neuropsychology of language.* Hillsdale, NJ: Erlbaum. (p. 400)

**Schwartz, S. H., & Gottlieb, A.** (1980). Bystander anonymity and reactions to emergencies. *Journal of Personality and Social Psychology, 39,* 418–430. (p. 544)

**Schwartzman, H.** (1978). *Transformations: The anthropology of children's play.* New York: Plenum. (p. 463)

**Scott, J. P.** (1963). The process of primary socialization in canine and human infants. *Monograph of the Society for Research in Child Development, 28,* 1–47. (p. 55)

**Scott, J. P., & Fuller, J. L.** (1965). *Genetics and the social behavior of the dog.* Chicago: University of Chicago Press. (p. 54)

**Scribner, S.** (1977). Modes of thinking and ways of speaking: Culture and logic reconsidered. In P. N. Johnson-Laird & P. C. Wason (Eds.), *Thinking: Readings in cognitive science.* Cambridge: Cambridge University Press. (p. 384)

**Scribner, S.** (1986). Thinking in action: Some characteristics of practical thought. In R. J. Sternberg & R. K. Wagner (Eds.), *Practical intelligence: Nature and origins of competence in the everyday world.* Cambridge: Cambridge University Press. (p. 383)

**Searle, L. V.** (1949). The organization of hereditary maze-brightness and maze-dullness. *Genetic Psychology Monographs, 39,* 279–325. (p. 66)

**Sears, R. R.** (1936). Experimental studies of projection: I. Attribution of traits. *Journal of Social Psychology, 7,* 151–163. (p. 572)

**Sechenov, I. M.** (1863; reprinted 1935). Reflexes of the brain. In A. A. Subkov (Ed. & trans.), *I. M. Sechenov: Selected works.* Moscow: State Publishing House for Biological and Medical Literature. (p. 6)

**Seeman, P., & Lee, T.** (1975). Antipsychotic drugs: Direct correlation between clinical potency and presynaptic action on dopamine neurons. *Science, 188,* 1271–1219. (p. 638)

**Seligman, M. E. P.** (1971). Phobias and preparedness. *Behavior Therapy, 193,* 323–325. (pp. 157, 617)

**Seligman, M. E. P., Abramson, L. Y., Semmel, A., & von Baeyer, C.** (1979). Depressive attributional style. *Journal of Abnormal Psychology, 88,* 242–247. (p. 630)

**Seligman, M. E. P., Castellon, C., Cacciola, J., Schulman, P., Luborsky, L., Ollove, M., & Downing, R.** (1988). Explanatory style change during cognitive therapy for unipolar depression. *Journal of Abnormal Psychology, 97,* 13–18. (p. 631)

**Seligman, M. E. P., Maier, S. F., & Geer, J. H.** (1968). Alleviation of learned helplessness in the dog. *Journal of Abnormal Psychology, 73,* 256–262. (p. 630)

**Selye, H.** (1956; reprinted 1976). *The stress of life* (rev. ed.). New York: McGraw-Hill. (p. 228)

**Semmel, A. K.** (1976). *Group dynamics and foreign policy process: The choice-shift phenomenon.* Paper presented to the Southern Political Science Association. (For description, see D. G. Myers, 1982.) (p. 550)

**Serbin, L., Sprafkin, C., Elman, M., & Doyle, A. B.** (1984). The early development of sex differentiated patterns and social influence. *Canadian Journal of Social Science, 14,* 350–363. (p. 469)

**Serbin, L. A., Conner, J. M., Burchardt, C. J., & Citron, C. C.** (1979). Effects of peer presence on sex-typing of children's behavior. *Journal of Experimental and Child Psychology, 27,* 303–309. (p. 468)

**Shallice, T., & Warrington, E. K.** (1970). Independent functioning of verbal memory stores: A neuropsychological study. *Quarterly Journal of Experimental Psychology, 22,* 261–273. (p. 359)

**Shapiro, C. M., Bortz, R., Mitchell, D., Bartell, P., & Jooste, P.** (1981). Slow-wave sleep: A recovery period after exercise. *Science, 214,* 1253–1254. (p. 220)

**Shapiro, S., Skinner, E. A., Kessler, L. G., Von Korff, M., German, P. S., Tischler, G. L., Leaf, P. J., Lee, B., Cottler, L., & Regier, D. A.** (1984) Utilization of health and mental health services: Three epidemiologic catchment area sites. *Archives of General Psychiatry, 41,* 971–978. (p. 648)

**Shaver, P., Hazen, C., & Bradshaw, D.** (1988). Love as attachment: The integration of three behavioral systems. In R. J. Sternberg & M. L. Barnes (Eds.), *The psychology of love.* New Haven, CT: Yale University Press. (p. 511)

**Sherif, M.** (1966). *In common predicament: Social psychology of intergroup conflict and cooperation.* Boston: Houghton Mifflin. (p. 553)

**Sherif, M., Harvey, O. J., White, B. J., Hood, W. E., & Sherif, C. W.** (1961). *Intergroup conflict and cooperation: The Robbers Cave experiment.* Norman, OK: University of Oklahoma Book Exchange. (p. 553)

**Sherman, P. W.** (1977). Nepotism and the evolution of alarm calls. *Science, 197,* 1246–1253. (pp. 112, 113)

**Sherry, D. F., & Schacter, D. L.** (1987). The evolution of multiple memory systems. *Psychological Review, 94,* 439–454. (p. 327)

**Shettleworth, S. J.** (1972). Constraints on learning. In D. S. Lehrman, R. A. Hinde, & E. Shaw (Eds.), *Advances in the study of behavior* (Vol. 4). New York: Academic Press. (p. 15)

**Shettleworth, S. J.** (1983, March). Memory in food-hoarding birds. *Scientific American,* 102–110. (p. 159)

**Shiffrin, R. M., & Schneider, W.** (1977). Controlled and automatic information processing: II. Perceptual learning, automatic attending, and a general theory. *Psychological Review, 84,* 127–190. (p. 302)

**Shoda, Y., Mischel, W., & Wright, J. C.** (1989). Intuitive interactionism in person perception: Effects of situation-behavior relations on dispositional judgments. *Journal of Personality and Social Psychology, 56,* 41–53. (p. 597)

**Shweder, R. A.** (1982). Fact and artifact in trait perception: The systematic distortion hypothesis. In B. A. Maher & W. B. Maher (Eds.), *Progress in experimental personality research, Vol. 11: Normal personality processes.* New York: Academic Press. (p. 600)

**Siegel, J. S.** (1980). Recent and prospective demographic trends for the elderly population and some implications for health care. In S. G. Haynes & M. Feinleib (Eds.), *Epidemiology of aging* (NIH Publication No. 80-969). Washington, DC: U.S. Government Printing Office. (p. 483)

**Siegel, S.** (1976). Morphine analgesia tolerance: Its situation specificity supports a Pavlovian conditioning model. *Science, 193,* 323–325. (p. 129)

**Siegel, S.** (1984). Pavlovian conditioning and heroin overdose: Reports by overdose victims. *Bulletin of the Psychonomic Society, 22,* 428–430. (p. 129)

**Siegel, S., Krank, M. D., & Hinson, R. E.** (1988). Anticipation of pharmacological and nonpharmacological events: Classical conditioning and addictive behavior. In S. Peele (Ed.), *Visions of addiction: Major contemporary perspectives on addiction and alcoholism.* Lexington, MA: Lexington Books. (pp. 129, 626)

**Siegler, R. S.** (1983). How knowledge influences learning. *American Scientist, 71,* 631–638. (pp. 442, 443)

**Simpson, E. L.** (1974). Moral development research: A case of scientific cultural bias. *Human development, 17,* 81–106. (p. 478)

**Sims, J. H., & Baumann, D. D.** (1972). The tornado threat: Coping styles of the north and south. *Science, 176,* 1386–1392. (p. 587)

**Singer, B., & Benassi, V. A.** (1981). Occult beliefs. *American Scientist, 69,* 49–55. (p. 27)

**Singer, J. E., Brush, C. A., & Lublin, S. C.** (1965). Some aspects of deindividuation and conformity. *Journal of Experimental Social Psychology, 1,* 356–378. (p. 545)

**Siqueland, R. R., & Lipsitt, L. P.** (1966). Conditioned head-turning in human newborns. *Journal of Experimental Child Psychology, 3,* 356–376. (p. 138)

**Sizemore, C. C.** (1989). *A mind of my own.* New York: William Morrow. (p. 623)

**Skarin, K.** (1977). Cognitive and contextual determinants of stranger fear in six- and eleven-month-old infants. *Child Development, 48,* 537–544. (p. 457)

**Skinner, B. F.** (1938). *The behavior of organisms.* New York: Appleton-Century-Crofts. (pp. 14, 122, 130, 133)

**Skinner, B. F.** (1953). *Science and human behavior.* New York: Macmillan. (pp. 136, 142)

**Skinner, B. F.** (1957). *Verbal behavior.* New York: Appleton-Century-Crofts. (pp. 18, 426, 520)

**Skinner, B. F.** (1971). *Beyond freedom and dignity.* New York: Knopf. (p. 14)

**Slater, E.** (1975). The diagnosis of "hysteria." *British Medical Journal, 1,* 1395–1399. (p. 620)

**Slavney, P. R., & Teitelbaum, M. L.** (1985). Patients with medically unexplained symptoms: DSM-III diagnoses and demographic characteristics. *General Hospital Psychiatry, 7,* 25–35. (p. 620)

**Sloane, M. C.** (1981). *A comparison of hypnosis vs. waking state and visual vs. non-visual recall instructions for witness/victim memory retrieval in actual major crimes.* Unpublished doctoral dissertation, Florida State University, Tallahassee. (p. 356)

**Sloane, R. B., Staples, F. R., Cristol, A. H., Yorkston, N. J., & Whipple, K.** (1975). *Psychotherapy versus behavior therapy.* Cambridge, MA: Harvard University Press. (p. 672)

**Slobin, D. I.** (1973). Cognitive prerequisites for the development of grammar. In C. H. Ferguson & D. I. Slobin (Eds.), *Studies of child language development.* New York: Holt, Rinehart & Winston. (p. 425)

**Slobin, D. I.** (1985). Introduction: Why study acquisition cross-linguistically? In D. I. Slobin (Ed.), *The crosslinguistic study of language acquisition, Vol. 1: The data.* Hillsdale, NJ: Erlbaum. (p. 425)

**Smith, B. D., Wilson, R. J., & Davidson, R.** (1984). Electrodermal activity and extraversion: Caffeine, preparatory signal and stimulus intensity effects. *Personality and Individual Differences, 5,* 59–65. (p. 594)

**Smith, D.** (1982). Trends in counseling and psychotherapy. *American Psychologist, 37,* 802–809. (p. 659)

**Smith, E. E., Shoben, E. J., & Rips, L. J.** (1974). Structure and process in semantic memory: A feature model for semantic decision. *Psychological Review, 81,* 214–241. (p. 344)

**Smith, M. B., Bruner, J. S., & White, R. W.** (1956). *Opinions and personality.* New York: Wiley. (p. 513)

**Smith, M. L., Glass, G. V., & Miller, T. I.** (1980). *The benefits of psychotherapy.* Baltimore: Johns Hopkins University Press. (p. 672)

**Smith, S. M., Brown, H. O., Toman, J. E. P., & Goodman, L. S.** (1947). The lack of cerebral effects of d-tubercurarine. *Anesthesiology, 8,* 1–14. (p. 401)

**Smyth, M. M., Morris, P. E., Levy, P., & Ellis, A. W.** (1987). *Cognition in action.* Hillsdale, NJ: Erlbaum. (p. 399)

**Snarey, J. R.** (1985). Cross-cultural universality of social-moral development: A critical review of Kohlbergian research. *Psychological Bulletin, 97,* 202–232. (p. 478)

**Snow, C. E.** (1984). Parent-child interaction and the development of communicative ability. In R. L. Schiefelbusch & J. Pickar (Eds.), *The acquisition of communicative competence.* Baltimore: University Park Press. (pp. 421, 427)

**Snow, C. P.** (1961, February). Either-or. *Progressive, 24.* (p. 535)

**Snyder, F., & Scott, J.** (1972). The psychophysiology of sleep. In N. S. Greenfield & R. A. Sternbach (Eds.), *Handbook of psychophysiology.* New York: Holt, Rinehart & Winston. (pp. 218, 219, 225)

**Snyder, M.** (1974). Self-monitoring of expressive behavior. *Journal of Personality and Social Psychology, 30,* 526–537. (pp. 508, 509)

**Snyder, M.** (1979). Self-monitoring processes. In L. Berkowitz (Ed.), *Advances in experimental social psychology* (Vol. 12). New York: Academic Press. (p. 509)

**Snyder, M., & DeBono, K. G.** (1987). A functional approach to attitudes and persuasion. In M. P. Zanna, J. M. Olson, & C. P. Herman (Eds.), *Social influence: The Ontario symposium, Vol. 5.* Hillsdale, NJ: Erlbaum. (pp. 514, 515)

**Snyder, M., & Monson, T. C.** (1975). Persons, situations, and the control of social behavior. *Journal of Personality and Social Psychology, 32,* 637–644. (p. 509)

**Snyder, M., & Smith, D.** (1986). Personality and friendship: The friendship worlds of self-monitoring. In V. Derlega & B. A. Winstead (Eds.), *Friendship and social interaction.* New York: Springer-Verlag. (p. 509)

**Snyder, M., & Swann, W. B.** (1976). When actions reflect attitudes: The politics of impression management. *Journal of Personality and Social Psychology, 34,* 1032–1042. (p. 521)

**Snyder, M., Tanke, E. D., & Berscheid, E.** (1977). Social perception and interpersonal behavior: On the self-fulfilling nature of social stereotypes. *Journal of Personality and Social Psychology, 35,* 656–666. (p. 502)

**Snyder, S. H.** (1985, October). The molecular basis of communication between cells. *Scientific American,* 132–141. (pp. 187, 191)

**Snyderman, M., & Rothman, S.** (1987). Survey of expert opinion on intelligence and aptitude testing. *American Psychologist, 42,* 137–144. (p. 365)

**Solomon, G. F., Amkraut, A. A., & Rubin, R. T.** (1985). Stress hormones, neuroregulation, and immunity. In S. R. Burchfield (Ed.), *Stress: Psychological and physiological interactions.* Washington, DC: Hemisphere. (p. 228)

**Sourkes, T. L.** (1989). Disorders of the basal ganglia. In G. J. Siegel, B. W. Agranoff, R. W. Albers, & P. B. Molinoff (Eds.), *Basic neurochemistry: Molecular, cellular, and medical aspects* (4th ed.). New York: Raven Press. (p. 179)

**Spalding, D. A.** (1873; reprinted 1954). Instinct with original observations on young animals. *British Journal of Animal Behavior, 2,* 2–11. (p. 158)

**Spanos, N. P., Weekes, J. R., & Bertrand, L. D.** (1985). Multiple personality: A social psychological perspective. *Journal of Abnormal Psychology, 94,* 362–376. (p. 623)

**Spearman, C.** (1904). The proof and measurement of association between two things. *American Journal of Psychology, 15,* 72–101. (p. 370)

**Spearman, C.** (1927). *The abilities of man.* New York: Macmillan. (p. 370)

**Spelke, E. S., Hirst, W. C., & Neisser, U.** (1976). Skills of divided attention. *Cognition, 4,* 215–230. (p. 299)

**Spence, K. W.** (1956). *Behavior theory and conditioning.* New Haven, CT: Yale University Press. (p. 147)

**Sperling, G.** (1960). The information available in brief visual presentations. *Psychological Monographs, 74* (Whole no. 498). (pp. 328–329)

**Spiro, M. E.** (1979). *Gender and culture: Kibbutz women revisited.* Durham, NC: Duke University Press. (p. 117)

**Spitzer, L., & Rodin, J.** (1983). Arousal-induced eating: Conventional wisdom or empirical finding? In J. T. Cacioppo & R. E. Petty (Eds.), *Social psychophysiology.* New York: Guilford. (p. 207)

**Spitzer, R. L., & Fleiss, J. L.** (1974). A reanalysis of the reliability of psychiatric diagnosis. *British Journal of Psychiatry, 125,* 341–347. (p. 610)

**Spitzer, R. L., Williams, J. B. W., & Gibbon, M.** (1987). *Instruction manual for the structured clinical interview for the DSM-III-R (SCID, 4/1/87 Revis.).* New York: NY State Psychiatric Institute. (p. 610)

**Spock, B., & Rothenberg, M. B.** (1985). *Dr. Spock's baby and child care* (rev. & updated ed.). New York: Pocket Books. (p. 456)

**Spohn, H., & Patterson, T.** (1980). Recent studies of psychophysiology in schizophrenia. *Schizophrenia–1980.* Washington, DC: NIMH. (p. 638)

**Springer, S. P., & Deutsch, G.** (1989). *Left brain, right brain* (3rd ed.). New York: Freeman. (p. 380)

**Squire, L. R.** (1987). *Memory and brain.* Oxford: Oxford University Press. (pp. 358, 359)

**Sroufe, L. A.** (1977). Wariness of strangers and the study of infant development. *Child Development, 48,* 731–746. (p. 457)

**Sroufe, L. A., & Fleeson, J.** (1986). Attachment and the construction of relationships. In W. H. Hartup & Z. Rubin (Eds.), *Relationships and development.* Hillsdale, NJ: Erlbaum. (p. 458)

**Stapp, J., Tucker, A. M., & VandenBos, G. R.** (1985). Census of psychological personnel: 1983. *American Psychologist, 40,* 1317–1351. (p. 21)

**Steinberg, L. D.** (1981). Transformations in family relations at puberty. *Developmental Psychology, 17,* 883–840. (p. 470)

**Steinberg, L., & Silverberg, S. B.** (1986). The vicissitudes of autonomy in early adolescence. *Child Development, 57,* 841–851. (p. 471)

**Steketee, G., & Foa, E. B.** (1985). Obsessive-compulsive disorder. In D. H. Barlow (Ed.), *Clinical handbook of psychological disorders: A step-by-step treatment manual.* New York: Guilford. (p. 618)

**Stellar, J. R., & Stellar, E.** (1985). *The neurobiology of motivation and reward.* New York: Springer-Verlag. (pp. 200, 203, 215, 216)

**Sternberg, R. J.** (1985a). *Beyond IQ: A triarchic theory of human intelligence.* Cambridge: Cambridge University Press. (pp. 375, 376, 377)

**Sternberg, R. J.** (1985b). General intellectual ability. In R. J. Sternberg (Ed.), *Human abilities: An information-processing approach.* New York: Freeman. (pp. 373, 377)

**Sternberg, R. J.** (1986a). *Intelligence applied: Understanding and increasing your intellectual skills.* San Diego: Harcourt Brace Jovanovich. (pp. 377, 390)

**Sternberg, R. J.** (1986b). Intelligence is mental self-government. In R. J. Sternberg & D. K. Detterman (Eds.), *What is intelligence? Contemporary viewpoints on its nature and definition.* Norwood, NJ: Ablex. (p. 375)

**Sternberg, R. J.** (1986c). A triangular theory of love. *Psychological Review, 93,* 119–135. (pp. 511, 512)

**Sternberg, R. J.** (1988). Triangulating love. In R. J. Sternberg & Michael Barnes (Eds.), *The psychology of love.* New Haven, CT: Yale University Press. (p. 511)

**Sternberg, R. J., & Gardner, M. K.** (1983). Unities in inductive reasoning. *Journal of Experimental Psychology: General, 112,* 80–116. (p. 376)

**Stevens, C. F.** (1979, September). The neuron. *Scientific American,* 54–65. (pp. 169, 170)

Stevens, S. S. (1962). The surprising simplicity of sensory metrics. *American Psychologist, 17,* 29–39. (p. 276)

Stevens, S. S. (1975). *Psychophysics: Introduction to its perceptual, neural, and social prospects.* New York: Wiley. (pp. 274, 276)

Steward, O. (1989). *Principles of cellular, molecular, and developmental neuroscience.* New York: Springer-Verlag. (p. 168)

Stewart, D. W., Netley, C. T., & Park, E. (1982). Summary of clinical findings of children with 47,XXY, 47,XYY and 47,XXX karyotypes. *Birth Defects: Original Aricle Series, 18,* 1–5. (p. 59)

Stewart, J., de Wit, H., & Eikelboom, R. (1984). Role of unconditioned and conditioned drug effects in the self-administration of opiates and stimulants. *Psychological Review, 91,* 251–268. (p. 215)

Stewart, R. B., & Marvin, R. S. (1984). Sibling relations: The role of conceptual perspective-taking in the ontogeny of sibling caregiving. *Child Development, 55,* 1322–1332. (p. 475)

Stiles, W. B., Shapiro, D. A., & Elliott, R. (1986). Are all psychotherapies equivalent? *American Psychologist, 41,* 165–180. (pp. 672, 673)

Stoner, J. A. F. (1961). *A comparison of individual and group decisions including risk.* Unpublished master's thesis, School of Industrial Management, Massachusetts Institute of Technology. (p. 549)

Storms, M. D. (1973). Videotape and the attribution process: Reversing actors' and observers' points of view. *Journal of Personality and Social Psychology, 27,* 165–175. (p. 501)

Stricker, E. M. (1973). Thirst, sodium appetite, and complementary physiological contributions to the regulation of intravascular fluid volume. In A. N. Epstein, H. R. Kissileff, & E. Stellar (Eds.), *The neuropsychology of thirst: New findings and advances in concepts.* Washington, DC: Winston. (p. 199)

Stricker, E. M. (1982). The central control of food intake: A role for insulin. In B. G. Hoebel & D. Novin (Eds.), *The neural basis of feeding and reward.* Brunswick, ME: Haer Institute. (p. 203)

Stroop, J. R. (1935). Studies of interference in serial verbal reactions. *Journal of Experimental Psychology, 18,* 643–662. (p. 300)

Struch, N., & Schwartz, S. H. (1989). Intergroup aggression: Its predictors and distinctness from in-group bias. *Journal of Personality and Social Psychology, 56,* 364–373. (p. 555)

Strupp, H. H. (1989). Psychotherapy: Can the practitioner learn from the researcher? *American Psychologist, 44,* 717–724. (p. 674)

Strupp, H. H., & Hadley, S. W. (1979). Specific vs. nonspecific factors in psychotherapy: A controlled study of outcome. *Archives of General Psychiatry, 36,* 1125–1136. (p. 674)

Sullivan, J. L., Sullivan, P. D., Mahorney, S., & Goldberg, R. L. (1984). Chemotherapy of anxiety. In J. L. Sullivan & P. D. Sullivan (Eds.), *Biochemical psychiatric therapeutics.* Boston: Butterworth. (p. 678)

Susman, R. L. (Ed.) (1984). *The pygmy chimpanzee: Evolutionary biology and behavior.* New York: Plenum. (p. 429)

Swann, W. B. (1985). The self as architect of social reality. In B. R. Schlenker (Ed.), *The self and social life.* New York: McGraw-Hill. (p. 508)

Swann, W. B. (1987). Identity negotiation: Where two roads meet. *Journal of Social Psychology, 53,* 1038–1051. (pp. 506, 508)

Swann, W. B., & Ely, R. J. (1984). A battle of wills: Self-verification versus behavioral confirmation. *Journal of Personality and Social Psychology, 46,* 1287–1302. (p. 508)

Swann, W. B., & Hill, C. A. (1982). When our identities are mistaken: Reaffirming self-conceptions through social interaction. *Journal of Personality and Social Psychology, 43,* 59–66. (p. 508)

Sweeney, P. D., & Gruber, K. L. (1984). Selective exposure: Voter information preferences and the Watergate affair. *Journal of Personality and Social Psychology, 46,* 1208–1221. (p. 517)

Tageson, C. W. (1982). *Humanistic psychology: A synthesis.* Homewood, IL: Dorsey. (p. 479)

Tajfel, H. (1982). Social psychology of intergroup relations. *Annual Review of Psychology, 33,* 1–39. (p. 498)

Tajfel, H., & Turner, J. (1979). An integrative theory of intergroup conflict. In W. G. Austin & S. Worchel (Eds.), *The social psychology of intergroup relations.* Monterey, CA: Brooks/Cole. (p. 556)

Takahashi, J. S., & Zatz, M. (1982). Regulation of circadian rhythmicity. *Science, 217,* 1104–1111. (pp. 221, 225, 226)

Taylor, H. F. (1980). *The IQ game.* New Brunswick, NJ: Rutgers University Press. (p. 71)

Teigen, K. H. (1984). A note on the origin of the term "nature and nurture": Not Shakespeare and Galton, but Mulcaster. *Journal of the History of the Behavioral Sciences, 20,* 363–364. (p. 47)

Tellegen, A., Lykken, D. T., Bouchard, T. J., Wilcox, K. J., Segal, N. L., & Rich, S. (1988). Personality similarity in twins reared apart and together. *Journal of Personality and Social Psychology, 54,* 1031–1039. (pp. 67, 599)

Terman, G. W., Shavit, Y., Lewis, J. W., Cannon, J. T., & Liebeskind, J. C. (1984). Intrinsic mechanisms of pain inhibition: Activation by stress. *Science, 226,* 1270–1277. (p. 269)

Terman, L. M. (1954). The discovery and encouragement of exceptional talent. *American Psychologist, 9,* 221–230. (p. 368)

Terrace, H. S. (1985). In the beginning was the "name." *American Psychologist, 40,* 1011–1028. (p. 429)

Terrace, H. S., Petitto, L. A., Sanders, R. J., & Bever, T. G. (1980). On the grammatical capacity of apes. In K. Nelson (Ed.), *Children's language* (Vol. 2). New York: Gardner Press. (p. 429)

Tetlock, P. E. (1984). Cognitive style and political belief systems in the British House of Commons. *Journal of Personality and Social Psychology, 46,* 365–375. (p. 523)

Therman, E. (1986). *Human chromosomes: Structure, behavior, effects.* New York: Springer-Verlag. (pp. 60, 61)

Thigpen, C. H., & Cleckley, H. M. (1957). *The three faces of Eve.* New York: Popular Library. (p. 623)

Thompson, R. F. (1985). *The brain: An introduction to neuroscience.* New York: Freeman. (p. 179)

Thorndike, E. L. (1898). Animal intelligence: An experimental study of associative processes in animals. *The Psychological Review Monograph Supplements, 2,* 4–160. (pp. 130, 131, 138)

Thorndike, E. L. (1913). *Educational psychology.* New York: Teachers College Press. (p. 350)

**Thorne, B.** (1986). Girls and boys together . . . but mostly apart: Gender arrangements in elementary schools. In W. H. Hartup & Z. Rubin (Eds.), *Relationships and development*. Hillsdale, NJ: Erlbaum. (p. 468)

**Thornhill, R., & Thornhill, N. W.** (1987). In C. Crawford, M. Smith, & D. Krebs (Eds.), *Sociobiology and psychology: Ideas, issues, and applications*. Hillsdale, NJ: Erlbaum. (p. 117)

**Thornton, B.** (1984). Defensive attribution of responsibility: Evidence for an arousal-based bias. *Journal of Personality and Social Psychology, 46*, 721–734. (p. 499)

**Thornton, B., Hogate, L., Moirs, K., Pinette, M., & Presby, W.** (1986). Physiological evidence of arousal-based motivational bias in the defensive attribution of responsibility. *Journal of Experimental Social Psychology, 22*, 148–162. (p. 499)

**Thurstone, L. L.** (1938). *Primary mental abilities*. Chicago: University of Chicago Press. (pp. 371, 372)

**Thurstone, L. L.** (1947). *Multiple factor analysis*. Chicago: University of Chicago Press. (p. 371)

**Tienari, P., Sorri, A., Lahti, I., Naarala, M., Wahlberg, K., Moring, J., Pohjola, J., & Wynne, L.** (1987). Genetic and psychosocial factors in schizophrenia: The Finnish adoptive family study. *Schizophrenia Bulletin, 13*, 477–484. (p. 639)

**Tiger, L., & Shepher, J.** (1975). *Women in the kibbutz*. New York: Harcourt Brace Jovanovich. (p. 117)

**Tilker, H. A.** (1970). Socially responsible behavior as a function of observer responsibility and victim feedback. *Journal of Personality and Social Psychology, 14*, 95–100. (p. 537)

**Tinbergen, N.** (1951). *The study of instinct*. New York: Oxford University Press. (pp. 89–90)

**Tinbergen, N.** (1952, December). The curious behavior of the stickleback. *Scientific American*, 22–26. (p. 89)

**Tinbergen, N.** (1960, December). The evolution of behavior in gulls. *Scientific American*, 118–130. (p. 98)

**Tinbergen, N.** (1968). On war and peace in animals and man. *Science, 160*, 1411–1418. (p. 115)

**Tizard, B., & Hodges, J.** (1978). The effect of early institutional rearing on the development of eight-year-old children. *Journal of Child Psychology and Psychiatry, 19*, 99–118. (p. 458)

**Tizard, B., & Rees, J.** (1974). A comparison of the effects of adoption, restoration to the natural mother and continued institutionalization. *Child Development, 45*, 92–99. (p. 458)

**Tolman, E. C.** (1948). Cognitive maps in rats and men. *The Psychological Review, 55*, 189–208. (pp. 150, 151)

**Tolman, E. C.** (1959). Principles of purposive behavior. In S. Koch (Ed.), *Psychology: A study of a science* (Vol. 2). New York: McGraw-Hill. (p. 147)

**Tolman, E. C., & Honzik, C. H.** (1930a). "Insight" in rats. *University of California Publications in Psychology, 4*, 215–232. (p. 150)

**Tolman, E. C., & Honzik, C. H.** (1930b). Introduction and removal of reward, and maze performance in rats. *University of California Publications in Psychology, 4*, 257–275. (pp. 150, 151)

**Tolstoy, L. N.** (1861; reprinted 1967). *Tolstoy on education.*

(A. Pinch & M. Armstrong, Eds. & Trans.). East Brunswick, NJ: Associated University Presses. (p. 465)

**Torrance, E. P.** (1954). Some consequences of power differences on decision-making in permanent and temporary three-man groups. *Research Studies, State College of Washington, 22*, 130–140. (p. 552)

**Torrey, E. F.** (1988). Stalking the schizovirus. *Schizophrenia Bulletin, 14*, 223–229. (p. 638)

**Townshend, B., Cotter, N., Van Compernolle, D., & White, R. L.** (1987). Pitch perception of cochlear implant subjects. *Journal of the Acoustical Society of America, 82*, 106–115. (p. 250)

**Travis, L. E.** (1925). The effect of a small audience upon eye-hand coordination. *Journal of Abnormal and Social Psychology, 20*, 142–146. (p. 540)

**Treisman, A.** (1969). Strategies and models of selective attention. *Psychological Review, 76*, 282–299. (p. 302)

**Treisman, A.** (1986, November). Features and objects in visual processing. *Scientific American*, 114B–125. (p. 290)

**Treisman, A., & Gormican, S.** (1988). Feature analysis in early vision: Evidence from search asymmetries. *Psychological Review, 95*, 15–48. (pp. 290, 291)

**Triplett, N.** (1898). The dynamogenic factors in peacemaking and competition. *American Journal of Psychology, 9*, 507–533. (p. 540)

**Trivers, R. L.** (1971). The evolution of reciprocal altruism. *Quarterly Review of Biology, 46*, 35–57. (pp. 112, 113)

**Trivers, R. L.** (1972). Parental investment and sexual selection. In B. Campbell (Ed.), *Sexual selection and the descent of man*. Chicago: Aldine. (pp. 105, 106, 107)

**Tryon, R. C.** (1942). Individual differences. In F. A. Moss (Ed.), *Comparative psychology* (rev. ed.). New York: Prentice Hall. (p. 65)

**Tucker, J. A., Vucinish, R. E., & Sobell, M. B.** (1981). Alcohol consumption as a self-handicapping strategy. *Journal of Abnormal Psychology, 90*, 220–230. (p. 507)

**Tulving, E.** (1974). Recall and recognition of semantically encoded words. *Journal of Experimental Psychology, 102*, 778–787. (p. 352)

**Tulving, E.** (1985). How many memory systems are there? *American Psychologist, 40*, 385–398. (pp. 327, 360)

**Tversky, A., & Kahneman, D.** (1974). Judgment under uncertainty: Heuristics and biases. *Science, 185*, 1124–1131. (p. 388)

———

**U.S. Bureau of the Census** (1986). Statistical abstract of the United States: 1986 (107th ed.). Washington, DC: U.S. Government Printing Office. (p. 483)

**Uttal, W. R.** (1973). *The psychobiology of sensory coding*. New York: Harper & Row. (p. 241)

———

**Vaillant, G. E.** (1977). *Adaptation to life*. Boston: Little, Brown. (p. 479)

**Vaillant, G. E.** (1983). *The natural history of alcoholism*. Cambridge, MA: Harvard University Press. (p. 627)

**Vaillant, G. E., & Milofsky, E.** (1980). Natural history of male psychological health: IX. Empirical evidence for Erikson's model of the life cycle. *American Journal of Psychiatry, 137,* 1348–1359. (p. 479)

**Valenstein, E. S.** (1973). *Brain control: A critical examination of brain stimulation and psychosurgery.* New York: Wiley. (p. 214)

**Valenstein, E. S. (Ed.)** (1980). *The psychosurgery debate: Scientific, legal, and ethical perspectives.* San Francisco: Freeman. (p. 679)

**Valenstein, E. S.** (1986). *Great and desperate cures: The rise and decline of psychosurgery and other radical treatments for mental illness.* New York: Basic Books. (p. 679)

**Valzelli, L.** (1981). *Psychobiology of aggression and violence.* New York: Raven Press. (p. 235)

**Vance, E. B., & Wagner, N. N.** (1976). Written descriptions of orgasm: A study of sex differences. *Archives of Sexual Behavior, 5,* 87–98. (p. 210)

**Van Dis, H., & Larsson, K.** (1971). Induction of sexual arousal in the castrated male rat by intracranial stimulation. *Physiology and Behavior, 6,* 85–86. (p. 209)

**Vanneman, R. D., & Pettigrew, T. F.** (1972). Race and relative deprivation in the urban United States. *Race, 13,* 461–486. (p. 555)

**Vaughn, B., Gove, F., & Egeland, B.** (1980). The relationship between out-of-home day care and the quality of infant-mother attachment in an economically deprived population. *Child Development, 51,* 1203–1214. (p. 458)

**Vernon, P. A.** (1987). New developments in reaction time research. In P. A. Vernon (Ed.), *Speed of information-processing and intelligence.* Norwood, NJ: Ablex. (pp. 374, 375)

**Vernon, P. A., & Kantor, L.** (1986). Reaction time correlations with intelligence test scores obtained under either timed or untimed conditions. *Intelligence, 9,* 357–374. (p. 374)

**Vernon, P. E.** (1961). *The structure of human abilities* (2nd ed.). London: Methuen. (p. 372)

**Vinokur, A., & Burnstein, E.** (1974). Effects of partially shared persuasive arguments on group-induced shifts: A group problem-solving approach. *Journal of Personality and Social Psychology, 29,* 305–315. (p. 550)

**Volkova, V. D.** (1953). On certain characteristics of the formation of conditioned reflexes to speech stimuli in children. *Fiziologicheskii Zhurnal USSR, 39,* 540–548. (p. 144)

**Vygotsky, L. S.** (1933; reprinted 1978). Play and its role in the mental development of the child. In M. Cole, V. John-Steiner, S. Scribner, & E. Souberman (Eds.), *Mind and society.* Cambridge, MA: Harvard University Press. (p. 464)

**Vygotsky, L. S.** (1934; reprinted 1962). *Thought and language* (E. Haufmann & G. Vaker, Eds. & trans.). Cambridge, MA: MIT Press. (pp. 401, 443, 444, 446)

**Wagstaff, G. F.** (1984). The enhancement of witness memory by hypnosis: A review and methodological critique of the experimental literature. *British Journal of Experimental and Clinical Hypnosis, 2,* 3–12. (p. 356)

**Wahl, O. F.** (1976). Monozygotic twins discordant for schizophrenia: A review. *Psychological Bulletin, 83,* 91–106. (pp. 76, 638)

**Walker, L. J.** (1984). Sex differences in the development of moral reasoning: A critical review. *Child Development, 55,* 677–691. (p. 478)

**Walker, L. J., de Vries, B., & Treverthan, S. D.** (1987). Moral stages and moral orientations in real-life and hypothetical dilemmas. *Child Development, 58,* 842–858. (p. 478)

**Walker, W. I.** (1973). Principles of organization of the ventrobasal complex in mammals. *Brain Behavior and Evolution, 7,* 253–336. (p. 182)

**Wallerstein, R. S.** (1989). The psychotherapy research project of the Menninger Foundation: An overview. *Journal of Consulting and Clinical Psychology, 57,* 195–205. (p. 674)

**Walster, E., Aronson, V., Abrahams, D., & Rottman, L.** (1966). Importance of physical attractiveness in dating behavior. *Journal of Personality and Social Psychology, 4,* 508–516. (p. 512)

**Ward, I. L., & Ward, O. B.** (1985). Sexual behavior differentiation: Effects of prenatal manipulation in rats. In N. T. Adler, D. Pfaff, & R. Goy (Eds.), *Handbook of behavioral neurobiology (Vol. 7: Reproduction).* New York: Plenum. (p. 209)

**Warner, R.** (1985). *Recovery from schizophrenia.* London: Routledge & Kegan Paul. (p. 677)

**Warren, R. M.** (1970). Perceptual restoration of missing speech sounds. *Science, 167,* 392–393. (p. 289)

**Warren, R. M.** (1984). Perceptual restoration of obliterated sounds. *Psychological Bulletin, 96,* 371–383. (pp. 290, 331)

**Warrington, E. K., & Weiskrantz, L.** (1973). An analysis of short-term and long-term memory deficits in man. In J. A. Deutsch (Ed.), *The physiological basis of memory.* New York: Academic Press. (p. 359)

**Waterman, A. S.** (1982). Identity development from adolescence to adulthood: An extension of theory and review of research. *Developmental Psychology, 18,* 341–358. (pp. 474, 475)

**Watson, J. B.** (1913). Psychology as the behaviorist views it. *The Psychological Review, 20,* 158–177. (pp. 13, 122)

**Watson, J. B.** (1924). *Behaviorism.* Chicago: University of Chicago Press. (pp. 122, 128, 145, 401, 617, 667)

**Watson, J. B.** (1936). John Broadus Watson. In C. Murchison (Ed.), *A history of psychology in autobiography* (Vol. 3). New York: Russell & Russell. (p. 14)

**Watson, J. B., & Rayner, R.** (1920). Conditioned emotional reactions. *Journal of Experimental Psychology, 3,* 1–14. (p. 128)

**Watson, J. S.** (1972). Smiling, cooing, and "the game." *Merrill-Palmer Quarterly, 18,* 323–339. (p. 417)

**Watson, R. I.** (1973). Investigation into deindividuation using a cross-cultural survey technique. *Journal of Personality and Social Psychology, 25,* 342–345. (p. 545)

**Watt, R. J.** (1988). *Visual processing: Computational, psychophysical, and cognitive research.* Hillsdale, NJ: Erlbaum. (p. 284)

**Waugh, N. C., & Norman, D. A.** (1965). Primary memory. *Psychological Review, 72,* 89–104. (pp. 323, 334)

**Waxler, N. E.** (1984). Culture and mental illness: A social labeling perspective. In J. E. Mezzich & C. E. Berganza (Eds.), *Culture and psychopathology.* New York: Columbia University Press. (p. 608)

**Webb, W. B.** (1982). Some theories about sleep and their clinical implications. *Psychiatric Annals, 11,* 415–422. (p. 220)

**Wechsler, D.** (1981). *Manual for the Wechsler Adult Intelligence Scale—Revised.* New York: Psychological Corporation. (p. 369)

**Wehr, R. A., Jacobsen, F. M., Sack, D. A., Arendt, J., Tamarkin, L., & Rosenthal, N. E.** (1986). Phototherapy of seasonal affective disorder. *Archives of General Psychiatry, 43,* 870–875. (p. 633)

**Weinberger, D. A., Schwartz, G. E., & Davidson, R. J.** (1979). Low-anxious, high-anxious, and repressive coping styles: Psychometric patterns and behavioral and physiological responses to stress. *Journal of Abnormal Psychology, 88,* 369–380. (p. 572)

**Weiner, R. D., & Coffey, C. E.** (1988). Indications for use of electroconvulsive therapy. In A. J. Frances & R. E. Hales (Eds.), *Review of psychiatry, Vol. 7.* Washington, DC: American Psychiatric Press. (pp. 678, 679)

**Weingartner, H., Miller, H., & Murphy, D. L.** (1977). Mood-state-dependent retrieval of verbal associations. *Journal of Abnormal Psychology, 86,* 276–284. (p. 354)

**Weiskrantz, L.** (1989). Remembering dissociations. In H. L. Roediger & F. I. Craik (Eds.), *Varieties of memory and consciousness: Essays in honour of Endel Tulving.* Hillsdale, NJ: Erlbaum. (pp. 358, 359)

**Weiss, J. M., Glazer, H. I., & Pohoresky, L. A.** (1976). Coping behavior and neurochemical change in rats: An alternative explanation for the "learned helplessness" experiments. In G. Serban & A. King (Eds.), *Animal models in human psychobiology.* New York: Plenum. (p. 630)

**Wender, P. H., Kety, S. S., Rosenthal, D., Schulsinger, F., Ortmann, J., & Lunde, I.** (1986). Psychiatric disorders in the biological and adoptive families of adopted individuals with affective disorders. *Archives of General Psychiatry,* 923–929. (p. 629)

**Werker, J. F., & Tees, R. C.** (1984). Cross-language speech perception: Evidence for perceptual reorganization during the first year of life. *Infant Behavior and Development, 7,* 49–64. (p. 421)

**Werner, H.** (1948). *Comparative psychology of mental development* (rev. ed.). Chicago: Follet. (p. 385)

**Wernicke, C.** (1874; reprinted 1977). The aphasia symptom complex: A psychological study on an anatomical basis. In G. H. Eggard (Ed. & trans.), *Wernicke's works on aphasia.* The Hague: Mouton. (p. 399)

**Wertheimer, M.** (1912; reprinted 1965). Experimentelle Studien über das Sehen von Bewegung (M. D. Boring, Trans.). In R. J. Herrnstein & E. G. Boring (Eds.), *A source book in the history of psychology.* Cambridge, MA: Harvard University Press. (p. 11)

**Wertheimer, M.** (1923; reprinted 1938). Principles of perceptual organization. In W. D. Ellis (Ed. & trans.), *A source-book of Gestalt psychology.* New York: Harcourt Brace. (pp. 285, 286)

**West, S. G.** (1975). Increasing the attractiveness of college cafeteria food: A reactance theory perspective. *Journal of Applied Psychology, 60,* 656–658. (p. 535)

**Whorf, B.** (1956). *Language, thought, and reality.* New York: Wiley. (p. 402)

**Wickens, D. D.** (1972). Characteristics of word encoding. In A. W. Melton & E. Martin (Eds.), *Coding processes in human memory.* Washington, DC: Winston & Sons. (p. 351)

**Wicker, A. W.** (1969). Attitudes versus actions: The relationship of verbal and overt behavioral responses to attitude objects. *Journal of Social Issues, 25,* 41–78. (p. 520)

**Wicker, A. W.** (1971). An examination of the "other variable" explanation of attitude-behavior inconsistency. *Journal of Personality and Social Psychology, 19,* 18–30. (p. 520)

**Wicklund, R. A.** (1974). *Freedom and reactance.* Potomac, MD: Erlbaum. (p. 534)

**Wicklund, R. A., & Frey, D.** (1980). Self-awareness theory: When the self makes a difference. In D. M. Wegner & R. R. Vallacher (Eds.), *The self in social psychology.* New York: Oxford University Press. (p. 521)

**Wicklund, R. A., Slattum, V., & Solomon, E.** (1970). Effects of implied pressure toward commitment on ratings of choice alternatives. *Journal of Experimental Social Psychology, 6,* 449–457. (p. 534)

**Wielgus, M. S., & Harvey, P. D.** (1988). Dichotic listening and recall in schizophrenia. *Schizophrenia Bulletin, 14,* 689–699. (p. 637)

**Wilkins, L., & Richter, C. P.** (1940). A great craving for salt by a child with cortico-adrenal insufficiency. *Journal of the American Medical Association, 114,* 866–868. (p. 199)

**Willerman, L.** (1979). *The psychology of individual and group differences.* San Francisco: Freeman. (p. 71)

**Williams, J. B. W., & Spitzer, R. L.** (1983). The issue of sex bias in DSM-III. *American Psychologist, 38,* 793–798. (p. 614)

**Williams, K., Harkins, S., & Latané, B.** (1981). Identifiability as a deterrent to social loafing: Two cheering experiments. *Journal of Personality and Social Psychology, 40,* 303–311. (p. 542)

**Willner, P.** (1985). *Depression: A psychobiological synthesis.* New York: Wiley. (p. 629)

**Wilson, E. O.** (1975). *Sociobiology.* Cambridge, MA: Belknap Press of Harvard University Press. (p. 113)

**Wimer, R. E., & Wimer, C. C.** (1985). Animal behavior genetics: A search for the biological foundations of behavior. *Annual Review of Psychology, 36,* 171–218. (p. 66)

**Wise, R. A., & Bozarth, M. A.** (1984). Brain reward circuitry: Four circuit elements "wired" in apparent series. *Brain Research Bulletin, 12,* 203–208. (p. 215)

**Wise, R. A., Spindler, J., & Legault, L.** (1978). Major attenuation of food reward with performance-sparing doses of pimozide in the rat. *Canadian Journal of Psychology, 32,* 77–85. (p. 215)

**Wishart, J. G., & Bower, T. G. R.** (1984). Spatial relations and the object concept: A normative study. In L. P. Lipsitt & C. Rovee-Collier (Eds.), *Advances in infancy research* (Vol. 3). Norwood, NJ: Ablex. (p. 419)

**Wissler, C.** (1901). The correlation of mental and physical tests. *Psychological Review, 3* (Whole no. 6). (p. 367)

**Witkin, H. A., Mednick, S. A., Schulsinger, F., Bakkestrom, E., Christiansen, K. O., Goodenough, D. R., Hirschhorn, K., Lundsteen, C., Owen, D. R., Philip, J., & others** (1976). Criminality in XYY and XXY men. *Science, 193,* 547–555. (p. 59)

**Witty, P. A., & Jenkins, M. D.** (1935). Intra-race testing and Negro intelligence. *The Journal of Psychology, 1,* 179–192. (p. 72)

**Wolfe, J. B.** (1936). Effectiveness of token-rewards for chimpanzees. *Comparative Psychology Monographs,* 12 (Whole no. 60). (p. 139)

**Wolpe, J.** (1958). *Psychotherapy by reciprocal inhibition.* Stanford: Stanford University Press. (p. 668)

**Woods, P. J. (Ed.)** (1987). *Is psychology the major for you?* Washington, DC: American Psychological Association. (p. 22)

**Wright, H. F.** (1937). *The influence of barriers upon strength of motivation.* Durham, NC: Duke University Press. (p. 535)

**Yasukawa, K.** (1981). Song repertoires in the red-winged blackbird *(Agelaius phoeniceus)*: A test of the Beau Geste hypothesis. *Animal Behaviour, 29,* 114–125. (p. 86)

**Yerkes, R. M., & Dodson, J. D.** (1908). The relation of strength of stimulus to rapidity of habit-formation. *Journal of Comparative and Neurological Psychology, 18,* 459–482. (p. 228)

**Yerkes, R. M., & Morgulis, S.** (1909). The method of Pavlov in animal psychology. *Psychological Bulletin, 6,* 257–273. (p. 124)

**Yuodelis, C., & Hendrickson, A.** (1986). A qualitative and quantitative analysis of the human fovea during development. *Vision Research, 26,* 847–856. (p. 415)

**Zajonc, R. B.** (1965). Social facilitation. *Science, 149,* 269–274. (p. 541)

**Zajonc, R. B.** (1980). Compresence. In P. B. Paulus (Ed.), *Psychology of group influence.* Hillsdale, NJ: Erlbaum. (p. 541)

**Zajonc, R. B., Murphy, S. T., & Inglehart, M.** (1989). Feeling and facial efference: Implications of the vascular theory of emotion. *Psychological Review, 96,* 395–416. (p. 234)

**Zelig, M., & Beidelman, W. B.** (1981). The investigative use of hypnosis: A word of caution. *International Journal of Clinical and Experimental Hypnosis, 29,* 401–412. (p. 356)

**Zelnick, M., & Kantner, J. F.** (1980). Sexual activity, contraceptive use and pregnancy among metropolitan area teenagers: 1970-1979. *Family Planning Perspectives, 12,* 230–237. (p. 472)

**Zelnick, M., Kantner, J. F., & Ford, K.** (1981). *Sex and pregnancy in adolescence.* Beverly Hills, CA: Sage. (p. 472)

**Zimbardo, P. G.** (1970). The human choice: Individuation, reason, and order versus deindividuation, impulse, and chaos. In W. J. Arnold & D. Levine (Eds.), *Nebraska symposium on motivation, 1969.* Lincoln, NE: University of Nebraska Press. (p. 545)

**Zucker, R. A., & Gomberg, E. S. L.** (1986). Etiology of alcoholism reconsidered: The case for a biopsychosocial process. *American Psychologist, 41,* 783–793. (p. 627)

**Zurif, E. B.** (1980). Language mechanisms: A neuropsychological perspective. *American Scientist, 68,* 305–311. (p. 400)

**Zwislocki, J. J.** (1981). Sound analysis in the ear: A history of discoveries. *American Scientist, 69,* 184–192. (p. 248)

# ILLUSTRATION CREDITS

**PART OPENERS**
1 Mary Joan Waid, *Dream Series V* (detail), 1984. Photo courtesy of G. W. Einstein Company, Inc., New York.
2 Rosamond Purcell, *Opata Masks*, 1989.
3 Paul Klee, *Senecio*, 1922. © 1991 A.R.S. NY/Cosmopress. Photograph by Hans Hinz.
4 Pablo Picasso, *Reading a Letter* (detail), 1921. Musee Picasso, Paris. © 1991 A.R.S. NY/S.P.A.D.E.M.
5 Paul Gauguin, *Tahitian Woman with Children*, 1901. Helen Birch Bartlett Memorial Collection, Art Institute of Chicago. © 1990 Art Institute of Chicago. All rights reserved.
6 Michael Leonard, *Afternoon of the Kites*, 1977.
7 Paul Giovanopolos, *Man 1/Man 2* (detail), 1987. Photo courtesy of Louis K. Meisel Gallery, New York.

**FRONT MATTER**
**p. ii** Mary Cassatt, *Two Women Reading*, 1901. Private collection. Photo courtesy of Valley House Gallery, Dallas, TX. **p. v** © Linda Haas Photography

**CHAPTER 1**
**Opener** © Mike Mazzaschi/Stock, Boston, Inc. **Fig. 1.1** The Bettmann Archive **Fig. 1.2** © Historical Picture Service **Fig. 1.3** Descartes, R. (1972). *Treatise of man.* Cambridge, MA: Harvard University Press **p. 7** © Paul Fusco/Magnum Photos **Fig. 1.4** Archives of the History of American Psychology, University of Akron, OH **Fig. 1.5** Archives of the History of American Psychology, University of Akron, OH **Fig. 1.6** Courtesy of the Harvard University Archive **p. 11** Giuseppe Arcimboldo, *The Garden.* © Scala/Art Resource **Fig. 1.7** © Edmund Engelman **Fig. 1.8** © Louis Fernandez/Black Star **Fig. 1.9** © Black Star **p. 15** © Nina Leen/Life Picture Service **p. 16** © Steve Krongard/The Image Bank **p. 17** Adapted from Rose, S. (1973). *The conscious brain.* New York: Alfred A. Knopf. Copyright © by Stephen Rose. Reprinted by permission of Alfred A. Knopf, Inc. **p. 20** © Peter Menzel **p. 22** Table 1.1 Copyright © 1983 by the American Psychological Association. Reprinted by permission.

**CHAPTER 2**
**Opener** © Rick Friedman/Black Star **Fig. 2.1** Pfungst, O. (1965). *Clever Hans: The horse of Mr. von Osten.* New York: Holt, Rinehart & Winston **Fig. 2.2** Hendricks, B., et al. (1990). The dimensions of psychological research. *Teaching of Psychology, 17,* 76–82. **Fig. 2.3** Di Mascio, A., et al. (1979). Differential symptom reduction by drugs and psychotherapy in acute depression. *Archives of General Psychiatry, 36,* 1453. Copyright © 1979, American Medical Association. **p. 30** © Rick Kopstein/Monkmeyer Press Photos **p. 31** © Ray Stott/The Image Works **p. 32** © Harold Takooshian **p. 37** © Peter Menzel **p. 39 (left)** © Jose Azel/Woodfin Camp & Associates; **(right)** © George Zimbel/Monkmeyer Press Photos **p. 41** © Joel Gordon

**CHAPTER 3**
**Opener** © Barbara J. Feigles/Stock, Boston, Inc. **p. 49** © Van Bucher/Photo Researchers **Fig. 3.2** Pueschel, S. M., & Goldstein, A. (1983). Genetic counseling. In J. L. Matson & J. A. Mulick (Eds.), *Handbook of mental retardation.* London: Pergamon. Copyright © 1983, Pergamon Press PLC. Reprinted with permission. **Fig. 3.4** Plomin, R., et al. (1990). *Behavior genetics: A primer* (2nd ed.). New York: Freeman.

**Fig. 3.7** Scott, J. P., & Fuller, J. L. (1965). *Genetics and social behavior of the dog.* Chicago: University of Chicago Press. **Fig. 3.10** Hay, D. (1985). *Essentials of behavior genetics.* Boston: Blackwell Scientific Publications. **p. 58** © Steve Uzzell **p. 59** © Linda Haas Photography **Fig. 3.11** © Mario Ruiz/Picture Group, Inc. **p. 64** © Ted Levin/Earth Scenes/Animals, Animals **Fig. 3.16** Cooper, R. M., & Zubek, J. P. (1958). Effects of enriched and restricted early environments on the learning ability of bright and dull rats. *Canadian Journal of Psychology, 12,* 159–164. **p. 68** AP Wire Photo/Wide World Photo **Fig. 3.17** Bouchard, T. J., & McGue, M. (1981). Familial studies of intelligence: A review. *Science, 212,* 1055–1059. Copyright © 1981 by the AAAS. **p. 73** © Jeff Albertson/Stock, Boston, Inc. **Fig. 3.18** Kety, S. S., et al. (1976). Mental illness in the biological and adoptive families of adopted individuals who have become schizophrenic. *Behavior Genetics, 6,* 219–225. **p. 75** Courtesy the Genain family

**CHAPTER 4**
**Opener** © Fritz Prenzel/Animals, Animals **Fig. 4.1 (left)** © W. F. Tweedie/Bruce Coleman; **(right)** © W. F. Tweedie/Photo Researchers **p. 85** © C. R. Carpenter **p. 86** © S. Nielson/Bruce Coleman **p. 88** © Raymond Attuil/Agence Vandystadt/Photo Researchers **Figs. 4.2 and 4.3** Tinbergen, N. (1951). *The study of instinct.* New York: Oxford University Press. Copyright © 1951 by N. Tinbergen. **Fig. 4.4** Eibl-Eibesfeldt, I. (1961, December). The fighting behavior of animals. *Scientific American, 205,* 7. Copyright © 1961 by Scientific American, Inc. All rights reserved. **Fig. 4.5** Emlen, S. T. (1975, August). The stellar orientation of a migrating bird. *Scientific American, 233,* 111. Copyright © 1975 by Scientific American, Inc. All rights reserved. **Fig. 4.6 (left)** © Joe McDonald/Animals, Animals; **(center)** © M. Tuttle/Photo Researchers; **(right)** © James Carmich/Bruce Coleman **Fig. 4.7** Lorenz, K. (1974). Analogy as a source of knowledge. *Science, 185,* 229–234. Copyright © 1973, Les Prix Nobel. **Fig. 4.8 (a)** © M. A. Chappell/Animals, Animals; **(b)** © D. M. Shale/Oxford Scientific Films/Animals, Animals **Fig. 4.9** Eibl-Eibesfeldt, I. (1975). *Ethology.* New York: Holt, Rinehart & Winston. **Fig. 4.10** © Dr. Eckart Pott/Bruce Coleman **Fig. 4.11** General Research Division, The New York Public Library, Astor, Lenox, and Tilden Foundations **Fig. 4.12** Ekman, P., & Friesen, W. (1975). *Unmasking the face.* Englewood Cliffs, NJ: Prentice Hall. **Fig. 4.13** Ekman, P., & Friesen, W. (1975). *Unmasking the face.* Englewood Cliffs, NJ: Prentice Hall. **Fig. 4.14** Lorenz, K. (1966). *On aggression.* New York: Harcourt Brace & World. Copyright © 1963 by Dr. G. Borotha-Schoeller Verlag, Wein. English translation copyright © 1966 by Konrad Lorenz. Copyright © 1983 by Deutscher Tashcenbuch Verlag GmbH & Co. KG, Munchen. Reprinted by permission of Harcourt Brace Jovanovich, Inc. **Fig. 4.15** Eibl-Eibesfeldt, I. (1989). *Human ethology.* Hawthorne, NY: Walter de Gruyter, Inc. **Fig. 4.16** Eibl-Eibesfeldt, I. (1975). *Ethology.* New York: Holt, Rinehart & Winston. **p. 104** Heltne, P. G., & Marquardt, L. (1989). *Understanding chimpanzees.* Cambridge, MA: Harvard University Press. **Fig. 4.18** © Rudie Kiuter/Animals, Animals/Oxford Scientific Films **p. 109** © Ken Regan/Camera Five, Inc. **Fig. 4.19** © Zig Leszcynski/Animals, Animals **Fig. 4.20** © L. and D. Klein/Photo Researchers **Fig. 4.21** © Bruce Coleman

**CHAPTER 5**
**Opener** © Comstock **p. 123** Archives of the History of American Psychology, University of Akron, OH **Fig. 5.1** Yerkes, R. M., & Morgulis, S. (1909). The method of Pavlov in animal psychology. *Psychological Bulletin, 6,* 257–273. **p. 125** © Benn Mitchell/The Image Bank **Fig. 5.4** Pavlov, I. P. (1927/1960). *Conditioned reflexes.* New

*Learning and Verbal Behavior*, 5, 358. **Fig. 10.7** Craik, F. I., & Watkins, M. J. (1973). The role of rehearsal in short-term memory. *Journal of Verbal Learning and Verbal Behavior*, 12, 602. **Fig. 10.8** Craik, F. I., & Tulving, E. (1975). Depth of processing and the retention of words in long-term memory. *Journal of Experimental Psychology: General*, 104, 274. Copyright © 1975 by the American Psychological Association. Adapted by permission. **p. 337 (left)** © Tony O'Brien/Picture Group, Inc.; **(right)** © Joel Gordon **p. 338 (left)** Bloom, F. E., & Lazerson, A. (1988). *Brain, mind, and behavior* (2nd ed.). New York: Freeman; **(right)** The Bettmann Archive **Fig. 10.9** Atkinson, R. C. (1975). Mnemotechnics in second language learning. *American Psychologist*, 30, 822. Copyright © 1975 by the American Psychological Association. Adapted by permission. **p. 341** © Culver Pictures, Inc. **Fig. 10.10** Kosslyn, S. M. (1980). *Image and mind.* Cambridge, MA: Harvard University Press. **Fig. 10.11** Cooper, L. A., & Shepard, R. N. (1973). Chronometric studies of the rotation of mental images. In W. G. Chase (Ed.), *Handbook of perception, Vol. III: Space and object perception.* New York: Academic Press. **Fig. 10.12** Luria, A. R. (1968). *The mind of a mnemonist.* London: Penguin. **Figs. 10.13 and 10.14** Collins, A. M., & Quillian, M. R. (1969). Retrieval times from semantic memory. *Journal of Verbal Learning and Verbal Behavior*, 8, 241 and 244, respectively. **Fig. 10.15** Halpern, A. R. (1986). Memory for tune titles after organized or unorganized presentation. *American Journal of Psychology*, 99, 60. **Fig. 10.16 (a)** Ebbinghaus, H. (1885/1913). *Memory: A contribution to experimental psychology* (H. A. Ruger & C. E. Bussenius, Trans.). New York: Teachers College Press; **(b)** Bahrick, H. P., et al. (1975). Fifty years of memory for names and faces. *Journal of Experimental Psychology*, 104, 54–75. Copyright © 1975 by the American Psychological Association. Adapted by permission. **Fig. 10.17** Keppel, G., et al. (1968). Studies of learning to learn: VIII. The influence of massive amounts of training upon learning and retention of paired-associate lists. *Journal of Verbal Learning and Verbal Behavior*, 7, 790–796. **p. 351** © Lawrence Migdale/Stock, Boston, Inc. **p. 352** © UPI/The Bettmann Archive **Fig. 10.18** Mäntylä, T. (1986). Optimizing cue effectiveness: Recall of 500 and 600 incidentally learned words. *Journal of Experimental Psychology: Learning, Memory, and Cognition*, 12, 69. Copyright © 1986 by the American Psychological Association. Reprinted by permission. **p. 356** News and Publications Service, Stanford University **p. 358** © Eve-Lucie Bourque

## CHAPTER 11

**Opener** © Bob Daemmrich/The Image Works **p. 366** The Bettmann Archive **p. 367** The Bettmann Archive **p. 368** © R. L. Thorndike, E. P. Hagen, & J. M. Sattler, Riverside Publishing Co., Chicago **p. 373 (left)** © Tom Sobolik/Black Star; **(right)** © N.A.S.A./Comstock **p. 374** © Photo Edit **Fig. 11.6** Sternberg, R. J., & Gardner, M. K. (1983). Unities in inductive reasoning. *Journal of Experimental Psychology: General*, 112, 80–116. Copyright © 1983 by the American Psychological Association. Adapted by permission. **p. 377** © Julie Houck/Stock, Boston, Inc. **Figs. 11.8 and 11.9** Gazzaniga, M. S. (1967, August). The split brain in man. *Scientific American*, 24–29. Copyright © 1967 by Scientific American, Inc. All rights reserved. **Fig. 11.10** Kolb, B., et al. (1990). *Fundamentals of human neuropsychology.* New York: Freeman (subsidiary of Scientific American). © 1990 **Fig. 11.11** Sackheim, H. A., & Gur, R. C. (1978). Lateral asymmetry in intensity of emotional expression. Reprinted with permission from *Neuropsychologia*, 16. © 1978, Pergamon Journals, Ltd. **Fig. 11.12** Kosslyn, S. M. (1987). Seeing and imaging in the cerebral hemisphere: A computational approach. *Psychological Review*, 94, 148–173. Copyright © 1987 by the American Psychological Association. Reprinted by permission. **p. 382** Selfe, L. (1979). *Nadia.* New York: Academic Press. Reprinted by permission. **p. 383 (left & right)** © Rick Friedman/Black Star **p. 384** © Rick Smolan/Stock, Boston, Inc. **p. 386** © 1990 Sidney Harris **p. 389** © Abe Rezny/The Image Works **p. 392** © Richard Hutchings/Info Edit **p. 395** © Cotton Coulson/Woodfin Camp & Associates **p. 397** © John F. Cook/Courtesy Noam Chomsky **Fig. 11.21** Smyth, M. M., et al. (1987). *Cognition in action.* Hillsdale, NJ: Erlbaum. **p. 402** © Pro Pix **p. 404** © New York Times News Service/NYT Pictures **p. 405 (left)** Scarry, R. (1963). *Best word book ever.* © 1963 by Western Publishing Company, Inc.; **(right)** © 1980 Richard Scarry. Used by permission.

## CHAPTER 12

**Opener** © G. G. Zimbel/Monkmeyer Press Photos **p. 412 (left)** © Nancy Sheehan/The Picture Cube; **(right)** © Info Edit **p. 414** © Julie O'Neil/The Picture Cube **Fig. 12.2** Cohen, L. B., & Younger, B. A. (1984). Infant perception of angular relations. *Infant Behavior and Development*, 7, 37–47. **Fig. 12.3** © Enrico Ferorelli/DOT **p. 418** © Anderson/Monkmeyer Press Photos **Fig. 12.4** Wishart, J. G., & Bower, T. G. R. (1984). Spatial relations and the object concept: A normative study. In L. P. Lipsitt & C. Rovee-Collier (Eds.), *Advances in Infancy Research*, Vol. 3. Norwood, NJ: Ablex. **Fig. 12.5** Baillargeon, R. (1987). Object permanence in 3½- and 4½-month-old infants. *Developmental Psychology*, 23, 655–664. Copyright © 1987 by the American Psychological Association. Adapted by permission. **p. 421** © Joel Gordon **p. 422** ©

Laura Dwight/Peter Arnold, Inc. **Fig. 12.6** Berko, J. (1958). The child's learning of English morphology. *Word*, 14, 150–177. **p. 427** © Ken Gaghan/Jeroboam, Inc. **Fig. 12.7** © Paul Fusco/Magnum Photos **Fig. 12.10** Courtesy Dr. Sue Savage-Rumbaugh, Yerkes Language Resource Center **p. 432** © Hazel Hankin **p. 434** From *Life in Hell* © 1984 by Matt Groening. All rights reserved. Reprinted by permission of Pantheon Books, a division of Random House, New York. **p. 435** © Bruce Plotkin/Image Works **p. 436 (top)** © George Goodwin/The Picture Cube; **(bottom)** © Susan Lapides/Design Conceptions **p. 437** © Amy Zuckerman/Impact Visuals **p. 441** © Paul Conklin/Monkmeyer Press Photos **Fig. 12.11** Chi, M. T. H. (1978). Knowledge structures and memory development. In R. S. Siegler (Ed.), *Children's thinking: What develops.* Hillsdale, NJ: Erlbaum. **Fig. 12.12** Siegler, R. S. (1983). How knowledge influences learning. *American Scientist*, 71, 631–638. Reprinted by permission of American Scientist, Journal of Sigma Pi, The Scientific Research Society. **p. 445 (left)** © Monkmeyer Press Photos; **(right)** © Beryl Goldberg

## CHAPTER 13

**Opener** © Henley and Savage/The Stock Market **p. 451** Harvard University News Office, Cambridge, MA **Fig. 13.1** Bronfenbrenner, U. (1979). Nature and nurture: A reinterpretation of the evidence. In A. Montague (Ed.), *Race and IQ.* New York: Oxford University Press. **p. 453** © Jim Carter/Photo Researchers **Fig. 13.2 (left)** Courtesy University of Wisconsin Primate Lab, Madison, WI; **(right)** © Sponholz/Monkmeyer Press Photos **Fig. 13.3** Harlow, H. (1959). Affectional responses in the infant monkey. *Science*, 130, 421–432. Copyright © 1959 by the AAAS. **p. 457 (top)** © Karen Webster, Psychology Dept., University of Virginia **Fig. 13.4** Courtesy Mary Ainsworth **Fig. 13.5** © Julie O'Neil/The Picture Cube **p. 459** © Joseph Schuyler/Stock, Boston, Inc. **p. 461** © Ed Koren/The New Yorker Magazine, 1988 **p. 463** © Alan Carey/The Image Works **p. 465** Courtesy Dr. Peter Gray/The Sudbury Valley School **p. 467** Courtesy Chuck Painter, News and Publications Service, Stanford University **p. 468** © Michael Siluk/The Image Works **Fig. 13.7** Jacklin, C. N., & Maccoby, E. E. (1978). Social behavior at 33 months in same-sex and mixed-sex dyads. *Child Development*, 49, 557–569. Copyright © The Society for Research in Child Development, Inc. **Fig. 13.8** Steinberg, L., & Silverberg, S. B. (1986). The vicissitudes of autonomy in early adolescence. *Child Development*, 57, 841–851. Copyright © The Society for Research in Child Development, Inc. **p. 473** © Ellen B. Neipris/Impact Visuals **p. 475** The FAR SIDE cartoon by Gary Larson is reprinted by permission of Chronicle Features, San Francisco, CA **p. 476** © Willie Hill Jr./The Image Works **Fig. 13.10** Colby, A., et al. (1983). A longitudinal study of moral judgment. *Monographs of the Society for Research in Child Development*, 148, 1–2. Copyright © The Society for Research in Child Development, Inc. **p. 479** © Marvin Lyons/The Image Bank **p. 480 (left)** © Frank Siteman/Stock, Boston, Inc.; **(right)** © Arthur Grace/Stock, Boston, Inc. **p. 481** © Bob Daemmrich/Stock, Boston, Inc. **p. 482** © Jodi Buren Photo **p. 483** © Anthony Jalandoni/Monkmeyer Press Photos

## CHAPTER 14

**Opener** © Cary Wolinsky/Stock, Boston, Inc. **p. 492** © Burton McNeely/The Image Bank **p. 494** © Burton McNeely/The Image Bank **Fig. 14.1** © Sandra Johnson/SAGA **Fig. 14.2** Berry, D. S., & McArthur, L. Z. (1988). What's in a face? Facial maturity and the attribution of legal responsibility. *Personality and Social Psychology Bulletin*, 14, 23–33. **p. 497** © Claus Meyer/Black Star **p. 498** © Bob Daemmrich/The Image Works **Fig. 14.3** Miller, J. G. (1984). Culture and the development of everyday social explanation. *Journal of Personality and Social Psychology*, 46, 961–978. Copyright © 1984 by the American Psychological Association. Reprinted by permission. **p. 502** © Robert Brenner/Photo Edit **Fig. 14.4** Miller, R. L., et al. (1975). Attribution versus persuasion as a means for modifying behavior. *Journal of Personality and Social Psychology*, 31, 430–441. Copyright © 1975 by the American Psychological Association. Adapted by permission. **p. 504** © Paula Lerner/The Picture Cube **p. 505** © Reuters/Bettmann News Photos **Fig. 14.6** McGuire, W. J., & McGuire, C. V. (1988). Content and process in the experience of self. In L. Berkowitz (Ed.), *Advances in experimental social psychology* (Vol. 21). New York: Academic Press. **p. 507** © Dan Ford Connolly/The Picture Group **p. 508** © Margot Granitsas/The Image Works **Table 14.1** Copyright © 1974 by the American Psychological Association. Reprinted by permission. **p. 511** © Joel Gordon **Fig. 14.7** Sternberg, R. J. (1986). A triangular theory of love. *Psychological Review*, 93, 119–135. Copyright © 1986 by the American Psychological Association. Adapted by permission. **Fig. 14.9** Petty, R. E., et al. (1981). Personal involvement as a determinant of argument-based persuasion. *Journal of Personality and Social Psychology*, 41, 847–855. Copyright © 1981 by the American Psychological Association. Reprinted by permission. **p. 520** © Comstock **Fig. 14.10** Ajzen, I. (1987). Attitudes, traits, and actions: Dispositional prediction of behavior in personality and social psychology. In L. Berkowitz (Ed.), *Advances in experimental social psychology* (Vol. 20). New York: Academic Press.

# Name Index

Abbot, W., 208
Abelson, R., 345, 445, 614
Abrahams, D., 512
Abramov, I., 265
Abramson, L., 630, 631
Adams, D., 211
Adams, N., 588, 671
Adamson, R., 391
Adelson, J., 470, 481
Adkins-Regan, E., 209
Adler, A., 576, 577, 582, 585, 601
Adler, K., 658
Agras, S., 142, 617
Aiken, L., 368
Ainsworth, M., 457, 458
Ajzen, I., 521–522
Akerstedt, T., 223
Akiyama, Y., 224
Albee, G., 608
Albert, M., 293
Alexander, R., 114
Allen, J., 222, 614
Allison, T., 220
Alloy, L., 630
Allport, D., 298
Allport, G., 491, 519, 541
Alpert, M., 637
Alphs, L., 676
Ambelas, A., 633
Ames, M., 210
Amkraut, A., 228
Anderson, J., 342
Anderson, M., 57
Anderson, S., 502
Andreasen, N., 633, 636
Angell, J., 25
Anglin, J., 423
Antonis, B., 298
Appenzeller, T., 360
Archer, J., 467
Arcimboldo, G., 11
Ardrey, R., 114, 115
Arendt, J., 633
Argyle, M., 510
Arieti, S., 635
Aristotle, 125, 165, 345–346, 491
Aronson, E., 555
Aronson, V., 512
Arregui, A., 639
Asanuma, H., 183
Asarnow, J., 77, 639
Asch, S., 492, 495, 545–548
Aschoff, T., 221

Ash, M., 12
Ashton, H., 629, 676, 677
Aslin, R., 415
Atkinson, R., 323, 333, 334, 339, 357
Atwater, J., 467
Auble, P., 335
Axelrod, R., 113
Ayllon, T., 670
Azrin, N., 670

Baddeley, A., 334, 352–353
Bahr, S., 479
Bahrick, B., 350
Bahrick, H., 350
Baillargeon, R., 418, 420
Bakkestrom, E., 59
Banaji, M., 361
Bancroft, J., 212
Bandura, A., 152, 270, 451, 452, 585, 588–589, 671
Barash, D., 86, 108
Barbano, H., 484
Barglow, P., 458
Barker, S., 675
Barlow, D., 618
Barnett, R., 483, 614, 622
Baron, R., 541
Barrett, A., 381
Barrett, K., 416
Barrington, B., 28
Barry, H., 456
Barsky, A., 622
Bartell, P., 220
Barth, J., 652
Bartlett, F., 345, 354, 362
Bartol, C., 594
Baruch, G., 483, 614
Basbaum, A., 268
Bassett, R., 532
Bassuk, E., 644
Batchelor, I., 621
Bates, J., 457
Bauer, C., 454
Baumann, D., 587
Baumeister, R., 506, 519, 541–542
Baumrind, D., 30, 461–462, 538
Baylor, D., 253, 254
Beach, D., 442
Beach, F., 473
Beagley, G., 216
Beaman, A., 521
Beauvais, F., 627
Beck, A., 616, 628, 630, 662, 664–665, 671

Beck, P., 485
Becklen, R., 297, 298–299
Bee, H., 481, 482
Beeghly, M., 60
Beidelman, W., 356
Beitman, B., 675
Békésy, G. von, 248–250
Bell, A., 473
Bell, C., 6
Bell, R., 462
Bell, S., 458
Belsky, J., 457, 458
Bem, S., 502
Ben-Porath, Y., 650
Benassi, V., 27
Benet, M., 633
Bengston, V., 484
Benson, H., 229
Berghe, P., 117
Berglas, S., 507
Berkeley, G., 314
Berko, J., 424
Bernstein, D., 658
Bernstein, I., 153
Bernstein, W., 501
Bernthal, P., 557
Berry, D., 495–496
Berry, J., 384, 385
Berscheid, E., 502
Bertelsen, A., 629, 633
Bertenthal, B., 416
Bertrand, L., 623
Beutler, L., 674
Bever, T., 424, 429
Beyer, J., 588
Bickerton, D., 425–426
Bickman, L., 543, 544
Biederman, I., 292–293, 294–295
Bieher, S., 598
Biener, L., 483, 614
Billings, A., 629, 630
Binet, A., 367
Bird, E., 639
Bishop, G., 550
Bishop, J., 83
Bitterman, M., 149
Bjork, R., 327
Blake, R., 554–555
Blaney, N., 555
Blaney, P., 248, 354
Blank, A., 531
Blasi, A., 477
Blazer, D., 616

Blehar, M., 457
Bleuler, E., 634, 635, 636
Blinn, N., 211
Bliss, E., 622, 623, 624
Block, J., 582
Block, J. H., 582
Blommel, J., 541
Bloom, A., 402
Bloom, F., 172, 175, 268
Bloom, L., 422
Blum, K., 626
Blumenthal, J., 8, 9, 17, 229
Blurton-Jones, N., 104, 456
Bogardus, C., 208
Bohman, M., 626
Bolen, D., 32, 503
Bolles, R., 157
Boor, M., 623
Booth, D., 204
Borbély, A., 222
Borges, M., 484
Boring, E., 307
Borker, R., 468
Borman, L., 485
Borson, S., 153
Bortz, R., 220
Botwinick, J., 483, 484
Bouchard, T., 67, 69, 70, 599
Boudreau, L., 614
Bowen, G., 479
Bower, G., 339, 353
Bower, T., 419
Bowlby, J., 454
Bowmaker, J., 263
Bowman, E., 623
Boyce, V., 208
Boyd, J., 612
Bozarth, M., 215
Bradshaw, D., 511
Bransford, J., 335, 340
Braun, B., 623
Bray, D., 482
Bray, G., 204
Bregman, E., 157
Brehm, J., 534
Brehm, S., 534
Breier, A., 619
Breuer, G., 116
Breuer, J., 653–654, 668–669
Brickman, P., 32, 503
Briggs, S., 509
Brinkman, C., 184
Brittain, R., 59
Broadbent, D., 301, 302
Broadhurst, P., 66
Broca, P., 7, 16, 399–400
Brocato, R., 541
Brody, G., 460
Brody, N., 368, 588
Bronfenbrenner, U., 71, 452, 462
Brooks-Gunn, J., 474
Brotzman, E., 540
Brown, A., 248
Brown, E., 222
Brown, G., 628
Brown, H., 401
Brown, L., 209, 478
Brown, N., 464
Brown, P., 645
Brown, R., 424, 427, 429, 430, 539, 549
Bruner, J., 427, 513
Brunton, M., 59
Brush, C., 545
Buhler, C., 578

Burchardt, C., 468
Burchfield, S., 228, 229
Burke, D., 210
Burke, J., 612, 634
Burkhard, B., 145
Burnstein, E., 550
Burt, A., 211
Bush, E., 468
Buss, A., 509
Bussey, K., 477
Butcher, J., 650
Butler, R., 485
Butler, S., 113
Butterfield, E., 422

———————

Cacciola, J., 631
Cacioppo, J., 515, 516, 532
Caggiula, A., 216
Caharack, G., 299
Caldwell, J., 194
Callaway, M., 552
Camargo, C., 211
Campbell, J., 547
Campbell, K., 5
Campbell, R., 484
Campos, J., 416
Candee, D., 477
Cann, A., 534
Cannon, J., 269
Cannon, W., 199, 226
Capman, M., 476
Cappell, H., 129
Caputo, C., 500
Card, J., 619
Carlsmith, J., 518
Carlson, N., 252, 639
Carpenter, C., 467
Carpenter, W., 676
Carroll, M., 40
Carter-Saltzman, L., 72
Case, R., 441
Castellon, C., 631
Cattell, R., 372, 592–593, 595, 599, 601, 650
Cavalli-Sforza, L., 76
Cavanaugh, J., 639
Cave, C., 381
Ceci, S., 383
Ceraso, J., 351
Cervone, D., 297, 298–299, 588
Chagnon, N., 116, 117
Chaiken, S., 515, 517
Chang, T., 348
Chanoff, D., 466, 582
Chanowitz, B., 531
Chapelle, A., 209
Chapman, L., 636, 637
Chappell, C., 479
Charcot, J., 654
Charney, D., 619
Chase, J., 557
Chase, M., 226
Chase, W., 338
Cheek, J., 509
Cheng, P., 389
Chen, S., 540
Cherry, E., 296
Chesler, P., 152
Chew, B., 208
Chi, M., 390, 392, 393, 441
Chinsky, J., 442
Chomsky, N., 17, 396–397, 425, 429

Christiansen, B., 626
Christiansen, K., 59
Christie, J., 463, 464
Christin, L., 208
Christy, M., 442
Cialdini, R., 530–532, 533
Cicchetti, D., 60, 220
Citron, C., 468
Clark, A., 209
Clark, D., 619
Clark, E., 423
Clark, G., 248
Clark, M., 156, 510
Clarke, A. D. B., 458
Clarke, A. M., 458
Cleckley, H., 623
Clement, C., 387–388
Clifford, M., 495
Cloninger, C., 626
Cody, S., 675
Coffey, C., 678, 679
Cohen, F., 60
Cohen, L., 415
Cohen, N., 359
Colby, A., 476, 477
Cole, M., 384
Collins, A., 345, 347–348, 362
Collins, J., 330, 472
Collins, W., 470
Conley, J., 598
Conneally, P., 57
Conner, J., 468
Connolly, J., 464
Cook, A., 467
Cook, K., 467
Cook, L., 83
Cooley, C., 502
Coons, P., 623
Cooper, H., 503
Cooper, J., 519, 522
Cooper, L., 343
Cooper, M., 626, 627
Cooper, R., 66
Corbett, S., 208
Coren, S., 263, 311
Corey, S., 520
Cornoni-Huntley, J., 484
Coryell, W., 611
Costa, P., 484, 595
Costello, N., 594
Cotter, N., 250
Cottler, L., 648
Cottrell, N., 541
Coward, W., 208
Cox, T., 229
Crago, M., 674
Craik, F., 334, 335, 336
Craske, M., 618
Creese, I., 639
Cristol, A., 671
Croft, J., 194
Cronkite, R., 629
Crow, T., 636
Crowder, R., 330, 361
Crowne, D., 587
Croyle, R., 522
Culbreth, L., 204
Culp, R., 467
Cumming, E., 484
Cunitz, A., 334
Curry, N., 464
Curtiss, S., 426
Cutting, J., 313
Czeisler, C., 222

Dallenbach, K., 350
Dalrymple, S., 540
Dalton, B., 557
Daly, M., 105, 106, 116, 117
Damon, W., 463, 471, 474, 478
Dana, R., 651
Dance, K., 504
Dardis, G., 557
Dark, V., 301
Dartnall, H., 263
Darwin, C., 7, 15, 23, 67, 81–82, 88 94–96, 97–99, 101, 103, 330, 366, 391
Dashiell, J., 542
Daubman, K., 391
Dauphinais, I., 638, 639
Davidson, J., 211
Davidson, R., 572, 594
Davidson, W., 468
Davis, C., 155
Davis, J., 638, 676
Davis, K., 511
Davis, M., 501
Davis, P., 572
Dawson, G., 148
Day, H., 475
Deaux, K., 467, 496
DeBono, K., 514, 515
DeCasper, A., 420
DeFries, J., 51, 58, 61, 71, 76, 467
de Groot, A., 338
DeKloet, E., 190
Delabar, J., 60
Delay, J., 675
DeLisi, L., 638, 639
Dement, W., 218, 222–223
Deniker, P., 675
Descartes, R., 4–5, 17, 385
DeSilva, P., 618
Deutsch, A., 644
Deutsch, G., 380
Deutsch, J., 204, 216
De Valois, K., 258, 259
De Valois, R., 258, 259, 265
de Villiers, J., 424
de Villiers, P., 424
Devine, P., 496–497, 499
de Vries, B., 478
de Wit, H., 215
Dewsbury, D., 107, 108, 116
Dickinson, A., 147, 148
Diener, E., 521, 544
Digman, J., 595
DiMascio, A., 29, 35, 40, 677
Dion, K., 495
Dix, D., 644, 645
Dodson, J., 228
Domjan, M., 145
Donovan, J., 475
Doob, A., 517
Dovidio, J., 543
Dowell, R., 248
Downing, R., 631
Doyle, A., 464, 469
Drenan, S., 557
DuBois, P., A-6
Duffy, J., 222
Duggan, J., 204
Dumais, S., 299, 300
Dumaret, A., 72
Duncan, B., 496
Duncan, C., 639
Duncan, J., 302
Duncker, K., 390
Dunphy, D., 471

Dutton, L., 484
Duyme, M., 72
Dweck, C., 468
Dworkin, R., 636
Dymond, R., 660

Eagle, M., 298
Easton, T., 177
Eaton, G., 112
Ebbinghaus, H., 8, 331–332, 350, 351, 361–362
Eccles, J., 468
Eckert, J., 199
Eckland, B., A-6
Eddy, R., 57, 263
Edelman, G., 182, 224
Edwards, D., 209, 211
Egeland, B., 458
Eibl-Eibesfeldt, I., 91, 96, 98, 102, 116
Eich, J., 353
Eichorn, D., 598
Eidelson, J., 628
Eikelboom, R., 215
Eimas, P., 421
Einstein, A., 388
Ekman, P., 99–101, 234, 235
Eldredge, N., 83
Elkes, R., 534
Elliott, R., 672, 673
Ellis, A., 399, 662–663
Ellis, L., 210
Elman, M., 469
Ely, R., 508
Emery, G., 616, 664
Emlen, S., 92
Endler, N., 628
Engel, M., 468
Enna, B., 468
Epstein, S., 597
Erberg, P., 651
Erckmann, W., 107
Erdelyi, M., 18, 572, 652
Erhardt, A., 211
Ericsson, K., 338
Eriksen, C., 330
Erikson, E., 450–451, 463, 470, 474, 475, 479, 484, 576, 577
Errera, P., 539
Ervin, F., 268
Ervin-Tripp, S., 403–404
Esser, J., 552
Essock-Vitale, S., 117
Etscorn, F., 154
Euler, L., 388
Evarts, E., 183
Eysenck, H., 69, 366, 591, 593–594, 595, 601, 616, 650
Eysenck, M., 594
Eysenck, S., 594

Fagot, B., 467
Fairey, P., 547
Falmagne, R., 387–388
Faloon, S., 338
Fancher, R., 69, 367
Fanselow, M., 269
Farina, A., 614
Farmer, A., 636
Farone, S., 176
Faust, I., 207
Favell, J., 142
Fazio, R., 521
Fechner, G., 8, 273–276, A-9

Feder, H., 189, 210, 211, 212
Feingold, J., 72
Feirtag, M., 167
Festinger, L., 504, 514, 516, 518
Feynman, R., 388
Field, T., 454, 455
Fields, H., 268, 270
Fiering, C., 458
Fieve, R., 632
Fifer, W., 420
Findley, M., 468
Finlay, B., 482
Firschein, O., 392
Fischler, M., 392
Fishbein, M., 522
Fisher, E., 209
Fisher, R., 573, 582
Fisher, S., 572, 573, 677
FitzGerald, K., 627
Flacks, R., 515
Flaherty, C., 149
Flavell, J., 439, 442
Fleeson, J., 458
Fleiss, J., 610
Fleminger, S., 677
Floody, O., 211
Flourens, P., 7
Foa, E., 618, 619, 668
Fobes, J., 216
Foch, T., 207, 601
Fodor, I., 617
Fong, G., 389
Foote, F., 617
Ford, C., 473, 621
Ford, K., 472
Ford, M., 478, 613
Forrest, G., 670
Forrest, J., 472
Foss, J., 394
Foulkes, D., 223, 224
Fox, N., 458
Frandsen, A., 387
Frank, M., 243
Frankel, G., 442
Frankl, V., 578
Franklin, B., 518
Franks, J., 335, 340
Fraser, S., 532–533
Fredrikson, M., 157
Freedman, B., 636
Freedman, J., 532–533
Frenkel, O., 517
Freud, A., 450, 569, 576
Freud, S., 12–13, 17, 22, 223, 449–450, 463, 479, 564–575, 582, 590, 601, 617, 621, 653–658, 668–669, 671
Frey, D., 517, 521
Freymond, D., 208
Friesen, W., 99–101, 234, 235
Fröberg, J., 223
Frohman, L., 204
Fromkin, V., 398
Frykholm, G., 313
Fulker, D., 66, 599
Fuller, J., 54–55, 64
Funk, S., 675
Futuyama, D., 82

Gabrieli, J., 381
Gage, D., 204
Galanter, E., 254
Galef, B., 156
Galen, 165

Gallagher, T., 204
Gallistel, C., 216
Galton, F., 47, 67–69, 366–367, 370, 371, 374, 385
Gantt, W., 123, 127
Garcia, J., 153, 154
Garcia, R., 454
Gardner, A., 428, 429
Gardner, B., 428, 429
Gardner, H., 377, 382–383
Gardner, M., 376
Garrett, M., 398, 400
Garvey, C., 464
Gauthier, R., 469
Gay, J., 384
Gazzaniga, M., 378–380
Gebhard, P., 213, 473
Geen, R., 541, 594
Geer, J., 630
Gelenberg, A., 679
Geliebter, A., 204
George, L., 612, 616
George, W., 626, 627
German, P., 648
Gershon, E., 638, 639
Gerson, S., 644
Geschwind, N., 400
Ghez, C., 184, 185
Gibbon, M., 610
Gibbons, F., 521
Gibbs, J., 476, 477
Gibson, E., 294, 416
Gibson, J., 315–316, 317–318, 320
Gilbert, D., 499
Gilgun, J., 472
Gilligan, C., 475, 478
Gillum, B., 598
Gillum, R., 598
Gilmore, R., 557
Gittelman, R., 677
Giuffra, L., 76
Glanzer, M., 334
Glaser, R., 390, 392, 393
Glass, D., 149
Glass, G., 672, 673
Glazer, H., 630
Glick, J., 384, 445
Gliha, D., 614
Glisky, E., 360
Godden, D., 353
Goethals, G., 500, 504
Goffman, E., 506
Gold, A., 211
Goldberg, J., 441
Goldberg, R., 678
Goldberg, S., 676
Goldfried, M., 675
Goldgaber, D., 60
Goldman, M., 626
Goldman, N., 472
Goldman, R., 516
Goldsmith, H., 67, 599
Gomberg, E., 627
Gonzalez, M., 204
Good, T., 468, 503
Goodall, J., 31, 108–109, 110, 112
Goodenough, D., 59
Goodman, L., 401
Goodman, P., 659
Goodwin, D., 626
Gordon, B., 677, 678
Gordon, C., 484
Gordon, N., 270
Gordon, S., 472

Gormican, S., 290
Gottesman, I., 73, 75, 636
Gottlieb, A., 544
Gottman, J., 479–480
Gould, J., 15
Gould, S., 83, 87, 88
Gouldner, A., 533
Gouze, M., 598
Gove, F., 458
Graham, J., 650
Graves, N., 540
Gray, P., 466, 582
Green, D., 272
Green, J., 500
Green, K., 153, 154
Green, M., 636, 637
Greenberg, D., 465, 466
Greenberg, J., 345
Greenberg, R., 572, 677
Greene, D., 149
Greenfield, P., 422, 424
Gregory, R., 308, 310
Griffith, J., 639
Groos, K., 463
Gross, T., 439
Grossman, S., 203
Grove, W., 611
Gruber, K., 517
Gruder, C., 544
Gruenberg, E., 612, 634
Grusch, J., 522
Grüsser, O., 256
Grüsser-Cornehls, U., 256
Guillemin, R., 268
Gur, R., 381
Gusella, J., 57
Guthrie, E., 147
Gutman, D., 297
Gutmann, D., 481
Guyote, M., 387
Gynther, M., 651

Hacker, S., 404
Hackman, J., 542
Hadley, S., 674
Hagestad, G., 453
Haines, J., 60
Hakes, D., 394
Halberstadt, L., 631
Hall, E., 481
Hall, G., 576
Hall, M., 677
Halliday, T., 109
Halpern, A., 348–349
Hamilton, V., 535, 544
Hamilton, W., 113
Hammersmith, S., 473
Hammond, E., 483
Haney, T., 229
Hanlon, C., 424, 427
Hansen, D., 471
Hanson, A., 588
Harbin, T., 229
Harbluk, J., 360
Harkins, S., 542
Harlow, H., 454, 455, 459
Harper, L., 156, 462
Harring, K., 557
Harrington, D., 582
Harris, M. J., 503
Hartshorne, H., 596, 597
Harvey, O., 553

Harvey, P., 637
Hashim, S., 204
Hasler, A., 159
Hassett, J., 217
Hatfield, E., 511, 512
Hathaway, S., 650
Hawkins, H., 296
Hay, D., 56, 57
Hayes, C., 428
Hayes, K., 428
Haynes, S., 229
Hazen, C., 511
Hécaen, H., 293
Hecht, S., 256
Hefferline, R., 133, 134, 659
Heider, F., 492–493, 499
Heiman, M., 336
Heimer, L., 209
Heinrichs, D., 676
Held, N., 639
Helmholtz, H. von, 239, 248, 262, 314
Helzer, J., 612, 634
Henderson, C., 416
Henderson, M., 510
Hendrick, C., 511, 540
Hendrick, S., 511
Hendricks, B., 28
Hendrickson, A., 415
Heninger, G., 619
Henry, J., 187, 268
Henry, W., 484
Henshaw, S., 472
Herek, G., 514
Hering, E., 264
Herman, C., 207
Herrnstein, R., 69, 144
Hershman, D., 633
Hess, E., 158
Hiatt, S., 416
Hilgard, E., 622
Hill, C., 508
Hill, J., 471
Hinson, R., 129, 626
Hippocrates, 606
Hirschhorn, K., 59
Hirst, W., 299
Hitch, G., 334
Hobbes, T., 6
Hobson, J., 219, 220, 224
Hochberg, J., 304
Hodges, J., 458
Hoebel, B., 205, 216
Hoelter, J., 504
Hoffer, A., 87
Hoffman, C., 404
Hoffman, L., 481
Hoffman, M., 460–461, 461, 462, 476
Hofling, C., 540
Hofstadter, R., 114
Hogarty, G., 676
Hogate, L., 499
Hogness, D., 57, 263
Hohmann, G., 232
Holder, J., 387
Holland, C., 539
Holton, B., 557
Holway, A., 307
Hong, G., 557
Honig, K., 459
Honzik, C., 150
Honzik, M., 598
Hood, W., 553
Hooff, J. van, 103–104

Hook, E., 59
Hopkins, B., 430
Horn, D., 483
Horn, J., 60, 70, 75
Horne, J., 222
Horney, K., 576, 577, 582, 590, 658
Horwitz, R., 465
Hosobuchi, Y., 268
Hothersall, D., 6, 13, 123, 125
Housley, P., 467
Houston, B., 675
Howard, A., 482
Howard, B., 208
Howard, K., 472
Hoyle, R., 557
Hrdy, S., 108, 116
Hsu, F., 511
Hubel, D., 258, 259, 265
Hudspeth, A., 247
Huff, O., 39
Hugdahl, K., 157
Hughes, D., 616
Hull, C., 14
Hume, D., 6
Hunt, E., 374
Huret, J., 60
Hurvich, L., 265
Husband, R., 541
Huston, A., 467
Huxley, J., 87
Hyde, J., 613

Inhelder, B., 432, 434
Inkster, J., 517
Inouye, J., 595
Insko, C., 557
Irons, W., 83, 116
Ironside, R., 621
Isabella, R., 458
Isen, A., 391
Isenberg, D., 551
Ison, J., 149
Ito, M., 177
Iverson, L., 639

Jacklin, C., 466, 467, 468, 469, 480
Jackson, D., 597
Jackson, J., 529
Jacobs, G., 265
Jacobs, P., 59
Jacobsen, F., 633
Jacobson, B., 74
Jacobson, C., 540
Jacobson, L., 502
James, W., 9–10, 12, 22, 23, 165, 230, 231, 232, 346, 391, 503, 506
Jameson, D., 265
Jamieson, D., 509
Janis, I., 551–552
Jaskir, J., 458
Jellison, J., 500
Jenkins, J., 350
Jenkins, M., 72
Jenner, P., 677
Jensen, A., 34, 71–72, 369, 370, 374
Jerome, J., 615
Jewett, M., 222
Johansson, G., 313
Johnson, D., 404
Johnson, J., 463, 464
Johnson, V., 210

Johnson-Laird, P., 387, 388
Johnston, D., 229
Johnston, T., 153
Johnston, W., 301
Jones, E., 472, 498, 499, 507, 519
Jones, M., 667
Jooste, P., 220
Jordan, N., 440
Jouvet, M., 226
Julien, R., 192
Jung, C., 484, 576, 577, 578, 593, 658
Jussim, L., 503

Kagan, J., 416, 440, 456, 457, 458
Kahneman, D., 301, 302, 320, 388–389
Kail, R., 442
Kalat, J., 154
Kallman, F., 77
Kamin, L., 69, 71, 147
Kanizsa, G., 289
Kant, I., 314–315
Kantner, J., 472
Kantor, L., 374
Kaplan, M., 549, 614
Karasu, T., 652
Karno, M., 612
Karon, B., 677
Karp, D., 485
Kastenbaum, R., 485
Katz, D., 513
Kaufman, L., 309
Kay, P., 402
Kearsley, R., 458
Keenan, J., 341
Keesey, R., 208
Keller, F., 139
Keller, H., 367
Kelley, H., 493
Kellogg, L., 428
Kellogg, W., 428
Kelly, D., 267
Kelly, G., 649
Kelly, J. A., 471
Kelman, H., 535, 544
Kempton, W., 402
Kendler, H., 8, 9
Kendler, T., 444
Kennedy, J., 76
Kessler, L., 648
Kessler, R., 614
Kettlewell, B., 83
Kety, S., 74, 75, 629
Kiesler, C., 644, 646, 647
Kihlstrom, J., 356, 357
Kilpatrick, G., 677
Kimura, D., 380
King, B., 204
Kinney, D., 633
Kinsey, A., 213, 473
Kirker, W., 336
Kirsch, I., 675
Kissin, B., 223
Kleiman, D., 107
Klein, D., 619, 677
Klein, G., 298
Kleinman, A., 608, 622
Kleitman, N., 218
Klentz, B., 521
Klerman, G., 29, 35, 40, 677
Kline, N., 608
Klinke, R., 245
Knowler, W., 208

Knox, R., 517
Koenig, K., 515
Koenig, O., 381
Koffka, K., 11, 12, 286
Kohlberg, L., 451, 469, 476–478
Köhler, W., 11, 12
Kohn, M., 462
Kolb, B., 180, 185, 265, 293, 380
Konner, M., 456
Kornhuber, H., 178, 183
Kosslyn, S., 342–343, 381
Kozak, M., 668
Kozlowski, L., 313
Kramer, M., 612
Krank, M., 129, 626
Krokoff, L., 479
Kronauer, R., 222
Krowitz, A., 416
Kruuk, H., 88
Kryter, K., 248, 249
Kübler-Ross, E., 485
Kubovy, M., 289
Kuczaj, S., 345
Kuffler, S., 258
Kuhl, P., 421
Kuhn, C., 454
Kuiper, N., 336, 504
Kurland, J., 117
Kurland, M., 441
Kutash, I., 658

Lack, D., 107
Lader, M., 678
Lafferty, R., 674
LaFreniere, P., 469
Lage, E., 547
Lahey, M., 422
Lahti, I., 639
Laird, J., 233, 234
Lakoff, G., 344
Lamarck, J., 82
Lamb, M., 458
Lamour, Y., 60
Lander, E., 57
Landry, P., 557
Lange, C., 230, 232
Langer, A., 416
Langer, E., 485, 531, 614
LaPiere, R., 520, 522
Larsen, B., 184
Larsen, J., 159
Larsen, N., 184
Larsson, K., 209
Latané, B., 528–530, 542, 543
Lau, I., 404
Lauer, J., 479, 512
Lauer, R., 479, 512
Lawson, J., 429
Layton, B., 149
Lazerson, A., 175
Leaf, P., 648
Leana, C., 552
LeBon, G., 544
Lee, B., 648
Lee, T., 638, 639
Legant, P., 500
Legault, L., 215
Lehman, D., 389
Leigh, G., 479
Leinhardt, G., 468
Lenneberg, E., 421, 426, 427
Lentz, R., 646, 651, 670, 676

Lenzenweger, M., 636
Leon, G., 206, 598
Lepper, M., 149
Lerner, M., 499–500
Lester, L., 269
Levenson, R., 234, 235
Levine, J., 270
Levinger, G., 551
Levinson, D., 479, 481
Levy, P., 399
Lewin, K., 11, 12, 527–528, 548–549, 557
Lewin, R., 191
Lewis, J., 269
Lewis, M., 458, 474
Lewontin, R., 69, 72, 87
Liberman, R., 646
Lickey, M., 677, 678
Lieb, J., 633
Lieberman, M., 476, 477, 485
Liebert, R., 477
Liebeskind, J., 268, 269
Liem, J., 482
Liem, R., 482
Light, W., 625
Liker, J., 383
Lillioja, S., 208
Lin, K., 608
Lin, Y., 557
Lincoln, R., 472
Linden, R., 676
Linder, D., 519
Lindsley, J., 226
Linkous, R., 541
Linville, P., 504
Lipet, J., 142
Lipman, R., 678
Lipowski, Z., 622
Lippmann, W., 496
Lipsitt, L., 138
Lisk, R., 211
Liverant, S., 587
Livingston, D., 269
Livingston, M., 265
Llinás, R., 172
Lloyd, B., 467
Locke, B., 484, 612
Locke, J., 6
Locke, J. L., 421
Lockhart, R., 336
Loeb, G., 248
Loehlin, J., 60, 70, 75
Loftus, E., 354, 355
Loftus, G., 355
Logue, A., 153
Lorenz, K., 15, 89, 94, 95, 100, 111, 158
Lott, B., 213
Lowery, C., 478
Lublin, S., 545
Luborsky, L., 631
Lucas, A., 208
Luchins, A., 495
Lunde, I., 629, 633
Lundsteen, C., 59
Luria, A., 343, 378
Luria, Z., 467
Lustman, P., 677
Lydon, J., 509
Lykken, D., 67, 599
Lynch, J., 485

Macciocchi, S., 652
Maccoby, E., 466, 467, 468, 469, 480

MacDonald, N., 636
Mackay, A., 639
Mackie, D., 551
Mackintosh, N., 147
MacWhinney, B., 341
Maddox, G., 484
Mahorney, S., 678
Maier, N., 552
Maier, S., 630
Maltz, D., 468
Mandelbaum, M., 256
Mani, G., 83
Manis, J., 481
Mann, L., 545
Mann, S., 677
Mäntylä, T., 352, 353
Manuck, S., 613
Marcel, A., 302
Marcia, J., 474, 475
Mardon, G., 209
Marecek, J., 500
Maret, E., 482
Margules, D., 124, 215
Mark, V., 268
Marks, I., 617, 618, 619, 667, 668
Marler, P., 92
Marr, D., 375
Marriott, R., 552
Marsden, C., 677
Martin, C., 213, 473
Martin, J., 267
Marvel, M., 28
Marvin, R., 475
Marx, K., 443
Masangkay, Z., 439
Maslow, A., 578, 582–584, 590
Mason, J., 156
Masters, W., 210
Matarazzo, J., 610, 611
Matlin, M., 244, 246, 257
Matthews, D., 211
Matthews, K., 229
Maughan, B., 477
Maurer, C., 414
Maurer, D., 414
May, M., 596, 597
May, R., 578
Mayhew, D., 341
Mayr, E., 82, 87
McArthur, L., 495–496
McCabe, M., 472
McCallum, D., 557
McClearn, G., 51, 58, 61, 71, 76, 207
McClelland, J., 424
McClemont, W., 59
McCloskey, M., 355–356
McCluskey, K., 439
McCrae, R., 484, 595
McDonald, K., 430
McDuff, D., 499
McEwen, B., 189, 190
McGillivray, B., 209
McGowan, B., 153, 154
McGue, M., 69, 70
McGuffin, P., 636
McGuffog, C., 458
McGuire, C., 505
McGuire, M., 117
McGuire, W., 505, 514
McIntyre, C., 439
McKay, D., 296
McKellar, P., 623
McKenna, R., 206, 207

McKim, W., 194
McKinley, J., 650
McLachlan, D., 360
McNally, R., 617
McRae, J., 614
McReynolds, P., 611
McShane, D., 385
Mead, M., 467
Meador, B., 660
Means, B., 384
Meddis, R., 223
Mednick, S., 59
Meiselman, K., 117
Melville, M., 59
Melzack, R., 266, 267, 268, 269
Mendel, G., 53
Mercer, D., 134
Meredith, W., 598
Merzel, A., 633
Metalsky, G., 630, 631
Mezynski, K., 335
Michaels, J., 541
Miczek, K., 269
Milgram, S., 535–539
Mill, J., 69
Mill, J. S., 6, 69
Miller, A., 537
Miller, D., 499
Miller, G. A., 423
Miller, G. E., 337
Miller, H., 354
Miller, J. A., 532
Miller, J. G., 500
Miller, L., 522
Miller, N., 41, 141
Miller, R., 32
Miller, R. L., 503
Miller, T., 672, 673
Milner, B., 357–358, 359, 378, 380
Milner, P., 214
Milofsky, E., 479
Milstein, V., 623
Minix, D., 550
Mintz, S., 637
Mirsky, A., 639
Mischel, W., 585, 596–597, 601
Mishkin, M., 360
Mitchell, D., 220
Modianos, D., 211
Moirs, K., 499
Moises, H., 76
Molitor, N., 458
Money, J., 211
Moniz, E., 679
Monson, T., 509
Moore, H., 541
Moos, R., 629
Morales, F., 226
Moray, N., 296
Morgan, C., 202
Moriarty, T., 530, 544
Moring, J., 639
Morris, P., 399
Morris, R., 150
Moscovici, S., 547
Mosher, R., 209
Mouton, J., 554–555
Mowrer, O., 140, 147
Mugny, G., 547
Mulcaster, R., 47
Müller, J., 7
Müller-Lyer, F., 308
Muntz, W., 277

Murdock, G., 116
Murphy, D., 354
Murphy, G., 677
Murray, E., 617
Mussen, P., 598
Myers, D., 549, 550
Myers, J., 612
Myers, L., 211

Naarala, M., 639
Naffrechoux, M., 547
Nathans, J., 57, 253, 263
Nauta, W., 167
Naylor, S., 57
Neale, M., 599
Nee, L., 60
Neill, A., 465
Neisser, U., 298, 299, 316, 361
Nelson, K., 445
Nelson, S., 468
Nemeth, C., 548
Netley, C., 59
Neu, C., 29, 35, 40
Neugarten, B., 453, 479, 484
Newcomb, T., 514–515
Newman, J., 149
Newson, C., 142
Nias, D., 599
Nicole, A., 60
Nida, S., 543
Nietzel, M., 658
Niijima, A., 204
Nisbett, R., 389, 500
Noble, E., 626
Norcross, J., 675
Norman, D., 323, 334
Novin, D., 204
Nowicki, G., 391
Nowlis, G., 243
Nue, C., 677
Nuechterlein, K., 639
Nystrom, J., 454

Oates, J., 639
O'Brien, E., 597
Ochs, E., 427
Oden, S., 471
Oetting, E., 627
Offer, D., 472
Öhman, A., 157
Okin, R., 645
Olds, J., 214, 215, 216
Oliveau, D., 617
Ollove, M., 631
Olson, S., 636
Olton, D., 158–159
Orne, M., 539
Orthner, D., 479
Ortmann, J., 629
Orvaschel, H., 612, 634
Osmond, H., 87
Ostrov, E., 472
Ottina, K., 57
Owen, D., 59
Ozarow, B., 618, 619

Padawer-Singer, A., 505
Page, D., 209
Palmer, J., 354
Palmer, S., 288, 289

Papousek, H., 417
Park, B., 498
Park, E., 59
Parkin, A., 358
Parmelee, A., 224
Partridge, L., 109
Pascual-Leone, J., 441
Passingham, R., 183
Passman, R., 459
Pastor, D., 458
Pate, J., 429
Patterson, F., 429
Patterson, T., 638
Patzer, G., 495
Paul, G., 646, 651, 670, 676
Paul, L., 268
Paunonen, S., 597
Pavlov, I., 123–129, 130, 145, 666
Paxson, L., 456
Peake, P., 596–597
Pearson, K., 366
Peckhan, W., 210
Peele, S., 627
Penfield, W., 224
Perfetto, G., 335
Perls, F., 659
Perot, P., 224
Perry, V., 183
Pervin, L., 651
Peter, A., 150
Peterson, C., 501
Peterson, L., 332–333, 359
Peterson, M., 332–333, 359
Petitto, L., 429
Pettigrew, T., 555
Petty, R., 515, 516
Petursson, H., 678
Pfaff, D., 209, 211
Pfeifle, J., 209
Pfungst, O., 25–27, 29, 38
Phares, E., 587, 588
Philip, J., 59
Piaget, J., 17, 401, 414, 417–420, 431–440, 443–444, 446, 451, 464, 476
Piantanida, T., 57, 263
Pick, A., 442
Pickles, J., 247, 249, 250
Pierce, C., 540
Pierrel, R., 139
Pietrewicz, A., 153
Pinel, P., 643
Pinette, M., 499
Pinkley, R., 557
Plomin, R., 51, 58, 61, 71, 76, 467, 601
Pohjola, J., 639
Pohoresky, L., 630
Polefrone, J., 613
Polinsky, R., 60
Pollack, J., 209
Pomerantz, J., 289
Pomeroy, W., 213, 473
Ponzo, M., 308
Porterfield, A., 480
Poulos, C., 129
Powers, B., 209
Powley, T., 205
Premack, A., 429
Premack, D., 429
Prentice-Dunn, S., 544, 545
Presby, W., 499
Pressin, J., 541
Presson, J., 296
Proffitt, D., 313

Provenzano, F., 467
Provine, W., 82
Prusoff, B., 29, 35, 40, 677
Ptolemy, 309
Pucey, A., 110

Quattrone, A., 498
Quillian, M., 345, 347–348, 362
Quitkin, F., 677

Rabkin, J., 619
Rachman, S., 618, 668
Radke-Yarrow, M., 476
Radloff, C., 500, 504
Rae, D., 612
Ramsay, D., 416
Rank, S., 540
Rapaport, J., 618
Rasmussen, E., 541
Rasmussen, T., 379
Raugh, M., 339
Ravussin, E., 208
Rayner, R., 14, 128, 141, 157
Razran, G., 144
Reaves, C., 299
Redican, W., 98, 104
Reedy, M., 484
Reese, L., 671
Rees, J., 458
Regier, D., 612, 634, 648
Reidlinger, R., 156
Reis, H., 510
Reisenzein, R., 233
Rescorla, R., 146, 147, 148
Rest, J., 476
Reynolds, D., 268
Reynolds, P., 298
Reznick, J., 416
Rheingold, H., 467
Rhodes, S., 481
Rich, S., 67, 599
Richards, R., 633
Richardson-Klavehn, A., 327
Richter, C., 199
Rifkin, A., 677
Riley, J., 485
Rimmö, 157
Rincover, A., 142
Rips, L., 344
Riskind, J., 628
Rittle, R., 541
Roberts, S., 208
Robins, L., 612, 634
Robinson, B., 204
Robinson, D., 165
Rock, I., 297, 308, 309, 310, 311, 317
Rodgers, D., 651
Rodin, J., 207, 484, 543
Roehling, P., 626
Rogers, A., 478
Rogers, C., 578, 580, 581–582, 601, 659–662, 671
Rogers, R., 544
Rogers, T., 336
Rokeach, M., 522–523
Roland, P., 184
Rolls, E., 203
Romer, D., 544
Ronda, J., 222
Rosch, E., 344, 345, 402
Rose, S., 17, 69
Rosen, J., 149

Rosenbaum, S., 429
Rosenberg, S., 504
Rosenhan, D., 621, 645–646
Rosenthal, D., 74, 75, 629
Rosenthal, N., 633
Rosenthal, R., 27, 502, 503
Rosoff, J., 472
Ross, L., 499
Rossier, J., 268
Rossor, M., 639
Rostene, W., 190
Roth, L., 206
Roth, M., 77
Rothbart, M., 498
Rothblum, E., 608
Rothenberg, M., 456
Rothman, S., 365
Rotter, J., 585, 586–587, 590, 601
Rottman, L., 512
Routtenberg, A., 215
Rovine, M., 457, 458
Rowe, R., 541
Rozin, P., 154
Rubin, J., 467
Rubin, R., 228
Rubin, Z., 510
Rubinstein, J., 676
Rudy, J., 150
Ruffin, P., 557
Rumbaugh, D., 429
Rumelhart, D., 424
Rundus, D., 262
Runeson, S., 313
Rupert, E., 430
Rupniak, N., 677
Rushton, J., 599
Russek, M., 204
Russell, M., 626, 627
Rutkowski, G., 544
Ryan, W., 499

Saccone, A., 675
Sachs, G., 679
Sachs, J., 340
Sack, D., 633
Sackeim, H., 678
Sackheim, H., 381
Sacks, O., 265
St. Clair, S., 475
St. George-Hyslop, P., 60
Sajwaj, T., 142
Sakaguchi, A., 57
Sakata, H., 183
Sakuma, Y., 209
Saltzstein, H., 461, 462
Sande, G., 500, 504
Sanders, K., 156
Sanders, R., 429
Savage, J., 208
Savage-Rumbaugh, S., 429, 430
Scafidi, F., 454
Scarr, S., 72, 459, 600
Schachter, S., 206, 207, 231, 232, 233
Schacter, D., 327, 360
Schanberg, S., 454, 455
Schank, R., 345, 445
Scharf, B., 249
Scheff, T., 608
Scher, S., 519
Schieffelin, B., 427
Schiff, M., 72
Schifter, D., 521

Schildkraut, J., 629
Schlenker, B., 506
Schmidt, R., 185
Schnapf, J., 253, 254
Schneider, D., 551
Schneider, H., 40
Schneider, J., 404, 587
Schneider, W., 299, 300, 301, 302
Schnell, S., 477
Schoenfeld, W., 139
Schopler, J., 557
Schulman, P., 631
Schulsinger, F., 59, 74, 629
Schultz, M., 224
Schunk, D., 588
Schwartz, G., 572
Schwartz, M., 400
Schwartz, S., 544, 555
Schwartzman, H., 463
Scott, J., 54–55, 218, 219, 225
Scribner, S., 383, 384
Searle, L., 66
Sears, R., 572
Sechenov, I. M., 6
Seeman, P., 638, 639
Seewald, A., 468
Segal, N., 67, 599
Sekerak, G., 541
Seligman, E., 501
Seligman, M., 157, 617, 621, 630, 631
Seligman, P., 248
Selye, H., 228
Semmel, A., 550, 630
Serbin, L., 468, 469
Sevcik, R., 430
Sever, P., 194
Shaffer, D., 460
Shallice, T., 359
Shapiro, C., 220
Shapiro, D., 672, 673
Shapiro, S., 648
Sharp, D., 384
Shaver, P., 511
Shavut, Y., 269
Shaw, G., 502
Shebalin, V., 377, 382
Shepard, R., 343
Shepher, J., 117
Sherif, C., 553
Sherif, M., 553–554
Sherman, J., 139
Sherman, M., 614
Sherman, P., 112
Sherman, S., 534
Sherrington, C., 166
Sherry, D., 327
Shettleworth, S., 15, 159
Shields, J., 73, 75
Shiffrar, M., 294
Shiffrin, R., 299, 300, 301, 302, 323, 333, 334, 357
Shoben, E., 344
Shoda, Y., 597
Shostakovich, D., 377
Showers, C., 542
Shows, T., 57, 263
Shuster, L., 269
Shweder, R., 600
Sibulkin, A., 644, 646, 647
Siegel, J., 483
Siegel, S., 129, 626
Siegler, R., 442, 443
Sigvardsson, S., 626
Sikes, J., 555

Silverberg, S., 471
Simmons, C., 499
Simon, H., 338
Simon, T., 367
Simons, A., 677
Simpson, E., 209, 477
Sims, J., 587
Sims-Knight, J., 439
Singer, B., 27
Singer, J., 545
Siperstein, G., 422
Siqueland, R., 138
Sizemore, C., 623
Skinhoj, E., 184
Skinner, B., 14, 15, 17, 23, 122, 130–143, 426–427, 520, 666
Skinner, E., 648
Slater, E., 620
Slattum, V., 534
Slavney, P., 620
Slim, R., 557
Sloane, M., 356
Sloane, R., 671
Slobin, D., 425
Smith, B., 594
Smith, D., 509, 659, 675
Smith, E., 211, 344
Smith, G., 626
Smith, J., 422, 424
Smith, L., 415
Smith, M. B., 513
Smith, M. L., 672, 673
Smith, R., 204
Smith, S., 401
Smith, T., 429
Smyth, M., 399
Snapp, M., 555
Snarey, J., 477
Snow, C., 421, 427, 535
Snyder, F., 218, 219, 225
Snyder, M., 502, 508–509, 514, 515, 521
Snyder, S., 187, 191, 639
Snyderman, M., 365
Sobell, M., 507
Solem, A., 552
Solomon, E., 534
Solomon, G., 228
Solomon, L., 608
Sophocles, 571
Sorri, A., 639
Spalding, D., 158
Spanos, N., 623
Spearman, C., 370–372
Spelke, E., 299, 420
Spence, K., 147
Spence, M., 420
Spencer, H., 114
Sperling, G., 328–330
Sperry, R., 378–379
Spindler, J., 215
Spiro, M., 117
Spitz, R., 454
Spitzer, L., 207, 485
Spitzer, R., 610, 614
Spivey, C., 545
Spock, B., 456
Spohn, H., 638
Spokes, P., 639
Spooner, W., 398
Sprafkin, C., 469
Sprecher, S., 512
Springer, S., 379
Squire, L., 358, 359

Sroufe, L., 458
Stadler-Morris, S., 150
Stangor, C., 517
Staples, F., 671
Stapp, J., 21
Steer, R., 628
Stein, B., 335
Steinberg, L., 470, 471
Steinhilber, A., 541–542
Steketee, G., 617, 618, 619
Stellar, E., 200, 203, 215, 216
Stellar, J., 200, 203, 215, 216
Stephan, C., 555
Stephan, W., 501
Stephens, R., 154
Stern, E., 224
Sternberg, R., 372–377, 387, 390, 511–512
Stevens, C., 169, 170
Stevens, S., 274–276
Steward, O., 168
Stewart, D., 59
Stewart, J., 72, 215
Stewart, R., 475
Stiles, W., 672, 673
Stoner, J., 549
Storms, M., 500
Strayer, F., 469
Stricker, E., 199, 203
Stroop, J., 300
Struch, N., 555
Strupp, H., 674
Sullivan, J., 678
Sullivan, P., 678
Susman, R., 429
Svanum, S., 521
Svejda, M., 416
Swann, W., 506, 508, 521
Sweeney, P., 517
Sylvester, D., 617
Szasz, T., 578
Szeminska, A., 432
Szymanski, K., 542

Tageson, C., 579
Tajfel, H., 498, 556
Takahashi, J., 221, 225, 226
Tamarkin, L., 633
Tang, J., 381
Tanke, E., 502
Tanzi, R., 57, 60
Taylor, H., 71
Taylor, L., 380
Taylor, W., 296
Tees, R., 421
Teigen, K., 47
Teitelbaum, M., 620
Teitelbaum, P., 205
Tellegen, A., 67, 599
Tennen, H., 675
Terman, G., 269
Terman, L., 368
Terrace, H., 429
Tesser, A., 547
Tetlock, P., 523
Therman, E., 60, 61
Thibaut, J., 557
Thigpen, C., 623
Thomas, W., 129
Thompson, M., 269
Thompson, R., 179
Thompson, W., 64
Thorndike, E., 10, 23, 130–131, 138, 157, 350

Thorne, B., 468–469
Thornhill, N., 117
Thornhill, R., 117
Thornton, B., 499
Thurstone, L., 371–372
Tice, D., 506, 519
Tiemann, B., 59
Tienari, P., 639
Tiger, L., 117
Tilker, H., 537
Tinbergen, N., 15, 89, 98, 115
Tischler, G., 648
Titchener, E., 9, 11, 12, 13, 14, 22
Tittnich, E., 464
Tizard, B., 458
Todd, M., 511
Tolman, E., 14, 147, 150, 151, 152
Tolstoy, L., 465
Toman, J., 401
Tomkiewicz, S., 72
Tordoff, M., 204
Torrey, E., 638
Townes, B., 459
Townshend, B., 250
Travis, L., 540
Treisman, A., 290–292, 299, 301, 302, 320
Treverthan, S., 478
Triplett, N., 540
Trivers, R., 105, 106, 107, 112, 113
Tryon, R., 65–66
Tsuang, M., 76
Tucker, A., 21
Tucker, J., 507
Tulving, E., 327, 336, 352, 360
Turner, J., 556
Turvey, M., 330
Tversky, A., 388–389

Uttal, W., 165, 241

Vaillant, G., 479, 627
Valenstein, E., 209, 214, 679
Valzelli, L., 235
Van Compernolle, D., 250
Van Dis, H., 209
Vance, E., 210
VandenBos, G., 21
Vanneman, R., 555
Vaughn, B., 439, 458
Vega-Lahr, N., 454
Vernon, P. A., 375
Vernon, P. E., 372, 374–375
Vinokur, A., 550
Volkova, V., 144
Voltaire, 87
Vomachka, A., 211
von Baeyer, C., 630
von Eye, A., 458
Von Korff, M., 648
von Osten, 25–27
Vucinish, R., 507
Vye, N., 335
Vygotsky, L., 401, 443–444, 446, 464

Wachtler, J., 548
Wack, D., 541
Waddell, B., 510
Wagner, A., 147
Wagner, N., 210
Wagstaff, G., 356

Wahl, O., 76, 638
Wahlberg, K., 639
Walk, R., 416
Walker, E., 636, 637
Walker, L., 477, 478
Walker, W., 182
Wall, P., 266, 267, 268, 269
Wall, S., 457
Wallace, M., 57
Wallerstein, R., 674
Walster, E., 495
Walster, G., 511, 512
Ward, I., 209–210
Ward, L., 263
Ward, O., 209
Warner, R., 677
Warren, R., 289, 290, 331
Warrington, E., 359
Warwick, D., 515
Wasserman, S., 420
Waterman, A., 474–475
Waters, E., 457
Watkins, M., 334, 335
Watkins, P., 57
Watson, J. B., 13–14, 23, 121, 126, 128, 141, 145, 157, 401, 617, 666, 667
Watson, J. S., 417
Watson, R., 545
Watt, R., 284
Waugh, N., 323, 334
Waxler, N., 608
Webb, W., 220
Weber, E., 8, 273, A-9
Weber, P., 600
Wechsler, D., 368
Weekes, J., 623
Wehr, T., 633
Weinberg, M., 473
Weinberg, R., 72, 600
Weinberger, D., 572
Weiner, R., 678, 679
Weingartner, H., 354
Weinman, C., 485
Weisberg, P., 459
Weiskrantz, L., 358
Weiss, J., 630
Weissman, M., 29, 35, 40, 612, 634, 677
Wender, P., 74, 629
Wenner, W., 224
Werker, J., 421
Werner, H., 385
Wernicke, C., 399
Wertheimer, M., 10, 12, 285, 286
Wesley, G., 40
West, S., 535
Westoff, C., 472
Westreich, S., 204
Wethington, E., 636
Wetzel, R., 677
Wexler, N., 57, 58
Wheatstone, C., 304
Whipple, K., 671
Whishaw, I., 180, 185, 265, 293
White, B., 445, 553
White, R., 250, 513
Whorf, B., 401–402
Wickens, D., 351
Wicker, A., 520
Wickless, C., 675
Wicklund, R., 521, 534
Widiger, T., 613
Wielgus, M., 637
Wiesel, T., 258, 259

Wilcock, J., 66
Wilcox, K., 67, 599
Wilkins, L., 199
Wilkinson, F., 183
Willerman, L., 60, 70, 71, 75
Williams, C., 650
Williams, J., 610, 614
Williams, K., 542
Willner, P., 629
Wilson, E., 113
Wilson, G., 668
Wilson, M., 105, 106, 116, 117
Wilson, R., 594
Wimer, C., 66
Wimer, R., 66
Wise, R., 215
Wishart, J., 419
Wissler, C., 367
Witkin, H., 59
Wittig, M., 600
Wittlinger, R., 350

Witty, P., 72
Wolf, A., 658
Wolfe, J., 139
Wolitzky, D., 298
Wolpe, J., 668
Woods, P., 22
Wright, H., 535
Wright, J., 597
Wulf, D., 472
Wundt, W., 8, 9, 11, 12, 17, 22, 361, 362
Wynne, L., 639
Wyshak, G., 622

Yakovlev, P., 268
Yasukawa, K., 86
Yawkey, T., 463, 464
Yerkes, R., 124, 228
Yorkston, N., 671
Youdelis, C., 415
Young, J., 665

Young, T., 262
Younger, B., 415

Zahn-Waxler, C., 476
Zajonc, R., 234, 541, 542
Zanna, M., 509
Zaragoza, M., 355–356
Zatz, M., 221, 225, 226
Zelazo, P., 458
Zelig, M., 356
Zelnick, M., 472
Zimbardo, P., 545
Zimmerman, M., 611
Zonderman, A., 484
Zubek, J., 66
Zucker, R., 627
Zurif, E., 400
Zwilling, M., 29, 35, 40, 677
Zwislocki, J., 248

# Subject index

ABC theory of emotions, 663
abnormal behavior. *See* mental disorder
abnormal psychology, 21
absolute threshold, 270–271
accommodation, defined, 438–439
acetylcholine, 191
action potential, 168, 169–170
adolescence
    identity formation in, 474–475
    peer group in, 471
    relationships in, 470–471
    sexuality in, 472–473
adulthood
    aging, 483–486
    employment, 481–483
    marriage and family, 479–480
aggression
    and dominance, 111–112
    group versus group, 552–557
    as motivation, 565
    observational learning of, 152
    territorial, 110–111
aging, 483–484
    approaching death, 485–486
    coping with, 484–485
    nursing home treatment, 647
    theories of, 484
agoraphobia, 619
alcohol abuse, 624
    amnesia induced by, 625
    antabuse to combat, 670
    genetic predisposition to, 625–626
algorithm, 393
allele, defined, 52
altruism, 112–113
Alzheimer's disease, brain plaques in, 60
amino acid, defined, 48
amnesia
    alcohol-induced, 625
    psychogenic, 622
amphetamines, 192, 194
anal stage of development, 570–571
analogy, 94
androgens, 88
anger, acceptability of, 613
animal experiments
    beehive building, 94–96
    behaviorism, 13–14
    bird migration, 92–93
    brain experiments, 178, 183
    brain stimulation, 201–202, 203, 215–216
    chimpanzee behavior, 31
    Clever Hans, 26–27, 29, 38

deprivation experiments, 91–93
discriminative stimuli, 144–145
ethics of, 41
ethology, 15
fear-based learning, 157
food preferences, 153–155
genetics of behavioral traits, 54–55
homeostasis, 199
imprinting, 157–158
language acquisition in primates, 428–431
learned helplessness, 630
mother-child attachment in monkeys, 454–455
negative reinforcement, 140–141
Pavlovian, 123–129
place learning, 150–151, 158–159
problem solving, 11–12
puzzle box, 130–132
reward contrast effects, 149
*S-R* vs. *S-S* theories and, 145–146
selective breeding, 65–67
Skinner box, 132–133
stickleback mating, 89–90
stress-induced analgesia, 269
anorexia nervosa, 608, 609
antidepressants, 193, 677
antipsychotic drugs, 193, 676–677
antithesis, principle of, 98
anxiety, 568
    basic, 577
    defense mechanisms and, 568–570
    drug therapy for, 677–678
    as neurotic symptom, 610
    tranquilizers and, 677–678
anxiety disorders, 611, 615
    generalized, 616
    obsessive-compulsive disorder, 617–618
    panic disorder, 618–619
    phobias, 616–617
    post-traumatic stress, 619
arithmetic mean (average), A-3
arousal, 226–228
    debilitation by, 228–229
    emotion and, 229–233
    performance and, 541–542
    sympathetic nervous system and, 174
arousal theory, 541–542
artificial selection, 82
assertiveness training, 671
assessment
    interviews, 649
    neuropsychological, 652
    projective tests, 651
    psychometric tests, 650–651

questionnaires, 649–650
assimilation, defined, 438
attachment, 454, 456–457
    to inanimate objects, 459
    multiple, 458–459
    romantic love and, 511
    secure, 457–458
attention, deficit in, 636
attitudes
    and behavior, 519–522
    cognitive dissonance and, 516–519
    construction of, 515–516
    functions of, 513
    planned behavior theory, 521
    reference group influence on, 514–515
    values and, 522–523
attribution, 492–494
    error of fundamental, 499–500
    means for modifying behavior, 32, 503
    styles of, 631
audience effects, 540–542
auditory masking, 249
authoritarian parenting, 461
authoritative parenting, 461, 462
authority, obedience to, 535–540
autonomic motor system, 173
aversion therapy, 669–670
avoidance learning, 140
axon, 166, 169–170
axon terminal, 166

basal ganglia, 178
Beck Depression Inventory, 649–650
behavior therapy, 134, 666
    assertiveness and social skills training, 671
    aversion treatment, 669–670
    biofeedback training, 134
    contingency contract, 670–671
    effectiveness of, 672, 673
    modeling, 671
    phobias treated by exposure, 667–669
    token economy, 670
behavioral genetics, defined, 47
behavioral monitoring, 651–652
behaviorism, 6, 13–14, 121–122
    contrasted with ethology, 15
    radical, 14
    *See also* classical conditioning, operant conditioning
Bennington College study, 514–515
benzodiazepines, 678
between-groups experiment, 29
bias, in person perception

actor-observer discrepancy, 500–501
ageism, 497
blaming the victim, 498
in diagnosis of mental disorder, 613–614
ethnocentrism, 498
favoritism, 498
fundamental attribution error, 499–500
ingroup-outgroup, 497–498
just-world bias, 499
prejudice, 496
primacy effect, 495
self-serving, 501
sexism and language, 404–405
stereotypes, 496–498
surface characteristics, 495–496
bias, in research results, defined, 36
bimodal frequency distribution, A-3
biofeedback training, 134
biological treatments
drugs, 675–678
psychosurgery, 679
shock therapy, 678–679
bipolar disorders, 632–633
lithium therapy for, 677
bird songs
in courtship, 86
dialects of, 92
blind experiment, 38
brain, 177–187
blood-brain barrier, 190
contralateral connections in, 182
control of hormones by, 188–189
control of movement by, 183–185
control of sleep by, 225–226
emotions and, 235
hearing and, 250
hemispheres, 180
and hunger drive, 202–205
and motivation, 200–202
neuropsychological study of, 16, 377–382, 399–401
neurotransmitters in, 678
organic disorders of, 610, 611
organizational principles of, 181–183
pituitary and, 188–189
pleasure centers in, 214–216
schizophrenia and, 628
and sex drive, 209–210
symmetry and asymmetry in, 182–183

care. See treatment
career cycle, 481
catatonic schizophrenia, 635
catharsis, 654, 668–669
cell body of neuron, defined, 166
cell membrane, 186
depolarization of, 186
repolarization of, 187
central drive systems, 200–201
location of, 201
central nervous system, 166
depressants, 193
functional approach to, 175
pain transduction and, 266–267
See also brain, spinal cord
central tendency, defined, 33, A-3
cerebellum, 178
cerebral cortex, 180
movement controlled by, 183–187
organization of, 181
children
cognitive development of, 411–446
discipline of, 460–462
egocentrism of, 431, 443, 444

language use by, 423–426, 429–430
parenting of, 460–462
play behavior, 463–464
reasoning by, 431–435
self-concept of, 505
social development of, 449–469
See also infancy
chromosome, 49
crossing over in reproduction, 50–51
disorders caused by, 58–61
chunking, 337–338
cingulotomy, 679
circadian rhythm, 221–222
hypothalamus and, 225–226
classical conditioning, 122–129
cognitive interpretations of, 145–147
and drug reactions, 129
emotions and, 128–129
expectancy theory on, 146–147
extinction and recovery, 126–127
generalization and discrimination, 127–128
higher-order, 128
Pavlov and, 123–129
phobias treated by, 667
stimulus-response theory of, 145
stimulus-stimulus theory of, 145
Clever Hans, 25–27, 29, 38
client-centered therapy, 659–662
clinical psychologist, defined, 648
clinical psychology, 21
cloning, 51
cocaine. See substance abuse
cocktail-party phenomenon, 296
coding, 242–243
of pain, 267–268
of sound frequency, 248–250
of visual contrast and contour, 257–260
cognitive-behavioral therapy, 666
effectiveness of, 673
cognitive constructs, as personality variables, 586
cognitive development, 411–446
control processes, 441–442
infant, 417–418
object permanence, 418–419
Piagetian view of, 435–438
short-term memory, 440–441
social context of, 445
and social development, 451
Vygotsky's view of, 443–444
cognitive dissonance, 516–519
avoiding, 517
techniques to achieve compliance, 531–533
cognitive map, 150
cognitive psychology, 7, 14
learning and, 143–152
observational learning and, 152
place learning and, 150–151, 158–159
rise of, 16–18
See also intelligence, language, memory, perception, problem solving
cognitive therapy, 662–666
effectiveness of, 673
color blindness, 263–264
genetic cause of, 56–57
color mixing, 260–262
color vision, 262–265
opponent-process theory of, 264–265
trichromatic theory of, 262–264
community mental health centers, 648
competition, factors affecting, 552–557
prisoner's-dilemma games, 556
compliance
cognitive dissonance and, 531–533
downward negotiation, 533

obedience, 535–540
principles of, 530–531
reactance and, 534–535
reciprocity principle, 533
component analysis, object recognition and, 292–293
compulsion, defined, 617
computerized axial tomography (CAT) scan of brain, 652
concentration, deficit in, 636–637
concordance, defined, 75
concrete-operational stage of childhood, 436–437
conditioning. See classical conditioning, operant conditioning
conformity, 545–546
group discussion and, 548–549
minority's influence on, 547–548
reasons for, 546–547
conservation, principle of, 432–433
constancy, visual, 316–318
context-dependent memory, 353
contiguity, 345–346
controlled experimentation, 27
convergence, visual, 304
convergent evolution, 94
conversion disorder, 620, 621
cooperation, 112
coparticipant effects, 542–545
corpus callosum, 182, 183, 378–379
correlates of structure, 88
correlation coefficient, 30, 34, A-7–A-8
correlational studies, limits of, 30
counseling psychologist, defined, 648
counselor, defined, 648
counter-conditioning, 667–668
counterfactual arguments, 402–403
couple therapy, 652
creativity, cyclothymia and, 633
creole languages, 425
criterion validity, 37
critical-period hypothesis, 426
crossing over, defined, 50
cultural adaptation, 85
cultural context, defined, 453
culture(s)
alcoholism and, 627
developmental effects of, 427–428, 452, 453, 462
emotions constant across, 99–103
fundamental attribution error and, 500
incidence of mental disorder by, 608
infant care, variations by, 456
in intelligence testing, 384–385
linguistic relativity, 402–404
moral reasoning in, 478
perceptions of mental disorder by, 608
reasoning style, variations by, 71–73, 384–385, 445
romantic love, variations by, 511
cycloid curve, 312
cyclothymia, 632, 633

data-collection methods, 31, 38
deception, in research, 40
decision making
group, 551–552
rules for, 515
declarative memory, 359
deductive reasoning, 386–388
visual imagery in, 386–387
defense mechanisms, 568–570
research on, 572
defense reactions, 157
deindividuation, 544–545
deinstitutionalization, 644
delirium tremens, 625

delusions, 634
dendrites, 166
dependent variable, 28
depolarization, 168, 169
depressants, 193
depression, 628–632
  attributional helplessness theory of, 630–631
  behaviorist perspective on, 629–630
  defined, 628
  learned helplessness theory of, 630
  monoamine theory of, 629
  self-perpetuation of, 631–632
  treatment for, 677, 678–679
deprivation experiments, 91
depth perception, 303–306
depth-processing theory, 308–310
descriptive statistics, 33–34
descriptive studies, 30–31
development, 411–486
  continuity of, 412–413
  cross-sectional method of assessing, 412
  individual, 412
  information-processing view of, 440–443
  of knowledge, 417–420
  of language, 420–431
  longitudinal method of assessing, 412
  normative, 411–412
  orderliness of, 411–412
  of perception, 414–417
  of personality, 570–572
  Piagetian view of, 417–418
  of reasoning, 431–445
  of short-term memory, 440–441
  social, 449–486
  sociocultural approach to, 443–445
  sources of change, 413–414
  *See also* cognitive development, social development
developmental psychology, 21, 411
  interactionist perspective, 414
  maturationist vs. learning perspectives, 413–414
deviation
  standard, A-5
  statistical, A-4
*Diagnostic and Statistical Manual of Mental Disorders.*
  *See* DSM-III-R
dichotic listening, 296
direct-perception theory, 303, 314, 315–319
discrepancy principle, 416
discrimination training, 127, 138
displacement, 569
dissociative disorders, 611, 622–624
DNA (deoxyribonucleic acid), 48
dominance hierarchies, 111
dominant gene, 52
door-in-the-face technique, 533–534
dopamine, 192, 629
  and schizophrenia, 638–639
double blind experiment, 38–39
Down syndrome, 60–61
downward negotiation, 533–534
dreams, 223–225
  Freudian interpretation of, 566
  in psychoanalysis, 655
  reasons, for, 224–225
drive. *See* motivation
drugs
  addiction to, 194
  antianxiety, 677–678
  antidepressants, 677
  antipsychotic, 676–677
  behavior control and, 191–192
  and blood-brain barrier, 190
  brain stimulation by, 215
  conditioned response to, 129

intoxicating effects of, 625
mental disorders caused by use of, 611, 624–627
opiates, 268
pain-inhibiting, 268
permanent effects of, 625
psychoactive, 192, 193
synaptic transmission and, 191
tolerance to, 192
withdrawal from, 192, 625
DSM-III-R, 610–611
dualism, 4–5

ear, anatomy of, 246–248
echoic memory, 330
eclectic therapies, 675
ecological perspective
  on child development, 452–453
  on intelligence, 383–385
  on learning, 153–156
  on memory, 362
  on perception, 314–316
education, self theory on, 581
ego, 567
  social needs of, 577
egocentrism, 431, 443, 444
elaboration, 335–337
electra crisis, 571
electroconvulsive shock therapy (ECT), 678–679
electroencephalogram (EEG), 217–219, 652
electromagnetic spectrum, 251
emotion, 228–238
  ABC theory of, 663
  arousal and, 229–233
  brain role in, 180, 235
  classical conditioning and, 128–129
  defined, 229
  disorders of, 615–633
  facial expression and, 223–225
  James-Lange theory of, 230, 233–234
  as species-specific behavior, 97–104
  spectrum of, 230
  theories of, 230–231
empathy, 476, 660
empiricism, 15
  defined, 6
  and perceptual theories, 314
employment
  career cycle, 481
  life satisfaction and, 482–483
encoding
  hierarchical, 348–349
  rehearsal, 335
endocrine glands, 187
endorphins, 187, 268, 270
environment
  control over, 484
  defined, 48
  immediate, 452
  learning, 586
  opposed to heredity, 47
  social, 443, 445
environmentality, 64
enzyme, defined, 48
episodic memory, 360
epistemology, 431
Eriksonian stages of development, 450–451, 453
erogenous zones, 570
error, defined, 36
escape response, 140
ethics, 40–41
  in human experimentation, 538–539
ethnocentrism, 498
ethology, 14–16, 89–104

distinguished from sociobiology, 104
related to behaviorism, 15
Euler circles, 388, 391
evolution(ary), 81–119
  adaptation, meaning of, 85
  convergent, 94
  Darwin's theory of, 7, 81–82
  environmental change and, 83–84
  nondirectional, 84
  origins of nonverbal signals, 97–99
  and specialized learning mechanisms, 153–156
  of species-specific behaviors, 93–96, 101–102
experiment
  between-groups, 29
  controlled, 27
  double blind, 38–39
  field, 32
  within-subject, 29
  *See also* research
experimental psychology, origin of, 8
exposure treatments, 668
extinction
  in classical conditioning, 126
  in operant conditioning, 135
extroversion, 593–594
eye
  anatomy of, 252–254
  role in vision, 254–255
eyebrow flash, 102
Eysenck Personality Inventory, 593

face validity, 37
facial expression, 99–104
  blended, 100–101
  deceptive, 100–101
  microexpression, 101
  primate homologies to, 103–104
  universality of, 101–103
family
  marriage, 479–480
  parenting, 481
family therapy, 652
favoritism, 498
fear, 229
feature analysis, object recognition and, 290–295
feature theory of memory, 344
Fechner's law, 273–276, A-9–A-10
fetal alcohol syndrome, 625
field experiment, 32
field study, defined, 32
field theory, 527–530
fixation, 570
fixed action pattern, 89
flooding, 667
food-preference learning, 153–156
foot-in-the-door technique, 532–533
forgetting, 349–354
  causes of, 350
  Freudian interpretation of, 567
  interference theories of, 350–352
  retrieval-cue theories of, 352–354
formal-operational stage of childhood, 437–438
founder effect, 87
four-walls technique, 531
frame illusion, 310
free association, 565, 655
frequency distribution, A-1–A-2
  mode of, A-3
  normal, A-2–A-3
  skew of, A-3
Freudian slips, 566–567
friendship
  contrasted with love, 510–511

perception of, 492
rules of, 510
fugue, psychogenic, 622
functionalism, 86
  defined, 10
  origin of, 9–10
fundamental attribution error, 499–500, 596

gate-control theory of pain, 268
gender
  alcoholism and, 626, 627
  bias and language, 404–405
  "daughter track," 482
  differential treatment by adults, 467–468
  electra and oedipal crises, 571
  genetic disorders and, 56–57
  identity, 469, 474–475
  longevity and, 483
  moral reasoning and, 478
  penis envy, 571
  play styles, differences in, 468–469
  prevalence of mental disorder
    correlated by, 612–614, 617, 623
  segregation by, causes of, 469
  and sexual behavior, 472
  and social development, 466–468
  stress and, 614
  violence correlated to, 116
general adaptation syndrome, 228
generalization, stimulus, 127
generalized anxiety disorder, 616
generative-transformational theory of language, 397
genes
  dominant vs. recessive, 52
  effect on behavior, 48, 53–73
  Mendelian effects in humans, 56–58
  and schizophrenia, 73–77
  See also chromosomes
genetic drift, 87
genetics, 47
  animal experiments, 54–55
  behavioral, defined, 47
  Darwinism and, 82–83
  quantitative, 61
  See also heredity, heritability
genital stage of development, 571
genotype, defined, 48–49
geons, 292–293
Gestalt movement, 285
  on perception, 315
  principles, 286
Gestalt psychology, 10–11, 22
Gestalt therapy, 659
glial cells, 168
goal interdependence, 554–555
grasp reflex, 96
group influences
  conformity and, 548–549
  decision making, 551–552
  intergroup conflict, 552–557
  polarization in, 549–551
group therapy, 652
groupthink, 551

habit, defined, 669
habituation, 123, 667
halfway houses, 647
hallucinations, 634–635, 637
hallucinogens, 193
Halstead-Reitan battery, 652
hearing, 244–250

brain role in, 250
coding of sound, 248–250
deafness, 248
ear and, 246–248
memory of, 330–331
sound and, 244–246
helping behavior, 112–113
  kin selection theory of, 113, 117
  reciprocity theory of, 113
helplessness, and depression, 630–631
heredity
  chromosomal disorders, 58–61
  and intelligence, 366
  Mendelian disorders, 56–58
  Mendelian patterns of, 53
  opposed to environmental influences, 47
  patterns of, 49–55
heritability, 62–77
  adoptive method of studying, 68
  application of concept, 62–63
  coefficient of, 62
  defined, 62
  and environmental diversity, 63–64
  and genetic diversity, 63
  of mood disorders, 633
  of traits, 599–600
  twin method of studying, 68
heterozygous, defined, 52
heuristics, 393, 515
hierarchical encoding, 348–349
hierarchy
  of motor control, 185–186
  of needs, 582–584
homeostasis, 199–200
homology, 93, 95
homosexuality, 472–473
  attitudes towards, 514
  cultural perspectives on, 608
homozygous, defined, 52
horizontal décalage, 439
hormones, 187
  affecting behavior, 189–190
  brain control of, 188–189
  neurotransmitters and, 187–188
  and sex drive, 209–212
  and stress, 228–229
hospitals. See mental hospitals
human development. See development
humanistic theories of personality, 578–579, 601
  criticisms of, 584–585
  hierarchy of needs, 582–584
  self theory, 581–582, 601
  tenets of, 579–580, 601
humanistic therapy, 659
  effectiveness of, 673
  Rogerian, 659–662
hunger, 202, 229
  hypothalamus and, 202–204
  obesity and, 205–208
  reward mechanisms and, 216
  stimuli of, 204–205
Huntington's disease, 57–58
hypnosis, 654
  effect on memory, 356–357
  post-hypnotic suggestion, 564
hypochondriasis, 620
hypothalamus, 180
  and circadian rhythms, 225–226
  and hunger, 202–204
  motivation and, 200–201
  and sex drive, 209
hypothesis, 35
  construction of, 386

hysteria, 620

iconic memory, 329
id, 567
identity, 473
  asserting and validating, 508
  crisis of, 474
  formation of, 474–475
  occupational and ideological commitment, 474
  roots of, 474
  social comparison and, 504–506
  See also self
illusions
  auditory, 289–290
  illusory conjunctions, 292
  of motion, 312
  of shape, size, and depth, 289, 308–331
impression management, 506
  self-handicapping, 507–508
  self-monitoring, 508–509
imprinting, 157–158
incest avoidance, 109–110, 116–117
independent variable, 28
index case, defined, 75
induction, as discipline, 460
inductive reasoning, 386, 388–389
  biases in, 388–389
infancy
  attachment in, 454, 456–459
  cultural differences in care of, 456
  defined, 414
  early speech, 422–423
  multiple caregivers in, 458–459
  perceptual development in, 414–417
  physical contact in, 454–455
  speech perception, 420–422
inferential statistics, 35–36
inferiority complex, 577
information
  conceptual, 344–345
  memory processing of, 323–328
  primacy effect, 495
  representation of, 391–393
  speed of processing, 374
  types of, 327
  verbal, 340–341
  visual, 378
  visual-spatial, 341–343
  See also knowledge, memory
information-processing approach, 17
  to cognitive development, 440–443
  to intelligence, 373–377
instrumental conditioning. See operant conditioning
insufficient-justification effect, 518
intellect. See intelligence
intelligence
  brain hemispheres and, 378–381
  cognitive correlates of, 374–375
  components and metacomponents of, 375
  conceptions of, 365–366
  cultural variations, 384–385
  development of thought, 431–445
  distinguished from talent, 382
  ecological approach to, 383–385
  environment and, 367
  factor analysis of, 370–372
  fluid vs. crystallized, 372
  heredity and, 366
  information-processing approach to, 373–377
  logical reasoning, 385–389
  mental age, 367
  multiple, 382–383

neuropsychological approach to, 377–382
practical-mechanical vs. verbal-educational, 372
primary mental abilities, 371
problem solving, 390–393
psychometric approach to, 366–372
quotient of. *See* IQ
intelligence tests. *See* IQ
interactionism, 4
interference, proactive and retroactive, 350–352
interneurons, 167
interview, defined, 31
interviewing, for assessment, 649
introspection, defined, 9
introversion, 593–594
IQ
  cultural and racial studies of, 71–73
  cultural variability of, 384
  of Down syndrome individuals, 60
  expectations affecting, 502–503
  family studies of, 69–71
  heritability vs. environmentality of, 67–73
  reaction times correlated with, 374
  related to grade-point average, 34
  reliability of tests, 36, 368–369
  standardization of test, A-7
  Stanford-Binet Scale, 368
  twin studies of, 68, 69–70
  validity of tests, 36, 370
  Wechsler scales, 368–370

James-Lange theory of emotion, 230, 233–234
just-noticeable difference, 273, A-9
just-world bias, 499

karyotype, defined, 49
keyword learning method, 339
kin selection, 113, 117
Klinefelter's syndrome, 58
knowledge
  child's acquisition of, 418–420
  infant acquisition of, 417–418
  *See also* information
Kohlberg's stages of moral reasoning, 476–478
Korsakoff's syndrome, 358, 625

L-dopa, 191–192
laboratory study, defined, 32
language
  -acquisition device (LAD), 425
  -acquisitions support system (LASS), 427
  bilingualism, 403–404
  children's vs. lower primate use, 429–430
  Chomsky's view of, 17
  as cognitive system, 394–401
  counterfactual argument, 402–403
  creole, 425
  critical period for learning, 426
  deep structure of, 397
  development of, 421–426
  and development of reasoning, 443–444
  disorders of, 399–400
  errors of, 398–399
  first words, 422
  grammar, 424, 425–426, 427
  infant's perception of, 420–421
  learning theories of, 426–428
  linguistic relativity, 401–404
  morphemes and phonemes of, 394–396
  nativist theories of, 425–426
  neuropsychological approach to, 399–401

pidgin, 425
primate experiments, 428–431
psycholinguistics, defined, 17, 20
related to thought, 401–406
sexism in, 404–405
speech production, 398–399
spoonerisms, 398
syntax and morphology, 396
transformational grammar, 397
vocabulary learning, 423–424
latency stage of development, 571
learning, 121–160
  classical conditioning and, 122–129
  cognitive perspective, 143–152
  defined, 121
  ecological perspective, 153–159
  fear-related, 157
  food avoidance and preference, 153–156
  imprinting, 157–158
  language, 421–426
  latent, 151
  observational, 151–152
  operant conditioning and, 130–143
  place, 150–151, 158–159
  social, basic tenets of, 585–586, 601
levels-of-processing theory of memory, 336
libido, 565
light, defined, 251
  *See also* vision
limbic system, 179
linguistics, relation to psychology, 17, 20
listening
  dichotic, 296
  selective, 296
  *See also* hearing
lithium therapy, 677
lobotomy, 679
localization of brain functions, 7
locus of control, 586–588
logic
  deductive, 386–388
  inductive, 386, 388–389
  symbolic, 388
long-term memory, 325–326
  analogue theory, 342–343
  associationist view of, 345–346
  of concepts, 344–345
  encoding into, 335–339
  feature theory of, 344
  hierarchical encoding, 348–349
  knowledge organization, 345–346
  propositional theory, 342
  prototype theory of, 344
  retrieval problems, 349–357
  separation from short-term memory, 357–358
  verbal information, 340–341
  visual-spatial information, 341–343
  *See also* memory, short-term memory
love
  contrasted with friendship, 510–511
  romantic, 510–512
  withdrawal of, 460
low-ball technique, 532

magnetic resonance imaging (MRI) of brain, 652
maintenance rehearsal, 335
mania, 633
manic-depression, 632–633
marriage, 479–480
marriage counseling, 652
materialism, defined, 6
mean, arithmetic, 33, A-3

measurement, problems in, 37–38
median, 33, A-3
medical students' disease, 615
medulla, 178
meiosis, defined, 50
memory, 323–362
  auditory, 330–331
  chunking, 337–338
  context-dependent, 353
  control processes, 326
  distortion of, 354–356
  echoic, 330
  episodic, 327
  episodic vs. semantic, 360
  hypnosis's effects on, 356–357
  iconic, 329
  information-processing model of, 323–328
  levels-of-processing theory, 336
  long-term, 325–326, 340–349
  mental imagery, 339
  mnemonic devices, 338–339
  multiple systems, evidence for, 357–360
  problems with, 349–357
  procedural, 327
  procedural vs. declarative, 359–360
  repression of, 568
  retrieval cues, 352–354
  semantic, 327, 346–348
  sensory, 324, 328–331
  short- vs. long-term, 357–358
  short-term, 325, 331–339, 440–441
  working, 325
Mendelian disorders, 56–58
menstrual cycle, 211
mental age, 367
mental disorder, 605–641
  anxiety disorders, 615–619
  behavioral perspective on, 607
  categorizing, 609
  cognitive perspective on, 607
  described, 605–606
  diagnosis of, 609–611
  dissociative, 611, 622–624
  labeling of, 608, 614–615
  medical model of, 606–607
  mood disorders, 627–633
  multiple causation of, 608–609
  prevalence of, 612
  schizophrenia, 633–639
  sociocultural perspective on, 607–608
  somatoform, 611, 620–622
  treatment of. *See* treatment
mental health system structure, 646–648
mental hospitals
  in Middle Ages, 643
  modern, problems with, 644–646
  programs in, 646
mental imagery, 339
mental set, 390
milieu therapy, 646
Minnesota Multiphasic Personality Inventory (MMPI)
  and MMPI-2, 650–651
mitosis, defined, 50
mnemonic devices, 338–339
modal model of the mind, 323–324
mode, of frequency distribution, A-3
modeling, in behavior therapy, 671
monoamines, 629
monogamy, 105, 107–108
mood disorders, 611
  bipolar, 632–633
  depression, 628–632
  heritability of, 633

moon illusion, 308
moon-cloud illusion, 312
moral behavior, 596–597
moral reasoning, 475
  Gilligan's approach, 478–479
  justice and caring, 478
  Kohlberg's stages, 476–478
morpheme
  characteristics of, 395–396
  defined, 394
motion
  and depth perception, 305
  illusions of, 312
  perception of, 311–313
  role in object identification, 312–313
motion parallax, 305
motivation, 197–216
  brain and, 200–202
  central-state theory of, 200
  incentives, 198
  Maslow's hierarchy of needs, 582
  and personality theories, 563, 601
  regulatory and nonregulatory drives, 200
  reward mechanisms, 214–216
  social needs, 577
  tissue needs, 199–200
  types of, 197–198
  unconscious, 564–565
motor neurons, 166–167
movement, brain control of, 183–187
Müller-Lyer illusion, 308, 309, 310–311
multiple intelligences theory, 382–383
multiple personality disorder, 622–624
mutation, 82
myelin sheath, 166

nativism, defined, 6
natural selection, 81–82
  of behavior, 84
naturalistic observation, 31
nature and nurture
  and animal development, 91–93
  defined, 47
  and human development, 413–414
  IQ and, 67–73
  and language acquisition, 426–429
  and learning theories, 153–159
  schizophrenia and, 73–77
nepotism, 113, 117
nervous system
  central, 166, 175
  functional organization of, 172–187
  hierarchical organization of, 185–186
  peripheral, 166, 173–174
neural impulses, speed of, 8
neurohormones, 188
neurons, 165–172
  A-delta fibers, 267
  action potential of, 168, 169–170
  C fibers, 266, 268
  free nerve endings of, 266
  interneuron, 167
  motor, 166–167
  rhythm generator, 172
  sensory, 167–168, 242
  structure and function of, 166–168
  synaptic transmission, 170–172
neuropsychology, 16, 357
  assessment, 652
  interpretations of intelligence, 377–382
  on language, 399–401
neurosis, defined, 610

neurotic symptom, 610
neurotransmitters
  in alcoholism, 626
  and brain reward mechanisms, 215
  chemical similarity to hormones, 187–188
  in mood disorders, 629
  psychoactive drugs and, 191–192, 193, 678
  in schizophrenia, 638–639
  and sleep, 228
  and synaptic transmission, 170–171
nonverbal communication, 97–99
  facial expression, 99–104
norepinephrine, 187, 192, 629
normal distribution, A-2–A-3
  defined, 61

obedience, 535
  Milgram's experiments, 535–539
  and rebellion, 539–540
obesity, theories of, 205–208
observer-expectancy effects, 27, 38
obsessive-compulsive disorder, 617–618
oedipal crisis, 571
operant conditioning, 130–143
  animal experiments, 130–133
  aversion treatment, 669–670
  chaining, 139
  cognitive interpretations of, 147–149
  history of, 130–132
  human experiments, 133–134
  language acquisition, 426–427
  means-end interpretation of, 147–148
  overjustification effect, 149
  punishment, 141–143
  reward contrast effects in, 148–149
  schedules of reinforcement, 136–137
  secondary reinforcement and tokens, 139
  shaping, 135
  stimulus and, 137–138
opiates, 193, 268
oral stage of development, 570
organic mental syndromes and disorders, 611

pain, 266–270
  disorder, 620
  gate-control theory of, 268
  inhibition of, 268–270
  pathways of, 267–268
  placebo effect on, 269–270
  religious belief inhibiting, 269
  stress-induced analgesia, 269
  transduction of, 266–267
panic disorder, 618–619
paranoid schizophrenia, 635
parasympathetic division of nervous system, 174
parenting
  adolescence and, 470–471
  parental imperative, 481
  self theory on, 581
  studies of, 30
  styles of discipline, 460–462
pattern recognition, 284–295
  development of, 415–416
peer group
  and adolescence, 471
  and gender identity, 468–469
penis envy, 571
peptides, 190
percentile ranking, A-5–A-6
  related to standardized scores, A-7
perception, 283–321

automatization of, 299–301
bottom-up processing, 284, 290–295
defined, 239
depth, 303–306
development of, 414–417
direct-perception theory, 303, 314, 315–319
distinctive features, 294
distinguished from sensation, 283
feature-integration theory of, 290–292
of figure and ground 286–287
frame of reference and, 312–313
geons, 292–293
Gestalt principles, 285–287
holistic, 285
illusions, 289–290
of motion, 311–313
parallel and serial processing, 291
perceptual set, 287–288
of person, 492–501
phonemic restoration, 289–290
recognition-by-components theory of, 292–293
reversible figure, 287
of size, 306–311
top-down processing, 284, 289–290
unconscious-inference theory of, 303, 314, 315, 316–319
visual-object agnosia, 293
perceptual reorganization, 391
periaqueductal gray (PAG), 268
peripheral nervous system, 166
  components of, 173–174
  sympathetic and parasympathetic divisions of, 174
permissive parenting, 461, 462
person perception
  behavior and, 492–494
  biases in, 494–501
  schema for, 492, 494
personality, 563–602
  cognitive aspects of, 586
  consistency across situation, 595–597
  consistency over time, 597–598
  disorders of, 611
  Freudian theory of, 449, 564–575
  humanistic views of, 578–584
  multiple, 622–624
  psychodynamic theories of, 576–578, 601
  psychosexual developmental stages, 570–572
  situational aspects of, 586
  social learning theories of, 585–590, 601
  trait theories of, 590–601
persuasion. See social influence
phallic stage of development, 571
phenomenology, 579
phenothiazines, 676
phenotype, defined, 48
phi phenomenon, 10
phobia
  agoraphobia, 619
  behavior therapy to treat, 667–669
  simple, 616, 617
  social, 616, 617
phonemes, 396, 420
phonemic restoration, 289–290
physiological psychology, 16
pidgin languages, 425
pituitary, 188–189
PKU (phenylketonuria), 56
placebo effects, 38–39, 269–270, 674–675
play
  role in social development, 463–464
  types of, 463
polyandry, 105, 106–107
polygenic characteristics, 61–73

polygyny, 105–106
pons, 178
Ponzo illusion, 308
post-hypnotic suggestion, 564
prejudice, 496–498
preoperational stage of childhood, 435–436
primacy effect, 333, 495
primary process, 567
prisoner's-dilemma games, 556
problem solving
  acquisition of rules, 442–443
  experiments in, 11–12
  selective attention, 441–442
  strategies for, 390–393
procedural memory, 360
projection, 570
projective tests, 573–574, 651
promiscuity, 105, 108–109
propositional theory of memory, 342
protein, defined, 48
prototype theory of memory, 344
proximate explanations, defined, 86
psychiatric nurse, defined, 648
psychiatric social worker, defined, 648
psychiatrist, defined, 648
psychoactive substance abuse, 611, 624–627
psychoanalysis, 12–13, 564–575, 607, 653–659
  basics of, 654–656
  case study, 656–658
  and cognitive psychology, 17
  effectiveness of, 672, 673
  insight in, 656–657
  post-Freudian, 658
  resistance and, 656
  transference in, 656, 658
psychoanalytic theory, 449
psychodynamic theory of personality, 564–578, 601
  critiques of Freud, 574–575
  Freudian symbols, 565–566
  on mental disorder, 607
  mind components, 567–570
  on personality development, 570–572
  post-Freudian, 576–578, 601
  on sex and aggression, 565
  on somatoform disorders, 620–621
  unconscious and, 564, 565–567
psycholinguistics. See language
psychologist
  clinical, 648
  counseling, 648
psychometric tests, 650–651
psychopharmacology, 675–678
psychophysics, 8, 241, 270–276
  absolute thresholds and, 270–271
  difference thresholds and Weber's law, 272–273
  scaling, 273–276, A-9–A-10
  signal detection theory and, 271–272
psychosis, defined, 610
psychosurgery, 679
psychotherapy
  behavior, 666–671
  cognitive, 662–666
  eclectic, 675
  evaluation of, 671–675
  humanistic, 659–662
  psychoanalysis, 654–658
  types of, 652–653
punishment, 141–143

questionnaires, 31
  for assessment, 649–650

racism. See stereotyping
rational-emotive therapy, 662–663
rationalization, 570
reactance 534–535
reaction formation, 569–570
reaction time, 8
reasoning
  algorithmic, 392–393
  cause-and-effect, 433–434
  cultural variations in, 71–73
  deductive, 386–388
  development of, 431–445
  hypothetico-deductive, 434–435
  inductive, 386, 388–389
  language and development of, 443–444
  moral, 475–479
  Piagetian theory of, 435–438
recency effect, 333
receptor cells, 242
receptor potential, 243
recessive gene, 52
reciprocity norms, 533
reciprocity theory of helping behavior, 113
reductionism, defined, 579
reference group, 504
reflex(es)
  conditioned, 124
  defined, 122
  physiology of, 176
  types of, 176–177, 178
  unconditioned, 124
reflexology, 6, 17
rehearsal
  elaborative, 335–337
  maintenance vs. encoding, 334–335
reinforcement, 133
  positive vs. negative, 140–141
  primary, 139
  secondary, 139
reinforcement schedules, 135–137
  extinction and, 135
  fixed-interval, 136
  fixed-ratio, 136
  variable-interval, 137
  variable-ratio, 136
reliability, defined, 36
REM (rapid eye movement) sleep, 219, 223–225, 226
repression, 568, 569
  research on, 572
research
  data-collection methods, 31
  designs for, 28–29
  error and bias in, 36–39
  ethics of, 40–41, 538–539
  generalization in, 39
  setting of, 28, 32
  strategies for, 28–32
  See also experiment
response, conditioned vs. unconditioned, 124
resting potential of neuron, 168
retrieval cues, 352–354
reward mechanisms, 214–216
rhodopsin, 253
rhythm generator neuron, 172
ribonucleic acid (RNA), 48
ritualization, 97
Robbers Cave experiment, 553–554
Rogerian therapy, 659–662
romantic love. See love
Rorschach inkblot, 573
Rorschach test, 651
rote rehearsal, 331–332

scatter plot, 34, A-8
Schachter theory of emotion, 231
schema, 416
  person, 492, 494
scheme, Piagetian, 17, 418, 438–439
schizophrenia, 73, 611, 634
  adoption studies of, 73–75
  attention deficit and, 636–637
  causes of, 638–639
  characterization of, 634–635
  delusions in, 634
  drug treatment of, 675–677
  electrical stimulation as treatment for, 214–215
  environmental prevention of, 76–77
  hallucination and, 634–635, 637
  heritability of, 74
  incidence of, 87, 634
  twin studies of, 75–76
  types of, 635–636
Scholastic Aptitude Test (SAT), 368, A-6
school
  and attitude change, 514–515
  experimental, 465–466
  implicit vs. explicit curriculum, 464
  open classrooms, 465
  See also education
seasonally affective disorder (SAD), 633
secondary process, 567
security, as need, 577
selective breeding, 64–67
  natural selection as, 81–82
selective viewing, 297–298
self
  actualization of, 580, 582, 583–584
  conditions of worth, 581
  handicapping, 507–508
  ideal vs. real, 577
  Jungian view of, 578
  monitoring of, 508–509
  others' expectations and, 502–503
  social presentation of, 506–509
  as social product, 501–502
  social roles and, 503–504
self-actualization, 580, 582, 583–584
self-concept, 579
  See also identity
self-efficacy, 588–589
self-esteem, 577–578
self-monitoring, 652
self-reporting, 31
sensation, 239–278
  See also hearing, pain, vision
sensitivity, defined, 36
sensorimotor stage of infant development, 417, 435
sensory adaptation, 244
sensory neurons, 167–168, 242
sensory physiological psychology, 241
sensory physiology, 241
serotonin, 629
sex drive, 208–213
  brain and, 209–210
  external stimuli and, 212–213
  hormones and, 209–212
  mating patterns, 105–110
sex-linked traits, 57
sexual differentiation, 209–210
sexual orientation, 472–473
sexual reproduction, genetic basis of, 49–51
sexuality
  adolescent development, 472–473
  childhood experience of and neurosis, 655
  disorders, 611
  as motivation, 565
shaping, 135

short-term memory
    development of, 440–441
    memory stores, 440
sign stimulus, 89
skeletal motor system, 173
skew, of frequency distribution, A-3
Skinner box, 132–133
sleep, 216–228
    biological rhythm of, 221–222
    deprivation of, 222–223
    disorders of, 611
    dreaming, 223–225
    EEG of, 217–219
    function of, 219–220
    insomniacs, 223
    as motivation, 216
    need for, 220
    nonsomniacs, 223
    preservation and protection explanation of, 220
    REM (rapid eye movement), 219, 223–225, 226
    restoration theory of, 219–220
    spindles, 218
    thought during, 224
social cognition, 491–525
social comparison, 504–506
social context, defined, 452
social Darwinism, 113–114
social development, 449–487
    in adolescence, 470–479
    in adulthood, 479–485
    in childhood, 460–469
    cognitive theories of, 451
    Erikson's stages, 450–451, 453
    Freudian view of, 449–450
    gender and, 466–469
    identity formation, 473–474
    in infancy, 453–459
    play's role in, 463–464
    school's role in, 464–466
    social clock, 453
    social ecology theory of, 452–453
    social learning theories of, 451–452
social facilitation, 540–541
social influence
    arousal theory, 541–542
    audience and coparticipation effects, 540–545
    compliance, 530–540
    conformity, 545–548
    deindividuation, 544–545
    field theory of, 527–530
    group interactions, 548–557
    social impact theory, 528–530
    unresponsive-bystander phenomenon, 542–544
social inhibition, 541
social learning theories of personality
    critiques of, 589–590
    locus of control, 586–588
    self-efficacy, 588–589
    tenets of, 585–586, 601
    therapy using, 646
    on traits, 596–597
social loafing, 542
social psychology, 21, 491–559
sociobiology, 104–117
    on aggression, 110–112
    on altruism, 112–113
    approaches in, 104–105
    fallacies associated with, 114–115
    on human behavior, 113–114, 115–117
    on mating, 105–110
    origins of, 104
sodium-potassium pump, 169
somatization disorder, 620

somatoform disorders, 611, 620–622
somatosensation, 173
S-O-R model, 14, 16, 143
sound, 244–245
    characteristics of, 246
    coding of, 248–250
    See also hearing
species-specific behavior, 89
    biological preparedness and, 90–91
    described, 89–91
    development of, 91–97
    human emotion as, 97–104
speech
    cooing and babbling, 421–422
    early, 422–423
    first words, 422
    perception of, 420–422
spinal cord, 175–177
spontaneous recovery, defined, 127
S-R paradigm, 14, 122–123
standard deviation, 33, A-5
standardized score, A-6–A-7
statistical significance, 35
statistical methods, 31–36, A-1–A-10
    analysis using, A-1–A-10
    correlational studies, 30
    descriptive, 33–34
    inferential, 35–36
    meta-analysis, 672–673
stereotyping, 496–498, 504
    by group, 553
    minimization of, 555
steroids, 190
Stevens's law, 274–276, A-10
stimulants, 193
stimulus
    cognitive view of, 143–146
    conditioned vs. unconditioned, 124
    discriminative, 138, 144–145
stimulus-response paradigm, 14, 122–123
strange-situation test, 457
stress, 228–229
    analgesia caused by, 269
    correlated with gender, 614
    eating, affected by, 206
    post-traumatic, 619
    precipitation of mental disorders, 609
    schizophrenia and, 639
structuralism, origin of, 9
subject-expectancy effects, 38–39
sublimation, 569
substance abuse, 611, 624
    behavioral perspective, 626
    cognitive perspective, 626–627
    dependence, 624
    effects of, 624–626
    sociocultural perspective, 627
Sudbury Valley School, 465–466, 582
suicide baiting, 544–545
Summerhill, 465
superego, 567–568
superiority complex, 577
sympathetic division of nervous system, 174
symptom
    defined, 605
    psychotic vs. neurotic, 610
synapse, 170
    drugs and, 191
    excitatory vs. inhibitory, 171
    fast vs. slow, 172
    transmission across, 170–172
syndrome, defined, 605
systematic desensitization, 668

tardive dyskinesia, 677
temporal lobe amnesia, 358
test(s)
    defined, 31
    Eysenck Personality Inventory, 593
    IQ, 34, 60, 67–73, 368–370, 374, 384, 502–503, A-7
    of logic, 445
    MMPI and MMPI-2, 650–651
    percentile ranking, A-5–A-6, A-7
    projective, 573–574, 651
    psychometric, 590–600, 650–651
    SAT, 368, A-6
    statistical analysis of, A-1–A-10
    TAT, 573, 651
testosterone, 211, 212
thalamus, 178
    ventrobasal complex, 267
Thematic Apperception Test (TAT), 573, 651
thought. See reasoning
three-mountains experiment, 432
top-down processing, 284
    and attention, 302
    illusions deriving from, 289–290
trait
    consistency of, 595–598
    defined, 590
    distinguished from state, 591
    heritability of, 599–600
    surface vs. source, 591
trait theories of personality, 590
    basics of, 590–591
    Big Five theory, 595
    critiques of, 600–601
    sixteen-dimensional, 592–593
    two-dimensional, 593–594, 601
tranquilizers, 193, 677–678
transduction. See coding
transference, 656, 658
treatment
    assessment for, 649–652
    aversion, 669–670
    behavior therapy, 666–671
    cognitive therapy, 662–666
    consumers of, 648
    couple therapy, 652
    drug, 675–678
    eclectic, 675
    ego-oriented psychodynamic, 658
    evaluation of, 671–675
    exposure, 668
    family therapy, 652
    group therapy, 652
    history of, 643–644
    humanistic therapy, 659–662
    loci of, 647–648
    nonspecific factors affecting, 673–674
    placebo effect and, 674–675
    post-Freudian psychoanalytic, 658
    psychoanalysis, 654–658
    psychodynamic, 658
    types of, 646
tricyclic antidepressants, 677
trisomy-21, 60–61
Turner's syndrome, 58
twins, genetic basis for, 51–52
Type A and Type B personalities, 229

ultimate explanations, defined, 86
unconscious
    defined, 12
    motivation, 564–565
    neurosis and, 654

routes to, 565–567
unconscious-inference theory of perception, 303, 314, 315, 316–319
undifferentiated schizophrenia, 636
unimodal frequency distribution, A-3
unipolar disorders, 632
unresponsive-bystander phenomenon, 542–544

validity, defined, 37
variability
  defined, 33
  measures of, A-4–A-5
  within-group, 35
variable, dependent vs. independent, 28
variance, A-4
vestigial behavior, 96–97
vision, 251–265
  coding of information, 257–260

color blindness, 263–264
color mixing, 260–262
development of, 414–415
duplex nature of, 254–255
eye in, 252–255
feature detection, 265
light and dark adaptation, 256
memory of, 329–330
opponent-process theory of, 264–265
parallax, 305
pictorial cues, 305
rod and cone, 254–255
stereo, 304-305
trichromatic theory of, 262–264
visual adaptation, 256
visual constancies, 316–318
visual fields, 378–379
visual cliff, 416–417

WAIS-R (Wechsler Adult Intelligence Scale, Revised), 368, 369
Weber fraction, 273
Weber's law, 273
Wechsler intelligence scales, 368–370, 372
Wernicke's aphasia, 400
Wernicke's area, 400
WISC-R (Wechsler Intelligence Scale for Children, Revised), 368
within-subject experiment, 29
working memory, 325
  See also short-term memory

Yerkes-Dodson law, 228

z score, A-6
zygote, defined, 51